Crime in the United States

2002

Uniform Crime Reports

BOOK SALE
Solano College Library

Printed Annually
Federal Bureau of Investigation
U.S. Department of Justice
Washington, D.C. 20535

Advisory:
Criminal Justice Information Systems Committee,
International Association of Chiefs of Police;
Criminal Justice Information Services Committee,
National Sheriffs' Association;
Criminal Justice Information Services Advisory Policy Board

Foreword

The concept of collecting national crime statistics and using them to explore the complexion and scope of the country's crimes originated with discussions among law enforcement officials in the late 1800s. The topic continued to be of interest at national meetings of law enforcement, and the idea gained momentum as the International Association of Chiefs of Police (IACP) took a leading role in promoting it. Finally, in January 1930, 400 cities from 43 of the 48 United States and the territories of Alaska, Hawaii, and Puerto Rico submitted their data to the IACP. The association compiled the information into the first national database of crime statistics and subsequently published them in a nine-page report. The IACP published the statistics that they collected thereafter in a monthly pamphlet titled *Uniform Crime Reports for the United States and Its Possessions* and distributed it to participating agencies and other interested parties.

Later in 1930, the years of planning further culminated in the IACP's successful implementation of a data collection program that we now know as the Uniform Crime Reporting (UCR) Program. By August 1930, the Bureau of Investigation (renamed the Federal Bureau of Investigation [FBI] in 1935) had assumed oversight of the UCR Program. At the time the IACP transferred the responsibilities of collecting and publishing crime statistics to the FBI, participation in the Program had grown to include 786 cities. In September, the fledgling UCR Program compiled the data into the first monthly report under the auspice of the FBI.

Although the Program experienced many changes throughout the decades that followed, its primary objective has never changed—to provide reliable criminal statistics for use by law enforcement, criminologists, sociologists, legislators, municipal planners, the media, and the general public. As the UCR Program developed through the years, crime categories were added and additional information pertaining to particular crimes were included. Consequently, the resulting reports grew in magnitude and scope. Today, the original pamphlet-sized publication, now titled *Crime in the United States,* has evolved into the current document that exceeds 450 pages and provides crime information from over 17,000 local and state law enforcement agencies.

Despite its long, rich history, the UCR Program is in many ways still in its infancy, and more changes lie ahead as it continues its development. FBI executives are exploring additional ways that the Program's data can be used to support the Nation's law enforcement and other governmental agencies as they struggle to combat crime in a new global environment. Moreover, as the FBI's Criminal Justice Information Services Division joins the current movement to more efficiently use and share data, officials are focusing on the UCR Program's potential to enhance the Nation's criminal justice information network.

Robert S. Mueller, III
Director

Data users are cautioned against comparing crime trends presented in this report and those estimated by the National Crime Victimization Survey (NCVS), administered by the Bureau of Justice Statistics. Because of differences in methodology and crime coverage, the two programs examine the Nation's crime problem from somewhat different perspectives, and their results are not strictly comparable. The definitional and procedural differences can account for many of the apparent discrepancies in results from the two programs.

The national Uniform Crime Reporting (UCR) Program would like to hear from you.

The staff at the national UCR Program are continually striving to improve their publications. We would appreciate it if the primary user of this publication would complete the evaluation form at the end of this book and either mail it to us at the indicated address or fax it: 304-625-5394.

Each year when *Crime in the United States* is published, many entities—news media, tourism agencies, and other groups with an interest in crime in our Nation—use reported Crime Index figures to compile rankings of cities and counties. These rankings, however, are merely a quick choice made by the data user; they provide no insight into the many variables that mold the crime in a particular town, city, county, state, or region. Consequently, these rankings lead to simplistic and/or incomplete analyses that often create misleading perceptions adversely affecting cities and counties, along with their residents. To assess criminality and law enforcement's response from jurisdiction to jurisdiction, one must consider many variables, some of which, while having significant impact on crime, are not readily measurable nor applicable pervasively among all locales. Geographic and demographic factors specific to each jurisdiction must be considered and applied if one is going to make an accurate and complete assessment of crime in that jurisdiction. Several sources of information are available that may assist the responsible researcher in exploring the many variables that affect crime in a particular locale. The U.S. Bureau of the Census data, for example, can be used to better understand the makeup of a locale's population. The transience of the population, its racial and ethnic makeup, its composition by age and gender, education levels, and prevalent family structures are all key factors in assessing and comprehending the crime issue.

Local chambers of commerce, planning offices, or similar entities provide information regarding the economic and cultural makeup of cities and counties. Understanding a jurisdiction's industrial/economic base; its dependence upon neighboring jurisdictions; its transportation system; its economic dependence on nonresidents (such as tourists and convention attendees); its proximity to military installations, correctional facilities, etc.; all contribute to accurately gauging and interpreting the crime known to and reported by law enforcement.

The strength (personnel and other resources) and the aggressiveness of a jurisdiction's law enforcement agency are also key factors. Although information pertaining to the number of sworn and civilian law enforcement employees can be found in this publication, it cannot alone be used as an assessment of the emphasis that a community places on enforcing the law. For example, one city may report more crime than a comparable one, not because there is more crime, but rather because its law enforcement agency through proactive efforts identifies more offenses. Attitudes of the citizens toward crime and their crime reporting practices, especially concerning more minor offenses, have an impact on the volume of crimes known to police.

It is incumbent upon all data users to become as well educated as possible about how to understand and quantify the nature and extent of crime in the United States and in any of the more than 17,000 jurisdictions represented by law enforcement contributors to this Program. Valid assessments are possible only with careful study and analysis of the various unique conditions affecting each local law enforcement jurisdiction.

Historically, the causes and origins of crime have been the subjects of investigation by many disciplines. Some factors that are known to affect the volume and type of crime occurring from place to place are:

- Population density and degree of urbanization.

- Variations in composition of the population, particularly youth concentration.

- Stability of population with respect to residents' mobility, commuting patterns, and transient factors.

- Modes of transportation and highway system.

- Economic conditions, including median income, poverty level, and job availability.

- Cultural factors and educational, recreational, and religious characteristics.

- Family conditions with respect to divorce and family cohesiveness.

- Climate.

- Effective strength of law enforcement agencies.

- Administrative and investigative emphases of law enforcement.

- Policies of other components of the criminal justice system (i.e., prosecutorial, judicial, correctional, and probational).

- Citizens' attitudes toward crime.

- Crime reporting practices of the citizenry.

Crime in the United States provides a nationwide view of crime based on statistics contributed by state and local law enforcement agencies. Population size is the only correlate of crime presented in this publication. Although many of the listed factors equally affect the crime of a particular area, the UCR Program makes no attempt to relate them to the data presented. The reader is, therefore, cautioned against comparing statistical data of individual reporting units from cities, counties, metropolitan areas, states, or colleges and universities solely on the basis of their population coverage or student enrollment. Until data users examine all the variables that affect crime in a town, city, county, state, region, or college or university, they can make no meaningful comparisons.

Contents

Tables—Continued

Tables—Continued

Tables—Continued

SECTION I

Summary of the Uniform Crime Reporting (UCR) Program

The Uniform Crime Reporting Program is a nationwide, cooperative statistical effort of more than 17,000 city, county, and state law enforcement agencies voluntarily reporting data on crimes brought to their attention. During 2002, law enforcement agencies active in the UCR Program represented 93.4 percent of the total population as established by the Bureau of Census. The coverage amounted to 94.3 percent of the United States population in Metropolitan Statistical Areas (MSAs), 89.9 percent of the population in cities outside metropolitan areas, and 89.5 percent in rural counties.

Since 1930, the FBI has administered the Uniform Crime Reporting Program and issued periodic assessments of the nature and type of crime in the Nation. The Program's primary objective is to generate a reliable set of criminal statistics for use in law enforcement administration, operation, and management; however, its data have over the years become one of the country's leading social indicators. The American public looks to Uniform Crime Reports for information on fluctuations in the level of crime, and criminologists, sociologists, legislators, municipal planners, the media, and other students of criminal justice use the statistics for varied research and planning purposes.

Historical Background

Recognizing a need for national crime statistics, the International Association of Chiefs of Police (IACP) formed the Committee on Uniform Crime Records in the 1920s to develop a system of uniform police statistics. Establishing offenses known to law enforcement as the appropriate measure, the Committee evaluated various crimes on the basis of their seriousness, frequency of occurrence, pervasiveness in all geographic areas of the country, and likelihood of being reported to law enforcement. After studying state criminal codes and

making an evaluation of the recordkeeping practices in use, the Committee completed a plan for crime reporting that became the foundation of the UCR Program in 1929.

Seven main classifications of crime were chosen to gauge fluctuations in the overall volume and rate of crime. These seven classifications that eventually became known as the Crime Index included the violent crimes of murder and non-negligent manslaughter, forcible rape, robbery, and aggravated assault and the property crimes of burglary, larceny-theft, and motor vehicle theft. By congressional mandate, arson was added as the eighth Index offense in 1979.

During the early planning of the Program, it was recognized that the differences among criminal codes precluded a mere aggregation of state statistics to arrive at a national total. Further, because of the variances in punishment for the same offenses in different state codes, no distinction between felony and misdemeanor crimes was possible. To avoid these problems and provide nationwide uniformity in crime reporting, standardized offense definitions by which law enforcement agencies were to submit data without regard for local statutes were formulated. The definitions used by the Program are set forth in Appendix II of this publication.

In January 1930, 400 cities representing 20 million inhabitants in 43 states began participating in the UCR Program. Congress enacted Title 28, Section 534, of the United States Code authorizing the Attorney General to gather crime information that same year. The Attorney General, in turn, designated the FBI to serve as the national clearinghouse for the data collected. Since that time, data based on uniform classifications and procedures for reporting have been obtained from the Nation's law enforcement agencies every year.

Advisory Groups

Providing vital links between local law enforcement and the FBI in the conduct of the UCR Program are the Criminal Justice Information Systems Committees of the IACP and the National Sheriffs' Association (NSA). The IACP, as it has since the Program began, represents the thousands of police departments nationwide. The NSA encourages sheriffs throughout the country to participate fully in the Program. Both committees serve in advisory capacities concerning the UCR Program's operation.

To function in an advisory capacity concerning UCR policy and to provide suggestions on UCR data usage, a Data Providers' Advisory Policy Board (APB) was established in August 1988. The Board operated until 1993 when a new Board, designed to address all FBI criminal justice information services, was approved. The Board functions in an advisory capacity concerning UCR policy and data collection and use. The UCR Subcommittee of the Board ensures continuing emphasis on UCR-related issues.

The Association of State Uniform Crime Reporting Programs and committees focuses on UCR within individual state law enforcement associations and are also active in promoting interest in the UCR Program. These organizations foster widespread and more intelligent use of uniform crime statistics and lend assistance to contributors when needed.

Redesign of UCR

Although UCR data collection had originally been conceived as a tool for law enforcement administration, by the 1980s, the data were widely used by other entities involved in various forms of social planning. Recognizing the need for more detailed crime statistics, law enforcement called for a thorough evaluative study that would modernize the UCR Program. The FBI fully concurred with the need for an updated Program and lent its complete support, formulating a comprehensive three-phase redesign effort. The Bureau of Justice Statistics (BJS), the Department of Justice agency responsible for funding criminal justice information projects, agreed to underwrite the first two phases. Conducted by an independent contractor, these phases were structured to determine what, if any, changes should be made to the current Program. The third phase would involve implementation of the changes identified. Abt Associates Inc. of Cambridge, Massachusetts, overseen by the FBI, BJS, and a Steering Committee comprised of prestigious individuals representing a myriad of disciplines, commenced the first phase in 1982.

During the first phase, the historical evolution of the UCR Program was examined. All aspects of the Program, including the objectives and intended user audience, data items, reporting mechanisms, quality control issues, publications and user services, and relationships with other criminal justice data systems, were studied.

Early in 1984, a conference on the future of UCR, held in Elkridge, Maryland, launched the second phase of the study that examined the potential of UCR and concluded with a set of recommended changes. Attendees at this conference reviewed work conducted during the first phase and discussed the recommendations that should be considered during phase two.

Findings from the evaluation's first phase and input on alternatives for the future were also major topics of discussion at the seventh National UCR Conference in July 1984. A survey of law enforcement agencies overlapped phases one and two.

Phase two ended in early 1985 with the production of a draft, *Blueprint for the Future of the Uniform Crime Reporting Program*. The study's Steering Committee reviewed the draft report at a March 1985 meeting and made various recommendations for revision. The Committee members, however, endorsed the report's concepts.

In April 1985, the phase two recommendations were presented at the eighth National UCR Conference. Various considerations for the final report were set forth, and the overall concept for the revised Program was unanimously approved. The joint IACP/NSA Committee on UCR also issued a resolution endorsing the *Blueprint*.

The final report, the *Blueprint for the Future of the Uniform Crime Reporting Program*, was released in the summer of 1985. It specifically outlined recommendations for an expanded, improved UCR Program to meet future informational needs. There were three recommended areas of enhancement to the UCR Program. First, offenses and arrests would be reported using an incident-based system. Second, data would be collected on two levels. Agencies in level one would report important details about those offenses comprising the current Crime Index, their victims, and arrestees. Law enforcement agencies covering populations of over 100,000 and a sampling of smaller agencies that would collect expanded detail on all significant offenses would be included in level two. The third proposal involved introducing a quality assurance program.

To begin implementation, the FBI awarded a contract to develop new offense definitions and data elements for the redesigned system. The work involved (a) revising the definitions of certain Index offenses, (b) identifying additional significant offenses to be reported, (c) refining definitions for both, and (d) developing data elements (incident details) for all UCR offenses in order to fulfill the requirements of incident-based reporting versus the current summary system.

Concurrent with the preparation of the data elements, the FBI studied the various state systems to select an experimental site for implementing the re-designed Program. In view of its long-standing incident-based Program and well-established staff dedicated solely to UCR, the South Carolina Law Enforcement Division (SLED) was chosen. SLED agreed to adapt its existing system to meet the requirements of the redesigned Program and collect data on both offenses and arrests relating to the newly defined offenses.

To assist SLED with the pilot project, offense definitions and data elements developed under the private contract were put at the staff's disposal. Also, FBI automated data processing personnel developed Automated Data Capture Specifications for use in adapting the state's data processing procedures to incorporate the revised system. The BJS supplied funding to facilitate software revisions needed by the state. SLED completed its testing of the new Program in late 1987.

Following the completion of the pilot project conducted by SLED, the FBI produced a draft of guidelines for an enhanced UCR Program. Law enforcement executives from around the country were then invited to a conference in Orange Beach, Alabama, where the guidelines were presented for final review.

During the conference, three overall recommendations were passed without dissent: first, that there be established a new, incident-based national crime reporting system; second, that the FBI manage this Program; and third, that an Advisory Policy Board composed of law enforcement executives be formed to assist in directing and implementing the new Program.

Information about the redesigned UCR Program, called the National Incident-Based Reporting System, or NIBRS, is contained in three documents. *Data Collection Guidelines* contains a system overview and descriptions of the offenses, offense codes, reports, data elements, and data values used in the system. *Data Submission Specifications* is for the use of state and local systems personnel who are responsible for preparing magnetic media for submission to the FBI. *Error Message Manual* contains designations of mandatory and optional data elements, data element edits, and error messages.

A NIBRS edition of the *UCR Handbook* was published to assist law enforcement agency data contributors implementing NIBRS within their departments. This document is geared toward familiarizing local and state law enforcement personnel with the definitions, policies, and procedures of NIBRS. It does not contain the technical coding and data transmission requirements presented in the other three NIBRS publications.

NIBRS collects data on each single incident and arrest within 22 crime categories. For each offense known to police within these categories, incident, victim, property, offender, and arrestee information are gathered when available. The goal of the redesign is to modernize crime information by collecting data presently maintained in law enforcement records; the enhanced UCR Program is, therefore, a by-product of current records systems. The integrity of UCR's long-running statistical series will, of course, be maintained.

It became apparent during the development of the prototype system that the level one and level two reporting proposed in the *Blueprint* might not be the most practical approach. Many state and local law enforcement administrators indicated that the collection of data on all pertinent offenses could be handled with more ease than could the extraction of selected ones. Although

"Limited" participation, equivalent to the *Blueprint's* level one, remains an option, most reporting jurisdictions, upon implementation, go immediately to "Full" participation, meeting all NIBRS' data submission requirements.

Implementation of NIBRS is occurring at a pace commensurate with the resources, abilities, and limitations of the contributing law enforcement agencies. The FBI was able to accept NIBRS data as of January 1989, and to date, the following 24 state Programs have been certified for NIBRS participation: Arkansas, Colorado, Connecticut, Delaware, Idaho, Iowa, Kansas, Kentucky, Louisiana, Massachusetts, Michigan, Nebraska, New Hampshire, North Dakota, Ohio, South Carolina, South Dakota, Tennessee, Texas, Utah, Vermont, Virginia, West Virginia, and Wisconsin.

Twelve state Programs are in various stages of testing NIBRS. Nine other state agencies, as well as agencies in the District of Columbia, are in various stages of planning and development.

Recent Developments

Quality Assurance Review

Effective October 1, 2003, the CJIS Audit Unit will include the Quality Assurance Reviews (QARs) in the newly revised triennial audit of all systems managed by the FBI's Criminal Justice Information Services (CJIS) Division. Although the QAR will remain voluntary, this change will make the review available to each state UCR Program once every 3 years. Agencies are encouraged to avail themselves of the

opportunity to assess the integrity of their data and to receive assistance in complying with Program requirements.

Missouri State UCR Program

On July 1, 2002, the state of Missouri officially became a UCR State Program following a substantial review of the state's crime reporting practices by the national Program. The state Program will be managed by the Missouri State Highway Patrol, which has demonstrated an ability to consistently meet the standards under which state Programs must operate in order to guarantee the consistency and comparability of UCR data submissions.

NIBRS

The detailed, accurate, and meaningful data produced by NIBRS benefit local agencies. Armed with comprehensive crime data, local agencies can better make their case to acquire and effectively allocate the resources needed to fight crime. Currently, 4,239 law enforcement agencies contribute NIBRS data to the national UCR Program. The data submitted by these agencies represent 17 percent of the U.S. population and 18 percent of the crime statistics collected by the UCR Program.

NIBRS Publication Series

As part of the CJIS Division's continuing efforts to showcase the potential uses of NIBRS data, Section V of this publication presents a study entitled *Bank Robbery in the United States*, which examines three different databases; UCR Summary, NIBRS, and Bank Crime Statistics.

CRIME CLOCK

Every 2.7 seconds
One Crime Index Offense

Every 22.1 seconds One Violent Crime

Every 35.3 seconds One Aggravated Assault

Every 1.2 minutes One Robbery

Every 5.5 minutes One Forcible Rape

Every 32.4 minutes One Murder

Every 3.0 seconds One Property Crime

Every 4.5 seconds One Larceny-theft

Every 14.7 seconds One Burglary

Every 25.3 seconds One Motor Vehicle Theft

SECTION II

Definition

The Uniform Crime Reporting (UCR) Program's Crime Index is composed of selected offenses used to gauge fluctuations in the volume and rate of crime reported to law enforcement. The UCR Crime Index was first recommended to the FBI Director J. Edgar Hoover in the report *Uniform Crime Reporting: Report of the Consultant Committee* (September 1958). This recommendation was accepted by the FBI and the term Crime Index first appeared in *Crime in the United States, 1960.*

The offenses selected to make up the Crime Index were the Part I crimes—the violent crimes of murder and nonnegligent manslaughter, forcible rape, robbery, and aggravated assault and the property crimes of burglary, larceny-theft, and motor vehicle theft. These crimes were considered by experts of the time to be the most serious and the most commonly reported crimes occurring in the Nation. The UCR Program created the Modified Crime Index to include arson, which was added to the Program in 1979 by congressional mandate. The definition of these offenses can be found in Appendix II of this report.

Trend

Year	Number of offenses	Rate per 100,000 inhabitants
2001	11,876,669	4,162.6
2002	11,877,218	4,118.8
Percent change	*	-1.1

*Less than one-tenth of 1 percent

National Volume, Trends, and Rates

Nationally, the 2002 Crime Index, with an estimated 11,877,218 offenses, rose by less than one-tenth of a percent when compared to the 2001 Index. Five- and 10-year trend data showed that in 2002 the Crime Index was 4.9 percent lower than the estimate from 1998 and 16.0 percent below the 1993 estimate. The Crime Index for 2002 was comprised of 12.0 percent violent crime and 88.0 percent property crime. The offense of larceny-theft accounted for the greatest part of the Crime Index, 59.4 percent. Murder, the least often committed crime in the Index, contributed slightly more than one-tenth of a percent to the total.

The Crime Index rate, which reflects the number of Index offenses per 100,000 inhabitants, for the Nation was 4,118.8. Two-, 5-, and 10-year trend data indicated that in 2002 this rate represented a 1.1 percent decrease over the 2001 Crime Index rate, a 10.9 percent drop from the rate in 1998, and a 24.9 percent decline from the estimated rate for 1993. (See Table 1.)

Figure 2.2

Crime Index
Percent Change from 1998

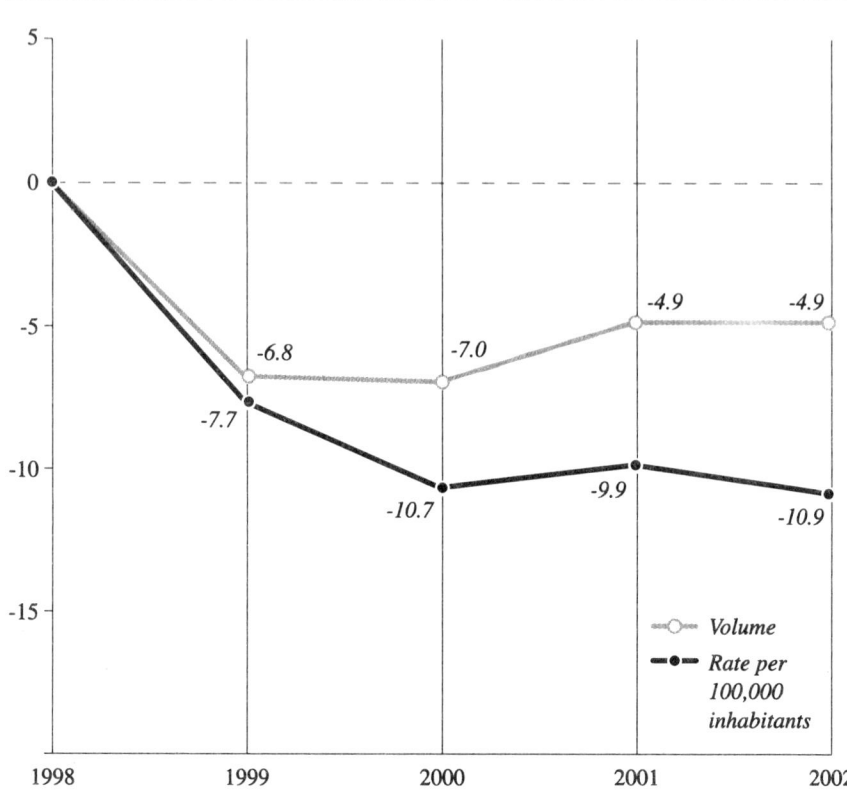

Community Types

The UCR Program defines three community types: Metropolitan Statistical Areas (MSAs), cities outside the MSAs, and rural counties which are discussed in detail in Appendix III of this report. MSAs are comprised of a central city of at least 50,000 people, the county in which the city is located, and any other adjacent counties with solid economic or social links to the central city and county. In 2002, 80 percent of the U.S. population lived within an MSA. MSAs as a community type posted an estimated Crime Index rate of 4,409.1 offenses per 100,000 people. Cities outside the MSAs, accounting for 8 percent of the Nation's inhabitants, experienced a Crime Index rate of 4,524.0. Rural counties, with 12 percent of the country's population, had an estimated Crime Index rate of 1,908.7 per 100,000 inhabitants. (See Table 2.)

Regional Offense Trends and Rates

The UCR Program divides the Nation into four regional areas: the Northeast, the South, the Midwest, and the West. (A map depicting the regions and divisions of the United States is presented in Appendix III.) The characteristics of the 2002 Crime Index in the regions of the Nation were as follows:

The Northeast

The Northeastern Region, which comprised 18.8 percent of the Nation's population, accounted for an estimated 13.2

Table 2.1

Crime Index by Month
Percent Distribution, 1998-2002

Month	1998	1999	2000	2001	2002
January	8.5	8.0	7.8	7.8	8.2
February	7.5	7.2	7.3	6.8	7.0
March	8.2	8.0	8.1	7.8	7.8
April	8.0	7.9	7.9	7.9	8.1
May	8.4	8.4	8.6	8.5	8.5
June	8.5	8.6	8.6	8.5	8.4
July	9.0	9.1	9.2	9.1	9.2
August	9.0	9.2	9.2	9.1	9.1
September	8.4	8.5	8.5	8.5	8.7
October	8.5	8.7	8.8	9.2	8.8
November	7.8	8.2	8.1	8.5	8.0
December	8.2	8.4	8.0	8.5	8.2

---

percent of the Crime Index offenses committed. This reflected a 3.2 percent decrease in offenses compared to the 2001 estimate. This region experienced an estimated rate of 2,889.0 Crime Index offenses per 100,000 in population. In 2002, this was the lowest rate of occurrence among the four regions. (See Tables 3 and 4.)

The Midwest

The region of the Midwest, home to 22.6 percent of the U.S. population, had an estimated 21.3 percent of the Crime Index offenses committed, a 1.9 percent decrease from 2001. The Midwest had an estimated Crime Index rate of 3,883.1 offenses per 100,000 inhabitants. (See Tables 3 and 4.)

The South

The South, with 35.8 percent of the country's inhabitants, was the region with the most population. Accordingly, it also had the highest volume of Crime Index offenses, an estimated 41.1 percent. This was a 0.1 percent rise in offenses compared to the 2001. The rate of Crime Index offenses per 100,000 individuals in the Southern region was 4,721.9, the highest estimated rate among the regions. (See Tables 3 and 4.)

The West

The West, with 22.8 percent of the population of the United States in 2002, registered an estimated 24.4 percent of Crime Index offenses. A two-year trend (2001-2002) showed a 3.3 percent increase that was the largest increase among of the four regions. An examination of the Crime Index rate showed 4,418.8 offenses per 100,000 people. (See Tables 3 and 4.)

Population Groups: Trends and Rates

Population groups in the UCR Program are comprised of city designations, aggregated by population, plus suburban and rural counties. Nationally, cities as a whole experienced a 0.5 percent decrease in offenses making up the

Crime Index. A review of the Crime Index within population groups in 2002 revealed that cities with populations 250,000 to 499,999 had the largest decrease at 1.8 percent. Slight increases in the Crime Index occurred in both cities with a population range of 100,000 to 249,999 (0.8 percent) and cities with 50,000 to 99,999 inhabitants (0.6 percent). Both suburban and rural counties counted increases in the Crime Index of 1.0 percent and 0.5 percent, respectively. (See Table 12.)

Collectively, U.S. cities reported a Crime Index rate of 5,047.2 offenses per 100,000 persons. The Nation's largest cities, those with populations of 250,000 and over, had the highest rate, 6,243.3 per 100,000. Among city agencies, smaller cities—those with a population of 10,000 to 24,999—reported the lowest Crime Index rate of 3,837.2 per 100,000 persons. Suburban counties had a rate of 3,047.4 Crime Index offenses per 100,000 individuals and rural counties, a rate of 2,054.8. (See Table 16.)

Clearances

An offense is cleared by UCR standards when an arrest is made and charges have been brought against the arrestee. A clearance by exceptional means can also be made when the offender has been identified and located and there is enough evidence to support an arrest, but conditions beyond the control of law enforcement preclude arresting, charging, and prosecuting the offender. Additionally, if an offender under the age of 18 is cited to appear before juvenile authorities, the UCR Program accepts that incident as cleared by arrest, even though a physical arrest may not have occurred. (More information about clearances can be obtained in Section III of this report.)

In the United States in 2002, 20.0 percent of all Crime Index offenses were cleared by arrest or exceptional means. Within those offenses, 46.8 percent of violent crime and 16.5 percent of property crime were cleared. Murder, the most serious offense in the Index, had the largest percentage of offenses cleared (64.0 percent), and burglary had the smallest percentage of cleared offenses (13.0 percent). (See Table 25.)

Clearances and Juveniles

Of all the Crime Index offenses cleared in 2002, 18.0 percent involved only persons under 18 years of age. (According to UCR guidelines, any clearance that involves both adults and juveniles is listed as an adult clearance.) A study of clearances among juveniles revealed that persons under age 18 accounted for 11.9 percent of violent crime clearances and 20.3 percent of property crime clearances. In 2002, as in previous years, the single offense that demonstrated the largest percentage of clearances involving juveniles was the Modified Crime Index offense of arson at 43.0 percent, followed by the Crime Index offense of larceny-theft at 21.2 percent. (See Table 28.)

Arrests

Total Arrests

The Nation's law enforcement made an estimated 2,234,464 arrests for Crime Index offenses, including arrests for arson, in 2002. This represented an estimated 16.3 percent of the total number of arrests made. (See Table 29.) The arrest rate for Crime Index offenses was 788.4 offenses per 100,000 inhabitants. This figure reflected a violent crime arrest rate of 217.9 and a property crime arrest rate (including arson) of 570.5 arrests per 100,000 persons. (See Table 30.)

The Nation's four regions experienced the following arrest rates for Crime Index offenses per 100,000 persons: the West recorded an arrest rate of 871.9; the South posted a rate of 790.0; the Midwest reported a rate of 777.2; and the Northeast had a rate of 658.5 arrests per 100,000 population. (See Table 30.)

A review of arrests within UCR population groups revealed that the Nation's largest cities, those with more than 250,000 inhabitants, recorded the highest arrest rate for Crime Index offenses at 1,069.9 per 100,000 persons. Smaller cities, those with a population range of 10,000 to 24,999, reported the lowest Crime Index arrest rate among city agencies at 791.6 per 100,000 inhabitants. Suburban counties had an arrest rate of 528.7, and rural counties had a rate of 413.2 Crime Index arrests per 100,000 individuals. (See Table 31.)

Arrest Trends

A comparison of 2002 arrests to the previous year's arrest figures for all Crime Index offenses showed a slight increase, 0.2 percent. Five- and 10-year trends presented a decline in arrests of 11.1 percent and 22.2 percent, respectively. (See Tables 32, 34, and 36.) Within the Crime Index, property crime arrests during 2002 increased 0.6 percent, and violent crime arrests declined 0.8 percent in comparison to arrests in 2001. Property crime arrests in 2002 were 12.5 percent lower than the 1998 figure and 25.2 percent below the 1993 number. Five- and 10-year trends for violent crime arrests also showed decreases of 7.3 percent and 13.4 percent, respectively.

Figure 2.3

Crime Index Offenses
Percent Distribution[1] 2002

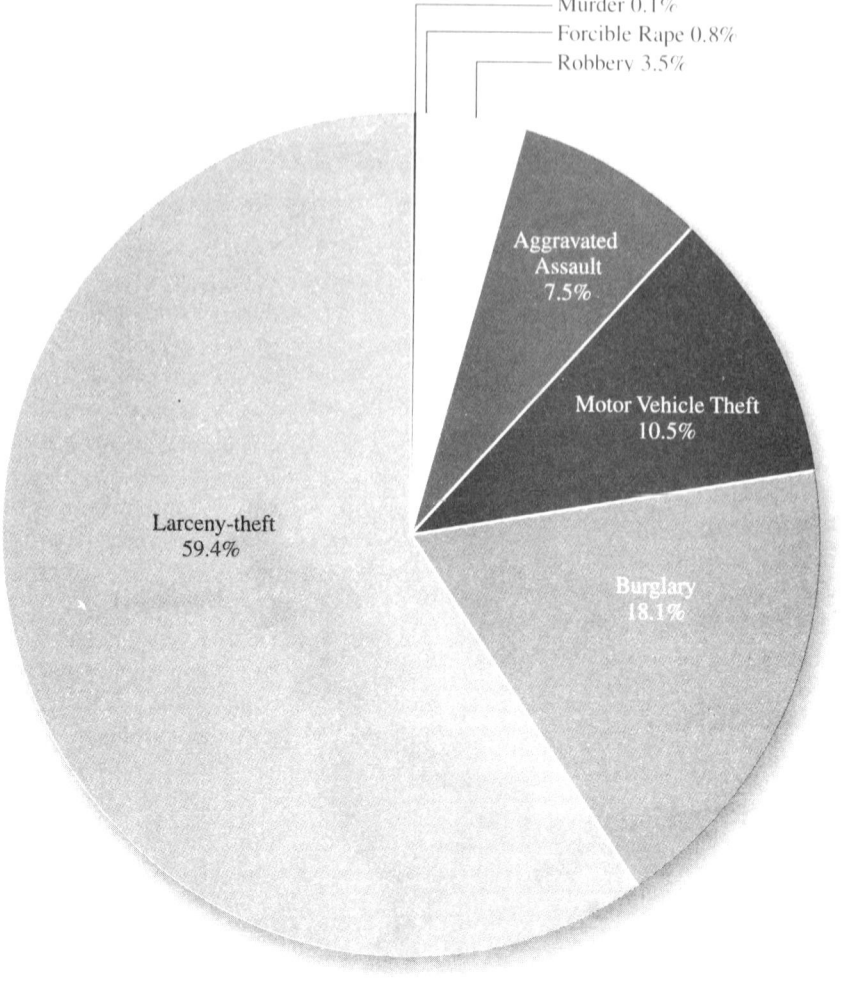

- Murder 0.1%
- Forcible Rape 0.8%
- Robbery 3.5%
- Aggravated Assault 7.5%
- Motor Vehicle Theft 10.5%
- Burglary 18.1%
- Larceny-theft 59.4%

[1] Due to rounding, the percentages do not add to 100.0.

Figure 2.4

Regional Crime Rates 2002

Violent and Property Crimes per 100,000 Inhabitants

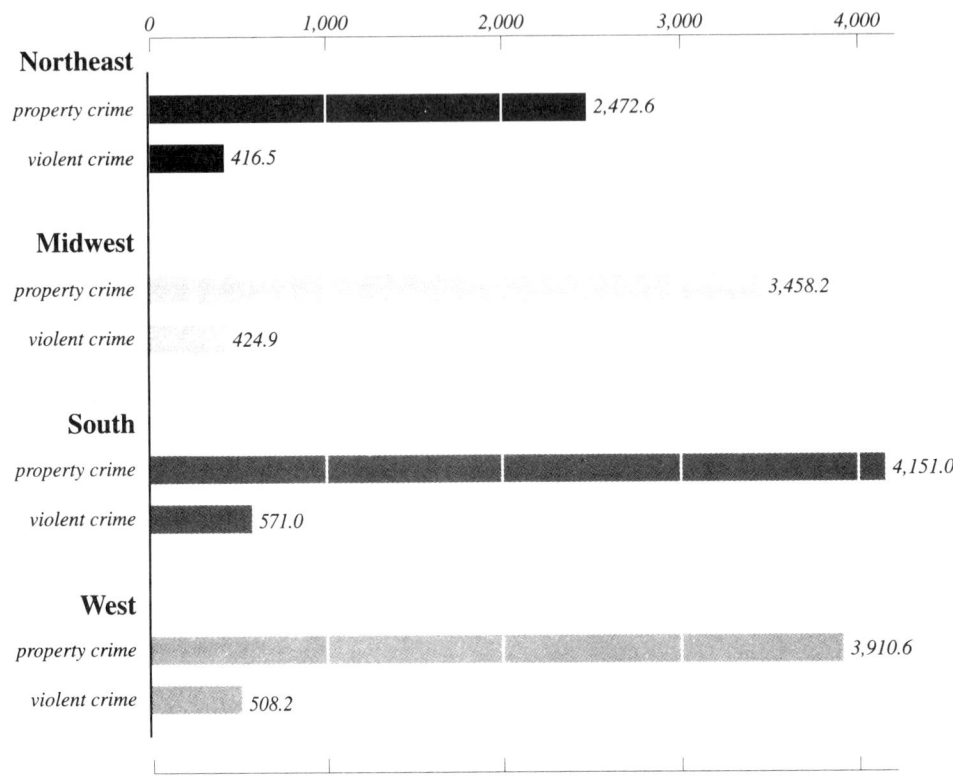

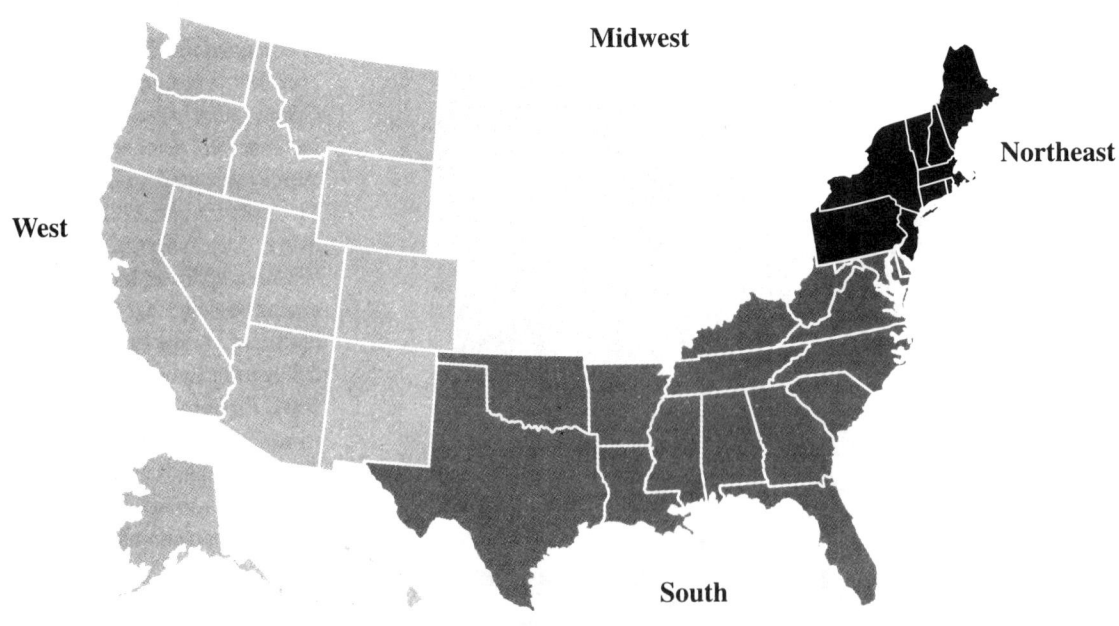

By gender, arrests of females for Crime Index offenses increased in 2002 by 0.8 percent when compared to figures from the previous year. At the same time, arrests of males declined 0.1 percent. Violent crime arrests within the Crime Index demonstrated a 0.8 percent decline in arrests for both males and females. Property crime, however, experienced a 1.2 percent increase in the arrests of females and a 0.3 percent rise in the arrests of males. (See Table 37.)

A review of 2002 data by age of arrestees revealed that, although arrests of adults for Crime Index offenses in 2002 rose 1.5 percent over the previous year's arrests, arrests of juveniles fell 3.5 percent. (See Table 36.)

Distribution

Adults accounted for 74.3 percent of all arrestees of Crime Index offenses in 2002 and juveniles, 25.7 percent. (Based on Table 38.) Males accounted for the majority of Crime Index offense arrestees at 72.9 percent. (See Table 42.)

By race, 65.5 percent of arrestees were white, 31.9 percent were black, and 2.5 percent were other races (Asian or Pacific Islander and American Indian or Alaskan Native). An examination of violent crime arrest data showed that 59.7 percent of arrests were of white individuals, 38.0 percent were of black persons, and 2.3 percent were individuals of other races. Property crime arrests were distributed as follows: 67.7 percent were white arrestees, 29.6 were black, and the remaining 2.7 percent were other races. (See Table 43.)

Definition

Violent crime is composed of four offenses: murder and nonnegligent manslaughter, forcible rape, robbery, and aggravated assault. According to the Uniform Crime Reporting Program's definition, violent crimes involve force or threat of force.

Trend

Year	Number of offenses	Rate per 100,000 inhabitants
2001	1,439,480	504.5
2002	1,426,325	494.6
Percent change	-0.9	-2.0

National Volume, Trends, and Rates

During 2002, the number of violent crimes declined nationally by 0.9 percent from the 2001 estimate. An examination of 5- and 10-year trend data showed that the 2002 estimate of 1.4 million violent crimes was 7.0 percent lower than the 1998 approximation and 25.9 percent below the 1993 figure. (See Table 1.)

As in previous years, aggravated assaults accounted for the largest share of the violent crime distribution, 62.7 percent. Robbery made up 29.5 percent of the total; forcible rape, 6.7 percent; and murder, 1.1 percent. (Based on Table 1.)

The violent crime rate for 2002 was estimated at 494.6 offenses per 100,000 persons, a decrease of 2.0 percent from the previous year's rate. The current estimate was a decrease of 12.9 percent when compared to the 1998 rate and 33.8 percent when compared to the 1993 violent crime rate. (See Table 1.)

Community Types

Metropolitan Statistical Areas, or MSAs, are those community types made up of a central city or urbanized area of at least 50,000 inhabitants, the county containing that city or area, and any other adjacent suburban counties with close cultural and economic ties to the area. In 2002, an estimated 80 percent of the U.S. population resided in MSAs, where approximately 88.5 percent of the Nation's violent crimes occurred. The estimated offense total of 1,262,359 violent crimes resulted in a rate of 545.6 per 100,000 MSA residents. The cities outside MSAs accounted for 8 percent of the population in 2002, and they accounted for 6.4 percent of the Nation's total violent crimes. The rate of 403.1 offenses per 100,000 inhabitants of those cities was based on an estimated 90,586 violent crimes. Twelve percent of the U.S. population lived in rural counties in 2002, and 5.1 percent of the Nation's total violent crimes occurred in those areas. Rural counties had an estimated 73,380 violent crimes, or a rate of 212.6 violent offenses per 100,000 rural county inhabitants. (Based on Table 2.)

Regional Offense Trends and Rates

The UCR Program divides the United States into four regions: the

Figure 2.5

Violent Crime
Percent Change from 1998

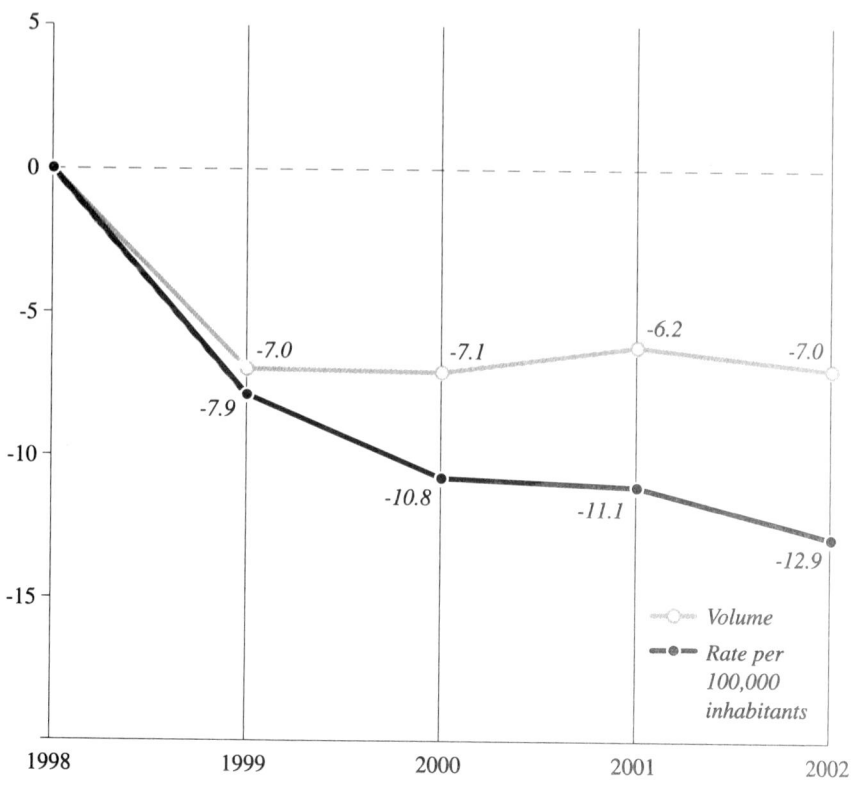

Northeast, the Midwest, the South, and the West. A map of the United States delineating the regions is included in Appendix III. Estimated crime volume, rates, and percent changes by region are published in Table 4.

The Northeast

The Northeastern Region, accounting for approximately 18.8 percent of the U.S. population in 2002, had an estimated 15.8 percent of the Nation's violent crimes. The estimated number of violent crimes, 225,841, was down 2.3 percent from the prior year's estimate. The 2002 violent crime rate of 416.5 per 100,000 inhabitants was also down, 2.8 percent, since 2001. The Northeastern Region had the lowest murder rate among the four regions. The estimated rate of 4.1 murders per 100,000 persons was a 3.7 percent decrease from the 2001 rate. (See Tables 3 and 4.)

The Midwest

Accounting for 22.6 percent of the population in 2002, the Midwestern Region experienced 19.4 percent of the Nation's estimated violent crimes, a decline of 0.9 percent from the previous year's numbers. The region had an estimated 276,763 offenses, or a violent crime rate of 424.9 per 100,000 persons, a 1.4 percent decrease from 2001. The estimated murder rate of 5.1 per 100,000 in population reflected a 3.5 percent decrease from the prior year's figures. (See Tables 3 and 4.)

The South

The Southern Region, the most populous section of the country accounting for 35.8 percent of the total U.S. population in 2002, had 41.4 percent of the total violent crimes, an estimated 590,086 offenses. The estimated violent crime rate of 571.0 per 100,000 persons was 2.0 percent lower than the 2001 rate. However, the South's murder rate increased slightly to 6.8 murders per 100,000 inhabitants, up 0.7 percent from the previous year's rate. (See Tables 3 and 4.)

The West

Approximately 22.8 percent of the U.S. population resided in the Western Region of the country; the West accounted for 23.4 percent of total violent crimes. The volume of violent crimes, 333,635, decreased 0.5 percent from the 2001 figure. The violent crime rate was measured at 508.2 per 100,000 inhabitants, a decrease of 2.1 percent from the rate calculated for 2001. The estimated murder rate, however, increased 4.1 percent from the 2001 rate to 5.8 murders per 100,000 inhabitants. (See Tables 3 and 4.)

Population Groups: Trends and Rates

The Nation's cities experienced a cumulative decline of 1.9 percent since 2001 in the number of violent crimes that occurred. Those cities with populations of 500,000 to 999,999 showed the greatest decline, 3.9 percent. The smallest decline was recorded by cities in the 50,000 to 99,999 population group range, 1.0 percent. In 2002, violent crimes decreased 1.2 percent in the Nation's rural counties from the 2001 estimate; however, suburban counties experienced a 1.0 percent increase. (See Table 12.)

Cities collectively had a rate of 624.6 violent crimes per 100,000 individuals. The violent crime rate in cities ranged from 326.5 in those with populations of 10,000 to 24,999 to 1,029.9 in those with populations in excess of 250,000. Rural counties had a rate of 232.2 violent crimes per 100,000 persons, and suburban counties had a rate of 352.1. (See Table 16.)

Weapons Distribution

The UCR Program collects data on the weapons used to commit murder, robbery, and aggravated assault. During 2002, hands, fists, feet, etc. were the predominant weapons used to commit these offenses. Such personal weapons were used in 31.2 percent of the violent crimes, firearms were involved in 26.8 percent, and knives or cutting instruments were used in 14.9 percent. Other types of weapons were used in 27.1 percent of these violent offenses. (Based on Tables 19 and 2.10.) The UCR Program does not collect data on weapons for the crime of forcible rape.

Clearances '

In the UCR Program, a crime is considered cleared when it is resolved either by arrest or by exceptional means, i.e., when some reason outside the control of law enforcement prevents the offender's arrest. In 2002, law enforcement cleared 46.8 percent of violent crime offenses. The highest percentage of clearances involved the crime of murder, 64.0 percent. Law enforcement cleared 56.5 percent of aggravated assaults, 44.5 percent of forcible rapes, and 25.7 percent of robberies. (See Table 25.)

A review of clearance data by population group indicated that the Nation's cities collectively cleared 44.5 percent of violent crimes, suburban counties cleared 54.0 percent, and rural counties cleared 61.4 percent of the violent crimes brought to the attention of law enforcement. Among cities, those under 10,000 in population cleared the greatest percentage of violent crimes, 58.9 percent. (See Table 25.) Regionally, the highest percentage of violent crime clearances for 2002 was reported by the Northeastern states, 52.2 percent. Law enforcement in the South cleared 47.2 percent of violent crimes; in the West, 46.0 percent; and in the Midwest, 42.9 percent of violent crimes. (See Table 26.)

Clearances and Juveniles

When an offender under the age of 18 is cited to appear in juvenile court or

Table 2.2

Violent Crime by Month
Percent Distribution, 1998-2002

Month	1998	1999	2000	2001	2002
January	8.4	8.2	7.9	7.7	7.9
February	7.2	7.1	7.2	6.7	6.7
March	8.1	7.9	8.1	7.9	7.9
April	8.0	8.1	8.1	8.1	8.1
May	8.7	8.8	8.9	8.7	8.7
June	8.5	8.5	8.6	8.7	8.8
July	9.1	9.3	9.3	9.3	9.3
August	9.2	9.1	9.1	8.9	9.3
September	8.6	8.4	8.6	8.7	9.2
October	8.5	8.6	8.7	9.0	8.6
November	7.7	8.0	7.8	8.2	7.7
December	7.8	8.0	7.7	8.1	7.7

before other juvenile authorities, the UCR Program records that incident as cleared by arrest, even though a physical arrest may not have occurred. In addition, as defined by the Program, clearances involving both adult and juvenile offenders are classified as adult clearances.

Approximately 11.9 percent of violent crime clearances for 2002 involved only juvenile offenders. Of those crimes cleared by the Nation's cities, collectively, 12.1 percent involved only juveniles. In suburban counties, juvenile clearances accounted for 12.3 percent of the overall violent crime clearances, and in rural counties, juvenile clearances accounted for 9.6 percent of offenses cleared. (See Table 28.)

Arrests

During 2002, law enforcement made an estimated 620,510 arrests for violent crimes. Approximately 76.1 percent of violent crime arrestees were charged with aggravated assault, 17.0 percent with robbery, 4.6 percent with forcible rape, and 2.3 percent with murder. The estimated number of arrests for violent crimes comprised 4.5 percent of all arrests nationally and 27.8 percent of the eight Part I offenses. (See Table 29 and Appendix II.)

For every 100,000 inhabitants, law enforcement effected 217.9 arrests for violent crime overall. A breakdown of violent crime arrests showed 4.9 arrests for murder, 9.8 arrests for forcible rape, 37.7 arrests for robbery, and 165.5 arrests for aggravated assault. (See Table 31.) An examination of the violent crime arrest rates for 2002 by city population size showed that the arrest rate in the Nation's cities ranged from 357.9 in cities with more than 250,000 inhabitants to 158.5 arrests per 100,000 inhabitants in cities with 10,000 to 24,999 residents. Suburban counties experienced a violent crime arrest rate of 168.7 arrests for every 100,000 persons, and rural counties a rate of 132.1 arrests. (See Table 31.)

Regionally, the Western states reported 275.6 violent crime arrests for each 100,000 inhabitants. The Southern states had a rate of 196.8 arrests; the Midwestern states, 193.5 arrests; and the Northeastern states, 188.9 violent crime arrests per 100,000 individuals. (See Table 30.)

Arrestees

Nationally, violent crime arrests were down 0.8 percent from the 2001 figure. The number of adults arrested for violent crimes decreased 0.4 percent, and the number of juveniles arrested decreased 3.0 percent from the 2001 number. (See Table 36.)

By gender, males made up 82.6 percent of violent crime arrestees. Females accounted for 10.8 percent of all murder arrestees, 1.4 percent of forcible rape arrestees, 10.3 percent of robbery arrestees, and 20.2 percent of aggravated assault arrestees. (See Table 42.)

A review of arrest data by race showed that whites made up 59.7 percent of all violent crime arrestees, with blacks comprising 38.0 percent, and other races, 2.3 percent. Fifty percent of the murder arrestees during 2002 were black, and 47.7 percent of arrestees were white. The remainder were individuals of other races. (See Table 43.)

By age, 43.7 percent of violent crime arrestees in 2002 were under the age of 25, and 14.9 percent were under age 18. (See Table 41.)

Definition

Murder and nonnegligent manslaughter, as defined in the Uniform Crime Reporting (UCR) Program, is the willful (nonnegligent) killing of one human being by another.

The classification of this offense, as for all other offenses that make up the Crime Index, is based solely on police investigation as opposed to the determination of a court, medical examiner, coroner, jury, or other judicial body. The Program does not include the following situations in the count for this offense classification: deaths caused by negligence, suicide, or accident; justifiable homicides; and attempts to murder or assaults to murder, which are scored as aggravated assaults.

Trend

Year	Number of offenses	Rate per 100,000 inhabitants
2001	16,037	5.6
2002	16,204	5.6
Percent change	+1.0	*

* Less than one-tenth of 1 percent.

National Volume, Trends, and Rates

An estimated 16,204 murders took place in 2002. This figure represents a 1.0 percent increase over the 2001 volume. A comparison of the data from 5 and 10 years ago showed that the 2002 estimated volume decreased 4.5 percent from the 1998 estimate, and it fell 33.9 percent from the estimate for 1993. (See Table 1.)

During 2002, the murder rate was estimated at 5.6 crimes per 100,000 inhabitants. The rate remained virtually unchanged from the rate for 2001. Five-year and 10-year trend analyses revealed that the 2002 murder rate was 10.5 percent lower than the rate in 1998 and 40.9 percent below the estimated murder rate in 1993. (See Table 1.)

Murder accounted for less than 1 percent of the offenses that make up the Crime Index reported in 2002. Among violent crimes, 1.1 percent were the offense of murder. (Based on Table 1.)

Community Types

When presenting crime data, the UCR Program designates three types of communities: Metropolitan Statistical Areas (MSAs), cities outside of MSAs, and rural counties. In 2002, MSAs, accounting for an estimated 80 percent of the Nation's population, had an estimated 87.8 percent of the Nation's murders. This equated to a murder rate of 6.2 offenses per 100,000 persons in MSAs. Cities outside of MSAs, with 8 percent of the population, had 4.4 percent of total murder offenses with a rate of 3.2 murder offenses per 100,000 inhabitants. Rural areas, making up 12 percent of the overall population, had an estimated 7.7 percent of murder offenses. Rural areas had an estimated rate of

Figure 2.6

Murder

Percent Change from 1998

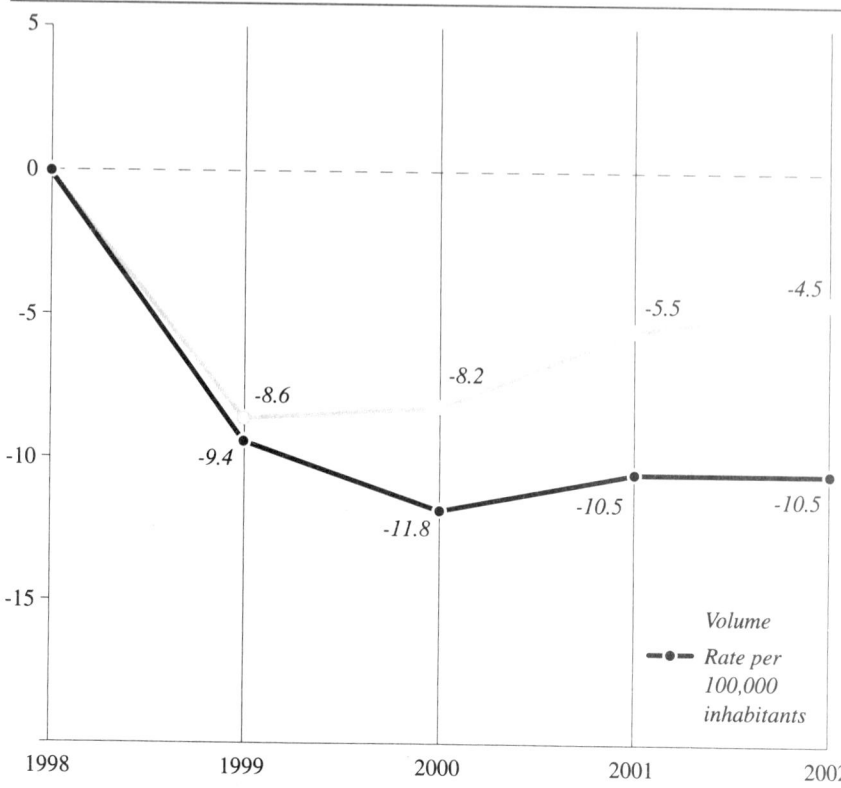

Volume

—•— Rate per 100,000 inhabitants

3.6 murders per 100,000 in population. (See Table 2.)

Regional Offense Trends and Rates

The UCR Program divides the United States into four regions for data analysis: the Northeast, the Midwest, the South, and the West. (Appendix III provides more information on UCR regional definitions.) An examination of 2002 murder data showed the following information regarding the Nation's four regions.

The Northeast

Nearly 19 percent (18.8) of the Nation's population in 2002 resided in the Northeast; 13.6 percent of the estimated murder offenses for the same year were reported there. The Northeast had 2,203 murder offenses, a 3.2 percent decrease from the 2001 estimate. The 2002 murder rate per 100,000 inhabitants was 4.1, which was an estimated 3.7 percent rate decrease when compared to the rate of the previous year. (See Tables 3 and 4.)

Table 2.3

Murder by Month
Percent Distribution, 1998-2002

Month	1998	1999	2000	2001¹	2002
January	9.1	8.8	8.4	7.9	8.2
February	7.2	7.1	7.3	6.2	6.8
March	8.3	7.6	7.6	7.1	7.8
April	7.7	7.7	7.7	7.9	7.8
May	8.4	8.3	8.5	8.3	8.1
June	8.4	8.1	8.5	8.5	8.2
July	8.7	9.1	9.3	9.5	9.6
August	9.2	9.1	9.4	9.0	9.1
September	8.3	8.7	8.3	8.6	9.6
October	8.3	8.4	8.7	9.3	8.5
November	7.6	8.2	7.7	8.5	7.8
December	8.8	8.8	8.7	9.2	8.5

¹ The murder and nonnegligent homicides that occurred as a result of the events of September 11, 2001, are not included.

Table 2.4

Murder Victims
by Race and Sex, 2002

Race	Total	Sex		
		Male	Female	Unknown
White	6,757	4,852	1,905	0
Black	6,730	5,544	1,184	2
Other race	377	256	121	0
Unknown race	190	127	41	22
Total	14,054	10,779	3,251	24

The Midwest

With 22.6 percent of the U.S. population, the Midwest accounted for 20.4 percent of the country's murders. The estimated 3,298 murders in the Midwest represented a 3.0 percent decrease from the region's murder total in 2001. The 2002 murder rate per 100,000 population was 5.1, a decrease of 3.5 percent from the previous year's rate. (See Tables 3 and 4.)

The South

The South, the Nation's most populous region (35.8 percent of the total population), accounted for 43.1 percent of the murders in the United States. The estimated 6,982 murders in the South during 2002 were an increase of 2.0 percent over the previous year's estimate. The murder rate during 2002 was 6.8 murders per 100,000 inhabitants, an increase of 0.7 percent when compared to the 2001 rate. (See Tables 3 and 4.)

The West

With 22.8 percent of the country's population, the West accounted for 23.0 percent of the national murder volume, or an estimated 3,721 murder offenses. This volume was a 5.8 percent increase from the 2001 estimate. The West's 2002 murder rate was 5.7 murder offenses per 100,000 persons, a 4.1 percent increase from the 2001 rate. (See Tables 3 and 4.)

Population Groups: Trends and Rates

Murder trends in 2002 varied greatly among cities, suburban counties, and rural counties. Two-year trend data (2001–2002) indicated that the Nation's cities collectively experienced a 0.6 percent decrease in murder offenses. Among population groups labeled *city*, cities with less than 10,000 inhabitants had the largest decline in murder, 15.3 percent, and cities with populations of 50,000 to 99,999 had the largest increase, 7.2 percent. Suburban counties had an 11.7 percent increase in murder. In rural counties, however, murder decreased from 2001 to 2002 by 2.3 percent. (See Table 12.)

Among city population groups, rate of murder in 2002 ranged from a high of 13.2 murders per 100,000 inhabitants in cities with populations of 250,000 and over to a low of 2.4 murders per 100,000 in cities with under 10,000 in population. Collectively, the Nation's cities had a rate of 7.0 murders per 100,000 inhabitants. Suburban counties had a rate of 4.0 murder offenses per 100,000 population and rural counties, 3.8 murder offenses per 100,000 inhabitants. (See Table 16.)

Supplementary Homicide Reports

During 2002, law enforcement agencies contributing data to the UCR Program submitted Supplementary Homicide Reports (SHRs) for 14,054 homicides. The SHR supplies data on the age, sex, and race of both the victim and the offender; the type of weapon used; the relationship of the victim to the offender; and the circumstance surrounding the incident.

Victims

Based on 2002 SHR data provided (where age, sex, or race were known for the victims), 90.1 percent of murder victims were adults. Males accounted for 76.8 percent of murder victims. Just over 8 percent (8.2 percent) of male victims and 15.3 percent of female victims were under the age of 18. By race, 48.7 percent of murder victims were white, 48.5 percent were black, and 2.7 percent were other races. (Based on Table 2.5.)

Offenders

Of those who committed murder in 2002, 90.3 percent were identified as male; 91.7 percent of the male offenders were over 18 years of age. A racial breakdown of murder offenders for whom race was known showed that 49.8 percent were black, 47.8 percent were white, and 2.4 percent were persons of other races. (See Table 2.6.)

Data from single victim/single offender incidents indicated that 92.3 percent of black victims were slain by black offenders. Similarly, the majority of white victims—84.7 percent—were

Table 2.5

Murder Victims
by Age, Sex, and Race, 2002

Age	Total	Sex			Race			
		Male	Female	Unknown	White	Black	Other	Unknown
Total	14,054	10,779	3,251	24	6,757	6,730	377	190
Percent distribution [1]	100.0	76.7	23.1	0.2	48.1	47.9	2.7	1.4
Under 18 [2]	1,357	867	489	1	689	610	45	13
Under 22 [2]	3,398	2,624	772	2	1,581	1,683	104	30
18 and over [2]	12,406	9,703	2,699	4	5,945	6,009	331	121
Infant (under 1)	180	96	84	0	102	71	4	3
1 to 4	328	180	147	1	176	134	14	4
5 to 8	86	35	51	0	50	33	3	0
9 to 12	92	50	42	0	53	35	4	0
13 to 16	390	281	109	0	180	196	11	3
17 to 19	1,184	1,018	166	0	519	615	39	11
20 to 24	2,756	2,356	398	2	1,115	1,560	58	23
25 to 29	2,059	1,746	313	0	809	1,173	48	29
30 to 34	1,587	1,212	375	0	667	851	54	15
35 to 39	1,337	976	359	2	676	624	23	14
40 to 44	1,137	812	325	0	621	470	40	6
45 to 49	856	624	232	0	487	337	25	7
50 to 54	566	412	154	0	333	214	16	3
55 to 59	353	246	107	0	237	98	14	4
60 to 64	245	181	64	0	170	60	10	5
65 to 69	162	103	59	0	116	44	2	0
70 to 74	156	96	60	0	115	35	4	2
75 and over	289	146	143	0	208	69	7	5
Unknown	291	209	63	19	123	111	1	56

[1] Because of rounding, the percentages may not add to 100.0.
[2] Does not include unknown ages.

Table 2.6

Murder Offenders
by Age, Sex, and Race, 2002

Age	Total	Sex			Race			
		Male	Female	Unknown	White	Black	Other	Unknown
Total	15,813	10,285	1,108	4,420	5,356	5,579	274	4,604
Percent distribution [1]	100.0	65.0	7.0	28.0	33.9	35.3	1.7	29.1
Under 18 [2]	848	770	77	1	389	424	26	9
Under 22 [2]	3,402	3,128	269	5	1,499	1,770	94	39
18 and over [2]	9,525	8,511	996	18	4,714	4,464	241	106
Infant (under 1)	0	0	0	0	0	0	0	0
1 to 4	1	0	1	0	0	1	0	0
5 to 8	1	1	0	0	0	1	0	0
9 to 12	26	18	7	1	7	18	0	1
13 to 16	446	401	45	0	227	198	15	6
17 to 19	1,507	1,412	92	3	648	802	42	15
20 to 24	2,916	2,656	256	4	1,265	1,547	73	31
25 to 29	1,644	1,492	150	2	769	819	37	19
30 to 34	1,120	986	132	2	573	506	27	14
35 to 39	865	749	116	0	460	385	13	7
40 to 44	638	522	115	1	367	242	21	8
45 to 49	493	425	68	0	298	172	20	3
50 to 54	311	262	44	5	195	103	7	6
55 to 59	168	150	18	0	117	41	6	4
60 to 64	83	72	11	0	59	22	2	0
65 to 69	49	41	8	0	38	9	2	0
70 to 74	45	38	6	1	32	12	0	1
75 and over	60	56	4	0	48	10	2	0
Unknown	5,440	1,004	35	4,401	253	691	7	4,489

[1] Because of rounding, the percentages may not add to 100.0.
[2] Does not include unknown ages.

murdered by white offenders. (See Table 2.8.)

Weapons

The SHRs where weapon type was provided showed that 71.1 percent of murder incidents involved a firearm. Among the homicides in which firearms were the weapon, 76.6 percent involved handguns; 5.1 percent, rifles; 5.1 percent, shotguns; and 13.2 percent, other type or unknown firearms. Offenders used knives or cutting instruments in 13.4 percent of the murders they committed, personal weapons (hands, fists, feet, etc.) in 7.1 percent, and blunt objects in 5.1 percent of the incidents. Other weapon types (poison, arson, narcotics, etc.) accounted for the remainder of weapon types used in the commission of murder. (See Table 2.10.)

Victim/Offender Relationships

Of the 14,054 homicides for which 2002 SHR data were submitted, the relationship of the victim to the offender was unknown for 42.8 percent of the

victims. An analysis of the 57.2 percent of the victims for whom the relationships to their offenders were known revealed the following: 24.4 percent of victims were murdered by strangers, and 75.6 percent of the victims knew their assailants. Among the incidents in which the victims knew their killers, 12.7 percent of the victims were related to their murderer, and 30.5 percent of the victims were acquainted with their offenders. Husbands and boyfriends killed 32.1 percent of female victims, and wives and girlfriends murdered 2.7 percent of male victims. (Based on Table 2.12.)

Circumstances

Supplemental data submitted in 2002 indicated that felonies (rape, robbery, arson, etc.) accounted for 16.5 percent of the circumstances surrounding murder offenses; another 0.5 percent of murder offense circumstances were suspected of being felonious in nature. Arguments resulted in 27.5 percent of the murders, and 23.0 percent of the murders involved other types of circumstances (brawls due to the influence of drugs or alcohol, juvenile gang killings, sniper attacks, etc.). Circumstances were unknown in 32.6 percent of the incidents. (Based on Table 2.14.)

Clearances

Clearances occur either by arrest or by exceptional means, i.e., when elements beyond the control of law enforcement

prevent the placing of formal charges against the offender. (Section III provides more information regarding clearances.) During 2002, law enforcement cleared 64.0 percent of the murders nationwide, making murder the most frequently cleared Crime Index offense. (See Table 25.) Juveniles accounted for 5.0 percent of the total clearances for murder, the lowest percentage of juvenile involvement among the individual Crime Index offenses. (See Table 28.)

Law enforcement in the Nation's cities collectively cleared 62.0 percent of the murder offenses reported within their jurisdictions. Among city population groupings, cities with populations under 10,000 had the greatest murder clearance percentage, 73.7 percent. The largest cities, those with populations of 250,000 and greater, cleared 57.8 percent of the murders reported in their jurisdictions, the least of all city population groupings. Additionally, suburban counties and rural counties cleared 66.6 percent and 78.9 percent, respectively, of reported murders. (See Table 25.)

Arrests

Total Arrests

During 2002, there were an estimated 14,158 arrests nationwide for the offense of murder. (See Table 29.) Adults accounted for 90.4 percent of murder arrestees. (Based on Table 38.) Overall, 51.1 percent of those arrested

---

Table 2.7

Murder Victim/Offender Relationship
by Age, 2002

[Single victim/single offender]

| Age of victim | Total | Age of offender | | |
		Under 18	18 and over	Unknown
Total	7,005	344	6,106	555
Under 18	758	98	624	36
18 and over	6,144	243	5,402	499
Unknown	103	3	80	20

Table 2.8

Murder Victim/Offender Relationship
by Race and Sex, 2002

[Single victim/single offender]

| Race of victim | Total | Race of offender | | | | Sex of offender | | |
		White	Black	Other	Unknown	Male	Female	Unknown
White victims	3,582	3,000	483	58	41	3,169	372	41
Black victims	3,137	227	2,852	11	47	2,768	320	49
Other race victims	192	51	28	109	4	169	19	4
Unknown race	94	31	23	2	38	45	11	38

| Sex of victim | Total | Race of offender | | | | Sex of offender | | |
		White	Black	Other	Unknown	Male	Female	Unknown
Male victims	4,931	2,192	2,545	121	73	4,328	528	75
Female victims	1,980	1,086	818	57	19	1,778	183	19
Unknown sex	94	31	23	2	38	45	11	38

Table 2.9

Murder, Types of Weapons Used
Percent Distribution by Region, 2002

Region	Total all weapons[1]	Firearms	Knives or cutting instruments	Unknown or other dangerous weapons	Personal weapons (hands, fists, feet, etc.)[2]
Total	100.0	66.7	12.6	14.1	6.6
Northeast	100.0	62.6	17.4	12.6	7.5
Midwest	100.0	66.4	10.3	16.5	6.8
South	100.0	66.9	12.1	14.6	6.4
West	100.0	68.9	12.3	12.4	6.4

[1] Because of rounding, the percentages may not add to 100.0.
[2] Pushed is included in personal weapons.

Table 2.10

Murder Victims
by Weapon, 1998-2002

Weapons	1998	1999	2000	2001[1]	2002
Total	14,209	13,011	13,230	14,061	14,054
Total firearms:	9,220	8,480	8,661	8,890	9,369
Handguns	7,405	6,658	6,778	6,931	7,176
Rifles	546	400	411	386	480
Shotguns	626	531	485	511	476
Other guns	16	92	53	59	74
Firearms, type not stated	627	799	934	1,003	1,163
Knives or cutting instruments	1,890	1,712	1,782	1,831	1,767
Blunt objects (clubs, hammers, etc.)	750	756	617	680	666
Personal weapons (hands, fists, feet, etc.)[2]	959	885	927	961	933
Poison	6	11	8	12	23
Explosives	10	0	9	4	11
Fire	132	133	134	109	104
Narcotics	33	26	20	37	48
Drowning	28	28	15	23	18
Strangulation	213	190	166	153	143
Asphyxiation	99	106	92	116	103
Other weapons or weapons not stated	869	684	799	1,245	869

[1] The murder and nonnegligent homicides that occurred as a result of the events of September 11, 2001, are not included.
[2] Pushed is included in personal weapons.

Table 2.11

Murder Victims by Age
by Weapon, 2002

Age	Total murder victims	Firearms	Knives or cutting instruments	Blunt objects (clubs, hammers, etc.)	Personal weapons (hands, fists, feet, etc.)[1]	Poison	Explosives	Fire	Narcotics	Strangulation	Asphyxiation	Other weapon or weapon not stated[2]
Total	14,054	9,369	1,767	666	933	23	11	104	48	143	103	887
Percent distribution[3]	100.0	66.7	12.6	4.7	6.6	0.2	0.1	0.7	0.3	1.0	0.7	6.3
Under 18[4]	1,357	661	90	52	299	5	5	21	11	16	41	156
Under 22[4]	3,398	2,358	256	94	345	6	5	29	14	23	47	221
18 and over[4]	12,406	8,568	1,646	595	607	18	6	76	36	125	58	671
Infant (under 1)	180	9	4	12	91	0	1	0	3	0	19	41
1 to 4	328	45	10	19	166	2	1	7	3	2	12	61
5 to 8	86	26	14	2	11	2	2	7	1	2	7	12
9 to 12	92	56	11	2	4	1	0	2	0	3	0	13
13 to 16	390	299	30	11	17	0	0	5	3	6	2	17
17 to 19	1,184	972	101	23	32	1	1	3	4	6	3	38
20 to 24	2,756	2,244	250	55	72	0	3	9	7	7	5	104
25 to 29	2,059	1,628	227	42	56	0	0	11	2	16	7	70
30 to 34	1,587	1,168	197	45	57	0	2	14	5	15	4	80
35 to 39	1,337	864	193	74	78	2	0	7	5	25	11	78
40 to 44	1,137	663	221	63	84	3	1	9	1	13	8	71
45 to 49	856	461	151	80	74	0	0	8	1	15	3	63
50 to 54	566	312	101	48	50	2	0	3	2	3	1	44
55 to 59	353	172	66	46	23	0	0	1	0	7	2	36
60 to 64	245	107	41	37	16	0	0	7	1	7	4	25
65 to 69	162	67	27	20	15	1	0	0	3	5	5	19
70 to 74	156	53	35	28	14	0	0	0	0	6	2	18
75 and over	289	83	57	40	46	9	0	4	6	3	4	37
Unknown	291	140	31	19	27	0	0	7	1	2	4	60

[1] Pushed is included in personal weapons.
[2] Includes drowning.
[3] Because of rounding, the percentages may not add to 100.0.
[4] Does not include unknown ages.

Table 2.12

Murder Circumstances by Relationship,[1] 2002

Circumstances	Total murder victims	Husband	Wife	Mother	Father	Son	Daughter	Brother	Sister	Other family	Acquaintance	Friend	Boyfriend	Girlfriend	Neighbor	Employee	Employer	Stranger	Unknown
Total	14,054	133	601	113	110	239	210	87	20	271	3,217	352	154	444	110	5	10	1,963	6,015
Felony type total:	2,314	4	17	4	3	8	9	4	1	32	586	50	8	18	16	0	1	595	958
Rape	43	0	0	0	0	0	1	0	1	3	11	2	0	0	1	0	0	7	17
Robbery	1,092	0	0	0	2	0	0	2	0	13	221	10	4	1	11	0	0	396	432
Burglary	96	0	1	0	0	0	0	0	0	4	21	1	0	1	1	0	1	39	26
Larceny-theft	15	0	0	0	0	0	0	0	0	0	2	0	0	0	0	0	0	8	5
Motor vehicle theft	16	0	0	1	0	0	0	0	0	0	1	1	0	0	0	0	0	7	6
Arson	59	0	1	1	0	1	2	0	0	1	9	3	0	3	0	0	0	17	21
Prostitution and commercialized vice	8	0	0	0	0	0	0	0	0	0	3	0	0	0	0	0	0	2	3
Other sex offenses	8	0	0	0	0	1	1	0	0	0	3	0	0	2	0	0	0	0	1
Narcotic drug laws	657	0	1	0	1	0	0	1	0	1	245	22	2	2	0	0	0	67	315
Gambling	5	0	0	0	0	0	0	0	0	0	2	0	0	0	0	0	0	1	2
Other - not specified	315	4	14	2	0	6	5	1	0	10	68	11	1	9	3	0	0	51	130
Suspected felony type	67	0	0	1	0	0	0	0	0	0	6	1	0	0	0	0	0	2	57
Other than felony type total:	7,097	109	516	93	88	199	184	69	17	202	2,179	257	134	348	77	4	7	999	1,615
Romantic triangle	130	1	9	0	0	1	0	1	0	9	57	10	2	14	1	0	0	15	10
Child killed by babysitter	38	0	0	0	0	1	2	0	0	7	23	3	0	0	0	0	0	1	1
Brawl due to influence of alcohol	153	1	6	0	3	0	2	0	0	5	68	10	1	4	0	0	0	41	12
Brawl due to influence of narcotics	84	0	2	0	1	0	0	2	0	3	36	3	0	3	1	0	0	8	25
Argument over money or property	203	0	4	5	1	0	0	0	0	7	104	13	0	3	8	0	1	17	40
Other arguments	3,527	81	334	45	47	52	29	51	11	111	1,154	170	105	243	48	4	3	496	543
Gangland killings	73	0	0	0	0	0	0	0	0	0	23	0	0	0	0	0	0	20	30
Juvenile gang killings	911	0	0	0	0	0	0	0	0	1	221	0	0	0	0	0	0	200	489
Institutional killings	12	0	0	0	0	0	0	0	0	0	9	0	0	0	0	0	0	1	2
Sniper attack	11	0	1	0	0	0	0	0	0	0	0	0	0	0	0	0	0	7	3
Other - not specified	1,955	26	160	43	36	145	151	15	6	59	484	48	26	81	19	0	3	193	460
Unknown	4,576	20	68	15	19	32	17	14	2	37	446	44	12	78	17	1	2	367	3,385

[1] Relationship is that of victim to offender.

Figure 2.7

Murder by relationship[1]

Percent Distribution, Volume by Known Relationship, 2002

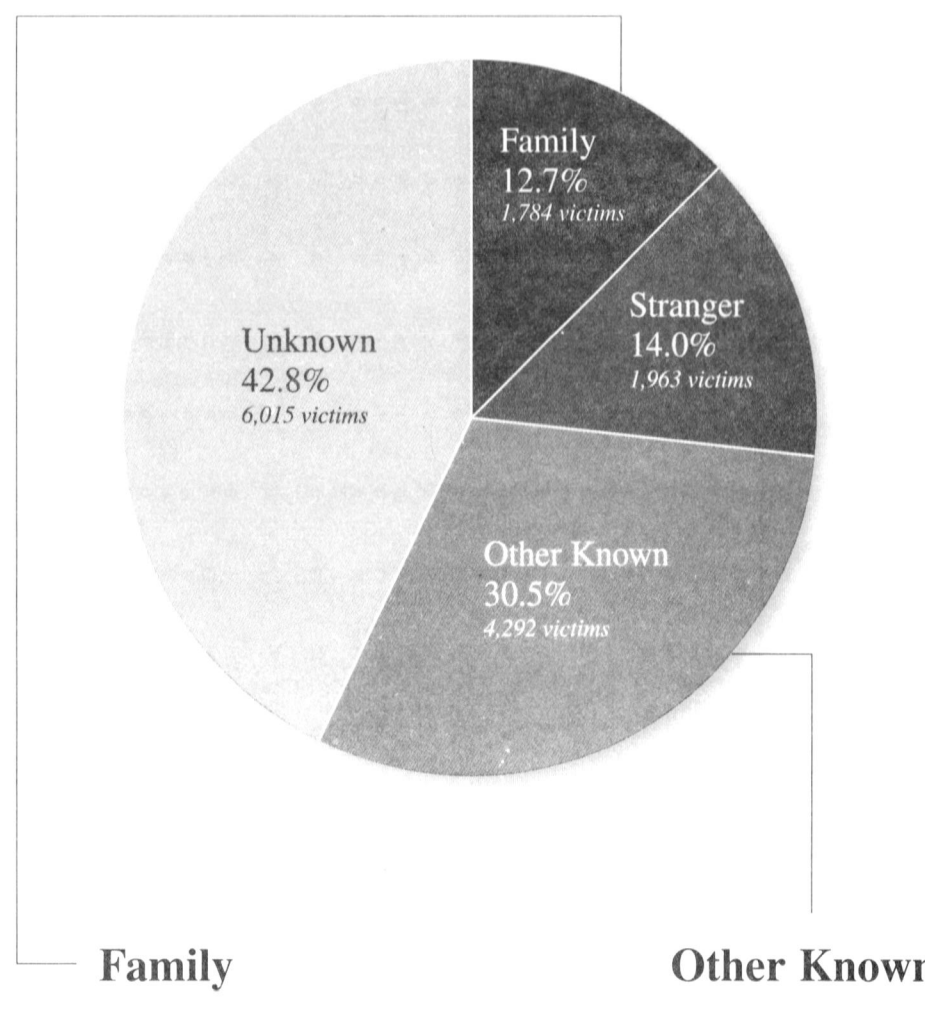

Family

Husband	133
Wife	601
Mother	113
Father	110
Son	239
Daughter	210
Brother	87
Sister	20
Other Family	271

0 100 200 300 400 500 600

Other Known

Acquaintance	3,217
Friend	352
Boyfriend	154
Girlfriend	444
Neighbor	110
Employee	5
Employer	10

0 100 200 300 400 500 600

[1] Relationship is that of victim to offender.
Figures are based on 14,054 murder victims for whom Supplementary Homicide Report data were received.

Table 2.13

Murder Circumstances by Weapon, 2002

Circumstances	Total murder victims	Total firearms	Handguns	Rifles	Shotguns	Other guns or type not stated	Knives or cutting instruments	Blunt objects (clubs, hammers, etc.)	Personal weapons (hands, fists, feet, etc.)	Poison	Pushed or thrown out window	Explosives	Fire	Narcotics	Drowning	Strangulation	Asphyxiation	Other
Total	14,054	9,369	7,176	480	476	1,237	1,767	666	929	23	4	11	104	48	18	143	103	869
Felony type total:	2,314	1,640	1,304	63	64	209	198	116	99	1	1	5	44	12	0	38	26	134
Rape	43	6	4	0	0	2	9	5	9	0	0	0	0	0	0	9	5	0
Robbery	1,092	797	664	24	34	75	93	74	47	0	0	0	3	0	0	17	10	51
Burglary	96	56	45	2	6	3	18	10	5	0	0	0	0	0	0	1	1	5
Larceny-theft	15	9	8	0	0	1	2	2	1	0	0	0	0	0	0	0	0	1
Motor vehicle theft	16	9	4	2	1	2	2	0	0	0	0	1	0	0	0	0	0	4
Arson	59	3	3	0	0	0	0	0	1	0	0	4	35	0	0	4	0	12
Prostitution and commercialized vice	8	1	1	0	0	0	2	2	0	0	0	0	0	0	0	1	0	2
Other sex offenses	8	0	0	0	0	0	1	1	5	0	0	0	0	0	0	0	1	0
Narcotic drug laws	657	553	425	22	14	92	39	13	11	0	1	0	2	12	0	1	2	23
Gambling	5	5	5	0	0	0	0	0	0	0	0	0	0	0	0	0	0	0
Other - not specified	315	201	145	13	9	34	32	9	20	1	0	0	4	0	0	5	7	36
Suspected felony type	67	53	40	7	1	5	7	2	0	0	0	0	0	0	0	1	0	4
Other than felony type total:	7,097	4,522	3,532	281	284	425	1,072	330	639	20	1	6	29	26	12	69	55	316
Romantic triangle	130	92	64	11	4	13	27	3	3	0	1	0	0	1	0	0	1	2
Child killed by babysitter	38	0	0	0	0	0	0	4	27	0	0	0	0	0	0	0	1	6
Brawl due to influence of alcohol	153	72	60	2	5	5	38	12	23	0	0	0	0	0	0	2	0	6
Brawl due to influence of narcotics	84	65	50	4	4	7	5	6	2	0	0	0	0	0	0	3	0	3
Argument over money or property	203	134	110	6	8	10	42	12	9	0	0	2	0	2	2	0	0	1
Other arguments	3,527	2,166	1,726	134	149	157	733	196	253	4	0	2	11	0	2	35	17	108
Gangland killings	73	68	59	2	0	7	3	0	1	0	0	0	0	0	0	0	0	1
Juvenile gang killings	911	870	752	37	18	63	23	4	3	0	0	0	0	0	0	0	0	11
Institutional killings	12	1	0	0	1	0	1	1	7	0	0	0	0	0	0	0	2	0
Sniper attack	11	11	3	7	0	1	0	0	0	0	0	0	0	0	0	0	0	0
Other - not specified	1,955	1,043	708	78	95	162	200	92	311	16	0	2	18	23	10	28	34	178
Unknown	4,576	3,154	2,300	129	127	598	490	218	191	2	2	0	31	10	6	35	22	415

for murder were under the age of 25. (See Table 41.)

Arrest Rates

Based upon 2002 arrest data and population figures, the Nation's rate of arrest for murder was 4.9 arrests per 100,000 inhabitants. By region, the South and the Midwest each had murder arrest rates of 5.7, the West had a rate of 4.6, and the Northeast experienced 3.2 murder arrests per 100,000 population. (See Table 30.)

Among population groups, the Nation's cities collectively had a murder arrest rate of 5.2 per 100,000 persons. The largest cities, those with 250,000 and over in population, registered the highest rate—10.4 murder arrests per 100,000 inhabitants. The lowest rate, 2.2 murder arrests per 100,000, was calculated for cities with 10,000 to 24,999 residents. Murder arrest rates for rural counties and suburban counties were, respectively, 4.0 and 4.3 arrests per 100,000 persons. (See Table 31.)

Arrest Trends

A comparison of 2002 murder arrest data to those of 2001 indicated a 1.9 percent decrease for the period. Arrests of adults also decreased, 2.2 percent. However, juvenile arrests increased 1.5 percent. By gender, murder arrests of males increased 0.1 percent, and those of females fell 15.2 percent. (See Tables 36 and 37.)

The 5-year trend data showed that overall murder arrests for 2002 fell 10.7 percent from the 1998 arrest level. Arrests of juveniles dropped 35.6 percent, but arrests of adults decreased 7.0 percent. An analysis of gender data for 1998 through 2002 showed that arrests of males for murder declined 10.6 percent, and arrests of females for murder dropped 11.0 percent. (See Tables 34 and 35.)

From 1993 to 2002, murder arrests fell 40.9 percent. Arrests of juveniles were 64.3 percent under the 1993 figure, and arrests of adults were 36.3 percent lower. The 10-year trend also revealed that arrests of males for murder were down 41.5 percent; arrests of

Table 2.14

Murder Circumstances, 1998–2002

Circumstances	1998	1999	2000	2001[1]	2002
Total	14,209	13,011	13,230	14,061	14,054
Felony type total:	2,510	2,215	2,229	2,364	2,314
Rape	62	47	58	61	43
Robbery	1,243	1,057	1,077	1,080	1,092
Burglary	92	81	76	80	96
Larceny-theft	17	14	23	17	15
Motor vehicle theft	15	12	25	22	16
Arson	83	66	81	71	59
Prostitution and commercialized vice	15	8	6	5	8
Other sex offenses	20	19	10	7	8
Narcotic drug laws	682	581	589	575	657
Gambling	12	17	12	3	5
Other—not specified	269	313	272	443	315
Suspected felony type	104	65	60	72	67
Other than felony type total:	7,203	6,880	6,871	7,073	7,097
Romantic triangle	187	137	122	118	130
Child killed by babysitter	23	34	30	37	38
Brawl due to influence of alcohol	211	203	188	152	153
Brawl due to influence of narcotics	117	127	99	118	84
Argument over money or property	241	213	206	198	203
Other arguments	4,115	3,471	3,589	3,618	3,527
Gangland killings	73	122	65	76	73
Juvenile gang killings	625	580	653	862	911
Institutional killings	15	13	10	8	12
Sniper attack	16	5	8	7	11
Other—not specified	1,580	1,975	1,901	1,879	1,955
Unknown	4,392	3,851	4,070	4,552	4,576

[1] The murder and nonnegligent homicides that occurred as a result of the events of September 11, 2001, are not included.

Table 2.15

Murder Circumstances
by Victim Sex, 2002

Circumstances	Total murder victims	Male	Female	Unknown
Total	14,054	10,779	3,251	24
Felony type total:	2,314	1,894	419	1
Rape	43	3	40	0
Robbery	1,092	936	156	0
Burglary	96	68	28	0
Larceny-theft	15	14	1	0
Motor vehicle theft	16	14	2	0
Arson	59	28	31	0
Prostitution and commercialized vice	8	3	5	0
Other sex offenses	8	1	7	0
Narcotic drug laws	657	595	61	1
Gambling	5	5	0	0
Other—not specified	315	227	88	0
Suspected felony type	67	56	11	0
Other than felony type total:	7,097	5,193	1,897	7
Romantic triangle	130	89	41	0
Child killed by babysitter	38	15	23	0
Brawl due to influence of alcohol	153	131	22	0
Brawl due to influence of narcotics	84	72	12	0
Argument over money or property	203	165	38	0
Other arguments	3,527	2,567	957	3
Gangland killings	73	69	4	0
Juvenile gang killings	911	869	42	0
Institutional killings	12	11	1	0
Sniper attack	11	8	3	0
Other—not specified	1,955	1,197	754	4
Unknown	4,576	3,636	924	16

Table 2.16

Justifiable Homicide
by Weapon, Law Enforcement,[1] 1998-2002

Year	Total	Total firearms	Handguns	Rifles	Shotguns	Firearms, type not stated	Knives or cutting instruments	Other dangerous weapons	Personal weapons
1998	369	367	322	15	18	12	0	0	2
1999	308	305	274	11	15	5	0	1	2
2000	309	308	274	14	13	7	0	1	0
2001	378	375	318	25	11	21	0	3	0
2002	339	335	294	18	7	16	1	3	0

[1] The killing of a felon by a law enforcement officer in the line of duty.

Table 2.17

Justifiable Homicide
by Weapon, Private Citizen,[1] 1998-2002

Year	Total	Total firearms	Handguns	Rifles	Shotguns	Firearms, type not stated	Knives or cutting instruments	Other dangerous weapons	Personal weapons
1998	196	170	150	6	14	0	17	5	4
1999	192	158	137	5	10	6	18	9	7
2000	164	138	123	4	7	4	15	8	3
2001	222	183	143	10	13	17	26	6	7
2002	225	184	154	11	13	6	26	9	6

[1] The killing of a felon, during the commission of a felony, by a private citizen.

females were 35.5 percent lower than arrests of females for murder in 1993. (See Tables 32 and 33.)

Arrest Distribution by Age, Sex, and Race

According to 2002 arrest data, by sex, males comprised 89.2 percent of all those arrested for murder. (See Table 42.) By race, blacks accounted for 50.0 percent of the murder arrestees; whites, 47.7 percent; and other races (American Indian or Alaskan Native; and Asian or Pacific Islander) made up 2.3 percent of the murder arrestees. (See Table 43.)

Justifiable Homicide

Justifiable homicide is defined in the UCR Program as the killing of a felon by a law enforcement officer in the line of duty or the killing of a felon, during the commission of a felony, by a private citizen. Because these willful killings are determined through law enforcement investigation to be justifiable, or excusable, they are tabulated separately from the murder counts.

During 2002, contributing law enforcement agencies provided supplemental data for 564 justifiable homicides. According to those data, law enforcement officers justifiably slew 339 felons, and private citizens justifiably killed 225 felons. Tables 2.16 and 2.17 provide additional information about justifiable homicides.

Information regarding the UCR Program's statistical methodology and table construction can be found in Appendix I.

Forcible Rape

Definition

Forcible rape, as defined in the Uniform Crime Reporting (UCR) Program, is the carnal knowledge of a female forcibly and against her will. Assaults or attempts to commit rape by force or threat of force are also included; however, statutory rape (without force) and other sex offenses are excluded.

Trend

Year	Number of offenses	Rate per 100,000 inhabitants
2001	90,863	31.8
2002	95,136	33.0
Percent change	+4.7	+3.6

National Volume, Trends, and Rates

Marking the third consecutive year of increase, the UCR Program's estimate of female forcible rapes for 2002 was 95,136 offenses. This estimate was 4.7 percent higher than the 2001 approximation, and it was 2.1 percent higher than the offense estimate for 1998. However, the volume of forcible rapes in 2002 was 10.3 percent below the 1993 estimate. (See Table 1.)

The UCR Program has traditionally collected rape data only for female victims. The rape rates listed above and in subsequent tables are based upon estimates of the total U.S. population. In this narrative, however, the rape rate is based on the 2002 estimate of the Nation's female population provided by the U. S. Bureau of the Census. That calculation yielded a rate of 64.8 forcible rapes per 100,000 females, which was an increase of 3.5 percent from the 2001 rate of 62.6. In comparison with the rates of 5 and 10 years ago, the 2002 female forcible rape rate was 3.9 percent below the 1998 rate of 67.5, and it was 19.4 percent below the 1993 estimate of 80.4 per 100,000 females.

Community Types

The UCR Program aggregates data for three types of communities: Metropolitan Statistical Areas (MSAs), cities outside metropolitan areas, and rural counties. (For a detailed explanation of the composition of these community types, see Appendix III.) During 2002, the estimated rate of female forcible rapes increased for all community types. The greatest increase was seen in cities outside MSAs, where forcible rapes occurred at the estimated rate of 75.9 per 100,000 females, an increase of 12.1 percent since 2001. MSAs had an estimated rate of 66.5 forcible rapes for each 100,000 segment of the female population, a 3.3 percent increase over the prior year's estimate. In rural counties, female rapes occurred at an estimated rate of 46.8 per 100,000 females, up 6.8 percent from 2001. (Based on Table 2.)

Regional Offense Trends and Rates

The UCR Program aggregates statistics for four regions within the United States: the Northeast, the Midwest, the South, and the West. A map delineating these regions is published in Appendix III. By region, the data on female forcible rapes reflected the following:

Figure 2.8

Forcible Rape
Percent Change from 1998

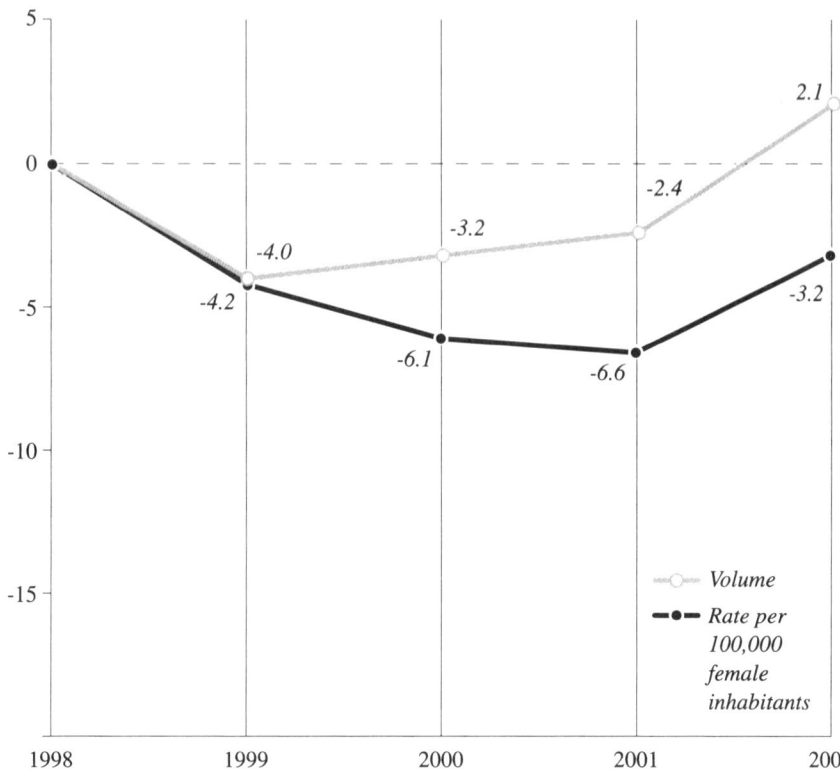

The Northeast

The Northeast had an estimated 13.5 percent of the Nation's forcible rapes during 2002, the lowest proportion of the four regions. Additionally, this group of states had the only decline in the estimated rate of 46.4 forcible rapes per 100,000 females. This figure was the lowest regional rate, and it reflected a 5.5 percent decrease from the Northeast's 2001 estimate.

The Midwest

Approximately 25.3 percent of the Nation's estimated forcible rapes occurred in the Midwestern states. In 2002, this region had an estimated 72.7 forcible rape rate per 100,000 females, which was an increase of 5.4 percent over 2001 estimates.

The South

The Nation's most populous region, the South, had the highest percentage of female rapes—37.5 percent. During 2002, the Southern states experienced an estimated 2.1 percent increase over the 2001 figure for the rate of forcible rapes, 67.9 for every 100,000 females.

The West

Of the Nation's rape offenses, an estimated 23.7 percent occurred in the Western Region during 2002. The West also had an increase of 3.2 percent in the rate of forcible rapes, with 67.4 rapes per 100,000 females. (Based on Table 4.)

Offense Analysis

The UCR Program counts each offense in which a female of any age is forcibly

| Table 2.18 |

Forcible Rape by Month
Percent Distribution, 1998-2002

Month	1998	1999	2000	2001	2002
January	7.9	8.1	8.0	7.7	7.6
February	7.4	7.3	7.5	7.1	7.0
March	8.6	8.2	8.5	8.4	7.8
April	8.2	8.2	8.0	8.3	8.6
May	8.8	8.6	9.0	8.8	9.0
June	8.7	8.8	9.1	8.7	9.0
July	9.6	9.6	9.5	9.7	9.6
August	9.3	9.5	9.3	9.4	9.6
September	8.8	8.3	8.4	8.6	9.2
October	7.9	8.3	8.3	8.5	8.4
November	7.6	7.9	7.5	7.6	7.4
December	7.1	7.2	6.9	7.2	6.8

raped or upon whom an assault to rape or attempt to rape is made. Of the total rapes reported for 2002, 91.0 percent were classified as rapes, and the remainder were attempts. (See Table 19.) The UCR Program classifies all sex offenses (except forcible rape) as Part II offenses and, as such, collects only arrest data, which are presented in an aggregated total. (See Appendix II.) Consequently, statutory rapes of female victims where no force is used and the victim is under the age of consent are included in sex offenses. Sexual attacks on males are classified as assaults or sex offenses depending on the nature of the crime and the extent of injury.

Clearances

Forcible rapes had a national clearance rate of 44.5 percent during 2002. Collectively, the Nation's cities cleared 43.4 percent of forcible rapes, with clearance rates ranging from 40.4 percent in cities with populations of 25,000 to 49,999 to 46.2 percent in those with fewer than 10,000 residents. The Nation's largest cities, those with populations of 250,000 and over, cleared 44.0 percent. Rural counties cleared 49.8 percent of the reported forcible rapes in their communities, and suburban counties cleared 47.0 percent. (See Table 25.)

The Northeast recorded the highest regional rape clearance rate, 50.7 percent of reported offenses. In 2002, the South cleared 48.4 percent of female rapes; the West, 40.1 percent; and the Midwest, 39.2 percent. (See Table 26.)

Clearances and Juveniles

When an offender under the age of 18 is cited to appear in juvenile court or before other juvenile authorities, the UCR Program records the incident as a clearance by arrest even though a physical arrest may not have occurred. In addition, according to Program definitions, clearances involving both adult and juvenile offenders are classified as adult clearances.

In 2002, juveniles made up 12.0 percent of the total clearances for forcible rape. Among the Nation's cities,

11.6 percent of forcible rape clearances were the result of a juvenile arrest or an exceptional clearance. The highest percentage of forcible rape clearances involving only juvenile offenders, 16.0 percent, were reported in cities with populations of 10,000 to 24,999; the lowest percentage of juvenile clearances, 9.1 percent, were reported by agencies in cities with more than 250,000 in population. During 2002, 13.8 percent of forcible rape clearances in rural counties involved only persons under age 18, as did 12.8 percent of those in suburban counties. (See Table 28.)

Arrests

Arrests for forcible rape in 2002 were estimated at 28,288. (See Table 29.) During 2002, 16.7 percent of all forcible rape arrests were of persons under the age of 18 and 46.1 percent were of persons under the age of 25. Adults (over the age of 18) made up 83.3 percent of arrests. (See Tables 38 and 41.) By race, 63.4 percent of arrestees for this offense were white, 34.0 percent were black, and the remainder were of other races. (See Table 43.) Regarding juvenile forcible rape arrests, 62.0 percent of the juvenile arrestees were white, 36.0 percent were black, and the remainder were of other races. (See Table 43.)

Two-, 5-, and 10-year trend data showed that the number of forcible rape arrests in 2002 was 1.8 percent higher than the 2001 arrest total; however, that figure was 7.2 percent lower than the 1998 total and 26.0 percent lower than the number of rape arrests in 1993. In 2002, arrests of adults for forcible rape increased 2.5 percent from the 2001 number, and arrests of juveniles decreased 1.4 percent when compared to 2001 arrest totals. Comparing the 2002 estimates with those of 5 years ago showed that adult arrests fell 5.8 percent and juvenile arrests dropped 13.8 percent from 1998. Adult arrests for forcible rape in 2002 declined 25.9 percent, and juvenile arrests decreased 26.5 percent when compared to arrests in 1993. (See Tables 32, 34, and 36.)

Robbery

Definition

The Uniform Crime Reporting Program defines robbery as the taking or attempting to take anything of value from the care, custody, or control of a person or persons by force or threat of force or violence and/or by putting the victim in fear.

Trend

Year	Number of offenses	Rate per 100,000 inhabitants
2001	423,557	148.5
2002	420,637	145.9
Percent change	-0.7	-1.7

National Volume, Trends, and Rates

In 2002, there were an estimated 420,637 robberies in the Nation. This estimate indicated a decrease of 0.7 percent when compared to the 2001 offense estimate and 5.9 percent and 36.3 percent decreases when compared to the 1998 and the 1993 estimates, respectively. (See Table 1.) Robbery accounted for 3.5 percent of the Crime Index in 2002 and comprised an estimated 29.5 percent of the violent crimes. (Based on Table 1.)

The 2002 robbery rate of 145.9 offenses per 100,000 inhabitants reflected a 1.7 percent decrease from the 2001 rate. Robbery rates in 2002 compared to figures from 1998 showed an 11.8 percent decline. Compared to 1993 rates, 2002 rates demonstrated a 43.0 percent decrease.

Regional Offense Trends and Rates

The UCR Program divides the United States into four regions: the Northeast, the Midwest, the South, and the West. (More information concerning UCR area definitions can be found in Appendix III.) In 2002, robbery data collected regarding the Nation's four regions reflected the following:

The Northeast

The Northeast, which comprised 18.8 percent of the total United States population in 2002, experienced 19.2 percent of the Nation's estimated robberies. The estimated number of robberies remained virtually unchanged from the 2001 figure; however, the robbery rate of 148.7 offenses per 100,000 population reflected a slight decrease (0.5 percent) from the 2001 rate. (See Tables 3 and 4.)

The Midwest

The Midwest, accounting for 22.6 percent of the Nation's population, had an estimated 19.5 percent of the country's robberies. The number of robberies that occurred in this region decreased by 1.1 percent from the 2001 figure, and the rate per 100,000 inhabitants (126.1) declined by 1.6 percent. (See Tables 3 and 4.)

The South

With 35.8 percent of the Nation's population, the South experienced an estimated 38.5 percent of the country's robbery volume. The number of robbery offenses in this region declined 0.7 percent from the 2001 figure, and the rate per 100,000 inhabitants (156.8)

Figure 2.9

Robbery
Percent Change from 1998

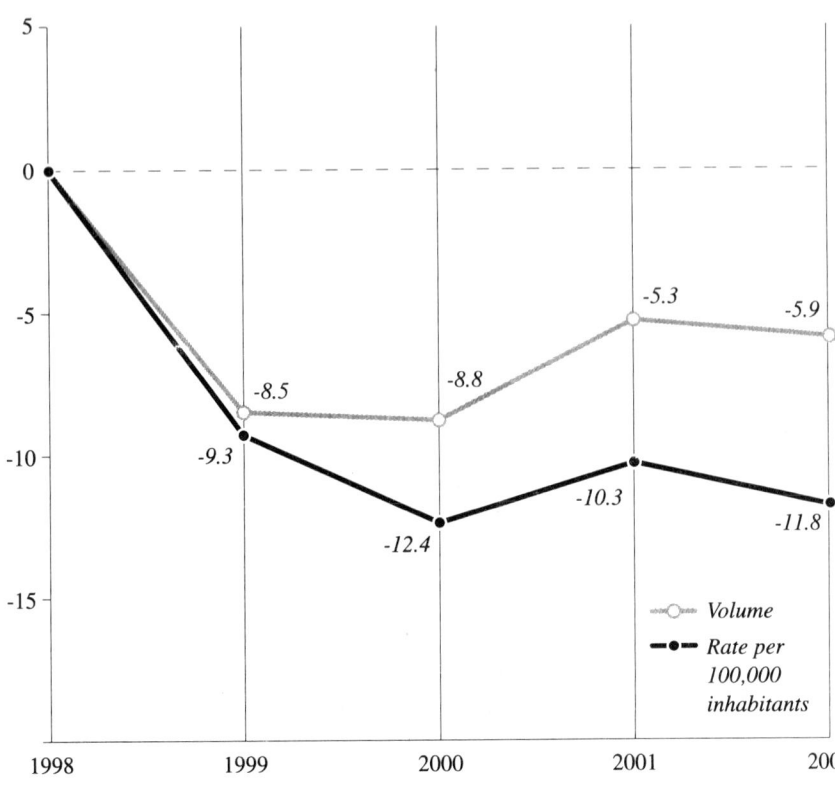

decreased 2.0 percent from the 2001 rate. (See Tables 3 and 4.)

The West

The West, comprising 22.8 percent of the U.S. population, accounted for an estimated 22.8 percent of the robbery volume. This percentage reflected a 0.9 percent decrease from the 2001 figure. The region reported a robbery rate of 146.0 offenses per 100,000, showing a 2.5 percent decline from the 2001 rate. (See Tables 3 and 4.)

Population Groups: Trends and Rates

The UCR Program often presents crime statistics in aggregations representing various population groups. An explanation of these population group classifications can be found in Appendix III.

Cumulatively, the Nation's cities experienced a 1.5 percent decrease in robberies in 2002. Among the Nation's cities, those with populations of 250,000 or more inhabitants reported the largest decline in robbery offenses—2.1 percent. Cities with popula-

tions of 10,000 to 24,999 inhabitants reflected a 3.3 percent increase from the number of robberies in 2001, and cities with 10,000 or fewer people experienced a 0.7 percent increase. Also in 2002, the country's suburban counties experienced a 1.8 percent increase; rural counties reported a 0.8 percent decline in the number of robberies. Additional data for population groups can be found in Table 12.

Collectively, the Nation's cities reported a robbery rate of 208.1 offenses per 100,000 inhabitants. Among the Nation's cities, those with populations of 250,000 or more people experienced the highest rate of occurrence for robbery—395.2 offenses per 100,000 inhabitants. Cities with populations of less than 10,000 people reported the lowest rate of robbery in 2002—54.2 offenses per 100,000 inhabitants. The country's suburban counties had a rate of 70.7 robberies per 100,000 people; rural counties experienced a rate of 17.7 robberies per 100,000 population. Rates for population groups can be found in Table 16.

Offense Analysis

Supplemental data concerning robberies reported by law enforcement to the national UCR Program in 2002 revealed the following:

Robbery by Weapon

Firearms continued to be the weapon used most often in the commission of robberies. In 2002, offenders used firearms in 42.1 percent of the robberies reported to the UCR Program. Another 39.9 percent of robberies

involved strong-arm tactics—hands, fists, feet, etc. Offenders used knives or cutting instruments in 8.7 percent of the offenses and other weapons in 9.3 percent of robberies. (See Table 2.22.) A state-by-state breakdown of weapons used in robberies in 2002 is provided in Table 21.

Dollar Loss

In 2002, offenders took an estimated $539 million from victims. Nationwide, the average monetary value of property stolen during a robbery was $1,281. Banks lost an average of $4,763 for each robbery,'and commercial houses (including supermarkets, department stores, restaurants, taverns, finance companies, hotels, motels, etc.) lost an average of $1,676 per robbery offense. The estimated value of losses incurred from robberies of residences averaged $1,340, and robberies on streets/highways averaged a loss of $1,045 per robbery offense. Additionally, losses from gas or service stations and convenience stores averaged $679 and $665, respectively, per robbery. (Based on Tables 1 and 23.)

Robbery Trends by Location

When compared to 2001 volumes, the number of robberies that occurred in 2002 decreased at every location type except residences. Residential robberies increased 4.4 percent from the 2001 figure. The greatest decline in the number of robberies—7.6 percent—occurred at gas or service stations, and the smallest decrease—1.3 percent—occurred at commercial houses. Unspecified locations (denoted as miscellaneous) showed an increase of 2.7 percent. (See Table 23.)

Percent Distribution

Robberies of victims on the street or highway accounted for 42.8 percent of the total number of robberies that occurred during 2002. Robberies that happened in commercial houses (restaurants, taverns, hotels, etc.) and residences accounted for 14.6 percent and 13.5 percent, respectively, of reported robberies. Robberies perpetrated in convenience stores, gas or service stations, and banks

---

Table 2.19

Robbery by Month
Percent Distribution, 1998–2002

Month	1998	1999	2000	2001	2002
January	9.5	8.9	8.6	8.3	8.8
February	7.5	7.3	7.1	6.5	6.7
March	8.0	7.7	7.7	7.6	7.6
April	7.6	7.6	7.5	7.4	7.5
May	7.9	8.1	8.1	8.1	8.0
June	7.7	8.1	7.9	8.0	8.0
July	8.5	8.7	8.7	8.7	8.8
August	8.7	8.8	9.0	8.7	9.0
September	8.5	8.3	8.5	8.5	8.8
October	9.0	8.8	9.1	9.7	9.1
November	8.3	8.6	8.7	9.2	8.6
December	8.8	9.2	9.0	9.4	9.2

Table 2.20

Robbery
Percent Distribution by Region, 2002

Type	United States total	Northeast	Midwest	South	West
Total [1]	100.0	100.0	100.0	100.0	100.0
Street/highway	42.8	57.7	48.4	36.3	42.9
Commercial house	14.6	9.5	10.8	14.9	18.3
Gas or service station	2.7	3.3	3.2	2.4	2.5
Convenience store	6.5	6.0	4.8	7.8	5.4
Residence	13.5	9.4	11.0	18.0	9.7
Bank	2.3	2.3	2.1	2.0	2.9
Miscellaneous	17.7	11.8	19.7	18.6	18.3

[1] Because of rounding, the percentages may not add to 100.0.

Figure 2.10

Robbery Categories
Percent Change from 1998

Street/Highway

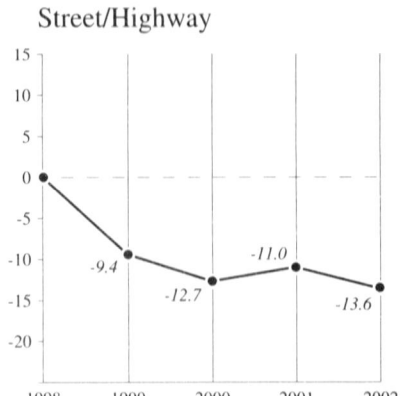

Commercial house

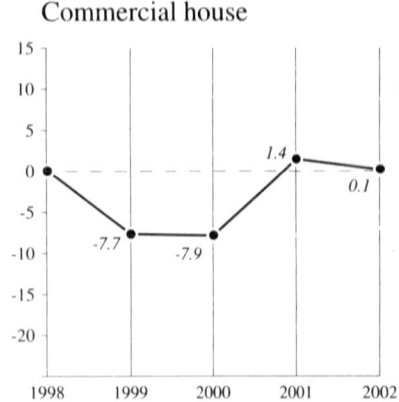

Gas or service station

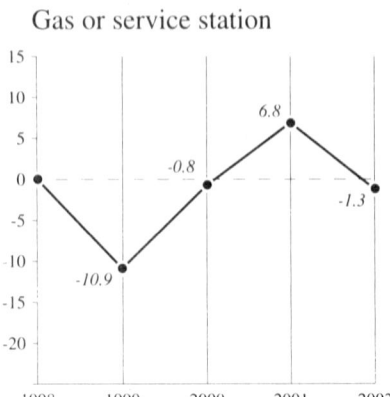

Convenience store

Residence

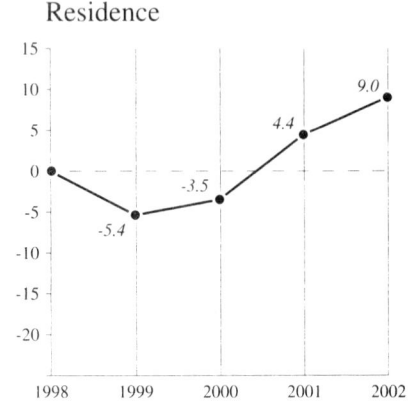

Bank

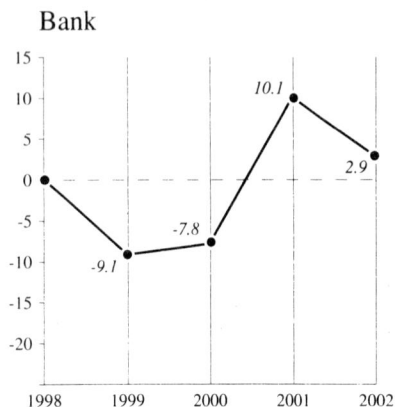

comprised 6.5 percent, 2.7 percent, and 2.3 percent, respectively, of the total number of robberies. The remaining 17.7 percent of robberies occurred at other venues. (See Table 23.)

Clearances

In 2002, law enforcement agencies cleared by arrest or exceptional means 25.7 percent of robberies reported to the national Program. (More information concerning clearances, including what constitutes a clearance by exceptional means, can be found in Section III of this report.) Collectively, the Nation's cities cleared 25.0 percent of robbery offenses. Law enforcement in suburban and rural counties cleared 29.5 percent and 41.4 percent, respectively, of reported robberies. (See Table 25.)

Regionally, the Northeast had the highest rate of clearance for robbery— 31.0 percent—followed by the South at 26.0 percent. Law enforcement in the West cleared 24.7 percent of reported robberies, and the Midwest cleared 21.5 percent of this offense. (See Table 26.)

Clearances and Juveniles

According to UCR Program reporting procedures, clearances involving both adult and juvenile offenders are classified as adult clearances. Therefore, the statistics provided in this narrative are for clearances which involved only

juveniles. In 2002, juvenile offenders (those under 18 years of age) accounted for 14.1 percent of the Nation's robbery clearances. In cities collectively, juveniles comprised 14.2 percent of robbery clearances. Additionally, arrests of juveniles for reported robbery offenses in suburban and rural counties, cleared 14.4 percent and 7.4 percent, respectively. Table 28 provides additional information concerning juvenile clearance data.

Arrests

Total Arrests

Law enforcement made an estimated 105,774 arrests for robbery offenses in 2002. Robbery arrests accounted for an estimated 4.7 percent of the arrests for Crime Index offenses and 17.0 percent of the arrests for violent crimes. (See Table 29.)

Arrest Trends

Robbery arrests for 2002 decreased 0.8 percent nationwide from the 2001 arrest total. Arrests of adults (persons 18 years of age and older) decreased 0.8 percent, and arrests of juveniles (persons under age 18) declined 0.9 percent over the 2-year period. (See Table 36.) By gender, the 2-year trend showed that there was a 1.1 percent decrease in the number of males who were arrested for robbery

and a 1.6 percent increase in the number of females arrested for that offense. (See Table 37.)

A 5-year comparison of robbery arrests for the Nation showed an overall 8.3 percent decline. The number of adults and juveniles arrested for robbery in 1998 compared to the number arrested in 2002 reflected decreases of 3.8 and 20.7 percent, respectively. (See Table 34.) By gender, the 5-year trend showed that there was an 8.5 percent decrease in the number of males who were arrested for robbery and a 6.8 percent decrease in the number of females arrested for that offense. (See Table 35.)

A 10-year overall comparison revealed that robbery arrests fell 28.4 percent since 1993. (See Table 32.) The number of adults arrested for robbery was down 24.6 percent, and the number of juveniles arrested during the same period declined 38.4 percent. (See Table 32.) By gender, the 10-year trend showed that there was a 29.4 percent decrease in the number of males who were arrested for robbery and a 17.3 percent decrease in the number of females arrested for that offense. (See Table 33.)

Arrest Rates

Nationally, the robbery arrest rate for 2002 was 37.7 arrests per 100,000

Table 2.21

Robbery
Percent Distribution by Population Group, 2002

Type	Group I (62 cities, 250,000 and over; population 39,124,731)	Group II (148 cities, 100,000 to 249,999; population 22,295,369)	Group III (380 cities, 50,000 to 99,999; population 26,354,653)	Group IV (698 cities, 25,000 to 49,999; population 24,398,552)	Group V (1,573 cities, 10,000 to 24,999; population 24,942,945)	Group VI (6,170 cities, under 10,000; population 20,386,464)	County agencies (3,493 agencies; population 79,119,438)
Total [1]	100.0	100.0	100.0	100.0	100.0	100.0	100.0
Street/highway	51.7	42.1	40.3	32.8	28.8	24.5	29.6
Commercial house	12.2	16.9	16.0	16.0	17.5	15.8	17.1
Gas or service station	1.8	2.7	3.2	3.9	4.2	4.4	3.8
Convenience store	4.6	6.5	7.2	8.4	9.1	10.4	9.2
Residence	12.2	13.7	11.5	13.5	14.9	14.2	19.3
Bank	1.6	2.4	2.8	3.2	3.8	3.9	2.8
Miscellaneous	16.0	15.6	19.1	22.2	21.8	26.8	18.2

[1] Because of rounding, the percentages may not add to 100.0.

inhabitants. (See Table 31.) Collectively, the Nation's cities experienced a robbery arrest rate of 46.9 per 100,000 people. Suburban and rural counties reported 20.8 robbery arrests per 100,000 inhabitants and 9.2 per 100,000 population, respectively.

Regionally, the robbery arrest rates were 44.7 arrests per 100,000 inhabitants in the Northeast; 32.1 arrests per 100,000 inhabitants in the Midwest; 35.5 arrests per 100,000 inhabitants in the South; and 40.0 arrests for robbery offenses per 100,000 individuals in the West. (See Table 30.)

Distribution by Age, Sex, and Race

During 2002, a total of 76.9 percent of all persons arrested for robbery were adults (persons 18 years of age and older). (See Table 38.) Further, 61.4 percent of the persons arrested for robbery were under the age of 25. (See Table 41.) The majority of the arrestees, 89.7 percent, were males. By race, 54.1 percent of persons arrested for robbery were black, 44.1 percent were white, and 1.7 percent were of other races (American Indian, Alaskan Native, Asian, or Pacific Islander.) (See Tables 41, 42, and 43.) Breakdowns of male and female arrestees by age are presented in Tables 39 and 40.

Table 2.22

Robbery, Types of Weapons Used
Percent Distribution by Region, 2002

| Region | Total all weapons[1] | Armed | | | |
		Firearms	Knives or cutting instruments	Other weapons	Strongarm
Total	100.0	42.1	8.7	9.3	39.9
Northeast	100.0	34.0	10.8	8.3	46.9
Midwest	100.0	43.8	6.5	9.7	40.0
South	100.0	47.8	7.8	9.7	34.7
West	100.0	36.3	10.3	9.1	44.3

[1] Because of rounding, the percentages may not add to 100.0.

Aggravated Assault

Definition

According to the Uniform Crime Reporting Program, an aggravated assault is an unlawful attack by one person upon another for the purpose of inflicting severe or aggravated bodily injury. This type of assault is usually accompanied by the use of a weapon or by means likely to produce death or great bodily harm. Attempts involving the display or threat of a gun, knife, or other weapon are included because serious personal injury would likely result if the assault were completed.

Trend

Year	Number of offenses	Rate per 100,000 inhabitants
2001	909,023	318.6
2002	894,348	310.1
Percent change	-1.6	-2.7

National Volume, Trends, and Rates

Nationally, an estimated 894,348 offenses of aggravated assault accounted for 62.7 percent of the violent crimes in 2002. The estimated number of aggravated assault offenses in 2002 marked the 9th consecutive year of decline for that offense. (See Table 1.)

In 2002, there were an estimated 310.1 reported victims of aggravated assault per 100,000 inhabitants. Two-, 5-, and 10-year trend data showed that the estimated rate was 2.7 percent lower than in 2001, 14.2 percent lower than in 1998, and 29.6 percent lower than in 1993. (See Table 1.)

When compared to 2001 data, the 2002 estimate of aggravated assaults showed a 1.6 percent decline. A 5- and 10-year trend analysis showed that the number of estimated aggravated assaults decreased 8.4 percent from the 1998 estimate and declined 21.2 percent from the 1993 estimate. (See Table 1.)

Community Types

The UCR Program categorizes communities as Metropolitan Statistical Areas (MSAs), cities outside of MSAs, and rural counties. MSAs are those community types made up of a central city of at least 50,000 inhabitants, the county containing that city, and adjacent areas with strong economic or cultural ties to the central city. Cities outside MSAs are mostly incorporated, and rural counties are composed of mostly unincorporated areas.

In 2002, the Nation's MSAs experienced an estimated rate of 332.3 aggravated assaults per 100,000 inhabitants. Cities outside MSAs had a rate of 300.1 aggravated assaults per 100,000 inhabitants, and rural counties had an estimated rate of 168.5 aggravated assaults per 100,000 persons. (See Table 2.)

Regional Offense Trends and Rates

The UCR Program divides the United States into four regions: the Northeast, the Midwest, the South, and the West. (See Appendix III.)

Figure 2.11

Aggravated Assault
Percent Change from 1998

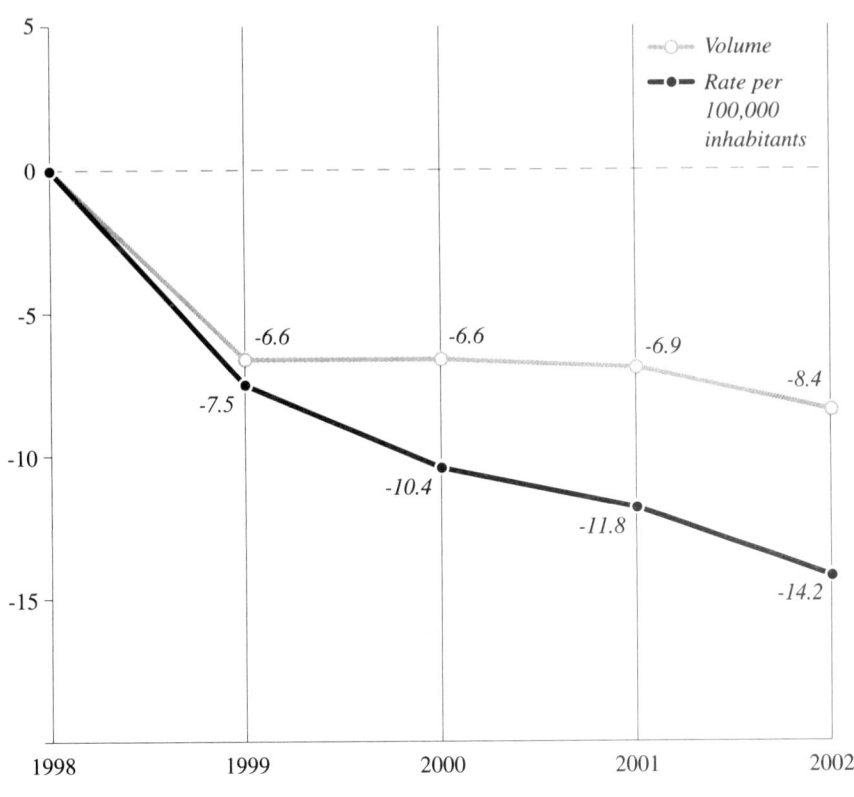

The Northeast

In 2002, the estimated number of aggravated assaults in the Northeast, which comprised 18.8 percent of the U.S. population, accounted for 14.6 percent of the Nation's total for that offense. (See Table 3.) The estimated rate for Northeastern states, collectively, was 240.1 per 100,000 persons; this represented a 4.8 percent decrease from the 2001 rate. (See Table 4.)

The Midwest

The Midwest, accounting for 22.6 percent of the Nation's population, had an estimated 18.7 percent of the estimated aggravated assaults in 2002. (See Table 3.) The Midwest had an estimated rate of 256.7 per 100,000 persons, which was a 2.1 percent decrease from the 2001 estimated aggravated assault rate. (See Table 4.)

The South

In 2002, the South, the Nation's most populous region (35.8 percent of the population), accounted for an estimated 43.1 percent of the aggravated assaults in the United States. (See Table 3.) The South had a rate of 372.9 aggravated assaults per 100,000 inhabitants, which represented a 2.3 percent decline from the rate in 2001. (See Table 4.)

The West

The West, accounting for 22.8 percent of the population, had an estimated 23.7 percent of the aggravated assaults in the Nation in 2002. (See Table 3.) The region experienced an estimated rate of 322.2 aggravated assaults per 100,000 people. The rate was a decrease of 2.6 percent from the 2001 rate. (See Table 4.)

Population Groups: Trends and Rates

During 2002, the Nation's cities collectively had a 2.6 percent decrease in the number of aggravated assaults when compared to the 2001 figure. The largest decrease in aggravated assaults among the country's cities occurred in cities with 10,000 to 24,999 inhabitants, a 3.3 percent decline in volume from 2001 to 2002. The Nation's largest cities, those with populations of 250,000 and over, showed a 2.9 percent drop in aggravated assaults. Rural counties experienced a decrease of 1.9 percent. Suburban counties were the only population group with an increase, 0.1 percent. (See Table 12.)

The Nation's cities collectively had an aggravated assault rate of 372.4 per 100,000 inhabitants. Among the Nation's cities, those cities with populations 250,000 and over had the highest aggravated assault rate at 577.5 offenses per 100,000 persons. Cities with populations from 10,000 to 24,999 had the lowest rate at 219.1 per 100,000. Suburban counties had a rate of 249.3 aggravated assaults per 100,000 in population, and rural counties had a rate of 186.0 per 100,000 persons. (See Table 16.)

Offense Analysis

By weapon type, personal weapons such as hands, fists, feet, etc. were used in 27.7 percent of the aggravated assaults, firearms in 19.0 percent, and knives or other cutting instruments in 17.8 percent. Other weapon types were used in 35.4 percent of the aggravated assaults in 2002. (See Table 2.24.)

In comparison to 2001 data, 2002 data showed that the use of firearms in aggravated assaults increased 2.1 percent. The three remaining weapon categories showed decreases in their use during aggravated assaults compared to 2001 figures. The use of personal weapons (hands, fists, feet, etc.) decreased 3.7 percent, the use of knives or other cutting instruments dropped 2.0 percent, and the use of other weapon types declined 2.4 percent. (See Table 15.)

Clearances

Nationwide in 2002, law enforcement agencies cleared 56.5 percent of reported aggravated assaults. Collectively, cities cleared 54.6 percent of aggravated assaults. Law enforcement agencies in the Nation's smallest cities, those with less than 10,000 in population, cleared 65.1 percent of their aggravated assaults. Law enforcement agencies in the Nation's largest cities, those with populations of 250,000 and over, cleared 49.1 percent of the aggravated assaults that came to their attention. Those agencies in rural and suburban counties cleared 64.5 and 61.6 percent, respectively, of the reported aggravated assaults in their jurisdictions. (See Table 25.)

The Nation's law enforcement cleared 63.3 percent of the aggravated assaults involving personal weapons such as hands, fists, or feet and 62.2 percent of aggravated assaults involv-

Table 2.23

Aggravated Assault by Month
Percent Distribution, 1998-2002

Month	1998	1999	2000	2001	2002
January	7.9	7.9	7.5	7.5	7.5
February	7.0	7.0	7.2	6.7	6.7
March	8.1	8.0	8.3	8.1	8.0
April	8.3	8.3	8.4	8.5	8.4
May	9.1	9.1	9.3	9.0	9.0
June	8.9	8.8	8.9	8.9	9.1
July	9.4	9.5	9.5	9.6	9.6
August	9.4	9.2	9.1	9.0	9.4
September	8.7	8.5	8.6	8.8	9.4
October	8.3	8.6	8.6	8.7	8.4
November	7.4	7.7	7.3	7.7	7.3
December	7.4	7.5	7.2	7.5	7.1

Table 2.24

Aggravated Assault, Types of Weapons Used
Percent Distribution by Region, 2002

Region	Total all weapons[1]	Firearms	Knives or cutting instruments	Other weapons (clubs, blunt objects, etc.)	Personal weapons
Total	100.0	19.0	17.8	35.4	27.7
Northeast	100.0	14.1	18.4	34.4	33.1
Midwest	100.0	18.0	17.2	34.7	30.1
South	100.0	21.0	19.5	37.6	21.9
West	100.0	18.0	15.2	32.6	34.3

[1]Because of rounding, the percentages may not add to 100.0.

ing a knife or cutting instrument. In addition, agencies cleared 41.3 percent of the aggravated assaults that involved firearms and 55.5 percent of those that involved other weapon types. (See Table 27.)

Law enforcement in the Northeastern Region cleared the highest percentage of aggravated assaults, 64.7 percent. Law enforcement in the Western Region cleared 56.1 percent of aggravated assaults, followed by the Southern Region with 55.8 percent, and the Midwestern Region with 53.3 percent. (See Table 26.)

Clearances and Juveniles

When an offender under the age of 18 is arrested or cited to appear in juvenile court or before other juvenile authorities, the UCR Program records that incident as a clearance by arrest. However, according to Program definitions, clearances involving both adult and juvenile offenders are classified as adult clearances.

Of all aggravated assault clearances reported nationally in 2002, 11.6 percent involved only persons under the age of 18. In the Nation's cities, collec-tively, 11.7 percent of clearances for aggravated assault involved only juveniles. In suburban counties, 12.1 percent of aggravated assault clearances involved only persons under the age of 18; in rural counties, 9.5 percent of aggravated assault clearances were of juveniles. (See Table 28.)

Arrests

In 2002, approximately 472,290 persons were arrested for aggravated assault. (See Table 29.) The rate for aggravated assault arrests nationwide was 165.5 per 100,000 persons. Collectively, cities had a rate of 182.9 aggravated assault arrests per 100,000 inhabitants. The highest arrest rate for aggravated assault among the Nation's cities was in the Nation's largest cities (those with 250,000 and over in population) at 257.1 arrests per 100,000 inhabitants, and the lowest rate was in cities from 10,000 to 24,999 at 121.7 arrests per 100,000 persons. Rural counties had a rate of 109.0 aggravated assault arrests per 100,000 inhabitants, and suburban counties had a rate of 135.1 aggravated assault arrests per 100,000 in population. (See Table 31.)

Of the reported arrests for aggravated assault, 79.8 percent were of males. (See Table 42.) By race, 63.4 percent of those arrested during 2002 for aggravated assault were white, 34.2 percent were black, 2.4 percent were of all other races. (See Table 43.)

Aggravated assault arrests in 2002 were down 0.9 percent when compared to 2001 arrests; arrests of juveniles (persons under 18 years of age) for aggravated assault decreased 4.0 percent and arrests of adults decreased 0.4 percent. (See Table 36.) A comparison of 1998 and 2002 data revealed a 6.9 percent decrease in the number of aggravated assault arrests, a 15.0 percent decrease in the number of juveniles arrested for aggravated assault, and a 5.5 percent decline in the number of adults arrested for this offense. (See Table 34.) An examination of the 10-year trend data showed a decline of 6.7 percent in the number of arrests for aggravated assault, with a 23.0 percent decrease in the number of juveniles arrested and a 3.8 percent decline in the number of adults arrested. (See Table 32.)

Property Crime

Definition

In the Uniform Crime Reporting Program, property crime includes the offenses of burglary, larceny-theft, motor vehicle theft, and arson. The object of the theft-type offenses is the taking of money or property, but there is no force or threat of force against the victims. The property crime category includes arson because the offense involves the destruction of property; however, arson victims may be subjected to force. Because of limited participation and varying collection procedures by local agencies, only limited data are available for arson. Arson statistics are included in trend, clearance, and arrest tables throughout *Crime in the United States*, but they are not included in any estimated volume data. The arson section in this report provides more information on that offense.

Trend

Year	Number of offenses[1]	Rate per 100,000 inhabitants[1]
2001	10,437,189	3,658.1
2002	10,450,893	3,624.1
Percent change	+0.1	-0.9

[1]Does not include arson. See Crime Index Tabulations.

National Volume, Trends, and Rates

Volume

In 2002, law enforcement reported an estimated 10,450,893 property crimes.

The figure was 0.1 percent higher than the 2001 estimate. Further trend analyses of 5- and 10-year volumes for property crime indicated that the 2002 figure was 4.6 percent lower than the 1998 number and 14.5 percent lower than the number in 1993.

Among individual property crimes in 2002, burglary offenses rose 1.7 percent, and motor vehicle theft increased 1.4 percent when compared to the 2001 estimates. Larceny-theft decreased 0.6 percent. As previously noted, arson is excluded from the estimated property crime volume totals. (See Table 1.)

Rate

The Nation's rate of property crime offenses in 2002 was estimated at 3,624.1 offenses per 100,000 inhabitants. The 2002 rate decreased 0.9 percent compared to the previous year's rate. When measured against the rates from 5 and 10 years ago, property crime rates declined 10.6 percent from the 1998 rate and fell 23.5 percent from the 1993 level. (See Table 1.)

Distribution

Property crimes reported in 2002 accounted for 88.0 percent of the Crime Index. (Based on Table 1.) The highest volume of offenses was attributed to larceny-theft, which made up 67.5 percent of property crimes and 59.4 percent of the Crime Index. (Based on Table 1.)

Community Types

When presenting crime data the UCR Program designates three types of

Figure 2.12

Property Crime
Percent Change from 1998

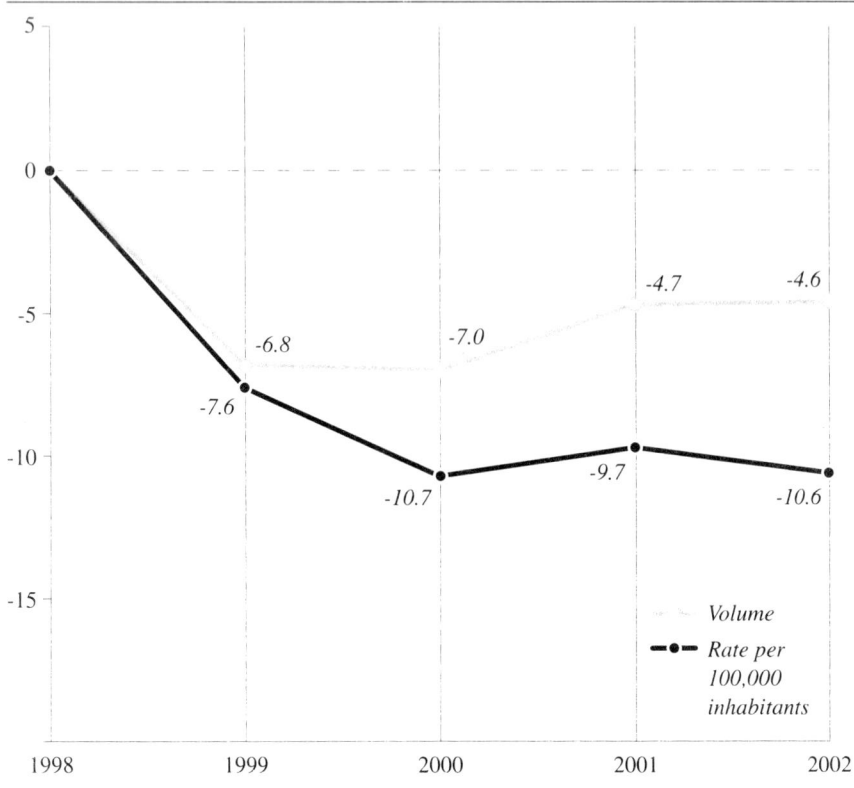

communities: Metropolitan Statistical Areas (MSAs), cities outside of MSAs, and rural counties. In 2002, MSAs, accounting for an estimated 80 percent of the Nation's population, had an estimated property crime rate of 3,863.5 offenses per 100,000 persons. Cities outside of MSAs, with 8 percent of the population, had a rate of 4,121.0 property crime offenses per 100,000 inhabitants. Rural areas, making up 12 percent of the overall population, had a rate of 1,696.1 property crimes per 100,000 in population. (See Table 2.)

Regional Offense Trends and Rates

The UCR Program divides the United States into four regions for data analyses: the Northeast, the Midwest, the South, and the West. (Appendix III provides more information on UCR area definitions.) An examination of 2002 data showed the following information regarding the Nation's four regions.

The Northeast

Property crimes reported by law enforcement agencies in the Northeast accounted for an estimated 12.8 percent of property crime nationwide. (See Table 3.) This category of offenses comprised 85.6 percent of the 2002 Index crimes in the Northeast. (Based on Table 4.) Compared to the 2001 volume, property crime decreased 3.3 percent in the Northeast in 2002. The rate of property crime offenses in the Northeast—2,472.6 per 100,000 inhabitants—also

Table 2.25

Property Crime by Month
Percent Distribution, 1998-2002

Month	1998	1999	2000	2001	2002
January	8.6	8.0	7.8	7.8	8.3
February	7.5	7.2	7.3	6.8	7.0
March	8.2	8.0	8.2	7.8	7.8
April	8.0	7.9	7.9	7.9	8.0
May	8.4	8.3	8.6	8.5	8.5
June	8.5	8.6	8.6	8.5	8.4
July	8.9	9.1	9.1	9.1	9.1
August	9.0	9.2	9.2	9.1	9.1
September	8.4	8.5	8.5	8.5	8.6
October	8.5	8.7	8.8	9.2	8.8
November	7.9	8.2	8.1	8.5	8.1
December	8.2	8.4	8.0	8.5	8.2

showed a decline, 3.8 percent from the previous year's rate. (See Table 4.)

The Midwest

Law enforcement agencies in the Midwest reported an estimated 21.6 percent of the Nation's property crime. (See Table 3.) Property crime comprised 89.1 percent of the Midwest's 2002 Index offenses. (Based on Table 4.) The estimated number of property crime offenses in the Midwest decreased 2.0 percent from the estimated number for 2001. The Midwest's property crime rate of 3,458.2 offenses per 100,000 population was 2.5 percent below the rate for the previous year. (See Table 4.)

The South

Property crimes reported by the South's law enforcement agencies made up 41.0 percent of the Nation's property crime total. (See Table 3.) Property crime offenses accounted for an estimated 87.9 percent of the Index crimes in the South for the year. (Based on Table 4.) The region's volume showed a 0.2 percent increase over the 2001 volume. When compared to the 2001 rate, the South's property crime rate declined 1.1 percent at 4,151.0 property crimes per 100,000 inhabitants. (See Table 4.)

The West

Law enforcement agencies in the West reported 24.6 percent of the property crime nationwide. (See Table 3.) This offense category made up 88.5 percent of the Index crimes in the West. (Based on Table 4.) A comparison to the previous year's volume showed that property crime for 2002 increased 3.8 percent in the West. The estimated property crime rate of 3,910.6 offenses per 100,000 population in the West increased 2.2 percent over the 2001 rate. (See Table 4.)

Population Groups: Trends and Rates

Among population groups, property crime for 2002 decreased by 0.3 percent in the Nation's cities collectively. Changes from the 2001 volume for city

groupings ranged from a 1.1 percent increase in cities with populations of 100,000 to 249,999 to a 1.7 percent decrease in cities of 250,000 to 499,999 inhabitants. Additionally, rural counties showed an increase of 0.7 percent in 2002, and suburban counties had an increase of 1.0 percent. (See Table 12.)

The Nation's cities collectively had a property crime rate of 4,422.6 per 100,000 population. Rural counties had a property crime rate of 1,822.6 per 100,000 people, and suburban counties had a rate of 2,695.3 property crime offenses per 100,000 inhabitants. (See Table 16.)

Offense Analysis

In 2002, the estimated dollar loss attributable to property crimes (excluding arson) was $16.6 billion. This figure remained virtually unchanged from the 2001 estimated dollar loss for property crime, up less than three-tenths of one percent. (Based on Tables 1 and 23.)

Among individual property crimes, the 2002 estimated dollar losses were $3.3 billion for burglary, $4.9 billion for larceny-theft, and $8.4 billion for motor vehicle theft. (Based on Tables 1 and 23.) Arson (which is excluded from the estimated property crime tabulations because of limited coverage and participation) had an average dollar loss of $11,253 for the 66,308 offenses for which monetary values were reported. (See Table 2.32.)

Clearances

Clearances occur either by arrest or by exceptional means, i.e., when elements beyond the control of law enforcement prevent the placing of formal charges against the offender. (Section III provides more information regarding clearances.) During 2002, property crime clearances totaled 16.5 percent nationwide. (See Table 25.)

By region, 21.1 percent of property crimes in the Northeast were cleared in 2002, 15.8 percent in the Midwest, 16.7 percent in the South, and 14.7 percent in the West. (See Table 26.)

Law enforcement in the Nation's cities collectively cleared 16.4 percent of property crimes in 2002. Among the Nation's cities, those with populations of 10,000 to 24,999 had the greatest percentage of clearances, 21.1 percent, for property crimes. Cities with populations of 500,000 to 999,999 inhabitants cleared the lowest percentage of property crimes during 2002, 11.9 percent. (See Table 25.)

In rural counties, law enforcement cleared 18.3 percent of property crimes and in suburban counties, 16.4 percent. (See Table 25.)

Clearances and Juveniles

When an offender under the age of 18 is cited to appear before juvenile authorities, the UCR Program clears the incident by arrest, even though a physical arrest may not have occurred. Additionally, the Program classifies clearances involving both adult and juvenile offenders as adult clearances.

In 2002, clearances involving only juveniles (persons under the age of 18) comprised 20.3 percent of all property crime clearances. By offense breakdown, this age group accounted for 17.3 percent of burglary clearances, 21.2 percent of larceny-theft clearances, and 18.2 percent of motor vehicle theft clearances.

Juvenile clearances accounted for 20.9 percent of all property crime clearances in the Nation's cities during 2002. In the rural counties, 16.5 percent of the clearances involved juveniles and in the suburban counties, 18.1 percent. (See Table 28.)

Arrests

Total Arrests

Law enforcement made an estimated 1.6 million arrests during 2002 for property crime offenses (including arson). Property crime arrests accounted for an estimated 11.7 percent of all the arrests in 2002. Of all the arrests for property crimes, an estimated 1.2 million arrests (71.9 percent) were for larceny-theft offenses. (Additional arrest breakdowns can be found in Table 29.)

Arrest Rates

In 2002, the United States experienced a rate of 570.5 property crime arrests per 100,000 inhabitants. Among the regions, the West had the highest arrest rate for property crimes with 596.3 arrests per 100,000 persons. The South had the second highest rate for property crime arrests with 593.2, followed by the Midwest with 583.6 and the Northeast with 469.6 property crime arrests per 100,000 inhabitants. (See Table 30.)

Collectively, the Nation's cities recorded an overall property crime arrest rate of 675.4 arrests per 100,000 inhabitants. Among those population groups labeled as city, the rate of arrests per 100,000 residents ranged from a low of 616.2 in cities with populations under 10,000 to a high of 716.5 in cities with 100,000 to 249,999 in population. The Nation's suburban counties had an arrest rate of 360.0 property crime arrests per 100,000 people, and rural counties experienced 281.2 property crime arrests per 100,000 residents. (See Table 31.)

Arrest Trends

A comparison of the volume of property crime arrests from 2002 to 2001 showed a 0.6 percent increase in the overall category. Individual property crime arrests increased for motor vehicle theft by 3.9 percent, for burglary by 0.6 percent, and for larceny-theft by 0.4 percent. Arson arrests decreased by 12.0 percent. Arrests of adults for property crime in 2002 were up 2.4 percent when compared to the 2001 figure, but arrests of juveniles were down 3.6 percent when compared to the previous years' arrests. (See Table 36.)

An analysis of 5-year and 10-year trend data revealed a nationwide decline in property crime arrests over the last decade. Property crime arrests in 2002 were 12.5 percent less than in 1998 and 25.2 percent fewer than in 1993. Tables 32 and 34 provide more information regarding trend data.

Distribution by Age, Sex, and Race

Tables 38-43 in Section IV of this report furnish information on the age, sex, and race of those arrested for property crimes. In 2002, a total of 70.2 percent of property crime arrestees were adults (persons 18 years and older). (See Table 38.) By gender, 69.3 percent of all property crime arrestees were males. (See Table 42.) By race, 67.7 percent of all property crime arrests were of whites, 29.6 percent were of blacks, and 2.7 percent were of other races. (See Table 43.)

Information regarding the UCR Program's statistical methodology and table construction can be found in Appendix I.

Burglary

Definition

Burglary is defined in the Uniform Crime Reporting Program as the unlawful entry of a structure to commit a felony or theft. The use of force to gain entry is not required to classify an offense as a burglary. Burglary in the Program is categorized into three subclassifications: forcible entry, unlawful entry where no force is used, and attempted forcible entry.

Trend

Year	Number of offenses	Rate per 100,000 inhabitants
2001	2,116,531	741.8
2002	2,151,875	746.2
Percent change	+1.7	+0.6

National Volume, Trends, and Rates

Burglary offenses nationwide in 2002 were estimated at 2,151,875, marking a 1.7 percent increase when compared to the 2001 estimate. Burglary offenses made up 18.1 percent of the Crime Index and 20.6 percent of all property crimes. Five- and 10-year trends showed that the estimated burglary volume decreased 7.8 percent when compared to the 1998 estimate, and it was down 24.1 percent when compared to 1993 data. (See Table 1.)

Two-, 5-, and 10-year trend data showed that in 2002 the burglary rate was estimated at 746.2 offenses per 100,000 inhabitants. This was an increase of 0.6 percent when compared to the burglary rate in 2001, a 13.5 percent decrease from the 1998 rate, and a 32.1 percent decrease from the 1993 rate. (See Table 1.)

Community Types

Metropolitan Statistical Areas (MSAs), which made up approximately 80 percent of the total U.S. population, accounted for 82.6 percent of the Nation's burglaries and had an estimated burglary rate of 768.5 per 100,000 persons in 2002. Cities outside of MSAs, which comprised approximately 8 percent of the Nation's population, accounted for an estimated 8.4 percent of the burglaries and had a burglary rate of 805.4 per 100,000 in population. Rural areas, comprising approximately 12 percent of the U.S. population, had an estimated 9.0 percent of the country's burglaries, or a rate of 558.2 burglaries per 100,000 inhabitants. (Based on Table 2.)

Regional Offense Trends and Rates

The UCR Program divides the United States into four regions: the Northeast, the Midwest, the South, and the West. (See Appendix III.) In 2002, data collected regarding the Nation's four regions reflected the following:

The Northeast

The Northeast, accounting for 18.8 percent of the U.S. population, had an estimated 11.5 percent of the burglaries nationwide. A comparison with 2001 data showed that in 2002 the Northeast was the only region to experience a decrease in the volume of burglaries (1.8 percent). The burglary rate per

Figure 2.13

Burglary
Percent Change from 1998

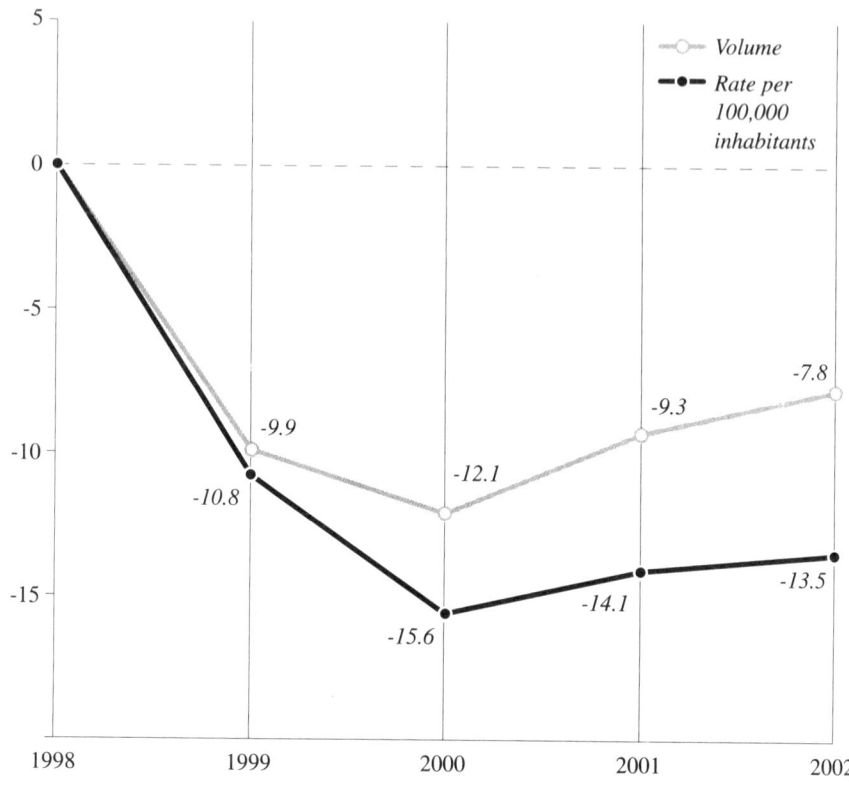

100,000 persons for 2002 was estimated at 457.8 offenses per 100,000 persons–a 2.3 percent decrease from the 2001 rate. (See Tables 3 and 4.)

The Midwest

The Midwest, comprising 22.6 percent of the country's population, had an estimated 20.7 percent of all burglaries. In 2002, the region experienced a 1.8 percent increase in the volume of burglaries over the 2001 estimate. The burglary rate per 100,000 inhabitants for 2002 was 685.4, which was a 1.3 percent increase over the 2001 estimate. (See Tables 3 and 4.)

The South

In 2002, the South, which makes up 35.8 percent of the U.S. population, experienced an estimated 44.8 percent of the Nation's burglaries, a 1.5 percent increase in the volume of burglaries from the 2001 estimate. The burglary rate per 100,000 inhabitants was 932.6, a 0.1 percent increase when compared to the 2001 rate. (See Tables 3 and 4.)

The West

The West, with 22.8 percent of the Nation's population, had an estimated 22.9 percent of all burglaries. In 2002, the region experienced a 3.9 percent increase in the volume of burglaries over the 2001 volume. The burglary rate per 100,000 in population in 2002 was estimated at 751.5, an increase of 2.2 percent when compared to the estimated rate in 2001. (See Tables 3 and 4.)

Table 2.26

Burglary by Month
Percent Distribution, 1998-2002

Month	1998	1999	2000	2001	2002
January	8.9	8.3	8.1	7.9	8.6
February	7.5	7.2	7.2	6.6	6.9
March	8.2	7.9	8.0	7.6	7.7
April	8.0	7.7	7.8	7.7	7.9
May	8.3	8.2	8.5	8.3	8.5
June	8.2	8.4	8.4	8.2	8.2
July	9.0	9.0	9.2	9.1	9.1
August	9.0	9.1	9.2	9.1	9.0
September	8.4	8.7	8.6	8.6	8.7
October	8.4	8.6	8.7	9.3	8.8
November	7.9	8.4	8.3	8.9	8.2
December	8.2	8.5	8.1	8.8	8.5

Population Groups: Trends and Rates

An examination of the data by population group showed that those cities with populations under 10,000, as well as those with populations from 10,000 to 24,999, experienced a 2.8 percent increase in reported burglaries in 2002. Those cities with populations of 250,000 and over were the only population group to experience a decline, 0.3 percent, from 2001. The Nation's cities collectively saw a 1.0 percent increase in the number of burglaries reported in 2002 when compared to the 2001 estimate. Suburban counties had an increase of 2.6 percent, and rural counties had an increase in burglaries of 2.4 percent. (See Table 12.)

In 2002, the Nation's cities collectively had a burglary rate of 840.8 offenses per 100,000 persons. Those cities with populations from 500,000 to 999,999 had a burglary rate of 1,213.6 offenses per 100,000 inhabitants, the highest among all population groups. Cities with populations of 10,000 to 24,999 had the lowest rate among the Nation's cities, 645.6 per 100,000 persons. Suburban counties had a rate of 652.6 burglaries per 100,000 in population, and rural counties had a rate of 595.9 per 100,000 persons. (See Table 16.)

Offense Analysis

Among those agencies that reported burglary statistics for all 12 months of 2002, the data showed that forcible entry burglaries accounted for 62.8 percent of the burglary offenses, unlawful entry comprised 30.8 percent, and attempted forcible entry accounted for approximately 6.5 percent. (Based on Table 19.)

The majority of burglaries, 65.8 percent, were residential, and the remaining 34.2 percent were of nonresidences, such as stores, offices, etc. A review of burglary data in which the time of the offense was known showed that most residential burglaries, 61.7 percent,

occurred during daytime hours, and most nonresidential burglaries, 57.7 percent, occurred at night. The time of occurrence for 24.1 percent of burglaries was unknown. (Based on Table 23.)

Losses due to burglary totaled an estimated $3.3 billion in 2002, with an estimated average value of $1,549 per offense. Residential burglaries averaged $1,482 per offense, and nonresidential burglaries averaged $1,678 per offense. (Based on Table 23.)

Clearances

Law enforcement cleared 13.0 percent of reported burglaries by arrest or exceptional means in 2002. Cities with under 10,000 in population cleared 16.3 percent of burglaries, the highest percentage of clearances among the Nation's cities. Those cities with populations of 500,000 to 999,999 cleared the lowest percentage of burglaries, 9.4 percent. Cities overall cleared 12.3 percent of burglaries in 2002. Rural counties cleared 16.6 percent of burglary offenses, and suburban counties cleared 14.0 percent. (See Table 25.)

Regionally, law enforcement agencies in the Northeast cleared 17.7 percent of the burglaries brought to the attention of law enforcement. Those in the South cleared 13.4 percent of burglaries, in the West 11.8 percent, and in the Midwest 11.0 percent. (See Table 26.)

Burglaries involving unlawful entry without use of force were cleared by arrest or exceptional means in 14.1 percent of the reported cases during 2002. Approximately 10.8 percent of attempted forcible entry burglaries and 12.3 percent of forcible entry burglaries were cleared. (See Table 27.)

Clearances and Juveniles

The UCR Program considers an incident involving only offenders under the age of 18 to be cleared by arrest when an offender is cited to appear in juvenile court or before other juvenile authorities, even though a physical arrest may not have occurred. Clearances involving

Figure 2.14

Burglary
Percent Change from 1998

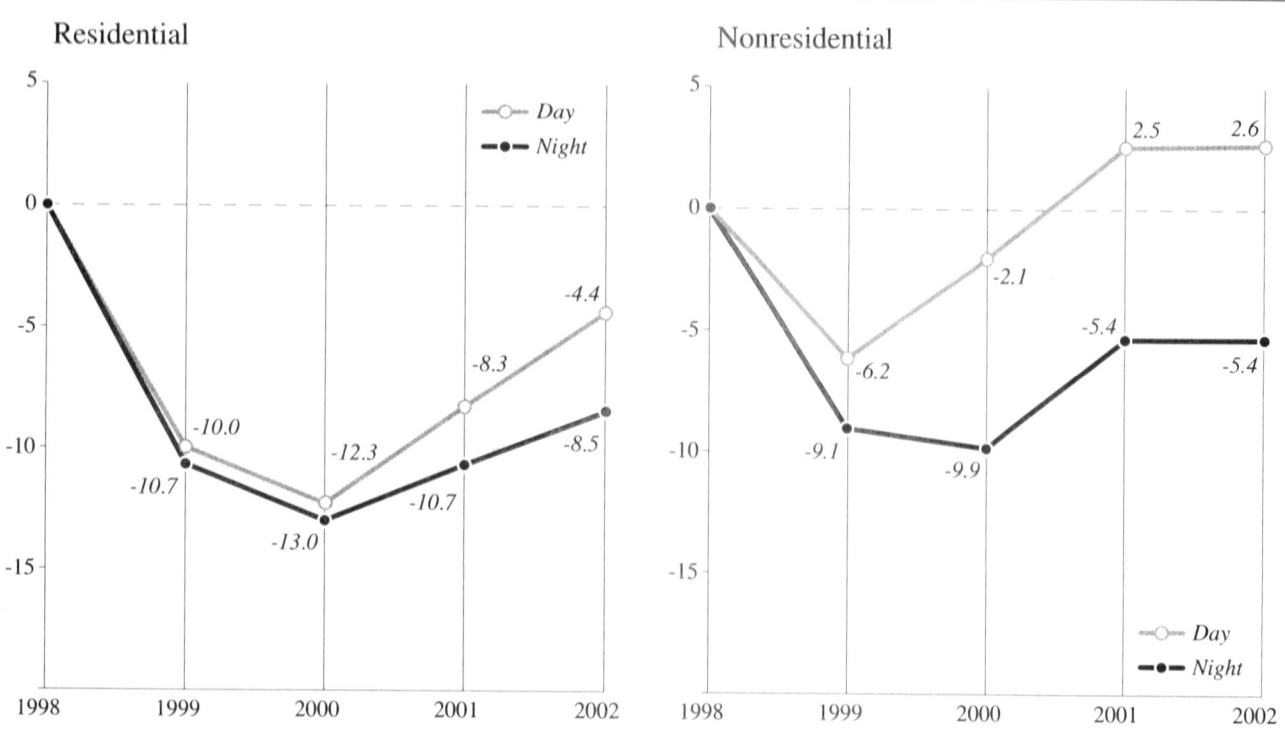

Residential

Nonresidential

Arrests

both adult and juvenile offenders are classified as adult clearances. Therefore, juveniles who may be participating in a burglary with an adult were not included in these figures.

In 2002, persons under 18 years of age comprised 17.3 percent of the burglaries cleared by arrest or exceptional means. A review of the data by population group showed that cities with populations under 10,000 had the highest percentage of clearances for burglary involving juveniles at 21.5 percent. Cities 250,000 and over in population had the lowest percentage of clearances for burglary involving juveniles at 14.4 percent. Rural county agencies reported that 16.6 percent of the burglary clearances in their jurisdictions were of juveniles, and suburban county agencies reported that juveniles accounted for 17.6 percent of clearances. (See Table 28.)

The estimated number of burglary arrests for 2002 was 288,291. Burglary arrests accounted for an estimated 12.9 percent of the arrests for Crime Index offenses and an estimated 17.9 percent of the arrests for property crimes. (Based on Table 29.)

In 2002, law enforcement agencies in the West reported 121.2 burglary arrests per 100,000 inhabitants. Agencies in the South reported an arrest rate of 103.5, the Northeast a rate of 83.3, and the Midwest a rate of 81.5 burglary arrests per 100,000 in population. (See Table 30.)

The Nation's cities collectively reported a burglary arrest rate per 100,000 inhabitants of 106.3. Those cities with populations of 25,000 to 49,999 reported the fewest arrests per 100,000 inhabitants, 89.1. Cities with 100,000 to 249,999 inhabitants reported

the highest number of arrests per 100,000 population, 123.4. Rural and suburban counties reported arrest rates of 95.2 and 83.1, respectively. (See Table 31.)

When compared to 2001 data, overall arrests for burglaries in 2002 increased 0.6 percent. Arrests of adults increased 2.9 percent; however, arrests of juveniles declined 4.4 percent. (See Table 36.)

Five- and 10-year trend data showed that burglary arrests overall declined 12.0 percent since 1998 and 29.7 percent since 1993. Additionally, in 2002 arrests of adults for burglary declined 4.2 percent since 1998 and 24.4 percent since 1993; arrests of juveniles declined 26.1 percent since 1998 and 39.2 percent since 1993. (See Tables 32 and 34.)

Adults (persons aged 18 and over) comprised 70.0 percent of those individuals arrested for burglary in 2002.

(Based on Table 38.) Males accounted for 86.7 percent of burglary arrestees. (See Table 42.) Of the male arrestees, 30.7 percent were juveniles (under 18 years of age). (Based on Table 39.) Of the female arrestees, 25.3 percent were juveniles. (Based on Table 40.)

By race, 70.4 percent of all burglary arrestees were white, 27.5 percent were black, and 2.1 percent were of other races. Of those adults arrested for burglary, 69.6 percent were white, 28.5 percent were black, and 1.9 percent were of other races. Of burglary arrestees under age 18, 72.4 percent were white, 25.2 percent were black, and 2.4 were of other races. (See Table 43.)

Larceny-theft

Definition

Larceny-theft is the unlawful taking, carrying, leading, or riding away of property from the possession or constructive possession of another. It includes crimes such as shoplifting, pocket-picking, purse-snatching, thefts from motor vehicles, thefts of motor vehicle parts and accessories, bicycle thefts, etc., in which no use of force, violence, or fraud occurs. In the Uniform Crime Reporting Program, this crime category does not include embezzlement, confidence games, forgery, and worthless checks. Motor vehicle theft is also excluded from this category inasmuch as it is a separate Crime Index offense.

Trend

Year	Number of offenses	Rate per 100,000 inhabitants
2001	7,092,267	2,485.7
2002	7,052,922	2,445.8
Percent change	-0.6	-1.6

National Volume, Trends, and Rates

In the Nation in 2002, the number of larceny-theft offenses was estimated at over 7 million and cost victims an estimated $4.9 billion in losses. (See Tables 1 and 23.)

The larceny-theft offenses in the Nation accounted for 59.4 percent of the 2002 Crime Index total and 67.5 percent of the property crime total. An examination of trends showed a 0.6 percent decrease in larceny-theft volume when 2002 data are compared to 2001 data, a 4.4 percent decrease from 1998 figures, and a decrease of 9.8 percent from the 1993 total. (See Table 1.)

In 2002, the larceny-theft rate for the Nation was an estimated 2,445.8 offenses per 100,000 in population, a 1.6 percent decrease from the 2001 rate. Five- and 10-year trends showed the rate fell 10.4 percent from the 1998 rate and 19.4 percent from the 1993 rate. (See Table 1.)

Community Types

By community type, Metropolitan Statistical Areas (MSAs) had an estimated a rate of 2,596.4 larceny offenses per 100,000 inhabitants. Cities outside MSAs had a rate of 3,107.9, and rural counties experienced a rate of 1,005.0 per 100,000 population. (See Table 2.) The UCR Program's definition of these community types can be found in Appendix III.

Regional Offense Trends and Rates

The UCR Program divides the United States into four regions: the Northeast, the Midwest, the South, and the West. (See Appendix III.) Regionally in 2002, the South, the Nation's most populous region with 35.8 percent of the population, accounted for 40.9 percent of the larceny-thefts nationwide. The West accounted for 23.6 percent of the total larceny-thefts, followed by the Midwest

Figure 2.15

Larceny-theft
Percent Change from 1998

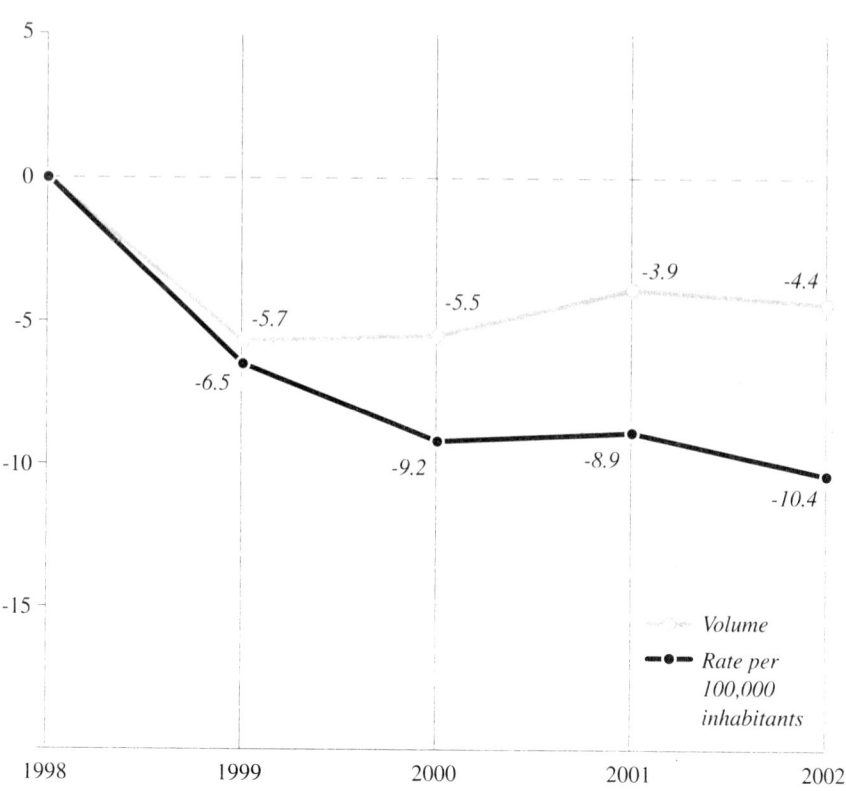

	-5.7	-5.5	-3.9	-4.4
	-6.5	-9.2	-8.9	-10.4

Volume
Rate per 100,000 inhabitants

1998   1999   2000   2001   2002

with 22.3 percent, and the Northeast with 13.2 percent. (See Table 3.)

An examination of 2002 regional volumes for larceny-theft compared to 2001 data revealed that the West was the only region that had an increase (2.5 percent). Larceny-theft offenses decreased an estimated 3.4 percent in the Northeast, 2.6 percent in the Midwest, and 0.2 percent in the South. Among the geographic regions in 2002, the South had an estimated larceny-theft rate per 100,000 inhabitants of 2,794.1 and the West a rate of 2,534.0. The Midwest had a rate of 2,413.5 per 100,000 inhabitants and the Northeast, a rate of 1,714.0 per 100,000 population. Rate trends comparing 2001 and 2002 data showed that the larceny-theft rate per 100,000 inhabitants was up 0.8 percent in the West; the rate declined 3.9 percent in the Northeast, 3.1 percent in the Midwest, and 1.5 percent in the South. (See Table 4.)

Population Groups: Trends and Rates

Collectively in 2002, the Nation's cities reported a decrease of 0.7 percent in larceny-thefts from 2001. Cities with populations of 250,000 to 499,999 reported a decrease of 2.3 percent, and cities with populations of 100,000 to 249,999 reported an increase of 0.8 percent. Both rural and suburban counties reported decreases of 0.6 percent for larceny-theft offenses. (See Table 12.) Cities collectively had a larceny-theft rate of 3,017.1 per 100,000 in population. Cities with populations of 500,000 to 999,999 showed a rate of 3,907.2 larceny-theft offenses per 100,000 inhabitants, and the Nation's largest cities (those 1 million and over in population) had a larceny-theft rate of 2,615.8. Suburban counties had a rate of 1,740.0 per 100,000 inhabitants, and rural counties registered a rate of 1,083.3. (See Table 16.)

Offense Analysis

Distribution

In 2002, thefts from motor vehicles accounted for 26.5 percent of reported larceny-thefts, followed by shoplifting with 14.0 percent. Thefts from buildings made up 12.5 percent of the larceny-theft total; thefts of motor vehicle accessories accounted for 10.7 percent; and thefts of bicycles, 3.9 percent. Pocket-pickings, purse-snatchings, thefts from coin-operated machines, and other miscellaneous types of larceny-thefts comprised the remainder. (See Table 23.)

Loss by Dollar Value

In 2002, an estimated $4.9 billion in property was lost due to larceny-theft. The average value of property stolen per offense was $699, down from the 2001 average value of $730. (See Table 23.)

Thefts from buildings in 2002 was the larceny-theft offense with the highest average loss, $1,013. For thefts from motor vehicles, the average value loss was $692, and for thefts of motor vehicle accessories, $432. Purse-snatchings had an average value loss of $332, and pocket-pickings an average loss of $328. Thefts of bicycles resulted in an average value loss of $257, and in thefts from coin-operated machines, the average loss was $250. Shoplifting was the category with the lowest average dollar loss, $187. (See Table 23.)

Losses of property valued over $200 accounted for 39.6 percent of reported larceny-thefts. Stolen property valued under $50 comprised 37.8 percent of the reported larceny-theft offenses, and 22.6 percent involved losses ranging from $50 to $200. (See Table 23.)

Clearances

Nationwide in 2002, 18.0 percent of larceny-theft offenses were cleared by arrest or exceptional means. Collectively the Nation's cities had a larceny-theft clearance rate of 18.1 percent. Those cities with 10,000 to 24,999 inhabitants had the highest rate of clearances for larceny-theft offenses among the Nation's cities, 22.6 percent, and cities with 500,000 to 999,999 inhabitants had the lowest clearance rate for larceny-theft offenses, 13.1 percent. Rural county agencies cleared 17.9 percent of larceny-thefts, and law enforcement in suburban counties cleared 17.4 percent. (See Table 25.)

Regionally, the highest rate of larceny-theft clearances in 2002 occurred in the Northeast with 22.9 percent of offenses cleared. Agencies in the South cleared 17.9 percent of the larceny-thefts reported. The Midwest and West had clearance rates of 17.3 and 16.6 percent, respectively. (See Table 26.)

Table 2.27

Larceny-theft by Month
Percent Distribution, 1998-2002

Month	1998	1999	2000	2001	2002
January	8.4	7.8	7.6	7.7	8.1
February	7.5	7.2	7.3	6.8	7.0
March	8.2	8.0	8.2	7.8	7.8
April	8.1	8.0	7.9	8.0	8.1
May	8.4	8.4	8.6	8.6	8.6
June	8.6	8.7	8.8	8.6	8.5
July	9.0	9.1	9.2	9.1	9.2
August	9.0	9.2	9.2	9.1	9.1
September	8.4	8.5	8.5	8.4	8.6
October	8.5	8.7	8.8	9.1	8.9
November	7.8	8.1	8.0	8.3	8.0
December	8.2	8.3	7.9	8.4	8.1

Table 2.28

Larceny-theft
Percent Distribution by Region, 2002

Type	United States total	Northeast	Midwest	South	West
Total¹	100.0	100.0	100.0	100.0	100.0
Pocket-picking	0.5	1.0	0.4	0.4	0.4
Purse-snatching	0.6	1.2	0.5	0.4	0.5
Shoplifting	14.0	15.2	13.1	13.5	14.8
From motor vehicles (except accessories)	26.5	21.5	23.8	25.0	32.7
Motor vehicle accessories	10.7	8.2	10.9	10.7	11.7
Bicycles	3.9	5.8	4.6	3.1	4.0
From buildings	12.5	16.3	14.6	10.5	12.9
From coin-operated machines	0.7	0.7	0.6	0.9	0.7
All others	30.7	30.3	31.5	35.4	22.3

¹ Because of rounding, the percentages may not add to 100.0.

Figure 2.16

Larceny-theft categories
Percent Change from 1998

Pocket-picking

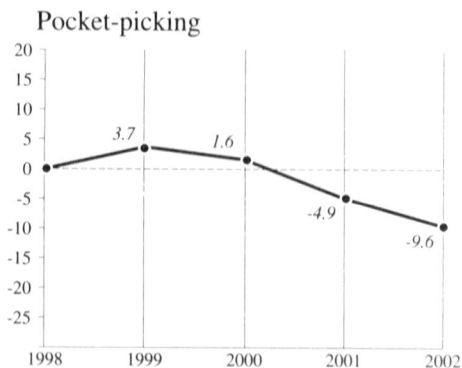

Purse-snatching

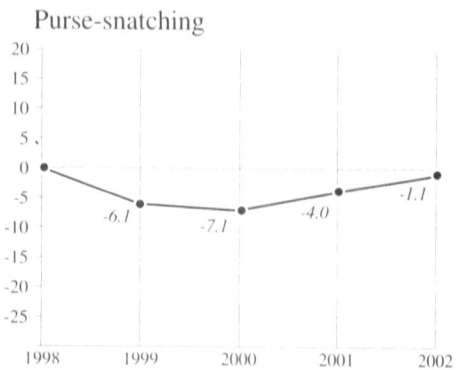

Shoplifting

From motor vehicles

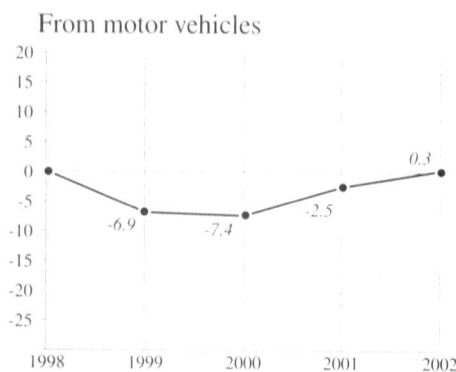

Motor vehicle accessories

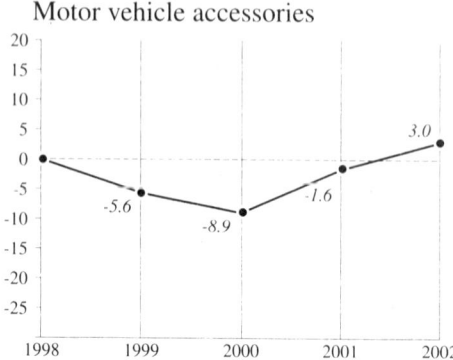

Bicycles

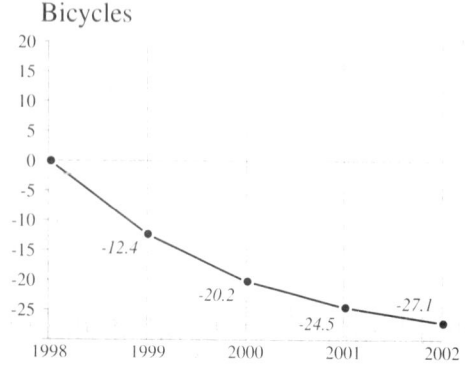

From buildings

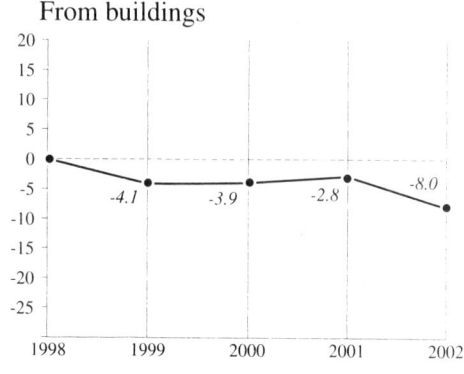

From coin-operated machines

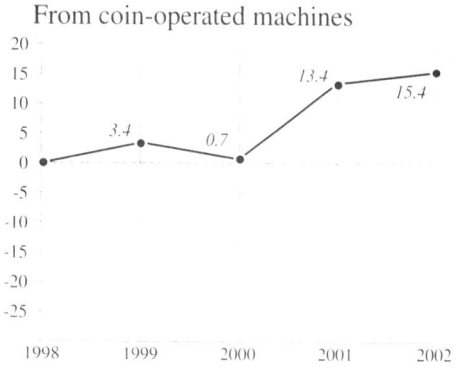

Just over 21 percent (21.2) of all larceny-theft clearances were of juveniles (persons under 18 years of age). Juveniles comprised 21.9 percent of offense clearances in the Nation's cities. By population group, cities with populations of 50,000 to 99,999 inhabitants had the largest percentage of juvenile clearances—25.0. Rural counties reported juvenile clearances at 15.9 percent, and suburban counties reported juvenile clearances at 18.6 percent. (See Table 28.)

Arrests

In 2002, the estimated number of arrests for larceny-thefts in the Nation was 1,160,085, the highest arrest total among the eight Crime Index offenses. Larceny-theft arrests accounted for an estimated 51.9 percent of the Crime Index arrests, and an estimated 71.9 percent of the property crime arrests. (Based on Table 29.) Law enforcement agencies in the South experienced the highest rate of larceny-theft arrests, 444.9 per 100,000 inhabitants. Those in the Midwestern states had an arrest

rate of 441.4, followed by the West, 394.4, and the Northeast, 345.8 arrests per 100,000 population. (See Table 30.) Among the population groups, larceny-theft arrest rates were 503.0 per 100,000 inhabitants in the Nation's cities collectively, 234.2 in suburban counties, and 151.6 in rural counties. (See Table 31.)

Larceny-theft arrests in 2002 were up slightly, 0.4 percent, when compared to 2001 arrests. Larceny-theft arrests of juveniles declined 3.0 percent from the previous year's number. Arrests of adults for larceny-thefts showed an increase, 1.8 percent. (See Table 36.) Arrests for males were down 0.2 percent, and arrests of females increased by 1.3 percent. (See Table 37.)

In 2002, arrests of juveniles accounted for 29.5 percent of reported larceny-theft arrests. (See Table 41.) Of the juveniles arrested for larceny-theft, 70.1 percent were white, 26.5 percent were black, and the remainder were other races. (See Table 43.) By race, 67.9 percent of persons arrested for larceny-theft were white and 29.3 percent were black. The remaining 2.8 percent were of other races. (See Table 43.)

Males accounted for 63.0 percent of the total arrestees for larceny-theft. (See Table 42.)

Figure 2.17

Larceny-theft
Percent Distribution[1] 2002

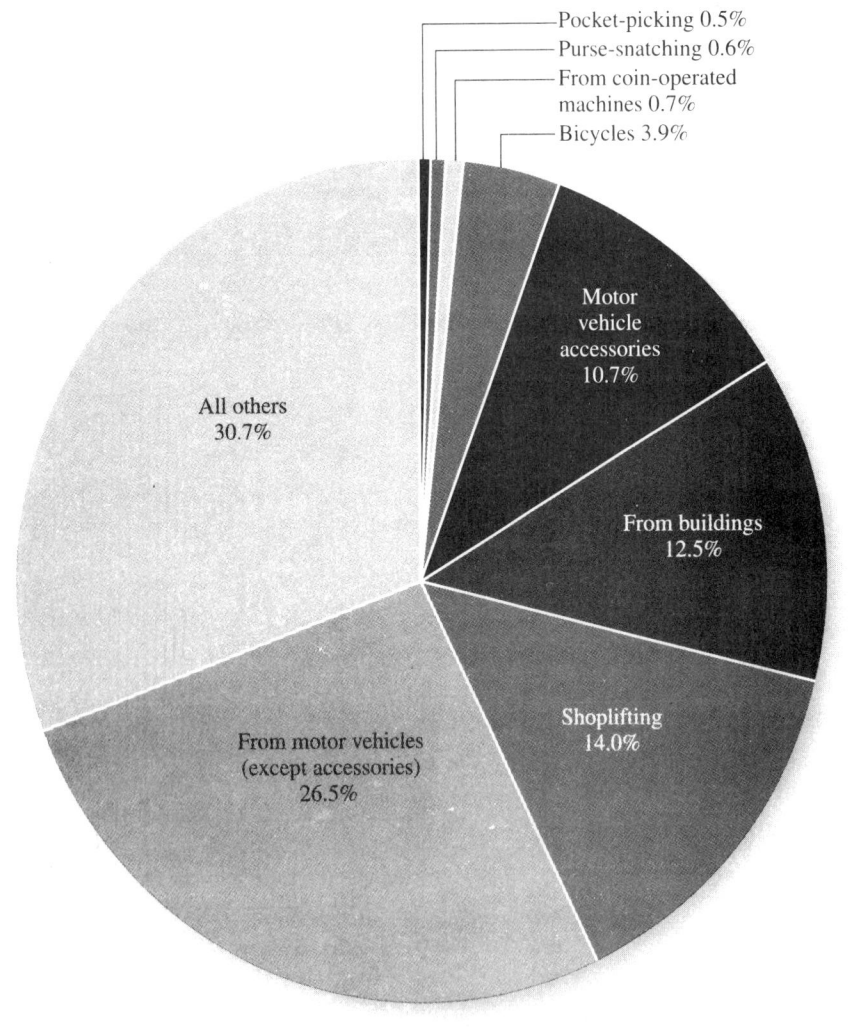

- Pocket-picking 0.5%
- Purse-snatching 0.6%
- From coin-operated machines 0.7%
- Bicycles 3.9%

Motor vehicle accessories 10.7%

All others 30.7%

From buildings 12.5%

Shoplifting 14.0%

From motor vehicles (except accessories) 26.5%

[1] Due to rounding, the percentages may not add to 100.0.

Motor Vehicle Theft

Definition

The Uniform Crime Reporting (UCR) Program defines motor vehicle theft as the theft or attempted theft of a motor vehicle. This offense includes the stealing of automobiles, trucks, buses, motorcycles, motorscooters, snowmobiles, etc. The taking of a motor vehicle for temporary use by persons having lawful access is excluded from this definition.

Trend

Year	Number of offenses	Rate per 100,000 inhabitants
2001	1,228,391	430.5
2002	1,246,096	432.1
Percent change	+1.4	+0.4

National Volume, Trends, and Rates

There were an estimated 1,246,096 motor vehicle thefts in the United States during 2002, which was a 1.4 percent increase in volume when compared to the 2001 estimate and a 0.3 percent increase over the 1998 estimate. The estimated number of motor vehicle thefts decreased 20.3 percent

when compared to the 1993 estimate. (See Table 1.)

The rate of motor vehicle thefts in the Nation in 2002 was an estimated 432.1 offenses per 100,000 inhabitants, which was a 0.4 percent increase over the 2001 rate. The rate of motor vehicle thefts per 100,000 inhabitants decreased 6.0 percent when compared to the 1998 rate and 28.7 percent from the 1993 rate. (See Table 1.)

Community Types

The UCR Program defines three community types: Metropolitan Statistical Areas (MSAs), cities outside MSAs, and rural counties. Additional information regarding community types is presented in Appendix III.

The estimated motor vehicle theft rate per 100,000 inhabitants during 2002 was 498.6 in MSAs, 207.6 in cities outside MSAs, and 132.8 in rural counties. (See Table 2.)

Regional Offense Trends and Rates

As shown in Appendix III, the UCR Program divides the Nation into four regions: the Northeast, the Midwest, the South, and the West. An examination of motor vehicle theft data by region indicated the following:

The Northeast

In 2002, 18.8 percent of the Nation's population resided in the Northeast. This region accounted for an estimated 13.1 percent of all motor vehicle thefts. (See Table 3.) The rate of stolen vehicles in the Northeast was an estimated 300.8 offenses per 100,000 inhabitants, a 5.4 percent decrease from the previous year's data. (See Table 4.)

The Midwest

The Midwestern Region, accounting for 22.6 percent of the U.S. population, had an estimated 18.8 percent of all motor vehicle thefts in the Nation. (See Table 3.) In 2002, the Midwest had an estimated rate of 359.4 motor vehicle

Figure 2.18

Motor Vehicle Theft
Percent Change from 1998

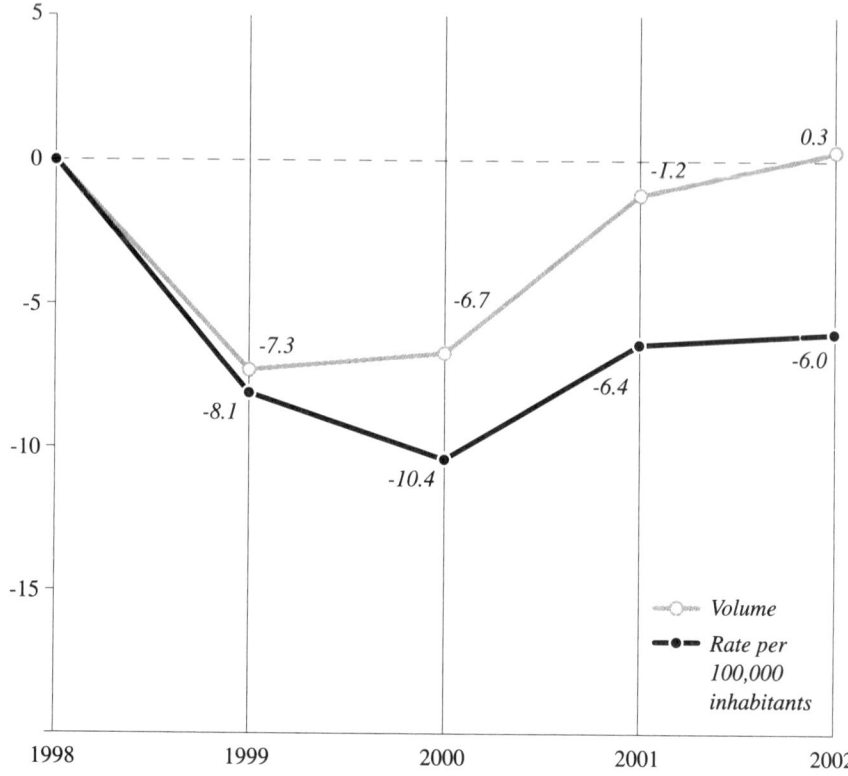

thefts per 100,000 inhabitants, which was a 5.2 percent decline from the previous year's rate. (See Table 4.)

The South

The most populous region, with 35.8 percent of the Nation's inhabitants, the South had the highest percentage of motor vehicle thefts, 35.2 percent. (See Table 3.) In 2002, the South had a rate of 424.3 motor vehicle thefts per 100,000 in population, which was a 1.1 percent decrease from the 2001 estimate. (See Table 4.)

The West

The Western Region, with 22.8 percent of the Nation's population, had an estimated 32.9 percent of the motor vehicle theft offenses. (See Table 3.) The region had the highest estimated rate, 625.1 motor vehicle thefts per 100,000 inhabitants. The region had the only increase, 8.0 percent, in rate from 2001 to 2002. (See Table 4.)

Table 2.29

Motor Vehicle Theft by Month
Percent Distribution, 1998–2002

Month	1998	1999	2000	2001	2002
January	9.1	8.5	8.1	8.1	8.6
February	7.9	7.3	7.4	6.9	7.2
March	8.5	7.9	8.0	7.7	8.1
April	7.9	7.7	7.6	7.6	7.8
May	8.3	8.0	8.2	8.0	8.1
June	8.1	8.2	8.3	8.2	8.1
July	8.7	8.8	8.9	9.0	9.0
August	8.8	9.0	9.1	8.9	8.8
September	8.3	8.5	8.5	8.5	8.6
October	8.4	8.8	8.7	9.3	8.8
November	7.9	8.5	8.5	8.9	8.4
December	8.1	8.8	8.6	9.0	8.6

Table 2.30

Motor Vehicle Theft
Percent Distribution by Region, 2002

Region	Total [1]	Autos	Trucks and buses	Other vehicles
Total	100.0	73.6	18.6	7.8
Northeast	100.0	88.5	5.2	6.2
Midwest	100.0	78.5	14.2	7.3
South	100.0	69.8	20.2	10.0
West	100.0	70.8	22.9	6.4

[1] Because of rounding, the percentages may not add to 100.0.

Population Groups: Trends and Rates

In the UCR Program, cities are grouped according to population size and counties are classified as either suburban or rural. (Additional information about population groups is located in Appendix III.) In 2002, the Nation's cities collectively had a 0.2 percent increase in the number of motor vehicle thefts. Cities with populations of 50,000 to 99,999 inhabitants had the largest increase of motor vehicle thefts, 2.7 percent, from the previous years' total.

Both suburban and rural counties had increases in the number of motor vehicle theft offenses when comparing 2001 to 2002 data—6.8 percent in suburban counties and 3.4 percent in rural counties. (See Table 12.)

During 2002, cities overall had a rate of 564.7 motor vehicle thefts per 100,000 inhabitants. Cities with populations of 250,000 and over had the highest rate at 927.8, and cities with fewer than 10,000 inhabitants had the lowest rate at 229.9 motor vehicle thefts per 100,000 in population. Suburban counties had a rate of 302.7 motor vehicle theft offenses per 100,000 inhabitants. In rural counties, the rate was 143.4. (See Table 16.)

Offense Analysis

By vehicle type, automobiles were stolen at a rate of 337.5 cars per 100,000 inhabitants. Trucks and buses (commercial vehicles) were stolen at a rate of 85.2 vehicles per 100,000 in population, and other types of vehicles at a rate of 35.9. (See Table 19.)

In the Nation, 73.6 percent of stolen vehicles were automobiles. Of the vehicles stolen in the Northeast, 88.5 percent were automobiles; in the Midwest, 78.5 percent, and in the West, 70.8 percent. In the South, 69.8 percent of the motor vehicles stolen in that region were automobiles. (See Table 2.30.)

The average value of motor vehicles reported stolen in 2002 was $6,701. The estimated total value of all motor vehicles stolen was $8.4 billion. (Based on Tables 1 and 23.)

Clearances

The UCR Program considers an offense to be cleared by arrest or "solved" when at least one person is arrested, charged with the commission of the offense, and turned over to the court for prosecution. A clearance by exceptional means can be recorded when the offender has been identified and located and there is enough evidence to support an arrest, but conditions beyond law enforcement's control prevent an agency from bringing charges. More information about clearances is available in Section III of this publication.

Of the motor vehicle thefts committed in the Nation in 2002, 13.8 percent were cleared by arrest or exceptional means. Cities overall had a motor vehicle theft clearance rate of 12.8 percent. Of all the city population groupings, cities with populations under 10,000 persons had the highest clearance rate at 26.3 percent; the Nation's largest cities, those with 250,000 or more inhabitants, had the lowest clearance rate at 10.3 percent. Rural counties cleared 27.9 percent of motor vehicle thefts by arrest or exceptional means, and suburban counties cleared 15.7 percent. (See Table 25.)

By region, the Northeast had the highest clearance rate, 15.7 percent. The South cleared 15.6 percent of the motor vehicle theft offenses reported in that region and the Midwest, 14.9 percent. The West cleared 10.8 percent of the motor vehicle thefts brought to law enforcement's attention. (See Table 26.)

Clearances and Juveniles

The UCR Program also considers an incident cleared by arrest if an offender under the age of 18 is physically arrested or if the individual is cited to appear before juvenile authorities. According to UCR guidelines, any clearance that involves both adult and juvenile offenders is listed as an adult clearance. Clearances involving only juveniles (those under age 18) accounted for 18.2 percent of all motor vehicle theft clearances. In cities overall, 18.5 percent of motor vehicle theft clearances involved juveniles only. Among the population groups labeled as city, those cities with populations of 500,000 to 999,999 inhabitants had the highest percentage of juvenile clearances at 21.1 percent. Cities with populations of 100,000 to 249,999 and those with 10,000 to 24,999 inhabitants had the lowest percentage of juvenile clearances at 17.1 percent each. Law enforcement agencies in rural counties reported 19.7 percent of clearances involved juveniles; suburban county law enforcement officials reported 16.1 percent of motor vehicle theft clearances involved only juveniles. (See Table 28.)

Arrests

Throughout the United States in 2002, there were an estimated 148,943 arrests for motor vehicle theft. (See Table 29.) Two-, 5-, and 10-year trend data showed that the number of motor vehicle theft arrests in the Nation was 3.9 percent higher than in 2001 but 0.8 percent lower than the number of motor vehicle theft arrests in 1998. The number of motor vehicle theft arrests during 2002 was 26.4 percent lower than in 1993. (See Tables 32, 34, and 36.)

The rate of motor vehicle theft arrests was 52.3 per 100,000 inhabitants in the United States. Among the four geographic regions, the West had the highest arrest rate for motor vehicle theft at 74.9 per 100,000 inhabitants; the Midwest, 54.9; the South, 39.2; and the Northeast, 34.6. (See Table 30.)

An examination of arrests by those population groups labeled as city showed that the Nation's largest cities, those with 250,000 inhabitants or greater, had the highest arrest rate for motor vehicle theft at 109.1 per 100,000 in population. Cities with populations of 25,000 to 49,999 had the lowest arrest rate at 31.8 per 100,000 in population. Law enforcement agencies in suburban counties reported a motor vehicle theft arrest rate of 36.9 per 100,000 inhabitants; rural law enforcement agencies reported a rate of 29.5. (See Table 31.)

By age, of those persons arrested for motor vehicle thefts in 2002, 63.8 percent were under the age of 25 and 30.4 percent were under the age of 18. Adults comprised 69.6 percent of motor vehicle theft arrestees. (See Tables 38 and 41.)

By sex, 83.5 percent of motor vehicle theft arrestees were males. (See Table 42.) Overall arrests of males for motor vehicle theft during 2002 increased 3.9 percent when compared to 2001 arrest totals; arrests of male juveniles decreased 5.6 percent. Arrests of females increased 4.0 percent from 2001 to 2002; however, arrests of female juveniles from 2001 to 2002 decreased 6.2 percent. (See Table 37.)

During 2002, 60.4 percent of arrestees for motor vehicle theft were white, 36.5 percent were black, and the remainder were of other races. Of juvenile arrestees, whites accounted for 58.3 percent and blacks accounted for 38.3 percent. The remaining percentage was comprised of juveniles of other races. (See Table 43.)

Arson

Definition

The Uniform Crime Reporting (UCR) Program defines arson as any willful or malicious burning or attempt to burn, with or without intent to defraud, a dwelling house, public building, motor vehicle or aircraft, personal property of another, etc.

Only fires determined through investigation to have been willfully or maliciously set are classified as arsons. Fires of suspicious or unknown origins are excluded.

National Coverage

During 2002, 12,454 law enforcement agencies provided from 1 to 12 months of arson data and reported 74,921 offenses to the UCR Program. Of the 12,454 agencies, 12,414 submitted additional information (such as structure type and estimated value of property damage) for 66,308 arsons. Of those agencies submitting supplemental information, 9,413 agencies provided 12 months of data covering 72.7 percent of the population.

Because of limited reporting of arson offenses by law enforcement, the UCR Program does not estimate for this offense and, therefore, does not include arson offenses in tables that contain offense estimates. (Tables 1 through 7, inclusive.) Tables 8–11 in this report present the total number of arsons reported by individual law enforcement agencies. The number of arson offenses are listed separately in the Arson column and aggregated with the Crime Index offenses for presentation in the Modified Crime Index column presented in those tables. Arson is not included in the national rate calculations; arson rates are computed separately and presented in Table 2.31. Tables 12-15 in this publication provide 2-year arson trend data. Arson clearance data are located in Table 2.32 and Tables 25-28. Additional information regarding the specific composition of each table is provided in the Table Methodology section of Appendix I.

Characteristics

Type

The UCR Program identifies arson by type of property burned: structure, mobile, and other. In 2002, structural arsons (residential, commercial, industrial, etc.) were the type most frequently reported, and accounted for 41.3 percent of those arsons for which supplemental data were received. Mobile properties, such as motor vehicles and trailers, made up 33.1 percent of arsons, and other properties (crops, timber, etc.) accounted for 25.7 percent of arson offenses. (See Table 2.32.)

Within structural arsons, the burning of residential properties accounted for 60.7 percent of those offenses. Single occupancy residences comprised 71.0 percent of the residential arsons. At the time of the arson, 18.2 percent of structural properties were uninhabited or not in use. In terms of mobile property arsons, motor vehicles comprised 94.6 percent of that type of arson. (See Table 2.32.)

During 2002, structural arsons declined 6.9 percent and arson incidents involving mobile property decreased 2.5 percent when compared to 2001 arson data. Arsons of other type property decreased 5.5 percent from the 2001 number. (See Table 15.)

Dollar Loss

In 2002, the average dollar loss associated with arson offenses was $11,253. The average dollar loss for structural property arsons was $20,818, and the average dollar loss for mobile property arson offenses was $6,073. Other property type arson offenses had an average dollar loss of $2,536. (See Table 2.32.)

Population Groups: Trends and Rates

The UCR Program determines population groups using several factors, one of which includes population size. These groups are further discussed in Appendix III. An examination of 2-year trend data showed that arsons in the Nation in 2002 declined 3.7 percent from 2001 data. In the Nation's cities collectively, arsons declined 3.1 percent from the previous year's number. Among the population groups labeled as *city*, cities with 100,000 to 249,999 in population had the only increase in the number of arson offenses, a rise of 0.7 percent when compared with 2001 data. Law enforcement agencies in suburban

Table 2.31

Arson Rate
by Population Group, 2002

[9,413 agencies; 2002 estimated population 209,674,400; rate per 100,000 inhabitants]

Population group	Rate
Total	32.4
Total cities	36.5
Group I (cities 250,000 and over)	58.6
(cities 1,000,000 and over)	52.3
(cities 500,000 to 999,999)	57.3
(cities 250,000 to 499,999)	68.3
Group II (cities 100,000 to 249,999)	38.8
Group III (cities 50,000 to 99,999)	28.6
Group IV (cities 25,000 to 49,999)	24.3
Group V (cities 10,000 to 24,999)	20.0
Group VI (cities under 10,000)	25.2
Suburban counties	27.0
Rural counties	16.6
Suburban area[1]	24.2

[1] Suburban area includes law enforcement agencies in cities with less than 50,000 inhabitants and county law enforcement agencies that are within a Metropolitan Statistical Area (see Appendix III). Suburban area excludes all metropolitan agencies associated with a central city. The agencies associated with suburban areas also appear in other groups within this table.

Table 2.32

Arson
by Type of Property, 2002
[12,414 agencies; 2002 estimated population 225,428,667]

Property classification	Number of offenses	Percent distribution [1]	Percent not in use	Average damage	Total clearances	Percent of offenses cleared [2]	Percent of clearances under 18
Total	66,308	100.0		$11,253	11,190	16.9	42.1
Total structure:	27,373	41.3	18.2	20,818	6,139	22.4	40.3
Single occupancy residential	11,789	17.8	19.7	18,535	2,631	22.3	31.2
Other residential	4,821	7.3	14.8	21,846	1,071	22.2	30.7
Storage	1,940	2.9	19.7	15,627	391	20.2	54.0
Industrial/manufacturing	333	0.5	22.8	71,376	62	18.6	29.0
Other commercial	2,735	4.1	15.4	45,927	485	17.7	27.6
Community/public	3,140	4.7	13.6	11,181	1,036	33.0	71.8
Other structure	2,615	3.9	24.3	11,933	463	17.7	47.1
Total mobile:	21,920	33.1		6,073	1,584	7.2	23.6
Motor vehicles	20,736	31.3		5,781	1,423	6.9	21.9
Other mobile	1,184	1.8		11,183	161	13.6	39.1
Other	17,015	25.7		2,536	3,467	20.4	53.5

[1] Because of rounding, the percentages may not add to 100.0.
[2] Includes offenses cleared by arrest or exceptional means.

counties reported a 5.4 percent decrease, and rural county law enforcement agencies had a 5.0 percent decrease in the number of arsons when compared to 2001 data. (See Table 12.)

Rates

Collectively, law enforcement agencies in the Nation reported an arson rate of 32.4 offenses per 100,000 inhabitants. Cities overall reported a rate of 36.5 arsons per 100,000 inhabitants. Among city population groupings, cities with populations of 250,000 and over posted the highest arson rate at 58.6 per 100,000 persons, and cities of 10,000 to 24,999 inhabitants had the lowest rate, 20.0 arsons per 100,000 inhabitants. Rural counties had an arson rate of 16.6 incidents per 100,000 inhabitants, and suburban counties had a rate of 27.0 per 100,000 in population. (See Table 2.31.)

Clearances

According to the UCR Program definition, an offense is cleared when an arrest is made and charges have been brought against the arrestee. A clearance by exceptional means can also be made when the offender has been identified and located and there is enough evidence to support an arrest, but conditions beyond the control of law enforcement personnel preclude the arrest,

charging, and prosecuting the offender. Section III of this report contains additional information regarding clearances.

In 2002, law enforcement agencies in the Nation cleared 16.5 percent of arson offenses either by arrest or exceptional means; those in cities collectively cleared 15.9 percent of arsons. Law enforcement agencies in rural counties cleared 23.0 percent of arson offenses, and 17.1 percent in suburban counties. (See Table 25.) By geographic region, the Northeast cleared 19.8 percent of the arson incidents brought to law enforcement's attention; the South, 18.9 percent; the Midwest, 14.8 percent; and the West, 13.9 percent of the arsons reported in that region. (See Table 26.)

A review of the data within city population groupings showed that cities with less than 10,000 in population had the highest percentage of both structural arsons and mobile property arsons cleared by arrest at 29.0 percent and 18.1 percent, respectively. Cities with 10,000 to 24,999 inhabitants had the highest percentage—25.9 percent—of arsons of other property types cleared by arrest. (See Table 27.)

During 2002, 12,414 law enforcement agencies provided supplemental clearance data for arson. Of the arsons for which supplemental clearance data were received, 22.4 percent

of all structural arsons were cleared by arrest or exceptional means. The highest percentage of structural arson clearances—33.0 percent—were for those offenses committed against community/public structures. The lowest percentage of structural arson clearances—17.7 percent—were for those offenses committed against other commercial properties. Law enforcement also cleared 7.2 percent of mobile property arsons and 20.4 percent of the arsons committed against other properties. (See Table 2.32.)

Clearances and Juveniles

The UCR Program lists any clearance involving both adults (those aged 18 and over) and juveniles (persons under age 18) as an adult clearance. In addition, if an offender under the age of 18 is cited to appear before juvenile authorities, the UCR Program considers that incident as cleared by arrest even though a physical arrest may not have occurred. Forty-three percent of arsons cleared in the Nation in 2002 involved juvenile offenders. In cities collectively, 45.6 percent of arsons cleared involved juveniles. By population group, juvenile clearances accounted for 50.3 percent of arsons cleared in cities with less than 10,000 in population and 42.1 percent in cities of 250,000 and over in population. Juvenile clearances accounted for 28.6 percent of arsons cleared in rural counties and 39.1 percent in suburban counties. (See Table 28.)

As shown in Table 2.32, community/public structures had the highest percentage—71.8 percent—of clearances involving juveniles, and motor vehicle arsons had the lowest—21.9 percent—of clearances involving juveniles.

Arrests

Total Arrests and Rates

In 2002, an estimated 16,635 people were arrested for arson. (See Table 29.) The arson arrest rate in the Nation was 5.8 arrests per 100,000 inhabitants. By geographic region, the Northeast and Midwest each had an arson arrest rate of 5.9 per 100,000 inhabitants, the West had a rate of 5.8 per 100,000 persons, and the South had a rate of 5.6 arson arrests per 100,000 inhabitants. (See Table 30.) Among population groups labeled *city*, law enforcement agencies in cities with less than 10,000 inhabitants had the highest arson arrest rate at 7.2 per 100,000 persons, and cities with populations of 250,000 and over along with cities with 25,000 to 49,999 in population had the lowest rates at 5.3. Rural counties had an arson arrest rate of 4.9, and suburban counties had an arrest rate of 5.9 per 100,000 inhabitants. (See Table 31.)

Arrest Trends

In 2002, arson arrests declined 12.0 percent from the number of arrests reported in 2001. Overall, arrests of adults for arson declined 13.8 percent. Arrests of juveniles decreased 10.2 percent from the previous year's number and included a 10.4 percent decline in arrests of juveniles under 15 years of age. (See Table 36.) The number of females arrested for arson was down 16.1 percent from the 2001 figure, and arson arrests of males declined 11.2 percent. Arrests of female juveniles for arson fell 15.8 percent, and the number of male juveniles arrested for arson declined 9.4 percent from the 2001 figure. (See Table 37.)

Law enforcement agencies in the Nation's cities collectively reported that arrests declined 15.1 percent from the 2001 number, including a 10.8 percent decrease in juvenile arrests for arson and a 19.8 percent drop in adult arson arrests. (See Table 44.) In the Nation's suburban counties, law enforcement officials reported a 0.3 percent decline in total arson arrests. Juvenile arson arrests in suburban counties declined 5.2 percent while adult arson arrests in suburban counties increased 4.1 percent. (See Table 50.) In rural counties, the number of arson arrests decreased 10.8 percent in 2002 from the 2001 total. Juvenile arson arrests in rural counties

fell 17.7 percent; adult arson arrests declined 7.3 percent. (See Table 56.)

An examination of arson arrests over a 5-year period indicated that nationwide, arson arrests decreased 5.6 percent from the 1998 figure. From 1998 to 2002, law enforcement agencies reported an 11.3 percent decrease in juvenile arson arrests and a 1.2 percent increase in the number of adults arrested for arson. (See Table 34.)

Over the 10-year period from 1993 to 2002, total arson arrests declined 20.5 percent—adult arrests decreased 17.7 percent and juvenile arrests declined 23.2 percent. (See Table 32.)

Distribution

Nearly half (49.4 percent) of arrestees for arson during 2002 were under the age of 18. Overall, 67.8 percent of arson arrestees were under age 25. (See Table 41.) Males accounted for 84.8 percent of those persons arrested for arson. (See Table 42.) Of the males arrested for arson, 51.7 percent were under age 18. (See Table 39.) Thirty-seven percent of females arrested for arson were under age 18. (See Table 40.)

An examination of arson arrests by race indicated that 76.8 percent of arson arrestees were white, 21.5 percent were black, and 1.7 percent were of other races. (See Table 43.)

Hate Crime

Definition

A hate crime, also known as a bias crime, is a criminal offense committed against a person, property, or society which is motivated, in whole or in part, by the offender's bias against a race, religion, disability, sexual orientation, or ethnicity/national origin.

Background

In response to mounting national concern over crimes motivated by bias, Congress enacted the Hate Crime Statistics Act of 1990 on April 23 of that year. This law required the Attorney General to collect data "about crimes that manifest evidence of prejudice based on race, religion, sexual orientation, or ethnicity." The Attorney General delegated the responsibilities of developing the procedures for and implementing, collecting, and managing hate crime data to the Director of the FBI, who in turn assigned the tasks to the Uniform Crime Reporting (UCR) Program. In September 1994, the Violent Crime Control and Law Enforcement Act amended the Hate Crime Statistics Act to include both physical and mental disabilities as potential bias factors, and the actual collection of disability-bias data began in January 1997. Additionally, the Church Arson Prevention Act of 1996 mandated that hate crime data collection become a permanent part of the UCR Program.

Those who developed the guidelines for hate crime data collection recognized that hate crimes are not separate, distinct crimes; instead they are traditional offenses motivated by the offender's bias. After much consideration, the developers decided that hate crime data could be derived by capturing the additional element of bias in those offenses already being reported to the UCR Program. Appending the collection of hate crime statistics to the established UCR data collection procedures, they concluded, would fulfill the directives of the Hate Crime Statistics Act without placing an undue additional reporting burden on law enforcement and, in time, develop a substantial body of data about the nature and frequency of bias crimes occurring throughout the Nation. Accordingly, the law enforcement agencies that participate in the national hate crime program collect details about an offender's bias motivation associated with the following offense types: murder and nonnegligent manslaughter, forcible rape, aggravated assault, simple assault, intimidation, robbery, burglary, larceny-theft, motor vehicle theft, arson, and destruction/damage/vandalism of property. (The law enforcement agencies participating in the National Incident-Based Reporting System also collect additional offense types for crimes against persons and crimes against property, which the UCR

Figure 2.19

Bias-motivated Offenses
Percent Distribution,[1] 2002

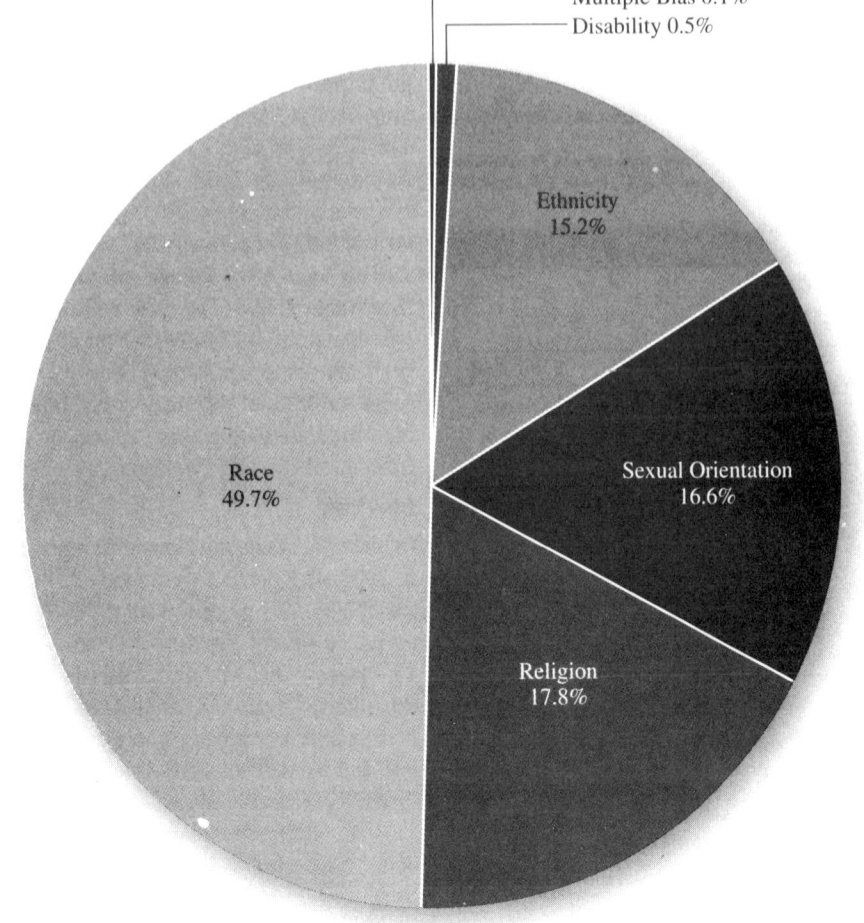

Multiple Bias 0.1%
Disability 0.5%
Ethnicity 15.2%
Sexual Orientation 16.6%
Religion 17.8%
Race 49.7%

[1] Due to rounding, the percentages may not add to 100.0.

Table 2.33

Incidents, Offenses, Victims, and Known Offenders
by Bias Motivation, 2002

Bias motivation	Incidents	Offenses	Victims[1]	Known offenders[2]
Total	7,462	8,832	9,222	7,314
Single-Bias Incidents	7,459	8,825	9,211	7,311
Race:	3,642	4,393	4,580	4,011
Anti-White	719	888	910	1,064
Anti-Black	2,486	2,967	3,076	2,510
Anti-American Indian/Alaskan Native	62	68	72	52
Anti-Asian/Pacific Islander	217	268	280	242
Anti-Multiple Races, Group	158	202	242	143
Religion:	1,426	1,576	1,659	568
Anti-Jewish	931	1,039	1,084	317
Anti-Catholic	53	58	71	21
Anti-Protestant	55	57	58	34
Anti-Islamic	155	170	174	103
Anti-Other Religion	198	217	237	73
Anti-Multiple Religions, Group	31	32	32	18
Anti-Atheism/Agnosticism/etc.	3	3	3	2
Sexual Orientation:	1,244	1,464	1,513	1,438
Anti-Male Homosexual	825	957	984	1,022
Anti-Female Homosexual	172	207	221	172
Anti-Homosexual	222	259	267	225
Anti-Heterosexual	10	26	26	6
Anti-Bisexual	15	15	15	13
Ethnicity/National Origin:	1,102	1,345	1,409	1,247
Anti-Hispanic	480	601	639	656
Anti-Other Ethnicity/National Origin	622	744	770	591
Disability:	45	47	50	47
Anti-Physical	20	20	20	21
Anti-Mental	25	27	30	26
Multiple-Bias Incidents[3]	3	7	11	3

[1]The term *victim* may refer to a person, business, institution, or society as a whole.
[2]The term *known offender* does not imply that the identity of the suspect is known, but only that an attribute of the suspect is identified, which distinguishes him/her from an unknown offender.
[3]A multiple-bias incident only occurs when two or more offense types are committed in a single incident. In a situation when there is more than one offense type, the agency can indicate a different bias type for each offense. In the case of a single offense type, only one bias type can be indicated.

Table 2.34

Incidents, Offenses, Victims, and Known Offenders
by Offense Type, 2002

Offense type	Incidents[1]	Offenses	Victims[2]	Known offenders[3]
Total	7,462	8,832	9,222	7,314
Crimes against persons:	4,784	5,960	5,960	6,090
Murder and nonnegligent manslaughter	11	11	11	15
Forcible rape	8	8	8	16
Aggravated assault	800	1,035	1,035	1,498
Simple assault	1,473	1,791	1,791	2,436
Intimidation	2,484	3,105	3,105	2,117
Other[4]	8	10	10	8
Crimes against property:	2,823	2,823	3,213	1,423
Robbery	131	131	179	269
Burglary	131	131	163	86
Larceny-theft	151	151	157	95
Motor vehicle theft	9	9	9	3
Arson	38	38	47	27
Destruction/damage/vandalism	2,347	2,347	2,642	927
Other[4]	16	16	16	16
Crimes against society[4]	49	49	49	61

[1]The actual number of incidents is 7,462. However, the column figures will not add to the total because incidents may include more than one offense type, and these are counted in each appropriate offense type category.
[2]The term *victim* may refer to a person, business, institution, or society as a whole.
[3]The term *known offender* does not imply that the identity of the suspect is known, but only that an attribute of the suspect is identified, which distinguishes him/her from an unknown offender. The actual number of known offenders is 7,314. However, the column figures will not add to the total because some offenders are responsible for more than one offense type, and they are, therefore, counted more than once in this table.
[4]Includes additional offenses collected in NIBRS.

Program publishes as "other." In addition, these agencies collect hate crime data for another category called "crimes against society.")

An abstract based on the information received from law enforcement agencies that provided 1 to 12 months of hate crime reports during 2002 follows. More detailed information concerning the characteristics of hate crime can be found in the UCR Program's annual publication *Hate Crime Statistics*.

Participation

A total of 12,073 law enforcement agencies participated in the hate crime program during 2002. Of these agencies, 1,868 agencies (15.5 percent) submitted 7,462 hate crime incident reports to the FBI. (See Table 2.36.) The following hate crime abstract is based on the data received from those law enforcement agencies that provided 1 to 12 months of hate crime reports.

Law Enforcement Reports

The UCR Program data collection guidelines stipulate that a hate crime may involve multiple offenses, victims, and offenders within one incident. Accordingly, in 2002, the 7,462 hate crime incidents reported to the FBI involved 8,832 separate offenses, 9,222 victims, and 7,314 known offenders. (See Table 2.33.) (The term *known offender* does not imply that the identity of the suspect is known but only that some attribute of the suspect has been identified, distinguishing him or her from an unknown offender.)

Incidents

Of the total single-bias incidents reported in 2002, 48.8 percent were motivated by racial bias, 19.1 percent were driven by prejudice against a particular religion, 16.7 percent involved a sexual-orientation bias, 14.8 percent resulted from a bias against an ethnicity or national origin, and 0.6 percent were motivated by a disability bias. (Based on Table 2.33.)

In addition to single-bias incidents, hate crime data collection guidelines permit the identification of multiple-bias incidents. These are incidents in which two or more offense types were committed as a result of two or more bias motivations. Only 3 of the 7,462 incidents reported in 2002 met that criteria. (See Table 2.33.)

Offenses

A victim of an offense, according to the UCR definition, may be either a person, a business, an institution, or society as a whole. When aggregating the number of hate crime offenses committed against individuals, the program counts one offense for each victim. The offense types of murder, rape, aggravated assault, simple assault, and intimidation are possible crimes against persons. When counting crimes against property, the program allots one offense for each distinct incident regardless of the number of victims. Robbery, burglary, larceny-theft, motor vehicle theft, arson, and destruction/damage/vandalism comprise the offense types that are possible crimes against property.

During 2002, a total of 5,960 (67.5 percent) of reported hate crime offenses were crimes against persons, and 2,823 (32.0 percent) were crimes against property. (Crimes against society comprised 0.6 percent of the reported offenses.) Intimidation continued to be the most frequently reported hate crime against individuals and accounted for 52.1 percent of all crimes against persons. Destruction/damage/vandalism of property was the most frequently reported crime against property. Of the instances of crimes against property, 83.1 percent were for the offenses of destruction/damage/vandalism. (Based on Table 2.34.)

Victims

A total of 9,222 individuals, businesses, institutions, or society as a whole were victims of hate crimes in 2002. Approximately 49.7 percent of all single-bias hate crime victims were targets of racial prejudice. Of these victims, 67.2 percent were attacked because of an anti-black bias motivation, and 19.9 percent were attacked because of an anti-white bias motivation. Eighteen percent of single-bias hate crime victims were targets because of the offender's bias toward the victim's religion. Of these, 65.3 percent were targeted because of an anti-Jewish bias motivation. Additionally, 16.4 percent of to-

tal single-bias hate crime victims were attacked because of the offender's prejudice against the victim's sexual-orientation; among these victims, 65.0 percent were victims of an anti-male homosexual bias motivation. Approximately 15.3 percent of hate crime victims were targets of ethnicity/national origin bias. Of these, 45.4 percent were victims of anti-Hispanic sentiment. (Based on Table 2.33.)

Offenders

In 2002, there were 7,314 known offenders who committed crimes motivated by biases. The majority of these known hate crime offenders were white,

Table 2.35

Race of Known Offenders, 2002[1]

Known offender's race	
Total	7,314
White	4,517
Black	1,592
American Indian/Alaskan Native	43
Asian/Pacific Islander	87
Multiple Races, Group[2]	355
Unknown Race	720

[1] The term *known offender* does not imply that the identity of the suspect is known, but only that an attribute of the suspect is identified, which distinguishes him/her from an unknown offender.
[2] The term *multiple races, group* is used to describe a group of offenders comprised of individuals of varying races.

Table 2.36

Agency Hate Crime Reporting by State, 2002

Participating state	Number of participating agencies	Population covered	Agencies submitting incident reports	Total number of incidents reported
Total	12,073	247,246,683	1,868	7,462
Alabama	31	259,938	2	2
Alaska	1	267,280	1	7
Arizona	88	5,023,657	29	238
Arkansas	7	387,957	0	0
California	726	35,056,859	243	1,648
Colorado	190	4,251,762	30	96
Connecticut	84	2,838,717	50	129
Delaware	50	806,717	8	13
District of Columbia	2	570,898	2	14
Florida	489	16,660,424	93	257
Georgia	76	1,558,760	10	31
Idaho	117	1,330,416	14	43
Illinois	59	4,639,084	46	155
Indiana	163	4,476,334	25	77
Iowa	221	2,863,046	18	46
Kansas	339	2,366,821	13	55
Kentucky	341	3,663,360	38	76
Louisiana	159	3,418,556	13	15
Maine	180	1,291,128	14	36
Maryland	148	5,458,137	26	211
Massachusetts	305	5,822,308	90	430
Michigan	619	9,814,593	164	416
Minnesota	279	4,843,609	71	203
Mississippi	66	942,735	3	3
Missouri	144	2,955,399	19	64
Montana	93	881,473	6	13
Nebraska	203	1,362,661	17	74
Nevada	35	2,173,491	7	62
New Hampshire	107	654,470	19	27
New Jersey	557	8,590,300	220	570
New Mexico	49	1,180,982	3	15
New York	505	19,154,571	63	693
North Carolina	446	8,242,488	29	62
North Dakota	74	562,980	7	18
Ohio	400	8,244,818	63	263
Oklahoma	301	3,493,714	19	44
Oregon	172	3,509,432	24	61
Pennsylvania	849	11,086,040	26	92
Rhode Island	48	1,069,725	7	38
South Carolina	310	4,103,856	35	70
South Dakota	130	734,731	4	4
Tennessee	443	5,796,102	54	129
Texas	969	21,698,160	82	347
Utah	59	1,790,393	17	54
Vermont	57	565,746	10	18
Virginia	399	7,258,150	54	291
Washington	246	6,036,923	47	174
West Virginia	336	1,758,307	16	41
Wisconsin	370	5,438,068	13	32
Wyoming	31	290,607	4	5

61.8 percent; 21.8 percent were black; 1.2 percent were Asian or Pacific Islander; 0.6 percent were American Indian or Alaskan Native; 9.8 percent were of unknown race; and 4.9 percent were groups of offenders consisting of multiple races. (Based on Table 2.35.)

Crime Index Tabulations

The tables in Section II—Crime Index Offenses Reported—organize crime data in many ways. First, for the Nation as a whole, then categorized by geographic divisions; individual states; Metropolitan Statistical Areas (MSAs); and cities, towns, and counties. The data are presented as crime volume and/or crime rate (occurrence per 100,000 U.S. inhabitants).

Although the exact number of crimes occurring within the United States is unknown, criminal activity can be gauged by studying those crimes reported to law enforcement. The reader is cautioned, however, that many factors affect crime volumes and crime types and can cause them to vary from time to time and from place to place. Even though one of these factors, population, is used in computing crime rates, all communities are affected to some degree by seasonal or transient population. Because current, permanent population counts are used in their computation, crime rates do not account for short-term population variables, such as an influx of day workers, tourists, shoppers, etc. Other factors contributing to the amount of crime in a given area are discussed in Crime Factors (page iv).

One tool law enforcement administrators can use in analyzing the volume of local crime and the performance of the law enforcement agencies is national data. That analysis, however, should not end with a comparison based solely on data presented in this publica-

tion. A true assessment of a community's crime problem or the effectiveness of law enforcement operations can be made only by including all the variables that shape local crime.

Brief Description of the Tables

Table 1 is a 20-year table that sets forth national estimates of volume and rate per 100,000 population for the offenses that make up the Crime Index. Table 2 shows estimates of crime volume and rates for 2002 for the Nation as a whole and for the Nation disaggregated by community type: MSAs, rural counties, and cities and towns outside metropolitan areas. Definitions of these community types can be found in Appendix III.

Data showing the regional distribution of estimated Index crimes along with proportional population estimates are provided in Table 3. A map of the United States illustrating the regions and divisions employed by the UCR Program appears in Appendix III.

Table 4 offers a 2-year trend in the volume and rate estimates by region, geographic division, and state. The estimated volume and rate of Crime Index offenses for each state and for individual MSAs are shown in Tables 5 and 6. Table 7 provides breakdowns for the offenses of robbery (by location), burglary (by time of day), and larceny-theft (by type) over the past 5 years.

Offenses known to police for cities over 10,000 in population are

presented in Table 8, and Table 9 shows the number of offenses occurring on college and university campuses as reported by college and university law enforcement agencies. The UCR Program does not assign population to educational institutions.

Offenses reported by suburban and rural county law enforcement agencies are presented in Tables 10 and 11. Tables 12–19 supply crime trends and rates by population groupings. The UCR Program's definition of the population groups can be found in Appendix III.

Data concerning weapons used in the violent crimes of murder, robbery, and aggravated assault are presented in Tables 20–22. Tables 23 and 24 analyze the value of property lost through the crimes of robbery, burglary, and larceny-theft, and offer breakdowns by type and value of property stolen and recovered.

Note

Because the UCR Program does not estimate for arson, arson offenses are not included in the tables containing offense estimates. However, the number of arson offenses reported by individual law enforcement agencies are displayed in Tables 8–11. Two-year arson trends are shown in Tables 12–15. An in-depth discussion of table construction methodology can be found in Appendix I.

Table 1

Index of Crime[1]
United States, 1983-2002

Population[2]	Crime Index	Modified Crime Index[3]	Violent crime[4]	Property crime[4]	Murder and non-negligent man-slaughter	Forcible rape	Robbery	Aggravated assault	Burglary	Larceny-theft	Motor vehicle theft	Arson[3]
					Number of Offenses							
Population by year:												
1983-233,791,994	12,108,630		1,258,087	10,850,543	19,308	78,918	506,567	653,294	3,129,851	6,712,759	1,007,933	
1984-235,824,902	11,881,755		1,273,282	10,608,473	18,692	84,233	485,008	685,349	2,984,434	6,591,874	1,032,165	
1985-237,923,795	12,430,357		1,327,767	11,102,590	18,976	87,671	497,874	723,246	3,073,348	6,926,380	1,102,862	
1986-240,132,887	13,211,869		1,489,169	11,722,700	20,613	91,459	542,775	834,322	3,241,410	7,257,153	1,224,137	
1987-242,288,918	13,508,708		1,483,999	12,024,709	20,096	91,111	517,704	855,088	3,236,184	7,499,851	1,288,674	
1988-244,498,982	13,923,086		1,566,221	12,356,865	20,675	92,486	542,968	910,092	3,218,077	7,705,872	1,432,916	
1989-246,819,230	14,251,449		1,646,037	12,605,412	21,500	94,504	578,326	951,707	3,168,170	7,872,442	1,564,800	
1990-249,464,396	14,475,613		1,820,127	12,655,486	23,438	102,555	639,271	1,054,863	3,073,909	7,945,670	1,635,907	
1991-252,153,092	14,872,883		1,911,767	12,961,116	24,703	106,593	687,732	1,092,739	3,157,150	8,142,228	1,661,738	
1992-255,029,699	14,438,191		1,932,274	12,505,917	23,760	109,062	672,478	1,126,974	2,979,884	7,915,199	1,610,834	
1993-257,782,608	14,144,794		1,926,017	12,218,777	24,526	106,014	659,870	1,135,607	2,834,808	7,820,909	1,563,060	
1994-260,327,021	13,989,543		1,857,670	12,131,873	23,326	102,216	618,949	1,113,179	2,712,774	7,879,812	1,539,287	
1995-262,803,276	13,862,727		1,798,792	12,063,935	21,606	97,470	580,509	1,099,207	2,593,784	7,997,710	1,472,441	
1996-265,228,572	13,493,863		1,688,540	11,805,323	19,645	96,252	535,594	1,037,049	2,506,400	7,904,685	1,394,238	
1997-267,783,607	13,194,571		1,636,096	11,558,475	18,208	96,153	498,534	1,023,201	2,460,526	7,743,760	1,354,189	
1998-270,248,003	12,485,714		1,533,887	10,951,827	16,974	93,144	447,186	976,583	2,332,735	7,376,311	1,242,781	
1999-272,690,813	11,634,378		1,426,044	10,208,334	15,522	89,411	409,371	911,740	2,100,739	6,955,520	1,152,075	
2000-281,421,906	11,608,070		1,425,486	10,182,584	15,586	90,178	408,016	911,706	2,050,992	6,971,590	1,160,002	
2001-285,317,559[5]	11,876,669		1,439,480	10,437,189	16,037	90,863	423,557	909,023	2,116,531	7,092,267	1,228,391	
2002-288,368,698	11,877,218		1,426,325	10,450,893	16,204	95,136	420,637	894,348	2,151,875	7,052,922	1,246,096	
Percent change, number of offenses:												
2002/2001	*		-0.9	+0.1	+1.0	+4.7	-0.7	-1.6	+1.7	-0.6	+1.4	
2002/1998	-4.9		-7.0	-4.6	-4.5	+2.1	-5.9	-8.4	-7.8	-4.4	+0.3	
2002/1993	-16.0		-25.9	-14.5	-33.9	10.3	-36.3	-21.2	-24.1	-9.8	-20.3	
					Rate per 100,000 Inhabitants							
Year:												
1983	5,179.2		538.1	4,641.1	8.3	33.8	216.7	279.4	1,338.7	2,871.3	431.1	
1984	5,038.4		539.9	4,498.5	7.9	35.7	205.7	290.6	1,265.5	2,795.2	437.7	
1985	5,224.5		558.1	4,666.4	8.0	36.8	209.3	304.0	1,291.7	2,911.2	463.5	
1986	5,501.9		620.1	4,881.8	8.6	38.1	226.0	347.4	1,349.8	3,022.1	509.8	
1987	5,575.5		612.5	4,963.0	8.3	37.6	213.7	352.9	1,335.7	3,095.4	531.9	
1988	5,694.5		640.6	5,054.0	8.5	37.8	222.1	372.2	1,316.2	3,151.7	586.1	
1989	5,774.0		666.9	5,107.1	8.7	38.3	234.3	385.6	1,283.6	3,189.6	634.0	
1990	5,802.7		729.6	5,073.1	9.4	41.1	256.3	422.9	1,232.2	3,185.1	655.8	
1991	5,898.4		758.2	5,140.2	9.8	42.3	272.7	433.4	1,252.1	3,229.1	659.0	
1992	5,661.4		757.7	4,903.7	9.3	42.8	263.7	441.9	1,168.4	3,103.6	631.6	
1993	5,487.1		747.1	4,740.0	9.5	41.1	256.0	440.5	1,099.7	3,033.9	606.3	
1994	5,373.8		713.6	4,660.2	9.0	39.3	237.8	427.6	1,042.1	3,026.9	591.3	
1995	5,274.9		684.5	4,590.5	8.2	37.1	220.9	418.3	987.0	3,043.2	560.3	
1996	5,087.6		636.6	4,451.0	7.4	36.3	201.9	391.0	945.0	2,980.3	525.7	
1997	4,927.3		611.0	4,316.3	6.8	35.9	186.2	382.1	918.8	2,891.8	505.7	
1998	4,620.1		567.6	4,052.5	6.3	34.5	165.5	361.4	863.2	2,729.5	459.9	
1999	4,266.5		523.0	3,743.6	5.7	32.8	150.1	334.3	770.4	2,550.7	422.5	
2000	4,124.8		506.5	3,618.3	5.5	32.0	145.0	324.0	728.8	2,477.3	412.2	
2001[5]	4,162.6		504.5	3,658.1	5.6	31.8	148.5	318.6	741.8	2,485.7	430.5	
2002	4,118.8		494.6	3,624.1	5.6	33.0	145.9	310.1	746.2	2,445.8	432.1	
Percent change, rate per 100,000 inhabitants:												
2002/2001	-1.1		-2.0	-0.9	*	+3.6	-1.7	-2.7	+0.6	-1.6	+0.4	
2002/1998	-10.9		-12.9	-10.6	-10.5	-4.3	-11.8	-14.2	-13.5	-10.4	-6.0	
2002/1993	-24.9		-33.8	-23.5	-40.9	-19.8	-43.0	-29.6	-32.1	-19.4	-28.7	

[1] The murder and nonnegligent homicides that occurred as a result of the events of September 11, 2001, were not included in this table.

[2] Populations are Bureau of the Census provisional estimates as of July 1 for each year except 1990 and 2000 which are decennial census counts.

[3] Although arson data are included in the trend and clearance tables, sufficient data are not available to estimate totals for this offense.

[4] Violent crimes are offenses of murder, forcible rape, robbery, and aggravated assault. Property crimes are offenses of burglary, larceny-theft, and motor vehicle theft.

[5] The 2001 crime figures have been adjusted. See Crime Trends, Appendix I, for details.

* Less than one-tenth of 1 percent.

Table 2

Index of Crime

United States, 2002

Area	Population[1]	Crime Index	Modified Crime Index[2]	Violent crime[3]	Property crime[3]	Murder and non-negligent man-slaughter	Forcible rape	Robbery	Aggravated assault	Burglary	Larceny-theft	Motor vehicle theft	Arson[2]
United States Total	288,368,698	11,877,218		1,426,325	10,450,893	16,204	95,136	420,637	894,348	2,151,875	7,052,922	1,246,096	
Rate per 100,000													
inhabitants		4,118.8		494.6	3,624.1	5.6	33.0	145.9	310.1	746.2	2,445.8	432.1	
Metropolitan Statistical													
Area	231,376,218												
Area actually reporting[4]	94.3%	9,482,136		1,163,636	8,318,500	13,100	72,708	369,834	707,994	1,658,078	5,570,764	1,089,658	
Estimated total	100.0%	10,201,622		1,262,359	8,939,263	14,235	78,236	401,140	768,748	1,778,174	6,007,505	1,153,584	
Rate per 100,000													
inhabitants		4,409.1		545.6	3,863.5	6.2	33.8	173.4	332.3	768.5	2,596.4	498.6	
Cities outside metropolitan													
areas	22,475,044												
Area actually reporting[4]	85.5%	881,650		79,845	801,805	617	7,464	11,981	59,783	157,232	603,408	41,165	
Estimated total	100.0%	1,016,773		90,586	926,187	717	8,679	13,746	67,444	181,014	698,507	46,666	
Rate per 100,000													
inhabitants		4,524.0		403.1	4,121.0	3.2	38.6	61.2	300.1	805.4	3,107.9	207.6	
Rural Counties	34,517,436												
Area actually reporting[4]	84.7%	582,496		65,962	516,534	1,046	6,937	5,045	52,934	169,192	306,754	40,588	
Estimated total	100.0%	658,823		73,380	585,443	1,252	8,221	5,751	58,156	192,687	346,910	45,846	
Rate per 100,000													
inhabitants		1,908.7		212.6	1,696.1	3.6	23.8	16.7	168.5	558.2	1,005.0	132.8	

[1] Populations are Bureau of the Census provisional estimates as of July 1, 2002.

[2] Although arson data are included in the trend and clearance tables, sufficient data are not available to estimate totals for this offense.

[3] Violent crimes are offenses of murder, forcible rape, robbery, and aggravated assault. Property crimes are offenses of burglary, larceny-theft, and motor vehicle theft.

[4] The percentage reported under "Area actually reporting" is based upon the population covered by agencies providing 3 months or more of crime reports to the FBI.

Table 3

Index of Crime

Offense and Population Distribution by Region, 2002

Region	Population	Crime Index	Modified Crime Index[1]	Violent crime[2]	Property crime[2]	Murder and non-negligent man-slaughter	Forcible rape	Robbery	Aggravated assault	Burglary	Larceny-theft	Motor vehicle theft	Arson[1]
United States Total[3]	100.0	100.0		100.0	100.0	100.0	100.0	100.0	100.0	100.0	100.0	100.0	
Northeast	18.8	13.2		15.8	12.8	13.6	13.5	19.2	14.6	11.5	13.2	13.1	
Midwest	22.6	21.3		19.4	21.6	20.4	25.3	19.5	18.7	20.7	22.3	18.8	
South	35.8	41.1		41.4	41.0	43.1	37.5	38.5	43.1	44.8	40.9	35.2	
West	22.8	24.4		23.4	24.6	23.0	23.7	22.8	23.7	22.9	23.6	32.9	

[1] Although arson data are included in the trend and clearance tables, sufficient data are not available to estimate totals for this offense.

[2] Violent crimes are offenses of murder, forcible rape, robbery, and aggravated assault. Property crimes are offenses of burglary, larceny-theft, and motor vehicle theft.

[3] Because of rounding, the percentages may not add to 100.0.

Table 4

Index of Crime[1]
by Region, Geographic Division, and State, 2001-2002

Area	Year	Population[2]	Crime Index		Modified Crime Index[3]		Violent crime[4]		Property crime[4]		Murder and non-negligent manslaughter	
			Number	Rate per 100,000	Number	Rate per 100,000	Number	Rate per 100,000	Number	Rate per 100,000	Number	Rate per 100,000
United States Total[5, 6, 7]	2001	285,317,559	11,876,669	4,162.6			1,439,480	504.5	10,437,189	3,658.1	16,037	5.6
	2002	288,368,698	11,877,218	4,118.8			1,426,325	494.6	10,450,893	3,624.1	16,204	5.6
Percent change			*	-1.1			-0.9	-2.0	+0.1	-0.9	+1.0	*
Northeast[5]	2001	53,950,802	1,617,785	2,998.6			231,126	428.4	1,386,659	2,570.2	2,277	4.2
	2002	54,227,064	1,566,645	2,889.0			225,841	416.5	1,340,804	2,472.6	2,203	4.1
Percent change			-3.2	-3.7			-2.3	-2.8	-3.3	-3.8	-3.2	-3.7
New England[5]	2001	14,052,232	424,275	3,019.3			49,578	352.8	374,697	2,666.5	330	2.3
	2002	14,144,141	419,289	2,964.4			49,065	346.9	370,224	2,617.5	333	2.4
Percent change			-1.2	-1.8			-1.0	-1.7	-1.2	-1.8	+0.9	+0.3
Connecticut	2001	3,434,602	106,791	3,109.3			11,492	334.6	95,299	2,774.7	105	3.1
	2002	3,460,503	103,719	2,997.2			10,767	311.1	92,952	2,686.1	80	2.3
Percent change			-2.9	-3.6			-6.3	-7.0	-2.5	-3.2	-23.8	-24.4
Maine[5]	2001	1,284,470	34,589	2,692.9			1,435	111.7	33,154	2,581.1	19	1.5
	2002	1,294,464	34,381	2,656.0			1,396	107.8	32,985	2,548.2	14	1.1
Percent change			-0.6	-1.4			-2.7	-3.5	-0.5	-1.3	-26.3	-26.9
Massachusetts[5]	2001	6,401,164	197,664	3,087.9			30,585	477.8	167,079	2,610.1	143	2.2
	2002	6,427,801	198,890	3,094.2			31,137	484.4	167,753	2,609.8	173	2.7
Percent change			+0.6	+0.2			+1.8	+1.4	+0.4	*	+21.0	+20.5
New Hampshire	2001	1,259,359	29,233	2,321.3			2,144	170.2	27,089	2,151.0	17	1.3
	2002	1,275,056	28,306	2,220.0			2,056	161.2	26,250	2,058.7	12	0.9
Percent change			-3.2	-4.4			-4.1	-5.3	-3.1	-4.3	-29.4	-30.3
Rhode Island	2001	1,059,659	39,020	3,682.3			3,278	309.3	35,742	3,373.0	39	3.7
	2002	1,069,725	38,393	3,589.1			3,051	285.2	35,342	3,303.8	41	3.8
Percent change			-1.6	-2.5			-6.9	-7.8	-1.1	-2.0	+5.1	+4.1
Vermont	2001	612,978	16,978	2,769.8			644	105.1	16,334	2,664.7	7	1.1
	2002	616,592	15,600	2,530.0			658	106.7	14,942	2,423.3	13	2.1
Percent change			-8.1	-8.7			+2.2	+1.6	-8.5	-9.1	+85.7	+84.6
Middle Atlantic[5]	2001	39,898,570	1,193,510	2,991.4			181,548	455.0	1,011,962	2,536.3	1,947	4.9
	2002	40,082,923	1,147,356	2,862.5			176,776	441.0	970,580	2,421.4	1,870	4.7
Percent change			-3.9	-4.3			-2.6	-3.1	-4.1	-4.5	-4.0	-4.4
New Jersey	2001	8,511,116	273,645	3,215.1			33,094	388.8	240,551	2,826.3	336	3.9
	2002	8,590,300	259,789	3,024.2			32,168	374.5	227,621	2,649.7	337	3.9
Percent change			-5.1	-5.9			-2.8	-3.7	-5.4	-6.2	+0.3	-0.6
New York[5]	2001	19,084,350	556,025	2,913.5			98,022	513.6	458,003	2,399.9	960	5.0
	2002	19,157,532	537,121	2,803.7			95,030	496.0	442,091	2,307.7	909	4.7
Percent change			-3.4	-3.8			-3.1	-3.4	-3.5	-3.8	-5.3	-5.7
Pennsylvania	2001	12,303,104	363,840	2,957.3			50,432	409.9	313,408	2,547.4	651	5.3
	2002	12,335,091	350,446	2,841.0			49,578	401.9	300,868	2,439.1	624	5.1
Percent change			-3.7	-3.9			-1.7	-1.9	-4.0	-4.3	-4.1	-4.4
Midwest[5, 6]	2001	64,819,817	2,577,704	3,976.7			279,218	430.8	2,298,486	3,546.0	3,401	5.2
	2002	65,141,893	2,529,508	3,883.1			276,763	424.9	2,252,745	3,458.2	3,298	5.1
Percent change			-1.9	-2.4			-0.9	-1.4	-2.0	-2.5	-3.0	-3.5
East North Central[5, 6]	2001	45,448,968	1,810,525	3,983.6			209,937	461.9	1,600,588	3,521.7	2,711	6.0
	2002	45,672,597	1,772,509	3,880.9			206,887	453.0	1,565,622	3,427.9	2,669	5.8
Percent change			-2.1	-2.6			-1.5	-1.9	-2.2	-2.7	-1.5	-2.0
Illinois[5, 6]	2001	12,520,227	513,918	4,104.7			79,270	633.1	434,648	3,471.6	982	7.8
	2002	12,600,620	506,086	4,016.4			78,214	620.7	427,872	3,395.6	949	7.5
Percent change			-1.5	-2.2			-1.3	-2.0	-1.6	-2.2	-3.4	-4.0

See footnotes at end of table.

Forcible rape		Robbery		Aggravated assault		Burglary		Larceny-theft		Motor vehicle theft		Arson[3]	
Number	Rate per 100,000	Number	Rate per 100,000	Number	Rate per 100,000	Number	Rate per 100,000	Number	Rate per 100,000	Number	Rate per 100,000	Number	Rate per 100,000
90,863	31.8	423,557	148.5	909,023	318.6	2,116,531	741.8	7,092,267	2,485.7	1,228,391	430.5		
95,136	33.0	420,637	145.9	894,348	310.1	2,151,875	746.2	7,052,922	2,445.8	1,246,096	432.1		
+4.7	+3.6	-0.7	-1.7	-1.6	-2.7	+1.7	+0.6	-0.6	-1.6	+1.4	+0.4		
12,093	22.4	80,626	149.4	136,130	252.3	252,907	468.8	962,226	1,783.5	171,526	317.9		
12,814	23.6	80,626	148.7	130,198	240.1	248,246	457.8	929,458	1,714.0	163,100	300.8		
+6.0	+5.4	0.0	-0.5	-4.4	-4.8	-1.8	-2.3	-3.4	-3.9	-4.9	-5.4		
3,802	27.1	12,461	88.7	32,985	234.7	71,350	507.7	253,529	1,804.2	49,818	354.5		
3,851	27.2	12,905	91.2	31,976	226.1	72,038	509.3	251,008	1,774.6	47,178	333.6		
+1.3	+0.6	+3.6	+2.9	-3.1	-3.7	+1.0	+0.3	-1.0	-1.6	-5.3	-5.9		
639	18.6	4,183	121.8	6,565	191.1	17,159	499.6	65,762	1,914.7	12,378	360.4		
730	21.1	4,060	117.3	5,897	170.4	17,088	493.8	64,292	1,857.9	11,572	334.4		
+14.2	+13.4	-2.9	-3.7	-10.2	-10.8	-0.4	-1.2	-2.2	-3.0	-6.5	-7.2		
326	25.4	264	20.6	826	64.3	6,898	537.0	24,585	1,914.0	1,671	130.1		
377	29.1	270	20.9	735	56.8	6,965	538.1	24,591	1,899.7	1,429	110.4		
+15.6	+14.8	+2.3	+1.5	-11.0	-11.7	+1.0	+0.2	*	-0.7	-14.5	-15.1		
1,856	29.0	6,476	101.2	22,110	345.4	32,430	506.6	106,821	1,668.8	27,828	434.7		
1,777	27.6	7,169	111.5	22,018	342.5	33,243	517.2	107,922	1,679.0	26,588	413.6		
-4.3	-4.7	+10.7	+10.2	-0.4	-0.8	+2.5	+2.1	+1.0	+0.6	-4.5	-4.9		
458	36.4	445	35.3	1,224	97.2	4,889	388.2	20,060	1,592.9	2,140	169.9		
446	35.0	413	32.4	1,185	92.9	4,838	379.4	19,468	1,526.8	1,944	152.5		
-2.6	-3.8	-7.2	-8.3	-3.2	-4.4	-1.0	-2.3	-3.0	-4.1	-9.2	-10.3		
416	39.3	986	93.0	1,837	173.4	6,824	644.0	23,875	2,253.1	5,043	475.9		
395	36.9	916	85.6	1,699	158.8	6,415	599.7	24,051	2,248.3	4,876	455.8		
-5.0	-5.9	-7.1	-8.0	-7.5	-8.4	-6.0	-6.9	+0.7	-0.2	-3.3	-4.2		
107	17.5	107	17.5	423	69.0	3,150	513.9	12,426	2,027.2	758	123.7		
126	20.4	77	12.5	442	71.7	3,489	565.9	10,684	1,732.8	769	124.7		
+17.8	+17.1	-28.0	-28.5	+4.5	+3.9	+10.8	+10.1	-14.0	-14.5	+1.5	+0.9		
8,291	20.8	68,165	170.8	103,145	258.5	181,557	455.0	708,697	1,776.2	121,708	305.0		
8,963	22.4	67,721	169.0	98,222	245.0	176,208	439.6	678,450	1,692.6	115,922	289.2		
+8.1	+7.6	-0.7	-1.1	-4.8	-5.2	-2.9	-3.4	-4.3	-4.7	-4.8	-5.2		
1,278	15.0	14,110	165.8	17,370	204.1	46,812	550.0	156,031	1,833.3	37,708	443.0		
1,347	15.7	13,905	161.9	16,579	193.0	43,898	511.0	147,984	1,722.7	35,739	416.0		
+5.4	+4.4	-1.5	-2.4	-4.6	-5.4	-6.2	-7.1	-5.2	-6.0	-5.2	-6.1		
3,546	18.6	36,555	191.5	56,961	298.5	80,400	421.3	329,316	1,725.6	48,287	253.0		
3,885	20.3	36,653	191.3	53,583	279.7	76,700	400.4	318,025	1,660.1	47,366	247.2		
+9.6	+9.1	+0.3	-0.1	-5.9	-6.3	-4.6	-5.0	-3.4	-3.8	-1.9	-2.3		
3,467	28.2	17,500	142.2	28,814	234.2	54,345	441.7	223,350	1,815.4	35,713	290.3		
3,731	30.2	17,163	139.1	28,060	227.5	55,610	450.8	212,441	1,722.2	32,817	266.0		
+7.6	+7.3	-1.9	-2.2	-2.6	-2.9	+2.3	+2.1	-4.9	-5.1	-8.1	-8.3		
22,757	35.1	83,079	128.2	169,981	262.2	438,675	676.8	1,614,095	2,490.1	245,716	379.1		
24,109	37.0	82,144	126.1	167,212	256.7	446,471	685.4	1,572,181	2,413.5	234,093	359.4		
+5.9	+5.4	-1.1	-1.6	-1.6	-2.1	+1.8	+1.3	-2.6	-3.1	-4.7	-5.2		
16,598	36.5	66,682	146.7	123,946	272.7	317,791	699.2	1,102,007	2,424.7	180,790	397.8		
17,551	38.4	66,315	145.2	120,352	263.5	321,788	704.6	1,072,742	2,348.8	171,092	374.6		
+5.7	+5.2	-0.6	-1.0	-2.9	-3.4	+1.3	+0.8	-2.7	-3.1	-5.4	-5.8		
4,010	32.0	24,931	199.1	49,347	394.1	79,158	632.2	306,757	2,450.1	48,733	389.2		
4,298	34.1	25,272	200.6	47,695	378.5	81,123	643.8	301,892	2,395.9	44,857	356.0		
+7.2	+6.5	+1.4	+0.7	-3.3	-4.0	+2.5	+1.8	-1.6	-2.2	-8.0	-8.5		

Table 4

Index of Crime[1]

by Region, Geographic Division, and State, 2001-2002—Continued

Area	Year	Population[2]	Crime Index Number	Crime Index Rate per 100,000	Modified Crime Index[3] Number	Modified Crime Index[3] Rate per 100,000	Violent crime[4] Number	Violent crime[4] Rate per 100,000	Property crime[4] Number	Property crime[4] Rate per 100,000	Murder and non-negligent manslaughter Number	Murder and non-negligent manslaughter Rate per 100,000
Indiana	2001	6,126,743	234,282	3,823.9			22,734	371.1	211,548	3,452.9	413	6.7
	2002	6,159,068	230,966	3,750.0			22,001	357.2	208,965	3,392.8	362	5.9
Percent change			-1.4	-1.9			-3.2	-3.7	-1.2	-1.7	-12.3	-12.8
Michigan	2001	10,006,266	407,777	4,075.2			55,424	553.9	352,353	3,521.3	672	6.7
	2002	10,050,446	389,366	3,874.1			54,306	540.3	335,060	3,333.8	678	6.7
Percent change			-4.5	-4.9			-2.0	-2.4	-4.9	-5.3	+0.9	+0.4
Ohio	2001	11,389,785	475,138	4,171.6			40,023	351.4	435,115	3,820.2	452	4.0
	2002	11,421,267	469,104	4,107.3			40,128	351.3	428,976	3,755.9	526	4.6
Percent change			-1.3	-1.5			+0.3	*	-1.4	-1.7	+16.4	+16.1
Wisconsin	2001	5,405,947	179,410	3,318.8			12,486	231.0	166,924	3,087.8	192	3.6
	2002	5,441,196	176,987	3,252.7			12,238	224.9	164,749	3,027.8	154	2.8
Percent change			-1.4	-2.0			-2.0	-2.6	-1.3	-1.9	-19.8	-20.3
West North Central	2001	19,370,849	767,179	3,960.5			69,281	357.7	697,898	3,602.8	690	3.6
	2002	19,469,296	756,999	3,888.2			69,876	358.9	687,123	3,529.3	629	3.2
Percent change			-1.3	-1.8			+0.9	+0.3	-1.5	-2.0	-8.8	-9.3
Iowa	2001	2,931,967	96,499	3,291.3			7,865	268.2	88,634	3,023.0	50	1.7
	2002	2,936,760	101,265	3,448.2			8,388	285.6	92,877	3,162.6	44	1.5
Percent change			+4.9	+4.8			+6.6	+6.5	+4.8	+4.6	-12.0	-12.1
Kansas	2001	2,702,125	116,446	4,309.4			10,909	403.7	105,537	3,905.7	92	3.4
	2002	2,715,884	110,997	4,087.0			10,229	376.6	100,768	3,710.3	78	2.9
Percent change			-4.7	-5.2			-6.2	-6.7	-4.5	-5.0	-15.2	-15.6
Minnesota	2001	4,984,535	178,191	3,574.9			13,145	263.7	165,046	3,311.2	119	2.4
	2002	5,019,720	177,454	3,535.1			13,428	267.5	164,026	3,267.6	112	2.2
Percent change			-0.4	-1.1			+2.2	+1.4	-0.6	-1.3	-5.9	-6.5
Missouri	2001	5,637,309	268,883	4,769.7			30,472	540.5	238,411	4,229.2	372	6.6
	2002	5,672,579	261,077	4,602.4			30,557	538.7	230,520	4,063.8	331	5.8
Percent change			-2.9	-3.5			+0.3	-0.3	-3.3	-3.9	-11.0	-11.6
Nebraska	2001	1,720,039	74,177	4,312.5			5,214	303.1	68,963	4,009.4	43	2.5
	2002	1,729,180	73,606	4,256.7			5,428	313.9	68,178	3,942.8	48	2.8
Percent change			-0.8	-1.3			+4.1	+3.6	-1.1	-1.7	+11.6	+11.0
North Dakota	2001	636,550	15,339	2,409.7			505	79.3	14,834	2,330.4	7	1.1
	2002	634,110	15,258	2,406.2			496	78.2	14,762	2,328.0	5	0.8
Percent change			-0.5	-0.1			-1.8	-1.4	-0.5	-0.1	-28.6	-28.3
South Dakota	2001	758,324	17,644	2,326.7			1,171	154.4	16,473	2,172.3	7	0.9
	2002	761,063	17,342	2,278.7			1,350	177.4	15,992	2,101.3	11	1.4
Percent change			-1.7	-2.1			+15.3	+14.9	-2.9	-3.3	+57.1	+56.6
South[5, 6, 7]	**2001**	**101,953,947**	**4,873,007**	**4,779.6**			**593,711**	**582.3**	**4,279,296**	**4,197.3**	**6,842**	**6.7**
	2002	**103,347,425**	**4,880,003**	**4,721.9**			**590,086**	**571.0**	**4,289,917**	**4,151.0**	**6,982**	**6.8**
Percent change			**+0.1**	**-1.2**			**-0.6**	**-2.0**	**+0.2**	**-1.1**	**+2.0**	**+0.7**
South Atlantic[5, 7]	2001	52,801,462	2,539,042	4,808.7			328,088	621.4	2,210,954	4,187.3	3,411	6.5
	2002	53,632,623	2,513,263	4,686.1			322,521	601.4	2,190,742	4,084.7	3,611	6.7
Percent change			-1.0	-2.5			-1.7	-3.2	-0.9	-2.4	+5.9	+4.2
Delaware	2001	796,599	32,267	4,050.6			4,868	611.1	27,399	3,439.5	23	2.9
	2002	807,385	31,803	3,939.0			4,836	599.0	26,967	3,340.0	26	3.2
Percent change			-1.4	-2.8			-0.7	-2.0	-1.6	-2.9	+13.0	+11.5
District of Columbia[5, 7]	2001	573,822	44,427	7,742.3			9,195	1,602.4	35,232	6,139.9	231	40.3
	2002	570,898	45,799	8,022.3			9,322	1,632.9	36,477	6,389.4	264	46.2
Percent change			+3.1	+3.6			+1.4	+1.9	+3.5	+4.1	+14.3	+14.9

See footnotes at end of table.

Forcible rape		Robbery		Aggravated assault		Burglary		Larceny-theft		Motor vehicle theft		Arson[1]	
Number	Rate per 100,000	Number	Rate per 100,000	Number	Rate per 100,000	Number	Rate per 100,000	Number	Rate per 100,000	Number	Rate per 100,000	Number	Rate per 100,000
1,716	28.0	7,171	117.0	13,434	219.3	42,758	697.9	147,291	2,404.1	21,499	350.9		
1,843	29.9	6,612	107.4	13,184	214.1	42,605	691.7	146,073	2,371.7	20,287	329.4		
+7.4	+6.8	-7.8	-8.3	-1.9	-2.4	-0.4	-0.9	-0.8	-1.3	-5.6	-6.1		
5,264	52.6	12,937	129.3	36,551	365.3	72,038	719.9	226,708	2,265.7	53,607	535.7		
5,364	53.4	11,847	117.9	36,417	362.3	70,970	706.1	214,367	2,132.9	49,723	494.7		
+1.9	+1.5	-8.4	-8.8	-0.4	-0.8	-1.5	-1.9	-5.4	-5.9	-7.2	-7.7		
4,466	39.2	17,199	151.0	17,906	157.2	96,910	850.9	295,976	2,598.6	42,229	370.8		
4,809	42.1	17,871	156.5	16,922	148.2	99,164	868.2	287,045	2,513.3	42,767	374.5		
+7.7	+7.4	+3.9	+3.6	-5.5	-5.8	+2.3	+2.0	-3.0	-3.3	+1.3	+1.0		
1,142	21.1	4,444	82.2	6,708	124.1	26,927	498.1	125,275	2,317.4	14,722	272.3		
1,237	22.7	4,713	86.6	6,134	112.7	27,926	513.2	123,365	2,267.2	13,458	247.3		
+8.3	+7.6	+6.1	+5.4	-8.6	-9.1	+3.7	+3.0	-1.5	-2.2	-8.6	-9.2		
6,159	31.8	16,397	84.6	46,035	237.7	120,884	624.1	512,088	2,643.6	64,926	335.2		
6,558	33.7	15,829	81.3	46,860	240.7	124,683	640.4	499,439	2,565.3	63,001	323.6		
+6.5	+5.9	-3.5	-4.0	+1.8	+1.3	+3.1	+2.6	-2.5	-3.0	-3.0	-3.5		
649	22.1	1,154	39.4	6,012	205.1	16,885	575.9	66,244	2,259.4	5,505	187.8		
797	27.1	1,169	39.8	6,378	217.2	18,643	634.8	68,411	2,329.5	5,823	198.3		
+22.8	+22.6	+1.3	+1.1	+6.1	+5.9	+10.4	+10.2	+3.3	+3.1	+5.8	+5.6		
945	35.0	2,423	89.7	7,449	275.7	20,514	759.2	77,038	2,851.0	7,985	295.5		
1,035	38.1	2,165	79.7	6,951	255.9	19,679	724.6	73,877	2,720.2	7,212	265.5		
+9.5	+9.0	-10.6	-11.1	-6.7	-7.2	-4.1	-4.6	-4.1	-4.6	-9.7	-10.1		
2,236	44.9	3,758	75.4	7,032	141.1	25,496	511.5	124,519	2,498.1	15,031	301.6		
2,273	45.3	3,937	78.4	7,106	141.6	28,034	558.5	122,150	2,433.4	13,842	275.8		
+1.7	+0.9	+4.8	+4.0	+1.1	+0.3	+10.0	+9.2	-1.9	-2.6	-7.9	-8.6		
1,383	24.5	7,771	137.8	20,946	371.6	42,977	762.4	167,420	2,969.9	28,014	496.9		
1,465	25.8	7,024	123.8	21,737	383.2	42,721	753.1	159,921	2,819.2	27,878	491.5		
+5.9	+5.3	-9.6	-10.2	+3.8	+3.1	-0.6	-1.2	-4.5	-5.1	-0.5	-1.1		
431	25.1	1,128	65.6	3,612	210.0	9,760	567.4	52,713	3,064.6	6,490	377.3		
464	26.8	1,359	78.6	3,557	205.7	10,329	597.3	51,440	2,974.8	6,409	370.6		
+7.7	+7.1	+20.5	+19.8	-1.5	-2.0	+5.8	+5.3	-2.4	-2.9	-1.2	-1.8		
164	25.8	60	9.4	274	43.0	2,165	340.1	11,583	1,819.7	1,086	170.6		
163	25.7	58	9.1	270	42.6	2,243	353.7	11,501	1,813.7	1,018	160.5		
-0.6	-0.2	-3.3	-3.0	-1.5	-1.1	+3.6	+4.0	-0.7	-0.3	-6.3	5.9		
351	46.3	103	13.6	710	93.6	3,087	407.1	12,571	1,657.7	815	107.5		
361	47.4	117	15.4	861	113.1	3,034	398.7	12,139	1,595.0	819	107.6		
+2.8	+2.5	+13.6	+13.2	+21.3	+20.8	-1.7	-2.1	-3.4	-3.8	+0.5	+0.1		
34,526	**33.9**	**163,093**	**160.0**	**389,250**	**381.8**	**949,916**	**931.7**	**2,892,143**	**2,836.7**	**437,237**	**428.9**		
35,706	**34.5**	**162,002**	**156.8**	**385,396**	**372.9**	**963,804**	**932.6**	**2,887,621**	**2,794.1**	**438,492**	**424.3**		
+3.4	**+2.0**	**-0.7**	**-2.0**	**-1.0**	**-2.3**	**+1.5**	**+0.1**	**-0.2**	**-1.5**	**+0.3**	**-1.1**		
16,813	31.8	92,588	175.4	215,276	407.7	485,202	918.9	1,492,066	2,825.8	233,686	442.6		
17,173	32.0	90,015	167.8	211,722	394.8	486,178	906.5	1,467,227	2,735.7	237,337	442.5		
+2.1	+0.6	-2.8	-4.3	-1.7	-3.2	+0.2	-1.4	-1.7	-3.2	+1.6	*		
420	52.7	1,156	145.1	3,269	410.4	5,144	645.7	19,476	2,444.9	2,779	348.9		
358	44.3	1,154	142.9	3,298	408.5	5,355	663.3	18,555	2,298.2	3,057	378.6		
-14.8	-15.9	-0.2	-1.5	+0.9	-0.5	+4.1	+2.7	-4.7	-6.0	+10.0	+8.5		
181	31.5	3,780	658.7	5,003	871.9	4,949	862.5	22,313	3,888.5	7,970	1,388.9		
262	45.9	3,834	671.6	4,962	869.2	5,170	905.6	21,708	3,802.4	9,599	1,681.4		
+44.8	+45.5	+1.4	+1.9	-0.8	-0.3	+4.5	+5.0	-2.7	-2.2	+20.4	+21.1		

Table 4

Index of Crime[1]
by Region, Geographic Division, and State, 2001-2002—Continued

Area	Year	Population[2]	Crime Index Number	Crime Index Rate per 100,000	Modified Crime Index[3] Number	Modified Crime Index[3] Rate per 100,000	Violent crime[4] Number	Violent crime[4] Rate per 100,000	Property crime[4] Number	Property crime[4] Rate per 100,000	Murder and non-negligent manslaughter Number	Murder and non-negligent manslaughter Rate per 100,000
Florida	2001	16,373,330	913,230	5,577.5			130,713	798.3	782,517	4,779.2	874	5.3
	2002	16,713,149	905,957	5,420.6			128,721	770.2	777,236	4,650.4	911	5.5
Percent change			-0.8	-2.8			-1.5	-3.5	-0.7	-2.7	+4.2	+2.1
Georgia	2001	8,405,677	389,543	4,634.3			41,671	495.7	347,872	4,138.5	598	7.1
	2002	8,560,310	385,830	4,507.2			39,271	458.8	346,559	4,048.4	606	7.1
Percent change			-1.0	-2.7			-5.8	-7.5	-0.4	-2.2	+1.3	-0.5
Maryland	2001	5,386,079	261,600	4,857.0			42,088	781.4	219,512	4,075.5	446	8.3
	2002	5,458,137	259,120	4,747.4			42,015	769.8	217,105	3,977.6	513	9.4
Percent change			-0.9	-2.3			-0.2	-1.5	-1.1	-2.4	+15.0	+13.5
North Carolina	2001	8,206,105	404,242	4,926.1			40,465	493.1	363,777	4,433.0	505	6.2
	2002	8,320,146	392,826	4,721.4			39,118	470.2	353,708	4,251.2	548	6.6
Percent change			-2.8	-4.2			-3.3	-4.7	﹀ -2.8	-4.1	+8.5	+7.0
South Carolina[5]	2001	4,062,125	219,168	5,395.4			33,114	815.2	186,054	4,580.2	330	8.1
	2002	4,107,183	217,569	5,297.3			33,761	822.0	183,808	4,475.3	298	7.3
Percent change			-0.7	-1.8			+2.0	+0.8	-1.2	-2.3	-9.7	-10.7
Virginia	2001	7,196,750	228,445	3,174.3			20,939	291.0	207,506	2,883.3	364	5.1
	2002	7,293,542	229,039	3,140.3			21,256	291.4	207,783	2,848.9	388	5.3
Percent change			+0.3	-1.1			+1.5	+0.2	+0.1	-1.2	+6.6	+5.2
West Virginia	2001	1,800,975	46,120	2,560.8			5,035	279.6	41,085	2,281.3	40	2.2
	2002	1,801,873	45,320	2,515.2			4,221	234.3	41,099	2,280.9	57	3.2
Percent change			-1.7	-1.8			-16.2	-16.2	*	*	+42.5	+42.4
East South Central[5, 6]	2001	17,146,859	726,084	4,234.5			82,874	483.3	643,210	3,751.2	1,265	7.4
	2002	17,248,470	729,533	4,229.6			82,769	479.9	646,764	3,749.7	1,171	6.8
Percent change			+0.5	-0.1			-0.1	-0.7	+0.6	*	-7.4	-8.0
Alabama	2001	4,468,912	192,835	4,315.0			19,582	438.2	173,253	3,876.8	379	8.5
	2002	4,486,508	200,331	4,465.2			19,931	444.2	180,400	4,020.9	303	6.8
Percent change			+3.9	+3.5			+1.8	+1.4	+4.1	+3.7	-20.1	-20.4
Kentucky[5, 6]	2001	4,068,816	117,866	2,896.8			10,510	258.3	107,356	2,638.5	181	4.4
	2002	4,092,891	118,799	2,902.6			11,418	279.0	107,381	2,623.6	184	4.5
Percent change			+0.8	+0.2			+8.6	+8.0	*	-0.6	+1.7	+1.1
Mississippi	2001	2,859,733	119,615	4,182.7			10,006	349.9	109,609	3,832.8	282	9.9
	2002	2,871,782	119,442	4,159.2			9,858	343.3	109,584	3,815.9	264	9.2
Percent change			-0.1	-0.6			-1.5	-1.9	*	-0.4	-6.4	-6.8
Tennessee[5]	2001	5,749,398	295,768	5,144.3			42,776	744.0	252,992	4,400.3	423	7.4
	2002	5,797,289	290,961	5,018.9			41,562	716.9	249,399	4,302.0	420	7.2
Percent change			-1.6	-2.4			-2.8	-3.6	-1.4	-2.2	-0.7	-1.5
West South Central	2001	32,005,626	1,607,881	5,023.7			182,749	571.0	1,425,132	4,452.8	2,166	6.8
	2002	32,466,332	1,637,207	5,042.8			184,796	569.2	1,452,411	4,473.6	2,200	6.8
Percent change			+1.8	+0.4			+1.1	-0.3	+1.9	+0.5	+1.6	+0.1
Arkansas	2001	2,694,698	111,296	4,130.2			12,190	452.4	99,106	3,677.8	148	5.5
	2002	2,710,079	112,672	4,157.5			11,501	424.4	101,171	3,733.1	142	5.2
Percent change			+1.2	+0.7			-5.7	-6.2	+2.1	+1.5	-4.1	-4.6
Louisiana	2001	4,470,368	238,371	5,332.2			30,678	686.3	207,693	4,646.0	501	11.2
	2002	4,482,646	228,528	5,098.1			29,690	662.3	198,838	4,435.7	593	13.2
Percent change			-4.1	-4.4			-3.2	-3.5	-4.3	-4.5	+18.4	+18.0
Oklahoma	2001	3,469,577	159,405	4,594.4			17,726	510.9	141,679	4,083.5	185	5.3
	2002	3,493,714	165,715	4,743.2			17,587	503.4	148,128	4,239.8	163	4.7
Percent change			+4.0	+3.2			-0.8	-1.5	+4.6	+3.8	-11.9	-12.5

See footnotes at end of table.

Forcible rape		Robbery		Aggravated assault		Burglary		Larceny-theft		Motor vehicle theft		Arson[1]	
Number	Rate per 100,000	Number	Rate per 100,000	Number	Rate per 100,000	Number	Rate per 100,000	Number	Rate per 100,000	Number	Rate per 100,000	Number	Rate per 100,000
6,641	40.6	32,867	200.7	90,331	551.7	176,052	1,075.2	516,548	3,154.8	89,917	549.2		
6,753	40.4	32,581	194.9	88,476	529.4	177,242	1,060.5	511,478	3,060.3	88,516	529.6		
+1.7	-0.4	-0.9	-2.9	-2.1	-4.0	+0.7	-1.4	-1.0	-3.0	-1.6	-3.6		
2,180	25.9	14,402	171.3	24,491	291.4	71,799	854.2	238,484	2,837.2	37,589	447.2		
2,108	24.6	13,432	156.9	23,125	270.1	73,932	863.7	234,591	2,740.4	38,036	444.3		
-3.3	-5.0	-6.7	-8.4	-5.6	-7.3	+3.0	+1.1	-1.6	-3.4	+1.2	-0.6		
1,449	26.9	13,525	251.1	26,668	495.1	41,553	771.5	145,934	2,709.5	32,025	594.6		
1,370	25.1	13,417	245.8	26,715	489.5	39,765	728.5	143,320	2,625.8	34,020	623.3		
-5.5	-6.7	-0.8	-2.1	+0.2	-1.1	-4.3	-5.6	-1.8	-3.1	+6.2	+4.8		
2,083	25.4	13,304	162.1	24,573	299.4	101,889	1,241.6	237,241	2,891.0	24,647	300.3		
2,196	26.4	12,205	146.7	24,169	290.5	99,535	1,196.3	229,307	2,756.0	24,866	298.9		
+5.4	+4.0	-8.3	-9.5	-1.6	-3.0	-2.3	-3.6	-3.3	-4.7	+0.9	-0.5		
1,769	43.5	5,987	147.4	25,028	616.1	42,611	1,049.0	126,742	3,120.1	16,701	411.1		
1,959	47.7	5,774	140.6	25,730	626.5	43,745	1,065.1	123,196	2,999.5	16,867	410.7		
+10.7	+9.5	-3.6	-4.6	+2.8	+1.7	+2.7	+1.5	-2.8	-3.9	+1.0	-0.1		
1,770	24.6	6,860	95.3	11,945	166.0	31,604	439.1	157,060	2,182.4	18,842	261.8		
1,839	25.2	6,961	95.4	12,068	165.5	31,757	435.4	157,548	2,160.1	18,478	253.3		
+3.9	+2.5	+1.5	+0.1	+1.0	-0.3	+0.5	-0.8	+0.3	-1.0	-1.9	-3.2		
320	17.8	707	39.3	3,968	220.3	9,601	533.1	28,268	1,569.6	3,216	178.6		
328	18.2	657	36.5	3,179	176.4	9,677	537.1	27,524	1,527.5	3,898	216.3		
+2.5	+2.4	-7.1	-7.1	-19.9	-19.9	+0.8	+0.7	-2.6	-2.7	+21.2	+21.1		
5,763	33.6	22,366	130.4	53,480	311.9	157,132	916.4	426,770	2,488.9	59,308	345.9		
6,169	35.8	21,794	126.4	53,635	311.0	161,274	935.0	426,786	2,474.3	58,704	340.3		
+7.0	+6.4	-2.6	-3.1	+0.3	-0.3	+2.6	+2.0	*	-0.6	-1.0	-1.6		
1,369	30.6	5,584	125.0	12,250	274.1	40,642	909.4	119,992	2,685.0	12,619	282.4		
1,664	37.1	5,962	132.9	12,002	267.5	42,578	949.0	123,932	2,762.3	13,890	309.6		
+21.5	+21.1	+6.8	+6.4	-2.0	-2.4	+4.8	+4.4	+3.3	+2.9	+10.1	+9.6		
1,051	25.8	3,269	80.3	6,009	147.7	26,964	662.7	71,448	1,756.0	8,944	219.8		
1,088	26.6	3,063	74.8	7,083	173.1	27,855	680.6	70,776	1,729.2	8,750	213.8		
+3.5	+2.9	-6.3	-6.9	+17.9	+17.2	+3.3	+2.7	-0.9	-1.5	-2.2	-2.7		
1,147	40.1	3,294	115.2	5,283	184.7	29,821	1,042.8	70,315	2,458.8	9,473	331.3		
1,127	39.2	3,356	116.9	5,111	178.0	29,593	1,030.5	70,468	2,453.8	9,523	331.6		
-1.7	-2.2	+1.9	+1.5	-3.3	-3.7	-0.8	1.2	+0.2	-0.2	+0.5	+0.1		
2,196	38.2	10,219	177.7	29,938	520.7	59,705	1,038.5	165,015	2,870.1	28,272	491.7		
2,290	39.5	9,413	162.4	29,439	507.8	61,248	1,056.5	161,610	2,787.7	26,541	457.8		
+4.3	+3.4	-7.9	-8.6	-1.7	-2.5	+2.6	+1.7	-2.1	-2.9	-6.1	-6.9		
11,950	37.3	48,139	150.4	120,494	376.5	307,582	961.0	973,307	3,041.0	144,243	450.7		
12,364	38.1	50,193	154.6	120,039	369.7	316,352	974.4	993,608	3,060.4	142,451	438.8		
+3.5	+2.0	+4.3	+2.8	-0.4	-1.8	+2.9	+1.4	+2.1	+0.6	-1.2	-2.6		
892	33.1	2,181	80.9	8,969	332.8	22,196	823.7	69,590	2,582.5	7,320	271.6		
754	27.8	2,524	93.1	8,081	298.2	23,229	857.1	71,129	2,624.6	6,813	251.4		
-15.5	-16.0	+15.7	+15.1	-9.9	-10.4	+4.7	+4.1	+2.2	+1.6	-6.9	-7.5		
1,403	31.4	7,864	175.9	20,910	467.7	46,451	1,039.1	139,555	3,121.8	21,687	485.1		
1,529	34.1	7,123	158.9	20,445	456.1	45,350	1,011.7	133,302	2,973.7	20,186	450.3		
+9.0	+8.7	-9.4	-9.7	-2.2	-2.5	-2.4	-2.6	-4.5	-4.7	-6.9	-7.2		
1,486	42.8	2,746	79.1	13,309	383.6	34,573	996.5	94,537	2,724.7	12,569	362.3		
1,573	45.0	2,966	84.9	12,885	368.8	35,171	1,006.7	100,185	2,867.6	12,772	365.6		
+5.9	+5.1	+8.0	+7.3	-3.2	-3.9	+1.7	+1.0	+6.0	+5.2	+1.6	+0.9		

Table 4

Index of Crime[1]

by Region, Geographic Division, and State, 2001-2002—Continued

Area	Year	Population[2]	Crime Index Number	Crime Index Rate per 100,000	Modified Crime Index[3] Number	Modified Crime Index[3] Rate per 100,000	Violent crime[4] Number	Violent crime[4] Rate per 100,000	Property crime[4] Number	Property crime[4] Rate per 100,000	Murder and non-negligent manslaughter Number	Murder and non-negligent manslaughter Rate per 100,000
Texas	2001	21,370,983	1,098,809	5,141.6			122,155	571.6	976,654	4,570.0	1,332	6.2
	2002	21,779,893	1,130,292	5,189.6			126,018	578.6	1,004,274	4,611.0	1,302	6.0
Percent change			+2.9	+0.9			+3.2	+1.2	+2.8	+0.9	-2.3	-4.1
West[5]	**2001**	**64,592,993**	**2,808,173**	**4,347.5**			**335,425**	**519.3**	**2,472,748**	**3,828.2**	**3,517**	**5.4**
	2002	**65,652,316**	**2,901,062**	**4,418.8**			**333,635**	**508.2**	**2,567,427**	**3,910.6**	**3,721**	**5.7**
Percent change			**+3.3**	**+1.6**			**-0.5**	**-2.1**	**+3.8**	**+2.2**	**+5.8**	**+4.1**
Mountain	2001	18,665,045	884,609	4,739.4			83,798	449.0	800,811	4,290.4	977	5.2
	2002	19,057,088	931,833	4,889.7			87,096	457.0	844,737	4,432.7	1,013	5.3
Percent change			+5.3	+3.2			+3.9	+1.8	+5.5	+3.3	+3.7	+1.6
Arizona	2001	5,306,966	322,549	6,077.8			28,675	540.3	293,874	5,537.5	400	7.5
	2002	5,456,453	348,467	6,386.3			30,171	552.9	318,296	5,833.4	387	7.1
Percent change			+8.0	+5.1			+5.2	+2.3	+8.3	+5.3	-3.3	-5.9
Colorado	2001	4,430,989	186,379	4,206.3			15,492	349.6	170,887	3,856.6	158	3.6
	2002	4,506,542	195,936	4,347.8			15,882	352.4	180,054	3,995.4	179	4.0
Percent change			+5.1	+3.4			+2.5	+0.8	+5.4	+3.6	+13.3	+11.4
Idaho	2001	1,320,585	41,392	3,134.4			3,211	243.1	38,181	2,891.2	30	2.3
	2002	1,341,131	42,547	3,172.5			3,419	254.9	39,128	2,917.5	36	2.7
Percent change			+2.8	+1.2			+6.5	+4.8	+2.5	+0.9	+20.0	+18.2
Montana	2001	905,382	33,362	3,684.9			3,187	352.0	30,175	3,332.8	34	3.8
	2002	909,453	31,948	3,512.9			3,197	351.5	28,751	3,161.4	16	1.8
Percent change			-4.2	-4.7			+0.3	-0.1	-4.7	-5.1	-52.9	-53.2
Nevada	2001	2,097,722	89,845	4,283.0			12,359	589.2	77,486	3,693.8	180	8.6
	2002	2,173,491	97,752	4,497.5			13,856	637.5	83,896	3,860.0	181	8.3
Percent change			+8.8	+5.0			+12.1	+8.2	+8.3	+4.5	+0.6	-2.9
New Mexico	2001	1,830,935	97,383	5,318.8			14,288	780.4	83,095	4,538.4	99	5.4
	2002	1,855,059	94,196	5,077.8			13,719	739.5	80,477	4,338.2	152	8.2
Percent change			-3.3	-4.5			-4.0	-5.2	-3.2	-4.4	+53.5	+51.5
Utah	2001	2,278,712	96,307	4,226.4			5,314	233.2	90,993	3,993.2	67	2.9
	2002	2,316,256	103,129	4,452.4			5,488	236.9	97,641	4,215.5	47	2.0
Percent change			+7.1	+5.3			+3.3	+1.6	+7.3	+5.6	-29.9	-31.0
Wyoming	2001	493,754	17,392	3,522.4			1,272	257.6	16,120	3,264.8	9	1.8
	2002	498,703	17,858	3,580.9			1,364	273.5	16,494	3,307.4	15	3.0
Percent change			+2.7	+1.7			+7.2	+6.2	+2.3	+1.3	+66.7	+65.0
Pacific[5]	2001	45,927,948	1,923,564	4,188.2			251,627	547.9	1,671,937	3,640.3	2,540	5.5
	2002	46,595,228	1,969,229	4,226.2			246,539	529.1	1,722,690	3,697.1	2,708	5.8
Percent change			+2.4	+0.9			-2.0	-3.4	+3.0	+1.6	+6.6	+5.1
Alaska	2001	633,630	26,895	4,244.6			3,735	589.5	23,160	3,655.1	39	6.2
	2002	643,786	27,745	4,309.7			3,627	563.4	24,118	3,746.3	33	5.1
Percent change			+3.2	+1.5			-2.9	-4.4	+4.1	+2.5	-15.4	-16.7
California[5]	2001	34,600,463	1,347,056	3,893.2			212,867	615.2	1,134,189	3,278.0	2,206	6.4
	2002	35,116,033	1,384,872	3,943.7			208,388	593.4	1,176,484	3,350.3	2,395	6.8
Percent change			+2.8	+1.3			-2.1	-3.5	+3.7	+2.2	+8.6	+7.0
Hawaii	2001	1,227,024	65,947	5,374.5			3,117	254.0	62,830	5,120.5	32	2.6
	2002	1,244,898	75,238	6,043.7			3,262	262.0	71,976	5,781.7	24	1.9
Percent change			+14.1	+12.5			+4.7	+3.1	+14.6	+12.9	-25.0	-26.1
Oregon	2001	3,473,441	175,174	5,043.2			10,650	306.6	164,524	4,736.6	84	2.4
	2002	3,521,515	171,443	4,868.4			10,298	292.4	161,145	4,576.0	72	2.0
Percent change			-2.1	-3.5			-3.3	-4.6	-2.1	-3.4	-14.3	-15.5

See footnotes at end of table.

	Forcible rape		Robbery		Aggravated assault		Burglary		Larceny-theft		Motor vehicle theft		Arson[1]	
	Number	Rate per 100,000	Number	Rate per 100,000	Number	Rate per 100,000	Number	Rate per 100,000	Number	Rate per 100,000	Number	Rate per 100,000	Number	Rate per 100,000
	8,169	38.2	35,348	165.4	77,306	361.7	204,362	956.3	669,625	3,133.3	102,667	480.4		
	8,508	39.1	37,580	172.5	78,628	361.0	212,602	976.1	688,992	3,163.4	102,680	471.4		
	+4.1	+2.2	+6.3	+4.3	+1.7	-0.2	+4.0	+2.1	+2.9	+1.0	*	-1.9		
	21,487	**33.3**	**96,759**	**149.8**	**213,662**	**330.8**	**475,033**	**735.4**	**1,623,803**	**2,513.9**	**373,912**	**578.9**		
	22,507	**34.3**	**95,865**	**146.0**	**211,542**	**322.2**	**493,354**	**751.5**	**1,663,662**	**2,534.0**	**410,411**	**625.1**		
	+4.7	**+3.1**	**-0.9**	**-2.5**	**-1.0**	**-2.6**	**+3.9**	**+2.2**	**+2.5**	**+0.8**	**+9.8**	**+8.0**		
	6,843	36.7	21,806	116.8	54,172	290.2	148,079	793.3	546,277	2,926.7	106,455	570.3		
	7,454	39.1	20,659	108.4	57,970	304.2	157,652	827.3	568,436	2,982.8	118,649	622.6		
	+8.9	+6.7	-5.3	-7.2	+7.0	+4.8	+6.5	+4.3	+4.1	+1.9	+11.5	+9.2		
	1,518	28.6	8,868	167.1	17,889	337.1	54,821	1,033.0	186,850	3,520.8	52,203	983.7		
	1,608	29.5	8,000	146.6	20,176	369.8	59,087	1,082.9	201,541	3,693.6	57,668	1,056.9		
	+5.9	+3.0	-9.8	-12.3	+12.8	+9.7	+7.8	+4.8	+7.9	+4.9	+10.5	+7.4		
	1,930	43.6	3,555	80.2	9,849	222.3	28,533	643.9	121,360	2,738.9	20,994	473.8		
	2,066	45.8	3,579	79.4	10,058	223.2	31,678	702.9	125,193	2,778.0	23,183	514.4		
	+7.0	+5.3	+0.7	-1.0	+2.1	+0.4	+11.0	+9.2	+3.2	+1.4	+10.4	+8.6		
	425	32.2	245	18.6	2,511	190.1	7,507	568.5	28,285	2,141.9	2,389	180.9		
	497	37.1	240	17.9	2,646	197.3	7,441	554.8	29,060	2,166.8	2,627	195.9		
	+16.9	+15.1	-2.0	-3.5	+5.4	+3.8	-0.9	-2.4	+2.7	+1.2	+10.0	+8.3		
	188	20.8	230	25.4	2,735	302.1	3,670	405.4	24,684	2,726.4	1,821	201.1		
	237	26.1	283	31.1	2,661	292.6	3,289	361.6	23,679	2,603.7	1,783	196.1		
	+26.1	+25.5	+23.0	+22.5	-2.7	-3.1	-10.4	-10.8	-4.1	-4.5	-2.1	-2.5		
	883	42.1	4,932	235.1	6,364	303.4	17,711	844.3	45,073	2,148.7	14,702	700.9		
	928	42.7	5,118	235.5	7,629	351.0	18,951	871.9	47,459	2,183.5	17,486	804.5		
	+5.1	+1.4	+3.8	+0.2	+19.9	+15.7	+7.0	+3.3	+5.3	+1.6	+18.9	+14.8		
	850	46.4	2,695	147.2	10,644	581.3	19,552	1,067.9	56,406	3,080.7	7,137	389.8		
	1,027	55.4	2,206	118.9	10,334	557.1	19,634	1,058.4	53,406	2,878.9	7,437	400.9		
	+20.8	+19.3	-18.1	-19.2	-2.9	-4.2	+0.4	-0.9	-5.3	-6.5	+4.2	+2.8		
	896	39.3	1,197	52.5	3,154	138.4	13,804	605.8	70,676	3,101.6	6,513	285.8		
	943	40.7	1,140	49.2	3,358	145.0	15,124	653.0	74,795	3,229.1	7,722	333.4		
	+5.2	+3.5	-4.8	-6.3	+6.5	+4.7	+9.6	+7.8	+5.8	+4.1	+18.6	+16.6		
	153	31.0	84	17.0	1,026	207.8	2,481	502.5	12,943	2,621.3	696	141.0		
	148	29.7	93	18.6	1,108	222.2	2,448	490.9	13,303	2,667.5	743	149.0		
	-3.3	-4.2	+10.7	+9.6	+8.0	+6.9	-1.3	-2.3	+2.8	+1.8	+6.8	+5.7		
	14,644	31.9	74,953	163.2	159,490	347.3	326,954	711.9	1,077,526	2,346.1	267,457	582.3		
	15,053	32.3	75,206	161.4	153,572	329.6	335,702	720.5	1,095,226	2,350.5	291,762	626.2		
	+2.8	+1.3	+0.3	-1.1	-3.7	-5.1	+2.7	+1.2	+1.6	+0.2	+9.1	+7.5		
	501	79.1	514	81.1	2,681	423.1	3,847	607.1	16,695	2,634.8	2,618	413.2		
	511	79.4	489	76.0	2,594	402.9	3,908	607.0	17,739	2,755.4	2,471	383.8		
	+2.0	+0.4	-4.9	-6.4	-3.2	-4.8	+1.6	*	+6.3	+4.6	-5.6	-7.1		
	9,960	28.8	64,614	186.7	136,087	393.3	232,273	671.3	697,739	2,016.6	204,177	590.1		
	10,198	29.0	64,968	185.0	130,827	372.6	238,428	679.0	715,692	2,038.1	222,364	633.2		
	+2.4	+0.9	+0.5	-0.9	-3.9	-5.3	+2.6	+1.1	+2.6	+1.1	+8.9	+7.3		
	409	33.3	1,142	93.1	1,534	125.0	11,162	909.7	44,925	3,661.3	6,743	549.5		
	372	29.9	1,210	97.2	1,656	133.0	12,722	1,021.9	49,344	3,963.7	9,910	796.0		
	-9.0	-10.4	+6.0	+4.4	+8.0	+6.4	+14.0	+12.3	+9.8	+8.3	+47.0	+44.9		
	1,174	33.8	2,749	79.1	6,643	191.3	26,648	767.2	123,034	3,542.1	14,842	427.3		
	1,238	35.2	2,742	77.9	6,246	177.4	25,696	729.7	118,925	3,377.1	16,524	469.2		
	+5.5	+4.0	-0.3	-1.6	-6.0	-7.3	-3.6	-4.9	-3.3	-4.7	+11.3	+9.8		

Table 4

Index of Crime[1]

by Region, Geographic Division, and State, 2001-2002—Continued

Area	Year	Population[2]	Crime Index		Modified Crime Index[3]		Violent crime[4]		Property crime[4]		Murder and non-negligent manslaughter	
			Number	Rate per 100,000	Number	Rate per 100,000	Number	Rate per 100,000	Number	Rate per 100,000	Number	Rate per 100,000
Washington	2001	5,993,390	308,492	5,147.2			21,258	354.7	287,234	4,792.5	179	3.0
	2002	6,068,996	309,931	5,106.8			20,964	345.4	288,967	4,761.4	184	3.0
Percent change			+0.5	-0.8			-1.4	-2.6	+0.6	-0.6	+2.8	+1.5
Puerto Rico	2001	3,839,810	70,117	1,826.1			11,403	297.0	58,714	1,529.1	744	19.4
	2002	3,858,806	90,783	2,352.6			13,471	349.1	77,312	2,003.5	774	20.1
Percent change			+29.5	+28.8			+18.1	+17.6	+31.7	+31.0	+4.0	+3.5

[1] The murder and nonnegligent homicides that occurred as a result of the events of September 11, 2001, were not included in this table.

[2] Populations are Bureau of the Census provisional estimates as of July 1, 2002, and July 1, 2001.

[3] Although arson data are included in the trend and clearance tables, sufficient data are not available to estimate totals for this offense.

[4] Violent crimes are offenses of murder, forcible rape, robbery, and aggravated assault. Property crimes are offenses of burglary, larceny-theft, and motor vehicle theft.

[5] The 2001 crime figures have been adjusted. See Crime Trends, Appendix I, for details.

[6] Limited data for 2002 were available. See Offense Estimation, Appendix I, for details.

[7] Includes offenses reported by the Zoological Police and the Metro Transit Police.

* Less than one-tenth of 1 percent.

NOTE: Offense totals are based on all data received from reporting agencies and estimates for unreported areas.

Forcible rape		Robbery		Aggravated assault		Burglary		Larceny-theft		Motor vehicle theft		Arson[3]	
Number	Rate per 100,000	Number	Rate per 100,000	Number	Rate per 100,000	Number	Rate per 100,000	Number	Rate per 100,000	Number	Rate per 100,000	Number	Rate per 100,000
2,600	43.4	5,934	99.0	12,545	209.3	53,024	884.7	195,133	3,255.8	39,077	652.0		
2,734	45.0	5,797	95.5	12,249	201.8	54,948	905.4	193,526	3,188.8	40,493	667.2		
+5.2	+3.8	-2.3	-3.5	-2.4	-3.6	+3.6	+2.3	-0.8	-2.1	+3.6	+2.3		
187	4.9	7,999	208.3	2,473	64.4	19,931	519.1	26,140	680.8	12,643	329.3		
241	6.2	8,978	232.7	3,478	90.1	24,737	641.1	39,640	1,027.3	12,935	335.2		
+28.9	+28.2	+12.2	+11.7	+40.6	+39.9	+24.1	+23.5	+51.6	+50.9	+2.3	+1.8		

Table 5

Index of Crime
by State, 2002

Area	Population	Crime Index	Modified Crime Index[1]	Violent crime[2]	Property crime[2]	Murder and non-negligent man-slaughter	Forcible rape	Robbery	Aggravated assault	Burglary	Larceny-theft	Motor vehicle theft	Arson[1]
ALABAMA													
Metropolitan Statistical Area	3,136,510												
Area actually reporting	93.2%	146,135		14,368	131,767	231	1,197	4,970	7,970	30,511	90,531	10,725	
Estimated total	100.0%	155,153		15,126	140,027	240	1,256	5,210	8,420	32,145	96,566	11,316	
Cities outside metropolitan areas	539,598												
Area actually reporting	82.2%	25,276		2,469	22,807	24	195	484	1,766	4,993	16,610	1,204	
Estimated total	100.0%	30,749		3,003	27,746	29	237	589	2,148	6,074	20,207	1,465	
Rural	810,400												
Area actually reporting	73.6%	10,626		1,327	9,299	25	126	120	1,056	3,210	5,272	817	
Estimated total	100.0%	14,429		1,802	12,627	34	171	163	1,434	4,359	7,159	1,109	
State Total	**4,486,508**	**200,331**		**19,931**	**180,400**	**303**	**1,664**	**5,962**	**12,002**	**42,578**	**123,932**	**13,890**	
Rate per 100,000 inhabitants		4,465.2		444.2	4,020.9	6.8	37.1	132.9	267.5	949.0	2,762.3	309.6	
ALASKA													
Metropolitan Statistical Area	267,280												
Area actually reporting	100.0%	13,670		1,721	11,949	18	254	382	1,067	1,521	9,255	1,173	
Cities outside metropolitan areas	167,350												
Area actually reporting	95.0%	8,727		1,122	7,605	5	134	73	910	1,015	5,901	689	
Estimated total	100.0%	9,181		1,180	8,001	5	141	77	957	1,068	6,208	725	
Rural	209,156												
Area actually reporting	100.0%	4,894		726	4,168	10	116	30	570	1,319	2,276	573	
State Total	**643,786**	**27,745**		**3,627**	**24,118**	**33**	**511**	**489**	**2,594**	**3,908**	**17,739**	**2,471**	
Rate per 100,000 inhabitants		4,309.7		563.4	3,746.3	5.1	79.4	76.0	402.9	607.0	2,755.4	383.8	
ARIZONA													
Metropolitan Statistical Area	4,814,487												
Area actually reporting	98.3%	322,139		27,408	294,731	364	1,499	7,804	17,741	53,694	185,611	55,426	
Estimated total	100.0%	327,109		27,729	299,380	367	1,520	7,876	17,966	54,662	188,571	56,147	
Cities outside metropolitan areas	305,238												
Area actually reporting	98.8%	13,860		1,146	12,714	8	54	91	993	2,353	9,487	874	
Estimated total	100.0%	14,030		1,160	12,870	8	55	92	1,005	2,382	9,603	885	
Rural	336,728												
Area actually reporting	100.0%	7,328		1,282	6,046	12	33	32	1,205	2,043	3,367	636	
State Total	**5,456,453**	**348,467**		**30,171**	**318,296**	**387**	**1,608**	**8,000**	**20,176**	**59,087**	**201,541**	**57,668**	
Rate per 100,000 inhabitants		6,386.3		552.9	5,833.4	7.1	29.5	146.6	369.8	1,082.9	3,693.6	1,056.9	
ARKANSAS													
Metropolitan Statistical Area	1,339,146												
Area actually reporting	100.0%	74,398		7,326	67,072	95	525	2,044	4,662	13,879	48,670	4,523	
Cities outside metropolitan areas	509,713												
Area actually reporting	98.4%	26,046		2,878	23,168	20	132	393	2,333	5,668	16,197	1,303	
Estimated total	100.0%	26,468		2,924	23,544	20	134	399	2,371	5,760	16,460	1,324	
Rural	861,220												
Area actually reporting	97.1%	11,467		1,215	10,252	26	92	79	1,018	3,487	5,827	938	
Estimated total	100.0%	11,806		1,251	10,555	27	95	81	1,048	3,590	5,999	966	
State Total	**2,710,079**	**112,672**		**11,501**	**101,171**	**142**	**754**	**2,524**	**8,081**	**23,229**	**71,129**	**6,813**	
Rate per 100,000 inhabitants		4,157.5		424.4	3,733.1	5.2	27.8	93.1	298.2	857.1	2,624.6	251.4	
CALIFORNIA													
Metropolitan Statistical Area	33,953,585												
Area actually reporting	100.0%	1,348,339		204,139	1,144,200	2,352	9,809	64,453	127,525	229,182	696,315	218,703	
Cities outside metropolitan areas	501,198												
Area actually reporting	100.0%	21,249		2,323	18,926	20	202	375	1,726	4,468	12,416	2,042	
Rural	661,250												
Area actually reporting	100.0%	15,284		1,926	13,358	23	187	140	1,576	4,778	6,961	1,619	
State Total	**35,116,033**	**1,384,872**		**208,388**	**1,176,484**	**2,395**	**10,198**	**64,968**	**130,827**	**238,428**	**715,692**	**222,364**	
Rate per 100,000 inhabitants		3,943.7		593.4	3,350.3	6.8	29.0	185.0	372.6	679.0	2,038.1	633.2	

See footnotes at end of table.

Table 5

Index of Crime

by State, 2002—Continued

Area	Population	Crime Index	Modified Crime Index[1]	Violent crime[2]	Property crime[2]	Murder and non-negligent man-slaughter	Forcible rape	Robbery	Aggravated assault	Burglary	Larceny-theft	Motor vehicle theft	Arson[1]
COLORADO													
Metropolitan Statistical Area	3,779,831												
Area actually reporting	95.6%	166,005		13,589	152,416	158	1,740	3,314	8,377	27,280	103,999	21,137	
Estimated total	100.0%	174,593		14,220	160,373	164	1,821	3,464	8,771	28,431	109,651	22,291	
Cities outside metropolitan areas	313,320												
Area actually reporting	86.6%	13,287		992	12,295	5	151	83	753	1,801	10,007	487	
Estimated total	100.0%	15,351		1,146	14,205	6	174	96	870	2,081	11,561	563	
Rural	413,391												
Area actually reporting	87.9%	5,061		449	4,612	8	62	15	364	1,005	3,333	274	
Estimated total	100.0%	5,992		516	5,476	9	71	19	417	1,166	3,981	329	
State Total	**4,506,542**	**195,936**		**15,882**	**180,054**	**179**	**2,066**	**3,579**	**10,058**	**31,678**	**125,193**	**23,183**	
Rate per 100,000 inhabitants		4,347.8		352.4	3,995.4	4.0	45.8	79.4	223.2	702.9	2,778.0	514.4	
CONNECTICUT													
Metropolitan Statistical Area	2,897,041												
Area actually reporting	100.0%	93,997		9,455	84,542	75	661	3,926	4,793	14,651	58,934	10,957	
Cities outside metropolitan areas	60,995												
Area actually reporting	100.0%	2,628		235	2,393	2	13	56	164	539	1,711	143	
Rural	502,467												
Area actually reporting	100.0%	7,094		1,077	6,017	3	56	78	940	1,898	3,647	472	
State Total	**3,460,503**	**103,719**		**10,767**	**92,952**	**80**	**730**	**4,060**	**5,897**	**17,088**	**64,292**	**11,572**	
Rate per 100,000 inhabitants		2,997.2		311.1	2,686.1	2.3	21.1	117.3	170.4	493.8	1,857.9	334.4	
DELAWARE													
Metropolitan Statistical Area	645,993												
Area actually reporting	99.9%	26,417		3,961	22,456	19	266	1,035	2,641	4,222	15,409	2,825	
Estimated total	100.0%	26,458		3,966	22,492	19	266	1,036	2,645	4,228	15,437	2,827	
Cities outside metropolitan areas	37,573												
Area actually reporting	100.0%	2,303		293	2,010	2	15	69	207	408	1,517	85	
Rural	123,819												
Area actually reporting	100.0%	3,042		577	2,465	5	77	49	446	719	1,601	145	
State Total	**807,385**	**31,803**		**4,836**	**26,967**	**26**	**358**	**1,154**	**3,298**	**5,355**	**18,555**	**3,057**	
Rate per 100,000 inhabitants		3,939.0		599.0	3,340.0	3.2	44.3	142.9	408.5	663.3	2,298.2	378.6	
DISTRICT OF COLUMBIA[3]													
Metropolitan Statistical Area	570,898												
Area actually reporting	100.0%	45,799		9,322	36,477	264	262	3,834	4,962	5,170	21,708	9,599	
Cities outside metropolitan areas	None												
Rural	None												
Total	**570,898**	**45,799**		**9,322**	**36,477**	**264**	**262**	**3,834**	**4,962**	**5,170**	**21,708**	**9,599**	
Rate per 100,000 inhabitants		8,022.3		1,632.9	6,389.4	46.2	45.9	671.6	869.2	905.6	3,802.4	1,681.4	
FLORIDA													
Metropolitan Statistical Area	15,515,922												
Area actually reporting	99.2%	854,239		121,332	732,907	869	6,225	31,484	82,754	164,155	483,463	85,289	
Estimated total	100.0%	859,847		122,124	737,723	874	6,273	31,647	83,330	165,296	486,611	85,816	
Cities outside metropolitan areas	240,207												
Area actually reporting	98.8%	16,556		2,120	14,436	9	105	457	1,549	3,610	9,962	864	
Estimated total	100.0%	16,750		2,144	14,606	9	106	462	1,567	3,653	10,079	874	
Rural	957,020												
Area actually reporting	100.0%	29,360		4,453	24,907	28	374	472	3,579	8,293	14,788	1,826	
State Total	**16,713,149**	**905,957**		**128,721**	**777,236**	**911**	**6,753**	**32,581**	**88,476**	**177,242**	**511,478**	**88,516**	
Rate per 100,000 inhabitants		5,420.6		770.2	4,650.4	5.5	40.4	194.9	529.4	1,060.5	3,060.3	529.6	

See footnotes at end of table.

Table 5

Index of Crime
by State, 2002—Continued

Area	Population	Crime Index	Modified Crime Index[1]	Violent crime[2]	Property crime[2]	Murder and non-negligent man-slaughter	Forcible rape	Robbery	Aggravated assault	Burglary	Larceny-theft	Motor vehicle theft	Arson[1]
GEORGIA													
Metropolitan Statistical Area	5,925,447												
Area actually reporting	99.0%	283,284		28,554	254,730	473	1,535	11,664	14,882	53,571	169,095	32,064	
Estimated total	100.0%	286,953		28,856	258,097	476	1,548	11,767	15,065	54,153	171,571	32,373	
Cities outside metropolitan areas	915,341												
Area actually reporting	92.3%	50,888		5,642	45,246	47	303	1,155	4,137	8,539	34,476	2,231	
Estimated total	100.0%	55,159		6,115	49,044	51	328	1,252	4,484	9,256	37,370	2,418	
Rural	1,719,522												
Area actually reporting	90.4%	39,504		3,885	35,619	71	210	373	3,231	9,509	23,178	2,932	
Estimated total	100.0%	43,718		4,300	39,418	79	232	413	3,576	10,523	25,650	3,245	
State Total	**8,560,310**	**385,830**		**39,271**	**346,559**	**606**	**2,108**	**13,432**	**23,125**	**73,932**	**234,591**	**38,036**	
Rate per 100,000 inhabitants		4,507.2		458.8	4,048.4	7.1	24.6	156.9	270.1	863.7	2,740.4	444.3	
HAWAII													
Metropolitan Statistical Area	900,433												
Area actually reporting	100.0%	57,271		2,601	54,670	18	304	1,072	1,207	8,932	37,250	8,488	
Cities outside metropolitan areas	None												
Rural	344,465												
Area actually reporting	100.0%	17,967		661	17,306	6	68	138	449	3,790	12,094	1,422	
State Total	**1,244,898**	**75,238**		**3,262**	**71,976**	**24**	**372**	**1,210**	**1,656**	**12,722**	**49,344**	**9,910**	
Rate per 100,000 inhabitants		6,043.7		262.0	5,781.7	1.9	29.9	97.2	133.0	1,021.9	3,963.7	796.0	
IDAHO													
Metropolitan Statistical Area	526,430												
Area actually reporting	100.0%	20,859		1,682	19,177	13	267	153	1,249	3,443	14,390	1,344	
Cities outside metropolitan areas	379,717												
Area actually reporting	97.9%	14,642		1,010	13,632	9	126	69	806	2,284	10,572	776	
Estimated total	100.0%	14,949		1,031	13,918	9	129	70	823	2,332	10,794	792	
Rural	434,984												
Area actually reporting	98.9%	6,665		699	5,966	14	100	17	568	1,647	3,833	486	
Estimated total	100.0%	6,739		706	6,033	14	101	17	574	1,666	3,876	491	
State Total	**1,341,131**	**42,547**		**3,419**	**39,128**	**36**	**497**	**240**	**2,646**	**7,441**	**29,060**	**2,627**	
Rate per 100,000 inhabitants		3,172.5		254.9	2,917.5	2.7	37.1	17.9	197.3	554.8	2,166.8	195.9	
ILLINOIS[4]													
State Total	**12,600,620**	**506,086**		**78,214**	**427,872**	**949**	**4,298**	**25,272**	**47,695**	**81,123**	**301,892**	**44,857**	
Rate per 100,000 inhabitants		4,016.4		620.7	3,395.6	7.5	34.1	200.6	378.5	643.8	2,395.9	356.0	
INDIANA													
Metropolitan Statistical Area	4,446,634												
Area actually reporting	89.7%	173,239		17,786	155,453	305	1,391	5,971	10,119	31,422	107,426	16,605	
Estimated total	100.0%	183,586		18,576	165,010	312	1,470	6,102	10,692	33,404	114,178	17,428	
Cities outside metropolitan areas	590,072												
Area actually reporting	81.7%	23,587		1,183	22,404	19	149	259	756	3,547	17,616	1,241	
Estimated total	100.0%	28,872		1,447	27,425	23	182	317	925	4,342	21,564	1,519	
Rural	1,122,362												
Area actually reporting	56.0%	10,372		1,108	9,264	15	107	108	878	2,723	5,790	751	
Estimated total	100.0%	18,508		1,978	16,530	27	191	193	1,567	4,859	10,331	1,340	
State Total	**6,159,068**	**230,966**		**22,001**	**208,965**	**362**	**1,843**	**6,612**	**13,184**	**42,605**	**146,073**	**20,287**	
Rate per 100,000 inhabitants		3,750.0		357.2	3,392.8	5.9	29.9	107.4	214.1	691.7	2,371.7	329.4	

See footnotes at end of table.

Table 5

Index of Crime

by State, 2002—Continued

Area	Population	Crime Index	Modified Crime Index[1]	Violent crime[2]	Property crime[2]	Murder and non-negligent man-slaughter	Forcible rape	Robbery	Aggravated assault	Burglary	Larceny-theft	Motor vehicle theft	Arson[1]
IOWA													
Metropolitan Statistical Area	1,330,865												
Area actually reporting	98.4%	67,221		5,761	61,460	30	555	1,026	4,150	11,123	46,145	4,192	
Estimated total	100.0%	67,944		5,801	62,143	30	559	1,032	4,180	11,213	46,711	4,219	
Cities outside metropolitan areas	710,725												
Area actually reporting	91.8%	23,511		1,904	21,607	5	180	119	1,600	4,475	16,101	1,031	
Estimated total	100.0%	25,622		2,075	23,547	5	196	130	1,744	4,877	17,546	1,124	
Rural	895,170												
Area actually reporting	98.5%	7,582		504	7,078	9	41	7	447	2,514	4,091	473	
Estimated total	100.0%	7,699		512	7,187	9	42	7	454	2,553	4,154	480	
State Total	**2,936,760**	**101,265**		**8,388**	**92,877**	**44**	**797**	**1,169**	**6,378**	**18,643**	**68,411**	**5,823**	
Rate per 100,000 inhabitants		3,448.2		285.6	3,162.6	1.5	27.1	39.8	217.2	634.8	2,329.5	198.3	
KANSAS													
Metropolitan Statistical Area	1,536,604												
Area actually reporting	95.8%	64,646		5,817	58,829	48	560	1,523	3,686	10,711	43,642	4,476	
Estimated total	100.0%	69,861		6,592	63,269	58	586	1,837	4,111	11,738	46,324	5,207	
Cities outside metropolitan areas	682,033												
Area actually reporting	91.7%	28,872		2,384	26,488	11	288	263	1,822	4,887	20,322	1,279	
Estimated total	100.0%	31,474		2,599	28,875	12	314	287	1,986	5,327	22,154	1,394	
Rural	497,247												
Area actually reporting	95.4%	9,219		991	8,228	8	129	39	815	2,494	5,151	583	
Estimated total	100.0%	9,662		1,038	8,624	8	135	41	854	2,614	5,399	611	
State Total	**2,715,884**	**110,997**		**10,229**	**100,768**	**78**	**1,035**	**2,165**	**6,951**	**19,679**	**73,877**	**7,212**	
Rate per 100,000 inhabitants		4,087.0		376.6	3,710.3	2.9	38.1	79.7	255.9	724.6	2,720.2	265.5	
KENTUCKY[4]													
State Total	**4,092,891**	**118,799**		**11,418**	**107,381**	**184**	**1,088**	**3,063**	**7,083**	**27,855**	**70,776**	**8,750**	
Rate per 100,000 inhabitants		2,902.6		279.0	2,623.6	4.5	26.6	74.8	173.1	680.6	1,729.2	213.8	
LOUISIANA													
Metropolitan Statistical Area	3,380,522												
Area actually reporting	98.8%	186,021		22,968	163,053	529	1,262	6,409	14,768	36,188	108,417	18,448	
Estimated total	100.0%	188,429		23,226	165,203	530	1,274	6,459	14,963	36,620	110,010	18,573	
Cities outside metropolitan areas	372,005												
Area actually reporting	67.2%	15,170		2,156	13,014	12	77	284	1,783	2,849	9,641	524	
Estimated total	100.0%	22,579		3,210	19,369	18	115	423	2,654	4,240	14,349	780	
Rural	730,119												
Area actually reporting	88.7%	15,539		2,886	12,653	40	124	214	2,508	3,982	7,932	739	
Estimated total	100.0%	17,520		3,254	14,266	45	140	241	2,828	4,490	8,943	833	
State Total	**4,482,646**	**228,528**		**29,690**	**198,838**	**593**	**1,529**	**7,123**	**20,445**	**45,350**	**133,302**	**20,186**	
Rate per 100,000 inhabitants		5,098.1		662.3	4,435.7	13.2	34.1	158.9	456.1	1,011.7	2,973.7	450.3	
MAINE													
Metropolitan Statistical Area	488,483												
Area actually reporting	99.9%	15,213		610	14,603	7	167	156	280	2,678	11,351	574	
Estimated total	100.0%	15,225		610	14,615	7	167	156	280	2,680	11,361	574	
Cities outside metropolitan areas	428,325												
Area actually reporting	99.4%	13,414		575	12,839	4	141	94	336	2,231	10,107	501	
Estimated total	100.0%	13,502		579	12,923	4	142	95	338	2,246	10,173	504	
Rural	377,656												
Area actually reporting	100.0%	5,654		207	5,447	3	68	19	117	2,039	3,057	351	
State Total	**1,294,464**	**34,381**		**1,396**	**32,985**	**14**	**377**	**270**	**735**	**6,965**	**24,591**	**1,429**	
Rate per 100,000 inhabitants		2,656.0		107.8	2,548.2	1.1	29.1	20.9	56.8	538.1	1,899.7	110.4	

See footnotes at end of table.

Table 5

Index of Crime

by State, 2002—Continued

Area	Population	Crime Index	Modified Crime Index[1]	Violent crime[2]	Property crime[2]	Murder and non-negligent man-slaughter	Forcible rape	Robbery	Aggravated assault	Burglary	Larceny-theft	Motor vehicle theft	Arson[1]
MARYLAND													
Metropolitan Statistical Area	5,060,926												
Area actually reporting	100.0%	244,746		39,609	205,137	493	1,240	13,033	24,843	37,148	134,608	33,381	
Cities outside metropolitan areas	108,964												
Area actually reporting	100.0%	8,287		1,303	6,984	9	63	276	955	1,314	5,386	284	
Rural	288,247												
Area actually reporting	100.0%	6,087		1,103	4,984	11	67	108	917	1,303	3,326	355	
State Total	**5,458,137**	**259,120**		**42,015**	**217,105**	**513**	**1,370**	**13,417**	**26,715**	**39,765**	**143,320**	**34,020**	
Rate per 100,000 inhabitants		4,747.4		769.8	3,977.6	9.4	25.1	245.8	489.5	728.5	2,625.8	623.3	
MASSACHUSETTS													
Metropolitan Statistical Area	6,166,938												
Area actually reporting	95.5%	184,978		29,255	155,723	168	1,642	6,944	20,501	30,464	99,669	25,590	
Estimated total	100.0%	190,894		29,971	160,923	170	1,689	7,054	21,058	31,503	103,287	26,133	
Cities outside metropolitan areas	251,236												
Area actually reporting	87.4%	6,918		962	5,956	3	77	99	783	1,517	4,044	395	
Estimated total	100.0%	7,970		1,153	6,817	3	88	113	949	1,736	4,629	452	
Rural	9,627												
Area actually reporting	100.0%	26		13	13	0	0	2	11	4	6	3	
State Total	**6,427,801**	**198,890**		**31,137**	**167,753**	**173**	**1,777**	**7,169**	**22,018**	**33,243**	**107,922**	**26,588**	
Rate per 100,000 inhabitants		3,094.2		484.4	2,609.8	2.7	27.6	111.5	342.5	517.2	1,679.0	413.6	
MICHIGAN													
Metropolitan Statistical Area	8,261,532												
Area actually reporting	99.4%	340,257		49,949	290,308	643	4,059	11,668	33,579	59,841	183,112	47,355	
Estimated total	100.0%	341,916		50,097	291,819	644	4,074	11,697	33,682	60,103	184,194	47,522	
Cities outside metropolitan areas	590,393												
Area actually reporting	89.2%	18,818		1,261	17,557	7	336	66	852	2,545	14,336	676	
Estimated total	100.0%	21,099		1,414	19,685	8	377	74	955	2,853	16,074	758	
Rural	1,198,521												
Area actually reporting	98.3%	25,898		2,747	23,151	26	897	75	1,749	7,876	13,857	1,418	
Estimated total	100.0%	26,351		2,795	23,556	26	913	76	1,780	8,014	14,099	1,443	
State Total	**10,050,446**	**389,366**		**54,306**	**335,060**	**678**	**5,364**	**11,847**	**36,417**	**70,970**	**214,367**	**49,723**	
Rate per 100,000 inhabitants		3,874.1		540.3	3,333.8	6.7	53.4	117.9	362.3	706.1	2,132.9	494.7	
MINNESOTA													
Metropolitan Statistical Area	3,533,926												
Area actually reporting	99.4%	138,855		11,309	127,546	95	1,599	3,816	5,799	20,598	95,543	11,405	
Estimated total	100.0%	139,550		11,342	128,208	95	1,606	3,824	5,817	20,688	96,073	11,447	
Cities outside metropolitan areas	559,457												
Area actually reporting	99.4%	22,009		1,158	20,851	5	335	74	744	2,861	16,956	1,034	
Estimated total	100.0%	22,137		1,164	20,973	5	337	74	748	2,878	17,055	1,040	
Rural	926,337												
Area actually reporting	100.0%	15,767		922	14,845	12	330	39	541	4,468	9,022	1,355	
State Total	**5,019,720**	**177,454**		**13,428**	**164,026**	**112**	**2,273**	**3,937**	**7,106**	**28,034**	**122,150**	**13,842**	
Rate per 100,000 inhabitants		3,535.1		267.5	3,267.6	2.2	45.3	78.4	141.6	558.5	2,433.4	275.8	
MISSISSIPPI													
Metropolitan Statistical Area	1,033,431												
Area actually reporting	82.8%	51,618		3,950	47,668	104	478	1,917	1,451	11,734	30,627	5,307	
Estimated total	100.0%	57,587		4,309	53,278	116	540	2,007	1,646	13,124	34,402	5,752	
Cities outside metropolitan areas	657,437												
Area actually reporting	79.3%	32,095		2,402	29,693	52	264	738	1,348	7,177	20,882	1,634	
Estimated total	100.0%	40,481		3,030	37,451	66	333	931	1,700	9,052	26,338	2,061	
Rural	1,180,914												
Area actually reporting	41.4%	8,850		1,043	7,807	34	105	173	731	3,071	4,028	708	
Estimated total	100.0%	21,374		2,519	18,855	82	254	418	1,765	7,417	9,728	1,710	
State Total	**2,871,782**	**119,442**		**9,858**	**109,584**	**264**	**1,127**	**3,356**	**5,111**	**29,593**	**70,468**	**9,523**	
Rate per 100,000 inhabitants		4,159.2		343.3	3,815.9	9.2	39.2	116.9	178.0	1,030.5	2,453.8	331.6	

See footnotes at end of table.

Table 5

Index of Crime

by State, 2002—Continued

Area	Population	Crime Index	Modified Crime Index[1]	Violent crime[2]	Property crime[2]	Murder and non-negligent man-slaughter	Forcible rape	Robbery	Aggravated assault	Burglary	Larceny-theft	Motor vehicle theft	Arson[1]
MISSOURI													
Metropolitan Statistical Area	3,847,277												
Area actually reporting	99.7%	211,121		23,892	187,229	267	1,089	6,644	15,892	32,331	129,332	25,566	
Estimated total	100.0%	211,647		23,936	187,711	267	1,091	6,653	15,925	32,403	129,699	25,609	
Cities outside metropolitan areas	761,234												
Area actually reporting	99.3%	31,434		3,494	27,940	20	193	300	2,981	4,904	21,876	1,160	
Estimated total	100.0%	31,662		3,519	28,143	20	194	302	3,003	4,940	22,035	1,168	
Rural	1,064,068												
Area actually reporting	100.0%	17,768		3,102	14,666	44	180	69	2,809	5,378	8,187	1,101	
State Total	**5,672,579**	**261,077**		**30,557**	**230,520**	**331**	**1,465**	**7,024**	**21,737**	**42,721**	**159,921**	**27,878**	
Rate per 100,000 inhabitants		4,602.4		538.7	4,063.8	5.8	25.8	123.8	383.2	753.1	2,819.2	491.5	
MONTANA													
Metropolitan Statistical Area	307,963												
Area actually reporting	87.3%	13,675		914	12,761	6	57	192	659	1,343	10,616	802	
Estimated total	100.0%	14,565		1,017	13,548	6	62	202	747	1,438	11,245	865	
Cities outside metropolitan areas	178,045												
Area actually reporting	72.6%	6,349		573	5,776	3	59	34	477	508	4,971	297	
Estimated total	100.0%	8,744		789	7,955	4	81	47	657	700	6,846	409	
Rural	423,445												
Area actually reporting	64.8%	5,601		902	4,699	4	61	22	815	746	3,623	330	
Estimated total	100.0%	8,639		1,391	7,248	6	94	34	1,257	1,151	5,588	509	
State Total	**909,453**	**31,948**		**3,197**	**28,751**	**16**	**237**	**283**	**2,661**	**3,289**	**23,679**	**1,783**	
Rate per 100,000 inhabitants		3,512.9		351.5	3,161.4	1.8	26.1	31.1	292.6	361.6	2,603.7	196.1	
NEBRASKA													
Metropolitan Statistical Area	909,259												
Area actually reporting	97.3%	50,855		4,452	46,403	35	307	1,242	2,868	6,214	34,840	5,349	
Estimated total	100.0%	51,466		4,486	46,980	35	310	1,248	2,893	6,303	35,277	5,400	
Cities outside metropolitan areas	412,276												
Area actually reporting	90.4%	14,890		592	14,298	8	105	85	394	2,284	11,431	583	
Estimated total	100.0%	16,475		655	15,820	9	116	94	436	2,527	12,648	645	
Rural	407,645												
Area actually reporting	93.1%	5,273		267	5,006	4	35	16	212	1,395	3,272	339	
Estimated total	100.0%	5,665		287	5,378	4	38	17	228	1,499	3,515	364	
State Total	**1,729,180**	**73,606**		**5,428**	**68,178**	**48**	**464**	**1,359**	**3,557**	**10,329**	**51,440**	**6,409**	
Rate per 100,000 inhabitants		4,256.7		313.9	3,942.8	2.8	26.8	78.6	205.7	597.3	2,974.8	370.6	
NEVADA													
Metropolitan Statistical Area	1,901,003												
Area actually reporting	100.0%	90,821		13,043	77,778	174	845	5,047	6,977	17,449	43,289	17,040	
Cities outside metropolitan areas	46,975												
Area actually reporting	100.0%	1,849		115	1,734	2	15	15	83	380	1,248	106	
Rural	225,513												
Area actually reporting	100.0%	5,082		698	4,384	5	68	56	569	1,122	2,922	340	
State Total	**2,173,491**	**97,752**		**13,856**	**83,896**	**181**	**928**	**5,118**	**7,629**	**18,951**	**47,459**	**17,486**	
Rate per 100,000 inhabitants		4,497.5		637.5	3,860.0	8.3	42.7	235.5	351.0	871.9	2,183.5	804.5	
NEW HAMPSHIRE													
Metropolitan Statistical Area	772,025												
Area actually reporting	80.5%	15,278		1,244	14,034	7	224	323	690	2,487	10,359	1,188	
Estimated total	100.0%	17,848		1,435	16,413	7	261	347	820	2,911	12,120	1,382	
Cities outside metropolitan areas	441,658												
Area actually reporting	66.8%	6,778		385	6,393	2	116	42	225	1,221	4,815	357	
Estimated total	100.0%	10,153		577	9,576	3	174	63	337	1,829	7,212	535	
Rural	61,373												
Area actually reporting	100.0%	305		44	261	2	11	3	28	98	136	27	
State Total	**1,275,056**	**28,306**		**2,056**	**26,250**	**12**	**446**	**413**	**1,185**	**4,838**	**19,468**	**1,944**	
Rate per 100,000 inhabitants		2,220.0		161.2	2,058.7	0.9	35.0	32.4	92.9	379.4	1,526.8	152.5	

See footnotes at end of table.

Table 5

Index of Crime

by State, 2002—Continued

Area	Population	Crime Index	Modified Crime Index[1]	Violent crime[2]	Property crime[2]	Murder and non-negligent man-slaughter	Forcible rape	Robbery	Aggravated assault	Burglary	Larceny-theft	Motor vehicle theft	Arson[1]
NEW JERSEY													
Metropolitan Statistical Area	8,590,300												
Area actually reporting	99.9%	258,903		32,110	226,793	337	1,347	13,882	16,544	43,877	147,217	35,699	
Estimated total	100.0%	259,789		32,168	227,621	337	1,347	13,905	16,579	43,898	147,984	35,739	
Cities outside metropolitan areas	None												
Rural	None												
State Total	**8,590,300**	**259,789**		**32,168**	**227,621**	**337**	**1,347**	**13,905**	**16,579**	**43,898**	**147,984**	**35,739**	
Rate per 100,000 inhabitants		3,024.2		374.5	2,649.7	3.9	15.7	161.9	193.0	511.0	1,722.7	416.0	
NEW MEXICO													
Metropolitan Statistical Area	1,060,156												
Area actually reporting	87.0%	55,962		7,558	48,404	76	527	1,672	5,283	10,584	32,541	5,279	
Estimated total	100.0%	59,826		8,381	51,445	83	583	1,774	5,941	11,519	34,292	5,634	
Cities outside metropolitan areas	442,777												
Area actually reporting	90.3%	24,373		3,616	20,757	35	242	334	3,005	5,156	14,624	977	
Estimated total	100.0%	26,984		4,004	22,980	39	268	370	3,327	5,708	16,190	1,082	
Rural	352,126												
Area actually reporting	82.8%	6,118		1,105	5,013	25	146	51	883	1,994	2,422	597	
Estimated total	100.0%	7,386		1,334	6,052	30	176	62	1,066	2,407	2,924	721	
State Total	**1,855,059**	**94,196**		**13,719**	**80,477**	**152**	**1,027**	**2,206**	**10,334**	**19,634**	**53,406**	**7,437**	
Rate per 100,000 inhabitants		5,077.8		739.5	4,338.2	8.2	55.4	118.9	557.1	1,058.4	2,878.9	400.9	
NEW YORK													
Metropolitan Statistical Area	17,639,788												
Area actually reporting	90.5%	470,354		88,373	381,981	862	3,215	35,621	48,675	64,789	272,759	44,433	
Estimated total	100.0%	502,782		91,371	411,411	894	3,478	36,332	50,667	69,911	295,019	46,481	
Cities outside metropolitan areas	607,003												
Area actually reporting	86.1%	16,156		1,387	14,769	3	132	197	1,055	2,462	11,889	418	
Estimated total	100.0%	18,760		1,611	17,149	4	153	229	1,225	2,859	13,805	485	
Rural	910,741												
Area actually reporting	92.1%	14,346		1,886	12,460	10	234	85	1,557	3,619	8,473	368	
Estimated total	100.0%	15,579		2,048	13,531	11	254	92	1,691	3,930	9,201	400	
State Total	**19,157,532**	**537,121**		**95,030**	**442,091**	**909**	**3,885**	**36,653**	**53,583**	**76,700**	**318,025**	**47,366**	
Rate per 100,000 inhabitants		2,803.7		496.0	2,307.7	4.7	20.3	191.3	279.7	400.4	1,660.1	247.2	
NORTH CAROLINA													
Metropolitan Statistical Area	5,619,995												
Area actually reporting	99.3%	282,298		28,800	253,498	373	1,543	9,864	17,020	65,851	168,529	19,118	
Estimated total	100.0%	284,500		28,953	255,547	374	1,552	9,909	17,118	66,280	170,055	19,212	
Cities outside metropolitan areas	810,696												
Area actually reporting	95.6%	54,791		5,224	49,567	52	291	1,519	3,362	12,354	34,847	2,366	
Estimated total	100.0%	57,283		5,461	51,822	54	304	1,588	3,515	12,916	36,432	2,474	
Rural	1,889,455												
Area actually reporting	95.8%	48,895		4,506	44,389	115	326	678	3,387	19,483	21,860	3,046	
Estimated total	100.0%	51,043		4,704	46,339	120	340	708	3,536	20,339	22,820	3,180	
State Total	**8,320,146**	**392,826**		**39,118**	**353,708**	**548**	**2,196**	**12,205**	**24,169**	**99,535**	**229,307**	**24,866**	
Rate per 100,000 inhabitants		4,721.4		470.2	4,251.2	6.6	26.4	146.7	290.5	1,196.3	2,756.0	298.9	
NORTH DAKOTA													
Metropolitan Statistical Area	280,387												
Area actually reporting	99.1%	9,430		299	9,131	2	94	41	162	1,282	7,218	631	
Estimated total	100.0%	9,528		301	9,227	2	95	41	163	1,297	7,294	636	
Cities outside metropolitan areas	144,198												
Area actually reporting	88.3%	3,666		128	3,538	2	41	15	70	477	2,859	202	
Estimated total	100.0%	4,149		144	4,005	2	46	17	79	540	3,236	229	
Rural	209,525												
Area actually reporting	84.5%	1,336		44	1,292	1	19	0	24	343	820	129	
Estimated total	100.0%	1,581		51	1,530	1	22	0	28	406	971	153	
State Total	**634,110**	**15,258**		**496**	**14,762**	**5**	**163**	**58**	**270**	**2,243**	**11,501**	**1,018**	
Rate per 100,000 inhabitants		2,406.2		78.2	2,328.0	0.8	25.7	9.1	42.6	353.7	1,813.7	160.5	

See footnotes at end of table.

Table 5

Index of Crime
by State, 2002—Continued

Area	Population	Crime Index	Modified Crime Index[1]	Violent crime[2]	Property crime[2]	Murder and non-negligent man-slaughter	Forcible rape	Robbery	Aggravated assault	Burglary	Larceny-theft	Motor vehicle theft	Arson[1]
OHIO													
Metropolitan Statistical Area	9,269,065												
Area actually reporting	87.5%	376,175		35,708	340,467	468	4,018	16,627	14,595	79,941	222,822	37,704	
Estimated total	100.0%	408,945		37,428	371,517	486	4,304	17,253	15,385	85,684	245,901	39,932	
Cities outside metropolitan areas	795,592												
Area actually reporting	79.5%	30,482		1,474	29,008	15	268	404	787	5,256	22,644	1,108	
Estimated total	100.0%	38,347		1,854	36,493	19	337	508	990	6,612	28,487	1,394	
Rural	1,356,610												
Area actually reporting	62.5%	13,640		529	13,111	13	105	69	342	4,295	7,915	901	
Estimated total	100.0%	21,812		846	20,966	21	168	110	547	6,868	12,657	1,441	
State Total	**11,421,267**	**469,104**		**40,128**	**428,976**	**526**	**4,809**	**17,871**	**16,922**	**99,164**	**287,045**	**42,767**	
Rate per 100,000 inhabitants		4,107.3		351.3	3,755.9	4.6	42.1	156.5	148.2	868.2	2,513.3	374.5	
OKLAHOMA													
Metropolitan Statistical Area	2,123,513												
Area actually reporting	100.0%	122,845		12,688	110,157	104	1,124	2,614	8,846	24,466	75,589	10,102	
Cities outside metropolitan areas	699,127												
Area actually reporting	100.0%	32,564		3,524	29,040	24	327	313	2,860	7,285	20,109	1,646	
Rural	671,074												
Area actually reporting	100.0%	10,306		1,375	8,931	35	122	39	1,179	3,420	4,487	1,024	
State Total	**3,493,714**	**165,715**		**17,587**	**148,128**	**163**	**1,573**	**2,966**	**12,885**	**35,171**	**100,185**	**12,772**	
Rate per 100,000 inhabitants		4,743.2		503.4	4,239.8	4.7	45.0	84.9	368.8	1,006.7	2,867.6	365.6	
OREGON													
Metropolitan Statistical Area	2,575,588												
Area actually reporting	99.9%	137,598		8,793	128,805	53	989	2,444	5,307	19,095	95,330	14,380	
Estimated total	100.0%	137,645		8,795	128,850	53	989	2,445	5,308	19,101	95,364	14,385	
Cities outside metropolitan areas	443,276												
Area actually reporting	97.1%	23,232		1,030	22,202	5	160	240	625	3,658	17,228	1,316	
Estimated total	100.0%	23,933		1,061	22,872	5	165	247	644	3,768	17,748	1,356	
Rural	502,651												
Area actually reporting	100.0%	9,865		442	9,423	14	84	50	294	2,827	5,813	783	
State Total	**3,521,515**	**171,443**		**10,298**	**161,145**	**72**	**1,238**	**2,742**	**6,246**	**25,696**	**118,925**	**16,524**	
Rate per 100,000 inhabitants		4,868.4		292.4	4,576.0	2.0	35.2	77.9	177.4	729.7	3,377.1	469.2	
PENNSYLVANIA													
Metropolitan Statistical Area	10,437,252												
Area actually reporting	90.6%	289,525		43,374	246,151	564	3,005	16,123	23,682	44,675	172,421	29,055	
Estimated total	100.0%	312,507		45,563	266,944	584	3,166	16,685	25,128	47,667	188,670	30,607	
Cities outside metropolitan areas	805,839												
Area actually reporting	76.1%	16,064		1,795	14,269	10	195	264	1,326	2,271	11,265	733	
Estimated total	100.0%	21,122		2,360	18,762	13	256	347	1,744	2,986	14,812	964	
Rural	1,092,000												
Area actually reporting	100.0%	16,817		1,655	15,162	27	309	131	1,188	4,957	8,959	1.246	
State Total	**12,335,091**	**350,446**		**49,578**	**300,868**	**624**	**3,731**	**17,163**	**28,060**	**55,610**	**212,441**	**32,817**	
Rate per 100,000 inhabitants		2,841.0		401.9	2,439.1	5.1	30.2	139.1	227.5	450.8	1,722.2	266.0	
PUERTO RICO													
Metropolitan Statistical Area	3,252,499												
Area actually reporting	100.0%	79,618		11,997	67,621	698	207	8,184	2,908	20,346	35,251	12,024	
Cities outside metropolitan areas	606,307												
Area actually reporting	100.0%	11,165		1,474	9,691	76	34	794	570	4,391	4,389	911	
Total	**3,858,806**	**90,783**		**13,471**	**77,312**	**774**	**241**	**8,978**	**3,478**	**24,737**	**39,640**	**12,935**	
Rate per 100,000 inhabitants		2,352.6		349.1	2,003.5	20.1	6.2	232.7	90.1	641.1	1,027.3	335.2	

See footnotes at end of table.

Table 5

Index of Crime

by State, 2002—Continued

Area	Population	Crime Index	Modified Crime Index[1]	Violent crime[2]	Property crime[2]	Murder and non-negligent man-slaughter	Forcible rape	Robbery	Aggravated assault	Burglary	Larceny-theft	Motor vehicle theft	Arson[1]
RHODE ISLAND													
Metropolitan Statistical Area	1,003,857												
Area actually reporting	100.0%	35,952		2,827	33,125	37	356	892	1,542	5,980	22,362	4,783	
Cities outside metropolitan areas	65,868												
Area actually reporting	100.0%	2,358		188	2,170	1	23	23	141	431	1,660	79	
Rural	None												
Area actually reporting	100.0%	83		36	47	3	16	1	16	4	29	14	
State Total	**1,069,725**	**38,393**		**3,051**	**35,342**	**41**	**395**	**916**	**1,699**	**6,415**	**24,051**	**4,876**	
Rate per 100,000 inhabitants		3,589.1		285.2	3,303.8	3.8	36.9	85.6	158.8	599.7	2,248.3	455.8	
SOUTH CAROLINA													
Metropolitan Statistical Area	2,873,545												
Area actually reporting	99.8%	158,519		22,943	135,576	205	1,384	4,509	16,845	30,200	92,031	13,345	
Estimated total	100.0%	158,894		22,985	135,909	205	1,386	4,517	16,877	30,257	92,285	13,367	
Cities outside metropolitan areas	311,683												
Area actually reporting	98.4%	23,583		4,386	19,197	31	147	606	3,602	4,114	14,118	965	
Estimated total	100.0%	23,972		4,458	19,514	32	149	616	3,661	4,182	14,351	981	
Rural	921,955												
Area actually reporting	100.0%	34,703		6,318	28,385	61	424	641	5,192	9,306	16,560	2,519	
State Total	**4,107,183**	**217,569**		**33,761**	**183,808**	**298**	**1,959**	**5,774**	**25,730**	**43,745**	**123,196**	**16,867**	
Rate per 100,000 inhabitants		5,297.3		822.0	4,475.3	7.3	47.7	140.6	626.5	1,065.1	2,999.5	410.7	
SOUTH DAKOTA													
Metropolitan Statistical Area	263,131												
Area actually reporting	93.8%	8,988		725	8,263	3	215	82	425	1,448	6,428	387	
Estimated total	100.0%	9,439		753	8,686	3	226	84	440	1,519	6,764	403	
Cities outside metropolitan areas	214,373												
Area actually reporting	88.6%	5,222		301	4,921	4	71	16	210	849	3,820	252	
Estimated total	100.0%	5,893		340	5,553	5	80	18	237	958	4,311	284	
Rural	283,559												
Area actually reporting	65.7%	1,321		169	1,152	2	36	10	121	366	699	87	
Estimated total	100.0%	2,010		257	1,753	3	55	15	184	557	1,064	132	
State Total	**761,063**	**17,342**		**1,350**	**15,992**	**11**	**361**	**117**	**861**	**3,034**	**12,139**	**819**	
Rate per 100,000 inhabitants		2,278.7		177.4	2,101.3	1.4	47.4	15.4	113.1	398.7	1,595.0	107.6	
TENNESSEE													
Metropolitan Statistical Area	3,935,464												
Area actually reporting	100.0%	228,278		33,438	194,840	340	1,820	8,726	22,552	46,561	125,860	22,419	
Cities outside metropolitan areas	656,434												
Area actually reporting	99.9%	36,531		4,236	32,295	28	244	532	3,432	6,679	23,639	1,977	
Estimated total	100.0%	36,574		4,241	32,333	28	244	533	3,436	6,687	23,667	1,979	
Rural	1,205,391												
Area actually reporting	100.0%	26,109		3,883	22,226	52	226	154	3,451	8,000	12,083	2,143	
State Total	**5,797,289**	**290,961**		**41,562**	**249,399**	**420**	**2,290**	**9,413**	**29,439**	**61,248**	**161,610**	**26,541**	
Rate per 100,000 inhabitants		5,018.9		716.9	4,302.0	7.2	39.5	162.4	507.8	1,056.5	2,787.7	457.8	
TEXAS													
Metropolitan Statistical Area	18,479,316												
Area actually reporting	99.9%	1,035,510		116,035	919,475	1,165	7,536	36,665	70,669	188,088	633,518	97,869	
Estimated total	100.0%	1,036,268		116,090	920,178	1,165	7,541	36,679	70,705	188,238	634,024	97,916	
Cities outside metropolitan areas	1,486,837												
Area actually reporting	99.2%	62,401		6,215	56,186	50	623	696	4,846	13,294	40,038	2,854	
Estimated total	100.0%	62,653		6,244	56,409	50	625	697	4,872	13,341	40,202	2,866	
Rural	1,813,740												
Area actually reporting	100.0%	31,371		3,684	27,687	87	342	204	3,051	11,023	14,766	1,898	
State Total	**21,779,893**	**1,130,292**		**126,018**	**1,004,274**	**1,302**	**8,508**	**37,580**	**78,628**	**212,602**	**688,992**	**102,680**	
Rate per 100,000 inhabitants		5,189.6		578.6	4,611.0	6.0	39.1	172.5	361.0	976.1	3,163.4	471.4	

See footnotes at end of table.

Table 5

Index of Crime

by State, 2002—Continued

Area	Population	Crime Index	Modified Crime Index[1]	Violent crime[3]	Property crime[2]	Murder and non-negligent man-slaughter	Forcible rape	Robbery	Aggravated assault	Burglary	Larceny-theft	Motor vehicle theft	Arson[1]
UTAH													
Metropolitan Statistical Area	1,772,063												
Area actually reporting	99.8%	88,281		4,596	83,685	34	723	1,096	2,743	12,621	64,067	6,997	
Estimated total	100.0%	88,399		4,601	83,798	34	724	1,097	2,746	12,639	64,153	7,006	
Cities outside metropolitan areas	293,306												
Area actually reporting	96.5%	9,775		563	9,212	6	152	28	377	1,521	7,263	428	
Estimated total	100.0%	10,127		583	9,544	6	157	29	391	1,576	7,525	443	
Rural	250,887												
Area actually reporting	96.6%	4,447		294	4,153	7	60	14	213	878	3,011	264	
Estimated total	100.0%	4,603		304	4,299	7	62	14	221	909	3,117	273	
State Total	**2,316,256**	**103,129**		**5,488**	**97,641**	**47**	**943**	**1,140**	**3,358**	**15,124**	**74,795**	**7,722**	
Rate per 100,000 inhabitants		4,452.4		236.9	4,215.5	2.0	40.7	49.2	145.0	653.0	3,229.1	333.4	
VERMONT													
Metropolitan Statistical Area	163,177												
Area actually reporting	100.0%	5,417		216	5,201	8	16	34	158	1,128	3,858	215	
Cities outside metropolitan areas	206,092												
Area actually reporting	99.4%	6,187		272	5,915	1	68	33	170	1,013	4,653	249	
Estimated total	100.0%	6,224		273	5,951	1	68	33	171	1,019	4,681	251	
Rural	247,323												
Area actually reporting	100.0%	3,959		169	3,790	4	42	10	113	1,342	2,145	303	
State Total	**616,592**	**15,600**		**658**	**14,942**	**13**	**126**	**77**	**442**	**3,489**	**10,684**	**769**	
Rate per 100,000 inhabitants		2,530.0		106.7	2,423.3	2.1	20.4	12.5	71.7	565.9	1,732.8	124.7	
VIRGINIA													
Metropolitan Statistical Area	5,695,993												
Area actually reporting	99.6%	195,402		18,151	177,251	304	1,435	6,492	9,920	25,657	134,985	16,609	
Estimated total	100.0%	196,372		18,251	178,121	305	1,443	6,520	9,983	25,768	135,664	16,689	
Cities outside metropolitan areas	449,150												
Area actually reporting	92.7%	14,081		1,174	12,907	15	125	216	818	1,902	10,393	612	
Estimated total	100.0%	15,185		1,266	13,919	16	135	233	882	2,051	11,208	660	
Rural	1,148,399												
Area actually reporting	99.4%	17,378		1,729	15,649	67	259	207	1,196	3,915	10,612	1,122	
Estimated total	100.0%	17,482		1,739	15,743	67	261	208	1,203	3,938	10,676	1,129	
State Total	**7,293,542**	**229,039**		**21,256**	**207,783**	**388**	**1,839**	**6,961**	**12,068**	**31,757**	**157,548**	**18,478**	
Rate per 100,000 inhabitants		3,140.3		291.4	2,848.9	5.3	25.2	95.4	165.5	435.4	2,160.1	253.3	
WASHINGTON													
Metropolitan Statistical Area	5,044,509												
Area actually reporting	97.9%	257,184		18,287	238,897	146	2,166	5,365	10,610	44,484	157,459	36,954	
Estimated total	100.0%	261,666		18,554	243,112	148	2,210	5,433	10,763	45,291	160,226	37,595	
Cities outside metropolitan areas	463,899												
Area actually reporting	90.7%	29,773		1,372	28,401	10	285	262	815	4,782	21,958	1,661	
Estimated total	100.0%	32,838		1,513	31,325	11	314	289	899	5,274	24,219	1,832	
Rural	560,588												
Area actually reporting	100.0%	15,427		897	14,530	25	210	75	587	4,383	9,081	1,066	
State Total	**6,068,996**	**309,931**		**20,964**	**288,967**	**184**	**2,734**	**5,797**	**12,249**	**54,948**	**193,526**	**40,493**	
Rate per 100,000 inhabitants		5,106.8		345.4	4,761.4	3.0	45.0	95.5	201.8	905.4	3,188.8	667.2	
WEST VIRGINIA													
Metropolitan Statistical Area	762,826												
Area actually reporting	91.8%	22,873		1,968	20,905	19	166	416	1,367	4,570	14,150	2,185	
Estimated total	100.0%	25,084		2,156	22,928	20	180	458	1,498	4,938	15,629	2,361	
Cities outside metropolitan areas	278,400												
Area actually reporting	81.1%	6,428		567	5,861	6	39	88	434	1,185	4,369	307	
Estimated total	100.0%	7,921		699	7,222	8	48	108	535	1,460	5,384	378	
Rural	760,647												
Area actually reporting	97.3%	11,978		1,329	10,649	28	97	89	1,115	3,189	6,333	1,127	
Estimated total	100.0%	12,315		1,366	10,949	29	100	91	1,146	3,279	6,511	1,159	
State Total	**1,801,873**	**45,320**		**4,221**	**41,099**	**57**	**328**	**657**	**3,179**	**9,677**	**27,524**	**3,898**	
Rate per 100,000 inhabitants		2,515.2		234.3	2,280.9	3.2	18.2	36.5	176.4	537.1	1,527.5	216.3	

See footnotes at end of table.

Table 5

Index of Crime

by State, 2002—Continued

Area	Population	Crime Index	Modified Crime Index[1]	Violent crime[2]	Property crime[2]	Murder and non-negligent man-slaughter	Forcible rape	Robbery	Aggravated assault	Burglary	Larceny-theft	Motor vehicle theft	Arson[1]
WISCONSIN													
Metropolitan Statistical Area	3,692,594												
Area actually reporting	97.4%	134,920		10,363	124,557	135	956	4,572	4,700	19,851	93,057	11,649	
Estimated total	100.0%	136,716		10,437	126,279	136	967	4,588	4,746	20,143	94,399	11,737	
Cities outside metropolitan areas	718,125												
Area actually reporting	99.0%	25,127		1,012	24,115	2	147	85	778	3,156	20,105	854	
Estimated total	100.0%	25,371		1,022	24,349	2	148	86	786	3,187	20,300	862	
Rural	1,030,477												
Area actually reporting	97.6%	14,547		761	13,786	16	119	38	588	4,487	8,460	839	
Estimated total	100.0%	14,900		779	14,121	16	122	39	602	4,596	8,666	859	
State Total	**5,441,196**	**176,987**		**12,238**	**164,749**	**154**	**1,237**	**4,713**	**6,134**	**27,926**	**123,365**	**13,458**	
Rate per 100,000 inhabitants		3,252.7		224.9	3,027.8	2.8	22.7	86.6	112.7	513.2	2,267.2	247.3	
WYOMING													
Metropolitan Statistical Area	149,614												
Area actually reporting	100.0%	6,626		367	6,259	5	54	51	257	988	4,957	314	
Cities outside metropolitan areas	208,723												
Area actually reporting	98.4%	8,560		649	7,911	4	56	35	554	994	6,592	325	
Estimated total	100.0%	8,697		660	8,037	4	57	36	563	1,010	6,697	330	
Rural	140,366												
Area actually reporting	100.0%	2,535		337	2,198	6	37	6	288	450	1,649	99	
State Total	**498,703**	**17,858**		**1,364**	**16,494**	**15**	**148**	**93**	**1,108**	**2,448**	**13,303**	**743**	
Rate per 100,000 inhabitants		3,580.9		273.5	3,307.4	3.0	29.7	18.6	222.2	490.9	2,667.5	149.0	

[1] Although arson data are included in the trend and clearance tables, sufficient data are not available to estimate totals for this offense.

[2] Violent crimes are offenses of murder, forcible rape, robbery, and aggravated assault. Property crimes are offenses of burglary, larceny-theft, and motor vehicle theft.

[3] Includes offenses reported by the Zoological Police and the Metro Transit Police.

[4] Limited data for 2002 were available. See Offense Estimation, Appendix I, for details.

NOTE: Offense totals are based on all data received from reporting agencies and estimates for unreported areas.

Table 6

Index of Crime
by Metropolitan Statistical Area, 2002

Metropolitan Statistical Area	Population	Crime Index	Modified Crime Index[1]	Violent crime[2]	Property crime[2]	Murder and non-negligent man-slaughter	Forcible rape	Robbery	Aggravated assault	Burglary	Larceny-theft	Motor vehicle theft	Arson[1]
Abilene, TX M.S.A.	**132,188**												
(Includes Taylor County.)													
City of Abilene	115,356	5,140		423	4,717	4	60	106	253	1,228	3,271	218	
Total area actually reporting	100.0%	5,471		452	5,019	5	62	109	276	1,362	3,418	239	
Rate per 100,000 inhabitants		4,138.8		341.9	3,796.9	3.8	46.9	82.5	208.8	1,030.4	2,585.7	180.8	
Albany, GA M.S.A.	**126,341**												
(Includes Dougherty and Lee Counties.)													
City of Albany	80,452	5,430		514	4,916	7	49	220	238	1,297	3,319	300	
Total area actually reporting	100.0%	6,706		559	6,147	7	50	232	270	1,577	4,202	368	
Rate per 100,000 inhabitants		5,307.9		442.5	4,865.4	5.5	39.6	183.6	213.7	1,248.2	3,325.9	291.3	
Albuquerque, NM M.S.A.	**726,846**												
(Includes Bernalillo, Sandoval, and Valencia Counties.)													
City of Albuquerque	457,488	35,762		4,889	30,873	51	293	1,295	3,250	5,452	21,371	4,050	
Total area actually reporting	94.5%	43,726		6,401	37,325	68	396	1,470	4,467	6,999	25,526	4,800	
Estimated total	100.0%	44,816		6,644	38,172	70	412	1,501	4,661	7,271	25,998	4,903	
Rate per 100,000 inhabitants		6,165.8		914.1	5,251.7	9.6	56.7	206.5	641.3	1,000.3	3,576.8	674.6	
Alexandria, LA M.S.A.	**126,723**												
(Includes Rapides Parish.)													
City of Alexandria	46,483	5,554		959	4,595	11	17	199	732	1,117	3,285	193	
Total area actually reporting	97.4%	8,280		1,269	7,011	18	35	223	993	2,055	4,584	372	
Estimated total	100.0%	8,474		1,290	7,184	18	36	227	1,009	2,090	4,712	382	
Rate per 100,000 inhabitants		6,687.0		1,018.0	5,669.1	14.2	28.4	179.1	796.2	1,649.3	3,718.3	301.4	
Allentown-Bethlehem-Easton, PA M.S.A.	**640,766**												
(Includes Carbon, Lehigh, and Northampton Counties.)													
City of:													
Allentown	107,101	5,944		615	5,329	9	58	294	254	1,212	3,615	502	
Bethlehem	71,643	2,418		245	2,173	2	31	98	114	398	1,616	159	
Total area actually reporting	86.1%	17,066		1,701	15,365	18	180	516	987	2,674	11,595	1,096	
Estimated total	100.0%	19,167		1,901	17,266	20	195	567	1,119	2,948	13,080	1,238	
Rate per 100,000 inhabitants		2,991.3		296.7	2,694.6	3.1	30.4	88.5	174.6	460.1	2,041.3	193.2	
Altoona, PA M.S.A.	**129,712**												
(Includes Blair County.)													
City of Altoona	49,741	2,058		177	1,881	2	20	74	81	540	1,218	123	
Total area actually reporting	79.4%	3,073		302	2,771	2	39	99	162	842	1,763	166	
Estimated total	100.0%	3,703		362	3,341	3	43	114	202	924	2,208	209	
Rate per 100,000 inhabitants		2,854.8		279.1	2,575.7	2.3	33.2	87.9	155.7	712.3	1,702.2	161.1	
Amarillo, TX M.S.A.	**227,555**												
(Includes Potter and Randall Counties.)													
City of Amarillo	181,355	13,473		1,479	11,994	7	109	330	1,033	2,468	8,566	960	
Total area actually reporting	100.0%	14,573		1,556	13,017	7	116	334	1,099	2,756	9,231	1,030	
Rate per 100,000 inhabitants		6,404.2		683.8	5,720.4	3.1	51.0	146.8	483.0	1,211.1	4,056.6	452.6	
Anchorage, AK M.S.A.	**267,280**												
(Includes Anchorage Borough.)													
Total area actually reporting	100.0%	13,670		1,721	11,949	18	254	382	1,067	1,521	9,255	1,173	
Rate per 100,000 inhabitants		5,114.5		643.9	4,470.6	6.7	95.0	142.9	399.2	569.1	3,462.7	438.9	
Ann Arbor, MI M.S.A.	**585,259**												
(Includes Lenawee, Livingston, and Washtenaw Counties.)													
City of Ann Arbor	115,309	3,727		301	3,426	5	26	87	183	859	2,385	182	
Total area actually reporting	100.0%	16,995		1,507	15,488	18	212	293	984	3,341	10,963	1,184	
Rate per 100,000 inhabitants		2,903.8		257.5	2,646.3	3.1	36.2	50.1	168.1	570.9	1,873.2	202.3	
Anniston, AL M.S.A.	**113,244**												
(Includes Calhoun County.)													
City of Anniston	24,491	3,617		572	3,045	7	35	164	366	900	1,995	150	
Total area actually reporting	100.0%	6,614		780	5,834	11	53	223	493	1,516	4,005	313	
Rate per 100,000 inhabitants		5,840.5		688.8	5,151.7	9.7	46.8	196.9	435.3	1,338.7	3,536.6	276.4	
Appleton-Oshkosh-Neenah, WI M.S.A.	**363,218**												
(Includes Calumet, Outagamie, and Winnebago Counties.)													
City of:													
Appleton	71,100	1,967		127	1,840	0	18	18	91	245	1,520	75	
Oshkosh	63,825	2,440		143	2,297	1	9	18	115	288	1,936	73	
Neenah	24,861	495		18	477	0	2	0	16	55	405	17	
Total area actually reporting	100.0%	8,790		388	8,402	2	57	45	284	1,011	7,081	310	
Rate per 100,000 inhabitants		2,420.0		106.8	2,313.2	0.6	15.7	12.4	78.2	278.3	1,949.5	85.3	

See footnotes at end of table.

Table 6

Index of Crime
by Metropolitan Statistical Area, 2002—Continued

Metropolitan Statistical Area	Population	Crime Index	Modified Crime Index[1]	Violent crime[2]	Property crime[2]	Murder and non-negligent man-slaughter	Forcible rape	Robbery	Aggravated assault	Burglary	Larceny-theft	Motor vehicle theft	Arson[1]
Asheville, NC M.S.A.	233,567												
(Includes Buncombe and Madison Counties.)													
City of Asheville	71,207	4,861		476	4,385	12	44	197	223	790	3,112	483	
Total area actually reporting	99.1%	8,304		786	7,518	21	57	228	480	1,808	4,947	763	
Estimated total	100.0%	8,432		796	7,636	21	58	231	486	1,833	5,035	768	
Rate per 100,000 inhabitants		3,610.1		340.8	3,269.3	9.0	24.8	98.9	208.1	784.8	2,155.7	328.8	
Athens, GA M.S.A.	160,451												
(Includes Clarke, Madison, and Oconee Counties.)													
City of Athens-Clarke County	105,007	6,693		441	6,252	7	53	158	223	1,042	4,779	431	
Total area actually reporting	99.7%	8,511		518	7,993	9	57	172	280	1,346	6,067	580	
Estimated total	100.0%	8,543		521	8,022	9	57	173	282	1,351	6,088	583	
Rate per 100,000 inhabitants		5,324.4		324.7	4,999.7	5.6	35.5	107.8	175.8	842.0	3,794.3	363.4	
Atlanta, GA M.S.A.	4,299,988												
(Includes Barrow, Bartow, Carroll, Cherokee, Clayton, Cobb, Coweta, DeKalb, Douglas, Fayette, Forsyth, Fulton, Gwinnett, Henry, Newton, Paulding, Pickens, Rockdale, Spalding, and Walton Counties.)													
City of Atlanta	435,494	49,451		9,969	39,482	152	276	4,168	5,373	8,554	23,706	7,222	
Total area actually reporting	98.8%	196,234		22,313	173,921	354	1,041	9,137	11,781	37,109	112,403	24,409	
Estimated total	100.0%	199,455		22,579	176,876	357	1,053	9,228	11,941	37,620	114,576	24,680	
Rate per 100,000 inhabitants		4,638.5		525.1	4,113.4	8.3	24.5	214.6	277.7	874.9	2,664.6	574.0	
Atlantic-Cape May, NJ M.S.A.	362,299												
(Includes Atlantic and Cape May Counties.)													
City of Atlantic City	41,364	5,346		663	4,683	5	21	283	354	482	4,031	170	
Total area actually reporting	100.0%	17,419		1,708	15,711	12	91	596	1,009	2,633	12,435	643	
Rate per 100,000 inhabitants		4,807.9		471.4	4,336.5	3.3	25.1	164.5	278.5	726.7	3,432.2	177.5	
Auburn-Opelika, AL M.S.A.	116,111												
(Includes Lee County.)													
City of:													
Auburn	43,368	2,282		166	2,116	2	17	48	99	516	1,506	94	
Opelika	23,706	2,063		357	1,706	2	29	70	256	422	1,276	8	
Total area actually reporting	100.0%	6,584		677	5,907	7	60	156	454	1,670	4,006	231	
Rate per 100,000 inhabitants		5,670.4		583.1	5,087.4	6.0	51.7	134.4	391.0	1,438.3	3,450.1	198.9	
Augusta-Aiken, GA-SC M.S.A.	495,578												
(Includes Columbia, McDuffie, and Richmond Counties, GA and Aiken and Edgefield Counties, SC.)													
City of Aiken, SC	25,938	1,334		100	1,234	4	9	23	64	163	1,018	53	
Total area actually reporting	99.9%	21,823		1,564	20,259	23	236	634	671	4,153	14,332	1,774	
Estimated total	100.0%	21,836		1,565	20,271	23	236	634	672	4,155	14,341	1,775	
Rate per 100,000 inhabitants		4,406.2		315.8	4,090.4	4.6	47.6	127.9	135.6	838.4	2,893.8	358.2	
Austin-San Marcos, TX M.S.A.	1,305,388												
(Includes Bastrop, Caldwell, Hays, Travis, and Williamson Counties.)													
City of:													
Austin	685,784	42,979		3,203	39,776	25	256	1,174	1,748	6,916	29,725	3,135	
San Marcos	36,279	1,593		146	1,447	0	34	34	78	234	1,133	80	
Total area actually reporting	100.0%	62,158		4,838	57,320	39	501	1,403	2,895	10,985	42,237	4,098	
Rate per 100,000 inhabitants		4,761.6		370.6	4,391.0	3.0	38.4	107.5	221.8	841.5	3,235.6	313.9	
Bakersfield, CA M.S.A.	685,953												
(Includes Kern County.)													
City of Bakersfield	256,134	11,846		1,071	10,775	22	47	355	647	2,436	6,941	1,398	
Total area actually reporting	100.0%	29,148		3,371	25,777	51	220	779	2,321	6,515	15,842	3,420	
Rate per 100,000 inhabitants		4,249.3		491.4	3,757.8	7.4	32.1	113.6	338.4	949.8	2,309.5	498.6	
Baltimore, MD M.S.A.	2,630,914												
(Includes Baltimore City and Anne Arundel, Baltimore, Carroll, Harford, Howard, and Queen Anne's Counties.)													
City of:													
Baltimore	671,028	55,820		13,789	42,031	253	178	4,714	8,644	8,759	26,716	6,556	
Annapolis	36,932	2,330		421	1,909	4	15	149	253	414	1,380	115	
Total area actually reporting	100.0%	134,817		26,049	108,768	317	631	7,743	17,358	20,892	74,924	12,952	
Rate per 100,000 inhabitants		5,124.3		990.1	4,134.2	12.0	24.0	294.3	659.8	794.1	2,847.8	492.3	

See footnotes at end of table.

Table 6

Index of Crime
by Metropolitan Statistical Area, 2002—Continued

Metropolitan Statistical Area	Population	Crime Index	Modified Crime Index[1]	Violent crime[2]	Property crime[2]	Murder and non-negligent man-slaughter	Forcible rape	Robbery	Aggravated assault	Burglary	Larceny-theft	Motor vehicle theft	Arson[1]
Bangor, ME M.S.A.	69,434												
(Includes part of Penobscot and Waldo Counties.)													
City of Bangor	31,956	1,630		39	1,591	0	4	18	17	158	1,378	55	
Total area actually reporting	99.2%	2,635		53	2,582	0	7	21	25	302	2,201	79	
Estimated total	100.0%	2,647		53	2,594	0	7	21	25	304	2,211	79	
Rate per 100,000 inhabitants		3,812.3		76.3	3,735.9	0.0	10.1	30.2	36.0	437.8	3,184.3	113.8	
Baton Rouge, LA M.S.A.[3]	604,739												
(Includes Ascension, East Baton Rouge, Livingston, and West Baton Rouge Parishes.)													
City of Baton Rouge[3]	228,515	18,949		2,670	16,279	59	133	1,107	1,371	4,070	10,763	1,446	
Total area actually reporting	99.5%	40,212		4,358	35,854	86	260	1,404	2,608	8,347	25,008	2,499	
Estimated total	100.0%	40,401		4,378	36,023	86	261	1,408	2,623	8,381	25,133	2,509	
Rate per 100,000 inhabitants		6,680.7		723.9	5,956.8	14.2	43.2	232.8	433.7	1,385.9	4,156.0	414.9	
Beaumont-Port Arthur, TX M.S.A.	402,229												
(Includes Hardin, Jefferson, and Orange Counties.)													
City of:													
Beaumont	118,934	10,443		1,150	9,293	7	172	408	563	1,722	7,015	556	
Port Arthur	60,326	2,883		368	2,515	6	14	170	178	866	1,357	292	
Total area actually reporting	100.0%	21,438		2,316	19,122	19	312	701	1,284	4,342	13,336	1,444	
Rate per 100,000 inhabitants		5,329.8		575.8	4,754.0	4.7	77.6	174.3	319.2	1,079.5	3,315.5	359.0	
Bellingham, WA M.S.A.	171,763												
(Includes Whatcom County.)													
City of Bellingham	69,164	5,108		164	4,944	2	22	71	69	678	3,972	294	
Total area actually reporting	100.0%	8,996		422	8,574	4	103	90	225	1,685	6,350	539	
Rate per 100,000 inhabitants		5,237.4		245.7	4,991.8	2.3	60.0	52.4	131.0	981.0	3,697.0	313.8	
Benton Harbor, MI M.S.A.	164,284												
(Includes Berrien County.)													
City of Benton Harbor	11,308	993		303	690	1	17	32	253	249	364	77	
Total area actually reporting	99.6%	6,941		876	6,065	8	112	101	655	1,275	4,376	414	
Estimated total	100.0%	6,960		877	6,083	8	112	101	656	1,278	4,389	416	
Rate per 100,000 inhabitants		4,236.6		533.8	3,702.7	4.9	68.2	61.5	399.3	777.9	2,671.6	253.2	
Bergen-Passaic, NJ M.S.A.	1,401,881												
(Includes Bergen and Passaic Counties.)													
Total area actually reporting	100.0%	33,533		3,495	30,038	28	98	1,594	1,775	5,476	19,916	4,646	
Rate per 100,000 inhabitants		2,392.0		249.3	2,142.7	2.0	7.0	113.7	126.6	390.6	1,420.7	331.4	
Billings, MT M.S.A.	130,387												
(Includes Yellowstone County.)													
City of Billings	90,569	4,846		215	4,631	0	13	59	143	407	3,943	281	
Total area actually reporting	100.0%	6,020		322	5,698	0	16	69	237	520	4,829	349	
Rate per 100,000 inhabitants		4,617.0		247.0	4,370.1	0.0	12.3	52.9	181.8	398.8	3,703.6	267.7	
Biloxi-Gulfport-Pascagoula, MS M.S.A.	367,459												
(Includes Hancock, Harrison, and Jackson Counties.)													
City of:													
Biloxi	51,127	3,852		329	3,523	2	29	120	178	921	2,305	297	
Gulfport	71,805	5,818		326	5,492	11	48	165	102	1,168	3,856	468	
Pascagoula	26,450	2,344		153	2,191	2	14	84	53	505	1,436	250	
Total area actually reporting	92.3%	20,136		1,295	18,841	32	156	505	602	4,648	12,598	1,595	
Estimated total	100.0%	20,881		1,340	19,541	34	164	512	630	4,846	13,041	1,654	
Rate per 100,000 inhabitants		5,682.5		364.7	5,317.9	9.3	44.6	139.3	171.4	1,318.8	3,549.0	450.1	
Binghamton, NY M.S.A.	254,727												
(Includes Broome and Tioga Counties.)													
City of Binghamton	47,832	2,366		205	2,161	6	21	80	98	260	1,856	45	
Total area actually reporting	89.5%	6,079		474	5,605	9	54	127	284	855	4,574	176	
Estimated total	100.0%	6,717		529	6,188	9	57	145	318	939	5,033	216	
Rate per 100,000 inhabitants		2,636.9		207.7	2,429.3	.5	22.4	56.9	124.8	368.6	1,975.8	84.8	
Birmingham, AL M.S.A.	929,271												
(Includes Blount, Jefferson, St. Clair, and Shelby Counties.)													
City of Birmingham	244,972	21,265		3,187	18,078	65	239	1,186	1,697	4,389	11,640	2,049	
Total area actually reporting	90.7%	39,487		4,642	34,845	81	380	1,729	2,452	7,941	23,407	3,497	
Estimated total	100.0%	43,580		4,983	38,597	85	405	1,841	2,652	8,632	26,204	3,761	
Rate per 100,000 inhabitants		4,689.7		536.2	4,153.5	9.1	43.6	198.1	285.4	928.9	2,819.8	404.7	
Bismarck, ND M.S.A.	93,525												
(Includes Burleigh and Morton Counties.)													
City of Bismarck	54,832	1,698		45	1,653	1	5	14	25	181	1,356	116	
Total area actually reporting	100.0%	2,416		83	2,333	2	21	19	41	296	1,862	175	
Rate per 100,000 inhabitants		2,583.3		88.7	2,494.5	2.1	22.5	20.3	43.8	316.5	1,990.9	187.1	

See footnotes at end of table.

Table 6

Index of Crime
by Metropolitan Statistical Area, 2002—Continued

Metropolitan Statistical Area	Population	Crime Index	Modified Crime Index[1]	Violent crime[2]	Property crime[2]	Murder and non-negligent man-slaughter	Forcible rape	Robbery	Aggravated assault	Burglary	Larceny-theft	Motor vehicle theft	Arson[1]
Bloomington, IN M.S.A.	**122,121**												
(Includes Monroe County.)													
City of Bloomington	70,186	2,744		109	2,635	2	35	32	40	437	2,053	145	
Total area actually reporting	100.0%	4,225		258	3,967	7	52	42	157	676	3,063	228	
Rate per 100,000 inhabitants		3,459.7		211.3	3,248.4	5.7	42.6	34.4	128.6	553.5	2,508.2	186.7	
Boise, ID M.S.A.	**448,110**												
(Includes Ada and Canyon Counties.)													
City of:													
Boise	192,561	8,748		679	8,069	6	92	84	497	1,318	6,209	542	
Nampa	53,759	2,871		261	2,610	1	71	27	162	449	1,912	249	
Total area actually reporting	100.0%	18,494		1,435	17,059	12	239	145	1,039	3,119	12,681	1,259	
Rate per 100,000 inhabitants		4,127.1		320.2	3,806.9	2.7	53.3	32.4	231.9	696.0	2,829.9	281.0	
Boston, MA-NH M.S.A.	**3,448,359**												
(Includes part of Bristol, Essex, Middlesex, Norfolk, Plymouth, Suffolk, and Worcester Counties, MA and part of Rockingham County, NH.)													
City of:													
Boston, MA	596,444	35,706		6,956	28,750	60	369	2,533	3,994	3,830	17,824	7,096	
Cambridge, MA	102,611	4,306		497	3,809	6	11	195	285	720	2,664	425	
Lynn, MA	90,156	3,924		857	3,067	3	9	180	665	561	1,463	1,043	
Waltham, MA	59,960	1,126		92	1,034	1	5	19	67	144	779	111	
Gloucester, MA	30,648	738		72	666	0	6	7	59	142	496	28	
Total area actually reporting	96.0%	97,790		15,269	82,521	90	782	4,299	10,098	13,305	55,738	13,478	
Estimated total	100.0%	100,675		15,612	85,063	91	806	4,351	10,364	13,810	57,512	13,741	
Rate per 100,000 inhabitants		2,919.5		452.7	2,466.8	2.6	23.4	126.2	300.5	400.5	1,667.8	398.5	
Brazoria, TX M.S.A.	**252,527**												
(Includes Brazoria County.)													
Total area actually reporting	99.7%	7,583		677	6,906	11	109	123	434	1,564	4,835	507	
Estimated total	100.0%	7,622		680	6,942	11	109	124	436	1,571	4,861	510	
Rate per 100,000 inhabitants		3,018.3		269.3	2,749.0	4.4	43.2	49.1	172.7	622.1	1,924.9	202.0	
Bremerton, WA M.S.A.	**238,852**												
(Includes Kitsap County.)													
City of Bremerton	38,365	2,917		407	2,510	1	82	64	260	519	1,659	332	
Total area actually reporting	100.0%	9,147		924	8,223	1	185	116	622	2,039	5,476	708	
Rate per 100,000 inhabitants		3,829.6		386.9	3,442.7	0.4	77.5	48.6	260.4	853.7	2,292.6	296.4	
Bridgeport, CT M.S.A.	**451,581**												
(Includes part of Fairfield and New Haven Counties.)													
City of Bridgeport	141,780	8,551		1,695	6,856	12	65	555	1,063	1,401	3,920	1,535	
Total area actually reporting	100.0%	16,044		2,046	13,998	17	115	715	1,199	2,544	9,259	2,195	
Rate per 100,000 inhabitants		3,552.9		453.1	3,099.8	3.8	25.5	158.3	265.5	563.4	2,050.4	486.1	
Brockton, MA M.S.A.	**258,627**												
(Includes part of Bristol, Norfolk, and Plymouth Counties.)													
City of Brockton	95,473	5,167		1,071	4,096	9	44	251	767	681	2,252	1,163	
Total area actually reporting	77.2%	7,372		1,377	5,995	9	53	285	1,030	990	3,637	1,368	
Estimated total	100.0%	8,618		1,528	7,090	10	63	308	1,147	1,209	4,399	1,482	
Rate per 100,000 inhabitants		3,332.2		590.8	2,741.4	3.9	24.4	119.1	443.5	467.5	1,700.9	573.0	
Brownsville-Harlingen-San Benito, TX M.S.A.	**350,147**												
(Includes Cameron County.)													
City of:													
Brownsville	145,941	12,759		806	11,953	1	32	181	592	1,207	10,266	480	
Harlingen	60,126	4,041		289	3,752	5	27	54	203	795	2,730	227	
San Benito	24,488	2,089		43	2,046	0	6	13	24	265	1,698	83	
Total area actually reporting	100.0%	22,627		1,508	21,119	11	108	279	1,110	3,159	17,005	955	
Rate per 100,000 inhabitants		6,462.1		430.7	6,031.5	3.1	30.8	79.7	317.0	902.2	4,856.5	272.7	
Bryan-College Station, TX M.S.A.	**159,199**												
(Includes Brazos County.)													
City of:													
Bryan	68,583	4,447		490	3,957	3	60	81	346	858	2,879	220	
College Station	70,911	2,972		141	2,831	2	37	16	86	354	2,374	103	
Total area actually reporting	100.0%	8,539		700	7,839	6	106	98	490	1,402	6,093	344	
Rate per 100,000 inhabitants		5,363.7		439.7	4,924.0	3.8	66.6	61.6	307.8	880.7	3,827.3	216.1	

See footnotes at end of table.

Table 6

Index of Crime
by Metropolitan Statistical Area, 2002—Continued

Metropolitan Statistical Area	Population	Crime Index	Modified Crime Index[1]	Violent crime[2]	Property crime[2]	Murder and non-negligent man-slaughter	Forcible rape	Robbery	Aggravated assault	Burglary	Larceny-theft	Motor vehicle theft	Arson[1]
Buffalo-Niagara Falls, NY M.S.A.	1,181,277												
(Includes Erie and Niagara Counties.)													
City of:													
Buffalo	295,441	19,017		3,757	15,260	43	185	1,627	1,902	3,857	9,115	2,288	
Niagara Falls	56,123	3,847		559	3,288	3	30	167	359	827	2,078	383	
Total area actually reporting	84.3%	37,760		5,300	32,460	48	299	2,068	2,885	6,771	22,123	3,566	
Estimated total	100.0%	41,495		5,641	35,854	52	326	2,155	3,108	7,337	24,715	3,802	
Rate per 100,000 inhabitants		3,512.7		477.5	3,035.2	4.4	27.6	182.4	263.1	621.1	2,092.2	321.9	
Burlington, VT M.S.A.	163,177												
(Includes part of Chittenden, Franklin, and Grand Isle Counties.)													
City of Burlington	39,385	1,871		115	1,756	1	5	18	91	324	1,349	83	
Total area actually reporting	100.0%	5,417		216	5,201	8	16	34	158	1,128	3,858	215	
Rate per 100,000 inhabitants		3,319.7		132.4	3,187.3	4.9	9.8	20.8	96.8	691.3	2,364.3	131.8	
Casper, WY M.S.A.	67,196												
(Includes Natrona County.)													
City of Casper	50,139	2,725		148	2,577	2	14	16	116	505	1,936	136	
Total area actually reporting	100.0%	3,360		184	3,176	3	14	18	149	667	2,317	192	
Rate per 100,000 inhabitants		5,000.3		273.8	4,726.5	4.5	20.8	26.8	221.7	992.6	3,448.1	285.7	
Cedar Rapids, IA M.S.A.	192,385												
(Includes Linn County.)													
City of Cedar Rapids	121,189	7,233		430	6,803	2	57	104	267	1,111	5,387	305	
Total area actually reporting	96.6%	8,226		481	7,745	2	65	109	305	1,382	5,994	369	
Estimated total	100.0%	8,441		493	7,948	2	66	111	314	1,409	6,162	377	
Rate per 100,000 inhabitants		4,387.6		256.3	4,131.3	1.0	34.3	57.7	163.2	732.4	3,203.0	196.0	
Charleston, WV M.S.A.	250,758												
(Includes Kanawha and Putnam Counties.)													
City of Charleston	53,230	4,463		553	3,910	7	25	162	359	838	2,615	457	
Total area actually reporting	88.6%	8,914		918	7,996	7	56	203	652	1,755	5,352	889	
Estimated total	100.0%	9,962		987	8,975	7	58	213	709	1,903	6,121	951	
Rate per 100,000 inhabitants		3,972.8		393.6	3,579.1	2.8	23.1	84.9	282.7	758.9	2,441.0	379.3	
Charleston-North Charleston, SC M.S.A.	562,057												
(Includes Berkeley, Charleston, and Dorchester Counties.)													
City of:													
Charleston	98,942	6,997		850	6,147	13	37	259	541	1,021	4,254	872	
North Charleston	81,530	8,884		1,354	7,530	16	103	441	794	1,357	4,891	1,282	
Total area actually reporting	99.7%	32,512		4,712	27,800	52	278	1,069	3,313	5,525	18,579	3,696	
Estimated total	100.0%	32,617		4,724	27,893	52	279	1,071	3,322	5,541	18,650	3,702	
Rate per 100,000 inhabitants		5,803.1		840.5	4,962.7	9.3	49.6	190.6	591.0	985.8	3,318.2	658.7	
Chattanooga, TN-GA M.S.A.	477,446												
(Includes Hamilton and Marion Counties, TN and Catoosa, Dade, and Walker Counties, GA.)													
City of Chattanooga, TN	158,507	15,867		2,399	13,468	24	112	625	1,638	2,574	9,462	1,432	
Total area actually reporting	100.0%	26,278		3,388	22,890	38	168	727	2,455	4,759	16,003	2,128	
Rate per 100,000 inhabitants		5,503.9		709.6	4,794.3	8.0	35.2	152.3	514.2	996.8	3,351.8	445.7	
Cheyenne, WY M.S.A.	82,418												
(Includes Laramie County.)													
City of Cheyenne	53,539	2,476		108	2,368	2	15	26	65	219	2,061	88	
Total area actually reporting	100.0%	3,266		183	3,083	2	40	33	108	321	2,640	122	
Rate per 100,000 inhabitants		3,962.7		222.0	3,740.7	2.4	48.5	40.0	131.0	389.5	3,203.2	148.0	
Chico-Paradise, CA M.S.A.	210,636												
(Includes Butte County.)													
City of:													
Chico	62,157	2,665		270	2,395	2	47	75	146	647	1,242	506	
Paradise	27,378	1,005		68	937	2	3	7	56	265	616	56	
Total area actually reporting	100.0%	8,337		675	7,662	4	74	148	449	2,078	4,129	1,455	
Rate per 100,000 inhabitants		3,958.0		320.5	3,637.6	1.9	35.1	70.3	213.2	986.5	1,960.3	690.8	
Cincinnati, OH-KY-IN M.S.A.	1,659,096												
(Includes Brown, Clermont, Hamilton, and Warren Counties, OH, Boone, Campbell, Gallatin, Grant, Kenton, and Pendleton Counties, KY, and Dearborn and Ohio Counties, IN.)													
City of Cincinnati, OH	333,273	29,205		4,193	25,012	64	388	2,412	1,329	6,461	14,526	4,025	
Total area actually reporting	75.7%	56,233		5,691	50,542	78	655	2,938	2,020	10,613	34,283	5,646	
Estimated total	100.0%	75,349		7,163	68,186	82	768	3,226	3,087	13,441	47,933	6,812	
Rate per 100,000 inhabitants		4,541.6		431.7	4,109.8	4.9	46.3	194.4	186.1	810.1	2,889.1	410.6	

See footnotes at end of table.

Table 6

Index of Crime

by Metropolitan Statistical Area, 2002—Continued

Metropolitan Statistical Area	Population	Crime Index	Modified Crime Index[1]	Violent crime[2]	Property crime[2]	Murder and non-negligent man-slaughter	Forcible rape	Robbery	Aggravated assault	Burglary	Larceny-theft	Motor vehicle theft	Arson[1]
Clarksville-Hopkinsville, TN-KY M.S.A.	**210,505**												
(Includes Christian County, KY and Montgomery County, TN.)													
City of:													
Clarksville, TN	105,419	5,962		594	5,368	6	44	82	462	768	4,330	270	
Hopkinsville, KY	30,469	2,008		119	1,889	3	25	58	33	515	1,300	74	
Total area actually reporting	79.7%	8,830		796	8,034	9	74	147	566	1,509	6,133	392	
Estimated total	100.0%	10,410		967	9,443	10	84	167	706	1,799	7,137	507	
Rate per 100,000 inhabitants		4,945.3		459.4	4,485.9	4.8	39.9	79.3	335.4	854.6	3,390.4	240.8	
Colorado Springs, CO M.S.A.	**541,600**												
(Includes El Paso County.)													
City of Colorado Springs	378,114	21,817		2,032	19,785	25	275	497	1,235	4,063	14,137	1,585	
Total area actually reporting	99.7%	25,438		2,395	23,043	39	303	552	1,501	4,898	16,295	1,850	
Estimated total	100.0%	25,528		2,402	23,126	39	304	554	1,505	4,910	16,354	1,862	
Rate per 100,000 inhabitants		4,713.4		443.5	4,269.9	7.2	56.1	102.3	277.9	906.6	3,019.6	343.8	
Columbia, MO M.S.A.	**137,327**												
(Includes Boone County.)													
City of Columbia	85,700	3,837		410	3,427	2	31	90	287	432	2,801	194	
Total area actually reporting	100.0%	5,326		488	4,838	3	37	105	343	663	3,910	265	
Rate per 100,000 inhabitants		3,878.3		355.4	3,523.0	2.2	26.9	76.5	249.8	482.8	2,847.2	193.0	
Columbia, SC M.S.A.	**549,421**												
(Includes Lexington and Richland Counties.)													
City of Columbia	119,036	10,307		1,539	8,768	10	83	497	949	1,639	6,213	916	
Total area actually reporting	100.0%	32,741		4,829	27,912	41	272	1,156	3,360	6,239	18,819	2,854	
Rate per 100,000 inhabitants		5,959.2		878.9	5,080.3	7.5	49.5	210.4	611.6	1,135.6	3,425.2	519.5	
Columbus, GA-AL M.S.A.	**285,336**												
(Includes Chattahoochee, Harris, and Muscogee Counties, GA and Russell County, AL.)													
City of Columbus, GA	194,265	12,382		831	11,551	20	25	359	427	1,937	8,595	1,019	
Total area actually reporting	99.4%	14,279		1,007	13,272	25	33	405	544	2,396	9,685	1,191	
Estimated total	100.0%	14,386		1,015	13,371	25	33	408	549	2,413	9,758	1,200	
Rate per 100,000 inhabitants		5,041.8		355.7	4,686.1	8.8	11.6	143.0	192.4	845.7	3,419.8	420.6	
Columbus, OH M.S.A.	**1,549,398**												
(Includes Delaware, Fairfield, Franklin, Licking, Madison, and Pickaway Counties.)													
City of:													
Columbus	715,739	66,261		6,499	59,762	81	673	3,503	2,242	16,066	36,063	7,633	
Newark	46,556	2,598		99	2,499	2	19	41	37	552	1,843	104	
Lancaster	35,547	1,320		79	1,241	0	19	35	25	280	882	79	
Total area actually reporting	93.5%	93,682		7,738	85,944	102	937	4,053	2,646	21,976	54,671	9,297	
Estimated total	100.0%	96,581		7,891	88,690	103	962	4,109	2,717	22,467	56,731	9,492	
Rate per 100,000 inhabitants		6,233.5		509.3	5,724.2	6.6	62.1	265.2	175.4	1,450.0	3,661.5	612.6	
Corpus Christi, TX M.S.A.	**397,732**												
(Includes Nueces and San Patricio Counties.)													
City of Corpus Christi	289,803	21,237		2,063	19,174	19	243	511	1,290	3,581	14,147	1,446	
Total area actually reporting	100.0%	25,395		2,442	22,953	23	288	559	1,572	4,483	16,845	1,625	
Rate per 100,000 inhabitants		6,385.0		614.0	5,771.0	5.8	72.4	140.5	395.2	1,127.1	4,235.3	408.6	
Cumberland, MD-WV M.S.A.	**104,197**												
(Includes Allegany County, MD and Mineral County, WV.)													
City of Cumberland, MD	22,175	1,262		133	1,129	0	15	15	103	245	837	47	
Total area actually reporting	99.3%	2,881		293	2,588	1	28	24	240	604	1,866	118	
Estimated total	100.0%	2,909		295	2,614	1	28	24	242	608	1,886	120	
Rate per 100,000 inhabitants		2,791.8		283.1	2,508.7	1.0	26.9	23.0	232.3	583.5	1,810.0	115.2	
Dallas, TX M.S.A.	**3,675,809**												
(Includes Collin, Dallas, Denton, Ellis, Henderson, Hunt, Kaufman, and Rockwall Counties.)													
City of:													
Dallas	1,241,481	112,040		17,018	95,022	196	656	8,041	8,125	20,351	56,306	18,365	
Irving	200,144	10,812		803	10,009	5	47	250	501	1,634	7,077	1,298	
Denton	84,121	3,880		374	3,506	2	65	78	229	673	2,655	178	
Total area actually reporting	99.9%	215,925		25,073	190,852	285	1,373	10,019	13,396	40,175	123,053	27,624	
Estimated total	100.0%	216,112		25,086	191,026	285	1,374	10,022	13,405	40,208	123,181	27,637	
Rate per 100,000 inhabitants		5,879.3		682.5	5,196.8	7.8	37.4	272.6	364.7	1,093.9	3,351.1	751.9	

See footnotes at end of table.

Table 6

Index of Crime
by Metropolitan Statistical Area, 2002—Continued

Metropolitan Statistical Area	Population	Crime Index	Modified Crime Index[1]	Violent crime[2]	Property crime[2]	Murder and non-negligent man-slaughter	Forcible rape	Robbery	Aggravated assault	Burglary	Larceny-theft	Motor vehicle theft	Arson[1]
Danbury, CT M.S.A.	**195,751**												
(Includes part of Fairfield and Litchfield Counties.)													
City of Danbury	76,055	2,198		153	2,045	2	23	66	62	281	1,577	187	
Total area actually reporting	100.0%	3,411		214	3,197	3	34	78	99	513	2,444	240	
Rate per 100,000 inhabitants		1,742.5		109.3	1,633.2	1.5	17.4	39.8	50.6	262.1	1,248.5	122.6	
Danville, VA M.S.A.	**113,502**												
(Includes Pittsylvania County and Danville City.)													
City of Danville	49,882	2,265		301	1,964	3	13	69	216	289	1,575	100	
Total area actually reporting	100.0%	2,825		389	2,436	8	26	80	275	483	1,806	147	
Rate per 100,000 inhabitants		2,488.9		342.7	2,146.2	7.0	22.9	70.5	242.3	425.5	1,591.2	129.5	
Daytona Beach, FL M.S.A.	**515,725**												
(Includes Flagler and Volusia Counties.)													
City of Daytona Beach	67,043	7,181		935	6,246	15	85	404	431	1,790	3,566	890	
Total area actually reporting	99.1%	23,534		3,229	20,305	32	250	713	2,234	5,587	12,810	1,908	
Estimated total	100.0%	23,774		3,257	20,517	32	251	721	2,253	5,630	12,956	1,931	
Rate per 100,000 inhabitants		4,609.8		631.5	3,978.3	6.2	48.7	139.8	436.9	1,091.7	2,512.2	374.4	
Dayton-Springfield, OH M.S.A.	**956,261**												
(Includes Clark, Greene, Miami, and Montgomery Counties.)													
City of:													
Dayton	167,176	15,932		2,029	13,903	42	193	1,066	728	3,903	7,311	2,689	
Springfield	65,750	7,226		587	6,639	7	79	287	214	1,620	4,425	594	
Fairborn	32,244	1,672		87	1,585	1	26	27	33	277	1,211	97	
Total area actually reporting	93.4%	45,165		3,597	41,568	56	504	1,804	1,233	9,374	27,112	5,082	
Estimated total	100.0%	47,131		3,702	43,429	57	520	1,843	1,282	9,676	28,542	5,211	
Rate per 100,000 inhabitants		4,928.7		387.1	4,541.5	6.0	54.4	192.7	134.1	1,011.9	2,984.7	544.9	
Decatur, AL M.S.A.	**147,160**												
(Includes Lawrence and Morgan Counties.)													
City of Decatur	54,324	3,803		217	3,586	4	17	105	91	771	2,701	114	
Total area actually reporting	98.1%	5,177		290	4,887	6	23	119	142	1,153	3,531	203	
Estimated total	100.0%	5,313		302	5,011	6	24	123	149	1,176	3,623	212	
Rate per 100,000 inhabitants		3,610.4		205.2	3,405.1	4.1	16.3	83.6	101.3	799.1	2,461.9	144.1	
Denver, CO M.S.A.	**2,232,454**												
(Includes Adams, Arapahoe, Denver, Douglas, and Jefferson Counties.)													
City of Denver	581,105	32,132		3,107	29,025	51	324	1,193	1,539	6,117	15,467	7,441	
Total area actually reporting	93.9%	100,584		8,104	92,480	97	986	2,338	4,683	15,788	59,749	16,943	
Estimated total	100.0%	107,627		8,621	99,006	102	1,052	2,461	5,006	16,732	64,384	17,890	
Rate per 100,000 inhabitants		4,821.0		386.2	4,434.9	4.6	47.1	110.2	224.2	749.5	2,884.0	801.4	
Des Moines, IA M.S.A.	**457,650**												
(Includes Dallas, Polk, and Warren Counties.)													
City of Des Moines	199,390	13,776		776	13,000	9	113	290	364	1,676	10,313	1,011	
Total area actually reporting	97.3%	21,670		1,278	20,392	12	152	347	767	2,866	16,068	1,458	
Estimated total	100.0%	22,071		1,300	20,771	12	154	350	784	2,916	16,382	1,473	
Rate per 100,000 inhabitants		4,822.7		284.1	4,538.6	2.6	33.7	76.5	171.3	637.2	3,579.6	321.9	
Detroit, MI M.S.A.	**4,491,605**												
(Includes Lapeer, Macomb, Monroe, Oakland, St. Clair, and Wayne Counties.)													
City of:													
Detroit	961,987	85,035		19,940	65,095	402	708	6,288	12,542	14,399	26,839	23,857	
Dearborn	98,877	5,681		1,109	4,572	3	29	131	946	536	3,099	937	
Pontiac	67,085	4,004		1,094	2,910	5	79	193	817	989	1,464	457	
Port Huron	32,703	1,379		193	1,186	0	47	30	116	191	898	97	
Total area actually reporting	99.3%	191,946		31,566	160,380	490	1,907	8,564	20,605	31,535	92,079	36,766	
Estimated total	100.0%	193,042		31,665	161,377	491	1,917	8,584	20,673	31,708	92,793	36,876	
Rate per 100,000 inhabitants		4,297.8		705.0	3,592.9	10.9	42.7	191.1	460.3	705.9	2,065.9	821.0	
Dover, DE M.S.A.	**130,543**												
(Includes Kent County.)													
City of Dover	33,110	1,923		183	1,740	1	15	50	117	105	1,528	107	
Total area actually reporting	99.5%	5,029		823	4,206	3	66	107	647	760	3,214	232	
Estimated total	100.0%	5,070		828	4,242	3	66	108	651	766	3,242	234	
Rate per 100,000 inhabitants		3,883.8		634.3	3,249.5	2.3	50.6	82.7	498.7	586.8	2,483.5	179.3	
Dubuque, IA M.S.A.	**89,461**												
(Includes Dubuque County.)													
City of Dubuque	57,891	2,095		160	1,935	1	16	8	135	402	1,407	126	
Total area actually reporting	100.0%	2,420		200	2,220	1	20	8	171	482	1,584	154	
Rate per 100,000 inhabitants		2,705.1		223.6	2,481.5	1.1	22.4	8.9	191.1	538.8	1,770.6	172.1	

See footnotes at end of table.

Table 6

Index of Crime
by Metropolitan Statistical Area, 2002—Continued

Metropolitan Statistical Area	Population	Crime Index	Modified Crime Index[1]	Violent crime[2]	Property crime[2]	Murder and non-negligent man-slaughter	Forcible rape	Robbery	Aggravated assault	Burglary	Larceny-theft	Motor vehicle theft	Arson[1]
Duluth-Superior, MN-WI M.S.A.	**248,526**												
(Includes St. Louis County, MN and Douglas County, WI.)													
City of:													
Duluth, MN	88,689	5,340		383	4,957	3	54	93	233	780	3,867	310	
Superior, WI	27,764	1,803		72	1,731	0	16	15	41	274	1,380	77	
Total area actually reporting	100.0%	10,541		625	9,916	4	126	122	373	2,020	7,286	610	
Rate per 100,000 inhabitants		4,241.4		251.5	3,989.9	1.6	50.7	49.1	150.1	812.8	2,931.7	245.4	
Dutchess County, NY M.S.A.	**282,823**												
(Includes Dutchess County.)													
City of Poughkeepsie	30,156	1,306		284	1,022	3	17	123	141	209	742	71	
Total area actually reporting	97.2%	5,920		684	5,236	6	49	191	438	890	4,060	286	
Estimated total	100.0%	6,109		700	5,409	6	50	196	448	915	4,196	298	
Rate per 100,000 inhabitants		2,160.0		247.5	1,912.5	2.1	17.7	69.3	158.4	323.5	1,483.6	105.4	
Eau Claire, WI M.S.A.	**150,481**												
(Includes Chippewa and Eau Claire Counties.)													
City of Eau Claire	62,596	2,792		155	2,637	1	14	17	123	475	2,017	145	
Total area actually reporting	99.0%	4,513		202	4,311	1	28	22	151	721	3,359	231	
Estimated total	100.0%	4,556		204	4,352	1	28	23	152	726	3,393	233	
Rate per 100,000 inhabitants		3,027.6		135.6	2,892.1	0.7	18.6	15.3	101.0	482.5	2,254.8	154.8	
Elkhart-Goshen, IN M.S.A.	**185,154**												
(Includes Elkhart County.)													
City of:													
Elkhart	52,545	4,288		214	4,074	7	28	154	25	877	2,943	254	
Goshen	29,763	1,430		185	1,245	0	2	4	179	136	1,063	46	
Total area actually reporting	100.0%	7,821		509	7,312	8	38	182	281	1,662	5,151	499	
Rate per 100,000 inhabitants		4,224.1		274.9	3,949.1	4.3	20.5	98.3	151.8	897.6	2,782.0	269.5	
El Paso, TX M.S.A.	**709,871**												
(Includes El Paso County.)													
City of El Paso	588,750	26,998		3,892	23,106	14	221	575	3,082	2,221	18,887	1,998	
Total area actually reporting	100.0%	30,012		4,300	25,712	17	272	601	3,410	2,711	20,754	2,247	
Rate per 100,000 inhabitants		4,227.8		605.7	3,622.1	2.4	38.3	84.7	480.4	381.9	2,923.6	316.5	
Enid, OK M.S.A.	**58,534**												
(Includes Garfield County.)													
City of Enid	47,632	2,985		251	2,734	0	34	25	192	638	1,969	127	
Total area actually reporting	100.0%	3,171		255	2,916	0	35	25	195	685	2,096	135	
Rate per 100,000 inhabitants		5,417.4		435.6	4,981.7	0.0	59.8	42.7	333.1	1,170.3	3,580.8	230.6	
Erie, PA M.S.A.	**282,078**												
(Includes Erie County.)													
City of Erie	104,173	3,560		450	3,110	4	71	196	179	702	2,241	167	
Total area actually reporting	98.1%	6,975		751	6,224	7	112	236	396	1,439	4,459	326	
Estimated total	100.0%	7,098		763	6,335	7	113	239	404	1,455	4,546	334	
Rate per 100,000 inhabitants		2,516.3		270.5	2,245.8	2.5	40.1	84.7	143.2	515.8	1,611.6	118.4	
Eugene-Springfield, OR M.S.A.	**332,409**												
(Includes Lane County.)													
City of:													
Eugene	141,928	9,308		469	8,839	2	56	155	256	1,209	6,824	806	
Springfield	54,411	4,063		118	3,945	0	11	29	78	464	3,071	410	
Total area actually reporting	100.0%	16,667		817	15,850	6	97	221	493	2,486	11,858	1,506	
Rate per 100,000 inhabitants		5,014.0		245.8	4,768.2	1.8	29.2	66.5	148.3	747.9	3,567.3	453.1	
Fargo-Moorhead, ND-MN M.S.A.	**173,858**												
(Includes Cass County, ND and Clay County, MN.)													
City of:													
Fargo, ND	89,458	3,266		124	3,142	0	49	14	61	396	2,547	199	
Moorhead, MN	32,833	1,264		83	1,181	0	20	6	57	142	968	71	
Total area actually reporting	100.0%	5,629		248	5,381	0	78	20	150	766	4,276	339	
Rate per 100,000 inhabitants		3,237.7		142.6	3,095.1	0.0	44.9	11.5	86.3	440.6	2,459.5	195.0	
Fayetteville, NC M.S.A.[3]	**313,156**												
(Includes Cumberland County.)													
City of Fayetteville[3]	125,087	10,594		1,143	9,451	20	54	435	634	2,273	6,480	698	
Total area actually reporting	100.0%	19,468		1,998	17,470	40	98	678	1,182	5,084	11,223	1,163	
Rate per 100,000 inhabitants		6,216.7		638.0	5,578.7	12.8	31.3	216.5	377.4	1,623.5	3,583.8	371.4	

See footnotes at end of table.

Table 6

Index of Crime
by Metropolitan Statistical Area, 2002—Continued

Metropolitan Statistical Area	Population	Crime Index	Modified Crime Index[1]	Violent crime[2]	Property crime[2]	Murder and non-negligent man-slaughter	Forcible rape	Robbery	Aggravated assault	Burglary	Larceny-theft	Motor vehicle theft	Arson[1]
Fitchburg-Leominster, MA M.S.A.	144,047												
(Includes part of Middlesex and Worcester Counties.)													
City of:													
Fitchburg	39,587	1,699		293	1,406	3	40	67	183	361	915	130	
Leominster	41,815	1,195		63	1,132	0	6	28	29	151	888	93	
Total area actually reporting	80.5%	3,536		465	3,071	3	49	100	313	668	2,131	272	
Estimated total	100.0%	4,128		537	3,591	3	54	111	369	772	2,493	326	
Rate per 100,000 inhabitants		2,865.7		372.8	2,492.9	2.1	37.5	77.1	256.2	535.9	1,730.7	226.3	
Flagstaff, AZ-UT M.S.A.	129,978												
(Includes Coconino County, AZ and Kane County, UT.)													
City of Flagstaff, AZ	56,253	5,597		535	5,062	1	48	62	424	720	4,042	300	
Total area actually reporting	95.7%	7,568		711	6,857	2	70	69	570	1,090	5,388	379	
Estimated total	100.0%	7,853		727	7,126	2	72	73	580	1,141	5,571	414	
Rate per 100,000 inhabitants		6,041.8		559.3	5,482.5	1.5	55.4	56.2	446.2	877.8	4,286.1	318.5	
Flint, MI M.S.A.[3]	441,056												
(Includes Genesee County.)													
City of Flint[3]	126,351	9,714		1,713	8,001	30	101	449	1,133	2,261	4,398	1,342	
Total area actually reporting	99.9%	21,554		2,762	18,792	39	241	662	1,820	4,612	11,787	2,393	
Estimated total	100.0%	21,566		2,763	18,803	39	241	662	1,821	4,614	11,795	2,394	
Rate per 100,000 inhabitants		4,889.6		626.5	4,263.2	8.8	54.6	150.1	412.9	1,046.1	2,674.3	542.8	
Florence, AL M.S.A.	144,217												
(Includes Colbert and Lauderdale Counties.)													
City of Florence	36,585	1,869		173	1,696	1	16	33	123	327	1,327	42	
Total area actually reporting	99.2%	4,189		281	3,908	4	24	56	197	818	2,976	114	
Estimated total	100.0%	4,247		286	3,961	4	24	58	200	828	3,015	118	
Rate per 100,000 inhabitants		2,944.9		198.3	2,746.6	2.8	16.6	40.2	138.7	574.1	2,090.6	81.8	
Florence, SC M.S.A.	128,744												
(Includes Florence County.)													
City of Florence	30,966	3,635		387	3,248	3	19	113	252	540	2,524	184	
Total area actually reporting	98.7%	8,449		1,120	7,329	4	63	243	810	1,531	5,239	559	
Estimated total	100.0%	8,542		1,131	7,411	4	64	245	818	1,545	5,302	564	
Rate per 100,000 inhabitants		6,634.9		878.5	5,756.4	3.1	49.7	190.3	635.4	1,200.1	4,118.3	438.1	
Fort Collins-Loveland, CO M.S.A.	263,497												
(Includes Larimer County.)													
City of:													
Fort Collins	124,315	5,371		436	4,935	0	99	35	302	738	3,990	207	
Loveland	53,023	2,169		119	2,050	0	23	18	78	256	1,706	88	
Total area actually reporting	100.0%	9,901		714	9,187	0	165	68	481	1,408	7,375	404	
Rate per 100,000 inhabitants		3,757.5		271.0	3,486.6	0.0	62.6	25.8	182.5	534.4	2,798.9	153.3	
Fort Lauderdale, FL M.S.A.	1,697,228												
(Includes Broward County.)													
City of Fort Lauderdale	159,365	11,681		1,407	10,274	12	39	669	687	2,482	6,418	1,374	
Total area actually reporting	100.0%	73,096		9,247	63,849	90	468	2,979	5,710	12,717	42,822	8,310	
Rate per 100,000 inhabitants		4,306.8		544.8	3,762.0	5.3	27.6	175.5	336.4	749.3	2,523.1	489.6	
Fort Myers-Cape Coral, FL M.S.A.	461,047												
(Includes Lee County.)													
City of:													
Fort Myers	50,412	5,118		1,074	4,044	16	28	369	661	742	2,508	794	
Cape Coral	106,963	4,086		389	3,697	3	17	42	327	1,081	2,394	222	
Total area actually reporting	100.0%	21,515		2,977	18,538	42	165	794	1,976	4,773	11,453	2,312	
Rate per 100,000 inhabitants		4,666.6		645.7	4,020.8	9.1	35.8	172.2	428.6	1,035.3	2,484.1	501.5	
Fort Pierce-Port St. Lucie, FL M.S.A.	334,032												
(Includes Martin and St. Lucie Counties.)													
City of:													
Fort Pierce	39,232	4,329		823	3,506	8	41	236	538	964	2,152	390	
Port St. Lucie	92,827	2,922		270	2,652	1	19	30	220	737	1,812	103	
Total area actually reporting	100.0%	14,622		2,064	12,558	17	128	433	1,486	3,398	8,217	943	
Rate per 100,000 inhabitants		4,377.4		617.9	3,759.5	5.1	38.3	129.6	444.9	1,017.3	2,459.9	282.3	
Fort Smith, AR-OK M.S.A.	210,086												
(Includes Crawford and Sebastian Counties, AR and Sequoyah County, OK.)													
City of Fort Smith, AR	81,369	7,498		714	6,784	8	52	152	502	1,183	5,296	305	
Total area actually reporting	100.0%	10,200		1,122	9,078	13	73	163	873	1,745	6,854	479	
Rate per 100,000 inhabitants		4,855.2		534.1	4,321.1	6.2	34.7	77.6	415.5	830.6	3,262.5	228.0	

See footnotes at end of table.

Table 6

Index of Crime
by Metropolitan Statistical Area, 2002—Continued

Metropolitan Statistical Area	Population	Crime Index	Modified Crime Index[1]	Violent crime[2]	Property crime[2]	Murder and non-negligent man-slaughter	Forcible rape	Robbery	Aggravated assault	Burglary	Larceny-theft	Motor vehicle theft	Arson[1]
Fort Walton Beach, FL M.S.A.	**178,294**												
(Includes Okaloosa County.)													
City of Fort Walton Beach	20,887	879		109	770	0	11	15	83	130	594	46	
Total area actually reporting	100.0%	5,449		616	4,833	4	58	108	446	911	3,644	278	
Rate per 100,000 inhabitants		3,056.2		345.5	2,710.7	2.2	32.5	60.6	250.1	511.0	2,043.8	155.9	
Fort Wayne, IN M.S.A.	**508,631**												
(Includes Adams, Allen, DeKalb, Huntington, Wells, and Whitley Counties.)													
City of Fort Wayne	208,386	12,152		846	11,306	24	113	454	255	2,030	8,268	1,008	
Total area actually reporting	84.7%	16,442		1,088	15,354	28	153	529	378	2,838	11,214	1,302	
Estimated total	100.0%	18,166		1,221	16,945	29	167	550	475	3,173	12,333	1,439	
Rate per 100,000 inhabitants		3,571.5		240.1	3,331.5	5.7	32.8	108.1	93.4	623.8	2,424.7	282.9	
Fort Worth-Arlington, TX M.S.A.	**1,778,405**												
(Includes Hood, Johnson, Parker, and Tarrant Counties.)													
City of:													
Fort Worth	558,447	44,797		4,243	40,554	53	321	1,648	2,221	9,736	26,881	3,937	
Arlington	347,789	23,594		2,202	21,392	14	152	794	1,242	3,638	15,746	2,008	
Total area actually reporting	100.0%	102,500		8,608	93,892	89	713	2,859	4,947	19,809	65,783	8,300	
Rate per 100,000 inhabitants		5,763.6		484.0	5,279.6	5.0	40.1	160.8	278.2	1,113.9	3,699.0	466.7	
Fresno, CA M.S.A.[3]	**956,408**												
(Includes Fresno and Madera Counties.)													
City of:													
Fresno	443,363	33,909		3,780	30,129	42	158	1,479	2,101	4,476	18,478	7,175	
Madera	44,795	2,605		475	2,130	5	21	104	345	426	1,320	384	
Total area actually reporting	100.0%	54,884		5,855	49,029	69	314	1,921	3,551	8,799	29,875	10,355	
Rate per 100,000 inhabitants		5,738.6		612.2	5,126.4	7.2	32.8	200.9	371.3	920.0	3,123.7	1,082.7	
Gadsden, AL M.S.A.	**104,375**												
(Includes Etowah County.)													
City of Gadsden	39,323	3,934		716	3,218	4	31	97	584	741	2,170	307	
Total area actually reporting	100.0%	5,421		805	4,616	5	37	104	659	1,071	3,178	367	
Rate per 100,000 inhabitants		5,193.8		771.3	4,422.5	4.8	35.4	99.6	631.4	1,026.1	3,044.8	351.6	
Gainesville, FL M.S.A.	**227,920**												
(Includes Alachua County.)													
City of Gainesville	99,811	6,016		765	5,251	7	65	185	508	1,248	3,530	473	
Total area actually reporting	100.0%	12,955		1,863	11,092	7	160	335	1,361	2,768	7,429	895	
Rate per 100,000 inhabitants		5,684.0		817.4	4,866.6	3.1	70.2	147.0	597.1	1,214.5	3,259.5	392.7	
Gary, IN M.S.A.	**639,521**												
(Includes Lake and Porter Counties.)													
City of:													
Gary	104,074	5,812		757	5,055	60	58	420	219	1,543	2,271	1,241	
East Chicago	32,833	2,489		642	1,847	11	11	107	513	380	1,058	409	
Total area actually reporting	96.7%	25,818		2,735	23,083	94	131	955	1,555	4,121	15,404	3,558	
Estimated total	100.0%	26,747		2,796	23,951	95	136	972	1,593	4,241	16,081	3,629	
Rate per 100,000 inhabitants		4,182.3		437.2	3,745.1	14.9	21.3	152.0	249.1	663.2	2,514.5	567.5	
Glens Falls, NY M.S.A.	**125,531**												
(Includes Warren and Washington Counties.)													
City of Glens Falls	14,491	668		36	632	0	2	4	30	117	502	13	
Total area actually reporting	96.2%	2,938		316	2,622	3	37	9	267	487	2,075	60	
Estimated total	100.0%	3,053		326	2,727	3	38	12	273	502	2,158	67	
Rate per 100,000 inhabitants		2,432.1		259.7	2,172.4	2.4	30.3	9.6	217.5	399.9	1,719.1	53.4	
Goldsboro, NC M.S.A.	**117,143**												
(Includes Wayne County.)													
City of Goldsboro	40,357	3,219		316	2,903	6	3	90	217	664	2,048	191	
Total area actually reporting	99.8%	5,789		518	5,271	9	7	122	380	1,530	3,423	318	
Estimated total	100.0%	5,804		519	5,285	9	7	122	381	1,533	3,433	319	
Rate per 100,000 inhabitants		4,954.6		443.0	4,511.6	7.7	6.0	104.1	325.2	1,308.7	2,930.6	272.3	
Grand Forks, ND-MN M.S.A.	**97,284**												
(Includes Grand Forks County, ND and Polk County, MN.)													
City of Grand Forks, ND	48,700	2,442		60	2,382	0	15	7	38	342	1,859	181	
Total area actually reporting	97.5%	3,725		143	3,582	0	52	13	78	575	2,756	251	
Estimated total	100.0%	3,823		145	3,678	0	53	13	79	590	2,832	256	
Rate per 100,000 inhabitants		3,929.7		149.0	3,780.7	0.0	54.5	13.4	81.2	606.5	2,911.1	263.1	

See footnotes at end of table.

Table 6

Index of Crime
by Metropolitan Statistical Area, 2002—Continued

Metropolitan Statistical Area	Population	Crime Index	Modified Crime Index[1]	Violent crime[2]	Property crime[2]	Murder and non-negligent man-slaughter	Forcible rape	Robbery	Aggravated assault	Burglary	Larceny-theft	Motor vehicle theft	Arson[1]
Grand Junction, CO M.S.A.	**121,803**												
(Includes Mesa County.)													
City of Grand Junction	43,989	2,617		151	2,466	0	19	18	114	372	1,952	142	
Total area actually reporting	94.1%	3,919		225	3,694	1	20	22	182	665	2,786	243	
Estimated total	100.0%	4,298		253	4,045	1	24	29	199	716	3,035	294	
Rate per 100,000 inhabitants		3,528.6		207.7	3,320.9	0.8	19.7	23.8	163.4	587.8	2,491.7	241.4	
Grand Rapids-Muskegon-Holland, MI M.S.A.[3]	**1,100,780**												
(Includes Allegan, Kent, Muskegon, and Ottawa Counties.)													
City of:													
Grand Rapids[3]	200,029	11,292		2,179	9,113	8	75	508	1,588	2,309	6,124	680	
Muskegon	40,557	3,482		466	3,016	4	58	83	321	471	2,135	410	
Holland	35,443	1,309		109	1,200	0	26	7	76	208	944	48	
Total area actually reporting	99.9%	41,376		4,923	36,453	23	557	824	3,519	7,916	25,811	2,726	
Estimated total	100.0%	41,395		4,924	36,471	23	557	824	3,520	7,919	25,824	2,728	
Rate per 100,000 inhabitants		3,760.5		447.3	3,313.2	2.1	50.6	74.9	319.8	719.4	2,346.0	247.8	
Great Falls, MT M.S.A.	**81,004**												
(Includes Cascade County.)													
City of Great Falls	57,146	4,529		267	4,262	4	16	32	215	333	3,765	164	
Total area actually reporting	100.0%	5,044		316	4,728	4	21	37	254	373	4,162	193	
Rate per 100,000 inhabitants		6,226.9		390.1	5,836.7	4.9	25.9	45.7	313.6	460.5	5,138.0	238.3	
Greeley, CO M.S.A.	**189,571**												
(Includes Weld County.)													
City of Greeley	80,601	5,275		315	4,960	1	55	49	210	637	3,972	351	
Total area actually reporting	90.0%	8,203		595	7,608	8	113	68	406	1,374	5,615	619	
Estimated total	100.0%	9,202		668	8,534	9	122	85	452	1,508	6,273	753	
Rate per 100,000 inhabitants		4,854.1		352.4	4,501.7	4.7	64.4	44.8	238.4	795.5	3,309.1	397.2	
Green Bay, WI M.S.A.	**230,055**												
(Includes Brown County.)													
City of Green Bay	103,791	3,762		389	3,373	1	63	73	252	635	2,468	270	
Total area actually reporting	100.0%	6,654		459	6,195	4	81	86	288	1,070	4,740	385	
Rate per 100,000 inhabitants		2,892.4		199.5	2,692.8	1.7	35.2	37.4	125.2	465.1	2,060.4	167.4	
Greensboro–Winston-Salem–High Point, NC M.S.A.	**1,293,618**												
(Includes Alamance, Davidson, Davie, Forsyth, Guilford, Randolph, Stokes, and Yadkin Counties.)													
City of:													
Greensboro	231,424	15,128		1,639	13,489	28	103	702	806	2,946	9,392	1,151	
Winston-Salem	192,027	14,669		1,614	13,055	15	116	549	934	3,311	8,757	987	
High Point	88,727	6,413		700	5,713	5	37	269	389	1,483	3,641	589	
Burlington	46,428	3,722		293	3,429	4	12	82	195	726	2,542	161	
Total area actually reporting	99.2%	63,274		5,767	57,507	81	376	1,902	3,408	14,145	39,360	4,002	
Estimated total	100.0%	63,859		5,807	58,052	81	378	1,914	3,434	14,259	39,766	4,027	
Rate per 100,000 inhabitants		4,936.5		448.9	4,487.6	6.3	29.2	148.0	265.5	1,102.3	3,074.0	311.3	
Greenville, NC M.S.A.	**138,300**												
(Includes Pitt County.)													
City of Greenville	62,511	5,225		557	4,668	4	24	208	321	1,204	3,226	238	
Total area actually reporting	100.0%	8,451		889	7,562	12	38	271	568	2,027	5,154	381	
Rate per 100,000 inhabitants		6,110.6		642.8	5,467.8	8.7	27.5	196.0	410.7	1,465.7	3,726.7	275.5	
Greenville-Spartanburg-Anderson, SC M.S.A.	**985,271**												
(Includes Anderson, Cherokee, Greenville, Pickens, and Spartanburg Counties.)													
City of:													
Greenville	57,331	4,652		672	3,980	9	45	172	446	622	3,075	283	
Spartanburg	40,615	4,582		778	3,804	3	22	152	601	727	2,754	323	
Anderson	26,120	1,758		238	1,520	3	10	49	176	331	1,051	138	
Total area actually reporting	99.9%	46,484		6,971	39,513	63	454	1,149	5,305	9,181	26,945	3,387	
Estimated total	100.0%	46,562		6,980	39,582	63	454	1,151	5,312	9,193	26,997	3,392	
Rate per 100,000 inhabitants		4,725.8		708.4	4,017.4	6.4	46.1	116.8	539.1	933.0	2,740.1	344.3	
Hagerstown, MD M.S.A.	**135,950**												
(Includes Washington County.)													
City of Hagerstown	37,807	1,764		240	1,524	2	10	90	138	345	1,047	132	
Total area actually reporting	100.0%	3,600		473	3,127	6	29	111	327	759	2,115	253	
Rate per 100,000 inhabitants		2,648.0		347.9	2,300.1	4.4	21.3	81.6	240.5	558.3	1,555.7	186.1	

See footnotes at end of table.

Table 6

Index of Crime
by Metropolitan Statistical Area, 2002—Continued

Metropolitan Statistical Area	Population	Crime Index	Modified Crime Index[1]	Violent crime[2]	Property crime[2]	Murder and non-negligent man-slaughter	Forcible rape	Robbery	Aggravated assault	Burglary	Larceny-theft	Motor vehicle theft	Arson[1]
Hamilton-Middletown, OH M.S.A.	**334,804**												
(Includes Butler County.)													
City of:													
Hamilton	61,054	5,513		569	4,944	4	73	189	303	1,129	3,362	453	
Middletown	49,871	3,607		161	3,446	1	19	74	67	600	2,710	136	
Total area actually reporting	88.7%	15,501		1,154	14,347	6	148	336	664	2,873	10,579	895	
Estimated total	100.0%	16,676		1,216	15,460	7	157	359	693	3,054	11,434	972	
Rate per 100,000 inhabitants		4,980.8		363.2	4,617.6	2.1	46.9	107.2	207.0	912.2	3,415.1	290.3	
Harrisburg-Lebanon-Carlisle, PA M.S.A.	**632,171**												
(Includes Cumberland, Dauphin, Lebanon, and Perry Counties.)													
City of:													
Harrisburg	49,165	2,928		670	2,258	12	40	345	273	577	1,575	106	
Lebanon	24,569	1,275		164	1,111	1	16	59	88	186	843	82	
Carlisle	18,049	558		41	517	1	7	16	17	68	431	18	
Total area actually reporting	91.5%	14,938		1,694	13,244	23	209	629	833	2,285	10,310	649	
Estimated total	100.0%	16,205		1,815	14,390	24	218	660	913	2,450	11,205	735	
Rate per 100,000 inhabitants		2,563.4		287.1	2,276.3	3.8	34.5	104.4	144.4	387.6	1,772.5	116.3	
Hartford, CT M.S.A.	**992,269**												
(Includes part of Hartford, Litchfield, Middlesex, New London, Tolland, and Windham Counties.)													
City of:													
Hartford	123,540	10,870		1,547	9,323	25	57	891	574	1,572	5,571	2,180	
Middletown	43,863	1,108		52	1,056	0	2	20	30	148	792	116	
Total area actually reporting	100.0%	33,997		3,149	30,848	30	195	1,480	1,444	4,996	21,310	4,542	
Rate per 100,000 inhabitants		3,426.2		317.4	3,108.8	3.0	19.7	149.2	145.5	503.5	2,147.6	457.7	
Hattiesburg, MS M.S.A.	**112,739**												
(Includes Forrest and Lamar Counties.)													
City of Hattiesburg	45,206	3,526		239	3,287	10	17	149	63	770	2,358	159	
Total area actually reporting	79.8%	4,353		285	4,068	11	28	168	78	991	2,849	228	
Estimated total	100.0%	4,952		322	4,630	13	34	174	101	1,150	3,204	276	
Rate per 100,000 inhabitants		4,392.4		285.6	4,106.8	11.5	30.2	154.3	89.6	1,020.1	2,842.0	244.8	
Hickory-Morganton-Lenoir, NC M.S.A.	**353,354**												
(Includes Alexander, Burke, Caldwell, and Catawba Counties.)													
City of:													
Hickory	38,474	3,143		227	2,916	3	20	71	133	482	2,275	159	
Morganton	17,892	864		33	831	0	6	18	9	175	622	34	
Lenoir	17,358	708		46	662	1	1	24	20	131	501	30	
Total area actually reporting	99.4%	12,312		829	11,483	16	56	187	570	3,160	7,703	620	
Estimated total	100.0%	12,425		836	11,589	16	56	189	575	3,182	7,782	625	
Rate per 100,000 inhabitants		3,516.3		236.6	3,279.7	4.5	15.8	53.5	162.7	900.5	2,202.3	176.9	
Honolulu, HI M.S.A.	**900,433**												
(Includes Honolulu County.)													
City of Honolulu	900,433	57,271		2,601	54,670	18	304	1,072	1,207	8,932	37,250	8,488	
Total area actually reporting	100.0%	57,271		2,601	54,670	18	304	1,072	1,207	8,932	37,250	8,488	
Rate per 100,000 inhabitants		6,360.4		288.9	6,071.5	2.0	33.8	119.1	134.0	992.0	4,136.9	942.7	
Houma, LA M.S.A.	**195,072**												
(Includes Lafourche and Terrebonne Parishes.)													
City of Houma	32,492	2,125		386	1,739	0	28	70	288	335	1,304	100	
Total area actually reporting	98.7%	8,705		986	7,719	6	79	150	751	1,809	5,512	398	
Estimated total	100.0%	8,857		1,002	7,855	6	80	153	763	1,836	5,613	406	
Rate per 100,000 inhabitants		4,540.4		513.7	4,026.7	3.1	41.0	78.4	391.1	941.2	2,877.4	208.1	
Houston, TX M.S.A.	**4,363,586**												
(Includes Chambers, Fort Bend, Harris, Liberty, Montgomery, and Waller Counties.)													
City of:													
Houston	2,040,583	149,247		24,958	124,289	256	892	11,212	12,598	26,905	73,445	23,939	
Baytown	69,387	3,303		245	3,058	2	33	79	131	617	2,159	282	
Conroe	38,450	3,044		353	2,691	2	25	139	187	540	1,973	178	
Total area actually reporting	99.9%	240,211		35,529	204,682	365	1,584	14,053	19,527	45,475	126,398	32,809	
Estimated total	100.0%	240,233		35,530	204,703	365	1,584	14,053	19,528	45,479	126,413	32,811	
Rate per 100,000 inhabitants		5,505.4		814.2	4,691.2	8.4	36.3	322.1	447.5	1,042.2	2,897.0	751.9	

See footnotes at end of table.

Table 6

Index of Crime

by Metropolitan Statistical Area, 2002—Continued

Metropolitan Statistical Area	Population	Crime Index	Modified Crime Index[1]	Violent crime[2]	Property crime[2]	Murder and non-negligent man-slaughter	Forcible rape	Robbery	Aggravated assault	Burglary	Larceny-theft	Motor vehicle theft	Arson[1]
Huntsville, AL M.S.A.	**345,410**												
(Includes Limestone and Madison Counties.)													
City of Huntsville	159,618	10,167		961	9,206	5	82	315	559	1,714	6,718	774	
Total area actually reporting	99.9%	14,637		1,253	13,384	14	117	383	739	2,721	9,575	1,088	
Estimated total	100.0%	14,659		1,255	13,404	14	117	384	740	2,725	9,590	1,089	
Rate per 100,000 inhabitants		4,243.9		363.3	3,880.6	4.1	33.9	111.2	214.2	788.9	2,776.4	315.3	
Iowa City, IA M.S.A.	**111,402**												
(Includes Johnson County.)													
City of Iowa City	62,442	2,194		344	1,850	0	39	44	261	312	1,465	73	
Total area actually reporting	100.0%	3,854		477	3,377	0	53	58	366	562	2,679	136	
Rate per 100,000 inhabitants		3,459.5		428.2	3,031.4	0.0	47.6	52.1	328.5	504.5	2,404.8	122.1	
Jackson, MI M.S.A.	**160,207**												
(Includes Jackson County.)													
City of Jackson	37,819	2,821		445	2,376	5	43	76	321	426	1,764	186	
Total area actually reporting	95.6%	5,842		772	5,070	8	114	95	555	1,022	3,613	435	
Estimated total	100.0%	6,082		793	5,289	8	116	99	570	1,060	3,770	459	
Rate per 100,000 inhabitants		3,796.3		495.0	3,301.4	5.0	72.4	61.8	355.8	661.6	2,353.2	286.5	
Jackson, MS M.S.A.	**445,012**												
(Includes Hinds, Madison, and Rankin Counties.)													
City of Jackson	186,012	17,648		1,802	15,846	49	182	1,074	497	4,377	8,669	2,800	
Total area actually reporting	81.3%	23,208		2,190	21,018	59	270	1,177	684	5,571	12,341	3,106	
Estimated total	100.0%	26,515		2,388	24,127	64	304	1,237	783	6,280	14,503	3,344	
Rate per 100,000 inhabitants		5,958.3		536.6	5,421.7	14.4	68.3	278.0	176.0	1,411.2	3,259.0	751.4	
Jackson, TN M.S.A.	**109,415**												
(Includes Chester and Madison Counties.)													
City of Jackson	60,775	4,661		685	3,976	3	38	182	462	836	2,788	352	
Total area actually reporting	100.0%	6,033		895	5,138	6	57	191	641	1,151	3,531	456	
Rate per 100,000 inhabitants		5,513.9		818.0	4,695.9	5.5	52.1	174.6	585.8	1,052.0	3,227.2	416.8	
Jacksonville, FL M.S.A.	**1,150,811**												
(Includes Clay, Duval, Nassau, and St. Johns Counties.)													
City of Jacksonville	769,253	51,021		7,043	43,978	90	277	2,016	4,660	9,173	29,391	5,414	
Total area actually reporting	90.1%	61,789		8,888	52,901	97	364	2,213	6,214	11,129	35,701	6,071	
Estimated total	100.0%	66,995		9,633	57,362	102	410	2,363	6,758	12,198	38,604	6,560	
Rate per 100,000 inhabitants		5,821.5		837.1	4,984.5	8.9	35.6	205.3	587.2	1,059.9	3,354.5	570.0	
Jacksonville, NC M.S.A.	**155,414**												
(Includes Onslow County.)													
City of Jacksonville	68,960	955		130	825	3	11	19	97	88	709	28	
Total area actually reporting	99.4%	3,814		262	3,552	5	49	48	160	943	2,244	365	
Estimated total	100.0%	3,864		265	3,599	5	49	49	162	953	2,279	367	
Rate per 100,000 inhabitants		2,486.3		170.5	2,315.8	3.2	31.5	31.5	104.2	613.2	1,466.4	236.1	
Jamestown, NY M.S.A.	**141,084**												
(Includes Chautauqua County.)													
City of Jamestown	32,032	1,258		162	1,096	1	11	40	110	269	762	65	
Total area actually reporting	100.0%	3,527		336	3,191	2	29	57	248	653	2,407	131	
Rate per 100,000 inhabitants		2,499.9		238.2	2,261.8	1.4	20.6	40.4	175.8	462.8	1,706.1	92.9	
Janesville-Beloit, WI M.S.A.	**154,508**												
(Includes Rock County.)													
City of:													
Janesville	60,358	3,499		147	3,352	1	15	52	79	497	2,714	141	
Beloit	36,292	2,144		139	2,005	0	17	52	70	263	1,626	116	
Total area actually reporting	100.0%	6,791		369	6,422	1	40	114	214	1,050	5,055	317	
Rate per 100,000 inhabitants		4,395.2		238.8	4,156.4	0.6	25.9	73.8	138.5	679.6	3,271.7	205.2	
Jersey City, NJ M.S.A.	**621,709**												
(Includes Hudson County.)													
City of:													
Jersey City	245,075	12,182		2,907	9,275	21	86	1,381	1,419	2,285	4,694	2,296	
Bayonne	63,135	1,099		208	891	4	3	93	108	186	584	121	
Total area actually reporting	100.0%	23,157		4,177	18,980	30	108	1,972	2,067	4,193	10,527	4,260	
Rate per 100,000 inhabitants		3,724.7		671.9	3,052.9	4.8	17.4	317.2	332.5	674.4	1,693.2	685.2	

See footnotes at end of table.

Table 6

Index of Crime
by Metropolitan Statistical Area, 2002—Continued

Metropolitan Statistical Area	Population	Crime Index	Modified Crime Index[1]	Violent crime[2]	Property crime[2]	Murder and non-negligent manslaughter	Forcible rape	Robbery	Aggravated assault	Burglary	Larceny-theft	Motor vehicle theft	Arson[1]
Johnson City-Kingsport-Bristol, TN-VA M.S.A.	**490,253**												
(Includes Carter, Hawkins, Sullivan, Unicoi, and													
Washington Counties, TN and Bristol City and													
Scott and Washington Counties, VA.)													
City of:													
Johnson City, TN	56,522	3,896		364	3,532	4	20	77	263	538	2,767	227	
Kingsport, TN	45,757	3,248		369	2,879	2	29	43	295	477	2,267	135	
Bristol, TN	25,292	1,475		121	1,354	1	4	13	103	189	1,083	82	
Bristol, VA	17,894	760		92	668	0	3	9	80	69	565	34	
Total area actually reporting	100.0%	17,961		1,963	15,998	17	135	204	1,607	3,380	11,614	1,004	
Rate per 100,000 inhabitants		3,663.6		400.4	3,263.2	3.5	27.5	41.6	327.8	689.4	2,369.0	204.8	
Johnstown, PA M.S.A.	**233,644**												
(Includes Cambria and Somerset Counties.)													
City of Johnstown	28,714	1,207		149	1,058	2	5	55	87	326	660	72	
Total area actually reporting	78.6%	3,436		409	3,027	7	40	85	277	864	1,960	203	
Estimated total	100.0%	4,612		521	4,091	8	48	114	351	1,017	2,792	282	
Rate per 100,000 inhabitants		1,973.9		223.0	1,751.0	3.4	20.5	48.8	150.2	435.3	1,195.0	120.7	
Jonesboro, AR M.S.A.	**83,275**												
(Includes Craighead County.)													
City of Jonesboro	56,276	3,252		261	2,991	2	8	72	179	507	2,324	160	
Total area actually reporting	100.0%	3,862		286	3,576	3	9	76	198	652	2,694	230	
Rate per 100,000 inhabitants		4,637.6		343.4	4,294.2	3.6	10.8	91.3	237.8	782.9	3,235.1	276.2	
Joplin, MO M.S.A.	**159,498**												
(Includes Jasper and Newton Counties.)													
City of Joplin	46,133	3,689		206	3,483	1	32	63	110	618	2,649	216	
Total area actually reporting	100.0%	7,394		856	6,538	2	53	81	720	1,272	4,814	452	
Rate per 100,000 inhabitants		4,635.8		536.7	4,099.1	1.3	33.2	50.8	451.4	797.5	3,018.2	283.4	
Kalamazoo-Battle Creek, MI M.S.A.	**457,954**												
(Includes Calhoun, Kalamazoo, and Van Buren													
Counties.)													
City of:													
Kalamazoo	78,014	6,315		852	5,463	6	40	158	648	1,171	3,696	596	
Battle Creek	53,965	4,715		840	3,875	5	79	139	617	810	2,780	285	
Total area actually reporting	99.0%	24,016		2,957	21,059	26	310	424	2,197	4,466	14,891	1,702	
Estimated total	100.0%	24,181		2,972	21,209	26	312	427	2,207	4,492	14,998	1,719	
Rate per 100,000 inhabitants		5,280.2		649.0	4,631.3	5.7	68.1	93.2	481.9	980.9	3,275.0	375.4	
Kenosha, WI M.S.A.[3]	**151,739**												
(Includes Kenosha County.)													
City of Kenosha[3]	91,658	2,785		207	2,578	1	28	80	98	502	1,899	177	
Total area actually reporting	100.0%	4,275		266	4,009	3	46	90	127	708	3,043	258	
Rate per 100,000 inhabitants		2,817.3		175.3	2,642.0	2.0	30.3	59.3	83.7	466.6	2,005.4	170.0	
Killeen-Temple, TX M.S.A.	**326,881**												
(Includes Bell and Coryell Counties.)													
City of:													
Killeen	90,779	6,505		711	5,794	3	77	155	476	1,756	3,700	338	
Temple	56,940	3,133		232	2,901	1	7	84	140	693	1,981	227	
Total area actually reporting	99.6%	14,057		1,363	12,694	7	135	276	945	3,405	8,519	770	
Estimated total	100.0%	14,109		1,366	12,743	7	135	277	947	3,414	8,555	774	
Rate per 100,000 inhabitants		4,316.2		417.9	3,898.4	2.1	41.3	84.7	289.7	1,044.4	2,617.2	236.8	
Knoxville, TN M.S.A.	**700,296**												
(Includes Anderson, Blount, Knox, Loudon, Sevier,													
and Union Counties.)													
City of:													
Knoxville	177,191	11,983		1,956	10,027	21	74	553	1,308	2,135	6,680	1,212	
Oak Ridge	25,078	1,679		148	1,531	0	15	43	90	293	1,167	71	
Total area actually reporting	100.0%	31,093		3,734	27,359	35	217	766	2,716	6,739	18,084	2,536	
Rate per 100,000 inhabitants		4,440.0		533.2	3,906.8	5.0	31.0	109.4	387.8	962.3	2,582.3	362.1	
Kokomo, IN M.S.A.	**102,853**												
(Includes Howard and Tipton Counties.)													
City of Kokomo	46,709	3,146		275	2,871	3	18	40	214	559	2,171	141	
Total area actually reporting	88.9%	3,948		352	3,596	5	24	49	274	737	2,667	192	
Estimated total	100.0%	4,154		369	3,785	5	26	51	287	784	2,792	209	
Rate per 100,000 inhabitants		4,038.8		358.8	3,680.0	4.9	25.3	49.6	279.0	762.3	2,714.6	203.2	

See footnotes at end of table.

Table 6

Index of Crime
by Metropolitan Statistical Area, 2002—Continued

Metropolitan Statistical Area	Population	Crime Index	Modified Crime Index[1]	Violent crime[2]	Property crime[2]	Murder and non-negligent man-slaughter	Forcible rape	Robbery	Aggravated assault	Burglary	Larceny-theft	Motor vehicle theft	Arson[1]
La Crosse, WI-MN M.S.A.	**128,788**												
(Includes La Crosse County, WI and Houston County, MN.)													
City of La Crosse, WI	52,567	1,798		114	1,684	0	14	26	74	210	1,400	74	
Total area actually reporting	100.0%	3,450		180	3,270	0	26	28	126	414	2,732	124	
Rate per 100,000 inhabitants		2,678.8		139.8	2,539.1	0.0	20.2	21.7	97.8	321.5	2,121.3	96.3	
Lafayette, IN M.S.A.[3]	**185,184**												
(Includes Clinton and Tippecanoe Counties.)													
City of Lafayette[3]	57,126	3,346		228	3,118	5	44	42	137	624	2,369	125	
Total area actually reporting	99.6%	6,610		414	6,196	6	83	55	270	1,217	4,718	261	
Estimated total	100.0%	6,640		416	6,224	6	83	56	271	1,221	4,740	263	
Rate per 100,000 inhabitants		3,585.6		224.6	3,361.0	3.2	44.8	30.2	146.3	659.3	2,559.6	142.0	
Lafayette, LA M.S.A.	**386,825**												
(Includes Acadia, Lafayette, St. Landry, and St. Martin Parishes.)													
City of Lafayette	110,594	8,431		1,043	7,388	3	85	171	784	1,391	5,503	494	
Total area actually reporting	93.3%	17,326		2,154	15,172	14	149	307	1,684	3,633	10,641	898	
Estimated total	100.0%	18,816		2,314	16,502	15	156	338	1,805	3,901	11,626	975	
Rate per 100,000 inhabitants		4,864.2		598.2	4,266.0	3.9	40.3	87.4	466.6	1,008.5	3,005.5	252.1	
Lake Charles, LA M.S.A.	**184,138**												
(Includes Calcasieu Parish.)													
City of Lake Charles	71,976	4,881		695	4,186	6	42	198	449	1,889	1,982	315	
Total area actually reporting	98.1%	11,374		1,250	10,124	13	109	322	806	3,268	6,182	674	
Estimated total	100.0%	11,570		1,271	10,299	13	110	326	822	3,303	6,312	684	
Rate per 100,000 inhabitants		6,283.3		690.2	5,593.1	7.1	59.7	177.0	446.4	1,793.8	3,427.9	371.5	
Lakeland-Winter Haven, FL M.S.A.	**506,050**												
(Includes Polk County.)													
City of:													
Lakeland	82,039	5,360		665	4,695	3	44	250	368	1,018	3,332	345	
Winter Haven	27,698	2,504		206	2,298	1	34	78	93	436	1,654	208	
Total area actually reporting	99.4%	25,818		2,847	22,971	27	203	660	1,957	5,780	15,271	1,920	
Estimated total	100.0%	25,980		2,866	23,114	27	204	665	1,970	5,809	15,370	1,935	
Rate per 100,000 inhabitants		5,133.9		566.3	4,567.5	5.3	40.3	131.4	389.3	1,147.9	3,037.2	382.4	
Lancaster, PA M.S.A.	**472,729**												
(Includes Lancaster County.)													
City of Lancaster	56,596	3,725		477	3,248	4	43	239	191	613	2,294	341	
Total area actually reporting	89.8%	12,036		917	11,119	9	92	369	447	2,104	8,226	789	
Estimated total	100.0%	13,167		1,025	12,142	10	100	397	518	2,251	9,026	865	
Rate per 100,000 inhabitants		2,785.3		216.8	2,568.5	2.1	21.2	84.0	109.6	476.2	1,909.3	183.0	
Lansing-East Lansing, MI M.S.A.	**452,774**												
(Includes Clinton, Eaton, and Ingham Counties.)													
City of:													
Lansing	120,471	6,601		1,292	5,309	11	169	245	867	1,065	3,837	407	
East Lansing	47,049	1,455		186	1,269	0	25	30	131	184	1,038	47	
Total area actually reporting	99.3%	16,247		2,069	14,178	12	356	373	1,328	2,740	10,624	814	
Estimated total	100.0%	16,355		2,079	14,276	12	357	375	1,335	2,757	10,694	825	
Rate per 100,000 inhabitants		3,612.2		459.2	3,153.0	2.7	78.8	82.8	294.8	608.9	2,361.9	182.2	
Laredo, TX M.S.A.	**201,712**												
(Includes Webb County.)													
City of Laredo	184,435	12,952		1,107	11,845	7	58	203	839	1,898	9,064	883	
Total area actually reporting	100.0%	13,468		1,186	12,282	8	59	203	916	2,074	9,288	920	
Rate per 100,000 inhabitants		6,676.8		588.0	6,088.9	4.0	29.2	100.6	454.1	1,028.2	4,604.6	456.1	
Las Vegas, NV-AZ M.S.A.[3]	**1,696,624**												
(Includes Clark and Nye Counties, NV and Mohave County, AZ.)													
City of Las Vegas Metropolitan Police Department, NV[3]	1,153,546	56,810		8,981	47,829	137	494	3,776	4,574	11,136	24,204	12,489	
Total area actually reporting	100.0%	81,627		11,518	70,109	168	681	4,527	6,142	17,029	37,010	16,070	
Rate per 100,000 inhabitants		4,811.1		678.9	4,132.3	9.9	40.1	266.8	362.0	1,003.7	2,181.4	947.2	
Lawrence, KS M.S.A.	**100,984**												
(Includes Douglas County.)													
City of Lawrence	80,916	3,939		321	3,618	2	32	43	244	668	2,775	175	
Total area actually reporting	100.0%	4,668		376	4,292	2	37	45	292	848	3,249	195	
Rate per 100,000 inhabitants		4,622.5		372.3	4,250.2	2.0	36.6	44.6	289.2	839.7	3,217.3	193.1	

See footnotes at end of table.

Table 6

Index of Crime

by Metropolitan Statistical Area, 2002—Continued

Metropolitan Statistical Area	Population	Crime Index	Modified Crime Index[1]	Violent crime[2]	Property crime[2]	Murder and non-negligent man-slaughter	Forcible rape	Robbery	Aggravated assault	Burglary	Larceny-theft	Motor vehicle theft	Arson[1]
Lawrence, MA-NH M.S.A.	**403,684**												
(Includes part of Essex County, MA and part of Rockingham County, NH.)													
City of Lawrence, MA	72,936	3,195		528	2,667	2	27	155	344	382	776	1,509	
Total area actually reporting	88.3%	8,591		1,086	7,505	5	73	228	780	1,626	3,737	2,142	
Estimated total	100.0%	9,398		1,147	8,251	5	85	236	821	1,759	4,289	2,203	
Rate per 100,000 inhabitants		2,328.1		284.1	2,043.9	1.2	21.1	58.5	203.4	435.7	1,062.5	545.7	
Lawton, OK M.S.A.	**115,396**												
(Includes Comanche County.)													
City of Lawton	93,915	5,515		666	4,849	6	57	151	452	1,281	3,247	321	
Total area actually reporting	100.0%	5,889		736	5,153	8	60	157	511	1,357	3,436	360	
Rate per 100,000 inhabitants		5,103.3		637.8	4,465.5	6.9	52.0	136.1	442.8	1,176.0	2,977.6	312.0	
Lewiston-Auburn, ME M.S.A.	**102,108**												
(Includes part of Androscoggin County.)													
City of:													
Lewiston	36,237	1,789		79	1,710	1	28	27	23	337	1,322	51	
Auburn	23,559	849		25	824	0	9	8	8	121	677	26	
Total area actually reporting	100.0%	3,392		134	3,258	2	49	37	46	641	2,487	130	
Rate per 100,000 inhabitants		3,322.0		131.2	3,190.7	2.0	48.0	36.2	45.1	627.8	2,435.7	127.3	
Lima, OH M.S.A.	**156,014**												
(Includes Allen and Auglaize Counties.)													
City of Lima	40,321	3,286		449	2,837	5	66	126	252	755	1,861	221	
Total area actually reporting	85.9%	5,031		510	4,521	5	86	143	276	1,028	3,212	281	
Estimated total	100.0%	5,713		545	5,168	5	91	156	293	1,133	3,709	326	
Rate per 100,000 inhabitants		3,661.9		349.3	3,312.5	3.2	58.3	100.0	187.8	726.2	2,377.4	209.0	
Lincoln, NE M.S.A.	**252,912**												
(Includes Lancaster County.)													
City of Lincoln	227,943	15,005		1,275	13,730	6	98	179	992	2,014	11,190	526	
Total area actually reporting	100.0%	15,956		1,302	14,654	6	102	185	1,009	2,209	11,886	559	
Rate per 100,000 inhabitants		6,308.9		514.8	5,794.1	2.4	40.3	73.1	399.0	873.4	4,699.7	221.0	
Little Rock-North Little Rock, AR M.S.A.	**591,859**												
(Includes Faulkner, Lonoke, Pulaski, and Saline Counties.)													
City of:													
Little Rock	185,646	20,680		2,411	18,269	41	116	884	1,370	4,826	11,930	1,513	
North Little Rock	61,262	5,840		520	5,320	6	47	179	288	657	4,207	456	
Conway	43,759	2,463		90	2,373	4	23	20	43	269	2,046	58	
Jacksonville	30,326	1,731		140	1,591	0	7	34	99	328	1,194	69	
Total area actually reporting	100.0%	40,284		3,890	36,394	61	257	1,196	2,376	7,956	25,745	2,693	
Rate per 100,000 inhabitants		6,806.4		657.3	6,149.1	10.3	43.4	202.1	401.4	1,344.2	4,349.9	455.0	
Longview-Marshall, TX M.S.A.	**218,072**												
(Includes Gregg, Harrison, and Upshur Counties.)													
City of:													
Longview	76,608	5,771		575	5,196	6	147	171	251	1,047	3,654	495	
Marshall	25,000	1,493		109	1,384	0	18	30	61	306	982	96	
Total area actually reporting	99.5%	11,328		964	10,364	12	181	236	535	2,474	7,082	808	
Estimated total	100.0%	11,380		967	10,413	12	181	237	537	2,483	7,118	812	
Rate per 100,000 inhabitants		5,218.5		443.4	4,775.0	5.5	83.0	108.7	246.2	1,138.6	3,264.1	372.4	
Los Angeles-Long Beach, CA M.S.A.	**9,869,056**												
(Includes Los Angeles County.)													
City of:													
Los Angeles	3,830,561	190,992		51,695	139,297	654	1,415	17,197	32,429	25,374	79,813	34,110	
Long Beach	478,478	19,303		3,626	15,677	67	144	1,505	1,910	3,405	8,530	3,742	
Pasadena	138,857	4,881		657	4,224	3	25	255	374	959	2,803	462	
Lancaster	123,079	5,123		1,362	3,761	12	57	313	980	1,179	1,893	689	
Total area actually reporting	100.0%	394,590		89,058	305,532	1,162	2,894	29,994	55,008	62,055	171,510	71,967	
Rate per 100,000 inhabitants		3,998.3		902.4	3,095.9	11.8	29.3	303.9	557.4	628.8	1,737.9	729.2	
Louisville, KY-IN M.S.A.[3]	**1,038,641**												
(Includes Bullitt, Jefferson, and Oldham Counties, KY and Clark, Floyd, Harrison, and Scott Counties, IN.)													
City of:													
Lousiville, KY	259,472	15,439		2,037	13,402	35	49	995	958	3,519	7,710	2,173	
New Albany, IN	38,089	3,109		226	2,883	3	8	79	136	614	2,083	186	
Total area actually reporting	80.9%	39,500		4,473	35,027	59	143	1,353	2,918	8,467	22,553	4,007	
Estimated total	100.0%	48,780		5,308	43,472	62	196	1,479	3,571	9,936	28,937	4,599	
Rate per 100,000 inhabitants		4,696.5		511.1	4,185.5	6.0	18.9	142.4	343.8	956.6	2,786.0	442.8	

See footnotes at end of table.

Table 6

Index of Crime
by Metropolitan Statistical Area, 2002—Continued

Metropolitan Statistical Area	Population	Crime Index	Modified Crime Index[1]	Violent crime[2]	Property crime[2]	Murder and non-negligent manslaughter	Forcible rape	Robbery	Aggravated assault	Burglary	Larceny-theft	Motor vehicle theft	Arson[1]
Lowell, MA-NH M.S.A.	**305,639**												
(Includes part of Middlesex County, MA and Hillsborough County, NH.)													
City of Lowell, MA	106,472	4,258		849	3,409	7	47	158	637	630	1,957	822	
Total area actually reporting	99.1%	6,846		1,030	5,816	8	56	206	760	1,023	3,687	1,106	
Estimated total	100.0%	6,907		1,037	5,870	8	56	207	766	1,034	3,724	1,112	
Rate per 100,000 inhabitants		2,259.9		339.3	1,920.6	2.6	18.3	67.7	250.6	338.3	1,218.4	363.8	
Lubbock, TX M.S.A.	**253,427**												
(Includes Lubbock County.)													
City of Lubbock	208,447	14,371		2,514	11,857	11	133	303	2,067	2,979	8,307	571	
Total area actually reporting	100.0%	16,001		2,665	13,336	11	152	304	2,198	3,281	9,387	668	
Rate per 100,000 inhabitants		6,313.8		1,051.6	5,262.3	4.3	60.0	120.0	867.3	1,294.7	3,704.0	263.6	
Lynchburg, VA M.S.A.	**221,438**												
(Includes Bedford and Lynchburg Cities and Amherst, Bedford, and Campbell Counties.)													
City of Lynchburg	67,251	2,641		309	2,332	6	25	87	191	419	1,714	199	
Total area actually reporting	100.0%	5,333		534	4,799	13	77	111	333	880	3,532	387	
Rate per 100,000 inhabitants		2,408.3		241.2	2,167.2	5.9	34.8	50.1	150.4	397.4	1,595.0	174.8	
Macon, GA M.S.A.	**337,280**												
(Includes Bibb, Houston, Jones, Peach, and Twiggs Counties.)													
City of Macon	101,696	10,433		638	9,795	16	63	240	319	2,288	6,296	1,211	
Total area actually reporting	99.9%	20,860		1,309	19,551	19	88	408	794	4,490	13,108	1,953	
Estimated total	100.0%	20,872		1,310	19,562	19	88	408	795	4,492	13,116	1,954	
Rate per 100,000 inhabitants		6,188.3		388.4	5,799.9	5.6	26.1	121.0	235.7	1,331.8	3,888.8	579.3	
Madison, WI M.S.A.	**432,691**												
(Includes Dane County.)													
City of Madison	211,061	8,847		755	8,092	3	90	266	396	1,564	5,898	630	
Total area actually reporting	83.4%	13,890		970	12,920	4	117	327	522	2,145	9,942	833	
Estimated total	100.0%	14,944		1,018	13,926	5	125	333	555	2,352	10,684	890	
Rate per 100,000 inhabitants		3,453.7		235.3	3,218.5	1.2	28.9	77.0	128.3	543.6	2,469.2	205.7	
Manchester, NH M.S.A.	**204,682**												
(Includes part of Hillsborough, Merrimack, and Rockingham Counties.)													
City of Manchester	110,406	3,545		242	3,303	0	44	116	82	617	2,441	245	
Total area actually reporting	85.1%	4,482		312	4,170	0	66	127	119	746	3,100	324	
Estimated total	100.0%	5,001		350	4,651	0	73	132	145	832	3,456	363	
Rate per 100,000 inhabitants		2,443.3		171.0	2,272.3	0.0	35.7	64.5	70.8	406.5	1,688.5	177.3	
Mansfield, OH M.S.A.	**176,873**												
(Includes Crawford and Richland Counties.)													
City of Mansfield	49,642	4,006		174	3,832	6	48	78	42	951	2,697	184	
Total area actually reporting	89.6%	7,058		244	6,814	8	72	97	67	1,616	4,904	294	
Estimated total	100.0%	7,631		274	7,357	8	77	108	81	1,704	5,321	332	
Rate per 100,000 inhabitants		4,314.4		154.9	4,159.5	4.5	43.5	61.1	45.8	963.4	3,008.4	187.7	
McAllen-Edinburg-Mission, TX M.S.A.	**594,808**												
(Includes Hidalgo County.)													
City of:													
McAllen	111,150	8,982		533	8,449	4	12	178	339	1,074	6,684	691	
Edinburg	50,622	5,189		284	4,905	3	18	45	218	605	4,051	249	
Mission	47,429	2,849		80	2,769	2	2	19	57	519	1,970	280	
Total area actually reporting	99.8%	34,122		2,892	31,230	46	176	611	2,059	6,479	22,481	2,270	
Estimated total	100.0%	34,183		2,896	31,287	46	176	612	2,062	6,490	22,523	2,274	
Rate per 100,000 inhabitants		5,746.9		486.9	5,260.0	7.7	29.6	102.9	346.7	1,091.1	3,786.6	382.3	
Medford-Ashland, OR M.S.A.	**186,573**												
(Includes Jackson County.)													
City of:													
Medford	65,002	4,434		254	4,180	0	24	39	191	503	3,484	193	
Ashland	20,093	947		15	932	0	5	9	1	147	739	46	
Total area actually reporting	100.0%	8,349		493	7,856	1	48	74	370	1,232	6,188	436	
Rate per 100,000 inhabitants		4,474.9		264.2	4,210.7	0.5	25.7	39.7	198.3	660.3	3,316.7	233.7	
Melbourne-Titusville-Palm Bay, FL M.S.A.	**498,005**												
(Includes Brevard County.)													
City of:													
Melbourne	74,646	5,329		1,074	4,255	1	35	164	874	793	3,218	244	
Titusville	42,530	2,146		364	1,782	2	22	95	245	550	1,043	189	
Palm Bay	83,044	4,129		693	3,436	2	64	89	538	917	2,340	179	
Total area actually reporting	100.0%	23,277		4,088	19,189	12	247	636	3,193	4,827	13,058	1,304	
Rate per 100,000 inhabitants		4,674.0		820.9	3,853.2	2.4	49.6	127.7	641.2	969.3	2,622.1	261.8	

See footnotes at end of table.

Table 6

Index of Crime

by Metropolitan Statistical Area, 2002—Continued

Metropolitan Statistical Area	Population	Crime Index	Modified Crime Index[1]	Violent crime[2]	Property crime[2]	Murder and non-negligent man-slaughter	Forcible rape	Robbery	Aggravated assault	Burglary	Larceny-theft	Motor vehicle theft	Arson[1]
Merced, CA M.S.A.	218,289												
(Includes Merced County.)													
City of Merced	66,241	5,080		498	4,582	6	21	115	356	840	3,175	567	
Total area actually reporting	100.0%	11,141		1,409	9,732	18	77	193	1,121	2,702	5,707	1,323	
Rate per 100,000 inhabitants		5,103.8		645.5	4,458.3	8.2	35.3	88.4	513.5	1,237.8	2,614.4	606.1	
Miami, FL M.S.A.	2,356,396												
(Includes Miami-Dade County.)													
City of:													
Miami	379,044	33,952		7,228	26,724	65	96	2,706	4,361	5,962	15,886	4,876	
Miami Beach	91,954	10,390		1,077	9,313	7	51	507	512	1,464	6,639	1,210	
Total area actually reporting	100.0%	168,968		26,303	142,665	204	837	8,435	16,827	26,120	95,340	21,205	
Rate per 100,000 inhabitants		7,170.6		1,116.2	6,054.4	8.7	35.5	358.0	714.1	1,108.5	4,046.0	899.9	
Middlesex-Somerset-Hunterdon, NJ M.S.A.	1,194,099												
(Includes Hunterdon, Middlesex, and Somerset Counties.)													
Total area actually reporting	99.9%	26,364		2,082	24,282	15	123	785	1,159	4,639	16,987	2,656	
Estimated total	100.0%	26,397		2,085	24,312	15	123	786	1,161	4,645	17,007	2,660	
Rate per 100,000 inhabitants		2,210.6		174.6	2,036.0	1.3	10.3	65.8	97.2	389.0	1,424.3	222.8	
Minneapolis-St. Paul, MN-WI M.S.A.	3,028,704												
(Includes Anoka, Carver, Chisago, Dakota, Hennepin, Isanti, Ramsey, Scott, Sherburne, Washington, and Wright Counties, MN and Pierce and St. Croix Counties, WI.)													
City of:													
Minneapolis, MN	390,415	26,630		4,123	22,507	47	362	1,794	1,920	4,433	14,641	3,433	
St. Paul, MN	293,002	17,803		2,359	15,444	13	192	973	1,181	3,232	10,041	2,171	
Total area actually reporting	99.3%	121,169		10,021	111,148	91	1,271	3,615	5,044	17,835	82,937	10,376	
Estimated total	100.0%	121,940		10,056	111,884	91	1,278	3,624	5,063	17,934	83,529	10,421	
Rate per 100,000 inhabitants		4,026.1		332.0	3,694.1	3.0	42.2	119.7	167.2	592.1	2,757.9	344.1	
Mobile, AL M.S.A.[4]	545,046												
(Includes Baldwin and Mobile Counties.)													
City of Mobile[4]	256,542	17,949		1,376	16,573	40	107	752	477	3,590	11,534	1,449	
Total area actually reporting	91.4%	27,719		2,569	25,150	58	211	1,031	1,269	6,019	16,984	2,147	
Estimated total	100.0%	29,946		2,755	27,191	60	225	1,092	1,378	6,395	18,506	2,290	
Rate per 100,000 inhabitants		5,494.2		505.5	4,988.8	11.0	41.3	200.4	252.8	1,173.3	3,395.3	420.1	
Modesto, CA M.S.A.	463,419												
(Includes Stanislaus County.)													
City of:													
Modesto	195,795	12,981		1,013	11,968	5	71	344	593	1,819	8,426	1,723	
Turlock	57,861	3,769		281	3,488	0	18	78	185	709	1,985	794	
Total area actually reporting	100.0%	27,932		2,493	25,439	15	174	638	1,666	4,837	16,358	4,244	
Rate per 100,000 inhabitants		6,027.4		538.0	5,489.4	3.2	37.5	137.7	359.5	1,043.8	3,529.9	915.8	
Monmouth-Ocean, NJ M.S.A.	1,149,767												
(Includes Monmouth and Ocean Counties.)													
City of Dover Township	91,582	2,542		189	2,353	11	9	46	123	432	1,829	92	
Total area actually reporting	100.0%	26,398		2,326	24,072	27	122	689	1,488	4,393	18,280	1,399	
Rate per 100,000 inhabitants		2,295.9		202.3	2,093.6	2.3	10.6	59.9	129.4	382.1	1,589.9	121.7	
Montgomery, AL M.S.A.	336,006												
(Includes Autauga, Elmore, and Montgomery Counties.)													
City of Montgomery	203,355	17,617		1,475	16,142	30	118	698	629	3,812	10,640	1,690	
Total area actually reporting	91.0%	21,848		1,784	20,064	32	159	780	813	4,610	13,574	1,880	
Estimated total	100.0%	22,752		1,861	20,891	33	166	801	861	4,816	14,132	1,943	
Rate per 100,000 inhabitants		6,771.3		553.9	6,217.4	9.8	49.4	238.4	256.2	1,433.3	4,205.9	578.3	
Muncie, IN M.S.A.	120,304												
(Includes Delaware County.)													
City of Muncie	68,301	3,214		284	2,930	2	49	75	158	509	2,232	189	
Total area actually reporting	100.0%	4,320		353	3,967	2	75	83	193	706	3,025	236	
Rate per 100,000 inhabitants		3,590.9		293.4	3,297.5	1.7	62.3	69.0	160.4	586.8	2,514.5	196.2	
Myrtle Beach, SC M.S.A.	201,293												
(Includes Horry County.)													
City of Myrtle Beach	23,299	4,869		475	4,394	2	42	158	273	835	3,106	453	
Total area actually reporting	99.8%	16,236		1,901	14,335	17	129	352	1,403	2,970	10,058	1,307	
Estimated total	100.0%	16,264		1,904	14,360	17	129	353	1,405	2,974	10,077	1,309	
Rate per 100,000 inhabitants		8,079.8		945.9	7,133.9	8.4	64.1	175.4	698.0	1,477.4	5,006.1	650.3	

See footnotes at end of table.

Table 6

Index of Crime
by Metropolitan Statistical Area, 2002—Continued

Metropolitan Statistical Area	Population	Crime Index	Modified Crime Index[1]	Violent crime[2]	Property crime[2]	Murder and non-negligent man-slaughter	Forcible rape	Robbery	Aggravated assault	Burglary	Larceny-theft	Motor vehicle theft	Arson[1]
Naples, FL M.S.A.	**262,871**												
(Includes Collier County.)													
City of Naples	21,935	1,103		76	1,027	0	4	20	52	266	718	43	
Total area actually reporting	100.0%	9,738		1,415	8,323	7	89	280	1,039	2,301	5,517	505	
Rate per 100,000 inhabitants		3,704.5		538.3	3,166.2	2.7	33.9	106.5	395.3	875.3	2,098.7	192.1	
Nashville, TN M.S.A.	**1,254,684**												
(Includes Cheatham, Davidson, Dickson, Robertson, Rutherford, Sumner, Williamson, and Wilson Counties.)													
City of:													
Nashville	560,596	46,018		8,683	37,335	61	403	2,081	6,138	7,468	25,082	4,785	
Murfreesboro	70,122	3,688		473	3,215	0	22	64	387	471	2,544	200	
Total area actually reporting	100.0%	69,766		11,632	58,134	80	648	2,370	8,534	11,634	40,231	6,269	
Rate per 100,000 inhabitants		5,560.4		927.1	4,633.4	6.4	51.6	188.9	680.2	927.2	3,206.5	499.6	
Newark, NJ M.S.A.	**2,075,500**												
(Includes Essex, Morris, Sussex, Union, and Warren Counties.)													
City of Newark	279,269	17,814		3,193	14,621	65	88	1,567	1,473	2,253	6,033	6,335	
Total area actually reporting	100.0%	72,485		10,752	61,733	134	394	5,256	4,968	11,227	33,954	16,552	
Rate per 100,000 inhabitants		3,492.4		518.0	2,974.4	6.5	19.0	253.2	239.4	540.9	1,635.9	797.5	
Newburgh, NY-PA M.S.A.	**391,130**												
(Includes Orange County, NY and Pike County, PA.)													
City of Newburgh, NY	28,529	1,889		587	1,302	7	23	179	378	349	860	93	
Total area actually reporting	94.8%	8,824		1,184	7,640	17	72	302	793	1,430	5,838	372	
Estimated total	100.0%	9,310		1,227	8,083	17	75	315	820	1,494	6,186	403	
Rate per 100,000 inhabitants		2,380.3		313.7	2,066.6	4.3	19.2	80.5	209.6	382.0	1,581.6	103.0	
New Orleans, LA M.S.A.	**1,341,821**												
(Includes Jefferson, Orleans, Plaquemines, St. Bernard, St. Charles, St. James, St. John the Baptist, and St. Tammany Parishes.)													
City of:													
New Orleans	486,157	31,206		4,556	26,650	258	162	1,994	2,142	4,759	14,325	7,566	
Slidell	25,774	2,398		206	2,192	3	16	41	146	259	1,773	160	
Total area actually reporting	99.9%	69,399		9,279	60,120	327	392	3,068	5,492	10,798	38,265	11,057	
Estimated total	100.0%	69,512		9,291	60,221	327	393	3,070	5,501	10,818	38,340	11,063	
Rate per 100,000 inhabitants		5,180.4		692.4	4,488.0	24.4	29.3	228.8	410.0	806.2	2,857.3	824.5	
New York, NY M.S.A.	**9,403,110**												
(Includes Bronx, Kings, New York, Putnam, Queens, Richmond, Rockland, and Westchester Counties.)													
City of:													
New York	8,084,693	250,630		63,839	186,791	587	1,689	27,229	34,334	30,102	129,655	27,034	
White Plains	53,584	2,033		198	1,835	3	5	71	119	158	1,564	113	
Total area actually reporting	99.7%	278,880		67,375	211,505	622	1,798	28,520	36,435	33,871	148,225	29,409	
Estimated total	100.0%	279,590		67,436	212,154	622	1,801	28,540	36,473	33,964	148,737	29,453	
Rate per 100,000 inhabitants		2,973.4		717.2	2,256.2	6.6	19.2	303.5	387.9	361.2	1,581.8	313.2	
Norfolk-Virginia Beach-Newport News, VA-NC M.S.A.	**1,617,279**												
(Includes Chesapeake, Hampton, Newport News, Norfolk, Poquoson, Portsmouth, Suffolk, Virginia Beach, and Williamsburg Cities, Gloucester, Isle of Wight, James City, Mathews, and York Counties, VA and Currituck County, NC.)													
City of:													
Norfolk, VA	241,523	15,476		1,353	14,123	41	115	709	488	1,758	10,738	1,627	
Virginia Beach, VA	438,175	16,067		954	15,113	3	132	443	376	2,290	11,981	842	
Newport News, VA	185,622	9,936		1,351	8,585	20	106	420	805	1,636	5,715	1,234	
Hampton, VA	150,885	6,209		607	5,602	9	38	291	269	961	3,772	869	
Portsmouth, VA	103,620	7,015		998	6,017	11	38	425	524	1,316	4,058	643	
Suffolk, VA	65,612	3,368		430	2,938	4	24	110	292	482	2,282	174	
Total area actually reporting	100.0%	72,434		7,490	64,944	99	564	2,799	4,028	10,603	48,075	6,266	
Rate per 100,000 inhabitants		4,478.8		463.1	4,015.6	6.1	34.9	173.1	249.1	655.6	2,972.6	387.4	

See footnotes at end of table.

Table 6

Index of Crime

by Metropolitan Statistical Area, 2002—Continued

Metropolitan Statistical Area	Population	Crime Index	Modified Crime Index[1]	Violent crime[2]	Property crime[2]	Murder and non-negligent man-slaughter	Forcible rape	Robbery	Aggravated assault	Burglary	Larceny-theft	Motor vehicle theft	Arson[1]
Oakland, CA M.S.A.	2,480,456												
(Includes Alameda and Contra Costa Counties.)													
City of:													
Oakland	414,161	29,875		5,661	24,214	108	249	2,452	2,852	4,252	13,703	6,259	
Berkeley	106,518	10,271		729	9,542	7	28	407	287	1,514	6,687	1,341	
Alameda	74,914	2,928		299	2,629	2	9	90	198	408	1,884	337	
Total area actually reporting	100.0%	121,462		13,930	107,532	194	683	5,765	7,288	18,040	67,219	22,273	
Rate per 100,000 inhabitants		4,896.8		561.6	4,335.2	7.8	27.5	232.4	293.8	727.3	2,709.9	897.9	
Ocala, FL M.S.A.	270,754												
(Includes Marion County.)													
City of Ocala	48,044	4,159		671	3,488	6	45	151	469	929	2,350	209	
Total area actually reporting	100.0%	10,784		2,126	8,658	16	145	230	1,735	2,613	5,492	553	
Rate per 100,000 inhabitants		3,983.0		785.2	3,197.7	5.9	53.6	84.9	640.8	965.1	2,028.4	204.2	
Odessa-Midland, TX M.S.A.	247,686												
(Includes Ector and Midland Counties.)													
City of:													
Odessa	94,990	5,747		539	5,208	3	33	89	414	948	4,020	240	
Midland	99,224	4,143		561	3,582	2	69	74	416	839	2,545	198	
Total area actually reporting	100.0%	12,228		1,266	10,962	7	110	171	978	2,296	8,097	569	
Rate per 100,000 inhabitants		4,936.9		511.1	4,425.8	2.8	44.4	69.0	394.9	927.0	3,269.1	229.7	
Oklahoma City, OK M.S.A.	1,096,867												
(Includes Canadian, Cleveland, Logan, McClain, Oklahoma, and Pottawatomie Counties.)													
City of:													
Oklahoma City	512,448	49,929		4,214	45,715	38	445	1,169	2,562	8,314	33,686	3,715	
Norman	96,888	3,769		224	3,545	1	34	44	145	1,057	2,352	136	
Shawnee	29,050	1,724		199	1,525	0	22	22	155	582	751	192	
Total area actually reporting	100.0%	70,930		5,960	64,970	51	656	1,414	3,839	13,406	46,562	5,002	
Rate per 100,000 inhabitants		6,466.6		543.4	5,923.2	4.6	59.8	128.9	350.0	1,222.2	4,245.0	456.0	
Olympia, WA M.S.A.	213,507												
(Includes Thurston County.)													
City of Olympia	43,775	2,791		144	2,647	0	25	50	69	437	2,005	205	
Total area actually reporting	99.7%	8,899		624	8,275	2	127	111	384	1,770	5,885	620	
Estimated total	100.0%	8,932		626	8,306	2	127	112	385	1,775	5,906	625	
Rate per 100,000 inhabitants		4,183.5		293.2	3,890.3	0.9	59.5	52.5	180.3	831.4	2,766.2	292.7	
Omaha, NE-IA M.S.A.	723,899												
(Includes Cass, Douglas, Sarpy, and Washington Counties, NE and Pottawatomie County, IA.)													
City of:													
Omaha, NE	394,090	28,781		2,829	25,952	26	173	998	1,632	3,220	18,490	4,242	
Council Bluffs, IA	58,475	6,865		521	6,344	3	68	78	372	941	4,641	762	
Total area actually reporting	96.2%	41,925		3,683	38,242	33	280	1,130	2,240	5,100	27,508	5,634	
Estimated total	100.0%	42,643		3,723	38,920	33	284	1,137	2,269	5,202	28,029	5,689	
Rate per 100,000 inhabitants		5,890.7		514.3	5,376.4	4.6	39.2	157.1	313.4	718.6	3,871.9	785.9	
Orange County, CA M.S.A.[3]	2,950,856												
(Includes Orange County.)													
City of:													
Santa Ana	350,393	12,038		1,930	10,108	23	66	871	970	1,225	6,485	2,398	
Anaheim	340,065	12,198		1,389	10,809	17	80	465	827	1,995	6,945	1,869	
Irvine	148,328	3,624		161	3,463	1	20	62	78	867	2,339	257	
Total area actually reporting	100.0%	82,277		8,206	74,071	77	448	2,789	4,892	13,253	49,949	10,869	
Rate per 100,000 inhabitants		2,788.2		278.1	2,510.2	2.6	15.2	94.5	165.8	449.1	1,692.7	368.3	
Orlando, FL M.S.A.	1,719,756												
(Includes Lake, Orange, Osceola, and Seminole Counties.)													
City of Orlando	194,454	21,133		3,619	17,514	15	121	1,034	2,449	3,710	11,602	2,202	
Total area actually reporting	100.0%	98,196		14,045	84,151	78	684	3,362	9,921	20,159	54,085	9,907	
Rate per 100,000 inhabitants		5,709.9		816.7	4,893.2	4.5	39.8	195.5	576.9	1,172.2	3,144.9	576.1	
Owensboro, KY M.S.A.	92,703												
(Includes Daviess County.)													
City of Owensboro	54,751	2,582		141	2,441	4	17	43	77	435	1,913	93	
Total area actually reporting	100.0%	3,189		219	2,970	4	22	49	144	591	2,256	123	
Rate per 100,000 inhabitants		3,440.0		236.2	3,203.8	4.3	23.7	52.9	155.3	637.5	2,433.6	132.7	
Panama City, FL M.S.A.	154,994												
(Includes Bay County.)													
City of Panama City	38,082	3,107		325	2,782	3	33	90	199	536	2,107	139	
Total area actually reporting	100.0%	9,673		1,160	8,513	8	113	180	859	1,722	6,392	399	
Rate per 100,000 inhabitants		6,240.9		748.4	5,492.5	5.2	72.9	116.1	554.2	1,111.0	4,124.0	257.4	

See footnotes at end of table.

Table 6

Index of Crime

by Metropolitan Statistical Area, 2002—Continued

Metropolitan Statistical Area	Population	Crime Index	Modified Crime Index[1]	Violent crime[2]	Property crime[2]	Murder and non-negligent man-slaughter	Forcible rape	Robbery	Aggravated assault	Burglary	Larceny-theft	Motor vehicle theft	Arson[1]
Pensacola, FL M.S.A.	**430,998**												
(Includes Escambia and Santa Rosa Counties.)													
City of Pensacola	58,827	3,121		460	2,661	1	36	101	322	622	1,912	127	
Total area actually reporting	100.0%	18,235		2,580	15,655	20	221	540	1,799	4,275	10,479	901	
Rate per 100,000 inhabitants		4,230.9		598.6	3,632.3	4.6	51.3	125.3	417.4	991.9	2,431.3	209.0	
Philadelphia, PA-NJ M.S.A.	**5,144,034**												
(Includes Bucks, Chester, Delaware, Montgomery, and Philadelphia Counties, PA and Burlington, Camden, Gloucester, and Salem Counties, NJ.)													
City of:													
Philadelphia, PA	1,524,226	83,392		20,057	63,335	288	1,035	8,869	9,865	11,244	38,789	13,302	
Camden, NJ	81,575	6,125		1,482	4,643	33	45	607	797	1,155	2,407	1,081	
Total area actually reporting	97.8%	171,700		30,020	141,680	399	1,697	11,970	15,954	24,864	95,927	20,889	
Estimated total	100.0%	174,365		30,274	144,091	401	1,716	12,035	16,122	25,211	97,811	21,069	
Rate per 100,000 inhabitants		3,389.7		588.5	2,801.1	7.8	33.4	234.0	313.4	490.1	1,901.4	409.6	
Phoenix-Mesa, AZ M.S.A.[3]	**3,458,385**												
(Includes Maricopa and Pinal Counties.)													
City of:													
Phoenix	1,404,938	109,916		10,223	99,693	177	410	4,075	5,561	16,855	57,214	25,624	
Mesa[3]	421,547	33,335		2,887	30,448	22	129	590	2,146	4,957	20,405	5,086	
Tempe	168,699	17,819		1,240	16,579	10	75	344	811	2,360	11,004	3,215	
Scottsdale	215,578	10,134		483	9,651	1	63	171	248	2,786	5,487	1,378	
Total area actually reporting	98.2%	232,994		19,542	213,452	281	935	6,070	12,256	40,003	128,322	45,127	
Estimated total	100.0%	236,785		19,787	216,998	283	951	6,125	12,428	40,741	130,580	45,677	
Rate per 100,000 inhabitants		6,846.7		572.1	6,274.5	8.2	27.5	177.1	359.4	1,178.0	3,775.8	1,320.8	
Pine Bluff, AR M.S.A.	**85,434**												
(Includes Jefferson County.)													
City of Pine Bluff	55,841	5,286		750	4,536	10	47	230	463	1,012	3,116	408	
Total area actually reporting	100.0%	6,020		810	5,210	14	49	233	514	1,147	3,579	484	
Rate per 100,000 inhabitants		7,046.4		948.1	6,098.3	16.4	57.4	272.7	601.6	1,342.6	4,189.2	566.5	
Pittsburgh, PA M.S.A.	**2,369,073**												
(Includes Allegheny, Beaver, Butler, Fayette, Washington, and Westmoreland Counties.)													
City of Pittsburgh	342,529	19,737		3,794	15,943	47	148	1,616	1,983	3,298	10,108	2,537	
Total area actually reporting	86.2%	57,987		8,057	49,930	107	528	2,647	4,775	9,653	34,904	5,373	
Estimated total	100.0%	65,671		8,789	56,882	114	582	2,835	5,258	10,653	40,337	5,892	
Rate per 100,000 inhabitants		2,772.0		371.0	2,401.0	4.8	24.6	119.7	221.9	449.7	1,702.6	248.7	
Pocatello, ID M.S.A.	**78,320**												
(Includes Bannock County.)													
City of Pocatello	53,318	1,692		146	1,546	1	21	6	118	264	1,208	74	
Total area actually reporting	100.0%	2,365		247	2,118	1	28	8	210	324	1,709	85	
Rate per 100,000 inhabitants		3,019.7		315.4	2,704.3	1.3	35.8	10.2	268.1	413.7	2,182.1	108.5	
Portland, ME M.S.A.	**259,783**												
(Includes part of Cumberland and York Counties.)													
City of Portland	65,234	3,525		190	3,335	3	42	60	85	636	2,547	152	
Total area actually reporting	100.0%	8,180		390	7,790	5	105	90	190	1,546	5,909	335	
Rate per 100,000 inhabitants		3,148.8		150.1	2,998.7	1.9	40.4	34.6	73.1	595.1	2,274.6	129.0	
Portland-Vancouver, OR-WA M.S.A.[3]	**1,974,272**												
(Includes Clackamas, Columbia, Multnomah, Washington, and Yamhill Counties, OR and Clark County, WA.)													
City of:													
Portland, OR	544,604	43,327		4,512	38,815	20	354	1,294	2,844	5,702	27,933	5,180	
Vancouver, WA[3]	147,819	7,773		532	7,241	1	100	155	276	1,196	5,189	856	
Total area actually reporting	100.0%	100,596		7,350	93,246	41	855	2,144	4,310	14,392	67,720	11,134	
Rate per 100,000 inhabitants		5,095.3		372.3	4,723.1	2.1	43.3	108.6	218.3	729.0	3,430.1	564.0	
Portsmouth-Rochester, NH-ME M.S.A.	**267,432**												
(Includes part of York County, ME and Rockingham and Strafford Counties, NH.)													
City of:													
Portsmouth, NH	21,444	860		55	805	0	20	13	22	97	653	55	
Rochester, NH	29,366	834		61	773	0	41	3	17	82	658	33	
Total area actually reporting	80.8%	4,924		300	4,624	3	97	41	159	718	3,643	263	
Estimated total	100.0%	5,800		365	5,435	3	110	49	203	862	4,244	329	
Rate per 100,000 inhabitants		2,168.8		136.5	2,032.3	1.1	41.1	18.3	75.9	322.3	1,586.9	123.0	

See footnotes at end of table.

Table 6

Index of Crime

by Metropolitan Statistical Area, 2002—Continued

Metropolitan Statistical Area	Population	Crime Index	Modified Crime Index[1]	Violent crime[2]	Property crime[2]	Murder and non-negligent manslaughter	Forcible rape	Robbery	Aggravated assault	Burglary	Larceny-theft	Motor vehicle theft	Arson[1]
Providence-Fall River-Warwick, RI-MA M.S.A.	**1,180,900**												
(Includes part of Bristol, Kent, Newport, Providence, and Washington Counties, RI and part of Bristol County, MA.)													
City of:													
Providence, RI	177,162	13,864		1,302	12,562	23	109	550	620	2,186	7,515	2,861	
Fall River, MA	93,078	4,869		926	3,943	3	48	233	642	738	2,620	585	
Warwick, RI	87,560	2,931		129	2,802	2	17	34	76	384	2,084	334	
Pawtucket, RI	74,448	3,209		260	2,949	1	34	78	147	574	1,917	458	
Woonsocket, RI	44,107	1,551		207	1,344	2	51	48	106	327	894	123	
Attleboro, MA	42,589	973		123	850	0	7	17	99	197	547	106	
Total area actually reporting	100.0%	43,210		4,134	39,076	40	425	1,157	2,512	7,131	26,353	5,592	
Rate per 100,000 inhabitants		3,659.1		350.1	3,309.0	3.4	36.0	98.0	212.7	603.9	2,231.6	473.5	
Provo-Orem, UT M.S.A.	**382,248**												
(Includes Utah County.)													
City of:													
Provo	109,079	3,657		165	3,492	0	37	23	105	514	2,789	189	
Orem	87,462	3,649		66	3,583	1	16	17	32	372	3,042	169	
Total area actually reporting	100.0%	13,761		402	13,359	3	80	55	264	2,076	10,598	685	
Rate per 100,000 inhabitants		3,600.0		105.2	3,494.9	0.8	20.9	14.4	69.1	543.1	2,772.5	179.2	
Pueblo, CO M.S.A.	**148,224**												
(Includes Pueblo County.)													
City of Pueblo	106,995	6,145		725	5,420	6	27	164	528	1,144	3,893	383	
Total area actually reporting	100.0%	7,410		764	6,646	7	31	174	552	1,461	4,755	430	
Rate per 100,000 inhabitants		4,999.2		515.4	4,483.8	4.7	20.9	117.4	372.4	985.7	3,208.0	290.1	
Punta Gorda, FL M.S.A.	**148,102**												
(Includes Charlotte County.)													
City of Punta Gorda	15,000	466		31	435	0	4	3	24	150	274	11	
Total area actually reporting	100.0%	4,839		490	4,349	2	34	54	400	1,081	3,013	255	
Rate per 100,000 inhabitants		3,267.3		330.9	2,936.5	1.4	23.0	36.5	270.1	729.9	2,034.4	172.2	
Racine, WI M.S.A.	**191,560**												
(Includes Racine County.)													
City of Racine	83,038	4,758		406	4,352	2	26	226	152	967	3,027	358	
Total area actually reporting	100.0%	7,157		473	6,684	2	41	256	174	1,284	4,931	469	
Rate per 100,000 inhabitants		3,736.2		246.9	3,489.2	1.0	21.4	133.6	90.8	670.3	2,574.1	244.8	
Raleigh-Durham-Chapel Hill, NC M.S.A.	**1,227,913**												
(Includes Chatham, Durham, Franklin, Johnston, Orange, and Wake Counties.)													
City of:													
Raleigh	285,383	17,833		1,966	15,867	19	106	697	1,144	3,836	10,692	1,339	
Durham	193,328	14,461		1,810	12,651	30	75	942	763	3,088	8,483	1,080	
Chapel Hill	50,354	2,505		236	2,269	1	6	81	148	403	1,747	119	
Total area actually reporting	99.5%	59,442		5,562	53,880	72	285	2,149	3,056	13,494	36,446	3,940	
Estimated total	100.0%	59,822		5,589	54,233	72	287	2,157	3,073	13,568	36,709	3,956	
Rate per 100,000 inhabitants		4,871.8		455.2	4,416.7	5.9	23.4	175.7	250.3	1,105.0	2,989.5	322.2	
Rapid City, SD M.S.A.	**89,294**												
(Includes Pennington County.)													
City of Rapid City	60,098	2,930		214	2,716	0	53	25	136	515	2,070	131	
Total area actually reporting	100.0%	4,405		299	4,106	2	92	30	175	646	3,292	168	
Rate per 100,000 inhabitants		4,933.1		334.8	4,598.3	2.2	103.0	33.6	196.0	723.5	3,686.7	188.1	
Reading, PA M.S.A.	**375,282**												
(Includes Berks County.)													
City of Reading	81,565	6,218		1,087	5,131	19	55	510	503	1,503	2,802	826	
Total area actually reporting	89.0%	10,932		1,429	9,503	21	71	603	734	2,126	6,222	1,155	
Estimated total	100.0%	11,904		1,522	10,382	22	78	627	795	2,252	6,909	1,221	
Rate per 100,000 inhabitants		3,172.0		405.6	2,766.5	5.9	20.8	167.1	211.8	600.1	1,841.0	325.4	
Redding, CA M.S.A.	**169,254**												
(Includes Shasta County.)													
City of Redding	83,836	3,389		426	2,963	0	57	79	290	801	1,788	374	
Total area actually reporting	100.0%	5,669		825	4,844	5	109	101	610	1,460	2,782	602	
Rate per 100,000 inhabitants		3,349.4		487.4	2,862.0	3.0	64.4	59.7	360.4	862.6	1,643.7	355.7	
Reno, NV M.S.A.[3]	**369,256**												
(Includes Washoe County.)													
City of Reno[3]	196,307	11,626		1,484	10,142	9	126	450	899	1,288	7,748	1,106	
Total area actually reporting	100.0%	17,477		2,045	15,432	12	188	573	1,272	2,429	11,382	1,621	
Rate per 100,000 inhabitants		4,733.0		553.8	4,179.2	3.2	50.9	155.2	344.5	657.8	3,082.4	439.0	

See footnotes at end of table.

Table 6

Index of Crime

by Metropolitan Statistical Area, 2002—Continued

Metropolitan Statistical Area	Population	Crime Index	Modified Crime Index[1]	Violent crime[2]	Property crime[2]	Murder and non-negligent man-slaughter	Forcible rape	Robbery	Aggravated assault	Burglary	Larceny-theft	Motor vehicle theft	Arson[1]
Richland-Kennewick-Pasco, WA M.S.A.	**197,514**												
(Includes Benton and Franklin Counties.)													
City of:													
Richland	39,857	1,363		62	1,301	2	8	13	39	224	982	95	
Kennewick	56,316	2,851		178	2,673	2	22	39	115	463	1,962	248	
Pasco	33,017	1,696		151	1,545	2	16	31	102	262	1,149	134	
Total area actually reporting	100.0%	7,382		505	6,877	6	59	87	353	1,296	5,011	570	
Rate per 100,000 inhabitants		3,737.5		255.7	3,481.8	3.0	29.9	44.0	178.7	656.2	2,537.0	288.6	
Richmond-Petersburg, VA M.S.A.	**1,026,785**												
(Includes Colonial Heights, Hopewell, Petersburg, and Richmond Cities and Charles City, Chesterfield, Dinwiddie, Goochland, Hanover, Henrico, New Kent, Powhatan, and Prince George Counties.)													
City of:													
Richmond	203,799	18,002		2,606	15,396	77	118	1,289	1,122	2,966	9,926	2,504	
Petersburg	34,765	2,497		260	2,237	6	18	79	157	278	1,676	283	
Total area actually reporting	99.9%	46,681		4,573	42,108	115	277	1,984	2,197	6,897	30,801	4,410	
Estimated total	100.0%	46,701		4,575	42,126	115	277	1,985	2,198	6,899	30,815	4,412	
Rate per 100,000 inhabitants		4,548.3		445.6	4,102.7	11.2	27.0	193.3	214.1	671.9	3,001.1	429.7	
Riverside-San Bernardino, CA M.S.A.	**3,374,398**												
(Includes Riverside and San Bernardino Counties.)													
City of:													
Riverside	264,540	15,161		2,026	13,135	20	94	616	1,296	2,525	8,140	2,470	
San Bernardino	192,212	13,755		2,484	11,271	42	102	886	1,454	2,340	6,226	2,705	
Palm Springs	44,380	3,908		397	3,511	3	22	112	260	993	2,061	457	
Hemet	60,972	2,794		247	2,547	1	23	112	111	828	1,368	351	
Temecula	59,837	2,151		216	1,935	0	19	28	169	452	1,249	234	
Palm Desert	42,667	2,193		151	2,042	0	9	37	105	536	1,325	181	
Total area actually reporting	100.0%	142,954		19,496	123,458	253	1,021	5,359	12,863	29,621	69,543	24,294	
Rate per 100,000 inhabitants		4,236.4		577.8	3,658.7	7.5	30.3	158.8	381.2	877.8	2,060.9	720.0	
Rochester, MN M.S.A.	**126,809**												
(Includes Olmsted County.)													
City of Rochester	87,555	3,003		232	2,771	1	44	43	144	455	2,136	180	
Total area actually reporting	100.0%	3,440		261	3,179	1	52	46	162	561	2,406	212	
Rate per 100,000 inhabitants		2,712.7		205.8	2,506.9	0.8	41.0	36.3	127.8	442.4	1,897.3	167.2	
Rochester, NY M.S.A.	**1,108,681**												
(Includes Genesee, Livingston, Monroe, Ontario, Orleans, and Wayne Counties.)													
City of Rochester	221,871	16,911		1,786	15,125	42	107	972	665	2,467	9,853	2,805	
Total area actually reporting	97.4%	37,387		2,743	34,644	51	231	1,240	1,221	5,194	25,612	3,838	
Estimated total	100.0%	38,078		2,802	35,276	51	234	1,259	1,258	5,285	26,110	3,881	
Rate per 100,000 inhabitants		3,434.5		252.7	3,181.8	4.6	21.1	113.6	113.5	476.7	2,355.1	350.1	
Rocky Mount, NC M.S.A.	**147,839**												
(Includes Edgecombe and Nash Counties.)													
City of Rocky Mount	57,774	5,710		452	5,258	4	13	174	261	1,148	3,835	275	
Total area actually reporting	99.4%	8,228		664	7,564	10	23	229	402	1,971	5,180	413	
Estimated total	100.0%	8,278		667	7,611	10	23	230	404	1,981	5,215	415	
Rate per 100,000 inhabitants		5,599.3		451.2	5,148.2	6.8	15.6	155.6	273.3	1,340.0	3,527.5	280.7	
Sacramento, CA M.S.A.	**1,688,014**												
(Includes El Dorado, Placer, and Sacramento Counties.)													
City of Sacramento	421,971	30,780		3,547	27,233	47	185	1,734	1,581	5,019	15,548	6,666	
Total area actually reporting	100.0%	81,534		9,144	72,390	87	596	3,151	5,310	14,979	42,928	14,483	
Rate per 100,000 inhabitants		4,830.2		541.7	4,288.5	5.2	35.3	186.7	314.6	887.4	2,543.1	858.0	
Saginaw-Bay City-Midland, MI M.S.A.	**407,613**												
(Includes Bay, Midland, and Saginaw Counties.)													
City of:													
Saginaw	62,496	4,848		1,511	3,337	17	86	215	1,193	1,129	1,830	378	
Bay City	37,232	1,618		167	1,451	0	20	27	120	309	1,037	105	
Midland	42,154	955		76	879	0	27	7	42	131	721	27	
Total area actually reporting	100.0%	15,340		2,517	12,823	19	250	332	1,916	2,934	8,968	921	
Rate per 100,000 inhabitants		3,763.4		617.5	3,145.9	4.7	61.3	81.4	470.1	719.8	2,200.1	225.9	
Salem, OR M.S.A.	**357,375**												
(Includes Marion and Polk Counties.)													
City of Salem	140,931	12,389		344	12,045	6	79	156	103	1,415	9,277	1,353	
Total area actually reporting	99.7%	22,622		858	21,764	8	132	226	492	2,919	16,299	2,546	
Estimated total	100.0%	22,669		860	21,809	8	132	227	493	2,925	16,333	2,551	
Rate per 100,000 inhabitants		6,343.2		240.6	6,102.6	2.2	36.9	63.5	138.0	818.5	4,570.3	713.8	

See footnotes at end of table.

Table 6

Index of Crime

by Metropolitan Statistical Area, 2002—Continued

Metropolitan Statistical Area	Population	Crime Index	Modified Crime Index[1]	Violent crime[2]	Property crime[2]	Murder and non-negligent manslaughter	Forcible rape	Robbery	Aggravated assault	Burglary	Larceny-theft	Motor vehicle theft	Arson[1]
Salinas, CA M.S.A.	**416,522**												
(Includes Monterey County.)													
City of:													
Salinas	156,609	6,834		1,138	5,696	20	59	367	692	757	4,013	926	
Monterey	30,764	1,369		132	1,237	0	15	31	86	255	907	75	
Total area actually reporting	100.0%	14,426		1,953	12,473	28	141	574	1,210	2,527	8,557	1,389	
Rate per 100,000 inhabitants		3,463.4		468.9	2,994.6	6.7	33.9	137.8	290.5	606.7	2,054.4	333.5	
Salt Lake City-Ogden, UT M.S.A.	**1,383,544**												
(Includes Davis, Salt Lake, and Weber Counties.)													
City of:													
Salt Lake City	188,504	19,059		1,233	17,826	11	109	478	635	2,512	13,337	1,977	
Ogden	80,099	5,332		473	4,859	5	89	93	286	914	3,505	440	
Clearfield	26,941	980		50	930	0	17	5	28	180	685	65	
Total area actually reporting	99.9%	74,458		4,189	70,269	31	642	1,041	2,475	10,535	53,423	6,311	
Estimated total	100.0%	74,476		4,190	70,286	31	642	1,041	2,476	10,538	53,436	6,312	
Rate per 100,000 inhabitants		5,383.0		302.8	5,080.1	2.2	46.4	75.2	179.0	761.7	3,862.3	456.2	
San Angelo, TX M.S.A.	**108,640**												
(Includes Tom Green County.)													
City of San Angelo	92,375	5,718		392	5,326	0	55	50	287	1,048	4,055	223	
Total area actually reporting	100.0%	6,144		407	5,737	0	63	50	294	1,157	4,335	245	
Rate per 100,000 inhabitants		5,655.4		374.6	5,280.7	0.0	58.0	46.0	270.6	1,065.0	3,990.2	225.5	
San Antonio, TX M.S.A.	**1,663,258**												
(Includes Bexar, Comal, Guadalupe, and Wilson Counties.)													
City of:													
San Antonio	1,195,592	94,132		9,769	84,363	100	464	2,114	7,091	13,368	65,251	5,744	
New Braunfels	38,119	2,726		292	2,434	1	18	24	249	327	2,001	106	
Total area actually reporting	100.0%	112,691		11,259	101,432	121	610	2,323	8,205	16,796	77,978	6,658	
Rate per 100,000 inhabitants		6,775.3		676.9	6,098.4	7.3	36.7	139.7	493.3	1,009.8	4,688.3	400.3	
San Diego, CA M.S.A.	**2,917,208**												
(Includes San Diego County.)													
City of:													
San Diego	1,268,346	50,124		7,193	42,931	47	330	1,627	5,189	7,639	24,577	10,715	
Escondido	138,466	5,495		608	4,887	4	40	165	399	960	3,111	816	
Coronado	24,986	403		23	380	0	7	7	9	101	233	46	
Total area actually reporting	100.0%	105,363		14,028	91,335	87	798	3,342	9,801	18,199	53,252	19,884	
Rate per 100,000 inhabitants		3,611.8		480.9	3,130.9	3.0	27.4	114.6	336.0	623.8	1,825.4	681.6	
San Francisco, CA M.S.A.	**1,794,784**												
(Includes Marin, San Francisco, and San Mateo Counties.)													
City of San Francisco	805,269	42,671		6,059	36,612	68	210	3,208	2,573	5,947	24,468	6,197	
Total area actually reporting	100.0%	69,039		8,664	60,375	93	409	4,058	4,104	9,953	41,187	9,235	
Rate per 100,000 inhabitants		3,846.6		482.7	3,363.9	5.2	22.8	226.1	228.7	554.6	2,294.8	514.5	
San Jose, CA M.S.A.	**1,744,400**												
(Includes Santa Clara County.)													
City of:													
San Jose	927,821	24,139		4,134	20,005	26	379	827	2,902	3,026	13,642	3,337	
Sunnyvale	136,601	2,569		192	2,377	2	24	70	96	322	1,837	218	
Santa Clara	106,121	3,228		311	2,917	4	19	62	226	417	2,188	312	
Palo Alto	60,751	1,778		107	1,671	1	7	45	54	223	1,353	95	
Gilroy	42,987	1,754		314	1,440	0	26	69	219	185	1,083	172	
Total area actually reporting	100.0%	46,147		6,232	39,915	37	543	1,298	4,354	6,094	28,793	5,028	
Rate per 100,000 inhabitants		2,645.4		357.3	2,288.2	2.1	31.1	74.4	249.6	349.3	1,650.6	288.2	
San Luis Obispo-Atascadero-Paso Robles, CA M.S.A.	**255,744**												
(Includes San Luis Obispo County.)													
City of:													
San Luis Obispo	45,796	2,093		160	1,933	0	32	19	109	318	1,489	126	
Atascadero	27,381	922		89	833	1	13	14	61	185	592	56	
Paso Robles	25,190	978		116	862	0	11	12	93	321	483	58	
Total area actually reporting	100.0%	7,603		699	6,904	3	95	78	523	1,493	4,913	498	
Rate per 100,000 inhabitants		2,972.9		273.3	2,699.6	1.2	37.1	30.5	204.5	583.8	1,921.1	194.7	

See footnotes at end of table.

Table 6

Index of Crime

by Metropolitan Statistical Area, 2002—Continued

Metropolitan Statistical Area	Population	Crime Index	Modified Crime Index[1]	Violent crime[2]	Property crime[2]	Murder and non-negligent man-slaughter	Forcible rape	Robbery	Aggravated assault	Burglary	Larceny-theft	Motor vehicle theft	Arson[1]
Santa Cruz-Watsonville, CA M.S.A.	264,993												
(Includes Santa Cruz County.)													
City of:													
Santa Cruz	56,599	3,569		460	3,109	4	43	97	316	534	2,371	204	
Watsonville	45,891	2,259		322	1,937	0	23	84	215	293	1,533	111	
Total area actually reporting	100.0%	10,136		1,099	9,037	6	109	238	746	1,676	6,844	517	
Rate per 100,000 inhabitants		3,825.0		414.7	3,410.3	2.3	41.1	89.8	281.5	632.5	2,582.7	195.1	
Santa Fe, NM M.S.A.	155,169												
(Includes Los Alamos and Santa Fe Counties.)													
City of Santa Fe	63,435	4,929		406	4,523	8	38	90	270	2,059	2,251	213	
Total area actually reporting	94.3%	6,596		687	5,909	8	66	110	503	2,639	2,974	296	
Estimated total	100.0%	6,928		731	6,197	8	70	113	540	2,700	3,177	320	
Rate per 100,000 inhabitants		4,464.8		471.1	3,993.7	5.2	45.1	72.8	348.0	1,740.0	2,047.4	206.2	
Santa Rosa, CA M.S.A.	475,463												
(Includes Sonoma County.)													
City of:													
Santa Rosa	153,018	6,531		625	5,906	6	93	167	359	974	4,213	719	
Petaluma	56,552	1,607		78	1,529	2	7	17	52	225	1,209	95	
Total area actually reporting	100.0%	16,061		1,472	14,589	16	188	295	973	3,107	9,985	1,497	
Rate per 100,000 inhabitants		3,378.0		309.6	3,068.4	3.4	39.5	62.0	204.6	653.5	2,100.1	314.9	
Sarasota-Bradenton, FL M.S.A.	616,934												
(Includes Manatee and Sarasota Counties.)													
City of:													
Sarasota	55,125	4,699		632	4,067	1	40	219	372	955	2,819	293	
Bradenton	51,768	3,758		458	3,300	8	32	151	267	769	2,180	351	
Total area actually reporting	100.0%	31,396		3,854	27,542	22	223	855	2,754	6,660	19,098	1,784	
Rate per 100,000 inhabitants		5,089.0		624.7	4,464.3	3.6	36.1	138.6	446.4	1,079.5	3,095.6	289.2	
Savannah, GA M.S.A.	306,380												
(Includes Bryan, Chatham, and Effingham Counties.)													
City of Savannah	137,516	11,595		1,189	10,406	32	58	650	449	1,985	6,884	1,537	
Total area actually reporting	98.4%	17,960		1,873	16,087	42	85	818	928	3,353	10,680	2,054	
Estimated total	100.0%	18,257		1,897	16,360	42	86	826	943	3,400	10,881	2,079	
Rate per 100,000 inhabitants		5,958.9		619.2	5,339.8	13.7	28.1	269.6	307.8	1,109.7	3,551.5	678.6	
Scranton--Wilkes-Barre--Hazelton, PA M.S.A.	627,525												
(Includes Columbia, Lackawanna, Luzerne, and Wyoming Counties.)													
City of:													
Scranton	76,751	2,549		222	2,327	1	39	92	90	503	1,636	188	
Wilkes-Barre	43,312	2,329		252	2,077	3	15	113	121	378	1,485	214	
Total area actually reporting	76.0%	12,399		1,282	11,117	18	139	349	776	2,093	8,112	912	
Estimated total	100.0%	15,943		1,620	14,323	21	164	436	999	2,554	10,618	1,151	
Rate per 100,000 inhabitants		2,540.6		258.2	2,282.5	3.3	26.1	69.5	159.2	407.0	1,692.0	183.4	
Seattle-Bellevue-Everett, WA M.S.A.	2,486,255												
(Includes Island, King, and Snohomish Counties.)													
City of:													
Seattle	580,089	46,432		4,092	42,340	26	152	1,576	2,338	7,290	26,742	8,308	
Bellevue	112,819	4,640		140	4,500	0	26	48	66	606	3,349	545	
Everett	94,203	6,745		507	6,238	3	54	185	265	839	3,724	1,675	
Total area actually reporting	96.4%	126,151		8,563	117,588	71	860	2,959	4,673	19,936	74,686	22,966	
Estimated total	100.0%	129,769		8,785	120,984	73	897	3,013	4,802	20,615	76,891	23,478	
Rate per 100,000 inhabitants		5,219.5		353.3	4,866.1	2.9	36.1	121.2	193.1	829.2	3,092.6	944.3	
Sharon, PA M.S.A.	120,822												
(Includes Mercer County.)													
City of Sharon	16,400	791		158	633	0	8	24	126	148	448	37	
Total area actually reporting	83.3%	2,551		270	2,281	1	19	45	205	495	1,656	130	
Estimated total	100.0%	3,026		315	2,711	1	22	57	235	557	1,992	162	
Rate per 100,000 inhabitants		2,504.5		260.7	2,243.8	0.8	18.2	47.2	194.5	461.0	1,648.7	134.1	
Sheboygan, WI M.S.A.	114,274												
(Includes Sheboygan County.)													
City of Sheboygan	51,526	2,460		89	2,371	0	36	16	37	281	2,004	86	
Total area actually reporting	100.0%	3,495		133	3,362	0	40	17	76	415	2,824	123	
Rate per 100,000 inhabitants		3,058.4		116.4	2,942.1	0.0	35.0	14.9	66.5	363.2	2,471.3	107.6	

See footnotes at end of table.

Table 6

Index of Crime
by Metropolitan Statistical Area, 2002—Continued

Metropolitan Statistical Area	Population	Crime Index	Modified Crime Index[1]	Violent crime[2]	Property crime[2]	Murder and non-negligent man-slaughter	Forcible rape	Robbery	Aggravated assault	Burglary	Larceny-theft	Motor vehicle theft	Arson[1]
Sherman-Denison, TX M.S.A.	115,518												
(Includes Grayson County.)													
City of:													
Sherman	36,643	2,378		180	2,198	0	12	56	112	359	1,742	97	
Denison	23,787	1,267		69	1,198	0	0	22	47	240	861	97	
Total area actually reporting	100.0%	4,889		318	4,571	3	22	81	212	943	3,357	271	
Rate per 100,000 inhabitants		4,232.2		275.3	3,957.0	2.6	19.0	70.1	183.5	816.3	2,906.0	234.6	
Shreveport-Bossier City, LA M.S.A.	393,503												
(Includes Bossier, Caddo, and Webster Parishes.)													
City of:													
Shreveport	200,757	16,389		2,044	14,345	40	119	667	1,218	3,350	9,346	1,649	
Bossier City	56,634	4,187		525	3,662	7	32	95	391	762	2,572	328	
Total area actually reporting	100.0%	24,145		2,947	21,198	55	180	798	1,914	4,835	14,209	2,154	
Rate per 100,000 inhabitants		6,135.9		748.9	5,387.0	14.0	45.7	202.8	486.4	1,228.7	3,610.9	547.4	
Sioux City, IA-NE M.S.A.	124,712												
(Includes Woodbury County, IA and Dakota County, NE.)													
City of Sioux City, IA	85,316	5,933		554	5,379	3	45	72	434	1,235	3,770	374	
Total area actually reporting	100.0%	6,788		617	6,171	3	51	78	485	1,409	4,349	413	
Rate per 100,000 inhabitants		5,442.9		494.7	4,948.2	2.4	40.9	62.5	388.9	1,129.8	3,487.2	331.2	
Sioux Falls, SD M.S.A.	173,837												
(Includes Lincoln and Minnehaha Counties.)													
City of Sioux Falls	124,997	4,189		396	3,793	1	115	52	228	652	2,946	195	
Total area actually reporting	90.6%	4,583		426	4,157	1	123	52	250	802	3,136	219	
Estimated total	100.0%	5,034		454	4,580	1	134	54	265	873	3,472	235	
Rate per 100,000 inhabitants		2,895.8		261.2	2,634.7	0.6	77.1	31.1	152.4	502.2	1,997.3	135.2	
South Bend, IN M.S.A.	268,991												
(Includes St. Joseph County.)													
City of South Bend	109,182	8,203		820	7,383	20	93	354	353	1,826	4,983	574	
Total area actually reporting	99.5%	15,019		1,088	13,931	22	125	435	506	2,898	10,030	1,003	
Estimated total	100.0%	15,081		1,092	13,989	22	125	436	509	2,906	10,075	1,008	
Rate per 100,000 inhabitants		5,606.5		406.0	5,200.5	8.2	46.5	162.1	189.2	1,080.3	3,745.5	374.7	
Spokane, WA M.S.A.	430,339												
(Includes Spokane County.)													
City of Spokane	201,433	15,895		1,302	14,593	20	83	379	820	2,660	10,248	1,685	
Total area actually reporting	98.0%	24,322		1,764	22,558	20	146	481	1,117	4,336	15,775	2,447	
Estimated total	100.0%	24,780		1,788	22,992	20	150	488	1,130	4,404	16,073	2,515	
Rate per 100,000 inhabitants		5,758.3		415.5	5,342.8	4.6	34.9	113.4	262.6	1,023.4	3,735.0	584.4	
Springfield, MO M.S.A.	330,225												
(Includes Christian, Greene, and Webster Counties.)													
City of Springfield	153,675	12,066		1,061	11,005	4	102	222	733	1,882	8,352	771	
Total area actually reporting	100.0%	16,160		1,542	14,618	6	118	239	1,179	2,747	10,833	1,038	
Rate per 100,000 inhabitants		4,893.6		467.0	4,426.7	1.8	35.7	72.4	357.0	831.9	3,280.5	314.3	
Stamford-Norwalk, CT M.S.A.	359,259												
(Includes part of Fairfield County.)													
City of:													
Stamford	118,971	2,398		280	2,118	2	14	147	117	249	1,571	298	
Norwalk	84,289	2,949		333	2,616	2	12	106	213	410	1,944	262	
Total area actually reporting	100.0%	6,785		654	6,131	4	33	268	349	860	4,609	662	
Rate per 100,000 inhabitants		1,888.6		182.0	1,706.6	1.1	9.2	74.6	97.1	239.4	1,282.9	184.3	
State College, PA M.S.A.	136,356												
(Includes Centre County.)													
City of State College	51,792	925		45	880	2	7	10	26	87	777	16	
Total area actually reporting	100.0%	2,782		159	2,623	4	38	22	95	321	2,233	69	
Rate per 100,000 inhabitants		2,040.2		116.6	1,923.6	2.9	27.9	16.1	69.7	235.4	1,637.6	50.6	
St. Cloud, MN M.S.A.	170,803												
(Includes Benton and Stearns Counties.)													
City of St. Cloud	54,208	2,911		172	2,739	0	46	33	93	275	2,310	154	
Total area actually reporting	100.0%	5,545		327	5,218	1	111	41	174	627	4,317	274	
Rate per 100,000 inhabitants		3,246.4		191.4	3,055.0	0.6	65.0	24.0	101.9	367.1	2,527.5	160.4	

See footnotes at end of table.

Table 6

Index of Crime

by Metropolitan Statistical Area, 2002—Continued

Metropolitan Statistical Area	Population	Crime Index	Modified Crime Index[1]	Violent crime[2]	Property crime[2]	Murder and non-negligent man-slaughter	Forcible rape	Robbery	Aggravated assault	Burglary	Larceny-theft	Motor vehicle theft	Arson[1]
Steubenville-Weirton, OH-WV M.S.A.	132,244												
(Includes Jefferson County, OH and Brooke and Hancock Counties, WV.)													
City of:													
Steubenville, OH	19,129	1,227		158	1,069	0	16	46	96	150	851	68	
Weirton, WV	20,338	359		22	337	0	2	7	13	75	251	11	
Total area actually reporting	88.7%	2,350		279	2,071	1	24	66	188	388	1,548	135	
Estimated total	100.0%	2,718		308	2,410	1	26	69	212	462	1,774	174	
Rate per 100,000 inhabitants		2,055.3		232.9	1,822.4	0.8	19.7	52.2	160.3	349.4	1,341.5	131.6	
St. Joseph, MO M.S.A.	103,907												
(Includes Andrew and Buchanan Counties.)													
City of St. Joseph	75,013	4,738		193	4,545	0	20	67	106	689	3,652	204	
Total area actually reporting	99.7%	5,222		222	5,000	0	22	69	131	787	3,976	237	
Estimated total	100.0%	5,233		223	5,010	0	22	69	132	788	3,984	238	
Rate per 100,000 inhabitants		5,036.2		214.6	4,821.6	0.0	21.2	66.4	127.0	758.4	3,834.2	229.1	
Stockton-Lodi, CA M.S.A.	584,304												
(Includes San Joaquin County.)													
City of:													
Stockton	252,727	21,114		3,693	17,421	36	141	1,171	2,345	2,965	11,003	3,453	
Lodi	59,093	3,293		288	3,005	4	6	75	203	436	2,083	486	
Total area actually reporting	100.0%	37,878		5,475	32,403	59	211	1,540	3,665	6,110	20,329	5,964	
Rate per 100,000 inhabitants		6,482.6		937.0	5,545.6	10.1	36.1	263.6	627.2	1,045.7	3,479.2	1,020.7	
Sumter, SC M.S.A.	107,128												
(Includes Sumter County.)													
City of Sumter	40,583	3,592		528	3,064	4	20	120	384	671	2,095	298	
Total area actually reporting	99.0%	6,584		1,082	5,502	9	46	205	822	1,509	3,408	585	
Estimated total	100.0%	6,642		1,088	5,554	9	46	206	827	1,518	3,448	588	
Rate per 100,000 inhabitants		6,200.1		1,015.6	5,184.5	8.4	42.9	192.3	772.0	1,417.0	3,218.6	548.9	
Syracuse, NY M.S.A.	739,104												
(Includes Cayuga, Madison, Onondaga, and Oswego Counties.)													
City of:													
Syracuse	148,712	9,791		1,519	8,272	23	43	551	902	1,930	5,060	1,282	
Auburn	28,846	1,147		70	1,077	1	14	14	41	196	861	20	
Total area actually reporting	98.3%	23,530		2,382	21,148	33	140	728	1,481	4,374	15,090	1,684	
Estimated total	100.0%	23,825		2,407	21,418	33	141	736	1,497	4,413	15,303	1,702	
Rate per 100,000 inhabitants		3,223.5		325.7	2,897.8	4.5	19.1	99.6	202.5	597.1	2,070.5	230.3	
Tacoma, WA M.S.A.	721,613												
(Includes Pierce County.)													
City of Tacoma	199,299	20,182		2,182	18,000	19	171	715	1,277	3,032	11,728	3,240	
Total area actually reporting	99.0%	44,237		3,997	40,240	29	402	1,097	2,469	7,525	26,360	6,355	
Estimated total	100.0%	44,610		4,016	40,594	29	405	1,103	2,479	7,580	26,603	6,411	
Rate per 100,000 inhabitants		6,182.0		556.5	5,625.5	4.0	56.1	152.9	343.5	1,050.4	3,686.6	888.4	
Tallahassee, FL M.S.A.	297,549												
(Includes Gadsden and Leon Counties.)													
City of Tallahassee	157,511	11,880		1,617	10,263	9	151	384	1,073	2,262	7,188	813	
Total area actually reporting	100.0%	17,508		2,452	15,056	14	230	526	1,682	3,784	10,165	1,107	
Rate per 100,000 inhabitants		5,884.1		824.1	5,060.0	4.7	77.3	176.8	565.3	1,271.7	3,416.2	372.0	
Tampa-St. Petersburg-Clearwater, FL M.S.A.	2,505,551												
(Includes Hernando, Hillsborough, Pasco, and Pinellas Counties.)													
City of:													
Tampa	317,322	35,380		6,289	29,091	37	204	2,334	3,714	6,283	16,088	6,720	
St. Petersburg	259,582	20,914		4,423	16,491	23	124	1,027	3,249	3,628	10,550	2,313	
Clearwater	113,761	6,544		1,123	5,421	7	51	270	795	1,181	3,799	441	
Total area actually reporting	100.0%	147,810		22,255	125,555	134	1,135	5,638	15,348	28,455	80,175	16,925	
Rate per 100,000 inhabitants		5,899.3		888.2	5,011.1	5.3	45.3	225.0	612.6	1,135.7	3,199.9	675.5	
Texarkana, TX-Texarkana, AR M.S.A.	134,279												
(Includes Bowie County, TX and Miller County, AR.)													
City of:													
Texarkana, TX	36.330	2,983		361	2.622	5	31	97	228	602	1,863	157	
Texarkana, AR	26,811	1,916		183	1,733	2	10	35	136	285	1,349	99	
Total area actually reporting	100.0%	6,508		732	5,776	8	50	151	523	1,254	4,146	376	
Rate per 100,000 inhabitants		4,846.6		545.1	4,301.5	6.0	37.2	112.5	389.5	933.9	3,087.6	280.0	

See footnotes at end of table.

Table 6

Index of Crime

by Metropolitan Statistical Area, 2002—Continued

Metropolitan Statistical Area	Population	Crime Index	Modified Crime Index[1]	Violent crime[2]	Property crime[2]	Murder and non-negligent man-slaughter	Forcible rape	Robbery	Aggravated assault	Burglary	Larceny-theft	Motor vehicle theft	Arson[1]
Toledo, OH M.S.A.[3]	**621,914**												
(Includes Fulton, Lucas, and Wood Counties.)													
City of:													
Toledo[3]	315,501	26,717		3,183	23,534	28	185	1,378	1,592	5,811	14,510	3,213	
Bowling Green	29,814	1,102		44	1,058	0	6	13	25	185	829	44	
Total area actually reporting	91.3%	36,344		3,527	32,817	31	231	1,490	1,775	7,291	21,793	3,733	
Estimated total	100.0%	37,569		3,590	33,979	32	244	1,512	1,802	7,575	22,580	3,824	
Rate per 100,000 inhabitants		6,040.9		577.3	5,463.6	5.1	39.2	243.1	289.8	1,218.0	3,630.7	614.9	
Topeka, KS M.S.A.[3]	**171,606**												
(Includes Shawnee County.)													
City of Topeka[3]	123,627	11,294		989	10,305	8	73	409	499	1,767	7,863	675	
Total area actually reporting	99.2%	12,572		1,108	11,464	8	82	429	589	2,073	8,652	739	
Estimated total	100.0%	12,621		1,110	11,511	8	82	429	591	2,080	8,688	743	
Rate per 100,000 inhabitants		7,354.6		646.8	6,707.8	4.7	47.8	250.0	344.4	1,212.1	5,062.8	433.0	
Trenton, NJ M.S.A.	**358,096**												
(Includes Mercer County.)													
City of Trenton	87,189	6,199		1,531	4,668	19	67	706	739	1,173	2,400	1,095	
Total area actually reporting	100.0%	13,255		1,951	11,304	21	101	895	934	2,375	7,162	1,767	
Rate per 100,000 inhabitants		3,701.5		544.8	3,156.7	5.9	28.2	249.9	260.8	663.2	2,000.0	493.4	
Tucson, AZ M.S.A.	**897,329**												
(Includes Pima County.)													
City of Tucson	517,607	50,171		4,709	45,462	47	338	1,350	2,974	6,717	32,539	6,206	
Total area actually reporting	100.0%	67,685		5,668	62,017	73	437	1,557	3,601	9,491	43,822	8,704	
Rate per 100,000 inhabitants		7,542.9		631.7	6,911.3	8.1	48.7	173.5	401.3	1,057.7	4,883.6	970.0	
Tulsa, OK M.S.A.	**813,257**												
(Includes Creek, Osage, Rogers, Tulsa, and Wagoner Counties.)													
City of Tulsa	397,953	30,119		4,323	25,796	26	243	901	3,153	6,313	15,918	3,565	
Total area actually reporting	100.0%	41,749		5,458	36,291	41	362	1,015	4,040	8,773	22,983	4,535	
Rate per 100,000 inhabitants		5,133.6		671.1	4,462.4	5.0	44.5	124.8	496.8	1,078.7	2,826.0	557.6	
Tuscaloosa, AL M.S.A.	**166,336**												
(Includes Tuscaloosa County.)													
City of Tuscaloosa	78,596	5,774		469	5,305	5	49	185	230	1,012	4,036	257	
Total area actually reporting	100.0%	9,330		874	8,456	9	84	246	535	1,867	6,012	577	
Rate per 100,000 inhabitants		5,609.1		525.4	5,083.7	5.4	50.5	147.9	321.6	1,122.4	3,614.4	346.9	
Tyler, TX M.S.A.	**182,482**												
(Includes Smith County.)													
City of Tyler	87,373	6,614		644	5,970	4	58	140	442	1,008	4,512	450	
Total area actually reporting	98.9%	9,062		914	8,148	8	127	179	600	1,864	5,682	602	
Estimated total	100.0%	9,153		921	8,232	8	128	181	604	1,880	5,744	608	
Rate per 100,000 inhabitants		5,015.8		504.7	4,511.1	4.4	70.1	99.2	331.0	1,030.2	3,147.7	333.2	
Utica-Rome, NY M.S.A.	**302,757**												
(Includes Herkimer and Oneida Counties.)													
City of:													
Utica	61,230	3,168		365	2,803	5	21	190	149	790	1,866	147	
Rome	35,284	770		63	707	1	8	28	26	200	472	35	
Total area actually reporting	86.3%	8,215		917	7,298	7	85	256	569	1,748	5,276	274	
Estimated total	100.0%	9,048		993	8,055	8	91	275	619	1,875	5,854	326	
Rate per 100,000 inhabitants		2,988.5		328.0	2,660.5	2.6	30.1	90.8	204.5	619.3	1,933.6	107.7	
Vallejo-Fairfield-Napa, CA M.S.A.	**537,881**												
(Includes Napa and Solano Counties.)													
City of:													
Vallejo	121,049	7,117		1,082	6,035	7	45	326	704	1,194	3,768	1,073	
Fairfield	99,711	5,353		578	4,775	6	28	213	331	678	3,426	671	
Napa	75,252	2,326		258	2,068	0	22	32	204	285	1,587	196	
Total area actually reporting	100.0%	21,527		2,575	18,952	18	154	705	1,698	3,321	12,836	2,795	
Rate per 100,000 inhabitants		4,002.2		478.7	3,523.5	3.3	28.6	131.1	315.7	617.4	2,386.4	519.6	
Ventura, CA M.S.A.	**780,869**												
(Includes Ventura County.)													
City of Ventura	104,623	3,648		286	3,362	2	30	90	164	621	2,478	263	
Total area actually reporting	100.0%	17,694		2,021	15,673	21	131	632	1,237	3,267	10,854	1,552	
Rate per 100,000 inhabitants		2,265.9		258.8	2,007.1	2.7	16.8	80.9	158.4	418.4	1,390.0	198.8	
Victoria, TX M.S.A.	**87,831**												
(Includes Victoria County.)													
City of Victoria	63,300	3,890		478	3,412	9	44	108	317	645	2,602	165	
Total area actually reporting	100.0%	4,583		588	3,995	15	59	115	399	825	2,985	185	
Rate per 100,000 inhabitants		5,218.0		669.5	4,548.5	17.1	67.2	130.9	454.3	939.3	3,398.6	210.6	

See footnotes at end of table.

Table 6

Index of Crime
by Metropolitan Statistical Area, 2002—Continued

Metropolitan Statistical Area	Population	Crime Index	Modified Crime Index[1]	Violent crime[2]	Property crime[2]	Murder and non-negligent man-slaughter	Forcible rape	Robbery	Aggravated assault	Burglary	Larceny-theft	Motor vehicle theft	Arson[1]
Vineland-Millville-Bridgeton, NJ M.S.A.	**149,500**												
(Includes Cumberland County.)													
City of:													
Vineland	57,448	3,733		453	3,280	4	8	221	220	809	2,265	206	
Millville	27,409	1,590		180	1,410	0	15	61	104	386	951	73	
Bridgeton	23,247	1,297		304	993	3	12	103	186	268	643	82	
Total area actually reporting	100.0%	7,547		1,034	6,513	8	38	404	584	1,761	4,305	447	
Rate per 100,000 inhabitants		5,048.2		691.6	4,356.5	5.4	25.4	270.2	390.6	1,177.9	2,879.6	299.0	
Visalia-Tulare-Porterville, CA M.S.A.[3]	**381,542**												
(Includes Tulare County.)													
City of:													
Visalia	94,929	6,309		862	5,447	12	46	130	674	1,094	3,521	832	
Tulare	45,611	3,022		486	2,536	2	20	57	407	1,041	1,257	238	
Porterville	41,070	1,817		175	1,642	1	15	46	113	350	979	313	
Total area actually reporting	100.0%	18,592		2,512	16,080	29	145	350	1,988	4,318	9,279	2,483	
Rate per 100,000 inhabitants		4,872.9		658.4	4,214.5	7.6	38.0	91.7	521.0	1,131.7	2,432.0	650.8	
Waco, TX M.S.A.	**223,020**												
(Includes McLennan County.)													
City of Waco	118,788	11,001		945	10,056	14	58	277	596	2,197	7,143	716	
Total area actually reporting	100.0%	14,878		1,294	13,584	15	103	311	865	3,044	9,664	876	
Rate per 100,000 inhabitants		6,671.2		580.2	6,090.9	6.7	46.2	139.4	387.9	1,364.9	4,333.2	392.8	
Washington, D.C.-MD-VA-WV M.S.A.	**5,050,449**												
(Includes District of Columbia, Calvert, Charles, Frederick, Montgomery, and Prince George's Counties, MD, Alexandria, Fairfax City, Falls Church, Fredericksburg, Manassas, and Manassas Park Cities, and Arlington, Clarke, Culpeper, Fairfax, Fauquier, King George, Loudoun, Prince William, Spotsylvania, Stafford, and Warren Counties, VA, and Berkeley and Jefferson Counties, WV.)													
City of:													
Washington, D.C.	570,898	44,349		9,111	35,238	264	262	3,731	4,854	5,167	20,903	9,168	
Frederick, MD	54,378	2,710		656	2,054	3	24	125	504	321	1,604	129	
Fredericksburg, VA	19,865	979		143	836	0	7	47	89	70	680	86	
Total area actually reporting	99.4%	203,156		25,413	177,743	474	1,146	10,217	13,576	25,162	118,381	34,200	
Estimated total	100.0%	204,399		25,531	178,868	475	1,155	10,247	13,654	25,312	119,261	34,295	
Rate per 100,000 inhabitants		4,047.1		505.5	3,541.6	9.4	22.9	202.9	270.4	501.2	2,361.4	679.0	
Waterbury, CT M.S.A.	**192,142**												
(Includes part of Litchfield and New Haven Counties.)													
City of Waterbury	109,002	6,524		583	5,941	4	48	283	248	1,246	3,926	769	
Total area actually reporting	100.0%	7,958		641	7,317	5	58	300	278	1,475	4,991	851	
Rate per 100,000 inhabitants		4,141.7		333.6	3,808.1	2.6	30.2	156.1	144.7	767.7	2,597.6	442.9	
Waterloo-Cedar Falls, IA M.S.A.	**128,469**												
(Includes Black Hawk County.)													
City of:													
Waterloo	68,993	4,245		326	3,919	1	37	91	197	1,064	2,604	251	
Cedar Falls	36,274	1,149		111	1,038	0	11	7	93	129	860	49	
Total area actually reporting	100.0%	6,124		465	5,659	1	64	100	300	1,428	3,904	327	
Rate per 100,000 inhabitants		4,766.9		362.0	4,405.0	0.8	49.8	77.8	233.5	1,111.6	3,038.9	254.5	
Wausau, WI M.S.A.	**127,653**												
(Includes Marathon County.)													
City of Wausau	38,982	1,532		89	1,443	0	23	17	49	253	1,106	84	
Total area actually reporting	100.0%	2,767		141	2,626	0	26	23	92	472	2,036	118	
Rate per 100,000 inhabitants		2,167.6		110.5	2,057.1	0.0	20.4	18.0	72.1	369.8	1,594.9	92.4	
West Palm Beach-Boca Raton, FL M.S.A.	**1,182,905**												
(Includes Palm Beach County.)													
City of:													
West Palm Beach	85,857	10,603		1,190	9,413	7	56	497	630	1,729	6,525	1,159	
Boca Raton	78,183	2,890		205	2,685	2	11	63	129	545	1,927	213	
Total area actually reporting	100.0%	75,037		8,833	66,204	36	471	2,513	5,813	15,095	43,302	7,807	
Rate per 100,000 inhabitants		6,343.5		746.7	5,596.7	3.0	39.8	212.4	491.4	1,276.1	3,660.6	660.0	

See footnotes at end of table.

Table 6

Index of Crime
by Metropolitan Statistical Area, 2002—Continued

Metropolitan Statistical Area	Population	Crime Index	Modified Crime Index[1]	Violent crime[2]	Property crime[2]	Murder and non-negligent man-slaughter	Forcible rape	Robbery	Aggravated assault	Burglary	Larceny-theft	Motor vehicle theft	Arson[1]
Wichita, KS M.S.A.	**550,790**												
(Includes Butler, Harvey, and Sedgwick Counties.)													
City of Wichita	347,801	24,104		2,368	21,736	20	208	796	1,344	4,459	15,523	1,754	
Total area actually reporting	97.1%	29,490		2,845	26,645	26	272	844	1,703	5,531	19,083	2,031	
Estimated total	100.0%	30,064		2,881	27,183	26	276	849	1,730	5,609	19,499	2,075	
Rate per 100,000 inhabitants		5,458.3		523.1	4,935.3	4.7	50.1	154.1	314.1	1,018.4	3,540.2	376.7	
Wichita Falls, TX M.S.A.	**146,772**												
(Includes Archer and Wichita Counties.)													
City of Wichita Falls	108,834	8,532		998	7,534	11	31	246	710	1,726	5,327	481	
Total area actually reporting	100.0%	9,346		1,079	8,267	11	41	256	771	1,953	5,764	550	
Rate per 100,000 inhabitants		6,367.7		735.2	5,632.5	7.5	27.9	174.4	525.3	1,330.6	3,927.2	374.7	
Williamsport, PA M.S.A.	**120,573**												
(Includes Lycoming County.)													
City of Williamsport	30,841	1,473		128	1,345	1	10	66	51	221	1,061	63	
Total area actually reporting	93.1%	2,789		207	2,582	2	25	83	97	536	1,915	131	
Estimated total	100.0%	2,985		225	2,760	2	26	88	109	562	2,054	144	
Rate per 100,000 inhabitants		2,475.7		186.6	2,289.1	1.7	21.6	73.0	90.4	466.1	1,703.5	119.4	
Wilmington, NC M.S.A.	**241,305**												
(Includes Brunswick and New Hanover Counties.)													
City of Wilmington	78,389	8,811		998	7,813	10	51	357	580	1,851	5,215	747	
Total area actually reporting	98.9%	15,703		1,332	14,371	12	89	439	792	4,290	8,978	1,103	
Estimated total	100.0%	15,863		1,343	14,520	12	90	442	799	4,321	9,089	1,110	
Rate per 100,000 inhabitants		6,573.8		556.6	6,017.3	5.0	37.3	183.2	331.1	1,790.7	3,766.6	460.0	
Yakima, WA M.S.A.	**229,185**												
(Includes Yakima County.)													
City of Yakima	73,977	6,845		353	6,492	4	59	106	184	1,407	4,415	670	
Total area actually reporting	100.0%	14,319		621	13,698	10	121	175	315	3,487	8,847	1,364	
Rate per 100,000 inhabitants		6,247.8		271.0	5,976.8	4.4	52.8	76.4	137.4	1,521.5	3,860.2	595.2	
Yolo, CA M.S.A.	**174,856**												
(Includes Yolo County.)													
City of:													
Davis	62,524	1,864		128	1,736	0	16	31	81	331	1,155	250	
Woodland	50,957	1,512		209	1,303	2	13	37	157	364	705	234	
Total area actually reporting	100.0%	6,853		838	6,015	5	62	167	604	1,452	3,543	1,020	
Rate per 100,000 inhabitants		3,919.2		479.3	3,440.0	2.9	35.5	95.5	345.4	830.4	2,026.2	583.3	
Yuba City, CA M.S.A.	**144,261**												
(Includes Sutter and Yuba Counties.)													
City of Yuba City	38,109	2,296		180	2,116	4	26	33	117	409	1,454	253	
Total area actually reporting	100.0%	6,357		686	5,671	7	65	94	520	1,451	3,334	886	
Rate per 100,000 inhabitants		4,406.6		475.5	3,931.1	4.9	45.1	65.2	360.5	1,005.8	2,311.1	614.2	
Yuma, AZ M.S.A.[3]	**170,189**												
(Includes Yuma County.)													
City of Yuma[3]	82,437				3,186	2	32	42		598	2,199	389	
Total area actually reporting	90.4%				4,699	2	34	55		1,111	3,022	566	
Estimated total	100.0%				5,629	3	38	69		1,305	3,614	710	
Rate per 100,000 inhabitants					3,307.5	1.8	22.3	40.5		766.8	2,123.5	417.2	
Aguadilla, Puerto Rico M.S.A.	**149,166**												
Total area actually reporting	100.0%	2,561		286	2,275	11	12	169	94	767	1,403	105	
Rate per 100,000 inhabitants		1,716.9		191.7	1,525.1	7.4	8.0	113.3	63.0	514.2	940.6	70.4	
Arecibo, Puerto Rico M.S.A.	**177,293**												
Total area actually reporting	100.0%	3,402		283	3,119	6	1	186	90	1,047	1,620	452	
Rate per 100,000 inhabitants		1,918.9		159.6	1,759.2	3.4	0.6	104.9	50.8	590.5	913.7	254.9	
Caguas, Puerto Rico M.S.A.	**313,101**												
Total area actually reporting	100.0%	6,002		1,124	4,878	56	20	811	237	1,977	1,862	1,039	
Rate per 100,000 inhabitants		1,917.0		359.0	1,558.0	17.9	6.4	259.0	75.7	631.4	594.7	331.8	
Mayaguez, Puerto Rico M.S.A.	**256,318**												
Total area actually reporting	100.0%	4,973		439	4,534	14	16	266	143	1,364	2,962	208	
Rate per 100,000 inhabitants		1,940.2		171.3	1,768.9	5.5	6.2	103.8	55.8	532.2	1,155.6	81.1	
Ponce, Puerto Rico M.S.A.	**364,849**												
Total area actually reporting	100.0%	6,867		929	5,938	83	25	525	296	1,588	3,803	547	
Rate per 100,000 inhabitants		1,882.1		254.6	1,627.5	22.7	6.9	143.9	81.1	435.2	1,042.3	149.9	
San Juan-Bayamon, Puerto Rico M.S.A.	**1,991,772**												
Total area actually reporting	100.0%	55,813		8,936	46,877	528	133	6,227	2,048	13,603	23,601	9,673	
Rate per 100,000 inhabitants		2,802.2		448.6	2,353.5	26.5	6.7	312.6	102.8	683.0	1,184.9	485.6	

[1] Although arson data are included in the trend and clearance tables, sufficient data are not available to estimate totals for this offense.

[2] Violent crimes are offenses of murder, forcible rape, robbery, and aggravated assault. Property crimes are offenses of burglary, larceny-theft, and motor vehicle theft.

[3] Due to changes in reporting practices, annexations, and/or incomplete data, figures are not comparable to previous years' data.

[4] The population for the city of Mobile, Alabama, includes 55,864 inhabitants from the jurisdiction of the Mobile County Sheriff's Department.

Table 7

Offense Analysis[1]
United States, 1998-2002

Classification	1998	1999	2000	2001[2]	2002
Murder	16,974	15,522	15,586	16,037	16,204
Forcible rape	93,144	89,411	90,178	90,863	95,136
Robbery:					
Total	**447,186**	**409,371**	**408,016**	**423,557**	**420,637**
Street/highway	219,689	197,770	187,688	187,571	179,985
Commercial house	61,232	55,678	56,714	61,152	61,288
Gas or service station	9,861	8,844	11,832	12,084	11,249
Convenience store	25,972	24,712	26,113	27,783	27,172
Residence	54,497	49,793	49,778	53,268	56,700
Bank	8,640	8,021	8,568	10,262	9,689
Miscellaneous	67,295	64,552	67,323	71,436	74,554
Burglary:					
Total	**2,332,735**	**2,100,739**	**2,050,992**	**2,116,531**	**2,151,875**
Residence (dwelling):	1,563,086	1,394,868	1,337,247	1,380,472	1,415,971
Night	448,988	402,548	399,943	410,071	418,215
Day	668,619	612,429	617,349	642,264	673,976
Unknown	445,479	379,891	319,955	328,137	323,780
Nonresidence (store, office, etc.):	769,649	705,871	713,745	736,059	735,904
Night	328,218	296,303	299,445	310,596	312,607
Day	190,412	186,166	219,456	224,538	228,764
Unknown	251,018	223,402	194,844	200,925	194,533
Larceny-theft (except motor vehicle theft):					
Total	**7,376,311**	**6,955,520**	**6,971,590**	**7,092,267**	**7,052,922**
By type:					
Pocket-picking	44,315	43,035	34,858	33,346	32,431
Purse-snatching	42,484	40,377	34,858	38,550	38,872
Shoplifting	1,094,412	1,002,576	962,079	978,802	985,673
From motor vehicles (except accessories)	1,936,742	1,788,630	1,756,841	1,832,934	1,865,743
Motor vehicle accessories	738,231	723,720	676,244	723,419	755,772
Bicycles	375,348	325,683	313,722	291,203	276,828
From buildings	990,467	946,419	913,278	943,631	883,289
From coin-operated machines	44,129	46,479	48,801	52,039	52,341
All others	2,110,183	2,038,602	2,230,909	2,198,344	2,161,973
By value:					
Over $200	2,886,866	2,692,746	2,711,949	2,792,231	2,794,699
$50 to $200	1,715,250	1,609,400	1,631,352	1,630,567	1,591,824
Under $50	2,774,195	2,653,374	2,628,289	2,669,469	2,666,399
Motor vehicle theft	1,242,781	1,152,075	1,160,002	1,228,391	1,246,096

[1] The murder and nonnegligent homicides that occurred as a result of the events of September 11, 2001, were not included in this table.
[2] The 2001 crime figures have been adjusted.

Table 8

Offenses Known to Law Enforcement
by City 10,000 and over in Population, 2002

City by state	Population	Crime Index	Modified Crime Index[1]	Murder and non-negligent man-slaughter	Forcible rape	Robbery	Aggravated assault	Burglary	Larceny-theft	Motor vehicle theft	Arson[1]
ALABAMA											
Alabaster	22,819	142		1	0	10	12	15	90	14	
Albertville	17,400	973		0	9	6	55	293	565	45	
Alexander City	15,141	987		2	8	23	81	129	724	20	
Anniston	24,491	3,617	3,635	7	35	164	366	900	1,995	150	18
Athens	19,135	761		2	1	10	10	119	584	35	
Auburn	43,368	2,282		2	17	48	99	516	1,506	94	
Birmingham	244,972	21,265	21,476	65	239	1,186	1,697	4,389	11,640	2,049	211
Cullman	14,119	907		0	3	2	10	150	698	44	
Daphne	16,728	456		2	3	7	14	58	343	29	
Decatur	54,407	3,810		4	17	105	91	773	2,706	114	
Dothan	58,248	3,072		1	40	90	81	568	2,152	140	
Enterprise	21,366	909		1	9	20	43	’151	631	54	
Eufaula	14,031	614		1	6	18	23	80	452	34	
Fairfield	12,491	1,730		0	6	68	52	209	1,155	240	
Florence	36,585	1,869	1,882	1	16	33	123	327	1,327	42	13
Fort Payne	13,052	581		0	5	4	41	79	450	2	
Gadsden	39,323	3,934		4	31	97	584	741	2,170	307	
Gardendale	11,729	475		0	1	3	12	67	374	18	
Hartselle	12,126	361		0	2	2	2	55	295	5	
Homewood	25,265	1,560		1	9	61	32	229	1,150	78	
Hoover	63,298	1,916		1	19	82	105	254	1,309	146	
Hueytown	15,500	481		0	5	27	21	92	292	44	
Huntsville	159,618	10,167	10,212	5	82	315	559	1,714	6,718	774	45
Leeds	10,547	465		0	6	18	11	76	332	22	
Madison	29,589	930		2	6	21	27	192	635	47	
Mobile[2]	256,542	17,949		40	107	752	477	3,590	11,534	1,449	
Montgomery	203,355	17,617		30	118	698	629	3,812	10,640	1,690	
Mountain Brook	20,787	384		0	0	2	5	65	305	7	
Muscle Shoals	12,029	591		0	1	2	25	113	442	8	
Northport	19,607	897		2	9	20	66	140	617	43	
Opelika	23,706	2,063		2	29	70	256	422	1,276	8	
Oxford	14,722	1,317		0	2	33	49	173	939	121	
Pelham	14,496	398	399	0	0	7	2	37	327	25	1
Phenix City	28,516	1,156		0	5	39	81	279	638	114	
Prattville	24,518	1,393		0	19	36	50	176	1,062	50	
Prichard	28,886	2,925		7	19	180	279	771	1,279	390	
Scottsboro	14,892	541		0	2	2	13	108	391	25	
Selma	20,694	3,158		2	33	97	237	840	1,737	212	
Talladega	15,277	1,439		1	12	34	23	243	1,052	74	
Troy	14,058	970		0	1	23	41	167	701	37	
Trussville	13,038	733		0	1	20	20	73	592	27	
Tuscaloosa	78,596	5,774	5,791	5	49	185	230	1,012	4,036	257	17
Tuskegee	11,951	1,343		1	9	30	43	353	839	68	
Vestavia Hills	24,693	323		0	2	4	16	61	214	26	
ALASKA											
Anchorage	267,280	13,670	13,811	18	254	382	1,067	1,521	9,255	1,173	141
Fairbanks	31,037	1,606	1,611	3	37	33	211	226	964	132	5
ARIZONA											
Apache Junction	33,834	1,908	1,913	0	4	20	84	514	1,082	204	5
Camp Verde	10,051	380	380	1	2	4	27	61	263	22	0
Casa Grande	26,826	2,173		2	0	15	241	582	1,158	175	
Chandler	187,795	11,204	11,267	3	46	149	321	1,893	7,447	1,345	63
Flagstaff	56,253	5,597	5,613	1	48	62	424	720	4,042	300	16
Gilbert	116,663	5,284	5,330	5	23	44	112	1,378	3,249	473	46
Glendale	232,707	15,475	15,566	17	65	405	866	2,438	7,889	3,795	91
Goodyear	20,112	1,239	1,241	1	8	14	55	524	429	208	2
Kingman	21,344	1,975	1,979	1	13	15	55	409	1,347	135	4
Lake Havasu City	44,601	1,819	1,832	1	1	2	78	323	1,272	142	13
Marana	14,417	1,214	1,219	0	4	17	9	134	913	137	5
Mesa[3]	421,547	33,335	33,402	22	129	590	2,146	4,957	20,405	5,086	67
Nogales	22,204	921	922	0	1	11	63	152	575	119	1

See footnotes at end of table.

Table 8

Offenses Known to Law Enforcement
by City 10,000 and over in Population, 2002—Continued

City by state	Population	Crime Index	Modified Crime Index[1]	Murder and non-negligent man-slaughter	Forcible rape	Robbery	Aggravated assault	Burglary	Larceny-theft	Motor vehicle theft	Arson[1]
ARIZONA—Continued											
Oro Valley	31,586	523	525	0	2	3	16	52	413	37	2
Paradise Valley	14,532	546	546	0	0	1	5	346	155	39	0
Payson	14,485	531	539	1	3	1	29	75	405	17	8
Peoria	115,245	5,877	5,892	0	34	64	184	955	3,439	1,201	15
Phoenix	1,404,938	109,916	110,417	177	410	4,075	5,561	16,855	57,214	25,624	501
Prescott	36,093	2,034	2,049	2	7	19	113	339	1,391	163	15
Prescott Valley	25,030	976	983	0	2	2	81	131	690	70	7
Scottsdale	215,578	10,134	10,185	1	63	171	248	2,786	5,487	1,378	51
Sierra Vista	40,174	1,660	1,672	1	6	15	101	187	1,248	102	12
Surprise	32,807	1,220	1,226	1	1	13	60	245	750	150	6
Tempe	168,699	17,819	17,860	10	75	344	811	2,360	11,004	3,215	41
Tucson	517,607	50,171	50,499	47	338	1,350	2,974	6,717	32,539	6,206	328
Winslow	10,124	652	662	0	7	4	60	72	490	19	10
Yuma[1]	82,437			2	32	42		598	2,199	389	30
ARKANSAS											
Benton	22,207	1,565	1,571	1	8	13	79	376	1,027	61	6
Bentonville	20,001	881	883	0	15	2	25	272	542	25	2
Blytheville	18,523	1,969	1,976	3	9	49	256	382	1,194	76	7
Cabot	15,471	1,020	1,022	0	1	1	39	88	871	20	2
Conway	43,759	2,463	2,467	4	23	20	43	269	2,046	58	4
El Dorado	21,826	1,517	1,519	1	9	41	125	439	791	111	2
Fayetteville	58,843	3,027	3,042	0	42	31	149	355	2,352	98	15
Fort Smith	81,369	7,498	7,531	8	52	152	502	1,183	5,296	305	33
Harrison	12,319	528	529	0	5	4	12	70	412	25	1
Jacksonville	30,326	1,731	1,732	0	7	34	99	328	1,194	69	1
Jonesboro	56,276	3,252	3,256	2	8	72	179	507	2,324	160	4
Little Rock	185,646	20,680	20,828	41	116	884	1,370	4,826	11,930	1,513	148
Magnolia	11,007	677	680	0	4	17	167	106	365	18	3
Maumelle	10,702	171	171	0	2	3	8	57	88	13	0
Mountain Home	11,163	249	249	0	0	0	4	15	226	4	0
North Little Rock	61,262	5,840	5,855	6	47	179	288	657	4,207	456	15
Pine Bluff	55,841	5,286	5,337	10	47	230	463	1,012	3,116	408	51
Russellville	24,007	1,302	1,302	0	8	6	153	165	916	54	0
Searcy	19,188	1,049	1,050	0	2	7	11	83	897	49	1
Siloam Springs	10,991	455	456	0	1	1	21	41	377	14	1
Springdale	46,426	2,197	2,213	1	24	175	116	362	1,447	72	16
Texarkana	26,811	1,916	1,928	2	10	35	136	285	1,349	99	12
Van Buren	19,246	754	756	0	6	4	28	105	575	36	2
CALIFORNIA											
Adelanto	18,796	623	632	1	4	15	87	223	197	96	9
Agoura Hills	21,292	356	358	0	6	11	18	114	171	36	2
Alameda	74,914	2,928	2,949	2	9	90	198	408	1,884	337	21
Albany	17,048	831	834	0	3	41	4	154	496	133	3
Alhambra	88,956	2,594	2,611	2	11	142	73	502	1,334	530	17
Aliso Viejo	41,641	624	628	0	3	8	35	100	444	34	4
American Canyon	10,133	312	314	0	0	8	9	86	166	43	2
Anaheim	340,065	12,198	12,248	17	80	465	827	1,995	6,945	1,869	50
Antioch	93,858	3,418	3,473	1	23	187	473	553	1,365	816	55
Apple Valley	56,232	2,241	2,259	4	13	69	162	593	1,162	238	18
Arcadia	55,004	1,622	1,628	2	6	69	73	382	947	143	6
Arcata	17,262	809	818	2	3	20	22	143	584	35	9
Arroyo Grande	16,433	411	413	0	4	5	14	63	302	23	2
Artesia	16,981	583	592	4	6	46	71	119	232	105	9
Arvin	13,432	515	537	1	19	23	35	129	264	44	22
Atascadero	27,381	922	931	1	13	14	61	185	592	56	9
Atwater	23,962	1,156	1,165	0	4	17	140	376	513	106	9
Auburn	12,920	375	377	0	3	7	32	52	253	28	2
Avenal	15,213	190	205	0	3	9	22	75	72	9	15
Azusa	46,355	1,475	1,487	5	15	73	90	320	748	224	12
Bakersfield	256,134	11,846	11,995	22	47	355	647	2,436	6,941	1,398	149
Baldwin Park	78,623	1,908	1,915	6	19	101	174	364	751	493	7

See footnotes at end of table.

Table 8

Offenses Known to Law Enforcement

by City 10,000 and over in Population, 2002—Continued

City by state	Population	Crime Index	Modified Crime Index[1]	Murder and non-negligent man-slaughter	Forcible rape	Robbery	Aggravated assault	Burglary	Larceny-theft	Motor vehicle theft	Arson[1]
CALIFORNIA—Continued											
Banning	24,428	708	708	3	5	19	150	230	191	110	0
Barstow	21,894	1,050	1,052	3	14	57	100	244	479	153	2
Beaumont	11,802	450	453	0	5	14	33	106	229	63	3
Bell	38,011	874	877	2	12	83	148	118	262	249	3
Bellflower	75,555	2,954	2,983	1	18	222	216	542	1,266	689	29
Bell Gardens	45,673	1,243	1,248	4	12	107	196	192	390	342	5
Belmont	26,046	553	553	0	10	10	70	199	224	40	0
Benicia	27,852	552	561	0	4	14	28	139	309	58	9
Berkeley	106,518	10,271	10,319	7	28	407	287	1,514	6,687	1,341	48
Beverly Hills	35,025	1,333	1,335	1	2	80	50	316	822	62	2
Blythe	12,602	849	860	1	7	14	118	206	460	43	11
Brawley	22,862	1,057	1,062	1	1	29	107	232	566	121	5
Brea	36,711	1,532	1,534	0	4	41	27	260	1,058	142	2
Brentwood	24,158	1,046	1,062	0	7	14	61	177	673	114	16
Buena Park	81,158	2,371	2,395	4	20	90	122	441	1,233	461	24
Burbank	104,001	3,216	3,240	1	10	100	162	501	1,851	591	24
Burlingame	29,193	1,010	1,011	2	5	24	50	139	694	96	1
Calabasas	20,769	348	352	0	3	7	33	90	186	29	4
Calexico	28,105	1,110	1,123	1	3	35	31	302	398	340	13
Camarillo	59,174	1,091	1,105	1	12	27	82	152	749	68	14
Campbell	39,540	1,176	1,191	0	19	20	40	208	783	106	15
Canyon Lake	10,317	156	157	0	0	0	12	33	95	16	1
Capitola	10,402	984	985	0	12	17	38	102	787	28	1
Carlsbad	81,122	2,273	2,286	1	16	49	144	426	1,396	241	13
Carpinteria	14,715	236	238	0	3	8	17	48	151	9	2
Carson	93,027	3,446	3,476	13	21	209	502	606	1,392	703	30
Cathedral City	44,214	1,932	1,932	7	7	53	152	495	807	411	0
Ceres	35,881	2,470	2,479	2	5	53	129	435	1,424	422	9
Cerritos	53,380	2,430	2,442	1	3	86	105	398	1,396	441	12
Chico	62,157	2,665	2,738	2	47	75	146	647	1,242	506	73
Chino	69,635	2,464	2,511	1	12	101	210	468	1,244	428	47
Chino Hills	69,241	1,140	1,149	0	3	20	53	207	718	139	9
Chowchilla	11,535	440	461	0	3	5	24	115	249	44	21
Chula Vista	179,932	7,463	7,549	5	50	257	579	1,068	3,733	1,771	86
Claremont	35,248	1,075	1,085	0	3	35	49	282	621	85	10
Clayton	11,158	162	163	0	0	2	0	30	115	15	1
Clearlake	13,625	914	919	2	14	8	45	275	477	93	5
Clovis	70,983	3,242	3,269	0	15	40	62	573	2,111	441	27
Coachella	23,559	1,165	1,173	2	2	44	118	294	506	199	8
Coalinga	12,097	414	415	0	4	4	18	83	281	24	1
Colton	49,413	2,286	2,298	3	15	103	94	490	1,083	498	12
Commerce	13,029	1,289	1,303	7	9	81	96	138	562	396	14
Compton	96,928	4,530	4,666	52	37	482	1,239	738	1,188	794	136
Concord	126,254	5,661	5,665	3	22	143	260	767	3,490	976	4
Corcoran	14,989	405	412	0	4	3	46	114	207	31	7
Corona	129,557	4,430	4,463	8	24	169	148	736	2,551	794	33
Coronado	24,986	403	405	0	7	7	9	101	233	46	2
Costa Mesa	112,718	3,826	3,842	2	14	98	156	511	2,620	425	16
Covina	48,558	2,267	2,273	2	9	78	109	373	1,359	337	6
Cudahy	25,097	671	674	3	7	40	154	91	190	186	3
Culver City	40,242	1,448	1,448	0	3	101	28	183	971	162	0
Cupertino	52,403	1,218	1,226	0	5	25	48	200	904	36	8
Cypress	47,928	1,090	1,098	0	8	29	42	190	705	116	8
Daly City	107,428	2,199	2,210	2	27	113	160	221	1,232	444	11
Dana Point	36,399	687	691	0	4	17	44	106	455	61	4
Danville	43,248	647	650	1	6	5	3	88	515	29	3
Davis	62,524	1,864	1,918	0	16	31	81	331	1,155	250	54
Delano	40,250	2,412	2,456	1	8	51	23	370	1,531	428	44
Desert Hot Springs	17,191	1,581	1,581	2	31	55	175	488	676	154	0
Diamond Bar	58,355	909	911	2	12	41	54	202	488	110	2
Dinuba	17,462	1,052	1,060	0	11	22	109	298	497	115	8
Dixon	16,694	683	690	1	9	7	79	88	420	79	7
Downey	111,266	3,651	3,667	1	17	195	224	556	1,594	1,064	16
Duarte	22,275	598	601	1	2	32	75	126	280	82	3
Dublin	31,074	722	723	0	1	11	31	136	422	121	1

See footnotes at end of table.

Table 8

Offenses Known to Law Enforcement
by City 10,000 and over in Population, 2002—Continued

City by state	Population	Crime Index	Modified Crime Index[1]	Murder and non-negligent man-slaughter	Forcible rape	Robbery	Aggravated assault	Burglary	Larceny-theft	Motor vehicle theft	Arson[1]
CALIFORNIA—Continued											
East Palo Alto	30,590	1,200	1,200	7	16	132	113	236	493	203	0
El Cajon	98,354	4,776	4,812	3	56	125	359	785	2,556	892	36
El Centro	39,225	1,590	1,599	1	14	49	257	564	504	201	9
El Cerrito	24,023	1,716	1,723	0	1	90	41	223	1,026	335	7
El Monte	120,225	3,592	3,605	7	39	265	437	647	1,392	805	13
El Segundo	16,622	609	612	0	5	21	11	133	358	81	3
Encinitas	60,145	1,597	1,604	0	13	42	122	358	873	189	7
Escondido	138,466	5,495	5,516	4	40	165	399	960	3,111	816	21
Eureka	27,088	2,323	2,341	3	25	46	155	419	1,461	214	18
Fairfield	99,711	5,353	5,412	6	28	213	331	678	3,426	671	59
Fillmore	14,145	300	305	0	0	10	59	50	168	13	5
Folsom	53,790	1,685	1,715	0	21	36	74	248	1,182	124	30
Fontana	133,665	4,312	4,349	7	45	274	587	843	1 337	1,219	37
Fortuna	10,883	265	271	0	5	5	9	61	165	20	6
Foster City	29,861	502	506	0	5	7	24	87	341	38	4
Fountain Valley	56,998	1,604	1,616	0	6	33	54	262	1,072	177	12
Fremont	210,886	5,704	5,729	3	32	134	221	1,018	3,686	610	25
Fresno	443,363	33,909	34,616	42	158	1,479	2,101	4,476	18,478	7,175	707
Fullerton	130,632	4,774	4,806	1	33	124	203	778	3,055	580	32
Galt	20,187	774	781	0	6	14	40	126	448	140	7
Gardena	59,868	2,492	2,499	5	15	288	316	526	941	401	7
Garden Grove	171,266	5,430	5,465	6	18	218	550	848	2,875	915	35
Gilroy	42,987	1,754	1,756	0	26	69	219	185	1,083	172	2
Glendale	202,136	4,535	4,585	9	21	186	279	913	2,392	735	50
Glendora	51,230	1,253	1,260	3	14	28	39	221	821	127	7
Grand Terrace	12,053	315	315	0	2	17	8	59	163	66	0
Grass Valley	11,323	632	633	0	4	4	38	103	433	50	1
Greenfield	13,046	273	274	2	6	20	52	39	128	26	1
Grover Beach	13,547	365	368	1	2	7	30	63	235	27	3
Half Moon Bay	12,277	217	217	0	2	3	14	29	156	13	0
Hanford	43,218	1,698	1,706	3	12	33	98	283	1,085	184	8
Hawaiian Gardens	15,322	634	642	0	8	43	65	94	302	122	8
Hawthorne	87,202	3,067	3,077	5	35	307	319	618	1,169	614	10
Hayward	145,174	5,508	5,583	9	42	324	225	791	2,756	1,361	75
Healdsburg	11,116	374	376	0	4	6	15	115	211	23	2
Hemet	60,972	2,794	2,806	1	23	112	111	828	1,368	351	12
Hercules	20,204	620	624	0	2	14	29	82	361	132	4
Hermosa Beach	19,248	758	761	0	3	17	48	143	479	68	3
Hesperia	64,882	2,079	2,089	1	13	50	123	584	980	328	10
Highland	46,244	1,775	1,784	4	14	101	60	376	872	348	9
Hillsborough	11,223	97	97	0	0	2	4	20	69	2	0
Hollister	35,677	1,114	1,119	1	15	26	83	160	692	137	5
Huntington Beach	196,559	4,385	4,418	3	36	84	216	856	2,715	475	33
Huntington Park	63,602	2,963	2,985	6	15	287	170	298	1,178	1,009	22
Imperial Beach	27,984	836	845	0	20	28	114	170	316	188	9
Indio	50,921	2,332	2,333	9	28	117	342	616	663	557	1
Inglewood[1]	116,716	4,107	4,131	28	61	507	329	690	1,522	970	24
Irvine	148,328	3,624	3,640	1	20	62	78	867	2,339	257	16
King City	11,502	644	656	3	5	9	31	201	374	21	12
La Canada Flintridge	21,064	438	439	0	1	9	14	185	207	22	1
Lafayette	24,786	578	581	0	0	14	9	103	394	58	3
Laguna Beach	24,599	692	695	1	2	4	39	146	470	30	3
Laguna Hills	32,324	790	790	0	6	11	38	136	560	39	0
Laguna Niguel	64,165	1,085	1,093	1	4	12	52	176	786	54	8
Laguna Woods	17,113	115	115	0	0	1	3	16	85	10	0
La Habra	61,141	1,824	1,847	0	11	40	106	298	1,114	255	23
Lake Elsinore	29,990	1,406	1,410	6	10	25	196	312	653	204	4
Lake Forest	78,790	1,400	1,424	3	8	36	80	235	921	117	24
Lakewood	82,260	3,112	3,130	1	14	132	191	419	1,836	519	18
La Mesa	56,760	2,357	2,369	2	11	89	105	375	1,410	365	12
La Mirada	48,502	1,040	1,048	1	4	57	94	191	502	191	8
Lancaster	123,079	5,123	5,186	12	57	313	980	1,179	1,893	689	63
La Palma	15,975	332	334	0	2	13	15	86	184	32	2
La Puente	42,572	932	941	6	14	62	147	159	353	191	9
La Quinta	24,565	1,380	1,383	2	3	17	90	349	798	121	3

See footnotes at end of table.

Table 8

Offenses Known to Law Enforcement
by City 10,000 and over in Population, 2002—Continued

City by state	Population	Crime Index	Modified Crime Index[1]	Murder and non-negligent man-slaughter	Forcible rape	Robbery	Aggravated assault	Burglary	Larceny-theft	Motor vehicle theft	Arson[1]
CALIFORNIA—Continued											
La Verne	32,801	770	771	0	7	26	64	146	469	58	1
Lawndale	32,876	975	981	1	8	89	163	274	294	146	6
Lemon Grove	25,833	983	987	0	8	57	89	249	386	194	4
Lemoore	20,436	845	855	0	9	15	57	107	546	111	10
Lincoln	11,617	494	498	0	6	2	35	126	283	42	4
Lindsay	10,676	557	558	1	4	4	95	110	253	90	1
Livermore	76,039	2,209	2,243	3	13	43	89	421	1,379	261	34
Livingston	10,857	396	405	1	9	3	58	106	167	52	9
Lodi	59,093	3,293	3,304	4	6	75	203	436	2,083	486	11
Loma Linda	19,367	823	827	2	1	19	25	150	438	188	4
Lomita	20,782	598	601	0	5	34	76	135	288	60	3
Lompoc	42,613	1,380	1,394	0	23	33	115	211	912	86	14
Long Beach	478,478	19,303	19,556	67	144	1,505	1,910	3,405	8,530	3,742	253
Los Alamitos	11,960	285	288	0	2	6	24	54	159	40	3
Los Altos	28,711	265	267	0	1	10	10	74	164	6	2
Los Angeles	3,830,561	190,992	193,083	654	1,415	17,197	32,429	25,374	79,813	34,110	2,091
Los Banos	26,820	776	776	0	10	11	96	132	460	67	0
Los Gatos	29,642	605	618	0	2	8	34	148	382	31	13
Lynwood	72,411	2,570	2,622	14	30	310	536	371	643	666	52
Madera	44,795	2,605	2,614	5	21	104	345	426	1,320	384	9
Malibu	13,037	335	339	0	0	5	30	90	191	19	4
Manhattan Beach	35,095	1,113	1,118	0	4	34	45	279	644	107	5
Manteca	51,068	2,570	2,589	2	12	63	102	399	1,576	416	19
Marina	26,023	499	501	0	5	26	47	86	320	15	2
Martinez	37,184	1,321	1,324	0	1	20	34	238	821	207	3
Marysville	12,719	851	851	0	14	24	87	133	462	131	0
Maywood	29,114	584	585	1	10	55	66	82	207	163	1
Menlo Park	31,916	742	745	0	8	26	37	128	500	43	3
Merced	66,241	5,080	5,126	6	21	115	356	840	3,175	567	46
Millbrae	21,479	373	382	1	4	23	13	63	229	40	9
Mill Valley	14,100	320	325	1	5	4	15	76	194	25	5
Milpitas	65,001	2,229	2,235	0	16	38	145	280	1,558	192	6
Mission Viejo	96,522	1,670	1,678	1	7	19	89	216	1,241	97	8
Modesto[3]	195,795	12,981	13,027	5	71	344	593	1,819	8,426	1,723	46
Monrovia	38,286	1,079	1,087	0	7	51	82	195	609	135	8
Montclair	34,263	2,139	2,144	1	8	78	152	303	1,180	417	5
Montebello	64,433	2,419	2,456	4	13	126	166	300	1,151	659	37
Monterey	30,764	1,369	1,371	0	15	31	86	255	907	75	2
Monterey Park	62,257	1,739	1,743	1	5	114	59	413	755	392	4
Moorpark	32,569	260	263	0	1	2	15	50	159	33	3
Moraga	16,889	256	257	0	5	2	17	41	179	12	1
Moreno Valley	147,612	6,902	6,937	7	51	278	907	1.446	3,087	1,126	35
Morgan Hill	34,789	1,035	1,061	1	8	18	49	178	705	76	26
Morro Bay	10,731	221	221	0	4	0	20	53	132	12	0
Mountain View	73,305	2,112	2,120	1	5	66	256	221	1.448	115	8
Murrieta	45,909	1,074	1,088	0	2	17	42	304	610	99	14
Napa	75,252	2,326	2,343	0	22	32	204	285	1,587	196	17
National City	56,254	2,736	2,746	4	32	156	358	397	1,100	689	10
Newark	44,031	2,015	2,027	1	9	46	92	247	1,403	217	12
Newport Beach	72,605	2,554	2,570	2	5	26	67	535	1,751	168	16
Norco	25,045	1,010	1,019	0	4	30	69	233	557	117	9
Norwalk	107,093	3,576	3,596	10	22	194	520	639	1,340	851	20
Novato	49,380	1,260	1,273	1	12	24	36	321	734	132	13
Oakdale	16,073	1,178	1,188	0	6	21	27	305	724	95	10
Oakland	414,161	29,875	30,229	108	249	2,452	2,852	4,252	13.703	6,259	354
Oakley	26,560	850	855	1	9	17	57	115	546	105	5
Oceanside	166,945	6,964	7,004	5	75	285	751	1,109	3,824	915	40
Ontario	163,812	8,296	8,404	7	55	391	595	1,139	4,390	1,719	108
Orange	133,554	3,872	3,897	1	17	108	151	628	2,435	532	25
Orinda	18,246	321	321	1	0	3	3	91	202	21	0
Oroville	13,482	1,233	1,248	0	1	47	14	308	690	173	15
Oxnard	176,617	5,373	5,414	10	36	353	449	913	3,034	578	41
Pacifica	39,800	818	819	0	5	15	70	133	498	97	1
Pacific Grove	16,092	325	326	1	7	2	18	91	198	8	1
Palmdale	120,956	5,374	5,456	7	56	245	847	961	2,521	737	82

See footnotes at end of table.

Table 8

Offenses Known to Law Enforcement

by City 10,000 and over in Population, 2002—Continued

City by state	Population	Crime Index	Modified Crime Index[1]	Murder and non-negligent man-slaughter	Forcible rape	Robbery	Aggravated assault	Burglary	Larceny-theft	Motor vehicle theft	Arson[1]
CALIFORNIA—Continued											
Palm Desert	42,667	2,193	2,198	0	9	37	105	536	1,325	181	5
Palm Springs	44,380	3,908	3,928	3	22	112	260	993	2,061	457	20
Palo Alto	60,751	1,778	1,795	1	7	45	54	223	1,353	95	17
Palos Verdes Estates	13,830	119	120	0	0	1	3	43	65	7	1
Paradise	27,378	1,005	1,010	2	3	7	56	265	616	56	5
Paramount	57,296	2,290	2,329	5	18	186	222	321	848	690	39
Parlier	11,555	747	760	2	9	25	57	138	393	123	13
Pasadena	138,857	4,881	4,941	3	25	255	374	959	2,803	462	60
Paso Robles	25,190	978	985	0	11	12	93	321	483	58	7
Patterson	12,033	389	389	0	9	5	5	80	259	31	0
Perris	37,519	1,749	1,761	1	7	56	173	343	757	412	12
Petaluma	56,552	1,607	1,636	2	7	17	52	225	1,209	95	29
Pico Rivera	65,758	1,655	1,671	13	15	93	287	243	615	389	16
Piedmont	11,355	224	225	0	1	7	2	53	115	46	1
Pinole	19,739	1,140	1,148	0	2	50	43	105	665	275	8
Pittsburg	58,854	2,922	2,929	6	14	84	105	417	1,680	616	7
Placentia	48,196	952	956	0	3	25	121	207	503	93	4
Pleasant Hill	34,044	2,102	2,111	0	10	62	80	345	1,384	221	9
Pleasanton	65,993	1,795	1,805	2	8	19	52	192	1,365	157	10
Pomona	154,964	6,132	6,160	18	77	448	805	886	2,681	1,217	28
Porterville	41,070	1,817	1,822	1	15	46	113	350	979	313	5
Port Hueneme	22,648	551	560	1	6	37	37	93	315	62	9
Poway	49,809	971	982	0	5	11	81	243	537	94	11
Rancho Cucamonga	132,436	3,966	4,001	2	29	99	149	744	2,372	571	35
Rancho Mirage	13,736	637	638	0	2	1	18	180	375	61	1
Rancho Palos Verdes	42,656	572	575	0	5	13	54	181	290	29	3
Rancho Santa Margarita	48,949	561	567	0	7	5	21	103	385	40	6
Red Bluff	13,630	703	708	1	8	8	116	101	418	51	5
Redding	83,836	3,389	3,410	0	57	79	290	801	1,788	374	21
Redlands	65,927	2,997	3,011	0	33	87	307	456	1,672	442	14
Redondo Beach	65,585	1,884	1,885	2	9	70	118	436	1,050	199	1
Redwood City	78,172	2,482	2,502	1	25	72	243	307	1,640	194	20
Reedley	21,519	939	947	2	7	22	104	162	534	108	8
Rialto	95,248	3,847	3,871	18	30	256	586	591	1,375	991	24
Richmond	102,861	7,838	7,926	29	38	471	660	1,051	3,534	2,055	88
Ridgecrest	25,842	753	776	0	7	6	73	249	363	55	23
Ripon	10,518	395	396	0	0	2	32	29	286	46	1
Riverbank	16,408	813	818	0	1	5	20	155	528	104	5
Riverside	264,540	15,161	15,399	20	94	616	1,296	2,525	8,140	2,470	238
Rocklin	37,665	1,059	1,064	0	6	4	37	194	694	124	5
Rohnert Park	43,788	1,828	1,836	1	8	21	93	710	819	176	8
Rosemead	55,470	1,518	1,526	2	10	103	173	380	524	326	8
Roseville	82,858	3,821	3,834	0	18	50	147	549	2,634	423	13
Sacramento	421,971	30,780	31,113	47	185	1,734	1,581	5,019	15,548	6,666	333
Salinas	156,609	6,834	6,892	20	59	367	692	757	4,013	926	58
San Anselmo	12,832	236	236	0	2	6	11	61	143	13	0
San Bernardino	192,212	13,755	13,864	42	102	886	1,454	2,340	6,226	2,705	109
San Bruno	41,640	1,221	1,227	5	14	31	46	127	840	158	6
San Carlos	28,736	578	578	0	0	8	22	112	405	31	0
San Clemente	51,770	877	886	1	5	17	44	155	572	83	9
San Diego	1,268,346	50,124	50,330	47	330	1,627	5,189	7,639	24,577	10,715	206
San Dimas	36,265	886	902	0	6	27	68	200	508	77	16
San Fernando	24,430	907	910	0	2	49	74	144	420	218	3
San Francisco	805,269	42,671	42,898	68	210	3,208	2,573	5,947	24,468	6,197	227
San Gabriel	41,266	1,054	1,062	0	3	62	121	241	474	153	8
Sanger	19,626	810	816	2	2	37	77	122	425	145	6
San Jacinto	24,653	714	714	3	13	21	88	274	165	150	0
San Jose	927,821	24,139	24,397	26	379	827	2,902	3,026	13,642	3,337	258
San Juan Capistrano	35,069	596	600	2	3	16	45	88	375	67	4
San Leandro	82,371	4,606	4,626	5	22	227	245	619	2,493	995	20
San Luis Obispo	45,796	2,093	2,128	0	32	19	109	318	1,489	126	35
San Marcos	56,997	1,472	1,478	1	8	46	138	437	643	199	6
San Marino	13,421	173	173	0	0	7	6	57	97	6	0
San Mateo	95,880	2,846	2,870	0	17	98	227	348	1,937	219	24
San Pablo	31,325	2,052	2,059	1	6	116	165	291	864	609	7

See footnotes at end of table.

Table 8

Offenses Known to Law Enforcement
by City 10,000 and over in Population, 2002—Continued

City by state	Population	Crime Index	Modified Crime Index[1]	Murder and non-negligent man-slaughter	Forcible rape	Robbery	Aggravated assault	Burglary	Larceny-theft	Motor vehicle theft	Arson[1]
CALIFORNIA--Continued											
San Rafael	58,122	1,883	1,891	2	10	67	62	313	1,102	327	8
San Ramon	46,365	1,127	1,134	0	1	10	28	146	861	81	7
Santa Ana	350,393	12,038	12,197	23	66	871	970	1,225	6,485	2,398	159
Santa Barbara	95,717	3,072	3,110	3	41	86	388	621	1,786	147	38
Santa Clara	106,121	3,228	3,257	4	19	62	226	417	2,188	312	29
Santa Clarita	156,639	3,195	3,229	6	24	90	185	611	1,844	435	34
Santa Cruz	56,599	3,569	3,596	4	43	97	316	534	2,371	204	27
Santa Fe Springs	18,078	1,386	1,389	1	1	65	73	186	751	309	3
Santa Monica	87,173	4,701	4,749	8	35	299	317	739	2,811	492	48
Santa Paula	29,648	893	901	6	4	32	55	297	426	73	8
Santa Rosa	153,018	6,531	6,574	6	93	167	359	974	4,213	719	43
Santee	54,921	1,380	1,388	0	11	18	109	285	769	188	8
Saratoga	30,939	348	349	0	3	2	18	83	230	12	1
Scotts Valley	11,803	329	331	0	1	1	10	45	260	12	2
Seal Beach	25,045	459	461	0	2	29	36	101	245	46	2
Seaside	32,860	935	943	1	10	38	101	225	507	53	8
Selma	20,158	1,297	1,303	1	5	24	50	250	731	236	6
Shafter	13,204	403	417	0	1	4	47	91	213	47	14
Sierra Madre	10,967	157	157	0	2	4	6	54	82	9	0
Simi Valley	115,442	1,756	1,776	0	7	26	105	355	1,100	163	20
Solana Beach	13,456	401	403	0	1	13	14	112	212	49	2
Soledad	11,676	323	323	0	4	7	33	104	144	31	0
South El Monte	21,921	749	759	0	4	52	99	182	255	157	10
South Gate	99,916	3,423	3,440	3	12	334	168	641	1,083	1,182	17
South Lake Tahoe	24,476	731	736	0	13	24	173	167	310	44	5
South Pasadena	25,185	612	617	0	3	18	16	164	315	96	5
South San Francisco	62,777	1,541	1,555	1	8	41	64	240	963	224	14
Stanton	38,777	888	908	2	6	40	86	141	425	188	20
Stockton	252,727	21,114	21,188	36	141	1,171	2,345	2,965	11,003	3,453	74
Suisun City	27,078	908	939	0	2	17	44	133	564	148	31
Sunnyvale	136,601	2,569	2,599	2	24	70	96	322	1,837	218	30
Susanville	14,038	407	410	0	8	4	54	74	261	6	3
Temecula	59,837	2,151	2,155	0	19	28	169	452	1,249	234	4
Temple City	34,603	528	534	0	1	25	42	199	211	50	6
Thousand Oaks	121,304	2,030	2,054	0	18	35	105	364	1,359	149	24
Torrance	143,014	4,541	4,564	2	23	211	248	708	2,712	637	23
Tracy	59,021	2,537	2,548	2	10	55	71	369	1,706	324	11
Truckee	14,373	423	423	0	1	3	26	123	245	25	0
Tulare	45,611	3,022	3,068	2	20	57	407	1,041	1,257	238	46
Turlock	57,861	3,769	3,802	0	18	78	185	709	1,985	794	33
Tustin	69,983	2,197	2,209	1	9	52	155	341	1,393	246	12
Twentynine Palms	15,307	536	550	2	9	8	46	135	285	51	14
Twin Cities	21,891	569	569	0	1	2	3	126	365	72	0
Ukiah	16,066	953	960	1	13	10	130	154	594	51	7
Union City	69,326	2,566	2,588	4	14	95	135	409	1,442	467	22
Upland	70,906	2,795	2,839	1	15	103	200	441	1,643	392	44
Vacaville	91,881	2,482	2,507	1	32	66	171	304	1,630	278	25
Vallejo	121,049	7,117	7,163	7	45	326	704	1,194	3,768	1,073	46
Ventura	104,623	3,648	3,657	2	30	90	164	621	2,478	263	9
Victorville	66,382	3,634	3,658	6	21	137	137	721	2,082	530	24
Visalia	94,929	6,309	6,339	12	46	130	674	1,094	3,521	832	30
Vista	93,158	3,184	3,197	4	23	112	257	786	1,590	412	13
Walnut	31,107	396	400	0	4	16	33	88	174	81	4
Walnut Creek	66,658	2,779	2,798	0	12	24	99	469	1,939	236	19
Watsonville	45,891	2,259	2,268	0	23	84	215	293	1,533	111	9
West Covina	108,940	4,238	4,268	2	25	136	199	532	2,573	771	30
West Hollywood	37,028	2,078	2,089	2	13	174	225	278	1,107	279	11
Westminster	91,448	3,114	3,161	4	19	151	193	524	1,772	471	47
West Sacramento	32,776	2,052	2,085	2	24	96	309	503	700	418	33
Whittier	86,755	2,578	2,586	3	8	105	191	329	1,530	412	8
Windsor	23,579	504	506	1	8	6	43	77	337	32	2
Woodland	50,957	1,512	1,553	2	13	37	157	364	705	234	41
Yorba Linda	61,083	1,005	1,017	0	6	15	22	177	736	49	12
Yuba City	38,109	2,296	2,317	4	26	33	117	409	1,454	253	21
Yucaipa	42,721	899	904	0	5	16	34	200	543	101	5
Yucca Valley	17,485	636	648	1	6	10	65	159	339	56	12

See footnotes at end of table.

Table 8

Offenses Known to Law Enforcement
by City 10,000 and over in Population, 2002—Continued

City by state	Population	Crime Index	Modified Crime Index[1]	Murder and non-negligent man-slaughter	Forcible rape	Robbery	Aggravated assault	Burglary	Larceny-theft	Motor vehicle theft	Arson[1]
COLORADO											
Arvada	107,028	4,148	4,196	2	17	48	107	519	3,098	357	48
Aurora	289,584	18,075	18,205	16	256	549	1,031	2,161	10,745	3,317	130
Boulder	99,191	3,743	3,773	5	48	45	133	536	2,787	189	30
Canon City	16,167	777	781	0	8	8	47	114	570	30	4
Castle Rock	21,189	517	517	1	1	6	15	230	209	55	0
Colorado Springs	378,114	21,817	21,956	25	275	497	1,235	4,063	14,137	1,585	139
Commerce City	21,993	1,710	1,710	0	10	17	124	274	875	410	0
Denver	581,105	32,132	32,415	51	324	1,193	1,539	6,117	15,467	7,441	283
Durango	14,587	1,074	1,089	0	21	8	25	99	887	34	15
Englewood	33,241	2,228	2,238	3	15	24	14	283	1,536	353	10
Federal Heights	12,641	1,147	1,150	0	3	16	19	173	825	111	3
Fort Collins	124,315	5,371	5,402	0	99	35	302	738	3,990	207	31
Fort Morgan	11,561	592	593	0	3	7	10	84	463	25	1
Golden	17,978	761	768	0	0	5	56	75	545	80	7
Grand Junction	43,989	2,617	2,645	0	19	18	114	372	1,952	142	28
Greeley	80,601	5,275	5,292	1	55	49	210	637	3,972	351	17
Greenwood Village	11,562	847	850	0	3	11	48	110	610	65	3
Lafayette	24,304	845	862	1	10	9	149	125	515	36	17
Lakewood	151,005	8,938	8,978	1	80	144	207	1,277	6,084	1,145	40
Littleton	42,266	1,551	1,558	3	8	16	37	219	1,083	185	7
Louisville	19,841	402	402	0	4	4	18	61	288	27	0
Loveland	53,023	2,169	2,178	0	23	18	78	256	1,706	88	9
Montrose	12,933	776	783	0	13	6	29	110	585	33	7
Northglenn	33,082	1,955	1,965	3	11	30	122	241	1,258	290	10
Parker	24,683	669	680	0	1	4	7	127	496	34	11
Pueblo	106,995	6,145	6,208	6	27	164	528	1,144	3,893	383	63
Steamboat Springs	10,283	438	440	0	6	2	17	58	334	21	2
Sterling	11,903	639	651	0	4	1	27	128	456	23	12
Thornton	86,316	5,502	5,515	1	41	58	344	702	3,676	680	13
Wheat Ridge	34,484	2,045	2,061	3	25	31	113	252	1,321	300	16
Windsor	10,368	64	67	0	0	1	4	17	35	7	3
CONNECTICUT											
Ansonia	18,853	481	481	1	9	16	14	59	337	45	0
Avon	16,087	196	196	0	1	2	0	26	161	6	0
Berlin	18,509	484	485	0	4	4	12	84	333	47	1
Bethel	18,358	184	185	0	1	3	3	44	123	10	1
Bloomfield	19,903	722	725	1	8	21	95	54	488	55	3
Branford	29,146	886	887	0	5	10	17	60	714	80	1
Bridgeport	141,780	8,551	8,680	17	65	555	1,063	1,401	3,920	1,535	129
Bristol	61,031	1,883	1,889	2	32	43	177	292	1,214	123	6
Brookfield	15,917	217	219	0	2	3	9	31	160	12	2
Clinton	13,306	274	275	0	1	2	2	63	197	9	1
Coventry	11,689	110	111	0	0	2	7	27	67	7	1
Cromwell	13,079	258	259	0	0	3	4	35	196	20	1
Danbury	76,055	2,198	2,208	2	23	66	62	281	1,577	187	10
Darien	19,923	165	165	0	1	3	1	25	122	13	0
Derby	12,591	406	406	0	0	9	5	90	272	30	0
East Hampton	13,568	68	69	0	0	1	2	12	46	7	1
East Haven	28,643	856	858	0	11	23	32	126	561	103	2
Enfield	45,941	1,194	1,208	0	2	28	36	212	766	150	14
Fairfield	58,265	1,190	1,195	0	3	13	7	205	887	75	5
Farmington	24,023	528	528	0	3	5	5	65	416	34	0
Glastonbury	32,390	421	422	0	0	7	8	70	319	17	1
Granby	10,514	157	158	0	3	1	3	17	123	10	1
Greenwich	62,087	554	556	0	2	3	11	72	414	52	2
Groton	10,171	290	293	1	7	7	17	67	181	10	3
Groton Town	29,702	595	597	0	45	15	26	69	419	21	2
Guilford	21,743	399	401	0	3	3	10	65	306	12	2
Hamden	57,831	1,268	1,274	0	2	26	33	160	918	129	6
Hartford	123,540	10,870	11,034	25	57	891	574	1,572	5,571	2,180	164
Madison	18,146	214	216	0	0	1	4	60	140	9	2
Meriden	59,184	2,622	2,628	0	4	81	48	592	1,787	110	6
Middletown	43,863	1,108	1,109	0	2	20	30	148	792	116	1

See footnotes at end of table.

Table 8

Offenses Known to Law Enforcement
by City 10,000 and over in Population, 2002—Continued

City by state	Population	Crime Index	Modified Crime Index[1]	Murder and non-negligent man-slaughter	Forcible rape	Robbery	Aggravated assault	Burglary	Larceny-theft	Motor vehicle theft	Arson[1]
CONNECTICUT—Continued											
Milford	53,149	2,027	2,031	2	16	28	31	238	1,543	169	4
Monroe	19,557	192	192	0	4	0	2	28	144	14	0
Naugatuck	31,489	602	604	0	7	12	18	96	423	46	2
New Britain	72,692	3,481	3,483	0	14	158	148	637	2,009	515	2
New Canaan	19,708	105	105	0	1	0	2	33	65	4	0
Newington	29,779	764	764	1	4	18	24	76	586	55	0
New Milford	27,558	342	344	1	6	4	13	69	232	17	2
Newtown	25,434	277	278	0	1	1	6	61	198	10	1
North Branford	14,131	122	122	0	0	0	6	25	78	13	0
North Haven	23,406	466	467	0	1	6	5	65	348	41	1
Norwalk	84,289	2,949	2,954	2	12	106	213	410	1,944	262	5
Norwich	36,700	1,257	1,262	4	23	53	71	216	788	102	5
Old Saybrook	10,534	276	276	0	1	4	3	25	235	8	0
Orange	13,447	201	201	0	0	3	0	24	165	9	0
Plainfield	14,855	279	280	0	0	0	30	70	168	11	1
Plainville	17,608	599	600	0	0	14	13	81	451	40	1
Plymouth	11,821	232	232	0	0	1	12	49	158	12	0
Ridgefield	24,025	129	136	0	0	1	2	12	112	2	7
Rocky Hill	18,256	395	397	0	7	2	10	36	284	56	2
Seymour	15,704	217	217	0	1	6	24	43	130	13	0
Shelton	38,716	437	438	0	5	7	8	111	241	65	1
Simsbury	23,609	218	221	0	2	4	2	25	183	2	3
Southington	40,369	905	912	0	3	13	44	158	621	66	7
South Windsor	24,806	236	239	0	1	2	14	42	152	25	3
Stamford	118,971	2,398	2,401	2	14	147	117	249	1,571	298	3
Stonington	18,195	472	474	0	1	7	5	73	367	19	2
Stratford	50,782	1,584	1,593	2	11	61	40	294	975	201	9
Suffield	13,771	148	148	0	0	0	3	27	105	13	0
Torrington	35,770	1,117	1,130	1	6	16	126	215	693	60	13
Trumbull	34,795	925	934	0	1	20	5	58	794	47	9
Vernon	28,515	821	823	0	0	17	22	105	631	46	2
Wallingford	43,720	1,077	1,089	0	5	9	17	136	849	61	12
Waterbury	109,002	6,524	6,536	4	48	283	248	1,246	3,926	769	12
Waterford	19,461	626	629	0	4	14	11	62	511	24	3
Watertown	22,011	399	399	1	0	0	5	49	329	15	0
West Hartford	64,615	1,914	1,918	0	3	81	39	278	1,383	130	4
West Haven[3]	53,204	1,989	1,998	1	18	58	41	305	1,259	307	9
Weston	10,199	75	75	0	0	0	1	11	60	3	0
Wethersfield	26,695	606	608	1	1	27	8	74	441	54	2
Willimantic	16,078	933	935	1	1	37	31	164	647	52	2
Wilton	17,917	137	137	0	0	3	1	24	100	9	0
Winchester	10,836	151	152	0	1	3	2	14	130	1	1
Windsor	28,693	546	551	0	1	13	3	56	421	52	5
Windsor Locks	12,238	236	237	0	1	1	2	32	145	55	1
DELAWARE											
Dover	33,110	1,923	1,935	1	15	50	117	105	1,528	107	12
Newark	29,414	1,391	1,410	0	13	54	115	223	873	113	19
DISTRICT OF COLUMBIA											
Washington	570,898	44,349	44,458	264	262	3,731	4,854	5,167	20,903	9,168	109
FLORIDA											
Altamonte Springs	43,084	2,084	2,091	1	21	53	109	308	1,307	279	7
Apopka	27,860	2,061	2,064	2	11	79	176	586	1,069	138	3
Atlantic Beach	13,979	562	563	0	6	20	57	123	321	35	1
Auburndale	11,537	872	873	0	4	21	65	199	540	43	1
Aventura	26,422	2,335	2,335	0	3	39	36	134	2,020	103	0
Bartow	16,041	1,324	1,324	0	10	27	128	260	788	111	0
Belle Glade	15,588	1,961	1,968	0	14	96	397	531	829	94	7
Boca Raton	78,183	2,890	2,892	2	11	63	129	545	1,927	213	2
Boynton Beach	63,150	5,277	5,284	2	10	204	380	853	3,269	559	7

See footnotes at end of table.

Table 8

Offenses Known to Law Enforcement

by City 10,000 and over in Population, 2002—Continued

City by state	Population	Crime Index	Modified Crime Index[1]	Murder and non-negligent man-slaughter	Forcible rape	Robbery	Aggravated assault	Burglary	Larceny-theft	Motor vehicle theft	Arson[1]
FLORIDA—Continued											
Bradenton	51,768	3,758	3,758	8	32	151	267	769	2,180	351	0
Cape Coral	106,963	4,086	4,111	3	17	42	327	1,081	2,394	222	25
Casselberry	23,664	1,192	1,195	1	16	40	82	223	756	74	3
Clearwater	113,761	6,544	6,581	7	51	270	795	1,181	3,799	441	37
Cocoa	17,162	2,002	2,003	1	16	94	269	466	1,015	141	1
Cocoa Beach	13,052	1,120	1,121	1	8	16	87	128	832	48	1
Coconut Creek	45,558	1,236	1,243	1	17	19	92	249	733	125	7
Cooper City	29,216	816	817	0	3	12	37	169	552	43	1
Coral Gables	44,180	2,863	2,863	1	11	55	117	485	1,978	216	0
Coral Springs	122,923	3,918	3,926	2	25	87	178	681	2,613	332	8
Crestview	15,441	599	600	0	11	14	43	72	433	26	1
Dania	20,979	1,301	1,303	2	6	57	112	193	731	200	2
Davie	79,182	3,699	3,711	5	11	77	224	702	2,313	367	12
Daytona Beach	67,043	7,181	7,212	15	85	404	431	1,790	3,566	890	31
Deerfield Beach	67,536	1,928	1,934	5	16	65	201	281	1,134	226	6
Deland	21,859	1,636	1,638	5	10	53	145	299	1,038	86	2
Delray Beach	62,764	4,665	4,672	1	22	139	429	698	2,870	506	7
Dunedin	37,323	1,087	1,090	0	11	25	64	242	698	47	3
Edgewater	19,522	713	715	0	9	6	39	146	468	45	2
Eustis	15,797	378	380	1	5	10	42	53	235	32	2
Fernandina Beach	11,031	531	536	0	7	8	39	95	359	23	5
Fort Lauderdale	159,365	11,681	11,735	12	39	669	687	2,482	6,418	1,374	54
Fort Myers	50,412	5,118	5,140	16	28	369	661	742	2,508	794	22
Fort Pierce	39,232	4,329	4,358	8	41	236	538	964	2,152	390	29
Fort Walton Beach	20,887	879	879	0	11	15	83	130	594	46	0
Gainesville	99,811	6,016	6,029	7	65	185	508	1,248	3,530	473	13
Greenacres City	28,829	1,782	1,784	3	13	46	124	276	1,176	144	2
Gulfport	13,099	727	733	0	3	45	54	179	393	53	6
Haines City	13,776	1,465	1,467	2	5	17	35	292	1,011	103	2
Hallandale	35,850	2,134	2,139	2	20	117	310	379	1,122	184	5
Hialeah	236,772	12,217	12,261	9	48	431	1,012	1,609	7,029	2,079	44
Hialeah Gardens	20,179	1,042	1,043	0	1	20	28	165	679	149	1
Holly Hill	12,673	1,199	1,201	2	12	40	61	292	691	101	2
Hollywood	145,729	9,171	9,206	11	44	392	576	1,205	5,917	1,026	35
Homestead	33,368	3,793	3,796	6	22	296	402	577	2,214	276	3
Jacksonville	769,253	51,021	51,318	90	277	2,016	4,660	9,173	29,391	5,414	297
Jacksonville Beach	21,949	1,367	1,372	3	13	47	105	196	922	81	5
Jupiter	41,126	1,717	1,719	0	2	41	102	365	1,112	95	2
Key Biscayne	10,987	373	374	0	0	0	7	38	308	20	1
Key West	26,643	2,199	2,199	0	26	61	94	384	1,377	257	0
Kissimmee	50,001	3,471	3,480	1	26	126	318	668	2,098	234	9
Lady Lake	12,368	227	228	0	0	2	28	59	126	12	1
Lake City	10,436	1,348	1,355	0	10	34	154	198	907	45	7
Lakeland	82,039	5,360	5,376	3	44	250	368	1,018	3,332	345	16
Lake Mary	11,982	265	265	0	2	6	11	62	176	8	0
Lake Wales	10,660	1,248	1,251	0	6	33	47	253	814	95	3
Lake Worth	36,739	3,424	3,433	8	24	223	234	705	1,841	389	9
Largo	72,543	3,050	3,054	3	29	55	173	547	2,083	160	4
Lauderdale Lakes	33,155	1,002	1,009	1	15	69	140	141	441	195	7
Lauderhill	60,218	2,949	2,960	6	27	152	327	663	1,306	468	11
Leesburg	16,685	1,236	1,240	1	5	47	267	258	607	51	4
Lighthouse Point	11,259	286	287	0	0	7	13	50	195	21	1
Longwood	14,373	939	939	0	2	15	315	132	427	48	0
Lynn Haven	13,021	417	417	0	1	7	36	99	252	22	0
Maitland	12,569	452	453	1	2	27	24	114	241	43	1
Marco Island	15,559	282	285	0	2	2	10	66	192	10	3
Margate	56,374	1,768	1,772	0	11	45	138	381	1,013	180	4
Melbourne	74,646	5,329	5,349	1	35	164	874	793	3,218	244	20
Miami	379,044	33,952	34,180	65	96	2,706	4,361	5,962	15,886	4,876	228
Miami Beach	91,954	10,390	10,398	7	51	507	512	1,464	6,639	1,210	8
Miami Lakes	23,713	1,313	1,313	0	5	25	78	178	838	189	0
Miami Shores	10,855	763	765	0	5	41	34	145	478	60	2
Miami Springs	14,339	713	715	1	2	37	39	120	456	58	2
Miramar	76,065	3,437	3,462	6	36	145	266	856	1,721	407	25
Naples	21,935	1,103	1,104	0	4	20	52	266	718	43	1

See footnotes at end of table.

Table 8

Offenses Known to Law Enforcement
by City 10,000 and over in Population, 2002—Continued

City by state	Population	Crime Index	Modified Crime Index[1]	Murder and non-negligent man-slaughter	Forcible rape	Robbery	Aggravated assault	Burglary	Larceny-theft	Motor vehicle theft	Arson[1]
FLORIDA—Continued											
New Port Richey	16,854	1,109	1,115	0	14	40	124	248	638	45	6
New Smyrna Beach	20,964	1,042	1,043	2	8	19	85	214	670	44	1
Niceville	12,218	188	188	0	3	5	17	41	110	12	0
North Lauderdale	33,739	758	761	2	16	43	106	130	365	96	3
North Miami	62,618	5,605	5,618	5	38	338	502	1,114	2,936	672	13
North Miami Beach	42,651	2,793	2,806	5	15	152	154	584	1,502	381	13
North Palm Beach	12,616	485	486	0	2	25	31	104	285	38	1
North Port	23,840	692	695	0	11	7	46	156	436	36	3
Oakland Park	32,381	1,598	1,600	6	8	81	143	247	878	235	2
Ocala	48,044	4,159	4,176	6	45	151	469	929	2,350	209	17
Ocoee	25,507	1,674	1,678	0	7	29	141	260	1,103	134	4
Oldsmar	12,454	558	560	1	1	9	35	117	362	33	2
Opa Locka	15,635	2,517	2,525	8	25	286	633	435	860	270	8
Orlando	194,454	21,133	21,186	15	121	1,034	2,449	3,710	11,602	2,202	53
Ormond Beach	37,961	1,223	1,225	0	0	21	83	361	701	57	2
Oviedo	27,520	748	757	0	12	9	85	133	487	22	9
Palatka	10,491	1,459	1,467	1	8	36	158	271	922	63	8
Palm Bay	83,044	4,129	4,157	2	64	89	538	917	2,340	179	28
Palm Beach	10,947	264	264	0	0	3	3	53	192	13	0
Palm Beach Gardens	36,661	1,872	1,875	0	10	51	66	346	1,285	114	3
Palmetto	13,146	956	959	0	1	42	108	195	564	46	3
Palm Springs	12,234	839	842	0	1	24	47	124	539	104	3
Panama City	38,082	3,107	3,118	5	33	90	199	536	2,107	139	11
Parkland	14,467	362	363	0	0	0	14	89	243	16	1
Pembroke Pines	143,711	4,751	4,780	3	20	121	234	675	3,091	607	29
Pensacola	58,827	3,121	3,128	1	36	101	322	622	1,912	127	7
Pinellas Park	47,746	3,134	3,155	2	40	54	183	587	2,075	193	21
Plantation	86,726	4,435	4,442	3	13	117	127	648	3,096	431	7
Plant City	31,283	2,432	2,438	1	9	80	178	355	1,495	314	6
Pompano Beach	81,767	4,178	4,185	5	44	242	493	653	2,285	456	7
Port Orange	47,918	1,128	1,129	0	2	8	19	167	887	45	1
Port St. Lucie	92,827	2,922	2,933	1	19	30	220	737	1,812	103	11
Punta Gorda	15,000	466	467	0	4	3	24	150	274	11	1
Riviera Beach	31,250	4,437	4,449	5	30	180	327	1,111	1,785	999	12
Rockledge	21,092	807	810	0	6	17	42	152	549	41	3
Royal Palm Beach	22,507	1,429	1,431	0	1	28	61	568	685	86	2
Safety Harbor	17,990	438	440	0	6	4	31	91	293	13	2
Sanford	40,042	3,283	3,283	3	22	117	129	553	2,112	347	0
Sarasota	55,125	4,699	4,712	1	40	219	372	955	2,819	293	13
Satellite Beach	10,015	289	290	0	0	2	23	62	194	8	1
Sebastian	16,921	472	474	0	4	2	54	111	288	13	2
Sebring	10,109	973	980	0	1	34	45	229	602	62	7
Seminole	11,388	614	617	0	2	11	31	121	422	27	3
South Daytona	13,779	560	564	0	4	15	44	145	304	48	4
South Miami	11,232	849	849	0	1	40	71	138	564	35	0
St. Augustine	12,122	936	938	0	9	24	99	85	676	43	2
St. Cloud	20,992	1,187	1,189	0	7	12	88	254	771	55	2
St. Pete Beach	10,383	545	545	0	2	11	23	93	392	24	0
St. Petersburg	259,582	20,914	21,033	23	124	1,027	3,249	3,628	10,550	2,313	119
Stuart	15,302	1,030	1,034	0	5	16	79	196	669	65	4
Sunny Isles Beach	16,016	758	761	0	3	11	24	142	495	83	3
Sunrise	89,701	4,290	4,296	4	11	145	280	551	2,896	403	6
Sweetwater	14,876	242	244	0	0	12	33	39	121	37	2
Tallahassee	157,511	11,880	11,914	9	151	384	1,073	2,262	7,188	813	34
Tamarac	58,130	1,129	1,131	2	11	58	79	151	684	144	2
Tampa	317,322	35,380	35,514	37	204	2,334	3,714	6,283	16,088	6,720	134
Tarpon Springs	21,964	912	917	2	12	7	115	166	549	47	5
Tavares	10,143	249	249	0	5	1	24	51	143	25	0
Temple Terrace	21,875	870	873	3	12	34	46	156	522	97	3
Titusville	42,530	2,146	2,154	2	22	95	245	550	1,043	189	8
Venice	18,577	452	453	0	3	7	24	62	334	22	1
Vero Beach	18,514	946	947	1	10	18	62	207	616	32	1
Village of Pinecrest	19,926	894	895	1	1	12	36	133	660	51	1
Wellington	39,964	1,743	1,747	0	12	12	109	303	1,046	261	4
West Melbourne	10,273	377	380	0	1	7	31	72	258	8	3

See footnotes at end of table.

Table 8

Offenses Known to Law Enforcement
by City 10,000 and over in Population, 2002—Continued

City by state	Population	Crime Index	Modified Crime Index[1]	Murder and non-negligent man-slaughter	Forcible rape	Robbery	Aggravated assault	Burglary	Larceny-theft	Motor vehicle theft	Arson[1]
FLORIDA—Continued											
Weston	51,540	563	567	0	3	6	41	117	333	63	4
West Palm Beach	85,857	10,603	10,631	7	56	497	630	1,729	6,525	1,159	28
Wilton Manors	13,278	866	869	2	1	35	47	174	529	78	3
Winter Garden	15,007	674	676	0	7	26	95	120	334	92	2
Winter Haven	27,698	2,504	2,516	1	34	78	93	436	1,654	208	12
Winter Park	25,191	1,123	1,125	0	4	41	50	163	791	74	2
Winter Springs	33,114	623	624	0	4	8	70	125	376	40	1
Zephyrhills	11,328	689	693	0	4	17	44	160	399	65	4
GEORGIA											
Acworth	14,035	466	466	0	1	8	15	47	360	35	0
Albany	80,452	5,430	5,449	7	49	220	238	1,297	3,319	300	19
Alpharetta	36,445	1,565		0	4	18	99	241	1,096	107	
Americus	17,790	1,594		1	12	34	105	256	1,141	45	
Athens-Clarke County	105,007	6,693	6,728	7	53	158	223	1,042	4,779	431	35
Atlanta	435,494	49,451	49,602	152	276	4,168	5,373	8,554	23,706	7,222	151
Bainbridge	12,257	941	941	2	12	26	28	156	699	18	0
Calhoun	11,154	1,072		0	3	17	27	138	842	45	
Carrollton	20,749	1,518	1,521	3	6	30	199	179	1,007	94	3
Cartersville	16,652	1,343	1,344	3	10	34	43	246	855	152	1
College Park	21,313	2,091		4	10	112	136	443	1,086	300	
Columbus	194,265	12,382	12,432	20	25	359	427	1,937	8,595	1,019	50
Conyers	11,177	1,494	1,498	2	10	43	107	156	1,048	128	4
Cordele	12,138	1,258	1,262	1	4	46	71	139	956	41	4
Covington	12,074	1,008		0	6	18	46	186	707	45	
Dalton	29,186	2,111		3	10	42	136	272	1,530	118	
Decatur	18,976	695	698	1	4	26	22	138	423	81	3
Doraville	10,312	549	549	0	0	40	22	78	358	51	0
Douglas	11,125	1,415	1,416	0	9	14	90	182	1,038	82	1
Douglasville	20,981	2,115	2,123	5	4	42	90	197	1,644	133	8
Duluth	23,132	430	430	0	3	10	18	84	278	37	0
East Point	41,403	2,852		8	17	159	161	785	1,346	376	
Fayetteville	11,658	612		2	0	4	5	39	537	25	
Forest Park	22,426	1,812	1,821	2	11	86	47	367	1,067	232	9
Gainesville	26,746	2,162	2,165	1	13	38	167	241	1,575	127	3
Garden City	11,804	890	896	0	7	31	138	181	429	104	6
Griffin	24,522	1,777		4	4	46	122	247	1,232	122	
Hinesville	31,780	1,812		6	13	45	90	316	1,277	65	
Kennesaw	22,664	535		0	2	4	19	60	426	24	
Kingsland	10,985	589	589	0	13	12	70	132	337	25	0
LaGrange	27,185	2,372	2,384	1	10	47	81	249	1,893	91	12
Lawrenceville	23,420	934	937	1	6	24	34	165	604	100	3
Macon	101,696	10,433	10,513	16	63	240	319	2,288	6,296	1,211	80
Marietta	61,431	3,170		1	16	158	119	554	1,994	328	
Milledgeville	19,613	883	883	0	3	16	27	141	663	33	0
Monroe	11,927	737	737	3	1	17	67	114	480	55	0
Moultrie	15,044	1,694	1,701	2	7	55	119	353	1,033	125	7
Newnan	16,984	960	963	1	3	25	56	128	685	62	3
Perry	10,040	325	327	0	1	6	25	48	214	31	2
Powder Springs	13,051	316	316	0	1	8	8	70	210	19	0
Riverdale	13,048	1,204	1,205	0	4	48	59	179	760	154	1
Rome	36,578	2,129	2,141	0	11	76	145	448	1,323	126	12
Roswell	82,957	2,033	2,033	1	5	48	172	380	1,291	136	0
Savannah	137,516	11,595	11,622	32	58	650	449	1,985	6,884	1,537	27
Smyrna	42,871	2,191		0	13	89	69	422	1,389	209	
Snellville	16,052	620	620	0	2	8	5	46	530	29	0
Statesboro	23,735	1,080	1,081	1	3	40	25	204	773	34	1
St. Marys	14,390	603	613	0	4	16	27	94	436	26	10
Thomasville	18,991	1,390	1,396	0	4	28	35	333	936	54	6
Tifton	15,747	1,390	1,390	5	6	26	75	221	999	58	0
Union City	12,152	1,179	1,179	0	0	33	43	182	720	201	0
Valdosta	45,721	3,028		4	30	70	158	498	2,138	130	
Vidalia	10,970	661	668	1	1	19	66	83	467	24	7
Warner Robins	51,033	3,384	3,389	2	12	76	124	673	2,329	168	5

See footnotes at end of table.

Table 8

Offenses Known to Law Enforcement
by City 10,000 and over in Population, 2002—Continued

City by state	Population	Crime Index	Modified Crime Index[1]	Murder and non-negligent man-slaughter	Forcible rape	Robbery	Aggravated assault	Burglary	Larceny-theft	Motor vehicle theft	Arson[1]
GEORGIA—Continued											
Waycross	16,034	1,236	1,241	1	9	35	38	168	934	51	5
Winder	10,667	802	802	0	3	17	23	115	592	52	0
HAWAII											
Honolulu	900,433	57,271	57,700	18	304	1,072	1,207	8,932	37,250	8,488	429
IDAHO											
Blackfoot	10,798	458	458	1	4	0	19	47	372	15	0
Boise	192,561	8,748	8,826	6	92	84	497	1,318	6,209	542	78
Caldwell	26,913	2,169	2,178	2	24	11	97	328	1,541	166	9
Chubbuck	10,054	443	445	0	3	2	58	22	352	6	2
Coeur d'Alene	35,772	2,246	2,269	1	14	13	144	317	1,590	167	23
Garden City	11,012	759	767	0	15	7	69	176	434	58	8
Idaho Falls	52,580	2,209	2,221	1	16	4	128	364	1,582	114	12
Lewiston	32,031	1,286	1,293	1	6	7	34	214	970	54	7
Meridian	36,192	1,211	1,227	0	6	3	22	139	1,006	35	16
Moscow	22,067	642	643	1	7	5	13	45	552	19	1
Mountain Home	11,549	477	483	0	6	1	31	53	357	29	6
Nampa	53,759	2,871	2,889	1	71	27	162	449	1,912	249	18
Pocatello	53,342	1,692	1,703	1	21	6	118	264	1,208	74	11
Post Falls	17,876	677	685	1	5	0	23	81	535	32	8
Rexburg	17,886	287	289	0	2	1	14	20	243	7	2
Twin Falls	35,725	2,292	2,303	0	20	24	145	396	1,598	109	11
ILLINOIS[4, 5]											
Aurora	145,078			25		158	538	1,017	3,979	317	40
Chicago	2,938,299			648		18,532	24,842	25,552	96,380	25,245	1,022
Joliet	107,772			7		183	405	851	3,025	290	70
Naperville	130,232			1		13	62	334	1,921	93	15
Peoria	114,585			9		380	437	1,841	5,590	860	85
Rockford	152,307			20		518	631	3,234	8,015	1,197	37
Springfield	113,081			5		342	846	1,736	6,095	349	60
INDIANA											
Auburn[3]	12,230	609	610	0	5	5	12	61	509	17	1
Bedford	13,946	540	541	2	3	3	10	69	419	34	1
Beech Grove	15,072	640	643	1	4	9	12	124	385	105	3
Bloomington	70,186	2,744	2,754	2	35	32	40	437	2,053	145	10
Brownsburg	14,707	251	252	0	1	1	12	48	179	10	1
Carmel	38,221	718	735	0	6	10	5	81	568	48	17
Chesterton	10,624	311	312	0	0	4	8	37	237	25	1
Clarksville	21,677	2,121	2,123	0	4	32	16	173	1,713	183	2
Columbus	39,564	2,251	2,263	1	6	13	58	204	1,891	78	12
Connersville	15,610	1,026	1,028	0	1	3	13	128	852	29	2
Crawfordsville	15,440	771	772	1	2	4	10	142	593	19	1
Crown Point	20,062	349	354	0	1	2	24	40	253	29	5
Dyer	14,075	316	316	0	2	2	9	38	238	27	0
East Chicago	32,833	2,489		11	11	107	513	380	1,058	409	
Elkhart	52,545	4,288	4,311	7	28	154	25	877	2,943	254	23
Evansville	123,153	6,154	6,219	2	53	134	473	1,112	4,067	313	65
Fishers	38,324	682	682	0	1	10	54	79	509	29	0
Fort Wayne	208,386	12,152	12,269	24	113	454	255	2,030	8,268	1,008	117
Frankfort	16,878	824	826	0	11	–	28	155	591	37	2
Franklin	19,714	1,030	1,032	0	9	2	3	131	839	46	2
Gary	104,074	5,812		60	58	420	219	1,543	2,271	1,241	
Goshen	29,763	1,430	1,432	0	2	4	179	136	1,063	46	2
Greenfield	14,789	382	384	0	4	3	16	49	287	23	2
Greenwood	36,503	2,012	2,017	0	6	25	174	207	1,487	113	5
Griffith	17,558	681	693	0	3	8	25	74	491	80	12
Hammond[3]	84,121	5,394	5,460	12	12	273	321	852	3,234	690	66
Highland	23,850	1,070	1,073	1	2	26	18	111	809	103	3

See footnotes at end of table.

Table 8

Offenses Known to Law Enforcement
by City 10,000 and over in Population, 2002—Continued

City by state	Population	Crime Index	Modified Crime Index[1]	Murder and non-negligent man-slaughter	Forcible rape	Robbery	Aggravated assault	Burglary	Larceny-theft	Motor vehicle theft	Arson[1]
INDIANA—Continued											
Hobart	25,691	1,399	1,405	0	7	28	81	107	1,045	131	6
Huntington	17,676	522	524	0	9	3	12	55	429	14	2
Indianapolis[3]	804,034	48,503	48,892	112	441	2,937	4,028	9,662	24,821	6,502	389
Jasper	12,256	131	131	0	0	1	5	12	103	10	0
Jeffersonville	27,715	1,479	1,485	3	8	36	32	350	906	144	6
Kokomo	46,709	3,146	3,153	3	18	40	214	559	2,171	141	7
Lafayette[3]	57,126	3,346	3,367	5	44	42	137	624	2,369	125	21
La Porte	21,900	1,312	1,312	0	15	11	49	146	1,030	61	0
Lawrence	39,418	1,101	1,109	0	13	44	107	211	568	158	8
Logansport	19,939	801	801	0	4	3	9	147	575	63	0
Madison	12,159	543	543	1	3	0	16	163	331	29	0
Marion	31,725	2,166	2,175	1	20	64	189	359	1,417	116	9
Martinsville	11,849	742	743	0	1	3	24	66	608	40	1
Merrillville	30,954	1,077	1,080	2	2	25	5	77	795	171	3
Michigan City	33,325	2,386	2,423	3	21	52	53	351	1,669	237	37
Mishawaka	47,159	4,119	4,142	0	18	48	83	525	3,217	228	23
Muncie	68,301	3,214	3,226	2	49	75	158	509	2,232	189	12
Munster	21,789	575	575	0	2	14	26	40	440	53	0
New Albany	38,089	3,109	3,144	3	8	79	136	614	2,083	186	35
New Castle	18,010	1,857	1,862	1	6	9	5	372	1,373	91	5
New Haven	12,566	409	410	0	2	16	17	71	265	38	1
Noblesville	28,960	671	679	0	11	5	25	123	481	26	8
Plainfield	18,634	881	883	0	4	7	14	131	686	39	2
Portage	33,929	1,559	1,563	0	8	9	69	236	1,137	100	4
Richmond	39,630	2,220	2,303	6	31	56	103	426	1,455	143	83
Schererville	25,172	650	650	0	2	8	13	46	523	58	0
Seymour	18,335	1,224	1,229	0	9	4	79	110	953	69	5
South Bend	109,182	8,203	8,272	20	93	354	353	1,826	4,983	574	69
Speedway[3]	13,047	569	571	3	7	31	9	71	349	99	2
Valparaiso	27,783	881	883	2	5	5	67	88	680	34	2
Vincennes	18,942	1,242	1,245	0	6	12	8	245	906	65	3
Wabash	11,894	206	206	0	0	0	7	34	154	11	0
Warsaw	12,575	338	338	0	3	2	14	59	249	11	0
West Lafayette	29,150	610	612	0	7	3	13	94	470	23	2
IOWA											
Altoona	10,382	482	486	0	0	4	8	54	399	17	4
Ames	50,912	2,075	2,084	0	35	13	86	244	1,624	73	9
Ankeny	27,213	653	656	0	2	5	14	95	512	25	3
Bettendorf	31,386	968	980	0	10	7	98	104	708	41	12
Boone	12,849	270	278	0	0	0	9	30	225	6	8
Burlington	26,935	1,308	1,316	0	13	18	121	248	850	58	8
Carroll	10,142	232	234	0	2	0	3	28	186	13	2
Cedar Falls	36,274	1,149	1,157	0	11	7	93	129	860	49	8
Cedar Rapids	121,189	7,233	7,248	2	57	104	267	1,111	5,387	305	15
Clive	12,901	449	453	0	4	4	28	57	328	28	4
Coralville	15,177	753	756	0	10	9	14	79	621	20	3
Council Bluffs	58,475	6,865	6,904	3	68	78	372	941	4,641	762	39
Davenport	98,710	9,558	9,607	7	63	244	1,223	1,697	5,908	416	49
Des Moines	199,390	13,776	13,848	9	113	290	364	1,676	10,313	1,011	72
Dubuque	57,891	2,095	2,119	1	16	8	135	402	1,407	126	24
Fort Dodge	25,225	2,005	2,023	0	15	29	163	426	1,254	118	18
Fort Madison	10,754	462	469	0	1	2	13	68	362	16	7
Indianola	13,044	353	353	0	1	1	15	30	295	11	0
Iowa City	62,442	2,194	2,201	0	39	44	261	312	1,465	73	7
Keokuk	11,468	703	707	0	7	3	152	82	425	34	4
Marion	26,388	361	368	0	0	3	15	86	248	9	7
Marshalltown	26,102	1,625	1,640	1	7	8	203	356	993	57	15
Mason City	29,276	1,688	1,700	0	3	9	20	308	1,291	57	12
Muscatine	22,778	1,071	1,077	1	33	3	130	317	540	47	6
Newton	15,635	776	776	0	0	3	17	231	502	23	0
Oskaloosa	10,977	408	411	0	4	3	11	83	289	18	3
Ottumwa	25,087	1,373	1,380	0	5	11	161	262	868	66	7
Sioux City	85,316	5,933	5,965	3	45	72	434	1,235	3,770	374	32

See footnotes at end of table.

Table 8

Offenses Known to Law Enforcement
by City 10,000 and over in Population, 2002—Continued

City by state	Population	Crime Index	Modified Crime Index[1]	Murder and non-negligent man-slaughter	Forcible rape	Robbery	Aggravated assault	Burglary	Larceny-theft	Motor vehicle theft	Arson[1]
IOWA—Continued											
Spencer	11,358	357	359	0	0	0	2	55	288	12	2
Storm Lake	10,112	420	422	0	5	3	24	59	307	22	2
Urbandale	29,176	1,049	1,050	0	4	8	55	122	818	42	1
Waterloo	68,993	4,245	4,276	1	37	91	197	1,064	2,604	251	31
West Des Moines	46,568	1,810	1,816	1	4	15	28	217	1,469	76	6
KANSAS											
Arkansas City	12,085	660	664	0	8	11	48	104	462	27	4
Atchison	10,336	427	428	0	3	3	27	57	313	24	1
Coffeyville	11,133	759	767	1	12	11	62	165	485	23	8
Derby	17,989	539	548	0	3	5	26	96	385	24	9
Dodge City	25,433	1,552	1,561	3	17	23	79	267	1,087	76	9
El Dorado	12,180	560	561	1	7	1	11	100	420	20	1
Emporia	27,033	1,609	1,620	2	21	10	66	249	1,214	47	11
Garden City	28,742	2,018	2,039	3	24	24	132	341	1,408	86	21
Junction City	19,079	1,571	1,580	0	18	43	186	236	1,032	56	9
Lawrence	80,916	3,939	3,951	2	32	43	244	668	2,775	175	12
Leavenworth	35,782	1,489	1,518	1	22	41	147	204	994	80	29
Leawood	27,939	566	572	1	2	4	47	112	372	28	6
Liberal	19,867	1,272	1,282	0	13	8	55	208	922	66	10
McPherson	13,910	290	292	0	4	3	33	44	195	11	2
Merriam	11,120	953	961	0	5	15	21	81	727	104	8
Newton	17,366	662	669	1	9	5	40	106	484	17	7.
Olathe	93,912	3,240	3,267	4	46	28	240	260	2,414	248	27
Ottawa	12,043	516	517	0	5	2	34	86	364	25	1
Overland Park	150,603	5,186	5,213	2	26	46	290	559	3,712	551	27
Parsons	11,632	561	566	0	2	10	57	131	342	19	5
Pittsburg	19,439	2,088	2,107	1	19	15	107	471	1,402	73	19
Prairie Village	22,298	434	442	0	2	14	10	102	275	31	8
Salina	46,146	2,955	2,987	0	18	20	113	296	2,402	106	32
Topeka[3]	123,627	11,294		8	73	409	499	1,767	7,863	675	
Wichita	347,801	24,104		20	208	796	1,344	4,459	15,523	1,754	
KENTUCKY[5]											
Bowling Green	49,920	3,498	3,501	1	40	81	238	675	2,262	201	3
Florence	23,849	1,556	1,559	0	5	24	59	180	1,185	103	3
Hopkinsville	30,469	2,008	2,027	3	25	58	33	515	1,300	74	19
Lexington	263,807	12,521	12,552	15	117	626	671	2,439	8,004	649	31
Louisville	259,472	15,439	15,655	35	49	995	958	3,519	7,710	2,173	216
Madisonville	19,551	932	936	0	6	22	42	187	642	33	4
Murray	15,139	592	594	0	1	7	10	145	399	30	2
Owensboro	54,751	2,582	2,591	4	17	43	77	435	1,913	93	9
Paducah	26,640	1,948	1,953	3	18	51	98	318	1,312	148	5
Radcliff	22,239	704	707	0	15	13	50	140	473	13	3
Richmond	27,496	1,649	1,655	0	12	22	105	264	1,154	92	6
LOUISIANA											
Alexandria	46,483	5,554	5,554	11	17	199	732	1,117	3,285	193	0
Baker	13,835	729	733	1	5	11	31	116	536	29	4
Baton Rouge[3]	228,515	18,949	19,142	59	133	1,107	1,371	4,070	10,763	1,446	193
Bogalusa	13,406	1,152	1,160	1	7	36	110	308	629	61	8
Bossier City	56,634	4,187	4,210	7	32	95	391	762	2,572	328	23
Crowley	14,268	885	885	0	1	7	50	272	535	20	0
Eunice	11,535	960	963	0	1	10	153	185	578	33	3
Gretna	17,476	995	1,001	0	8	62	86	131	567	141	6
Houma	32,492	2,125	2,131	0	28	70	288	335	1,304	100	6
Jennings	11,019	743	746	0	1	17	92	199	419	15	3
Kenner	70,733	3,357	3,369	3	12	88	210	435	2,309	300	12
Lafayette	110,594	8,431	8,463	3	85	171	784	1,391	5,503	494	32
Lake Charles	71,976	4,881	4,895	6	42	198	449	1,889	1,982	315	14
Mandeville	10,521	493	496	0	1	15	26	67	365	19	3
Minden	13,067	356	357	1	1	6	30	73	228	17	1

See footnotes at end of table.

Table 8

Offenses Known to Law Enforcement
by City 10,000 and over in Population, 2002—Continued

City by state	Population	Crime Index	Modified Crime Index[1]	Murder and non-negligent man-slaughter	Forcible rape	Robbery	Aggravated assault	Burglary	Larceny-theft	Motor vehicle theft	Arson[1]
LOUISIANA—Continued											
Morgan City	12,742	737	737	0	4	22	73	135	464	39	0
Natchitoches	17,920	1,291	1,294	1	9	28	151	303	760	39	3
New Iberia	32,723	2,178	2,189	0	6	47	223	308	1,488	106	11
New Orleans	486,157	31,206		258	162	1,994	2,142	4,759	14,325	7,566	
Pineville	13,871	595	595	2	8	7	10	244	301	23	0
Ruston	20,608	1,209	1,209	1	6	22	103	266	772	39	0
Shreveport	200,757	16,389	16,535	40	119	667	1,218	3,350	9,346	1,649	146
Slidell	25,774	2,398	2,398	3	16	41	146	259	1,773	160	0
Thibodaux	14,475	572	575	1	6	21	57	119	359	9	3
West Monroe	13,290	1,359	1,366	1	10	21	80	217	976	54	7
Westwego	10,796	315	319	0	2	15	32	45	196	25	4
Zachary	11,310	542	544	0	1	6	49	80	382	24	2
MAINE											
Auburn	23,559	849	859	0	9	8	8	121	677	26	10
Augusta	18,844	1,233	1,245	0	29	16	17	202	944	25	12
Bangor	31,956	1,630	1,646	0	4	18	17	158	1,378	55	16
Biddeford	21,263	771	779	1	16	14	24	123	573	20	8
Brunswick	21,497	480	488	0	7	8	1	55	386	23	8
Falmouth	10,468	168	169	0	1	1	2	26	136	2	1
Gorham	14,358	237	239	0	11	2	8	48	149	19	2
Kennebunk	10,636	199	202	0	6	0	4	48	136	5	3
Lewiston	36,237	1,789	1,798	1	28	27	23	337	1,322	51	9
Portland	65,234	3,525	3,551	3	42	60	85	636	2,547	152	26
Saco	17,080	661	662	1	0	5	22	133	482	18	1
Sanford	21,125	527	532	0	7	4	12	59	423	22	5
Scarborough	17,230	357	357	0	0	1	9	86	254	7	0
South Portland	23,682	1,025	1,033	0	7	11	12	116	853	26	8
Waterville	15,844	619	621	0	4	9	17	77	493	19	2
Westbrook	16,390	500	502	0	6	3	18	67	386	20	2
Windham	15,133	440	446	0	0	3	3	84	342	8	6
York	13,051	210	210	0	5	2	0	36	165	2	0
MARYLAND											
Aberdeen	14,264	979	983	1	4	61	60	104	709	40	4
Annapolis	36,932	2,330	2,357	4	15	149	253	414	1,380	115	27
Baltimore	671,028	55,820	56,164	253	178	4,714	8,644	8,759	26,716	6,556	344
Bel Air	10,388	613	625	0	0	14	53	52	461	33	12
Cambridge	11,244	858	862	3	9	20	110	141	536	39	4
Cumberland	22,175	1,262	1,276	0	15	15	103	245	837	47	14
Easton	12,065	623	623	0	8	11	36	95	467	6	0
Elkton	12,256	938	957	0	7	23	91	127	625	65	19
Frederick	54,378	2,710	2,727	3	24	125	504	321	1,604	129	17
Greenbelt	22,111	1,727	1,727	1	14	106	71	160	957	418	0
Hagerstown	37,807	1,764	1,790	2	10	90	138	345	1,047	132	26
Havre de Grace	11,677	685	689	1	2	28	74	88	467	25	4
Hyattsville	15,182	1,017	1,017	2	2	54	33	140	568	218	0
Laurel	20,570	1,429	1,429	0	8	60	66	159	852	284	0
Ocean Pines	10,817	93	93	0	0	0	7	20	65	1	0
Takoma Park	17,827	1,099	1,099	0	6	92	26	107	639	229	0
Westminster	17,242	883	889	1	3	19	91	119	620	30	6
MASSACHUSETTS											
Abington[6]	14,786			0	5	4		60	177	31	8
Acton	20,583	277	282	0	1	1	1	61	197	16	5
Acushnet	10,287	146	150	0	3	1	20	33	79	10	4
Agawam	28,493	843	848	0	4	7	70	385	297	80	5
Amesbury	16,654	308	311	0	10	3	56	49	172	18	3
Amherst	35,306	663		0	17	9	70	221	311	35	
Andover	31,634	457	457	1	3	0	8	83	328	34	0
Arlington	42,915	476	477	0	6	18	44	127	244	37	1
Ashland	14,856	137	137	0	2	1	33	33	64	4	0

See footnotes at end of table.

Table 8

Offenses Known to Law Enforcement

by City 10,000 and over in Population, 2002—Continued

City by state	Population	Crime Index	Modified Crime Index[1]	Murder and non-negligent man-slaughter	Forcible rape	Robbery	Aggravated assault	Burglary	Larceny-theft	Motor vehicle theft	Arson[1]
MASSACHUSETTS—Continued											
Athol	11,439	304	309	0	4	5	79	98	104	14	5
Attleboro	42,589	973		0	7	17	99	197	547	106	
Barnstable	48,412	1,643	1,675	3	28	36	268	446	743	119	32
Bedford	12,751	42	42	0	0	0	1	2	36	3	0
Belchertown	13,128	214	215	0	5	1	20	72	88	28	1
Bellingham	15,504	363	365	0	3	5	12	126	206	11	2
Belmont	24,494	197	197	0	0	2	19	51	111	14	0
Beverly	40,356	853	855	0	8	15	90	139	554	47	2
Billerica	39,465	524	530	0	2	3	16	46	410	47	6
Boston	596,444	35,706		60	369	2,533	3,994	3,830	17,824	7,096	
Bourne[6]	18,954			1	5	9		235	322	37	10
Braintree	34,247	1,285	1,289	0	2	27	85	100	945	126	4
Brewster	10,219	111	111	0	0	0	5	20	83	3	0
Brockton	95,473	5,167		9	44	251	767	681	2,252	1,163	
Brookline	57,815	1,269		1	9	54	116	213	772	104	
Burlington	23,160	921		0	0	10	11	53	789	58	
Cambridge	102,611	4,306		6	11	195	285	720	2,664	425	
Canton	21,032	229	229	0	1	4	5	33	170	16	0
Charlton[6]	11,402			0	2	0		28	89	10	1
Chelmsford	34,278	552	554	0	1	2	30	47	441	31	2
Chelsea	35,515	1,867	1,880	4	39	134	488	281	481	440	13
Chicopee	55,330	2,447	2,460	1	20	51	345	534	1,139	357	13
Clinton	13,601	95	96	0	0	4	14	13	58	6	1
Concord	17,203	199	201	0	0	2	15	12	168	2	2
Danvers	25,525	1,069	1,077	0	3	11	35	67	873	80	8
Dartmouth	31,046	1,066	1,072	1	10	11	86	210	677	71	6
Dedham	23,754	429	429	0	0	7	13	30	334	45	0
Dennis	16,171	628	629	1	1	4	93	164	345	20	1
Dracut	28,916	419	420	1	2	4	15	101	227	69	1
East Bridgewater	13,134	87	87	0	1	1	5	11	64	5	0
Easthampton	16,192	216	219	0	5	1	37	71	86	16	3
East Longmeadow	14,275	501	502	0	2	2	16	81	358	42	1
Easton	22,576	253	253	0	0	6	13	52	166	16	0
Everett	38,509	1,079	1,082	0	5	41	65	119	643	206	3
Fairhaven	16,360	615	617	2	6	17	81	141	340	28	2
Fall River	93,078	4,869		3	48	233	642	738	2,620	585	
Falmouth	33,065	1,122	1,126	0	5	8	88	190	795	36	4
Fitchburg	39,587	1,699		3	40	67	183	361	915	130	
Framingham	67,740	1,775		0	25	25	107	332	1,060	226	
Franklin	29,926	115	115	0	3	0	7	3	97	5	0
Gloucester	30,648	738	741	0	6	7	59	142	496	28	3
Greenfield[6]	18,393			0	18	15		225	350	40	7
Hanover	13,327	226	226	0	1	6	3	38	167	11	0
Harwich	12,540	295	297	0	0	0	29	61	194	11	2
Haverhill	59,700	1,776		2	20	43	213	611	638	249	
Holbrook	10,918	236		0	3	9	8	63	131	22	
Holden	15,815	124	128	0	3	0	20	21	74	6	4
Holliston	13,972	99	99	0	0	1	5	17	68	8	0
Holyoke	40,332	3,346	3,370	3	35	92	332	433	2,049	402	24
Hudson	18,338	255	259	0	0	1	3	22	216	13	4
Hull	11,187	146	148	0	8	3	39	25	54	17	2
Ipswich	13,148	201	201	0	2	0	7	47	138	7	0
Kingston	11,926	325	325	0	0	7	3	15	275	25	0
Lawrence	72,936	3,195		2	27	155	344	382	776	1,509	
Leicester	10,601	129	130	0	3	2	20	22	74	8	1
Leominster	41,815	1,195	1,195	0	6	28	29	151	888	93	0
Lexington[6]	30,731			0	0	2		22	256	3	2
Longmeadow	15,827	186	187	0	0	0	1	11	168	6	1
Lowell	106,472	4,258		7	47	158	637	630	1,957	822	
Ludlow	21,472	412	415	0	1	6	35	80	253	37	3
Lynn	90,156	3,924		3	9	180	665	561	1,463	1,043	
Lynnfield[6]	11,685			0	0	0		66	133	13	0
Mansfield	22,692	273	279	0	4	5	54	53	135	22	6
Marblehead	20,629	233	234	0	0	3	16	13	194	7	1
Marlborough	36,704	700	702	0	2	8	63	89	502	36	2

See footnotes at end of table.

Table 8

Offenses Known to Law Enforcement
by City 10,000 and over in Population, 2002—Continued

City by state	Population	Crime Index	Modified Crime Index[1]	Murder and non-negligent man-slaughter	Forcible rape	Robbery	Aggravated assault	Burglary	Larceny-theft	Motor vehicle theft	Arson[1]
MASSACHUSETTS—Continued											
Marshfield	24,625	251	251	0	3	2	31	27	172	16	0
Mashpee	13,106	178	178	0	0	1	4	48	114	11	0
Maynard	10,563	74	74	0	1	0	5	20	46	2	0
Medford	56,456	1,486		0	8	45	25	196	1,041	171	
Medway	12,602	46	46	0	0	0	9	6	31	0	0
Melrose	27,471	340	342	0	2	8	13	73	212	32	2
Methuen	44,332	1,231	1,235	0	5	14	67	138	799	208	4
Middleboro	20,189	446	451	0	2	7	30	72	287	48	5
Millbury[6]	12,943			0	1	3		49	76	22	3
Natick	32,569	776		0	2	16	10	75	639	34	
Needham	29,269	252	255	0	1	1	7	27	203	13	3
Norfolk	10,590	42	42	0	1	0	1	16	20	4	0
North Adams	14,863	600	604	0	15	7	73	178	303	24	4
North Andover	27,539	225	225	0	1	2	8	58	146	10	0
North Attleboro	27,480	991	993	0	1	2	14	97	754	123	2
Northborough	14,187	161	162	0	0	1	3	28	117	12	1
Northbridge	13,345	264	265	0	9	2	28	84	129	12	1
Norton	18,260	124	124	0	2	0	2	20	94	6	0
Oxford	13,517	221	224	0	5	8	52	50	89	17	3
Palmer	12,651	372	381	0	6	2	47	89	199	29	9
Peabody	48,726	1,467	1,468	0	5	22	75	361	865	139	1
Pembroke	17,137	316	321	0	4	2	37	73	189	11	5
Pepperell	11,280	125	125	0	0	0	6	28	86	5	0
Plymouth	52,342	1,208	1,217	0	9	29	110	224	750	86	9
Quincy	89,118	2,455		5	17	86	156	434	1,518	239	
Randolph	31,347	803	804	0	6	18	40	105	540	94	1
Reading	24,001	161	161	0	0	1	2	30	118	10	0
Rehoboth	10,298	165	165	0	1	1	14	46	89	14	0
Revere	47,869	1,945	1,951	0	11	51	170	278	1,064	371	6
Rockland	17,889	379		0	6	11	44	65	180	73	
Salem	40,908	1,057	1,057	0	7	22	51	117	743	117	0
Sandwich	20,385	315	318	0	2	4	50	28	226	5	3
Saugus[6]	26,401			0	3	23		247	776	139	1
Scituate	18,084	131	132	0	2	0	16	34	67	12	1
Seekonk	13,591	657	657	0	2	3	39	91	484	38	0
Sharon	17,624	130		0	2	2	3	22	96	5	
Somerset	18,461	452	455	0	4	8	69	62	286	23	3
Somerville	78,438	2,559		3	27	125	193	427	1,361	433	
Southbridge	17,427	561	571	1	11	11	103	154	245	36	10
South Hadley	17,409	343	347	1	1	2	30	76	204	29	4
Springfield	153,967	14,299	14,424	12	107	585	2,400	3,808	5,117	2,270	125
Stoughton	27,486	517	524	2	9	17	70	113	240	66	7
Sudbury	17,050	139	139	0	0	1	7	18	111	2	0
Swansea[6]	16,098			1	1	6		41	260	39	0
Taunton	56,670	1,641	1,641	0	11	39	230	261	934	166	0
Tyngsboro	11,218	281	282	0	1	1	21	67	151	40	1
Uxbridge	11,294	143	146	0	3	0	10	42	75	13	3
Walpole	23,107	268	268	0	2	2	7	22	213	22	0
Waltham	59,960	1,126		1	5	19	67	144	779	111	
Watertown	33,395	636		0	0	10	34	81	470	41	
Wayland	13,262	117	117	0	2	2	4	24	82	3	0
Webster	16,619	509	512	1	5	6	35	58	370	34	3
Wellesley	26,943	336	336	0	1	2	17	74	231	11	0
Westborough	18,221	358	358	0	4	2	45	44	226	37	0
Westfield[6]	40,569			3	11	14		188	516	99	6
Westford	21,011	109	109	0	0	3	3	5	95	3	0
Westport	14,359	285	288	0	8	0	48	70	127	32	3
West Springfield	28,245	1,759	1,762	0	5	23	75	292	1,106	258	3
Westwood	14,292	155	156	0	1	4	6	21	115	8	1
Weymouth	54,658	1,005		0	5	24	192	117	563	104	
Wilbraham	13,640	330	330	0	1	2	25	38	223	41	0
Wilmington	21,628	466		0	7	5	49	64	312	29	
Winchester	21,068	239	239	1	0	0	4	32	191	11	0
Winthrop[6]	18,530			0	0	3		75	98	12	3
Woburn	37,720	992	997	0	2	22	67	106	708	87	5
Wrentham	10,685	74	74	0	2	0	1	6	65	0	0

See footnotes at end of table.

Table 8

Offenses Known to Law Enforcement

by City 10,000 and over in Population, 2002—Continued

City by state	Population	Crime Index	Modified Crime Index[1]	Murder and non-negligent man-slaughter	Forcible rape	Robbery	Aggravated assault	Burglary	Larceny-theft	Motor vehicle theft	Arson[1]
MICHIGAN											
Adrian	21,817	1,073	1,081	1	24	16	56	130	793	53	8
Allen Park	29,707	688	693	0	2	11	24	147	415	89	5
Alpena	11,431	467	469	0	14	4	23	70	341	15	2
Ann Arbor	115,309	3,727	3,762	5	26	87	183	859	2,385	182	35
Auburn Hills	20,060	1,378	1,380	1	14	12	47	136	1,091	77	2
Battle Creek	53,965	4,715	4,745	5	79	139	617	810	2,780	285	30
Bay City	37,232	1,618	1,625	0	20	27	120	309	1,037	105	7
Benton Harbor	11,308	993	1,008	1	17	32	253	249	364	77	15
Benton Township	16,589	1,721	1,736	3	15	32	118	286	1,154	113	15
Berkley	15,706	237	238	0	1	7	6	48	157	18	1
Beverly Hills	10,554	114	114	0	1	3	6	19	83	2	0
Big Rapids	10,971	402	407	0	9	6	21	67	281	18	5
Birmingham	19,509	443	444	0	4	7	5	71	322	34	1
Blackman Township	23,057	618	628	1	10	4	30	84	443	46	10
Bloomfield Township	43,508	796	806	0	8	15	27	110	594	42	10
Bridgeport Township	11,841	331	336	0	7	7	42	62	186	27	5
Brownstown Township	23,248	798	801	0	5	14	72	175	452	80	3
Buena Vista Township	10,434	810	823	0	5	32	88	225	403	57	13
Burton	30,650	1,951	1,964	0	14	38	102	384	1,267	146	13
Cadillac	10,112	530	535	0	17	4	43	65	379	22	5
Canton Township	77,226	1,661	1,680	0	30	17	52	264	1,157	141	19
Chesterfield Township	37,826	701	702	0	1	4	7	88	535	66	1
Clawson	12,876	101	101	0	0	1	2	12	80	6	0
Clinton Township[3]	96,726	2,655	2,663	2	28	46	264	424	1,613	278	8
Coldwater	12,840	609	616	1	10	2	37	59	479	21	7
Davison Township	17,922	462	463	0	5	1	20	98	296	42	1
Dearborn	98,877	5,681	5,700	3	29	131	946	536	3,099	937	19
Detroit	961,987	85,035	87,464	402	708	6,288	12,542	14,399	26,839	23,857	2,429
Dewitt Township	12,280	268	268	1	7	3	10	62	168	17	0
East Grand Rapids	10,885	136	136	0	1	0	8	27	95	5	0
East Lansing	47,049	1,455	1,474	0	25	30	131	184	1,038	47	19
Eastpointe	34,461	1,350	1,357	2	5	55	108	169	748	263	7
Emmett Township	12,114	831	838	0	9	17	57	113	581	54	7
Farmington	10,540	247	247	0	1	4	7	31	188	16	0
Farmington Hills	83,036	1,799	1,811	0	13	36	125	345	1,172	108	12
Fenton	10,701	285	289	0	3	4	13	46	202	17	4
Ferndale	22,354	916	921	0	11	34	46	165	496	164	5
Flint[3]	126,351	9,714	9,801	30	101	449	1,133	2,261	4,398	1,342	87
Flint Township	34,071	2,663	2,671	5	21	70	114	391	1,797	265	8
Flushing Township	10,345	107	107	0	2	0	4	31	65	5	0
Fraser	15,469	477	480	0	8	3	18	47	363	38	3
Garden City	30,386	814	823	2	7	14	71	169	459	92	9
Genesee Township	24,397	854	859	2	18	17	93	206	443	75	5
Grand Blanc Township	30,164	770	774	0	6	5	34	137	509	79	4
Grand Haven	11,294	467	469	0	8	1	24	107	310	17	2
Grand Rapids[3]	200,029	11,292	11,391	8	75	508	1,588	2,309	6,124	680	99
Grandville	16,446	1,100	1,103	0	19	3	28	114	903	33	3
Green Oak Township	15,794	211	211	0	2	2	9	49	118	31	0
Grosse Ile Township	11,016	87	87	0	0	0	0	8	79	0	0
Grosse Pointe Park	12,583	306	307	0	0	8	2	26	207	63	1
Grosse Pointe Woods	17,273	281	285	0	0	5	11	30	216	19	4
Hamburg Township	20,860	210	213	0	2	2	10	38	140	18	3
Hampton Township	10,014	276	276	0	4	2	9	30	219	12	0
Hamtramck	23,235	1,582	1,592	1	6	141	195	349	371	519	10
Harper Woods	14,414	633	633	0	5	15	1	57	391	164	0
Hazel Park	19,176	703	708	1	9	25	53	126	357	132	5
Holland	35,443	1,309	1,317	0	26	7	76	208	944	48	8
Huron Township	13,892	334	338	0	3	2	23	96	171	39	4
Inkster	30,455	1,465	1,486	0	25	74	312	347	436	271	21
Ionia	10,688	336	336	0	16	4	11	45	244	16	0
Jackson	37,819	2,821	2,864	5	43	76	321	426	1,764	186	43
Kalamazoo	78,014	6,315	6,393	6	40	158	648	1,171	3,696	596	78
Kalamazoo Township	21,919	1,121	1,126	2	11	11	73	226	697	101	5
Kentwood	45,765	1,671	1,690	1	22	29	69	367	1,105	78	19
Lansing	120,471	6,601	6,653	11	169	245	867	1,065	3,837	407	52

See footnotes at end of table.

Table 8

Offenses Known to Law Enforcement
by City 10,000 and over in Population, 2002—Continued

City by state	Population	Crime Index	Modified Crime Index[1]	Murder and non-negligent man-slaughter	Forcible rape	Robbery	Aggravated assault	Burglary	Larceny-theft	Motor vehicle theft	Arson[1]
MICHIGAN—Continued											
Leoni Township	13,611	411	412	0	4	1	10	77	304	15	1
Lincoln Park	40,459	1,969	1,978	0	9	47	95	360	1,146	312	9
Lincoln Township	14,109	309	312	0	5	1	20	74	202	7	3
Livonia	101,678	2,779	2,804	7	33	61	112	400	1,938	228	25
Madison Heights	31,451	1,304	1,312	1	9	32	38	171	874	179	8
Marquette	19,882	489	492	0	10	1	15	63	377	23	3
Melvindale	10,856	417	420	0	0	15	17	65	222	98	3
Meridian Township	39,557	1,350	1,359	0	8	13	55	210	1,035	29	9
Midland	42,154	955	963	0	27	7	42	131	721	27	8
Milford	15,443	181	189	0	2	1	5	45	111	17	8
Monroe	22,325	822	830	0	16	15	70	115	549	57	8
Mount Clemens	17,507	697	700	1	2	26	35	90	467	76	3
Mount Morris Township	23,992	1,389	1,398	2	23	41	124	413	607	179	9
Mount Pleasant	26,238	899	902	3	13	3	43	105	703	29	3
Mundy Township	12,328	391	393	0	1	2	16	58	299	15	2
Muskegon	40,557	3,482	3,504	4	58	83	321	471	2,135	410	22
Muskegon Heights	12,185	1,551	1,577	4	23	51	235	213	771	254	26
Muskegon Township	17,937	1,239	1,241	0	13	8	48	164	912	94	2
Niles	12,341	843	849	0	11	13	38	108	628	45	6
Northville Township	21,274	392	393	0	1	3	7	37	323	21	1
Norton Shores	22,781	1,128	1,133	0	6	11	41	103	893	74	5
Novi	47,920	1,492	1,497	1	5	8	36	189	1,183	70	5
Oak Park	30,128	1,076	1,077	1	8	53	60	194	562	198	1
Owosso	15,890	562	565	0	12	5	25	85	409	26	3
Pittsfield Township	30,507	1,120	1,124	0	4	19	45	149	812	91	4
Plymouth Township	28,112	428	430	0	1	7	15	66	302	37	2
Pontiac	67,085	4,004	4,046	5	79	193	817	989	1,464	457	42
Portage	45,403	2,177	2,181	1	13	13	90	269	1,710	81	4
Port Huron	32,703	1,379	1,390	0	47	30	116	191	898	97	11
Redford Township	52,203	1,918	1,924	0	19	68	76	330	990	435	6
Riverview	13,422	324	325	0	1	3	10	34	243	33	1
Rochester	10,585	181	182	0	1	0	1	26	146	7	1
Romulus	23,238	1,345	1,356	1	24	28	90	243	730	229	11
Roseville	48,671	2,500	2,522	2	12	58	98	169	1,812	349	22
Royal Oak	60,739	1,508	1,517	0	10	35	60	289	971	143	9
Saginaw	62,496	4,848	4,952	17	86	215	1,193	1,129	1,830	378	104
Saginaw Township	40,104	1,178	1,184	1	4	12	77	135	896	53	6
Sault Ste. Marie	16,729	350	353	0	2	0	22	39	276	11	3
Shelby Township	65,894	830	834	1	9	5	49	137	570	59	4
Southfield	79,178	4,543	4,556	6	25	128	693	567	2,329	795	13
Southgate	30,476	1,389	1,395	1	5	15	46	151	1,041	130	6
South Lyon	10,149	165	165	0	5	4	12	16	126	2	0
St. Clair Shores	63,807	1,734	1,741	0	11	31	123	326	1,088	155	7
Sterling Heights	125,873	3,377	3,397	1	30	35	180	397	2,489	245	20
St. Joseph Township	10,156	212	212	0	1	0	16	45	141	9	0
Sturgis	11,412	458	461	0	8	3	24	71	340	12	3
Summit Township	21,777	424	428	0	9	4	30	99	245	37	4
Sumpter Township	11,990	263	268	0	10	1	25	64	137	26	5
Taylor	66,610	3,418	3,447	3	45	60	186	672	1,972	480	29
Thomas Township	12,011	354	354	0	0	0	22	44	282	6	0
Traverse City	14,696	632	635	0	5	1	35	52	511	28	3
Trenton	19,805	368	369	0	2	3	25	50	262	26	1
Troy	81,871	2,077	2,087	1	17	21	55	346	1,512	125	10
Van Buren Township	23,825	491	493	0	4	6	10	69	335	67	2
Walker	22,088	1,175	1,183	0	13	4	30	153	931	44	8
Warren	139,805	5,358	5,410	8	68	204	577	870	2,483	1,148	52
Waterford Township	73,974	1,783	1,794	3	6	30	94	336	1,172	142	11
Wayne	19,266	1,059	1,068	1	9	23	95	153	614	164	9
West Bloomfield Township	65,591	767	773	1	2	6	4	116	614	24	6
Westland	87,578	3,042	3,075	1	36	56	205	532	1,746	466	33
White Lake Township	28,537	612	615	0	11	0	24	88	456	33	3
Wixom	13,413	465	466	1	6	2	12	56	370	18	1
Woodhaven	12,672	539	541	0	1	5	13	56	423	41	2
Wyoming	70,149	2,713	2,730	0	41	50	232	706	1,461	223	17
Ypsilanti	22,614	1,301	1,316	1	19	45	118	270	707	141	15

See footnotes at end of table.

Table 8

Offenses Known to Law Enforcement
by City 10,000 and over in Population, 2002—Continued

City by state	Population	Crime Index	Modified Crime Index[1]	Murder and non-negligent man-slaughter	Forcible rape	Robbery	Aggravated assault	Burglary	Larceny-theft	Motor vehicle theft	Arson[1]
MINNESOTA											
Albert Lea	18,730	548	548	0	1	3	15	46	456	27	0
Andover	27,130	733	738	0	3	1	14	93	595	27	5
Anoka	18,444	782	785	0	23	9	25	98	570	57	3
Apple Valley	46,455	1,380		0	7	19	35	145	1,113	61	
Austin	23,789	1,219	1,226	0	22	3	50	186	907	51	7
Bemidji	12,160	1,002	1,004	1	8	2	25	57	830	79	2
Blaine	45,857	2,376	2,385	0	23	16	46	252	1,927	112	9
Bloomington	86,907	4,008	4,023	1	16	71	80	350	3,248	242	15
Brainerd	13,446	979	994	1	23	7	35	138	719	56	15
Brooklyn Center	29,767	2,040	2,071	2	36	40	58	203	1,508	193	31
Brooklyn Park	68,761	3,204	3,218	2	31	84	122	569	2,116	280	14
Buffalo	10,303	394	397	0	7	1	10	29	332	15	3
Burnsville	61,447	2,187	2,190	1	26	33	46	286	1,665	130	3
Centennial Lakes	10,284	317	318	0	4	5	13	32	251	12	1
Champlin	22,645	532	533	0	8	3	13	68	417	23	1
Chanhassen	20,735	311	311	0	0	1	9	46	238	17	0
Chaska	17,805	394	404	0	2	2	15	44	320	11	10
Cloquet	11,429	465	465	0	1	1	25	53	353	32	0
Columbia Heights	18,897	892	898	0	14	28	40	105	636	69	6
Coon Rapids	62,863	2,762	2,783	2	29	26	41	251	2,274	139	21
Cottage Grove	31,205	818	826	0	10	4	28	123	636	17	8
Crystal	23,160	916	925	0	2	12	24	130	693	55	9
Duluth	88,689	5,340	5,350	3	54	93	233	780	3,867	310	10
Eagan	64,852	1,774	1,784	2	7	30	19	269	1,359	88	10
East Bethel	11,164	363	368	0	6	2	10	58	256	31	5
Eden Prairie	56,020	1,312	1,331	0	11	21	35	176	1,012	57	19
Edina	48,391	1,217	1,220	0	7	23	18	187	940	42	3
Elk River	16,782	782	782	0	3	1	14	113	626	25	0
Fairmont	11,111	578	580	0	5	0	29	80	444	20	2
Faribault	21,242	1,036	1,053	0	17	6	37	186	739	51	17
Farmington	12,617	304	307	0	6	1	4	40	241	12	3
Fergus Falls	13,745	582	589	0	10	0	35	89	430	18	7
Fridley	28,008	1,632	1,650	1	13	32	45	168	1,264	109	18
Golden Valley	20,694	639	645	0	6	12	16	109	462	34	6
Ham Lake	12,969	378	378	0	0	1	7	66	272	32	0
Hastings	18,575	524	530	0	7	2	21	63	410	21	6
Hibbing	17,419	314	315	0	5	1	6	77	204	21	1
Hopkins	17,495	398	402	0	8	6	15	68	264	37	4
Hutchinson	13,347	558	562	0	17	2	26	103	395	15	4
Inver Grove Heights	30,357	1,032	1,045	1	14	7	31	156	746	77	13
Lakeville	44,006	949	958	0	0	7	17	103	794	28	9
Lino Lakes	17,133	331	331	0	4	0	8	35	255	29	0
Mankato	33,088	1,998	1,998	0	26	6	35	237	1,617	77	0
Maple Grove	51,391	1,238	1,249	4	7	7	43	170	964	43	11
Maplewood	35,659	2,562	2,582	0	17	26	57	233	2,074	155	20
Marshall	12,994	579	579	0	10	2	19	71	460	17	0
Minneapolis	390,415	26.630	26,891	47	362	1,794	1,920	4,433	14,641	3,433	261
Minnetonka	52,346	1,270	1,278	0	11	15	19	224	945	56	8
Moorhead	32,833	1,264	1,271	0	20	6	57	142	968	71	7
Mounds View	12,997	584	587	0	8	5	16	62	447	46	3
New Brighton	22,659	666	671	1	0	9	6	98	507	45	5
New Hope	21,298	616	617	1	5	7	22	77	468	36	1
New Ulm	13,871	353	357	0	2	1	9	52	272	17	4
Northfield	17,497	615	617	0	2	3	20	91	462	37	2
North Mankato	12,038	283	285	0	6	0	0	13	244	20	2
North St. Paul	12,172	455	456	0	4	3	13	54	338	43	1
Oakdale	27,196	1,259	1,268	0	20	8	38	115	981	97	9
Orono	11,949	289	290	0	0	1	4	31	231	22	1
Owatonna	22,891	836	853	0	12	3	27	200	558	36	17
Plymouth	67,236	1,926	1,942	0	18	13	42	378	1,383	92	16
Prior Lake	16,241	594	594	1	11	7	25	81	429	40	0
Ramsey	18,887	593	595	0	9	3	10	83	453	35	2
Red Wing	16,444	775	783	0	9	4	25	90	605	42	8
Richfield	35,140	1,363	1,380	1	16	53	76	207	887	123	17
Robbinsdale	14,411	666	668	1	4	25	21	149	411	55	2

See footnotes at end of table.

Table 8

Offenses Known to Law Enforcement

by City 10,000 and over in Population, 2002—Continued

City by state	Population	Crime Index	Modified Crime Index[1]	Murder and non-negligent man-slaughter	Forcible rape	Robbery	Aggravated assault	Burglary	Larceny-theft	Motor vehicle theft	Arson[1]
MINNESOTA—Continued											
Rochester	87,555	3,003	3,050	1	44	43	144	455	2,136	180	47
Rosemount	14,917	603	607	0	8	5	10	90	465	25	4
Roseville	34,377	1,659	1,659	0	5	17	26	146	1,344	121	0
Sauk Rapids	10,421	334	343	0	7	2	4	32	285	4	9
Savage	21,545	624	632	0	7	5	27	123	424	38	8
Shakopee	20,987	747	750	0	5	5	21	95	576	45	3
Shoreview	26,452	471	483	0	5	3	8	48	385	22	12
South Lake Minnetonka	12,315	269	272	0	3	3	5	50	202	6	3
South St. Paul	20,578	775	779	1	7	7	35	105	553	67	4
St. Cloud	60,312	3,238		0	51	37	103	306	2,570	171	
Stillwater	15,451	511	514	0	3	4	12	69	395	28	3
St. Louis Park	45,026	1,398	1,416	0	9	26	20	164	1,084	95	18
St. Paul	293,002	17,803	18,011	13	192	973	1,181	3,232	10,041	2,171	208
Vadnais Heights	13,335	321	326	0	3	0	5	37	252	24	5
West St. Paul	19,801	1,091	1,093	1	6	24	36	114	847	63	2
White Bear Lake	24,821	889	896	0	1	6	14	179	635	54	7
Willmar	18,725	852	861	0	28	2	39	102	648	33	9
Winona	27,621	828	829	0	1	4	14	115	656	38	1
Woodbury	47,409	1,154	1,163	0	8	6	26	149	904	61	9
Worthington	11,513	363	364	0	2	3	17	66	268	7	1
MISSISSIPPI											
Biloxi	51,127	3,852	3,873	2	29	120	178	921	2,305	297	21
Brandon	16,593	270	274	0	6	4	5	41	205	9	4
Columbus	26,191	1,732	1,741	3	12	18	35	280	1,298	86	9
Greenwood	18,601	1,470	1,471	4	7	37	38	324	990	70	1
Grenada	15,021	850	856	1	5	22	60	189	524	49	6·
Gulfport	71,805	5,818	5,843	11	48	165	102	1,168	3,856	468	25
Hattiesburg	45,206	3,526	3,536	10	17	149	63	770	2,358	159	10
Horn Lake	14,234	981	987	0	11	16	27	91	754	82	6
Indianola	12,181	812	817	2	7	16	43	205	520	19	5
Jackson	186,012	17,648	17,721	49	182	1,074	497	4,377	8,669	2,800	73
Laurel	18,568	1,920	1,924	1	10	63	90	271	1,424	61	4
Long Beach	17,485	665	671	1	2	14	3	159	442	44	6
Madison	14,832	176	177	0	6	1	3	25	139	2	1
McComb	13,464	806	806	0	1	19	47	140	534	65	0
Meridian	40,349	1,812	1,836	2	22	63	81	534	955	155	24
Ocean Springs	17,389	821	821	1	5	20	11	147	595	42	0
Olive Branch	21,255	883	885	1	11	16	39	259	474	83	2
Pascagoula	26,450	2,344	2,353	2	14	84	53	505	1,436	250	9
Pearl	22,170	953	955	0	38	24	57	317	451	66	2
Picayune	10,636	747	751	0	9	9	19	111	553	46	4
Ridgeland	20,365	1,029	1,031	1	6	27	10	78	867	40	2
Southaven	29,254	2,057	2,060	1	2	35	21	174	1,611	213	3
Starkville	22,078	1,110	1,113	2	4	10	50	193	820	31	3
Tupelo	34,537	2,230	2,233	1	23	55	47	489	1,433	182	3
Vicksburg	26,659	2,400	2,412	5	31	56	235	348	1,551	174	12
West Point	12,260	455	455	0	12	20	31	142	246	4	0
MISSOURI											
Arnold	20,241	1,213	1,219	0	6	10	145	51	965	36	6
Ballwin	31,715	352	354	0	0	0	18	76	241	17	2
Bellefontaine Neighbors	11,427	572	574	0	0	15	21	82	348	106	2
Belton	22,030	644	651	2	8	1	47	76	476	34	7
Berkeley	10,202	774	780	2	2	28	85	116	336	205	6
Blue Springs	48,745	1,972	1,983	0	13	30	56	268	1,459	146	11
Bridgeton	15,765	1,136	1,136	1	9	24	50	140	787	125	0
Cape Girardeau	35,838	2,179	2,179	1	16	42	6	250	1,820	44	0
Carthage	12,843	496	496	0	4	4	23	69	379	17	0
Chesterfield	47,449	1,018	1,024	0	4	13	23	169	786	23	6
Clayton	13,002	449	451	0	0	4	7	35	372	31	2
Columbia	85,700	3,837	3,850	2	31	90	287	432	2,801	194	13
Crestwood	12,027	965	966	0	5	3	47	35	847	28	1

See footnotes at end of table.

Table 8

Offenses Known to Law Enforcement
by City 10,000 and over in Population, 2002—Continued

City by state	Population	Crime Index	Modified Crime Index[1]	Murder and non-negligent man-slaughter	Forcible rape	Robbery	Aggravated assault	Burglary	Larceny-theft	Motor vehicle theft	Arson[1]
MISSOURI—Continued											
Creve Coeur	16,728	387	389	0	0	8	17	49	284	29	2
Excelsior Springs[3]	10,997	562	574	0	5	2	72	109	332	42	12
Farmington	14,117	713	719	0	4	3	141	59	476	30	6
Ferguson	22,716	1,559	1,560	1	12	44	36	247	973	246	1
Florissant	51,195	1,287	1,287	0	2	39	31	171	919	125	0
Fulton	12,295	325	328	0	6	2	20	51	231	15	3
Gladstone	26,729	795	802	0	12	16	i5	111	554	87	7
Grandview	25,225	1,070	1,074	0	11	50	89	280	466	174	4
Hannibal	18,003	1,071	1,076	1	11	11	59	211	739	39	5
Hazelwood	26,568	786	786	0	7	16	73	132	444	114	0
Independence	114,854	8,483	8,531	6	33	124	489	1,210	5,833	788	48
Jackson	12,112	303	304	0	1	5	17	41	226	13	1
Jefferson City	40,184	1,596	1,613	1	10	37	237	213	1,025	73	17
Jennings	15,683	1,402	1,407	3	8	50	72	241	799	229	5
Joplin	46,133	3,689	3,713	1	32	63	!10	618	2,649	216	24
Kansas City	447,650	44,942	45,420	83	300	2,011	3,660	7,978	24,161	6,749	478
Kennett	11,416	445	447	0	5	14	18	101	292	15	2
Kirksville	17,223	704	705	1	6	6	30	110	530	21	1
Kirkwood	27,702	732	742	0	5	7	32	62	600	26	10
Lake St. Louis	10,310	208	211	0	0	1	18	16	160	13	3
Lebanon	12,323	854	857	0	2	1	104	112	605	30	3
Lee's Summit	71,678	2,040	2,047	1	9	42	15	248	1,594	131	7
Liberty	26,594	671	678	1	4	12	90	99	400	65	7
Manchester	19,426	203	203	0	0	0	5	31	159	8	0
Marshall	12,605	287	287	2	2	0	3	50	221	9	0
Maryland Heights	26,112	1,089	1,092	0	2	14	15	145	843	70	3
Maryville	10,728	172	175	0	1	0	26	15	123	7	3
Mexico	11,476	354	356	1	0	7	18	68	247	13	2
Moberly	12,110	740	742	0	3	4	31	121	567	14	2
Neosho	10,650	673	675	0	2	2	100	98	442	29	2
Nixa	12,291	295	295	0	0	1	6	66	217	5	0
O'Fallon	46,807	1,904	1,910	0	7	9	53	200	1,591	44	6
Overland	17,071	616	616	0	0	20	38	142	396	20	0
Poplar Bluff	16,881	1,095	1,111	2	12	11	54	151	813	52	16
Raymore	11,300	258	260	0	2	4	10	29	204	9	2
Raytown	30,809	1,161	1,166	0	9	32	41	268	675	136	5
Rolla	16,593	867	871	0	7	14	21	122	678	25	4
Sedalia	20,620	1,670	1,678	0	3	17	178	281	1,150	41	8
Sikeston	17,227	787	791	2	8	23	23	118	582	31	4
Springfield	153,675	12,066	12,150	4	102	222	733	1,882	8,352	771	84
St. Ann	13,795	1,242	1,244	0	6	14	55	77	981	109	2
St. Charles	61,155	1,842	1,857	1	16	27	69	250	1,350	129	15
St. Joseph	75,013	4,738	4,758	0	20	67	106	689	3,652	204	20
St. Louis	353,004	50,429	51,014	111	136	2,818	4,434	7,059	26,036	9,835	585
St. Peters	52,092	1,672	1,672	2	14	33	107	166	1,296	54	0
Town and Country	11,045	261	265	0	1	2	17	19	214	8	4
University City	37,946	2,220	2,236	4	13	65	76	392	1,467	203	16
Warrensburg	16,566	574	577	0	4	8	21	81	430	30	3
Washington	13,426	366	369	0	3	2	13	29	295	24	3
Webster Groves	23,551	320	322	0	1	6	15	40	222	36	2
West Plains	11,016	797	800	0	4	1	77	127	548	40	3
MONTANA											
Billings	90,569	4,846		0	13	59	143	407	3,943	281	
Bozeman	27,730	1,764		0	22	12	77	121	1,460	72	
Great Falls	57,146	4,529		4	16	32	215	333	3,765	164	
Kalispell	14,337	949		1	0	5	48	74	779	42	
NEBRASKA											
Beatrice	12,627	823	827	0	3	2	21	160	591	46	4
Bellevue	44,847	1,678	1,698	0	12	19	24	181	1,286	156	20
Columbus	21,191	561	563	0	5	4	3	76	449	24	2
Fremont	25,437	1,083	1,088	0	5	9	8	170	859	32	5

See footnotes at end of table.

Table 8

Offenses Known to Law Enforcement
by City 10,000 and over in Population, 2002—Continued

City by state	Population	Crime Index	Modified Crime Index[1]	Murder and non-negligent man-slaughter	Forcible rape	Robbery	Aggravated assault	Burglary	Larceny-theft	Motor vehicle theft	Arson[1]
NEBRASKA—Continued											
Grand Island	43,389	2,894	2,895	2	16	22	94	474	2,169	117	1
Hastings	24,316	1,266	1,269	0	13	10	18	154	1,018	53	3
Kearney	27,719	1,346	1,358	0	15	4	54	232	1,000	41	12
La Vista	11,821	403	409	0	3	8	5	37	310	40	6
Lexington	10,115	413	414	0	0	2	15	47	327	22	1
Lincoln	227,943	15,005	15,031	6	98	179	992	2,014	11,190	526	26
Norfolk	23,763	1,439	1,443	6	19	9	17	190	1,136	62	4
Omaha	394,090	28,781	29,049	26	173	998	1,632	3,220	18,490	4,242	268
Papillion	16,534	351	352	0	3	1	4	22	302	19	1
Scottsbluff	14,887	965	967	0	6	9	36	125	758	31	2
South Sioux City	12,050	431	433	0	2	6	5	47	351	20	2
NEVADA											
Boulder City	16,278	323	326	0	0	6	55	87	150	25	3
Elko	18,174	632	641	1	7	6	23	148	419	28	9
Henderson	190,761	5,781	5,837	4	104	200	146	1,470	2,705	1,152	56
Las Vegas Metropolitan Police Department[3]	1,153,546	56,810	57,080	137	494	3,776	4,574	11,136	24,204	12,489	270
Mesquite	10,212	243	243	0	0	4	10	17	173	39	0
North Las Vegas	125,616	7,367	7,435	19	57	449	769	1,525	3,029	1,519	68
Reno[3]	196,307	11,626	11,690	9	126	450	899	1,288	7,748	1,106	64
Sparks	72,164	3,741		2	52	102	193	673	2,407	312	
NEW HAMPSHIRE											
Amherst	11,111	190	191	0	1	3	1	6	178	1	1
Bedford	18,855	228	230	0	3	3	4	23	181	14	2
Berlin	10,659	174	175	0	13	1	10	18	118	14	1
Claremont	13,569	325	330	0	4	4	16	36	242	23	5
Derry	35,102	829	875	0	9	5	55	164	523	73	46
Exeter	14,505	192	197	0	2	3	5	21	153	8	5
Hampton	15,412	512	516	0	13	7	21	78	363	30	4
Hanover	11,195	106	111	0	1	1	2	14	82	6	5
Hooksett	12,094	298	300	0	10	2	2	26	247	11	2
Hudson	23,656	373	377	0	7	8	21	59	247	31	4
Keene	23,280	762	774	0	12	4	23	110	576	37	12
Lebanon	12,968	542	546	1	4	2	22	63	434	16	4
Londonderry	23,974	285	294	0	9	6	23	51	155	41	9
Manchester	110,406	3,545	3,599	0	44	116	82	617	2,441	245	54
Merrimack	25,917	284	285	0	0	0	0	36	237	11	1
Milford	13,965	219	221	0	8	2	17	26	149	17	2
Portsmouth	21,444	860	871	0	20	13	22	97	653	55	11
Rochester	29,366	834	837	0	41	3	17	82	658	33	3
Somersworth	11,842	539	548	0	0	2	19	56	420	42	9
Windham	11,049	160	164	0	1	3	5	34	103	14	4
NEW JERSEY											
Aberdeen Township	17,819	377	381	0	2	13	18	57	256	31	4
Asbury Park	17,284	1,259	1,265	3	9	171	163	246	525	142	6
Atlantic City	41,364	5,346	5,402	5	21	283	354	482	4,031	170	56
Barnegat Township	15,590	178	180	0	2	7	14	29	117	9	2
Bayonne	63,135	1,099	1,103	4	3	93	108	186	584	121	4
Beachwood	10,592	239	239	0	0	1	11	28	193	6	0
Belleville	36,679	1,142	1,148	0	11	57	57	213	560	244	6
Bellmawr	11,498	246	246	0	1	6	10	27	176	26	0
Bergenfield	26,796	322	323	1	0	10	15	42	234	20	1
Berkeley Heights Township	13,687	79	79	0	0	0	3	22	42	12	0
Berkeley Township	40,827	659	665	0	4	11	52	155	424	13	6
Bernards Township	25,089	232	234	0	0	2	12	49	157	12	2
Bloomfield	48,680	2,066	2,071	0	11	106	49	287	1,083	530	5
Bound Brook	10,368	301	302	0	3	13	8	88	180	9	1
Branchburg Township	14,871	162	168	0	0	0	0	29	123	10	6
Brick Township	77,710	1,410	1,415	0	1	28	63	221	1,039	58	5

See footnotes at end of table.

Table 8

Offenses Known to Law Enforcement
by City 10,000 and over in Population, 2002—Continued

City by state	Population	Crime Index	Modified Crime Index[1]	Murder and non-negligent man-slaughter	Forcible rape	Robbery	Aggravated assault	Burglary	Larceny-theft	Motor vehicle theft	Arson[1]
NEW JERSEY—Continued											
Bridgeton	23,247	1,297	1,301	3	12	103	186	268	643	82	4
Bridgewater Township	43,838	712	714	0	0	7	12	97	549	47	2
Brigantine	12,858	254	256	0	0	4	24	58	161	7	2
Burlington Township	20,718	624	633	1	4	25	19	70	453	52	9
Camden	81,575	6,125	6,347	33	45	607	797	1,155	2,407	1,081	222
Carteret	21,142	445	446	1	4	20	25	84	256	55	1
Cedar Grove Township	12,557	225	226	0	1	0	12	24	175	13	1
Chatham Township	10,297	58	59	0	0	1	0	8	47	2	1
Cherry Hill Township	71,428	2,274	2,277	1	8	56	67	257	1,774	111	3
Cinnaminson Township	14,900	319	321	0	0	11	9	51	224	24	2
Clark Township	14,902	204	204	1	0	3	3	17	159	21	0
Cliffside Park	23,489	278	278	0	0	6	21	69	157	25	0
Clifton	80,317	2,627	2,633	0	7	117	82	417	1,572	432	6
Clinton Township	13,228	123	123	0	0	1	0	29	92	1	0
Collingswood	14,626	416	417	0	0	19	12	86	263	36	1
Colts Neck Township	12,589	145	146	0	0	2	17	29	93	4	1
Cranford Township	23,050	448	449	0	2	5	11	70	320	40	1
Delran Township	15,861	404	405	0	1	8	10	79	273	33	1
Denville Township	16,155	222	224	0	0	2	13	23	167	17	2
Deptford Township	27,323	1,741	1,748	0	1	63	86	269	1,199	123	7
Dover	18,568	495	500	1	1	15	33	96	309	40	5
Dover Township	91,582	2,542	2,564	11	9	46	123	432	1,829	92	22
Dumont	17,869	264	264	1	4	3	20	69	158	9	0
East Brunswick Township	47,734	1,102	1,107	0	7	9	27	122	879	58	5
East Hanover Township	11,631	269	271	0	0	1	6	27	207	28	2
East Orange	71,284	5,954	6,063	16	54	698	752	912	1,999	1,523	109
East Windsor Township	25,441	523	524	0	1	11	18	107	364	22	1
Eatontown	14,301	688	690	1	3	14	10	77	552	31	2
Edison Township	99,731	2,578	2,588	0	15	70	138	358	1,600	397	10
Egg Harbor Township	31,368	1,348	1,364	0	8	31	63	213	959	74	16
Elizabeth	123,088	7,149	7,165	13	30	571	291	1,050	3,400	1,794	16
Elmwood Park	19,321	519	519	1	0	20	26	75	317	80	0
Englewood	26,751	661	665	1	1	25	41	167	375	51	4
Evesham Township	43,159	675	685	1	11	18	9	124	490	22	10
Ewing Township	36,454	1,139	1,142	0	7	37	37	159	707	192	3
Fair Lawn	32,299	567	567	0	5	26	21	151	336	28	0
Fairview	13,532	118	118	0	0	5	11	24	42	36	0
Florence Township	10,971	211	212	0	0	3	7	48	142	11	1
Fort Lee	36,203	814	816	1	1	14	2	91	653	52	2
Franklin Lakes	10,640	144	144	0	0	0	1	23	118	2	0
Franklin Township (Gloucester County)	15,790	423	428	0	3	3	24	116	248	29	5
Franklin Township (Somerset County)	51,967	1,141	1,157	0	5	41	40	228	682	145	16
Freehold	11,205	484	491	1	1	36	52	57	313	24	7
Freehold Township	32,197	1,043	1,049	0	1	22	28	68	885	39	6
Galloway Township	31,862	938	958	1	7	15	34	223	625	33	20
Garfield	30,409	583	586	1	1	18	18	92	346	107	3
Glassboro	19,466	801	810	0	9	33	37	132	554	36	9
Glen Rock	11,788	136	137	0	0	1	1	13	117	4	1
Gloucester City	11,724	266	267	1	2	12	17	31	184	19	1
Gloucester Township	65,696	1,625	1,642	0	16	55	115	302	1,035	102	17
Guttenberg	11,033	266	268	0	0	20	38	72	103	33	2
Hackensack	43,562	1,317	1,320	1	0	45	79	87	974	131	3
Hackettstown	10,621	172	172	0	0	3	11	22	129	7	0
Haddonfield	11,903	213	215	0	0	1	5	15	186	6	2
Haddon Township	14,957	419	421	0	1	12	16	82	283	25	2
Hamilton Township (Atlantic County)	20,928	1,028	1,041	1	5	36	65	152	728	41	13
Hamilton Township (Mercer County)	88,931	2,235	2,240	1	7	89	61	448	1,371	258	5
Hammonton	12,868	253	256	2	3	6	16	55	148	23	3
Hanover Township	13,167	125	125	0	1	2	13	31	59	19	0
Harrison	14,726	473	474	0	1	24	25	109	207	107	1
Hasbrouck Heights	11,906	196	196	0	0	4	0	29	133	30	0

See footnotes at end of table.

Table 8

Offenses Known to Law Enforcement

by City 10,000 and over in Population, 2002—Continued

City by state	Population	Crime Index	Modified Crime Index[1]	Murder and non-negligent man-slaughter	Forcible rape	Robbery	Aggravated assault	Burglary	Larceny-theft	Motor vehicle theft	Arson[1]
NEW JERSEY—Continued											
Hawthorne	18,599	344	346	0	3	3	3	46	260	29	2
Hazlet Township	21,825	305	306	0	0	4	6	42	236	17	1
Highland Park	14,292	260	260	0	1	1	2	54	186	16	0
Hillsborough Township	37,400	360	364	0	5	3	11	82	251	8	4
Hillsdale	10,298	100	101	0	0	0	3	10	85	2	1
Hillside Township	22,202	1,043	1,045	0	4	72	33	212	445	277	2
Hoboken	39,384	1,530	1,532	1	0	68	109	285	872	195	2
Holmdel Township	16,111	233	237	0	0	1	11	28	189	4	4
Hopatcong	16,221	153	153	0	0	0	7	24	114	8	0
Hopewell Township	16,442	125	126	0	0	3	13	34	73	2	1
Howell Township	49,925	731	735	0	2	6	44	122	511	46	4
Irvington	61,964	5,415	5,468	15	45	862	776	1,077	1,123	1,517	53
Jackson Township	43,711	546	552	0	1	7	42	98	357	41	6
Jefferson Township	20,130	200	200	0	1	0	8	54	123	14	0
Jersey City	245,075	12,182	12,213	21	86	1,381	1,419	2,285	4,694	2,296	31
Keansburg	10,956	413	416	2	3	6	31	95	255	21	3
Kearny	41,360	1,210	1,220	0	5	38	56	184	724	203	10
Lacey Township	25,876	504	505	1	0	3	22	56	408	14	1
Lakewood Township	61,614	1,785	1,800	2	13	90	116	426	1,004	134	15
Lawrence Township	29,768	1,177	1,181	0	6	31	31	156	853	100	4
Lincoln Park	11,159	132	133	0	1	3	5	11	107	5	1
Linden	40,218	1,879	1,880	1	8	79	57	212	1,126	396	1
Lindenwold	17,778	788	797	3	8	38	67	238	346	88	9
Little Egg Harbor Township	16,278	464	466	0	6	3	24	70	347	14	2
Little Falls Township	11,082	415	415	0	1	4	13	42	272	83	0
Little Ferry	11,026	135	135	1	1	5	13	21	67	27	0
Livingston Township	27,964	685	686	0	0	7	13	39	570	56	1
Lodi	24,473	529	532	0	0	11	43	64	335	76	3
Long Branch	31,995	1,046	1,047	1	2	43	97	262	586	55	1
Lower Township	23,425	565	565	0	5	2	31	86	419	22	0
Lumberton Township	10,679	373	380	1	4	11	11	55	273	18	7
Lyndhurst Township	19,788	402	403	0	4	13	14	55	275	41	1
Madison	16,876	190	190	0	0	3	6	16	158	7	0
Mahwah Township	24,565	280	280	0	0	5	1	29	215	30	0
Manalapan Township	34,122	327	327	0	0	3	28	69	212	15	0
Manchester Township	39,742	336	341	1	2	1	24	80	204	24	5
Mantua Township	14,514	303	306	0	1	5	8	39	235	15	3
Manville	10,559	222	222	0	0	3	4	35	165	15	0
Maple Shade Township	19,478	599	602	1	7	25	43	97	347	79	3
Maplewood Township	24,367	672	674	0	2	52	39	111	324	144	2
Marlboro Township	37,160	459	461	1	1	8	20	94	316	19	2
Medford Township	22,718	376	376	1	0	2	9	76	275	13	0
Metuchen	13,109	284	287	0	0	5	9	58	194	18	3
Middlesex	14,004	151	151	0	0	3	11	25	101	11	0
Middle Township	16,748	612	623	0	5	10	42	117	401	37	11
Middletown Township	67,714	856	859	0	2	4	40	127	626	57	3
Millburn Township	20,178	810	810	0	2	10	9	58	665	66	0
Millville	27,409	1,590	1,603	0	15	61	104	386	951	73	13
Monroe Township (Gloucester County)	29,573	879	884	1	6	12	29	193	577	61	5
Monroe Township (Middlesex County)	28,584	307	311	0	2	5	10	46	232	12	4
Montclair	39,792	1,355	1,357	0	6	52	72	320	682	223	2
Montgomery Township	17,847	171	171	0	0	1	1	22	142	5	0
Montville Township	21,275	256	259	0	1	2	8	42	165	38	3
Moorestown Township	19,415	531	532	0	5	11	11	48	428	28	1
Morristown	18,932	749	750	0	13	47	57	81	487	64	1
Morris Township	22,252	212	213	0	1	5	24	23	131	28	1
Mount Holly Township	10,952	576	584	1	2	35	71	87	347	33	8
Mount Laurel Township	41,063	864	871	0	9	34	14	202	560	45	7
Mount Olive Township	24,699	373	373	0	8	0	25	76	250	14	0
Neptune Township	32,614	1,445	1,449	2	1	50	67	251	930	144	4
Newark	279,269	17,814	18,061	65	88	1,567	1,473	2,253	6,033	6,335	247
New Brunswick	49,589	2,940	2,945	3	14	219	122	636	1,625	321	5
New Milford	16,743	136	136	0	0	2	8	23	97	6	0

See footnotes at end of table.

Table 8

Offenses Known to Law Enforcement
by City 10,000 and over in Population, 2002—Continued

City by state	Population	Crime Index	Modified Crime Index[1]	Murder and non-negligent man-slaughter	Forcible rape	Robbery	Aggravated assault	Burglary	Larceny-theft	Motor vehicle theft	Arson[1]
NEW JERSEY—Continued											
New Providence	12,156	150	150	0	0	0	2	25	116	7	0
North Arlington	15,499	193	193	0	0	5	13	23	137	15	0
North Bergen Township	59,307	1,493	1,498	0	4	66	58	226	869	270	5
North Brunswick Township	37,045	1,220	1,223	0	4	44	60	169	849	94	3
North Plainfield	21,545	664	664	0	3	28	13	151	415	54	0
Nutley Township	27,934	567	570	0	0	9	39	126	309	84	3
Oakland	12,726	136	139	0	0	0	8	27	93	8	3
Ocean City	15,700	972	973	1	0	7	23	151	784	6	1
Ocean Township (Monmouth County)	27,523	652	654	0	1	5	12	92	515	27	2
Old Bridge Township	61,720	1,025	1,033	0	12	16	34	215	601	147	8
Orange	33,555	2,354	2,361	4	8	275	170	437	795	665	7
Palisades Park	17,430	189	189	0	1	5	8	77	81	17	0
Paramus	26,275	2,209	2,218	0	4	50	50	118	1,781	206	9
Parsippany-Troy Hills Township	51,708	912	916	0	3	21	37	244	491	116	4
Passaic	69,280	3,345	3,353	4	5	374	482	464	1,396	620	8
Paterson	152,340	6,842	6,861	15	29	653	468	1,595	2,645	1,437	19
Pemberton Township	29,291	722	729	1	7	28	45	164	421	56	7
Pennsauken Township	36,484	1,383	1,386	1	6	76	83	265	766	186	3
Pennsville Township	13,470	361	364	0	0	1	10	55	281	14	3
Pequannock Township	14,179	205	208	0	0	1	7	21	158	18	3
Perth Amboy	48,292	1,697	1,703	1	10	95	139	358	883	211	6
Phillipsburg	15,483	280	283	1	2	8	11	56	182	20	3
Pine Hill	11,107	263	265	0	0	9	20	46	168	20	2
Piscataway Township	51,538	1,124	1,141	1	4	28	41	140	796	114	17
Plainfield	48,829	2,413	2,424	1	19	255	241	449	1,135	313	11
Plainsboro Township	20,637	197	200	0	0	2	7	29	148	11	3
Pleasantville	19,410	860	870	1	1	75	86	161	472	64	10
Point Pleasant	19,710	396	396	0	4	1	12	76	294	9	0
Pompton Lakes	10,862	173	173	0	0	2	6	34	120	11	0
Princeton	14,500	527	527	0	1	8	10	100	404	4	0
Princeton Township	16,362	243	246	0	1	2	5	57	161	17	3
Rahway	27,054	863	868	0	2	32	33	133	519	144	5
Ramsey	14,651	221	221	0	1	4	12	19	167	18	0
Randolph Township	25,367	246	246	0	0	1	9	26	200	10	0
Raritan Township	20,223	196	197	0	0	1	8	38	138	11	1
Readington Township	16,134	158	159	0	0	0	3	48	99	8	1
Red Bank	12,091	360	361	0	5	19	19	27	276	14	1
Ridgefield	11,057	97	97	0	0	3	4	25	42	23	0
Ridgefield Park	13,142	304	321	0	0	9	10	45	190	50	17
Ridgewood	25,458	310	312	0	2	4	10	57	230	7	2
Ringwood	12,656	93	93	0	1	0	4	16	67	5	0
River Edge	11,175	113	114	0	0	2	3	18	87	3	1
Rockaway Township	23,410	468	471	0	9	9	18	50	346	36	3
Roselle	21,719	620	624	1	1	39	24	172	276	107	4
Roselle Park	13,559	252	252	0	0	10	4	56	140	42	0
Roxbury Township	24,383	311	312	2	0	0	14	46	236	13	1
Rutherford	18,488	352	353	0	0	6	11	41	244	50	1
Saddle Brook Township	13,430	314	315	0	1	5	5	38	222	43	1
Sayreville	41,221	835	849	0	11	19	48	168	493	96	14
Scotch Plains Township	23,207	300	300	0	1	16	4	38	232	9	0
Secaucus	16,264	666	666	0	0	9	5	19	483	150	0
Somers Point	11,857	352	354	0	4	14	17	58	254	5	2
Somerville	12,683	298	299	0	1	16	19	39	208	15	1
South Brunswick Township	38,523	639	644	2	2	14	22	162	396	41	5
South Orange	17,319	724	724	1	0	51	22	130	360	160	0
South Plainfield	22,266	542	544	1	3	13	18	60	406	41	2
South River	15,642	199	200	1	1	7	18	58	105	9	1
Sparta Township	18,458	84	86	0	0	1	4	21	54	4	2
Springfield	14,731	354	356	0	1	8	3	49	220	73	2
Stafford Township	23,003	589	590	0	4	3	22	84	457	19	1
Summit	21,573	480	480	0	1	13	9	82	347	28	0
Teaneck Township	40,080	885	901	0	1	40	34	237	506	67	16
Tenafly	14,095	141	147	0	0	1	0	65	62	13	6
Tinton Falls	15,368	314	318	1	2	2	9	46	220	34	4

See footnotes at end of table.

Table 8

Offenses Known to Law Enforcement

by City 10,000 and over in Population, 2002—Continued

City by state	Population	Crime Index	Modified Crime Index[1]	Murder and non-negligent man-slaughter	Forcible rape	Robbery	Aggravated assault	Burglary	Larceny-theft	Motor vehicle theft	Arson[1]
NEW JERSEY—Continued											
Totowa	10,099	426	427	0	0	5	6	28	299	88	1
Trenton	87,189	6,199	6,246	19	67	706	739	1,173	2,400	1,095	47
Union City	68,491	2,212	2,213	3	5	177	125	474	899	529	1
Union Township	55,543	2,273	2,277	1	11	119	72	329	1,302	439	4
Ventnor City	13,179	315	315	0	1	8	12	91	193	10	0
Vernon Township	25,202	292	293	0	1	2	15	67	192	15	1
Verona	13,816	223	225	1	2	3	8	33	145	31	2
Vineland	57,448	3,733	3,757	4	8	221	220	809	2,265	206	24
Voorhees Township	28,714	879	888	0	3	19	48	94	677	38	9
Wallington	11,825	184	186	0	1	5	16	29	118	15	2
Wall Township	25,790	342	344	0	3	5	22	74	228	10	2
Wanaque	10,481	127	127	0	0	1	6	47	66	7	0
Warren Township	14,557	155	155	0	1	0	4	16	125	9	0
Washington Township (Gloucester County)	48,099	1,264	1,278	0	7	20	44	465	651	77	14
Washington Township (Mercer County)	10,490	145	147	0	3	1	1	26	102	12	2
Washington Township (Morris County)	17,960	144	144	0	0	0	7	16	111	10	0
Waterford Township	10,714	202	203	1	6	2	15	34	126	18	1
Wayne Township	55,200	1,648	1,651	0	3	20	19	167	1,209	230	3
Weehawken Township	13,783	501	502	1	1	8	9	72	320	90	1
West Caldwell Township	11,468	128	128	0	0	1	4	20	93	10	0
West Deptford Township	19,773	464	464	1	4	12	18	87	314	28	0
Westfield	30,264	334	334	0	1	1	2	60	263	7	0
West Milford Township	26,963	386	390	0	0	9	17	96	254	10	4
West New York	46,725	1,457	1,463	0	3	86	111	266	738	253	6
West Orange	45,883	1,347	1,353	0	0	49	37	250	713	298	6
West Paterson	11,216	248	248	0	3	8	11	30	162	34	0
West Windsor Township	22,365	572	575	1	2	6	9	67	437	50	3
Westwood	11,229	146	147	0	3	4	12	18	105	4	1
Willingboro Township	33,699	917	923	0	8	61	58	213	511	66	6
Winslow Township	35,335	1,010	1,021	5	8	43	126	210	555	63	11
Woodbridge Township	99,236	3,481	3,505	3	8	72	212	537	2,130	519	24
Woodbury	10,523	546	546	0	0	30	22	67	394	33	0
Wyckoff Township	16,853	130	130	0	2	0	3	17	106	2	0
NEW MEXICO											
Alamogordo	36,287	1,215	1,217	1	18	7	78	127	943	41	2
Albuquerque	457,488	35,762	35,839	51	293	1,295	3,250	5,452	21,371	4,050	77
Artesia	10,904	519	521	2	1	5	102	136	267	6	2
Carlsbad	26,132	1,727	1,739	1	10	28	110	349	1,146	83	12
Clovis	33,314	2,239	2,255	4	16	34	142	633	1,320	90	16
Deming	14,395	929	941	2	13	11	94	220	533	56	12
Gallup	20,609	2,613	2,614	6	14	64	319	250	1,844	116	1
Hobbs	29,224	2,061	2,064	4	16	27	304	355	1,320	35	3
Las Vegas	14,853	1,019	1,029	2	11	11	176	260	516	43	10
Los Alamos	18,706	257	260	0	0	0	10	122	112	13	3
Los Lunas	10,233	663	664	2	9	3	214	92	256	87	1
Portales	11,352	540	543	0	4	0	41	114	364	17	3
Rio Rancho	52,789	1,443	1,458	1	23	15	101	266	938	99	15
Roswell	46,190	3,633	3,651	9	36	35	422	704	2,290	137	18
Santa Fe	63,435	4,929	4,958	8	38	90	270	2,059	2,251	213	29
Silver City	10,754	853		1	2	7	28	273	527	15	
Sunland Park	13,573	209		0	0	6	33	55	102	13	
NEW YORK											
Amherst Town	112,024	1,940		0	9	44	48	194	1,558	87	
Amsterdam	18,530	290		0	2	4	31	60	190	3	
Auburn	28,846	1,147		1	14	14	41	196	861	20	
Bethlehem Town	31,603	623		0	2	8	16	108	471	18	
Binghamton	47,832	2,366		6	21	80	98	260	1,856	45	
Brighton Town	35,927	1,032		0	5	13	3	111	847	53	

See footnotes at end of table.

Table 8

Offenses Known to Law Enforcement
by City 10,000 and over in Population, 2002—Continued

City by state	Population	Crime Index	Modified Crime Index[1]	Murder and non-negligent man-slaughter	Forcible rape	Robbery	Aggravated assault	Burglary	Larceny-theft	Motor vehicle theft	Arson[1]
NEW YORK—Continued											
Buffalo	295,441	19,017	19,423	43	185	1,627	1,902	3,857	9,115	2,288	406
Camillus Town and Village	23,373	366		0	0	7	16	32	307	4	
Canandaigua	11,371	255		0	5	4	4	31	206	5	
Carmel Town	33,321	397		0	0	3	21	86	263	24	
Cicero Town	26,360	826		0	1	12	16	70	694	33	
Clarkstown Town	78,409	2,112		1	8	48	96	184	1,675	100	
Clay Town	54,327	412		0	0	7	3	69	329	4	
Cohoes	15,669	224		0	0	1	40	41	126	16	
Colonie Town	76,068	2,795		0	8	32	37	364	2,265	89	
Cortland	18,919	693		0	11	9	24	99	523	27	
Dewitt Town	21,093	707		0	2	8	14	113	532	38	
Dunkirk	13,257	495		0	6	14	38	61	362	14	
Eastchester Town	18,742	298		0	0	3	11	35	223	26	
East Fishkill Town	25,833	344		0	0	2	8	48	265	21	
East Greenbush Town	15,708	364		0	2	6	9	58	282	7	
East Hampton Town	17,627	584		0	1	3	16	169	368	27	
Endicott Village	13,162	574		0	11	13	33	79	424	14	
Fallsburg Town	11,441	213		0	1	6	13	96	81	16	
Fishkill Town	18,699	275		0	2	2	12	33	213	13	
Floral Park Village	16,120	118		0	0	6	1	24	75	12	
Fredonia Village	10,808	313		0	3	1	18	20	266	5	
Freeport Village	44,201	1,212		1	4	72	111	94	712	218	
Fulton City	11,968	677		0	2	11	12	94	544	14	
Garden City Village	21,879	333		0	2	8	6	32	265	20	
Gates Town	29,554	1,172		1	4	20	7	112	920	108	
Geddes Town	10,999	210		0	0	6	1	26	169	8	
Geneva	13,747	412		0	2	4	13	55	330	8	
Glen Cove	26,876	275		1	0	13	4	35	197	25	
Glens Falls	14,491	668		0	2	4	30	117	502	13	
Gloversville	15,560	589		0	2	2	35	85	439	26	
Greenburgh Town	42,228	1,115		0	3	27	27	135	841	82	
Haverstraw Town	23,919	414		1	2	6	104	74	208	19	
Hempstead Village	57,094	1,455		4	10	177	201	122	512	429	
Hyde Park Town	21,050	206		0	2	6	4	29	154	11	
Irondequoit Town	52,854	2,294		0	4	55	15	265	1,820	135	
Jamestown	32,032	1,258		1	11	40	110	269	762	65	
Kent Town	14,143	246		1	1	0	2	43	193	6	
Lewisboro Town	12,442	138		0	0	0	1	12	124	1	
Lloyd Town	10,036	111		0	1	2	5	28	70	5	
Lynbrook Village	20,101	248		3	3	9	7	37	150	39	
Mamaroneck Town	11,430	143		0	0	2	5	23	98	15	
Mamaroneck Village	18,931	268		0	0	3	7	42	188	28	
Manlius Town	24,566	368		2	0	0	12	58	285	11	
Massena Village	11,316	185		1	0	2	7	24	145	6	
Middletown	25,630	865		0	15	32	33	114	622	49	
Mount Kisco Village	10,078	295		0	0	13	25	24	213	20	
Newburgh	28,529	1,889		7	23	179	378	349	860	93	
Newburgh Town	27,831	1,104		1	4	18	19	114	921	27	
New Castle Town	17,657	148		0	0	0	6	23	112	7	
New Hartford Town and Village	19,611	821		0	2	5	7	56	744	7	
New Rochelle	72,870	1,854		2	3	125	132	218	1,194	180	
New York	8,084,693	250,630		587	1,689	27,229	34,334	30,102	129,655	27,034	
Niagara Falls	56,123	3,847		3	30	167	359	827	2,078	383	
Niskayuna Town	20,488	336		0	2	1	8	38	275	12	
North Castle Town	10,953	142		0	2	3	2	32	96	7	
North Tonawanda	33,579	639		0	3	9	38	121	440	28	
Ogdensburg	12,482	522		0	1	1	11	87	402	20	
Ogden Town	18,668	390		0	1	3	11	56	312	7	
Olean	15,493	527		0	9	1	11	68	431	7	
Oneida	11,091	524		0	2	3	5	91	409	14	
Ossining Village	24,240	433		0	5	46	73	44	236	29	
Port Washington	17,921	305		0	1	6	10	38	237	13	
Poughkeepsie	30,156	1,306		3	17	123	141	209	742	71	
Poughkeepsie Town	42,233	1,349		0	5	21	78	101	1,107	37	
Ramapo Town	71,919	936		0	1	24	54	162	651	44	

See footnotes at end of table.

Table 8

Offenses Known to Law Enforcement
by City 10,000 and over in Population, 2002—Continued

City by state	Population	Crime Index	Modified Crime Index[1]	Murder and non-negligent man-slaughter	Forcible rape	Robbery	Aggravated assault	Burglary	Larceny-theft	Motor vehicle theft	Arson[1]
NEW YORK—Continued											
Rochester	221,871	16,911	17,241	42	107	972	665	2,467	9,853	2,805	330
Rockville Centre Village	24,803	439		0	0	22	45	68	254	50	
Rome	35,284	770		1	8	28	26	200	472	35	
Schodack Town	10,956	206		0	0	0	5	53	144	4	
Shawangunk Town	12,136	112		0	0	0	18	14	76	4	
Stony Point Town	14,380	101		0	0	0	2	23	74	2	
Suffern Village	11,111	116		0	0	1	10	20	82	3	
Syracuse	148,712	9,791	9,909	23	43	551	902	1,930	5,060	1,282	118
Tarrytown Village	11,196	197		0	6	2	12	41	115	21	
Troy	49,640	2,496		3	28	118	165	521	1,411	250	
Utica	61,230	3,168		5	21	190	149	790	1,866	147	
Watertown	26,960	791		1	28	16	28	122	584	12	
Webster Town and Village	38,288	584		0	5	3	1	63	477	35	
West Seneca Town	46,358	1,024		0	5	24	108	119	717	51	
White Plains	53,584	2,033		3	5	71	119	158	1,564	113	
Yonkers	197,957	4,676	4,723	13	11	419	450	746	2,225	812	47
NORTH CAROLINA											
Albemarle	16,207	1,243	1,252	5	6	45	79	290	725	93	9
Apex	20,892	442	443	0	1	7	33	80	293	28	1
Asheboro	22,401	1,986	1,987	1	3	29	20	419	1,431	83	1
Asheville	71,207	4,861	4,914	12	44	197	223	790	3,112	483	53
Boone	13,925	498	500	0	2	3	12	57	404	20	2
Burlington	46,428	3,722	3,730	4	12	82	195	726	2,542	161	8
Carrboro	17,347	953	954	0	2	15	41	121	742	32	1
Cary	97,716	2,253	2,257	0	7	44	61	384	1,655	102	4
Chapel Hill	50,354	2,505	2,516	1	6	81	148	403	1,747	119	11
Charlotte-Mecklenburg	646,864	48,597	49,052	67	289	2,893	4,334	10,516	25,860	4,638	455
Concord	57,860	2,894	2,904	1	16	81	75	499	2,065	157	10
Cornelius	12,372	197	197	0	4	13	21	47	111	1	0
Durham	193,328	14,461	14,499	30	75	942	763	3,088	8,483	1,080	38
Elizabeth City	17,767	1,124	1,131	1	4	42	102	214	715	46	7
Fayetteville[3]	125,087	10,594	10,637	20	54	435	634	2,273	6,480	698	43
Garner	18,355	1,463	1,466	0	4	29	46	204	1,132	48	3
Goldsboro	40,357	3,219	3,236	6	3	90	217	664	2,048	191	17
Graham	13,265	803	805	0	3	12	48	191	511	38	2
Greensboro	231,424	15,128	15,232	28	103	702	806	2,946	9,392	1,151	104
Greenville	62,511	5,225	5,230	4	24	208	321	1,204	3,226	238	5
Havelock	23,197	592	592	0	0	11	27	115	427	12	0
Hickory	38,474	3,143	3,161	3	20	71	133	482	2,275	159	18
High Point	88,727	6,413	6,454	5	37	269	389	1,483	3,641	589	41
Hope Mills	11,615	1,006	1,011	3	3	24	27	152	752	45	5
Huntersville	25,800	835	842	0	9	12	30	162	590	32	7
Jacksonville	68,960	955	957	3	11	19	97	88	709	28	2
Kannapolis	38,152	1,136	1,143	2	15	52	88	212	704	63	7
Kernersville	17,703	1,250	1,254	1	4	15	66	177	942	45	4
Kings Mountain	10,019	997	997	0	2	25	32	181	752	5	0
Kinston	24,485	2,655	2,655	4	18	75	179	637	1,650	92	0
Laurinburg	16,408	1,090	1,104	1	11	39	69	313	606	51	14
Lenoir	17,358	708	710	1	1	24	20	131	501	30	2
Lexington	20,625	1,393	1,401	6	9	46	87	373	791	81	8
Lumberton	21,495	3,238	3,246	1	12	125	192	696	2,067	145	8
Matthews	22,871	1,029	1,046	0	3	20	22	154	764	66	17
Morganton	17,892	864	866	0	6	18	9	175	622	34	2
New Bern	23,907	1,778	1,780	2	12	54	155	382	1,117	56	2
Newton	12,983	643	647	0	3	19	5	153	432	31	4
Pinehurst	10,033	158	158	0	0	0	0	28	118	12	0
Raleigh	285,383	17,833	17,923	19	106	697	1,144	3,836	10,692	1,339	90
Roanoke Rapids	17,527	1,168	1,172	2	1	40	53	251	752	69	4
Rocky Mount	57,774	5,710	5,734	4	13	174	261	1,148	3,835	275	24
Salisbury	27,352	1,763	1,774	4	20	79	97	331	1,136	96	11
Sanford	24,001	2,608	2,620	5	10	88	104	514	1,765	122	12
Shelby	20,132	1,845	1,857	4	20	88	124	424	1,120	65	12
Smithfield	11,897	1,473	1,478	2	1	45	97	268	986	74	5

See footnotes at end of table.

Table 8

Offenses Known to Law Enforcement
by City 10,000 and over in Population, 2002—Continued

City by state	Population	Crime Index	Modified Crime Index[1]	Murder and non-negligent man-slaughter	Forcible rape	Robbery	Aggravated assault	Burglary	Larceny-theft	Motor vehicle theft	Arson[1]
NORTH CAROLINA—Continued											
Southern Pines	11,286	905	906	0	1	35	48	264	520	37	1
Statesville	24,104	2,022	2,024	1	8	49	139	334	1,402	89	2
Tarboro	11,513	497	499	0	4	14	47	106	313	13	2
Thomasville	20,453	1,172	1,176	1	7	27	101	269	722	45	4
Wake Forest	13,011	427	428	0	2	14	26	87	286	12	1
Wilmington	78,389	8,811	8,839	10	51	357	580	1,851	5,215	747	28
Wilson	45,899	3,147	3,154	1	12	103	235	687	1,918	191	7
Winston-Salem	192,027	14,669	14,784	15	116	549	934	3,311	8,757	987	115
NORTH DAKOTA											
Bismarck	54,832	1,698	1,705	1	5	14	25	181	1,356	116	7
Dickinson	15,808	459	459	1	1	5	4	48	376	24	0
Fargo	89,458	3,266	3,281	0	49	14	61	396	2,547	199	15
Grand Forks	48,700	2,442	2,453	0	15	7	38	342	1,859	181	11
Jamestown	15,331	448	448	0	15	3	11	55	345	19	0
Mandan	16,507	427	433	0	8	4	9	40	332	34	6
Minot	36,106	1,189	1,198	0	12	4	24	191	881	77	9
West Fargo	14,752	493	497	0	2	0	7	105	353	26	4
Williston	12,354	281	282	0	9	1	4	18	220	29	1
OHIO											
Akron	218,377	13,101	13,213	19	156	655	361	3,069	7,383	1,458	112
Alliance	23,392	1,389	1,411	5	19	34	37	269	975	50	22
Ashtabula	21,088	14	14	1	0	1	3	2	7	0	0
Athens	21,470	713	714	0	15	6	4	94	568	26	1
Aurora	13,638	243	245	0	1	2	2	19	210	9	2
Avon	11,515	184	185	0	0	2	4	21	155	2	1
Avon Lake	18,254	262	262	0	0	2	0	65	188	7	0
Bainbridge Township	10,966	266	266	0	3	0	12	35	209	7	0
Barberton	28,066	1,420	1,430	0	19	23	26	268	1,014	70	10
Beavercreek	38,212	1,544	1,553	0	14	24	8	156	1,258	84	9
Bedford Heights	11,444	305	306	2	3	7	25	42	177	49	1
Bellefontaine	13,147	638	638	0	7	7	3	126	475	20	0
Berea	19,084	392	392	0	0	4	10	35	320	23	0
Bexley	13,283	501	506	0	2	16	1	173	276	33	5
Bowling Green	29,814	1,102	1,104	0	6	13	25	185	829	44	2
Brecksville	13,462	92	93	0	0	2	1	19	66	4	1
Broadview Heights	16,063	40	41	0	0	0	2	12	23	3	1
Brookfield Township	10,066	280	280	0	7	3	13	69	173	15	0
Brooklyn	11,655	537	539	1	1	19	10	37	434	35	2
Brook Park	21,345	117	117	1	0	0	4	14	58	40	0
Cambridge	11,589	1,074	1,075	0	10	12	46	184	760	62	1
Celina	10,365	408	417	0	1	4	11	57	313	22	9
Centerville	23,162	556	559	0	4	5	9	117	378	43	3
Chillicothe	21,926	2,461	2,473	0	11	32	14	456	1,858	90	12
Cincinnati	333,273	29,205	29,657	64	388	2,412	1,329	6,461	14,526	4,025	452
Circleville	13,566	959	964	0	2	9	18	175	710	45	5
Cleveland	481,274	33,209	33,698	80	619	3,263	2,402	8,096	13,250	5,499	489
Cleveland Heights	50,258	768	768	0	0	23	2	88	564	91	0
Columbus	715,739	66,261	66,484	81	673	3,503	2,242	16,066	36,063	7,633	223
Conneaut	12,560	390	390	0	1	3	12	65	297	12	0
Copley Township	13,704	373	373	1	2	9	5	37	293	26	0
Cuyahoga Falls	49,670	1,919	1,925	0	18	14	40	229	1,519	99	6
Dayton	167,176	15,932	16,108	42	193	1,066	728	3,903	7,311	2,689	176
Delaware	25,394	1,052	1,081	2	41	13	31	196	720	49	29
Delhi Township	30,241	493	493	0	1	8	8	54	400	22	0
Dover	12,283	231	237	0	4	2	10	42	163	10	6
Dublin	31,580	760	766	0	9	5	5	127	574	40	6
East Cleveland	27,380	1,846	1,846	6	36	191	152	487	407	567	0
Eastlake	20,376	391	394	0	2	7	5	51	294	32	3
East Liverpool	13,167	450	451	0	2	11	6	104	298	29	1
Englewood	12,308	561	562	1	4	10	15	48	450	33	1
Euclid	53,033	2,477	2,480	2	30	100	40	449	1,559	297	3

See footnotes at end of table.

Table 8

Offenses Known to Law Enforcement

by City 10,000 and over in Population, 2002—Continued

City by state	Population	Crime Index	Modified Crime Index[1]	Murder and non-negligent man-slaughter	Forcible rape	Robbery	Aggravated assault	Burglary	Larceny-theft	Motor vehicle theft	Arson[1]
OHIO—Continued											
Fairborn	32,244	1,672	1,680	1	26	27	33	277	1,211	97	8
Fairfield	42,350	1,931	1,945	0	16	21	128	273	1,380	113	14
Forest Park	19,580	724	726	0	8	26	8	96	546	40	2
Franklin Township	14,596	214	226	0	2	3	2	84	107	16	12
Fremont	17,479	1,589	1,596	2	6	20	36	179	1,301	45	7
Gahanna[3]	32,831	1,040	1,047	0	11	13	12	210	752	42	7
Garfield Heights	30,918	463	463	0	1	13	36	88	278	47	0
Genoa Township	11,344	202	203	2	0	1	1	27	163	8	1
Girard	10,967	436	436	0	2	5	6	102	275	46	0
Goshen Township	13,726	328	338	0	2	2	36	93	171	24	10
Greenville	13,374	418	420	0	2	3	36	51	316	10	2
Hamilton	61,054	5,513	5,543	4	73	189	303	1,129	3,362	453	30
Hilliard	24,375	768	780	0	3	4	8	120	613	20	12
Huber Heights	38,441	1,889	1,907	0	11	48	21	293	1,391	125	18
Hudson	22,573	171	179	0	1	1	3	39	124	3	8
Kettering	57,847	2,164	2,182	1	25	43	22	324	1,609	140	18
Lakewood	56,986	1,128	1,131	1	5	25	33	230	771	63	3
Lancaster	35,547	1,320	1,340	0	19	35	25	280	882	79	20
Lebanon	17,064	494	496	0	13	4	17	71	366	23	2
Lima	40,321	3,286	3,310	5	66	126	252	755	1,861	221	24
Lorain	69,064	2,901	2,923	2	14	109	146	787	1,746	97	22
Lyndhurst	15,370	78	78	0	1	0	12	8	52	5	0
Madison Township	15,574	398	401	0	0	4	24	45	308	17	3
Mansfield	49,642	4,006	4,048	6	48	78	42	951	2,697	184	42
Marietta	14,602	458	465	0	17	5	10	78	318	30	7
Marion	35,530	1,874	1,890	0	11	33	26	432	1,312	60	16
Marysville	16,037	502	503	1	2	3	34	71	370	21	1
Mason	22,148	393	393	0	3	1	3	56	323	7	0
Maumee	15,328	924	927	1	1	19	5	120	754	24	3
Mayfield Heights	19,503	259	260	1	1	3	16	18	196	24	1
Mentor	50,579	1,578	1,585	0	8	20	17	162	1,284	87	7
Miamisburg	19,606	1,147	1,159	0	8	19	11	218	777	114	12
Miami Township	36,799	944	949	0	10	7	52	105	725	45	5
Middletown	51,915	3,753	3,762	1	20	77	70	624	2,820	141	9
Montgomery	10,224	235	235	0	0	6	3	22	193	11	0
Newark	46,556	2,598	2,631	2	19	41	37	552	1,843	104	33
Niles	21,058	2,610	2,655	1	6	32	97	179	2,164	131	45
North Canton	16,467	257	262	0	3	10	0	72	161	11	5
North College Hill	10,143	610	615	0	4	29	16	97	413	51	5
North Olmsted	34,318	668	668	1	0	11	12	24	567	53	0
North Ridgeville	22,472	433	433	0	4	6	24	70	305	24	0
North Royalton	28,819	407	407	2	9	1	8	34	334	19	0
Norton	11,592	435	435	0	0	6	4	83	304	38	0
Norwalk	16,335	459	463	0	0	3	1	80	364	11	4
Norwood	21,805	1,553	1,555	1	21	65	39	197	1,128	102	2
Oregon	19,471	1,205	1,210	1	2	10	30	144	955	63	5
Parma	86,169	1,774	1,792	2	17	41	55	382	1,147	130	18
Parma Heights	21,789	433	439	0	7	9	8	63	326	20	6
Perkins Township	12,636	372	373	0	0	5	10	10	344	3	1
Perrysburg[3]	17,047	486	489	0	1	6	11	72	385	11	3
Perry Township (Stark County)	29,300	644	651	1	3	9	37	123	406	65	7
Pierce Township	12,282	246	249	0	1	3	4	34	188	16	3
Piqua	20,863	1,267	1,281	0	5	22	14	211	988	27	14
Portsmouth	21,034	2,276	2,279	3	34	80	68	484	1,424	183	3
Ravenna	11,842	600	600	0	4	3	29	37	491	36	0
Reading	11,359	332	337	3	8	8	11	49	226	27	5
Reynoldsburg	32,262	1,216	1,228	0	7	27	17	177	932	56	12
Richmond Heights	11,009	431	431	0	0	10	5	19	366	31	0
Salem	12,270	64	64	0	0	0	6	12	42	4	0
Sandusky	28,011	2,081	2,082	1	10	37	74	337	1,552	70	1
Seven Hills	12,152	130	130	0	0	0	3	15	108	4	0
Shaker Heights	29,582	790	794	0	1	33	14	125	536	81	4
Sharonville	13,887	706	710	1	5	14	10	73	552	51	4
Solon	21,932	342	344	0	0	3	2	50	281	6	2
South Euclid	23,678	560	577	0	8	23	11	72	391	55	17

See footnotes at end of table.

Table 8

Offenses Known to Law Enforcement
by City 10,000 and over in Population, 2002—Continued

City by state	Population	Crime Index	Modified Crime Index[1]	Murder and non-negligent man-slaughter	Forcible rape	Robbery	Aggravated assault	Burglary	Larceny-theft	Motor vehicle theft	Arson[1]
OHIO—Continued											
Springboro	12,454	230	230	0	1	5	5	38	171	10	0
Springdale	10,626	1,229	1,232	0	6	35	5	59	1,042	82	3
Springfield	65,750	7,226	7,243	7	79	287	214	1,620	4,425	594	17
Springfield Township (Hamilton County)	37,759	822	822	0	3	21	25	187	524	62	0
Steubenville	19,129	1,227	1,229	0	16	46	96	150	851	68	2
Stow	32,332	773	786	1	2	18	7	132	592	21	13
Streetsboro	12,385	342	343	0	0	3	1	28	299	11	1
Sylvania	18,782	308	310	0	1	1	5	56	238	7	2
Sylvania Township	25,674	838	840	0	1	10	4	114	673	36	2
Tallmadge	16,488	476	480	0	6	8	15	87	341	19	4
Tiffin	18,244	797	798	0	9	3	6	146	613	20	1
Toledo[3]	315,501	26,717	27,204	28	185	1,378	1,592	5,811	14,510	3,213	487
Troy	22,131	831	831	1	18	10	7	102	650	43	0
University Heights	14,231	244	244	0	4	5	51	23	143	18	0
Urbana	11,682	522	528	0	4	3	11	86	406	12	6
Vandalia	14,690	567	573	0	11	7	5	101	409	34	6
Vermilion	10,992	481	483	0	3	2	5	75	371	25	2
Wadsworth	18,548	390	392	0	9	2	8	84	269	18	2
Warren	47,113	2,728	2,789	5	38	110	245	707	1,377	246	61
Warrensville Heights	15,200	504	505	0	5	21	41	96	270	71	1
Washington Court House	13,606	392	394	1	7	10	7	144	208	15	2
West Carrollton	13,901	692	708	0	8	9	7	108	465	95	16
West Chester Township	52,907	1,690	1,705	0	15	29	21	309	1,245	71	15
Westerville	35,530	1,129	1,139	1	2	18	12	192	867	37	10
Westlake	31,909	453	453	0	3	5	4	63	359	19	0
Whitehall	19,316	1,657	1,672	0	12	81	26	308	1,071	159	15
Willoughby	22,757	421	422	0	4	11	11	58	299	38	1
Willowick	14,447	282	282	0	1	5	11	57	174	34	0
Worthington	14,210	399	401	0	1	10	12	106	249	21	2
Xenia	24,309	1,259	1,264	0	4	27	1	189	1,011	27	5
Youngstown	82,518	5,915	6,196	33	54	298	574	1,832	2,631	493	281
Zanesville	25,740	2,358	2,374	1	25	64	57	383	1,729	99	16
OKLAHOMA											
Ada	15,887	994	1,003	3	13	5	69	226	630	48	9
Altus	21,715	1,165	1,167	2	16	17	22	439	637	32	2
Ardmore	24,007	1,977	1,984	2	9	26	252	325	1,301	62	7
Bartlesville	35,182	1,592	1,593	1	20	15	92	305	1,079	80	1
Bethany	20,560	853	859	1	9	16	47	174	555	51	6
Bixby	13,502	370	377	1	2	5	25	64	239	34	7
Broken Arrow	75,794	2,281	2,281	3	31	24	108	427	1,532	156	0
Chickasha	16,048	1,300	1,307	0	15	19	199	254	757	56	7
Claremore	16,071	623	625	1	8	2	46	79	449	38	2
Del City	22,404	1,044	1,055	0	14	35	58	239	599	99	11
Duncan	22,785	1,139	1,143	0	10	6	41	185	846	51	4
Durant	13,718	940	944	1	15	6	41	204	611	62	4
Edmond	69,168	1,761	1,772	1	15	14	43	385	1,229	74	11
Elk City	10,642	274	275	0	1	1	4	26	231	11	1
El Reno	16,414	594	596	1	4	9	46	109	380	45	2
Enid	47,632	2,985	2,989	0	34	25	192	638	1,969	127	4
Guthrie	10,048	438	447	1	5	6	48	94	272	12	9
Guymon	10,602	345	345	0	4	1	10	40	267	23	0
Lawton	93,915	5,515	5,550	6	57	151	452	1,281	3,247	321	35
McAlester	18,005	932	934	0	4	12	43	217	589	67	2
Miami	13,875	747	749	2	11	4	54	150	503	23	2
Midwest City	54,763	2,318	2,328	1	20	36	117	574	1,395	175	10
Moore	41,652	1,729	1,736	0	17	14	104	332	1,138	124	7
Muskogee	38,788	2,318	2,334	0	18	68	198	685	1,199	150	16
Mustang	13,320	454	454	2	0	2	37	63	332	18	0
Norman	96,888	3,769	3,783	1	34	44	145	1,057	2,352	136	14
Oklahoma City	512,448	49,929	50,157	38	445	1,169	2,562	8,314	33,686	3,715	228
Okmulgee	13,184	687	687	0	0	10	48	152	444	33	0
Owasso	18,732	645	650	0	4	5	30	94	462	50	5

See footnotes at end of table.

Table 8

Offenses Known to Law Enforcement

by City 10,000 and over in Population, 2002—Continued

City by state	Population	Crime Index	Modified Crime Index[1]	Murder and non-negligent man-slaughter	Forcible rape	Robbery	Aggravated assault	Burglary	Larceny-theft	Motor vehicle theft	Arson[1]
OKLAHOMA—Continued											
Ponca City	26,242	1,542	1,564	0	29	18	156	291	952	96	22
Sand Springs	17,669	704	709	0	9	14	33	128	451	69	5
Sapulpa	19,405	831	846	1	1	11	35	149	569	65	15
Shawnee	29,050	1,724	1,728	0	22	22	155	582	751	192	4
Stillwater	39,552	1,432	1,435	0	24	7	66	262	1,005	68	3
Tahlequah	14,638	650	652	1	8	8	36	137	422	38	2
The Village	10,284	629	630	0	1	5	31	136	430	26	1
Tulsa	397,953	30,119	30,365	26	243	901	3,153	6,313	15,918	3,565	246
Woodward	12,001	628	629	0	14	1	90	152	349	22	1
Yukon	21,305	653	656	1	1	3	19	118	486	25	3
OREGON											
Albany	42,047	2,783	2,791	0	10	37	26	288	2,230	192	8
Ashland	20,093	947	960	0	5	9	1	147	739	46	13
Baker City	10,149	398	399	0	10	3	13	56	295	21	1
Beaverton	78,357	3,350	3,375	0	19	53	114	420	2,410	334	25
Bend	53,551	3,344	3,362	2	17	28	98	509	2,506	184	18
Canby	13,165	465	475	0	1	5	8	48	369	34	10
Central Point	12,859	493	503	0	0	5	0	69	396	23	10
Coos Bay	15,824	686	697	0	16	5	14	133	472	46	11
Dallas	12,824	396	397	0	8	2	29	56	273	28	1
Eugene	141,928	9,308	9,408	2	56	155	256	1,209	6,824	806	100
Gladstone	11,773	583	584	0	1	5	1	66	431	79	1
Grants Pass	23,676	1,611	1,624	0	9	26	33	212	1,233	98	13
Gresham	92,844	6,154	6,212	3	62	141	276	817	3,956	899	58
Hermiston	13,539	785	787	0	5	4	0	107	618	51	2
Hillsboro	72,240	3,759	3,794	2	37	60	84	376	2,755	445	35
Keizer	33,145	1,426	1,429	0	7	13	30	147	1,091	138	3
Klamath Falls	20,031	841	846	0	7	25	29	204	503	73	5
La Grande	12,688	376	377	0	0	4	5	64	288	15	1
Lake Oswego	36,311	824	842	0	3	8	22	153	585	53	18
Lebanon	13,329	920	923	0	5	10	12	105	749	39	3
McMinnville	27,274	1,164	1,167	1	19	14	19	217	825	69	3
Medford	65,002	4,434	4,472	0	24	39	191	503	3,484	193	38
Milwaukie	21,090	1,071	1,081	0	9	13	22	148	752	127	10
Ontario	11,306	872	872	0	8	6	46	81	691	40	0
Oregon City	26,508	1,246	1,255	3	6	16	27	145	947	102	9
Pendleton	16,833	780	784	0	2	11	7	130	577	53	4
Portland	544,604	43,327	43,823	20	354	1,294	2,844	5,702	27,933	5,180	496
Redmond	13,875	1,224	1,226	1	13	5	8	166	959	72	2
Roseburg	20,602	1,148	1,167	0	8	9	16	160	898	57	19
Salem	140,931	12,389	12,412	6	79	156	103	1,415	9,277	1,353	23
Sherwood	12,136	346	348	0	2	0	0	45	288	11	2
Springfield	54,411	4,063	4,098	0	11	29	78	464	3,071	410	35
St. Helens	10,312	392	397	0	2	3	8	65	296	18	5
The Dalles	12,512	715	719	0	2	8	9	104	549	43	4
Tigard	42,429	2,442	2,457	0	14	41	54	288	1,858	187	15
Troutdale	14,181	564	567	0	2	13	10	74	423	42	3
Tualatin	23,458	1,028	1,028	0	2	11	28	130	748	109	0
West Linn	22,913	484	485	0	1	8	3	78	377	17	1
Wilsonville	14,401	697	698	0	7	6	9	82	515	78	1
Woodburn	20,688	1,579	1,587	1	5	15	21	192	1,131	214	8
PENNSYLVANIA											
Abington Township	56,350	1,197	1,201	2	5	29	21	187	867	86	4
Aliquippa	11,786	362	362	1	4	10	53	78	193	23	0
Allentown	107,101	5,944	6,025	9	58	294	254	1,212	3,615	502	81
Altoona	49,741	2,058	2,063	2	20	74	81	540	1,218	123	5
Aston Township	16,274	262	262	0	0	5	25	30	171	31	0
Baldwin Borough	20,087	275	275	1	7	9	13	52	164	29	0
Bensalem Township	58,691	2,197	2,213	0	11	55	62	264	1,505	300	16
Berks-Lehigh Regional	20,471	243	245	0	1	2	9	38	179	14	2
Bethel Park	33,703	388	388	0	3	9	12	66	282	16	0
Bethlehem	71,643	2,418	2,424	2	31	98	114	398	1,616	159	6

See footnotes at end of table.

Table 8

Offenses Known to Law Enforcement
by City 10,000 and over in Population, 2002—Continued

City by state	Population	Crime Index	Modified Crime Index[1]	Murder and non-negligent man-slaughter	Forcible rape	Robbery	Aggravated assault	Burglary	Larceny-theft	Motor vehicle theft	Arson[1]
PENNSYLVANIA—Continued											
Bethlehem Township	21,264	452	452	1	5	11	26	17	375	17	0
Bloomsburg Town	12,429	299	301	0	6	5	10	41	219	18	2
Brecknock Township	11,025	44	44	0	1	0	0	7	31	5	0
Bristol Township	55,766	2,098	2,125	1	12	74	84	268	1,393	266	27
Buckingham Township	16,515	169	169	0	1	0	5	21	137	5	0
Butler	15,187	953	956	0	15	24	142	119	623	30	3
Butler Township (Butler County)	17,261	479	481	0	6	13	16	45	384	15	2
Caln Township	11,968	397	397	0	2	10	54	37	275	19	0
Carlisle	18,049	558	561	1	7	16	17	68	431	18	3
Center Township	11,543	380	380	0	3	3	24	50	295	5	0
Chambersburg	17,941	881	888	1	17	24	232	120	457	30	7
Cheltenham Township	37,037	1,221	1,224	0	5	64	43	195	750	164	3
Chester	37,016	1,874	1,905	12	31	162	472	239	646	312	31
Chippewa Township	10,866	273	274	0	2	3	6	30	221	11	1
Coatesville	10,885	396	401	0	4	35	74	73	170	40	5
Colonial Regional	17,577	475	475	0	3	2	26	21	410	13	0
Columbia	10,357	287	287	0	3	18	26	50	161	29	0
Cranberry Township	23,729	425	427	0	2	9	19	32	354	9	2
Darby	10,344	683	688	1	13	29	238	103	227	72	5
Derry Township (Dauphin County)	21,366	573	575	0	5	6	21	68	451	22	2
Doylestown Township	17,697	254	256	0	2	2	8	24	205	13	2
Dunmore	14,080	140	140	0	0	1	2	15	114	8	0
East Hempfield Township	21,493	799	799	1	2	3	9	136	628	20	0
East Lampeter Township	13,615	842	844	0	1	15	3	62	741	20	2
East Norriton Township	13,269	257	257	1	1	4	4	21	212	14	0
Easton	26,378	1,193	1,204	1	21	52	143	158	753	65	11
East Pennsboro Township	18,335	407	411	0	4	18	10	60	296	19	4
Easttown Township	10,315	135	135	0	1	3	14	26	79	12	0
Elizabeth Township	13,900	157	157	0	0	0	21	37	85	14	0
Emmaus	11,362	321	325	1	3	2	20	39	252	4	4
Ephrata	13,271	278	280	0	3	2	23	39	195	16	2
Erie	104,173	3,560	3,601	4	71	196	179	702	2,241	167	41
Exeter Township (Berks County)	23,074	551	554	0	2	9	24	56	429	31	3
Fairview Township (York County)	14,384	418	420	1	6	4	32	45	318	12	2
Falls Township (Bucks County)	35,019	1,186	1,189	0	5	29	20	119	849	164	3
Ferguson Township	14,125	208	208	0	1	0	8	22	168	9	0
Franconia Township	11,574	69	69	0	2	0	11	9	40	7	0
Franklin Park	11,414	88	89	0	0	1	4	7	66	10	1
Greensburg	15,959	516	519	0	2	7	25	58	392	32	3
Hampden Township	24,241	361	362	0	0	8	6	49	281	17	1
Hampton Township	17,603	238	238	0	1	3	13	25	189	7	0
Hanover	14,599	550	566	0	7	7	16	62	444	14	16
Hanover Township (Luzerne County)	11,539	407	408	0	2	12	32	61	282	18	1
Harrisburg	49,165	2,928	2,957	12	40	345	273	577	1,575	106	29
Harrison Township	10,982	343	343	0	0	4	7	40	278	14	0
Hatfield Township	19,403	352	358	0	0	5	8	27	284	28	6
Haverford Township	48,711	689	689	0	1	15	12	71	550	40	0
Hazleton	23,432	540	544	0	5	20	27	97	319	72	4
Hermitage	16,228	596	598	0	0	6	20	51	505	14	2
Hilltown Township	12,156	223	223	0	2	4	18	26	158	15	0
Horsham Township	24,339	272	276	1	1	5	3	33	199	30	4
Indiana	14,961	356	356	0	11	9	24	45	258	9	0
Johnstown	28,714	1,207	1,221	2	5	55	87	326	660	72	14
Kingston	13,916	643	643	0	2	13	63	91	439	35	0
Lancaster	56,596	3,725	3,773	4	43	239	191	613	2,294	341	48
Lancaster Township (Lancaster County)	14,005	624	630	0	5	26	13	134	409	37	6
Lansdale	16,142	333	338	0	3	10	18	33	258	11	5
Lansdowne	11,093	281	283	0	3	10	50	37	162	19	2
Lebanon	24,569	1,275	1,282	1	16	59	88	186	843	82	7
Limerick Township	13,593	274	274	0	4	1	6	47	202	14	0
Logan Township	11,977	317	318	0	1	13	11	98	184	10	1
Lower Allen Township	17,513	318	319	0	1	8	5	49	249	6	1
Lower Burrell	12,664	194	194	1	2	8	11	23	134	15	0
Lower Gwynedd Township	10,468	157	163	0	0	1	9	16	121	10	6

See footnotes at end of table.

Table 8

Offenses Known to Law Enforcement

by City 10,000 and over in Population, 2002—Continued

City by state	Population	Crime Index	Modified Crime Index[1]	Murder and non-negligent man-slaughter	Forcible rape	Robbery	Aggravated assault	Burglary	Larceny-theft	Motor vehicle theft	Arson[1]
PENNSYLVANIA—Continued											
Lower Makefield Township	32,825	442	442	0	1	3	2	98	314	24	0
Lower Merion Township	60,113	942	943	5	0	32	15	145	678	67	1
Lower Moreland Township	11,330	238	240	0	3	1	18	52	153	11	2
Lower Paxton Township	44,620	1,107	1,121	1	11	34	23	131	858	49	14
Lower Pottsgrove Township	11,262	225	226	0	1	3	9	31	164	17	1
Lower Providence Township	22,488	314	316	1	3	5	5	39	231	30	2
Lower Salford Township	12,950	65	65	0	2	1	4	9	46	3	0
Lower Southampton Township	19,361	386	388	0	1	4	19	32	301	29	2
Manheim Township	33,846	1,088	1,093	2	1	15	20	191	805	54	5
Marple Township	23,842	338	342	0	0	2	16	36	268	16	4
McCandless	29,150	384	388	0	0	4	8	40	323	9	4
McKeesport	24,146	1,239	1,241	2	11	57	250	275	574	70	2
Meadville	13,746	401	408	0	7	15	20	64	277	18	7
Middletown Township	44,335	1,502	1,520	1	10	20	53	175	1,141	102	18
Millcreek Township	52,359	1,021	1,021	2	6	18	31	225	695	44	0
Monroeville	29,478	951	965	0	4	23	67	78	656	123	14
Montgomery Township	22,122	557	559	0	0	10	5	30	494	18	2
Moon Township	22,388	419	419	1	2	6	11	55	323	21	0
Mount Lebanon	33,162	355	356	1	0	3	33	71	237	10	1
Muhlenberg Township	16,376	658	667	1	1	17	8	55	519	57	9
Munhall	12,318	165	165	0	0	3	1	35	106	20	0
Murrysville	18,955	257	258	1	2	6	2	55	175	16	1
Nanticoke	11,004	302	302	0	5	9	5	44	225	14	0
Nether Providence Township	13,515	160	161	0	0	2	19	23	109	7	1
Newberry Township	14,395	291	291	1	3	1	0	54	198	34	0
New Britain Township	10,745	149	149	0	2	1	6	12	126	2	0
New Castle	26,425	1,398	1,419	2	12	82	117	357	747	81	21
New Kensington	14,765	585	588	1	5	21	45	101	350	62	3
Newtown Township (Bucks County)	18,286	244	245	0	0	2	29	10	196	7	1
Newtown Township (Delaware County)	11,751	161	162	0	0	1	10	23	124	3	1
Norristown	31,419	1,851	1,865	5	27	167	176	389	864	223	14
Northampton Township	39,558	326	326	1	3	1	10	41	261	9	0
Northern York Regional	49,951	1,065	1,071	2	4	19	13	133	842	52	6
North Fayette Township	12,308	412	413	0	0	3	6	28	359	16	1
North Huntingdon Township	29,251	332	333	0	1	4	15	70	211	31	1
North Lebanon Township	10,676	441	441	0	6	3	21	24	369	18	0
North Middleton Township	10,242	81	82	1	1	3	1	12	57	6	1
North Strabane Township	10,101	227	227	0	1	1	20	30	163	12	0
North Versailles Township	11,174	351	351	1	2	13	41	26	245	23	0
Oil City	11,555	365	368	0	5	3	15	33	295	14	3
Patton Township	11,471	220	226	0	4	3	0	24	183	6	6
Penn Hills	47,015	1,353	1,359	5	17	53	73	277	790	138	6
Penn Township (Westmoreland County)	19,677	52	52	0	0	1	8	12	31	0	0
Penn Township (York County)	14,656	220	223	0	0	3	16	24	164	13	3
Peters Township	17,644	223	228	1	3	5	12	34	162	6	5
Philadelphia	1,524,226	83,392		288	1,035	8,869	9,865	11,244	38,789	13,302	
Phoenixville	14,854	520	521	0	2	9	31	39	426	13	1
Pine-Marshall-Bradford Woods	14,894	338	338	0	1	0	12	33	281	11	0
Pittsburgh	342,529	19,737	19,851	47	148	1,616	1,983	3,298	10,108	2,537	114
Plains Township	10,954	347	347	3	6	6	44	45	221	22	0
Plumstead Township	11,459	198	200	0	2	1	2	29	148	16	2
Plymouth Township (Montgomery County)	16,116	766	771	0	4	18	37	86	557	64	5
Pocono Mountain Regional	29,210	813	821	0	11	11	22	276	431	62	8
Pottstown	21,955	1,336	1,347	1	13	60	125	185	865	87	11
Pottsville	15,617	376	378	1	6	8	40	34	253	34	2
Radnor Township	31,013	488	494	0	1	8	12	68	379	20	6
Reading	81,565	6,218	6,289	19	55	510	503	1,503	2,802	826	71
Richland Township (Cambria County)	12,654	330	331	0	3	7	48	34	225	13	1
Ridley Township	30,926	644	644	1	5	18	65	62	429	64	0
Robinson Township (Allegheny County)	12,343	463	463	0	2	9	5	42	384	21	0

See footnotes at end of table.

Table 8

Offenses Known to Law Enforcement
by City 10,000 and over in Population, 2002—Continued

City by state	Population	Crime Index	Modified Crime Index[1]	Murder and non-negligent man-slaughter	Forcible rape	Robbery	Aggravated assault	Burglary	Larceny-theft	Motor vehicle theft	Arson[1]
PENNSYLVANIA—Continued											
Ross Township	32,694	912	915	0	0	10	23	70	760	49	3
Salisbury Township	13,557	392	394	0	1	3	33	28	301	26	2
Sandy Township	11,607	185	186	0	0	0	27	21	127	10	1
Scranton	76,751	2,549	2,549	1	39	92	90	503	1,636	188	0
Shaler Township	29,888	424	424	0	1	9	18	46	319	31	0
Sharon	16,400	791	792	0	8	24	126	148	448	37	1
Silver Spring Township	10,639	254	256	0	1	2	1	17	222	11	2
South Fayette Township	12,325	115	117	0	1	1	11	22	72	8	2
South Park Township	14,403	54	55	0	2	1	2	18	26	5	1
South Whitehall Township	18,107	623	624	0	0	5	15	58	523	22	1
Springettsbury Township	23,988	1,088	1,088	0	2	13	6	82	953	32	0
Springfield Township (Delaware County)	23,782	751	751	1	2	9	38	60	568	73	0
Springfield Township (Montgomery County)	19,619	207	209	2	0	8	7	24	153	13	2
Spring Garden Township	12,026	379	382	0	1	15	5	39	303	16	3
Spring Township (Berks County)	21,901	250	253	0	1	5	7	32	185	20	3
State College	51,792	925	931	2	7	10	26	87	777	16	6
St. Marys City	14,566	319	319	0	1	1	17	44	239	17	0
Stroud Area Regional	29,752	917	917	3	6	21	15	108	714	50	0
Sunbury	10,657	549	555	0	11	2	87	70	361	18	6
Susquehanna Township (Dauphin County)	21,991	702	717	0	7	25	5	83	562	20	15
Towamencin Township	17,675	198	205	0	1	2	12	20	154	9	7
Tredyffrin Township	29,190	696	699	1	4	5	24	59	588	15	3
Uniontown	12,476	663	675	1	3	37	33	110	417	62	12
Upper Allen Township	15,406	192	194	0	2	3	4	41	135	7	2
Upper Chichester Township	16,916	597	601	0	6	22	27	59	415	68	4
Upper Darby Township	82,181	1,542	1,542	4	7	91	65	139	1,030	206	0
Upper Dublin Township	25,991	302	302	0	2	3	18	41	225	13	0
Upper Gwynedd Township	14,306	193	197	0	0	3	8	23	150	9	4
Upper Merion Township	26,981	1,443	1,444	0	2	19	16	79	1,238	89	1
Upper Moreland Township	25,103	395	402	1	3	6	15	42	306	22	7
Upper Providence Township (Delaware County)	10,555	58	58	0	2	0	4	17	31	4	0
Upper Providence Township (Montgomery County)	15,466	186	186	0	0	0	5	30	137	14	0
Upper Saucon Township	11,991	112	115	0	1	0	5	17	83	6	3
Upper Southampton Township	15,833	223	223	0	1	1	21	26	159	15	0
Upper St. Clair Township	20,141	103	104	0	0	3	2	14	79	5	1
Uwchlan Township	16,649	287	287	0	4	5	24	49	188	17	0
Warminster Township	31,521	613	621	1	4	20	24	58	467	39	8
Warren	10,304	152	153	0	1	0	7	38	103	3	1
Warrington Township	17,658	269	273	0	3	3	21	33	198	11	4
Warwick Township (Bucks County)	12,030	120	122	0	1	0	1	21	94	3	2
Warwick Township (Lancaster County)	15,543	83	83	0	0	0	1	12	64	6	0
Washington Township (Franklin County)	11,610	204	204	0	3	4	13	28	144	12	0
West Chester	17,940	678	681	0	12	43	46	120	388	69	3
West Goshen Township	20,585	565	566	0	3	6	24	48	466	18	1
West Hempfield Township	15,194	355	356	0	1	1	4	53	275	21	1
West Lampeter Township	13,203	196	196	0	0	2	3	27	153	11	0
West Manchester Township	17,110	797	797	0	5	20	18	75	651	28	0
West Norriton Township	14,967	328	328	0	2	3	33	46	228	16	0
Westtown-East Goshen Township	13,088	381	382	0	2	1	39	73	250	16	1
West Whiteland Township	16,572	585	587	0	1	5	6	49	506	18	2
Whitehall	14,508	57	57	0	2	2	4	9	33	7	0
Whitehall Township	25,006	1,118	1,137	0	2	18	33	109	886	70	19
Whitpain Township	18,643	232	232	0	2	2	6	40	169	13	0
Wilkes-Barre	43,312	2,329	2,343	3	15	113	121	378	1,485	214	14
Wilkinsburg	19,280	909	916	1	12	81	97	239	293	186	7
Williamsport	30,841	1,473	1,478	1	10	66	51	221	1,061	63	5
Yeadon	11,814	342	349	0	5	16	35	45	183	58	7
York Area Regional	44,731	819	820	1	5	14	49	148	578	24	1

See footnotes at end of table.

Table 8

Offenses Known to Law Enforcement
by City 10,000 and over in Population, 2002—Continued

City by state	Population	Crime Index	Modified Crime Index[1]	Murder and non-negligent man-slaughter	Forcible rape	Robbery	Aggravated assault	Burglary	Larceny-theft	Motor vehicle theft	Arson[1]
RHODE ISLAND											
Barrington	17,162	369	385	0	4	2	5	86	268	4	16
Bristol	22,928	440	444	0	2	1	24	38	349	26	4
Burrillville	16,119	244	249	0	3	1	18	45	169	8	5
Central Falls	19,315	674	681	2	16	29	71	128	324	104	7
Coventry	34,355	603	613	1	9	9	31	135	391	27	10
Cranston	80,887	2,632	2,648	0	27	44	76	454	1,745	286	16
Cumberland	32,490	538	549	0	10	9	12	82	415	10	11
East Greenwich	13,212	186	187	0	0	1	4	38	135	8	1
East Providence	49,683	1,025	1,037	0	13	21	51	191	675	74	12
Glocester	10,152	94	98	0	0	0	11	25	53	5	4
Johnston	28,771	1,003	1,021	0	4	10	42	154	698	95	18
Lincoln	21,325	465	465	0	0	6	1	65	332	61	0
Middletown	17,688	444	445	1	7	2	13	69	348	4	1
Narragansett	16,695	356	357	0	4	0	13	56	270	13	1
Newport	27,013	1,576	1,589	0	13	20	109	307	1,066	61	13
North Kingstown	26,864	571	576	1	4	0	12	93	431	30	5
North Providence	33,073	663	665	0	5	21	44	100	415	78	2
North Smithfield	10,835	228	232	0	0	0	9	37	178	4	4
Pawtucket	74,448	3,209	3,241	1	34	78	147	574	1,917	458	32
Portsmouth	17,500	253	256	0	2	1	17	39	189	5	3
Providence	177,162	13,864	14,188	23	109	550	620	2,186	7,515	2,861	324
Scituate	10,535	155	157	0	1	0	6	36	106	6	2
Smithfield	21,034	382	388	0	2	4	9	44	314	9	6
South Kingstown	28,491	394	405	0	7	3	17	87	268	12	11
Tiverton	15,572	245	247	0	2	2	5	60	156	20	2
Warren	11,592	336	341	0	2	1	13	35	277	8	5
Warwick	87,560	2,931	2,962	2	17	34	76	384	2,084	334	31
Westerly	23,435	365	366	1	2	2	5	58	278	19	1
West Warwick	30,185	726	743	1	9	10	49	148	495	14	17
Woonsocket	44,107	1,551	1,579	2	51	48	106	327	894	123	28
SOUTH CAROLINA											
Aiken	25,938	1,334	1,337	4	9	23	64	163	1,018	53	3
Anderson	26,120	1,758		3	10	49	176	331	1,051	138	
Beaufort	13,257	999	1,001	1	6	40	124	161	614	53	2
Cayce	12,438	850	851	1	3	17	62	143	571	53	1
Charleston	98,942	6,997	7,002	13	37	259	541	1,021	4,254	872	5
Clemson	12,222	393	395	0	1	9	8	66	264	45	2
Columbia	119,036	10,307		10	83	497	949	1,639	6,213	916	
Conway	12,067	1,438	1,440	2	6	37	127	235	962	69	2
Easley	18,175	757	760	0	7	13	35	126	526	50	3
Florence	30,966	3,635	3,653	3	19	113	252	540	2,524	184	18
Forest Acres	10,809	985		0	0	29	66	116	737	37	
Gaffney	13,276	842	844	1	11	30	72	195	493	40	2
Goose Creek	29,901	846	851	1	3	22	52	148	570	50	5
Greenville	57,331	4,652	4,659	9	45	172	446	622	3,075	283	7
Greenwood	22,595	1,828	1,838	2	9	53	325	284	1,092	63	10
Greer	17,242	836	846	1	8	32	56	124	556	59	10
Hanahan	13,244	658	660	0	4	13	36	128	402	75	2
Irmo	11,301	385	387	0	8	9	42	62	249	15	2
Laurens	10,151	630	635	1	3	26	140	100	340	20	5
Lexington	10,025	405	407	0	0	7	26	37	325	10	2
Mauldin	15,585	533	540	0	5	14	56	63	365	30	7
Mount Pleasant	48,739	1,796	1,804	0	1	34	55	169	1,427	110	8
Myrtle Beach	23,299	4,869		2	42	158	273	835	3,106	453	
Newberry	10,831	575	576	0	3	11	86	50	411	14	1
North Augusta	17,991	902	903	1	6	29	55	140	610	61	1
North Charleston	81,530	8,884	8,935	16	103	441	794	1,357	4,891	1,282	51
North Myrtle Beach	11,234	1,390	1,391	0	18	39	43	245	942	103	1
Orangeburg	13,067	1,284	1,287	1	15	33	165	262	739	69	3
Rock Hill	50,946	3,633	3,638	5	21	115	403	708	2,173	208	5
Simpsonville	14,692	684	686	0	4	11	77	79	484	29	2
Spartanburg	40,615	4,582	4,599	3	22	152	601	727	2,754	323	17
Summerville	28,411	1,495		0	7	35	146	247	973	87	

See footnotes at end of table.

Table 8

Offenses Known to Law Enforcement
by City 10,000 and over in Population, 2002—Continued

City by state	Population	Crime Index	Modified Crime Index[1]	Murder and non-negligent man-slaughter	Forcible rape	Robbery	Aggravated assault	Burglary	Larceny-theft	Motor vehicle theft	Arson[1]
SOUTH CAROLINA—Continued											
Sumter	40,583	3,592		4	20	120	384	671	2,095	298	
West Columbia	13,374	1,498	1,501	1	6	64	247	195	879	106	3
SOUTH DAKOTA											
Aberdeen	24,861	573	574	0	10	0	19	114	409	21	1
Brookings	18,656	482	484	0	3	0	6	76	389	8	2
Mitchell	14,678	497	501	0	8	2	28	77	367	15	4
Pierre	13,990	537	537	0	7	1	22	38	446	23	0
Rapid City	60,098	2,930	2,941	0	53	25	136	515	2,070	131	11
Sioux Falls	124,997	4,189	4,242	1	115	52	228	652	2,946	195	53
Watertown	20,403	789	791	0	12	2	30	158	547	40	2
Yankton	13,639	405	405	0	13	2	15	34	322	19	0
TENNESSEE											
Athens	13,471	1,166	1,168	0	7	18	186	217	665	73	2
Brentwood	23,890	558	565	1	1	5	8	68	462	13	7
Bristol	25,292	1,475	1,477	1	4	13	103	189	1,083	82	2
Brownsville	10,952	718	719	0	8	23	145	124	377	41	1
Chattanooga	158,507	15,867	15,939	24	112	625	1,638	2,574	9,462	1,432	72
Clarksville	105,419	5,962	5,982	6	44	82	462	768	4,330	270	20
Cleveland	37,898	2,373	2,378	3	29	29	210	340	1,653	109	5
Collierville	32,477	651	656	0	2	8	47	63	473	58	5
Columbia	33,682	2,407	2,417	1	10	57	281	459	1,496	103	10
Cookeville	24,377	1,437	1,445	2	6	23	51	214	1,059	82	8
Dickson	12,476	930	932	0	10	8	59	100	697	56	2
Dyersburg	17,783	1,450	1,454	0	15	28	192	207	950	58	4
East Ridge	21,032	1,286	1,292	0	6	17	77	223	869	94	6
Elizabethton	13,626	833	836	0	7	1	63	140	586	36	3
Franklin	42,636	1,136	1,140	0	8	15	55	128	852	78	4
Gallatin	23,671	1,515	1,522	0	17	23	132	195	1,083	65	7
Germantown	38,057	861	866	0	2	10	21	140	652	36	5
Goodlettsville	14,042	1,081	1,081	0	1	23	51	129	779	98	0
Greeneville	15,487	954	956	0	13	20	61	113	686	61	2
Hendersonville	41,391	1,086	1,093	0	12	3	114	189	719	49	7
Jackson	60,775	4,661	4,676	3	38	182	462	836	2,788	352	15
Johnson City	56,522	3,896	3,911	4	20	77	263	538	2,767	227	15
Kingsport	45,757	3,248	3,263	2	29	43	295	477	2,267	135	15
Knoxville	177,191	11,983	12,121	21	74	553	1,308	2,135	6,680	1,212	138
La Vergne	19,041	643	654	0	3	6	103	91	393	47	11
Lawrenceburg	11,001	963	972	0	10	10	157	125	639	22	9
Lebanon	20,619	1,388	1,389	2	15	25	140	312	804	90	1
Lewisburg	10,611	439	441	0	3	4	37	100	279	16	2
Martin	10,715	315	317	0	5	7	17	34	239	13	2
Maryville	23,559	809	819	1	12	10	39	156	544	47	10
McMinnville	12,991	756	758	0	5	9	41	142	502	57	2
Memphis	662,441	65,846	66,121	151	517	4,240	5,538	16,340	29,841	9,219	275
Millington	10,631	748	750	0	4	15	60	144	476	49	2
Morristown	25,439	1,921	1,938	4	7	33	124	211	1,426	116	17
Mount Juliet	12,601	547	548	0	4	4	48	82	380	29	1
Murfreesboro	70,122	3,688	3,695	0	22	64	387	471	2,544	200	7
Nashville	560,596	46,018	46,180	61	403	2,081	6,138	7,468	25,082	4,785	162
Oak Ridge	27,907	1,868	1,876	0	17	48	100	326	1,298	79	8
Red Bank	12,654	561	563	1	7	8	85	135	292	33	2
Sevierville	11,980	1,015	1,018	0	4	6	43	152	742	68	3
Shelbyville	16,411	684	688	1	3	^)	68	151	409	32	4
Smyrna	26,054	1,128	1,135	1	7	11	79	144	826	60	7
Soddy-Daisy	11,749	402	402	0	1	4	43	93	236	25	0
Springfield	14,601	953	954	0	15	25	157	75	633	48	1
Tullahoma	18,335	1,251	1,254	0	2	21	60	270	838	60	3
Union City	11,083	939	947	0	2	10	84	145	654	44	8

See footnotes at end of table.

Table 8

Offenses Known to Law Enforcement
by City 10,000 and over in Population, 2002—Continued

City by state	Population	Crime Index	Modified Crime Index[1]	Murder and non-negligent man-slaughter	Forcible rape	Robbery	Aggravated assault	Burglary	Larceny-theft	Motor vehicle theft	Arson[1]
TEXAS											
Abilene	121,089	5,394	5,431	4	63	111	266	1,289	3,432	229	37
Addison	14,797	1,105	1,112	1	4	24	36	156	763	121	7
Alamo	15,416	942	945	0	0	17	31	104	736	54	3
Alice	19,856	1,635	1,652	0	6	4	197	318	1,059	51	17
Allen	45,492	1,506	1,509	0	8	14	49	404	989	42	3
Alvin	22,366	938	944	0	9	24	56	159	623	67	6
Amarillo	181,355	13,473	13,539	7	109	330	1,033	2,468	8,566	960	66
Andrews	10,081	293	293	0	0	0	24	63	195	11	0
Angleton	18,937	621	621	3	11	2	88	105	378	34	0
Arlington	347,789	23,594	23,667	14	152	794	1,242	3,638	15,746	2,008	73
Athens	11,800	650	653	0	3	16	101	152	344	34	3
Austin	685,784	42,979	43,131	25	256	1,174	1,748	6,916	29,725	3,135	152
Azle	10,027	435	437	0	1	1	35	70	316	12	2
Balch Springs	20,237	1,364	1,367	3	4	42	83	263	811	158	3
Bay City	19,498	1,181	1,184	0	0	31	76	256	777	41	3
Baytown	69,387	3,303	3,325	2	33	79	131	617	2,159	282	22
Beaumont	118,934	10,443	10,509	7	172	408	563	1,722	7,015	556	66
Bedford	49,251	1,913	1,923	0	18	26	43	316	1,377	133	10
Beeville	13,713	470	472	0	7	3	32	92	318	18	2
Bellaire	16,338	522	524	0	2	34	7	124	329	26	2
Belton	15,274	637	639	0	0	7	29	130	459	12	2
Benbrook	21,107	483	488	2	5	9	9	107	308	43	5
Big Spring	26,356	1,105	1,111	1	16	8	43	318	667	52	6
Bonham	10,435	558	563	0	6	2	49	105	359	37	5
Borger	14,938	811	816	1	14	6	25	161	580	24	5
Brenham	14,108	769	775	0	9	10	80	152	457	61	6
Brownsville	145,941	12,759	12,785	1	32	181	592	1,207	10,266	480	26
Brownwood	19,650	1,578	1,582	0	15	11	193	288	915	156	4
Bryan	68,583	4,447	4,470	3	60	81	346	858	2,879	220	23
Burkburnett	11,413	246	249	0	0	2	14	66	162	2	3
Burleson	21,909	1,087	1,092	0	6	11	19	157	836	58	5
Canyon	13,448	214	214	0	2	0	2	29	178	3	0
Carrollton	114,453	4,289	4,329	1	18	90	148	819	2,802	411	40
Cedar Hill	33,521	1,401	1,411	0	17	16	121	358	776	113	10
Cedar Park	27,209	580	584	0	9	13	42	114	378	24	4
Cleburne	27,162	1,778	1,784	1	28	14	85	230	1,333	87	6
Clute	10,888	662	664	0	8	6	49	106	440	53	2
College Station	70,911	2,972	2,975	2	37	16	86	354	2,374	103	3
Colleyville	20,510	348	350	0	2	2	9	60	269	6	2
Conroe	38,450	3,044	3,051	2	25	139	187	540	1,973	178	7
Converse	12,021	303	303	0	11	2	7	69	191	23	0
Coppell	37,558	923	924	0	5	9	15	245	620	29	1
Copperas Cove	30,909	1,275	1,277	0	4	14	118	282	804	53	2
Corinth	11,829	235	235	0	4	1	4	56	162	8	0
Corpus Christi	289,803	21,237	21,386	19	243	511	1,290	3,581	14,147	1,446	149
Corsicana	25,575	1,652	1,659	0	17	31	42	349	1,123	90	7
Dallas	1,241,481	112,040	113,607	196	656	8,041	8,125	20,351	56,306	18,365	1,567
Deer Park	29,789	596	598	0	5	12	16	108	409	46	2
Del Rio	35,374	1,254	1,255	2	2	10	54	190	913	83	1
Denison	23,787	1,267	1,269	0	0	22	47	240	861	97	2
Denton	84,121	3,880	3,912	2	65	78	229	673	2,655	178	32
DeSoto	39,321	1,901	1,910	2	11	35	92	513	1,116	132	9
Dickinson	17,854	594	594	0	6	18	30	130	349	61	0
Donna	15,426	1,089	1,100	1	4	27	54	180	765	58	11
Dumas	14,359	582	590	0	9	8	46	74	423	22	8
Duncanville	37,687	1,928	1,935	5	13	57	104	386	1,119	244	7
Eagle Pass	23,411	941	947	0	0	4	32	94	734	77	6
Edinburg	50,622	5,189	5,228	3	18	45	218	605	4,051	249	39
El Campo	11,433	555	557	1	7	3	44	125	350	25	2
El Paso	588,750	26,998	27,108	14	221	575	3,082	2,221	18,887	1,998	110
Ennis	16,759	908	913	1	16	14	51	134	652	40	5
Euless	48,052	1,714	1,727	1	6	30	70	262	1,207	138	13
Farmers Branch	28,732	1,382	1,382	1	4	37	30	224	864	222	0
Flower Mound	52,958	765	766	2	8	10	30	161	529	25	1
Forest Hill	13,525	582	582	3	5	27	57	141	281	68	0

See footnotes at end of table.

Table 8

Offenses Known to Law Enforcement
by City 10,000 and over in Population, 2002—Continued

City by state	Population	Crime Index	Modified Crime Index[1]	Murder and non-negligent man-slaughter	Forcible rape	Robbery	Aggravated assault	Burglary	Larceny-theft	Motor vehicle theft	Arson[1]
TEXAS—Continued											
Fort Worth	558,493	44,797	45,065	53	321	1,648	2,221	9,736	26,881	3,937	268
Freeport	13,273	598	601	2	13	13	32	169	337	32	3
Friendswood	30,329	474	481	1	8	11	25	100	301	28	7
Frisco	35,214	1,482	1,482	1	13	16	48	398	953	53	0
Gainesville	16,230	1,017	1,019	1	1	13	118	197	624	63	2
Galena Park	11,064	335	335	0	10	6	24	93	176	26	0
Garland	225,371	9,734	9,777	11	44	286	287	1,868	6,349	889	43
Gatesville	16,285	262	262	1	5	0	44	54	154	4	0
Georgetown	29,601	599	601	1	2	11	28	82	432	43	2
Grand Prairie	133,099	7,924	7,958	3	68	193	259	1,291	4,804	1,306	34
Grapevine	43,931	1,898	1,925	2	9	27	60	272	1,331	197	27
Greenville	25,027	2,447	2,457	0	14	63	240	474	1,539	117	10
Groves	16,434	745	745	0	1	28	13	157	487	59	0
Haltom City	40,754	2,007	2,026	0	9	30	108	500	1,207	153	19
Harker Heights	18,078	849	850	1	10	6	26	158	602	46	1
Harlingen	60,126	4,041	4,051	5	27	54	203	795	2,730	227	10
Henderson	11,775	954	955	2	17	9	159	123	619	25	1
Hereford	15,246	658	661	0	3	3	70	170	393	19	3
Hewitt	11,578	288	288	0	1	2	8	54	215	8	0
Highland Village	12,715	151	152	1	0	1	10	40	92	7	1
Houston	2,040,583	149,247	150,943	256	892	11,212	12,598	26,905	73,445	23,939	1,696
Humble	15,228	1,630	1,632	0	14	56	48	136	1,151	225	2
Huntsville	36,639	1,138	1,143	0	7	34	127	193	712	65	5
Hurst	37,887	2,649	2,655	1	19	48	82	272	2,081	146	6
Irving	200,144	10,812	10,861	5	47	250	501	1,634	7,077	1,298	49
Jacinto City	10,760	464	467	0	0	24	18	82	269	71	3
Jacksonville	14,485	721	725	1	25	13	43	174	423	42	4
Katy	12,299	631	633	0	6	7	59	39	490	30	2
Keller	28,562	608	613	0	4	4	76	113	394	17	5
Kerrville	21,335	729	734	0	6	5	15	133	535	35	5
Kilgore	11,804	1,066	1,066	0	14	7	43	179	785	38	0
Killeen	90,779	6,505	6,532	3	77	155	476	1,756	3,700	338	27
Kingsville	26,714	1,712	1,712	3	18	17	199	267	1,154	54	0
Lake Jackson	27,560	1,005	1,006	0	4	7	27	134	797	36	1
La Marque	14,291	901	903	3	11	24	36	220	530	77	2
Lamesa	10,395	307	307	0	5	2	42	73	177	8	0
Lancaster	27,047	1,741	1,751	0	7	44	175	408	925	182	10
La Porte	33,299	762	776	2	14	14	49	191	427	65	14
Laredo	184,435	12,952	13,029	7	58	203	839	1,898	9,064	883	77
League City	47,466	1,249	1,249	2	2	14	15	225	918	73	0
Levelland	13,438	375	377	0	5	4	36	69	247	14	2
Lewisville	81,196	4,231	4,239	4	41	69	97	617	2,950	453	8
Lockhart	12,132	417	417	0	10	4	45	88	256	14	0
Longview	76,608	5,771	5,794	6	147	171	251	1,047	3,654	495	23
Lubbock	208,447	14,371	14,436	11	133	303	2,067	2,979	8,307	571	65
Lufkin	34,164	2,013	2,021	1	18	35	118	443	1,286	112	8
Mansfield	29,279	1,067	1,074	0	4	13	42	305	667	36	7
Marshall	25,000	1,493	1,495	0	18	30	61	306	982	96	2
McAllen	111,150	8,982	9,040	4	12	178	339	1,074	6,684	691	58
McKinney	56,789	2,596	2,622	2	54	46	91	528	1,715	160	26
Memorial Villages	11,916	174	174	0	0	2	2	45	115	10	0
Mercedes	14,257	301	301	0	1	1	23	41	216	19	0
Mesquite	130,065	6,480	6,532	9	5	135	298	689	4,528	816	52
Midland	99,224	4,143	4,158	2	69	74	416	839	2,545	198	15
Mineral Wells	17,700	793	797	0	16	9	14	139	562	53	4
Mission	47,429	2,849	2,849	2	2	19	57	519	1,970	280	0
Missouri City	55,268	1,459	1,474	5	13	⟨⟩	74	325	866	116	15
Mount Pleasant	14,555	777	784	0	0	6	55	124	543	49	7
Nacogdoches	31,246	1,229	1,233	0	13	18	184	220	755	39	4
Nederland	18,198	805	805	1	4	10	18	130	586	56	0
New Braunfels	38,119	2,726	2,736	1	18	24	249	327	2,001	106	10
North Richland Hills	58,111	2,957	2,957	1	25	35	97	422	2,236	141	0
Odessa	94,990	5,747	5,778	3	33	89	414	948	4,020	240	31
Orange	19,473	1,294	1,302	1	15	32	125	260	767	94	8
Palestine	18,381	1,029	1,039	1	10	14	45	202	707	50	10

See footnotes at end of table.

Table 8

Offenses Known to Law Enforcement

by City 10,000 and over in Population, 2002—Continued

City by state	Population	Crime Index	Modified Crime Index[1]	Murder and non-negligent man-slaughter	Forcible rape	Robbery	Aggravated assault	Burglary	Larceny-theft	Motor vehicle theft	Arson[1]
TEXAS—Continued											
Pampa	18,683	1,521	1,524	0	10	20	76	431	956	28	3
Paris	27,051	3,272	3,277	3	58	43	314	536	2,222	96	5
Pasadena	147,979	7,184	7,268	7	68	154	390	1,379	4,402	784	84
Pearland	39,315	1,387	1,393	2	25	25	45	214	971	105	6
Pflugerville	17,062	436	443	0	1	2	13	74	321	25	7
Pharr	48,737	3,086	3,095	7	22	81	194	524	2,178	80	9
Plainview	23,330	1,344	1,347	0	11	18	73	267	947	28	3
Plano	231,912	9,020	9,042	6	40	145	478	1,326	6,505	520	22
Port Arthur	60,326	2,883	2,912	6	14	170	178	866	1,357	292	29
Portland	15,487	484	486	0	7	1	24	76	361	15	2
Port Lavaca	12,571	495	497	0	15	3	19	117	306	35	2
Port Neches	14,207	588	589	0	4	3	25	111	411	34	1
Raymondville	10,166	572	578	1	0	10	51	215	279	16	6
Richardson	95,888	3,812	3,813	0	15	97	170	716	2,487	327	1
Richmond	11,574	578	586	1	4	14	38	102	400	19	8
Rio Grande City	12,454	414	415	2	3	3	65	79	210	52	1
Robstown	13,294	770	775	0	4	21	81	214	416	34	5
Rockwall	18,777	694	696	0	8	12	19	129	464	62	2
Roma	10,045	290	290	1	4	0	22	82	127	54	0
Rosenberg	25,113	1,185	1,195	0	15	34	75	216	771	74	10
Round Rock	63,857	1,813	1,817	0	20	31	65	278	1,361	58	4
Rowlett	46,484	1,065	1,069	0	10	9	26	265	694	61	4
Sachse	10,185	202	204	0	6	1	15	59	112	9	2
Saginaw	12,925	411	413	0	7	0	9	90	282	23	2
San Angelo	92,375	5,718	5,745	0	55	50	287	1,048	4,055	223	27
San Antonio	1,195,592	94,132	94,665	100	464	2,114	7,091	13,368	65,251	5,744	533
San Benito	24,488	2,089	2,089	0	6	13	24	265	1,698	83	0
San Juan	27,396	1,286	1,295	1	0	24	54	242	901	64	9
San Marcos	36,279	1,593	1,602	0	34	34	78	234	1,133	80	9
Schertz	19,526	515	515	0	5	8	25	75	390	12	0
Seagoville	11,304	605	605	0	10	9	32	128	338	88	0
Seguin	22,991	1,687	1,688	3	7	19	73	281	1,262	42	1
Sherman	36,643	2,378	2,385	0	12	56	112	359	1,742	97	7
Snyder	11,262	277	279	0	1	3	10	77	172	14	2
Socorro	28,360	425	428	0	5	2	42	95	241	40	3
South Houston	16,537	975	975	3	6	45	61	195	503	162	0
Southlake	22,477	377	378	0	0	6	12	53	295	11	1
Stafford	16,379	1,027	1,028	0	11	35	11	145	745	80	1
Stephenville	15,585	641	646	0	7	5	13	80	518	18	5
Sugar Land	66,147	1,937	1,937	1	12	61	107	256	1,387	113	0
Sulphur Springs	15,198	505	510	1	2	4	29	118	315	36	5
Sweetwater	11,923	410	418	1	8	3	31	144	198	25	8
Taylor	14,179	432	435	1	9	5	29	71	302	15	3
Temple	56,940	3,133	3,171	1	7	84	140	693	1,981	227	38
Terrell	14,212	1,449	1,454	3	9	45	173	213	876	130	5
Texarkana	36,330	2,983	3,007	5	31	97	228	602	1,863	157	24
Texas City	43,369	3,915	3,944	5	26	101	439	734	2,322	288	29
The Colony	27,712	1,040	1,059	0	12	5	32	224	717	50	19
Tyler	87,373	6,614	6,616	4	58	140	442	1,008	4,512	450	2
Universal City	15,510	459	465	1	5	7	34	94	299	19	6
University Park	24,362	652	654	1	0	15	9	120	484	23	2
Uvalde	15,594	875	892	1	1	7	57	213	554	42	17
Vernon	12,179	748	748	0	13	5	25	149	533	23	0
Victoria	63,300	3,890	3,894	9	44	108	317	645	2,602	165	4
Vidor	11,949	584	590	0	5	9	25	136	371	38	6
Waco	118,788	11,001	11,033	14	58	277	596	2,197	7,143	716	32
Watauga	22,883	768	769	0	10	9	58	170	483	38	1
Waxahachie	22,379	1,133	1,137	0	1	8	53	256	751	64	4
Weatherford	19,846	962	964	0	9	8	26	173	720	26	2
Weslaco	28,134	2,216	2,219	0	7	37	104	376	1,495	197	3
West University Place	14,844	284	284	0	1	2	3	87	179	12	0
White Settlement	15,491	860	864	1	0	12	28	182	570	67	4
Wichita Falls	108,834	8,532	8,567	11	31	246	710	1,726	5,327	481	35
Wylie	15,806	427	430	0	14	3	8	121	268	13	3

See footnotes at end of table.

Table 8

Offenses Known to Law Enforcement
by City 10,000 and over in Population, 2002—Continued

City by state	Population	Crime Index	Modified Crime Index[1]	Murder and non-negligent man-slaughter	Forcible rape	Robbery	Aggravated assault	Burglary	Larceny-theft	Motor vehicle theft	Arson[1]
UTAH											
Alpine/Highland	15,888	271	271	0	1	0	4	76	179	11	0
American Fork	22,757	1,024	1,026	0	4	0	19	162	786	53	2
Bountiful	42,837	1,069	1,069	0	5	5	22	138	850	49	0
Brigham City	18,059	632	635	0	7	1	17	125	445	37	3
Cedar City	21,291	690	694	0	1	2	19	101	545	22	4
Centerville	15,127	431	433	0	2	0	9	72	326	22	2
Clearfield	26,941	980	991	0	17	5	28	180	685	65	11
Clinton	13,054	225	227	0	0	0	5	40	170	10	2
Farmington	12,530	354	356	0	3	1	7	44	290	9	2
Kaysville	21,108	493	500	0	8	3	10	96	363	13	7
Layton	60,650	2,566	2,582	1	24	21	72	387	1,930	131	16
Lehi	19,736	560	561	0	2	3	14	186	319	36	1
Logan	44,257	1,190	1,190	0	19	0	29	141	976	25	0
Midvale	28,034	1,611	1,613	0	23	20	74	206	1,104	184	2
Murray	35,290	3,703	3,709	1	24	51	86	461	2,782	298	6
North Ogden	15,585	301	301	0	2	0	5	43	247	4	0
Ogden	80,099	5,332	5,332	5	89	93	286	914	3,505	440	0
Orem	87,462	3,649	3,655	1	16	17	32	372	3,042	169	6
Payson	13,189	432	432	0	3	1	5	69	316	38	0
Provo	109,079	3,657	3,674	0	37	23	105	514	2,789	189	17
Roy	34,109	944	951	0	16	6	56	132	680	54	7
Salt Lake City	188,504	19,059	19,146	11	109	478	635	2,512	13,337	1,977	87
Sandy	91,707	3,593	3,608	1	18	31	126	547	2,649	221	15
South Jordan	30,532	855	857	2	3	4	24	209	578	35	2
South Ogden	14,912	691	695	0	4	6	3	82	568	28	4
South Salt Lake	22,857	1,968	1,971	1	42	40	78	344	1,117	346	3
Springville	21,184	913	913	1	4	0	26	188	660	34	0
St. George	51,511	1,664	1,667	2	59	1	81	226	1,203	92	3
Tooele	23,339	817	820	0	13	10	70	203	440	81	3
West Jordan	70,879	3,513	3,524	1	24	32	130	446	2,614	266	11
West Valley[1]	112,948	6,889	6,924	3	59	98	275	883	4,843	728	35
VERMONT											
Bennington	16,172	554	556	0	10	2	13	121	381	27	2
Brattleboro	12,158	471	473	1	6	1	19	124	301	19	2
Burlington	39,385	1,871	1,874	1	5	18	91	324	1,349	83	3
Colchester	17,203	510	511	0	0	3	7	71	410	19	1
Essex	18,864	591	593	0	4	0	7	153	415	12	2
Hartford	10,500	183	183	0	3	1	5	29	135	10	0
Rutland	17,513	917	924	0	6	16	27	118	713	37	7
South Burlington	16,016	645	647	0	1	3	4	96	507	34	2
VIRGINIA											
Alexandria	132,180	5,165	5,181	3	21	176	212	482	3,532	739	16
Blacksburg	40,775	758	761	2	4	12	55	165	490	30	3
Bristol	17,894	760	769	0	3	9	80	69	565	34	9
Chesapeake	205,235	8,756	8,774	6	65	321	971	1,438	5,351	604	18
Chesapeake State Police		8	8	0	0	0	5	0	3	0	0
Colonial Heights	17,410	968	980	0	5	21	18	89	790	45	12
Danville	49,882	2,265	2,285	3	13	69	216	289	1,575	100	20
Falls Church	10,692	453	457	0	0	5	11	37	343	57	4
Fredericksburg	19,865	979	982	0	7	47	89	70	680	86	3
Fredericksburg State Police		7	7	0	0	0	4	0	3	0	0
Front Royal	14,002	598	601	0	13	9	19	74	446	37	3
Hampton	150,885	6,209	6,244	9	38	29.	269	961	3,772	869	35
Hampton State Police		14	14	0	0	0	9	0	3	2	0
Harrisonburg	41,697	1,239	1,252	0	19	10	100	195	847	68	13
Harrisonburg State Police		11	11	0	0	0	1	0	8	2	0
Herndon	22,313	636	636	0	10	24	31	35	503	33	0
Leesburg	29,171	917	921	6	12	22	46	58	719	54	4
Lynchburg	67,251	2,641	2,660	6	25	87	191	419	1,714	199	19
Martinsville	15,884	671	673	2	7	13	43	54	522	30	2
Newport News	185,622	9,936	10,053	20	106	420	805	1,636	5,715	1,234	117

See footnotes at end of table.

Table 8

Offenses Known to Law Enforcement
by City 10,000 and over in Population, 2002—Continued

City by state	Population	Crime Index	Modified Crime Index[1]	Murder and non-negligent man-slaughter	Forcible rape	Robbery	Aggravated assault	Burglary	Larceny-theft	Motor vehicle theft	Arson[1]
VIRGINIA—Continued											
Newport News State Police		10	10	0	0	0	8	0	0	2	0
Norfolk	241,523	15,476	15,499	41	115	709	488	1,758	10,738	1,627	23
Norfolk State Police		12	12	0	0	0	10	0	2	0	0
Petersburg	34,765	2,497	2,510	6	18	79	157	278	1,676	283	13
Petersburg State Police		1	1	0	0	0	1	0	0	0	0
Poquoson	11,917	131	138	0	2	0	5	17	101	6	7
Portsmouth	103,620	7,015	7,035	11	38	425	524	1,316	4,058	643	20
Portsmouth State Police		8	8	0	0	0	4	0	3	1	0
Richmond	203,799	18,002	18,193	77	118	1,289	1,122	2,966	9,926	2,504	191
Richmond State Police		21	21	0	0	0	5	0	12	4	0
Salem	25,498	658	664	0	3	13	11	53	539	39	6
Staunton	24,577	919	924	0	6	6	41	136	680	50	5
Staunton State Police		3	3	0	0	0	0	0	3	0	0
Suffolk	65,612	3,368	3,399	4	24	110	292	482	2,282	174	31
Virginia Beach	438,175	16,067	16,242	3	132	443	376	2,290	11,981	842	175
Virginia Beach State Police		15	15	0	0	0	12	0	2	1	0
Waynesboro	20,113	879	886	0	8	18	126	121	572	34	7
Williamsburg	12,362	312	312	0	3	12	8	26	244	19	0
Williamsburg State Police		1	1	0	0	0	0	0	1	0	0
Winchester	24,302	1,474	1,479	0	16	30	41	131	1,214	42	5
Winchester State Police		1	1	0	0	0	0	0	1	0	0
WASHINGTON											
Aberdeen	16,949	1,716	1,720	0	23	12	32	224	1,344	81	4
Anacortes	14,989	587	590	0	4	4	11	119	428	21	3
Arlington	12,060	1,003	1,008	0	3	12	41	121	701	125	5
Auburn	41,510	3,955	4,002	5	31	68	169	575	2,231	876	47
Bainbridge Island	20,910	418	423	0	3	0	7	132	260	16	5
Bellevue	112,819	4,640	4,679	0	26	48	66	606	3,349	545	39
Bellingham	69,164	5,108	5,137	2	22	71	69	678	3,972	294	29
Bothell	31,045	878	885	0	10	9	24	136	585	114	7
Bremerton	38,365	2,917	2,939	1	82	64	260	519	1,659	332	22
Burien	32,827	2,374	2,385	1	32	49	106	400	1,243	543	11
Camas	12,906	373	377	0	0	1	6	57	287	22	4
Centralia	15,179	1,224	1,230	2	9	24	55	195	855	84	6
Covington	14,192	586	590	0	8	6	17	76	378	101	4
Des Moines	30,135	1,030	1,035	0	13	29	37	158	511	282	5
Edmonds	40,688	1,160	1,168	0	5	11	14	168	832	130	8
Ellensburg	15,872	1,157	1,174	1	15	4	12	197	888	40	17
Enumclaw	11,446	335	336	0	1	6	17	34	220	57	1
Everett	94,203	6,745	6,771	3	54	185	265	839	3,724	1,675	26
Federal Way	85,729	5,496	5,525	4	34	108	120	677	3,347	1,206	29
Issaquah	11,545	746	750	1	5	6	4	91	567	72	4
Kelso	12,248	1,275	1,283	0	13	16	42	197	914	93	8
Kenmore	19,233	513	523	0	6	3	12	114	324	54	10
Kennewick	56,316	2,851	2,864	2	22	39	115	463	1,962	248	13
Kent	81,883	5,861	5,920	4	19	125	132	910	3,282	1,389	59
Kirkland	46,391	1,614	1,634	2	15	22	25	236	1,102	212	20
Lacey	32,153	1,529	1,535	0	19	26	45	244	1,112	83	6
Lake Forest Park	13,532	234	236	0	1	2	3	42	165	21	2
Lakewood	59,938	4,204	4,232	1	58	134	249	763	2,549	450	28
Longview	35,689	3,157	3,192	1	14	43	127	592	2,084	296	35
Lynnwood	34,851	2,613	2,622	1	14	46	38	191	1,951	372	9
Maple Valley	14,630	422	425	0	5	4	10	112	221	70	3
Marysville	26,066	1,189	1,201	1	9	14	30	160	716	259	12
Mercer Island	22,690	403	408	0	1	2	8	68	296	28	5
Mill Creek	11,867	490	491	0	4	2	7	48	367	62	1
Moses Lake	15,397	1,621	1,627	1	25	19	54	220	1,210	92	6
Mountlake Terrace	20,966	772	783	0	8	7	19	92	530	116	11
Mount Vernon	27,010	2,171	2,187	2	24	14	29	216	1,774	112	16
Mukilteo	18,553	482	490	0	2	6	8	84	302	80	8
Olympia	43,775	2,791	2,795	0	25	50	69	437	2,005	205	4
Pasco	33,017	1,696	1,696	2	16	31	102	262	1,149	134	0
Port Angeles	18,943	801	815	0	4	15	32	133	566	51	14

See footnotes at end of table.

Table 8

Offenses Known to Law Enforcement
by City 10,000 and over in Population, 2002—Continued

City by state	Population	Crime Index	Modified Crime Index[1]	Murder and non-negligent man-slaughter	Forcible rape	Robbery	Aggravated assault	Burglary	Larceny-theft	Motor vehicle theft	Arson[1]
WASHINGTON—Continued											
Puyallup	33,990	2,776	2,791	0	20	27	35	262	2,022	410	15
Redmond	46,599	1,972	1,979	0	17	19	43	192	1,531	170	7
Renton	51,537	4,584	4,606	0	23	99	119	756	2,719	868	22
Richland	39,857	1,363	1,376	2	8	13	39	224	982	95	13
Sammamish	35,115	488	497	0	12	2	16	104	323	31	9
SeaTac	26,252	1,600	1,604	0	16	45	62	280	765	432	4
Seattle	580,089	46,432	46,643	26	152	1,576	2,338	7,290	26,742	8,308	211
Shoreline	54,598	1,918	1,936	1	15	41	65	275	1,259	262	18
Spokane	201,433	15,895	15,957	20	83	379	820	2,660	10,248	1,685	62
Sunnyside	14,317	1,218	1,226	0	2	8	16	207	923	62	8
Tacoma	199,299	20,182	20,297	19	171	715	1,277	3,032	11,728	3,240	115
Tukwila	17,690	2,763	2,773	2	22	64	63	223	1,904	485	10
Tumwater	13,075	587	593	0	27	4	17	99	391	49	6
University Place	30,821	1,204	1,214	1	17	34	47	185	772	148	10
Vancouver[3]	147,819	7,773	7,812	1	100	155	276	1,196	5,189	856	39
Walla Walla	30,567	1,691	1,694	0	36	22	69	271	1,231	62	3
Wenatchee	28,682	2,074	2,084	1	19	26	76	325	1,538	89	10
Yakima	73,977	6,845	6,899	4	59	106	184	1,407	4,415	670	54
WEST VIRGINIA											
Bluefield	11,410	395	401	2	4	12	27	82	246	22	6
Charleston	53,230	4,463	4,517	7	25	162	359	838	2,615	457	54
Clarksburg	16,683	312	317	0	6	5	38	64	181	18	5
Fairmont	19,028	578	582	1	2	20	30	102	379	44	4
Martinsburg	14,918	984	990	0	1	23	53	160	691	56	6
Vienna	10,822	308	309	0	1	1	7	31	256	12	1
Weirton	20,338	359	362	0	2	7	13	75	251	11	3
WISCONSIN											
Appleton	71,100	1,967	1,976	0	18	18	91	245	1,520	75	9
Ashwaubenon	17,889	816	816	0	1	4	2	56	726	27	0
Baraboo	10,865	290	290	0	0	4	7	24	241	14	0
Beaver Dam	15,389	620	623	0	0	5	10	58	536	11	3
Beloit	36,292	2,144	2,157	0	17	52	70	263	1,626	116	13
Brookfield	39,208	1,108	1,108	0	1	11	5	102	958	31	0
Brown Deer	12,346	677	677	0	4	13	2	21	612	25	0
Burlington	10,079	415	418	0	2	0	0	33	371	9	3
Caledonia	23,955	329	330	0	0	4	3	77	220	25	1
Cedarburg	11,066	161	162	0	0	1	0	10	150	0	1
Chippewa Falls	13,112	339	340	0	8	0	5	41	264	21	1
Cudahy	18,695	547	548	0	5	8	7	98	399	30	1
De Pere	20,856	395	395	0	0	0	10	51	327	7	0
Eau Claire	62,596	2,792	2,805	1	14	17	123	475	2,017	145	13
Everest	14,401	396	400	0	1	3	7	63	306	16	4
Fitchburg	20,798	569	569	1	5	8	13	81	418	43	0
Fond du Lac	42,813	1,669	1,671	0	11	13	37	180	1,382	46	2
Fort Atkinson	11,789	442	443	0	0	0	10	40	373	19	1
Fox Valley	16,862	411	411	0	0	0	1	38	359	13	0
Franklin	29,920	555	557	0	6	7	25	98	389	30	2
Germantown	18,524	300	304	0	1	5	1	43	238	12	4
Glendale	13,560	873	873	0	0	29	7	28	756	53	0
Grafton	10,461	237	237	0	0	0	1	17	214	5	0
Grand Chute	18,658	809	812	1	4	5	4	25	745	25	3
Green Bay	103,791	3,762	3,784	1	63	73	252	635	2,468	270	22
Greendale	14,614	440	441	1	0		4	21	386	23	1
Greenfield	35,989	1,259	1,261	0	7	19	4	155	995	79	2
Hartford	11,063	360	360	0	1	2	8	23	310	16	0
Janesville	60,358	3,499	3,514	1	15	52	79	497	2,714	141	15
Kaukauna	13,170	283	283	0	1	0	4	14	249	15	0
Kenosha[3]	91,658	2,785	2,800	1	28	80	98	502	1,899	177	15
La Crosse	52,567	1,798	1,811	0	14	26	74	210	1,400	74	13
Madison	211,061	8,847	8,974	3	90	266	396	1,564	5,898	630	127
Manitowoc	34,545	1,317	1,317	0	3	4	33	207	1,023	47	0

See footnotes at end of table.

Table 8

Offenses Known to Law Enforcement

by City 10,000 and over in Population, 2002—Continued

City by state	Population	Crime Index	Modified Crime Index[1]	Murder and non-negligent man-slaughter	Forcible rape	Robbery	Aggravated assault	Burglary	Larceny-theft	Motor vehicle theft	Arson[1]
WISCONSIN—Continued											
Marinette	11,919	515	516	1	1	4	5	77	410	17	1
Marshfield	19,072	581	583	0	5	2	10	104	448	12	2
Menasha	16,567	460	462	0	3	0	15	53	378	11	2
Menomonee Falls	33,119	545	547	1	2	9	6	69	442	16	2
Menomonie	15,153	583	587	0	6	1	16	85	444	31	4
Mequon	22,138	182	186	0	0	4	19	42	116	1	4
Merrill	10,293	411	411	0	4	0	11	59	320	17	0
Middleton	15,998	554	555	0	1	5	1	63	469	15	1
Milwaukee	605,600	46,315	46,697	111	326	3,197	2,148	6,922	26,424	7,187	382
Monroe	10,999	323	324	0	0	0	4	38	269	12	1
Mount Pleasant	23,476	722	726	0	9	13	12	82	571	35	4
Neenah	24,861	495	501	0	2	0	16	55	405	17	6
New Berlin	38,772	619	628	1	0	2	12	103	478	23	9
Oak Creek	28,867	947	958	0	12	11	10	125	744	45	11
Onalaska	15,054	571	572	0	0	0	22	44	498	7	1
Oshkosh	63,825	2,440	2,445	1	9	18	115	288	1,936	73	5
Pewaukee Township	11,953	129	129	0	0	1	2	11	110	5	0
Platteville	10,134	398	398	0	3	0	9	31	346	9	0
Pleasant Prairie	16,369	424	424	0	5	3	1	30	377	8	0
Plover	10,672	193	194	0	5	1	12	28	139	8	1
Port Washington	10,618	225	225	0	0	0	0	25	196	4	0
Racine	83,038	4,758	4,774	2	26	226	152	967	3,027	358	16
River Falls	12,742	551	554	0	1	0	7	51	475	17	3
Sheboygan	51,526	2,460	2,481	0	36	16	37	281	2,004	86	21
Shorewood	13,961	443	443	0	4	10	1	41	382	5	0
South Milwaukee	21,564	586	589	0	2	11	15	83	447	28	3
Stevens Point	24,905	1,050	1,051	0	7	2	31	120	852	38	1
Stoughton	12,532	305	305	0	0	2	6	78	211	8	0
Sun Prairie	20,664	585	585	0	0	2	14	67	481	21	0
Superior	27,764	1,803	1,820	0	16	15	41	274	1,380	77	17
Town of Menasha	16,087	268	269	0	5	1	1	34	216	11	1
Watertown	21,910	629	647	0	5	4	22	137	438	23	18
Waupun	10,872	262	262	0	0	0	4	30	226	2	0
Wausau	38,982	1,532	1,542	0	23	17	49	253	1,106	84	10
Wauwatosa	47,955	2,386	2,386	0	7	60	20	292	1,861	146	0
West Allis	62,140	2,689	2,725	0	8	66	81	493	1,850	191	36
West Bend	28,559	698	699	0	1	5	8	30	633	21	1
Whitefish Bay	14,368	216	217	0	1	5	2	11	192	5	1
Whitewater	13,631	320	321	0	3	3	8	30	258	18	1
Wisconsin Rapids	18,701	905	910	0	4	1	1	151	724	24	5
WYOMING											
Casper	50,139	2,725	2,747	2	14	16	116	505	1,936	136	22
Cheyenne	53,539	2,476	2,484	2	15	26	65	219	2,061	88	8
Evanston	11,621	593	594	0	4	0	7	40	523	19	1
Gillette	19,842	1,317	1,323	0	4	4	27	112	1,135	35	6
Green River	11,925	393	395	0	0	3	10	47	318	15	2
Laramie	27,475	1,018	1,021	0	5	0	141	125	693	54	3
Rock Springs	18,895	909	911	0	8	4	54	97	698	48	2
Sheridan	15,961	496	497	0	1	3	13	43	422	14	1

[1] The Modified Crime Index is the sum of the seven offenses making up the Crime Index, with the addition of arson. If the FBI does not receive 12 months of arson data from either the agency or the state, no arson or Modified Crime Index will be shown.

[2] The population for the city of Mobile, Alabama, includes 55,864 inhabitants from the jurisdiction of the Mobile County Sheriff's Department.

[3] Due to changes in reporting practices, annexations, and/or incomplete data, figures are not comparable to previous years' data.

[4] Forcible rape figures furnished by the state Uniform Crime Reporting (UCR) Program administered by the Illinois State Police were not in accordance with national UCR guidelines; therefore, the figures were excluded from the forcible rape, Crime Index, and Modified Crime Index categories.

[5] Limited data for 2002 were available for Illinois and Kentucky.

[6] Aggravated assault figures furnished by these agencies were not in accordance with national UCR guidelines; therefore, the figures were excluded from the aggravated assault, Crime Index, and Modified Crime Index categories.

Table 9

Offenses Known to Law Enforcement
by University and College, 2002

University/College by state	Student enrollment[1]	Violent crime[2]	Murder and non-negligent man-slaughter	Forcible rape	Robbery	Aggravated assault	Property crime[1]	Burglary	Larceny-theft	Motor vehicle theft	Arson[1]
ALABAMA											
Alabama State University	4,348	9	0	0	5	4	259	8	249	2	
Auburn University:											
Main Campus	18,326	2	0	1	0	1	292	26	257	9	
Montgomery	4,098	1	0	0	1	0	88	6	82	0	
Troy State University	7,613	1	0	0	0	1	108	12	95	1	1
University of Alabama:											
Huntsville	5,220	0	0	0	0	0	81	4	76	1	
Tuscaloosa	15,318	7	0	1	5	1	344	22	312	10	
University of Montevallo	2,557	0	0	0	0	0	7	1	6	0	
University of North Alabama	4,944	1	0	0	0	1	58	17	41	0	
University of South Alabama	9,232	0	0	0	0	0	133	21	110	2	1
ALASKA											
University of Alaska, Fairbanks	6,359	6	0	2	0	4	140	10	127	3	0
ARIZONA											
Arizona State University:											
Main Campus	33,985	31	0	6	2	23	1,264	153	1,007	104	9
West	3,785	0	0	0	0	0	55	0	54	1	0
Central Arizona College	4,536	2	0	1	0	1	36	8	26	2	0
Northern Arizona University	13,905	22	0	3	4	15	470	69	392	9	11
Pima Community College	28,078	2	0	0	0	2	245	39	199	7	0
University of Arizona	26,404	26	3	6	4	13	1,405	114	1,240	51	7
Yavapai College	7,915	1	0	0	0	1	60	8	50	2	0
ARKANSAS											
Southern Arkansas University	2,781	0	0	0	0	0	43	6	36	1	0
University of Arkansas:											
Fayetteville	12,502	11	0	5	1	5	251	21	225	5	0
Medical Sciences	599	1	0	0	0	1	218	3	211	4	0
University of Central Arkansas	7,471	2	0	0	0	2	164	27	137	0	0
CALIFORNIA											
Allan Hancock College	12,110	0	0	0	0	0	38	8	30	0	3
California State Polytechnic University:											
Pomona	16,436	7	0	0	5	2	313	41	226	46	0
San Luis Obispo	15,867	4	0	1	0	3	253	24	224	5	1
California State University:											
Bakersfield	4,809	1	0	0	1	0	67	13	51	3	0
Channel Islands[4]		0	0	0	0	0	15	3	12	0	0
Chico	13,907	3	0	2	0	1	243	33	203	7	0
Dominguez Hills	7,733	1	0	0	1	0	96	27	59	10	0
Fresno	15,413	6	0	2	0	4	517	95	386	36	2
Fullerton	23,385	1	0	0	1	0	214	24	164	26	0
Hayward	9,337	3	0	0	2	1	117	35	69	13	0
Long Beach	25,153	3	0	0	0	3	289	45	197	47	0
Los Angeles	13,476	9	0	1	4	4	460	21	370	69	0
Monterey Bay	2,367	9	0	4	0	5	118	27	84	7	1
Northridge	22,553	8	0	1	1	6	271	20	214	37	1
Sacramento	20,342	8	0	3	1	4	306	15	258	33	0
San Bernardino	10,273	3	0	1	0	2	134	26	100	8	0
San Jose[4]		12	0	6	3	3	364	25	332	7	5
San Marcos	5,005	0	0	0	0	0	31	4	25	2	0
Stanislaus	5,353	1	0	0	0	1	76	1	66	9	0
College of the Sequoias	10,251	5	0	1	1	3	113	38	61	14	0
Contra Costa Community College	7,133	17	0	0	7	10	270	21	214	35	0
Cuesta College	9,496	0	0	0	0	0	53	11	40	2	0
El Camino College	24,067	3	0	0	1	2	231	6	206	19	3
Foothill-De Anza College	36,963	0	0	0	0	0	229	0	223	6	0
Humboldt State University	6,469	6	0	2	0	4	173	19	151	3	7

See footnotes at end of table.

Table 9

Offenses Known to Law Enforcement
by University and College, 2002—Continued

University/College by state	Student enrollment[1]	Violent crime[2]	Murder and non-negligent man-slaughter	Forcible rape	Robbery	Aggravated assault	Property crime[1]	Burglary	Larceny-theft	Motor vehicle theft	Arson[1]
CALIFORNIA—Continued											
Long Beach City College	20,926	1	0	0	1	0	159	49	87	23	1
Marin Community College	8,317	1	0	0	0	1	53	0	51	2	2
Pasadena Community College	22,948	2	0	0	1	1	187	12	157	18	10
Reedley College	9,081	1	0	0	0	1	35	1	30	4	0
Riverside Community College	22,107	3	0	0	1	2	148	16	117	15	0
San Bernardino Community College	12,025	3	0	0	2	1	92	6	71	15	0
San Diego State University	25,658	12	0	2	2	8	717	35	603	79	2
San Francisco State University	20,365	14	0	0	11	3	279	42	207	30	0
San Jose/Evergreen Community College	23,699	3	0	0	0	3	127	15	109	3	3
Santa Rosa Junior College	27,020	1	0	0	1	0	85	16	67	2	0
Sonoma State University	6,211	2	0	0	0	2	146	25	112	9	0
State Center Community College[4]		3	0	0	0	3	342	6	300	36	2
University of California:											
Berkeley	22,678	22	0	4	13	5	977	93	853	31	1
Davis	20,388	5	0	2	0	3	765	82	660	23	4
Hastings College of Law[4]		1	0	1	0	0	16	2	14	0	0
Irvine	16,223	8	0	1	2	5	604	57	518	29	1
Lawrence-Livermore Laboratory[4]		0	0	0	0	0	11	0	11	0	0
Los Angeles	25,011	50	0	4	18	28	1,433	262	1,092	79	0
Riverside	11,436	2	0	2	0	0	350	52	270	28	1
Sacramento[4]		1	0	0	0	1	226	13	181	32	0
San Diego	16,496	4	0	1	1	2	489	49	388	52	2
San Francisco	93	8	0	0	6	2	416	30	380	6	0
Santa Barbara	17,538	2	0	1	0	1	358	29	324	5	0
Santa Cruz	11,075	4	0	2	0	2	232	66	166	0	3
West Valley-Mission College	20,540	2	0	0	0	2	128	9	116	3	2
COLORADO											
Arapahoe Community College	7,436	1	0	0	1	0	32	0	32	0	0
Auraria Higher Education Center[4]		4	0	0	1	3	232	3	214	15	0
Colorado School of Mines	2,559	2	0	1	0	1	42	9	28	5	0
Colorado State University	20,728	30	0	16	1	13	535	25	505	5	5
Fort Lewis College	4,285	2	0	1	1	0	102	21	81	0	1
Pikes Peak Community College	9,997	1	0	0	1	0	42	6	36	0	0
University of Colorado:											
Boulder	23,612	17	0	3	3	11	631	130	479	22	14
Colorado Springs	4,967	3	0	1	1	1	84	15	67	2	0
Health Sciences Center	411	10	0	0	1	9	216	9	204	3	0
Health Sciences Center, Fitzsimons Campus[4]		0	0	0	0	0	50	2	45	3	0
University of Northern Colorado	10,213	4	0	3	0	1	231	12	216	3	0
CONNECTICUT											
Central Connecticut State University	9,443	5	0	3	0	2	119	19	72	28	0
Eastern Connecticut State University	4,821	2	0	2	0	0	89	9	79	1	0
Southern Connecticut State University	8,080	2	0	1	1	0	120	14	103	3	1
University of Connecticut:											
Health Center[4]		0	0	0	0	0	49	2	44	3	0
Storrs, Avery Point, and Hartford[4]		7	0	3	2	2	320	102	209	9	3
Western Connecticut State University	4,881	5	0	1	0	4	43	7	34	2	0
Yale University	5,351	6	0	1	4	1	360	58	296	6	0
DELAWARE											
University of Delaware	16,110	15	0	0	10	5	458	61	386	11	12
FLORIDA											
Florida A&M University	10,707	23	0	3	11	9	540	184	343	13	6
Florida Atlantic University	17,496	7	0	2	2	3	443	111	296	36	4
Florida Gulf Coast University	2,977	3	0	1	0	2	31	2	28	1	0
Florida International University	26,222	6	0	0	1	5	521	57	407	57	0

See footnotes at end of table.

Table 9

Offenses Known to Law Enforcement
by University and College, 2002—Continued

University/College by state	Student enrollment[1]	Violent crime[2]	Violent crime				Property crime[3]	Property crime			
			Murder and non-negligent man-slaughter	Forcible rape	Robbery	Aggravated assault		Burglary	Larceny-theft	Motor vehicle theft	Arson[3]
FLORIDA—Continued											
Florida State University:											
Panama City[4]		0	0	0	0	0	1	0	1	0	0
Tallahassee[4]		16	0	8	1	7	745	73	651	21	5
New College of Florida[4]		0	0	0	0	0	35	6	26	3	1
Pensacola Junior College	9,985	1	0	0	0	1	79	4	74	1	0
Santa Fe Community College	12,464	0	0	0	0	0	59	4	55	0	0
Tallahassee Community College	10,816	2	0	0	0	2	74	3	67	4	0
University of Central Florida	28,252	13	0	1	3	9	297	39	247	11	2
University of Florida	32,680	12	0	2	1	9	825	28	758	39	2
University of North Florida	10,663	3	0	2	0	1	153	17	131	5	2
University of South Florida:											
St. Petersburg[4]		0	0	0	0	0	30	1	25	4	0
Tampa[4]		6	0	1	0	5	507	124	329	54	0
University of West Florida	6,753	1	0	0	0	1	95	1	90	4	0
GEORGIA											
Abraham Baldwin Agricultural College	2,630	0	0	0	0	0	41	6	35	0	0
Agnes Scott College	892	0	0	0	0	0	41	5	34	2	0
Armstrong Atlantic State University	4,988	1	0	0	1	0	59	9	49	1	0
Augusta State University	4,440	0	0	0	0	0	32	0	31	1	0
Berry College	1,822	0	0	0	0	0	32	3	29	0	0
Clayton College and State University	4,455	0	0	0	0	0	67	16	49	2	0
Coastal Georgia Community College	1,912	1	0	0	0	1	20	8	12	0	0
Columbus State University	4,450	1	0	0	1	0	90	10	77	3	
Dalton State College	3,137	1	0	0	0	1	6	1	5	0	0
Emory University	6,316	8	0	0	3	5	447	19	420	8	
Fort Valley State University	2,212	2	0	0	2	0	97	7	87	3	0
Georgia College and State University	3,976	0	0	0	0	0	50	3	45	2	0
Georgia Institute of Technology	10,745	11	0	0	11	0	1,149	170	896	83	0
Georgia Perimeter College	13,708	2	0	0	1	1	134	2	129	3	0
Georgia Southern University	12,648	3	0	0	1	2	206	2	201	3	0
Georgia Southwestern State University	1,981	1	0	0	0	1	43	6	37	0	0
Georgia State University	16,444	16	0	2	11	3	542	27	504	11	1
Gordon College	2,890	0	0	0	0	0	15	10	5	0	0
Kennesaw State University	11,977	1	0	0	0	1	74	9	62	3	1
Medical College of Georgia	615	3	0	0	2	1	139	0	129	10	0
Mercer University	4,305	1	0	0	0	1	83	4	77	2	0
Middle Georgia College	1,938	1	0	1	0	0	32	23	9	0	
Morehouse College	2,970	4	0	0	4	0	130	0	123	7	0
Morris-Brown College	2,785	13	0	1	7	5	180	44	129	7	
North Georgia College	3,240	2	0	0	0	2	26	4	22	0	0
Piedmont College	1,026	0	0	0	0	0	0	0	0	0	0
Savannah State University	2,070	15	0	0	2	13	99	4	88	7	0
Southern Polytechnic State University	2,943	0	0	0	0	0	66	7	59	0	1
South Georgia College	1,267	0	0	0	0	0	21	3	17	1	0
University of Georgia	24,213	6	0	2	3	1	560	18	527	15	0
Valdosta State University	7,482	5	0	1	0	4	148	8	140	0	6
Wesleyan College	560	0	0	0	0	0	5	1	4	0	0
Young Harris College	620	0	0	0	0	0	0	0	0	0	0
ILLINOIS[5]											
INDIANA											
Ball State University	16,350	15	0	5	4	6	442	63	373	6	2
Indiana State University	9,537	2	0	1	0	1	275	47	221	7	1
Indiana University:											
Bloomington	29,383	18	0	4	5	9	606	51	552	3	0
Gary[4]		0	0	0	0	0	33	0	28	5	0
Indianapolis[4]		5	0	1	4	0	474	10	456	8	0
New Albany[4]		0	0	0	0	0	25	0	25	0	0
Marian College	1,271	0	0	0	0	0	11	2	8	1	0
Purdue University	32,669	7	0	5	1	1	562	29	526	7	1

See footnotes at end of table.

Table 9

Offenses Known to Law Enforcement

by University and College, 2002—Continued

University/College by state	Student enrollment[1]	Violent crime[2]	Murder and non-negligent man-slaughter	Forcible rape	Robbery	Aggravated assault	Property crime[3]	Burglary	Larceny-theft	Motor vehicle theft	Arson[1]
IOWA											
Iowa State University	22,087	8	0	4	0	4	342	26	308	8	11
University of Iowa	19,284	9	0	2	0	7	357	31	317	9	0
University of Northern Iowa	12,413	4	0	1	0	3	167	14	152	1	3
KANSAS											
Emporia State University	4,198	0	0	0	0	0	61	20	38	3	2
Fort Hays State University	4,418	1	0	1	0	0	62	29	33	0	0
Pittsburg State University	5,222	3	0	0	0	3	71	4	66	1	2
University of Kansas:											
Main Campus	19,698	4	0	1	0	3	301	80	218	3	0
Medical Center	452	2	0	0	1	1	203	1	197	5	1
KENTUCKY[5]											
University of Kentucky	16,897	15	1	0	5	9	770	72	684	14	5
LOUISIANA											
Delgado Community College	12,784	2	0	0	0	2	67	1	63	3	0
Grambling State University	4,289	9	0	0	3	6	239	100	136	3	0
Louisiana State University:											
Baton Rouge[4]		20	0	1	11	8	765	96	650	19	0
Eunice	2,704	0	0	0	0	0	0	0	0	0	0
Health Sciences Center, New Orleans[4]		0	0	0	0	0	64	0	64	0	0
Health Sciences Center, Shreveport[4]		0	0	0	0	0	122	0	111	11	0
Shreveport	3,422	2	0	0	1	1	15	2	13	0	0
Louisiana Tech University	8,921	3	0	0	3	0	119	39	73	7	2
McNeese State University	6,703	10	0	0	1	9	141	32	109	0	1
Nicholls State University	6,556	4	0	0	0	4	35	10	25	0	0
Northwestern State University	8,270	5	0	2	1	2	111	33	76	2	0
Southeastern Louisiana University	12,916	5	0	3	2	0	174	16	149	9	0
Southern University and A&M College:											
Baton Rouge	7,769	10	1	1	3	5	237	25	205	7	0
New Orleans	3,573	2	0	0	1	1	42	3	33	6	0
Shreveport	1,176	0	0	0	0	0	17	3	14	0	0
Tulane University	7,353	12	0	2	2	8	293	85	204	4	2
University of Louisiana:											
Lafayette	14,091	10	0	0	0	10	248	70	169	9	3
Monroe	8,033	4	0	0	1	3	163	37	126	0	0
University of New Orleans	12,260	5	0	2	1	2	229	5	209	15	0
MAINE											
University of Maine:											
Farmington	2,413	1	0	0	0	1	20	2	18	0	0
Orono	8,220	0	0	0	0	0	219	42	176	1	14
University of Southern Maine	8,726	6	0	4	0	2	103	11	92	0	0
MARYLAND											
Bowie State University	3,109	1	0	0	0	1	70	7	60	3	0
Coppin State College	3,092	19	0	0	10	9	72	14	53	5	1
Frostburg State University	4,430	5	0	0	0	5	117	37	80	0	0
Morgan State University	5,685	37	0	1	31	5	113	29	84	0	1
Salisbury University	5,883	4	0	2	2	0	175	6	163	6	0
St. Mary's College	1,547	2	0	0	0	2	55	5	50	0	0
Towson University	13,905	11	0	1	3	7	297	64	230	3	1
University of Baltimore	2,016	1	0	0	1	0	61	6	53	2	0
University of Maryland:											
Baltimore City	750	12	0	0	8	4	323	5	313	5	1
Baltimore County	9,101	1	0	0	1	0	185	21	158	6	0
College Park	24,638	24	0	4	9	11	1,015	141	787	87	4
Eastern Shore	2,969	5	0	1	1	3	136	38	97	1	2

See footnotes at end of table.

Table 9

Offenses Known to Law Enforcement
by University and College, 2002—Continued

University/College by state	Student enrollment[1]	Violent crime[2]	Violent crime				Property crime[3]	Property crime			
			Murder and non-negligent man-slaughter	Forcible rape	Robbery	Aggravated assault		Burglary	Larceny-theft	Motor vehicle theft	Arson[3]
MASSACHUSETTS											
Boston University	17,819	16	0	1	8	7	671	77	587	7	
Brandeis University	3,282	2	0	0	0	2	118	29	89	0	
Bristol Community College	6,054	0	0	0	0	0	31	0	29	2	
Emerson College	3,168	16	0	0	2	14	52	15	37	0	0
Fitchburg State College	3,238	3	0	1	0	2	93	1	91	1	0
Holyoke Community College	5,754	3	0	0	0	3	54	0	47	7	0
Massachusetts College of Art	2,221	0	0	0	0	0	35	0	35	0	0
Massachusetts College of Liberal Arts	1,387	1	0	0	0	1	21	4	17	0	0
Massachusetts Institute of Technology	4,258	9	0	1	2	6	640	34	600	6	
Northeastern University	19,588	23	0	0	7	16	379	26	347	6	
North Shore Community College	6,285	0	0	0	0	0	3	0	3	0	0
Quinsigamond Community College	5,617	1	0	0	0	1	22	0	18	4	
Springfield College	3,371	10	0	0	3	7	91	21	66	4	
Tufts University:											
Medford	4,886	7	0	2	0	5	186	18	167	1	
Suffolk[4]		0	0	0	0	0	75	3	72	0	
Worcester[4]		0	0	0	0	0	9	0	9	0	
University of Massachusetts:											
Amherst	19,061	27	1	12	7	7	390	149	223	18	4
Dartmouth	6,423	13	0	1	0	12	110	1	105	4	
Harbor Campus, Boston	10,442	1	0	0	0	1	123	7	116	0	1
Medical Center, Worcester[4]		12	0	0	0	12	98	1	96	1	0
Wellesley College	2,287	2	0	1	0	1	95	41	54	0	0
MICHIGAN											
Central Michigan University	18,620	7	0	6	0	1	299	9	288	2	2
Delta College	9,358	0	0	0	0	0	25	0	25	0	0
Eastern Michigan University	18,189	12	0	2	1	9	529	21	492	16	5
Ferris State University	9,235	8	0	1	0	7	248	12	234	2	0
Grand Rapids Community College	13,400	1	0	0	1	0	111	1	110	0	0
Grand Valley State University	15,211	1	0	1	0	0	155	4	151	0	0
Hope College	3,015	0	0	0	0	0	60	0	60	0	0
Lansing Community College	16,011	2	0	0	0	2	141	1	140	0	0
Macomb Community College	22,001	0	0	0	0	0	86	0	84	2	0
Michigan State University	34,342	21	0	5	6	10	969	135	817	17	3
Michigan Technological University	5,666	3	0	3	0	0	134	0	134	0	0
Northern Michigan University	7,575	2	0	0	0	2	176	0	176	0	1
Oakland Community College	23,188	2	0	0	0	2	56	1	52	3	0
Oakland University	12,002	0	0	0	0	0	101	9	91	1	1
Saginaw Valley State University	7,059	0	0	0	0	0	94	6	88	0	0
University of Michigan:											
Ann Arbor	24,412	27	0	4	8	15	1,454	134	1,304	16	13
Dearborn	6,615	0	0	0	0	0	69	1	65	3	0
Flint	5,786	0	0	0	0	0	81	1	80	0	0
Western Michigan University	22,756	13	0	5	3	5	320	11	298	11	2
MINNESOTA											
University of Minnesota:											
Duluth	8,400	0	0	0	0	0	97	3	94	0	0
Twin Cities	31,824	9	0	2	4	3	926	71	841	14	6
MISSISSIPPI											
Coahoma Community College	277	0	0	0	0	0	12	5	6	1	0
Hinds Community College	16,032	1	0	0	1	0	95	14	77	4	2
Jackson State University	5,471	1	0	0	0	1	244	56	180	8	0
Mississippi State University	13,307	2	0	0	0	2	228	14	211	3	0
University of Mississippi:											
Medical Center	603	4	0	0	2	2	191	7	179	5	0
Oxford	9,608	4	0	3	1	0	173	20	146	7	0
MISSOURI											
Central Missouri State University	9,150	2	0	1	0	1	132	43	89	0	2
Lincoln University	3,128	3	0	0	1	2	85	27	57	1	0

See footnotes at end of table.

Table 9

Offenses Known to Law Enforcement
by University and College, 2002—Continued

University/College by state	Student enrollment[1]	Violent crime[2]	Murder and non-negligent manslaughter	Forcible rape	Robbery	Aggravated assault	Property crime[3]	Burglary	Larceny-theft	Motor vehicle theft	Arson[1]
MISSOURI—Continued											
Northwest Missouri State University	5,568	0	0	0	0	0	46	13	33	0	0
Southeast Missouri State University	7,758	1	0	0	0	1	67	2	65	0	1
St. Louis Community College,											
Meramec	12,518	1	0	0	1	0	21	1	20	0	0
Truman State University	5,812	0	0	0	0	0	95	6	89	0	2
University of Missouri:											
Columbia	18,058	8	0	0	2	6	361	32	326	3	6
Kansas City	8,091	3	0	1	0	2	255	94	144	17	1
Rolla	3,698	1	0	0	0	1	75	11	64	0	1
St. Louis	12,737	4	0	1	3	0	171	29	133	9	0
Washington University	6,695	3	0	0	3	0	286	15	265	6	0
NEBRASKA											
University of Nebraska:											
Kearney	5,502	0	0	0	0	0	94	38	53	3	0
Lincoln	17,968	4	0	1	2	1	434	70	359	5	2
NEVADA											
Truckee Meadows Community College	9,930	0	0	0	0	0	22	7	14	1	0
University of Nevada:											
Las Vegas	17,327	12	0	2	4	6	474	84	319	71	5
Reno	10,134	5	0	3	0	2	194	39	149	6	1
NEW JERSEY											
Brookdale Community College	11,552	0	0	0	0	0	54	1	49	4	0
Essex County College	8,868	2	0	0	1	1	102	9	87	6	0
Kean University of New Jersey	9,300	5	0	1	1	3	172	10	148	14	0
Middlesex County College	10,398	0	0	0	0	0	67	2	61	4	0
Monmouth University	4,194	3	0	0	1	2	81	11	70	0	0
Montclair State University	10,188	4	0	0	1	3	179	26	128	25	0
New Jersey Institute of Technology	5,637	5	0	0	1	4	189	2	144	43	0
Richard Stockton College	5,976	3	0	0	0	3	78	9	66	3	1
Rowan University	8,051	3	0	2	1	0	122	9	112	1	1
Rutgers University:											
Camden	3,717	3	0	0	3	0	132	41	83	8	0
Newark	5,873	8	0	0	5	3	279	20	222	37	0
New Brunswick	27,938	13	0	1	2	10	637	71	530	36	1
The College of New Jersey	6,010	?	0	0	0	2	181	21	159	1	1
University of Medicine and Dentistry:											
Camden[4]		0	0	0	0	0	7	0	7	0	0
Newark	829	39	0	0	10	29	422	4	341	77	0
Piscataway[4]		0	0	0	0	0	53	0	51	2	0
William Paterson University	8,454	1	0	0	0	1	118	22	78	18	0
NEW MEXICO											
Eastern New Mexico University	2,942	2	0	1	0	1	60	28	30	2	0
New Mexico State University	12,453	12	0	1	1	10	330	41	276	13	0
University of New Mexico	16,414	30	0	2	2	26	781	100	644	37	2
NEW YORK											
Cornell University[4]		4	0	0	2	2	538	86	447	5	
Ithaca College	5,906	1	0	0	1	0	110	0	110	0	
State University of New York:											
Downstate Medical Center[4]		3	0	0	3	· 0	103	5	97	1	
Stony Brook	13,257	6	0	1	1	4	594	19	566	9	
State University of New York											
Agricultural and Technical College:											
Farmingdale	5,045	2	0	0	0	2	73	6	67	0	
Morrisville	3,033	5	0	0	2	3	136	36	100	0	

See footnotes at end of table.

Table 9

Offenses Known to Law Enforcement
by University and College, 2002—Continued

University/College by state	Student enrollment[1]	Violent crime[2]	Violent crime — Murder and non-negligent manslaughter	Violent crime — Forcible rape	Violent crime — Robbery	Violent crime — Aggravated assault	Property crime[3]	Property crime — Burglary	Property crime — Larceny-theft	Property crime — Motor vehicle theft	Arson[1]
NEW YORK—Continued											
State University of New York College:											
Buffalo	9,386	11	0	1	0	10	233	46	178	9	
Cortland	5,648	3	0	2	0	1	89	16	73	0	
Environmental Science and Forestry	1,166	0	0	0	0	0	19	3	16	0	
Geneseo	5,197	1	0	0	0	1	100	7	89	4	
New Paltz	6,028	2	0	0	1	1	118	2	115	1	
Oswego	6,989	3	0	2	1	0	163	21	141	1	
Plattsburgh	5,377	2	0	1	0	1	114	10	104	0	
Potsdam	3,580	1	0	1	0	0	93	14	79	0	
NORTH CAROLINA											
Appalachian State University	12,112	6	0	1	1	4	159	7	151	1	4
Duke University	6,325	22	0	5	4	13	1,048	58	982	8	0
East Carolina University	15,018	8	0	2	3	3	324	14	300	10	2
Elon University	3,900	2	0	0	0	2	91	18	71	2	0
Methodist College	2,134	0	0	0	0	0	45	17	27	1	0
North Carolina Agricultural and Technical State University	6,850	26	0	2	14	10	405	43	350	12	4
North Carolina Central University	4,057	8	0	2	4	2	126	26	98	2	0
North Carolina School of the Arts	692	0	0	0	0	0	27	1	26	0	1
North Carolina State University, Raleigh	21,990	13	1	1	2	9	649	67	573	9	1
Pfeiffer University	985	0	0	0	0	0	18	6	8	4	0
University of North Carolina:											
Asheville	3,245	1	0	0	0	1	59	11	44	4	0
Chapel Hill	15,608	5	0	2	2	1	498	19	464	15	0
Greensboro	10,109	14	0	0	2	12	273	38	231	4	0
Pembroke	3,076	2	0	0	2	0	72	13	58	1	0
Wilmington	9,343	1	0	1	0	0	260	25	231	4	1
Wake Forest University	4,086	3	0	1	2	0	114	28	86	0	0
NORTH DAKOTA											
North Dakota State University	8,973	0	0	0	0	0	133	31	102	0	2
University of North Dakota	9,122	7	0	3	1	3	256	17	233	6	2
OHIO											
Bowling Green State University	15,494	6	0	6	0	0	287	14	269	4	2
Cleveland State University	10,133	9	0	2	7	0	254	1	240	13	0
Columbus State Community College	18,094	0	0	0	0	0	233	5	219	9	0
Cuyahoga Community College	19,518	2	0	1	1	0	91	3	87	1	0
Kent State University	17,580	1	0	1	0	0	289	4	282	3	1
Lakeland Community College	7,722	3	0	0	0	3	19	0	19	0	0
Marietta College	1,187	1	0	1	0	0	39	9	29	1	1
Miami University	14,957	5	0	3	1	1	324	52	271	1	1
Ohio State University	35,749	25	0	5	15	5	1,264	307	941	16	8
Ohio University	16,712	6	0	4	1	1	204	25	176	3	3
University of Cincinnati	20,039	6	0	2	3	1	580	92	482	6	4
University of Toledo	15,950	12	0	2	4	6	459	52	389	18	1
Wright State University	10,618	7	0	2	3	2	272	19	233	20	1
Youngstown State University	10,619	1	0	0	1	0	136	0	130	6	0
OKLAHOMA											
Cameron University	4,543	0	0	0	0	0	6	0	5	1	0
East Central University	3,260	0	0	0	0	0	33	11	22	0	0
Murray State College	1,768	1	0	0	0	1	15	5	9	1	0
Northeastern Oklahoma A&M College	1,947	2	0	1	0	1	35	15	20	0	1
Northeastern State College	7,186	3	0	0	1	2	63	13	49	1	1
Oklahoma State University:											
Main Campus	16,574	6	0	3	1	2	261	42	213	6	1
Okmulgee	2,419	1	0	1	0	0	41	12	28	1	0
Tulsa[4]		0	0	0	0	0	25	1	22	2	0

See footnotes at end of table.

Table 9

Offenses Known to Law Enforcement
by University and College, 2002—Continued

University/College by state	Student enrollment[1]	Violent crime[2]	Violent crime Murder and non-negligent man-slaughter	Forcible rape	Robbery	Aggravated assault	Property crime[1]	Property crime Burglary	Larceny-theft	Motor vehicle theft	Arson[3]
OKLAHOMA—Continued											
Rogers State University	2,640	0	0	0	0	0	14	4	10	0	0
Seminole State College	2,033	0	0	0	0	0	26	3	23	0	0
Southeastern Oklahoma State University	3,393	7	0	2	0	5	32	3	29	0	0
Southwestern Oklahoma State University	4,231	0	0	0	0	0	49	27	22	0	0
Tulsa Community College	16,270	1	0	0	0	1	55	0	52	3	0
University of Central Oklahoma	11,790	1	0	0	1	0	88	9	77	2	1
University of Oklahoma:											
Health Sciences Center	601	23	0	0	2	21	262	64	195	3	0
Norman	17,771	6	0	2	3	1	325	39	275	11	4
PENNSYLVANIA											
Bloomsburg University	6,843	1	0	1	0	0	73	2	70	1	0
California University	5,003	1	0	0	0	1	59	1	58	0	0
Clarion University	5,687	1	0	0	0	1	60	14	46	0	3
Community College of Beaver County	2,188	0	0	0	0	0	5	5	0	0	0
East Stroudsburg University	4,732	0	0	0	0	0	88	0	88	0	0
Edinboro University	6,552	3	0	0	0	3	74	0	72	2	1
Elizabethtown College	1,825	0	0	0	0	0	26	9	17	0	0
Indiana University	11,735	9	0	3	5	1	121	15	106	0	0
Kutztown University	7,033	3	0	0	1	2	115	4	111	0	0
Lehigh University	4,685	5	0	3	0	2	99	0	97	2	1
Lock Haven University	3,839	0	0	0	0	0	46	0	46	0	0
Mansfield University	2,891	0	0	0	0	0	23	4	19	0	0
Millersville University	6,497	5	0	0	2	3	84	10	74	0	0
Moravian College	1,723	3	0	3	0	0	41	3	38	0	0
Pennsylvania State University:											
Altoona	3,749	2	0	0	0	2	37	10	27	0	0
Beaver	759	0	0	0	0	0	11	1	10	0	0
Behrend	3,606	0	0	0	0	0	39	5	34	0	0
Berks	2,186	0	0	0	0	0	43	4	37	2	0
Harrisburg	1,865	1	0	0	1	0	23	0	23	0	0
McKeesport	901	0	0	0	0	0	0	0	0	0	0
Mont Alto	1,176	0	0	0	0	0	21	1	20	0	0
University Park	34,406	3	0	0	1	2	584	24	553	7	1
Shippensburg University	5,990	0	0	0	0	0	55	1	54	0	0
Slippery Rock University	6,294	5	0	0	0	5	75	1	74	0	0
University of Pittsburgh:											
Bradford	1,204	0	0	0	0	0	11	1	10	0	0
Pittsburgh	17,424	8	0	0	5	3	480	59	410	11	0
West Chester University	10,324	11	0	0	0	11	82	0	79	3	0
RHODE ISLAND											
Brown University	6,029	8	0	2	2	4	298	82	216	0	0
University of Rhode Island	10,647	5	0	2	1	2	246	45	195	6	1
SOUTH CAROLINA											
Aiken Technical College	2,268	1	0	0	1	0	40	1	39	0	0
Benedict College	2,966	16	0	1	7	8	344	82	258	4	0
Bob Jones University[4]		0	0	0	0	0	2	1	1	0	0
Clemson University	14,066	3	0	1	1	1	120	21	91	8	0
Coastal Carolina University	4,405	0	0	0	0	0	65	8	56	1	1
College of Charleston	9,750	6	0	0	0	6	200	39	159	2	0
Columbia College	1,206	0	0	0	0	0	92	12	77	3	0
Denmark Technical College	1,240	0	0	0	0	0	1	0	1	0	0
Erskine College	502	1	0	1	0	0	6	3	3	0	0
Francis Marion University	2,793	1	0	0	0	1	63	3	60	0	0
Lander University	2,436	3	0	1	1	1	31	4	27	0	0
Medical University of South Carolina	406	2	0	0	1	1	213	2	210	1	0
Presbyterian College	1,148	2	0	1	0	1	6	0	6	0	0
South Carolina State University	3,639	18	0	0	6	12	195	39	152	4	0
The Citadel	1,995	0	0	0	0	0	18	0	18	0	0

See footnotes at end of table.

Table 9

Offenses Known to Law Enforcement
by University and College, 2002—Continued

University/College by state	Student enrollment[1]	Violent crime[2]	Violent crime				Property crime[3]	Property crime			
			Murder and non-negligent man-slaughter	Forcible rape	Robbery	Aggravated assault		Burglary	Larceny-theft	Motor vehicle theft	Arson[3]
SOUTH CAROLINA—Continued											
Trident Technical College	10,246	1	0	0	0	1	26	0	26	0	0
University of South Carolina:											
Aiken	3,148	0	0	0	0	0	10	2	7	1	0
Columbia	15,266	15	0	3	4	8	554	13	522	19	1
Spartanburg	3,585	0	0	0	0	0	24	0	24	0	0
Winthrop University	4,649	6	0	2	1	3	145	21	112	12	0
SOUTH DAKOTA											
South Dakota State University	7,448	0	0	0	0	0	2	2	0	0	0
TENNESSEE											
Austin Peay State University	6,658	3	0	0	0	3	68	4	63	1	0
Chattanooga State Technical Community College	7,873	0	0	0	0	0	32	0	32	0	0
Cleveland State Community College	3,056	0	0	0	0	0	0	0	0	0	0
Dyersburg State Community College	2,278	0	0	0	0	0	5	0	5	0	0
East Tennessee State University	9,125	5	0	0	4	1	168	38	129	1	0
Jackson State Community College	3,726	0	0	0	0	0	14	0	14	0	0
Middle Tennessee State University	17,247	7	0	0	2	5	199	39	156	4	3
Tennessee State University	7,142	14	0	0	8	6	230	9	198	23	0
Tennessee Technological University	6,876	4	0	1	0	3	174	21	153	0	0
University of Memphis	15,296	9	0	1	5	3	274	59	200	15	1
University of Tennessee:											
Chattanooga	6,993	4	0	2	2	0	219	91	127	1	1
Knoxville	20,009	13	1	1	4	7	502	30	458	14	4
Martin	5,472	4	0	0	0	4	64	5	59	0	0
Memphis[4]		0	0	0	0	0	136	7	116	13	0
Vanderbilt University	5,935	21	0	3	11	7	690	62	612	16	4
Volunteer State Community College	6,567	0	0	0	0	0	23	1	22	0	0
Walters State Community College	6,163	0	0	0	0	0	3	0	3	0	0
TEXAS											
Alamo Community College District[4]		5	0	1	2	2	259	48	201	10	0
Alvin Community College	3,665	1	0	0	0	1	13	1	11	1	0
Amarillo College	8,422	0	0	0	0	0	62	12	47	3	0
Angelo State University	5,773	2	0	1	0	1	92	17	72	3	0
Austin College	1,196	1	0	0	0	1	40	0	40	0	0
Baylor Health Care System[4]		1	0	0	0	1	385	20	351	14	0
Baylor University, Waco	11,806	2	0	0	0	2	282	31	249	2	1
Central Texas College	14,636	3	0	1	0	2	25	2	23	0	0
College of the Mainland	3,358	0	0	0	0	0	34	4	27	3	0
Eastfield College	7,873	1	0	0	0	1	47	0	44	3	0
El Paso Community College	18,001	1	0	0	1	0	89	2	85	2	1
Grayson County College	3,318	0	0	0	0	0	30	8	22	0	2
Hardin-Simmons University	1,910	0	0	0	0	0	26	14	12	0	0
Houston Baptist University	1,967	1	0	0	1	0	8	1	7	0	0
Lamar University, Beaumont	10,713	5	0	1	4	0	151	19	127	5	0
Laredo Community College	7,322	0	0	0	0	0	16	0	14	2	0
McLennan Community College	5,731	0	0	0	0	0	64	2	62	0	0
Midwestern State University	5,151	1	0	1	0	0	46	5	41	0	0
Mountain View College	5,491	0	0	0	0	0	80	4	67	9	0
North Lake College	8,615	0	0	0	0	0	58	4	50	4	0
Paris Junior College	2,942	0	0	0	0	0	27	9	18	0	1
Prairie View A&M University	5,285	15	0	4	1	10	279	77	189	13	4
Rice University	2,692	4	0	1	0	3	142	6	129	7	0
Richland College	12,537	0	0	0	0	0	98	10	79	9	0
Southern Methodist University	5,662	4	0	1	0	3	206	14	182	10	1
South Plains College	6,731	2	0	0	0	2	12	0	12	0	0
Southwestern University	1,309	0	0	0	0	0	24	5	19	0	1
Southwest Texas State University	19,412	5	0	3	0	2	252	37	211	4	0
Stephen F. Austin State University	10,246	4	0	1	0	3	191	31	158	2	1
St. Mary's University	2,618	2	0	1	0	1	118	24	88	6	0
Sul Ross State University	1,990	3	0	1	0	2	67	29	38	0	3

See footnotes at end of table.

Table 9

Offenses Known to Law Enforcement

by University and College, 2002—Continued

University/College by state	Student enrollment[1]	Violent crime[2]	Violent crime - Murder and non-negligent man-slaughter	Violent crime - Forcible rape	Violent crime - Robbery	Violent crime - Aggravated assault	Property crime[1]	Property crime - Burglary	Property crime - Larceny-theft	Property crime - Motor vehicle theft	Arson[3]
TEXAS—Continued											
Tarleton State University	6,222	1	0	1	0	0	64	17	46	1	0
Texas A&M International University	2,263	0	0	0	0	0	26	2	24	0	0
Texas A&M University:											
College Station	36,229	5	0	3	0	2	691	53	636	2	0
Commerce	4,362	4	0	1	0	3	172	55	114	3	1
Corpus Christi	5,329	7	0	1	0	6	116	8	107	1	3
Galveston	1,363	1	0	1	0	0	22	5	14	3	0
Kingsville	4,822	9	0	6	0	3	128	34	87	7	0
Texas Christian University	6,675	2	0	0	0	2	201	23	174	4	1
Texas Southern University	5,124	15	0	0	1	14	248	53	160	35	0
Texas State Technical College:											
Harlingen	3,265	0	0	0	0	0	59	3	53	3	0
Waco	3,814	9	0	1	0	8	160	53	101	6	0
Texas Technological University, Lubbock	20,518	12	0	3	0	9	491	13	469	9	0
Texas Woman's University	4,476	1	0	0	0	1	79	18	54	7	0
Trinity University	2,356	1	0	0	1	0	102	5	93	4	0
Tyler Junior College	8,319	2	0	1	0	1	82	14	68	0	0
University of Houston:											
Central Campus	24,350	12	0	2	5	5	460	25	378	57	0
Clearlake	3,946	0	0	0	0	0	23	0	23	0	0
Downtown Campus	8,932	4	0	0	1	3	54	0	49	5	0
University of Mary Hardin-Baylor	2,401	0	0	0	0	0	59	10	46	3	0
University of North Texas:											
Denton	21,059	6	0	1	1	4	258	58	190	10	0
Health Science Center[4]		0	0	0	0	0	27	1	26	0	0
University of Texas:											
Austin	38,162	9	0	1	3	5	689	58	624	7	4
Brownsville	8,385	1	0	0	0	1	99	1	92	6	0
Dallas	6,560	2	0	0	1	1	157	7	145	5	0
El Paso	12,955	6	0	3	1	2	153	1	143	9	0
Health Science Center, San Antonio	762	1	0	0	0	1	99	1	98	0	0
Health Science Center, Tyler	264	1	0	0	0	1	20	0	20	0	0
Houston[4]		7	0	2	3	2	353	2	346	5	0
Medical Branch	653	4	0	0	2	2	203	0	194	9	0
Pan American	11,186	1	0	1	0	0	111	6	103	2	1
Permian Basin	1,642	0	0	0	0	0	12	2	10	0	0
San Antonio	16,026	5	0	1	0	4	147	48	95	4	0
Southwestern Medical School	239	0	0	0	0	0	298	1	280	17	0
Tyler	2,602	1	0	0	0	1	23	6	17	0	0
West Texas A&M University	5,623	4	0	1	1	2	47	5	42	0	0
UTAH											
Brigham Young University	29,688	4	0	0	1	3	386	8	372	6	3
College of Eastern Utah	2,704	1	0	1	0	0	11	0	10	1	0
Salt Lake Community College	21,596	0	0	0	0	0	200	16	182	2	0
Southern Utah University	5,729	1	0	1	0	0	41	0	40	1	0
University of Utah	19,718	9	0	2	0	7	635	25	583	27	1
Utah State University	17,903	1	0	1	0	0	151	12	139	0	0
Utah Valley State College	20,946	7	0	0	0	7	95	2	93	0	0
Weber State University	15,853	8	0	1	0	7	125	19	104	2	0
VIRGINIA											
Christopher Newport University	5,101	3	0	2	0	1	102	1	99	2	1
College of William and Mary	5,585	7	0	0	2	5	240	9	227	4	3
George Mason University	15,185	2	0	0	1	1	335	16	306	13	2
Hampton University	4,891	3	0	0	1	2	101	27	70	4	0
James Madison University	14,280	6	0	3	0	3	178	16	162	0	4
Mary Washington College	4,103	0	0	0	0	0	65	0	65	0	1
Norfolk State University	5,890	9	0	1	8	0	224	61	148	15	7
Northern Virginia Community College	37,073	2	0	0	1	1	174	1	169	4	0
Radford University	7,622	7	0	1	0	6	121	6	114	1	3
Thomas Nelson Community College	7,379	0	0	0	0	0	25	0	25	0	0
University of Richmond	3,652	5	0	3	0	2	118	16	100	2	8

See footnotes at end of table.

Table 9

Offenses Known to Law Enforcement
by University and College, 2002—Continued

University/College by state	Student enrollment[1]	Violent crime[2]	Violent crime — Murder and non-negligent man-slaughter	Violent crime — Forcible rape	Violent crime — Robbery	Violent crime — Aggravated assault	Property crime[3]	Property crime — Burglary	Property crime — Larceny-theft	Property crime — Motor vehicle theft	Arson[3]
VIRGINIA—Continued											
University of Virginia	13,712	19	0	2	2	15	323	8	306	9	6
Virginia Commonwealth University	16,505	26	0	1	5	20	588	11	571	6	3
Virginia State University	3,473	8	0	2	4	2	119	3	114	2	0
WASHINGTON											
Central Washington University	7,603	2	0	2	0	0	229	56	165	8	2
Eastern Washington University	7,567	1	0	1	0	0	83	15	66	2	1
Evergreen State College	3,901	3	0	1	2	0	83	16	65	2	2
University of Washington	25,987	20	0	1	2	17	997	133	824	40	1
Washington State University:											
Pullman	16,839	10	0	2	0	8	335	59	276	0	1
Vancouver[4]		0	0	0	0	0	11	0	11	0	0
Western Washington University	11,564	2	0	0	0	2	165	8	155	2	0
WEST VIRGINIA											
Bluefield State College	2,648	0	0	0	0	0	8	1	7	0	0
Concord College	3,048	0	0	0	0	0	34	9	25	0	0
Fairmont State College	6,496	1	0	0	0	1	42	9	33	0	0
Glenville State College	2,126	0	0	0	0	0	3	0	3	0	0
Marshall University	11,621	2	0	0	0	2	146	4	140	2	1
Potomac State College	1,109	4	0	1	0	3	19	7	12	0	0
West Liberty State College	2,606	1	0	0	0	1	40	1	39	0	0
West Virginia State College	4,824	2	0	0	0	2	39	4	35	0	0
West Virginia Tech	2,311	0	0	0	0	0	16	3	13	0	1
West Virginia University	15,463	5	0	0	4	1	245	16	226	3	6
WISCONSIN											
University of Wisconsin:											
Eau Claire	10,165	0	0	0	0	0	83	0	83	0	0
Green Bay	5,349	0	0	0	0	0	54	1	52	1	0
La Crosse	8,465	1	0	1	0	0	63	8	53	2	0
Madison	29,697	12	0	3	4	5	591	57	502	32	0
Milwaukee	19,246	9	0	3	3	3	299	40	257	2	2
Oshkosh	9,105	4	0	3	1	0	101	6	94	1	0
Parkside	4,736	1	0	1	0	0	85	1	83	1	0
Platteville	5,302	5	0	3	1	1	93	11	80	2	0
Stevens Point	8,287	0	0	0	0	0	146	2	144	0	0
Stout	7,240	0	0	0	0	0	101	19	82	0	0
Superior	2,505	0	0	0	0	0	65	15	50	0	0
Whitewater	9,460	5	0	0	2	3	139	19	118	2	0
WYOMING											
Sheridan College	2,674	0	0	0	0	0	4	2	2	0	0
University of Wyoming	8,550	1	0	1	0	0	176	13	162	1	0

[1] The student enrollment figures provided by the United States Department of Education are for the 2000 school year, the most recent available. The enrollment figures include full-time and part-time students. See Appendix I for details.

[2] Violent crimes are offenses of murder, forcible rape, robbery, and aggravated assault.

[3] Property crimes are offenses of burglary, larceny-theft, and motor vehicle theft. Arson is not included in the property crime total. If the FBI does not receive 12 months of arson data from either the agency or the state, no arson will be shown.

[4] Student enrollment figures were not available.

[5] Limited data for 2002 were available for Illinois and Kentucky.

NOTE: Caution should be exercised in making any inter-campus comparisons or ranking schools, as university/college crime statistics are affected by a variety of factors. These include demographic characteristics of the surrounding community, ratio of male to female students, number of on-campus residents, accessibility of outside visitors, size of enrollment, etc.

Table 10

Offenses Known to Law Enforcement
by Suburban County, 2002

[The data shown in this table do not reflect county totals but are the number of offenses reported by the sheriff's office, county police department, or state police.]

County by state	Crime Index	Modified Crime Index[1]	Murder and non-negligent man-slaughter	Forcible rape	Robbery	Aggravated assault	Burglary	Larceny-theft	Motor vehicle theft	Arson[1]
ALABAMA										
Baldwin	851		0	34	9	49	264	491	4	
Blount	699		0	10	1	13	205	390	80	
Calhoun	700		3	5	8	10	222	427	25	
Colbert	201		2	0	4	9	69	107	10	
Elmore	750		1	12	9	11	228	446	43	
Etowah	472		1	4	1	4	162	267	33	
Houston	391		0	0	5	11	119	229	27	
Jefferson	4,742	4,746	7	29	129	211	1,339	2,651	376	4
Lauderdale	180		1	0	0	15	60	74	30	
Lawrence	268		1	1	3	7	66	157	33	
Lee	1,863		3	13	35	92	686	922	112	
Limestone	407		3	8	7	20	110	218	41	
Madison	2,167		2	20	29	114	556	1,267	179	
Mobile	2,684		5	24	48	277	781	1,398	151	
Montgomery	1,004		1	8	21	74	261	566	73	
Morgan	510		1	3	8	25	210	222	41	
Russell	311		3	2	4	15	112	155	20	
Shelby	655		0	19	14	35	237	268	82	
St. Clair	457		1	9	3	27	121	276	20	
Tuscaloosa	2,300		2	25	36	236	691	1,043	267	
ARIZONA										
Coconino	771	781	1	12	3	81	186	449	39	10
Maricopa	7,887	7,908	35	23	77	493	2,083	3,946	1,230	21
Mohave	2,582	2,612	3	6	12	139	868	1,328	226	30
Pima	13,196	13,357	22	82	138	509	2,290	7,954	2,201	161
Pinal	3,579	3,597	2	26	34	680	814	1,588	435	18
Yuma[2]			0	2	10		429	672	144	0
ARKANSAS										
Craighead	457	458	1	1	3	9	126	249	68	1
Faulkner	635	635	2	3	1	92	162	327	48	0
Miller	381	395	0	1	3	57	102	192	26	14
Pulaski	2,071	2,085	7	23	28	113	392	1,363	145	14
Sebastian	196	196	0	2	2	14	54	96	28	0
Washington	522	523	0	3	1	45	205	231	37	1
CALIFORNIA										
Alameda	3,961	4,021	2	40	217	288	742	1,861	811	60
Alameda Highway Patrol	205	206	0	0	0	0	1	28	176	1
Contra Costa	4,042	4,074	5	43	129	292	876	2,694	3	32
Contra Costa Highway Patrol	1,178	1,178	0	0	0	13	7	58	1,100	0
El Dorado	2,328	2,343	4	22	22	220	933	1,115	12	15
El Dorado Highway Patrol	318	318	0	0	0	0	0	45	273	0
Fresno[2]	5,954	6,384	13	65	140	393	1,452	2,912	979	430
Fresno Highway Patrol	105	105	0	0	0	0	1	7	97	0
Kern	12,276	12,641	26	129	331	1,432	3,032	6,051	1,275	365
Kern Highway Patrol	179	179	0	1	0	0	0	60	118	0
Los Angeles	27,934	28,497	135	270	1,918	6,181	5,124	8,871	5,435	563
Los Angeles Highway Patrol	355	355	0	0	7	33	19	64	232	0
Madera	1,701	1,714	2	20	17	202	596	846	18	13
Madera Highway Patrol	291	291	0	0	0	0	0	19	272	0
Marin	1,294	1,315	0	11	30	153	277	822	1	21
Marin Highway Patrol	99	99	0	0	0	0	0	0	99	0
Merced	2,811	2,824	11	29	41	423	1,158	1,133	16	13
Merced Highway Patrol	574	574	0	0	0	0	0	81	493	0
Monterey	2,304	2,330	0	23	64	139	668	1,398	12	26
Monterey Highway Patrol	205	205	0	0	0	1	1	1	202	0
Napa	506	507	1	4	6	22	139	328	6	1
Napa Highway Patrol	85	85	0	0	0	0	0	0	85	0
Orange[2]	1,655	1,673	1	8	37	166	303	933	207	18

See footnotes at end of table.

Table 10

Offenses Known to Law Enforcement

by Suburban County, 2002—Continued

[The data shown in this table do not reflect county totals but are the number of offenses reported by the sheriff's office, county police department, or state police.]

County by state	Crime Index	Modified Crime Index[1]	Murder and non-negligent man-slaughter	Forcible rape	Robbery	Aggravated assault	Burglary	Larceny-theft	Motor vehicle theft	Arson[1]
CALIFORNIA—Continued										
Orange Highway Patrol	72	72	0	0	0	4	6	25	37	0
Placer	2,282	2,294	0	21	22	113	756	1,325	45	12
Placer Highway Patrol	206	206	0	0	0	0	0	9	197	0
Riverside	14,326	14,411	37	114	326	1,953	3,073	6,452	2,371	85
Riverside Highway Patrol	95	95	0	0	0	7	7	19	62	0
Sacramento	29,528	29,728	36	279	1,227	2,776	6,537	17,478	1,195	200
Sacramento Highway Patrol	5,754	5,754	0	0	1	1	6	717	5,029	0
San Bernardino	8,405	8,541	35	75	240	759	2,326	3,433	1,537	136
San Bernardino Highway Patrol	147	147	0	0	0	1	0	3	143	0
San Diego	9,872	9,928	11	88	242	954	2,503	4,412	1,662	56
San Diego Highway Patrol	133	133	0	0	0	0	2	47	84	0
San Francisco Highway Patrol	125	125	0	0	0	2	3	13	107	0
San Joaquin	5,376	5,428	15	38	154	792	1,300	2,914	163	52
San Joaquin Highway Patrol	1,306	1,306	0	0	0	0	0	268	1,038	0
San Luis Obispo	1,525	1,533	1	25	11	119	377	990	2	8
San Luis Obispo Highway Patrol	218	218	0	0	0	5	0	54	159	0
San Mateo	1,853	1,864	2	8	58	23	185	1,347	230	11
San Mateo Highway Patrol	33	33	0	0	0	0	1	10	22	0
Santa Barbara	1,970	1,988	2	38	15	191	451	1,264	9	18
Santa Barbara Highway Patrol	112	112	0	0	0	0	0	12	100	0
Santa Clara	2,535	2,538	2	22	26	234	434	1,582	235	3
Santa Clara Highway Patrol	74	74	0	0	0	0	1	21	52	0
Santa Cruz	2,465	2,495	2	28	38	160	635	1,592	10	30
Santa Cruz Highway Patrol	247	247	0	0	0	0	0	95	152	0
Shasta	1,671	1,721	5	44	16	294	546	717	49	50
Shasta Highway Patrol	205	205	0	0	0	1	0	48	156	0
Solano	523	543	1	7	11	71	158	266	9	20
Solano Highway Patrol	112	112	0	0	0	0	2	3	107	0
Sonoma	3,168	3,189	6	60	56	320	726	1,955	45	21
Sonoma Highway Patrol	439	439	0	0	0	0	0	121	318	0
Stanislaus	5,510	5,863	8	59	129	672	1,217	2,591	834	353
Stanislaus Highway Patrol	183	183	0	0	0	0	0	29	154	0
Sutter	966	971	3	11	9	112	285	481	65	5
Sutter Highway Patrol	67	67	0	0	0	0	0	0	67	0
Tulare[2]			12	36	75	450	1,141	1,668		615
Tulare Highway Patrol	1,054	1,054	0	0	0	0	0	305	749	0
Ventura	1,404	1,424	1	13	16	148	318	786	122	20
Ventura Highway Patrol	35	35	0	0	0	0	0	13	22	0
Yolo	382	388	1	6	2	44	129	188	12	6
Yolo Highway Patrol	74	74	0	0	0	0	1	12	61	0
Yuba	1,783	1,808	0	14	28	199	617	923	2	25
Yuba Highway Patrol	368	368	0	0	0	1	1	0	366	0
COLORADO										
Adams	4,949	5,030	8	43	63	315	918	2,650	952	81
Arapahoe	2,184	2,219	1	27	31	196	462	1,205	262	35
Boulder	812	834	0	29	3	59	258	410	53	22
Broomfield	1,719	1,734	0	4	12	20	165	1,391	127	15
Douglas	2,562	2,586	0	61	10	60	446	1,852	133	24
El Paso	3,024	3,058	13	27	48	242	754	1,689	251	34
Jefferson	2,843	2,878	2	28	20	135	464	1,965	229	35
Larimer	1,549	1,583	0	27	13	74	359	977	99	34
Mesa	1,281	1,303	1	0	4	64	291	821	100	22
Pueblo	1,265	1,273	1	4	10	24	317	862	47	8
Weld	1,423	1,439	5	33	11	107	475	620	172	16
DELAWARE										
Kent State Police	2,067	2,067	2	40	45	403	500	984	93	0
New Castle Police Department	7,907	7,925	6	118	237	664	1,814	4,046	1,022	18
New Castle State Police	6,155	6,160	2	21	305	400	691	4,236	500	5

See footnotes at end of table.

Table 10

Offenses Known to Law Enforcement

by Suburban County, 2002—Continued

[The data shown in this table do not reflect county totals but are the number of offenses reported by the sheriff's office, county police department, or state police.]

County by state	Crime Index	Modified Crime Index¹	Murder and non-negligent man-slaughter	Forcible rape	Robbery	Aggravated assault	Burglary	Larceny-theft	Motor vehicle theft	Arson¹
FLORIDA										
Alachua	4,893	4,911	0	87	117	693	1,216	2,493	287	18
Bay	4,120	4,120	5	57	51	406	690	2,721	190	0
Brevard	6,787	6,837	5	94	150	1,055	1,610	3,440	433	50
Broward	3,525	3,548	10	66	183	666	633	1,525	442	23
Charlotte	4,367	4,377	2	30	51	375	931	2,735	243	10
Clay	3,954	3,968	2	37	61	423	693	2,526	212	14
Collier	8,347	8,383	7	83	258	975	1,969	4,603	452	36
Escambia	12,168	12,196	15	127	405	1,145	3,013	6,813	650	28
Flagler	1,158	1,160	2	8	13	119	270	680	66	2
Gadsden	784	788	2	12	33	99	192	407	39	4
Hernando	5,580	5,599	4	54	68	668	1,487	3,073	226	19
Hillsborough	36,708	36,835	31	268	1,053	3,697	6,556	20,828	4,275	127
Lake	3,860	3,872	3	27	37	624	1,088	1,790	291	12
Lee	12,090	12,189	23	119	382	976	2,924	6,379	1,287	99
Leon	2,433	2,461	0	39	68	328	868	944	186	28
Manatee	11,731	11,798	8	88	321	1,280	2,567	6,826	641	67
Marion	6,383	6,392	10	99	73	1,238	1,627	3,001	335	9
Martin	3,804	3,818	6	34	101	356	805	2,310	192	14
Miami-Dade	78,404	78,596	94	494	3,198	8,115	11,448	45,060	9,995	192
Nassau	1,918	1,926	2	5	20	675	579	447	190	8
Okaloosa	3,680	3,692	4	33	74	297	645	2,436	191	12
Orange	39,071	39,071	38	258	1,428	3,587	7,742	21,148	4,870	0
Osceola	5,184	5,189	6	67	81	413	1,908	2,349	360	5
Palm Beach	26,159	26,306	8	240	706	2,273	5,659	14,617	2,656	147
Pasco	11,856	11,911	12	116	205	988	3,314	6,371	850	55
Pinellas	10,135	10,176	7	147	188	866	2,158	6,088	681	41
Polk	12,015	12,015	20	96	206	1,085	3,062	6,601	945	0
Santa Rosa	2,214	2,220	4	50	27	276	553	1,202	102	6
Sarasota	8,648	8,669	5	47	107	630	1,870	5,608	381	21
Seminole	4,725	4,735	2	35	94	552	1,005	2,706	331	10
St. Lucie	2,478	2,498	2	29	50	281	686	1,240	190	20
Volusia	6,494	6,539	6	106	88	1,043	1,667	3,114	470	45
GEORGIA										
Augusta-Richmond	12,143	12,219	13	157	449	182	2,139	8,037	1,166	76
Barrow	1,008	1,014	2	2	9	50	270	575	100	6
Bartow	1,987	1,987	0	1	20	35	501	1,211	219	0
Bibb	2,870	2,882	0	0	43	88	630	1,797	312	12
Bryan	318	318	0	2	3	13	57	241	2	0
Carroll	1,130		3	14	17	73	281	646	96	
Catoosa	1,086		0	9	7	29	201	728	112	
Chatham County Police Department	2,695	2,717	6	9	92	126	665	1,547	250	22
Chattahoochee	53	55	1	0	0	6	23	15	8	2
Cherokee	2,056	2,062	0	16	17	108	443	1,396	76	6
Clayton County Police Department	8,873	8,911	13	49	332	397	2,379	4,357	1,346	38
Cobb County Police Department	13,796	13,853	13	104	414	602	2,659	8,508	1,496	57
Columbia	2,253	2,262	0	10	27	29	387	1,698	102	9
Coweta	1,216	1,218	2	1	12	48	339	686	128	2
Dade	175	177	0	2	2	11	41	97	22	2
DeKalb County Police Department	24,887	25,080	74	102	1,395	633	5,109	12,975	4,599	193
Douglas	1,916	1,924	4	7	33	110	378	1,190	194	8
Effingham	629	629	4	5	8	36	150	356	70	0
Fayette	537		0	0	3	15	98	369	52	
Forsyth	2,198		1	22	9	183	439	1,338	206	
Fulton	85	85	0	0	1	32	1	48	3	0
Fulton County Police Department	8,593	8,619	21	44	363	228	1,877	5,032	1,028	26
Gwinnett County Police Department	17,352	17,436	20	149	662	574	3,758	10,276	1,913	84
Harris	169	169	1	1	3	5	29	104	26	0
Henry County Police Department	2,594		1	22	38	100	532	1,604	297	
Houston	1,132	1,134	1	5	5	42	284	703	92	2
Jones	546	546	0	0	0	20	138	331	57	0
Lee	611	612	0	0	6	13	132	422	38	1
Madison	664		2	0	7	39	183	357	76	

See footnotes at end of table.

Table 10

Offenses Known to Law Enforcement

by Suburban County, 2002—Continued

[The data shown in this table do not reflect county totals but are the number of offenses reported by the sheriff's office, county police department, or state police.]

County by state	Crime Index	Modified Crime Index[1]	Murder and non-negligent man-slaughter	Forcible rape	Robbery	Aggravated assault	Burglary	Larceny-theft	Motor vehicle theft	Arson[1]
GEORGIA—Continued										
McDuffie	469	470	1	1	4	32	106	298	27	1
Newton	1,154	1,156	1	8	20	36	315	636	138	2
Oconee	454	454	0	2	2	14	87	297	52	0
Paulding	1,945	1,952	0	12	13	160	443	1,100	217	7
Rockdale	2,258	2,263	0	6	26	132	397	1,509	188	5
Spalding	1,519	1,519	0	8	16	98	350	877	170	0
Twiggs	48	48	0	0	0	2	40	6	0	0
Walker	1,290	1,321	4	3	11	21	383	785	83	31
Walton	1,045	1,048	3	1	8	43	273	610	107	3
IDAHO										
Ada	1,812	1,837	0	20	9	102	411	1,158	112	25
Bannock	230	233	0	4	0	34	38	149	5	3
Canyon	866	869	3	10	4	82	278	398	91	3
ILLINOIS[3]										
INDIANA										
Allen	1,725	1,732	2	20	34	35	422	1,068	144	7
Allen State Police	65	65	0	0	7	9	5	33	11	0
Clark	972	978	0	6	9	139	283	459	76	6
Clark State Police	100	100	0	3	2	19	13	40	23	0
Clay	220	223	0	2	0	12	72	120	14	3
Clay State Police	37	37	0	0	2	10	9	15	1	0
Clinton	345	348	0	2	2	45	78	201	17	3
Clinton State Police	20	20	0	3	1	3	3	9	1	0
Dearborn	248	248	0	0	0	19	135	87	7	0
Dearborn State Police	58	61	0	3	2	8	8	33	4	3
Delaware	616	619	0	20	3	21	129	407	36	3
Delaware State Police	33	33	0	1	1	8	5	13	5	0
Elkhart	1,835	1,850	0	7	22	63	618	947	178	15
Elkhart State Police	92	93	0	0	2	8	17	55	10	1
Hamilton	835	839	0	8	0	25	169	602	31	4
Hamilton State Police	20	20	0	0	0	0	3	15	2	0
Hancock	265	265	0	5	4	3	98	143	12	0
Hancock State Police	18	18	0	1	0	4	0	10	3	0
Harrison	1,096	1,098	0	5	4	11	436	601	39	2
Harrison State Police	80	80	0	2	2	16	18	35	7	0
Howard	607	612	1	5	8	45	132	370	46	5
Howard State Police	36	36	0	1	1	9	4	18	3	0
Huntington	187	188	1	2	0	0	41	136	7	1
Huntington State Police	22	22	0	0	0	0	2	15	5	0
Lake	821	825	3	8	10	33	159	468	140	4
Lake State Police	228	229	1	1	4	38	4	86	94	1
Marion State Police	191	191	0	4	4	25	2	92	64	0
Monroe	766	771	5	10	2	95	176	404	74	5
Monroe State Police	91	92	0	3	3	13	12	54	6	1
Porter	1,216	1,224	1	7	2	16	173	904	113	8
Porter State Police	38	38	1	0	0	1	0	26	10	0
Shelby	404		0	3	0	45	90	250	16	
Shelby State Police	11	11	0	0	0	2	i	4	4	0
St. Joseph	2,398	2,420	1	12	28	32	492	1,658	175	22
St. Joseph State Police	116	116	0	0	4	9	30	57	16	0
Tippecanoe	828	835	1	10	1	28	230	515	43	7
Tippecanoe State Police	68	69	0	1	3	15	4	37	8	1
Vanderburgh	1,376	1,378	0	6	7	146	112	1,062	43	2
Vanderburgh State Police	30	30	0	2	1	9	2	16	0	0
Warrick	615	620	1	5	0	87	104	402	16	5
Warrick State Police	28	28	0	1	2	7	1	13	4	0
Wells	154	154	0	1	0	3	61	71	18	0
Wells State Police	14	14	0	1	1	2	1	8	1	0

See footnotes at end of table.

Table 10

Offenses Known to Law Enforcement
by Suburban County, 2002—Continued

[The data shown in this table do not reflect county totals but are the number of offenses reported by the sheriff's office, county police department, or state police.]

County by state	Crime Index	Modified Crime Index[1]	Murder and non-negligent man-slaughter	Forcible rape	Robbery	Aggravated assault	Burglary	Larceny-theft	Motor vehicle theft	Arson[1]
IOWA										
Black Hawk	369	374	0	11	2	7	193	144	12	5
Dallas	196	196	0	0	0	3	48	137	8	0
Dubuque	279	283	0	4	0	36	76	140	23	4
Johnson	463	468	0	2	4	80	128	222	27	5
Linn	543	555	0	7	2	22	158	301	53	12
Polk	1,627	1,643	2	14	12	165	331	921	182	16
Pottawattamie	677	680	1	9	1	18	218	318	112	3
Scott	321	323	0	2	1	47	63	182	26	2
Warren	357	360	0	5	2	21	117	182	30	3
Woodbury	239	241	0	3	0	28	89	111	8	2
KANSAS										
Butler	465	470	2	5	3	27	125	263	40	5
Johnson	402	406	1	8	3	43	118	195	34	4
Leavenworth	298	309	1	4	2	48	107	109	27	11
Miami	257	270	0	9	1	19	82	131	15	13
Shawnee	1,225	1,247	0	6	20	78	300	760	61	22
KENTUCKY[3]										
Boone	1,219	1,224	0	31	10	63	225	771	119	5
Campbell County Police Department	336	341	3	11	0	33	69	185	35	5
Daviess	607	612	0	5	6	67	156	343	30	5
Jefferson County Police Department[2]	13,282	13,294	17	53	180	1,429	2,729	7,803	1,071	12
Woodford County Police Department	20	20	0	0	0	0	6	13	1	0
LOUISIANA										
Acadia	742	742	1	11	3	37	117	529	44	0
Ascension	3,149	3,171	2	29	31	312	964	1,571	240	22
Bossier	782	783	0	6	8	61	119	555	33	1
Caddo	1,627	1,627	6	17	16	139	427	921	101	0
Calcasieu	4,651	4,663	7	58	101	195	1,061	2,969	260	12
East Baton Rouge	11,430	11,446	16	57	175	333	1,883	8,423	543	16
Jefferson	19,392	19,626	38	125	670	1,480	2,945	12,126	2,008	234
Lafayette	1,626	1,635	2	12	24	143	468	848	129	9
Lafourche	1,925	1,927	1	8	22	135	271	1,378	110	2
Livingston	1,387	1,389	5	23	10	177	760	364	48	2
Ouachita	2,597	2,608	7	30	32	258	774	1,403	93	11
Plaquemines	535	536	0	3	4	49	131	284	64	1
Rapides	2,047	2,047	5	10	14	231	672	967	148	0
St. Bernard	1,505	1,509	3	5	29	169	256	879	164	4
St. Charles	1,821	1,831	3	13	26	259	395	1,018	107	10
St. James	1,060	1,064	2	4	15	458	173	384	24	4
St. John the Baptist	1,243	1,243	6	7	51	63	221	760	135	0
St. Landry	1,196	1,199	3	5	15	164	303	629	77	3
St. Tammany	3,242	3,257	10	27	36	236	724	1,946	263	15
Terrebonne	3,993	4,012	4	37	37	265	1,050	2,421	179	19
Webster	321	321	0	3	1	43	75	190	9	0
West Baton Rouge	1,001	1,001	1	4	12	86	70	779	48	0
MAINE										
Androscoggin	315	316	0	0	2	2	88	204	19	1
Androscoggin State Police	182	182	1	5	0	5	53	97	21	0
Cumberland	705	712	0	12	2	18	262	363	48	7
Cumberland State Police	141	141	0	5	0	10	37	77	12	0
MARYLAND										
Allegany	163	163	0	4	0	12	43	98	6	0
Allegany State Police	578	581	0	5	7	47	108	383	28	3
Anne Arundel Police Department	19,280	19,458	13	78	603	2,467	2,776	11,991	1,352	178

See footnotes at end of table.

Table 10

Offenses Known to Law Enforcement
by Suburban County, 2002—Continued

[The data shown in this table do not reflect county totals but are the number of offenses reported by the sheriff's office, county police department, or state police.]

County by state	Crime Index	Modified Crime Index[1]	Murder and non-negligent man-slaughter	Forcible rape	Robbery	Aggravated assault	Burglary	Larceny-theft	Motor vehicle theft	Arson[1]
MARYLAND—Continued										
Anne Arundel State Police	128	128	0	1	2	21	1	86	17	0
Baltimore County Police Department	36,407	36,769	29	234	1,700	4,568	5,633	20,778	3,465	362
Baltimore County State Police	53	53	0	1	1	13	1	20	17	0
Calvert	1,141	1,141	0	16	14	223	212	621	55	0
Calvert State Police	457	474	0	7	3	108	80	232	27	17
Carroll	142	142	0	1	0	10	23	105	3	0
Carroll State Police	1,674	1,683	4	27	31	166	337	1,017	92	9
Cecil	537	537	0	1	4	25	155	338	14	0
Cecil State Police	1,345	1,354	1	7	16	228	309	692	92	9
Charles	4,745	4,745	6	41	180	629	668	2,774	447	0
Charles State Police	31	71	0	0	1	6	1	18	5	40
Frederick	1,647	1,654	2	17	9	121	313	1,101	84	7
Frederick State Police	710	721	0	7	11	50	118	485	39	11
Harford	3,915	3,915	1	35	104	296	775	2,434	270	0
Harford State Police	714	743	2	4	30	71	131	406	70	29
Howard Police Department	7,784	7,784	7	37	212	202	1.293	5,422	611	0
Howard State Police	71	78	0	1	6	8	1	47	8	7
Montgomery	13	13	0	1	0	12	0	0	0	0
Montgomery Police Department	28,435	28,709	32	138	877	895	3,874	18,897	3,722	274
Montgomery State Police	23	23	0	0	0	11	1	7	4	0
Queen Anne's	657	657	0	5	5	119	122	386	20	0
Queen Anne's State Police	288	299	0	2	6	40	65	161	14	11
Washington	1,276	1,276	2	10	11	123	317	729	84	0
Washington State Police	436	462	2	9	9	47	74	265	30	26
MASSACHUSETTS										
Barnstable State Police	9	9	0	0	1	3	0	3	2	0
Bristol State Police	23		0	0	1	11	2	3	6	
Hampden State Police	69		0	0	2	24	3	21	19	
Middlesex State Police	3		0	0	0	1	0	0	2	
Norfolk State Police	11		0	0	0	0	4	2	5	
Plymouth State Police	15		0	0	4	9	0	1	1	
Suffolk State Police	80		0	6	2	24	0	20	28	
Worcester State Police	30	30	0	0	0	15	0	13	2	0
MICHIGAN										
Allegan	615	617	1	30	4	68	165	304	43	2
Allegan State Police	493	497	0	17	2	43	148	248	35	4
Bay	739	743	0	7	5	18	153	496	60	4
Bay State Police	632	634	0	21	5	45	135	376	50	2
Berrien	678	684	3	16	6	94	136	372	51	6
Berrien State Police	612	622	0	29	9	45	149	332	48	10
Calhoun	452	453	1	4	5	53	121	244	24	1
Calhoun State Police	351	356	0	16	1	26	118	160	30	5
Clinton	197	198	0	2	0	12	51	118	14	1
Clinton State Police	72	72	0	9	0	5	14	42	2	0
Eaton	1,957	1,965	0	43	26	78	350	1,366	94	8
Eaton State Police	24	25	0	3	0	3	1	16	1	1
Genesee	836	839	0	12	8	45	162	527	82	3
Genesee State Police	480	488	0	23	14	51	133	220	39	8
Ingham	1,311	1,326	0	50	20	65	396	682	98	15
Ingham State Police	91	93	0	17	1	4	3	64	2	2
Jackson	683	694	2	20	6	75	149	362	69	11
Jackson State Police	553	562	0	24	4	74	134	269	48	9
Kalamazoo	2,488	2,505	2	38	25	100	578	1,560	185	17
Kalamazoo State Police	50	55	0	3	0	3	7	32	5	5
Kent	4,928	4,952	4	44	25	248	1,186	3,168	253	24
Kent State Police	72	74	0	7	1	11	2	48	3	2
Lapeer	690	693	4	11	7	24	154	445	45	3
Lapeer State Police	235	238	0	12	0	26	59	127	11	3
Lenawee	532	534	0	11	3	33	115	345	25	2
Lenawee State Police	205	206	0	6	0	36	53	100	10	1

See footnotes at end of table.

Table 10

Offenses Known to Law Enforcement
by Suburban County, 2002—Continued

[The data shown in this table do not reflect county totals but are the number of offenses reported by the sheriff's office, county police department, or state police.]

County by state	Crime Index	Modified Crime Index[1]	Murder and non-negligent man-slaughter	Forcible rape	Robbery	Aggravated assault	Burglary	Larceny-theft	Motor vehicle theft	Arson[1]
MICHIGAN—Continued										
Livingston State Police	651	657	1	10	9	60	136	380	55	6
Macomb	2,314	2,330	2	82	8	89	384	1,574	175	16
Macomb State Police	59	59	0	3	0	14	7	29	6	0
Midland	614	622	0	24	0	53	174	341	22	8
Midland State Police	43	43	0	6	0	7	9	20	1	0
Monroe	3,020	3,082	3	50	25	164	698	1,842	238	62
Monroe State Police	313	319	2	10	5	29	66	175	26	6
Muskegon	1,785	1,802	0	11	10	87	266	1,304	107	17
Muskegon State Police	361	365	0	18	2	21	86	201	33	4
Oakland	5,087	5,180	5	88	46	404	832	3,352	360	93
Oakland State Police	322	325	1	12	3	24	72	192	18	3
Ottawa	3,150	3,178	0	79	13	158	775	1,955	170	28
Ottawa State Police	261	262	0	11	0	12	44	164	30	1
Saginaw	907	912	0	15	8	84	136	616	48	5
Saginaw State Police	562	569	0	21	7	68	107	310	49	7
St. Clair	2,147	2,174	0	44	14	136	489	1,325	139	27
St. Clair State Police	273	279	0	10	1	17	81	134	30	6
Van Buren	643	648	3	12	5	46	182	345	50	5
Van Buren State Police	787	790	3	28	5	98	250	341	62	3
Washtenaw	2,910	2,938	4	62	87	241	846	1,313	357	28
Washtenaw State Police	266	271	2	9	2	26	86	118	23	5
Wayne	232	232	5	4	16	26	34	74	73	0
Wayne State Police	301	311	5	16	23	65	30	135	27	10
MINNESOTA										
Anoka	516	522	0	19	0	15	100	339	43	6
Benton	328	330	0	12	0	10	75	206	25	2
Carver	340	341	1	5	0	25	59	223	27	1
Chisago	716	719	0	24	2	13	111	489	77	3
Clay	94	94	0	4	0	6	31	43	10	0
Dakota	253	256	0	10	0	17	71	136	19	3
Hennepin	192	193	1	3	1	15	35	113	24	1
Houston	146	147	0	3	0	3	19	109	12	1
Isanti	286	290	1	9	1	8	70	150	47	4
Olmsted	339	343	0	4	3	13	89	205	25	4
Polk	348	356	0	3	2	10	102	201	30	8
Ramsey	294	300	0	4	0	10	24	238	18	6
Scott	272	274	0	5	0	6	50	185	26	2
Sherburne	603	605	0	9	1	19	82	420	72	2
St. Louis	1,043	1,045	0	29	2	28	403	515	66	2
Washington	1,185	1,189	1	11	1	40	235	833	64	4
Wright	2,096	2,101	1	10	9	37	261	1,641	137	5
MISSISSIPPI										
Harrison	1,845	1,862	5	7	9	33	427	1,270	94	17
Jackson	2,293	2,293	5	28	14	103	572	1,335	236	0
Lamar	671	672	1	10	15	11	191	381	62	1
Madison	650	653	3	14	15	61	199	288	70	3
Rankin	891	898	5	6	7	31	300	499	43	7
MISSOURI										
Andrew	162	162	0	0	2	2	29	116	13	0
Boone	816	819	1	4	13	40	172	532	54	3
Buchanan	266	266	0	2	0	18	61	168	17	0
Cass	510	510	0	8	1	62	167	239	33	0
Christian	511	513	0	6	2	30	157	280	36	2
Clay	171	180	0	1	1	42	62	49	16	9
Clinton	182	185	0	3	3	44	62	59	11	3
Franklin	1,440	1,446	2	3	5	327	310	720	73	6
Greene	1,535	1,535	0	2	4	115	308	966	140	0
Jackson	711	711	0	3	6	74	185	360	83	0

See footnotes at end of table.

Table 10

Offenses Known to Law Enforcement

by Suburban County, 2002—Continued

[The data shown in this table do not reflect county totals but are the number of offenses reported by the sheriff's office, county police department, or state police.]

County by state	Crime Index	Modified Crime Index[1]	Murder and non-negligent man-slaughter	Forcible rape	Robbery	Aggravated assault	Burglary	Larceny-theft	Motor vehicle theft	Arson[1]
MISSOURI—Continued										
Jasper	439	439	0	0	3	5	138	254	39	0
Jefferson	4,269	4,282	5	34	14	288	498	3,053	377	13
Lafayette	172	172	0	2	1	28	61	75	5	0
Lincoln	620	630	1	0	2	182	140	266	29	10
Newton	1,303	1,311	0	4	2	385	214	589	109	8
Platte	423	431	0	1	1	42	105	233	41	8
Ray	146	156	1	1	0	10	62	41	31	10
St. Charles	1,523	1,541	1	7	11	144	321	946	93	18
St. Louis County Police Department	11,854	11,928	15	52	230	619	1,703	8,059	1,176	74
Warren	245	245	1	0	1	38	91	103	11	0
Webster	426	434	1	7	5	143	92	146	32	8
MONTANA										
Cascade	515		0	5	5	39	40	397	29	
Yellowstone	793		0	3	9	90	100	527	64	
NEBRASKA										
Dakota	83	83	0	0	0	2	17	54	10	0
Dakota State Patrol	2	2	0	0	0	2	0	0	0	0
Douglas	1,475	1,481	2	6	13	164	214	946	130	6
Douglas State Patrol	5	5	0	0	0	0	0	1	4	0
Lancaster	510	514	0	3	4	14	125	337	27	4
Lancaster State Patrol	3	3	0	0	0	2	0	0	1	0
Sarpy	892	896	1	5	8	10	120	654	94	4
Sarpy State Patrol	1	1	0	0	0	0	0	1	0	0
Washington	165	166	0	0	0	0	46	103	16	1
Washington State Patrol	0	0	0	0	0	0	0	0	0	0
NEVADA										
Nye	1,219	1,238	2	0	16	114	418	594	75	19
Washoe	1,708	1,716	1	6	17	171	409	911	193	8
NEW HAMPSHIRE										
Hillsborough State Police	18	18	4	1	0	4	9	0	0	0
Rockingham State Police	9	10	2	0	2	3	1	1	0	1
Strafford State Police	7	8	1	1	0	1	2	1	1	1
NEW JERSEY										
Atlantic State Police	822	826	0	2	14	25	80	682	19	4
Bergen State Police	230	231	0	0	3	5	6	152	64	1
Burlington State Police	583	590	3	3	16	31	137	346	47	7
Camden State Police	37	37	0	0	2	8	1	23	3	0
Cape May State Police	301	303	0	2	4	27	55	199	14	2
Cumberland State Police	927	940	1	3	19	74	298	446	86	13
Essex Police Department	232	234	1	18	52	30	13	101	17	2
Essex State Police	35	35	1	0	2	14	2	15	1	0
Gloucester State Police	18	18	0	0	1	9	2	6	0	0
Hudson State Police	21	21	0	0	1	0	4	12	4	0
Hunterdon State Police	245	249	1	1	2	11	75	143	12	4
Mercer State Police	204	205	0	4	0	5	24	165	6	1
Middlesex State Police	151	152	0	0	5	11	6	110	19	1
Monmouth State Police	233	233	0	2	1	5	31	179	15	0
Morris State Police	54	54	1	1	1	9	9	31	2	0
Ocean State Police	80	81	0	0	0	10	19	47	4	1
Passaic State Police	36	36	0	1	0	2	0	23	10	0
Salem State Police	449	504	0	1	13	31	116	259	29	55
Somerset State Police	11	11	0	0	1	1	1	8	0	0
Sussex State Police	454	456	0	2	4	31	79	307	31	2
Union State Police	56	56	0	0	4	12	4	31	5	0
Warren State Police	210	211	0	1	0	9	52	131	17	1

See footnotes at end of table.

Table 10

Offenses Known to Law Enforcement
by Suburban County, 2002—Continued

[The data shown in this table do not reflect county totals but are the number of offenses reported by the sheriff's office, county police department, or state police.]

County by state	Crime Index	Modified Crime Index[1]	Murder and non-negligent man-slaughter	Forcible rape	Robbery	Aggravated assault	Burglary	Larceny-theft	Motor vehicle theft	Arson[1]
NEW MEXICO										
Bernalillo	3,731	3,817	10	50	134	679	815	1,620	423	86
Sandoval	210		1	1	2	56	69	67	14	
Santa Fe	1,410	1,424	0	28	20	223	458	611	70	14
NEW YORK										
Albany	124		1	0	0	19	36	67	1	
Albany State Police	302		0	3	4	18	38	225	14	
Broome	1,044		2	8	8	51	158	766	51	
Broome State Police	677		1	9	11	59	104	468	25	
Cayuga	303		0	4	3	18	73	201	4	
Cayuga State Police	330		1	1	4	63	66	195	0	
Chautauqua	933		1	5	1	40	229	617	40	
Chautauqua State Police	196		0	3	0	20	41	128	4	
Chemung	312		0	4	3	31	42	221	11	
Chemung State Police	348		1	4	2	80	35	221	5	
Dutchess	978		0	4	9	42	184	668	71	
Dutchess State Police	745		3	15	5	93	136	469	24	
Erie State Police	615		0	4	2	35	111	444	19	
Herkimer State Police	318		1	6	4	17	98	184	8	
Livingston	799		0	5	2	13	113	651	15	
Livingston State Police	117		0	1	1	21	13	80	1	
Madison State Police	345		0	5	2	34	121	178	5	
Monroe	5,190	5,209	0	30	63	84	692	4,024	297	19
Monroe State Police	54		0	3	1	33	2	14	1	
Nassau	17,586		16	92	749	926	2,242	11,632	1,929	
Naussau State Police	34		0	0	1	14	1	16	2	
New York State Police	88		0	0	0	0	1	87	0	
Oneida	745		0	30	8	67	181	434	25	
Oneida State Police	688		0	7	4	68	185	404	20	
Onondaga	2,671	2,699	1	27	48	121	449	1,927	98	28
Onondaga State Police	1,024		2	10	17	59	166	744	26	
Ontario	1,030		0	2	13	27	191	751	46	
Ontario State Police	324		0	7	0	18	46	244	9	
Orange State Police	1,008		5	19	23	86	152	673	50	
Orleans	221		4	1	3	8	35	157	13	
Orleans State Police	68		0	4	0	18	11	31	4	
Oswego	445		1	1	2	19	139	247	36	
Oswego State Police	852		2	9	2	33	248	545	13	
Putnam	419		0	5	4	22	115	246	27	
Putnam State Police	181		0	1	3	7	22	133	15	
Rensselaer	452		0	1	3	55	102	285	6	
Rensselaer State Police	704		2	15	9	72	123	464	19	
Rockland	101		0	0	1	5	0	92	3	
Rockland State Police	7		0	0	0	1	0	6	0	
Saratoga	1,053	1,058	1	21	10	33	196	749	43	5
Schenectady	7		0	0	0	6	0	1	0	
Schenectady State Police	106		0	0	0	16	21	66	3	
Schoharie	146		0	4	0	3	41	96	2	
Schoharie State Police	216		0	12	0	31	36	131	6	
Suffolk	270		0	1	1	222	18	22	6	
Suffolk State Police	106		1	2	3	18	21	45	16	
Tioga	230		0	1	1	10	74	133	11	
Tioga State Police	163		0	1	0	7	32	116	7	
Warren	1,037		1	8	5	48	169	786	20	
Warren State Police	176		1	9	0	15	16	131	4	
Wayne	704		1	10	9	15	158	495	16	
Wayne State Police	478		1	4	2	33	94	330	14	
Westchester Public Safety	387		0	3	2	44	33	290	15	
Westchester State Police	654		2	3	10	45	128	424	42	
NORTH CAROLINA										
Alamance	1,387	1,394	4	2	18	42	548	699	74	7
Alexander	677	681	1	2	5	41	216	357	55	4

See footnotes at end of table.

Table 10

Offenses Known to Law Enforcement
by Suburban County, 2002—Continued

[The data shown in this table do not reflect county totals but are the number of offenses reported by the sheriff's office, county police department, or state police.]

County by state	Crime Index	Modified Crime Index[1]	Murder and non-negligent man-slaughter	Forcible rape	Robbery	Aggravated assault	Burglary	Larceny-theft	Motor vehicle theft	Arson[1]
NORTH CAROLINA—Continued										
Brunswick	2,129	2,135	2	13	33	59	1,030	837	155	6
Buncombe	2,904		6	9	27	228	864	1,522	248	
Cabarrus	983	987	1	5	21	19	428	478	31	4
Chatham	1,286	1,291	2	15	14	51	484	620	100	5
Cumberland	7,157	7,262	17	35	193	493	2,401	3,635	383	105
Currituck	574	578	1	2	4	47	157	347	16	4
Davidson	1,566	1,570	0	0	7	46	33	1,410	70	4
Davie	487	488	2	2	5	43	180	222	33	1
Durham	1,023	1,024	3	1	17	69	218	625	90	1
Forsyth	3,683	3,757	4	26	26	132	946	2,401	148	74
Franklin	912	917	0	2	0	27	450	341	92	5
Gaston Police Department	2,145	2,171	4	20	25	186	812	958	140	26
Guilford	2,550	2,572	3	13	42	159	824	1,358	151	22
Johnston	2,711	2,720	4	8	34	120	928	1,396	221	9
Madison	149	153	2	0	2	9	62	59	15	4
Nash	869	882	3	0	20	30	314	451	51	13
Orange	1,108	1,113	6	2	28	6	472	545	49	5
Pitt	1,982	1,993	7	9	38	180	574	1,083	91	11
Randolph	2,418	2,423	3	14	22	51	668	1,521	139	5
Stokes	1,038	1,059	2	6	8	147	334	462	79	21
Union	2,115	2,124	0	8	8	61	784	1,197	57	9
Wake	3,084	3,134	1	26	39	104	1,112	1,564	238	50
Wayne	2,087	2,090	3	2	22	112	766	1,081	101	3
Yadkin	521	523	0	4	3	32	189	256	37	2
NORTH DAKOTA										
Burleigh	201	207	1	2	1	6	65	109	17	6
Cass	264	266	0	2	0	11	60	164	27	2
Grand Forks	138	138	0	2	0	1	28	91	16	0
Morton	90	91	0	6	0	1	10	65	8	1
OHIO										
Allen	1,446	1,449	0	15	13	17	194	1,160	47	3
Auglaize	75	75	0	4	0	0	33	37	1	0
Belmont	512	520	6	9	3	13	131	294	56	8
Butler	1,419	1,444	1	14	15	94	378	851	66	25
Clermont	1,530	1,569	0	57	6	36	360	963	108	39
Columbiana	434	436	1	15	0	67	126	161	64	2
Crawford	226	226	0	1	0	2	76	135	12	0
Delaware	1,316	1,327	3	5	10	11	439	772	76	11
Fairfield	975	991	0	14	9	11	384	484	73	16
Franklin	4,471	4,495	6	51	158	75	1,015	2,711	455	24
Fulton	377	384	0	2	3	6	123	187	56	7
Greene	398	401	0	14	2	3	107	247	25	3
Hamilton	7,739	7,809	2	48	152	86	1,033	6,066	352	70
Jefferson	312	318	0	4	11	34	79	153	31	6
Licking	811	818	0	2	3	8	174	577	47	7
Lorain	1,212	1,238	0	13	19	37	679	442	22	26
Lucas	1,914	1,928	1	18	30	43	368	1,271	183	14
Miami	591	595	0	6	1	4	81	425	74	4
Montgomery	2,764	2,784	0	42	127	73	761	1,243	518	20
Richland	1,407	1,408	1	6	12	8	380	939	61	1
Stark	3,231	3,255	2	35	53	43	929	1,893	276	24
Summit	1,211	1,218	0	14	28	42	264	788	75	7
Trumbull	629	630	0	3	6	19	117	393	91	1
Warren	1,181	1,195	0	0	13	27	238	844	59	14
Washington	582	594	0	27	5	10	142	357	41	12
OKLAHOMA										
Canadian	103	105	0	1	0	10	30	50	12	2
Cleveland	354	359	0	20	1	37	128	150	18	5

See footnotes at end of table.

Table 10

Offenses Known to Law Enforcement
by Suburban County, 2002—Continued

[The data shown in this table do not reflect county totals but are the number of offenses reported by the sheriff's office, county police department, or state police.]

County by state	Crime Index	Modified Crime Index[1]	Murder and non-negligent man-slaughter	Forcible rape	Robbery	Aggravated assault	Burglary	Larceny-theft	Motor vehicle theft	Arson[1]
OKLAHOMA—Continued										
Comanche	368	373	2	3	6	59	76	184	38	5
Creek	736	743	3	8	1	146	212	283	83	7
Garfield	169	175	0	1	0	2	43	115	8	6
Logan	307	312	2	5	3	36	117	127	17	5
McClain	193	193	0	3	1	27	56	87	19	0
Oklahoma	233	233	1	0	0	33	78	103	18	0
Osage	561	570	0	12	6	50	197	260	36	9
Pottawatomie	580	595	1	15	1	44	164	310	45	15
Rogers	326	326	0	0	0	13	98	165	50	0
Sequoyah	440	447	1	2	1	99	133	170	34	7
Tulsa	1,618	1,627	3	14	30	185	323	891	172	9
Wagoner	423	432	1	6	1	25	138	192	60	9
OREGON										
Clackamas	7,839	7,864	2	61	106	107	1,231	5,518	814	25
Jackson	1,783	1,791	1	13	14	164	389	1,074	128	8
Lane	1,504	1,513	3	12	19	107	459	732	172	9
Marion	4,353	4,356	0	15	33	242	757	2,701	605	3
Multnomah	748	754	0	9	2	36	100	514	87	6
Polk	458	460	1	8	2	28	124	262	33	2
Washington	4,851	4,882	2	31	45	81	902	3,268	522	31
Yamhill	729	733	5	16	5	21	189	407	86	4
PENNSYLVANIA										
Allegheny	14	14	0	0	0	12	0	2	0	0
Allegheny State Police	84	87	0	3	0	41	8	29	3	3
Beaver	20	20	0	0	0	9	0	11	0	0
Beaver State Police	155	160	0	1	3	22	43	76	10	5
Berks State Police	673	683	1	9	14	68	159	352	70	10
Blair State Police	437	443	0	18	5	21	152	216	25	6
Bucks State Police	412	422	1	5	6	24	103	228	45	10
Butler State Police	1,055	1,076	3	36	14	42	258	626	76	21
Cambria State Police	334	338	2	6	5	48	106	133	34	4
Carbon State Police	368	377	0	9	2	30	109	195	23	9
Centre State Police	639	652	2	23	7	53	145	382	27	13
Chester State Police	1,418	1,436	1	28	31	124	420	685	129	18
Columbia State Police	225	227	0	4	2	12	67	125	15	2
Cumberland State Police	683	691	0	17	11	30	158	413	54	8
Delaware State Police	1,009	1,023	0	11	18	36	179	653	112	14
Elizabethville State Police	764	773	1	11	8	39	135	520	50	9
Erie State Police	1,702	1,719	1	25	19	118	430	1,004	105	17
Fayette State Police	2,020	2,164	7	46	35	84	580	1,004	264	144
Lackawanna State Police	239	261	0	8	4	5	87	111	24	22
Lancaster	2	2	0	0	0	2	0	0	0	0
Lancaster State Police	1,361	1,388	1	22	20	85	400	735	98	27
Lebanon State Police	485	493	1	8	5	50	102	299	20	8
Lehigh State Police	878	897	1	13	8	71	177	556	52	19
Luzerne State Police	1,000	1,043	9	14	17	153	221	509	77	43
Lycoming State Police	881	891	1	12	15	25	266	512	50	10
Mercer State Police	532	539	1	6	6	19	163	290	47	7
Northampton State Police	296	309	1	3	5	21	94	151	21	13
Perry State Police	678	683	0	31	3	56	169	386	33	5
Philadelphia State Police	10	10	0	0	0	0	0	8	2	0
Pike State Police	516	527	1	3	6	21	217	239	29	11
Skippack State Police	536	548	0	13	6	65	110	304	38	12
Somerset State Police	763	776	2	17	13	27	269	381	54	13
Washington State Police	852	900	4	22	26	79	210	432	79	48
Westmoreland State Police	2,288	2,322	2	23	45	102	550	1,378	188	34
Wyoming State Police	275	279	2	10	1	23	73	148	18	4
York State Police	1,000	1,037	0	27	11	171	253	471	67	37

See footnotes at end of table.

Table 10

Offenses Known to Law Enforcement

by Suburban County, 2002—Continued

[The data shown in this table do not reflect county totals but are the number of offenses reported by the sheriff's office, county police department, or state police.]

County by state	Crime Index	Modified Crime Index[1]	Murder and non-negligent man-slaughter	Forcible rape	Robbery	Aggravated assault	Burglary	Larceny-theft	Motor vehicle theft	Arson[1]
RHODE ISLAND										
Kent (Hope Valley State Police)	184	185	2	5	1	24	45	89	18	1
Providence (Chepachet State Police)	44	46	0	4	0	2	2	29	7	2
Providence (Lincoln Woods State Police)	92	92	0	2	1	6	1	63	19	0
Washington (Wickford State Police)	26	26	1	3	0	1	1	18	2	0
SOUTH CAROLINA										
Aiken	2,872	2,894	3	39	79	186	814	1,479	272	22
Anderson	6,389	6,440	11	57	102	715	1,361	3,584	559	51
Berkeley	3,940		10	53	77	526	978	1,831	465	
Charleston	4,066	4,080	8	41	103	730	740	1,961	483	14
Cherokee	1,610	1,612	3	9	21	165	420	882	110	2
Dorchester	2,175	2,181	4	20	54	322	515	1,095	165	6
Edgefield	401	404	0	6	6	23	127	212	27	3
Florence	3,670	3,673	1	39	97	370	809	2,031	323	3
Greenville	11,435	11,498	19	125	328	1,565	2,639	5,929	830	63
Horry Police Department	7,751	7,774	12	57	99	889	1,526	4,527	641	23
Lexington	5,383		7	49	117	507	1,472	2,747	484	
Pickens	1,708		1	26	11	217	489	835	129	
Richland	11,135	11,168	21	116	388	1,318	2,338	5,784	1,170	33
Spartanburg	7,805		12	101	161	861	1,461	4,590	619	
Sumter	2,972	2,994	5	26	85	436	836	1,297	287	22
York	4,441	4,467	5	46	50	848	1,014	2,239	239	26
SOUTH DAKOTA										
Minnehaha	303	308	0	7	0	17	126	131	22	5
Pennington	1,413	1,418	2	37	3	34	118	1,191	28	5
TENNESSEE										
Anderson	940	948	1	2	10	46	337	465	79	8
Blount	1,989	1,998	3	34	6	302	586	931	127	9
Carter	887	905	4	5	2	97	198	520	61	18
Cheatham	623	634	1	10	1	94	132	317	68	11
Chester	106	106	0	3	0	17	34	44	8	0
Dickson	759	764	4	33	7	79	250	329	57	5
Fayette	723	731	0	5	13	58	261	315	71	8
Hamilton	2,195	2,206	5	23	25	314	562	1,166	100	11
Hawkins	782	788	0	9	3	49	287	364	70	6
Knox	6,152	6,208	5	45	69	440	1,590	3,466	537	56
Loudon	630	630	1	2	6	69	129	378	45	0
Madison	1,022	1,026	3	14	5	137	243	535	85	4
Marion	490	494	1	0	0	120	79	209	81	4
Montgomery	788	795	0	5	7	67	222	440	47	7
Robertson	620	620	0	4	3	125	151	297	40	0
Rutherford	1,386	1,395	1	27	6	233	367	627	125	9
Sevier	1,373	1,375	0	7	3	87	458	734	84	2
Shelby	4,493	4,509	11	32	95	325	1,392	2,242	396	16
Shelby County Police Department	46	46	0	0	0	0	2	42	2	0
Sullivan	1,947	1,972	3	32	21	284	583	907	117	25
Sumner	802	814	1	18	8	77	248	400	50	12
Tipton	1,063	1,072	3	11	8	141	318	458	124	9
Unicoi	336	339	0	1	3	51	85	176	20	3
Union	358	358	1	1	2	52	162	113	27	0
Washington	1,130	1,141	0	4	9	168	337	515	97	11
Williamson	656	661	0	5	0	35	158	425	33	5
Wilson	1,001	1,002	2	5	4	155	383	375	77	1
TEXAS										
Archer	103	105	0	1	1	11	32	48	10	2
Bastrop	1,120	1,122	4	3	16	102	473	456	66	2
Bell	726	739	1	27	8	61	221	343	65	13

See footnotes at end of table.

Table 10

Offenses Known to Law Enforcement
by Suburban County, 2002—Continued

[The data shown in this table do not reflect county totals but are the number of offenses reported by the sheriff's office, county police department, or state police.]

County by state	Crime Index	Modified Crime Index[1]	Murder and non-negligent man-slaughter	Forcible rape	Robbery	Aggravated assault	Burglary	Larceny-theft	Motor vehicle theft	Arson[1]
TEXAS—Continued										
Bexar	5,500	5,611	10	49	66	382	1,317	3,325	351	111
Bowie	639	649	0	7	5	71	158	318	80	10
Brazoria	1,535	1,539	4	39	42	94	477	748	131	4
Brazos	424	429	1	6	1	56	137	204	19	5
Caldwell	307	310	0	11	4	53	126	106	7	3
Cameron	1,625	1,651	4	26	20	183	568	723	101	26
Chambers	568	575	0	4	11	49	202	283	19	7
Collin	881	882	3	39	6	50	276	430	77	1
Comal	1,026	1,036	2	20	5	74	266	607	52	10
Coryell	148	152	0	2	1	21	45	69	10	4
Dallas	501	519	3	5	12	88	129	220	44	18
Denton	863	875	1	17	9	89	174	492	81	12
Ector	1,498	1,499	0	8	6	119	343	933	89	1
Ellis	1,286	1,291	2	19	14	102	464	611	74	5
El Paso	1,540	1,560	3	43	18	215	310	762	189	20
Fort Bend	3,560	3,609	1	31	64	393	1,005	1,856	210	49
Galveston	1,267	1,281	3	20	36	169	378	512	149	14
Grayson	822	826	0	6	2	25	262	473	54	4
Gregg	762	765	3	2	12	36	148	499	62	3
Guadalupe	1,020	1,020	1	13	2	89	312	548	55	0
Hardin	572	580	0	4	2	84	182	229	71	8
Harris	42,494	43,071	68	297	1,717	4,058	9,065	22,207	5,082	577
Harrison	1,046	1,063	1	1	9	99	459	437	40	17
Hays	1,285	1,285	1	4	19	47	372	724	118	0
Henderson	1,690	1,691	3	9	6	255	636	604	177	1
Hidalgo	6,966	7,069	26	98	174	914	2,434	2,824	496	103
Hood	972	976	0	1	6	45	283	561	76	4
Hunt	1,170	1,171	0	0	11	47	488	561	63	1
Jefferson	603	607	0	21	10	14	176	321	61	4
Johnson	1,653	1,676	2	1	5	139	566	802	138	23
Kaufman	1,476	1,512	6	10	10	208	445	687	110	36
Liberty	1,229	1,231	1	22	7	145	512	421	121	2
Lubbock	716	721	0	12	1	75	221	331	76	5
McLennan	983	995	1	29	3	54	353	469	74	12
Midland	474	476	2	0	2	29	157	243	41	2
Montgomery	7,548	7,639	11	44	115	630	1,701	4,575	472	91
Nueces	418	418	0	25	8	36	108	201	40	0
Orange	1,298	1,304	3	63	10	151	311	645	115	6
Parker	1,125	1,126	2	1	6	61	412	551	92	1
Potter	275	279	0	1	1	10	62	184	17	4
Randall	498	501	0	3	2	52	180	214	47	3
Rockwall	261	261	1	4	4	43	76	107	26	0
San Patricio	388	390	2	0	3	15	142	204	22	2
Smith	1,958	2,000	4	57	35	135	770	819	138	42
Tarrant	1,025	1,031	0	17	11	65	339	530	63	6
Taylor	184	184	1	0	0	11	86	70	16	0
Tom Green	332	333	0	7	0	6	92	208	19	1
Travis	4,141	4,163	4	73	48	240	1,086	2,405	285	22
Upshur	549	550	2	2	4	28	252	225	36	1
Victoria	693	705	6	15	7	82	180	383	20	12
Waller	243	243	2	5	3	17	86	94	36	0
Webb	385	392	1	1	0	66	168	115	34	7
Wichita	159	167	0	4	2	18	49	65	21	8
Williamson	2,237	2,267	1	42	10	226	507	1,348	103	30
Wilson	246	246	0	0	4	26	88	114	14	0
UTAH										
Davis	177	182	0	3	2	14	42	93	23	5
Salt Lake	15,209	15,245	5	140	120	350	2,188	11,257	1,149	36
Utah	335	347	0	8	3	21	91	192	20	12
Weber	997	1,002	0	4	4	18	211	693	67	5

See footnotes at end of table.

Table 10

Offenses Known to Law Enforcement
by Suburban County, 2002—Continued

[The data shown in this table do not reflect county totals but are the number of offenses reported by the sheriff's office, county police department, or state police.]

County by state	Crime Index	Modified Crime Index[1]	Murder and non-negligent man-slaughter	Forcible rape	Robbery	Aggravated assault	Burglary	Larceny-theft	Motor vehicle theft	Arson[1]
VERMONT										
Grand Isle	60	61	0	0	0	1	11	47	1	1
Williston State Police	361	383	7	1	1	8	124	205	15	22
VIRGINIA										
Albemarle County Police Department	1,906	1,929	1	23	19	105	271	1,402	85	23
Albemarle State Police	5	5	0	0	0	0	0	5	0	0
Amherst	345	352	2	5	2	15	47	254	20	7
Arlington County Police Department	6,178	6,186	6	35	212	182	427	4,652	664	8
Arlington State Police	7	7	0	0	0	4	0	3	0	0
Bedford	914	920	0	19	3	34	164	630	64	6
Bedford State Police	20	20	0	0	0	3	0	8	9	0
Botetourt	346	347	2	4	1	13	37	265	24	1
Botetourt State Police	15	15	0	0	0	0	0	14	1	0
Campbell	1,009	1,018	3	13	13	57	195	651	77	9
Campbell State Police	19	19	0	1	0	1	4	11	2	0
Chesterfield County Police Department	8,321	8,390	9	53	213	281	1,348	5,985	432	69
Chesterfield State Police	29	29	0	0	0	12	1	14	2	0
Clarke	189	194	1	1	0	35	18	122	12	5
Clarke State Police	4	4	0	0	0	1	1	2	0	0
Culpeper	304	308	0	9	3	21	43	211	17	4
Culpeper State Police	20	20	0	0	0	8	0	10	2	0
Dinwiddie	670	673	3	5	9	18	91	514	30	3
Dinwiddie State Police	6	6	0	0	0	1	0	4	1	0
Fairfax County Police Department	17,830	17,915	6	44	296	127	1,552	14,547	1,258	85
Fairfax State Police	52	52	0	0	0	30	0	16	6	0
Fauquier	677	694	1	9	9	62	77	487	32	17
Fauquier State Police	24	24	0	0	0	4	2	14	4	0
Fluvanna	242	248	0	4	4	26	56	137	15	6
Fluvanna State Police	3	3	0	0	0	0	0	3	0	0
Gloucester	595	609	2	5	3	36	66	476	7	14
Gloucester State Police	8	8	0	0	0	0	1	7	0	0
Goochland	213	213	2	0	3	27	58	110	13	0
Greene	152	154	0	1	2	18	20	99	12	2
Hanover	1,132	1,142	3	15	26	34	139	834	81	10
Hanover State Police	5	5	0	0	0	2	0	3	0	0
Henrico County Police Department	10,836	10,980	8	30	252	279	1,408	8,074	785	144
Henrico State Police	10	10	0	0	0	1	1	8	0	0
Isle of Wight	449	454	0	6	11	9	86	310	27	5
Isle of Wight State Police	6	6	0	0	0	1	0	2	3	0
James City County Police Department	1,053	1,070	1	15	12	44	112	791	78	17
James City State Police	5	5	0	0	0	0	1	1	3	0
King George	438	442	1	8	8	27	68	292	34	4
Loudoun	3,090	3,158	1	32	41	200	260	2,391	165	68
Loudoun State Police	17	17	0	0	0	2	1	13	1	0
Mathews	100	102	1	1	1	3	16	75	3	2
New Kent	271	272	1	1	0	16	49	187	17	1
Powhatan	229	233	1	1	0	4	46	160	17	4
Powhatan State Police	4	4	0	0	0	3	0	0	1	0
Prince George County Police Department	569	576	1	6	11	24	95	393	39	7
Prince George State Police	1	1	0	0	1	0	0	0	0	0
Prince William County Police Department	8,013	8,093	6	39	194	363	1,018	5,699	694	80
Prince William State Police	29	30	0	1	1	12	0	13	2	1
Roanoke County Police Department	1,269	1,274	6	24	11	151	208	786	83	5
Roanoke State Police	9	9	0	0	0	6	0	2	1	0
Scott	364	370	1	5	2	20	74	243	19	6
Scott State Police	12	13	0	0	0	0	2	10	0	1
Spotsylvania	2,166	2,174	3	23	36	87	250	1,693	74	8
Spotsylvania State Police	47	47	0	0	0	8	1	31	7	0
Stafford	1,843	1,863	1	30	56	72	188	1,355	141	20
Stafford State Police	21	21	0	0	0	6	1	9	5	0
Warren	233	235	2	3	1	2	67	137	21	2
Warren State Police	7	7	0	1	0	1	0	2	3	0
York	1,177	1,203	0	8	24	79	112	912	42	26
York State Police	4	4	0	0	0	0	0	3	1	0

See footnotes at end of table.

Table 10

Offenses Known to Law Enforcement

by Suburban County, 2002—Continued

[The data shown in this table do not reflect county totals but are the number of offenses reported by the sheriff's office, county police department, or state police.]

County by state	Crime Index	Modified Crime Index[1]	Murder and non-negligent man-slaughter	Forcible rape	Robbery	Aggravated assault	Burglary	Larceny-theft	Motor vehicle theft	Arson[1]
WASHINGTON										
Benton	881	897	0	11	3	72	210	524	61	16
Clark	4,736	4,778	2	48	83	148	1,021	2,978	456	42
Franklin	213	214	0	0	1	9	69	117	17	1
King	10,256	10,477	14	94	197	398	2,342	5,372	1,839	221
Kitsap	5,000	5,041	0	86	44	317	1,255	2,962	336	41
Pierce	12,483	12,579	7	104	145	752	2,697	7,101	1,677	96
Snohomish	7,718	7,798	4	186	98	306	1,825	3,586	1,713	80
Spokane	8,179	8,243	0	60	98	293	1,644	5,337	747	64
Thurston	3,500	3,535	2	53	26	247	886	2,018	268	35
Whatcom	2,204	2,215	1	62	11	89	741	1,125	175	11
Yakima	2,964	3,027	5	35	23	62	1,216	1,257	366	63
WEST VIRGINIA										
Berkeley-Martinsburg State Police	856	862	2	6	12	89	227	427	93	6
Cabell	778	782	0	3	11	1	92	615	56	4
Jefferson	120	120	0	2	2	12	28	76	0	0
Jefferson-Kearneysville State Police	361	365	0	4	4	23	59	227	44	4
Mineral	58	58	0	0	0	9	13	29	7	0
Mineral-Keyser State Police	204	207	1	1	2	21	59	107	13	3
Putnam	789	797	0	12	5	40	205	468	59	8
Putnam-Teays Valley State Police	86	86	0	0	0	3	16	61	6	0
WISCONSIN										
Brown	1,503	1,509	3	17	9	20	307	1,073	74	6
Calumet	169	172	0	0	1	3	31	130	4	3
Chippewa	369	369	0	3	2	12	59	262	31	0
Douglas	324	326	0	2	1	4	150	147	20	2
Eau Claire	385	386	0	2	0	6	75	289	13	1
Kenosha	808	811	2	9	6	21	159	549	62	3
La Crosse	198	199	0	2	1	9	35	139	12	1
Marathon	489	493	0	2	2	30	118	327	10	4
Milwaukee	129	129	0	2	4	25	6	89	3	0
Outagamie	462	464	0	9	0	3	96	328	26	2
Pierce	250	250	0	0	2	3	99	123	23	0
Racine	715	716	0	3	10	5	102	564	31	1
Rock	580	586	0	6	0	41	188	310	35	6
Sheboygan	607	607	0	2	1	30	99	448	27	0
St. Croix	491	500	0	3	0	6	145	281	56	9
Washington	717	735	1	6	1	13	112	549	35	18
Waukesha	751	754	0	1	5	53	92	570	30	3
WYOMING										
Laramie	754	760	0	25	7	38	98	559	27	6
Natrona	413	414	1	0	1	17	107	249	38	1

[1] The Modified Crime Index is the sum of the seven offenses making up the Crime Index, with the addition of arson. If the FBI does not receive 12 months of arson data from either the agency or the state, no arson or Modified Crime Index will be shown.

[2] Due to changes in reporting practices, annexations, and/or incomplete data, figures are not comparable to previous years' data.

[3] Limited data for 2002 were available for Illinois and Kentucky.

Table 11

Offenses Known to Law Enforcement
by Rural County 25,000 and over in Population, 2002

[The data shown in this table do not reflect county totals but are the number of offenses reported by the sheriff's office, county police department, or state police.]

County by state	Crime Index	Modified Crime Index[1]	Murder and non-negligent man-slaughter	Forcible rape	Robbery	Aggravated assault	Burglary	Larceny-theft	Motor vehicle theft	Arson[1]
ALABAMA										
Chilton	812		0	8	4	321	159	307	13	
Cullman	2,228		1	32	10	66	551	1,372	196	
Dallas	707		0	6	11	71	232	332	55	
Jackson	696		3	6	4	41	237	318	87	
Marshall	387		2	9	4	37	118	185	32	
Walker	1,091		0	0	13	23	458	496	101	
ARIZONA										
Apache	273	273	0	3	2	71	66	128	3	0
Cochise	1,663	1,671	2	9	14	496	321	628	193	8
Navajo	666	680	0	4	1	57	293	256	55	14
Yavapai	2,574	2,583	7	9	8	362	698	1,271	219	9
ARKANSAS										
Garland	301	301	1	7	8	42	52	124	67	0
Independence	1,462	1,464	2	2	4	29	404	966	55	2
Pope	386	391	0	3	1	20	113	223	26	5
White	778	782	4	3	3	36	208	426	98	4
CALIFORNIA										
Calaveras	907	911	2	10	6	164	295	424	6	4
Calaveras Highway Patrol	175	175	0	0	0	1	0	34	140	0
Humboldt	1,280	1,311	7	26	25	126	344	742	10	31
Humboldt Highway Patrol	236	236	0	0	0	0	0	21	215	0
Imperial	868	894	0	7	11	112	236	472	30	26
Imperial Highway Patrol	144	144	0	0	0	0	0	15	129	0
Kings	491	495	1	10	9	49	213	203	6	4
Kings Highway Patrol	189	189	0	0	0	0	0	28	161	0
Lake	1,075	1,080	1	9	14	159	409	475	8	5
Lake Highway Patrol	115	115	0	0	0	0	0	28	87	0
Mendocino	1,265	1,282	3	27	14	242	459	509	11	17
Mendocino Highway Patrol	104	104	0	0	0	1	0	22	81	0
Nevada	1,118	1,123	3	15	6	81	351	650	12	5
Nevada Highway Patrol	110	110	0	0	0	0	0	17	93	0
Tehama	681	696	1	9	4	73	221	371	2	15
Tehama Highway Patrol	65	65	0	0	0	0	0	0	65	0
Tuolumne	1,038	1,062	2	13	13	90	530	386	4	24
Tuolumne Highway Patrol	185	185	0	0	1	2	0	25	157	0
COLORADO										
Eagle	584	587	0	6	0	30	59	479	10	3
Fremont	230	235	1	3	1	17	64	138	6	5
La Plata	435	435	0	14	3	14	127	254	23	0
DELAWARE										
Sussex State Police	3,042	3,045	5	77	49	446	719	1,601	145	3
FLORIDA										
Citrus	2,369	2,374	4	24	15	280	681	1,231	134	5
Columbia	1,588	1,595	5	12	24	187	548	677	135	7
Desoto	768	772	0	2	23	110	276	295	62	4
Hendry	925	925	2	11	35	139	245	405	88	0
Highlands	2,154	2,164	4	17	53	169	754	987	170	10
Indian River	3,175	3,190	1	49	45	210	634	2,064	172	15
Jackson	799	800	2	18	14	116	216	403	30	1
Levy	1,035	1,052	0	21	6	143	384	433	48	17
Monroe	2,992	3,001	2	11	39	245	468	2,076	151	9
Okeechobee	1,091	1,093	1	14	27	159	296	521	73	2
Putnam	2,803	2,812	1	61	40	480	1,061	983	177	9

See footnotes at end of table.

Table 11

Offenses Known to Law Enforcement
by Rural County 25,000 and over in Population, 2002—Continued

[The data shown in this table do not reflect county totals but are the number of offenses reported by the sheriff's office, county police department, or state police.]

County by state	Crime Index	Modified Crime Index[1]	Murder and non-negligent man-slaughter	Forcible rape	Robbery	Aggravated assault	Burglary	Larceny-theft	Motor vehicle theft	Arson[1]
FLORIDA—Continued										
Sumter	1,038	1,042	1	16	27	127	287	491	89	4
Suwannee	860	864	1	8	16	128	234	414	59	4
Walton	939	939	0	1	8	83	323	487	37	0
GEORGIA										
Baldwin	717		3	1	14	51	231	390	27	
Bulloch	860	860	2	2	12	43	175	575	51	0
Coffee	738	747	1	1	8	44	186	478	20	9
Colquitt	964	965	1	2	4	260	173	449	75	1
Floyd County Police Department	1,551		1	0	19	62	326	1,013	130	
Glynn County Police Department	4,408	4,414	2	2	62	248	502	3,419	173	6
Habersham	377	378	0	5	3	33	121	179	36	1
Hall	2,918	2,930	10	25	19	171	653	1,695	345	12
Jackson	753	760	5	1	4	30	235	415	63	7
Laurens	577	578	0	11	5	50	151	317	43	1
Liberty	712		3	4	14	37	161	463	30	
Lowndes	1,290		3	13	18	71	292	825	68	
Murray	838	838	1	1	2	79	255	433	67	0
Troup	1,003		0	2	6	20	112	823	40	
Whitfield	2,669	2,696	0	19	21	116	613	1,631	269	27
HAWAII										
Hawaii Police Department	6,936	6,985	5	35	48	133	1,539	4,663	513	49
Kauai Police Department	3,045	3,048	1	23	17	138	726	2,015	125	3
Maui Police Department[2]	7,986	8,032	0	10	73	178	1,525	5,416	784	46
IDAHO										
Bingham	234	237	0	6	0	13	58	139	18	3
Bonner	553	554	0	6	1	52	132	323	39	1
Bonneville	782	785	0	20	1	25	171	510	55	3
Kootenai	1,311	1,326	2	15	5	86	392	723	88	15
ILLINOIS[3]										
INDIANA										
Bartholomew	205	206	1	3	0	10	29	152	10	1
Bartholomew State Police	26	26	0	1	0	6	3	11	5	0
Grant	402	406	0	1	3	5	105	261	27	4
Grant State Police	8	8	0	1	0	2	1	2	2	0
Henry	833	833	0	4	2	9	224	548	46	0
Henry State Police	30	30	0	0	1	4	1	18	6	0
Kosciusko	917	921	0	5	4	5	193	681	29	4
Kosciusko State Police	42	42	0	0	1	6	8	20	7	0
LaGrange	193	193	1	1	1	8	54	110	18	0
LaGrange State Police	41	41	0	0	0	4	1	34	2	0
La Porte	981	984	2	8	6	30	241	635	59	3
La Porte State Police	64	65	1	1	1	8	1	35	17	1
Lawrence	275	279	0	1	1	2	100	154	17	4
Lawrence State Police	24	24	0	3	3	1	4	10	3	0
Putnam	533	536	0	3	4	150	160	177	39	3
Putnam State Police	76	77	0	1	0	11	11	40	13	1
Steuben	618	621	0	8	2	19	120	443	26	3
Steuben State Police	49	49	0	0	0	8	8	27	6	0
KANSAS										
Riley County Police Department	1,837	1,840	2	32	15	147	463	1,116	62	3
KENTUCKY[3]										

See footnotes at end of table.

Table 11

Offenses Known to Law Enforcement

by Rural County 25,000 and over in Population, 2002—Continued

[The data shown in this table do not reflect county totals but are the number of offenses reported by the sheriff's office, county police department, or state police.]

County by state	Crime Index	Modified Crime Index[1]	Murder and non-negligent man-slaughter	Forcible rape	Robbery	Aggravated assault	Burglary	Larceny-theft	Motor vehicle theft	Arson[1]
LOUISIANA										
Tangipahoa	3,081	3,085	8	21	57	517	1,011	1,355	112	4
Vermilion	342	342	2	5	2	45	68	201	19	0
MAINE										
Aroostook	124	125	0	0	0	0	57	60	7	1
Aroostook State Police	324	325	0	12	0	11	149	132	20	1
Hancock	244	244	0	0	0	2	59	171	12	0
Hancock State Police	182	182	0	4	1	5	69	94	9	0
Kennebec	352	352	0	3	0	2	86	235	26	0
Kennebec State Police	202	202	0	0	1	6	54	127	14	0
Penobscot	556	557	0	2	2	3	177	342	30	1
Penobscot State Police	408	408	0	11	2	7	149	216	23	0
Somerset	346	347	0	2	0	16	158	159	11	1
Somerset State Police	55	55	0	0	0	0	17	33	5	0
Waldo	292	292	0	5	2	13	72	179	21	0
Waldo State Police	61	61	1	0	0	0	22	35	3	0
York	466	468	0	0	2	12	174	241	37	2
York State Police	160	160	0	0	2	4	61	72	21	0
MARYLAND										
Garrett	261	261	0	0	0	20	45	188	8	0
Garrett State Police	196	198	0	2	1	21	45	116	11	2
St. Mary's	1,672	1,689	3	10	27	213	282	1,046	91	17
St. Mary's State Police	413	437	0	6	5	110	62	188	42	24
Wicomico	1,013	1,013	1	16	30	143	283	500	40	0
Wicomico State Police	424	445	1	4	16	62	121	183	37	21
MICHIGAN										
Barry	272	275	0	14	2	30	53	153	20	3
Barry State Police	579	583	1	17	1	42	204	275	39	4
Branch	153	155	0	6	0	11	43	91	2	2
Branch State Police	346	356	0	19	1	29	110	170	17	10
Cass	897	918	2	10	5	26	311	484	59	21
Cass State Police	98	103	0	4	1	6	26	53	8	5
Clare	861	867	1	6	3	63	345	405	38	6
Clare State Police	140	145	0	15	1	12	47	58	7	5
Grand Traverse	1,350	1,356	2	20	2	79	209	990	48	6
Grand Traverse State Police	333	335	0	16	0	17	45	244	11	2
Hillsdale	291	293	0	13	0	26	87	145	20	2
Hillsdale State Police	293	296	0	16	1	39	93	127	17	3
Ionia	409	413	0	12	1	18	102	245	31	4
Ionia State Police	442	448	0	31	1	34	130	222	24	6
Isabella	560	565	0	8	4	39	152	329	28	5
Isabella State Police	410	412	0	11	3	15	149	215	17	2
Mecosta	743	752	0	17	1	42	270	374	39	9
Mecosta State Police	114	116	0	10	0	8	48	44	4	2
Montcalm	599	603	1	23	0	40	176	301	58	4
Montcalm State Police	463	477	0	38	1	35	156	189	44	14
Newaygo	487	490	1	24	3	46	194	190	29	3
Newaygo State Police	438	443	1	20	0	25	137	229	26	5
Sanilac	273	285	0	5	1	15	62	166	24	12
Sanilac State Police	241	246	0	14	0	29	86	100	12	5
Shiawassee	528	535	1	27	3	46	103	319	29	7
Shiawassee State Police	268	272	0	6	3	19	63	156	21	4
St. Joseph	562	565	0	11	4	36	188	311	12	3
St. Joseph State Police	370	385	0	18	0	35	116	175	26	15
Tuscola	240	242	0	6	0	23	73	118	20	2
Tuscola State Police	263	267	0	35	0	22	70	103	33	4

See footnotes at end of table.

Table 11

Offenses Known to Law Enforcement
by Rural County 25,000 and over in Population, 2002—Continued

[The data shown in this table do not reflect county totals but are the number of offenses reported by the sheriff's office, county police department, or state police.]

County by state	Crime Index	Modified Crime Index[1]	Murder and non-negligent man-slaughter	Forcible rape	Robbery	Aggravated assault	Burglary	Larceny-theft	Motor vehicle theft	Arson[1]
MINNESOTA										
Beltrami	383	385	0	4	2	22	101	202	52	2
Cass	1,373	1,376	2	49	6	27	429	734	126	3
Crow Wing	830	830	1	8	1	16	294	452	58	0
Itasca	516	521	1	1	2	27	177	255	53	5
Otter Tail	660	663	1	18	1	30	181	375	54	3
Pine	1,137	1,142	0	30	8	38	341	609	111	5
MISSISSIPPI										
Lauderdale	586	586	3	8	16	12	250	260	37	0
Lee	693	703	0	6	9	44	300	298	36	10
Lowndes	794	804	1	14	13	52	265	418	31	10
Marshall	624	627	3	9	17	83	201	242	69	3
Panola	454	454	1	2	7	109	166	161	8	0
Pontotoc	195	195	0	0	3	0	71	105	16	0
MISSOURI										
Camden	499	502	1	7	0	39	149	284	19	3
Cole	352	352	1	9	1	60	80	186	15	0
Johnson	302	306	1	0	0	29	108	136	28	4
Pulaski	320	320	0	1	2	49	105	138	25	0
St. Francois	495	504	1	5	3	52	91	280	63	9
Taney	745	746	4	15	2	116	218	372	18	1
MONTANA										
Ravalli	378		0	8	1	88	58	202	21	
Silver Bow	1,693		2	19	11	133	213	1,206	109	
NEVADA										
Carson City	2,073	2,090	1	29	31	242	394	1,233	143	17
Douglas	964	968	1	0	13	45	199	650	56	4
Lyon	666	671	0	8	1	62	160	388	47	5
NEW MEXICO										
San Juan	1,291	1,298	3	38	8	175	238	752	77	7
NEW YORK										
Allegany	12		0	0	0	6	2	4	0	
Allegany State Police	313		0	11	1	36	123	140	2	
Cattaraugus	428		0	7	2	22	131	249	17	
Cattaraugus State Police	356		0	3	4	35	86	217	11	
Chenango	510		1	1	3	77	113	311	4	
Chenango State Police	217		0	2	2	16	58	130	9	
Clinton State Police	936		2	15	8	149	241	505	16	
Columbia	266		0	0	0	8	62	193	3	
Columbia State Police	340		0	1	3	26	82	223	5	
Cortland	349		0	4	1	19	49	270	6	
Cortland State Police	277		0	0	3	18	34	218	4	
Delaware	160		0	9	1	5	37	101	7	
Delaware State Police	379		0	3	1	58	122	183	12	
Essex	4		0	0	0	2	0	2	0	
Essex State Police	457		2	3	0	43	147	251	11	
Franklin State Police	436		1	3	3	108	137	177	7	
Fulton	384		0	3	1	13	72	274	21	
Fulton State Police	139		0	1	1	12	18	105	2	
Greene State Police	460		0	3	1	66	144	230	16	
Jefferson	477		0	10	2	26	100	329	10	
Jefferson State Police	623		0	37	0	59	103	411	13	
Otsego State Police	516		0	6	3	82	70	347	8	
Steuben	313		0	0	1	9	87	208	8	

See footnotes at end of table.

Table 11

Offenses Known to Law Enforcement
by Rural County 25,000 and over in Population, 2002—Continued

[The data shown in this table do not reflect county totals but are the number of offenses reported by the sheriff's office, county police department, or state police.]

County by state	Crime Index	Modified Crime Index[1]	Murder and non-negligent man-slaughter	Forcible rape	Robbery	Aggravated assault	Burglary	Larceny-theft	Motor vehicle theft	Arson[1]
NEW YORK—Continued										
Steuben State Police	500		0	14	7	54	132	277	16	
St. Lawrence	384		0	1	0	31	49	280	23	
St. Lawrence State Police	531		1	26	2	88	158	243	13	
Sullivan	570		0	7	2	30	115	400	16	
Sullivan State Police	501		0	10	6	66	162	240	17	
Tompkins	590		0	16	4	5	109	439	17	
Tompkins State Police	275		1	4	2	47	48	166	7	
Ulster State Police	791		0	11	9	166	169	414	22	
Wyoming	571		0	2	1	23	368	163	14	
Wyoming State Police	104		0	3	1	24	20	49	7	
NORTH CAROLINA										
Beaufort	965	971	0	7	18	59	355	474	52	6
Bladen	1,183	1,189	2	6	20	197	415	489	54	6
Carteret	716	718	1	7	6	42	238	372	50	2
Cleveland[2]			0	11	49		671	1,073	112	4
Columbus	2,021	2,030	4	14	28	284	822	791	78	9
Craven	1,396	1,401	0	13	26	118	373	820	46	5
Duplin	1,058	1,072	4	2	13	100	435	432	72	14
Granville	861	864	2	4	10	27	393	352	73	3
Halifax	1,048	1,051	4	9	19	50	499	393	74	3
Harnett	3,433	3,461	5	24	47	292	1,388	1,479	198	28
Haywood	791	793	0	4	3	59	281	399	45	2
Henderson	1,152	1,159	4	25	12	34	409	586	82	7
Hoke	1,377	1,401	2	11	29	82	561	568	124	24
Iredell	2,164	2,184	1	15	26	112	649	1,239	122	20
Lee	834	848	2	7	2	3	414	335	71	14
Lenoir	1,103	1,110	5	2	15	71	425	542	43	7
Macon	475	477	0	0	0	6	220	228	21	2
McDowell	613	617	4	6	2	29	232	298	42	4
Moore	1,136	1,146	6	0	14	45	587	399	85	10
Robeson	2,663	2,697	25	9	95	318	1,187	679	350	34
Rockingham	1,689	1,692	2	2	14	112	678	833	48	3
Rutherford[2]	1,040	1,045	2	7	11	68	386	499	67	5
Stanly	969	972	0	5	7	51	439	431	36	3
Surry	1,455	1,468	4	6	10	156	506	611	162	13
Vance	1,671	1,686	2	5	19	107	824	642	72	15
Watauga	603	604	0	1	1	34	267	272	28	1
Wilkes	1,001	1,003	5	3	9	78	346	472	88	2
Wilson	744	750	0	0	15	59	268	368	34	6
OHIO										
Champaign	495	503	1	4	0	15	153	305	17	8
Coshocton	705	706	0	0	2	1	74	605	23	1
Darke	259	269	0	2	1	15	100	128	13	10
Erie	478	485	0	1	3	28	158	256	32	7
Gallia	777	785	1	9	5	5	326	380	51	8
Highland	404	408	0	1	0	34	115	233	21	4
Huron	363	364	1	1	3	17	128	186	27	1
Logan	446	446	0	2	0	25	122	267	30	0
Marion	1,041	1,050	0	4	7	17	275	695	43	9
Morrow	314	315	0	1	1	11	111	163	27	1
Muskingum	1,397	1,404	3	11	13	5	372	865	128	7
Perry	343	347	0	3	0	2	140	174	24	4
Preble	482	484	0	19	2	44	122	254	41	2
Shelby	232	235	0	0	0	2	56	165	9	3
Tuscarawas	279	282	0	8	2	12	100	131	26	3
Williams	292	295	0	4	2	4	78	188	16	3
OKLAHOMA										
Cherokee	339	343	1	2	1	68	122	117	28	4
Delaware	419	428	2	3	1	34	184	147	48	9

See footnotes at end of table.

Table 11

Offenses Known to Law Enforcement

by Rural County 25,000 and over in Population, 2002—Continued

[The data shown in this table do not reflect county totals but are the number of offenses reported by the sheriff's office, county police department, or state police.]

County by state	Crime Index	Modified Crime Index[1]	Murder and non-negligent man-slaughter	Forcible rape	Robbery	Aggravated assault	Burglary	Larceny-theft	Motor vehicle theft	Arson[1]
OKLAHOMA—Continued										
Le Flore	310	312	1	13	0	50	105	91	50	2
Mayes	425	425	0	4	0	53	164	159	45	0
OREGON										
Deschutes	870	881	1	11	1	6	199	610	42	11
Douglas	1,384	1,388	0	8	3	22	389	854	108	4
Josephine	800	806	0	12	6	9	237	465	71	6
Klamath	1,014	1,020	2	13	18	47	276	587	71	6
Linn	1,320	1,327	0	5	3	1	379	836	96	7
PENNSYLVANIA										
Adams State Police	529	539	3	15	4	27	130	313	37	10
Armstrong State Police	400	405	0	8	6	21	136	195	34	5
Bedford State Police	723	728	3	9	3	24	204	441	39	5
Bradford State Police	586	601	0	13	1	16	223	283	50	15
Clarion State Police	564	570	1	14	1	22	157	332	37	6
Clearfield State Police	672	683	1	19	5	44	174	363	66	11
Crawford State Police	808	818	3	14	7	28	348	340	68	10
Franklin State Police	1,044	1,058	1	14	13	45	248	658	65	14
Greene State Police	526	542	3	10	5	12	180	273	43	16
Huntingdon State Police	430	432	2	14	8	43	135	197	31	2
Jefferson State Police	378	390	1	12	3	57	118	163	24	12
Lawrence State Police	745	860	0	5	8	44	207	411	70	115
Monroe State Police	1,267	1,280	1	17	13	73	368	688	107	13
Northumberland State Police	405	409	0	7	3	20	108	246	21	4
Schuylkill State Police	1,237	1,261	1	14	6	338	181	589	108	24
Snyder State Police	345	349	0	6	5	17	52	245	20	4
Susquehanna State Police	571	577	0	2	5	47	147	312	58	6
Tioga State Police	315	318	0	7	0	8	103	179	18	3
Union State Police	323	324	0	4	7	26	111	155	20	1
Venango State Police	570	577	0	11	4	18	180	325	32	7
Wayne State Police	691	711	0	24	1	46	189	364	67	20
SOUTH CAROLINA										
Beaufort	4,797		8	58	109	495	1,233	2,482	412	
Chester	1,171		1	9	23	142	252	681	63	
Chesterfield	1,107		4	12	7	190	370	439	85	
Clarendon	714		2	8	25	141	214	266	58	
Colleton	1,361	1,388	1	18	36	254	328	612	112	27
Darlington	2,357		5	32	46	315	630	1,129	200	
Georgetown	1,689	1,698	4	22	22	183	459	896	103	9
Greenwood	1,395		3	12	17	243	250	810	60	
Kershaw	1,454		1	37	19	200	371	705	121	
Lancaster	2,283	2,294	3	30	33	214	743	1,178	82	11
Laurens	1,934		1	22	31	331	455	981	113	
Oconee	1,375		4	21	8	203	359	679	101	
Orangeburg	3,891	3,905	7	30	114	659	1,095	1,678	308	14
Williamsburg	879		4	21	28	191	225	317	93	
TENNESSEE										
Bradley	1,370	1,375	2	12	5	172	372	708	99	5
Campbell	713	715	1	4	0	93	114	450	51	2
Claiborne	438	445	0	0	2	43	162	191	40	7
Cocke	828	841	7	3	11	115	279	306	107	13
Greene	1,318	1,335	1	11	13	201	422	542	128	17
Hamblen	686	694	1	7	7	78	184	354	55	8
Jefferson	799	807	1	6	6	91	253	363	79	8
Lawrence	581	593	1	7	1	90	188	249	45	12
Maury	835	839	2	23	9	102	167	461	71	4
McMinn	900	903	0	8	5	169	286	373	59	3
Monroe	885	899	0	16	6	220	189	386	68	14

See footnotes at end of table.

Table 11

Offenses Known to Law Enforcement
by Rural County 25,000 and over in Population, 2002—Continued

[The data shown in this table do not reflect county totals but are the number of offenses reported by the sheriff's office, county police department, or state police.]

County by state	Crime Index	Modified Crime Index[1]	Murder and non-negligent man-slaughter	Forcible rape	Robbery	Aggravated assault	Burglary	Larceny-theft	Motor vehicle theft	Arson[1]
TENNESSEE—Continued										
Putnam	687	690	0	6	2	59	154	412	54	3
Roane	791	801	0	4	0	76	293	351	67	10
Warren	459	463	2	1	2	54	121	230	49	4
TEXAS										
Anderson	628	630	3	9	6	54	283	255	18	2
Angelina	1,015	1,015	3	8	3	286	321	349	45	0
Cherokee	570	573	2	16	2	88	245	177	40	3
Jasper	665	665	0	6	3	60	234	339	23	0
Maverick	519	521	2	0	2	66	177	242	30	2
Medina	447	448	1	11	5	48	169	179	34	1
Nacogdoches	498	499	2	17	1	51	166	246	15	1
Polk	652	656	1	3	10	52	222	322	42	4
Rusk	650	652	0	15	2	83	234	292	24	2
Starr	407	412	3	4	9	51	195	105	40	5
Van Zandt	943	946	1	3	4	85	368	376	106	3
Walker	479	479	1	13	4	51	151	217	42	0
Wise	657	657	0	14	1	91	222	253	76	0
Wood	612	622	2	10	0	26	251	319	4	10
UTAH										
Cache	383	383	0	8	1	17	52	286	19	0
Washington	484	484	0	9	1	52	76	303	43	0
VERMONT										
Rutland State Police	540	544	0	1	2	13	184	325	15	4
St. Albans State Police	843	853	1	19	0	26	277	405	115	10
VIRGINIA										
Accomack	508	508	0	7	34	44	131	252	40	0
Accomack State Police	11	11	0	0	0	2	1	4	4	0
Buchanan	580	587	1	5	8	34	197	298	37	7
Buchanan State Police	73	75	6	1	1	0	14	44	7	2
Carroll	366	372	1	5	3	24	97	212	24	6
Carroll State Police	26	26	0	0	0	0	0	25	1	0
Franklin	516	517	2	7	5	27	81	371	23	1
Franklin State Police	11	11	1	0	0	1	0	6	3	0
Halifax	313	316	8	3	12	28	61	177	24	3
Halifax State Police	18	18	1	1	1	1	1	8	5	0
Henry	1,795	1,810	7	19	40	126	323	1,180	100	15
Henry State Police	28	28	0	0	0	8	1	9	10	0
Montgomery	502	507	1	5	2	23	137	310	24	5
Montgomery State Police	17	17	0	0	1	1	0	10	5	0
Rockingham	259	259	1	12	3	13	73	144	13	0
Rockingham State Police	38	38	0	0	0	3	4	12	19	0
Russell	339	343	0	2	0	4	74	236	23	4
Russell State Police	11	12	1	0	0	0	2	5	3	1
Tazewell	736	749	1	9	6	43	202	435	40	13
Tazewell State Police	26	26	0	0	1	1	1	18	5	0
Wise	453	460	0	5	2	51	123	238	34	7
Wise State Police	9	9	0	0	0	1	1	3	4	0
WASHINGTON										
Chelan	972	974	0	9	5	13	168	743	34	2
Clallam	847	854	0	7	5	30	263	482	60	7
Cowlitz	1,267	1,277	3	10	4	69	381	707	93	10
Douglas	722	723	1	6	2	18	149	502	44	1
Grant	1,414	1,427	1	18	15	49	349	846	136	13
Grays Harbor	427	437	3	0	2	24	171	195	32	10
Lewis	948	958	1	22	5	61	313	494	52	10

See footnotes at end of table.

Table 11

Offenses Known to Law Enforcement
by Rural County 25,000 and over in Population, 2002—Continued

[The data shown in this table do not reflect county totals but are the number of offenses reported by the sheriff's office, county police department, or state police.]

County by state	Crime Index	Modified Crime Index[1]	Murder and non-negligent man-slaughter	Forcible rape	Robbery	Aggravated assault	Burglary	Larceny-theft	Motor vehicle theft	Arson[1]
WASHINGTON—Continued										
Mason	1,894	1,905	3	47	11	67	621	943	202	11
Skagit	1,737	1,740	2	18	6	33	489	1,069	120	3
Stevens	513	514	3	3	3	6	162	299	37	1
WEST VIRGINIA										
Harrison	258	263	4	0	1	44	55	140	14	5
Harrison-Bridgeport State Police	196	200	0	0	1	13	22	149	11	4
Logan	108	109	0	1	1	3	23	73	7	1
Logan-Logan State Police	647	656	1	3	6	96	150	333	58	9
Monongalia	424	425	1	2	5	33	75	283	25	1
Monongalia-Morgantown State Police	532	536	0	2	5	21	170	271	63	4
WISCONSIN										
Barron	797	802	0	11	2	61	403	298	22	5
Clark	224	225	1	2	4	9	63	123	22	1
Columbia	408	411	0	1	0	16	102	263	26	3
Dodge	363	369	0	2	0	19	86	231	25	6
Fond du Lac	319	321	0	1	0	7	46	235	30	2
Grant	240	243	0	0	0	25	75	122	18	3
Jefferson	537	544	1	15	2	18	103	356	42	7
Manitowoc	358	362	0	16	1	22	85	208	26	4
Oconto	472	473	3	0	0	10	230	211	18	1
Polk	400	408	1	3	0	7	181	170	38	8
Portage	388	390	0	6	1	0	110	261	10	2
Sauk	667	670	0	0	3	16	108	499	41	3
Shawanno	568	569	0	6	1	16	126	395	24	1
Walworth	353	356	1	7	2	11	84	232	16	3
Waupaca	356	356	0	4	1	6	68	268	9	0
Wood	440	441	0	0	1	6	120	298	15	1
STATE AGENCIES										
Alaska State Police	4,894	4,950	10	116	30	570	1,319	2,276	573	56
Arizona Department of Public Safety	14	14	0	0	1	8	0	5	0	0
District of Columbia Metro Transit Police	1,426	1,429	0	0	103	108	3	782	430	3
Kansas Highway Patrol	110	113	0	0	0	18	0	66	26	3
Minnesota State Patrol	4	4	0	0	0	1	0	0	3	0
Nebraska State Patrol	0	0	0	0	0	0	0	0	0	0
New Mexico State Police	1,742	1,757	13	64	18	232	724	357	334	15
Port Authority of New York and New Jersey[4]	853	854	0	0	22	33	15	747	36	1
Port Authority of New York and New Jersey[5]	1,455		0	2	41	117	20	1,254	21	
Rhode Island State Police	70	70	3	14	1	15	2	23	12	0
OTHER AGENCIES										
American Samoa	492	494	6	22	2	124	235	98	5	2
National Institutes of Health	187	187	0	0	0	0	9	178	0	0
United States Department of the Interior:										
Bureau of Indian Affairs	28,482	29,234	106	1,219	186	9,892	4,585	9,752	2,742	752
Bureau of Land Management	749	838	3	0	0	3	42	641	60	89
Bureau of Reclamation	16	16	0	0	0	0	5	7	4	0
Fish and Wildlife Service	340	419	2	3	0	18	118	169	30	79
National Park Service	3,773	3,871	9	44	47	257	456	2,812	148	98

[1] The Modified Crime Index is the sum of the seven offenses making up the Crime Index, with the addition of arson. If the FBI does not receive 12 months of arson data from either the agency or the state, no arson or Modified Crime Index will be shown.

[2] Due to changes in reporting practices, annexations, and/or incomplete data, figures are not comparable to previous years' data.

[3] Limited data for 2002 were available for Illinois and Kentucky.

[4] Figures reported are the number of crimes occurring in New Jersey.

[5] Figures reported are the number of crimes occurring in New York.

Table 12

Crime Trends[1]
by Population Group, 2001-2002
[2002 estimated population]

Population group	Crime Index	Modified Crime Index[2]	Violent crime[3]	Property crime[4]	Murder and non-negligent man-slaughter	Forcible rape[5]	Robbery	Aggravated assault	Burglary	Larceny-theft	Motor vehicle theft	Arson
TOTAL ALL AGENCIES: **12,270 agencies;** **population 255,383,586**												
2001	10,781,626	10,857,692	1,327,864	9,453,762	14,888	80,223	400,324	832,429	1,915,952	6,394,800	1,143,010	76,066
2002	10,758,229	10,831,504	1,308,757	9,449,472	15,031	83,631	395,474	814,621	1,942,577	6,350,026	1,156,869	73,275
Percent change	-0.2	-0.2	-1.4	*	+1.0	+4.2	-1.2	-2.1	+1.4	-0.7	+1.2	-3.7
TOTAL CITIES: 8,618 cities; **population 171,734,038**												
2001	8,565,743	8,622,380	1,072,524	7,493,219	11,823	59,203	356,474	645,024	1,407,365	5,138,943	946,911	56,637
2002	8,523,610	8,578,483	1,052,260	7,471,350	11,750	61,551	350,974	627,985	1,420,872	5,101,814	948,664	54,873
Percent change	-0.5	-0.5	-1.9	-0.3	-0.6	+4.0	-1.5	-2.6	+1.0	-0.7	+0.2	-3.1
GROUP I												
69 cities, 250,000 and over; population 51,949,588												
2001	3,255,232	3,280,207	546,105	2,709,127	6,880	21,373	209,681	308,171	517,254	1,709,386	482,487	24,975
2002	3,220,348	3,244,348	532,902	2,687,446	6,823	21,773	205,183	299,123	515,935	1,692,484	479,027	24,000
Percent change	-1.1	-1.1	-2.4	-0.8	-0.8	+1.9	-2.1	-2.9	-0.3	-1.0	-0.7	-3.9
10 cities, 1,000,000 and over; population 24,682,265												
2001	1,298,118	1,306,349	262,710	1,035,408	3,222	7,239	103,827	148,422	188,589	648,583	198,236	8,231
2002	1,288,482	1,296,368	257,755	1,030,727	3,090	7,385	102,672	144,608	188,526	645,634	196,567	7,886
Percent change	-0.7	-0.8	-1.9	-0.5	-4.1	+2.0	-1.1	-2.6	*	-0.5	-0.8	-4.2
21 cities, 500,000 to 999,999; population 13,963,253												
2001	1,014,346	1,021,919	146,304	868,042	1,911	7,038	53,223	84,132	169,262	554,602	144,178	7,573
2002	1,005,707	1,013,362	140,595	865,112	1,926	7,303	50,280	81,086	169,540	552,076	143,496	7,655
Percent change	-0.9	-0.8	-3.9	-0.3	+0.8	+3.8	-5.5	-3.6	+0.2	-0.5	-0.5	+1.1
38 cities, 250,000 to 499,999; population 13,304,070												
2001	942,768	951,939	137,091	805,677	1,747	7,096	52,631	75,617	159,403	506,201	140,073	9,171
2002	926,159	934,618	134,552	791,607	1,807	7,085	52,231	73,429	157,869	494,774	138,964	8,459
Percent change	-1.8	-1.8	-1.9	-1.7	+3.4	-0.2	-0.8	-2.9	-1.0	-2.3	-0.8	-7.8
GROUP II												
166 cities, 100,000 to 249,999; population 24,834,622												
2001	1,398,173	1,407,385	158,920	1,239,253	1,850	9,252	55,373	92,445	241,215	837,554	160,484	9,212
2002	1,409,516	1,418,791	156,772	1,252,744	1,906	10,066	54,243	90,557	245,410	844,408	162,926	9,275
Percent change	+0.8	+0.8	-1.4	+1.1	+3.0	+8.8	-2.0	-2.0	+1.7	+0.8	+1.5	+0.7
GROUP III												
387 cities, 50,000 to 99,999; population 26,758,653												
2001	1,188,578	1,196,027	129,564	1,059,014	1,118	9,190	38,967	80,289	204,585	735,536	118,893	7,449
2002	1,195,535	1,202,579	128,209	1,067,326	1,198	9,456	38,858	78,697	205,909	739,275	122,142	7,044
Percent change	+0.6	+0.5	-1.0	+0.8	+7.2	+2.9	-0.3	-2.0	+0.6	+0.5	+2.7	-5.4
GROUP IV												
701 cities, 25,000 to 49,999; population 24,448,049												
2001	1,001,664	1,007,404	92,139	909,525	766	7,435	24,776	59,162	166,915	662,089	80,521	5,740
2002	989,433	995,103	90,670	898,763	763	7,683	24,372	57,852	168,453	650,184	80,126	5,670
Percent change	-1.2	-1.2	-1.6	-1.2	-0.4	+3.3	-1.6	-2.2	+0.9	-1.8	-0.5	-1.2

See footnotes at end of table.

Table 12

Crime Trends[1]

by Population Group, 2001-2002—Continued

[2002 estimated population]

Population group	Crime Index	Modified Crime Index[2]	Violent crime[3]	Property crime[4]	Murder and non-negligent man-slaughter	Forcible rape[5]	Robbery	Aggravated assault	Burglary	Larceny-theft	Motor vehicle theft	Arson
GROUP V												
1,538 cities, 10,000 to 24,999; population 24,424,834												
2001	925,269	930,000	79,164	846,105	666	6,753	17,481	54,264	150,759	634,399	60,947	4,731
2002	919,341	923,915	78,131	841,210	600	7,019	18,050	52,462	154,921	624,962	61,327	4,574
Percent change	-0.6	-0.7	-1.3	-0.6	-9.9	+3.9	+3.3	-3.3	+2.8	-1.5	+0.6	-3.3
GROUP VI												
5,757 cities, under 10,000; population 19,318,292												
2001	796,827	801,357	66,632	730,195	543	5,200	10,196	50,693	126,637	559,979	43,579	4,530
2002	789,437	793,747	65,576	723,861	460	5,554	10,268	49,294	130,244	550,501	43,116	4,310
Percent change	-0.9	-0.9	-1.6	-0.9	-15.3	+6.8	+0.7	-2.8	+2.8	-1.7	-1.1	-4.9
SUBURBAN COUNTIES												
1,259 agencies; population 55,661,496												
2001	1,672,347	1,687,324	193,253	1,479,094	2,050	14,739	39,076	137,388	354,044	965,598	159,452	14,977
2002	1,688,437	1,702,611	195,127	1,493,310	2,289	15,524	39,763	137,551	363,406	959,610	170,294	14,174
Percent change	+1.0	+0.9	+1.0	+1.0	+11.7	+5.3	+1.8	+0.1	+2.6	-0.6	+6.8	-5.4
RURAL COUNTIES[6]												
2,393 agencies; population 27,988,052												
2001	543,536	547,988	62,087	481,449	1,015	6,281	4,774	50,017	154,543	290,259	36,647	4,452
2002	546,182	550,410	61,370	484,812	992	6,556	4,737	49,085	158,299	288,602	37,911	4,228
Percent change	+0.5	+0.4	-1.2	+0.7	-2.3	+4.4	-0.8	-1.9	+2.4	-0.6	+3.4	-5.0
SUBURBAN AREA[7]												
5,893 agencies; population 101,022,671												
2001	3,279,354	3,303,201	325,394	2,953,960	3,082	25,157	72,353	224,802	605,950	2,060,715	287,295	23,847
2002	3,277,268	3,300,133	323,799	2,953,469	3,259	26,079	72,917	221,544	619,687	2,035,813	297,969	22,865
Percent change	-0.1	-0.1	-0.5	*	+5.7	+3.7	+0.8	-1.4	+2.3	-1.2	+3.7	-4.1

[1] The murder and nonnegligent homicides that occurred as a result of the events of September 11, 2001, were not included in this table.

[2] The Modified Crime Index is the sum of the seven offenses making up the Crime Index, with the addition of arson.

[3] Violent crimes are offenses of murder, forcible rape, robbery, and aggravated assault.

[4] Property crimes are offenses of burglary, larceny-theft, and motor vehicle theft.

[5] Forcible rape figures furnished by the state Uniform Crime Reporting (UCR) Program administered by the Illinois State Police were not in accordance with national UCR guidelines; therefore, the figures were excluded from the forcible rape, violent crime, Crime Index, and Modified Crime Index categories.

[6] Includes state police agencies that report aggregately for the entire state.

[7] Suburban area includes law enforcement agencies in cities with less than 50,000 inhabitants and county law enforcement agencies that are within a Metropolitan Statistical Area (see Appendix III). Suburban area excludes all metropolitan agencies associated with a central city. The agencies associated with suburban areas also appear in other groups within this table.

* Less than one-tenth of 1 percent.

Table 13

Crime Trends[1]

by Suburban and Nonsuburban Cities[2] by Population Group, 2001-2002
[2002 estimated population]

Population group	Crime Index	Modified Crime Index[3]	Violent crime[4]	Property crime[5]	Murder and non-negligent man-slaughter	Forcible rape	Robbery	Aggravated assault	Burglary	Larceny-theft	Motor vehicle theft	Arson
Suburban cities												
TOTAL SUBURBAN CITIES:												
4,634 cities;												
population 45,361,175												
2001	1,607,007	1,615,877	132,141	1,474,866	1,032	10,418	33,277	87,414	251,906	1,095,117	127,843	8,870
2002	1,588,831	1,597,522	128,672	1,460,159	970	10,555	33,154	83,993	256,281	1,076,203	127,675	8,691
Percent change	-1.1	-1.1	-2.6	-1.0	-6.0	+1.3	-0.4	-3.9	+1.7	-1.7	-0.1	-2.0
GROUP IV												
477 cities, 25,000 to 49,999;												
population 16,505,891												
2001	552,379	555,411	47,485	504,894	371	3,547	14,390	29,177	89,320	362,357	53,217	3,032
2002	544,674	547,719	45,379	499,295	357	3,542	13,857	27,623	89,659	356,528	53,108	3,045
Percent change	-1.4	-1.4	-4.4	-1.1	-3.8	-0.1	-3.7	-5.3	+0.4	-1.6	-0.2	+0.4
GROUP V												
1,136 cities, 10,000 to 24,999;												
population 18,149,800												
2001	600,705	603,758	50,817	549,888	420	4,144	12,355	33,898	96,333	407,322	46,233	3,053
2002	597,248	600,284	50,240	547,008	394	4,246	12,759	32,841	98,854	401,693	46,461	3,036
Percent change	-0.6	-0.6	-1.1	-0.5	-6.2	+2.5	+3.3	-3.1	+2.6	-1.4	+0.5	-0.6
GROUP VI												
3,021 cities, under 10,000;												
population 10,705,484												
2001	453,923	456,708	33,839	420,084	241	2,727	6,532	24,339	66,253	325,438	28,393	2,785
2002	446,909	449,519	33,053	413,856	219	2,767	6,538	23,529	67,768	317,982	28,106	2,610
Percent change	-1.5	-1.6	-2.3	-1.5	-9.1	+1.5	+0.1	-3.3	+2.3	-2.3	-1.0	-6.3
Nonsuburban cities												
TOTAL NONSUBURBAN CITIES:												
3,362 cities;												
population 22,830,000												
2001	1,116,753	1,122,884	105,794	1,010,959	943	8,970	19,176	76,705	192,405	761,350	57,204	6,131
2002	1,109,380	1,115,243	105,705	1,003,675	853	9,701	19,536	75,615	197,337	749,444	56,894	5,863
Percent change	-0.7	-0.7	-0.1	-0.7	-9.5	+8.1	+1.9	-1.4	+2.6	-1.6	-0.5	-4.4
GROUP IV												
224 cities, 25,000 to 49,999;												
population 7,942,158												
2001	449,285	451,993	44,654	404,631	395	3,888	10,386	29,985	77,595	299,732	27,304	2,708
2002	444,759	447,384	45,291	399,468	406	4,141	10,515	30,229	78,794	293,656	27,018	2,625
Percent change	-1.0	-1.0	+1.4	-1.3	+2.8	+6.5	+1.2	+0.8	+1.5	-2.0	-1.0	-3.1

See footnotes at end of table.

Table 13

Crime Trends[1]
by Suburban and Nonsuburban Cities[2] by Population Group, 2001-2002—Continued
[2002 estimated population]

Population group	Crime Index	Modified Crime Index[1]	Violent crime[4]	Property crime[5]	Murder and non-negligent man-slaughter	Forcible rape	Robbery	Aggravated assault	Burglary	Larceny-theft	Motor vehicle theft	Arson
TOTAL NONSUBURBAN CITIES—Continued:												
GROUP V												
402 cities, 10,000 to 24,999; population 6,275,034												
2001	324,564	326,242	28,347	296,217	246	2,609	5,126	20,366	54,426	227,077	14,714	1,678
2002	322,093	323,631	27,891	294,202	206	2,773	5,291	19,621	56,067	223,269	14,866	1,538
Percent change	-0.8	-0.8	-1.6	-0.7	-16.3	+6.3	+3.2	-3.7	+3.0	-1.7	+1.0	-8.3
GROUP VI												
2,736 cities, under 10,000; population 8,612,808												
2001	342,904	344,649	32,793	310,111	302	2,473	3,664	26,354	60,384	234,541	15,186	1,745
2002	342,528	344,228	32,523	310,005	241	2,787	3,730	25,765	62,476	232,519	15,010	1,700
Percent change	-0.1	-0.1	-0.8	*	-20.2	+12.7	+1.8	-2.2	+3.5	-0.9	-1.2	-2.6

[1] The murder and nonnegligent homicides that occurred as a result of the events of September 11, 2001, were not included in this table.

[2] Suburban includes law enforcement agencies in cities with less than 50,000 inhabitants that are within a Metropolitan Statistical Area (see Appendix III). Suburban excludes all metropolitan agencies associated with a central city. Nonsuburban includes law enforcement agencies in cities with less than 50,000 inhabitants that are not associated with a Metropolitan Statistical Area.

[3] The Modified Crime Index is the sum of the seven offenses making up the Crime Index, with the addition of arson.

[4] Violent crimes are offenses of murder, forcible rape, robbery, and aggravated assault.

[5] Property crimes are offenses of burglary, larceny-theft, and motor vehicle theft.

* Less than one-tenth of 1 percent.

Table 14

Crime Trends[1]
by Suburban and Nonsuburban Counties by Population Group, 2001-2002
[2002 estimated population]

Population group	Crime Index	Modified Crime Index[2]	Violent crime[3]	Property crime[4]	Murder and non-negligent man-slaughter	Forcible rape	Robbery	Aggravated assault	Burglary	Larceny-theft	Motor vehicle theft	Arson
SUBURBAN COUNTIES[5]												
100,000 and over												
134 counties; population 33,617,118												
2001	1,143,992	1,154,065	137,974	1,006,018	1,386	9,177	32,534	94,877	226,157	667,229	112,632	10,073
2002	1,152,964	1,162,562	138,350	1,014,614	1,554	9,595	33,049	94,152	231,680	663,052	119,882	9,598
Percent change	+0.8	+0.7	+0.3	+0.9	+12.1	+4.6	+1.6	-0.8	+2.4	-0.6	+6.4	-4.7
25,000 to 99,999												
365 counties; population 19,438,114												
2001	414,767	418,196	41,907	372,860	504	4,367	4,819	32,217	104,811	238,357	29,692	3,429
2002	421,898	425,198	42,955	378,943	567	4,627	4,894	32,867	109,735	237,690	31,518	3,300
Percent change	+1.7	+1.7	+2.5	+1.6	+12.5	+6.0	+1.6	+2.0	+4.7	-0.3	+6.1	-3.8
Under 25,000												
760 counties; population 2,606,264												
2001	113,588	115,063	13,372	100,216	160	1,195	1,723	10,294	23,076	60,012	17,128	1,475
2002	113,575	114,851	13,822	99,753	168	1,302	1,820	10,532	21,991	58,868	18,894	1,276
Percent change	*	-0.2	+3.4	-0.5	+5.0	+9.0	+5.6	+2.3	-4.7	-1.9	+10.3	-13.5
NONSUBURBAN COUNTIES[5]												
25,000 and over												
305 counties; population 11,981,976												
2001	248,095	250,044	27,687	220,408	430	2,685	2,655	21,917	71,249	133,412	15,747	1,949
2002	250,950	252,694	27,516	223,434	404	2,799	2,613	21,700	73,750	133,462	16,222	1,744
Percent change	+1.2	+1.1	-0.6	+1.4	-6.0	+4.2	-1.6	-1.0	+3.5	*	+3.0	-10.5
10,000 to 24,999												
643 counties; population 10,191,616												
2001	161,910	163,131	18,832	143,078	357	1,746	1,116	15,613	48,049	84,434	10,595	1,221
2002	163,921	165,119	18,685	145,236	368	1,800	1,133	15,384	49,307	84,880	11,049	1,198
Percent change	+1.2	+1.2	-0.8	+1.5	+3.1	+3.1	+1.5	-1.5	+2.6	+0.5	+4.3	-1.9
Under 10,000												
1,276 counties; population 4,129,322												
2001	86,179	87,110	10,502	75,677	175	1,271	492	8,564	24,025	45,107	6,545	931
2002	85,413	86,388	10,601	74,812	155	1,480	565	8,401	23,710	44,456	6,646	975
Percent change	-0.9	-0.8	+0.9	-1.1	-11.4	+16.4	+14.8	-1.9	-1.3	-1.4	+1.5	+4.7

[1] The murder and nonnegligent homicides that occurred as a result of the events of September 11, 2001, were not included in this table.
[2] The Modified Crime Index is the sum of the seven offenses making up the Crime Index, with the addition of arson.
[3] Violent crimes are offenses of murder, forcible rape, robbery, and aggravated assault.
[4] Property crimes are offenses of burglary, larceny-theft, and motor vehicle theft.
[5] Suburban counties include sheriffs and county law enforcement agencies associated with a Metropolitan Statistical Area (see Appendix III). Nonsuburban counties include sheriffs and county law enforcement agencies that are not associated with a Metropolitan Statistical Area. The offenses from state police agencies are not included in this table.
*Less than one-tenth of 1 percent.

Table 15

Crime Trends

Breakdown of Offenses Known by Population Group, 2001-2002
[2002 estimated population]

Population group	Forcible rape: Rape by force	Forcible rape: Assault to rape-attempts	Robbery: Firearm	Robbery: Knife or cutting instrument	Robbery: Other weapon	Robbery: Strong-arm	Aggravated assault: Firearm	Aggravated assault: Knife or cutting instrument	Aggravated assault: Other weapon	Aggravated assault: Hands, fists, feet, etc.	Burglary: Forcible entry	Burglary: Unlawful entry	Burglary: Attempted forcible entry	Motor vehicle theft: Autos	Motor vehicle theft: Trucks and buses	Motor vehicle theft: Other vehicles	Arson: Structure	Arson: Mobile	Arson: Other
TOTAL ALL AGENCIES: 12,195 agencies; population 238,281,718																			
2001	68,623	7,427	140,078	29,142	32,699	133,003	135,599	133,915	266,608	207,049	1,128,220	540,480	117,459	768,400	193,602	78,150	29,090	22,576	18,364
2002	72,090	7,173	138,468	29,247	30,985	133,289	138,436	131,232	260,337	199,342	1,138,883	558,353	118,618	780,164	197,040	83,121	27,088	22,013	17,347
Percent change	+5.1	-3.4	-1.1	+0.4	-5.2	+0.2	+2.1	-2.0	-2.4	-3.7	+0.9	+3.3	+1.0	+1.5	+1.8	+6.4	-6.9	-2.5	-5.5
TOTAL CITIES: 8,564 cities; population 156,683,004																			
2001	49,712	5,765	121,919	25,701	28,293	117,817	105,747	105,323	199,073	148,568	814,938	388,999	88,944	644,958	156,563	51,627	21,805	16,283	13,159
2002	52,101	5,610	119,817	25,840	26,586	117,684	107,848	102,923	192,626	142,545	820,540	399,941	89,454	650,995	157,707	53,154	20,295	15,766	12,591
Percent change	+4.8	-2.7	-1.7	+0.5	-6.0	-0.1	+2.0	-2.3	-3.2	-4.1	+0.7	+2.8	+0.6	+0.9	+0.7	+3.0	-6.9	-3.2	-4.3
GROUP I																			
65 cities, 250,000 and over; population 39,999,026																			
2001	16,501	2,331	67,851	13,099	13,742	59,144	56,501	44,624	85,001	46,606	300,073	111,320	25,679	297,291	92,531	18,975	8,710	8,508	3,962
2002	16,967	2,223	66,855	12,990	12,463	58,860	57,626	43,147	82,158	44,899	303,301	111,965	24,954	298,816	93,974	19,856	7,544	7,967	3,715
Percent change	+2.8	-4.6	-1.5	-0.8	-9.3	-0.5	+2.0	-3.3	-3.3	-3.7	+1.1	+0.6	-2.8	+0.5	+1.6	+4.6	-13.4	-6.4	-6.2
8 cities, 1,000,000 and over; population 13,659,273																			
2001	4,778	931	25,900	5,627	4,698	20,967	21,357	15,268	25,733	22,719	89,529	34,903	6,628	95,408	37,371	7,774	2,547	3,414	1,266
2002	4,870	826	25,949	5,544	4,508	20,910	22,239	15,111	25,348	22,734	91,761	34,490	6,621	97,763	38,496	8,029	2,251	3,414	1,199
Percent change	+1.9	-11.3	+0.2	-1.5	-4.0	-0.3	+4.1	-1.0	-1.5	+0.1	+2.5	-1.2	-0.1	+2.5	+3.0	+3.3	-11.6	0.0	-5.3
20 cities, 500,000 to 999,999; population 13,292,225																			
2001	6,019	723	21,380	3,887	4,896	17,313	18,497	15,343	29,763	12,029	111,271	36,663	10,429	99,984	29,830	6,189	2,407	1,817	1,156
2002	6,364	761	20,640	3,834	4,288	16,804	18,851	14,722	28,745	10,124	112,740	37,843	10,198	100,142	29,923	6,875	2,020	1,579	1,129
Percent change	+5.7	+5.3	-3.5	-1.4	-12.4	-2.9	+1.9	-4.0	-3.4	-15.8	+1.3	+3.2	-2.2	+0.2	+0.3	+11.1	-16.1	-13.1	-2.3
37 cities, 250,000 to 499,999; population 13,047,528																			
2001	5,704	677	20,571	3,585	4,148	20,864	16,647	14,013	29,505	11,858	99,273	39,754	8,622	101,899	25,330	5,012	3,756	3,277	1,540
2002	5,733	636	20,266	3,612	3,667	21,146	16,536	13,314	28,065	12,041	98,800	39,632	8,135	100,911	25,555	4,952	3,273	2,974	1,387
Percent change	+0.5	-6.1	-1.5	+0.8	-11.6	+1.4	-0.7	-5.0	-4.9	+1.5	-0.5	-0.3	-5.6	-1.0	+0.9	-1.2	-12.9	-9.2	-9.9

See footnotes at end of table.

Table 15

Crime Trends
Breakdown of Offenses Known
by Population Group, 2001-2002—Continued
[2002 estimated population]

Population group	Forcible rape: Rape by force	Forcible rape: Assault to rape-attempts	Robbery: Firearm	Robbery: Knife or cutting instrument	Robbery: Other weapon	Robbery: Strong-arm	Aggravated assault: Firearm	Aggravated assault: Knife or cutting instrument	Aggravated assault: Other weapon	Aggravated assault: Hands, fists, feet, etc.	Burglary: Forcible entry	Burglary: Unlawful entry	Burglary: Attempted forcible entry	Motor vehicle theft: Autos	Motor vehicle theft: Trucks and buses	Motor vehicle theft: Other vehicles	Arson: Structure	Arson: Mobile	Arson: Other
GROUP II																			
152 cities, 100,000 to 249,999; population 22,790,684																			
2001	7,616	804	20,986	4,300	5,333	19,107	16,359	16,638	34,197	16,685	138,308	60,961	14,616	114,415	24,120	7,671	3,575	2,806	1,937
2002	8,351	838	20,118	4,416	4,887	19,043	16,740	16,591	32,469	16,597	141,400	60,749	15,117	115,632	24,421	7,856	3,546	2,789	2,101
Percent change	+9.7	+4.2	-4.1	+2.7	-8.4	-0.3	+2.3	-0.3	-5.1	-0.5	+2.2	-0.3	+3.4	+1.1	+1.2	+2.4	-0.8	-0.6	+8.5
GROUP III																			
377 cities, 50,000 to 99,999; population 26,125,455																			
2001	8,155	790	14,304	3,512	3,591	16,589	12,643	14,816	28,739	22,209	120,955	63,522	15,551	91,187	15,546	7,600	3,042	1,976	2,204
2002	8,458	739	13,985	3,632	3,513	16,713	12,773	14,630	28,224	21,031	119,805	66,101	15,527	94,532	15,471	7,858	2,889	2,008	1,953
Percent change	+3.7	-6.5	-2.2	+3.4	-2.2	+0.7	+1.0	-1.3	-1.8	-5.3	-1.0	+4.1	-0.2	+3.7	-0.5	+3.4	-5.0	+1.6	-11.4
GROUP IV																			
695 cities, 25,000 to 49,999; population 24,225,048																			
2001	6,738	634	8,837	2,307	2,673	10,789	8,037	11,031	19,968	19,900	97,188	55,865	12,765	63,099	10,255	6,376	2,247	1,323	1,964
2002	6,995	615	8,461	2,310	2,715	10,741	8,397	10,826	19,271	18,999	96,276	57,789	13,222	63,011	10,225	6,233	2,275	1,350	1,865
Percent change	+3.8	-3.0	-4.3	+0.1	+1.6	-0.4	+4.5	-1.9	-3.5	-4.5	-0.9	+3.4	+3.6	-0.1	-0.3	-2.2	+1.2	+2.0	-5.0
GROUP V																			
1,531 cities, 10,000 to 24,999; population 24,284,679																			
2001	6,116	608	6,253	1,527	1,942	7,670	6,762	10,013	17,388	20,004	86,888	51,771	11,075	46,717	8,286	5,625	2,151	968	1,478
2002	6,401	588	6,685	1,549	1,967	7,766	6,639	9,612	17,035	19,086	87,951	54,831	11,037	47,281	7,861	5,834	2,099	905	1,450
Percent change	+4.7	-3.3	+6.9	+1.4	+1.3	+1.3	-1.8	-4.0	-2.0	-4.6	+1.2	+5.9	-0.3	+1.2	-5.1	+3.7	-2.4	-6.5	-1.9
GROUP VI																			
5,744 cities, under 10,000; population 19,258,112																			
2001	4,586	598	3,688	956	1,012	4,518	5,445	8,201	13,780	23,164	71,526	45,560	9,258	32,249	5,825	5,380	2,080	702	1,614
2002	4,929	607	3,713	943	1,041	4,561	5,673	8,117	13,469	21,933	71,807	48,506	9,597	31,723	5,755	5,517	1,942	747	1,507
Percent change	+7.5	+1.5	+0.7	-1.4	+2.9	+1.0	+4.2	-1.0	-2.3	-5.3	+0.4	+6.5	+3.7	-1.6	-1.2	+2.5	-6.6	+6.4	-6.6

See footnotes at end of table.

Table 15

Crime Trends
Breakdown of Offenses Known
by Population Group, 2001-2002—Continued
[2002 estimated population]

Population group	Forcible rape — Rape by force	Forcible rape — Assault to rape-attempts	Robbery — Firearm	Robbery — Knife or cutting instrument	Robbery — Other weapon	Robbery — Strong-arm	Aggravated assault — Firearm	Aggravated assault — Knife or cutting instrument	Aggravated assault — Other weapon	Aggravated assault — Hands, fists, feet, etc.	Burglary — Forcible entry	Burglary — Unlawful entry	Burglary — Attempted forcible entry	Motor vehicle theft — Autos	Motor vehicle theft — Trucks and buses	Motor vehicle theft — Other vehicles	Arson — Structure	Arson — Mobile	Arson — Other
SUBURBAN COUNTIES																			
1,251 agencies; population 53,980,743																			
2001	13,233	1,139	16,225	2,990	3,796	13,479	21,190	21,519	53,048	39,291	213,808	106,326	21,056	102,209	30,638	18,311	5,126	5,131	4,216
2002	13,923	1,133	16,642	2,992	3,849	13,925	21,894	21,363	53,675	38,043	216,708	111,559	21,731	107,551	32,669	21,083	4,645	5,196	3,805
Percent change	+5.2	-0.5	+2.6	+0.1	+1.4	+3.3	+3.3	-0.7	+1.2	-3.2	+1.4	+4.9	+3.2	+5.2	+6.6	+15.1	-9.4	+1.3	-9.7
RURAL COUNTIES																			
2,380 agencies; population 27,617,971																			
2001	5,678	523	1,934	451	610	1,707	8,662	7,073	14,487	19,190	99,474	45,155	7,459	21,233	6,401	8,212	2,159	1,162	989
2002	6,066	430	2,009	415	550	1,680	8,694	6,946	14,036	18,754	101,635	46,853	7,433	21,618	6,664	8,884	2,148	1,051	951
Percent change	+6.8	-17.8	+3.9	-8.0	-9.8	-1.6	+0.4	-1.8	-3.1	-2.3	+2.2	+3.8	-0.3	+1.8	+4.1	+8.2	-0.5	-9.6	-3.8
SUBURBAN AREA[1]																			
5,874 agencies; population 99,133,369																			
2001	22,535	2,211	28,476	5,939	7,240	28,007	31,025	36,153	80,616	74,399	354,964	196,274	41,062	202,523	46,673	29,307	8,765	7,026	7,379
2002	23,435	2,138	28,860	5,896	7,311	28,400	31,854	35,531	80,704	70,623	357,610	205,622	42,067	207,697	48,509	32,342	8,233	7,040	6,922
Percent change	+4.0	-3.3	+1.3	-0.7	+1.0	+1.4	+2.7	-1.7	+0.1	-5.1	+0.7	+4.8	+2.4	+2.6	+3.9	+10.4	-6.1	+0.2	-6.2

[1] Suburban area includes law enforcement agencies in cities with less than 50,000 inhabitants and county law enforcement agencies that are within a Metropolitan Statistical Area (see Appendix III). Suburban area excludes all metropolitan agencies associated with a central city. The agencies associated with suburban areas also appear in other groups within this table.

Table 16

Rate: Number of Crimes per 100,000 Inhabitants
by Population Group, 2002
[2002 estimated population]

Population group	Crime Index	Modified Crime Index[1]	Violent crime[2]	Property crime[3]	Murder and non-negligent man-slaughter	Forcible rape[4]	Robbery	Aggravated assault	Burglary	Larceny-theft	Motor vehicle theft	Arson[1]
TOTAL ALL AGENCIES: 11,843 agencies; population 249,310,858												
Number of offenses known	10,730,321		1,308,689	9,421,632	14,989	84,437	395,417	813,846	1,931,386	6,332,788	1,157,458	
Rate	4,304.0		524.9	3,779.1	6.0	33.9	158.6	326.4	774.7	2,540.1	464.3	
TOTAL CITIES: 8,402 cities; population 169,487,389												
Number of offenses known	8,554,405		1,058,628	7,495,777	11,822	62,911	352,690	631,205	1,425,111	5,113,632	957,034	
Rate	5,047.2		624.6	4,422.6	7.0	37.1	208.1	372.4	840.8	3,017.1	564.7	
GROUP I												
70 cities, 250,000 and over; population 52,797,055												
Number of offenses known	3,296,258		543,772	2,752,486	6,953	23,297	208,643	304,879	529,108	1,733,548	489,830	
Rate	6,243.3		1,029.9	5,213.3	13.2	44.1	395.2	577.5	1,002.2	3,283.4	927.8	
10 cities, 1,000,000 and over; population 24,682,265												
Number of offenses known	1,289,480		258,753	1,030,727	3,090	8,383	102,672	144,608	188,526	645,634	196,567	
Rate	5,224.3		1,048.3	4,176.0	12.5	34.0	416.0	585.9	763.8	2,615.8	796.4	
22 cities, 500,000 to 999,999; population 14,767,287												
Number of offenses known	1,054,317		148,116	906,201	2,038	7,747	53,219	85,112	179,220	576,984	149,997	
Rate	7,139.5		1,003.0	6,136.5	13.8	52.5	360.4	576.4	1,213.6	3,907.2	1,015.7	
38 cities, 250,000 to 499,999; population 13,347,503												
Number of offenses known	952,461		136,903	815,558	1,825	7,167	52,752	75,159	161,362	510,930	143,266	
Rate	7,135.9		1,025.7	6,110.2	13.7	53.7	395.2	563.1	1,208.9	3,827.9	1,073.4	
GROUP II												
165 cities, 100,000 to 249,999; population 24,763,634												
Number of offenses known	1,409,246		156,935	1,252,311	1,903	10,387	54,024	90,621	245,571	844,203	162,537	
Rate	5,690.8		633.7	5,057.1	7.7	41.9	218.2	365.9	991.7	3,409.0	656.4	
GROUP III												
372 cities, 50,000 to 99,999; population 25,659,637												
Number of offenses known	1,174,943		124,295	1,050,648	1,157	9,172	37,721	76,245	201,527	728,955	120,166	
Rate	4,579.0		484.4	4,094.6	4.5	35.7	147.0	297.1	785.4	2,840.9	468.3	
GROUP IV												
670 cities, 25,000 to 49,999; population 23,458,107												
Number of offenses known	966,736		89,293	877,443	754	7,494	24,012	57,033	164,353	633,953	79,137	
Rate	4,121.1		380.6	3,740.5	3.2	31.9	102.4	243.1	700.6	2,702.5	337.4	
GROUP V												
1,506 cities, 10,000 to 24,999; population 23,889,704												
Number of offenses known	916,703		77,998	838,705	603	7,029	18,034	52,332	154,233	622,594	61,878	
Rate	3,837.2		326.5	3,510.7	2.5	29.4	75.5	219.1	645.6	2,606.1	259.0	

See footnotes at end of table.

Table 16

Rate: Number of Crimes per 100,000 Inhabitants
by Population Group, 2002—Continued

[2002 estimated population]

Population group	Crime Index	Modified Crime Index[1]	Violent crime[2]	Property crime[3]	Murder and non-negligent man-slaughter	Forcible rape[4]	Robbery	Aggravated assault	Burglary	Larceny-theft	Motor vehicle theft	Arson[1]
GROUP VI												
5,619 cities, under 10,000; population 18,919,252												
Number of offenses known	790,519		66,335	724,184	452	5,532	10,256	50,095	130,319	550,379	43,486	
Rate	4,178.4		350.6	3,827.8	2.4	29.2	54.2	264.8	688.8	2,909.1	229.9	
SUBURBAN COUNTIES												
1,151 agencies; population 53,969,080												
Number of offenses known	1,644,668		190,040	1,454,628	2,181	15,163	38,148	134,548	352,209	939,074	163,345	
Rate	3,047.4		352.1	2,695.3	4.0	28.1	70.7	249.3	652.6	1,740.0	302.7	
RURAL COUNTIES[5]												
2,290 agencies; population 25,854,389												
Number of offenses known	531,248		60,021	471,227	986	6,363	4,579	48,093	154,066	280,082	37,079	
Rate	2,054.8		232.2	1,822.6	3.8	24.6	17.7	186.0	595.9	1,083.3	143.4	
SUBURBAN AREA[6]												
5,666 agencies; population 98,242,913												
Number of offenses known	3,229,740		319,748	2,909,992	3,167	25,687	71,495	219,399	607,961	2,010,328	291,703	
Rate	3,287.5		325.5	2,962.0	3.2	26.1	72.8	223.3	618.8	2,046.3	296.9	

[1] Arson rates are not presented in this table because fewer agencies furnished complete reports for arson than for the other seven offenses making up the Crime Index. Independently tabulated arson rates appear in the arson narrative.

[2] Violent crimes are offenses of murder, forcible rape, robbery, and aggravated assault.

[3] Property crimes are offenses of burglary, larceny-theft, and motor vehicle theft.

[4] Forcible rape figures furnished by the state Uniform Crime Reporting (UCR) Program administered by the Illinois State Police were not in accordance with national UCR guidelines; therefore, the figures were estimated for inclusion in the forcible rape, violent crime, and Crime Index categories. See Appendix I for details.

[5] Includes state police agencies that report aggregately for the entire state.

[6] Suburban area includes law enforcement agencies in cities with less than 50,000 inhabitants and county law enforcement agencies that are within a Metropolitan Statistical Area (see Appendix III). Suburban area excludes all metropolitan agencies associated with a central city. The agencies associated with suburban areas also appear in other groups within this table.

Table 17

Rate: Number of Crimes per 100,000 Inhabitants
by Suburban and Nonsuburban Cities[1] by Population Group, 2002
[2002 estimated population]

Population group	Crime Index	Modified Crime Index[2]	Violent crime[3]	Property crime[4]	Murder and non-negligent manslaughter	Forcible rape	Robbery	Aggravated assault	Burglary	Larceny-theft	Motor vehicle theft	Arson[2]
Suburban cities												
TOTAL SUBURBAN CITIES:												
4,515 cities;												
population 44,273,833												
Number of offenses known	1,585,072		129,708	1,455,364	986	10,524	33,347	84,851	255,752	1,071,254	128,358	
Rate	3,580.2		293.0	3,287.2	2.2	23.8	75.3	191.7	577.7	2,419.6	289.9	
Group IV												
459 cities, 25,000 to 49,999;												
population 15,943,212												
Number of offenses known	535,792		45,207	490,585	362	3,520	13,761	27,564	88,643	349,181	52,761	
Rate	3,360.6		283.6	3,077.1	2.3	22.1	86.3	172.9	556.0	2,190.2	330.9	
Group V												
1,120 cities, 10,000 to 24,999;												
population 17,866,303												
Number of offenses known	600,178		50,648	549,530	404	4,247	12,971	33,026	98,740	403,570	47,220	
Rate	3,359.3		283.5	3,075.8	2.3	23.8	72.6	184.9	552.7	2,258.8	264.3	
Group VI												
2,936 cities, under 10,000;												
population 10,464,318												
Number of offenses known	449,102		33,853	415,249	220	2,757	6,615	24,261	68,369	318,503	28,377	
Rate	4,291.7		323.5	3,968.2	2.1	26.3	63.2	231.8	653.4	3,043.7	271.2	
Nonsuburban cities												
TOTAL NONSUBURBAN CITIES:												
3,280 cities;												
population 21,993,230												
Number of offenses known	1,088,886		103,918	984,968	823	9,531	18,955	74,609	193,153	735,672	56,143	
Rate	4,951.0		472.5	4,478.5	3.7	43.3	86.2	339.2	878.2	3,345.0	255.3	
Group IV												
211 cities, 25,000 to 49,999;												
population 7,514,895												
Number of offenses known	430,944		44,086	386,858	392	3,974	10,251	29,469	75,710	284,772	26,376	
Rate	5,734.5		586.6	5,147.9	5.2	52.9	136.4	392.1	1,007.5	3,789.4	351.0	
Group V												
386 cities, 10,000 to 24,999;												
population 6,023,401												
Number of offenses known	316,525		27,350	289,175	199	2,782	5,063	19,306	55,493	219,024	14,658	
Rate	5,254.9		454.1	4,800.9	3.3	46.2	84.1	320.5	921.3	3,636.2	243.4	
Group VI												
2,683 cities, under 10,000;												
population 8,454,934												
Number of offenses known	341,417		32,482	308,935	232	2,775	3,641	25,834	61,950	231,876	15,109	
Rate	4,038.1		384.2	3,653.9	2.7	32.8	43.1	305.5	732.7	2,742.5	178.7	

[1] Suburban includes law enforcement agencies in cities with less than 50,000 inhabitants that are within a Metropolitan Statistical Area (see Appendix III). Suburban excludes all metropolitan agencies associated with a central city. Nonsuburban includes law enforcement agencies in cities with less than 50,000 inhabitants that are not associated with a Metropolitan Statistical Area.

[2] Arson rates are not presented in this table because fewer agencies furnished complete reports for arson than for the other seven offenses making up the Crime Index. Independently tabulated arson rates appear in the arson narrative.

[3] Violent crimes are offenses of murder, forcible rape, robbery, and aggravated assault.

[4] Property crimes are offenses of burglary, larceny-theft, and motor vehicle theft.

Table 18

Rate: Number of Crimes per 100,000 Inhabitants
by Suburban and Nonsuburban Counties by Population Group, 2002
[2002 estimated population]

Population group	Crime Index	Modified Crime Index[1]	Violent crime[3]	Property crime[4]	Murder and non-negligent man-slaughter	Forcible rape	Robbery	Aggravated assault	Burglary	Larceny-theft	Motor vehicle theft	Arson[2]
SUBURBAN COUNTIES[4]												
100,000 and over												
132 counties;												
population 33,608,314												
Number of offenses known	1,130,997		135,525	995,472	1,477	9,427	31,590	93,031	226,595	655,919	112,958	
Rate	3,365.2		403.2	2,962.0	4.4	28.0	94.0	276.8	674.2	1,951.7	336.1	
25,000 to 99,999												
338 counties;												
population 17,982,524												
Number of offenses known	407,169		41,781	365,388	540	4,554	4,871	31,816	105,106	229,253	31,029	
Rate	2,264.2		232.3	2,031.9	3.0	25.3	27.1	176.9	584.5	1,274.9	172.6	
Under 25,000												
681 counties;												
population 2,378,242												
Number of offenses known	106,502		12,734	93,768	164	1,182	1,687	9,701	20,508	53,902	19,358	
Rate	4,478.2		535.4	3,942.7	6.9	49.7	70.9	407.9	862.3	2,266.5	814.0	
NONSUBURBAN COUNTIES[4]												
25,000 and over												
289 counties;												
population 11,354,703												
Number of offenses known	251,262		26,932	224,330	392	2,697	2,588	21,255	72,876	134,985	16,469	
Rate	2,212.8		237.2	1,975.7	3.5	23.8	22.8	187.2	641.8	1,188.8	145.0	
10,000 to 24,999												
601 counties;												
population 9,586,654												
Number of offenses known	161,458		18,883	142,575	359	1,748	1,130	15,646	48,610	83,160	10,805	
Rate	1,684.2		197.0	1,487.2	3.7	18.2	11.8	163.2	507.1	867.5	112.7	
Under 10,000												
1,236 counties;												
population 3,897,322												
Number of offenses known	83,027		10,381	72,646	155	1,436	533	8,257	23,076	43,063	6,507	
Rate	2,130.4		266.4	1,864.0	4.0	36.8	13.7	211.9	592.1	1,104.9	167.0	

[1] Arson rates are not presented in this table because fewer agencies furnished complete reports for arson than for the other seven offenses making up the Crime Index. Independently tabulated arson rates appear in the arson narrative.

[2] Violent crimes are offenses of murder, forcible rape, robbery, and aggravated assault.

[3] Property crimes are offenses of burglary, larceny-theft, and motor vehicle theft.

[4] Suburban counties include sheriffs and county law enforcement agencies associated with a Metropolitan Statistical Area (see Appendix III). Nonsuburban counties include sheriffs and county law enforcement agencies that are not associated with a Metropolitan Statistical Area. The offenses from state police agencies are not included in this table.

Table 19

Rate: Number of Crimes per 100,000 Inhabitants
Breakdown of Offenses Known
by Population Group, 2002
[2002 estimated population]

Population group	Forcible rape — Rape by force	Forcible rape — Assault to rape-attempts	Robbery — Firearm	Robbery — Knife or cutting instrument	Robbery — Other weapon	Robbery — Strong-arm	Aggravated assault — Firearm	Aggravated assault — Knife or cutting instrument	Aggravated assault — Other weapon	Aggravated assault — Hands, fists, feet, etc.	Burglary — Forcible entry	Burglary — Unlawful entry	Burglary — Attempted forcible entry	Motor vehicle theft — Autos	Motor vehicle theft — Trucks and buses	Motor vehicle theft — Other vehicles	Arson[1] — Structure	Arson[1] — Mobile	Arson[1] — Other
TOTAL ALL AGENCIES: 11,781 agencies; population 232,068,946																			
Number of offenses known	71,689	7,117	139,657	28,929	31,021	132,398	137,704	129,249	256,872	200,928	1,136,350	557,074	117,126	783,209	197,821	83,244			
Rate	30.9	3.1	60.2	12.5	13.4	57.1	59.3	55.7	110.7	86.6	489.7	240.0	50.5	337.5	85.2	35.9			
TOTAL CITIES: 8,360 cities; population 154,572,211																			
Number of offenses known	52,343	5,623	122,144	25,700	26,634	117,625	108,547	102,430	193,357	145,019	829,572	402,643	89,393	658,332	160,600	54,292			
Rate	33.9	3.6	79.0	16.6	17.2	76.1	70.2	66.3	125.1	93.8	536.7	260.5	57.8	425.9	103.9	35.1			
GROUP I																			
64 cities, 250,000 and over; population 40,124,177																			
Number of offenses known	17,312	2,265	68,677	12,998	12,656	59,384	58,399	43,366	84,285	46,072	312,921	114,313	25,740	304,689	96,931	21,214			
Rate	43.1	5.6	171.2	32.4	31.5	148.0	145.5	108.1	210.1	114.8	779.9	284.9	64.2	759.4	241.6	52.9			
8 cities, 1,000,000 and over; population 13,659,273																			
Number of offenses known	4,870	826	25,949	5,544	4,508	20,910	22,239	15,111	25,348	22,734	91,761	34,490	6,621	97,763	38,496	8,029			
Rate	35.7	6.0	190.0	40.6	33.0	153.1	162.8	110.6	185.6	166.4	671.8	252.5	48.5	715.7	281.8	58.8			
21 cities, 500,000 to 999,999; population 14,096,259																			
Number of offenses known	6,741	825	22,368	3,975	4,416	17,744	19,606	15,352	30,375	11,137	119,695	39,634	11,114	104,199	31,330	7,913			
Rate	47.8	5.9	158.7	28.2	31.3	125.9	139.1	108.9	215.5	79.0	849.1	281.2	78.8	739.2	222.3	56.1			
35 cities, 250,000 to 499,999; population 12,368,645																			
Number of offenses known	5,701	614	20,360	3,479	3,732	20,730	16,554	12,903	28,562	12,201	101,465	40,189	8,005	102,727	27,105	5,272			
Rate	46.1	5.0	164.6	28.1	30.2	167.6	133.8	104.3	230.9	98.6	820.3	324.9	64.7	830.5	219.1	42.6			
GROUP II																			
152 cities, 100,000 to 249,999; population 22,954,609																			
Number of offenses known	8,548	819	20,694	4,399	4,884	18,973	17,277	16,502	32,265	16,803	144,833	62,228	14,813	116,586	24,434	7,803			
Rate	37.2	3.6	90.2	19.2	21.3	82.7	75.3	71.9	140.6	73.2	631.0	271.1	64.5	507.9	106.4	34.0			
GROUP III																			
368 cities, 50,000 to 99,999; population 25,420,252																			
Number of offenses known	8,307	732	13,897	3,564	3,531	16,355	12,369	14,273	27,650	20,934	117,676	66,437	15,461	94,665	15,384	7,767			
Rate	32.7	2.9	54.7	14.0	13.9	64.3	48.7	56.1	108.8	82.4	462.9	261.4	60.8	372.4	60.5	30.6			

See footnotes at end of table.

Table 19

Rate: Number of Crimes per 100,000 Inhabitants
Breakdown of Offenses Known
by Population Group, 2002—Continued
[2002 estimated population]

Population group	Forcible rape: Rape by force	Forcible rape: Assault to rape-attempts	Robbery: Firearm	Robbery: Knife or cutting instrument	Robbery: Other weapon	Robbery: Strong-arm	Aggravated assault: Firearm	Aggravated assault: Knife or cutting instrument	Aggravated assault: Other weapon	Aggravated assault: Hands, fists, feet, etc.	Burglary: Forcible entry	Burglary: Unlawful entry	Burglary: Attempted forcible entry	Motor vehicle theft: Autos	Motor vehicle theft: Trucks and buses	Motor vehicle theft: Other vehicles	Arson[1]: Structure	Arson[1]: Mobile	Arson[1]: Other
GROUP IV																			
668 cities, 25,000 to 49,999; population 23,381,470																			
Number of offenses known	6,853	605	8,378	2,277	2,567	10,625	8,166	10,714	18,986	18,993	94,240	56,377	13,007	62,634	10,062	5,990			
Rate	29.3	2.6	35.8	9.7	11.0	45.4	34.9	45.8	81.2	81.2	403.1	241.1	55.6	267.9	43.0	25.6			
GROUP V																			
1,503 cities, 10,000 to 24,999; population 23,833,515																			
Number of offenses known	6,423	592	6,786	1,521	1,966	7,726	6,730	9,482	16,726	19,370	88,211	54,557	10,825	47,856	7,953	5,890			
Rate	26.9	2.5	28.5	6.4	8.2	32.4	28.2	39.8	70.2	81.3	370.1	228.9	45.4	200.8	33.4	24.7			
GROUP VI																			
5,605 cities, under 10,000; population 18,858,188																			
Number of offenses known	4,900	610	3,712	941	1,030	4,562	5,606	8,093	13,445	22,847	71,691	48,731	9,547	31,892	5,836	5,628			
Rate	26.0	3.2	19.7	5.0	5.5	24.2	29.7	42.9	71.3	121.2	380.2	258.4	50.6	169.1	30.9	29.8			
SUBURBAN COUNTIES																			
1,142 agencies; population 52,016,888																			
Number of offenses known	13,457	1,073	15,600	2,833	3,849	13,192	20,637	20,082	49,855	37,560	208,351	109,201	20,562	104,040	30,878	20,408			
Rate	25.9	2.1	30.0	5.4	7.4	25.4	39.7	38.6	95.8	72.2	400.5	209.9	39.5	200.0	59.4	39.2			
RURAL COUNTIES																			
2,279 agencies; population 25,479,847																			
Number of offenses known	5,889	421	1,913	396	538	1,581	8,520	6,737	13,660	18,349	98,427	45,230	7,171	20,837	6,343	8,544			
Rate	23.1	1.7	7.5	1.6	2.1	6.2	33.4	26.4	53.6	72.0	386.3	177.5	28.1	81.8	24.9	33.5			
SUBURBAN AREA[2]																			
5,652 agencies; population 96,235,187																			
Number of offenses known	22,964	2,082	27,993	5,755	7,341	27,720	30,728	34,305	76,959	70,900	349,336	203,278	40,841	204,948	46,858	31,736			
Rate	23.9	2.2	29.1	6.0	7.6	28.8	31.9	35.6	80.0	73.7	363.0	211.2	42.4	213.0	48.7	33.0			

[1] Arson rates are not presented in this table because fewer agencies furnished complete reports for arson than for the other seven offenses making up the Crime Index. Independently tabulated arson rates appear in the arson narrative.

[2] Suburban area includes law enforcement agencies in cities with less than 50,000 inhabitants and county law enforcement agencies that are within a Metropolitan Statistical Area (see Appendix III). Suburban area excludes all metropolitan agencies associated with a central city. The agencies associated with suburban areas also appear in other groups within this table.

Table 20

Murder
by State, 2002
Type of Weapon

State	Total murders[1]	Total firearms	Handguns	Rifles	Shotguns	Firearms (type unknown)	Knives or cutting instruments	Other weapons	Hands, fists, feet, etc.[2]
Alabama	286	186	168	0	18	0	35	43	22
Alaska	33	18	16	0	2	0	6	6	3
Arizona	382	290	246	25	12	7	27	45	20
Arkansas	137	103	74	6	9	14	15	14	5
California	2,395	1,737	1,554	82	60	41	275	266	117
Colorado	166	108	75	6	6	21	23	18	17
Connecticut	75	45	32	1	4	8	17	6	7
Delaware	22	17	9	0	4	4	3	1	1
District of Columbia[3]									
Florida[3]									
Georgia	574	415	366	16	15	18	64	60	35
Hawaii	23	10	6	4	0	0	3	3	7
Idaho	36	18	8	3	0	7	6	5	7
Illinois[3]	648	481	216	7	9	249	44	88	35
Indiana	323	206	150	11	9	36	33	52	32
Iowa	44	22	13	4	1	4	7	7	8
Kansas	67	27	19	1	0	7	17	18	5
Kentucky[3]	82	53	42	2	5	4	7	16	6
Louisiana	556	431	371	26	24	10	46	51	28
Maine	14	6	6	0	0	0	4	2	2
Maryland	460	301	277	9	8	7	61	70	28
Massachusetts	162	80	49	1	2	28	39	35	8
Michigan	676	463	355	32	27	49	64	119	30
Minnesota	112	60	51	2	5	2	19	20	13
Mississippi	184	117	88	8	4	17	28	29	10
Missouri	331	229	114	11	16	88	43	50	9
Montana	9	4	2	1	0	1	2	3	0
Nebraska	16	7	4	0	2	1	4	4	1
Nevada	176	109	92	9	4	4	23	32	12
New Hampshire	11	8	7	0	0	1	2	0	1
New Jersey	335	205	180	7	9	9	63	36	31
New Mexico	122	66	50	4	3	9	28	11	17
New York	860	506	463	20	16	7	181	89	84
North Carolina	537	367	261	28	35	43	47	85	38
North Dakota	5	2	1	0	0	1	0	1	2
Ohio	476	289	222	12	12	43	44	93	50
Oklahoma	163	85	54	12	10	9	36	22	20
Oregon	65	40	18	4	6	12	9	14	2
Pennsylvania	599	434	342	19	8	65	52	92	21
Rhode Island	41	26	11	3	1	11	7	5	3
South Carolina	294	200	125	7	24	44	32	48	14
South Dakota	9	3	2	1	0	0	2	2	2
Tennessee	414	276	167	7	18	84	48	67	23
Texas	1,296	795	561	57	60	117	200	204	97
Utah	47	22	17	2	1	2	7	9	9
Vermont	13	10	8	1	0	1	2	0	1
Virginia	381	257	118	14	10	115	31	79	14
Washington	181	87	81	1	3	2	35	40	19
West Virginia	53	34	19	6	1	8	5	7	7
Wisconsin	149	108	63	7	11	27	17	16	8
Wyoming	14	6	3	1	2	0	4	2	2

[1] Total number of murders for which supplemental homicide data were received.

[2] Pushed is included in hands, fists, feet, etc.

[3] Limited or no supplemental homicide data were received.

Table 21

Robbery
by State, 2002
Type of Weapon

State	Total robberies[1]	Firearms	Knives or cutting instruments	Other weapons	Strong-arm	Agency count	Population
Alabama	4,388	2,528	233	499	1,128	268	3,719,249
Alaska	478	188	38	32	220	30	598,264
Arizona	7,816	3,716	783	685	2,632	84	5,146,764
Arkansas	2,096	1,046	83	147	820	105	1,673,500
California	64,434	23,318	6,566	5,715	28,835	720	34,762,918
Colorado	2,820	1,021	355	348	1,096	149	3,430,798
Connecticut	3,125	1,069	357	248	1,451	91	2,607,853
Delaware	840	348	65	60	367	36	721,039
District of Columbia	3,834	1,917	200	98	1,619	3	570,898
Florida	32,413	12,656	2,368	3,545	13,844	595	16,589,355
Georgia	12,090	6,903	632	1,156	3,399	427	7,166,137
Hawaii	1,137	130	97	19	891	3	1,113,277
Idaho	236	80	28	35	93	111	1,303,441
Illinois[2]							
Indiana	6,082	3,272	370	336	2,104	260	4,680,803
Iowa	1,148	267	119	185	577	190	2,638,836
Kansas	1,220	511	104	231	374	190	1,716,619
Kentucky[2]	2,151	953	173	192	833	21	1,321,725
Louisiana	6,678	3,928	407	473	1,870	160	3,971,556
Maine	269	58	37	34	140	180	1,291,128
Maryland	3,578	1,553	408	213	1,404	142	3,222,063
Massachusetts	6,014	1,570	1,116	770	2,558	253	4,953,523
Michigan	11,442	5,345	776	1,477	3,844	528	9,232,023
Minnesota	1,148	352	93	344	359	287	4,202,614
Mississippi	2,419	1,423	136	251	609	95	1,457,976
Missouri	6,962	3,020	465	562	2,915	532	5,546,857
Montana	159	47	21	21	70	67	598,495
Nebraska	1,342	637	109	108	488	223	1,564,711
Nevada	4,669	1,815	462	446	1,946	34	2,047,875
New Hampshire	232	53	31	43	105	118	859,866
New Jersey	13,825	4,553	1,434	1,028	6,810	494	8,345,025
New Mexico	1,903	856	282	160	605	71	1,425,666
New York	5,375	1,621	650	534	2,570	408	6,755,060
North Carolina	11,308	5,854	885	1,180	3,389	337	7,141,367
North Dakota	56	10	12	4	30	65	569,346
Ohio	16,271	6,067	911	1,355	7,938	343	8,303,709
Oklahoma	2,966	1,226	277	201	1,262	301	3,493,714
Oregon	2,509	684	243	241	1,341	134	3,116,138
Pennsylvania	16,158	6,443	1,209	1,031	7,475	766	10,763,082
Rhode Island	916	249	109	124	434	48	1,069,725
South Carolina	5,103	2,552	426	519	1,606	183	3,588,078
South Dakota	105	24	17	10	54	84	597,349
Tennessee	9,377	5,260	618	935	2,564	373	5,616,774
Texas	37,474	17,120	3,794	3,561	12,999	963	21,685,436
Utah	1,129	367	116	183	463	109	2,236,759
Vermont	51	14	5	11	21	48	465,200
Virginia	6,477	3,143	485	859	1,990	284	6,527,954
Washington	4,704	1,155	491	454	2,604	225	5,314,933
West Virginia	322	121	23	42	136	243	845,230
Wisconsin	4,666	2,571	300	302	1,493	338	5,010,946
Wyoming	90	43	10	14	23	62	487,292

[1] The number of robberies for which breakdowns by type of weapon were received for 12 months of 2002.

[2] Limited or no robbery by type of weapon data for 2002 were received.

Table 22

Aggravated Assault
by State, 2002
Type of Weapon

State	Total aggravated assaults[1]	Firearms	Knives or cutting instruments	Other weapons	Personal weapons	Agency count	Population
Alabama	9,095	2,402	1,284	2,110	3,299	268	3,719,249
Alaska	2,306	441	600	621	644	30	598,264
Arizona	18,857	4,604	2,759	5,355	6,139	84	5,146,764
Arkansas	5,661	1,322	1,024	1,647	1,668	105	1,673,500
California	130,064	22,889	17,925	42,631	46,619	720	34,762,918
Colorado	7,688	1,446	1,607	2,590	2,045	149	3,430,798
Connecticut	3,771	413	732	1,448	1,178	91	2,607,853
Delaware	2,517	414	539	1,272	292	36	721,039
District of Columbia	4,962	927	1,266	2,024	745	3	570,898
Florida	87,882	12,959	15,603	41,248	18,072	595	16,589,355
Georgia	19,567	4,648	3,800	6,525	4,594	427	7,166,137
Hawaii	1,478	156	159	426	737	3	1,113,277
Idaho	2,577	592	580	1,005	400	111	1,303,441
Illinois[2]							
Indiana	11,028	1,599	1,271	2,839	5,319	260	4,680,803
Iowa	6,134	557	1,085	1,645	2,847	190	2,638,836
Kansas	4,543	768	732	2,311	732	190	1,716,619
Kentucky[2]	4,035	605	515	1,221	1,694	21	1,321,725
Louisiana	17,843	4,879	3,445	5,278	4,241	160	3,971,556
Maine	733	17	99	233	384	180	1,291,128
Maryland	9,432	1,228	1,843	3,575	2,786	142	3,222,063
Massachusetts	18,102	1,365	3,593	8,914	4,230	253	4,953,523
Michigan	34,038	7,048	6,686	14,753	5,551	528	9,232,023
Minnesota	3,884	418	984	1,337	1,145	287	4,202,614
Mississippi	2,833	814	579	887	553	95	1,457,976
Missouri	21,270	3,954	3,010	6,345	7,961	532	5,546,857
Montana	1,761	230	220	525	786	67	598,495
Nebraska	3,411	507	660	1,615	629	223	1,564,711
Nevada	6,860	1,096	1,455	2,562	1,747	34	2,047,875
New Hampshire	660	87	193	204	176	118	859,866
New Jersey	16,301	2,372	3,465	5,368	5,096	494	8,345,025
New Mexico	8,492	1,783	1,400	2,555	2,754	71	1,425,666
New York	10,928	1,057	2,029	3,123	4,719	408	6,755,060
North Carolina	21,640	5,861	4,060	6,766	4,953	337	7,141,367
North Dakota	244	8	53	64	119	65	569,346
Ohio	14,767	3,105	2,638	4,354	4,670	343	8,303,709
Oklahoma	12,885	2,109	2,081	4,802	3,893	301	3,493,714
Oregon	5,925	751	867	2,050	2,257	134	3,116,138
Pennsylvania	25,316	5,335	3,769	6,648	9,564	766	10,763,082
Rhode Island	1,699	271	409	758	261	48	1,069,725
South Carolina	22,985	5,247	4,811	7,494	5,433	183	3,588,078
South Dakota	744	85	237	190	232	84	597,349
Tennessee	29,099	9,231	5,847	10,753	3,268	373	5,616,774
Texas	78,360	16,585	17,313	28,926	15,536	963	21,685,436
Utah	3,312	594	764	1,098	856	109	2,236,759
Vermont	305	46	55	73	131	48	465,200
Virginia	10,353	1,929	2,047	3,314	3,063	284	6,527,954
Washington	9,700	1,301	1,837	3,408	3,154	225	5,314,933
West Virginia	1,733	541	287	303	602	243	845,230
Wisconsin	5,884	1,008	874	1,347	2,655	338	5,010,946
Wyoming	1,089	100	158	332	499	62	487,292

[1] The number of aggravated assaults for which breakdowns by type of weapon were received for 12 months of 2002.

[2] Limited or no aggravated assault by type of weapon data for 2002 were received.

Table 23

Offense Analysis
Number and Percent Change, 2001-2002
[12,524 agencies; 2002 estimated population 236,622,152]

Classification	Number of offenses 2002	Percent change over 2001	Percent distribution[1]	Average value
Murder	12,904	+2.2	–	
Forcible rape	77,639	+4.2	–	
Robbery:				
Total	324,938	-1.1	100.0	$1,281
Street/highway	139,037	-2.9	42.8	1,045
Commercial house	47,344	-1.3	14.6	1,676
Gas or service station	8,690	-7.6	2.7	679
Convenience store	20,990	-4.8	6.5	665
Residence	43,800	+4.4	13.5	1,340
Bank	7,485	-6.5	2.3	4,763
Miscellaneous	57,592	+2.7	17.7	1,340
Burglary:				
Total	1,793,362	+2.0	100.0	1,549
Residence (dwelling):	1,180,063	+3.0	65.8	1,482
Night	348,538	+2.4	19.4	1,177
Day	561,688	+4.3	31.3	1,567
Unknown	269,837	+1.3	15.0	1,698
Nonresidence (store, office, etc.):	613,299	-0.1	34.2	1,678
Night	260,525	*	14.5	1,449
Day	190,651	+0.1	10.6	1,525
Unknown	162,123	-0.4	9.0	2,227
Larceny-theft (except motor vehicle theft):				
Total	5,808,133	*	100.0	699
By type:				
Pocket-picking	26,707	-5.0	0.5	328
Purse-snatching	32,011	+3.0	0.6	332
Shoplifting	811,709	+2.2	14.0	187
From motor vehicles (except accessories)	1,536,453	+2.9	26.5	692
Motor vehicle accessories	622,384	+4.7	10.7	432
Bicycles	227,970	-3.5	3.9	257
From buildings	727,395	-5.4	12.5	1,013
From coin-operated machines	43,103	+1.8	0.7	250
All others	1,780,401	-2.2	30.7	984
By value:				
Over $200	2,301,455	+0.7	39.6	1,682
$50 to $200	1,310,879	-1.5	22.6	114
Under $50	2,195,799	+0.1	37.8	18
Motor vehicle theft	1,039,490	+2.2	–	6,701

[1] Because of rounding, the percentages may not add to 100.0.
*Less than one-tenth of 1 percent.

Table 24

Property Stolen and Recovered
by Type and Value, 2002
[12,007 agencies; 2002 estimated population 228,033,072]

Type of property	Value of property		Percent recovered
	Stolen	Recovered	
Total	$13,731,306,278	$4,958,923,288	36.1
Currency, notes, etc.	977,139,529	40,078,922	4.1
Jewelry and precious metals	998,967,252	54,599,943	5.5
Clothing and furs	240,855,326	30,152,611	12.5
Locally stolen motor vehicles	6,569,478,599	4,146,165,060	63.1
Office equipment	466,027,464	25,132,680	5.4
Televisions, radios, stereos, etc.	932,644,149	39,517,884	4.2
Firearms	92,717,808	8,258,690	8.9
Household goods	205,369,049	9,693,633	4.7
Consumable goods	121,826,909	12,945,137	10.6
Livestock	17,122,092	3,253,959	19.0
Miscellaneous	3,109,158,101	589,124,769	18.9

SECTION III

Law enforcement agencies reporting offenses to the national UCR Program can clear these offenses in one of two ways: by arrest or by exceptional means. However, the administrative closing or "clearing" of a case by a local law enforcement agency does not necessarily mean that the agency can clear an offense according to UCR procedures. To clear an offense within the Program's guidelines, the reporting agency must adhere to certain criteria.

Cleared by Arrest

In the UCR Program, a reporting law enforcement agency clears, or solves, an offense by arrest only when all of the following conditions are met. At least one person must be:

- Arrested.
- Charged with the commission of an offense.
- Turned over to the court for prosecution.

The UCR Program counts in the clearances the number of offenses and not the number of persons arrested. The arrest of one person may clear several crimes. Conversely, the arrest of many persons may clear only one offense. In addition, the clearances that an agency recorded in a particular calendar year such as 2002 may include offenses that occurred in previous years.

Cleared by Exceptional Means

When elements beyond law enforcement's control prevent the agency from placing formal charges against the offender, the agency can clear the offense exceptionally. According to UCR Program guidelines, an agency can clear an offense exceptionally if it adheres to all of the following criteria. The agency must have:

- Identified the offender.
- Gathered enough evidence to support an arrest, make a charge, and turn over the offender to the court for prosecution.
- Identified the offender's exact location so that law enforcement can make an arrest.
- Encountered a circumstance outside the control of law enforcement that prohibits the agency from arresting, charging, and prosecuting an offender.

Examples of exceptional clearances include, but are not limited to, the death of the offender (suicide, justifiably killed by police or private citizens, etc.); the victim's refusal to cooperate with the prosecution after having identified the offender; or the denial of extradition because the offender committed a crime in another jurisdiction and is being prosecuted. In the UCR Program, the recovery of property does not clear an offense.

2002 National Clearances

Nationwide, law enforcement agencies in 2002 recorded a 20.0 percent Crime Index clearance rate in 2002. (The Crime Index is an aggregate of murder, forcible rape, robbery, aggravated assault, burglary, motor vehicle theft, and larceny-theft.) The Modified Crime Index (the Crime Index offenses plus arson) showed a 20.0 percent clearance rate for the year and included a 16.5 percent clearance rate for arson.

Violent crimes (murder, forcible rape, robbery, and aggravated assault)

often undergo a more vigorous investigative effort than crimes against property. Additionally, victims and/or witnesses often identify the perpetrators. Consequently, violent crimes tend to have higher clearance rates than property crimes. In 2002, that tendency continued with 46.8 percent of violent crimes cleared compared to 16.5 percent of property crimes cleared (excluding arson). An examination of violent crime clearances showed that the clearance rate for murder was 64.0 percent; for aggravated assault, 56.5 percent; for forcible rape, 44.5 percent, and for robbery, 25.7 percent. A review of the clearances for property crimes indicated that the clearance rate for larceny-theft was 18.0 percent; for motor vehicle theft, 13.8 percent, and for burglary, 13.0 percent. (See Table 25.)

2002 Regional Clearances

An examination of clearance rates by region showed that in 2002 law enforcement agencies in the Northeast recorded the highest Crime Index clearance rate among the regions in the Nation—24.9 percent. The South had a 20.4 percent clearance rate, the Midwest had an 18.5 percent clearance rate, and the West cleared 18.4 percent of reported Crime Index offenses. The Northeast had a 52.2 percent violent crime clearance rate, and the South cleared 47.2 percent of violent crimes, followed by the West at 46.0 percent and the Midwest at 42.9 percent. For property crime, the Northeast and the South showed clearance rates of 21.1 percent and 16.7 percent, respectively. The Midwest cleared 15.8 percent of property crimes and the West recorded a clearance rate of 14.7 percent. (See Table 26.)

Figure 3.1

Crimes Cleared by Arrest

Percent of crimes cleared by arrest, 2002

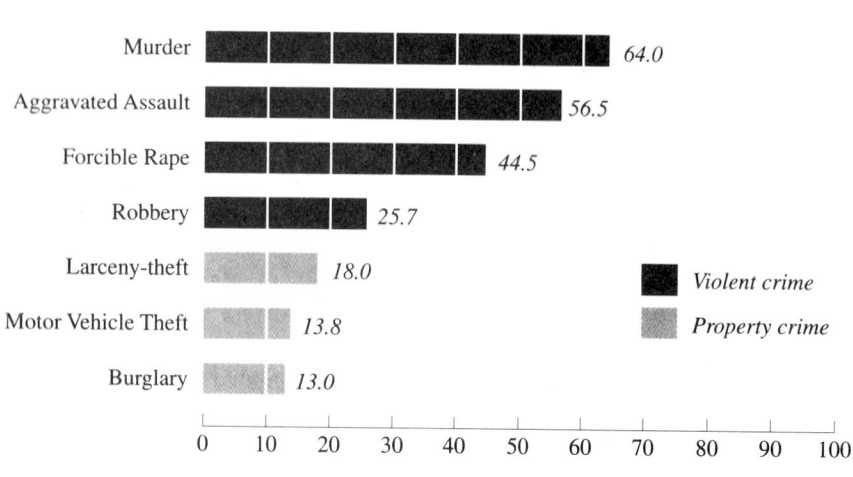

2002 Community Clearances

Among community types, cities collectively cleared 19.7 percent of Crime Index offenses, 44.5 percent of violent crimes, and 16.4 percent of property crimes. Among city groupings, cities with populations of 10,000 to 24,999 had the highest clearance rate for offenses that make up the Crime Index—23.9 percent. In 2002, these cities collectively also had the highest property crime clearance rate—21.1 percent. The highest percentage of violent crimes cleared—58.9 percent—occurred in cities with less than 10,000 inhabitants. Of the remaining community types, law enforcement in suburban counties cleared 20.8 percent of Crime Index offenses, 54.0 percent of violent crimes, and 16.4 percent of property crimes. Rural county law enforcement agencies recorded a 23.2 percent clearance rate for Crime Index offenses. Additionally, rural counties had a violent crime clearance rate of 61.4 percent and a property crime clearance rate of 18.3 percent. (See Table 25.)

Clearances Involving Only Persons Under 18 Years of Age

When an offender under the age of 18 is cited to appear in juvenile court or before other juvenile authorities, even though a physical arrest may not have occurred, the UCR Program considers that incident as a clearance by arrest. In addition, according to Program definitions, clearances involving both adult and juvenile offenders are classified as adult clearances. Therefore, because the juvenile clearance percentages in this publication include only the offenses in which there were no adults involved, these figures underestimate juvenile involvement in crime.

Of the Crime Index offenses law enforcement cleared, 18.0 percent involved only juveniles. In addition, juvenile offenders accounted for 11.9 percent of violent crime clearances and 20.3 percent of property crime clearances. Murder clearances showed the lowest percentage of juvenile involvement at 5.0 percent, and arson clearances showed the highest percentage of juvenile involvement at 43.0 percent. (See Table 28.)

By region, the Midwest had the largest percentage of Crime Index offenses involving only juveniles, clearing 22.7 percent. In the West, juveniles alone accounted for 20.0 percent of the clearances; in the Northeast, 16.2 percent; and in the South, 15.3 percent.

Table 25

Percent of Offenses Cleared by Arrest or Exceptional Means
by Population Group, 2002
[2002 estimated population]

Population group	Crime Index	Modified Crime Index[1]	Violent crime[2]	Property crime[3]	Murder and non-negligent man-slaughter	Forcible rape	Robbery	Aggravated assault	Burglary	Larceny-theft	Motor vehicle theft	Arson[1]
TOTAL ALL AGENCIES:												
12,862 agencies;												
population 240,070,262												
Offenses known	10,121,721	10,192,984	1,184,453	8,937,268	13,561	80,515	343,023	747,354	1,842,930	6,014,290	1,080,048	71,263
Percent cleared by arrest	20.0	20.0	46.8	16.5	64.0	44.5	25.7	56.5	13.0	18.0	13.8	16.5
TOTAL CITIES: 9,130 cities;												
population 159,128,836												
Offenses known	7,966,962	8,020,178	934,424	7,032,538	10,371	59,085	299,891	565,077	1,341,162	4,812,396	878,980	53,216
Percent cleared by arrest	19.7	19.6	44.5	16.4	62.0	43.4	25.0	54.6	12.3	18.1	12.8	15.9
GROUP I												
65 cities, 250,000 and over;												
population 40,220,526												
Offenses known	2,746,733	2,769,325	425,109	2,321,624	5,643	19,771	158,573	241,122	455,961	1,442,526	423,137	22,592
Percent cleared by arrest	16.8	16.7	38.6	12.8	57.8	44.0	21.4	49.1	10.5	14.3	10.3	10.5
8 cities, 1,000,000 and over;												
population 13,659,273												
Offenses known	846,653	853,517	149,894	696,759	1,855	5,696	56,911	85,432	132,872	419,599	144,288	6,864
Percent cleared by arrest	17.4	17.4	38.6	12.9	61.9	42.9	22.2	48.7	10.7	14.8	9.2	9.9
21 cities, 500,000 to 999,999;												
population 13,866,854												
Offenses known	997,046	1,004,672	145,515	851,531	2,020	7,443	52,147	83,905	170,288	539,734	141,509	7,626
Percent cleared by arrest	15.6	15.6	37.2	11.9	54.5	43.7	19.8	47.0	9.4	13.1	10.3	10.9
36 cities, 250,000 to 499,999;												
population 12,694,399												
Offenses known	903,034	911,136	129,700	773,334	1,768	6,632	49,515	71,785	152,801	483,193	137,340	8,102
Percent cleared by arrest	17.5	17.5	40.3	13.7	57.1	45.2	22.3	51.9	11.4	15.1	11.3	10.6
GROUP II												
158 cities, 100,000 to 249,999;												
population 23,822,400												
Offenses known	1,320,491	1,329,190	145,837	1,174,654	1,698	9,645	50,401	84,093	226,441	793,631	154,582	8,699
Percent cleared by arrest	18.6	18.5	44.4	15.3	61.7	43.1	26.4	55.0	11.4	17.1	11.9	15.7
GROUP III												
381 cities, 50,000 to 99,999;												
population 26,328,413												
Offenses known	1,187,713	1,194,733	126,887	1,060,826	1,189	9,443	38,358	77,897	203,511	738,564	118,751	7,020
Percent cleared by arrest	20.4	20.4	46.9	17.3	67.3	41.9	27.6	56.7	12.3	19.4	12.3	18.9

See footnotes at end of table.

Table 25

Percent of Offenses Cleared by Arrest or Exceptional Means
by Population Group, 2002—Continued
[2002 estimated population]

Population group	Crime Index	Modified Crime Index[1]	Violent crime[2]	Property crime[3]	Murder and non-negligent man-slaughter	Forcible rape	Robbery	Aggravated assault	Burglary	Larceny-theft	Motor vehicle theft	Arson[1]
GROUP IV												
682 cities, 25,000 to 49,999; population 23,803,053												
Offenses known	965,387	971,002	87,974	877,413	746	7,388	23,742	56,098	163,955	637,193	76,265	5,615
Percent cleared by arrest	21.7	21.6	49.8	18.8	72.3	40.4	30.9	58.7	12.8	20.8	15.4	20.1
GROUP V												
1,555 cities, 10,000 to 24,999; population 24,675,220												
Offenses known	929,803	934,563	79,815	849,988	612	7,156	18,290	53,757	156,697	631,531	61,760	4,760
Percent cleared by arrest	23.9	23.9	53.4	21.1	70.6	44.9	32.9	61.3	15.3	22.6	20.8	24.5
GROUP VI												
6,289 cities, under 10,000; population 20,279,224												
Offenses known	816,835	821,365	68,802	748,033	483	5,682	10,527	52,110	134,597	568,951	44,485	4,530
Percent cleared by arrest	22.9	22.9	58.9	19.6	73.7	46.2	34.9	65.1	16.3	19.8	26.3	24.6
SUBURBAN COUNTIES												
1,279 agencies; population 54,106,364												
Offenses known	1,636,611	1,650,437	191,377	1,445,234	2,227	15,051	38,727	135,372	349,563	930,563	165,108	13,826
Percent cleared by arrest	20.8	20.7	54.0	16.4	66.6	47.0	29.5	61.6	14.0	17.4	15.7	17.1
RURAL COUNTIES												
2,453 agencies; population 26,835,062												
Offenses known	518,148	522,369	58,652	459,496	963	6,379	4,405	46,905	152,205	271,331	35,960	4,221
Percent cleared by arrest	23.2	23.2	61.4	18.3	78.9	49.8	41.4	64.5	16.6	17.9	27.9	23.0
SUBURBAN AREA[4]												
6,120 agencies; population 99,561,928												
Offenses known	3,226,405	3,249,065	320,382	2,906,023	3,210	25,562	71,803	219,807	604,584	2,010,471	290,968	22,660
Percent cleared by arrest	21.3	21.3	53.4	17.8	67.5	45.7	29.9	61.7	14.1	19.1	16.2	19.1

[1] Because arson is reported to the FBI separately from other offenses, the number of agency reports used in arson clearance rates is less than those used in compiling other Crime Index offense clearance rates. The Modified Crime Index is the sum of the seven offenses making up the Crime Index, with the addition of arson.

[2] Violent crimes are offenses of murder, forcible rape, robbery, and aggravated assault.

[3] Property crimes are offenses of burglary, larceny-theft, and motor vehicle theft.

[4] Suburban area includes law enforcement agencies in cities with less than 50,000 inhabitants and county law enforcement agencies that are within a Metropolitan Statistical Area (see Appendix III). Suburban area excludes all metropolitan agencies associated with a central city. The agencies associated with suburban areas also appear in other groups within this table.

Table 26

Percent of Offenses Cleared by Arrest or Exceptional Means
by Geographic Region and Division, 2002

[2002 estimated population]

Geographic region/division	Crime Index	Modified Crime Index[1]	Violent crime[2]	Property crime[1]	Murder and non-negligent man-slaughter	Forcible rape	Robbery	Aggravated assault	Burglary	Larceny-theft	Motor vehicle theft	Arson[1]
TOTAL ALL AGENCIES:												
12,862 agencies;												
population 240,070,262												
Offenses known	10,121,721	10,192,984	1,184,453	8,937,268	13,561	80,515	343,023	747,354	1,842,930	6,014,290	1,080,048	71,263
Percent cleared by arrest	**20.0**	**20.0**	**46.8**	**16.5**	**64.0**	**44.5**	**25.7**	**56.5**	**13.0**	**18.0**	**13.8**	**16.5**
NEW ENGLAND												
761 agencies;												
population 11,657,696												
Offenses known	327,937	330,012	36,786	291,151	281	3,089	10,335	23,081	54,723	201,459	34,969	2,075
Percent cleared by arrest	21.1	21.0	51.0	17.3	61.6	42.2	27.0	62.8	14.2	18.6	14.3	17.4
MIDDLE ATLANTIC												
1,934 agencies;												
population 28,460,160												
Offenses known	805,251	811,181	103,821	701,430	1,203	6,569	38,295	57,754	132,198	485,894	83,338	5,930
Percent cleared by arrest	26.5	26.4	52.6	22.6	77.3	54.7	32.1	65.4	19.2	24.7	16.2	20.6
NORTHEAST												
2,695 agencies;												
population 40,117,856												
Offenses known	1,133,188	1,141,193	140,607	992,581	1,484	9,658	48,630	80,835	186,921	687,353	118,307	8,005
Percent cleared by arrest	**24.9**	**24.9**	**52.2**	**21.1**	**74.3**	**50.7**	**31.0**	**64.7**	**17.7**	**22.9**	**15.7**	**19.8**
EAST NORTH CENTRAL												
1,594 agencies;												
population 28,041,819												
Offenses known	1,131,786	1,142,662	119,161	1,012,625	1,559	12,013	38,528	67,061	213,619	683,068	115,938	10,876
Percent cleared by arrest	16.7	16.6	36.9	14.3	50.4	36.6	19.0	47.0	10.0	15.8	13.0	12.7
WEST NORTH CENTRAL												
1,712 agencies;												
population 17,287,696												
Offenses known	646,246	651,021	57,263	588,983	526	5,451	11,337	39,949	104,790	431,723	52,470	4,775
Percent cleared by arrest	21.7	21.7	55.4	18.4	74.0	45.0	29.9	63.9	13.1	19.6	19.2	19.5
MIDWEST												
3,306 agencies;												
population 45,329,515												
Offenses known	1,778,032	1,793,683	176,424	1,601,608	2,085	17,464	49,865	107,010	318,409	1,114,791	168,408	15,651
Percent cleared by arrest	**18.5**	**18.5**	**42.9**	**15.8**	**56.3**	**39.2**	**21.5**	**53.3**	**11.0**	**17.3**	**14.9**	**14.8**

See footnotes at end of table.

Table 26

Percent of Offenses Cleared by Arrest or Exceptional Means
by Geographic Region and Division, 2002—Continued
[2002 estimated population]

Geographic region/division	Crime Index	Modified Crime Index[1]	Violent crime[2]	Property crime[1]	Murder and non-negligent man-slaughter	Forcible rape	Robbery	Aggravated assault	Burglary	Larceny-theft	Motor vehicle theft	Arson[1]
SOUTH ATLANTIC												
2,569 agencies; population 49,147,598												
Offenses known	2,308,418	2,320,488	298,964	2,009,454	3,346	15,558	84,173	195,887	444,889	1,347,608	216,957	12,070
Percent cleared by arrest	21.4	21.4	49.3	17.2	64.7	51.3	26.3	58.7	14.8	18.3	15.9	19.7
EAST SOUTH CENTRAL												
814 agencies; population 12,043,974												
Offenses known	585,742	588,288	68,775	516,967	885	4,686	18,549	44,655	124,081	344,455	48,431	2,546
Percent cleared by arrest	18.8	18.8	41.9	15.7	70.5	37.9	23.0	49.6	11.3	17.4	15.2	17.6
WEST SOUTH CENTRAL												
1,625 agencies; population 31,725,162												
Offenses known	1,600,557	1,611,457	180,150	1,420,407	2,161	12,137	49,469	116,383	309,213	970,928	140,266	10,900
Percent cleared by arrest	19.5	19.5	45.9	16.2	70.4	48.8	26.6	53.3	12.2	17.6	15.2	18.3
SOUTH												
5,008 agencies; population 92,916,734												
Offenses known	**4,494,717**	**4,520,233**	**547,889**	**3,946,828**	**6,392**	**32,381**	**152,191**	**356,925**	**878,183**	**2,662,991**	**405,654**	**25,516**
Percent cleared by arrest	**20.4**	**20.4**	**47.2**	**16.7**	**67.4**	**48.4**	**26.0**	**55.8**	**13.4**	**17.9**	**15.6**	**18.9**
MOUNTAIN												
735 agencies; population 17,875,995												
Offenses known	879,016	883,998	81,454	797,562	961	6,931	19,841	53,721	147,067	536,222	114,273	4,982
Percent cleared by arrest	18.4	18.4	43.6	15.8	56.6	35.9	22.8	52.1	11.3	17.7	12.9	19.4
PACIFIC												
1,118 agencies; population 43,830,162												
Offenses known	1,836,768	1,853,877	238,079	1,598,689	2,639	14,081	72,496	148,863	312,350	1,012,933	273,406	17,109
Percent cleared by arrest	18.4	18.3	46.8	14.2	58.6	42.2	25.2	57.5	12.0	16.0	9.9	12.3
WEST												
1,853 agencies; population 61,706,157												
Offenses known	**2,715,784**	**2,737,875**	**319,533**	**2,396,251**	**3,600**	**21,012**	**92,337**	**202,584**	**459,417**	**1,549,155**	**387,679**	**22,091**
Percent cleared by arrest	**18.4**	**18.4**	**46.0**	**14.7**	**58.1**	**40.1**	**24.7**	**56.1**	**11.8**	**16.6**	**10.8**	**13.9**

[1] Because arson is reported to the FBI separately from other offenses, the number of agency reports used in arson clearance rates is less than those used in compiling other Crime Index offense clearance rates. The Modified Crime Index is the sum of the seven offenses making up the Crime Index, with the addition of arson.
[2] Violent crimes are offenses of murder, forcible rape, robbery, and aggravated assault.
[3] Property crimes are offenses of burglary, larceny-theft, and motor vehicle theft.

Table 27

Percent of Offenses Cleared by Arrest or Exceptional Means
Breakdown of Offenses Known
by Population Group, 2002
[2002 estimated population]

Population group	Forcible rape		Robbery				Aggravated assault				Burglary			Motor vehicle theft			Arson[1]		
	Rape by force	Assault to rape-attempts	Firearm	Knife or cutting instrument	Other weapon	Strong-arm	Firearm	Knife or cutting instrument	Other weapon	Hands, fists, feet, etc.	Forcible entry	Unlawful entry	Attempted forcible entry	Autos	Trucks and buses	Other vehicles	Structure	Mobile	Other
TOTAL ALL AGENCIES: 12,246 agencies; population 221,558,621																			
Offenses known	66,158	6,699	129,309	26,942	27,999	119,904	126,072	115,673	218,827	186,326	1,033,712	504,385	106,502	724,754	179,072	72,167	25,943	21,219	16,725
Percent cleared by arrest	43.7	44.2	20.3	28.2	28.0	29.8	41.3	62.2	55.5	63.3	12.3	14.1	10.8	14.1	11.6	12.9	22.4	7.2	20.7
TOTAL CITIES: 8,791 cities; population 149,851,350																			
Offenses known	49,715	5,401	114,535	24,235	24,673	108,368	102,154	94,871	172,141	137,495	771,293	374,776	82,678	615,915	147,974	48,424	19,758	15,270	12,398
Percent cleared by arrest	43.0	43.6	19.8	27.4	27.1	29.2	38.2	61.0	53.9	62.5	11.7	13.6	10.3	13.1	10.8	12.6	22.1	6.9	20.3
GROUP I																			
60 cities, 250,000 and over; population 37,824,297																			
Offenses known	16,567	2,209	65,643	12,528	12,064	55,482	55,660	41,090	76,223	43,587	289,956	108,236	23,765	288,125	90,209	18,655	7,413	7,643	3,574
Percent cleared by arrest	43.5	45.2	17.1	23.3	23.7	25.4	32.9	57.9	50.4	58.2	9.8	11.3	9.2	10.6	8.4	10.8	18.2	4.0	15.8
8 cities, 1,000,000 and over; population 13,659,273																			
Offenses known	4,870	826	25,949	5,544	4,508	20,910	22,239	15,111	25,348	22,734	91,761	34,490	6,621	97,763	38,496	8,029	2,251	3,414	1,199
Percent cleared by arrest	41.7	49.9	17.4	22.9	23.6	27.6	29.0	56.3	49.3	62.3	10.3	12.0	9.7	10.6	6.4	7.0	15.3	3.0	19.2
19 cities, 500,000 to 999,999; population 12,426,573																			
Offenses known	6,176	809	21,193	3,752	4,155	16,315	18,188	14,199	28,177	10,039	106,399	35,939	10,000	95,797	27,948	5,795	1,994	1,431	966
Percent cleared by arrest	42.7	39.9	14.4	22.1	21.5	22.5	33.4	55.4	47.8	49.4	8.2	9.5	8.2	9.9	9.8	4.5	25.5	6.3	14.2
33 cities, 250,000 to 499,999; population 11,738,451																			
Offenses known	5,521	574	18,501	3,232	3,401	18,257	15,233	11,780	22,698	10,814	91,796	37,807	7,144	94,565	23,765	4,831	3,168	2,798	1,409
Percent cleared by arrest	45.9	46.0	19.8	25.2	26.6	25.4	38.0	63.2	54.9	58.0	11.1	12.3	10.2	11.3	10.0	24.7	15.7	3.9	14.0
GROUP II																			
147 cities, 100,000 to 249,999; population 22,100,981																			
Offenses known	8,065	810	19,545	4,162	4,584	17,681	16,367	15,039	28,404	15,537	135,452	57,819	13,420	109,806	23,537	7,092	3,380	2,740	2,040
Percent cleared by arrest	42.6	40.9	21.4	29.1	27.2	30.2	38.9	61.4	53.3	62.1	10.8	13.1	10.0	12.1	10.9	9.0	19.8	5.6	21.0
GROUP III																			
350 cities, 50,000 to 99,999; population 24,172,113																			
Offenses known	7,794	669	12,466	3,246	3,020	14,464	11,326	12,968	23,815	19,303	107,314	58,523	13,891	86,352	13,191	6,710	2,733	1,933	1,884
Percent cleared by arrest	41.3	39.2	22.3	29.5	30.3	31.6	40.7	60.8	55.9	63.8	11.7	13.3	9.9	12.1	12.8	11.6	23.9	9.6	20.6

See footnotes at end of table.

Table 27

Percent of Offenses Cleared by Arrest or Exceptional Means

Breakdown of Offenses Known
by Population Group, 2002—Continued

[2002 estimated population]

Population group	Forcible rape — Rape by force	Forcible rape — Assault to rape-attempts	Robbery — Firearm	Robbery — Knife or cutting instrument	Robbery — Other weapon	Robbery — Strong-arm	Aggravated assault — Firearm	Aggravated assault — Knife or cutting instrument	Aggravated assault — Other weapon	Aggravated assault — Hands, fists, feet, etc.	Burglary — Forcible entry	Burglary — Unlawful entry	Burglary — Attempted forcible entry	Motor vehicle theft — Autos	Motor vehicle theft — Trucks and buses	Motor vehicle theft — Other vehicles	Arson[1] — Structure	Arson[1] — Mobile	Arson[1] — Other
GROUP IV																			
646 cities, 25,000 to 49,999; population 22,508,549																			
Offenses known	6,252	534	7,342	1,997	2,250	9,308	7,315	9,331	16,313	17,536	85,548	51,940	11,879	54,902	8,668	5,306	2,130	1,279	1,869
Percent cleared by arrest	40.1	46.3	25.8	32.0	32.1	35.5	46.8	64.2	57.8	62.4	12.4	13.8	9.4	15.4	16.4	12.3	24.5	10.4	21.9
GROUP V																			
1,481 cities, 10,000 to 24,999; population 23,534,294																			
Offenses known	6,177	573	6,057	1,423	1,791	7,131	6,166	8,728	14,886	18,386	83,057	50,855	10,250	45,388	6,869	5,264	2,105	901	1,498
Percent cleared by arrest	44.7	42.2	27.4	38.2	33.6	37.7	52.1	65.4	59.2	65.1	14.9	16.8	12.9	21.5	19.5	17.3	27.9	15.1	25.9
GROUP VI																			
6,107 cities, under 10,000; population 19,711,116																			
Offenses known	4,860	606	3,482	879	964	4,302	5,320	7,715	12,500	23,146	69,966	47,403	9,473	31,342	5,500	5,397	1,997	774	1,533
Percent cleared by arrest	46.4	45.5	29.1	43.3	33.5	38.2	58.3	68.0	61.1	67.7	16.5	16.5	12.4	27.6	25.5	20.2	29.0	18.1	21.9
SUBURBAN COUNTIES																			
1,127 agencies; population 46,036,211																			
Offenses known	10,868	906	13,102	2,349	2,843	10,190	16,394	15,155	34,905	30,955	168,682	87,928	16,873	88,919	25,268	15,891	4,079	4,946	3,429
Percent cleared by arrest	44.6	45.3	22.1	35.1	33.3	34.6	50.8	67.1	61.4	66.3	12.8	15.0	10.3	16.4	12.7	11.4	22.7	6.6	21.6
RURAL COUNTIES																			
2,328 agencies; population 25,671,060																			
Offenses known	5,575	392	1,672	358	483	1,346	7,524	5,647	11,781	17,876	93,737	41,681	6,951	19,920	5,830	7,852	2,106	1,003	898
Percent cleared by arrest	48.8	49.0	38.3	39.7	44.5	43.0	62.1	69.0	62.3	63.9	16.0	16.5	17.2	31.4	26.3	17.9	25.3	15.8	22.5
SUBURBAN AREA[2]																			
5,737 agencies; population 89,073,699																			
Offenses known	19,562	1,841	23,775	4,904	5,759	22,811	25,040	27,269	57,125	61,223	294,622	172,469	35,227	179,863	38,871	25,971	7,542	6,745	6,517
Percent cleared by arrest	44.3	43.9	22.9	34.9	32.7	35.0	50.3	66.3	60.8	66.6	13.2	15.2	10.6	16.8	13.9	12.7	24.6	8.4	22.2

[1] Because arson is reported to the FBI separately from other offenses, the number of agency reports used in arson clearance rates is less than those used in compiling other Crime Index offense clearance rates. It is necessary to report arson clearances by detailed property classification as specified on the *Monthly Return of Arson Offenses Known to Law Enforcement* to be included in this table: therefore, clearances in this table may differ from other clearance tables.

[2] Suburban area includes law enforcement agencies in cities with less than 50,000 inhabitants and county law enforcement agencies that are within a Metropolitan Statistical Area (see Appendix III). Suburban area excludes all metropolitan agencies associated with a central city. The agencies associated with suburban areas also appear in other groups within this table.

Table 28

Number of Offenses Cleared by Arrest or Exceptional Means
of Persons Under 18 Years of Age
by Population Group, 2002
[2002 estimated population]

Population group	Crime Index	Modified Crime Index[1]	Violent crime[2]	Property crime[3]	Murder and non-negligent man-slaughter	Forcible rape	Robbery	Aggravated assault	Burglary	Larceny-theft	Motor vehicle theft	Arson[1]
TOTAL ALL AGENCIES:												
11,912 agencies;												
population 212,703,198												
Total clearances	1,715,344	1,725,968	460,834	1,254,510	7,473	30,521	73,815	349,025	199,395	929,658	125,457	10,624
Percent under 18	18.0	18.2	11.9	20.3	5.0	12.0	14.1	11.6	17.3	21.2	18.2	43.0
TOTAL CITIES: 8,647 cities;												
population 144,084,799												
Total clearances	1,366,819	1,374,546	356,903	1,009,916	5,599	22,632	64,405	264,267	142,839	769,020	98,057	7,727
Percent under 18	18.6	18.8	12.1	20.9	5.4	11.6	14.2	11.7	17.3	21.9	18.5	45.6
GROUP I												
56 cities, 250,000 and over;												
population 35,189,022												
Total clearances	391,212	393,253	138,430	252,782	2,774	7,594	29,021	99,041	39,903	175,057	37,822	2,041
Percent under 18	15.2	15.3	10.2	17.8	5.1	9.1	13.8	9.4	14.4	18.3	19.3	42.1
8 cities, 1,000,000 and over;												
population 13,659,273												
Total clearances	147,518	148,197	57,801	89,717	1,148	2,443	12,617	41,593	14,217	62,174	13,326	679
Percent under 18	13.8	13.9	9.2	16.8	5.1	8.5	13.8	7.9	13.2	17.6	16.8	40.4
15 cities, 500,000 to 999,999;												
population 9,791,298												
Total clearances	101,556	102,114	34,923	66,633	680	2,355	6,396	25,492	10,067	46,297	10,269	558
Percent under 18	14.9	15.0	10.5	17.2	3.7	8.9	14.9	9.8	14.7	16.8	21.1	45.0
33 cities, 250,000 to 499,999;												
population 11,738,451												
Total clearances	142,138	142,942	45,706	96,432	946	2,796	10,008	31,956	15,619	66,586	14,227	804
Percent under 18	16.7	16.9	11.4	19.3	6.0	9.9	13.1	11.2	15.3	20.0	20.2	41.7
GROUP II												
140 cities, 100,000 to 249,999;												
population 21,144,564												
Total clearances	208,095	209,321	54,414	153,681	935	3,543	11,455	38,481	22,045	116,431	15,205	1,226
Percent under 18	18.2	18.3	11.6	20.5	5.7	9.4	13.8	11.3	16.2	21.8	17.1	43.4
GROUP III												
342 cities, 50,000 to 99,999;												
population 23,701,295												
Total clearances	211,407	212,629	51,078	160,329	713	3,454	9,113	37,798	21,363	126,249	12,717	1,222
Percent under 18	21.1	21.2	13.5	23.5	5.8	13.1	16.3	13.0	17.6	25.0	19.2	44.8

See footnotes at end of table.

Table 28

Number of Offenses Cleared by Arrest or Exceptional Means
of Persons Under 18 Years of Age
by Population Group, 2002—Continued
[2002 estimated population]

Population group	Crime Index	Modified Crime Index[1]	Violent crime[2]	Property crime[3]	Murder and non-negligent man-slaughter	Forcible rape	Robbery	Aggravated assault	Burglary	Larceny-theft	Motor vehicle theft	Arson[1]
GROUP IV												
628 cities, 25,000 to 49,999; population 21,868,627												
Total clearances	184,190	185,258	38,302	145,888	458	2,640	6,269	28,935	18,054	117,778	10,056	1,068
Percent under 18	21.1	21.2	13.9	22.9	5.9	13.3	15.2	13.7	19.4	23.8	19.2	49.0
GROUP V												
1,429 cities, 10,000 to 24,999; population 22,716,911												
Total clearances	197,861	198,958	37,283	160,578	385	2,898	5,239	28,761	21,259	128,035	11,284	1,097
Percent under 18	20.0	20.2	13.7	21.5	5.2	16.0	13.6	13.5	18.0	22.5	17.1	47.7
GROUP VI												
6,052 cities, under 10,000; population 19,464,380												
Total clearances	174,054	175,127	37,396	136,658	334	2,503	3,308	31,251	20,215	105,470	10,973	1,073
Percent under 18	19.6	19.8	14.2	21.1	5.7	13.2	13.5	14.5	21.5	21.3	17.6	50.3
SUBURBAN COUNTIES												
1,053 agencies; population 44,134,049												
Total clearances	244,872	246,881	72,856	172,016	1,185	5,088	7,968	58,615	34,919	118,309	18,788	2,009
Percent under 18	16.4	16.5	12.3	18.1	4.0	12.8	14.4	12.1	17.6	18.6	16.1	39.1
RURAL COUNTIES												
2,212 agencies; population 24,484,350												
Total clearances	103,653	104,541	31,075	72,578	689	2,801	1,442	26,143	21,637	42,329	8,612	888
Percent under 18	14.5	14.6	9.6	16.5	4.2	13.8	7.4	9.5	16.6	15.9	19.7	28.6
SUBURBAN AREA[4]												
5,581 agencies; population 85,992,422												
Total clearances	548,995	552,871	130,615	418,380	1,768	9,178	16,460	103,209	65,999	314,949	37,432	3,876
Percent under 18	18.5	18.7	13.6	20.0	4.8	13.9	14.6	13.5	18.6	20.7	16.5	45.9

[1] Because arson is reported to the FBI separately from other offenses, the number of agency reports used in arson clearance rates is less than those used in compiling other Crime Index offense clearance rates. The Modified Crime Index is the sum of the seven offenses making up the Crime Index, with the addition of arson.

[2] Violent crimes are offenses of murder, forcible rape, robbery, and aggravated assault.

[3] Property crimes are offenses of burglary, larceny-theft, and motor vehicle theft.

[4] Suburban area includes law enforcement agencies in cities with less than 50,000 inhabitants and county law enforcement agencies that are within a Metropolitan Statistical Area (see Appendix III). Suburban area excludes all metropolitan agencies associated with a central city. The agencies associated with suburban areas also appear in other groups within this table.

SECTION IV

As the ultimate goal of criminal investigations, arrests are often viewed by the public as a primary gauge of law enforcement's response to crime. Arrest practices, policies, and enforcement emphasis vary from place to place and even within an agency from time to time. The arrest practices for certain unlawful conduct such as disorderly conduct, vagrancy, and related violations also may differ among agencies. However, arrest practices for cases involving crimes, such as murder, rape, and robbery, are more likely to be uniform and consistent throughout all jurisdictions.

In the UCR Program, one arrest is counted for each separate occasion in which an individual is arrested, cited, or summoned for criminal acts in Part I and Part II crimes. (See Appendix II.) An individual may be arrested several times during the year, so the arrest figures in this section should not be viewed as an annual accounting of the number of persons arrested, but rather, as the number of arrests reported by law enforcement.

National Volume, Trends, and Rates

In 2002, law enforcement agencies nationwide made an estimated 13.7 million arrests for criminal infractions excluding traffic violations. (See Table 29.) Arrests for drug abuse violations and driving under the influence, estimated at 1.5 million arrests for each offense in 2002, accounted for 21.8 percent of all arrests. (Based on Table 29.) Arrests for simple assaults totaled 1.3 million, and larceny-theft arrests totaled 1.2 million. (See Table 29.)

The total number of arrests for all offenses in 2002 increased 0.5 percent nationally when compared to the number of arrests in 2001. Arrests for offenses that make up the Crime Index rose 0.2 percent. Arrests for violent crime decreased 0.8 percent, and arrests for property crime increased 0.6 percent. (See Table 36.)

The 5-year trend (1998-2002) showed that total arrests (for both Part I and Part II crimes) decreased 7.9 percent. When compared to 1998 arrest data, violent crime arrests in 2002 were down 7.3 percent and property crime arrests fell 12.5 percent. (See Table 34.) A comparison of the number of arrests for the 10 years, 1993 to 2002, revealed a 1.9 percent decline in total arrests. In 2002, arrests for violent crime were down 13.4 percent and arrests for property crime fell 25.2 percent from the 1993 numbers. (See Table 32.)

In relation to the total U.S. population, the arrest rate was 4,783.4 arrests per 100,000 inhabitants. Nationally, law enforcement personnel arrested persons for offenses that make up the Crime Index at a rate of 788.4 per 100,000 in population. In 2002, the violent crime arrest rate was 217.9 per 100,000 persons, and the property crime arrest rate was 570.5 per 100,000 inhabitants. (See Table 30.)

By Age, Sex, and Race

Nationwide, adults accounted for 83.5 percent of persons arrested in 2002. Juveniles were most often arrested for larceny-theft, and adults were most often arrested for driving under the influence. (See Table 38.) Overall, arrests of adults increased 1.2 percent, and arrests of juveniles decreased 3.0 percent when compared to the number of arrests during 2001. (See Table 36.)

In 2002, males comprised 77.0 percent of the persons arrested in the United States. Further, males accounted for 82.6 percent of violent crime arrestees and 69.3 percent of property crime arrestees. The offenses for which males were most frequently arrested were drug abuse violations and driving under the influence. The offenses for which females were most frequently arrested were larceny-theft. (See Table 42.)

A comparison of 2001 arrest data to 2002 data revealed that the number of males arrested remained virtually unchanged, but the number of females ar-

rested increased 2.1 percent. (See Table 37.) The 5-year trend (1998-2002) showed a 9.1 percent decline in the number of males arrested and a 3.4 percent decrease in the number of females arrested. (See Table 35.) In 2002, the number of males arrested was 5.9 percent below the number arrested in 1993, but the number of females arrested increased 14.1 percent from the 1993 number. (See Table 33.)

By race, 70.7 percent of arrestees in 2002 were white, 26.9 percent were black, and the remainder were of other races. Whites accounted for 65.5 percent of the individuals arrested for Index crimes. The offense for which whites were arrested most often was driving under the influence. The offense for which blacks were arrested most often was drug abuse violations. (See Table 43.)

Regional Arrest Rates

The UCR Program divides the United States into four regions: the Northeast, the Midwest, the South, and the West. (See Appendix III.) In 2002, data collected regarding the Nation's four regions reflected the following:

The Northeast

The Northeast recorded a rate of 3,942.3 arrests per 100,000 inhabitants. The arrest rate for violent crime was 188.9 per 100,000 in population. By offense within violent crime, law enforcement agencies in the region reported a murder arrest rate of 3.2; a forcible rape arrest rate of 10.0; a robbery arrest rate of 44.7; and an aggravated assault arrest rate of 131.1. Property crime arrests in the region were calculated at a rate of 469.6 per 100,000. A breakdown of property crime showed that the burglary rate in the region was 83.3; larceny-theft, 345.8; and motor vehicle theft, 34.6. For the offense of arson, there were 5.9 arrests per 100,000 persons. (See Table 30.)

The Midwest

The law enforcement agencies in the Midwest reported an overall arrest rate of 5,041.1 per 100,000 in population. Violent crime arrests were recorded at a rate of 193.5 per 100,000 residents. By violent crime offense type, the rates were murder, 5.7; forcible rape, 11.2; robbery, 32.1, and aggravated assault, 144.5 arrests per 100,000 inhabitants. For property crimes, the region had a rate of 583.6 arrests per 100,000 persons. Among property crimes, the burglary arrest rate was 81.5 per 100,000, the larceny-theft arrest rate was 441.4, the motor vehicle theft rate was 54.9, and the arson arrest rate was 5.9 per 100,000 inhabitants. (See Table 30.)

The South

The Nation's most populated region, the South, had 5,217.7 arrests per 100,000 inhabitants. The region had a violent crime rate of 196.8 per 100,000 people.

Within the category of violent crime, the murder arrest rate was 5.7; forcible rape, 10.1; robbery, 35.5; and aggravated assault, 145.5 arrests per 100,000 individuals. Property crime arrests were registered at a rate of 593.2. Among property crimes, burglary arrests were recorded at a rate of 103.5 per 100,000; larceny-theft, 444.9; motor vehicle theft, 39.2; and the arson arrest rate was 5.6 per 100,000 in population. (See Table 30.)

The West

Arrests were reported at a rate of 4,628.0 for every 100,000 persons in the West. The violent crime arrest rate in the region was 275.6. Within the violent crime category, the arrest rates per 100,000 inhabitants were murder, 4.6; forcible rape, 8.4; robbery, 40.0; and aggravated assault, 222.6 arrests per 100,000 inhabitants. The overall property crime arrest rate in the region was 596.3. Among the property crimes, the burglary arrest rate per 100,000 persons was 121.2, larceny-theft was 394.4, motor vehicle theft calculated at 74.9, and the arson arrest rate was 5.8 per 100,000 persons. (See Table 30.)

Population Groups: Trends and Rates

In 2002, cities, as a whole, recorded 5,170.2 arrests per 100,000 persons. Among population groups labeled *city*, cities with less than 10,000 inhabitants recorded the highest arrest rate per

100,000 persons at 6,365.5. Cities with 25,000 to 49,999 population recorded the lowest rate at 4,465.8 arrests per 100,000 inhabitants. The arrest rate for suburban counties was 3,841.5 per 100,000 in population and the arrest rate for rural counties was 4,025.6. (See Table 31.)

In the Nation's cities collectively, juveniles accounted for 18.0 percent of all arrestees. Juveniles comprised 15.7 percent of persons arrested for violent crime and 30.7 percent of persons arrested for property crime. Of all persons arrested in cities in 2002, 48.0 percent were under age 25. As for violent crimes, 44.9 percent of arrestees were under 25, and for property crime, 58.3 percent of arrestees were from this age group. (Based on Table 46.)

A comparison of total arrests in the Nation's cities collectively for 2001 and 2002 indicated a 0.2 percent increase. (See Table 44.) Suburban and rural counties each had an increase of 1.4 percent in arrests. In suburban counties, juveniles comprised 13.1 percent of arrestees, including 12.8 percent of violent crime arrestees and 26.3 percent of property crime arrestees. In rural counties, juveniles accounted for 10.2 percent of arrestees, 9.6 percent of the violent crime arrestees and 24.5 percent of the property crime arrestees. (See Tables 50, 52, 56 and 58.)

Table 4.1

Arrests for Drug Abuse Violations
by Region, 2002

Drug abuse violations	United States total	Northeast	Midwest	South	West
Total[1]	100.0	100.0	100.0	100.0	100.0
Sale/Manufacturing:[1]	19.7	27.9	23.1	17.2	16.4
Heroin or cocaine and their derivatives	8.8	19.1	6.0	7.8	6.2
Marijuana	5.4	6.5	7.4	4.8	4.4
Synthetic or manufactured drugs	1.4	1.0	1.3	2.6	0.8
Other dangerous nonnarcotic drugs	4.0	1.3	8.3	2.0	5.0
Possession:[1]	80.3	72.1	76.9	82.8	83.6
Heroin or cocaine and their derivatives	21.3	23.4	11.5	22.0	24.4
Marijuana	39.9	41.6	49.4	48.6	27.1
Synthetic or manufactured drugs	3.0	1.8	2.7	4.4	2.5
Other dangerous nonnarcotic drugs	16.0	5.4	13.3	7.8	29.7

[1] Because of rounding, the percentages may not add to 100.0.

Table 29

Estimated Arrests
United States, 2002

Total[1]	**13,741,438**	Embezzlement	18,552
		Stolen property; buying, receiving, possessing	126,422
Murder and nonnegligent manslaughter	14,158	Vandalism	276,697
Forcible rape	28,288	Weapons; carrying, possessing, etc.	164,446
Robbery	105,774	Prostitution and commercialized vice	79,733
Aggravated assault	472,290	Sex offenses (except forcible rape and prostitution)	95,066
Burglary	288,291	Drug abuse violations	1,538,813
Larceny-theft	1,160,085	Gambling	10,506
Motor vehicle theft	148,943	Offenses against the family and children	140,286
Arson	16,635	Driving under the influence	1,461,746
		Liquor laws	653,819
Violent crime[2]	620,510	Drunkenness	572,735
Property crime[3]	1,613,954	Disorderly conduct	669,938
Crime Index[4]	2,234,464	Vagrancy	27,295
		All other offenses	3,662,159
Other assaults	1,288,682	Suspicion	8,899
Forgery and counterfeiting	115,735	Curfew and loitering law violations	141,252
Fraud	337,404	Runaways	125,688

[1] Does not include suspicion.
[2] Violent crimes are offenses of murder, forcible rape, robbery, and aggravated assault.
[3] Property crimes are offenses of burglary, larceny-theft, motor vehicle theft, and arson.
[4] Includes arson.

Table 30

Number and Rate of Arrests
by Geographic Region, 2002
[Rate: Number of arrests per 100,000 inhabitants]

Offense charged	United States total (10,372 agencies; population 205,122,185)	Northeast (2,329 agencies; population 35,850,159)	Midwest (2,711 agencies; population 43,772,777)	South (3,658 agencies; population 65,086,583)	West (1,674 agencies; population 60,412,666)
TOTAL[1]	**9,811,831**	**1,413,312**	**2,206,610**	**3,396,013**	**2,795,896**
Rate	**4,783.4**	**3,942.3**	**5,041.1**	**5,217.7**	**4,628.0**
Murder and nonnegligent manslaughter	10,107	1,130	2,514	3,710	2,753
Rate	4.9	3.2	5.7	5.7	4.6
Forcible rape	20,162	3,569	4,924	6,581	5,088
Rate	9.8	10.0	11.2	10.1	8.4
Robbery	77,342	16,013	14,034	23,128	24,167
Rate	37.7	44.7	32.1	35.5	40.0
Aggravated assault	339,437	47,014	63,245	94,699	134,479
Rate	165.5	131.1	144.5	145.5	222.6
Burglary	206,136	29,874	35,675	67,372	73,215
Rate	100.5	83.3	81.5	103.5	121.2
Larceny-theft	845,009	123,967	193,198	289,561	238,283
Rate	412.0	345.8	441.4	444.9	394.4
Motor vehicle theft	107,187	12,390	24,022	25,526	45,249
Rate	52.3	34.6	54.9	39.2	74.9
Arson	11,833	2,114	2,571	3,625	3,523
Rate	5.8	5.9	5.9	5.6	5.8
Violent crime[2]	447,048	67,726	84,717	128,118	166,487
Rate	217.9	188.9	193.5	196.8	275.6
Property crime[3]	1,170,165	168,345	255,466	386,084	360,270
Rate	570.5	469.6	583.6	593.2	596.3
Crime Index[4]	1,617,213	236,071	340,183	514,202	526,757
Rate	788.4	658.5	777.2	790.0	871.9
Other assaults	921,676	145,638	191,176	366,274	218,588
Rate	449.3	406.2	436.7	562.7	361.8
Forgery and counterfeiting	83,111	11,440	14,471	31,969	25,231
Rate	40.5	31.9	33.1	49.1	41.8
Fraud	233,087	32,519	39,272	138,948	22,348
Rate	113.6	90.7	89.7	213.5	37.0
Embezzlement	13,416	1,038	2,337	6,932	3,109
Rate	6.5	2.9	5.3	10.7	5.1
Stolen property; buying, receiving, possessing	91,280	17,324	23,265	22,311	28,380
Rate	44.5	48.3	53.1	34.3	47.0
Vandalism	198,550	41,216	49,077	45,759	62,498
Rate	96.8	115.0	112.1	70.3	103.5
Weapons; carrying, possessing, etc.	118,312	15,043	26,469	38,232	38,568
Rate	57.7	42.0	60.5	58.7	63.8
Prostitution and commercialized vice	58,758	8,474	13,838	14,451	21,995
Rate	28.6	23.6	31.6	22.2	36.4
Sex offenses (except forcible rape and prostitution)	67,833	10,658	15,905	16,169	25,101
Rate	33.1	29.7	36.3	24.8	41.5
Drug abuse violations	1,103,017	179,848	229,915	324,869	368,385
Rate	537.7	501.7	525.2	499.1	609.8
Gambling	7,525	923	3,452	2,310	840
Rate	3.7	2.6	7.9	3.5	1.4
Offenses against the family and children	97,716	19,454	34,673	31,469	12,120
Rate	47.6	54.3	79.2	48.3	20.1
Driving under the influence	1,020,377	117,194	242,664	321,878	338,641
Rate	497.4	326.9	554.4	494.5	560.5
Liquor laws	463,849	56,010	177,925	101,769	128,145
Rate	226.1	156.2	406.5	156.4	212.1
Drunkenness	413,808	30,089	34,856	240,362	108,501
Rate	201.7	83.9	79.6	369.3	179.6
Disorderly conduct	482,827	113,258	161,294	133,567	74,708
Rate	235.4	315.9	368.5	205.2	123.7
Vagrancy	19,678	3,870	1,852	5,780	8.176
Rate	9.6	10.8	4.2	8.9	13.5
All other offenses (except traffic)	2,606,294	335,562	564,293	983,695	722,744
Rate	1,270.6	936.0	1,289.1	1,511.4	1,196.3
Suspicion	7,670	527	698	1,427	5,018
Rate	3.7	1.5	1.6	2.2	8.3
Curfew and loitering law violations	103,155	28,915	19,745	23.005	31,490
Rate	50.3	80.7	45.1	35.3	52.1
Runaways	90,349	8,768	19,948	32,062	29,571
Rate	44.0	24.5	45.6	49.3	48.9

[1] Does not include suspicion.

[2] Violent crimes are offenses of murder, forcible rape, robbery, and aggravated assault.

[3] Property crimes are offenses of burglary, larceny-theft, motor vehicle theft, and arson.

[4] Includes arson.

PERSONS ARRESTED   235

Table 31

Number and Rate of Arrests
by Population Group, 2002
[Rate: Number of arrests per 100,000 inhabitants]

Offense charged	Total (10,372 agencies; population 205,122,185)	Total cities (7,507 cities; population 142,375,961)	Cities — Group I (54 cities, 250,000 and over; population 38,631,295)	Group II (134 cities, 100,000 to 249,999; population 20,337,915)	Group III (322 cities, 50,000 to 99,999; population 22,278,495)	Group IV (625 cities, 25,000 to 49,999; population 21,842,796)	Group V (1,368 cities, 10,000 to 24,999; population 21,747,999)	Group VI (5,004 cities, under 10,000; population 17,537,461)	Counties — Suburban counties[1] (916 agencies; population 40,822,218)	Rural counties (1,949 agencies; population 21,924,006)	Suburban area[2] (5,060 agencies; population 85,923,394)
TOTAL[3]	9,811,831	7,361,064	2,124,721	994,018	1,094,374	975,460	1,056,146	1,116,345	1,568,199	882,568	3,627,108
Rate	4,783.4	5,170.2	5,500.0	4,887.5	4,912.2	4,465.8	4,856.3	6,365.5	3,841.5	4,025.6	4,221.3
Murder and nonnegligent manslaughter	10,107	7,467	4,022	1,093	862	529	471	490	1,754	886	2,660
Rate	4.9	5.2	10.4	5.4	3.9	2.4	2.2	2.8	4.3	4.0	3.1
Forcible rape	20,162	14,515	4,980	2,059	2,062	1,797	1,857	1,760	3,476	2,171	6,893
Rate	9.8	10.2	12.9	10.1	9.3	8.2	8.5	10.0	8.5	9.9	8.0
Robbery	77,342	66,834	29,940	11,185	9,638	6,858	5,682	3,531	8,494	2,014	20,577
Rate	37.7	46.9	77.5	55.0	43.3	31.4	26.1	20.1	20.8	9.2	23.9
Aggravated assault	339,437	260,392	99,328	41,276	37,833	30,000	26,458	25,497	55,158	23,887	110,807
Rate	165.5	182.9	257.1	203.0	169.8	137.3	121.7	145.4	135.1	109.0	129.0
Burglary	206,136	151,343	42,217	25,095	25,204	19,458	19,884	19,485	33,920	20,873	72,415
Rate	100.5	106.3	109.3	123.4	113.1	89.1	91.4	111.1	83.1	95.2	84.3
Larceny-theft	845,009	716,186	188,616	106,453	122,677	108,759	109,372	80,309	95,596	33,227	293,756
Rate	412.0	503.0	488.2	523.4	550.7	497.9	502.9	457.9	234.2	151.6	341.9
Motor vehicle theft	107,187	85,662	42,141	12,934	9,569	6,953	7,058	7,007	15,052	6,473	29,520
Rate	52.3	60.2	109.1	63.6	43.0	31.8	32.5	40.0	36.9	29.5	34.4
Arson	11,833	8,372	2,064	1,242	1,273	1,152	1,371	1,270	2,392	1,069	4,894
Rate	5.8	5.9	5.3	6.1	5.7	5.3	6.3	7.2	5.9	4.9	5.7
Violent crime[4]	447,048	349,208	138,270	55,613	50,395	39,184	34,468	31,278	68,882	28,958	140,937
Rate	217.9	245.3	357.9	273.4	226.2	179.4	158.5	178.3	168.7	132.1	164.0
Property crime[5]	1,170,165	961,563	275,038	145,724	158,723	136,322	137,685	108,071	146,960	61,642	400,585
Rate	570.5	675.4	712.0	716.5	712.4	624.1	633.1	616.2	360.0	281.2	466.2
Crime Index[6]	1,617,213	1,310,771	413,308	201,337	209,118	175,506	172,153	139,349	215,842	90,600	541,522
Rate	788.4	920.6	1,069.9	990.0	938.7	803.5	791.6	794.6	528.7	413.2	630.2
Other assaults	921,676	691,820	201,815	103,551	100,389	91,462	96,509	98,094	151,178	78,678	329,934
Rate	449.3	485.9	522.4	509.2	450.6	418.7	443.8	559.3	370.3	358.9	384.0
Forgery and counterfeiting	83,111	63,725	15,285	9,175	10,653	9,329	10,627	8,656	12,866	6,520	30,751
Rate	40.5	44.8	39.6	45.1	47.8	42.7	48.9	49.4	31.5	29.7	35.8
Fraud	233,087	121,969	18,506	13,595	18,624	18,389	25,464	27,391	71,794	39,324	112,608
Rate	113.6	85.7	47.9	66.8	83.6	84.2	117.1	156.2	175.9	179.4	131.1
Embezzlement	13,416	10,337	2,005	1,848	2,209	1,578	1,606	1,091	2,151	928	4,727
Rate	6.5	7.3	5.2	9.1	9.9	7.2	7.4	6.2	5.3	4.2	5.5
Stolen property; buying, receiving, possessing	91,280	71,788	22,776	10,286	12,384	10,287	9,034	7,021	13,977	5,515	33,825
Rate	44.5	50.4	59.0	50.6	55.6	47.1	41.5	40.0	34.2	25.2	39.4
Vandalism	198,550	155,656	40,568	21,305	23,714	21,473	24,252	24,344	27,787	15,107	72,884
Rate	96.8	109.3	105.0	104.8	106.4	98.3	111.5	138.8	68.1	68.9	84.8
Weapons; carrying, possessing, etc.	118,312	93,030	34,824	14,098	13,284	10,551	9,767	10,506	17,307	7,975	38,959
Rate	57.7	65.3	90.1	69.3	59.6	48.3	44.9	59.9	42.4	36.4	45.3
Prostitution and commercialized vice	58,758	56,686	40,661	8,620	4,189	2,062	862	292	1,929	143	4,773
Rate	28.6	39.8	105.3	42.4	18.8	9.4	4.0	1.7	4.7	0.7	5.6

See footnotes at end of table.

Table 31

Number and Rate of Arrests

by Population Group, 2002—Continued

[Rate: Number of arrests per 100,000 inhabitants]

Offense charged	Total (16,372 agencies; population 205,122,185)	Total cities (7,507 cities; population 142,375,961)	Group I (54 cities, 250,000 and over; population 38,631,295)	Group II (134 cities, 100,000 to 249,999; population 20,337,915)	Group III (322 cities, 50,000 to 99,999; population 22,278,495)	Group IV (625 cities, 25,000 to 49,999; population 21,842,796)	Group V (1,368 cities, 10,000 to 24,999; population 21,747,999)	Group VI (5,004 cities, under 10,000; population 17,537,461)	Suburban counties[1] (916 agencies; population 40,822,218)	Rural counties (1,949 agencies; population 21,924,006)	Suburban area[2] (5,060 agencies; population 85,923,394)
Sex offenses (except forcible rape and prostitution)	67,833	49,745	19,639	6,735	7,164	5,653	5,471	5,083	11,865	6,223	22,771
Rate	33.1	34.9	50.8	33.1	32.2	25.9	25.2	29.0	29.1	28.4	26.5
Drug abuse violations	1,103,017	838,900	305,079	130,137	118,287	97,171	92,402	95,824	172,912	91,205	372,988
Rate	537.7	589.2	789.7	639.9	530.9	444.9	424.9	546.4	423.6	416.0	434.1
Gambling	7,525	6,216	4,222	439	618	264	296	377	658	651	1,281
Rate	3.7	4.4	10.9	2.2	2.8	1.2	1.4	2.1	1.6	3.0	1.5
Offenses against the family and children	97,716	53,532	10,108	6,588	9,340	9,117	9,656	8,723	29,443	14,741	47,539
Rate	47.6	37.6	26.2	32.4	41.9	41.7	44.4	49.7	72.1	67.2	55.3
Driving under the influence	1,020,377	632,092	133,013	70,136	84,470	93,099	115,918	135,456	215,764	172,521	442,751
Rate	497.4	444.0	344.3	344.9	379.2	426.2	533.0	772.4	528.5	786.9	515.3
Liquor laws	463,849	368,132	60,397	36,373	53,809	46,070	69,035	102,448	49,729	45,988	176,569
Rate	226.1	258.6	156.3	178.8	241.5	210.9	317.4	584.2	121.8	209.8	205.5
Drunkenness	413,808	347,469	83,907	49,505	51,344	49,840	53,590	59,283	41,471	24,868	140,222
Rate	201.7	244.1	217.2	243.4	230.5	228.2	246.4	338.0	101.6	113.4	163.2
Disorderly conduct	482,827	415,817	101,985	43,442	62,883	53,946	71,839	81,722	40,754	26,256	174,655
Rate	235.4	292.1	264.0	213.6	282.3	247.0	330.3	466.0	99.8	119.8	203.3
Vagrancy	19,678	17,378	9,294	1,995	1,621	946	1,388	2,134	1,713	587	4,941
Rate	9.6	12.2	24.1	9.8	7.3	4.3	6.4	12.2	4.2	2.7	5.8
All other offenses (except traffic)	2,606,294	1,892,117	541,924	245,919	284,227	261,584	265,427	293,036	466,910	247,267	1,018,349
Rate	1,270.6	1,329.0	1,402.8	1,209.2	1,275.8	1,197.6	1,220.5	1,670.9	1,143.8	1,127.8	1,185.2
Suspicion	7,670	6,781	4,887	274	315	224	593	488	730	159	1,617
Rate	3.7	4.8	12.7	1.3	1.4	1.0	2.7	2.8	1.8	0.7	1.9
Curfew and loitering law violations	103,155	97,467	49,158	6,936	13,397	7,998	10,888	9,090	4,654	1,034	22,511
Rate	50.3	68.5	127.2	34.1	60.1	36.6	50.1	51.8	11.4	4.7	26.2
Runaways	90,349	66,417	16,247	11,998	12,650	9,135	9,962	6,425	17,495	6,437	32,548
Rate	44.0	46.6	42.1	59.0	56.8	41.8	45.8	36.6	42.9	29.4	37.9

[1] Includes only suburban county law enforcement agencies.

[2] Suburban area includes law enforcement agencies in cities with less than 50,000 inhabitants and county law enforcement agencies that are within a Metropolitan Statistical Area (see Appendix III). Suburban area excludes all metropolitan agencies associated with a central city. The agencies associated with suburban areas also appear in other groups within this table.

[3] Does not include suspicion.

[4] Violent crimes are offenses of murder, forcible rape, robbery, and aggravated assault.

[5] Property crimes are offenses of burglary, larceny-theft, motor vehicle theft, and arson.

[6] Includes arson.

Table 32

Ten-Year Arrest Trends

Totals, 1993-2002

[7,596 agencies; 2002 estimated population 175,384,794; 1993 estimated population 157,011,564]

	Number of persons arrested								
	Total all ages			Under 18 years of age			18 years of age and over		
Offense charged	1993	2002	Percent change	1993	2002	Percent change	1993	2002	Percent change
TOTAL[1]	8,581,290	8,413,983	-1.9	1,564,326	1,393,752	-10.9	7,016,964	7,020,231	*
Murder and nonnegligent manslaughter	15,125	8,933	-40.9	2,485	886	-64.3	12,640	8,047	-36.3
Forcible rape	23,509	17,394	-26.0	3,928	2,887	-26.5	19,581	14,507	-25.9
Robbery	96,877	69,405	-28.4	26,505	16,338	-38.4	70,372	53,067	-24.6
Aggravated assault	320,814	299,286	-6.7	49,427	38,082	-23.0	271,387	261,204	-3.8
Burglary	253,751	178,477	-29.7	89,511	54,393	-39.2	164,240	124,084	-24.4
Larceny-theft	959,452	729,825	-23.9	307,926	216,434	-29.7	651,526	513,391	-21.2
Motor vehicle theft	128,552	94,608	-26.4	57,740	28,664	-50.4	70,812	65,944	-6.9
Arson	12,646	10,055	-20.5	6,451	4,957	-23.2	6,195	5,098	-17.7
Violent crime[2]	456,325	395,018	-13.4	82,345	58,193	-29.3	373,980	336,825	-9.9
Property crime[3]	1,354,401	1,012,965	-25.2	461,628	304,448	-34.0	892,773	708,517	-20.6
Crime Index[4]	1,810,726	1,407,983	-22.2	543,973	362,641	-33.3	1,266,753	1,045,342	-17.5
Other assaults	733,037	782,294	+6.7	126,489	143,933	+13.8	606,548	638,361	+5.2
Forgery and counterfeiting	66,364	71,842	+8.3	5,341	3,070	-42.5	61,023	68,772	+12.7
Fraud	218,695	195,925	-10.4	6,449	5,258	-18.5	212,246	190,667	-10.2
Embezzlement	7,910	11,815	+49.4	510	883	+73.1	7,400	10,932	+47.7
Stolen property; buying, receiving, possessing	101,613	76,137	-25.1	28,808	15,766	-45.3	72,805	60,371	-17.1
Vandalism	209,095	169,842	-18.8	97,968	65,360	-33.3	111,127	104,482	-6.0
Weapons; carrying, possessing, etc.	175,998	104,418	-40.7	42,530	22,615	-46.8	133,468	81,803	-38.7
Prostitution and commercialized vice	61,811	51,275	-17.0	755	958	+26.9	61,056	50,317	-17.6
Sex offenses (except forcible rape and prostitution)	69,072	59,193	-14.3	13,387	12,198	-8.9	55,685	46,995	-15.6
Drug abuse violations	710,922	974,082	+37.0	73,413	116,781	+59.1	637,509	857,301	+34.5
Gambling	10,348	6,500	-37.2	1,715	1,053	-38.6	8,633	5,447	-36.9
Offenses against the family and children	67,930	79,059	+16.4	3,520	5,208	+48.0	64,410	73,851	+14.7
Driving under the influence	984,141	879,210	-10.7	8,878	12,921	+45.5	975,263	866,289	-11.2
Liquor laws	316,919	385,611	+21.7	75,836	88,574	+16.8	241,083	297,037	+23.2
Drunkenness	509,543	362,979	-28.8	11,705	11,452	-2.2	497,838	351,527	-29.4
Disorderly conduct	483,676	398,728	-17.6	103,747	112,844	+8.8	379,929	285,884	-24.8
Vagrancy	13,581	15,702	+15.6	2,254	1,346	-40.3	11,327	14,356	+26.7
All other offenses (except traffic)	1,834,511	2,209,668	+20.4	221,650	239,171	+7.9	1,612,861	1,970,497	+22.2
Suspicion	6,231	2,252	-63.9	1,239	708	-42.9	4,992	1,544	-69.1
Curfew and loitering law violations	68,042	91,984	+35.2	68,042	91,984	+35.2	–	–	–
Runaways	127,356	79,736	-37.4	127,356	79,736	-37.4	–	–	–

[1] Does not include suspicion.

[2] Violent crimes are offenses of murder, forcible rape, robbery, and aggravated assault.

[3] Property crimes are offenses of burglary, larceny-theft, motor vehicle theft, and arson.

[4] Includes arson.

* Less than one-tenth of 1 percent.

Table 33

Ten-Year Arrest Trends
by Sex, 1993-2002

[7,596 agencies; 2002 estimated population 175,384,794; 1993 estimated population 157,011,564]

| | Male | | | | | | Female | | | | | |
| | Total | | | Under 18 | | | Total | | | Under 18 | | |
Offense charged	1993	2002	Percent change	1993	2002	Percent change	1993	2002	Percent change	1993	2002	Percent change
TOTAL[1]	6,891,398	6,486,470	-5.9	1,186,822	992,153	-16.4	1,689,892	1,927,513	+14.1	377,504	401,599	+6.4
Murder and nonnegligent manslaughter	13,656	7,986	-41.5	2,326	795	-65.8	1,469	947	-35.5	159	91	-42.8
Forcible rape	23,201	17,141	-26.1	3,856	2,782	-27.9	308	253	-17.9	72	105	+45.8
Robbery	88,326	62,330	-29.4	24,263	14,908	-38.6	8,551	7,075	-17.3	2,242	1,430	-36.2
Aggravated assault	272,381	238,780	-12.3	41,055	29,127	-29.1	48,433	60,506	+24.9	8,372	8,955	+7.0
Burglary	227,422	154,642	-32.0	80,681	48,136	-40.3	26,329	23,835	-9.5	8,830	6,257	-29.1
Larceny-theft	645,065	459,358	-28.8	212,145	130,798	-38.3	314,387	270,467	-14.0	95,781	85,636	-10.6
Motor vehicle theft	112,582	78,955	-29.9	49,534	23,777	-52.0	15,970	15,653	-2.0	8,206	4,887	-40.4
Arson	10,847	8,507	-21.6	5,685	4,393	-22.7	1,799	1,548	-14.0	766	564	-26.4
Violent crime[2]	397,564	326,237	-17.9	71,500	47,612	-33.4	58,761	68,781	+17.1	10,845	10,581	-2.4
Property crime[3]	995,916	701,462	-29.6	348,045	207,104	-40.5	358,485	311,503	-13.1	113,583	97,344	-14.3
Crime Index[4]	1,393,480	1,027,699	-26.2	419,545	254,716	-39.3	417,246	380,284	-8.9	124,428	107,925	-13.3
Other assaults	600,914	596,196	-0.8	93,725	97,759	+4.3	132,123	186,098	+40.9	32,764	46,174	+40.9
Forgery and counterfeiting	42,342	43,190	+2.0	3,482	1,949	-44.0	24,022	28,652	+19.3	1,859	1,121	-39.7
Fraud	120,506	105,140	-12.8	4,270	3,472	-18.7	98,189	90,785	-7.5	2,179	1,786	-18.0
Embezzlement	4,631	5,898	+27.4	296	506	+70.9	3,279	5,917	+80.5	214	377	+76.2
Stolen property; buying, receiving, possessing	88,634	63,261	-28.6	25,671	13,551	-47.2	12,979	12,876	-0.8	3,137	2,215	-29.4
Vandalism	183,817	141,782	-22.9	88,566	56,527	-36.2	25,278	28,060	+11.0	9,402	8,833	-6.1
Weapons; carrying, possessing, etc.	162,611	96,141	-40.9	39,160	20,123	-48.6	13,387	8,277	-38.2	3,370	2,492	-26.1
Prostitution and commercialized vice	22,728	18,078	-20.5	320	331	+3.4	39,083	33,197	-15.1	435	627	+44.1
Sex offenses (except forcible rape and prostitution)	63,068	54,249	-14.0	12,148	11,084	-8.8	6,004	4,944	-17.7	1,239	1,114	-10.1
Drug abuse violations	594,006	798,695	+34.5	65,051	98,383	+51.2	116,916	175,387	+50.0	8,362	18,398	+120.0
Gambling	9,314	5,954	-36.1	1,670	1,022	-38.8	1,034	546	-47.2	45	31	-31.1
Offenses against the family and children	55,344	59,802	+8.1	2,242	3,229	+44.0	12,586	19,257	+53.0	1,278	1,979	+54.9
Driving under the influence	846,497	727,089	-14.1	7,584	10,416	+37.3	137,644	152,121	+10.5	1,294	2,505	+93.6
Liquor laws	252,565	289,770	+14.7	54,032	58,648	+8.5	64,354	95,841	+48.9	21,804	29,926	+37.3
Drunkenness	452,805	313,451	-30.8	9,842	9,047	-8.1	56,738	49,528	-12.7	1,863	2,405	+29.1
Disorderly conduct	384,867	301,613	-21.6	80,673	79,064	-2.0	98,809	97,115	-1.7	23,074	33,780	+46.4
Vagrancy	11,470	12,696	+10.7	1,893	1,023	-46.0	2,111	3,006	+42.4	361	323	-10.5
All other offenses (except traffic)	1,498,770	1,730,296	+15.4	173,623	175,833	+1.3	335,741	479,372	+42.8	48,027	63,338	+31.9
Suspicion	5,200	1,748	-66.4	1,024	512	-50.0	1,031	504	-51.1	215	196	-8.8
Curfew and loitering law violations	49,007	63,454	+29.5	49,007	63,454	+29.5	19,035	28,530	+49.9	19,035	28,530	+49.9
Runaways	54,022	32,016	-40.7	54,022	32,016	-40.7	73,334	47,720	-34.9	73,334	47,720	-34.9

[1] Does not include suspicion.
[2] Violent crimes are offenses of murder, forcible rape, robbery, and aggravated assault.
[3] Property crimes are offenses of burglary, larceny-theft, motor vehicle theft, and arson.
[4] Includes arson.

Table 34

Five-Year Arrest Trends

Totals, 1998-2002

[7,779 agencies; 2002 estimated population 169,318,197; 1998 estimated population 158,699,352]

Offense charged	Number of persons arrested								
	Total all ages			Under 18 years of age			18 years of age and over		
	1998	2002	Percent change	1998	2002	Percent change	1998	2002	Percent change
TOTAL[1]	8,870,062	8,170,655	-7.9	1,620,158	1,307,660	-19.3	7,249,904	6,862,995	-5.3
Murder and nonnegligent manslaughter	8,836	7,893	-10.7	1,134	730	-35.6	7,702	7,163	-7.0
Forcible rape	18,238	16,926	-7.2	3,218	2,774	-13.8	15,020	14,152	5.8
Robbery	71,175	65,235	-8.3	19,236	15,253	-20.7	51,939	49,982	-3.8
Aggravated assault	303,458	282,472	-6.9	44,009	37,405	-15.0	259,449	245,067	-5.5
Burglary	199,917	175,882	-12.0	71,389	52,755	-26.1	128,528	123,127	-4.2
Larceny-theft	825,616	709,622	-14.0	267,930	206,580	-22.9	557,686	503,042	-9.8
Motor vehicle theft	93,419	92,650	-0.8	32,830	27,855	-15.2	60,589	64,795	+6.9
Arson	10,173	9,607	-5.6	5,483	4,861	-11.3	4,690	4,746	+1.2
Violent crime[2]	401,707	372,526	-7.3	67,597	56,162	-16.9	334,110	316,364	-5.3
Property crime[3]	1,129,125	987,761	-12.5	377,632	292,051	-22.7	751,493	695,710	-7.4
Crime Index[4]	1,530,832	1,360,287	-11.1	445,229	348,213	-21.8	1,085,603	1,012,074	-6.8
Other assaults	818,346	782,242	-4.4	145,757	143,235	-1.7	672,589	639,007	-5.0
Forgery and counterfeiting	67,922	69,469	+2.3	4,376	3,006	-31.3	63,546	66,463	+4.6
Fraud	214,488	197,253	-8.0	6,908	5,527	-20.0	207,580	191,726	-7.6
Embezzlement	10,744	11,555	+7.5	1,020	834	-18.2	9,724	10,721	+10.3
Stolen property; buying, receiving, possessing	82,208	75,374	-8.3	21,137	15,616	-26.1	61,071	59,758	-2.1
Vandalism	186,930	163,225	-12.7	80,167	62,363	-22.2	106,763	100,862	-5.5
Weapons; carrying, possessing, etc.	115,949	98,120	-15.4	27,720	21,031	-24.1	88,229	77,089	-12.6
Prostitution and commercialized vice	59,775	49,597	-17.0	890	839	-5.7	58,885	48,758	-17.2
Sex offenses (except forcible rape and prostitution)	56,192	55,040	-2.1	9,692	10,577	+9.1	46,500	44,463	-4.4
Drug abuse violations	946,065	945,334	-0.1	126,219	112,787	-10.6	819,846	832,547	+1.5
Gambling	7,398	6,092	-17.7	1,006	924	-8.2	6,392	5,168	-19.1
Offenses against the family and children	79,458	77,818	-2.1	5,841	5,120	-12.3	73,617	72,698	-1.2
Driving under the influence	864,669	840,384	-2.8	13,037	12,278	-5.8	851,632	828,106	-2.8
Liquor laws	395,831	357,222	-9.8	102,175	79,758	-21.9	293,656	277,464	-5.5
Drunkenness	455,225	378,102	-16.9	16,062	11,822	-26.4	439,163	366,280	-16.6
Disorderly conduct	426,915	347,576	-18.6	117,096	98,956	-15.5	309,819	248,620	-19.8
Vagrancy	18,704	17,681	-5.5	1,891	1,192	-37.0	16,813	16,489	-1.9
All other offenses (except traffic)	2,316,119	2,187,182	-5.6	277,643	222,480	-19.9	2,038,476	1,964,702	-3.6
Suspicion	3,543	1,756	-50.4	931	846	-9.1	2,612	910	-65.2
Curfew and loitering law violations	113,717	76,525	-32.7	113,717	76,525	-32.7	–	–	–
Runaways	102,575	74,577	-27.3	102,575	74,577	-27.3	–	–	–

[1] Does not include suspicion.

[2] Violent crimes are offenses of murder, forcible rape, robbery, and aggravated assault.

[3] Property crimes are offenses of burglary, larceny-theft, motor vehicle theft, and arson.

[4] Includes arson.

Table 35

Five-Year Arrest Trends

by Sex, 1998-2002

[7,779 agencies; 2002 estimated population 169,318,197; 1998 estimated population 158,699,352]

Offense charged	Male Total 1998	Male Total 2002	Male Total Percent change	Male Under 18 1998	Male Under 18 2002	Male Under 18 Percent change	Female Total 1998	Female Total 2002	Female Total Percent change	Female Under 18 1998	Female Under 18 2002	Female Under 18 Percent change
TOTAL[1]	6,935,191	6,301,422	-9.1	1,184,101	932,601	-21.2	1,934,871	1,869,233	-3.4	436,057	375,059	-14.0
Murder and nonnegligent manslaughter	7,892	7,053	-10.6	1,043	661	-36.6	944	840	-11.0	91	69	-24.2
Forcible rape	18,015	16,694	-7.3	3,165	2,682	-15.3	223	232	+4.0	53	92	+73.6
Robbery	63,905	58,459	-8.5	17,544	13,872	-20.9	7,270	6,776	-6.8	1,692	1,381	-18.4
Aggravated assault	245,349	226,080	-7.9	34,518	28,692	-16.9	58,109	56,392	-3.0	9,491	8,713	-8.2
Burglary	174,096	151,719	-12.9	63,232	46,668	-26.2	25,821	24,163	-6.4	8,157	6,087	-25.4
Larceny-theft	536,764	446,853	-16.8	174,404	125,073	-28.3	288,852	262,769	-9.0	93,526	81,507	-12.9
Motor vehicle theft	78,637	77,278	-1.7	27,087	23,162	-14.5	14,782	15,372	+4.0	5,743	4,693	-18.3
Arson	8,697	8,169	-6.1	4,894	4,310	-11.9	1,476	1,438	-2.6	589	551	-6.5
Violent crime[2]	335,161	308,286	-8.0	56,270	45,907	-18.4	66,546	64,240	-3.5	11,327	10,255	-9.5
Property crime[3]	798,194	684,019	-14.3	269,617	199,213	-26.1	330,931	303,742	-8.2	108,015	92,838	-14.1
Crime Index[4]	1,133,355	992,305	-12.4	325,887	245,120	-24.8	397,477	367,982	-7.4	119,342	103,093	-13.6
Other assaults	635,264	594,588	-6.4	101,364	97,167	-4.1	183,082	187,654	+2.5	44,393	46,068	+3.8
Forgery and counterfeiting	41,721	41,688	-0.1	2,799	1,926	-31.2	26,201	27,781	+6.0	1,577	1,080	-31.5
Fraud	118,529	108,615	-8.4	4,669	3,774	-19.2	95,959	88,638	-7.6	2,239	1,753	-21.7
Embezzlement	5,472	5,767	+5.4	587	479	-18.4	5,272	5,788	+9.8	433	355	-18.0
Stolen property; buying, receiving, possessing	69,284	61,769	-10.8	18,401	13,097	-28.8	12,924	13,605	+5.3	2,736	2,519	-7.9
Vandalism	159,058	136,308	-14.3	70,677	53,901	-23.7	27,872	26,917	-3.4	9,490	8,462	-10.8
Weapons; carrying, possessing, etc.	106,958	90,406	-15.5	25,247	18,785	-25.6	8,991	7,714	-14.2	2,473	2,246	-9.2
Prostitution and commercialized vice	24,334	16,820	-30.9	427	299	-30.0	35,441	32,777	-7.5	463	540	+16.6
Sex offenses (except forcible rape and prostitution)	52,142	51,162	-1.9	9,034	9,838	+8.9	4,050	3,878	-4.2	658	739	+12.3
Drug abuse violations	779,388	773,509	-0.8	108,704	94,770	-12.8	166,677	171,825	+3.1	17,515	18,017	+2.9
Gambling	6,602	5,480	-17.0	982	894	-9.0	796	612	-23.1	24	30	+25.0
Offenses against the family and children	61,587	58,960	-4.3	3,645	3,133	-14.0	17,871	18,858	+5.5	2,196	1,987	-9.5
Driving under the influence	728,757	695,338	-4.6	10,747	9,932	-7.6	135,912	145,046	+6.7	2,290	2,346	+2.4
Liquor laws	308,994	270,938	-12.3	71,229	53,385	-25.1	86,837	86,284	-0.6	30,946	26,373	-14.8
Drunkenness	397,428	326,029	-18.0	13,142	9,326	-29.0	57,797	52,073	-9.9	2,920	2,496	-14.5
Disorderly conduct	328,902	263,971	-19.7	84,575	69,152	-18.2	98,013	83,605	-14.7	32,521	29,804	-8.4
Vagrancy	15,170	14,540	-4.2	1,561	927	-40.6	3,534	3,141	-11.1	330	265	-19.7
All other offenses (except traffic)	1,841,042	1,710,202	-7.1	209,220	163,669	-21.8	475,077	476,980	+0.4	68,423	58,811	-14.0
Suspicion	2,825	1,346	-52.4	708	592	-16.4	718	410	-42.9	223	254	+13.9
Curfew and loitering law violations	78,678	53,181	-32.4	78,678	53,181	-32.4	35,039	23,344	-33.4	35,039	23,344	-33.4
Runaways	42,526	29,846	-29.8	42,526	29,846	-29.8	60,049	44,731	-25.5	60,049	44,731	-25.5

[1] Does not include suspicion.

[2] Violent crimes are offenses of murder, forcible rape, robbery, and aggravated assault.

[3] Property crimes are offenses of burglary, larceny-theft, motor vehicle theft, and arson.

[4] Includes arson.

Table 36

Current Year Over Previous Year Arrest Trends
Totals, 2001-2002
[8,787 agencies; 2002 estimated population 179,500,199; 2001 estimated population 177,579,561]

	Number of persons arrested											
	Total all ages			Under 15 years of age			Under 18 years of age			18 years of age and over		
Offense charged	2001	2002	Percent change	2001	2002	Percent change	2001	2002	Percent change	2001	2002	Percent change
TOTAL[1]	8,465,363	8,505,348	+0.5	455,386	438,291	-3.8	1,421,948	1,379,049	-3.0	7,043,415	7,126,299	+1.2
Murder and nonnegligent manslaughter	8,680	8,515	-1.9	98	93	-5.1	799	811	+1.5	7,881	7,704	-2.2
Forcible rape	17,225	17,539	+1.8	1,086	1,042	-4.1	2,883	2,842	-1.4	14,342	14,697	+2.5
Robbery	67,093	66,523	-0.8	3,455	3,452	-0.1	14,994	14,856	-0.9	52,099	51,667	-0.8
Aggravated assault	303,711	300,953	-0.9	14,765	13,780	-6.7	40,147	38,539	-4.0	263,564	262,414	-0.4
Burglary	183,009	184,162	+0.6	21,331	19,690	-7.7	57,018	54,504	-4.4	125,991	129,658	+2.9
Larceny-theft	734,476	737,112	+0.4	86,587	83,245	-3.9	224,099	217,422	-3.0	510,377	519,690	+1.8
Motor vehicle theft	85,125	88,449	+3.9	6,892	6,539	-5.1	27,470	25,910	-5.7	57,655	62,539	+8.5
Arson	12,043	10,597	-12.0	3,821	3,423	-10.4	5,962	5,353	-10.2	6,081	5,244	-13.8
Violent crime[2]	396,709	393,530	-0.8	19,404	18,367	-5.3	58,823	57,048	-3.0	337,886	336,482	-0.4
Property crime[3]	1,014,653	1,020,320	+0.6	118,631	112,897	-4.8	314,549	303,189	-3.6	700,104	717,131	+2.4
Crime Index[4]	1,411,362	1,413,850	+0.2	138,035	131,264	-4.9	373,372	360,237	-3.5	1,037,990	1,053,613	+1.5
Other assaults	813,792	812,891	-0.1	63,669	63,338	-0.5	146,451	148,433	+1.4	667,341	664,458	-0.4
Forgery and counterfeiting	73,133	72,972	-0.2	408	395	-3.2	3,838	3,174	-17.3	69,295	69,798	+0.7
Fraud	198,522	198,718	+0.1	878	861	-1.9	5,478	5,084	-7.2	193,044	193,634	+0.3
Embezzlement	13,341	12,601	-5.5	93	74	-20.4	1,241	926	-25.4	12,100	11,675	-3.5
Stolen property; buying, receiving, possessing	84,481	84,233	-0.3	4,735	4,540	-4.1	18,088	17,109	-5.4	66,393	67,124	+1.1
Vandalism	170,208	171,794	+0.9	29,287	28,335	-3.3	66,718	65,433	-1.9	103,490	106,361	+2.8
Weapons; carrying, possessing, etc.	102,187	101,676	-0.5	7,602	7,370	-3.1	22,549	21,383	-5.2	79,638	80,293	+0.8
Prostitution and commercialized vice	46,777	47,129	+0.8	124	132	+6.5	793	826	+4.2	45,984	46,303	+0.7
Sex offenses (except forcible rape and prostitution)	56,089	56,528	+0.8	6,155	6,020	-2.2	11,354	11,426	+0.6	44,735	45,102	+0.8
Drug abuse violations	940,129	941,842	+0.2	20,648	18,328	-11.2	119,191	110,659	-7.2	820,938	831,183	+1.2
Gambling	4,566	4,481	-1.9	66	96	+45.5	399	464	+16.3	4,167	4,017	-3.6
Offenses against the family and children	84,167	86,132	+2.3	2,107	1,977	-6.2	5,934	5,563	-6.3	78,233	80,569	+3.0
Driving under the influence	859,550	878,767	+2.2	323	317	-1.9	12,628	13,142	+4.1	846,922	865,625	+2.2
Liquor laws	396,347	391,744	-1.2	8,625	8,346	-3.2	90,297	87,676	-2.9	306,050	304,068	-0.6
Drunkenness	398,449	376,854	-5.4	1,737	1,567	-9.8	13,281	12,376	-6.8	385,168	364,478	-5.4
Disorderly conduct	384,237	379,551	-1.2	44,155	45,897	+3.9	108,029	110,994	+2.7	276,208	268,557	-2.8
Vagrancy	17,647	18,908	+7.1	396	365	-7.8	1,621	1,378	-15.0	16,026	17,530	+9.4
All other offenses (except traffic)	2,235,995	2,291,178	+2.5	69,336	65,623	-5.4	246,302	239,267	-2.9	1,989,693	2,051,911	+3.1
Suspicion	2,032	2,590	+27.5	199	234	+17.6	625	933	+49.3	1,407	1,657	+17.8
Curfew and loitering law violations	86,077	82,003	-4.7	24,170	23,269	-3.7	86,077	82,003	-4.7	–	–	–
Runaways	88,307	81,496	-7.7	32,837	30,177	-8.1	88,307	81,496	-7.7	–	–	–

[1] Does not include suspicion.
[2] Violent crimes are offenses of murder, forcible rape, robbery, and aggravated assault.
[3] Property crimes are offenses of burglary, larceny-theft, motor vehicle theft, and arson.
[4] Includes arson.

Table 37

Current Year Over Previous Year Arrest Trends

by Sex, 2001-2002

[8,787 agencies; 2002 estimated population 179,500,199; 2001 estimated population 177,579,561]

	Male						Female					
	Total			Under 18			Total			Under 18		
Offense charged	2001	2002	Percent change	2001	2002	Percent change	2001	2002	Percent change	2001	2002	Percent change
TOTAL[1]	6,541,353	6,540,340	*	1,012,899	977,219	-3.5	1,924,010	1,965,008	+2.1	409,049	401,830	-1.8
Murder and nonnegligent manslaughter	7,557	7,563	+0.1	710	724	+2.0	1,123	952	-15.2	89	87	-2.2
Forcible rape	17,019	17,343	+1.9	2,840	2,793	-1.7	206	196	-4.9	43	49	+14.0
Robbery	60,195	59,516	-1.1	13,692	13,498	-1.4	6,898	7,007	+1.6	1,302	1,358	+4.3
Aggravated assault	242,573	240,305	-0.9	30,781	29,513	-4.1	61,138	60,648	-0.8	9,366	9,026	-3.6
Burglary	157,719	158,932	+0.8	50,063	48,168	-3.8	25,290	25,230	-0.2	6,955	6,336	-8.9
Larceny-theft	463,925	463,111	-0.2	136,458	131,809	-3.4	270,551	274,001	+1.3	87,641	85,613	-2.3
Motor vehicle theft	71,080	73,837	+3.9	22,593	21,334	-5.6	14,045	14,612	+4.0	4,877	4,576	-6.2
Arson	10,118	8,982	-11.2	5,235	4,741	-9.4	1,925	1,615	-16.1	727	612	-15.8
Violent crime[2]	327,344	324,727	-0.8	48,023	46,528	-3.1	69,365	68,803	-0.8	10,800	10,520	-2.6
Property crime[3]	702,842	704,862	+0.3	214,349	206,052	-3.9	311,811	315,458	+1.2	100,200	97,137	-3.1
Crime Index[4]	1,030,186	1,029,589	-0.1	262,372	252,580	-3.7	381,176	384,261	+0.8	111,000	107,657	-3.0
Other assaults	622,322	617,297	-0.8	100,278	100,612	+0.3	191,470	195,594	+2.2	46,173	47,821	+3.6
Forgery and counterfeiting	43,716	43,760	+0.1	2,446	2,026	-17.2	29,417	29,212	-0.7	1,392	1,148	-17.5
Fraud	108,347	107,450	-0.8	3,623	3,373	-6.9	90,175	91,268	+1.2	1,855	1,711	-7.8
Embezzlement	6,729	6,310	-6.2	706	535	-24.2	6,612	6,291	-4.9	535	391	-26.9
Stolen property; buying, receiving, possessing	69,350	69,215	-0.2	15,148	14,422	-4.8	15,131	15,018	-0.7	2,940	2,687	-8.6
Vandalism	142,512	142,967	+0.3	57,962	56,483	-2.6	27,696	28,827	+4.1	8,756	8,950	+2.2
Weapons; carrying, possessing, etc.	93,886	93,550	-0.4	20,224	19,075	-5.7	8,301	8,126	-2.1	2,325	2,308	-0.7
Prostitution and commercialized vice	16,376	16,575	+1.2	260	299	+15.0	30,401	30,554	+0.5	533	527	-1.1
Sex offenses (except forcible rape and prostitution)	52,118	52,596	+0.9	10,509	10,566	+0.5	3,971	3,932	-1.0	845	860	+1.8
Drug abuse violations	770,247	767,873	-0.3	99,623	92,127	-7.5	169,882	173,969	+2.4	19,568	18,532	-5.3
Gambling	3,981	3,841	-3.5	375	441	+17.6	585	640	+9.4	24	23	-4.2
Offenses against the family and children	64,309	65,150	+1.3	3,780	3,401	-10.0	19,858	20,982	+5.7	2,154	2,162	+0.4
Driving under the influence	714,540	724,469	+1.4	10,340	10,607	+2.6	145,010	154,298	+6.4	2,288	2,535	+10.8
Liquor laws	301,748	296,394	-1.8	60,992	58,568	-4.0	94,599	95,350	+0.8	29,305	29,108	-0.7
Drunkenness	343,540	323,737	-5.8	10,464	9,678	-7.5	54,909	53,117	-3.3	2,817	2,698	-4.2
Disorderly conduct	290,123	284,538	-1.9	75,390	76,639	+1.7	94,114	95,013	+1.0	32,639	34,355	+5.3
Vagrancy	14,448	15,529	+7.5	1,284	1,049	-18.3	3,199	3,379	+5.6	337	329	-2.4
All other offenses (except traffic)	1,757,527	1,790,117	+1.9	181,775	175,355	-3.5	478,468	501,061	+4.7	64,527	63,912	-1.0
Suspicion	1,560	1,981	+27.0	421	656	+55.8	472	609	+29.0	204	277	+35.8
Curfew and loitering law violations	59,527	56,826	-4.5	59,527	56,826	-4.5	26,550	25,177	-5.2	26,550	25,177	-5.2
Runaways	35,821	32,557	-9.1	35,821	32,557	-9.1	52,486	48,939	-6.8	52,486	48,939	-6.8

[1] Does not include suspicion.
[2] Violent crimes are offenses of murder, forcible rape, robbery, and aggravated assault.
[3] Property crimes are offenses of burglary, larceny-theft, motor vehicle theft, and arson.
[4] Includes arson.
* Less than one-tenth of 1 percent.

Table 38

Arrests

by Age, 2002

[10,372 agencies; 2002 estimated population 205,122,185]

Offense charged	Total all ages	Ages under 15	Ages under 18	Ages 18 and over	Under 10	10-12	13-14	15	16	17	18	19	20	21
TOTAL	**9,819,501**	**510,226**	**1,624,192**	**8,195,309**	**19,904**	**120,097**	**370,225**	**306,678**	**381,909**	**425,379**	**478,836**	**502,251**	**472,286**	**425,790**
Percent distribution[1]	**100.0**	**5.2**	**16.5**	**83.5**	**0.2**	**1.2**	**3.8**	**3.1**	**3.9**	**4.3**	**4.9**	**5.1**	**4.8**	**4.3**
Murder and nonnegligent manslaughter	10,107	101	973	9,134	0	17	84	140	274	458	568	676	698	658
Forcible rape	20,162	1,243	3,361	16,801	42	336	865	562	672	884	1,028	1,029	906	901
Robbery	77,342	4,323	17,893	59,449	85	789	3,449	3,408	4,532	5,630	6,228	5,617	4,671	4,187
Aggravated assault	339,437	15,846	44,281	295,156	699	4,350	10,797	7,948	9,722	10,765	12,052	12,786	13,018	13,725
Burglary	206,136	22,389	61,843	144,293	1,153	5,804	15,432	11,515	13,349	14,590	15,620	13,143	10,280	8,856
Larceny-theft	845,009	95,090	248,861	596,148	3,538	25,799	65,753	46,317	53,323	54,131	51,524	43,421	34,862	29,605
Motor vehicle theft	107,187	8,227	32,544	74,643	65	1,006	7,156	7,698	8,531	8,088	7,766	6,763	5,550	4,795
Arson	11,833	3,728	5,851	5,982	552	1,350	1,826	855	671	597	494	435	328	274
Violent crime[2]	447,048	21,513	66,508	380,540	826	5,492	15,195	12,058	15,200	17,737	19,876	20,108	19,293	19,471
Percent distribution[1]	100.0	4.8	14.9	85.1	0.2	1.2	3.4	2.7	3.4	4.0	4.4	4.5	4.3	4.4
Property crime[3]	1,170,165	129,434	349,099	821,066	5,308	33,959	90,167	66,385	75,874	77,406	75,404	63,762	51,020	43,530
Percent distribution[1]	100.0	11.1	29.8	70.2	0.5	2.9	7.7	5.7	6.5	6.6	6.4	5.4	4.4	3.7
Crime Index[4]	1,617,213	150,947	415,607	1,201,606	6,134	39,451	105,362	78,443	91,074	95,143	95,280	83,870	70,313	63,001
Percent distribution[1]	100.0	9.3	25.7	74.3	0.4	2.4	6.5	4.9	5.6	5.9	5.9	5.2	4.3	3.9
Other assaults	921,676	71,697	168,996	752,680	2,813	20,123	48,761	31,230	33,653	32,416	29,604	30,983	31,671	34,362
Forgery and counterfeiting	83,111	457	3,652	79,459	34	70	353	479	984	1,732	3,391	4,186	4,508	4,066
Fraud	233,087	1,178	6,434	226,653	102	225	851	885	1,611	2,760	5,610	8,342	9,519	9,377
Embezzlement	13,416	90	1,005	12,411	2	20	68	72	259	584	876	926	774	718
Stolen property; buying, receiving, possessing	91,280	5,044	18,819	72,461	138	982	3,924	3,550	4,600	5,625	6,133	5,937	5,175	4,527
Vandalism	198,550	32,888	75,955	122,595	2,565	10,049	20,274	13,179	14,988	14,900	13,082	10,862	8,599	8,437
Weapons; carrying, possessing, etc.	118,312	8,647	25,288	93,024	438	2,166	6,043	4,615	5,379	6,647	7,509	7,177	6,517	6,263
Prostitution and commercialized vice	58,758	165	1,095	57,663	2	24	139	170	281	479	1,567	1,802	1,795	1,888
Sex offenses (except forcible rape and prostitution)	67,833	7,226	13,877	53,956	427	2,144	4,655	2,352	2,128	2,171	2,565	2,534	2,337	2,281
Drug abuse violations	1,103,017	21,836	133,754	969,263	284	2,609	18,943	23,031	36,904	51,983	70,713	72,105	65,632	58,791
Gambling	7,525	171	1,114	6,411	0	32	139	200	308	435	456	486	440	377
Offenses against the family and children	97,716	2,442	6,572	91,144	343	612	1,487	1,279	1,406	1,445	1,959	2,232	2,464	2,977
Driving under the influence	1,020,377	370	15,214	1,005,163	113	23	234	631	3,810	10,403	24,662	33,317	37,656	50,189
Liquor laws	463,849	10,132	106,014	357,835	152	752	9,228	15,826	30,702	49,354	76,275	81,666	67,454	13,320
Drunkenness	413,808	1,679	13,529	400,279	87	143	1,449	2,101	3,245	6,504	12,401	13,721	13,853	18,425
Disorderly conduct	482,827	56,314	139,048	343,779	1,487	14,502	40,325	27,667	27,941	27,126	23,628	21,274	20,047	22,963
Vagrancy	19,678	402	1,519	18,159	10	62	330	297	369	451	685	581	540	551
All other offenses (except traffic)	2,606,294	76,025	282,025	2,324,269	3,118	15,459	57,448	54,407	70,007	81,586	102,123	119,925	122,713	122,989
Suspicion	7,670	294	1,171	6,499	6	52	236	220	298	359	317	325	279	288
Curfew and loitering law violations	103,155	29,070	103,155	–	523	5,127	23,420	23,323	29,066	21,696	–	–	–	–
Runaways	90,349	33,152	90,349	–	1,126	5,470	26,556	22,721	22,896	11,580	–	–	–	–

[1] Because of rounding, the percentages may not add to 100.0.

[2] Violent crimes are offenses of murder, forcible rape, robbery, and aggravated assault.

[3] Property crimes are offenses of burglary, larceny-theft, motor vehicle theft, and arson.

[4] Includes arson.

Table 38

Arrests

by Age, 2002—Continued

[10,372 agencies; 2002 estimated population 205,122,185]

Offense charged	22	23	24	25-29	30-34	35-39	40-44	45-49	50-54	55-59	60-64	65 and over
TOTAL	**393,201**	**346,552**	**312,996**	**1,212,258**	**1,073,614**	**1,023,543**	**876,049**	**543,956**	**281,008**	**132,915**	**61,634**	**58,420**
Percent distribution[1]	**4.0**	**3.5**	**3.2**	**12.3**	**10.9**	**10.4**	**8.9**	**5.5**	**2.9**	**1.4**	**0.6**	**0.6**
Murder and nonnegligent manslaughter	575	542	471	1,590	999	783	591	455	230	144	69	85
Forcible rape	722	733	622	2,465	2,429	2,158	1,622	994	520	304	166	202
Robbery	3,445	2,933	2,486	8,624	7,322	6,179	4,417	2,051	789	291	113	96
Aggravated assault	13,437	12,393	11,708	48,211	43,290	40,344	33,587	20,285	10,299	5,054	2,434	2,533
Burglary	7,520	6,274	5,588	20,067	17,854	16,388	12,323	6,379	2,479	903	317	302
Larceny-theft	26,005	22,331	19,294	77,250	75,980	74,348	62,966	39,451	20,386	9,403	4,527	4,795
Motor vehicle theft	4,235	3,565	3,176	11,525	9,745	8,067	5,213	2,582	1,048	395	134	84
Arson	245	201	194	781	735	754	649	450	232	107	61	42
Violent crime[2]	18,179	16,601	15,287	60,890	54,040	49,464	40,217	23,785	11,838	5,793	2,782	2,916
Percent distribution[1]	4.1	3.7	3.4	13.6	12.1	11.1	9.0	5.3	2.6	1.3	0.6	0.7
Property crime[3]	38,005	32,371	28,252	109,623	104,314	99,557	81,151	48,862	24,145	10,808	5,039	5,223
Percent distribution[1]	3.2	2.8	2.4	9.4	8.9	8.5	6.9	4.2	2.1	0.9	0.4	0.4
Crime Index[4]	56,184	48,972	43,539	170,513	158,354	149,021	121,368	72,647	35,983	16,601	7,821	8,139
Percent distribution[1]	3.5	3.0	2.7	10.5	9.8	9.2	7.5	4.5	2.2	1.0	0.5	0.5
Other assaults	33,987	31,248	29,302	121,664	113,791	107,750	88,571	51,417	25,272	11,800	5,494	5,764
Forgery and counterfeiting	3,967	3,721	3,350	14,226	12,699	10,649	7,633	4,079	1,884	647	259	194
Fraud	9,837	9,016	8,579	39,305	38,137	33,058	25,363	15,175	7,813	3,986	1,776	1,760
Embezzlement	604	524	460	1,890	1,661	1,488	1,172	620	382	194	84	38
Stolen property; buying, receiving, possessing	3,967	3,330	2,990	11,006	9,500	8,068	6,194	3,266	1,437	526	226	179
Vandalism	7,129	5,918	4,944	17,588	14,125	12,420	9,567	5,224	2,476	1,138	500	586
Weapons; carrying, possessing, etc.	5,634	4,888	4,182	14,878	10,399	8,515	6,861	4,620	2,697	1,466	681	737
Prostitution and commercialized vice	1,937	1,878	1,856	8,358	10,545	10,600	8,110	4,166	1,691	733	348	389
Sex offenses (except forcible rape and prostitution)	1,964	1,857	1,634	6,701	7,014	7,335	6,288	4,380	2,734	1,814	1,147	1,371
Drug abuse violations	53,195	45,625	40,327	147,495	120,515	110,963	93,072	54,064	23,606	8,348	3,024	1,788
Gambling	354	339	279	888	571	500	471	368	330	214	165	173
Offenses against the family and children	3,131	3,050	3,181	15,448	16,326	16,144	12,502	6,566	2,912	1,223	536	493
Driving under the influence	48,676	44,500	40,684	156,792	134,311	128,625	120,640	83,515	49,980	26,735	13,114	11,767
Liquor laws	9,180	6,662	5,554	18,374	15,404	17,138	17,855	13,396	7,935	4,089	1,907	1,626
Drunkenness	16,684	14,456	12,982	50,553	47,954	55,553	57,678	41,299	23,422	11,523	5,561	4,214
Disorderly conduct	19,922	16,285	14,034	48,603	39,438	39,193	35,128	21,893	11,175	5,236	2,548	2,412
Vagrancy	525	475	418	1,820	2,090	2,597	3,108	2,257	1,338	695	284	195
All other offenses (except traffic)	116,063	103,558	94,428	365,226	319,836	303,002	253,687	154,460	77,702	35,864	16,127	16,566
Suspicion	261	250	273	930	944	924	781	544	239	83	32	29
Curfew and loitering law violations	–	–	–	–	–	–	–	–	–	–	–	–
Runaways	–	–	–	–	–	–	–	–	–	–	–	–

Table 39

Arrests

Males, by Age, 2002
[10,372 agencies; 2002 estimated population 205,122,185]

Offense charged	Total all ages	Ages under 15	Ages under 18	Ages 18 and over	Under 10	10-12	13-14	15	16	17	18	19	20	21
TOTAL	**7,559,435**	**349,307**	**1,154,193**	**6,405,242**	**16,157**	**87,842**	**245,308**	**207,784**	**273,085**	**324,017**	**377,971**	**398,150**	**374,598**	**342,014**
Percent distribution[1]	**100.0**	**4.6**	**15.3**	**84.7**	**0.2**	**1.2**	**3.2**	**2.7**	**3.6**	**4.3**	**5.0**	**5.3**	**5.0**	**4.5**
Murder and nonnegligent manslaughter	9,015	84	872	8,143	0	13	71	122	247	419	529	632	642	604
Forcible rape	19,884	1,187	3,252	16,632	36	321	830	544	653	868	1,018	1,020	893	891
Robbery	69,369	3,843	16,310	53,059	77	721	3,045	3,074	4,169	5,224	5,749	5,163	4,266	3,785
Aggravated assault	270,905	11,886	33,820	237,085	612	3,502	7,772	5,865	7,421	8,648	9,866	10,439	10,513	11,158
Burglary	178,806	19,533	54,915	123,891	1,032	5,072	13,429	10,135	12,041	13,206	14,050	11,679	9,091	7,799
Larceny-theft	532,274	57,939	150,845	381,429	2,673	16,758	38,508	27,131	31,975	33,800	33,423	28,437	22,323	18,870
Motor vehicle theft	89,463	6,459	26,958	62,505	61	833	5,565	6,216	7,208	7,075	6,773	5,859	4,765	4,079
Arson	10,031	3,301	5,185	4,846	517	1,207	1,577	747	596	541	455	391	288	235
Violent crime[2]	369,173	17,000	54,254	314,919	725	4,557	11,718	9,605	12,490	15,159	17,162	17,254	16,314	16,438
Percent distribution[1]	100.0	4.6	14.7	85.3	0.2	1.2	3.2	2.6	3.4	4.1	4.7	4.7	4.4	4.5
Property crime[3]	810,574	87,232	237,903	572,671	4,283	23,870	59,079	44,229	51,820	54,622	54,699	46,366	36,467	30,983
Percent distribution[1]	100.0	10.8	29.3	70.7	0.5	2.9	7.3	5.5	6.4	6.7	6.7	5.7	4.5	3.8
Crime Index[4]	1,179,747	104,232	292,157	887,590	5,008	28,427	70,797	53,834	64,310	69,781	71,861	63,620	52,781	47,421
Percent distribution[1]	100.0	8.8	24.8	75.2	0.4	2.4	6.0	4.6	5.5	5.9	6.1	5.4	4.5	4.0
Other assaults	701,562	48,824	114,746	586,816	2,359	14,611	31,854	20,250	22,692	22,980	21,617	22,995	23,698	26,433
Forgery and counterfeiting	49,788	301	2,349	47,439	20	36	245	325	647	1,076	2,143	2,623	2,814	2,424
Fraud	127,896	777	4,323	123,573	58	155	564	591	1,081	1,874	3,321	4,732	5,336	5,233
Embezzlement	6,740	62	590	6,150	2	10	50	52	132	344	441	473	368	364
Stolen property; buying, receiving, possessing	74,958	4,091	15,858	59,100	118	813	3,160	2,987	3,902	4,878	5,250	5,034	4,318	3,779
Vandalism	165,574	28,253	65,664	99,910	2,294	8,727	17,232	11,374	13,046	12,991	11,375	9,294	7,291	7,105
Weapons; carrying, possessing, etc.	108,759	7,480	22,502	86,257	415	1,876	5,189	4,007	4,832	6,183	7,103	6,766	6,164	5,898
Prostitution and commercialized vice	20,127	71	366	19,761	2	18	51	43	101	151	306	449	520	591
Sex offenses (except forcible rape and prostitution)	62,234	6,565	12,601	49,633	381	1,978	4,206	2,095	1,926	2,015	2,318	2,281	2,126	2,044
Drug abuse violations	903,656	16,999	112,254	791,402	236	1,970	14,793	18,956	31,320	44,979	60,907	61,957	55,904	50,356
Gambling	6,749	163	1,081	5,668	0	27	136	194	301	423	439	451	415	360
Offenses against the family and children	73,756	1,446	3,996	69,760	207	378	861	708	878	964	1,422	1,608	1,753	2,118
Driving under the influence	842,770	254	12,270	830,500	93	17	144	490	3,024	8,502	20,443	27,740	31,647	41,632
Liquor laws	348,869	5,212	70,249	278,620	112	369	4,731	9,363	20,351	35,323	56,154	61,327	51,697	11,077
Drunkenness	355,973	1,050	10,607	345,366	74	96	880	1,546	2,563	5,448	10,629	11,913	12,132	16,314
Disorderly conduct	364,695	38,239	97,173	267,522	1,240	10,504	26,495	18,612	19,741	20,581	18,516	16,662	15,640	18,629
Vagrancy	16,158	286	1,162	14,996	9	48	229	218	304	354	579	485	439	434
All other offenses (except traffic)	2,036,108	52,758	206,197	1,829,911	2,443	11,517	38,798	37,852	51,788	63,799	82,890	97,475	99,329	99,562
Suspicion	6,103	217	835	5,268	5	40	172	154	220	244	257	265	226	240
Curfew and loitering law violations	70,874	18,999	70,874	–	392	3,489	15,118	15,466	20,376	16,033	–	–	–	–
Runaways	36,339	13,028	36,339	–	689	2,736	9,603	8,667	9,550	5,094	–	–	–	–

[1] Because of rounding, the percentages may not add to 100.0.
[2] Violent crimes are offenses of murder, forcible rape, robbery, and aggravated assault.
[3] Property crimes are offenses of burglary, larceny-theft, motor vehicle theft, and arson.
[4] Includes arson.

Table 39

Arrests

Males, by Age, 2002—Continued

[10,372 agencies; 2002 estimated population 205,122,185]

Offense charged	22	23	24	25-29	30-34	35-39	40-44	45-49	50-54	55-59	60-64	65 and over
TOTAL	**314,602**	**275,486**	**248,277**	**949,750**	**814,371**	**766,417**	**670,912**	**431,356**	**230,330**	**110,899**	**51,894**	**48,215**
Percent distribution[1]	**4.2**	**3.6**	**3.3**	**12.6**	**10.8**	**10.1**	**8.9**	**5.7**	**3.0**	**1.5**	**0.7**	**0.6**
Murder and nonnegligent manslaughter	524	497	429	1,437	872	652	482	390	198	127	61	67
Forcible rape	717	726	617	2,440	2,408	2,127	1,604	984	518	304	166	199
Robbery	3,104	2,621	2,240	7,659	6,348	5,348	3,834	1,785	699	265	103	90
Aggravated assault	10,921	10,038	9,511	38,744	34,048	31,397	26,616	16,465	8,667	4,315	2,131	2,256
Burglary	6,516	5,447	4,775	16,910	14,843	13,731	10,321	5,392	2,109	729	252	247
Larceny-theft	16,545	13,866	11,977	47,272	47,555	47,889	41,563	26,447	13,751	5,967	2,735	2,809
Motor vehicle theft	3,588	2,994	2,652	9,446	7,793	6,568	4,336	2,196	916	344	123	73
Arson	206	165	167	629	585	584	464	335	180	85	48	31
Violent crime[2]	15,266	13,882	12,797	50,280	43,676	39,524	32,536	19,624	10,082	5,011	2,461	2,612
Percent distribution[1]	4.1	3.8	3.5	13.6	11.8	10.7	8.8	5.3	2.7	1.4	0.7	0.7
Property crime[3]	26,855	22,472	19,571	74,257	70,776	68,772	56,684	34,370	16,956	7,125	3,158	3,160
Percent distribution[1]	3.3	2.8	2.4	9.2	8.7	8.5	7.0	4.2	2.1	0.9	0.4	0.4
Crime Index[4]	42,121	36,354	32,368	124,537	114,452	108,296	89,220	53,994	27,038	12,136	5,619	5,772
Percent distribution[1]	3.6	3.1	2.7	10.6	9.7	9.2	7.6	4.6	2.3	1.0	0.5	0.5
Other assaults	26,126	24,139	22,859	95,429	88,619	83,321	69,748	41,644	20,894	9,799	4,652	4,843
Forgery and counterfeiting	2,421	2,205	1,937	8,150	7,284	6,243	4,596	2,587	1,230	452	182	148
Fraud	5,332	4,779	4,434	20,315	19,985	17,752	14,475	8,765	4,638	2,367	1,073	1,036
Embezzlement	297	237	215	909	796	718	623	304	201	122	55	27
Stolen property; buying, receiving, possessing	3,293	2,732	2,381	8,767	7,474	6,303	5,038	2,712	1,217	446	199	157
Vandalism	5,941	4,850	4,000	13,932	11,063	9,460	7,542	4,160	2,023	953	426	495
Weapons; carrying, possessing, etc.	5,296	4,593	3,906	13,835	9,512	7,640	6,153	4,213	2,490	1,376	631	681
Prostitution and commercialized vice	700	627	654	3,132	3,189	3,004	2,589	1,691	1,029	599	308	373
Sex offenses (except forcible rape and prostitution)	1,772	1,691	1,486	6,048	6,385	6,698	5,766	4,131	2,620	1,781	1,130	1,356
Drug abuse violations	45,302	38,695	34,107	122,219	94,237	83,070	70,754	42,761	19,623	7,234	2,681	1,595
Gambling	330	322	256	821	486	408	377	289	267	175	132	140
Offenses against the family and children	2,278	2,150	2,346	11,614	12,202	12,463	10,018	5,467	2,437	1,027	436	421
Driving under the influence	40,661	37,334	34,460	133,664	111,113	101,969	95,014	67,587	42,174	23,158	11,542	10,362
Liquor laws	7,729	5,576	4,643	15,114	12,288	13,601	14,487	11,326	6,820	3,644	1,714	1,423
Drunkenness	14,845	12,879	11,564	44,537	40,578	45,789	48,047	35,582	20,866	10,597	5,187	3,907
Disorderly conduct	16,113	13,042	11,143	38,031	29,378	28,720	26,644	17,369	9,114	4,370	2,142	2,009
Vagrancy	425	390	349	1,465	1,585	2,070	2,579	1,960	1,165	620	268	183
All other offenses (except traffic)	93,420	82,688	74,943	286,486	243,008	228,149	196,604	124,352	64,278	29,979	13,487	13,261
Suspicion	200	203	226	745	737	743	638	462	206	64	30	26
Curfew and loitering law violations	—	—	—	—	—	—	—	—	—	—	—	—
Runaways	—	—	—	—	—	—	—	—	—	—	—	—

Table 40

Arrests
Females, by Age, 2002
[10,372 agencies; 2002 estimated population 205,122,185]

Offense charged	Total all ages	Ages under 15	Ages under 18	Ages 18 and over	Under 10	10-12	13-14	15	16	17	18	19	20	21
TOTAL	2,260,066	160,919	469,999	1,790,067	3,747	32,255	124,917	98,894	108,824	101,362	100,865	104,101	97,688	83,776
Percent distribution[1]	100.0	7.1	20.8	79.2	0.2	1.4	5.5	4.4	4.8	4.5	4.5	4.6	4.3	3.7
Murder and nonnegligent manslaughter	1,092	17	101	991	0	4	13	18	27	39	39	44	56	54
Forcible rape	278	56	109	169	6	15	35	18	19	16	10	9	13	10
Robbery	7,973	480	1,583	6,390	8	68	404	334	363	406	479	454	405	402
Aggravated assault	68,532	3,960	10,461	58,071	87	848	3,025	2,083	2,301	2,117	2,186	2,347	2,505	2,567
Burglary	27,330	2,856	6,928	20,402	121	732	2,003	1,380	1,308	1,384	1,570	1,464	1,189	1,057
Larceny-theft	312,735	37,151	98,016	214,719	865	9,041	27,245	19,186	21,348	20,331	18,101	14,984	12,539	10,735
Motor vehicle theft	17,724	1,768	5,586	12,138	4	173	1,591	1,482	1,323	1,013	993	904	785	716
Arson	1,802	427	666	1,136	35	143	249	108	75	56	41	44	40	39
Violent crime[2]	77,875	4,513	12,254	65,621	101	935	3,477	2,453	2,710	2,578	2,714	2,854	2,979	3,033
Percent distribution[1]	100.0	5.8	15.7	84.3	0.1	1.2	4.5	3.1	3.5	3.3	3.5	3.7	3.8	3.9
Property crime[3]	359,591	42,202	111,196	248,395	1,025	10,089	31,088	22.156	24,054	22,784	20,705	17,396	14,553	12,547
Percent distribution[1]	100.0	11.7	30.9	69.1	0.3	2.8	8.6	6.2	6.7	6.3	5.8	4.8	4.0	3.5
Crime Index[4]	437,466	46,715	123,450	314,016	1,126	11,024	34,565	24,609	26,764	25,362	123,419	20,250	17,532	15,580
Percent distribution[1]	100.0	10.7	28.2	71.8	0.3	2.5	7.9	5.6	6.1	5.8	5.4	4.6	4.0	3.6
Other assaults	220,114	22,873	54,250	165,864	454	5,512	16,907	10,980	10,961	9,436	7,987	7,988	7,973	7,929
Forgery and counterfeiting	33,323	156	1,303	32,020	14	34	108	154	337	656	1,248	1,563	1,694	1,642
Fraud	105,191	401	2,111	103,080	44	70	287	294	530	886	2,289	3,610	4,183	4,144
Embezzlement	6,676	28	415	6,261	0	10	18	20	127	240	435	453	406	354
Stolen property; buying, receiving, possessing	16,322	953	2,961	13,361	20	169	764	563	698	747	883	903	857	748
Vandalism	32,976	4,635	10,291	22,685	271	1,322	3,042	1,805	1,942	1,909	1,707	1,568	1,308	1,332
Weapons; carrying, possessing, etc.	9,553	1,167	2,786	6,767	23	290	854	608	547	464	406	411	353	365
Prostitution and commercialized vice	38,631	94	729	37,902	0	6	88	127	180	328	1,261	1,353	1,275	1,297
Sex offenses (except forcible rape and prostitution)	5,599	661	1,276	4,323	46	166	449	257	202	156	247	253	211	237
Drug abuse violations	199,361	4,837	21,500	177,861	48	639	4,150	4,075	5,584	7,004	9,806	10,148	9,728	8,435
Gambling	776	8	33	743	0	5	3	6	7	12	17	35	25	17
Offenses against the family and children	23,960	996	2,576	21,384	136	234	626	571	528	481	537	624	711	859
Driving under the influence	177,607	116	2,944	174,663	20	6	90	141	786	1,901	4,219	5,577	6,009	8,557
Liquor laws	114,980	4,920	35,765	79,215	40	383	4,497	6,463	10,351	14,031	20,121	20,339	15,757	2,243
Drunkenness	57,835	629	2,922	54,913	13	47	569	555	682	1,056	1,772	1,808	1,721	2,111
Disorderly conduct	118,132	18,075	41,875	76,257	247	3,998	13,830	9,055	8,200	6,545	5,112	4,612	4,407	4,334
Vagrancy	3,520	116	357	3,163	1	14	101	79	65	97	106	96	101	117
All other offenses (except traffic)	570,186	23,267	75,828	494,358	675	3,942	18,650	16,555	18,219	17,787	19,233	22,450	23,384	23,427
Suspicion	1,567	77	336	1,231	1	12	64	66	78	115	60	60	53	48
Curfew and loitering law violations	32,281	10,071	32,281	–	131	1,638	8,302	7,857	8,690	5,663	–	–	–	–
Runaways	54,010	20,124	54,010	–	437	2,734	16,953	14,054	13,346	6,486	–	–	–	–

[1] Because of rounding, the percentages may not add to 100.0.

[2] Violent crimes are offenses of murder, forcible rape, robbery, and aggravated assault.

[3] Property crimes are offenses of burglary, larceny-theft, motor vehicle theft, and arson.

[4] Includes arson.

Table 40

Arrests

Females, by Age, 2002—Continued

[10,372 agencies; 2002 estimated population 205,122,185]

Offense charged	22	23	24	25-29	30-34	35-39	40-44	45-49	50-54	55-59	60-64	65 and over
TOTAL	78,599	71,066	64,719	262,508	259,243	257,126	205,137	112,600	50,678	22,016	9,740	10,205
Percent distribution[1]	3.5	3.1	2.9	11.6	11.5	11.4	9.1	5.0	2.2	1.0	0.4	0.5
Murder and nonnegligent manslaughter	51	45	42	153	127	131	109	65	32	17	8	18
Forcible rape	5	7	5	25	21	31	18	10	2	0	0	3
Robbery	341	312	246	965	974	831	583	266	90	26	10	6
Aggravated assault	2,516	2,355	2,197	9,467	9,242	8,947	6,971	3,820	1,632	739	303	277
Burglary	1,004	827	813	3,157	3,011	2,657	2,002	987	370	174	65	55
Larceny-theft	9,460	8,465	7,317	29,978	28,425	26,459	21,403	13,004	6,635	3,436	1,792	1,986
Motor vehicle theft	647	571	524	2,079	1,952	1,499	877	386	132	51	11	11
Arson	39	36	27	152	150	170	185	115	52	22	13	11
Violent crime[2]	2,913	2,719	2,490	10,610	10,364	9,940	7,681	4,161	1,756	782	321	304
Percent distribution[1]	3.7	3.5	3.2	13.6	13.3	12.8	9.9	5.3	2.3	1.0	0.4	0.4
Property crime[3]	11,150	9,899	8,681	35,366	33,538	30,785	24,467	14,492	7,189	3,683	1,881	2,063
Percent distribution[1]	3.1	2.8	2.4	9.8	9.3	8.6	6.8	4.0	2.0	1.0	0.5	0.6
Crime Index[4]	14,063	12,618	11,171	45,976	43,902	40,725	32,148	18,653	8,945	4,465	2,202	2,367
Percent distribution[1]	3.2	2.9	2.6	10.5	10.0	9.3	7.3	4.3	2.0	1.0	0.5	0.5
Other assaults	7,861	7,109	6,443	26,235	25,172	24,429	18,823	9,773	4,378	2,001	842	921
Forgery and counterfeiting	1,546	1,516	1,413	6,076	5,415	4,406	3,037	1,492	654	195	77	46
Fraud	4,505	4,237	4,145	18,990	18,152	15,306	10,888	6,410	3,175	1,619	703	724
Embezzlement	307	287	245	981	865	770	549	316	181	72	29	11
Stolen property; buying, receiving, possessing	674	598	609	2,239	2,026	1,765	1,156	554	220	80	27	22
Vandalism	1,188	1,068	944	3,656	3,062	2,960	2,025	1,064	453	185	74	91
Weapons; carrying, possessing, etc.	338	295	276	1,043	887	875	708	407	207	90	50	56
Prostitution and commercialized vice	1,237	1,251	1,202	5,226	7,356	7,596	5,521	2,475	662	134	40	16
Sex offenses (except forcible rape and prostitution)	192	166	148	653	629	637	522	249	114	33	17	15
Drug abuse violations	7,893	6,930	6,220	25,276	26,278	27,893	22,318	11,303	3,983	1,114	343	193
Gambling	24	17	23	67	85	92	94	79	63	39	33	33
Offenses against the family and children	853	900	835	3,834	4,124	3,681	2,484	1,099	475	196	100	72
Driving under the influence	8,015	7,166	6,224	23,128	23,198	26,656	25,626	15,928	7,806	3,577	1,572	1,405
Liquor laws	1,451	1,086	911	3,260	3,116	3,537	3,368	2,070	1,115	445	193	203
Drunkenness	1,839	1,577	1,418	6,016	7,376	9,764	9,631	5,717	2,556	926	374	307
Disorderly conduct	3,809	3,243	2,891	10,572	10,060	10,473	8,484	4,524	2,061	866	406	403
Vagrancy	100	85	69	355	505	527	529	297	173	75	16	12
All other offenses (except traffic)	22,643	20,870	19,485	78,740	76,828	74,853	57,083	30,108	13,424	5,885	2,640	3,305
Suspicion	61	47	47	185	207	181	143	82	33	19	2	3
Curfew and loitering law violations	–	–	–	–	–	–	–	–	–	–	–	–
Runaways	–	–	–	–	–	–	–	–	–	–	–	–

Table 41

Arrests

of Persons Under 15, 18, 21, and 25 Years of Age, 2002
[10,372 agencies; 2002 estimated population 205,122,185]

Offense charged	Total all ages	Number of persons arrested				Percent of total all ages			
		Under 15	Under 18	Under 21	Under 25	Under 15	Under 18	Under 21	Under 25
TOTAL	**9,819,501**	**510,226**	**1,624,192**	**3,077,565**	**4,556,104**	**5.2**	**16.5**	**31.3**	**46.4**
Murder and nonnegligent manslaughter	10,107	101	973	2,915	5,161	1.0	9.6	28.8	51.1
Forcible rape	20,162	1,243	3,361	6,324	9,302	6.2	16.7	31.4	46.1
Robbery	77,342	4,323	17,893	34,409	47,460	5.6	23.1	44.5	61.4
Aggravated assault	339,437	15,346	44,281	82,137	133,400	4.7	13.0	24.2	39.3
Burglary	206,136	22,389	61,843	100,886	129,124	10.9	30.0	48.9	62.6
Larceny-theft	845,009	95,090	248,861	378,668	475,903	11.3	29.5	44.8	56.3
Motor vehicle theft	107,187	8,227	32,544	52,623	68,394	7.7	30.4	49.1	63.8
Arson	11,833	3,728	5,851	7,108	8,022	31.5	49.4	60.1	67.8
Violent crime[1]	447,048	21,513	66,508	125,785	195,323	4.8	14.9	28.1	43.7
Property crime[2]	1,170,165	129,434	349,099	539,285	681,443	11.1	29.8	46.1	58.2
Crime Index[3]	1,617,213	150,947	415,607	665,070	876,766	9.3	25.7	41.1	54.2
Other assaults	921,676	71,697	168,996	261,254	390,153	7.8	18.3	28.3	42.3
Forgery and counterfeiting	83,111	457	3,652	15,737	30,841	0.5	4.4	18.9	37.1
Fraud	233,087	1,178	6,434	29,905	66,714	0.5	2.8	12.8	28.6
Embezzlement	13,416	90	1,005	3,581	5,887	0.7	7.5	26.7	43.9
Stolen property; buying, receiving, possessing	91,280	5,044	18,819	36,064	50,878	5.5	20.6	39.5	55.7
Vandalism	198,550	32,888	75,955	108,498	134,926	16.6	38.3	54.6	68.0
Weapons; carrying, possessing, etc.	118,312	8,647	25,288	46,491	67,458	7.3	21.4	39.3	57.0
Prostitution and commercialized vice	58,758	165	1,095	6,259	13,818	0.3	1.9	10.7	23.5
Sex offenses (except forcible rape and prostitution)	67,833	7,226	13,877	21,313	29,049	10.7	20.5	31.4	42.8
Drug abuse violations	1,103,017	21,836	133,754	342,204	540,142	2.0	12.1	31.0	49.0
Gambling	7,525	171	1,114	2,496	3,845	2.3	14.8	33.2	51.1
Offenses against the family and children	97,716	2,442	6,572	13,227	25,566	2.5	6.7	13.5	26.2
Driving under the influence	1,020,377	370	15,214	110,849	294,898	*	1.5	10.9	28.9
Liquor laws	463,849	10,132	106,014	331,409	366,125	2.2	22.9	71.4	78.9
Drunkenness	413,808	1,679	13,529	53,504	116,051	0.4	3.3	12.9	28.0
Disorderly conduct	482,827	56,314	139,048	203,997	277,201	11.7	28.8	42.3	57.4
Vagrancy	19,678	402	1,519	3,325	5,294	2.0	7.7	16.9	26.9
All other offenses (except traffic)	2,606,294	76,025	282,025	626,786	1,063,824	2.9	10.8	24.0	40.8
Suspicion	7,670	294	1,171	2,092	3,164	3.8	15.3	27.3	41.3
Curfew and loitering law violations	103,155	29,070	103,155	103,155	103,155	28.2	100.0	100.0	100.0
Runaways	90,349	33,152	90,349	90,349	90,349	36.7	100.0	100.0	100.0

[1] Violent crimes are offenses of murder, forcible rape, robbery, and aggravated assault.
[2] Property crimes are offenses of burglary, larceny-theft, motor vehicle theft, and arson.
[3] Includes arson.
* Less than one-tenth of 1 percent.

Table 42

Arrests

by Sex, 2002

[10,372 agencies; 2002 estimated population 205,122,185]

Offense charged	Number of persons arrested			Percent male	Percent female	Percent distribution[1]		
	Total	Male	Female			Total	Male	Female
TOTAL	**9,819,501**	**7,559,435**	**2,260,066**	**77.0**	**23.0**	**100.0**	**100.0**	**100.0**
Murder and nonnegligent manslaughter	10,107	9,015	1,092	89.2	10.8	0.1	0.1	*
Forcible rape	20,162	19,884	278	98.6	1.4	0.2	0.3	*
Robbery	77,342	69,369	7,973	89.7	10.3	0.8	0.9	0.4
Aggravated assault	339,437	270,905	68,532	79.8	20.2	3.5	3.6	3.0
Burglary	206,136	178,806	27,330	86.7	13.3	2.1	2.4	1.2
Larceny-theft	845,009	532,274	312,735	63.0	37.0	8.6	7.0	13.8
Motor vehicle theft	107,187	89,463	17,724	83.5	16.5	1.1	1.2	0.8
Arson	11,833	10,031	1,802	84.8	15.2	0.1	0.1	0.1
Violent crime[2]	447,048	369,173	77,875	82.6	17.4	4.6	4.9	3.4
Property crime[3]	1,170,165	810,574	359,591	69.3	30.7	11.9	10.7	15.9
Crime Index[4]	1,617,213	1,179,747	437,466	72.9	27.1	16.5	15.6	19.4
Other assaults	921,676	701,562	220,114	76.1	23.9	9.4	9.3	9.7
Forgery and counterfeiting	83,111	49,788	33,323	59.9	40.1	0.8	0.7	1.5
Fraud	233,087	127,896	105,191	54.9	45.1	2.4	1.7	4.7
Embezzlement	13,416	6,740	6,676	50.2	49.8	0.1	0.1	0.3
Stolen property; buying, receiving, possessing	91,280	74,958	16,322	82.1	17.9	0.9	1.0	0.7
Vandalism	198,550	165,574	32,976	83.4	16.6	2.0	2.2	1.5
Weapons; carrying, possessing, etc.	118,312	108,759	9,553	91.9	8.1	1.2	1.4	0.4
Prostitution and commercialized vice	58,758	20,127	38,631	34.3	65.7	0.6	0.3	1.7
Sex offenses (except forcible rape and prostitution)	67,833	62,234	5,599	91.7	8.3	0.7	0.8	0.2
Drug abuse violations	1,103,017	903,656	199,361	81.9	18.1	11.2	12.0	8.8
Gambling	7,525	6,749	776	89.7	10.3	0.1	0.1	*
Offenses against the family and children	97,716	73,756	23,960	75.5	24.5	1.0	1.0	1.1
Driving under the influence	1,020,377	842,770	177,607	82.6	17.4	10.4	11.1	7.9
Liquor laws	463,849	348,869	114,980	75.2	24.8	4.7	4.6	5.1
Drunkenness	413,808	355,973	57,835	86.0	14.0	4.2	4.7	2.6
Disorderly conduct	482,827	364,695	118,132	75.5	24.5	4.9	4.8	5.2
Vagrancy	19,678	16,158	3,520	82.1	17.9	0.2	0.2	0.2
All other offenses (except traffic)	2,606,294	2,036,108	570,186	78.1	21.9	26.5	26.9	25.2
Suspicion	7,670	6,103	1,567	79.6	20.4	0.1	0.1	0.1
Curfew and loitering law violations	103,155	70,874	32,281	68.7	31.3	1.1	0.9	1.4
Runaways	90,349	36,339	54,010	40.2	59.8	0.9	0.5	2.4

[1] Because of rounding, the percentages may not add to 100.0.

[2] Violent crimes are offenses of murder, forcible rape, robbery, and aggravated assault.

[3] Property crimes are offenses of burglary, larceny-theft, motor vehicle theft, and arson.

[4] Includes arson.

* Less than one-tenth of 1 percent.

Table 43

Arrests

by Race, 2002

[10,370 agencies; 2002 estimated population 205,108,615]

Offense charged	Total arrests					Percent distribution[1]				
	Total	White	Black	American Indian or Alaskan Native	Asian or Pacific Islander	Total	White	Black	American Indian or Alaskan Native	Asian or Pacific Islander
TOTAL	**9,797,385**	**6,923,390**	**2,633,632**	**130,636**	**109,727**	**100.0**	**70.7**	**26.9**	**1.3**	**1.1**
Murder and nonnegligent manslaughter	10,099	4,814	5,047	115	123	100.0	47.7	50.0	1.1	1.2
Forcible rape	20,127	12,766	6,852	240	269	100.0	63.4	34.0	1.2	1.3
Robbery	77,280	34,109	41,837	471	863	100.0	44.1	54.1	0.6	1.1
Aggravated assault	338,850	214,992	115,789	4,069	4,000	100.0	63.4	34.2	1.2	1.2
Burglary	205,873	144,958	56,647	1,992	2,276	100.0	70.4	27.5	1.0	1.1
Larceny-theft	843,066	572,515	246,946	10,345	13,260	100.0	67.9	29.3	1.2	1.6
Motor vehicle theft	107,031	64,625	39,114	1,156	2,136	100.0	60.4	36.5	1.1	2.0
Arson	11,808	9,067	2,537	100	104	100.0	76.8	21.5	0.8	0.9
Violent crime[2]	446,356	266,681	169,525	4,895	5,255	100.0	59.7	38.0	1.1	1.2
Property crime[3]	1,167,778	791,165	345,244	13,593	17,776	100.0	67.7	29.6	1.2	1.5
Crime Index[4]	1,614,134	1,057,846	514,769	18,488	23,031	100.0	65.5	31.9	1.1	1.4
Other assaults	919,691	610,946	286,787	12,201	9,757	100.0	66.4	31.2	1.3	1.1
Forgery and counterfeiting	82,882	57,125	24,148	458	1,151	100.0	68.9	29.1	0.6	1.4
Fraud	232,336	157,763	71,538	1,431	1,604	100.0	67.9	30.8	0.6	0.7
Embezzlement	13,379	9,153	3,959	64	203	100.0	68.4	29.6	0.5	1.5
Stolen property; buying, receiving, possessing	91,150	53,535	35,986	611	1,018	100.0	58.7	39.5	0.7	1.1
Vandalism	198,139	150,437	42,757	2,804	2,141	100.0	75.9	21.6	1.4	1.1
Weapons; carrying, possessing, etc.	118,148	73,140	42,810	879	1,319	100.0	61.9	36.2	0.7	1.1
Prostitution and commercialized vice	58,659	33,650	23,455	364	1,190	100.0	57.4	40.0	0.6	2.0
Sex offenses (except forcible rape and prostitution)	67,761	50,378	15,745	680	958	100.0	74.3	23.2	1.0	1.4
Drug abuse violations	1,101,547	728,797	357,725	6,848	8,177	100.0	66.2	32.5	0.6	0.7
Gambling	7,525	2,033	5,136	38	318	100.0	27.0	68.3	0.5	4.2
Offenses against the family and children	97,393	66,440	28,180	1,266	1,507	100.0	68.2	28.9	1.3	1.5
Driving under the influence	1,017,504	893,395	99,548	15,460	9,101	100.0	87.8	9.8	1.5	0.9
Liquor laws	462,215	405,275	41,204	11,397	4,339	100.0	87.7	8.9	2.5	0.9
Drunkenness	412,735	345,448	55,598	9,563	2,126	100.0	83.7	13.5	2.3	0.5
Disorderly conduct	481,932	321,117	149,393	7,883	3,539	100.0	66.6	31.0	1.6	0.7
Vagrancy	19,669	12,223	6,888	419	139	100.0	62.1	35.0	2.1	0.7
All other offenses (except traffic)	2,599,658	1,751,450	778,558	37,377	32,273	100.0	67.4	29.9	1.4	1.2
Suspicion	7,647	4,130	3,128	108	281	100.0	54.0	40.9	1.4	3.7
Curfew and loitering law violations	103,054	70,738	29,717	1,083	1,516	100.0	68.6	28.8	1.1	1.5
Runaways	90,227	68,371	16,603	1,214	4,039	100.0	75.8	18.4	1.3	4.5

See footnotes at end of table.

Table 43

Arrests

by Race, 2002—Continued

[10,370 agencies; 2002 estimated population 205,108,615]

Offense charged	Arrests under 18					Percent distribution[1]				
	Total	White	Black	American Indian or Alaskan Native	Asian or Pacific Islander	Total	White	Black	American Indian or Alaskan Native	Asian or Pacific Islander
TOTAL	**1,620,594**	**1,158,776**	**415,854**	**20,383**	**25,581**	**100.0**	**71.5**	**25.7**	**1.3**	**1.6**
Murder and nonnegligent manslaughter	972	446	487	23	16	100.0	45.9	50.1	2.4	1.6
Forcible rape	3,355	2,079	1,207	37	32	100.0	62.0	36.0	1.1	1.0
Robbery	17,878	6,895	10,537	91	355	100.0	38.6	58.9	0.5	2.0
Aggravated assault	44,185	26,877	16,217	535	556	100.0	60.8	36.7	1.2	1.3
Burglary	61,754	44,680	15,558	689	827	100.0	72.4	25.2	1.1	1.3
Larceny-theft	248,202	173,910	65,667	3,443	5,182	100.0	70.1	26.5	1.4	2.1
Motor vehicle theft	32,487	18,949	12,428	445	665	100.0	58.3	38.3	1.4	2.0
Arson	5,837	4,711	1,026	48	52	100.0	80.7	17.6	0.8	0.9
Violent crime[2]	66,390	36,297	28,448	686	959	100.0	54.7	42.8	1.0	1.4
Property crime[3]	348,280	242,250	94,679	4,625	6,726	100.0	69.6	27.2	1.3	1.9
Crime Index[4]	414,670	278,547	123,127	5,311	7,685	100.0	67.2	29.7	1.3	1.9
Other assaults	168,641	106,119	58,518	1,942	2,062	100.0	62.9	34.7	1.2	1.2
Forgery and counterfeiting	3,644	2,845	711	33	55	100.0	78.1	19.5	0.9	1.5
Fraud	6,418	4,242	2,051	47	78	100.0	66.1	32.0	0.7	1.2
Embezzlement	1,004	696	287	1	20	100.0	69.3	28.6	0.1	2.0
Stolen property; buying, receiving, possessing	18,769	10,612	7,761	134	262	100.0	56.5	41.4	0.7	1.4
Vandalism	75,781	61,373	12,594	919	895	100.0	81.0	16.6	1.2	1.2
Weapons; carrying, possessing, etc.	25,239	16,945	7,751	207	336	100.0	67.1	30.7	0.8	1.3
Prostitution and commercialized vice	1,094	479	597	6	12	100.0	43.8	54.6	0.5	1.1
Sex offenses (except forcible rape and prostitution)	13,857	9,986	3,603	107	161	100.0	72.1	26.0	0.8	1.2
Drug abuse violations	133,494	97,766	33,208	1,152	1,368	100.0	73.2	24.9	0.9	1.0
Gambling	1,114	127	955	0	32	100.0	11.4	85.7	*	2.9
Offenses against the family and children	6,554	4,837	1,541	56	120	100.0	73.8	23.5	0.9	1.8
Driving under the influence	15,155	14,138	628	267	122	100.0	93.3	4.1	1.8	0.8
Liquor laws	105,652	97,372	4,629	2,656	995	100.0	92.2	4.4	2.5	0.9
Drunkenness	13,508	12,155	995	258	100	100.0	90.0	7.4	1.9	0.7
Disorderly conduct	138,847	88,761	47,261	1,708	1,117	100.0	63.9	34.0	1.2	0.8
Vagrancy	1,518	1,147	346	14	11	100.0	75.6	22.8	0.9	0.7
All other offenses (except traffic)	281,184	210,704	62,641	3,261	4,578	100.0	74.9	22.3	1.2	1.6
Suspicion	1,170	816	330	7	17	100.0	69.7	28.2	0.6	1.5
Curfew and loitering law violations	103,054	70,738	29,717	1,083	1,516	100.0	68.6	28.8	1.1	1.5
Runaways	90,227	68,371	16,603	1,214	4,039	100.0	75.8	18.4	1.3	4.5

See footnotes at end of table.

Table 43

Arrests

by Race, 2002—Continued

[10,370 agencies; 2002 estimated population 205,108,615]

Offense charged	Arrests 18 and over					Percent distribution[1]				
	Total	White	Black	American Indian or Alaskan Native	Asian or Pacific Islander	Total	White	Black	American Indian or Alaskan Native	Asian or Pacific Islander
TOTAL	**8,176,791**	**5,764,614**	**2,217,778**	**110,253**	**84,146**	**100.0**	**70.5**	**27.1**	**1.3**	**1.0**
Murder and nonnegligent manslaughter	9,127	4,368	4,560	92	107	100.0	47.9	50.0	1.0	1.2
Forcible rape	16,772	10,687	5,645	203	237	100.0	63.7	33.7	1.2	1.4
Robbery	59,402	27,214	31,300	380	508	100.0	45.8	52.7	0.6	0.9
Aggravated assault	294,665	188,115	99,572	3,534	3,444	100.0	63.8	33.8	1.2	1.2
Burglary	144,119	100,278	41,089	1,303	1,449	100.0	69.6	28.5	0.9	1.0
Larceny-theft	594,864	398,605	181,279	6,902	8,078	100.0	67.0	30.5	1.2	1.4
Motor vehicle theft	74,544	45,676	26,686	711	1,471	100.0	61.3	35.8	1.0	2.0
Arson	5,971	4,356	1,511	52	52	100.0	73.0	25.3	0.9	0.9
Violent crime[2]	379,966	230,384	141,077	4,209	4,296	100.0	60.6	37.1	1.1	1.1
Property crime[3]	819,498	548,915	250,565	8,968	11,050	100.0	67.0	30.6	1.1	1.3
Crime Index[4]	1,199,464	779,299	391,642	13,177	15,346	100.0	65.0	32.7	1.1	1.3
Other assaults	751,050	504,827	228,269	10,259	7,695	100.0	67.2	30.4	1.4	1.0
Forgery and counterfeiting	79,238	54,280	23,437	425	1,096	100.0	68.5	29.6	0.5	1.4
Fraud	225,918	153,521	69,487	1,384	1,526	100.0	68.0	30.8	0.6	0.7
Embezzlement	12,375	8,457	3,672	63	183	100.0	68.3	29.7	0.5	1.5
Stolen property; buying, receiving, possessing	72,381	42,923	28,225	477	756	100.0	59.3	39.0	0.7	1.0
Vandalism	122,358	89,064	30,163	1,885	1,246	100.0	72.8	24.7	1.5	1.0
Weapons; carrying, possessing, etc.	92,909	56,195	35,059	672	983	100.0	60.5	37.7	0.7	1.1
Prostitution and commercialized vice	57,565	33,171	22,858	358	1,178	100.0	57.6	39.7	0.6	2.0
Sex offenses (except forcible rape and prostitution)	53,904	40,392	12,142	573	797	100.0	74.9	22.5	1.1	1.5
Drug abuse violations	968,053	631,031	324,517	5,696	6,809	100.0	65.2	33.5	0.6	0.7
Gambling	6,411	1,906	4,181	38	286	100.0	29.7	65.2	0.6	4.5
Offenses against the family and children	90,839	61,603	26,639	1,210	1,387	100.0	67.8	29.3	1.3	1.5
Driving under the influence	1,002,349	879,257	98,920	15,193	8,979	100.0	87.7	9.9	1.5	0.9
Liquor laws	356,563	307,903	36,575	8,741	3,344	100.0	86.4	10.3	2.5	0.9
Drunkenness	399,227	333,293	54,603	9,305	2,026	100.0	83.5	13.7	2.3	0.5
Disorderly conduct	343,085	232,356	102,132	6,175	2,422	100.0	67.7	29.8	1.8	0.7
Vagrancy	18,151	11,076	6,542	405	128	100.0	61.0	36.0	2.2	0.7
All other offenses (except traffic)	2,318,474	1,540,746	715,917	34,116	27,695	100.0	66.5	30.9	1.5	1.2
Suspicion	6,477	3,314	2,798	101	264	100.0	51.2	43.2	1.6	4.1
Curfew and loitering law violations	–	–	–	–	–	–	–	–	–	–
Runaways	–	–	–	–	–	–	–	–	–	–

[1] Because of rounding, the percentages may not add to 100.0.

[2] Violent crimes are offenses of murder, forcible rape, robbery, and aggravated assault.

[3] Property crimes are offenses of burglary, larceny-theft, motor vehicle theft, and arson.

[4] Includes arson.

* Less than one-tenth of 1 percent.

Table 44

Arrest Trends

City, 2001-2002

[6,335 agencies; 2002 estimated population 123,260,979; 2001 estimated population 121,645,273]

Offense charged	Number of persons arrested								
	Total all ages			Under 18 years of age			18 years of age and over		
	2001	2002	Percent change	2001	2002	Percent change	2001	2002	Percent change
TOTAL[1]	6,321,725	6,332,176	+0.2	1,150,458	1,116,543	-2.9	5,171,267	5,215,633	+0.9
Murder and nonnegligent manslaughter	6,300	6,195	-1.7	663	656	-1.1	5,637	5,539	-1.7
Forcible rape	12,387	12,431	+0.4	2,142	2,090	-2.4	10,245	10,341	+0.9
Robbery	57,792	57,056	-1.3	13,275	13,098	-1.3	44,517	43,958	-1.3
Aggravated assault	231,162	228,557	-1.1	31,963	30,530	-4.5	199,199	198,027	-0.6
Burglary	133,512	134,899	+1.0	42,103	40,728	-3.3	91,409	94,171	+3.0
Larceny-theft	618,833	620,847	+0.3	194,724	188,883	-3.0	424,109	431,964	+1.9
Motor vehicle theft	66,139	68,554	+3.7	21,960	20,705	-5.7	44,179	47,849	+8.3
Arson	8,788	7,458	-15.1	4,567	4,074	-10.8	4,221	3,384	-19.8
Violent crime[2]	307,641	304,239	-1.1	48,043	46,374	-3.5	259,598	257,865	-0.7
Property crime[3]	827,272	831,758	+0.5	263,354	254,390	-3.4	563,918	577,368	+2.4
Crime Index[4]	1,134,913	1,135,997	+0.1	311,397	300,764	-3.4	823,516	835,233	+1.4
Other assaults	603,901	601,600	-0.4	112,978	114,887	+1.7	490,923	486,713	-0.9
Forgery and counterfeiting	56,229	56,059	-0.3	3,074	2,496	-18.8	53,155	53,563	+0.8
Fraud	101,858	102,630	+0.8	4,133	3,860	-6.6	97,725	98,770	+1.1
Embezzlement	10,215	9,632	-5.7	1,084	777	-28.3	9,131	8,855	-3.0
Stolen property; buying, receiving, possessing	67,619	66,873	-1.1	15,416	14,488	-6.0	52,203	52,385	+0.3
Vandalism	132,389	133,050	+0.5	52,467	51,667	-1.5	79,922	81,383	+1.8
Weapons; carrying, possessing, etc.	79,597	79,040	-0.7	18,383	17,525	-4.7	61,214	61,515	+0.5
Prostitution and commercialized vice	44,595	45,169	+1.3	735	762	+3.7	43,860	44,407	+1.2
Sex offenses (except forcible rape and prostitution)	41,067	40,985	-0.2	8,333	8,360	+0.3	32,734	32,625	-0.3
Drug abuse violations	703,801	703,273	-0.1	94,778	87,897	-7.3	609,023	615,376	+1.0
Gambling	3,494	3,357	-3.9	338	429	+26.9	3,156	2,928	-7.2
Offenses against the family and children	45,467	46,360	+2.0	4,593	4,022	-12.4	40,874	42,338	+3.6
Driving under the influence	547,301	553,775	+1.2	8,719	8,878	+1.8	538,582	544,897	+1.2
Liquor laws	309,089	309,141	*	67,442	65,704	-2.6	241,647	243,437	+0.7
Drunkenness	331,848	313,293	-5.6	11,391	10,539	-7.5	320,457	302,754	-5.5
Disorderly conduct	330,165	326,705	-1.0	93,268	95,954	+2.9	236,897	230,751	-2.6
Vagrancy	16,145	16,856	+4.4	1,206	1,008	-16.4	14,939	15,848	+6.1
All other offenses (except traffic)	1,616,517	1,651,531	+2.2	195,208	189,676	-2.8	1,421,309	1,461,855	+2.9
Suspicion	1,513	1,757	+16.1	449	853	+90.0	1,064	904	-15.0
Curfew and loitering law violations	80,456	77,138	-4.1	80,456	77,138	-4.1	–	–	–
Runaways	65,059	59,712	-8.2	65,059	59,712	-8.2	–	–	–

[1] Does not include suspicion.
[2] Violent crimes are offenses of murder, forcible rape, robbery, and aggravated assault.
[3] Property crimes are offenses of burglary, larceny-theft, motor vehicle theft, and arson.
[4] Includes arson.
* Less than one-tenth of 1 percent

Table 45

Arrest Trends
City
by Sex, 2001-2002
[6,335 agencies; 2002 estimated population 123,260,979; 2001 estimated population 121,645,273]

| | Male | | | | | | Female | | | | | |
| | Total | | | Under 18 | | | Total | | | Under 18 | | |
Offense charged	2001	2002	Percent change	2001	2002	Percent change	2001	2002	Percent change	2001	2002	Percent change
TOTAL[1]	4,863,870	4,851,656	-0.3	816,802	787,867	-3.5	1,457,855	1,480,520	+1.6	333,656	328,676	-1.5
Murder and nonnegligent manslaughter	5,661	5,552	-1.9	592	587	-0.8	639	643	+0.6	71	69	-2.8
Forcible rape	12,262	12,304	+0.3	2,117	2,052	-3.1	125	127	+1.6	25	38	+52.0
Robbery	51,774	50,965	-1.6	12,075	11,890	-1.5	6,018	6,091	+1.2	1,200	1,208	+0.7
Aggravated assault	183,062	180,931	-1.2	24,377	23,212	-4.8	48,100	47,626	-1.0	7,586	7,318	-3.5
Burglary	114,220	115,590	+1.2	36,666	35,622	-2.8	19,292	19,309	+0.1	5,437	5,106	-6.1
Larceny-theft	386,724	385,612	-0.3	116,939	112,689	-3.6	232,109	235,235	+1.3	77,785	76,194	-2.0
Motor vehicle theft	55,264	57,117	+3.4	18,208	17,055	-6.3	10,875	11,437	+5.2	3,752	3,650	-2.7
Arson	7,387	6,298	-14.7	3,988	3,610	-9.5	1,401	1,160	-17.2	579	464	-19.9
Violent crime[2]	252,759	249,752	-1.2	39,161	37,741	-3.6	54,882	54,487	-0.7	8,882	8,633	-2.8
Property crime[3]	563,595	564,617	+0.2	175,801	168,976	-3.9	263,677	267,141	+1.3	87,553	85,414	-2.4
Crime Index[4]	816,354	814,369	-0.2	214,962	206,717	-3.8	318,559	321,628	+1.0	96,435	94,047	-2.5
Other assaults	460,665	456,100	-1.0	76,889	77,280	+0.5	143,236	145,500	+1.6	36,089	37,607	+4.2
Forgery and counterfeiting	33,536	33,535	*	1,959	1,581	-19.3	22,693	22,524	-0.7	1,115	915	-17.9
Fraud	58,601	58,589	*	2,770	2,586	-6.6	43,257	44,041	+1.8	1,363	1,274	-6.5
Embezzlement	5,044	4,789	-5.1	610	451	-26.1	5,171	4,843	-6.3	474	326	-31.2
Stolen property; buying, receiving, possessing	55,177	54,819	-0.6	12,826	12,189	-5.0	12,442	12,054	-3.1	2,590	2,299	-11.2
Vandalism	110,401	110,163	-0.2	45,431	44,425	-2.2	21,988	22,887	+4.1	7,036	7,242	+2.9
Weapons; carrying, possessing, etc.	73,130	72,750	-0.5	16,490	15,656	-5.1	6,467	6,290	-2.7	1,893	1,869	-1.3
Prostitution and commercialized vice	15,219	15,572	+2.3	232	260	+12.1	29,376	29,597	+0.8	503	502	-0.2
Sex offenses (except forcible rape and prostitution)	37,831	37,835	*	7,684	7,691	+0.1	3,236	3,150	-2.7	649	669	+3.1
Drug abuse violations	577,411	574,962	-0.4	79,578	73,439	-7.7	126,390	128,311	+1.5	15,200	14,458	-4.9
Gambling	3,089	2,939	-4.9	322	410	+27.3	405	418	+3.2	16	19	+18.8
Offenses against the family and children	31,872	32,122	+0.8	2,906	2,452	-15.6	13,595	14,238	+4.7	1,687	1,570	-6.9
Driving under the influence	451,289	453,192	+0.4	7,157	7,192	+0.5	96,012	100,583	+4.8	1,562	1,686	+7.9
Liquor laws	236,160	234,277	-0.8	45,804	43,911	-4.1	72,929	74,864	+2.7	21,638	21,793	+0.7
Drunkenness	286,675	269,964	-5.8	8,972	8,260	-7.9	45,173	43,329	-4.1	2,419	2,279	-5.8
Disorderly conduct	249,337	245,020	-1.7	65,136	66,341	+1.8	80,828	81,685	+1.1	28,132	29,613	+5.3
Vagrancy	13,287	13,994	+5.3	978	806	-17.6	2,858	2,862	+0.1	228	202	-11.4
All other offenses (except traffic)	1,266,776	1,289,569	+1.8	144,080	139,124	-3.4	349,741	361,962	+3.5	51,128	50,552	-1.1
Suspicion	1,199	1,338	+11.6	333	607	+82.3	314	419	+33.4	116	246	+112.1
Curfew and loitering law violations	55,830	53,613	-4.0	55,830	53,613	-4.0	24,626	23,525	-4.5	24,626	23,525	-4.5
Runaways	26,186	23,483	-10.3	26,186	23,483	-10.3	38,873	36,229	-6.8	38,873	36,229	-6.8

[1] Does not include suspicion.
[2] Violent crimes are offenses of murder, forcible rape, robbery, and aggravated assault.
[3] Property crimes are offenses of burglary, larceny-theft, motor vehicle theft, and arson.
[4] Includes arson.
* Less than one-tenth of 1 percent.

Table 46

Arrests

City

by Age, 2002

[7,507 agencies; 2002 estimated population 142,375,961]

Offense charged	Total all ages	Ages under 15	Ages under 18	Ages 18 and over	Under 10	10-12	13-14	15	16	17	18	19	20	21
TOTAL	7,367,845	427,563	1,328,050	6,039,795	16,108	101,060	310,395	254,054	309,436	336,997	367,262	383,443	356,964	319,441
Percent distribution[1]	100.0	5.8	18.0	82.0	0.2	1.4	4.2	3.4	4.2	4.6	5.0	5.2	4.8	4.3
Murder and nonnegligent														
manslaughter	7,467	83	788	6,679	0	14	69	111	222	372	431	546	548	483
Forcible rape	14,515	949	2,507	12,008	39	258	652	429	488	641	720	702	651	670
Robbery	66,834	3,994	15,996	50,838	84	732	3,178	3,078	4,016	4,908	5,303	4,720	3,930	3,522
Aggravated assault	260,392	12,960	35,608	224,784	567	3,570	8,823	6,419	7,748	8,481	9,220	10,008	10,076	10,658
Burglary	151,343	17,470	46,577	104,766	899	4,538	12,033	8,921	9,885	10,301	10,600	9,002	7,075	6,194
Larceny-theft	716,186	84,717	217,533	498,653	3,172	23,106	58,439	40,674	46,168	45,974	43,069	36,129	28,969	24,604
Motor vehicle theft	85,662	6,795	26,768	58,894	51	836	5,908	6,396	6,986	6,591	6,216	5,295	4,431	3,776
Arson	8,372	2,921	4,497	3,875	424	1,084	1,413	671	499	406	309	286	197	175
Violent crime[2]	349,208	17,986	54,899	294,309	690	4,574	12,722	10,037	12,474	14,402	15,674	15,976	15,205	15,333
Percent distribution[1]	100.0	5.2	15.7	84.3	0.2	1.3	3.6	2.9	3.6	4.1	4.5	4.6	4.4	4.4
Property crime[3]	961,563	111,903	295,375	666,188	4,546	29,564	77,793	56,662	63,538	63,272	60,194	50,712	40,672	34,749
Percent distribution[1]	100.0	11.6	30.7	69.3	0.5	3.1	8.1	5.9	6.6	6.6	6.3	5.3	4.2	3.6
Crime Index[4]	1,310,771	129,889	350,274	960,497	5,236	34,138	90,515	66,699	76,012	77,674	75,868	66,688	55,877	50,082
Percent distribution[1]	100.0	9.9	26.7	73.3	0.4	2.6	6.9	5.1	5.8	5.9	5.8	5.1	4.3	3.8
Other assaults	691,820	57,568	132,955	558,865	2,219	16,221	39,128	24,811	25,885	24,691	22,199	23,752	24,086	26,334
Forgery and counterfeiting	63,725	350	2,861	60,864	23	55	272	391	774	1,346	2,685	3,266	3,590	3,105
Fraud	121,969	920	4,668	117,301	86	167	667	660	1,175	1,913	3,678	5,150	5,640	5,193
Embezzlement	10,337	88	846	9,491	2	20	66	60	209	489	719	759	620	605
Stolen property; buying,														
receiving, possessing	71,788	4,376	15,833	55,955	126	873	3,377	3,003	3,820	4,634	4,820	4,695	4,027	3,547
Vandalism	155,656	26,983	60,759	94,897	2,029	8,283	16,671	10,678	11,774	11,324	10,046	8,250	6,656	6,675
Weapons; carrying,														
possessing, etc.	93,030	7,203	21,056	71,974	337	1,781	5,085	3,908	4,492	5,453	6,146	5,879	5,256	5,017
Prostitution and														
commercialized vice	56,686	141	1,027	55,659	2	23	116	158	267	461	1,534	1,750	1,745	1,834
Sex offenses (except forcible														
rape and prostitution)	49,745	5,458	10,211	39,534	309	1,650	3,499	1,685	1,560	1,508	1,711	1,785	1,695	1,664
Drug abuse violations	838,900	18,224	108,530	730,370	228	2,128	15,868	19,264	30,094	40,948	53,798	54,477	49,097	44,161
Gambling	6,216	164	1,077	5,139	0	28	136	195	301	417	418	416	354	328
Offenses against the family														
and children	53,532	1,776	4,799	48,733	263	454	1,059	912	1,010	1,101	1,328	1,460	1,616	1,827
Driving under the influence	632,092	279	10,078	622,014	90	18	171	472	2,506	6,821	15,722	21,437	23,812	32,351
Liquor laws	368,132	8,118	79,928	288,204	131	605	7,382	12,257	23,040	36,513	59,127	64,839	53,694	10,818
Drunkenness	347,469	1,455	11,576	335,893	73	126	1,256	1,817	2,786	5,518	10,157	11,198	11,388	15,525
Disorderly conduct	415,817	49,493	120,733	295,084	1,243	12,776	35,474	24,001	23,887	23,352	20,272	18,570	17,596	20,264
Vagrancy	17,378	325	1,120	16,258	8	47	270	218	256	321	599	492	460	479
All other offenses														
(except traffic)	1,892,117	61,866	224,758	1,667,359	2,478	12,472	46,916	44,095	55,470	63,327	76,142	88,295	89,514	89,386
Suspicion	6,781	260	1,077	5,704	4	47	209	199	275	343	293	285	241	246
Curfew and loitering law														
violations	97,467	27,663	97,467	–	507	4,915	22,241	22,037	27,198	20,569	–	–	–	–
Runaways	66,417	24,964	66,417	–	714	4,233	20,017	16,534	16,645	8,274	–	–	–	–

See footnotes at end of table.

Table 46

Arrests

City

by Age, 2002—Continued

[7,507 agencies; 2002 estimated population 142,375,961]

Offense charged	22	23	24	25-29	30-34	35-39	40-44	45-49	50-54	55-59	60-64	65 and over
TOTAL	**293,923**	**257,550**	**230,919**	**884,967**	**776,100**	**741,089**	**638,895**	**400,910**	**205,831**	**96,389**	**44,178**	**41,934**
Percent distribution[1]	**4.0**	**3.5**	**3.1**	**12.0**	**10.5**	**10.1**	**8.7**	**5.4**	**2.8**	**1.3**	**0.6**	**0.6**
Murder and nonnegligent manslaughter	439	413	371	1,189	703	547	388	302	141	88	38	52
Forcible rape	536	522	458	1,795	1,739	1,548	1,175	692	361	192	115	132
Robbery	2,912	2,475	2,097	7,344	6,362	5,382	3,860	1,785	701	266	99	80
Aggravated assault	10,525	9,709	9,261	37,318	32,983	30,268	24,866	15,148	7,637	3,648	1,698	1,761
Burglary	5,284	4,462	4,042	14,532	13,410	12,469	9,581	5,033	1,940	693	245	204
Larceny-theft	21,468	18,481	15,787	63,659	63,189	62,515	53,560	33,803	17,492	8,005	3,816	4,107
Motor vehicle theft	3,302	2,786	2,516	9,020	7,736	6,411	4,126	2,033	792	304	94	56
Arson	169	134	114	497	473	509	409	309	156	75	39	24
Violent crime[2]	14,412	13,119	12,187	47,646	41,787	37,745	30,289	17,927	8,840	4,194	1,950	2,025
Percent distribution[1]	4.1	3.8	3.5	13.6	12.0	10.8	8.7	5.1	2.5	1.2	0.6	0.6
Property crime[3]	30,223	25,863	22,459	87,708	84,808	81,904	67,676	41,178	20,380	9,077	4,194	4,391
Percent distribution[1]	3.1	2.7	2.3	9.1	8.8	8.5	7.0	4.3	2.1	0.9	0.4	0.5
Crime Index[4]	44,635	38,982	34,646	135,354	126,595	119,649	97,965	59,105	29,220	13,271	6,144	6,416
Percent distribution[1]	3.4	3.0	2.6	10.3	9.7	9.1	7.5	4.5	2.2	1.0	0.5	0.5
Other assaults	26,282	24,010	22,386	92,350	83,880	78,104	63,994	37,463	18,140	8,192	3,763	3,930
Forgery and counterfeiting	3,028	2,914	2,565	10,817	9,663	8,015	5,788	3,150	1,491	455	195	137
Fraud	5,317	4,817	4,451	20,140	19,071	16,443	12,649	7,398	3,819	1,899	815	821
Embezzlement	480	427	340	1,455	1,241	1,070	878	423	269	123	53	29
Stolen property; buying, receiving, possessing	3,096	2,551	2,298	8,371	7,250	6,185	4,722	2,571	1,132	376	176	138
Vandalism	5,614	4,669	3,940	13,874	10,917	9,497	7,327	3,978	1,860	830	357	407
Weapons; carrying, possessing, etc.	4,489	3,887	3,310	11,608	7,839	6,280	5,003	3,305	1,934	1,035	481	505
Prostitution and commercialized vice	1,879	1,808	1,791	8,080	10,205	10,237	7,833	4,007	1,606	675	318	357
Sex offenses (except forcible rape and prostitution)	1,472	1,344	1,202	4,996	5,219	5,431	4,725	3,269	2,018	1,266	801	936
Drug abuse violations	39,877	34,238	30,169	110,074	90,588	83,707	70,555	41,490	18,141	6,373	2,307	1,318
Gambling	312	302	233	711	426	362	349	259	252	161	130	126
Offenses against the family and children	1,899	1,869	1,851	8,248	8,326	8,031	6,279	3,321	1,472	625	290	291
Driving under the influence	31,322	28,373	25,711	98,132	82,552	78,233	72,466	50,739	30,094	16,171	7,858	7,041
Liquor laws	7,458	5,425	4,492	14,793	12,519	14,372	15,277	11,749	6,965	3,603	1,684	1,389
Drunkenness	14,063	12,246	10,849	42,450	39,933	46,396	48,755	35,123	19,752	9,822	4,669	3,567
Disorderly conduct	17,656	14,365	12,216	41,874	33,329	32,981	29,708	18,564	9,396	4,310	2,060	1,923
Vagrancy	450	417	356	1,543	1,840	2,312	2,872	2,092	1,243	654	266	183
All other offenses (except traffic)	84,373	74,690	67,873	259,305	223,871	212,976	181,055	112,427	56,806	26,471	11,779	12,396
Suspicion	221	216	240	792	836	808	695	477	221	77	32	24
Curfew and loitering law violations	–	–	–	–	–	–	–	–	–	–	–	–
Runaways	–	–	–	–	–	–	–	–	–	–	–	–

[1] Because of rounding, the percentages may not add to 100.0.

[2] Violent crimes are offenses of murder, forcible rape, robbery, and aggravated assault.

[3] Property crimes are offenses of burglary, larceny-theft, motor vehicle theft, and arson.

[4] Includes arson.

Table 47

Arrests

City

of Persons Under 15, 18, 21, and 25 Years of Age, 2002

[7,507 agencies; 2002 estimated population 142,375,961]

Offense charged	Total all ages	Number of persons arrested				Percent of total all ages			
		Under 15	Under 18	Under 21	Under 25	Under 15	Under 18	Under 21	Under 25
TOTAL	**7,367,845**	**427,563**	**1,328,050**	**2,435,719**	**3,537,552**	**5.8**	**18.0**	**33.1**	**48.0**
Murder and nonnegligent manslaughter	7,467	83	788	2,313	4,019	1.1	10.6	31.0	53.8
Forcible rape	14,515	949	2,507	4,580	6,766	6.5	17.3	31.6	46.6
Robbery	66,834	3,994	15,996	29,949	40,955	6.0	23.9	44.8	61.3
Aggravated assault	260,392	12,960	35,608	64,912	105,065	5.0	13.7	24.9	40.3
Burglary	151,343	17,470	46,577	73,254	93,236	11.5	30.8	48.4	61.6
Larceny-theft	716,186	84,717	217,533	325,700	406,040	11.8	30.4	45.5	56.7
Motor vehicle theft	85,662	6,795	26,768	42,710	55,090	7.9	31.2	49.9	64.3
Arson	8,372	2,921	4,497	5,289	5,881	34.9	53.7	63.2	70.2
Violent crime[1]	349,208	17,986	54,899	101,754	156,805	5.2	15.7	29.1	44.9
Property crime[2]	961,563	111,903	295,375	446,953	560,247	11.6	30.7	46.5	58.3
Crime Index[3]	1,310,771	129,889	350,274	548,707	717,052	9.9	26.7	41.9	54.7
Other assaults	691,820	57,568	132,955	202,992	302,004	8.3	19.2	29.3	43.7
Forgery and counterfeiting	63,725	350	2,861	12,402	24,014	0.5	4.5	19.5	37.7
Fraud	121,969	920	4,668	19,136	38,914	0.8	3.8	15.7	31.9
Embezzlement	10,337	88	846	2,944	4,796	0.9	8.2	28.5	46.4
Stolen property; buying, receiving, possessing	71,788	4,376	15,833	29,375	40,867	6.1	22.1	40.9	56.9
Vandalism	155,656	26,983	60,759	85,711	106,609	17.3	39.0	55.1	68.5
Weapons; carrying, possessing, etc.	93,030	7,203	21,056	38,337	55,040	7.7	22.6	41.2	59.2
Prostitution and commercialized vice	56,686	141	1,027	6,056	13,368	0.2	1.8	10.7	23.6
Sex offenses (except forcible rape and prostitution)	49,745	5,458	10,211	15,402	21,084	11.0	20.5	31.0	42.4
Drug abuse violations	838,900	18,224	108,530	265,902	414,347	2.2	12.9	31.7	49.4
Gambling	6,216	164	1,077	2,265	3,440	2.6	17.3	36.4	55.3
Offenses against the family and children	53,532	1,776	4,799	9,203	16,649	3.3	9.0	17.2	31.1
Driving under the influence	632,092	279	10,078	71,049	188,806	*	1.6	11.2	29.9
Liquor laws	368,132	8,118	79,928	257,588	285,781	2.2	21.7	70.0	77.6
Drunkenness	347,469	1,455	11,576	44,319	97,002	0.4	3.3	12.8	27.9
Disorderly conduct	415,817	49,493	120,733	177,171	241,672	11.9	29.0	42.6	58.1
Vagrancy	17,378	325	1,120	2,671	4,373	1.9	6.4	15.4	25.2
All other offenses (except traffic)	1,892,117	61,866	224,758	478,709	795,031	3.3	11.9	25.3	42.0
Suspicion	6,781	260	1,077	1,896	2,819	3.8	15.9	28.0	41.6
Curfew and loitering law violations	97,467	27,663	97,467	97,467	97,467	28.4	100.0	100.0	100.0
Runaways	66,417	24,964	66,417	66,417	66,417	37.6	100.0	100.0	100.0

[1] Violent crimes are offenses of murder, forcible rape, robbery, and aggravated assault.

[2] Property crimes are offenses of burglary, larceny-theft, motor vehicle theft, and arson.

[3] Includes arson.

* Less than one-tenth of 1 percent.

Table 48

Arrests
City
by Sex, 2002
[7,507 agencies; 2002 estimated population 142,375,961]

Offense charged	Number of persons arrested			Percent male	Percent female	Percent distribution[1]		
	Total	Male	Female			Total	Male	Female
TOTAL	**7,367,845**	**5,650,215**	**1,717,630**	**76.7**	**23.3**	**100.0**	**100.0**	**100.0**
Murder and nonnegligent manslaughter	7,467	6,730	737	90.1	9.9	0.1	0.1	*
Forcible rape	14,515	14,319	196	98.6	1.4	0.2	0.3	*
Robbery	66,834	59,901	6,933	89.6	10.4	0.9	1.1	0.4
Aggravated assault	260,392	206,175	54,217	79.2	20.8	3.5	3.6	3.2
Burglary	151,343	130,543	20,800	86.3	13.7	2.1	2.3	1.2
Larceny-theft	716,186	446,007	270,179	62.3	37.7	9.7	7.9	15.7
Motor vehicle theft	85,662	71,392	14,270	83.3	16.7	1.2	1.3	0.8
Arson	8,372	7,083	1,289	84.6	15.4	0.1	0.1	0.1
Violent crime[2]	349,208	287,125	62,083	82.2	17.8	4.7	5.1	3.6
Property crime[3]	961,563	655,025	306,538	68.1	31.9	13.1	11.6	17.8
Crime Index[4]	1,310,771	942,150	368,621	71.9	28.1	17.8	16.7	21.5
Other assaults	691,820	525,945	165,875	76.0	24.0	9.4	9.3	9.7
Forgery and counterfeiting	63,725	38,064	25,661	59.7	40.3	0.9	0.7	1.5
Fraud	121,969	69,148	52,821	56.7	43.3	1.7	1.2	3.1
Embezzlement	10,337	5,152	5,185	49.8	50.2	0.1	0.1	0.3
Stolen property; buying, receiving, possessing	71,788	58,787	13,001	81.9	18.1	1.0	1.0	0.8
Vandalism	155,656	129,281	26,375	83.1	16.9	2.1	2.3	1.5
Weapons; carrying, possessing, etc.	93,030	85,550	7,480	92.0	8.0	1.3	1.5	0.4
Prostitution and commercialized vice	56,686	19,054	37,632	33.6	66.4	0.8	0.3	2.2
Sex offenses (except forcible rape and prostitution)	49,745	45,112	4,633	90.7	9.3	0.7	0.8	0.3
Drug abuse violations	838,900	689,595	149,305	82.2	17.8	11.4	12.2	8.7
Gambling	6,216	5,705	511	91.8	8.2	0.1	0.1	*
Offenses against the family and children	53,532	37,165	16,367	69.4	30.6	0.7	0.7	1.0
Driving under the influence	632,092	518,288	113,804	82.0	18.0	8.6	9.2	6.6
Liquor laws	368,132	277,453	90,679	75.4	24.6	5.0	4.9	5.3
Drunkenness	347,469	299,821	47,648	86.3	13.7	4.7	5.3	2.8
Disorderly conduct	415,817	314,636	101,181	75.7	24.3	5.6	5.6	5.9
Vagrancy	17,378	14,416	2,962	83.0	17.0	0.2	0.3	0.2
All other offenses (except traffic)	1,892,117	1,475,991	416,126	78.0	22.0	25.7	26.1	24.2
Suspicion	6,781	5,420	1,361	79.9	20.1	0.1	0.1	0.1
Curfew and loitering law violations	97,467	67,169	30,298	68.9	31.1	1.3	1.2	1.8
Runaways	66,417	26,313	40,104	39.6	60.4	0.9	0.5	2.3

[1] Because of rounding, the percentages may not add to 100.0.

[2] Violent crimes are offenses of murder, forcible rape, robbery, and aggravated assault.

[3] Property crimes are offenses of burglary, larceny-theft, motor vehicle theft, and arson.

[4] Includes arson.

* Less than one-tenth of 1 percent.

Table 49

Arrests

City

by Race, 2002

[7,505 agencies; 2002 estimated population 142,362,391]

Offense charged	Total arrests					Percent distribution[1]				
	Total	White	Black	American Indian or Alaskan Native	Asian or Pacific Islander	Total	White	Black	American Indian or Alaskan Native	Asian or Pacific Islander
TOTAL	**7,351,904**	**5,006,302**	**2,155,660**	**94,160**	**95,782**	**100.0**	**68.1**	**29.3**	**1.3**	**1.3**
Murder and nonnegligent manslaughter	7,463	3,073	4,225	56	109	100.0	41.2	56.6	0.8	1.5
Forcible rape	14,491	8,394	5,719	143	235	100.0	57.9	39.5	1.0	1.6
Robbery	66,784	28,509	37,104	362	809	100.0	42.7	55.6	0.5	1.2
Aggravated assault	259,904	156,085	97,791	2,585	3,443	100.0	60.1	37.6	1.0	1.3
Burglary	151,127	101,169	46,761	1,199	1,998	100.0	66.9	30.9	0.8	1.3
Larceny-theft	714,476	479,268	213,858	9,165	12,185	100.0	67.1	29.9	1.3	1.7
Motor vehicle theft	85,542	47,798	34,947	820	1,977	100.0	55.9	40.9	1.0	2.3
Arson	8,350	6,131	2,065	64	90	100.0	73.4	24.7	0.8	1.1
Violent crime[2]	348,642	196,061	144,839	3,146	4,596	100.0	56.2	41.5	0.9	1.3
Property crime[3]	959,495	634,366	297,631	11,248	16,250	100.0	66.1	31.0	1.2	1.7
Crime Index[4]	1,308,137	830,427	442,470	14,394	20,846	100.0	63.5	33.8	1.1	1.6
Other assaults	690,184	436,318	236,676	8,860	8,330	100.0	63.2	34.3	1.3	1.2
Forgery and counterfeiting	63,514	42,648	19,475	359	1,032	100.0	67.1	30.7	0.6	1.6
Fraud	121,544	79,736	39,815	730	1,263	100.0	65.6	32.8	0.6	1.0
Embezzlement	10,313	6,826	3,262	51	174	100.0	66.2	31.6	0.5	1.7
Stolen property; buying, receiving, possessing	71,676	39,420	30,923	424	909	100.0	55.0	43.1	0.6	1.3
Vandalism	155,325	114,440	36,907	2,099	1,879	100.0	73.7	23.8	1.4	1.2
Weapons; carrying, possessing, etc.	92,913	54,496	36,674	583	1,160	100.0	58.7	39.5	0.6	1.2
Prostitution and commercialized vice	56,590	32,164	22,974	345	1,107	100.0	56.8	40.6	0.6	2.0
Sex offenses (except forcible rape and prostitution)	49,696	35,208	13,161	488	839	100.0	70.8	26.5	1.0	1.7
Drug abuse violations	837,806	521,279	305,106	4,431	6,990	100.0	62.2	36.4	0.5	0.8
Gambling	6,216	1,260	4,648	36	272	100.0	20.3	74.8	0.6	4.4
Offenses against the family and children	53,340	35,434	15,613	879	1,414	100.0	66.4	29.3	1.6	2.7
Driving under the influence	630,312	549,723	64,823	9,119	6,647	100.0	87.2	10.3	1.4	1.1
Liquor laws	367,105	317,097	36,736	9,407	3,865	100.0	86.4	10.0	2.6	1.1
Drunkenness	346,480	286,560	49,843	8,127	1,950	100.0	82.7	14.4	2.3	0.6
Disorderly conduct	415,023	270,582	134,755	6,411	3,275	100.0	65.2	32.5	1.5	0.8
Vagrancy	17,373	10,688	6,160	394	131	100.0	61.5	35.5	2.3	0.8
All other offenses (except traffic)	1,887,888	1,223,700	610,826	24,990	28,372	100.0	64.8	32.4	1.3	1.5
Suspicion	6,773	3,687	2,698	107	281	100.0	54.4	39.8	1.6	4.1
Curfew and loitering law violations	97,377	66,156	28,883	1,010	1,328	100.0	67.9	29.7	1.0	1.4
Runaways	66,319	48,453	13,232	916	3,718	100.0	73.1	20.0	1.4	5.6

See footnotes at end of table.

Table 49

Arrests
City
by Race, 2002—Continued
[7,505 agencies; 2002 estimated population 142,362,391]

Offense charged	Arrests under 18					Percent distribution[1]				
	Total	White	Black	American Indian or Alaskan Native	Asian or Pacific Islander	Total	White	Black	American Indian or Alaskan Native	Asian or Pacific Islander
TOTAL	**1,325,223**	**925,182**	**360,857**	**16,185**	**22,999**	**100.0**	**69.8**	**27.2**	**1.2**	**1.7**
Murder and nonnegligent manslaughter	788	341	422	9	16	100.0	43.3	53.6	1.1	2.0
Forcible rape	2,502	1,411	1,039	23	29	100.0	56.4	41.5	0.9	1.2
Robbery	15,983	6,011	9,559	78	335	100.0	37.6	59.8	0.5	2.1
Aggravated assault	35,526	20,815	13,848	380	483	100.0	58.6	39.0	1.1	1.4
Burglary	46,511	32,072	13,242	480	717	100.0	69.0	28.5	1.0	1.5
Larceny-theft	216,960	150,757	58,284	3,137	4,782	100.0	69.5	26.9	1.4	2.2
Motor vehicle theft	26,732	14,436	11,362	332	602	100.0	54.0	42.5	1.2	2.3
Arson	4,484	3,527	869	39	49	100.0	78.7	19.4	0.9	1.1
Violent crime[2]	54,799	28,578	24,868	490	863	100.0	52.2	45.4	0.9	1.6
Property crime[3]	294,687	200,792	83,757	3,988	6,150	100.0	68.1	28.4	1.4	2.1
Crime Index[4]	349,486	229,370	108,625	4,478	7,013	100.0	65.6	31.1	1.3	2.0
Other assaults	132,643	80,911	48,488	1,459	1,785	100.0	61.0	36.6	1.1	1.3
Forgery and counterfeiting	2,855	2,197	580	28	50	100.0	77.0	20.3	1.0	1.8
Fraud	4,657	3,140	1,423	28	66	100.0	67.4	30.6	0.6	1.4
Embezzlement	845	574	252	1	18	100.0	67.9	29.8	0.1	2.1
Stolen property; buying, receiving, possessing	15,788	8,442	7,003	108	235	100.0	53.5	44.4	0.7	1.5
Vandalism	60,619	48,200	10,915	711	793	100.0	79.5	18.0	1.2	1.3
Weapons; carrying, possessing, etc.	21,015	13,849	6,714	150	302	100.0	65.9	31.9	0.7	1.4
Prostitution and commercialized vice	1,026	436	575	5	10	100.0	42.5	56.0	0.5	1.0
Sex offenses (except forcible rape and prostitution)	10,197	6,957	3,042	56	142	100.0	68.2	29.8	0.5	1.4
Drug abuse violations	108,335	76,464	29,864	837	1,170	100.0	70.6	27.6	0.8	1.1
Gambling	1,077	112	933	0	32	100.0	10.4	86.6	*	3.0
Offenses against the family and children	4,787	3,423	1,200	51	113	100.0	71.5	25.1	1.1	2.4
Driving under the influence	10,034	9,279	481	178	96	100.0	92.5	4.8	1.8	1.0
Liquor laws	79,698	72,719	4,027	2,083	869	100.0	91.2	5.1	2.6	1.1
Drunkenness	11,556	10,333	889	242	92	100.0	89.4	7.7	2.1	0.8
Disorderly conduct	120,547	76,616	41,487	1,408	1,036	100.0	63.6	34.4	1.2	0.9
Vagrancy	1,119	816	280	14	9	100.0	72.9	25.0	1.3	0.8
All other offenses (except traffic)	224,166	165,992	51,654	2,415	4,105	100.0	74.0	23.0	1.1	1.8
Suspicion	1,077	743	310	7	17	100.0	69.0	28.8	0.6	1.6
Curfew and loitering law violations	97,377	66,156	28,883	1,010	1,328	100.0	67.9	29.7	1.0	1.4
Runaways	66,319	48,453	13,232	916	3,718	100.0	73.1	20.0	1.4	5.6

See footnotes at end of table.

Table 49

Arrests
City
by Race, 2002—Continued
[7,505 agencies; 2002 estimated population 142,362,391]

Offense charged	Arrests 18 and over					Percent distribution[1]				
	Total	White	Black	American Indian or Alaskan Native	Asian or Pacific Islander	Total	White	Black	American Indian or Alaskan Native	Asian or Pacific Islander
TOTAL	**6,026,681**	**4,081,120**	**1,794,803**	**77,975**	**72,783**	**100.0**	**67.7**	**29.8**	**1.3**	**1.2**
Murder and nonnegligent manslaughter	6,675	2,732	3,803	47	93	100.0	40.9	57.0	0.7	1.4
Forcible rape	11,989	6,983	4,680	120	206	100.0	58.2	39.0	1.0	1.7
Robbery	50,801	22,498	27,545	284	474	100.0	44.3	54.2	0.6	0.9
Aggravated assault	224,378	135,270	83,943	2,205	2,960	100.0	60.3	37.4	1.0	1.3
Burglary	104,616	69,097	33,519	719	1,281	100.0	66.0	32.0	0.7	1.2
Larceny-theft	497,516	328,511	155,574	6,028	7,403	100.0	66.0	31.3	1.2	1.5
Motor vehicle theft	58,810	33,362	23,585	488	1,375	100.0	56.7	40.1	0.8	2.3
Arson	3,866	2,604	1,196	25	41	100.0	67.4	30.9	0.6	1.1
Violent crime[2]	293,843	167,483	119,971	2,656	3,733	100.0	57.0	40.8	0.9	1.3
Property crime[3]	664,808	433,574	213,874	7,260	10,100	100.0	65.2	32.2	1.1	1.5
Crime Index[4]	958,651	601,057	333,845	9,916	13,833	100.0	62.7	34.8	1.0	1.4
Other assaults	557,541	355,407	188,188	7,401	6,545	100.0	63.7	33.8	1.3	1.2
Forgery and counterfeiting	60,659	40,451	18,895	331	982	100.0	66.7	31.1	0.5	1.6
Fraud	116,887	76,596	38,392	702	1,197	100.0	65.5	32.8	0.6	1.0
Embezzlement	9,468	6,252	3,010	50	156	100.0	66.0	31.8	0.5	1.6
Stolen property; buying, receiving, possessing	55,888	30,978	23,920	316	674	100.0	55.4	42.8	0.6	1.2
Vandalism	94,706	66,240	25,992	1,388	1,086	100.0	69.9	27.4	1.5	1.1
Weapons; carrying, possessing, etc.	71,898	40,647	29,960	433	858	100.0	56.5	41.7	0.6	1.2
Prostitution and commercialized vice	55,564	31,728	22,399	340	1,097	100.0	57.1	40.3	0.6	2.0
Sex offenses (except forcible rape and prostitution)	39,499	28,251	10,119	432	697	100.0	71.5	25.6	1.1	1.8
Drug abuse violations	729,471	444,815	275,242	3,594	5,820	100.0	61.0	37.7	0.5	0.8
Gambling	5,139	1,148	3,715	36	240	100.0	22.3	72.3	0.7	4.7
Offenses against the family and children	48,553	32,011	14,413	828	1,301	100.0	65.9	29.7	1.7	2.7
Driving under the influence	620,278	540,444	64,342	8,941	6,551	100.0	87.1	10.4	1.4	1.1
Liquor laws	287,407	244,378	32,709	7,324	2,996	100.0	85.0	11.4	2.5	1.0
Drunkenness	334,924	276,227	48,954	7,885	1,858	100.0	82.5	14.6	2.4	0.6
Disorderly conduct	294,476	193,966	93,268	5,003	2,239	100.0	65.9	31.7	1.7	0.8
Vagrancy	16,254	9,872	5,880	380	122	100.0	60.7	36.2	2.3	0.8
All other offenses (except traffic)	1,663,722	1,057,708	559,172	22,575	24,267	100.0	63.6	33.6	1.4	1.5
Suspicion	5,696	2,944	2,388	100	264	100.0	51.7	41.9	1.8	4.6
Curfew and loitering law violations	–	–	–	–	–	–	–	–	–	–
Runaways	–	–	–	–	–	–	–	–	–	–

[1] Because of rounding, the percentages may not add to 100.0.
[2] Violent crimes are offenses of murder, forcible rape, robbery, and aggravated assault.
[3] Property crimes are offenses of burglary, larceny-theft, motor vehicle theft, and arson.
[4] Includes arson
* Less than one-tenth of 1 percent.

Table 50

Arrest Trends

Suburban Counties, 2001-2002

[793 agencies; 2002 estimated population 37,206,488; 2001 estimated population 37,000,588]

| | Number of persons arrested | | | | | | | | |
| | Total all ages | | | Under 18 years of age | | | 18 years of age and over | | |
Offense charged	2001	2002	Percent change	2001	2002	Percent change	2001	2002	Percent change
TOTAL[1]	1,410,244	1,429,611	+1.4	190,553	185,198	-2.8	1,219,691	1,244,413	+2.0
Murder and nonnegligent manslaughter	1,404	1,561	+11.2	91	100	+9.9	1,313	1,461	+11.3
Forcible rape	3,021	3,177	+5.2	473	486	+2.7	2,548	2,691	+5.6
Robbery	7,477	7,676	+2.7	1,504	1,557	+3.5	5,973	6,119	+2.4
Aggravated assault	51,006	51,241	+0.5	6,036	6,081	+0.7	44,970	45,160	+0.4
Burglary	31,263	30,819	-1.4	9,575	8,998	-6.0	21,688	21,821	+0.6
Larceny-theft	85,772	86,479	+0.8	22,239	22,055	-0.8	63,533	64,424	+1.4
Motor vehicle theft	13,572	14,126	+4.1	3,752	3,410	-9.1	9,820	10,716	+9.1
Arson	2,236	2,230	-0.3	1,051	996	-5.2	1,185	1,234	+4.1
Violent crime[2]	62,908	63,655	+1.2	8,104	8,224	+1.5	54,804	55,431	+1.1
Property crime[3]	132,843	133,654	+0.6	36,617	35,459	-3.2	96,226	98,195	+2.0
Crime Index[4]	195,751	197,309	+0.8	44,721	43,683	-2.3	151,030	153,626	+1.7
Other assaults	136,912	138,806	+1.4	24,562	24,965	+1.6	112,350	113,841	+1.3
Forgery and counterfeiting	11,419	11,188	-2.0	517	452	-12.6	10,902	10,736	-1.5
Fraud	57,765	60,232	+4.3	885	778	-12.1	56,880	59,454	+4.5
Embezzlement	2,186	2,101	-3.9	140	119	-15.0	2,046	1,982	-3.1
Stolen property; buying, receiving, possessing	11,823	12,394	+4.8	1,902	2,019	+6.2	9,921	10,375	+4.6
Vandalism	24,288	25,366	+4.4	9,498	9,430	-0.7	14,790	15,936	+7.7
Weapons; carrying, possessing, etc.	15,993	15,992	*	3,266	3,075	-5.8	12,727	12,917	+1.5
Prostitution and commercialized vice	2,047	1,828	-10.7	55	52	-5.5	1,992	1,776	-10.8
Sex offenses (except forcible rape and prostitution)	9,835	10,293	+4.7	2,011	2,033	+1.1	7,824	8,260	+5.6
Drug abuse violations	162,988	160,398	-1.6	17,952	16,396	-8.7	145,036	144,002	-0.7
Gambling	345	496	+43.8	32	24	-25.0	313	472	+50.8
Offenses against the family and children	26,201	26,633	+1.6	841	1,051	+25.0	25,360	25,582	+0.9
Driving under the influence	200,085	202,464	+1.2	2,177	2,225	+2.2	197,908	200,239	+1.2
Liquor laws	47,947	43,905	-8.4	12,705	12,087	-4.9	35,242	31,818	-9.7
Drunkenness	42,302	40,048	-5.3	1,280	1,227	-4.1	41,022	38,821	-5.4
Disorderly conduct	34,305	33,879	-1.2	10,322	10,634	+3.0	23,983	23,245	-3.1
Vagrancy	1,064	1,515	+42.4	179	112	-37.4	885	1,403	+58.5
All other offenses (except traffic)	404,750	424,563	+4.9	35,270	34,635	-1.8	369,480	389,928	+5.5
Suspicion	185	703	+280.0	135	62	-54.1	50	641	+1,182.0
Curfew and loitering law violations	4,879	4,065	-16.7	4,879	4,065	-16.7	–	–	–
Runaways	17,359	16,136	-7.0	17,359	16,136	-7.0	–	–	–

[1] Does not include suspicion.

[2] Violent crimes are offenses of murder, forcible rape, robbery, and aggravated assault.

[3] Property crimes are offenses of burglary, larceny-theft, motor vehicle theft, and arson.

[4] Includes arson.

* Less than one-tenth of 1 percent.

Table 51

Arrest Trends
Suburban Counties
by Sex, 2001-2002
[793 agencies; 2002 estimated population 37,206,488; 2001 estimated population 37,000,588]

Offense charged	Male Total 2001	2002	Percent change	Male Under 18 2001	2002	Percent change	Female Total 2001	2002	Percent change	Female Under 18 2001	2002	Percent change
TOTAL[1]	1,102,032	1,106,800	+0.4	136,791	133,051	-2.7	308,212	322,811	+4.7	53,762	52,147	-3.0
Murder and nonnegligent manslaughter	1,236	1,346	+8.9	82	87	+6.1	168	215	+28.0	9	13	+44.4
Forcible rape	2,972	3,135	+5.5	462	477	+3.2	49	42	-14.3	11	9	-18.2
Robbery	6,790	6,921	+1.9	1,413	1,423	+0.7	687	755	+9.9	91	134	+47.3
Aggravated assault	41,809	41,849	+0.1	4,750	4,754	+0.1	9,197	9,392	+2.1	1,286	1,327	+3.2
Burglary	27,319	26,958	-1.3	8,568	8,133	-5.1	3,944	3,861	-2.1	1,007	865	-14.1
Larceny-theft	55,569	56,024	+0.8	14,134	14,255	+0.9	30,203	30,455	+0.8	8,105	7,800	-3.8
Motor vehicle theft	11,327	11,873	+4.8	3,026	2,816	-6.9	2,245	2,253	+0.4	726	594	-18.2
Arson	1,898	1,912	+0.7	939	878	-6.5	338	318	-5.9	112	118	+5.4
Violent crime[2]	52,807	53,251	+0.8	6,707	6,741	+0.5	10,101	10,404	+3.0	1,397	1,483	+6.2
Property crime[3]	96,113	96,767	+0.7	26,667	26,082	-2.2	36,730	36,887	+0.4	9,950	9,377	-5.8
Crime Index[4]	148,920	150,018	+0.7	33,374	32,823	-1.7	46,831	47,291	+1.0	11,347	10,860	-4.3
Other assaults	105,189	105,360	+0.2	17,124	17,382	+1.5	31,723	33,446	+5.4	7,438	7,583	+1.9
Forgery and counterfeiting	6,988	6,946	-0.6	350	311	-11.1	4,431	4,242	-4.3	167	141	-15.6
Fraud	29,991	30,529	+1.8	576	507	-12.0	27,774	29,703	+6.9	309	271	-12.3
Embezzlement	1,162	1,094	-5.9	87	66	-24.1	1,024	1,007	-1.7	53	53	0.0
Stolen property; buying, receiving, possessing	9,911	10,237	+3.3	1,662	1,729	+4.0	1,912	2,157	+12.8	240	290	+20.8
Vandalism	20,509	21,537	+5.0	8,263	8,271	+0.1	3,779	3,829	+1.3	1,235	1,159	-6.2
Weapons; carrying, possessing, etc.	14,673	14,662	-0.1	2,930	2,703	-7.7	1,320	1,330	+0.8	336	372	+10.7
Prostitution and commercialized vice	1,075	919	-14.5	27	30	+11.1	972	909	-6.5	28	22	-21.4
Sex offenses (except forcible rape and prostitution)	9,367	9,757	+4.2	1,895	1,904	+0.5	468	536	+14.5	116	129	+11.2
Drug abuse violations	132,964	129,642	-2.5	14,826	13,499	-9.0	30,024	30,756	+2.4	3,126	2,897	-7.3
Gambling	292	380	+30.1	30	20	-33.3	53	116	+118.9	2	4	+100.0
Offenses against the family and children	22,066	22,194	+0.6	541	656	+21.3	4,135	4,439	+7.4	300	395	+31.7
Driving under the influence	168,581	168,958	+0.2	1,796	1,802	+0.3	31,504	33,506	+6.4	381	423	+11.0
Liquor laws	36,334	33,254	-8.5	8,592	8,117	-5.5	11,613	10,651	-8.3	4,113	3,970	-3.5
Drunkenness	36,107	33,822	-6.3	1,008	943	-6.4	6,195	6,226	+0.5	272	284	+4.4
Disorderly conduct	25,898	25,260	-2.5	7,137	7,273	+1.9	8,407	8,619	+2.5	3,185	3,361	+5.5
Vagrancy	835	1,160	+38.9	137	88	-35.8	229	355	+55.0	42	24	-42.9
All other offenses (except traffic)	320,716	331,569	+3.4	25,982	25,425	-2.1	84,034	92,994	+10.7	9,288	9,210	-0.8
Suspicion	89	536	+502.2	57	36	-36.8	96	167	+74.0	78	26	-66.7
Curfew and loitering law violations	3,235	2,687	-16.9	3,235	2,687	-16.9	1,644	1,378	-16.2	1,644	1,378	-16.2
Runaways	7,219	6,815	-5.6	7,219	6,815	-5.6	10,140	9,321	-8.1	10,140	9,321	-8.1

[1] Does not include suspicion.
[2] Violent crimes are offenses of murder, forcible rape, robbery, and aggravated assault.
[3] Property crimes are offenses of burglary, larceny-theft, motor vehicle theft, and arson.
[4] Includes arson.

Table 52

Arrests
Suburban Counties
by Age, 2002
[916 agencies; 2002 estimated population 40,822,218]

Offense charged	Total all ages	Ages under 15	Ages under 18	Ages 18 and over	Under 10	10-12	13-14	15	16	17	18	19	20	21
TOTAL	**1,568,929**	**60,508**	**205,950**	**1,362,979**	**2,576**	**13,871**	**44,061**	**37,797**	**49,760**	**57,885**	**68,525**	**73,595**	**72,023**	**67,731**
Percent distribution[1]	**100.0**	**3.9**	**13.1**	**86.9**	**0.2**	**0.9**	**2.8**	**2.4**	**3.2**	**3.7**	**4.4**	**4.7**	**4.6**	**4.3**
Murder and nonnegligent manslaughter	1,754	6	121	1,633	0	2	4	22	32	61	97	99	106	129
Forcible rape	3,476	192	553	2,923	2	51	139	93	125	143	172	190	153	149
Robbery	8,494	304	1,675	6,819	0	52	252	302	452	617	748	693	594	525
Aggravated assault	55,158	2,225	6,487	48,671	94	589	1,542	1,195	1,444	1,623	1,937	1,926	2,030	2,093
Burglary	33,920	3,310	9,842	24,078	163	844	2,303	1,694	2,233	2,605	2,819	2,433	1,943	1,621
Larceny-theft	95,596	8,043	24,023	71,573	269	2,052	5,722	4,438	5,489	6,053	5,944	5,290	4,336	3,579
Motor vehicle theft	15,052	902	3,735	11,317	10	95	797	840	1,014	979	1,061	1,023	826	746
Arson	2,392	633	1,033	1,359	91	200	342	138	133	129	120	98	87	52
Violent crime[2]	68,882	2,727	8,836	60,046	96	694	1,937	1,612	2,053	2,444	2,954	2,908	2,883	2,896
Percent distribution[1]	100.0	4.0	12.8	87.2	0.1	1.0	2.8	2.3	3.0	3.5	4.3	4.2	4.2	4.2
Property crime[3]	146,960	12,888	38,633	108,327	533	3,191	9,164	7,110	8,869	9,766	9,944	8,844	7,192	5,998
Percent distribution[1]	100.0	8.8	26.3	73.7	0.4	2.2	6.2	4.8	6.0	6.6	6.8	6.0	4.9	4.1
Crime Index[4]	215,842	15,615	47,469	168,373	629	3,885	11,101	8,722	10,922	12,210	12,898	11,752	10,075	8,894
Percent distribution[1]	100.0	7.2	22.0	78.0	0.3	1.8	5.1	4.0	5.1	5.7	6.0	5.4	4.7	4.1
Other assaults	151,178	10,987	26,781	124,397	456	3,060	7,471	4,865	5,608	5,321	4,800	4,695	5,085	5,356
Forgery and counterfeiting	12,866	83	527	12,339	10	11	62	66	123	255	459	596	638	603
Fraud	71,794	198	1,279	70,515	13	46	139	158	319	604	1,260	2,041	2,489	2,698
Embezzlement	2,151	1	123	2,028	0	0	1	6	40	76	125	135	123	82
Stolen property; buying, receiving, possessing	13,977	534	2,317	11,660	7	81	446	420	614	749	877	862	782	696
Vandalism	27,787	4,092	10,277	17,510	323	1,202	2,567	1,747	2,157	2,281	1,846	1,615	1,222	1,124
Weapons; carrying, possessing, etc.	17,307	1,156	3,303	14,004	70	304	782	545	695	907	984	973	932	903
Prostitution and commercialized vice	1,929	23	56	1,873	0	1	22	10	10	13	30	49	43	51
Sex offenses (except forcible rape and prostitution)	11,865	1,148	2,377	9,488	61	330	757	436	370	423	516	449	407	414
Drug abuse violations	172,912	2,627	17,866	155,046	28	333	2,266	2,743	4,852	7,644	10,843	11,366	10,598	9,349
Gambling	658	5	26	632	0	2	3	3	5	13	15	36	46	17
Offenses against the family and children	29,443	486	1,218	28,225	67	117	302	265	260	207	390	492	545	744
Driving under the influence	215,764	39	2,442	213,322	9	4	26	78	585	1,740	4,643	6,429	7,582	10,179
Liquor laws	49,729	1,129	13,951	35,778	7	88	1,034	1,922	4,006	6,894	8,843	8,671	6,984	1,269
Drunkenness	41,471	160	1,299	40,172	7	14	139	202	323	614	1,395	1,527	1,522	1,820
Disorderly conduct	40,754	4,833	12,512	28,242	135	1,215	3,483	2,559	2,672	2,448	2,061	1,698	1,496	1,619
Vagrancy	1,713	25	138	1,575	0	1	24	29	38	46	74	81	70	60
All other offenses (except traffic)	466,910	10,087	39,775	427,135	371	2,069	7,647	7,434	10,064	12,190	16,444	20,102	21,351	21,820
Suspicion	730	22	65	665	1	4	17	12	20	11	22	26	33	33
Curfew and loitering law violations	4,654	1,140	4,654	–	10	166	964	1,026	1,545	943	–	–	–	–
Runaways	17,495	6,118	17,495	–	372	938	4,808	4,549	4,532	2,296	–	–	–	–

[1] Because of rounding, the percentages may not add to 100.0.

[2] Violent crimes are offenses of murder, forcible rape, robbery, and aggravated assault.

[3] Property crimes are offenses of burglary, larceny-theft, motor vehicle theft, and arson.

[4] Includes arson.

Table 52

Arrests

Suburban Counties
by Age, 2002—Continued
[916 agencies; 2002 estimated population 40,822,218]

Offense charged	22	23	24	25-29	30-34	35-39	40-44	45-49	50-54	55-59	60-64	65 and over
TOTAL	**63,721**	**57,034**	**52,825**	**209,822**	**191,229**	**181,127**	**149,570**	**89,722**	**45,539**	**21,488**	**10,023**	**9,005**
Percent distribution[1]	**4.1**	**3.6**	**3.4**	**13.4**	**12.2**	**11.5**	**9.5**	**5.7**	**2.9**	**1.4**	**0.6**	**0.6**
Murder and nonnegligent manslaughter	90	96	67	267	189	146	125	96	52	37	16	21
Forcible rape	120	115	102	418	432	395	284	190	86	57	25	35
Robbery	395	366	311	979	761	654	452	228	69	20	11	13
Aggravated assault	1,986	1,859	1,730	7,636	7,213	7,070	6,051	3,528	1,742	908	482	480
Burglary	1,378	1,112	955	3,326	2,863	2,492	1,717	858	329	125	46	61
Larceny-theft	3,296	2,743	2,583	9,958	9,517	8,853	7,085	4,235	2,174	1,009	500	471
Motor vehicle theft	690	555	499	1,802	1,486	1,194	765	377	185	65	27	16
Arson	59	41	54	182	178	156	168	80	42	22	12	8
Violent crime[2]	2,591	2,436	2,210	9,300	8,595	8,265	6,912	4,042	1,949	1,022	534	549
Percent distribution[1]	3.8	3.5	3.2	13.5	12.5	12.0	10.0	5.9	2.8	1.5	0.8	0.8
Property crime[3]	5,423	4,451	4,091	15,268	14,044	12,695	9,735	5,550	2,730	1,221	585	556
Percent distribution[1]	3.7	3.0	2.8	10.4	9.6	8.6	6.6	3.8	1.9	0.8	0.4	0.4
Crime Index[4]	8,014	6,887	6,301	24,568	22,639	20,960	16,647	9,592	4,679	2,243	1,119	1,105
Percent distribution[1]	3.7	3.2	2.9	11.4	10.5	9.7	7.7	4.4	2.2	1.0	0.5	0.5
Other assaults	5,177	4,721	4,598	18,668	19,286	18,950	15,662	8,890	4,304	2,140	1,020	1,045
Forgery and counterfeiting	598	536	491	2,314	2,074	1,722	1,233	607	256	132	47	33
Fraud	2,903	2,653	2,641	12,320	12,282	10,868	8,310	5,089	2,528	1,293	595	545
Embezzlement	90	73	86	297	284	255	202	137	70	49	16	4
Stolen property; buying, receiving, possessing	653	554	480	1,889	1,628	1,332	1,059	492	195	105	31	25
Vandalism	997	787	647	2,378	2,060	1,890	1,392	807	374	186	89	96
Weapons; carrying, possessing, etc.	838	692	636	2,214	1,640	1,389	1,150	774	424	227	104	124
Prostitution and commercialized vice	51	61	58	261	321	347	263	149	78	54	28	29
Sex offenses (except forcible rape and prostitution)	325	314	272	1,117	1,204	1,330	1,075	750	460	336	233	286
Drug abuse violations	8,598	7,361	6,576	24,222	19,557	18,099	14,699	8,321	3,493	1,254	444	266
Gambling	17	12	10	70	61	71	70	68	51	39	20	29
Offenses against the family and children	786	764	874	4,764	5,317	5,464	4,180	2,241	960	425	169	110
Driving under the influence	10,040	9,461	8,765	34,697	29,789	27,943	25,772	17,300	10,413	5,444	2,632	2,233
Liquor laws	862	635	539	1,849	1,491	1,494	1,350	904	493	203	97	94
Drunkenness	1,642	1,363	1,309	5,141	4,980	5,849	5,490	3,922	2,273	1,046	529	364
Disorderly conduct	1,318	1,107	1,080	3,905	3,361	3,539	3,074	1,939	1,018	515	248	264
Vagrancy	72	43	49	219	203	235	198	145	76	32	9	9
All other offenses (except traffic)	20,708	18,983	17,389	68,810	62,965	59,289	47,665	27,538	13,378	5,760	2,593	2,340
Suspicion	32	27	24	119	87	101	79	57	16	5	0	4
Curfew and loitering law violations	–	–	–	–	–	–	–	–	–	–	–	–
Runaways	–	–	–	–	–	–	–	–	–	–	–	–

Table 53

Arrests

Suburban Counties
of Persons Under 15, 18, 21, and 25 Years of Age, 2002
[916 agencies; 2002 estimated population 40,822,218]

Offense charged	Total all ages	Number of persons arrested				Percent of total all ages			
		Under 15	Under 18	Under 21	Under 25	Under 15	Under 18	Under 21	Under 25
TOTAL	**1,568,929**	**60,508**	**205,950**	**420,093**	**661,404**	**3.9**	**13.1**	**26.8**	**42.2**
Murder and nonnegligent manslaughter	1,754	6	121	423	805	0.3	6.9	24.1	45.9
Forcible rape	3,476	192	553	1,068	1,554	5.5	15.9	30.7	44.7
Robbery	8,494	304	1,675	3,710	5,307	3.6	19.7	43.7	62.5
Aggravated assault	55,158	2,225	6,487	12,380	20,048	4.0	11.8	22.4	36.3
Burglary	33,920	3,310	9,842	17,037	22,103	9.8	29.0	50.2	65.2
Larceny-theft	95,596	8,043	24,023	39,593	51,794	8.4	25.1	41.4	54.2
Motor vehicle theft	15,052	902	3,735	6,645	9,135	6.0	24.8	44.1	60.7
Arson	2,392	633	1,033	1,338	1,544	26.5	43.2	55.9	64.5
Violent crime[1]	68,882	2,727	8,836	17,581	27,714	4.0	12.8	25.5	40.2
Property crime[2]	146,960	12,888	38,633	64,613	84,576	8.8	26.3	44.0	57.6
Crime Index[3]	215,842	15,615	47,469	82,194	112,290	7.2	22.0	38.1	52.0
Other assaults	151,178	10,987	26,781	41,361	61,213	7.3	17.7	27.4	40.5
Forgery and counterfeiting	12,866	83	527	2,220	4,448	0.6	4.1	17.3	34.6
Fraud	71,794	198	1,279	7,069	17,964	0.3	1.8	9.8	25.0
Embezzlement	2,151	1	123	506	837	*	5.7	23.5	38.9
Stolen property; buying, receiving, possessing	13,977	534	2,317	4,838	7,221	3.8	16.6	34.6	51.7
Vandalism	27,787	4,092	10,277	14,960	18,515	14.7	37.0	53.8	66.6
Weapons; carrying, possessing, etc.	17,307	1,156	3,303	6,192	9,261	6.7	19.1	35.8	53.5
Prostitution and commercialized vice	1,929	23	56	178	399	1.2	2.9	9.2	20.7
Sex offenses (except forcible rape and prostitution)	11,865	1,148	2,377	3,749	5,074	9.7	20.0	31.6	42.8
Drug abuse violations	172,912	2,627	17,866	50,673	82,557	1.5	10.3	29.3	47.7
Gambling	658	5	26	123	179	0.8	4.0	18.7	27.2
Offenses against the family and children	29,443	486	1,218	2,645	5,813	1.7	4.1	9.0	19.7
Driving under the influence	215,764	39	2,442	21,096	59,541	*	1.1	9.8	27.6
Liquor laws	49,729	1,129	13,951	38,449	41,754	2.3	28.1	77.3	84.0
Drunkenness	41,471	160	1,299	5,743	11,877	0.4	3.1	13.8	28.6
Disorderly conduct	40,754	4,833	12,512	17,767	22,891	11.9	30.7	43.6	56.2
Vagrancy	1,713	25	138	363	587	1.5	8.1	21.2	34.3
All other offenses (except traffic)	466,910	10,087	39,775	97,672	176,572	2.2	8.5	20.9	37.8
Suspicion	730	22	65	146	262	3.0	8.9	20.0	35.9
Curfew and loitering law violations	4,654	1,140	4,654	4,654	4,654	24.5	100.0	100.0	100.0
Runaways	17,495	6,118	17,495	17,495	17,495	35.0	100.0	100.0	100.0

[1] Violent crimes are offenses of murder, forcible rape, robbery, and aggravated assault.

[2] Property crimes are offenses of burglary, larceny-theft, motor vehicle theft, and arson.

[3] Includes arson.

* Less than one-tenth of 1 percent.

Table 54

Arrests

Suburban Counties
by Sex, 2002
[916 agencies; 2002 estimated population 40,822,218]

Offense charged	Number of persons arrested			Percent male	Percent female	Percent distribution[1]		
	Total	Male	Female			Total	Male	Female
TOTAL	**1,568,929**	**1,214,849**	**354,080**	**77.4**	**22.6**	**100.0**	**100.0**	**100.0**
Murder and nonnegligent manslaughter	1,754	1,509	245	86.0	14.0	0.1	0.1	0.1
Forcible rape	3,476	3,422	54	98.4	1.6	0.2	0.3	*
Robbery	8,494	7,644	850	90.0	10.0	0.5	0.6	0.2
Aggravated assault	55,158	44,930	10,228	81.5	18.5	3.5	3.7	2.9
Burglary	33,920	29,715	4,205	87.6	12.4	2.2	2.4	1.2
Larceny-theft	95,596	62,176	33,420	65.0	35.0	6.1	5.1	9.4
Motor vehicle theft	15,052	12,636	2,416	83.9	16.1	1.0	1.0	0.7
Arson	2,392	2,037	355	85.2	14.8	0.2	0.2	0.1
Violent crime[2]	68,882	57,505	11,377	83.5	16.5	4.4	4.7	3.2
Property crime[3]	146,960	106,564	40,396	72.5	27.5	9.4	8.8	11.4
Crime Index[4]	215,842	164,069	51,773	76.0	24.0	13.8	13.5	14.6
Other assaults	151,178	114,887	36,291	76.0	24.0	9.6	9.5	10.2
Forgery and counterfeiting	12,866	7,946	4,920	61.8	38.2	0.8	0.7	1.4
Fraud	71,794	38,568	33,226	53.7	46.3	4.6	3.2	9.4
Embezzlement	2,151	1,126	1,025	52.3	47.7	0.1	0.1	0.3
Stolen property; buying, receiving, possessing	13,977	11,559	2,418	82.7	17.3	0.9	1.0	0.7
Vandalism	27,787	23,544	4,243	84.7	15.3	1.8	1.9	1.2
Weapons; carrying, possessing, etc.	17,307	15,846	1,461	91.6	8.4	1.1	1.3	0.4
Prostitution and commercialized vice	1,929	980	949	50.8	49.2	0.1	0.1	0.3
Sex offenses (except forcible rape and prostitution)	11,865	11,233	632	94.7	5.3	0.8	0.9	0.2
Drug abuse violations	172,912	140,057	32,855	81.0	19.0	11.0	11.5	9.3
Gambling	658	501	157	76.1	23.9	*	*	*
Offenses against the family and children	29,443	24,490	4,953	83.2	16.8	1.9	2.0	1.4
Driving under the influence	215,764	179,903	35,861	83.4	16.6	13.8	14.8	10.1
Liquor laws	49,729	37,417	12,312	75.2	24.8	3.2	3.1	3.5
Drunkenness	41,471	35,048	6,423	84.5	15.5	2.6	2.9	1.8
Disorderly conduct	40,754	30,321	10,433	74.4	25.6	2.6	2.5	2.9
Vagrancy	1,713	1,326	387	77.4	22.6	0.1	0.1	0.1
All other offenses (except traffic)	466,910	364,971	101,939	78.2	21.8	29.8	30.0	28.8
Suspicion	730	548	182	75.1	24.9	*	*	0.1
Curfew and loitering law violations	4,654	3,054	1,600	65.6	34.4	0.3	0.3	0.5
Runaways	17,495	7,455	10,040	42.6	57.4	1.1	0.6	2.8

[1] Because of rounding, the percentages may not add to 100.0.
[2] Violent crimes are offenses of murder, forcible rape, robbery, and aggravated assault.
[3] Property crimes are offenses of burglary, larceny-theft, motor vehicle theft, and arson.
[4] Includes arson.
* Less than one-tenth of 1 percent.

Table 55

Arrests

Suburban Counties
by Race, 2002
[916 agencies; 2002 estimated population 40,822,218]

Offense charged	Total arrests					Percent distribution[1]				
	Total	White	Black	American Indian or Alaskan Native	Asian or Pacific Islander	Total	White	Black	American Indian or Alaskan Native	Asian or Pacific Islander
TOTAL	**1,565,444**	**1,189,168**	**357,113**	**10,558**	**8,605**	**100.0**	**76.0**	**22.8**	**0.7**	**0.5**
Murder and nonnegligent manslaughter	1,751	1,138	589	15	9	100.0	65.0	33.6	0.9	0.5
Forcible rape	3,469	2,639	774	37	19	100.0	76.1	22.3	1.1	0.5
Robbery	8,483	4,568	3,821	48	46	100.0	53.8	45.0	0.6	0.5
Aggravated assault	55,120	41,013	13,265	434	408	100.0	74.4	24.1	0.8	0.7
Burglary	33,898	26,635	6,913	177	173	100.0	78.6	20.4	0.5	0.5
Larceny-theft	95,422	65,934	28,210	490	788	100.0	69.1	29.6	0.5	0.8
Motor vehicle theft	15,026	11,329	3,496	98	103	100.0	75.4	23.3	0.7	0.7
Arson	2,391	2,017	346	16	12	100.0	84.4	14.5	0.7	0.5
Violent crime[2]	68,823	49,358	18,449	534	482	100.0	71.7	26.8	0.8	0.7
Property crime[3]	146,737	105,915	38,965	781	1,076	100.0	72.2	26.6	0.5	0.7
Crime Index[4]	215,560	155,273	57,414	1,315	1,558	100.0	72.0	26.6	0.6	0.7
Other assaults	151,002	112,076	37,122	895	909	100.0	74.2	24.6	0.6	0.6
Forgery and counterfeiting	12,853	9,277	3,457	31	88	100.0	72.2	26.9	0.2	0.7
Fraud	71,581	46,522	24,621	194	244	100.0	65.0	34.4	0.3	0.3
Embezzlement	2,144	1,541	575	6	22	100.0	71.9	26.8	0.3	1.0
Stolen property; buying, receiving, possessing	13,965	9,781	4,012	76	96	100.0	70.0	28.7	0.5	0.7
Vandalism	27,756	23,070	4,313	199	174	100.0	83.1	15.5	0.7	0.6
Weapons; carrying, possessing, etc.	17,284	12,250	4,811	98	125	100.0	70.9	27.8	0.6	0.7
Prostitution and commercialized vice	1,926	1,383	451	14	78	100.0	71.8	23.4	0.7	4.0
Sex offenses (except forcible rape and prostitution)	11,857	9,703	2,038	40	76	100.0	81.8	17.2	0.3	0.6
Drug abuse violations	172,714	131,754	39,381	809	770	100.0	76.3	22.8	0.5	0.4
Gambling	658	410	205	0	43	100.0	62.3	31.2	*	6.5
Offenses against the family and children	29,341	20,046	9,121	97	77	100.0	68.3	31.1	0.3	0.3
Driving under the influence	215,109	192,965	19,843	1,199	1,102	100.0	89.7	9.2	0.6	0.5
Liquor laws	49,382	45,145	3,313	613	311	100.0	91.4	6.7	1.2	0.6
Drunkenness	41,431	37,064	3,875	367	125	100.0	89.5	9.4	0.9	0.3
Disorderly conduct	40,685	29,571	10,609	319	186	100.0	72.7	26.1	0.8	0.5
Vagrancy	1,713	1,074	629	5	5	100.0	62.7	36.7	0.3	0.3
All other offenses (except traffic)	465,643	331,913	127,133	4,153	2,444	100.0	71.3	27.3	0.9	0.5
Suspicion	716	342	373	1	0	100.0	47.8	52.1	0.1	*
Curfew and loitering law violations	4,644	3,758	806	29	51	100.0	80.9	17.4	0.6	1.1
Runaways	17,480	14,250	3,011	98	121	100.0	81.5	17.2	0.6	0.7

See footnotes at end of table.

Table 55

Arrests

Suburban Counties
by Race, 2002—Continued
[916 agencies; 2002 estimated population 40,822,218]

	Arrests under 18					Percent distribution[1]				
Offense charged	Total	White	Black	American Indian or Alaskan Native	Asian or Pacific Islander	Total	White	Black	American Indian or Alaskan Native	Asian or Pacific Islander
TOTAL	**205,533**	**156,166**	**46,355**	**1,432**	**1,580**	**100.0**	**76.0**	**22.6**	**0.7**	**0.8**
Murder and nonnegligent manslaughter	120	73	47	0	0	100.0	60.8	39.2	*	*
Forcible rape	552	420	127	5	0	100.0	76.1	23.0	0.9	*
Robbery	1,673	762	888	5	18	100.0	45.5	53.1	0.3	1.1
Aggravated assault	6,483	4,425	1,944	66	48	100.0	68.3	30.0	1.0	0.7
Burglary	9,830	7,856	1,858	49	67	100.0	79.9	18.9	0.5	0.7
Larceny-theft	23,958	16,841	6,720	124	273	100.0	70.3	28.0	0.5	1.1
Motor vehicle theft	3,718	2,713	933	33	39	100.0	73.0	25.1	0.9	1.0
Arson	1,033	896	131	3	3	100.0	86.7	12.7	0.3	0.3
Violent crime[2]	8,828	5,680	3,006	76	66	100.0	64.3	34.1	0.9	0.7
Property crime[3]	38,539	28,306	9,642	209	382	100.0	73.4	25.0	0.5	1.0
Crime Index[4]	47,367	33,986	12,648	285	448	100.0	71.8	26.7	0.6	0.9
Other assaults	26,755	18,061	8,329	195	170	100.0	67.5	31.1	0.7	0.6
Forgery and counterfeiting	525	410	107	3	5	100.0	78.1	20.4	0.6	1.0
Fraud	1,279	693	573	5	8	100.0	54.2	44.8	0.4	0.6
Embezzlement	123	90	32	0	1	100.0	73.2	26.0	*	0.8
Stolen property; buying, receiving, possessing	2,315	1,598	677	15	25	100.0	69.0	29.2	0.6	1.1
Vandalism	10,262	8,754	1,375	65	68	100.0	85.3	13.4	0.6	0.7
Weapons; carrying, possessing, etc.	3,300	2,371	883	17	29	100.0	71.8	26.8	0.5	0.9
Prostitution and commercialized vice	56	35	18	1	2	100.0	62.5	32.1	1.8	3.6
Sex offenses (except forcible rape and prostitution)	2,374	1,908	450	9	7	100.0	80.4	19.0	0.4	0.3
Drug abuse violations	17,835	14,804	2,811	111	109	100.0	83.0	15.8	0.6	0.6
Gambling	26	8	18	0	0	100.0	30.8	69.2	*	*
Offenses against the family and children	1,217	903	306	2	6	100.0	74.2	25.1	0.2	0.5
Driving under the influence	2,434	2,345	74	6	9	100.0	96.3	3.0	0.2	0.4
Liquor laws	13,878	13,186	457	136	99	100.0	95.0	3.3	1.0	0.7
Drunkenness	1,299	1,201	86	6	6	100.0	92.5	6.6	0.5	0.5
Disorderly conduct	12,498	7,742	4,609	89	58	100.0	61.9	36.9	0.7	0.5
Vagrancy	138	91	46	0	1	100.0	65.9	33.3	*	0.7
All other offenses (except traffic)	39,663	29,920	9,026	360	357	100.0	75.4	22.8	0.9	0.9
Suspicion	65	52	13	0	0	100.0	80.0	20.0	*	*
Curfew and loitering law violations	4,644	3,758	806	29	51	100.0	80.9	17.4	0.6	1.1
Runaways	17,480	14,250	3,011	98	121	100.0	81.5	17.2	0.6	0.7

See footnotes at end of table.

Table 55

Arrests
Suburban Counties
by Race, 2002—Continued
[916 agencies; 2002 estimated population 40,822,218]

Offense charged	Arrests 18 and over					Percent distribution[1]				
	Total	White	Black	American Indian or Alaskan Native	Asian or Pacific Islander	Total	White	Black	American Indian or Alaskan Native	Asian or Pacific Islander
TOTAL	**1,359,911**	**1,033,002**	**310,758**	**9,126**	**7,025**	**100.0**	**76.0**	**22.9**	**0.7**	**0.5**
Murder and nonnegligent manslaughter	1,631	1,065	542	15	9	100.0	65.3	33.2	0.9	0.6
Forcible rape	2,917	2,219	647	32	19	100.0	76.1	22.2	1.1	0.7
Robbery	6,810	3,806	2,933	43	28	100.0	55.9	43.1	0.6	0.4
Aggravated assault	48,637	36,588	11,321	368	360	100.0	75.2	23.3	0.8	0.7
Burglary	24,068	18,779	5,055	128	106	100.0	78.0	21.0	0.5	0.4
Larceny-theft	71,464	49,093	21,490	366	515	100.0	68.7	30.1	0.5	0.7
Motor vehicle theft	11,308	8,616	2,563	65	64	100.0	76.2	22.7	0.6	0.6
Arson	1,358	1,121	215	13	9	100.0	82.5	15.8	1.0	0.7
Violent crime[2]	59,995	43,678	15,443	458	416	100.0	72.8	25.7	0.8	0.7
Property crime[3]	108,198	77,609	29,323	572	694	100.0	71.7	27.1	0.5	0.6
Crime Index[4]	168,193	121,287	44,766	1,030	1,110	100.0	72.1	26.6	0.6	0.7
Other assaults	124,247	94,015	28,793	700	739	100.0	75.7	23.2	0.6	0.6
Forgery and counterfeiting	12,328	8,867	3,350	28	83	100.0	71.9	27.2	0.2	0.7
Fraud	70,302	45,829	24,048	189	236	100.0	65.2	34.2	0.3	0.3
Embezzlement	2,021	1,451	543	6	21	100.0	71.8	26.9	0.3	1.0
Stolen property; buying, receiving, possessing	11,650	8,183	3,335	61	71	100.0	70.2	28.6	0.5	0.6
Vandalism	17,494	14,316	2,938	134	106	100.0	81.8	16.8	0.8	0.6
Weapons; carrying, possessing, etc.	13,984	9,879	3,928	81	96	100.0	70.6	28.1	0.6	0.7
Prostitution and commercialized vice	1,870	1,348	433	13	76	100.0	72.1	23.2	0.7	4.1
Sex offenses (except forcible rape and prostitution)	9,483	7,795	1,588	31	69	100.0	82.2	16.7	0.3	0.7
Drug abuse violations	154,879	116,950	36,570	698	661	100.0	75.5	23.6	0.5	0.4
Gambling	632	402	187	0	43	100.0	63.6	29.6	*	6.8
Offenses against the family and children	28,124	19,143	8,815	95	71	100.0	68.1	31.3	0.3	0.3
Driving under the influence	212,675	190,620	19,769	1,193	1,093	100.0	89.6	9.3	0.6	0.5
Liquor laws	35,504	31,959	2,856	477	212	100.0	90.0	8.0	1.3	0.6
Drunkenness	40,132	35,863	3,789	361	119	100.0	89.4	9.4	0.9	0.3
Disorderly conduct	28,187	21,829	6,000	230	128	100.0	77.4	21.3	0.8	0.5
Vagrancy	1,575	983	583	5	4	100.0	62.4	37.0	0.3	0.3
All other offenses (except traffic)	425,980	301,993	118,107	3,793	2,087	100.0	70.9	27.7	0.9	0.5
Suspicion	651	290	360	1	0	100.0	44.5	55.3	0.2	*
Curfew and loitering law violations	–	–	–	–	–	–	–	–	–	–
Runaways	–	–	–	–	–	–	–	–	–	–

[1] Because of rounding, the percentages may not add to 100.0.
[2] Violent crimes are offenses of murder, forcible rape, robbery, and aggravated assault.
[3] Property crimes are offenses of burglary, larceny-theft, motor vehicle theft, and arson.
[4] Includes arson.
* Less than one-tenth of 1 percent.

Table 56

Arrest Trends

Rural Counties, 2001-2002

[1,659 agencies; 2002 estimated population 19,032,732; 2001 estimated population 18,933,700]

Offense charged	Number of persons arrested								
	Total all ages			Under 18 years of age			18 years of age and over		
	2001	2002	Percent change	2001	2002	Percent change	2001	2002	Percent change
TOTAL[1]	**733,394**	**743,561**	**+1.4**	**80,937**	**77,308**	**-4.5**	**652,457**	**666,253**	**+2.1**
Murder and nonnegligent manslaughter	976	759	-22.2	45	55	+22.2	931	704	-24.4
Forcible rape	1,817	1,931	+6.3	268	266	-0.7	1,549	1,665	+7.5
Robbery	1,824	1,791	-1.8	215	201	-6.5	1,609	1,590	-1.2
Aggravated assault	21,543	21,155	-1.8	2,148	1,928	-10.2	19,395	19,227	-0.9
Burglary	18,234	18,444	+1.2	5,340	4,778	-10.5	12,894	13,666	+6.0
Larceny-theft	29,871	29,786	-0.3	7,136	6,484	-9.1	22,735	23,302	+2.5
Motor vehicle theft	5,414	5,769	+6.6	1,758	1,795	+2.1	3,656	3,974	+8.7
Arson	1,019	909	-10.8	344	283	-17.7	675	626	-7.3
Violent crime[2]	26,160	25,636	-2.0	2,676	2,450	-8.4	23,484	23,186	-1.3
Property crime[3]	54,538	54,908	+0.7	14,578	13,340	-8.5	39,960	41,568	+4.0
Crime Index[4]	80,698	80,544	-0.2	17,254	15,790	-8.5	63,444	64,754	+2.1
Other assaults	72,979	72,485	-0.7	8,911	8,581	-3.7	64,068	63,904	-0.3
Forgery and counterfeiting	5,485	5,725	+4.4	247	226	-8.5	5,238	5,499	+5.0
Fraud	38,899	35,856	-7.8	460	446	-3.0	38,439	35,410	-7.9
Embezzlement	940	868	-7.7	17	30	+76.5	923	838	-9.2
Stolen property; buying, receiving, possessing	5,039	4,966	-1.4	770	602	-21.8	4,269	4,364	+2.2
Vandalism	13,531	13,378	-1.1	4,753	4,336	-8.8	8,778	9,042	+3.0
Weapons; carrying, possessing, etc.	6,597	6,644	+0.7	900	783	-13.0	5,697	5,861	+2.9
Prostitution and commercialized vice	135	132	-2.2	3	12	+300.0	132	120	-9.1
Sex offenses (except forcible rape and prostitution)	5,187	5,250	+1.2	1,010	1,033	+2.3	4,177	4,217	+1.0
Drug abuse violations	73,340	78,171	+6.6	6,461	6,366	-1.5	66,879	71,805	+7.4
Gambling	727	628	-13.6	29	11	-62.1	698	617	-11.6
Offenses against the family and children	12,499	13,139	+5.1	500	490	-2.0	11,999	12,649	+5.4
Driving under the influence	112,164	122,528	+9.2	1,732	2,039	+17.7	110,432	120,489	+9.1
Liquor laws	39,311	38,698	-1.6	10,150	9,885	-2.6	29,161	28,813	-1.2
Drunkenness	24,299	23,513	-3.2	610	610	0.0	23,689	22,903	-3.3
Disorderly conduct	19,767	18,967	-4.0	4,439	4,406	-0.7	15,328	14,561	-5.0
Vagrancy	438	537	+22.6	236	258	+9.3	202	279	+38.1
All other offenses (except traffic)	214,728	215,084	+0.2	15,824	14,956	-5.5	198,904	200,128	+0.6
Suspicion	334	130	-61.1	41	18	-56.1	293	112	-61.8
Curfew and loitering law violations	742	800	+7.8	742	800	+7.8	–	–	–
Runaways	5,889	5,648	-4.1	5,889	5,648	-4.1	–	–	–

[1] Does not include suspicion.

[2] Violent crimes are offenses of murder, forcible rape, robbery, and aggravated assault.

[3] Property crimes are offenses of burglary, larceny-theft, motor vehicle theft, and arson.

[4] Includes arson.

Table 57

Arrest Trends
Rural Counties
by Sex, 2001-2002
[1,659 agencies; 2002 estimated population 19,032,732; 2001 estimated population 18,933,700]

| | Male | | | | | | Female | | | | | |
| | Total | | | Under 18 | | | Total | | | Under 18 | | |
Offense charged	2001	2002	Percent change	2001	2002	Percent change	2001	2002	Percent change	2001	2002	Percent change
TOTAL[1]	**575,451**	**581,884**	**+1.1**	**59,306**	**56,301**	**-5.1**	**157,943**	**161,677**	**+2.4**	**21,631**	**21,007**	**-2.9**
Murder and nonnegligent manslaughter	660	665	+0.8	36	50	+38.9	316	94	-70.3	9	5	-44.4
Forcible rape	1,785	1,904	+6.7	261	264	+1.1	32	27	-15.6	7	2	-71.4
Robbery	1,631	1,630	-0.1	204	185	-9.3	193	161	-16.6	11	16	+45.5
Aggravated assault	17,702	17,525	-1.0	1,654	1,547	-6.5	3,841	3,630	-5.5	494	381	-22.9
Burglary	16,180	16,384	+1.3	4,829	4,413	-8.6	2,054	2,060	+0.3	511	365	-28.6
Larceny-theft	21,632	21,475	-0.7	5,385	4,865	-9.7	8,239	8,311	+0.9	1,751	1,619	-7.5
Motor vehicle theft	4,489	4,847	+8.0	1,359	1,463	+7.7	925	922	-0.3	399	332	-16.8
Arson	833	772	-7.3	308	253	-17.9	186	137	-26.3	36	30	-16.7
Violent crime[2]	21,778	21,724	-0.2	2,155	2,046	-5.1	4,382	3,912	-10.7	521	404	-22.5
Property crime[3]	43,134	43,478	+0.8	11,881	10,994	-7.5	11,404	11,430	+0.2	2,697	2,346	-13.0
Crime Index[4]	64,912	65,202	+0.4	14,036	13,040	-7.1	15,786	15,342	-2.8	3,218	2,750	-14.5
Other assaults	56,468	55,837	-1.1	6,265	5,950	-5.0	16,511	16,648	+0.8	2,646	2,631	-0.6
Forgery and counterfeiting	3,192	3,279	+2.7	137	134	-2.2	2,293	2,446	+6.7	110	92	-16.4
Fraud	19,755	18,332	-7.2	277	280	+1.1	19,144	17,524	-8.5	183	166	-9.3
Embezzlement	523	427	-18.4	9	18	+100.0	417	441	+5.8	8	12	+50.0
Stolen property; buying, receiving, possessing	4,262	4,159	-2.4	660	504	-23.6	777	807	+3.9	110	98	-10.9
Vandalism	11,602	11,267	-2.9	4,268	3,787	-11.3	1,929	2,111	+9.4	485	549	+13.2
Weapons; carrying, possessing, etc.	6,083	6,138	+0.9	804	716	-10.9	514	506	-1.6	96	67	-30.2
Prostitution and commercialized vice	82	84	+2.4	1	9	+800.0	53	48	-9.4	2	3	+50.0
Sex offenses (except forcible rape and prostitution)	4,920	5,004	+1.7	930	971	+4.4	267	246	-7.9	80	62	-22.5
Drug abuse violations	59,872	63,269	+5.7	5,219	5,189	-0.6	13,468	14,902	+10.6	1,242	1,177	-5.2
Gambling	600	522	-13.0	23	11	-52.2	127	106	-16.5	6	0	-100.0
Offenses against the family and children	10,371	10,834	+4.5	333	293	-12.0	2,128	2,305	+8.3	167	197	+18.0
Driving under the influence	94,670	102,319	+8.1	1,387	1,613	+16.3	17,494	20,209	+15.5	345	426	+23.5
Liquor laws	29,254	28,863	-1.3	6,596	6,540	-0.8	10,057	9,835	-2.2	3,554	3,345	-5.9
Drunkenness	20,758	19,951	-3.9	484	475	-1.9	3,541	3,562	+0.6	126	135	+7.1
Disorderly conduct	14,888	14,258	-4.2	3,117	3,025	-3.0	4,879	4,709	-3.5	1,322	1,381	+4.5
Vagrancy	326	375	+15.0	169	155	-8.3	112	162	+44.6	67	103	+53.7
All other offenses (except traffic)	170,035	168,979	-0.6	11,713	10,806	-7.7	44,693	46,105	+3.2	4,111	4,150	+0.9
Suspicion	272	107	-60.7	31	13	-58.1	62	23	-62.9	10	5	-50.0
Curfew and loitering law violations	462	526	+13.9	462	526	+13.9	280	274	-2.1	280	274	-2.1
Runaways	2,416	2,259	-6.5	2,416	2,259	-6.5	3,473	3,389	-2.4	3,473	3,389	-2.4

[1] Does not include suspicion.

[2] Violent crimes are offenses of murder, forcible rape, robbery, and aggravated assault.

[3] Property crimes are offenses of burglary, larceny-theft, motor vehicle theft, and arson.

[4] Includes arson.

Table 58

Arrests

Rural Counties
by Age, 2002
[1,949 agencies; 2002 estimated population 21,924,006]

Offense charged	Total all ages	Ages under 15	Ages under 18	Ages 18 and over	Under 10	10-12	13-14	15	16	17	18	19	20	21
TOTAL	**882,727**	**22,155**	**90,192**	**792,535**	**1,220**	**5,166**	**15,769**	**14,827**	**22,713**	**30,497**	**43,049**	**45,213**	**43,299**	**38,618**
Percent distribution[1]	**100.0**	**2.5**	**10.2**	**89.8**	**0.1**	**0.6**	**1.8**	**1.7**	**2.6**	**3.5**	**4.9**	**5.1**	**4.9**	**4.4**
Murder and nonnegligent manslaughter	886	12	64	822	0	1	11	7	20	25	40	31	44	46
Forcible rape	2,171	102	301	1,870	1	27	74	40	59	100	136	137	102	82
Robbery	2,014	25	222	1,792	1	5	19	28	64	105	177	204	147	140
Aggravated assault	23,887	661	2,186	21,701	38	191	432	334	530	661	895	852	912	974
Burglary	20,873	1,609	5,424	15,449	91	422	1,096	900	1,231	1,684	2,201	1,708	1,262	1,041
Larceny-theft	33,227	2,330	7,305	25,922	97	641	1,592	1,205	1,666	2,104	2,511	2,002	1,557	1,422
Motor vehicle theft	6,473	530	2,041	4,432	4	75	451	462	531	518	489	445	293	273
Arson	1,069	174	321	748	37	66	71	46	39	62	65	51	44	47
Violent crime[2]	28,958	800	2,773	26,185	40	224	536	409	673	891	1,248	1,224	1,205	1,242
Percent distribution[1]	100.0	2.8	9.6	90.4	0.1	0.8	1.9	1.4	2.3	3.1	4.3	4.2	4.2	4.3
Property crime[3]	61,642	4,643	15,091	46,551	229	1,204	3,210	2,613	3,467	4,368	5,266	4,206	3,156	2,783
Percent distribution[1]	100.0	7.5	24.5	75.5	0.4	2.0	5.2	4.2	5.6	7.1	8.5	6.8	5.1	4.5
Crime Index[4]	90,600	5,443	17,864	72,736	269	1,428	3,746	3,022	4,140	5,259	6,514	5,430	4,361	4,025
Percent distribution[1]	100.0	6.0	19.7	80.3	0.3	1.6	4.1	3.3	4.6	5.8	7.2	6.0	4.8	4.4
Other assaults	78,678	3,142	9,260	69,418	138	842	2,162	1,554	2,160	2,404	2,605	2,536	2,500	2,672
Forgery and counterfeiting	6,520	24	264	6,256	1	4	19	22	87	131	247	324	280	358
Fraud	39,324	60	487	38,837	3	12	45	67	117	243	672	1,151	1,390	1,486
Embezzlement	928	1	36	892	0	0	1	6	10	19	32	32	31	31
Stolen property; buying, receiving, possessing	5,515	134	669	4,846	5	28	101	127	166	242	436	380	366	284
Vandalism	15,107	1,813	4,919	10,188	213	564	1,036	754	1,057	1,295	1,190	997	721	638
Weapons; carrying, possessing, etc.	7,975	288	929	7,046	31	81	176	162	192	287	379	325	329	343
Prostitution and commercialized vice	143	1	12	131	0	0	1	2	4	5	3	3	7	3
Sex offenses (except forcible rape and prostitution)	6,223	620	1,289	4,934	57	164	399	231	198	240	338	300	235	203
Drug abuse violations	91,205	985	7,358	83,847	28	148	809	1,024	1,958	3,391	6,072	6,262	5,937	5,281
Gambling	651	2	11	640	0	2	0	2	2	5	23	34	40	32
Offenses against the family and children	14,741	180	555	14,186	13	41	126	102	136	137	241	280	303	406
Driving under the influence	172,521	52	2,694	169,827	14	1	37	81	719	1,842	4,297	5,451	6,262	7,659
Liquor laws	45,988	885	12,135	33,853	14	59	812	1,647	3,656	5,947	8,305	8,156	6,776	1,233
Drunkenness	24,868	64	654	24,214	7	3	54	82	136	372	849	996	943	1,080
Disorderly conduct	26,256	1,988	5,803	20,453	109	511	1,368	1,107	1,382	1,326	1,295	1,006	955	1,080
Vagrancy	587	52	261	326	2	14	36	50	75	84	12	8	10	12
All other offenses (except traffic)	247,267	4,072	17,492	229,775	269	918	2,885	2,878	4,473	6,069	9,537	11,528	11,848	11,783
Suspicion	159	12	29	130	1	1	10	9	3	5	2	14	5	9
Curfew and loitering law violations	1,034	267	1,034	–	6	46	215	260	323	184	–	–	–	–
Runaways	6,437	2,070	6,437	–	40	299	1,731	1,638	1,719	1,010	–	–	–	–

See footnotes at end of table.

Table 58

Arrests

Rural Counties
by Age, 2002—Continued
[1,949 agencies; 2002 estimated population 21,924,006]

Offense charged	22	23	24	25-29	30-34	35-39	40-44	45-49	50-54	55-59	60-64	65 and over
TOTAL	**35,557**	**31,968**	**29,252**	**117,469**	**106,285**	**101,327**	**87,584**	**53,324**	**29,638**	**15,038**	**7,433**	**7,481**
Percent distribution[1]	**4.0**	**3.6**	**3.3**	**13.3**	**12.0**	**11.5**	**9.9**	**6.0**	**3.4**	**1.7**	**0.8**	**0.8**
Murder and nonnegligent manslaughter	46	33	33	134	107	90	78	57	37	19	15	12
Forcible rape	66	96	62	252	258	215	163	112	73	55	26	35
Robbery	138	92	78	301	199	143	105	38	19	5	3	3
Aggravated assault	926	825	717	3,257	3,094	3,006	2,670	1,609	920	498	254	292
Burglary	858	700	591	2,209	1,581	1,427	1,025	488	210	85	26	37
Larceny-theft	1,241	1,107	924	3,633	3,274	2,980	2,321	1,413	720	389	211	217
Motor vehicle theft	243	224	161	703	523	462	322	172	71	26	13	12
Arson	17	26	26	102	84	89	72	61	34	10	10	10
Violent crime[2]	1,176	1,046	890	3,944	3,658	3,454	3,016	1,816	1,049	577	298	342
Percent distribution[1]	4.1	3.6	3.1	13.6	12.6	11.9	10.4	6.3	3.6	2.0	1.0	1.2
Property crime[3]	2,359	2,057	1,702	6,647	5,462	4,958	3,740	2,134	1,035	510	260	276
Percent distribution[1]	3.8	3.3	2.8	10.8	8.9	8.0	6.1	3.5	1.7	0.8	0.4	0.4
Crime Index[4]	3,535	3,103	2,592	10,591	9,120	8,412	6,756	3,950	2,084	1,087	558	618
Percent distribution[1]	3.9	3.4	2.9	11.7	10.1	9.3	7.5	4.4	2.3	1.2	0.6	0.7
Other assaults	2,528	2,517	2,318	10,646	10,625	10,696	8,915	5,064	2,828	1,468	711	789
Forgery and counterfeiting	341	271	294	1,095	962	912	612	322	137	60	17	24
Fraud	1,617	1,546	1,487	6,845	6,784	5,747	4,404	2,688	1,466	794	366	394
Embezzlement	34	24	34	138	136	163	92	60	43	22	15	5
Stolen property; buying, receiving, possessing	218	225	212	746	622	551	413	203	110	45	19	16
Vandalism	518	462	357	1,336	1,148	1,033	848	439	242	122	54	83
Weapons; carrying, possessing, etc.	307	309	236	1,056	920	846	708	541	339	204	96	108
Prostitution and commercialized vice	7	9	7	17	19	16	14	10	7	4	2	3
Sex offenses (except forcible rape and prostitution)	167	199	160	588	591	574	488	361	256	212	113	149
Drug abuse violations	4,720	4,026	3,582	13,199	10,370	9,157	7,818	4,253	1,972	721	273	204
Gambling	25	25	36	107	84	67	52	41	27	14	15	18
Offenses against the family and children	446	417	456	2,436	2,683	2,649	2,043	1,004	480	173	77	92
Driving under the influence	7,314	6,666	6,208	23,963	21,970	22,449	22,402	15,476	9,473	5,120	2,624	2,493
Liquor laws	860	602	523	1,732	1,394	1,272	1,228	743	477	283	126	143
Drunkenness	979	847	824	2,962	3,041	3,308	3,433	2,254	1,397	655	363	283
Disorderly conduct	948	813	738	2,824	2,748	2,673	2,346	1,390	761	411	240	225
Vagrancy	3	15	13	58	47	50	38	20	19	9	9	3
All other offenses (except traffic)	10,982	9,885	9,166	37,111	33,000	30,737	24,967	14,495	7,518	3,633	1,755	1,830
Suspicion	8	7	9	19	21	15	7	10	2	1	0	1
Curfew and loitering law violations	–	–	–	–	–	–	–	–	–	–	–	–
Runaways	–	–	–	–	–	–	–	–	–	–	–	–

[1] Because of rounding, the percentages may not add to 100.0.

[2] Violent crimes are offenses of murder, forcible rape, robbery, and aggravated assault.

[3] Property crimes are offenses of burglary, larceny-theft, motor vehicle theft, and arson.

[4] Includes arson.

Table 59

Arrests

Rural Counties

of Persons Under 15, 18, 21, and 25 Years of Age, 2002

[1,949 agencies; 2002 estimated population 21,924,006]

Offense charged	Total all ages	Number of persons arrested				Percent of total all ages			
		Under 15	Under 18	Under 21	Under 25	Under 15	Under 18	Under 21	Under 25
TOTAL	**882,727**	**22,155**	**90,192**	**221,753**	**357,148**	**2.5**	**10.2**	**25.1**	**40.5**
Murder and nonnegligent manslaughter	886	12	64	179	337	1.4	7.2	20.2	38.0
Forcible rape	2,171	102	301	676	982	4.7	13.9	31.1	45.2
Robbery	2,014	25	222	750	1,198	1.2	11.0	37.2	59.5
Aggravated assault	23,887	661	2,186	4,845	8,287	2.8	9.2	20.3	34.7
Burglary	20,873	1,609	5,424	10,595	13,785	7.7	26.0	50.8	66.0
Larceny-theft	33,227	2,330	7,305	13,375	18,069	7.0	22.0	40.3	54.4
Motor vehicle theft	6,473	530	2,041	3,268	4,169	8.2	31.5	50.5	64.4
Arson	1,069	174	321	481	597	16.3	30.0	45.0	55.8
Violent crime[1]	28,958	800	2,773	6,450	10,804	2.8	9.6	22.3	37.3
Property crime[2]	61,642	4,643	15,091	27,719	36,620	7.5	24.5	45.0	59.4
Crime Index[3]	90,600	5,443	17,864	34,169	47,424	6.0	19.7	37.7	52.3
Other assaults	78,678	3,142	9,260	16,901	26,936	4.0	11.8	21.5	34.2
Forgery and counterfeiting	6,520	24	264	1,115	2,379	0.4	4.0	17.1	36.5
Fraud	39,324	60	487	3,700	9,836	0.2	1.2	9.4	25.0
Embezzlement	928	1	36	131	254	0.1	3.9	14.1	27.4
Stolen property; buying, receiving, possessing	5,515	134	669	1,851	2,790	2.4	12.1	33.6	50.6
Vandalism	15,107	1,813	4,919	7,827	9,802	12.0	32.6	51.8	64.9
Weapons; carrying, possessing, etc.	7,975	288	929	1,962	3,157	3.6	11.6	24.6	39.6
Prostitution and commercialized vice	143	1	12	25	51	0.7	8.4	17.5	35.7
Sex offenses (except forcible rape and prostitution)	6,223	620	1,289	2,162	2,891	10.0	20.7	34.7	46.5
Drug abuse violations	91,205	985	7,358	25,629	43,238	1.1	8.1	28.1	47.4
Gambling	651	2	11	108	226	0.3	1.7	16.6	34.7
Offenses against the family and children	14,741	180	555	1,379	3,104	1.2	3.8	9.4	21.1
Driving under the influence	172,521	52	2,694	18,704	46,551	*	1.6	10.8	27.0
Liquor laws	45,988	885	12,135	35,372	38,590	1.9	26.4	76.9	83.9
Drunkenness	24,868	64	654	3,442	7,172	0.3	2.6	13.8	28.8
Disorderly conduct	26,256	1,988	5,803	9,059	12,638	7.6	22.1	34.5	48.1
Vagrancy	587	52	261	291	334	8.9	44.5	49.6	56.9
All other offenses (except traffic)	247,267	4,072	17,492	50,405	92,221	1.6	7.1	20.4	37.3
Suspicion	159	12	29	50	83	7.5	18.2	31.4	52.2
Curfew and loitering law violations	1,034	267	1,034	1,034	1,034	25.8	100.0	100.0	100.0
Runaways	6,437	2,070	6,437	6,437	6,437	32.2	100.0	100.0	100.0

[1] Violent crimes are offenses of murder, forcible rape, robbery, and aggravated assault.

[2] Property crimes are offenses of burglary, larceny-theft, motor vehicle theft, and arson.

[3] Includes arson.

* Less than one-tenth of 1 percent.

Table 60

Arrests

Rural Counties
by Sex, 2002
[1,949 agencies; 2002 estimated population 21,924,006]

Offense charged	Number of persons arrested			Percent male	Percent female	Percent distribution[1]		
	Total	Male	Female			Total	Male	Female
TOTAL	**882,727**	**694,371**	**188,356**	**78.7**	**21.3**	**100.0**	**100.0**	**100.0**
Murder and nonnegligent manslaughter	886	776	110	87.6	12.4	0.1	0.1	0.1
Forcible rape	2,171	2,143	28	98.7	1.3	0.2	0.3	*
Robbery	2,014	1,824	190	90.6	9.4	0.2	0.3	0.1
Aggravated assault	23,887	19,800	4,087	82.9	17.1	2.7	2.9	2.2
Burglary	20,873	18,548	2,325	88.9	11.1	2.4	2.7	1.2
Larceny-theft	33,227	24,091	9,136	72.5	27.5	3.8	3.5	4.9
Motor vehicle theft	6,473	5,435	1,038	84.0	16.0	0.7	0.8	0.6
Arson	1,069	911	158	85.2	14.8	0.1	0.1	0.1
Violent crime[2]	28,958	24,543	4,415	84.8	15.2	3.3	3.5	2.3
Property crime[3]	61,642	48,985	12,657	79.5	20.5	7.0	7.1	6.7
Crime Index[4]	90,600	73,528	17,072	81.2	18.8	10.3	10.6	9.1
Other assaults	78,678	60,730	17,948	77.2	22.8	8.9	8.7	9.5
Forgery and counterfeiting	6,520	3,778	2,742	57.9	42.1	0.7	0.5	1.5
Fraud	39,324	20,180	19,144	51.3	48.7	4.5	2.9	10.2
Embezzlement	928	462	466	49.8	50.2	0.1	0.1	0.2
Stolen property; buying, receiving, possessing	5,515	4,612	903	83.6	16.4	0.6	0.7	0.5
Vandalism	15,107	12,749	2,358	84.4	15.6	1.7	1.8	1.3
Weapons; carrying, possessing, etc.	7,975	7,363	612	92.3	7.7	0.9	1.1	0.3
Prostitution and commercialized vice	143	93	50	65.0	35.0	*	*	*
Sex offenses (except forcible rape and prostitution)	6,223	5,889	334	94.6	5.4	0.7	0.8	0.2
Drug abuse violations	91,205	74,004	17,201	81.1	18.9	10.3	10.7	9.1
Gambling	651	543	108	83.4	16.6	0.1	0.1	0.1
Offenses against the family and children	14,741	12,101	2,640	82.1	17.9	1.7	1.7	1.4
Driving under the influence	172,521	144,579	27,942	83.8	16.2	19.5	20.8	14.8
Liquor laws	45,988	33,999	11,989	73.9	26.1	5.2	4.9	6.4
Drunkenness	24,868	21,104	3,764	84.9	15.1	2.8	3.0	2.0
Disorderly conduct	26,256	19,738	6,518	75.2	24.8	3.0	2.8	3.5
Vagrancy	587	416	171	70.9	29.1	0.1	0.1	0.1
All other offenses (except traffic)	247,267	195,146	52,121	78.9	21.1	28.0	28.1	27.7
Suspicion	159	135	24	84.9	15.1	*	*	*
Curfew and loitering law violations	1,034	651	383	63.0	37.0	0.1	0.1	0.2
Runaways	6,437	2,571	3,866	39.9	60.1	0.7	0.4	2.1

[1] Because of rounding, the percentages may not add to 100.0.
[2] Violent crimes are offenses of murder, forcible rape, robbery, and aggravated assault.
[3] Property crimes are offenses of burglary, larceny-theft, motor vehicle theft, and arson.
[4] Includes arson.
* Less than one-tenth of 1 percent.

Table 61

Arrests
Rural Counties
by Race, 2002
[1,949 agencies; 2002 estimated population 21,924,006]

	Total arrests					Percent distribution[1]				
Offense charged	Total	White	Black	American Indian or Alaskan Native	Asian or Pacific Islander	Total	White	Black	American Indian or Alaskan Native	Asian or Pacific Islander
TOTAL	**880,037**	**727,920**	**120,859**	**25,918**	**5,340**	**100.0**	**82.7**	**13.7**	**2.9**	**0.6**
Murder and nonnegligent manslaughter	885	603	233	44	5	100.0	68.1	26.3	5.0	0.6
Forcible rape	2,167	1,733	359	60	15	100.0	80.0	16.6	2.8	0.7
Robbery	2,013	1,032	912	61	8	100.0	51.3	45.3	3.0	0.4
Aggravated assault	23,826	17,894	4,733	1,050	149	100.0	75.1	19.9	4.4	0.6
Burglary	20,848	17,154	2,973	616	105	100.0	82.3	14.3	3.0	0.5
Larceny-theft	33,168	27,313	4,878	690	287	100.0	82.3	14.7	2.1	0.9
Motor vehicle theft	6,463	5,498	671	238	56	100.0	85.1	10.4	3.7	0.9
Arson	1,067	919	126	20	2	100.0	86.1	11.8	1.9	0.2
Violent crime[2]	28,891	21,262	6,237	1,215	177	100.0	73.6	21.6	4.2	0.6
Property crime[3]	61,546	50,884	8,648	1,564	450	100.0	82.7	14.1	2.5	0.7
Crime Index[4]	90,437	72,146	14,885	2,779	627	100.0	79.8	16.5	3.1	0.7
Other assaults	78,505	62,552	12,989	2,446	518	100.0	79.7	16.5	3.1	0.7
Forgery and counterfeiting	6,515	5,200	1,216	68	31	100.0	79.8	18.7	1.0	0.5
Fraud	39,211	31,505	7,102	507	97	100.0	80.3	18.1	1.3	0.2
Embezzlement	922	786	122	7	7	100.0	85.2	13.2	0.8	0.8
Stolen property; buying, receiving, possessing	5,509	4,334	1,051	111	13	100.0	78.7	19.1	2.0	0.2
Vandalism	15,058	12,927	1,537	506	88	100.0	85.8	10.2	3.4	0.6
Weapons; carrying, possessing, etc.	7,951	6,394	1,325	198	34	100.0	80.4	16.7	2.5	0.4
Prostitution and commercialized vice	143	103	30	5	5	100.0	72.0	21.0	3.5	3.5
Sex offenses (except forcible rape and prostitution)	6,208	5,467	546	152	43	100.0	88.1	8.8	2.4	0.7
Drug abuse violations	91,027	75,764	13,238	1,608	417	100.0	83.2	14.5	1.8	0.5
Gambling	651	363	283	2	3	100.0	55.8	43.5	0.3	0.5
Offenses against the family and children	14,712	10,960	3,446	290	16	100.0	74.5	23.4	2.0	0.1
Driving under the influence	172,083	150,707	14,882	5,142	1,352	100.0	87.6	8.6	3.0	0.8
Liquor laws	45,728	43,033	1,155	1,377	163	100.0	94.1	2.5	3.0	0.4
Drunkenness	24,824	21,824	1,880	1,069	51	100.0	87.9	7.6	4.3	0.2
Disorderly conduct	26,224	20,964	4,029	1,153	78	100.0	79.9	15.4	4.4	0.3
Vagrancy	583	461	99	20	3	100.0	79.1	17.0	3.4	0.5
All other offenses (except traffic)	246,127	195,837	40,599	8,234	1,457	100.0	79.6	16.5	3.3	0.6
Suspicion	158	101	57	0	0	100.0	63.9	36.1	*	*
Curfew and loitering law violations	1,033	824	28	44	137	100.0	79.8	2.7	4.3	13.3
Runaways	6,428	5,668	360	200	200	100.0	88.2	5.6	3.1	3.1

See footnotes at end of table.

Table 61

Arrests

Rural Counties
by Race, 2002—Continued
[1,949 agencies; 2002 estimated population 21,924,006]

Offense charged	Arrests under 18					Percent distribution[1]				
	Total	White	Black	American Indian or Alaskan Native	Asian or Pacific Islander	Total	White	Black	American Indian or Alaskan Native	Asian or Pacific Islander
TOTAL	**89,838**	**77,428**	**8,642**	**2,766**	**1,002**	**100.0**	**86.2**	**9.6**	**3.1**	**1.1**
Murder and nonnegligent manslaughter	64	32	18	14	0	100.0	50.0	28.1	21.9	*
Forcible rape	301	248	41	9	3	100.0	82.4	13.6	3.0	1.0
Robbery	222	122	90	8	2	100.0	55.0	40.5	3.6	0.9
Aggravated assault	2,176	1,637	425	89	25	100.0	75.2	19.5	4.1	1.1
Burglary	5,413	4,752	458	160	43	100.0	87.8	8.5	3.0	0.8
Larceny-theft	7,284	6,312	663	182	127	100.0	86.7	9.1	2.5	1.7
Motor vehicle theft	2,037	1,800	133	80	24	100.0	88.4	6.5	3.9	1.2
Arson	320	288	26	6	0	100.0	90.0	8.1	1.9	*
Violent crime[2]	2,763	2,039	574	120	30	100.0	73.8	20.8	4.3	1.1
Property crime[3]	15,054	13,152	1,280	428	194	100.0	87.4	8.5	2.8	1.3
Crime Index[4]	17,817	15,191	1,854	548	224	100.0	85.3	10.4	3.1	1.3
Other assaults	9,243	7,147	1,701	288	107	100.0	77.3	18.4	3.1	1.2
Forgery and counterfeiting	264	238	24	2	0	100.0	90.2	9.1	0.8	*
Fraud	482	409	55	14	4	100.0	84.9	11.4	2.9	0.8
Embezzlement	36	32	3	0	1	100.0	88.9	8.3	*	2.8
Stolen property; buying, receiving, possessing	666	572	81	11	2	100.0	85.9	12.2	1.7	0.3
Vandalism	4,900	4,419	304	143	34	100.0	90.2	6.2	2.9	0.7
Weapons; carrying, possessing, etc.	924	725	154	40	5	100.0	78.5	16.7	4.3	0.5
Prostitution and commercialized vice	12	8	4	0	0	100.0	66.7	33.3	*	*
Sex offenses (except forcible rape and prostitution)	1,286	1,121	111	42	12	100.0	87.2	8.6	3.3	0.9
Drug abuse violations	7,324	6,498	533	204	89	100.0	88.7	7.3	2.8	1.2
Gambling	11	7	4	0	0	100.0	63.6	36.4	*	*
Offenses against the family and children	550	511	35	3	1	100.0	92.9	6.4	0.5	0.2
Driving under the influence	2,687	2,514	73	83	17	100.0	93.6	2.7	3.1	0.6
Liquor laws	12,076	11,467	145	437	27	100.0	95.0	1.2	3.6	0.2
Drunkenness	653	621	20	10	2	100.0	95.1	3.1	1.5	0.3
Disorderly conduct	5,802	4,403	1,165	211	23	100.0	75.9	20.1	3.6	0.4
Vagrancy	261	240	20	0	1	100.0	92.0	7.7	*	0.4
All other offenses (except traffic)	17,355	14,792	1,961	486	116	100.0	85.2	11.3	2.8	0.7
Suspicion	28	21	7	0	0	100.0	75.0	25.0	*	*
Curfew and loitering law violations	1,033	824	28	44	137	100.0	79.8	2.7	4.3	13.3
Runaways	6,428	5,668	360	200	200	100.0	88.2	5.6	3.1	3.1

See footnotes at end of table.

Table 61

Arrests

Rural Counties
by Race, 2002—Continued
[1,949 agencies; 2002 estimated population 21,924,006]

Offense charged	Arrests 18 and over					Percent distribution[1]				
	Total	White	Black	American Indian or Alaskan Native	Asian or Pacific Islander	Total	White	Black	American Indian or Alaskan Native	Asian or Pacific Islander
TOTAL	**790,199**	**650,492**	**112,217**	**23,152**	**4,338**	**100.0**	**82.3**	**14.2**	**2.9**	**0.5**
Murder and nonnegligent manslaughter	821	571	215	30	5	100.0	69.5	26.2	3.7	0.6
Forcible rape	1,866	1,485	318	51	12	100.0	79.6	17.0	2.7	0.6
Robbery	1,791	910	822	53	6	100.0	50.8	45.9	3.0	0.3
Aggravated assault	21,650	16,257	4,308	961	124	100.0	75.1	19.9	4.4	0.6
Burglary	15,435	12,402	2,515	456	62	100.0	80.3	16.3	3.0	0.4
Larceny-theft	25,884	21,001	4,215	508	160	100.0	81.1	16.3	2.0	0.6
Motor vehicle theft	4,426	3,698	538	158	32	100.0	83.6	12.2	3.6	0.7
Arson	747	631	100	14	2	100.0	84.5	13.4	1.9	0.3
Violent crime[2]	26,128	19,223	5,663	1,095	147	100.0	73.6	21.7	4.2	0.6
Property crime[3]	46,492	37,732	7,368	1,136	256	100.0	81.2	15.8	2.4	0.6
Crime Index[4]	72,620	56,955	13,031	2,231	403	100.0	78.4	17.9	3.1	0.6
Other assaults	69,262	55,405	11,288	2,158	411	100.0	80.0	16.3	3.1	0.6
Forgery and counterfeiting	6,251	4,962	1,192	66	31	100.0	79.4	19.1	1.1	0.5
Fraud	38,729	31,096	7,047	493	93	100.0	80.3	18.2	1.3	0.2
Embezzlement	886	754	119	7	6	100.0	85.1	13.4	0.8	0.7
Stolen property; buying, receiving, possessing	4,843	3,762	970	100	11	100.0	77.7	20.0	2.1	0.2
Vandalism	10,158	8,508	1,233	363	54	100.0	83.8	12.1	3.6	0.5
Weapons; carrying, possessing, etc.	7,027	5,669	1,171	158	29	100.0	80.7	16.7	2.2	0.4
Prostitution and commercialized vice	131	95	26	5	5	100.0	72.5	19.8	3.8	3.8
Sex offenses (except forcible rape and prostitution)	4,922	4,346	435	110	31	100.0	88.3	8.8	2.2	0.6
Drug abuse violations	83,703	69,266	12,705	1,404	328	100.0	82.8	15.2	1.7	0.4
Gambling	640	356	279	2	3	100.0	55.6	43.6	0.3	0.5
Offenses against the family and children	14,162	10,449	3,411	287	15	100.0	73.8	24.1	2.0	0.1
Driving under the influence	169,396	148,193	14,809	5,059	1,335	100.0	87.5	8.7	3.0	0.8
Liquor laws	33,652	31,566	1,010	940	136	100.0	93.8	3.0	2.8	0.4
Drunkenness	24,171	21,203	1,860	1,059	49	100.0	87.7	7.7	4.4	0.2
Disorderly conduct	20,422	16,561	2,864	942	55	100.0	81.1	14.0	4.6	0.3
Vagrancy	322	221	79	20	2	100.0	68.6	24.5	6.2	0.6
All other offenses (except traffic)	228,772	181,045	38,638	7,748	1,341	100.0	79.1	16.9	3.4	0.6
Suspicion	130	80	50	0	0	100.0	61.5	38.5	*	*
Curfew and loitering law violations	–	–	–	–	–	–	–	–	–	–
Runaways	–	–	–	–	–	–	–	–	–	–

[1] Because of rounding, the percentages may not add to 100.0.

[2] Violent crimes are offenses of murder, forcible rape, robbery, and aggravated assault.

[3] Property crimes are offenses of burglary, larceny-theft, motor vehicle theft, and arson.

[4] Includes arson

* Less than one-tenth of 1 percent.

Table 62

Arrest Trends

Suburban Areas,[1] 2001-2002

[4,224 agencies; 2002 estimated population 73,073,161; 2001 estimated population 72,468,502]

Offense charged	Number of persons arrested								
	Total all ages			Under 18 years of age			18 years of age and over		
	2001	2002	Percent change	2001	2002	Percent change	2001	2002	Percent change
TOTAL[2]	2,923,694	2,957,098	+1.1	495,024	482,099	-2.6	2,428,670	2,474,999	+1.9
Murder and nonnegligent manslaughter	2,139	2,169	+1.4	149	147	-1.3	1,990	2,022	+1.6
Forcible rape	5,395	5,570	+3.2	951	937	-1.5	4,444	4,633	+4.3
Robbery	16,105	16,364	+1.6	3,669	3,563	-2.9	12,436	12,801	+2.9
Aggravated assault	94,112	92,620	-1.6	13,354	12,890	-3.5	80,758	79,730	-1.3
Burglary	59,845	60,116	+0.5	19,597	18,717	-4.5	40,248	41,399	+2.9
Larceny-theft	232,420	233,726	+0.6	69,178	67,477	-2.5	163,242	166,249	+1.8
Motor vehicle theft	24,737	25,443	+2.9	7,564	7,016	-7.2	17,173	18,427	+7.3
Arson	4,130	4,206	+1.8	2,301	2,304	+0.1	1,829	1,902	+4.0
Violent crime[3]	117,751	116,723	-0.9	18,123	17,537	-3.2	99,628	99,186	-0.4
Property crime[4]	321,132	323,491	+0.7	98,640	95,514	-3.2	222,492	227,977	+2.5
Crime Index[5]	438,883	440,214	+0.3	116,763	113,051	-3.2	322,120	327,163	+1.6
Other assaults	267,217	271,218	+1.5	53,495	54,667	+2.2	213,722	216,551	+1.3
Forgery and counterfeiting	24,672	24,311	-1.5	1,313	1,152	-12.3	23,359	23,159	-0.9
Fraud	84,163	87,199	+3.6	1,946	1,840	-5.4	82,217	85,359	+3.8
Embezzlement	4,235	4,019	-5.1	384	327	-14.8	3,851	3,692	-4.1
Stolen property; buying, receiving, possessing	26,700	27,247	+2.0	5,653	5,582	-1.3	21,047	21,665	+2.9
Vandalism	56,921	58,695	+3.1	24,954	25,064	+0.4	31,967	33,631	+5.2
Weapons; carrying, possessing, etc.	31,808	31,717	-0.3	7,806	7,322	-6.2	24,002	24,395	+1.6
Prostitution and commercialized vice	3,554	3,296	-7.3	84	95	+13.1	3,470	3,201	-7.8
Sex offenses (except forcible rape and prostitution)	17,453	18,042	+3.4	3,896	3,873	-0.6	13,557	14,169	+4.5
Drug abuse violations	313,424	313,079	-0.1	45,623	42,024	-7.9	267,801	271,055	+1.2
Gambling	718	921	+28.3	78	90	+15.4	640	831	+29.8
Offenses against the family and children	37,738	38,823	+2.9	2,049	2,185	+6.6	35,689	36,638	+2.7
Driving under the influence	376,460	379,772	+0.9	5,111	5,265	+3.0	371,349	374,507	+0.9
Liquor laws	139,823	138,690	-0.8	37,094	35,855	-3.3	102,729	102,835	+0.1
Drunkenness	118,153	113,566	-3.9	5,184	4,832	-6.8	112,969	108,734	-3.7
Disorderly conduct	125,723	124,939	-0.6	42,073	44,087	+4.8	83,650	80,852	-3.3
Vagrancy	3,905	4,191	+7.3	542	527	-2.8	3,363	3,664	+9.0
All other offenses (except traffic)	803,290	833,485	+3.8	92,122	90,587	-1.7	711,168	742,898	+4.5
Suspicion	864	1,420	+64.4	274	238	-13.1	590	1,182	+100.3
Curfew and loitering law violations	18,778	16,594	-11.6	18,778	16,594	-11.6	–	–	–
Runaways	30,076	27,080	-10.0	30,076	27,080	-10.0	–	–	–

[1] Suburban area includes law enforcement agencies in cities with less than 50,000 inhabitants and county law enforcement agencies that are within a Metropolitan Statistical Area (see Appendix III). Suburban area excludes all metropolitan agencies associated with a central city. The agencies associated with suburban areas also appear in other groups within this table.

[2] Does not include suspicion.

[3] Violent crimes are offenses of murder, forcible rape, robbery, and aggravated assault.

[4] Property crimes are offenses of burglary, larceny-theft, motor vehicle theft, and arson.

[5] Includes arson.

Table 63

Arrest Trends
Suburban Areas[1]
by Sex, 2001-2002
[4,224 agencies; 2002 estimated population 73,073,161; 2001 estimated population 72,468,502]

	Male						Female					
	Total			Under 18			Total			Under 18		
Offense charged	2001	2002	Percent change	2001	2002	Percent change	2001	2002	Percent change	2001	2002	Percent change
TOTAL[2]	2,272,269	2,282,769	+0.5	358,918	348,334	-2.9	651,425	674,329	+3.5	136,106	133,765	-1.7
Murder and nonnegligent manslaughter	1,899	1,872	-1.4	131	126	-3.8	240	297	+23.8	18	21	+16.7
Forcible rape	5,325	5,514	+3.5	935	924	-1.2	70	56	-20.0	16	13	-18.8
Robbery	14,563	14,683	+0.8	3,417	3,266	-4.4	1,542	1,681	+9.0	252	297	+17.9
Aggravated assault	76,699	75,338	-1.8	10,539	10,105	-4.1	17,413	17,282	-0.8	2,815	2,785	-1.1
Burglary	52,167	52,550	+0.7	17,446	16,815	-3.6	7,678	7,566	-1.5	2,151	1,902	-11.6
Larceny-theft	147,578	148,282	+0.5	43,635	42,535	-2.5	84,842	85,444	+0.7	25,543	24,942	-2.4
Motor vehicle theft	20,643	21,336	+3.4	6,136	5,769	-6.0	4,094	4,107	+0.3	1,428	1,247	-12.7
Arson	3,571	3,658	+2.4	2,090	2,057	-1.6	559	548	-2.0	211	247	+17.1
Violent crime[3]	98,486	97,407	-1.1	15,022	14,421	-4.0	19,265	19,316	+0.3	3,101	3,116	+0.5
Property crime[4]	223,959	225,826	+0.8	69,307	67,176	-3.1	97,173	97,665	+0.5	29,333	28,338	-3.4
Crime Index[5]	322,445	323,233	+0.2	84,329	81,597	-3.2	116,438	116,981	+0.5	32,434	31,454	-3.0
Other assaults	204,180	205,523	+0.7	37,435	38,050	+1.6	63,037	65,695	+4.2	16,060	16,617	+3.5
Forgery and counterfeiting	14,906	14,957	+0.3	865	780	-9.8	9,766	9,354	-4.2	448	372	-17.0
Fraud	44,877	45,676	+1.8	1,321	1,237	-6.4	39,286	41,523	+5.7	625	603	-3.5
Embezzlement	2,207	2,038	-7.7	229	187	-18.3	2,028	1,981	-2.3	155	140	-9.7
Stolen property; buying, receiving, possessing	22,135	22,466	+1.5	4,875	4,799	-1.6	4,565	4,781	+4.7	778	783	+0.6
Vandalism	48,636	49,947	+2.7	21,868	21,928	+0.3	8,285	8,748	+5.6	3,086	3,136	+1.6
Weapons; carrying, possessing, etc.	29,272	29,158	-0.4	7,054	6,550	-7.1	2,536	2,559	+0.9	752	772	+2.7
Prostitution and commercialized vice	1,854	1,602	-13.6	45	59	+31.1	1,700	1,694	-0.4	39	36	-7.7
Sex offenses (except forcible rape and prostitution)	16,644	17,171	+3.2	3,668	3,624	-1.2	809	871	+7.7	228	249	+9.2
Drug abuse violations	257,288	254,753	-1.0	37,807	34,631	-8.4	56,136	58,326	+3.9	7,816	7,393	-5.4
Gambling	607	740	+21.9	74	82	+10.8	111	181	+63.1	4	8	+100.0
Offenses against the family and children	30,314	30,841	+1.7	1,286	1,342	+4.4	7,424	7,982	+7.5	763	843	+10.5
Driving under the influence	312,360	312,323	*	4,237	4,247	+0.2	64,100	67,449	+5.2	874	1,018	+16.5
Liquor laws	105,494	103,879	-1.5	25,253	24,144	-4.4	34,329	34,811	+1.4	11,841	11,711	-1.1
Drunkenness	100,838	96,132	-4.7	4,085	3,771	-7.7	17,315	17,434	+0.7	1,099	1,061	-3.5
Disorderly conduct	95,416	94,292	-1.2	30,166	31,492	+4.4	30,307	30,647	+1.1	11,907	12,595	+5.8
Vagrancy	3,341	3,468	+3.8	436	406	-6.9	564	723	+28.2	106	121	+14.2
All other offenses (except traffic)	634,238	652,032	+2.8	68,668	66,870	-2.6	169,052	181,453	+7.3	23,454	23,717	+1.1
Suspicion	635	1,110	+74.8	155	165	+6.5	229	310	+35.4	119	73	-38.7
Curfew and loitering law violations	12,674	11,303	-10.8	12,674	11,303	-10.8	6,104	5,291	-13.3	6,104	5,291	-13.3
Runaways	12,543	11,235	-10.4	12,543	11,235	-10.4	17,533	15,845	-9.6	17,533	15,845	-9.6

[1] Suburban area includes law enforcement agencies in cities with less than 50,000 inhabitants and county law enforcement agencies that are within a Metropolitan Statistical Area (see Appendix III). Suburban area excludes all metropolitan agencies associated with a central city.
[2] Does not include suspicion.
[3] Violent crimes are offenses of murder, forcible rape, robbery, and aggravated assault.
[4] Property crimes are offenses of burglary, larceny-theft, motor vehicle theft, and arson.
[5] Includes arson.
* Less than one-tenth of 1 percent.

Table 64

Arrests
Suburban Areas[1]
by Age, 2002
[5,060 agencies; 2002 estimated population 85,923,394]

Offense charged	Total all ages	Ages under 15	Ages under 18	Ages 18 and over	Under 10	10-12	13-14	15	16	17	18	19	20	21
TOTAL	**3,628,725**	**185,389**	**602,934**	**3,025,791**	**7,428**	**43,858**	**134,103**	**111,357**	**143,256**	**162,932**	**187,805**	**193,005**	**178,352**	**157,840**
Percent distribution[2]	**100.0**	**5.1**	**16.6**	**83.4**	**0.2**	**1.2**	**3.7**	**3.1**	**3.9**	**4.5**	**5.2**	**5.3**	**4.9**	**4.3**
Murder and nonnegligent manslaughter	2,660	15	195	2,465	0	8	7	37	51	92	137	177	172	174
Forcible rape	6,893	429	1,209	5,684	13	121	295	193	272	315	376	377	314	314
Robbery	20,577	959	4,509	16,068	19	163	777	853	1,173	1,524	1,793	1,593	1,293	1,163
Aggravated assault	110,807	5,572	15,614	95,193	246	1,501	3,825	2,834	3,425	3,783	4,251	4,202	4,224	4,365
Burglary	72,415	7,817	22,557	49,858	396	1,994	5,427	4,026	5,081	5,633	5,896	4,930	3,845	3,166
Larceny-theft	293,756	30,938	85,918	207,838	1,096	8,148	21,694	15,995	19,074	19,911	19,031	16,090	12,899	10,690
Motor vehicle theft	29,520	2,121	8,448	21,072	25	260	1,836	1,927	2,280	2,120	2,173	1,884	1,572	1,415
Arson	4,894	1,642	2,621	2,273	226	565	851	389	318	272	234	204	136	85
Violent crime[3]	140,937	6,975	21,527	119,410	278	1,793	4,904	3,917	4,921	5,714	6,557	6,349	6,003	6,016
Percent distribution[2]	100.0	4.9	15.3	84.7	0.2	1.3	3.5	2.8	3.5	4.1	4.7	4.5	4.3	4.3
Property crime[4]	400,585	42,518	119,544	281,041	1,743	10,967	29,808	22,337	26,753	27,936	27,334	23,108	18,452	15,356
Percent distribution[2]	100.0	10.6	29.8	70.2	0.4	2.7	7.4	5.6	6.7	7.0	6.8	5.8	4.6	3.8
Crime Index[5]	541,522	49,493	141,071	400,451	2,021	12,760	34,712	26,254	31,674	33,650	33,891	29,457	24,455	21,372
Percent distribution[2]	100.0	9.1	26.1	73.9	0.4	2.4	6.4	4.8	5.8	6.2	6.3	5.4	4.5	3.9
Other assaults	329,934	27,185	64,375	265,559	1,086	7,555	18,544	11,906	13,008	12,276	10,930	11,006	11,163	11,710
Forgery and counterfeiting	30,751	189	1,429	29,322	19	31	139	196	355	689	1,230	1,582	1,549	1,523
Fraud	112,608	439	2,689	109,919	38	87	314	357	719	1,174	2,520	3,877	4,434	4,444
Embezzlement	4,727	46	390	4,337	1	12	33	29	104	211	320	324	271	233
Stolen property; buying, receiving, possessing	33,825	1,862	7,135	26,690	49	347	1,466	1,349	1,813	2,111	2,381	2,128	1,923	1,701
Vandalism	72,884	12,826	30,382	42,502	999	3,811	8,016	5,140	6,210	6,206	5,236	4,125	3,137	2,964
Weapons; carrying, possessing, etc.	38,959	3,185	8,824	30,135	188	825	2,172	1,538	1,867	2,234	2,541	2,348	2,125	1,962
Prostitution and commercialized vice	4,773	37	122	4,651	0	3	34	17	26	42	83	148	137	159
Sex offenses (except forcible rape and prostitution)	22,771	2,508	5,079	17,692	150	699	1,659	916	784	871	970	896	863	757
Drug abuse violations	372,988	7,816	50,450	322,538	104	976	6,736	8,299	14,080	20,255	27,409	27,374	23,901	20,726
Gambling	1,281	39	137	1,144	0	8	31	24	36	38	40	63	68	35
Offenses against the family and children	47,539	990	2,729	44,810	99	233	658	572	588	579	805	993	1,075	1,303
Driving under the influence	442,751	135	6,312	436,439	41	9	85	243	1,466	4,468	10,817	14,318	16,037	21,607
Liquor laws	176,569	3,980	45,995	130,574	63	275	3,642	6,545	13,246	22,224	33,456	34,079	26,523	4,598
Drunkenness	140,222	730	5,781	134,441	26	76	628	950	1,393	2,708	4,942	5,209	5,084	6,574
Disorderly conduct	174,655	24,016	57,901	116,754	662	6,437	16,917	11,300	11,791	10,794	9,207	7,709	7,132	7,832
Vagrancy	4,941	207	657	4,284	5	22	180	140	146	164	225	196	167	144
All other offenses (except traffic)	1,018,349	32,017	116,088	902,261	1,322	6,883	23,812	22,188	28,765	33,118	40,709	47,102	48,237	48,137
Suspicion	1,617	104	329	1,288	2	22	80	58	86	81	93	71	71	59
Curfew and loitering law violations	22,511	6,179	22,511	–	62	972	5,145	5,043	6,634	4,655	–	–	–	–
Runaways	32,548	11,406	32,548	–	491	1,815	9,100	8,293	8,465	4,384	–	–	–	–

[1] Suburban area includes law enforcement agencies in cities with less than 50,000 inhabitants and county law enforcement agencies that are within a Metropolitan Statistical Area (see Appendix III). Suburban area excludes all metropolitan agencies associated with a central city.

[2] Because of rounding, the percentages may not add to 100.0.

[3] Violent crimes are offenses of murder, forcible rape, robbery, and aggravated assault.

[4] Property crimes are offenses of burglary, larceny-theft, motor vehicle theft, and arson.

[5] Includes arson.

Table 64

Arrests

Suburban Areas[1]
by Age, 2002—Continued

[5,060 agencies; 2002 estimated population 85,923,394]

Offense charged	22	23	24	25-29	30-34	35-39	40-44	45-49	50-54	55-59	60-64	65 and over
TOTAL	**144,866**	**127,099**	**115,078**	**445,437**	**397,753**	**378,976**	**317,011**	**192,440**	**99,267**	**47,448**	**22,168**	**21,246**
Percent distribution[2]	**4.0**	**3.5**	**3.2**	**12.3**	**11.0**	**10.4**	**8.7**	**5.3**	**2.7**	**1.3**	**0.6**	**0.6**
Murder and nonnegligent manslaughter	141	145	103	407	277	231	183	137	70	51	25	35
Forcible rape	253	209	209	795	803	750	514	346	189	106	64	65
Robbery	908	816	714	2,280	1,967	1,576	1,129	510	199	72	27	28
Aggravated assault	4,215	3,810	3,595	15,014	13,764	13,427	11,148	6,546	3,255	1,668	844	865
Burglary	2,763	2,221	1,977	6,730	6,050	5,432	3,738	1,894	703	295	99	119
Larceny-theft	9,487	7,962	6,942	27,330	26,350	24,948	20,708	12,566	6,572	3,098	1,503	1,662
Motor vehicle theft	1,224	1,034	947	3,192	2,712	2,229	1,433	744	319	120	42	32
Arson	96	74	79	293	266	263	250	137	78	43	21	14
Violent crime[3]	5,517	4,980	4,621	18,496	16,811	15,984	12,974	7,539	3,713	1,897	960	993
Percent distribution[2]	3.9	3.5	3.3	13.1	11.9	11.3	9.2	5.3	2.6	1.3	0.7	0.7
Property crime[4]	13,570	11,291	9,945	37,545	35,378	32,872	26,129	15,341	7,672	3,556	1,665	1,827
Percent distribution[2]	3.4	2.8	2.5	9.4	8.8	8.2	6.5	3.8	1.9	0.9	0.4	0.5
Crime Index[5]	19,087	16,271	14,566	56,041	52,189	48,856	39,103	22,880	11,385	5,453	2,625	2,820
Percent distribution[2]	3.5	3.0	2.7	10.3	9.6	9.0	7.2	4.2	2.1	1.0	0.5	0.5
Other assaults	11,450	10,362	9,963	40,586	40,366	39,375	32,457	18,578	8,993	4,381	2,058	2,181
Forgery and counterfeiting	1,435	1,307	1,186	5,340	4,724	4,042	2,805	1,482	685	263	95	74
Fraud	4,653	4,280	4,097	18,919	18,730	16,489	12,495	7,459	3,827	1,962	903	830
Embezzlement	207	173	168	641	578	529	401	240	133	73	35	11
Stolen property; buying, receiving, possessing	1,538	1,279	1,102	4,091	3,538	2,864	2,255	1,101	453	194	82	60
Vandalism	2,431	1,899	1,633	5,648	4,692	4,170	3,226	1,727	817	391	176	230
Weapons; carrying, possessing, etc.	1,735	1,494	1,328	4,506	3,317	2,861	2,367	1,595	918	508	258	272
Prostitution and commercialized vice	141	139	160	643	820	810	623	368	185	113	57	65
Sex offenses (except forcible rape and prostitution)	614	593	545	2,078	2,299	2,405	1,922	1,352	836	617	421	524
Drug abuse violations	18,374	15,280	13,388	48,106	38,324	35,283	28,378	15,694	6,629	2,359	814	499
Gambling	37	22	26	134	113	119	119	116	96	67	36	53
Offenses against the family and children	1,363	1,370	1,484	7,507	8,091	8,265	6,420	3,460	1,511	671	275	217
Driving under the influence	20,793	19,171	17,462	67,771	58,553	56,821	53,070	36,583	21,565	11,501	5,547	4,823
Liquor laws	2,960	2,151	1,800	5,785	4,384	4,348	4,204	2,969	1,726	743	412	436
Drunkenness	5,873	4,975	4,359	17,615	16,304	18,603	18,400	12,738	7,337	3,437	1,705	1,286
Disorderly conduct	6,484	5,214	4,684	15,932	13,233	13,398	11,591	7,079	3,700	1,758	892	909
Vagrancy	167	137	117	553	520	626	593	390	251	121	52	25
All other offenses (except traffic)	45,466	40,926	36,954	143,336	126,807	118,949	96,443	56,539	28,186	12,826	5,720	5,924
Suspicion	58	56	56	205	171	163	139	90	34	10	5	7
Curfew and loitering law violations	–	–	–	–	–	–	–	–	–	–	–	–
Runaways	–	–	–	–	–	–	–	–	–	–	–	–

Table 65

Arrests

Suburban Areas[1]
of Persons Under 15, 18, 21, and 25 Years of Age, 2002
[5,060 agencies; 2002 estimated population 85,923,394]

Offense charged	Total all ages	Number of persons arrested				Percent of total all ages			
		Under 15	Under 18	Under 21	Under 25	Under 15	Under 18	Under 21	Under 25
TOTAL	**3,628,725**	**185,389**	**602,934**	**1,162,096**	**1,706,979**	**5.1**	**16.6**	**32.0**	**47.0**
Murder and nonnegligent manslaughter	2,660	15	195	681	1,244	0.6	7.3	25.6	46.8
Forcible rape	6,893	429	1,209	2,276	3,261	6.2	17.5	33.0	47.3
Robbery	20,577	959	4,509	9,188	12,789	4.7	21.9	44.7	62.2
Aggravated assault	110,807	5,572	15,614	28,291	44,276	5.0	14.1	25.5	40.0
Burglary	72,415	7,817	22,557	37,228	47,355	10.8	31.1	51.4	65.4
Larceny-theft	293,756	30,938	85,918	133,938	169,019	10.5	29.2	45.6	57.5
Motor vehicle theft	29,520	2,121	8,448	14,077	18,697	7.2	28.6	47.7	63.3
Arson	4,894	1,642	2,621	3,195	3,529	33.6	53.6	65.3	72.1
Violent crime[2]	140,937	6,975	21,527	40,436	61,570	4.9	15.3	28.7	43.7
Property crime[3]	400,585	42,518	119,544	188,438	238,600	10.6	29.8	47.0	59.6
Crime Index[4]	541,522	49,493	141,071	228,874	300,170	9.1	26.1	42.3	55.4
Other assaults	329,934	27,185	64,375	97,474	140,959	8.2	19.5	29.5	42.7
Forgery and counterfeiting	30,751	189	1,429	5,790	11,241	0.6	4.6	18.8	36.6
Fraud	112,608	439	2,689	13,520	30,994	0.4	2.4	12.0	27.5
Embezzlement	4,727	46	390	1,305	2,086	1.0	8.3	27.6	44.1
Stolen property; buying, receiving, possessing	33,825	1,862	7,135	13,567	19,187	5.5	21.1	40.1	56.7
Vandalism	72,884	12,826	30,382	42,880	51,807	17.6	41.7	58.8	71.1
Weapons; carrying, possessing, etc.	38,959	3,185	8,824	15,838	22,357	8.2	22.6	40.7	57.4
Prostitution and commercialized vice	4,773	37	122	490	1,089	0.8	2.6	10.3	22.8
Sex offenses (except forcible rape and prostitution)	22,771	2,508	5,079	7,808	10,317	11.0	22.3	34.3	45.3
Drug abuse violations	372,988	7,816	50,450	129,134	196,902	2.1	13.5	34.6	52.8
Gambling	1,281	39	137	308	428	3.0	10.7	24.0	33.4
Offenses against the family and children	47,539	990	2,729	5,602	11,122	2.1	5.7	11.8	23.4
Driving under the influence	442,751	135	6,312	47,484	126,517	*	1.4	10.7	28.6
Liquor laws	176,569	3,980	45,995	140,053	151,562	2.3	26.0	79.3	85.8
Drunkenness	140,222	730	5,781	21,016	42,797	0.5	4.1	15.0	30.5
Disorderly conduct	174,655	24,016	57,901	81,949	106,163	13.8	33.2	46.9	60.8
Vagrancy	4,941	207	657	1,245	1,810	4.2	13.3	25.2	36.6
All other offenses (except traffic)	1,018,349	32,017	116,088	252,136	423,619	3.1	11.4	24.8	41.6
Suspicion	1,617	104	329	564	793	6.4	20.3	34.9	49.0
Curfew and loitering law violations	22,511	6,179	22,511	22,511	22,511	27.4	100.0	100.0	100.0
Runaways	32,548	11,406	32,548	32,548	32,548	35.0	100.0	100.0	100.0

[1] Suburban area includes law enforcement agencies in cities with less than 50,000 inhabitants and county law enforcement agencies that are within a Metropolitan Statistical Area (see Appendix III). Suburban area excludes all metropolitan agencies associated with a central city.
[2] Violent crimes are offenses of murder, forcible rape, robbery, and aggravated assault.
[3] Property crimes are offenses of burglary, larceny-theft, motor vehicle theft, and arson.
[4] Includes arson.
* Less than one-tenth of 1 percent.

Table 66

Arrests

Suburban Areas[1]
by Sex, 2002
[5,060 agencies; 2002 estimated population 85,923,394]

Offense charged	Number of persons arrested			Percent male	Percent female	Percent distribution[2]		
	Total	Male	Female			Total	Male	Female
TOTAL	**3,628,725**	**2,789,848**	**838,877**	**76.9**	**23.1**	**100.0**	**100.0**	**100.0**
Murder and nonnegligent manslaughter	2,660	2,290	370	86.1	13.9	0.1	0.1	*
Forcible rape	6,893	6,813	80	98.8	1.2	0.2	0.2	*
Robbery	20,577	18,397	2,180	89.4	10.6	0.6	0.7	0.3
Aggravated assault	110,807	89,568	21,239	80.8	19.2	3.1	3.2	2.5
Burglary	72,415	63,444	8,971	87.6	12.4	2.0	2.3	1.1
Larceny-theft	293,756	185,275	108,481	63.1	36.9	8.1	6.6	12.9
Motor vehicle theft	29,520	24,701	4,819	83.7	16.3	0.8	0.9	0.6
Arson	4,894	4,239	655	86.6	13.4	0.1	0.2	0.1
Violent crime[3]	140,937	117,068	23,869	83.1	16.9	3.9	4.2	2.8
Property crime[4]	400,585	277,659	122,926	69.3	30.7	11.0	10.0	14.7
Crime Index[5]	541,522	394,727	146,795	72.9	27.1	14.9	14.1	17.5
Other assaults	329,934	249,781	80,153	75.7	24.3	9.1	9.0	9.6
Forgery and counterfeiting	30,751	18,676	12,075	60.7	39.3	0.8	0.7	1.4
Fraud	112,608	60,734	51,874	53.9	46.1	3.1	2.2	6.2
Embezzlement	4,727	2,375	2,352	50.2	49.8	0.1	0.1	0.3
Stolen property; buying, receiving,								
possessing	33,825	27,756	6,069	82.1	17.9	0.9	1.0	0.7
Vandalism	72,884	61,605	11,279	84.5	15.5	2.0	2.2	1.3
Weapons; carrying, possessing, etc.	38,959	35,629	3,330	91.5	8.5	1.1	1.3	0.4
Prostitution and commercialized vice	4,773	2,150	2,623	45.0	55.0	0.1	0.1	0.3
Sex offenses (except forcible rape and								
prostitution)	22,771	21,573	1,198	94.7	5.3	0.6	0.8	0.1
Drug abuse violations	372,988	303,862	69,126	81.5	18.5	10.3	10.9	8.2
Gambling	1,281	1,035	246	80.8	19.2	*	*	*
Offenses against the family and children	47,539	37,449	10,090	78.8	21.2	1.3	1.3	1.2
Driving under the influence	442,751	363,493	79,258	82.1	17.9	12.2	13.0	9.4
Liquor laws	176,569	131,374	45,195	74.4	25.6	4.9	4.7	5.4
Drunkenness	140,222	118,735	21,487	84.7	15.3	3.9	4.3	2.6
Disorderly conduct	174,655	131,265	43,390	75.2	24.8	4.8	4.7	5.2
Vagrancy	4,941	4,097	844	82.9	17.1	0.1	0.1	0.1
All other offenses (except traffic)	1,018,349	793,434	224,915	77.9	22.1	28.1	28.4	26.8
Suspicion	1,617	1,258	359	77.8	22.2	*	*	*
Curfew and loitering law violations	22,511	15,275	7,236	67.9	32.1	0.6	0.5	0.9
Runaways	32,548	13,565	18,983	41.7	58.3	0.9	0.5	2.3

[1] Suburban area includes law enforcement agencies in cities with less than 50,000 inhabitants and county law enforcement agencies that are within a Metropolitan Statistical Area (see Appendix III). Suburban area excludes all metropolitan agencies associated with a central city.
[2] Because of rounding, the percentages may not add to 100.0.
[3] Violent crimes are offenses of murder, forcible rape, robbery, and aggravated assault.
[4] Property crimes are offenses of burglary, larceny-theft, motor vehicle theft, and arson.
[5] Includes arson.
* Less than one-tenth of 1 percent

Table 67

Arrests

Suburban Areas[1]
by Race, 2002
[5,058 agencies; 2002 estimated population 85,883,296]

Offense charged	Total arrests					Percent distribution[2]				
	Total	White	Black	American Indian or Alaskan Native	Asian or Pacific Islander	Total	White	Black	American Indian or Alaskan Native	Asian or Pacific Islander
TOTAL	**3,615,828**	**2,782,303**	**782,253**	**24,226**	**27,046**	**100.0**	**76.9**	**21.6**	**0.7**	**0.7**
Murder and nonnegligent manslaughter	2,655	1,634	979	18	24	100.0	61.5	36.9	0.7	0.9
Forcible rape	6,876	5,045	1,720	60	51	100.0	73.4	25.0	0.9	0.7
Robbery	20,546	10,929	9,394	100	123	100.0	53.2	45.7	0.5	0.6
Aggravated assault	110,549	81,098	27,590	783	1,078	100.0	73.4	25.0	0.7	1.0
Burglary	72,302	55,893	15,529	351	529	100.0	77.3	21.5	0.5	0.7
Larceny-theft	292,150	207,164	79,719	1,822	3,445	100.0	70.9	27.3	0.6	1.2
Motor vehicle theft	29,414	21,522	7,347	211	334	100.0	73.2	25.0	0.7	1.1
Arson	4,882	4,147	669	30	36	100.0	84.9	13.7	0.6	0.7
Violent crime[3]	140,626	98,706	39,683	961	1,276	100.0	70.2	28.2	0.7	0.9
Property crime[4]	398,748	288,726	103,264	2,414	4,344	100.0	72.4	25.9	0.6	1.1
Crime Index[5]	539,374	387,432	142,947	3,375	5,620	100.0	71.8	26.5	0.6	1.0
Other assaults	328,973	244,642	79,658	2,165	2,508	100.0	74.4	24.2	0.7	0.8
Forgery and counterfeiting	30,587	22,036	8,181	85	285	100.0	72.0	26.7	0.3	0.9
Fraud	112,207	76,367	34,920	311	609	100.0	68.1	31.1	0.3	0.5
Embezzlement	4,708	3,323	1,319	9	57	100.0	70.6	28.0	0.2	1.2
Stolen property; buying, receiving, possessing	33,774	22,664	10,586	176	348	100.0	67.1	31.3	0.5	1.0
Vandalism	72,582	60,410	11,125	480	567	100.0	83.2	15.3	0.7	0.8
Weapons; carrying, possessing, etc.	38,857	27,774	10,535	177	371	100.0	71.5	27.1	0.5	1.0
Prostitution and commercialized vice	4,765	3,390	1,183	24	168	100.0	71.1	24.8	0.5	3.5
Sex offenses (except forcible rape and prostitution)	22,724	18,589	3,818	102	215	100.0	81.8	16.8	0.4	0.9
Drug abuse violations	372,099	287,395	80,984	1,535	2,185	100.0	77.2	21.8	0.4	0.6
Gambling	1,281	777	451	1	52	100.0	60.7	35.2	0.1	4.1
Offenses against the family and children	47,287	33,653	13,215	210	209	100.0	71.2	27.9	0.4	0.4
Driving under the influence	441,014	397,403	37,794	2,743	3,074	100.0	90.1	8.6	0.6	0.7
Liquor laws	175,359	159,228	12,443	1,865	1,823	100.0	90.8	7.1	1.1	1.0
Drunkenness	139,943	125,140	12,608	1,483	712	100.0	89.4	9.0	1.1	0.5
Disorderly conduct	174,151	131,394	40,429	1,158	1,170	100.0	75.4	23.2	0.7	0.7
Vagrancy	4,938	3,193	1,691	18	36	100.0	64.7	34.2	0.4	0.7
All other offenses (except traffic)	1,014,702	731,850	268,447	7,881	6,524	100.0	72.1	26.5	0.8	0.6
Suspicion	1,595	1,040	545	3	7	100.0	65.2	34.2	0.2	0.4
Curfew and loitering law violations	22,386	17,940	4,094	137	215	100.0	80.1	18.3	0.6	1.0
Runaways	32,522	26,663	5,280	288	291	100.0	82.0	16.2	0.9	0.9

See footnotes at end of table.

Table 67

Arrests

Suburban Areas[1]

by Race, 2002—Continued

[5,058 agencies; 2002 estimated population 85,883,296]

Offense charged	Arrests under 18					Percent distribution[2]				
	Total	White	Black	American Indian or Alaskan Native	Asian or Pacific Islander	Total	White	Black	American Indian or Alaskan Native	Asian or Pacific Islander
TOTAL	600,579	469,669	121,133	3,949	5,828	100.0	78.2	20.2	0.7	1.0
Murder and nonnegligent manslaughter	194	112	82	0	0	100.0	57.7	42.3	*	*
Forcible rape	1,205	858	332	10	5	100.0	71.2	27.6	0.8	0.4
Robbery	4,502	2,110	2,331	19	42	100.0	46.9	51.8	0.4	0.9
Aggravated assault	15,575	10,838	4,451	134	152	100.0	69.6	28.6	0.9	1.0
Burglary	22,526	17,799	4,408	128	191	100.0	79.0	19.6	0.6	0.8
Larceny-theft	85,377	61,835	21,588	601	1,353	100.0	72.4	25.3	0.7	1.6
Motor vehicle theft	8,402	5,993	2,186	78	145	100.0	71.3	26.0	0.9	1.7
Arson	2,619	2,278	311	13	17	100.0	87.0	11.9	0.5	0.6
Violent crime[3]	21,476	13,918	7,196	163	199	100.0	64.8	33.5	0.8	0.9
Property crime[4]	118,924	87,905	28,493	820	1,706	100.0	73.9	24.0	0.7	1.4
Crime Index[5]	140,400	101,823	35,689	983	1,905	100.0	72.5	25.4	0.7	1.4
Other assaults	64,189	45,527	17,791	395	476	100.0	70.9	27.7	0.6	0.7
Forgery and counterfeiting	1,423	1,145	249	11	18	100.0	80.5	17.5	0.8	1.3
Fraud	2,679	1,725	918	6	30	100.0	64.4	34.3	0.2	1.1
Embezzlement	389	291	91	0	7	100.0	74.8	23.4	*	1.8
Stolen property; buying, receiving, possessing	7,117	4,632	2,329	45	111	100.0	65.1	32.7	0.6	1.6
Vandalism	30,265	26,197	3,654	164	250	100.0	86.6	12.1	0.5	0.8
Weapons; carrying, possessing, etc.	8,804	6,645	2,035	34	90	100.0	75.5	23.1	0.4	1.0
Prostitution and commercialized vice	122	76	43	1	2	100.0	62.3	35.2	0.8	1.6
Sex offenses (except forcible rape and prostitution)	5,062	4,029	990	14	29	100.0	79.6	19.6	0.3	0.6
Drug abuse violations	50,260	42,743	6,902	241	374	100.0	85.0	13.7	0.5	0.7
Gambling	137	65	72	0	0	100.0	47.4	52.6	*	*
Offenses against the family and children	2,718	2,159	541	6	12	100.0	79.4	19.9	0.2	0.4
Driving under the influence	6,279	5,988	220	37	34	100.0	95.4	3.5	0.6	0.5
Liquor laws	45,669	42,965	1,790	482	432	100.0	94.1	3.9	1.1	0.9
Drunkenness	5,775	5,389	297	56	33	100.0	93.3	5.1	1.0	0.6
Disorderly conduct	57,776	41,168	15,946	270	392	100.0	71.3	27.6	0.5	0.7
Vagrancy	656	512	137	3	4	100.0	78.0	20.9	0.5	0.6
All other offenses (except traffic)	115,622	91,726	21,999	775	1,122	100.0	79.3	19.0	0.7	1.0
Suspicion	329	261	66	1	1	100.0	79.3	20.1	0.3	0.3
Curfew and loitering law violations	22,386	17,940	4,094	137	215	100.0	80.1	18.3	0.6	1.0
Runaways	32,522	26,663	5,280	288	291	100.0	82.0	16.2	0.9	0.9

See footnotes at end of table.

Table 67

Arrests

Suburban Areas[1]
by Race, 2002—Continued
[5,058 agencies; 2002 estimated population 85,883,296]

Offense charged	Arrests 18 and over					Percent distribution[2]				
	Total	White	Black	American Indian or Alaskan Native	Asian or Pacific Islander	Total	White	Black	American Indian or Alaskan Native	Asian or Pacific Islander
TOTAL	**3,015,249**	**2,312,634**	**661,120**	**20,277**	**21,218**	**100.0**	**76.7**	**21.9**	**0.7**	**0.7**
Murder and nonnegligent manslaughter	2,461	1,522	897	18	24	100.0	61.8	36.4	0.7	1.0
Forcible rape	5,671	4,187	1,388	50	46	100.0	73.8	24.5	0.9	0.8
Robbery	16,044	8,819	7,063	81	81	100.0	55.0	44.0	0.5	0.5
Aggravated assault	94,974	70,260	23,139	649	926	100.0	74.0	24.4	0.7	1.0
Burglary	49,776	38,094	11,121	223	338	100.0	76.5	22.3	0.4	0.7
Larceny-theft	206,773	145,329	58,131	1,221	2,092	100.0	70.3	28.1	0.6	1.0
Motor vehicle theft	21,012	15,529	5,161	133	189	100.0	73.9	24.6	0.6	0.9
Arson	2,263	1,869	358	17	19	100.0	82.6	15.8	0.8	0.8
Violent crime[3]	119,150	84,788	32,487	798	1,077	100.0	71.2	27.3	0.7	0.9
Property crime[4]	279,824	200,821	74,771	1,594	2,638	100.0	71.8	26.7	0.6	0.9
Crime Index[5]	398,974	285,609	107,258	2,392	3,715	100.0	71.6	26.9	0.6	0.9
Other assaults	264,784	199,115	61,867	1,770	2,032	100.0	75.2	23.4	0.7	0.8
Forgery and counterfeiting	29,164	20,891	7,932	74	267	100.0	71.6	27.2	0.3	0.9
Fraud	109,528	74,642	34,002	305	579	100.0	68.1	31.0	0.3	0.5
Embezzlement	4,319	3,032	1,228	9	50	100.0	70.2	28.4	0.2	1.2
Stolen property; buying, receiving, possessing	26,657	18,032	8,257	131	237	100.0	67.6	31.0	0.5	0.9
Vandalism	42,317	34,213	7,471	316	317	100.0	80.8	17.7	0.7	0.7
Weapons; carrying, possessing, etc.	30,053	21,129	8,500	143	281	100.0	70.3	28.3	0.5	0.9
Prostitution and commercialized vice	4,643	3,314	1,140	23	166	100.0	71.4	24.6	0.5	3.6
Sex offenses (except forcible rape and prostitution)	17,662	14,560	2,828	88	186	100.0	82.4	16.0	0.5	1.1
Drug abuse violations	321,839	244,652	74,082	1,294	1,811	100.0	76.0	23.0	0.4	0.6
Gambling	1,144	712	379	1	52	100.0	62.2	33.1	0.1	4.5
Offenses against the family and children	44,569	31,494	12,674	204	197	100.0	70.7	28.4	0.5	0.4
Driving under the influence	434,735	391,415	37,574	2,706	3,040	100.0	90.0	8.6	0.6	0.7
Liquor laws	129,690	116,263	10,653	1,383	1,391	100.0	89.6	8.2	1.1	1.1
Drunkenness	134,168	119,751	12,311	1,427	679	100.0	89.3	9.2	1.1	0.5
Disorderly conduct	116,375	90,226	24,483	888	778	100.0	77.5	21.0	0.8	0.7
Vagrancy	4,282	2,681	1,554	15	32	100.0	62.6	36.3	0.4	0.7
All other offenses (except traffic)	899,080	640,124	246,448	7,106	5,402	100.0	71.2	27.4	0.8	0.6
Suspicion	1,266	779	479	2	6	100.0	61.5	37.8	0.2	0.5
Curfew and loitering law violations	–	–	–	–	–	–	–	–	–	–
Runaways	–	–	–	–	–	–	–	–	–	–

[1] Suburban area includes law enforcement agencies in cities with less than 50,000 inhabitants and county law enforcement agencies that are within a Metropolitan Statistical Area (see Appendix III). Suburban area excludes all metropolitan agencies associated with a central city.

[2] Because of rounding, the percentages may not add to 100.0.

[3] Violent crimes are offenses of murder, forcible rape, robbery, and aggravated assault.

[4] Property crimes are offenses of burglary, larceny-theft, motor vehicle theft, and arson.

[5] Includes arson.

* Less than one-tenth of 1 percent.

Table 68

Police Disposition
of Juvenile Offenders Taken into Custody, 2002
[2002 estimated population]

Population group	Total[1]	Handled within department and released	Referred to juvenile court jurisdiction	Referred to welfare agency	Referred to other police agency	Referred to criminal or adult court
TOTAL AGENCIES: 6,073 agencies; population 130,229,927						
Number	732,282	132,825	532,940	4,779	10,183	51,555
Percent[2]	100.0	18.1	72.8	0.7	1.4	7.0
TOTAL CITIES: 4,577 cities; population 92,489,061						
Number	611,897	115,191	444,336	3,956	7,901	40,513
Percent[2]	100.0	18.8	72.6	0.6	1.3	6.6
GROUP I						
32 cities, 250,000 and over; population 23,601,703						
Number	122,767	24,627	93,612	525	1,638	2,365
Percent[2]	100.0	20.1	76.3	0.4	1.3	1.9
GROUP II						
88 cities, 100,000 to 249,999; population 13,193,782						
Number	81,448	13,344	61,791	636	1,143	4,534
Percent[2]	100.0	16.4	75.9	0.8	1.4	5.6
GROUP III						
235 cities, 50,000 to 99,999; population 16,120,073						
Number	111,816	26,075	78,439	533	1,822	4,947
Percent[2]	100.0	23.3	70.2	0.5	1.6	4.4
GROUP IV						
405 cities, 25,000 to 49,999; population 14,310,637						
Number	94,913	17,183	68,483	1,187	1,769	6,291
Percent[2]	100.0	18.1	72.2	1.3	1.9	6.6
GROUP V						
896 cities, 10,000 to 24,999; population 14,336,965						
Number	105,574	18,232	74,556	553	670	11,563
Percent[2]	100.0	17.3	70.6	0.5	0.6	11.0
GROUP VI						
2,921 cities, under 10,000; population 10,925,901						
Number	95,379	15,730	67,455	522	859	10,813
Percent[2]	100.0	16.5	70.7	0.5	0.9	11.3
SUBURBAN COUNTIES						
568 agencies; population 25,198,464						
Number	86,648	13,068	64,180	478	1,745	7,177
Percent[2]	100.0	15.1	74.1	0.6	2.0	8.3
RURAL COUNTIES						
928 agencies; population 12,542,402						
Number	33,737	4,566	24,424	345	537	3,865
Percent[2]	100.0	13.5	72.4	1.0	1.6	11.5
SUBURBAN AREA[3]						
3,286 agencies; population 62,227,924						
Number	321,746	60,621	227,447	1,826	3,557	28,295
Percent[2]	100.0	18.8	70.7	0.6	1.1	8.8

[1] Includes all offenses except traffic and neglect cases.

[2] Because of rounding, the percentages may not add to 100.0.

[3] Suburban area includes law enforcement agencies in cities with less than 50,000 inhabitants and county law enforcement agencies that are within a Metropolitan Statistical Area (see Appendix III). Suburban area excludes all metropolitan agencies associated with a central city. The agencies associated with suburban areas also appear in other groups within this table.

Table 69

Arrests
by State, 2002
[2002 estimated population]

State	Total all classes[1]	Crime Index[2]	Violent crime[3]	Property crime[4]	Murder and non-negligent man-slaughter	Forcible rape	Robbery	Aggra-vated assault	Burglary	Larceny-theft	Motor vehicle theft	Arson	Other assaults	Forgery and counter-feiting	Fraud
ALABAMA: 279 agencies; population 3,782,265															
Under 18	11,861	3,912	592	3,320	26	36	231	299	486	2,650	163	21	1,990	50	57
Total all ages	195,820	25,619	6,730	18,889	300	370	1,709	4,351	2,849	14,691	1,242	107	27,883	2,028	11,392
ALASKA: 27 agencies; population 585,475															
Under 18	5,102	2,212	216	1,996	3	14	38	161	260	1,501	225	10	542	8	14
Total all ages	31,730	5,626	1,272	4,354	27	78	144	1,023	492	3,401	442	19	3,734	75	148
ARIZONA: 84 agencies; population 5,164,982															
Under 18	50,583	13,508	1,592	11,916	19	17	266	1,290	1,638	8,918	1,189	171	4,678	116	87
Total all ages	298,631	48,900	9,040	39,860	271	191	1,497	7,081	4,903	29,643	5,055	259	23,478	2,908	2,046
ARKANSAS: 93 agencies; population 1,404,187															
Under 18	9,410	2,517	272	2,245	1	8	56	207	284	1,890	63	8	542	35	46
Total all ages	107,467	11,877	2,903	8,974	48	93	443	2,319	1,234	7,333	349	58	4,436	1,111	7,247
CALIFORNIA: 681 agencies; population 34,678,046															
Under 18	227,266	66,812	15,351	51,461	216	344	4,455	10,336	14,498	29,248	6,610	1,105	22,459	558	688
Total all ages	1,412,566	298,772	128,951	169,821	1,865	2,541	16,838	107,707	48,759	92,024	27,177	1,861	84,562	13,226	10,351
COLORADO: 144 agencies; population 3,653,314															
Under 18	44,035	10,300	973	9,327	8	55	183	727	994	6,765	1,373	195	3,034	75	101
Total all ages	222,108	33,788	5,842	27,946	120	436	800	4,486	2,841	21,889	2,895	321	20,311	1,340	1,616
CONNECTICUT: 88 agencies; population 2,420,548															
Under 18	14,345	3,795	556	3,239	2	38	162	354	490	2,402	269	78	2,169	35	45
Total all ages	99,005	17,013	3,753	13,260	52	221	1,015	2,465	1,893	10,285	943	139	14,076	770	1,417
DELAWARE: 36 agencies; population 687,929															
Under 18	5,206	1,288	245	1,043	2	21	57	165	258	702	55	28	1,197	9	58
Total all ages	25,217	4,986	1,228	3,758	12	117	231	868	826	2,729	156	47	5,225	275	1,293
DISTRICT OF COLUMBIA:[6,7] 2 agencies;															
Under 18	277	62	23	39	0	0	13	10	2	8	29	0	14	0	0
Total all ages	4,303	140	63	77	0	0	26	37	2	34	41	0	72	0	1
FLORIDA:[8] 595 agencies; population 16,589,355															
Under 18	123,260	47,936	9,222	38,714	44	310	2,120	6,748	9,542	24,824	4,103	245	18,011	218	607
Total all ages	912,998	182,530	53,630	128,900	730	2,218	9,470	41,212	27,271	88,464	12,593	572	92,244	5,466	12,801
GEORGIA: 271 agencies; population 4,188,014															
Under 18	26,900	7,792	1,295	6,497	69	43	356	827	1,150	4,752	529	66	3,169	136	503
Total all ages	232,233	39,589	11,249	28,340	493	377	2,168	8,211	4,647	21,408	2,023	262	20,309	3,719	11,137
HAWAII: 2 agencies; population 960,506															
Under 18	9,850	1,997	292	1,705	0	13	167	112	158	1,344	193	10	898	11	15
Total all ages	45,929	6,970	1,148	5,822	26	122	432	568	569	4,028	1,201	24	3,103	460	390
IDAHO: 111 agencies; population 1,303,441															
Under 18	16,699	4,004	260	3,744	3	17	24	216	421	3,060	181	82	1,379	44	57
Total all ages	72,595	9,121	1,362	7,759	33	107	135	1,087	1,027	6,229	395	108	6,601	430	731

See footnotes at end of table.

Embezzlement	Stolen property; buying, receiving, possessing	Vandalism	Weapons; carrying, possessing, etc.	Prostitution and commercialized vice	Sex offenses (except forcible rape and prostitution)	Drug abuse violations	Gambling	Offenses against the family and children	Driving under the influence	Liquor laws	Drunkenness[5]	Disorderly conduct	Vagrancy	All other offenses (except traffic)	Suspicion	Curfew and loitering law violations	Runaways
0	182	393	128	0	24	938	6	4	170	791	112	1,102	11	1,536	0	132	323
27	2,157	2,396	1,364	187	395	14,100	95	1,390	13,869	6,503	9,715	3,808	324	72,113	0	132	323
1	2	306	58	2	52	460	0	18	110	314	2	91	0	909	0	0	1
9	24	866	351	58	193	1,639	2	333	4,720	1,144	51	798	1	11,957	0	0	1
39	168	2,786	422	39	325	4,547	2	427	597	5,037	0	3,349	64	5,889	0	3,152	5,351
228	1,619	9,158	2,974	1,948	1,844	29,167	13	2,844	41,417	24,896	0	16,669	754	79,265	0	3,152	5,351
2	164	136	99	2	32	496	0	40	150	261	263	789	99	2,152	123	912	550
146	904	607	1,148	327	380	6,960	40	1,166	9,781	1,649	8,943	3,343	630	44,420	890	912	550
159	3,552	12,804	6,799	431	2,933	23,043	72	8	1,564	4,828	4,020	11,861	297	40,717	0	16,960	6,701
1,969	18,111	27,501	24,849	12,257	15,944	254,829	562	631	178,548	25,310	99,546	17,293	4,514	300,130	0	16,960	6,701
18	217	1,814	608	16	439	3,070	5	136	553	4,324	7	3,232	13	8,846	14	2,844	4,369
141	865	6,379	2,134	1,361	1,415	15,921	10	2,585	23,039	17,436	367	14,160	824	71,188	15	2,844	4,369
5	37	692	217	14	95	1,329	1	83	96	311	0	2,525	1	2,629	1	157	108
147	278	1,978	1,009	527	531	11,851	25	1,193	6,425	1,376	6	12,590	33	27,494	1	157	108
20	69	310	181	0	4	332	0	7	0	418	8	623	0	661	0	21	0
225	219	793	806	125	32	1,541	1	201	184	1,792	205	1,593	126	5,574	0	21	0
0	5	6	14	0	0	9	0	0	0	5	0	59	0	103	0	0	0
1	13	14	35	0	0	92	0	0	28	1,385	49	180	104	2,189	0	0	0
56	497	2,922	1,777	70	469	12,808	51		546	1,848				35,444			
893	4,078	7,682	5,970	7,742	4,070	126,087	448		60,574	35,508				366,905			
8	365	403	508	32	362	2,166	29	199	284	793	131	2,923	79	5,780	58	408	772
215	3,647	1,541	3,445	1,551	3,066	27,266	517	3,273	23,836	7,646	4,377	16,458	1,244	58,025	192	408	772
3	13	277	36	5	91	438	29	107	29	98	0	30	0	1,769	0	286	3,718
46	196	692	285	430	409	2,097	231	1,454	2,312	531	0	290	0	22,029	0	286	3,718
3	73	925	185	0	113	827	0	30	293	1,753	20	596	0	3,541	0	767	2,089
79	290	1,691	609	2	382	5,385	0	412	9,888	5,122	209	2,227	14	26,546	0	767	2,089

Table 69

Arrests
by State, 2002—Continued
[2002 estimated population]

State	Total all classes[1]	Crime Index[2]	Violent crime[3]	Property crime[4]	Murder and non-negligent man-slaughter	Forcible rape	Robbery	Aggra-vated assault	Burglary	Larceny-theft	Motor vehicle theft	Arson	Other assaults	Forgery and counter-feiting	Fraud
ILLINOIS:[6] 1 agency; population 2,938,299															
Under 18	38,810	10,983	3,062	7,921	49	119	1,180	1,714	1,225	3,170	3,459	67	7,628	6	222
Total all ages	199,430	41,490	9,885	31,605	520	630	2,995	5,740	3,395	18,487	9,542	181	30,809	233	2,146
INDIANA: 149 agencies; population 4,227,126															
Under 18	33,841	8,426	1,681	6,745	15	39	209	1,418	847	5,309	511	78	2,417	47	64
Total all ages	196,964	32,336	10,730	21,606	250	222	1,403	8,855	3,174	16,504	1,771	157	11,160	1,162	1,979
IOWA: 192 agencies; population 2,665,086															
Under 18	20,944	6,587	731	5,856	8	25	81	617	748	4,707	298	103	2,567	79	52
Total all ages	112,438	18,840	4,198	14,642	47	112	413	3,626	2,021	11,830	639	152	10,307	1,041	1,482
KANSAS: 183 agencies; population 1,318,620															
Under 18	9,500	2,154	262	1,892	2	28	25	207	317	1,415	114	46	1,475	35	19
Total all ages	54,136	6,050	1,251	4,799	19	98	97	1,037	751	3,734	242	72	7,095	268	1,222
KENTUCKY:[6] 18 agencies; population 953,247															
Under 18	5,717	1,925	289	1,636	1	4	73	211	332	1,091	191	22	415	27	34
Total all ages	61,176	10,226	3,202	7,024	51	99	524	2,528	1,255	4,916	800	53	4,350	970	3,375
LOUISIANA: 153 agencies; population 3,185,679															
Under 18	35,560	9,132	1,550	7,582	21	95	242	1,192	1,597	5,601	287	97	4,916	39	41
Total all ages	216,444	39,138	10,157	28,981	288	512	1,282	8,075	5,339	22,164	1,256	222	27,582	1,360	3,138
MAINE: 180 agencies; population 1,291,128															
Under 18	9,277	2,968	140	2,828	0	24	39	77	577	2,022	192	37	1,149	19	43
Total all ages	54,880	8,171	787	7,384	5	126	170	486	1,477	5,436	403	68	7,364	319	1,132
MARYLAND: 139 agencies; population 3,197,675															
Under 18	25,518	7,229	1,119	6,110	3	45	362	709	1,233	4,097	595	185	4,419	23	27
Total all ages	161,317	24,028	5,497	18,531	85	263	1,220	3,929	3,366	13,284	1,570	311	20,209	612	2,700
MASSACHUSETTS: 239 agencies; population 4,660,489															
Under 18	17,395	5,576	2,098	3,478	5	42	385	1,666	736	2,354	347	41	2,030	45	49
Total all ages	114,657	26,930	11,348	15,582	79	384	1,545	9,340	2,791	11,760	923	108	14,269	795	1,106
MICHIGAN: 557 agencies; population 9,625,166															
Under 18	46,096	13,115	1,986	11,129	21	161	360	1,444	1,732	8,442	824	131	3,833	63	447
Total all ages	371,037	51,794	18,103	33,691	607	1,008	2,560	13,928	6,043	25,140	2,075	433	33,005	1,262	6,445
MINNESOTA: 302 agencies; population 4,155,118															
Under 18	42,874	10,997	906	10,091	17	141	116	632	990	8,391	604	106	3,135	148	219
Total all ages	164,144	26,316	3,697	22,619	73	614	457	2,553	2,516	18,614	1,329	160	13,576	1,805	4,760
MISSISSIPPI: 92 agencies; population 1,542,712															
Under 18	14,003	3,458	223	3,235	10	25	100	88	632	2,405	168	30	1,536	27	60
Total all ages	116,670	15,033	2,414	12,619	135	238	653	1,388	2,290	9,451	641	237	12,386	1,250	2,380
MISSOURI: 302 agencies; population 4,763,516															
Under 18	38,813	10,907	1,637	9,270	32	98	358	1,149	1,470	6,512	1,075	213	5,267	103	81
Total all ages	304,921	54,487	15,112	39,375	393	582	2,180	11,957	5,937	29,220	3,686	532	33,064	2,918	4,754

See footnotes at end of table.

Embezzlement	Stolen property; buying, receiving, possessing	Vandalism	Weapons; carrying, possessing, etc.	Prostitution and commercialized vice	Sex offenses (except forcible rape and prostitution)	Drug abuse violations	Gambling	Offenses against the family and children	Driving under the influence	Liquor laws	Drunkenness[5]	Disorderly conduct	Vagrancy	All other offenses (except traffic)	Suspicion	Curfew and loitering law violations	Runaways
0	0	1,916	1,311	62	164	8,665	597	14	56	397	0	3,252	0	3,537	0	0	0
0	0	5,225	5,046	5,584	2,108	54,205	2,317	434	5,910	1,050	0	19,215	0	23,658	0	0	0
1	1,214	1,131	172	2	228	2,266	7	318	277	3,252	500	2,553	40	5,911	48	1,247	3,720
7	4,516	2,198	1,662	1,127	1,299	18,278	233	1,495	26,347	11,685	16,173	8,000	364	51,717	259	1,247	3,720
15	50	1,493	111	0	103	1,248	0	8	319	2,557	253	1,403	0	2,956	0	738	405
161	221	3,033	583	378	340	10,218	6	604	13,151	12,099	8,351	4,759	54	25,667	0	738	405
9	52	536	54	0	84	716	0	18	289	1,332	1	658	0	995	0	0	1,073
44	263	1,376	244	28	228	4,691	0	210	10,684	5,211	216	2,383	0	12,850	0	0	1,073
0	223	174	60	7	23	664	13	3	53	194	150	393	0	956	5	82	316
96	865	747	662	332	267	8,681	42	1,370	5,941	1,469	4,959	2,184	2	14,235	5	82	316
0	444	1,406	276	8	258	2,072	22	329	131	387	89	5,178	56	7,049	74	1,396	2,257
54	2,409	4,287	1,572	403	1,342	21,634	144	2,038	12,309	3,294	3,960	16,393	608	70,998	128	1,396	2,257
1	75	709	46	3	43	763	4	9	134	810	8	211	0	1,911	0	144	227
19	328	1,869	304	40	252	4,861	55	369	6,797	3,597	31	1,683	0	17,318	0	144	227
24	42	1,292	500	17	254	2,989	11	16	283	1,246	0	960	29	5,327	56	86	688
217	200	2,436	1,657	226	856	15,755	31	1,836	19,762	5,376	4	3,430	96	61,024	88	86	688
3	285	754	163	22	57	1,958	1	136	134	1,077	268	1,281	3	3,129	45	7	372
35	1,359	2,481	949	936	531	13,828	16	2,050	9,215	3,565	6,072	5,917	12	23,944	268	7	372
120	980	1,544	622	26	377	3,740	14	18	957	6,387	37	1,317	20	9,016	0	1,339	2,124
1,372	6,312	4,204	5,233	1,820	1,717	34,586	183	5,589	50,022	29,145	612	10,947	337	122,989	0	1,339	2,124
0	478	2,014	422	1	317	3,028	3	15	822	6,497	0	3,226	9	6,728	0	2,658	2,157
8	1,443	4,043	957	59	1,081	13,387	23	499	26,922	25,703	0	9,737	83	28,927	0	2,658	2,157
18	108	303	145	0	42	1,028	34	231	166	425	242	2,015	13	2,838	38	874	402
693	690	1,226	841	87	395	11,969	373	3,861	11,897	3,132	6,786	8,233	112	33,967	83	874	402
13	332	2,286	532	12	436	3,217	3	273	567	1,827	61	1,995	62	6,217	1	1,749	2,872
124	2,380	8,760	4,099	1,275	2,923	34,797	276	5,217	34,276	11,293	2,142	13,822	654	83,033	6	1,749	2,872

Table 69

Arrests
by State, 2002—Continued
[2002 estimated population]

State	Total all classes[1]	Crime Index[2]	Violent crime[3]	Property crime[4]	Murder and non-negligent man-slaughter	Forcible rape	Robbery	Aggra-vated assault	Burglary	Larceny-theft	Motor vehicle theft	Arson	Other assaults	Forgery and counter-feiting	Fraud
MONTANA: 67 agencies; population 598,495															
Under 18	5,953	1,656	111	1,545	1	3	12	95	114	1,296	117	18	393	15	9
Total all ages	21,579	4,440	782	3,658	10	33	64	675	271	3,127	234	26	2,033	84	198
NEBRASKA: 224 agencies; population 1,570,139															
Under 18	15,772	4,404	198	4,206	4	11	85	98	332	3,561	231	82	1,649	57	102
Total all ages	93,355	11,970	1,333	10,637	42	149	332	810	953	9,075	490	119	9,434	820	1,868
NEVADA:[6] 3 agencies; population 1,540,614															
Under 18	12,489	4,072	390	3,682	9	19	210	152	451	2,765	432	34	1,366	3	57
Total all ages	115,128	18,783	2,761	16,022	85	172	1,142	1,362	3,943	10,186	1,833	60	14,278	316	2,520
NEW HAMPSHIRE: 113 agencies; population 819,288															
Under 18	7,165	1,146	115	1,031	0	12	17	86	187	757	61	26	823	7	77
Total all ages	34,348	2,896	518	2,378	5	64	93	356	421	1,792	124	41	4,523	118	860
NEW JERSEY: 525 agencies; population 8,312,552															
Under 18	62,093	13,027	3,309	9,718	22	123	1,261	1,903	1,914	6,978	558	268	5,902	74	112
Total all ages	368,619	51,333	15,268	36,065	253	640	4,203	10,172	6,344	27,716	1,566	439	31,167	1,722	5,101
NEW MEXICO: 53 agencies; population 1,187,172															
Under 18	9,201	2,181	461	1,720	7	24	52	378	235	1,340	133	12	915	19	30
Total all ages	76,539	8,677	3,014	5,663	81	130	361	2,442	926	4,304	392	41	5,584	367	493
NEW YORK:[6] 361 agencies; population 6,333,908															
Under 18	43,790	12,590	2,196	10,394	24	75	730	1,367	2,183	7,075	914	222	4,009	282	397
Total all ages	264,833	47,530	11,190	36,340	208	587	2,535	7,860	6,138	27,418	2,380	404	23,682	3,906	10,090
NORTH CAROLINA: 356 agencies; population 6,907,574															
Under 18	45,879	14,336	2,370	11,966	50	69	658	1,593	2,863	8,414	514	175	7,198	78	602
Total all ages	447,259	76,017	21,729	54,288	622	685	3,768	16,654	13,929	37,819	2,115	425	54,352	4,271	37,456
NORTH DAKOTA: 65 agencies; population 569,346															
Under 18	7,025	1,420	39	1,381	0	15	8	16	151	1,074	143	13	407	34	18
Total all ages	25,221	2,810	161	2,649	6	32	20	103	276	2,113	237	23	1,421	176	1,651
OHIO: 317 agencies; population 6,468,915															
Under 18	46,858	9,741	1,397	8,344	16	152	370	859	1,560	5,866	718	200	5,270	67	52
Total all ages	247,868	38,944	9,534	29,410	200	687	1,892	6,755	5,210	22,081	1,733	386	21,858	2,111	2,495
OKLAHOMA: 297 agencies; population 3,424,485															
Under 18	22,805	6,770	958	5,812	13	55	157	733	978	4,205	528	101	1,248	37	84
Total all ages	161,363	22,663	6,098	16,565	173	426	745	4,754	3,013	11,577	1,739	236	10,186	1,005	3,146
OREGON: 125 agencies; population 2,943,092															
Under 18	24,840	6,500	440	6,060	5	27	146	262	818	4,614	466	162	1,709	80	68
Total all ages	111,337	25,543	2,795	22,748	77	220	881	1,617	2,554	17,514	2,454	226	11,543	2,009	1,092
PENNSYLVANIA: 728 agencies; population 10,433,778															
Under 18	100,243	19,298	4,641	14,657	38	283	1,504	2,816	2,770	9,615	1,922	350	8,407	145	371
Total all ages	421,600	74,338	23,269	51,069	492	1,362	6,196	15,219	9,663	35,048	5,571	787	43,603	3,514	11,359

See footnotes at end of table.

Embezzlement	Stolen property; buying, receiving, possessing	Vandalism	Weapons; carrying, possessing, etc.	Prostitution and commercialized vice	Sex offenses (except forcible rape and prostitution)	Drug abuse violations	Gambling	Offenses against the family and children	Driving under the influence	Liquor laws	Drunkenness	Disorderly conduct	Vagrancy	All other offenses (except traffic)	Suspicion	Curfew and loitering law violations	Runaways
0	7	398	23	0	16	191	0	13	58	725	0	524	0	1,238	0	408	279
10	17	778	70	2	56	725	0	291	2,659	1,998	0	2,019	6	5,506	0	408	279
7	252	1,027	127	1	111	1,242	1	25	364	2,670	0	818	1	2,282	0	388	244
141	1,175	2,805	1,079	406	588	11,758	15	1,567	12,855	13,132	0	4,162	5	18,942	1	388	244
14	67	412	112	77	75	553	0	5	37	817	0	126	12	1,019	300	2,697	668
250	1,178	1,061	1,196	3,698	1,281	5,988	3	508	5,186	6,321	0	1,919	1,801	45,176	300	2,697	668
1	111	396	15	0	19	704	3	19	90	634	568	168	45	2,056	0	10	273
13	310	952	114	23	137	2,953	5	177	4,075	3,171	4,191	862	83	8,602	0	10	273
23	1,897	3,802	1,669	40	433	7,131	26	38	319	2,902	0	6,072	94	8,276	1	5,703	4,552
181	6,591	7,900	5,578	2,712	1,887	54,560	458	9,937	23,933	9,526	8	22,902	2,285	120,545	38	5,703	4,552
15	108	325	214	2	16	820	0	31	253	1,104	73	467	3	1,924	2	132	567
172	695	731	609	424	70	4,370	0	750	10,772	3,149	1,922	2,086	17	34,925	27	132	567
6	1,218	3,727	674	11	935	4,938	10	510	295	1,100	0	2,428	126	10,534	0	0	0
255	4,763	11,123	3,004	1,101	3,961	37,534	88	3,375	22,831	5,394	0	13,208	985	72,003	0	0	0
107	1,030	2,124	1,178	23	210	3,189	9	73	712	1,567	0	4,772	14	7,682	0	3	972
2,168	5,979	8,962	6,089	1,190	1,829	34,206	403	6,743	58,210	13,804	0	15,400	248	118,957	0	3	972
0	79	477	27	0	33	245	0	75	59	1,404	0	637	0	1,211	0	245	654
4	138	703	81	0	77	1,342	4	219	3,329	5,113	274	1,447	2	5,531	0	245	654
78	1,133	1,869	499	15	290	2,606	5	1,541	313	3,196	142	2,895	41	12,333	46	2,873	1,853
215	4,429	4,257	2,927	2,055	1,411	20,091	61	14,535	20,585	14,907	6,430	14,185	199	71,284	163	2,873	1,853
38	280	637	326	8	82	1,730	2	29	461	623	919	809	0	3,477	0	3,060	2,185
620	1,549	1,476	2,440	316	858	21,773	23	1,229	21,649	3,031	23,792	2,955	3	37,404	0	3,060	2,185
1	76	1,433	193	12	234	1,727	0	10	163	3,441	0	1,239	0	3,362	0	2,186	2,406
31	374	3,432	1,410	269	1,114	13,056	3	517	13,214	11,276	0	5,278	0	16,584	0	2,186	2,406
18	771	5,176	1,144	31	764	6,570	22	112	584	7,793	258	15,144	86	7,763	0	22,855	2,931
234	3,324	12,964	3,597	2,749	3,219	48,674	250	1,334	38,947	27,596	19,588	52,391	462	47,671	0	22,855	2,931

Table 69

Arrests

by State, 2002—Continued

[2002 estimated population]

State	Total all classes[1]	Crime Index[2]	Violent crime[3]	Property crime[4]	Murder and non-negligent man-slaughter	Forcible rape	Robbery	Aggra-vated assault	Burglary	Larceny-theft	Motor vehicle theft	Arson	Other assaults	Forgery and counter-feiting	Fraud
RHODE ISLAND: 47 agencies; population 1,046,290															
Under 18	7,681	1,902	284	1,618	7	22	70	185	317	1,054	161	86	927	3	21
Total all ages	42,140	6,034	1,259	4,775	27	123	254	855	842	3,458	366	109	5,524	144	963
SOUTH CAROLINA:[6] 109 agencies; population 2,223,424															
Under 18	15,696	4,804	1,000	3,804	19	59	155	767	716	2,817	217	54	2,961	57	130
Total all ages	120,025	20,597	6,613	13,984	171	317	873	5,252	2,552	10,651	647	134	15,291	1,507	19,520
SOUTH DAKOTA: 82 agencies; population 527,406															
Under 18	5,954	1,144	52	1,092	0	4	2	46	167	848	53	24	347	17	4
Total all ages	28,112	2,917	494	2,423	6	82	30	376	405	1,854	132	32	2,332	159	827
TENNESSEE: 337 agencies; population 4,936,496															
Under 18	26,686	5,963	1,065	4,898	11	48	192	814	704	3,735	409	50	3,134	64	131
Total all ages	234,995	36,020	11,267	24,753	284	332	1,224	9,427	3,566	18,797	2,113	277	24,283	2,407	10,770
TEXAS: 948 agencies; population 21,447,682															
Under 18	180,017	42,091	5,175	36,916	67	420	1,449	3,239	6,419	27,717	2,432	348	21,981	352	457
Total all ages	1,036,323	154,229	31,844	122,385	801	2,310	6,865	21,868	18,498	93,853	9,187	847	103,491	8,586	16,171
UTAH: 107 agencies; population 2,201,721															
Under 18	28,450	7,658	506	7,152	8	42	64	392	488	6,224	338	102	2,095	78	74
Total all ages	121,200	20,091	1,768	18,323	48	163	291	1,266	1,488	15,821	857	157	9,932	1,297	1,154
VERMONT: 48 agencies; population 532,178															
Under 18	1,851	489	29	460	0	8	0	21	108	298	50	4	262	15	31
Total all ages	13,757	1,826	334	1,492	9	62	2	261	305	1,054	114	19	1,430	152	491
VIRGINIA: 279 agencies; population 6,286,697															
Under 18	32,989	6,927	897	6,030	17	57	247	576	903	4,449	481	197	4,620	102	124
Total all ages	251,047	30,532	6,276	24,256	222	405	1,341	4,308	3,525	18,915	1,449	367	32,569	2,639	8,537
WASHINGTON: 208 agencies; population 5,108,516															
Under 18	38,772	13,456	1,370	12,086	9	167	388	806	1,943	9,038	900	205	5,538	146	58
Total all ages	237,512	42,765	7,133	35,632	102	837	1,541	4,653	5,088	27,988	2,195	361	30,789	2,581	1,376
WEST VIRGINIA: 249 agencies; population 918,517															
Under 18	1,739	566	51	515	1	2	7	41	99	353	53	10	191	5	11
Total all ages	25,781	3,508	848	2,660	25	37	56	730	481	1,939	198	42	3,650	229	685
WISCONSIN: 337 agencies; population 4,944,040															
Under 18	114,131	20,771	2,040	18,731	112	209	566	1,153	2,243	15,188	1,133	167	4,282	172	375
Total all ages	409,682	52,229	10,219	42,010	351	708	1,655	7,505	4,994	34,546	2,146	324	17,115	2,516	9,643
WYOMING: 62 agencies; population 487,292															
Under 18	6,231	1,039	63	976	0	3	5	55	105	824	36	11	504	5	10
Total all ages	34,060	3,281	619	2,662	8	58	41	512	354	2,129	119	60	2,640	138	233

[1] Does not include traffic arrests.

[2] Includes arson.

[3] Violent crimes are offenses of murder, forcible rape, robbery, and aggravated assault.

[4] Property crimes are offenses of burglary, larceny-theft, motor vehicle theft, and arson.

[5] Drunkenness is not considered a crime in some states; therefore, the figures vary widely from state to state.

[6] See Arrest Data, Appendix I, for details.

[7] Includes offenses reported by the Zoological Police and the Metro Transit Police. These agencies have no population associated with them.

[8] The arrest category all other offenses includes the arrest counts for offenses against the family and children, drunkenness, disorderly conduct, vagrancy, suspicion, and curfew and loitering law violations.

NOTE: Direct comparisons of arrest totals listed in this table made with prior years' issues should be made with caution as participation levels may vary. Additionally, some Part II offenses are not considered crimes in some states; therefore, figures may vary widely from state to state.

Embezzlement	Stolen property; buying, receiving, possessing	Vandalism	Weapons; carrying, possessing, etc.	Prostitution and commercialized vice	Sex offenses (except forcible rape and prostitution)	Drug abuse violations	Gambling	Offenses against the family and children	Driving under the influence	Liquor laws	Drunkenness[5]	Disorderly conduct	Vagrancy	All other offenses (except traffic)	Suspicion	Curfew and loitering law violations	Runaways
7	50	604	152	2	31	638	0	460	27	166	15	627	0	1,588	117	39	305
123	237	1,567	477	384	113	4,077	26	684	1,933	1,066	190	2,872	6	15,156	220	39	305
14	220	615	348	12	144	1,562	0	110	41	396	60	2,021	0	1,837	0	36	328
267	1,349	2,103	1,304	448	510	13,945	87	928	3,596	3,712	4,073	7,523	146	22,755	0	36	328
3	23	177	49	1	23	387	0	69	87	1,354	13	370	0	1,148	0	227	511
30	80	429	105	3	214	2,303	3	233	4,100	6,000	265	1,352	8	6,014	0	227	511
24	67	716	452	12	143	2,026	27	53	217	1,302	376	3,421	0	4,337	0	1,950	2,271
429	517	2,755	2,611	1,876	643	21,769	160	904	25,350	6,519	18,589	9,765	46	65,361	0	1,950	2,271
69	165	5,434	1,635	88	932	14,356	51	597	1,307	6,586	4,400	18,584	62	32,241	31	11,505	17,093
602	835	12,017	10,898	6,879	4,500	101,266	364	5,711	89,750	32,069	131,896	36,727	1,993	289,700	41	11,505	17,093
6	236	1,499	303	4	339	1,628	0	43	206	2,967	133	2,195	174	6,428	1	1,572	811
18	933	3,328	1,297	276	789	8,654	6	1,361	7,847	12,723	5,113	6,021	188	37,788	1	1,572	811
2	28	151	9	0	4	198	0	9	37	216	0	156	0	244	0	0	0
31	134	382	11	2	27	1,510	0	335	3,038	719	3	833	4	2,829	0	0	0
55	142	1,171	508	4	247	2,589	3	20	240	1,809	281	1,267	0	6,483	0	2,503	3,894
1,122	845	3,901	3,114	417	1,012	22,288	30	756	21,664	9,242	21,426	5,231	97	79,228	0	2,503	3,894
16	705	2,203	547	34	289	2,949	1	7	538	4,184	11	648	12	4,807	80	57	2,486
145	3,965	6,289	2,657	1,268	1,466	23,824	8	268	34,671	13,668	28	4,524	44	60,017	4,616	57	2,486
3	14	91	21	0	3	116	0	0	26	162	12	6	0	464	0	37	11
50	133	498	246	87	84	1,624	0	63	4,052	1,146	1,588	344	1	7,745	0	37	11
36	996	4,833	1,349	17	1,631	5,162	101	264	675	12,260	75	21,687	49	26,700	80	8,281	4,335
231	2,308	12,044	4,453	1,103	3,919	24,259	331	4,071	34,483	42,587	393	71,285	146	113,681	269	8,281	4,335
0	14	248	45	0	17	488	0	12	71	1,315	21	345	4	1,489	50	429	125
11	113	592	127	2	138	2,730	2	166	4,368	4,571	1,265	1,424	13	11,633	59	429	125

SECTION V

Bank Robbery in the United States

Introduction

According to the Uniform Crime Reporting (UCR) Program, robbery is the taking or attempting to take anything of value from the care, custody, or control of a person or persons by force or threat of force or violence and/or by putting the victim in fear. The focus of this study, bank robbery, is a subtype of robbery targeted at banks. Because of this element of force or the threat of force, bank robbery is highly feared among the population.[1]

Some view robbery in the context of violence; others maintain that robbery offenders come from a subculture of theft.[2] Sometimes it is difficult to separate the two. The UCR Program classifies robbery as a crime against property and includes robbery in its violent crime total.

A bank robbery is indicated when the crime is robbery and the location is a financial institution. UCR-National Instant-Based Reporting System (NIBRS) standards state that the victims in a robbery can be either persons or entities, i.e., businesses, financial institutions, etc., or both.[3] In a bank robbery, the primary victim is the bank itself, but the teller being threatened or injured is also a victim.

A computation of UCR Summary data showed that a bank robbery occurred just under every 52 minutes in 2001, accounting for 2.4 percent of all robbery in the United States.[4] This represented a total loss of approximately $70 million. While this seems like a large amount of money taken, the average amount of money taken in a bank robbery over the period 1996 through 2000, according to NIBRS data is less than $5,000.

The crime of robbery showed a clearance rate of only 24.9 percent in 2001. The clearance for bank robbery was 57.7 percent in 2001.[5] This is a relatively high clearance rate when compared with that of other Part I crimes.[*] Only murder, at 62.4 percent, has a higher percentage of crimes cleared by arrest.

Even with such a high clearance rate, bank robbery remains prevalent. Bank robbery has been the subject of many studies.[6] Because of the number of incidents, the amount of money taken, and the fear engendered in the public, bank robbery is a serious problem in the United States. Dr. Yoshio Akiyama of the FBI addressed this question in 1983 in the *Crime Indicators System, Fourth Semiannual Briefing on Crime*. That study used a 10-year time series to show the prevalence and characteristics of bank robbery incidents, a profile of offenders, and an analysis of the length of time from the incident until clearance.

The present study will update and extend parts of that earlier study.

Objectives

The general objective of this study is to examine three different criminal justice databases maintained by the FBI. Their similarities and differences are pointed out and discussed with the purpose of producing a fuller picture of bank robbery than that created when using only one of these databases. A further and no less important objective is to provide some assessment of the NIBRS bank robbery data by comparing it with the Bank Crime Statistics database, even though the collection methods, the scope, and content of these databases are different.

To address these objectives, a time series from the Bank Crime Statistics (BCS), collected by the Violent Crimes/Fugitive Unit of the FBI, covering the period 1973 to 2001 was generated and compared to the time series for Summary UCR data and to NIBRS data. NIBRS data on bank robbery incidents used for this analysis is for 1996-2000. Although Summary data have been collected by the FBI since 1930, its comprehensiveness concerning bank robbery is limited. Therefore, only the crime counts and estimates from 1990 through 2001 were examined for comparison to BCS data from the same period.[†]

The study questions in this analysis are designed to compare and contrast the databases on the subject of bank robbery as it is reported to the FBI and are divided into two areas, characteristics of the incident and characteristics of the offender(s).

Further, this study will discuss the general compatibility of the Summary UCR data, the historical BCS database, and bank robbery incidents identified in the NIBRS. By using data from all three of these databases it will be possible to present a fuller picture of the crime of bank robbery in the United States and how it is reported.

Study Question 1— Characteristics of the Incident

The level of analysis here is the incident itself. Variables that describe the incident, such as the number of bank robbery incidents per year, the state, the region, the time of day and day of the week, the violence—deaths, injuries, hostages taken—and the type of weapons used are addressed in question 1.

Study Question 2—Offenders

Question 2 concerns the offender characteristics. What is the age, sex, and race of the offender (or offenders)? What is the average number of offend-

---

* Part I crimes are murder and nonnegligent manslaughter, forcible rape, robbery, aggravated assault, burglary, larceny-theft, motor vehicle theft, and arson. The first seven of these crimes make up the Crime Index. The Modified Crime Index consists of all eight Part I crimes.

† See Data & Methodology Section for a more complete discussion of the databases discussed in this section.

ers per incident? What is the previous bank robbery experience of offenders?

Data and Methodology

Data for the study come from three sources.

The UCR Program's data collections for the years 1990 and 2001. (Summary data)

The UCR Program is a law enforcement initiative that gives an annual depiction of crime in the United States. It is a nationwide cooperative statistical effort of over 17,000 city, county, and state law enforcement agencies that voluntarily report data on crimes that have been reported to them. The FBI has collected Summary data since 1930 with little change in the type of data collected and disseminated. Today, law enforcement agencies active in the UCR Program cover approximately 93.4 percent of the population of the United States.

The UCR's NIBRS data from 1996-2000

The NIBRS is the redesigned, expanded version of the Summary UCR system. NIBRS data differ from Summary data in that the NIBRS contains data on each single incident and arrest. While the Summary data are individual counts of seven Part I crimes, NIBRS collects data on 22 crime categories. Incident, offense, victim, offender, and arrest data are collected on each incident reported by a law enforcement agency. NIBRS is a richer, disaggregated database than the Summary database that can be used to enhance law enforcement and crime research as well as strategic and administrative decision-making. A limited number of agencies began submitting NIBRS data to the FBI's UCR Program in January 1989.

The BCS data collected by the FBI from 1970-2001

In 1934 Congress enacted the Bank Robbery and Incidental Crimes Statute, making it a federal crime to rob any national bank or state member bank of the Federal Reserve System. This statute was expanded to include bank burglary and bank larceny and similar crimes committed against federally-insured savings and loan associations and Federal credit unions. The investigative jurisdiction under this statute has been delegated to the FBI, which today investigates a bank crime concurrently with local law enforcement.[7]

The Violent Crimes/Fugitive Unit of the FBI has collected descriptive data on bank robberies since 1970. This is a database that FBI Special Agents in the 56 field offices use when investigating bank robberies. The variables concern the incident, the solution, the mode of operation, and offender characteristics. Although these data are primarily meant to be used as an investigative tool to clear the particular crime, much of the data contained in the BCS can be used for quantitative research as well. These data can be used alone by the researcher or in concert with other statistical databases, specifically, the NIBRS database, to present a fuller rendering of the bank robbery incident.

The BCS database contains a more comprehensive representation of the U.S. population than the NIBRS database. It also includes several incident-level elements not included in the

---

Figure 5.1

Number of Bank Robbery Incidents Reported in BCS Database and the Summary UCR, 1990–2001

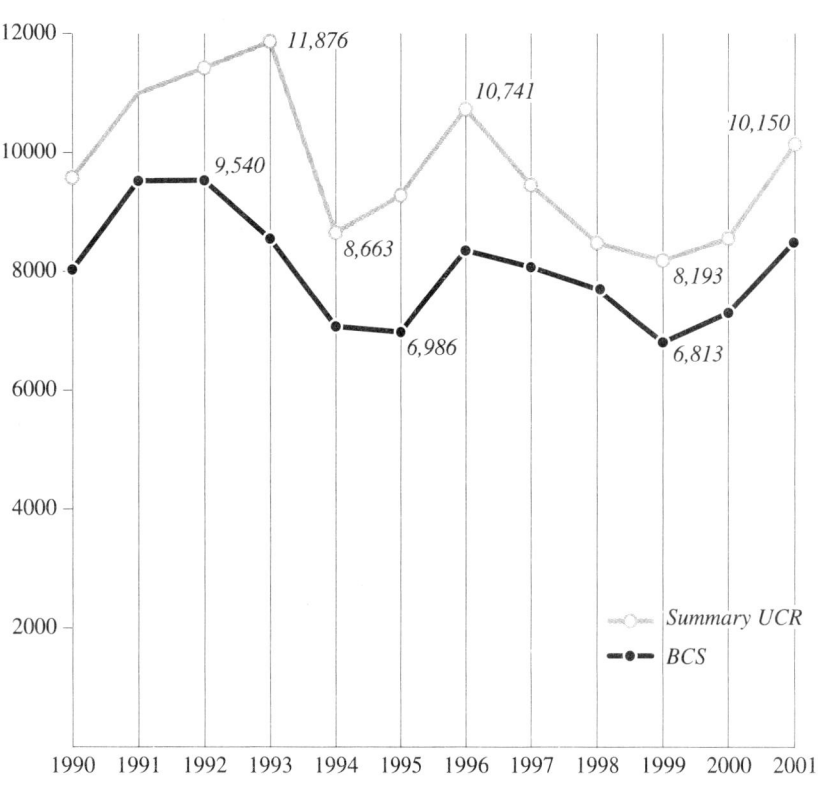

Table 5.1

Number of Bank Robbery Incidents Reported in BCS Database and the Summary UCR, 1990–2001

Year	BCS	Summary UCR
1990	8,042	9,589
1991	9,532	11,004
1992	9,540	11,432
1993	8,561	11,876
1994	7,081	8,663
1995	6,986	9,289
1996	8,362	10,741
1997	8,082	9,461
1998	7,711	8,486
1999	6,813	8,193
2000	7,310	8,565
2001	8,516	10,150

NIBRS. These are institution type, facility type, modus operandi, solution rates (analogous to clearance rates in the UCR Program definitions), types of security devices present in the incident, disguises used by the perpetrator(s), information on hostages that may have been taken, and the contents of any robbery notes.

Since the focus of BCS is a subset of all bank robberies collected by the UCR Program, care must be exercised when BCS statistics show deviations from those of Summary/NIBRS statistics. The definitions in the BCS data differ from those established by the UCR Program. It will be seen, however, that the two sets of statistics show striking similarities.

Methods

Frequency distributions and graphs are used to explore the consistencies and unique aspects of the databases to address the Study Questions.

Findings

Incident characteristics

Although the amount of money taken overall in any given year may seem high, approximately $70 million according to the BCS data for the period 1996 through 2000, the average amount netted from an individual bank robbery is less than $8,000 (BCS). The NIBRS data, covering less population than BCS, indicate an average of less than $5,000 per incident.

BCS reports the amount of money recovered is quite small. Over the period 1996-2000, $469,815,218.10

was reported as being taken and only $94,407,085.90 was recovered. This is only a 20 percent recovery rate.

Number of incidents

Table 5.1 shows the number of bank robbery incidents reported in the Summary UCR Program and in the BCS database of the FBI from 1990 through 2001. Figure 5.1 graphs the same data and makes the pattern easier to see. There was a substantial increase in the early 1990s, followed by an even more substantial decrease in the mid-1990s. Through 1999, the overall trend was down, but beginning in 2000 there was an upturn. The Summary UCR data always shows a greater number of incidents than the BCS database. There are two reasons for this. The first is measurement error, present in any data collection. The second reason may be

Table 5.2

Number of Bank Robbery Incidents,

NIBRS Data and BCS by State and Region, 2000

Region, State	BCS robberies 2000	NIBRS robberies 2000	Region, State	BCS robberies 2000	NIBRS robberies 2000
Southern			**Northeastern**		
(South)			**(Northeast)**		
Alabama	77		Connecticut	41	26
Arkansas	18	1	Massachusetts	156	47
DC	12		Maine	4	
Delaware	24		New Hampshire	15	
Florida	559		New Jersey	140	
Georgia	175		New York	304	
Kentucky	66	2	Pennsylvania	339	
Louisiana	87		Rhode Island	13	
Maryland	174		Vermont	13	7
Mississippi	64		**Regional Total**	**1,025**	**80**
North Carolina	288		**Regional %**	**14.18**	**7.70**
Oklahoma	31				
South Carolina	122	164	**Midwestern**		
Tennessee	138	127	**(North central)**		
Texas	342	32	Iowa	50	44
Virginia	149	161	Illinois	181	
West Virginia	17	23	Indiana	137	
Regional Total	**2,343**	**510**	Kansas	49	14
Regional %	**32.41**	**49.04**	Michigan	328	181
			Minnesota	88	
Western			Missouri	96	
(West)			North Dakota	1	1
Alaska	3		Nebraska	47	3
Arizona	184		Ohio	402	89
California	1,291		South Dakota	3	
Colorado	149	79	Wisconsin	115	
Hawaii	37		**Regional Total**	**1,497**	**332**
Idaho	12	16	**Regional %**	**20.71**	**31.92**
Montana	4				
New Mexico	54		**GRAND TOTAL**	**7,289**	**1,040**
Nevada	178				
Oregon	150				
Utah	47	23			
Washington	314				
Wyoming	1				
Regional Total	**2,424**	**118**			
Regional %	**33.53**	**11.35**			

Figure 5.2

**Bank Robbery Incidents by Day of the Week,
NIBRS Data and BCS, 1996–2000, in percent**

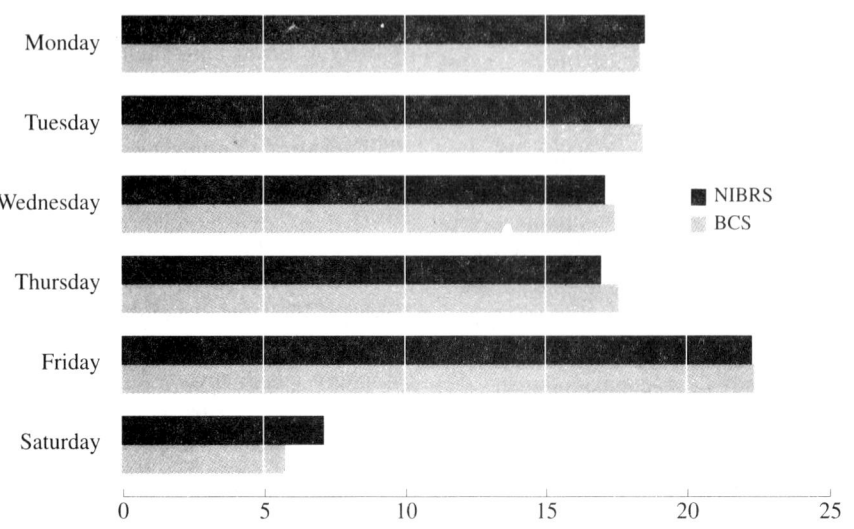

Table 5.4

Time of Day of Bank Robbery Incidents, NIBRS Data & BCS, 1996–2000

	NIBRS	NIBRS Percent	BCS	BCS Percent
6 AM - 8:59 AM	87	3.4	1,018	2.66
9 AM - 10:59 AM	711	28.0	10,955	28.65
11 AM - 12:59 PM	518	20.4	8,902	23.28
1 PM - 2:59 PM	502	19.8	8,710	22.78
3 PM - 5:59 PM	601	23.7	7,911	20.69
6 PM - 8 PM	119	4.7	741	1.94
Total	2,538	100.0	38,237	100.00

Figure 5.3

**Time of Day of Occurrence of Bank Robbery Incident,
NIBRS Data and BCS, 1996–2000, in percent**

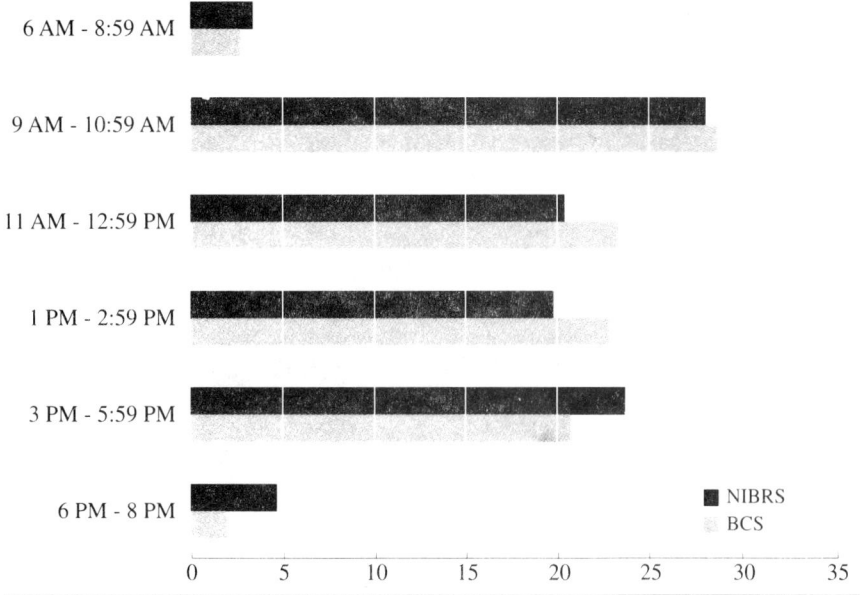

Table 5.3

**Bank Robbery Incidents by Day of
the Week, NIBRS Data and BCS,
1996–2000 (in percentages)**

Day	NIBRS	BCS
Monday	18.53	18.36
Tuesday	17.99	18.46
Wednesday	17.10	17.45
Thursday	16.96	17.59
Friday	22.29	22.37
Saturday	7.13	5.77
Total	100.00	100.00

because of the different, but overlapping, missions of the two databases. The Summary UCR number consists of all bank robbery incidents reported to the Program by local law enforcement. The BCS data includes bank robbery incidents reported to the Violent Crimes/Fugitive Unit of the FBI by the individual FBI field offices. Only in incidents where the FBI has investigative jurisdiction are the field offices required to collect and report data. FBI field offices do not report crime statistics to the UCR Program. Summary UCR data should contain these BCS incidents reported to UCR by the state or local law enforcement entity collaborating with the FBI on the investigation of the incident. Additionally, Summary data include incidents in which the FBI had no jurisdiction and, thus, no role. Therefore, the FBI became involved in the investigation of approximately 85 percent of all bank robbery incidents reported in the United States in 2000.

Although the time series of BCS is considered to reflect bank robbery trends in the Nation, the undulations in the number of bank robberies are also a result of the FBI involvements in the bank robbery investigations. The two time series track each other quite closely as we would expect. When one is moving downward, the other is moving downward as well, and when one turns up, so does the other.

Participation in the NIBRS has been more volatile over the period of the system's existence than either the Summary UCR or BCS participation over this same period of time. With only 17 percent of the U.S. population covered in 2000, the NIBRS reported 1,040 bank robberies. Summary UCR data showed approximately 8,565 bank robberies reported to the UCR Program by police agencies. The BCS recorded 7,310 bank robbery incidents with FBI involvement. A comparison of NIBRS data to Summary data to BCS data of this type is not meaningful. The Summary data and BCS data will drown out NIBRS data. However, other comparisons may be more fruitful between NIBRS and BCS data.

Regional breakdown

Table 5.2 shows a regional breakdown for NIBRS and BCS bank robberies in 2000. The UCR Program defines four regions in the United States and calls them Northeastern, Midwestern, Southern, and Western. The BCS also places states into four regions called Northeast, North Central, South, and West. The states in the UCR regions Northeastern, Southern, and Western are placed in the BCS regions Northeast, South, and West, respectively. The BCS region, North Central, contains the states that the UCR Program defines as Midwestern.

The percentages of bank robberies within the regions correspond somewhat between the two databases. Monotonically, they track from a low in the Northeastern, then the Midwestern, or North Central, through the South. The Western, or West region, is the odd one here, with the NIBRS showing it with only 11.3 percent of the bank robberies in 2000, while the BCS shows it with 33.3 percent. These disparities are due to the absence of major cities' participation in the NIBRS. It may also be that even though the Western region contains

13 states, only three of these report NIBRS data. Further, at least two of these three, Idaho and Utah, have small populations and thus would be expected to have fewer bank robberies. Moreover, California alone has more than one-half of the bank robberies in the entire 13-state region reported to BCS. California's 1,291 bank robbery incidents in 2000 are more than twice its closest competitor, Florida, and more than the entire Northeastern region. California drives the numbers in the Western region but is not represented in the NIBRS. On the other hand, 9 of 16 (17 when the District of Columbia is included) states in the Southern [South] region report NIBRS data. Further, 8 of 12 states in the Midwestern [North Central] region are NIBRS states.

Day of the week

Table 5.3 and Figure 5.2 show different presentations of the same data—bank robbery incidents by day of the week. The data are presented as percentages, i.e., the percentage of bank robberies reported in the NIBRS that happen on Sunday, on Monday, etc., and the same for the BCS data. In this way we can begin to make some comparisons between the two databases even though the difference in the absolute number of bank robberies in the two databases is quite high. The striking finding here is how closely the data in the two programs coincide. In both data series, Friday is the day on which most bank robbery incidents occur. Substantively, this may be because Friday has historically been payday for much of the United States and, thus, has required large deliveries of cash to branch banks. This may still be the case even in the modern world of electronic banking with direct deposit of paychecks and bill-paying either as an automatic withdrawal, by posted check, or over the Internet.

The second most prevalent days are Monday and Tuesday. The NIBRS reports a few more incidents on Monday than on Tuesday and BCS reports the opposite. Still, these differences are

Table 5.5

BCS Incidents Involving Shooting

Year	Incidents	Shooting	Percent
1996	8,362	172	2.06
1997	8,082	155	1.92
1998	7,711	159	2.06
1999	6,813	119	1.75
2000	7,310	132	1.81

Table 5.6

BCS Incidents Involving Firearms, 1996–2000

Year	Incidents involving firearms	Percentage of incidents in which firearm used	Incidents involving handguns	Percentage of incidents in which handgun used	Total incidents
1996	2,707	32.37	2,571	30.75	8,362
1997	2,718	33.63	2,539	31.42	8,082
1998	2,505	32.49	2,385	30.93	7,711
1999	2,047	30.05	1,953	28.67	6,813
2000	2,190	29.96	2,105	28.80	7,310
Total	12,167	31.79	11,553	30.18	38,278

Table 5.7

NIBRS Incidents Involving Firearms, 1996–2000

Year	Incidents involving firearms	Percentage of incidents in which firearm used	Incidents involving handguns	Percentage of incidents in which handgun used	Total incidents
1996	127	47.57	109	40.82	267
1997	206	46.29	156	35.06	445
1998	312	50.49	252	40.78	618
1999	312	46.43	238	35.42	672
2000	525	51.12	411	40.02	1,027
Total	1,482	48.93	1,166	38.49	3,029

negligible and speak well for the integrity of the NIBRS data.

Most bank robberies from 1996 through 2000 happened on workdays, Monday through Friday, with very few occurring on the weekend. The NIBRS reports that workdays accounted for 89.83 percent of bank robbery incidents, while in the BCS the percentage was 93.85 percent for the period.

Time of day

Both the NIBRS data and the BCS data show that the time period during which most bank robberies occur is 9 a.m. until 11 a.m. Table 5.4 and Figure 5.3 present the time of occurrence of bank robberies reported in the NIBRS and BCS from 1996 through 2000 as a percentage of bank robbery incidents reported. The prominent detail presented here is the clear similarity of the two databases on this variable.

Weapons, violence, injury, and other crimes

One obvious reason for an individual to engage in bank robbery is economic where the motive is to obtain money. Another is that because of the low amounts of cash actually stolen per robbery, bank robbers are interested in projecting a persona of violence.[8] Whichever is the case, the threat of violence is always present. Information on weapons used in the commission of a bank robbery, violence, injuries sustained, and other crimes is contained in the NIBRS data as well as the BCS data. The percentage involving an actual shooting reported in BCS is around 2 percent. Table 5.5 shows this percentage over the 1996–2000 period. BCS data displayed in Table 5.6 show that over this period, a firearm was present in about 32 percent of all bank robbery incidents. In almost all of those cases, 30 percent overall, that firearm was a handgun.

Table 5.7 presents NIBRS firearms data. Over the period 1996–2000, NIBRS reports firearms (including handguns) use in 49 percent of the 3,029 bank robbery incidents reported. Handguns were used in 38.5 percent of NIBRS incidents in which a firearm was used over the period.

It may be surprising that only between one-third and one-half of bank robbery incidents involve firearms. The perception one would tend to get from television or the movies is that a bank robber would never attempt a holdup without a firearm—and the more the better.

Table 5.8 holds another surprise. The incidence of violence and injury is very low. NIBRS data show that violence occurred in only 2.34 percent of incidents and BCS shows 4.84 percent over the time period. Given the low

---

Table 5.8

Percent of Bank Robbery Incidents Involving Violence, Injury, and Other Crimes, NIBRS Data & BCS, 1996–2000

Incidents Involving	NIBRS Incidents	Total NIBRS	Percent*	BCS Incidents	Total BCS	Percent*
Injury	169		5.58	764		2.00
Violence	71		2.34	2151		5.62
Explosives/Explosions	60		1.98	1557		4.07
Kidnapping/Hostages	49		1.62	230		0.60
Assault	19		0.63	1285		3.36
Murder	5		0.17	34		0.09
Total NIBRS Incidents		3,029				
Total BCS Incidents					38,278	

* Will not add to 100% because some incidents involved more than one other crime or weapon.

Figure 5.4

Race of Bank Robbers in Percentage, NIBRS Data and BCS, 1996–2000

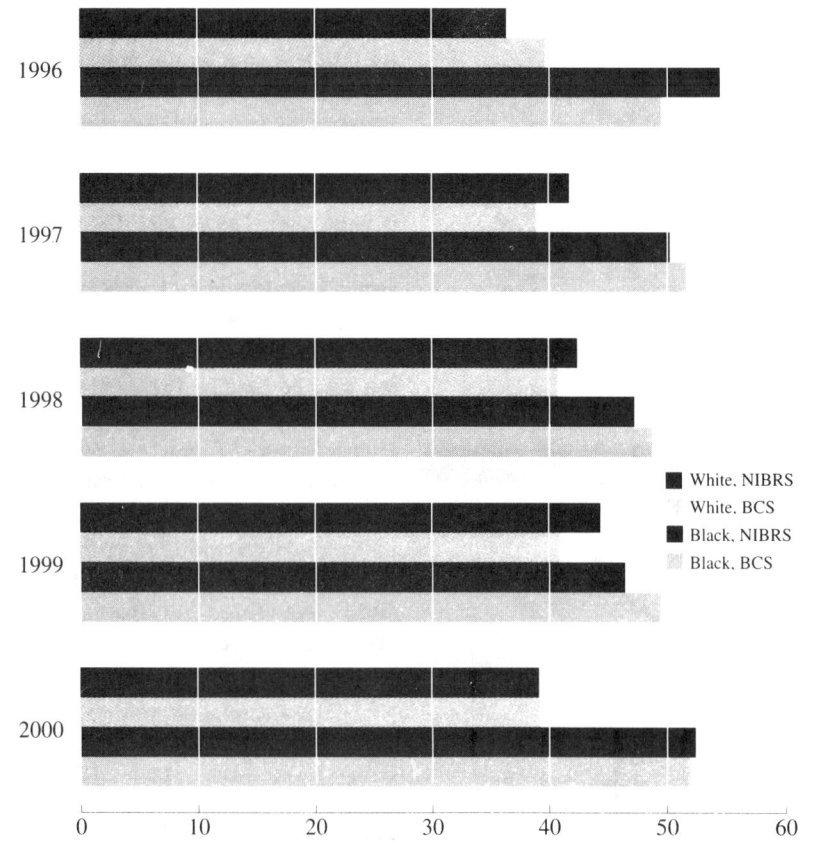

---

rates of violence, it should not be unexpected that the injury levels displayed in Table 5.8 are also quite low—5.58 percent for NIBRS data and 2.00 percent for BCS.

Regarding other crimes present in the incident, murder is very low at less than 1.0 percent in both databases, as are kidnapping and hostage-taking. Both NIBRS data and BCS data show that kidnapping/hostage-taking occurs in less than 2.0 percent of reported bank robberies.

Overall, the percentages in the table are close with neither database showing wildly divergent numbers; however, the numbers are so small for the NIBRS that we cannot take total comfort in the only-slight discrepancies the two databases show on these variables.

Offender characteristics

Despite what may be the popular perception, most bank robbery incidents, 79.9 percent in the NIBRS data over the period 1996–2000, were carried out by only one offender. Another

15 percent involved two offenders. Thus, over 95 percent of all the bank robbery incidents reported were attempted by two or fewer offenders.

Race

Bank robbery offenders may not be as many or as varied as one might at first think. Using NIBRS and BCS data, we can analyze their race, and sex, and using NIBRS data we can examine age. Figure 5.4 shows the race of bank robbers from NIBRS data and BCS from 1996 through 2000 as a percentage of all offenders. There are similar patterns evident in the figure. Whites account for between 35 and 45 percent of all offenders in each of the years. Both NIBRS and BCS data bear this out and overall show the same level. Black offenders are responsible for between 45 percent and 55 percent over the period. If we average offenders by race over the 5 years, there is virtually no difference with whites averaging 40.84 percent in the NIBRS data and 39.45 percent in the BCS data. Similarly, the percentage of black offenders in the NIBRS data is very close to that in the BCS at 50.14 percent and 50.26 percent, respectively.

Sex

There is a great disparity between the number of male bank robbery offenders and the number of female offenders in both the NIBRS and the BCS databases. However, there is very little discrepancy when comparing the percentage of male offenders in NIBRS data to that in BCS and when comparing the number of female offenders. Figure 5.5 shows both of these comparisons. Male offenders are shown in dark red (NIBRS) and light red (BCS) and female offenders are shown in either black (NIBRS) or gray (BCS). In both databases, over 95 percent of the offenders are males, and less than 5 percent are females.

The percentage of male offenders in both NIBRS data and BCS is virtually the same. Table 5.9 shows the percentages of offenders that are identified as male in NIBRS data and BCS as well

Table 5.9

Percentage of Offenders in NIBRS Data and BCS, by Sex, 1996–2000

	1996	1997	1998	1999	2000
Male - NIBRS	94.79	94.55	94.66	92.53	92.75
Male - BCS	95.56	94.83	94.41	94.75	93.99
Female - NIBRS	5.21	5.45	5.34	7.47	7.25
Female - BCS	4.44	5.17	5.59	5.25	6.01

Figure 5.5

Sex of Bank Robbers as Percentages, NIBRS Data and BCS, 1996–2000

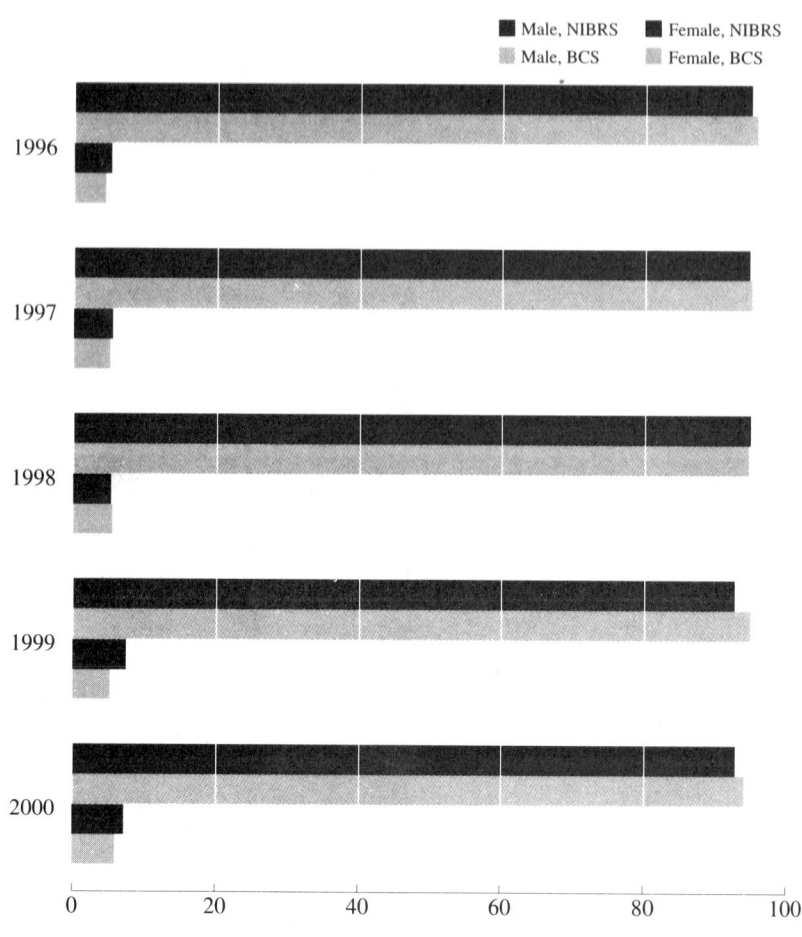

as the percentage identified as females. There is a strong correspondence between the two databases here.

Age

Figure 5.6 displays the age and gender of offenders reported to the NIBRS from 1996–2000. The same information is contained in Table 5.10. Nearly 20 per-cent of all offenders are male, between the ages of 18 and 24. Males, aged 25–29 account for another 14 percent. Summing the two groups, we see that one-third of all bank robbery offenders are between 18 and 29 years of age. This is all the more astonishing because there are 703 offenders contained in the denominator that are either unknown or listed as missing data. If we drop the unknown and missing data from the denominator and recalculate the percent-age, we find that 41.7 percent of bank robbery offenders reported in NIBRS data are 18–29-year-old males.

An examination of only male offenders shows these two age groups account for more then 45 percent of all male bank robbery offenders. Figure 5.6 shows a clear pulse in the late teens and early twenties that damps down in every subsequent age group.

Females show the same general pattern except that the numbers of female bank robbery offenders is much smaller than that of males.

Age, race, and sex are combined and presented in Table 5.11. The same patterns are visible in this table as shown earlier and separately. There are more males than females in every age group. There are more black males than white males in younger age groups and more white males than black in older (>35) age groups. There are more white females than black females. The number of Asian/Pacific Islanders and American Indians/Alaskan Natives are presented but are too small to analyze.

Prior bank robbery convictions

In *Crime Indicators System, Fourth Semiannual Briefing on Crime* (1983), Akiyama discussed the bank robber classifications of "professional" and "amateur." His discussion was based on a previous FBI report from 1977 that divided bank robbers into these cate-

Figure 5.6

Age and Gender of Offender, NIBRS Data, 1996–2000, in percent

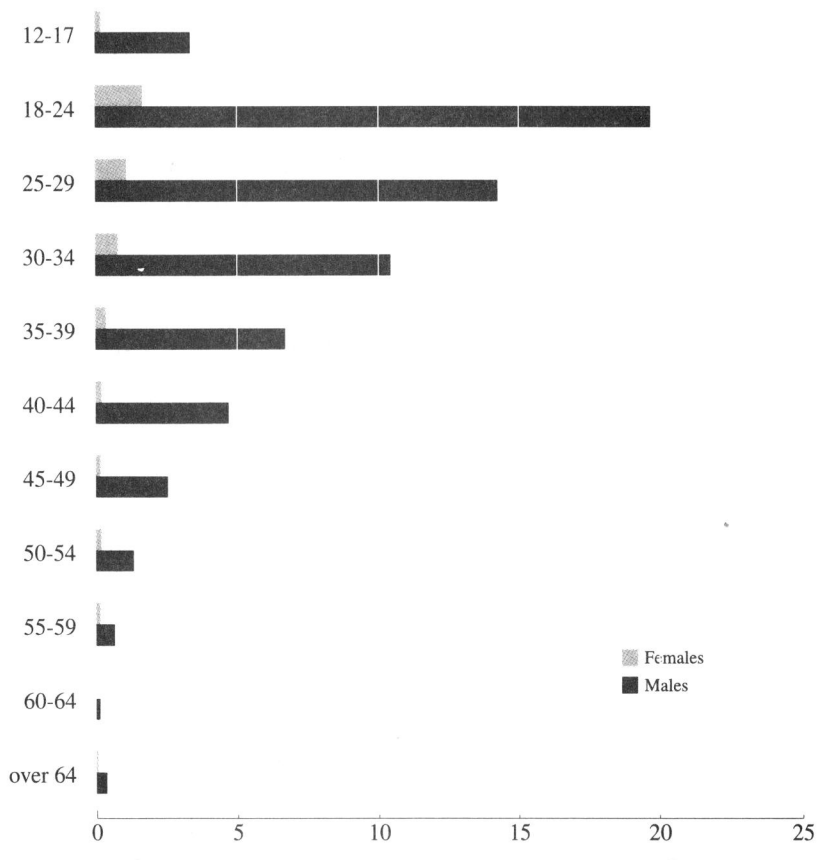

Table 5.10

Age and Gender of Offender, NIBRS Data, 1996–2000

Age	Female	Female %	Male	Male %	Unknown	Unknown %	Missing Values	Missing Values %	Total
12–17	8	0.21	131	3.39	1	0.03		0.00	140
18–24	65	1.68	766	19.80	5	0.13		0.00	836
25–29	42	1.09	554	14.32	7	0.18		0.00	603
30–34	31	0.80	406	10.49	4	0.10		0.00	441
35–39	14	0.36	261	6.75		0.00		0.00	275
40–44	8	0.21	183	4.73	1	0.03		0.00	192
45–49	6	0.16	99	2.56		0.00		0.00	105
50–54	7	0.18	51	1.32	8	0.21		0.00	66
55–59	5	0.13	25	0.65	1	0.03		0.00	31
60–64		0.00	5	0.13		0.00		0.00	5
over 64	2	0.05	14	0.36	1	0.03		0.00	17
Unknown	16	0.41	467	12.07	167	4.32	508	13.13	1,158
Total	204	5.27	2,962	76.56	195	5.04	508	13.13	3,869

gories. A "professional" in this classification scheme is a bank robber with a prior criminal record, despite his or her lack of success as evidenced by his/her incarceration. This professional is a bank robbery specialist. The "amateur" bank robber is a bank robber with no prior record. The amateur is presented as acting almost on a whim. The bank robbery to the amateur is almost a spur-of-the-moment undertaking with the robber engaging in very little planning. This individual robs banks to get the means to fulfill some more fundamental need, such as the need for drugs. Table 5.12 displays BCS data concerning the number and percent of subjects taken into custody for bank robbery who already have a conviction for bank robbery, bank burglary, bank larceny, or bank extortion. From 1996–2000, the average percent of "professional" bank robbers is 20 percent. This was more than the average in the earlier period from 1978–1982. Over that time period the average percent of "professional" bank robbers was 14 percent. This is still a clear indication that the great majority of bank robbers are amateurs and have not been convicted of a bank crime in the past.

Limitations

There are several limitations to this study. Although Summary data have been collected by the FBI since 1930 and cover virtually the entire population of the United States, their comprehensiveness concerning bank robbery is limited. The only information available is the number of bank robberies, the percent of total robberies that that number represents, region of occurrence, bank robberies by population group, month of occurrence, and the amount of money taken in the aggregate. It is not possible to disaggregate Summary data to the individual incident.

Some bank robberies may not be captured in the database because of the Hierarchy Rule that limits reporting of only that crime in the incident that is highest in the "hierarchy" of Part I crimes as defined by the UCR Program. Both murder and rape are higher on this ordering of crimes than robbery. Therefore, if a bank robbery included a murder, the only crime entered into the Summary database is the murder. This would also be the case for a rape occurring within the bank robbery incident. Only the rape would be recorded and the bank robbery would be lost information.

Table 5.11

Age, Race, and Sex of Offender, NIBRS Data, 1996–2000

Sex/Age of Offender		Race of Offender					
		Asian/ Pacific Islander	Black	American Indian/ Alaskan Native	Unknown Race	White	Total
Total Unknown Age, Sex, and Race							508
Female	12–17					8	8
	18–24		26			39	65
	25–29		22			20	42
	30–34		13			18	31
	35–39		6			8	14
	40–44		2			6	8
	45–49		1			5	6
	50–54		2			5	7
	55–59		1			4	5
	over 64		1			1	2
	unknown age		5		2	9	16
Total Female			79		2	123	204
Male	12–17		92		2	37	131
	18–24	5	465	1	8	287	766
	25–29		327		15	212	554
	30–34		221		6	179	406
	35–39	1	103		3	154	261
	40–44		61		1	121	183
	45–49		36	1	3	59	99
	50–54		15		1	35	51
	55–59		9		1	15	25
	60–64					5	5
	over 64		5			9	14
	unknown age	1	262		65	139	467
Total Male		7	1,596	2	105	1,252	2,962
Unknown sex							
	12–17					1	1
	18–24				5		5
	25–29		2		4	1	7
	30–34				4		4
	40–44				1		1
	50–54		1		7		8
	55–59				1		1
	over 64				1		1
	unknown age				163	4	167
Total unknown sex			3		186	6	195

Further, the bank robbery totals are collected on the form entitled Supplement to the Monthly Return of Offenses Known To The Police (Return A), but not on the Return A itself. If the supplement is not submitted, a robbery on the Return A cannot be counted as bank robbery. Thus, it may be the case that some robberies listed on the Return A and, therefore, in *Crime in the United States*, are bank robberies and are not captured in the Summary data.

Even though the NIBRS has distinct benefits as a data source, it is limited in its scope. Currently, agencies from 24 states, representing 17 percent of the U.S. population, participate in the program. These data lack the cross-sectional representation of incidents and cannot be treated as a sample. There are no cities participating that have populations greater than 1 million inhabitants. There are only 11 cities or consolidated counties that contribute NIBRS data whose population is more than 250,000. With this limitation, NIBRS data may not represent the crime experience in the entire United States.

Like the Summary UCR and NIBRS data, the BCS database also has its limitations. Only robberies of banks and financial institutions covered under the Bank Robbery and Incidental Crime Statute and its progeny are included. Further, the NIBRS includes, but BCS does not, specific information on each victim, offender, and arrestee. Finally, BCS is an investigative system; consequently the data are not available for use by the public.

Summary and Conclusions

The objective of depicting bank robbery from the data collected by the FBI has been met. Further, this realization of bank robbery through the use of these data has been an opportunity to compare and contrast elements in the databases—particularly the NIBRS data and the BCS data. These are preliminary findings and require further study.

The presentation of incident characteristics has emphasized the similarity of data submitted to the FBI's NIBRS program by local and state law enforcement to that submitted to the Violent Crimes/Fugitive Unit of the FBI by the separate FBI field offices. Both Summary UCR data and BCS indicate the same trends in the numbers of bank robberies over a 12-year period, 1990–2001.

Further, NIBRS data showing days of the week on which the greatest number of bank robberies occur and the hours during which they are most prevalent are very similar to BCS data, with Friday mornings generally the modal day and time for bank robberies.

In both databases, violence and injury are very low, an unexpected finding since one element of the crime is force or the threat of force. The similarity between the two databases concerning this unanticipated result adds further validation to the quality of NIBRS data.

Evidence of offender race and gender is also quite comparable between the two databases, with the number of whites committing bank robbery reported in NIBRS data very close to the number reported in BCS and the same for blacks. Reported gender of bank robbers is virtually identical in both databases.

Presenting the age data reported in NIBRS shows that a plurality of bank robberies are committed by offenders between 18 and 30 years of age.

Offenders are clearly amateurs and not bank robbery specialists as evidenced by the low number with previous convictions for a bank crime shown in the BCS statistics. That bank robberies do not involve the meticulously planned caper carried out by a group of highly experienced criminals is further borne out by the significant number of incidents involving only one or two offenders. NIBRS and BCS data show that the money obtained in a bank robbery is low, especially considering the amount of physical risk and the high probability of apprehension involved for the offender.

The money recovered is also not a very high percentage of that stolen. Both databases bear this out. This indicates that Akiyama (1983) was correct in his conclusion that most of these amateur bank robbers committed the crime to fulfill some more immediate need. More research is required, particularly into the aspect of drugs associated with this crime.

These findings are interesting and have significant implications for policymakers. This study and other research, such as which banks are most likely to be robbed, and which are more likely to be robbed more than once, in addition to spatial analyses adding variables such as location of the bank relative to escape routes, entrances to freeways, traffic patterns, location of nearest police station, etc., will allow law enforcement policymakers to develop better, more effective strategies for use in dealing with bank robberies.

The present study is also good news for the NIBRS program. The NIBRS has only 24 states that participate covering 17 percent of the population. Nevertheless, the percentages on

Table 5.12

Prior Bank Robbery Convictions, BCS, 1996–2000

Year	Subjects previously convicted		Subjects not previously convicted		Total	
	Number	Percent	Number	Percent	Number	Percent
1996	1,127	21.04	4,230	78.96	5,357	100.0
1997	917	18.03	4,169	81.97	5,086	100.0
1998	964	19.40	4,005	80.60	4,969	100.0
1999	912	20.75	3,483	79.25	4,395	100.0
2000	957	20.79	3,646	79.21	4,603	100.0
Total	4,877	19.98	19,533	80.02	24,410	100.0

the NIBRS variables examined here clearly accord with the percentages reported in the BCS. This should assure those who do not yet participate in the NIBRS program that they may reap large benefits from becoming a contributor to the Program.

Finally, since 9/11 the government has realized that information-sharing is a powerful tool with which to fight lawlessness. Databases such as those examined here should be examined to derive the maximum information toward this end.

[1] Garofalo, J. 1977. Public Opinion About Crime: The Attitudes of Victims and Nonvictims in Selected Cities. Washington, DC: USGPO.

[2] Wolfgang, M.E. and F. Ferracuti. 1967. The Subculture of Violence. London: Tavistock; Normandeau, A. 1968. "Patterns in Robbery," Criminoligica.

[3] U.S. Department of Justice. Federal Bureau of Investigation. (December 1999). NIBRS, Volume 1: Data Collection Guidelines, Washington D.C.: The Government Printing Office, p. 33.

[4] U.S. Department of Justice. Federal Bureau of Investigation. Crime in the United States, 2001, Washington D.C.: The Government Printing Office.

[5] Bank Crime Statistics Data, 2001.

[6] Baumer, T. and M. Carrington, 1986. The Robbery of Financial Institutions. U.S. Department of Justice; Tavistock; Normandeau, A. 1968. op. cit.; Katz, J. 1991. "The Motivation of the Persistent Robber." In Michael Tonry (Ed.), Crime and Justice: A Review of Research (Vol. 14, pp. 277–306). Chicago: University of Chicago Press.

[7] Crime Indicators System, Fourth Semiannual Briefing on Crime, 1983. Federal Bureau of Investigation.

[8] Katz, J. 1991. op. cit.

Special Report
Reported Sniper Attacks, 1982–2001

Introduction

For 23 days in October 2002, the world was shocked by media reports of attacks in and around the Nation's capital—a Metropolitan Statistical Area of nearly five million inhabitants—resulting from the actions of snipers. The first six victims were killed within the first 27 hours of the ordeal. By the end of the 23 days, 10 people would be dead, three others injured, and two men would be in police custody. (Cannon, A. and staff of U. S. News and World Report, (2003). *23 Days of Terror*. New York: Pocket Books.)

Because of the nationwide interest in sniper attacks and the terror the attacks in the fall of 2002 wreaked on the people living in the Washington, D.C. metropolitan area, the FBI's Uniform Crime Reporting (UCR) Program decided to look at the data law enforcement agencies throughout the United States submitted to the Program for the past 20 years and prepare a report summarizing that data. Several limitations to these data must be stated so that one can put this report in perspective. First, it must be noted that the data in this report are limited to those sniper attacks reported by law enforcement agencies participating in the UCR Program. Further, there is no uniform definition of sniper attack for law enforcement to follow, so the interpretation of this circumstance is left to the agency's discretion. The sniper-attack designation is a circumstance available on the Supplementary Homicide Report (SHR), a form law enforcement agencies voluntarily submit for the offense of murder only. Consequently, the UCR database does not contain those instances of sniper attacks in which the victim survived. Finally, even though there are other circumstances on the SHR from which the reporting agency can select, the agency is limited to reporting only one. It may be that a sniper attack occurred in conjunction with another circumstance, for example a romantic triangle or a gangland killing, and the agency selected that other circumstance to report, not the sniper attack.

Caution is urged when trying to draw any conclusions from the data presented in this report. The data are presented as a compilation of statistics and are of informational value only. The statistics in this report include only those instances in which 1) sniper attack was selected as the circumstance, 2) the victim was killed, and 3) the weapon reported by the agency on the SHR was a firearm.

Purpose of Report

The report presents the information submitted on the SHR about the characteristics involved in homicide incidents limited to murder by sniper attack with a firearm. Specifically, this report looks at:

1. the number of sniper attack incidents with a firearm involving murder, the number of victims, and the number of instances in which at least one characteristic (age, sex, race) of the offender was reported.

2. the number of incidents by situation.

3. the number of incidents by firearm type.

4. the number of incidents by geographical region of the United States.

Table 5.13

Sniper-attack Murder Incidents, Victims, and Offenders, 1982-2001

Year	Number of Incidents	Number of Victims	Offenders[1]
Total	327	379	224
1982	12	15	8
1983	17	17	8
1984	18	37	16
1985	10	10	5
1986	9	9	4
1987	28	36	17
1988	47	55	32
1989	46	49	28
1990	40	41	24
1991	10	12	5
1992	31	33	14
1993	6	6	3
1994	2	2	5
1995	11	12	6
1996	8	8	13
1997	4	4	1
1998	10	15	15
1999	5	5	4
2000	8	8	5
2001	5	5	11

[1] This represents the number of instances in which the age, sex, and/or race of the offender was reported by law enforcement.

Table 5.14

Sniper-attack Murder Incidents by Year and Situation, 1982-2001

Year	Total	Single Victim			Multiple Victims		
		Single Offender	Multiple Offenders	Unknown Offender(s)	Single Offender	Multiple Offenders	Unknown Offender(s)
Total	327	102	39	165	12	3	6
1982	12	5	0	5	1	1	0
1983	17	8	0	9	0	0	0
1984	18	9	1	5	3	0	0
1985	10	3	1	6	0	0	0
1986	9	4	0	5	0	0	0
1987	28	9	3	13	2	0	1
1988	47	13	6	25	1	0	2
1989	46	12	6	25	0	1	2
1990	40	13	5	21	1	0	0
1991	10	4	0	5	1	0	0
1992	31	5	4	20	1	0	1
1993	6	3	0	3	0	0	0
1994	2	0	2	0	0	0	0
1995	11	5	0	5	1	0	0
1996	8	2	4	2	0	0	0
1997	4	1	0	3	0	0	0
1998	10	0	2	6	1	1	0
1999	5	1	1	3	0	0	0
2000	8	5	0	3	0	0	0
2001	5	0	4	1	0	0	0

5. the number of incidents by population group.

6. the characteristics (age, sex, and race) of the victims and offenders when at least one characteristic is known.

7. the victim-to-offender relationship.

Focus of Report

This report focuses on incidents of criminal homicide in which the law enforcement agency has reported the circumstance as sniper attack in which the weapon was a firearm. Any murders involving a sniper in which the weapon was reported as something other than a firearm were excluded. For this report, 20 years (1982 to 2001) of SHR data were examined in order to acquire specific information regarding the victim, offender, their relationship, the weapon used, and the circumstance surrounding those incidents. The race categories considered in this report are the standard UCR categories of White, Black, Asian/Pacific Islander, and American Indian/Alaskan Native and unknown. Agencies submitting data on the SHR identify the age, sex, and/or race of the offender, if it is known. If none of these characteristics of the offender can be identified, the offender is, obviously, unknown. The selection of firearm categories available to law enforcement on the SHR are firearm, type not stated; handgun (pistol, revolver, etc.); rifle; shotgun; and other/unknown gun. The data in the tables are limited to those reported to UCR by law enforcement on the SHR.

Table 5.15

Sniper-attack Murder Incidents
by Year and Firearm Type, 1982–2001

Year	Total[1]	Firearm (type not stated)	Handgun (pistol, revolver, etc.)[3]	Rifle[3]	Shotgun	Other/Unknown Gun
Total	327	19	208	75	23	3
1982	12	2	6	2	2	0
1983	17	2	7	4	4	0
1984	18	0	7	7	4	0
1985	10	0	5	5	0	0
1986	9	2	1	6	0	0
1987	28	2	12	12	2	0
1988	47	0	32	9	6	0
1989	46	0	37	8	1	0
1990	40	4	29	4	3	0
1991	10	0	7	3	0	0
1992	31	2	26	3	0	0
1993	6	0	4	2	0	0
1994	2	0	1	0	0	1
1995	11	0	6	2	1	2
1996	8	3	4	1	0	0
1997	4	0	4	0	0	0
1998	10	0	7	3	0	0
1999	5	0	5	0	0	0
2000	8	0	7	1	0	0
2001	6	2	1	3	0	0

[1] In 2001, one incident involved more than one weapon type.

Table 5.16

Sniper-attack Murder Incidents
by Year and Region, 1982–2001

Year	Total	Northeast[1]	Midwest[2]	South[3]	West[4]
Total	327	35	83	60	149
1982	12	1	2	6	3
1983	17	1	4	6	6
1984	18	3	3	1	11
1985	10	1	2	3	4
1986	9	2	1	3	3
1987	28	3	1	4	20
1988	47	0	3	4	40
1989	46	1	0	2	43
1990	40	2	22	4	12
1991	10	1	4	4	1
1992	31	1	29	1	0
1993	6	0	2	3	1
1994	2	0	2	0	0
1995	11	0	5	6	0
1996	8	2	0	6	0
1997	4	2	0	2	0
1998	10	5	0	4	1
1999	5	1	1	0	3
2000	8	7	0	1	0
2001	5	2	2	0	1

[1] Includes incidents reported by Connecticut, Maine, Massachusetts, New Jersey, New York, and Pennsylvania.
[2] Includes incidents reported by Illinois, Indiana, Michigan, Minnesota, Missouri, Ohio, and Wisconsin.
[3] Includes incidents reported by Alabama, Arkansas, Florida, Georgia, Kentucky, Louisiana, Maryland, Mississippi, North Carolina, Oklahoma, South Carolina, Tennessee, Texas, Virginia, and West Virginia.
[4] Includes incidents reported by Alaska, Arizona, California, Colorado, New Mexico, Oregon, Utah, Washington, and Wyoming.

Discussion

Incidents

During the 20-year period from 1982 to 2001, law enforcement agencies contributing data to the UCR Program submitted supplemental information on 364,648 homicides in the United States. According to data from the SHRs from 1982 to 2001, there were a total of 327 incidents involving murder during a sniper attack in which the weapon was a firearm, or 0.1 percent of the 20-year total of 364,648 homicides for which supplementary data were received. Within those 327 incidents, there were 379 victims and 224 instances in which the age, sex, and/or race of the offender was identified. Law enforcement agencies nationwide reported as few as 2 incidents in 1994 and as many as 47 incidents in 1988 that fit the aforementioned criteria. (See Table 5.13.)

Single sniper victim incidents accounted for 306, or 93.6 percent, of the total incidents. Of the 306 single sniper victim incidents, most (53.9 percent) were committed by an unknown offender, 33.3 percent by a single offender, and the remaining by multiple offenders. Of the 21 incidents that involved multiple victims, 57.1 percent involved a single offender. (See Table 5.14.)

All but 1 of the 327 incidents involved a single firearm type. A handgun was involved in 63.6 percent (208) of the incidents. The next most commonly used firearm was a rifle (75 incidents), followed by shotgun, firearm (type not stated), and other/unknown gun, in that order. One incident involved two firearm types, a handgun and a rifle. (See Table 5.15.)

An analysis of the data by region showed that nearly one-half (45.6 percent) of the total instances of sniper attack reportedly occurred in the West. The Midwest followed in frequency with 25.4 percent, and then the South and Northeast with 18.3 percent and 10.7 percent, respectively. (See Table 5.16.)

A breakdown of the data by population showed that Population Group I, which includes cities with the population range of 250,000 and over, had the highest number of reported sniper attack murders with a firearm with 43.7 percent. Agencies classified as Group IX, Suburban Counties, reported 12.5 percent of the incidents. The remaining 143 of the 327 total incidents were reported by agencies in other population group sizes. (See Table 5.17.) (Refer to Appendix III of this publication for an explanation of the Population Groups.)

Victims

Of the 379 reported murder victims of a sniper attack with a firearm, 77.8 percent were male and 22.2 percent were female, dispersed over all age groups. (See Table 5.18.) More victims (55) were killed in 1988 than in any other year of the 20-year period under consideration. (See Table 5.13.) Fifty of the total number of victims were under the age of 18 (juveniles); the remaining 329 victims (86.8 percent) were age 18 or over or of unknown age. Of the 295 male victims, 155 (52.5 percent) were between the ages of 25 and 49. Females in that age range comprised 47.6 percent of the 84 total number of female victims. (See Table 5.18.)

A breakdown of the data by race of victims showed that 52.5 percent were white, 44.1 percent were black, and the remaining 3.4 percent were other races (American Indian/Alaskan Native or Asian/Pacific Islander) or unknown. (See Table 5.18.)

Offenders

There were 224 instances in the 327 reported sniper attacks in which at least one characteristic (age, sex, race) of the offender was reported. Of the 224 instances in which a characteristic was reported, 96.9 percent of the time the

Table 5.17

Sniper-attack Murder Incidents
by Year and Population Group, 1982–2001

Year	Total	Group I[1]	Group II[2]	Group III[3]	Group IV[4]	Group V[5]	Group VI[6]	Group VIII[7]	Group IX[8]
Total	327	143	37	34	20	20	11	21	41
1982	12	3	1	1	2	0	0	4	1
1983	17	4	2	2	1	4	3	0	1
1984	18	7	1	2	2	1	1	1	3
1985	10	3	1	0	1	1	0	2	2
1986	9	4	1	1	1	0	0	0	2
1987	28	6	4	7	2	2	0	4	3
1988	47	16	8	5	2	2	1	1	12
1989	46	22	8	3	3	2	1	2	5
1990	40	26	2	3	3	2	1	0	3
1991	10	5	0	2	0	0	1	0	2
1992	31	29	1	0	0	0	1	0	0
1993	6	0	1	1	0	1	0	2	1
1994	1	0	0	0	1	0	0	0	0
1995	11	3	1	2	0	1	0	2	2
1996	8	2	4	0	1	0	1	0	0
1997	4	2	2	0	0	0	0	0	0
1998	10	2	0	2	1	1	1	2	1
1999	5	3	0	1	0	0	0	1	0
2000	8	5	0	1	0	1	0	0	1
2001	6	1	0	1	0	2	0	0	2

[1] Includes cities with population range 250,000 and over.

[2] Includes cities with population range 100,000 to 249,999.

[3] Includes cities with population range 50,000 to 99,999.

[4] Includes cities with population range 25,000 to 49,999.

[5] Includes cities with population range 10,000 to 24,999.

[6] Includes cities with population range 9,999 and under and universities and colleges to which no population is attributed.

[7] Includes rural counties, population range not applicable and state police to which no population is attributed.

[8] Includes suburban counties, population range not applicable and state police to which no population is attributed.

Table 5.18

Sniper-attack Murder Victims
by Age, Sex, and Race, 1982–2001

Age	Total	Sex			Race				
		Male	Female	Unknown	White	Black	American Indian/ Alaskan Native	Asian/ Pacific Islander	Unknown
Total	379	295	84	0	199	167	1	9	3
Under 10	8	4	4	0	3	5	0	0	0
10 to 12	13	8	5	0	11	2	0	0	0
13	1	1	0	0	1	0	0	0	0
14	3	3	0	0	0	2	0	0	1
15	1	0	1	0	0	1	0	0	0
16	9	6	3	0	5	3	0	1	0
17	15	13	2	0	7	8	0	0	0
18	20	15	5	0	11	8	1	0	0
19	14	12	2	0	6	8	0	0	0
20	13	13	0	0	5	7	0	1	0
21	9	4	5	0	5	4	0	0	0
22	15	12	3	0	6	9	0	0	0
23	17	13	4	0	10	7	0	0	0
24	15	13	2	0	6	7	0	1	1
25 to 29	59	48	11	0	28	30	0	1	0
30 to 34	55	46	9	0	28	26	0	1	0
35 to 39	35	26	9	0	19	15	0	1	0
40 to 44	31	24	7	0	20	10	0	0	1
45 to 49	15	11	4	0	8	6	0	1	0
50 to 54	8	7	1	0	3	3	0	2	0
55 to 59	8	5	3	0	5	3	0	0	0
60 to 64	6	5	1	0	6	0	0	0	0
65 and over	7	4	3	0	5	2	0	0	0
Unknown	2	2	0	0	1	1	0	0	0

Table 5.19

Sniper-attack Murder Offenders
by Age, Sex, and Race, 1982–2001

Age	Total	Sex			Race				
		Male	Female	Unknown	White	Black	American Indian/ Alaskan Native	Asian/ Pacific Islander	Unknown
Total	224	217	7	0	117	94	2	2	9
Under 10	0	0	0	0	0	0	0	0	0
10 to 12	1	1	0	0	1	0	0	0	0
13	5	4	1	0	5	0	0	0	0
14	2	2	0	0	1	1	0	0	0
15	8	7	1	0	5	1	0	0	2
16	6	6	0	0	3	3	0	0	0
17	7	7	0	0	2	5	0	0	0
18	15	15	0	0	7	5	1	0	2
19	20	19	1	0	7	12	0	0	1
20	17	17	0	0	5	10	0	2	0
21	9	9	0	0	1	7	0	0	1
22	15	14	1	0	5	9	1	0	0
23	6	6	0	0	5	1	0	0	0
24	12	12	0	0	8	4	0	0	0
25 to 29	36	35	1	0	19	17	0	0	0
30 to 34	17	16	1	0	13	4	0	0	0
35 to 39	11	11	0	0	7	4	0	0	0
40 to 44	6	6	0	0	6	0	0	0	0
45 to 49	6	6	0	0	5	1	0	0	0
50 to 54	5	5	0	0	3	2	0	0	0
55 to 59	1	1	0	0	1	0	0	0	0
60 to 64	2	2	0	0	1	1	0	0	0
65 and over	3	3	0	0	2	1	0	0	0
Unknown	14	13	1	0	5	6	0	0	3

offender was reported as male and the remainder, female. Of the 217 instances in which the offender was reported to be male, 42.4 percent of the time the male was reportedly between the ages of 18 and 24. No particular age group was most frequent for those offenders reported to be female. The youngest identified female offender was reported to be 13 years old and the oldest was reported to be in the 30- to 34-year-old age group. The youngest reported offender overall was in the 10- to 12-year age category. (See Table 5.19.)

Of the 224 instances in which at least one characteristic of the offender was known, 215 of those instances identified the race of the offender. An analysis of the data by race showed that of the 215 instances in which the race was identified, 54.5 percent of the time the offender was white and 43.7 percent of the time the offender was black. In 4 instances the offender was either an American Indian/Alaskan Native or Asian/Pacific Islander. Of the 211 instances in which the offender was iden-

tified as either white or black, 87.2 percent showed the offender to be an adult (18 and over) or unknown and 12.8 percent a juvenile. (See Table 5.19.)

Confrontations

For this report, a confrontation is defined as the relationship of one or more victims to one or more offenders within the sniper attack. Of the 444 confrontations in the 327 total sniper attacks during the 20-year period, only 1 showed the relationship of the victim to the offender to be a family member—a father.

Stranger was reported as the relationship of victim to offender in 207 (46.6 percent) of the confrontations, and in 166 (37.4 percent) the relationship was reported as unknown. The remaining reported confrontations were dispersed over various victim-to-offender relationships. (See Table 5.20.)

Summary

The SHR data collected by the UCR Program show that sniper attack is a

unique circumstance that occurs infrequently in everyday life. The stealth of the offender and the randomness of the victim contribute to the uniqueness of those incidents. In the 20-year period studied in this report, there were a total of 327 circumstances of murder by a sniper with a firearm, involving 379 victims and 224 instances in which a characteristic about the offender was reported by law enforcement. Fifty-two percent of the incidents involved unknown offenders; the victims were dispersed over all age groups. The data show that most victims were between the ages of 25 and 49, male, and white. The offenders followed a similar pattern in that in most instances in which age, sex, and/or race were reported, the offender was reported as being between the ages of 25 and 49, male, and white. Most incidents involving snipers were reported by law enforcement agencies in the Western region, and the majority of the attacks involved a handgun.

Table 5.20

Sniper-attack Murder Victim/Offender Relationship
by Year, 1982–2001

Year	Total Confrontations	Within Family¹ Father	Neighbor	Acquaintance	Boyfriend	Girlfriend	Ex-Husband	Ex-Wife	Employee	Employer	Friend	Homosexual Relationship	Other	Stranger	Unknown Relationship
1982	18	0	0	3	0	0	0	0	0	0	0	0	0	13	2
1983	17	0	0	2	0	0	0	0	0	0	0	0	2	5	8
1984	40	0	0	8	0	0	0	0	0	0	0	0	0	29	3
1985	11	0	0	0	0	0	0	0	0	0	0	0	0	6	5
1986	9	0	0	0	0	0	0	0	0	0	0	0	0	4	5
1987	39	0	0	0	0	0	0	0	0	0	0	0	0	32	7
1988	67	0	0	1	0	0	0	0	0	0	5	0	3	27	31
1989	57	0	0	1	0	0	0	0	0	0	1	0	7	23	25
1990	46	0	1	1	0	0	0	0	0	0	1	0	2	19	22
1991	12	0	0	1	0	0	0	0	0	0	0	0	3	3	5
1992	37	0	0	4	0	0	0	0	0	0	0	0	0	11	22
1993	6	0	0	0	0	0	0	0	0	0	0	0	0	3	3
1994	5	0	0	3	0	0	0	0	0	0	0	0	0	2	0
1995	12	0	0	3	1	0	0	0	0	0	0	0	0	2	6
1996	15	0	0	4	0	0	0	0	0	0	0	0	0	9	2
1997	4	0	0	0	0	0	0	0	0	0	0	0	0	0	4
1998	22	0	0	7	0	0	0	0	0	0	0	0	0	9	6
1999	7	0	0	0	0	0	0	0	0	0	0	0	0	4	3
2000	8	0	1	1	0	0	0	0	0	0	0	0	0	0	6
2001	12	1	0	1	0	0	0	0	0	0	0	0	3	6	1
Total	444	1	2	40	1	0	0	0	0	0	7	0	20	207	166

¹ Possible relationships within the family are Husband, Wife, Common-Law Husband, Common-Law Wife, Mother, Father, Son, Daughter, Brother, Sister, In-Law, Stepfather, Stepmother, Stepson, Stepdaughter, and Other Family. All entries except Father were zero; therefore, they were omitted from the table.

SECTION VI

Law enforcement personnel provide services in cities, colleges and universities, suburban counties, rural counties, and states, each population with its own unique law enforcement needs. Even within a particular community type, such as cities, the law enforcement needs vary from locale to locale. For example, a small town positioned between two larger cities may need more law enforcement personnel than a same-sized community that does not have a nearby urban center. A city with legal gambling establishments may pose unique law enforcement challenges when compared to a similarly populated city with a neighboring military base.

Not only are the law enforcement needs of various locales different, but the functions of the officers serving those areas differ as well. In some areas, the county sheriff's officers may be responsible for a variety of civil functions such as tax collection; they may also be the enforcement authority for local and state courts; and they may administer jail facilities. In other locales, officers may be the only law enforcement agency in the county and, thus, responsible for providing all necessary services across what may be a large geographical area. State police and highway patrol officers may focus primarily on traffic enforcement on highways and interstates or investigative responsibilities of violent crimes throughout the state. Data users must consider the different service requirements and duties when attempting any comparison of law enforcement employee rates.

The data presented in the following tables should be viewed as guidelines or averages; they should not be considered recommended staffing

levels. Only after careful study and analysis of a myriad of conditions affecting service requirements can the appropriate personnel needs of any jurisdiction be determined.

The average number of law enforcement personnel collectively employed by agencies within each of the UCR population groups are presented in Tables 70–75. Table 76 reports the number of law enforcement employees working within state law enforcement agencies for each state; Tables 77–81 present the number of law enforcement employees for states, cities, colleges and universities, and suburban and rural counties. Table 82 offers data from county and city agencies serving the Nation's transit systems, parks and forests, schools and school districts, hospitals, etc., that usually share concurrent jurisdiction with local law enforcement.

Law Enforcement Rate

On average, there were 3.5 full-time law enforcement employees, officers and civilians, for every 1,000 inhabitants in the Nation in 2002. (Based on Table 74.) In the Nation during 2002, a total of 13,981 city, college and university, county, and state police agencies employed 665,555 full-time officers and 291,947 civilians providing law enforcement services for more than 271 million inhabitants. (See Table 74.)

Collectively, cities in the United States reported 3.1 law enforcement employees per 1,000 inhabitants in 2002. The highest average among cities, 4.1 law enforcement employees per 1,000 in population, was recorded in those with fewer than 10,000 in population. Those cities with a population of 250,000 or more inhabitants

had an average of 3.9 law enforcement employees per 1,000 inhabitants. (See Table 70.) Suburban counties reported the highest rate, an average of 4.7 law enforcement employees. Rural counties had an average of 4.2 law enforcement employees per 1,000 inhabitants. (Based on Table 74.)

By region, the cities in the Northeast and the South each posted a law enforcement employee rate of 3.5 per 1,000 in population. Cities in the Midwest recorded a rate of 2.8; in cities in the West, the rate was 2.4. (See Table 70.)

Sworn Personnel

When considering only sworn officers, the Nation's cities recorded a rate of 2.3 officers per 1,000 inhabitants. By population grouping, rates ranged from 1.8 officers per 1,000 inhabitants for cities with 25,000 to 99,999 in population to 3.2 officers for cities with fewer than 10,000 inhabitants. (See Table 71.) Suburban counties reported an average of 2.7 sworn officers per 1,000; rural counties had an average of 2.5. (Based on Table 74.)

In terms of geographic location, cities in the Northeast had the highest ratio of sworn officers to population with 2.7 officers for every 1,000 persons. The South followed with 2.6 officers for every 1,000 inhabitants, and the Midwest had a rate of 2.2 officers. The West had a rate of 1.7 sworn officers per 1,000 inhabitants. (See Table 71.)

Males comprised the majority of sworn officers, 88.7 percent, nationally and also in cities collectively. In rural counties, 92.1 percent of sworn officers were males; 86.9 percent in suburban counties were males. Females made up 11.3 percent of the

Nation's sworn officers in 2002. Cities with a population of 1 million inhabitants or more had the highest percentage of sworn female officers at 17.5 percent. (See Table 74.)

Civilian Employees

Civilians made up 30.5 percent of the total national law enforcement work force in 2002. In cities collectively, they represented 23.4 percent of law enforcement employees. In suburban counties, civilians constituted 41.0 percent of the law enforcement workforce; in rural counties, they accounted for 39.4 percent. (See Table 75.) Females comprised 62.1 percent of all civilian employees. (See Table 74.)

Law Enforcement Officers Killed and Assaulted

In 2002, 56 law enforcement officers were feloniously killed while carrying out their duties, which decreased from 2001 when 70 officers were feloniously slain. The 2001 figure does not include the 72 officers who lost their lives in the terrorist attacks on September 11, 2001.

Accidental law enforcement deaths also decreased from 2001—77 officers were accidentally killed in 2002; 78 officers lost their lives in accidents in 2001. More extensive data on line-of-duty deaths as well as assaults on city, county, state, and federal officers is contained in the Uniform Crime Reports annual publication *Law Enforcement Officers Killed and Assaulted.*

Table 70

Full-time Law Enforcement Employees[1] as of October 31, 2002

Number and Rate per 1,000 Inhabitants
by Geographic Region and Division by Population Group
[2002 estimated population]

Geographic region/division	Total (10,653 cities; population 182,456,027)	Group I (70 cities, 250,000 and over; population 52,879,728)	Group II (162 cities, 100,000 to 249,999; population 24,457,039)	Group III (389 cities, 50,000 to 99,999; population 26,808,264)	Group IV (760 cities, 25,000 to 49,999; population 26,374,112)	Group V (1,763 cities, 10,000 to 24,999; population 27,930,903)	Group VI (7,509 cities, under 10,000; population 24,005,981)
TOTAL CITIES: 10,653 cities; population 182,456,027:							
Number of employees	558,892	205,573	61,739	62,203	61,343	68,513	99,521
Average number of employees per 1,000 inhabitants	3.1	3.9	2.5	2.3	2.3	2.5	4.1
New England: 758 cities; population 12,313,029:							
Number of employees	32,668	2,771	4,785	5,904	6,782	7,061	5,365
Average number of employees per 1,000 inhabitants	2.7	4.6	3.6	2.4	2.3	2.2	2.9
Middle Atlantic: 1,567 cities; population 29,933,085:							
Number of employees	114,757	64,343	4,745	8,753	11,751	12,378	12,787
Average number of employees per 1,000 inhabitants	3.8	6.3	3.4	2.6	2.4	2.1	3.0
NORTHEAST: 2,325 cities; population 42,246,114:							
Number of employees	147,425	67,114	9,530	14,657	18,533	19,439	18,152
Average number of employees per 1,000 inhabitants	3.5	6.2	3.5	2.5	2.4	2.2	2.9
East North Central: 1,991 cities; population 31,512,235:							
Number of employees	91,525	31,322	7,334	10,367	12,012	14,769	15,721
Average number of employees per 1,000 inhabitants	2.9	4.4	2.5	2.2	2.1	2.3	3.3
West North Central: 1,159 cities; population 12,573,771:							
Number of employees	31,694	7,713	3,038	3,702	4,055	4,828	8,358
Average number of employees per 1,000 inhabitants	2.5	3.5	2.2	1.8	2.0	2.2	3.1
MIDWEST: 3,150 cities; population 44,086,006:							
Number of employees	123,219	39,035	10,372	14,069	16,067	19,597	24,079
Average number of employees per 1,000 inhabitants	2.8	4.2	2.4	2.1	2.1	2.3	3.2
South Atlantic: 1,660 cities; population 20,995,073:							
Number of employees	83,945	21,293	12,207	11,094	7,654	10,254	21,443
Average number of employees per 1,000 inhabitants	4.0	4.5	3.0	3.1	3.0	3.3	7.1
East South Central: 941 cities; population 8,764,850:							
Number of employees	32,425	6,860	4,348	2,045	3,551	5,480	10,141
Average number of employees per 1,000 inhabitants	3.7	3.4	3.5	3.3	2.9	3.1	5.2
West South Central: 1,210 cities; population 21,822,633:							
Number of employees	63,499	23,529	7,695	6,213	5,833	6,706	13,523
Average number of employees per 1,000 inhabitants	2.9	2.8	2.4	2.3	2.5	2.7	4.9
SOUTH: 3,811 cities; population 51,582,556:							
Number of employees	179,869	51,682	24,250	19,352	17,038	22,440	45,107
Average number of employees per 1,000 inhabitants	3.5	3.4	2.9	2.8	2.8	3.1	5.8
Mountain: 593 cities; population 13,392,422:							
Number of employees	35,833	14,733	5,979	3,552	2,968	2,915	5,686
Average number of employees per 1,000 inhabitants	2.7	2.8	2.2	2.1	2.3	2.5	4.3
Pacific: 774 cities; population 31,148,929:							
Number of employees	72,546	33,009	11,608	10,573	6,737	4,122	6,497
Average number of employees per 1,000 inhabitants	2.3	2.7	1.9	1.9	1.9	2.1	4.8
WEST: 1,367 cities; population 44,541,351:							
Number of employees	108,379	47,742	17,587	14,125	9,705	7,037	12,183
Average number of employees per 1,000 inhabitants	2.4	2.7	2.0	1.9	2.0	2.2	4.6

Suburban Area[2]: 6,528 agencies; population 108,747,307:		County[3]: 3,328 agencies; population 88,784,510:	
Number of employees	418,093	Number of employees	398,610
Average number of employees per 1,000 inhabitants	3.8	Average number of employees per 1,000 inhabitants	4.5

[1] Full-time law enforcement employees include civilians.

[2] Suburban area includes law enforcement agencies in cities with less than 50,000 inhabitants and county law enforcement agencies that are within a Metropolitan Statistical Area (see Appendix III). Suburban area excludes all metropolitan agencies associated with a central city. The agencies associated with suburban areas also appear in other groups within this table.

[3] County is a combination of both suburban and rural counties.

Table 71

Full-time Law Enforcement Officers as of October 31, 2002

Number and Rate per 1,000 Inhabitants

by Geographic Region and Division by Population Group

[2002 estimated population]

Geographic region/division	Total (10,653 cities; population 182,456,027)	Group I (70 cities, 250,000 and over; population 52,879,728)	Group II (162 cities, 100,000 to 249,999; population 24,457,039)	Group III (389 cities, 50,000 to 99,999; population 26,808,264)	Group IV (760 cities, 25,000 to 49,999; population 26,374,112)	Group V (1,763 cities, 10,000 to 24,999; population 27,930,903)	Group VI (7,509 cities, under 10,000; population 24,005,981)
TOTAL CITIES: 10,653 cities; population 182,456,027:							
Number of officers	428,365	154,116	46,124	47,762	47,960	54,413	77,990
Average number of officers per 1,000 inhabitants	2.3	2.9	1.9	1.8	1.8	1.9	3.2
New England: 758 cities; population 12,313,029:							
Number of officers	26,633	2,143	3,855	5,042	5,661	5,750	4,182
Average number of officers per 1,000 inhabitants	2.2	3.6	2.9	2.1	1.9	1.8	2.3
Middle Atlantic: 1,567 cities; population 29,933,085:							
Number of officers	89,216	46,603	3,959	7,236	9,818	10,555	11,045
Average number of officers per 1,000 inhabitants	3.0	4.6	2.8	2.2	2.0	1.8	2.5
NORTHEAST: 2,325 cities; population 42,246,114:							
Number of officers	115,849	48,746	7,814	12,278	15,479	16,305	15,227
Average number of officers per 1,000 inhabitants	2.7	4.5	2.8	2.1	2.0	1.8	2.5
East North Central: 1,991 cities; population 31,512,235:							
Number of officers	74,325	26,552	5,930	8,079	9,365	11,664	12,735
Average number of officers per 1,000 inhabitants	2.4	3.7	2.0	1.7	1.7	1.8	2.7
West North Central: 1,159 cities; population 12,573,771:							
Number of officers	24,577	5,480	2,384	2,907	3,143	3,803	6,860
Average number of officers per 1,000 inhabitants	2.0	2.5	1.7	1.4	1.5	1.8	2.5
MIDWEST: 3,150 cities; population 44,086,006:							
Number of officers	98,902	32,032	8,314	10,986	12,508	15,467	19,595
Average number of officers per 1,000 inhabitants	2.2	3.4	1.9	1.6	1.6	1.8	2.6
South Atlantic: 1,660 cities; population 20,995,073:							
Number of officers	63,780	15,791	9,093	8,399	5,907	8,012	16,578
Average number of officers per 1,000 inhabitants	3.0	3.3	2.3	2.3	2.3	2.6	5.5
East South Central: 941 cities; population 8,764,850:							
Number of officers	24,583	4,914	3,124	1,563	2,798	4,253	7,931
Average number of officers per 1,000 inhabitants	2.8	2.5	2.5	2.5	2.3	2.4	4.1
West South Central: 1,210 cities; population 21,822,633:							
Number of officers	48,083	18,353	5,747	4,759	4,340	5,135	9,749
Average number of officers per 1,000 inhabitants	2.2	2.2	1.8	1.8	1.9	2.1	3.5
SOUTH: 3,811 cities; population 51,582,556:							
Number of officers	136,446	39,058	17,964	14,721	13,045	17,400	34,258
Average number of officers per 1,000 inhabitants	2.6	2.6	2.1	2.1	2.2	2.4	4.4
Mountain: 593 cities; population 13,392,422:							
Number of officers	25,099	9,989	4,129	2,535	2,122	2,159	4,165
Average number of officers per 1,000 inhabitants	1.9	1.9	1.5	1.5	1.7	1.9	3.1
Pacific: 774 cities; population 31,148,929:							
Number of officers	52,069	24,291	7,903	7,242	4,806	3,082	4,745
Average number of officers per 1,000 inhabitants	1.7	2.0	1.3	1.3	1.3	1.5	3.5
WEST: 1,367 cities; population 44,541,351:							
Number of officers	77,168	34,280	12,032	9,777	6,928	5,241	8,910
Average number of officers per 1,000 inhabitants	1.7	2.0	1.3	1.3	1.4	1.7	3.3

Suburban Area[1]: 6,528 agencies; population 108,747,307:
Number of officers 275,584
Average number of officers per 1,000 inhabitants 2.5

County[2]: 3,328 agencies; population 88,784,510:
Number of officers 237,190
Average number of officers per 1,000 inhabitants 2.7

[1] Suburban area includes law enforcement agencies in cities with less than 50,000 inhabitants and county law enforcement agencies that are within a Metropolitan Statistical Area (see Appendix III). Suburban area excludes all metropolitan agencies associated with a central city. The agencies associated with suburban areas also appear in other groups within this table.

[2] County is a combination of both suburban and rural counties.

Table 72

Agencies with Full-time Law Enforcement Employees[1] as of October 31, 2002
Range in Rate per 1,000 Inhabitants
by Population Group
[2002 estimated population]

Rate range		Total cities[2] (9,781 cities; population 182,456,027)	Group I (70 cities, 250,000 and over; population 52,879,728)	Group II (162 cities, 100,000 to 249,999; population 24,457,039)	Group III (389 cities, 50,000 to 99,999; population 26,808,264)	Group IV (760 cities, 25,000 to 49,999; population 26,374,112)	Group V (1,763 cities, 10,000 to 24,999; population 27,930,903)	Group VI (6,637 cities, under 10,000; population 24,005,981)
.1-.5	Number	87	–	–	1	3	7	76
	Percent	0.9	–	–	0.3	0.4	0.4	1.1
.6-1.0	Number	381	–	–	2	11	39	329
	Percent	3.9	–	–	0.5	1.4	2.2	5.0
1.1-1.5	Number	1,007	–	11	34	82	158	722
	Percent	10.3	–	6.8	8.7	10.8	9.0	10.9
1.6-2.0	Number	1,752	6	46	130	196	368	1,006
	Percent	17.9	8.6	28.4	33.4	25.8	20.9	15.2
2.1-2.5	Number	1,982	18	43	117	225	480	1,099
	Percent	20.3	25.7	26.5	30.1	29.6	27.2	16.6
2.6-3.0	Number	1,481	17	25	51	129	361	898
	Percent	15.1	24.3	15.4	13.1	17.0	20.5	13.5
3.1-3.5	Number	958	9	17	24	71	164	673
	Percent	9.8	12.9	10.5	6.2	9.3	9.3	10.1
3.6-4.0	Number	637	5	13	15	23	100	481
	Percent	6.5	7.1	8.0	3.9	3.0	5.7	7.2
4.1-4.5	Number	420	3	3	7	13	38	356
	Percent	4.3	4.3	1.9	1.8	1.7	2.2	5.4
4.6-5.0	Number	263	5	4	6	4	22	222
	Percent	2.7	7.1	2.5	1.5	0.5	1.2	3.3
5.1 and over	Number	813	7	–	2	3	26	775
	Percent	8.3	10.0	–	0.5	0.4	1.5	11.7
Total Cities	Number	9,781	70	162	389	760	1,763	6,637
Percent[3]	Percent	100.0	100.0	100.0	100.0	100.0	100.0	100.0

[1] Full-time law enforcement employees include civilians.

[2] The number of agencies used to compile these figures differs from the other Law Enforcement Employee tables because agencies with no resident population are excluded from this table. These agencies include those associated with universities and colleges (see Table 79) and other agencies (see Table 82), as well as some state agencies that have concurrent jurisdiction with other local law enforcement.

[3] Because of rounding, the percentages may not add to 100.0.

Table 73

Agencies with Full-time Law Enforcement Officers as of October 31, 2002

Range in Rate per 1,000 Inhabitants
by Population Group
[2002 estimated population]

Rate range		Total cities[1] (9,781 cities; population 182,456,027)	Group I (70 cities, 250,000 and over; population 52,87>,728)	Group II (162 cities, 100,000 to 249,999; population 24,457,039)	Group III (389 cities, 50,000 to 99,999; population 26,808,264)	Group IV (760 cities, 25,000 to 49,999; population 26,374,112)	Group V (1,763 cities, 10,000 to 24,999; population 27,930,903)	Group VI (6,637 cities, under 10,000; population 24,005,981)
.1-.5	Number	105	–	–	1	3	9	92
	Percent	1.1	–	–	0.3	0.4	0.5	1.4
.6-1.0	Number	524	1	7	21	43	78	374
	Percent	5.4	1.4	4.3	5.4	5.7	4.4	5.6
1.1-1.5	Number	1,811	7	59	138	223	369	1,015
	Percent	18.5	10.0	36.4	35.5	29.3	20.9	15.3
1.6-2.0	Number	2,528	26	40	124	270	655	1,413
	Percent	25.8	37.1	24.7	31.9	35.5	37.2	21.3
2.1-2.5	Number	1,865	13	31	65	135	374	1,247
	Percent	19.1	18.6	19.1	16.7	17.8	21.2	18.8
2.6-3.0	Number	1,070	9	11	22	58	168	802
	Percent	10.9	12.9	6.8	5.7	7.6	9.5	12.1
3.1-3.5	Number	661	4	13	11	21	70	542
	Percent	6.8	5.7	8.0	2.8	2.8	4.0	8.2
3.6-4.0	Number	344	2	1	5	6	24	306
	Percent	3.5	2.9	0.6	1.3	0.8	1.4	4.6
4.1-4.5	Number	239	3	–	1	–	8	227
	Percent	2.4	4.3	–	0.3	–	0.5	3.4
4.6-5.0	Number	150	4	–	–	–	3	143
	Percent	1.5	5.7	–	–	–	0.2	2.2
5.1 and over	Number	484	1	–	1	1	5	476
	Percent	4.9	1.4	–	0.3	0.1	0.3	7.2
Total Cities	Number	9,781	70	162	389	760	1,763	6,637
Percent[2]	Percent	100.0	100.0	100.0	100.0	100.0	100.0	100.0

[1] The number of agencies used to compile these figures differs from the other Law Enforcement Officer tables because agencies with no resident population are excluded from this table. These agencies include those associated with universities and colleges (see Table 79) and other agencies (see Table 82), as well as some state agencies that have concurrent jurisdiction with other local law enforcement.

[2] Because of rounding, the percentages may not add to 100.0.

Table 74

Full-time Law Enforcement Employees as of October 31, 2002
Percent Male and Female
by Population Group
[2002 estimated population]

Population group	Total	Percent law enforcement employees		Total	Percent officers		Total	Percent civilians	
		Male	Female		Male	Female		Male	Female
TOTAL AGENCIES: 13,981 agencies; population 271,240,537	**957,502**	**73.2**	**26.8**	**665,555**	**88.7**	**11.3**	**291,947**	**37.9**	**62.1**
TOTAL CITIES: 10,653 cities; population 182,456,027	**558,892**	**75.1**	**24.9**	**428,365**	**88.7**	**11.3**	**130,527**	**30.2**	**69.8**
GROUP I 70 cities, 250,000 and over; population 52,879,728	205,573	70.5	29.5	154,116	83.5	16.5	51,457	31.8	68.2
10 cities, 1,000,000 and over; population 24,682,265	112,183	69.6	30.4	83,925	82.5	17.5	28,258	31.4	68.6
22 cities, 500,000 to 999,999; population 14,767,287	52,626	72.6	27.4	40,101	84.0	16.0	12,525	36.1	63.9
38 cities, 250,000 to 499,999; population 13,430,176	40,764	70.4	29.6	30,090	85.6	14.4	10,674	27.8	72.2
GROUP II 162 cities, 100,000 to 249,999; population 24,457,039	61,739	73.2	26.8	46,124	89.0	11.0	15,615	26.4	73.6
GROUP III 389 cities, 50,000 to 99,999; population 26,808,264	62,203	76.3	23.7	47,762	91.3	8.7	14,441	26.9	73.1
GROUP IV 760 cities, 25,000 to 49,999; population 26,374,112	61,343	78.0	22.0	47,960	92.2	7.8	13,383	27.3	72.7
GROUP V 1,763 cities, 10,000 to 24,999; population 27,930,903	68,513	79.4	20.6	54,413	93.1	6.9	14,100	26.5	73.5
GROUP VI 7,509 cities, under 10,000; population 24,005,981	99,521	79.9	20.1	77,990	92.1	7.9	21,531	35.8	64.2
SUBURBAN COUNTIES 964 agencies; population 57,536,474	268,044	69.8	30.2	158,104	86.9	13.1	109,940	45.3	54.7
RURAL COUNTIES 2,364 agencies; population 31,248,036	130,566	72.1	27.9	79,086	92.1	7.9	51,480	41.5	58.5
SUBURBAN AREA[1] 6,528 agencies; population 108,747,307	418,093	73.3	26.7	275,584	89.2	10.8	142,509	42.5	57.5

[1] Suburban area includes law enforcement agencies in cities with less than 50,000 inhabitants and county law enforcement agencies that are within a Metropolitan Statistical Area (see Appendix III). Suburban area excludes all metropolitan agencies associated with a central city. The agencies associated with suburban areas also appear in other groups within this table.

Table 75

Full-time Civilian Law Enforcement Employees as of October 31, 2002
Percent of Total
by Population Group
[2002 estimated population]

Population group	Percent civilian employees	Population group	Percent civilian employees
TOTAL AGENCIES: 13,981 agencies; **population 271,240,537**	**30.5**	GROUP IV 760 cities, 25,000 to 49,999; population 26,374,112	21.8
TOTAL CITIES: 10,653 cities; **population 182,456,027**	**23.4**	GROUP V 1,763 cities, 10,000 to 24,999; population 27,930,903	20.6
GROUP I 70 cities, 250,000 and over; population 52,879,728	25.0	GROUP VI 7,509 cities, under 10,000; population 24,005,981	21.6
10 cities, 1,000,000 and over; population 24,682,265	25.2		
22 cities, 500,000 to 999,999; population 14,767,287	23.8		
38 cities, 250,000 to 499,999; population 13,430,176	26.2	SUBURBAN COUNTIES 964 agencies; population 57,536,474	41.0
GROUP II 162 cities, 100,000 to 249,999; population 24,457,039	25.3	RURAL COUNTIES 2,364 agencies; population 31,248,036	39.4
GROUP III 389 cities, 50,000 to 99,999; population 26,808,264	23.2	SUBURBAN AREA[1] 6,528 agencies; population 108,747,307	34.1

[1] Suburban area includes law enforcement agencies in cities with less than 50,000 inhabitants and county law enforcement agencies that are within a Metropolitan Statistical Area (see Appendix III). Suburban area excludes all metropolitan agencies associated with a central city. The agencies associated with suburban areas also appear in other groups within this table.

Table 76

Full-time State Law Enforcement Employees as of October 31, 2002
by State

State	Total law enforcement employees	Total officers Male	Total officers Female	Total civilians Male	Total civilians Female
ALABAMA					
Department of Public Safety	1,248	616	15	182	435
Other state agencies	230	177	8	7	38
ALASKA					
State Police	585	323	18	94	150
ARIZONA					
Department of Public Safety	1,894	1,013	77	323	481
Other state agencies	70	24	5	26	15
CALIFORNIA					
Highway Patrol	10,317	6,245	602	1,544	1,926
Other state agencies	1,151	817	204	51	79
COLORADO					
State Patrol	962	672	40	67	183
Other state agencies	54	39	10	1	4
CONNECTICUT					
State Police	1,793	1,163	85	237	308
Other state agencies	32	23	1	6	2
DELAWARE					
State Police	859	561	64	98	136
Other state agencies	792	437	87	64	204
FLORIDA					
Highway Patrol	2,126	1,451	183	180	312
Other state agencies	1,491	1,040	103	105	243
GEORGIA					
Department of Public Safety	1,384	845	27	273	239
Other state agencies	1,622	701	57	313	551
IDAHO					
State Police	330	237	13	8	72
ILLINOIS					
State Police	3,840	1,932	204	637	1,067
Other state agencies	398	279	29	37	53
INDIANA					
State Police	1,916	1,164	66	283	403
Other state agencies	7	7	0	0	0
IOWA					
Department of Public Safety	894	582	37	107	168
KANSAS					
Highway Patrol	811	506	20	117	168
Other state agencies	454	262	14	57	121
KENTUCKY					
State Police	1,681	907	34	370	370
Other state agencies	536	410	11	54	61
LOUISIANA					
State Police	1,607	974	35	222	376
Other state agencies	3	2	0	1	0
MAINE					
State Police	478	307	20	64	87
Other state agencies	130	32	2	48	48
MARYLAND					
State Police	2,356	1,425	153	400	378
Other state agencies	1,835	1,032	188	345	270
MASSACHUSETTS					
State Police	2,742	2,135	219	198	190
MICHIGAN					
State Police	2,956	1,792	243	404	517
Other state agencies	20	17	3	0	0
MINNESOTA					
State Patrol	796	474	51	164	107
MISSISSIPPI					
Highway Safety Patrol	1,016	521	9	151	335
MISSOURI					
State Highway Patrol	2,167	1,037	38	516	576
Other state agencies	519	418	28	33	40
MONTANA					
Highway Patrol	270	196	9	21	44
Other state agencies	15	12	0	0	3
NEBRASKA					
State Patrol	670	464	21	57	128
NEVADA					
Highway Patrol	1,249	621	94	139	395
NEW HAMPSHIRE					
State Police	400	259	25	43	73
Other state agencies	32	17	3	3	9
NEW JERSEY					
State Police	3,982	2,638	97	568	679
Other state agencies	75	67	7	0	1
Port Authority of New York and New Jersey[1]	656	555	29	19	53
NEW MEXICO					
State Police	714	556	20	48	90
NEW YORK					
State Police	5,443	4,202	351	346	544
Other state agencies	225	196	12	8	9
Port Authority of New York and New Jersey[2]	880	801	56	1	22
NORTH CAROLINA					
Highway Patrol	1,804	1,340	28	266	170
Other state agencies	1,115	703	128	66	218
NORTH DAKOTA					
Highway Patrol	187	121	5	45	16
OHIO					
State Highway Patrol	2,638	1,386	140	511	601
Other state agencies	480	404	25	12	39
OKLAHOMA					
Department of Public Safety	1,451	830	22	268	331
OREGON					
State Police	1,160	682	71	136	271

Table 76

Full-time State Law Enforcement Employees as of October 31, 2002

by State—Continued

State	Total law enforcement employees	Total officers		Total civilians		State	Total law enforcement employees	Total officers		Total civilians	
		Male	Female	Male	Female			Male	Female	Male	Female
PENNSYLVANIA						**UTAH**					
State Police	5,859	3,971	169	834	885	Highway Patrol	458	416	11	7	24
Other state agencies	629	479	58	28	64	Other state agencies	176	162	6	2	6
RHODE ISLAND						**VERMONT**					
State Police	257	192	19	27	19	State Police	474	274	21	61	118
Other state agencies	37	26	4	3	4	**VIRGINIA**					
SOUTH CAROLINA						State Police	2,466	1,741	76	215	434
Highway Patrol	1,092	856	27	66	143	Other state agencies	873	584	73	92	124
Other state agencies	354	190	43	84	37	**WASHINGTON**					
SOUTH DAKOTA						State Patrol	2,034	1,020	85	422	507
Highway Patrol	221	144	1	56	20	**WEST VIRGINIA**					
Other state agencies	129	35	0	33	61	State Police	938	568	15	110	245
TENNESSEE						Other state agencies	151	137	1	0	13
Department of Safety	1,831	868	42	217	704	**WISCONSIN**					
Other state agencies	1,151	591	50	188	322	State Patrol	709	461	68	72	108
TEXAS						Other state agencies	302	237	21	22	22
Department of Public Safety	7,480	2,853	178	1,530	2,919	**WYOMING**					
						Highway Patrol	320	167	5	65	83

[1] Data reported are the number of law enforcement employees for the state of New Jersey.

[2] Data reported are the number of law enforcement employees for the state of New York.

NOTE: Caution should be used when comparing data from one state to that of another. The responsibilities of the various state police, highway patrol, and department of public safety agencies range from full law enforcement duties to only traffic patrol, which can impact both level of employment for agencies as well as the ratio of sworn officers to civilians employed. Any valid comparison must take these factors and the other identified crime factors (see page iv) into consideration.

Table 77

Full-time Law Enforcement Employees as of October 31, 2002
by State
[2002 estimated population]

State	Total law enforcement employees	Total officers Male	Female	Total civilians Male	Female
ALABAMA 297 agencies; population 3,930,746	13,613	8,664	687	1,519	2,743
ALASKA 41 agencies; population 642,955	1,857	1,052	109	219	477
ARIZONA 101 agencies; population 5,443,984	18,731	9,784	1,180	3,228	4,539
ARKANSAS 206 agencies; population 2,710,079	7,638	4,520	544	1,007	1,567
CALIFORNIA 462 agencies; population 30,685,929	113,827	65,011	9,163	14,557	25,096
COLORADO 233 agencies; population 4,403,008	15,489	9,388	1,316	1,404	3,381
CONNECTICUT 97 agencies; population 3,374,179	9,741	7,122	666	708	1,245
DELAWARE 51 agencies; population 807,385	3,101	1,948	258	349	546
DISTRICT OF COLUMBIA 3 agencies; population 570,898	4,923	3,084	939	281	619
FLORIDA 407 agencies; population 16,401,547	69,762	36,158	5,353	10,853	17,398
GEORGIA 431 agencies; population 7,226,657	26,651	16,336	2,417	2,819	5,079
HAWAII 4 agencies; population 1,244,898	3,553	2,530	269	217	537
IDAHO 114 agencies; population 1,311,796	3,502	2,223	135	217	927
ILLINOIS 751 agencies; population 12,542,030	50,441	31,109	5,280	6,181	7,871
INDIANA 253 agencies; population 6,049,242	17,292	9,945	797	2,954	3,596
IOWA 231 agencies; population 2,916,660	7,529	4,709	344	880	1,596
KANSAS 343 agencies; population 2,691,202	9,980	6,276	511	1,274	1,919
KENTUCKY 383 agencies; population 4,068,895	10,035	7,109	610	836	1,480
LOUISIANA 207 agencies; population 4,356,611	22,539	13,558	3,399	1,943	3,639
MAINE 134 agencies; population 1,291,698	2,927	2,062	133	334	398
MARYLAND 123 agencies; population 5,291,592	19,516	12,763	2,064	1,824	2,865
MASSACHUSETTS 328 agencies; population 6,268,238	19,749	15,132	1,293	1,420	1,904
MICHIGAN 606 agencies; population 9,976,197	28,080	18,175	2,831	2,882	4,192
MINNESOTA 285 agencies; population 4,859,720	12,583	7,220	884	1,809	2,670
MISSISSIPPI 170 agencies; population 2,426,944	8,381	4,862	415	1,195	1,909
MISSOURI 536 agencies; population 5,604,305	18,838	11,960	1,242	2,128	3,508
MONTANA 106 agencies; population 909,453	2,707	1,488	93	478	648
NEBRASKA 164 agencies; population 1,719,618	4,649	3,043	343	284	979
NEVADA 36 agencies; population 2,173,491	8,312	4,397	510	1,157	2,248
NEW HAMPSHIRE 131 agencies; population 925,055	2,523	1,794	123	177	429
NEW JERSEY 530 agencies; population 8,331,239	38,931	28,331	2,152	3,030	5,418
NEW MEXICO 110 agencies; population 1,851,009	5,660	3,779	363	432	1,086
NEW YORK 425 agencies; population 16,675,972	80,990	51,892	7,762	6,936	14,400
NORTH CAROLINA 513 agencies; population 8,313,727	27,852	17,510	2,181	3,372	4,789
NORTH DAKOTA 89 agencies; population 608,703	1,542	1,021	83	172	266
OHIO 555 agencies; population 10,878,422	33,621	21,099	2,565	3,935	6,022
OKLAHOMA 302 agencies; population 3,493,714	10,585	6,590	518	1,446	2,031
OREGON 164 agencies; population 3,492,816	7,679	5,066	551	441	1,621
PENNSYLVANIA 779 agencies; population 8,590,601	28,183	21,015	2,698	1,720	2,750
RHODE ISLAND 43 agencies; population 1,063,557	3,122	2,324	161	286	351
SOUTH CAROLINA 260 agencies; population 3,735,856	12,128	7,791	996	1,277	2,064
SOUTH DAKOTA 130 agencies; population 747,844	2,016	1,198	69	335	414
TENNESSEE 437 agencies; population 5,787,364	23,962	13,629	1,545	3,272	5,516
TEXAS 965 agencies; population 21,670,261	77,464	42,806	4,904	12,935	16,819
UTAH 124 agencies; population 2,315,689	6,872	4,260	376	969	1,267
VERMONT 58 agencies; population 364,545	1,343	888	68	132	255
VIRGINIA 278 agencies; population 7,292,028	21,540	14,787	1,765	1,470	3,518
WASHINGTON 251 agencies; population 6,064,698	13,747	8,910	958	1,225	2,654
WEST VIRGINIA 352 agencies; population 1,790,599	3,959	2,936	92	358	573
WISCONSIN 316 agencies; population 4,849,982	15,848	9,781	1,566	1,531	2,970
WYOMING 66 agencies; population 496,899	1,989	1,153	86	245	505

Table 78

Full-time Law Enforcement Employees as of October 31, 2002
by City by State

City by state	Total law enforcement employees	Total officers	Total civilians	City by state	Total law enforcement employees	Total officers	Total civilians
ALABAMA				**ALABAMA—Continued**			
Abbeville	19	11	8	Fairhope	36	24	12
Adamsville	30	18	12	Fayette	14	14	0
Alabaster	59	48	11	Flomaton	12	7	5
Albertville	53	35	18	Florala	5	5	0
Alexander City	65	48	17	Florence	116	92	24
Aliceville	11	7	4	Foley	55	35	20
Andalusia	35	26	9	Fort Payne	40	36	4
Anniston	112	83	29	Frisco City	2	2	0
Arab	34	24	10	Fultondale	24	18	6
Ardmore	11	6	5	Gadsden	137	104	33
Argo	4	4	0	Gardendale	32	25	7
Ashford	9	5	4	Geneva	16	11	5
Ashland	12	8	4	Glencoe	9	6	3
Ashville	5	5	0	Gordo	5	4	1
Athens	51	40	11	Grant	3	3	0
Atmore	30	26	4	Greensboro	9	9	0
Attalla	28	22	6	Greenville	38	30	8
Auburn	77	71	6	Grove Hill	6	6	0
Bay Minette	27	20	7	Gulf Shores	38	28	10
Bayou La Batre	22	17	5	Guntersville	35	26	9
Bear Creek	2	2	0	Hackleburg	4	4	0
Bessemer	134	114	20	Haleyville	19	14	5
Birmingham	1,125	833	292	Hamilton	14	13	1
Blountsville	8	8	0	Hanceville	12	8	4
Boaz	33	23	10	Hartford	12	7	5
Brantley	5	3	2	Hartselle	37	30	7
Brent	4	4	0	Headland	10	5	5
Brewton	30	20	10	Heflin	9	9	0
Bridgeport	11	7	4	Helena	20	15	5
Brighton	13	9	4	Hobson City	3	3	0
Brundidge	13	9	4	Hokes Bluff	9	6	3
Butler	8	5	3	Hollywood	3	2	1
Camden	8	8	0	Homewood	106	72	34
Carbon Hill	7	4	3	Hoover	189	137	52
Castleberry	2	1	1	Hueytown	28	23	5
Centreville	6	6	0	Huntsville	515	345	170
Chatom	6	6	0	Irondale	38	31	7
Chickasaw	21	16	5	Jackson	24	19	5
Citronelle	11	7	4	Jacksonville	28	23	5
Clanton	22	21	1	Jasper	72	49	23
Cleveland	2	2	0	Jemison	6	6	0
Clio	4	3	1	Killen	5	5	0
Coffeeville	1	1	0	Kimberly	4	4	0
Collinsville	9	5	4	Kinsey	3	3	0
Columbiana	14	10	4	Lafayette	17	15	2
Coosada	2	2	0	Lanett	22	21	1
Cordova	8	5	3	Leeds	31	25	6
Cottonwood	3	3	0	Leighton	3	3	0
Creola	12	8	4	Level Plains	5	4	1
Crossville	7	4	3	Lexington	2	2	0
Cullman	70	49	21	Lincoln	21	16	5
Dadeville	11	11	0	Linden	6	6	0
Daleville	23	17	6	Lipscomb	11	6	5
Daphne	61	37	24	Littleville	7	5	2
Dauphin Island	11	7	4	Livingston	12	8	4
Decatur	147	124	23	Lockhart	2	2	0
Demopolis	25	21	4	Louisville	3	3	0
Dora	6	3	3	Loxley	14	8	6
Dothan	200	135	65	Luverne	16	12	4
Dozier	1	1	0	Madison	70	50	20
East Brewton	6	4	2	Maplesville	4	4	0
Eclectic	10	5	5	McIntosh	6	6	0
Elba	28	19	9	McKenzie	2	1	1
Enterprise	54	48	6	Millbrook	27	20	7
Eufaula	51	36	15	Millport	2	2	0
Eutaw	13	8	5	Millry	4	4	0
Evergreen	22	16	6	Mobile	720	526	194
Fairfield	53	40	13	Monroeville	24	18	6

Table 78

Full-time Law Enforcement Employees as of October 31, 2002

by City by State—Continued

City by state	Total law enforcement employees	Total officers	Total civilians	City by state	Total law enforcement employees	Total officers	Total civilians
ALABAMA—Continued				**ALABAMA—Continued**			
Montevallo	19	14	5	Taylor	2	2	0
Montgomery	639	446	193	Thomasville	22	18	4
Moody	18	16	2	Thorsby	4	4	0
Morris	4	4	0	Town Creek	4	4	0
Mosses	1	1	0	Triana	1	1	0
Moulton	11	11	0	Trinity	5	5	0
Moundville	5	4	1	Troy	62	47	15
Mountain Brook	58	47	11	Tuscaloosa	303	236	67
Mount Vernon	9	8	1	Tuscumbia	26	20	6
Muscle Shoals	42	33	9	Tuskegee	40	28	12
Napier Field	1	1	0	Union Springs	13	8	5
New Hope	4	4	0	Valley	36	27	9
New Site	1	1	0	Valley Head	3	2	1
Newville	1	1	0	Vance	1	1	0
Northport	75	59	16	Vestavia Hills	67	65	2
Oneonta	18	17	1	Wadley	8	4	4
Opelika	91	76	15	Warrior	21	15	6
Opp	28	22	6	Weaver	11	8	3
Orange Beach	48	31	17	Wedowee	8	8	0
Owens Crossroads	3	3	0	Wetumpka	32	24	8
Oxford	55	44	11	Winfield	11	9	2
Ozark	48	42	6				
Pelham	74	60	14	**ALASKA**			
Pell City	32	30	2				
Phenix City	93	73	20	Anchorage	463	313	150
Phil Campbell	4	4	0	Bethel	25	14	11
Pickensville	2	2	0	Bristol Bay Borough	8	2	6
Piedmont	18	15	3	Cordova	11	5	6
Pinckard	2	2	0	Craig	10	5	5
Pine Hill	5	5	0	Dillingham	16	7	9
Pleasant Grove	20	16	4	Emmonak	12	5	7
Prattville	90	83	7	Fairbanks	56	41	15
Priceville	4	4	0	Haines	10	5	5
Prichard	77	60	17	Homer	25	11	14
Ragland	8	5	3	Hoonah	6	5	1
Rainbow City	33	22	11	Juneau	85	45	40
Rainsville	14	10	4	Kake	6	3	3
Ranburne	3	2	1	Kenai	25	16	9
Red Bay	10	6	4	Ketchikan	33	25	8
Reform	5	5	0	Klawock	2	2	0
Riverside	5	5	0	Kodiak	31	17	14
Roanoke	27	23	4	Kotzebue	18	8	10
Robertsdale	14	9	5	Nenana	2	2	0
Russellville	27	23	4	Nome	14	8	6
Samson	5	5	0	North Pole	16	11	5
Saraland	50	38	12	North Slope Borough	62	37	25
Sardis City	4	4	0	Palmer	22	7	15
Satsuma	18	14	4	Petersburg	13	8	5
Scottsboro	60	44	16	Sand Point	6	4	2
Section	1	1	0	Seldovia	1	1	0
Selma	105	57	48	Seward	21	9	12
Sheffield	38	32	6	Sitka	34	19	15
Shorter	4	4	0	Skagway	7	4	3
Silas	1	1	0	Soldotna	13	12	1
Silverhill	2	2	0	St. Paul	7	4	3
Snead	5	5	0	Unalaska	29	13	16
Southside	14	8	6	Valdez	21	11	10
Spanish Fort	8	7	1	Wasilla	20	19	1
Springville	7	7	0	Whittier	3	3	0
Steele	11	3	8	Wrangell	12	6	6
Stevenson	9	5	4				
St. Florian	3	3	0	**ARIZONA**			
Sumiton	14	9	5				
Summerdale	4	4	0	Apache Junction	78	51	27
Sylacauga	48	36	12	Avondale	92	71	21
Talladega	59	47	12	Benson	20	13	7
Tallassee	25	19	6	Bisbee	22	15	7
Tarrant City	29	23	6	Buckeye	33	25	8

Table 78

Full-time Law Enforcement Employees as of October 31, 2002

by City by State—Continued

City by state	Total law enforcement employees	Total officers	Total civilians	City by state	Total law enforcement employees	Total officers	Total civilians
ARIZONA—Continued				**ARIZONA—Continued**			
Bullhead City	114	75	39	Winslow	36	28	8
Camp Verde	29	18	11	Youngtown	11	10	1
Casa Grande	83	58	25	Yuma	195	126	69
Chandler	447	286	161				
Chino Valley	28	18	10	**ARKANSAS**			
Clarkdale	11	9	2				
Colorado City	6	5	1	Alma	15	8	7
Coolidge	40	31	9	Arkadelphia	27	22	5
Cottonwood	38	24	14	Ashdown	12	11	1
Douglas	43	30	13	Atkins	7	6	1
Eagar	11	8	3	Bald Knob	9	5	4
El Mirage	56	46	10	Barling	8	8	0
Eloy	44	30	14	Beebe	15	9	6
Flagstaff	138	92	46	Benton	69	59	10
Florence	24	15	9	Bentonville	62	41	21
Fredonia	5	5	0	Berryville	10	9	1
Gilbert	166	116	50	Blytheville	68	51	17
Glendale	379	271	108	Booneville	11	7	4
Globe	33	24	9	Brinkley	14	10	4
Goodyear	62	47	15	Bryant	32	25	7
Hayden	8	7	1	Bull Shoals	3	3	0
Holbrook	24	17	7	Cabot	40	29	11
Huachuca City	10	4	6	Caddo Valley	6	5	1
Jerome	4	4	0	Camden	39	26	13
Kearny	12	7	5	Carlisle	10	6	4
Kingman	67	45	22	Cherokee Village	7	6	1
Lake Havasu City	94	72	22	Clarksville	19	15	4
Mammoth	8	5	3	Clinton	7	6	1
Marana	69	52	17	Conway	118	95	23
Mesa	1,243	772	471	Corning	11	7	4
Miami	8	6	2	Crossett	25	17	8
Nogales	78	60	18	Danville	6	5	1
Oro Valley	90	65	25	Dardanelle	13	9	4
Page	29	18	11	De Queen	16	13	3
Paradise Valley	45	34	11	Dermott	16	9	7
Parker	15	11	4	Des Arc	4	4	0
Patagonia	3	3	0	De Witt	14	9	5
Payson	36	25	11	Dumas	25	11	14
Peoria	186	134	52	Earle	11	8	3
Phoenix	3,628	2,773	855	El Dorado	65	48	17
Pima	3	3	0	England	12	7	5
Pinetop-Lakeside	25	15	10	Etowah	1	1	0
Prescott	93	59	34	Eudora	12	8	4
Prescott Valley	52	41	11	Eureka Springs	15	10	5
Quartzsite	8	6	2	Fairfield Bay	16	7	9
Safford	20	17	3	Farmington	7	7	0
Sahuarita	12	11	1	Fayetteville	146	97	49
San Luis	37	28	9	Flippin	7	6	1
Scottsdale	577	347	230	Fordyce	12	8	4
Sedona	35	26	9	Forrest City	42	31	11
Show Low	36	24	12	Fort Smith	183	142	41
Sierra Vista	85	56	29	Greenbrier	16	10	6
Snowflake-Taylor	15	10	5	Green Forest	9	7	2
Somerton	27	19	8	Greenland	4	4	0
South Tucson	36	26	10	Greenwood	18	17	1
Springerville	10	8	2	Gurdon	5	4	1
St. Johns	11	8	3	Hamburg	7	6	1
Superior	13	8	5	Harrisburg	5	4	1
Surprise	89	66	23	Harrison	49	27	22
Tempe	534	339	195	Hazen	8	4	4
Thatcher	11	10	1	Heber Springs	21	13	8
Tolleson	28	19	9	Helena	17	12	5
Tombstone	8	6	2	Hermitage	4	4	0
Tucson	1,290	969	321	Hope	36	26	10
Wellton	4	4	0	Horseshoe Bend	7	6	1
Wickenburg	19	12	7	Hot Springs	123	92	31
Willcox	18	11	7	Hoxie	8	4	4
Williams	19	11	8	Jacksonville	76	65	11

Table 78

Full-time Law Enforcement Employees as of October 31, 2002
by City by State—Continued

City by state	Total law enforcement employees	Total officers	Total civilians	City by state	Total law enforcement employees	Total officers	Total civilians
ARKANSAS—Continued				**CALIFORNIA—Continued**			
Jonesboro	117	107	10	Angels Camp	9	8	1
Keiser	3	1	2	Antioch	145	97	48
Lake Village	15	9	6	Arcadia	110	75	35
Lincoln	5	5	0	Arcata	38	26	12
Little Rock	681	543	138	Arroyo Grande	36	26	10
Lonoke	17	12	5	Arvin	18	10	8
Lowell	12	11	1	Atascadero	39	30	9
Magnolia	27	20	7	Atherton	28	22	6
Malvern	26	22	4	Atwater	41	31	10
Marianna	16	11	5	Auburn	34	24	10
Marion	17	16	1	Azusa	84	60	24
Marked Tree	12	8	4	Bakersfield	439	316	123
Maumelle	27	18	9	Baldwin Park	104	75	29
Mayflower	5	4	1	Banning	48	34	14
McGehee	15	8	7	Barstow	51	31	20
Mena	17	15	2	Bear Valley	13	7	6
Monticello	27	20	7	Beaumont	30	23	7
Morrilton	28	17	11	Bell	46	37	9
Mountain Home	33	25	8	Bell Gardens	67	48	19
Mountain View	9	8	1	Belmont	45	30	15
Mulberry	3	3	0	Belvedere	8	7	1
Nashville	14	13	1	Benicia	49	35	14
Newport	22	16	6	Berkeley	293	181	112
North Little Rock	242	199	43	Beverly Hills	214	141	73
Osceola	38	23	15	Bishop	20	14	6
Ozark	9	8	1	Blue Lake	2	2	0
Paragould	44	37	7	Blythe	36	24	12
Paris	14	9	5	Brawley	44	31	13
Piggott	9	9	0	Brea	130	106	24
Pine Bluff	164	139	25	Brentwood	55	42	13
Pocahontas	14	13	1	Brisbane	20	17	3
Pottsville	4	3	1	Broadmoor	13	12	1
Prairie Grove	8	7	1	Buena Park	145	94	51
Prescott	9	8	1	Burbank	259	168	91
Rogers	102	73	29	Burlingame	71	50	21
Rose Bud	3	2	1	Calexico	61	45	16
Russellville	68	56	12	California City	20	14	6
Searcy	49	38	11	Calipatria	7	6	1
Sheridan	26	11	15	Calistoga	10	10	0
Sherwood	82	63	19	Campbell	65	44	21
Siloam Springs	43	26	17	Capitola	32	21	11
Smackover	5	4	1	Carlsbad	144	106	38
Springdale	134	93	41	Carmel	22	14	8
Star City	5	4	1	Cathedral City	82	52	30
Stuttgart	30	21	9	Ceres	56	40	16
Texarkana	116	79	37	Chico	139	85	54
Trumann	21	15	6	Chino	119	91	28
Tuckerman	6	5	1	Chowchilla	24	17	7
Van Buren	50	37	13	Chula Vista	332	226	106
Vilonia	6	6	0	Claremont	61	42	19
Waldron	7	7	0	Clayton	14	11	3
Walnut Ridge	12	8	4	Clearlake	33	24	9
Ward	7	6	1	Cloverdale	19	12	7
Warren	24	15	9	Clovis	132	86	46
West Fork	5	5	0	Coalinga	24	18	6
West Helena	25	19	6	Colma	23	18	5
West Memphis	91	76	15	Colton	89	61	28
White Hall	12	11	1	Colusa	8	7	1
Wynne	20	18	2	Concord	219	157	62
				Corcoran	28	19	9
CALIFORNIA				Corning	23	15	8
				Corona	236	153	83
Alameda	159	104	55	Coronado	56	41	15
Albany	29	24	5	Costa Mesa	233	159	74
Alhambra	131	83	48	Cotati	20	13	7
Alturas	11	10	1	Covina	89	58	31
Anaheim	552	400	152	Crescent City	14	13	1
Anderson	26	16	10	Culver City	174	124	50

Table 78

Full-time Law Enforcement Employees as of October 31, 2002

by City by State—Continued

City by state	Total law enforcement employees	Total officers	Total civilians	City by state	Total law enforcement employees	Total officers	Total civilians
CALIFORNIA—Continued				**CALIFORNIA—Continued**			
Cypress	75	57	18	Inglewood	250	188	62
Daly City	151	114	37	Ione	8	7	1
Davis	88	53	35	Irvine	212	142	70
Delano	65	45	20	Irwindale	31	24	7
Del Rey Oaks	6	6	0	Isleton	3	3	0
Desert Hot Springs	22	17	5	Jackson	13	10	3
Dinuba	31	23	8	Kensington	10	10	0
Dixon	26	22	4	Kerman	19	16	3
Dos Palos	8	8	0	King City	20	16	4
Downey	157	109	48	Kingsburg	20	15	5
Dublin	54	46	8	Laguna Beach	86	50	36
East Palo Alto	47	32	15	La Habra	108	64	44
El Cajon	209	139	70	Lakeport	17	13	4
El Centro	72	50	22	Lake Shastina	5	4	1
El Cerrito	41	34	7	La Mesa	90	64	26
El Monte	216	156	60	La Palma	35	26	9
El Segundo	96	65	31	La Verne	64	47	17
Emeryville	47	33	14	Lemoore	32	25	7
Escalon	10	7	3	Lincoln	27	23	4
Escondido	227	161	66	Lindsay	27	17	10
Etna	3	2	1	Livermore	136	93	43
Eureka	75	44	31	Livingston	23	18	5
Exeter	18	16	2	Lodi	113	78	35
Fairfax	17	12	5	Lompoc	68	47	21
Fairfield	164	107	57	Long Beach	1,366	869	497
Farmersville	15	14	1	Los Alamitos	27	24	3
Ferndale	5	5	0	Los Altos	45	30	15
Firebaugh	16	12	4	Los Angeles	12,178	9,056	3,122
Folsom	81	58	23	Los Banos	51	32	19
Fontana	202	141	61	Los Gatos	65	46	19
Fort Bragg	20	14	6	Madera	63	49	14
Fortuna	16	16	0	Mammoth Lakes	22	17	5
Foster City	59	40	19	Manhattan Beach	90	66	24
Fountain Valley	87	64	23	Manteca	91	64	27
Fowler	8	7	1	Marina	39	32	7
Fremont	316	199	117	Martinez	52	39	13
Fresno	1,046	688	358	Marysville	36	23	13
Fullerton	222	151	71	Maywood	43	32	11
Galt	34	23	11	Menlo Park	76	54	22
Gardena	105	83	22	Merced	105	76	29
Garden Grove	238	165	73	Millbrae	40	27	13
Gilroy	95	53	42	Mill Valley	25	19	6
Glendale	355	237	118	Milpitas	120	91	29
Glendora	89	58	31	Modesto	353	250	103
Gonzales	14	13	1	Monrovia	83	58	25
Grass Valley	32	22	10	Montclair	79	53	26
Greenfield	20	17	3	Montebello	129	84	45
Gridley	20	15	5	Monterey	79	56	23
Grover Beach	26	17	9	Monterey Park	117	74	43
Guadalupe	15	12	3	Moraga	13	12	1
Gustine	11	10	1	Morgan Hill	48	32	16
Half Moon Bay	23	18	5	Morro Bay	29	21	8
Hanford	61	43	18	Mountain View	130	95	35
Hawthorne	137	96	41	Mount Shasta	16	9	7
Hayward	323	205	118	Murrieta	64	46	18
Healdsburg	26	16	10	Napa	119	75	44
Hemet	96	67	29	National City	115	79	36
Hercules	24	21	3	Nevada City	10	9	1
Hermosa Beach	49	38	11	Newark	82	57	25
Hillsborough	32	24	8	Newman	15	12	3
Hollister	41	34	7	Newport Beach	234	148	86
Holtville	11	8	3	Novato	82	59	23
Hughson	5	4	1	Oakdale	29	26	3
Huntington Beach	371	222	149	Oakland	1,232	814	418
Huntington Park	110	73	37	Oceanside	263	178	85
Huron	12	8	4	Ontario	324	214	110
Imperial	13	12	1	Orange	224	153	71
Indio	81	52	29	Orland	11	10	1

Table 78

Full-time Law Enforcement Employees as of October 31, 2002

by City by State—Continued

City by state	Total law enforcement employees	Total officers	Total civilians	City by state	Total law enforcement employees	Total officers	Total civilians
CALIFORNIA—Continued				**CALIFORNIA—Continued**			
Oroville	30	22	8	Santa Paula	42	32	10
Oxnard	308	209	99	Santa Rosa	262	174	88
Pacifica	53	42	11	Sausalito	27	22	5
Pacific Grove	37	28	9	Scotts Valley	28	20	8
Palm Springs	133	79	54	Seal Beach	42	33	9
Palo Alto	174	101	73	Seaside	53	41	12
Palos Verdes Estates	33	24	9	Sebastopol	23	16	7
Paradise	37	22	15	Selma	40	27	13
Parlier	16	14	2	Shafter	24	18	6
Pasadena	387	248	139	Sierra Madre	22	18	4
Paso Robles	45	36	9	Signal Hill	39	24	15
Patterson	15	13	2	Simi Valley	185	122	63
Petaluma	66	66	0	Soledad	16	16	0
Piedmont	28	20	8	Sonoma	22	14	8
Pinole	41	27	14	Sonora	17	13	4
Pismo Beach	32	23	9	South Gate	120	83	37
Pittsburg	110	78	32	South Lake Tahoe	67	49	18
Placentia	71	55	16	South Pasadena	46	35	11
Placerville	30	18	12	South San Francisco	114	83	31
Pleasant Hill	67	45	22	Stallion Springs	3	3	0
Pleasanton	101	81	20	St. Helena	19	13	6
Pomona	294	165	129	Stockton	570	384	186
Porterville	62	41	21	Suisun City	38	28	10
Port Hueneme	23	23	0	Sunnyvale	308	205	103
Red Bluff	39	26	13	Susanville	23	20	3
Redding	162	111	51	Sutter Creek	8	7	1
Redlands	145	79	66	Taft	20	10	10
Redondo Beach	157	105	52	Tiburon	17	14	3
Redwood City	140	100	40	Torrance	359	234	125
Reedley	41	27	14	Tracy	113	72	41
Rialto	134	96	38	Trinidad	3	3	0
Richmond	281	198	83	Tulare	74	50	24
Ridgecrest	45	32	13	Tulelake	4	2	2
Rio Dell	6	6	0	Turlock	86	59	27
Rio Vista	14	12	2	Tustin	132	92	40
Ripon	27	19	8	Twin Cities	45	34	11
Riverbank	17	14	3	Ukiah	37	28	9
Riverside	526	358	168	Union City	124	74	50
Rocklin	63	43	20	Upland	120	80	40
Rohnert Park	101	67	34	Vacaville	169	107	62
Roseville	150	89	61	Vallejo	230	158	72
Ross	7	6	1	Ventura	195	125	70
Sacramento	1,055	680	375	Vernon	81	58	23
Salinas	215	159	56	Visalia	162	111	51
San Anselmo	26	19	7	Walnut Creek	111	78	33
San Bernardino	430	279	151	Watsonville	80	61	19
San Bruno	70	52	18	Weed	16	10	6
San Carlos	46	31	15	West Covina	160	116	44
Sand City	10	9	1	Westminster	143	99	44
San Diego	2,913	2,123	790	Westmorland	4	4	0
San Fernando	54	38	16	West Sacramento	87	57	30
San Francisco	2,661	2,274	387	Wheatland	8	8	0
San Gabriel	67	52	15	Whittier	199	129	70
Sanger	33	22	11	Williams	10	9	1
San Jacinto	33	24	9	Willits	24	15	9
San Jose	1,819	1,378	441	Willows	14	11	3
San Leandro	139	94	45	Winters	11	10	1
San Luis Obispo	86	60	26	Woodlake	15	13	2
San Marino	36	27	9	Woodland	86	65	21
San Mateo	158	113	45	Yreka	24	16	8
San Pablo	66	44	22	Yuba City	72	45	27
San Rafael	106	78	28				
Santa Ana	669	353	316	**COLORADO**			
Santa Barbara	222	144	78				
Santa Clara	200	148	52	Alamosa	30	25	5
Santa Cruz	127	95	32	Alma	1	1	0
Santa Maria	133	95	38	Antonito	3	3	0
Santa Monica	399	207	192	Arvada	209	135	74

Table 78

Full-time Law Enforcement Employees as of October 31, 2002
by City by State—Continued

City by state	Total law enforcement employees	Total officers	Total civilians	City by state	Total law enforcement employees	Total officers	Total civilians
COLORADO—Continued				**COLORADO—Continued**			
Aspen	36	26	10	Gunnison	26	15	11
Ault	6	6	0	Haxtun	3	3	0
Aurora	765	529	236	Hayden	4	4	0
Avon	17	15	2	Holyoke	3	3	0
Basalt	10	8	2	Hotchkiss	3	3	0
Bayfield	4	4	0	Hugo	3	3	0
Berthoud	7	6	1	Idaho Springs	8	7	1
Black Hawk	33	22	11	Ignacio	7	7	0
Boulder	253	167	86	Johnstown	12	11	1
Bow Mar	2	2	0	Kersey	3	3	0
Breckenridge	23	18	5	Kremmling	4	4	0
Brighton	58	45	13	Lafayette	47	36	11
Brush	15	12	3	La Jara	4	4	0
Buena Vista	9	7	2	La Junta	20	17	3
Burlington	11	10	1	Lakeside	5	5	0
Calhan	1	1	0	Lakewood	395	266	129
Canon City	48	33	15	Lamar	34	21	13
Carbondale	18	15	3	La Salle	5	5	0
Castle Rock	55	41	14	Las Animas	9	7	2
Cedaredge	6	5	1	La Veta	4	3	1
Center	6	5	1	Leadville	10	8	2
Central City	8	7	1	Limon	6	5	1
Cherry Hills Village	22	21	1	Littleton	98	70	28
Colorado Springs	940	651	289	Lochbuie	8	6	2
Columbine Valley	3	3	0	Log Lane Village	4	4	0
Commerce City	91	64	27	Lone Tree	9	9	0
Cortez	49	28	21	Longmont	143	111	32
Craig	27	22	5	Louisville	38	33	5
Crested Butte	8	6	2	Loveland	125	82	43
Cripple Creek	23	12	11	Mancos	3	3	0
Dacono	10	8	2	Manitou Springs	20	14	6
De Beque	1	1	0	Manzanola	1	1	0
Del Norte	6	5	1	Meeker	6	5	1
Delta	20	15	5	Milliken	10	9	1
Denver	1,778	1,451	327	Minturn	3	3	0
Dillon	9	8	1	Monte Vista	16	12	4
Dinosaur	1	1	0	Montrose	47	32	15
Durango	56	46	10	Monument	10	9	1
Eagle	9	7	2	Morrison	2	1	1
Eaton	9	7	2	Mountain View	7	6	1
Edgewater	18	15	3	Mount Crested Butte	8	7	1
Elizabeth	10	7	3	Nederland	6	5	1
Empire	1	1	0	New Castle	6	6	0
Englewood	113	75	38	Northglenn	81	61	20
Erie	18	15	3	Oak Creek	1	1	0
Estes Park	26	15	11	Olathe	4	4	0
Evans	25	21	4	Ouray	5	5	0
Fairplay	2	2	0	Pagosa Springs	7	7	0
Federal Heights	34	24	10	Palisade	8	6	2
Firestone	12	9	3	Palmer Lake	4	4	0
Florence	14	9	5	Paonia	4	4	0
Fort Collins	226	151	75	Parachute	5	5	0
Fort Lupton	18	14	4	Parker	53	42	11
Fort Morgan	34	25	9	Platteville	7	7	0
Fountain	46	31	15	Pueblo	255	194	61
Fowler	2	2	0	Rangely	13	8	5
Frederick	12	10	2	Ridgway	2	2	0
Frisco	14	11	3	Rifle	18	15	3
Fruita	11	9	2	Rocky Ford	11	9	2
Georgetown	3	3	0	Salida	15	15	0
Gilcrest	3	3	0	Sheridan	27	20	7
Glendale	40	26	14	Silt	7	6	1
Glenwood Springs	34	25	9	Silverthorne	22	18	4
Golden	52	37	15	Simla	2	2	0
Grand Junction	139	85	54	Snowmass Village	13	9	4
Greeley	202	112	90	Springfield	3	3	0
Green Mountain Falls	2	2	0	Steamboat Springs	35	24	11
Greenwood Village	80	60	20	Sterling	38	22	16

Table 78

Full-time Law Enforcement Employees as of October 31, 2002

by City by State—Continued

City by state	Total law enforcement employees	Total officers	Total civilians	City by state	Total law enforcement employees	Total officers	Total civilians
COLORADO—Continued				**CONNECTICUT—Continued**			
Stratton	1	1	0	Orange	52	40	12
Telluride	13	9	4	Plainfield	21	18	3
Thornton	160	128	32	Plainville	37	30	7
Trinidad	27	18	9	Plymouth	19	19	0
Vail	58	27	31	Portland	11	10	1
Victor	5	5	0	Putnam	19	15	4
Walsenburg	21	13	8	Redding	18	13	5
Westminster	218	151	67	Ridgefield	44	39	5
Wheat Ridge	91	63	28	Rocky Hill	38	35	3
Wiggins	2	2	0	Seymour	37	35	2
Windsor	19	16	3	Shelton	59	51	8
Woodland Park	27	19	8	Simsbury	44	34	10
Wray	7	6	1	Southington	73	58	15
Yuma	8	7	1	South Windsor	50	39	11
				Stamford	364	297	67
CONNECTICUT				Stonington	45	34	11
				Stratford	114	105	9
Ansonia	51	42	9	Suffield	20	15	5
Avon	37	30	7	Thomaston	16	12	4
Berlin	46	37	9	Torrington	81	74	7
Bethel	46	33	13	Vernon	65	51	14
Bloomfield	52	43	9	Wallingford	91	68	23
Branford	62	49	13	Waterbury	385	341	44
Bridgeport	560	457	103	Waterford	51	44	7
Bristol	126	115	11	Watertown	46	36	10
Brookfield	37	31	6	West Hartford	146	124	22
Canton	19	14	5	West Haven	126	111	15
Cheshire	56	46	10	Weston	16	15	1
Clinton	26	23	3	Westport	87	72	15
Coventry	18	13	5	Wethersfield	56	45	11
Cromwell	31	24	7	Willimantic	42	37	5
Danbury	152	146	6	Wilton	48	44	4
Darien	56	50	6	Winchester	33	24	9
Derby	26	26	0	Windsor	66	56	10
East Hampton	17	15	2	Windsor Locks	30	24	6
East Hartford	170	129	41	Wolcott	32	24	8
East Haven	51	48	3	Woodbridge	32	24	8
Easton	21	14	7				
Enfield	114	95	19	**DELAWARE**			
Fairfield	112	106	6				
Farmington	58	42	16	Bethany Beach	12	11	1
Glastonbury	74	59	15	Bridgeville	4	4	0
Granby	18	13	5	Camden	8	7	1
Greenwich	180	159	21	Cheswold	1	1	0
Groton	35	30	5	Clayton	4	4	0
Groton Long Point	5	5	0	Dagsboro	2	2	0
Groton Town	74	70	4	Delaware City	3	3	0
Guilford	41	34	7	Delmar	11	10	1
Hamden	123	102	21	Dewey Beach	8	8	0
Hartford	601	397	204	Dover	111	81	30
Manchester	151	119	32	Ellendale	2	2	0
Meriden	142	131	11	Elsmere	11	10	1
Middlebury	18	12	6	Felton	4	4	0
Middletown	113	99	14	Fenwick Island	6	5	1
Milford	120	104	16	Frederica	1	1	0
Monroe	49	38	11	Georgetown	15	13	2
Naugatuck	66	55	11	Greenwood	6	4	2
New Britain	161	148	13	Harrington	10	9	1
New Canaan	49	45	4	Laurel	10	9	1
New Haven	538	427	111	Lewes	14	13	1
Newington	56	45	11	Milford	34	26	8
New London	95	79	16	Millsboro	11	10	1
New Milford	62	47	15	Milton	7	5	2
Newtown	45	39	6	Newark	72	55	17
North Branford	28	21	7	New Castle	18	17	1
Norwalk	201	175	26	Newport	8	7	1
Norwich	100	81	19	Ocean View	8	7	1
Old Saybrook	31	26	5	Rehoboth Beach	25	18	7

Table 78

Full-time Law Enforcement Employees as of October 31, 2002

by City by State—Continued

City by state	Total law enforcement employees	Total officers	Total civilians	City by state	Total law enforcement employees	Total officers	Total civilians
DELAWARE—Continued				**FLORIDA—Continued**			
Seaford	27	20	7	Dade City	34	23	11
Selbyville	6	6	0	Dania	75	65	10
Smyrna	23	17	6	Davenport	7	6	1
South Bethany	6	6	0	Davie	221	166	55
Wilmington	352	279	73	Daytona Beach	292	213	79
Wyoming	2	2	0	Daytona Beach Shores	41	33	8
				Deerfield Beach	118	102	16
DISTRICT OF COLUMBIA				De Funiak Springs	16	14	2
				Deland	86	59	27
Washington	4,445	3,655	790	Delray Beach	220	149	71
				Dundee	16	10	6
FLORIDA				Dunnellon	11	9	2
				Eagle Lake	5	5	0
Alachua	25	20	5	Eatonville	12	11	1
Altamonte Springs	139	102	37	Edgewater	40	35	5
Altha	1	1	0	Edgewood	12	11	1
Apalachicola	8	7	1	El Portal	8	8	0
Apopka	81	72	9	Eustis	53	39	14
Arcadia	24	20	4	Fellsmere	9	8	1
Astatula	4	4	0	Fernandina Beach	44	35	9
Atlantic Beach	36	26	10	Flagler Beach	13	12	1
Atlantis	17	12	5	Florida City	36	24	12
Auburndale	41	32	9	Fort Lauderdale	751	494	257
Aventura	98	66	32	Fort Meade	19	14	5
Avon Park	40	25	15	Fort Myers	223	156	67
Baldwin	11	6	5	Fort Pierce	136	103	33
Bal Harbour Village	28	22	6	Fort Walton Beach	68	54	14
Bartow	75	50	25	Frostproof	15	10	5
Bay Harbor Island	29	22	7	Fruitland Park	10	9	1
Belleair	15	10	5	Gainesville	339	274	65
Belleair Beach	7	7	0	Golden Beach	20	15	5
Belle Glade	53	42	11	Graceville	11	9	2
Belleview	16	14	2	Greenacres City	69	48	21
Biscayne Park	10	9	1	Green Cove Springs	24	18	6
Blountstown	12	7	5	Greensboro	1	1	0
Boca Raton	243	154	89	Gretna	3	3	0
Bonifay	9	5	4	Groveland	14	9	5
Bowling Green	6	6	0	Gulf Breeze	25	18	7
Boynton Beach	182	134	48	Gulfport	37	27	10
Bradenton	127	101	26	Gulf Stream	10	10	0
Bradenton Beach	10	10	0	Haines City	59	42	17
Brooksville	25	15	10	Hallandale	119	88	31
Bunnell	12	10	2	Hampton	1	1	0
Bushnell	10	9	1	Havana	13	9	4
Cape Coral	224	146	78	Hialeah	465	348	117
Carrabelle	4	4	0	Hialeah Gardens	48	36	12
Casselberry	86	55	31	Highland Beach	14	13	1
Cedar Grove	6	5	1	High Springs	13	8	5
Cedar Key	3	3	0	Hillsboro Beach	16	14	2
Center Hill	3	3	0	Holly Hill	31	24	7
Chattahoochee	11	10	1	Hollywood	488	318	170
Chiefland	11	8	3	Holmes Beach	19	12	7
Chipley	10	9	1	Homestead	98	70	28
Clearwater	390	252	138	Howey-in-the-Hills	5	5	0
Clermont	39	29	10	Indialantic	18	12	6
Clewiston	23	15	8	Indian Creek Village	15	11	4
Cocoa	91	70	21	Indian Harbour Beach	23	16	7
Cocoa Beach	50	34	16	Indian River Shores	22	21	1
Coconut Creek	117	82	35	Indian Shores	13	11	2
Coleman	2	2	0	Inglis	6	5	1
Cooper City	78	55	23	Interlachen	3	3	0
Coral Gables	223	168	55	Inverness	15	14	1
Coral Springs	278	184	94	Jacksonville	2,592	1,562	1,030
Cottondale	4	4	0	Jacksonville Beach	68	50	18
Crescent City	10	9	1	Jasper	8	8	0
Crestview	46	37	9	Jennings	2	2	0
Cross City	5	5	0	Juno Beach	19	14	5
Crystal River	22	19	3	Jupiter	135	99	36

Table 78

Full-time Law Enforcement Employees as of October 31, 2002

by City by State—Continued

City by state	Total law enforcement employees	Total officers	Total civilians	City by state	Total law enforcement employees	Total officers	Total civilians
FLORIDA—Continued				**FLORIDA—Continued**			
Jupiter Inlet Colony	5	5	0	Orlando	968	680	288
Jupiter Island	20	16	4	Ormond Beach	98	68	30
Kenneth City	16	14	2	Oviedo	70	52	18
Key Biscayne	38	28	10	Pahokee	20	18	2
Key West	105	81	24	Palatka	39	32	7
Kissimmee	171	109	62	Palm Bay	198	131	67
Lady Lake	31	22	9	Palm Beach	127	78	49
Lake Alfred	14	11	3	Palm Beach Gardens	117	89	28
Lake City	51	38	13	Palm Beach Shores	14	9	5
Lake Clarke Shores	10	10	0	Palmetto	45	33	12
Lake Hamilton	7	6	1	Palm Springs	41	32	9
Lake Helen	6	6	0	Panama City	133	94	39
Lakeland	334	232	102	Panama City Beach	61	46	15
Lake Mary	46	32	14	Parker	8	7	1
Lake Placid	11	8	3	Parkland	32	29	3
Lake Wales	55	40	15	Pembroke Park	61	53	8
Lake Worth	135	91	44	Pembroke Pines	275	217	58
Lantana	38	30	8	Pensacola	220	159	61
Largo	177	118	59	Perry	25	23	2
Lauderhill	111	88	23	Pinellas Park	125	95	30
Leesburg	93	69	24	Plantation	290	182	108
Lighthouse Point	37	28	9	Plant City	90	67	23
Live Oak	20	16	4	Pompano Beach	292	210	82
Longboat Key	29	20	9	Ponce Inlet	17	11	6
Longwood	42	38	4	Port Orange	95	74	21
Lynn Haven	31	24	7	Port Richey	20	14	6
Madison	14	13	1	Port St. Joe	11	9	2
Maitland	51	40	11	Port St. Lucie	202	144	58
Manalapan	13	9	4	Punta Gorda	47	33	14
Mangonia Park	19	18	1	Quincy	40	29	11
Marco Island	28	26	2	Riviera Beach	129	95	34
Margate	176	112	64	Rockledge	63	46	17
Marianna	25	18	7	Royal Palm Beach	61	45	16
Mascotte	9	8	1	Sanford	136	111	25
Medley	39	32	7	Sanibel	42	18	24
Melbourne	210	155	55	Sarasota	265	194	71
Melbourne Beach	9	8	1	Satellite Beach	26	19	7
Melbourne Village	6	6	0	Sea Ranch Lakes	10	7	3
Mexico Beach	6	5	1	Sebastian	48	31	17
Miami	1,408	1,075	333	Sebring	49	36	13
Miami Beach	518	370	148	Sewall's Point	8	8	0
Miami Shores	42	32	10	Shalimar	4	4	0
Miami Springs	49	37	12	Sneads	9	5	4
Milton	27	19	8	South Bay	18	16	2
Miramar	205	152	53	South Daytona	38	28	10
Monticello	14	10	4	South Miami	66	56	10
Mount Dora	45	30	15	South Palm Beach	9	9	0
Mulberry	14	10	4	Springfield	22	15	7
Naples	117	77	40	Starke	28	20	8
Neptune Beach	25	18	7	St. Augustine	63	49	14
New Port Richey	38	31	7	St. Augustine Beach	13	11	2
New Smyrna Beach	56	47	9	St. Cloud	59	41	18
Niceville	25	20	5	St. Pete Beach	44	30	14
North Bay Village	32	25	7	St. Petersburg	773	507	266
North Miami	146	110	36	Stuart	59	42	17
North Miami Beach	140	102	38	Sunny Isles Beach	52	42	10
North Palm Beach	45	36	9	Sunrise	229	163	66
North Port	64	45	19	Surfside	28	19	9
Oak Hill	7	7	0	Sweetwater	31	23	8
Oakland	10	9	1	Tallahassee	477	336	141
Oakland Park	10	9	1	Tamarac	93	82	11
Ocala	234	151	83	Tampa	1,277	956	321
Ocean Ridge	20	15	5	Tarpon Springs	57	47	10
Ocoee	71	63	8	Tavares	22	21	1
Okeechobee	28	22	6	Temple Terrace	63	47	16
Opa Locka	45	33	12	Tequesta	22	18	4
Orange City	19	17	2	Titusville	115	81	34
Orange Park	27	22	5	Treasure Island	28	21	7

Table 78

Full-time Law Enforcement Employees as of October 31, 2002
by City by State—Continued

City by state	Total law enforcement employees	Total officers	Total civilians	City by state	Total law enforcement employees	Total officers	Total civilians
FLORIDA—Continued				**GEORGIA—Continued**			
Trenton	4	3	1	Centerville	17	14	3
Umatilla	9	8	1	Chamblee	45	31	14
Valparaiso	13	9	4	Chatsworth	15	13	2
Venice	71	52	19	Claxton	9	8	1
Vero Beach	90	63	27	Clayton	11	11	0
Village of Pinecrest	69	50	19	Cleveland	7	7	0
Virginia Gardens	9	7	2	Cochran	15	14	1
Waldo	9	8	1	Collins	1	1	0
Wauchula	18	14	4	Colquitt	9	8	1
Webster	3	3	0	Columbus	478	375	103
Welaka	1	1	0	Comer	2	2	0
West Melbourne	32	27	5	Commerce	23	19	4
West Miami	19	15	4	Conyers	57	40	17
West Palm Beach	370	269	101	Coolidge	1	1	0
White Springs	4	4	0	Cordele	37	30	7
Wildwood	19	14	5	Cornelia	21	18	3
Williston	19	11	8	Crawfordville	2	2	0
Wilton Manors	44	33	11	Cumming	20	14	6
Windermere	10	9	1	Cusseta	7	5	2
Winter Garden	48	38	10	Cuthbert	15	11	4
Winter Haven	113	76	37	Dallas	19	14	5
Winter Park	115	85	30	Dalton	100	85	15
Winter Springs	80	58	22	Damascus	1	1	0
Zephyrhills	40	27	13	Danielsville	1	1	0
Zolfo Springs	3	2	1	Darien	5	5	0
				Dawson	24	19	5
GEORGIA				Doerun	5	4	1
				Donalsonville	12	9	3
Acworth	44	28	16	Douglas	46	38	8
Adairsville	10	8	2	Dublin	56	48	8
Adel	21	17	4	Duluth	66	43	23
Adrian	2	2	0	Eastman	14	13	1
Alapaha	2	2	0	Edison	4	4	0
Albany	220	194	26	Ellijay	9	8	1
Alma	16	14	2	Enigma	1	1	0
Alpharetta	96	71	25	Eton	3	2	1
Americus	55	40	15	Euharlee	8	7	1
Aragon	5	4	1	Fairburn	31	24	7
Arcade	9	9	0	Fairmount	2	2	0
Arlington	3	3	0	Fayetteville	43	39	4
Ashburn	15	13	2	Fitzgerald	33	28	5
Athens-Clarke County	255	198	57	Flowery Branch	9	8	1
Atlanta	2,090	1,535	555	Folkston	6	5	1
Attapulgus	1	1	0	Forest Park	80	58	22
Auburn	19	14	5	Fort Gaines	6	5	1
Bainbridge	41	36	5	Fort Oglethorpe	28	23	5
Baldwin	9	7	2	Gainesville	114	94	20
Ball Ground	4	4	0	Garden City	38	34	4
Barnesville	16	14	2	Glenwood	4	3	1
Bartow	2	1	1	Gordon	11	7	4
Baxley	15	13	2	Grantville	5	5	0
Berlin	4	4	0	Gray	13	8	5
Blackshear	15	13	2	Greensboro	16	15	1
Blue Ridge	7	7	0	Greenville	8	7	1
Bowdon	14	10	4	Grovetown	26	17	9
Brooklet	3	3	0	Hagan	2	2	0
Broxton	5	5	0	Hahira	8	7	1
Brunswick	83	75	8	Hampton	12	11	1
Buena Vista	9	7	2	Hapeville	54	41	13
Byron	18	15	3	Harlem	14	8	6
Cairo	24	21	3	Hawkinsville	12	11	1
Calhoun	49	45	4	Hazlehurst	16	13	3
Camilla	25	19	6	Helen	13	9	4
Canton	42	35	7	Hephzibah	4	4	0
Carrollton	77	62	15	Hinesville	87	77	10
Cartersville	53	42	11	Hiram	7	6	1
Cave Spring	5	5	0	Hoboken	2	2	0
Cedartown	28	25	3	Hogansville	15	11	4

Table 78

Full-time Law Enforcement Employees as of October 31, 2002

by City by State—Continued

City by state	Total law enforcement employees	Total officers	Total civilians	City by state	Total law enforcement employees	Total officers	Total civilians
GEORGIA—Continued				**GEORGIA—Continued**			
Holly Springs	13	12	1	Pine Lake	3	3	0
Homerville	9	8	1	Pine Mountain	8	7	1
Hoschton	3	3	0	Pineview	1	1	0
Ideal	1	1	0	Pooler	24	21	3
Irwinton	1	1	0	Portal	2	2	0
Jackson	16	11	5	Porterdale	7	7	0
Jasper	11	10	1	Port Wentworth	18	16	2
Jefferson	20	17	3	Powder Springs	34	25	9
Jeffersonville	4	4	0	Ray City	3	2	1
Jesup	32	28	4	Reidsville	9	8	1
Kennesaw	61	40	21	Remerton	9	8	1
Kingsland	36	32	4	Richland	4	4	0
Lafayette	19	16	3	Richmond Hill	23	18	5
LaGrange	92	83	9	Rincon	13	11	2
Lake City	17	16	1	Roberta	3	3	0
Lakeland	9	7	2	Rochelle	8	4	4
Lake Park	3	3	0	Rockmart	17	15	2
Lawrenceville	67	51	16	Rome	108	95	13
Leary	2	2	0	Rossville	9	8	1
Leesburg	9	9	0	Royston	16	13	3
Lenox	2	1	1	Sardis	6	6	0
Leslie	1	1	0	Savannah	524	419	105
Locust Grove	15	13	2	Screven	2	2	0
Loganville	24	20	4	Sky Valley	6	6	0
Lookout Mountain	7	7	0	Smithville	4	4	0
Louisville	7	7	0	Smyrna	140	93	47
Lumpkin	6	5	1	Snellville	46	36	10
Lyons	15	14	1	Soperton	10	6	4
Macon	375	295	80	Springfield	8	7	1
Madison	13	12	1	Statesboro	63	53	10
Manchester	18	13	5	Statham	4	4	0
Marietta	164	135	29	Stillmore	2	1	1
Marshallville	3	2	1	St. Marys	36	33	3
Maysville	4	4	0	Stone Mountain	25	21	4
McCaysville	4	4	0	Suwanee	34	26	8
McDonough	33	31	2	Swainsboro	22	18	4
McRae	10	6	4	Sycamore	4	2	2
Meigs	7	6	1	Sylvania	15	12	3
Metter	12	11	1	Sylvester	25	20	5
Milledgeville	58	38	20	Tallapoosa	14	13	1
Milner	1	1	0	Tallulah Falls	3	2	1
Montezuma	17	12	5	Temple	6	6	0
Morrow	35	32	3	Tennille	7	7	0
Moultrie	45	40	5	Thomaston	46	37	9
Mt. Zion	6	6	0	Thomasville	58	53	5
Nahunta	4	4	0	Thomson	17	14	3
Nashville	20	13	7	Tifton	56	47	9
Nelson	2	1	1	Tignall	2	1	1
Newington	2	2	0	Toccoa	34	22	12
Newnan	69	59	10	Trenton	7	7	0
Newton	1	1	0	Trion	8	8	0
Nicholls	3	2	1	Tunnel Hill	5	3	2
Norcross	38	30	8	Twin City	4	4	0
Norman Park	2	2	0	Tybee Island	25	14	11
Oakwood	10	9	1	Tyrone	13	12	1
Ocilla	15	13	2	Union City	38	34	4
Oconee	1	1	0	Union Point	10	9	1
Oglethorpe	6	5	1	Valdosta	133	115	18
Omega	4	4	0	Vidalia	39	30	9
Palmetto	12	10	2	Vienna	8	7	1
Patterson	1	1	0	Villa Rica	45	37	8
Pavo	3	3	0	Wadley	6	4	2
Peachtree City	58	54	4	Warm Springs	2	1	1
Pearson	6	5	1	Warner Robins	134	104	30
Pelham	18	10	8	Warwick	4	4	0
Pembroke	8	7	1	Washington	17	16	1
Perry	43	32	11	Watkinsville	5	5	0
Pinehurst	1	1	0	Waynesboro	27	19	8

Table 78

Full-time Law Enforcement Employees as of October 31, 2002
by City by State—Continued

City by state	Total law enforcement employees	Total officers	Total civilians	City by state	Total law enforcement employees	Total officers	Total civilians
GEORGIA—Continued				**IDAHO—Continued**			
West Point	17	12	5	Spirit Lake	4	4	0
Whitesburg	4	4	0	St. Anthony	7	7	0
Willacoochee	5	5	0	St. Maries	6	5	1
Winterville	3	3	0	Sun Valley	10	9	1
Woodbine	4	4	0	Twin Falls	74	53	21
Woodbury	14	8	6	Weiser	12	10	2
Wrens	10	6	4	Wendell	3	3	0
Wrightsville	6	6	0	Wilder	4	4	0
Zebulon	9	8	1				
				ILLINOIS			
HAWAII				Abingdon	5	5	0
				Addison	88	63	25
Honolulu	2,455	1,973	482	Albany	1	1	0
				Albers	1	1	0
IDAHO				Albion	2	2	0
				Aledo	8	6	2
Aberdeen	8	5	3	Algonquin	55	42	13
American Falls	11	9	2	Alorton	4	4	0
Bellevue	3	3	0	Alsip	53	41	12
Blackfoot	25	22	3	Altamont	5	5	0
Boise	326	262	64	Alton	93	69	24
Bonners Ferry	8	8	0	Amboy	3	3	0
Buhl	10	8	2	Andalusia	3	3	0
Caldwell	59	46	13	Anna	9	9	0
Cascade	4	4	0	Annawan	3	3	0
Challis	1	1	0	Antioch	30	20	10
Chubbuck	26	17	9	Arcola	6	6	0
Coeur d'Alene	74	61	13	Arlington Heights	143	107	36
Cottonwood	1	1	0	Arthur	5	5	0
Emmett	13	12	1	Ashland	2	2	0
Filer	5	5	0	Assumption	1	1	0
Fruitland	9	8	1	Astoria	1	1	0
Garden City	33	28	5	Athens	3	3	0
Gooding	6	6	0	Atkinson	1	1	0
Grangeville	6	6	0	Atlanta	3	3	0
Hagerman	1	1	0	Auburn	9	5	4
Hailey	14	12	2	Augusta	1	1	0
Heyburn	7	6	1	Aurora	344	268	76
Homedale	5	5	0	Aviston	1	1	0
Idaho Falls	118	86	32	Bannockburn	7	7	0
Jerome	18	16	2	Barrington	43	34	9
Kamiah	4	4	0	Barrington Hills	27	19	8
Kellogg	8	7	1	Barry	1	1	0
Ketchum	21	10	11	Bartlett	64	47	17
Kimberly	7	6	1	Bartonville	16	11	5
Lewiston	65	45	20	Batavia	49	42	7
McCall	10	8	2	Beardstown	13	9	4
Meridian	53	45	8	Beckemeyer	1	1	0
Montpelier	6	6	0	Bedford Park	43	35	8
Moscow	46	35	11	Beecher	6	6	0
Mountain Home	25	21	4	Belleville	98	80	18
Nampa	105	80	25	Bellwood	61	47	14
Orofino	6	5	1	Belvidere	36	34	2
Osburn	2	2	0	Benld	4	4	0
Parma	4	4	0	Bensenville	52	38	14
Payette	13	11	2	Benton	15	10	5
Pinehurst	2	2	0	Berkeley	20	16	4
Pocatello	126	90	36	Berwyn	116	91	25
Ponderay	4	4	0	Bethalto	23	16	7
Post Falls	50	30	20	Bloomingdale	66	49	17
Preston	6	6	0	Bloomington	128	108	20
Rathdrum	13	10	3	Blue Island	65	40	25
Rexburg	37	31	6	Blue Mound	2	2	0
Rigby	7	7	0	Bolingbrook	145	100	45
Rupert	17	16	1	Bourbonnais	26	19	7
Sandpoint	37	20	17	Bradley	37	29	8
Shelley	8	8	0	Braidwood	22	14	8
Soda Springs	8	7	1				

Table 78

Full-time Law Enforcement Employees as of October 31, 2002

by City by State—Continued

City by state	Total law enforcement employees	Total officers	Total civilians	City by state	Total law enforcement employees	Total officers	Total civilians
ILLINOIS—Continued				**ILLINOIS—Continued**			
Breese	7	6	1	Crete	18	16	2
Bridgeport	2	2	0	Creve Coeur	10	8	2
Bridgeview	47	44	3	Crystal Lake	80	60	20
Brighton	5	3	2	Cuba	2	2	0
Broadview	45	36	9	Dallas City	1	1	0
Brookfield	37	30	7	Danvers	1	1	0
Brooklyn	6	6	0	Danville	81	64	17
Buffalo Grove	84	71	13	Darien	55	38	17
Bull Valley	2	2	0	Decatur	184	154	30
Bunker Hill	5	4	1	Deerfield	53	38	15
Burbank	65	49	16	De Kalb	69	56	13
Burnham	14	10	4	De Pue	2	2	0
Burr Ridge	29	25	4	De Soto	3	3	0
Byron	7	6	1	Des Plaines	131	107	24
Cahokia	46	35	11	Divernon	1	1	0
Cairo	12	7	5	Dixmoor	20	15	5
Calumet City	109	80	29	Dixon	30	26	4
Calumet Park	28	20	8	Dolton	66	50	16
Cambridge	1	1	0	Downers Grove	114	80	34
Camp Point	2	2	0	Dupo	6	6	0
Canton	32	23	9	Du Quoin	14	10	4
Carbon Cliff	3	3	0	Durand	1	1	0
Carbondale	75	59	16	Dwight	10	9	1
Carlinville	18	12	6	Earlville	3	3	0
Carlyle	8	7	1	East Alton	17	12	5
Carmi	10	9	1	East Carondelet	2	2	0
Carol Stream	86	60	26	East Dubuque	7	7	0
Carpentersville	71	60	11	East Dundee	15	14	1
Carrier Mills	2	2	0	East Galesburg	1	1	0
Carrollton	6	6	0	East Hazel Crest	12	10	2
Carterville	7	7	0	East Moline	50	39	11
Carthage	4	4	0	East Peoria	50	37	13
Cary	32	24	8	East St. Louis	88	67	21
Casey	9	8	1	Edwardsville	48	35	13
Caseyville	13	9	4	Effingham	37	24	13
Catlin	1	1	0	Elburn	8	7	1
Central City	4	4	0	Eldorado	12	8	4
Centralia	38	26	12	Elgin	227	170	57
Centreville	20	15	5	Elizabeth	1	1	0
Chadwick	1	1	0	Elk Grove Village	109	96	13
Champaign	148	117	31	Elmhurst	91	69	22
Channahon	15	13	2	Elmwood	1	1	0
Charleston	36	33	3	Elmwood Park	48	37	11
Chatham	17	12	5	El Paso	5	5	0
Chenoa	4	4	0	Energy	4	4	0
Cherry Valley	15	15	0	Enfield	1	1	0
Chester	13	10	3	Erie	3	3	0
Chicago	14,932	13,609	1,323	Essex	2	2	0
Chicago Heights	116	81	35	Eureka	5	5	0
Chicago Ridge	34	30	4	Evanston	207	159	48
Chillicothe	14	10	4	Evergreen Park	65	53	12
Christopher	4	4	0	Fairbury	7	7	0
Cicero	152	131	21	Fairfield	17	13	4
Clarendon Hills	15	15	0	Fairmont City	8	5	3
Clinton	15	14	1	Fairview	1	1	0
Coal City	11	11	0	Fairview Heights	51	40	11
Coal Valley	7	6	1	Farmer City	6	3	3
Cobden	2	2	0	Farmington	4	4	0
Collinsville	47	37	10	Fisher	2	2	0
Colona	11	9	2	Flora	16	11	5
Columbia	19	14	5	Flossmoor	25	19	6
Cordova	2	2	0	Ford Heights	23	14	9
Cortland	2	2	0	Forest Park	54	38	16
Coulterville	1	1	0	Forest View	11	8	3
Country Club Hills	42	31	11	Fox Lake	32	26	6
Countryside	29	23	6	Fox River Grove	11	11	0
Crest Hill	28	25	3	Fox River Valley Gardens	1	1	0
Crestwood	3	2	1	Frankfort	28	25	3

Table 78

Full-time Law Enforcement Employees as of October 31, 2002

by City by State—Continued

City by state	Total law enforcement employees	Total officers	Total civilians	City by state	Total law enforcement employees	Total officers	Total civilians
ILLINOIS—Continued				**ILLINOIS—Continued**			
Franklin Park	65	48	17	Hopedale	1	1	0
Freeburg	9	8	1	Hopkins Park	5	5	0
Freeport	76	58	18	Huntley	25	21	4
Fulton	8	7	1	Indian Head Park	13	10	3
Galena	12	10	2	Island Lake	17	12	5
Galesburg	81	53	28	Itasca	38	28	10
Galva	3	3	0	Jacksonville	51	42	9
Geneseo	21	14	7	Jerome	6	6	0
Geneva	47	35	12	Jerseyville	19	13	6
Genoa	8	8	0	Johnsburg	9	8	1
Georgetown	4	4	0	Johnston City	5	5	0
Germantown	2	2	0	Joliet	347	262	85
Gibson City	11	6	5	Jonesboro	3	3	0
Gifford	1	1	0	Justice	32	26	6
Gilberts	6	5	1	Kankakee	98	73	25
Gillespie	10	6	4	Kenilworth	14	10	4
Gilman	2	2	0	Kewanee	30	22	8
Girard	5	5	0	Kildeer	18	17	1
Glen Carbon	24	17	7	Kirkland	3	3	0
Glencoe	44	34	10	Knoxville	4	4	0
Glendale Heights	78	52	26	Lacon	3	3	0
Glen Ellyn	47	37	10	La Grange	34	28	6
Glenview	101	74	27	La Grange Park	29	24	5
Glenwood	26	19	7	Lake Bluff	20	15	5
Golf	4	4	0	Lake Forest	63	45	18
Grafton	2	2	0	Lake-in-the-Hills	49	36	13
Granite City	63	53	10	Lakemoor	9	8	1
Grant Park	6	5	1	Lake Villa	18	16	2
Granville	3	3	0	Lakewood	9	8	1
Grayslake	42	28	14	Lake Zurich	57	38	19
Grayville	7	3	4	La Moille	1	1	0
Greenfield	1	1	0	Lanark	2	2	0
Greenup	4	4	0	Lansing	81	62	19
Green Valley	3	3	0	La Salle	24	19	5
Greenville	14	10	4	Lebanon	9	9	0
Gridley	1	1	0	Leland	1	1	0
Gurnee	88	62	26	Leland Grove	6	6	0
Hamilton	5	5	0	Lemont	32	28	4
Hampshire	11	10	1	Lenzburg	1	1	0
Hampton	4	4	0	Le Roy	5	5	0
Hanover	2	2	0	Lewistown	3	3	0
Hanover Park	68	48	20	Lexington	3	3	0
Harrisburg	14	13	1	Libertyville	57	41	16
Hartford	4	3	1	Lincoln	32	28	4
Harvard	24	18	6	Lincolnshire	34	23	11
Harvey	93	56	37	Lincolnwood	45	34	11
Harwood Heights	36	27	9	Lindenhurst	16	14	2
Havana	14	9	5	Lisle	56	43	13
Hawthorn Woods	12	11	1	Litchfield	23	15	8
Hazel Crest	39	30	9	Livingston	1	1	0
Hebron	3	3	0	Lockport	34	30	4
Henry	4	4	0	Lombard	86	69	17
Herrin	20	14	6	Loves Park	39	30	9
Herscher	2	2	0	Ludlow	3	3	0
Hickory Hills	36	29	7	Lynwood	21	15	6
Highland	26	18	8	Lyons	28	22	6
Highland Park	75	53	22	Mackinaw	2	2	0
Highwood	15	13	2	Macomb	26	23	3
Hillsboro	8	8	0	Madison	17	13	4
Hillside	38	29	9	Mahomet	7	6	1
Hinckley	3	3	0	Manhattan	7	7	0
Hinsdale	39	28	11	Manito	5	5	0
Hodgkins	19	17	2	Manteno	15	14	1
Hoffman Estates	115	96	19	Marengo	17	12	5
Homer	1	1	0	Marion	32	22	10
Hometown	5	1	4	Marissa	5	5	0
Homewood	48	36	12	Markham	40	32	8
Hoopeston	17	11	6	Maroa	3	3	0

Table 78

Full-time Law Enforcement Employees as of October 31, 2002

by City by State—Continued

City by state	Total law enforcement employees	Total officers	Total civilians	City by state	Total law enforcement employees	Total officers	Total civilians
ILLINOIS—Continued				**ILLINOIS—Continued**			
Marquette Heights	5	5	0	Northlake	47	31	16
Marseilles	14	10	4	North Pekin	2	2	0
Marshall	11	10	1	North Riverside	38	30	8
Martinsville	2	2	0	Oak Brook	52	44	8
Maryville	15	10	5	Oakbrook Terrace	21	19	2
Mascoutah	14	12	2	Oak Forest	52	39	13
Mason City	4	4	0	Oak Lawn	153	105	48
Matteson	47	39	8	Oak Park	132	117	15
Mattoon	57	45	12	Oblong	2	2	0
Maywood	72	53	19	O'Fallon	63	43	20
McCook	19	15	4	Oglesby	19	9	10
McCullom Lake	1	1	0	Okawville	3	3	0
McHenry	57	43	14	Olney	19	13	6
McLean	1	1	0	Olympia Fields	20	18	2
McLeansboro	5	5	0	Oregon	8	7	1
Melrose Park	79	65	14	Orion	3	3	0
Mendota	20	15	5	Orland Hills	17	15	2
Meredosia	2	2	0	Orland Park	121	93	28
Metamora	6	6	0	Oswego	39	36	3
Metropolis	21	16	5	Ottawa	40	31	9
Midlothian	31	24	7	Palatine	140	110	30
Milan	22	13	9	Palestine	3	3	0
Milledgeville	2	2	0	Palmyra	1	1	0
Millstadt	5	5	0	Palos Heights	29	27	2
Minier	2	2	0	Palos Hills	38	35	3
Minonk	2	2	0	Palos Park	9	9	0
Minooka	15	13	2	Pana	13	9	4
Mokena	28	26	2	Paris	21	16	5
Moline	108	82	26	Park City	12	8	4
Momence	8	8	0	Park Forest	52	37	15
Monee	11	10	1	Park Ridge	68	54	14
Monmouth	26	17	9	Pawnee	10	6	4
Montgomery	23	15	8	Paxton	7	7	0
Monticello	7	6	1	Pecatonica	3	3	0
Morris	33	26	7	Pekin	59	53	6
Morrison	6	6	0	Peoria	280	234	46
Morton	29	22	7	Peoria Heights	14	10	4
Morton Grove	64	46	18	Peotone	11	10	1
Mound City	3	3	0	Peru	26	20	6
Mount Carmel	16	12	4	Petersburg	6	6	0
Mount Carroll	3	3	0	Phoenix	2	1	1
Mount Morris	6	5	1	Pinckneyville	11	8	3
Mount Olive	4	2	2	Piper City	1	1	0
Mount Prospect	102	82	20	Pittsfield	6	6	0
Mount Pulaski	4	4	0	Plainfield	40	34	6
Mount Sterling	10	5	5	Plano	16	14	2
Mount Vernon	60	46	14	Plymouth	1	1	0
Mount Zion	11	9	2	Polo	4	4	0
Moweaqua	2	2	0	Pontiac	25	22	3
Mundelein	56	39	17	Pontoon Beach	19	13	6
Murphysboro	25	16	9	Port Byron	2	2	0
Naperville	276	180	96	Posen	14	12	2
Nashville	7	6	1	Princeton	16	15	1
Nauvoo	3	3	0	Prophetstown	3	2	1
Neoga	3	3	0	Prospect Heights	34	26	8
New Athens	4	4	0	Quincy	90	72	18
New Baden	3	3	0	Ramsey	1	1	0
New Lenox	31	28	3	Rantoul	42	33	9
Newman	1	1	0	Raymond	1	1	0
Newton	8	7	1	Red Bud	5	5	0
Niles	70	54	16	Richmond	5	5	0
Nokomis	7	4	3	Richton Park	34	27	7
Normal	79	69	10	Ridge Farm	1	1	0
Norridge	54	39	15	Ridgway	3	3	0
North Aurora	25	23	2	Riverdale	49	35	14
Northbrook	91	62	29	River Forest	34	31	3
North Chicago	75	56	19	River Grove	30	23	7
Northfield	30	21	9	Riverside	25	19	6

Table 78

Full-time Law Enforcement Employees as of October 31, 2002
by City by State—Continued

City by state	Total law enforcement employees	Total officers	Total civilians	City by state	Total law enforcement employees	Total officers	Total civilians
ILLINOIS—Continued				**ILLINOIS—Continued**			
Robbins	13	6	7	Sullivan	10	8	2
Robinson	14	12	2	Summit	41	35	6
Rochelle	25	19	6	Sumner	2	2	0
Rochester	7	7	0	Swansea	21	16	5
Rockdale	3	3	0	Sycamore	32	22	10
Rock Falls	29	21	8	Tampico	1	1	0
Rockford	330	297	33	Taylorville	29	22	7
Rock Island	113	86	27	Thomasboro	2	2	0
Rockton	14	13	1	Thomson	1	1	0
Rolling Meadows	80	56	24	Thornton	11	10	1
Romeoville	66	52	14	Tilton	3	3	0
Roodhouse	5	5	0	Tinley Park	89	69	20
Roscoe	11	10	1	Tolono	4	4	0
Roselle	51	36	15	Tremont	3	3	0
Rosemont	84	70	14	Trenton	3	3	0
Rossville	2	2	0	Troy	20	15	5
Round Lake	19	15	4	Tuscola	7	6	1
Round Lake Beach	48	37	11	University Park	20	17	3
Round Lake Heights	4	4	0	Urbana	63	50	13
Round Lake Park	13	11	2	Valmeyer	1	1	0
Roxana	6	5	1	Vandalia	18	13	5
Royalton	2	2	0	Venice	7	4	3
Rushville	5	5	0	Vernon Hills	72	48	24
Salem	21	14	7	Vienna	3	3	0
Sandwich	19	13	6	Villa Grove	5	4	1
Sauget	13	12	1	Villa Park	53	38	15
Sauk Village	24	18	6	Virden	12	7	5
Savanna	8	8	0	Virginia	1	1	0
Schaumburg	203	134	69	Wamac	4	4	0
Schiller Park	38	31	7	Warren	3	3	0
Seneca	9	4	5	Warrensburg	1	1	0
Sesser	6	5	1	Warrenville	31	24	7
Shawneetown	4	4	0	Washburn	2	2	0
Shelbyville	8	7	1	Washington	26	17	9
Sheridan	2	2	0	Washington Park	14	10	4
Sherman	6	6	0	Waterloo	16	14	2
Shiloh	11	11	0	Waterman	1	1	0
Shorewood	22	19	3	Watseka	12	11	1
Silvis	21	14	7	Wauconda	34	20	14
Skokie	142	109	33	Waukegan	219	163	56
Sleepy Hollow	7	6	1	Wayne	4	4	0
Smithton	5	4	1	Wayne City	1	1	0
Somonauk	4	4	0	Westchester	50	38	12
South Barrington	20	16	4	West Chicago	58	47	11
South Beloit	12	9	3	West City	11	4	7
South Chicago Heights	11	9	2	West Dundee	23	20	3
South Elgin	35	27	8	Western Springs	27	21	6
Southern View	4	4	0	West Frankfort	20	14	6
South Holland	55	43	12	Westmont	60	44	16
South Jacksonville	6	5	1	West Salem	1	1	0
South Pekin	2	2	0	Westville	3	3	0
South Roxana	5	5	0	Wheaton	93	69	24
Sparta	17	12	5	Wheeling	87	63	24
Springfield	322	272	50	White Hall	7	4	3
Spring Grove	9	8	1	Williamsfield	1	1	0
Spring Valley	13	9	4	Williamsville	3	3	0
St. Anne	3	3	0	Willowbrook	29	25	4
Staunton	10	7	3	Willow Springs	19	14	5
St. Charles	60	49	11	Wilmette	57	40	17
Steger	23	16	7	Wilmington	19	13	6
Sterling	43	30	13	Winchester	4	4	0
Stickney	21	16	5	Winfield	22	20	2
Stockton	3	3	0	Winnebago	5	5	0
Stone Park	30	21	9	Winnetka	39	28	11
Stonington	1	1	0	Winthrop Harbor	17	10	7
Streamwood	67	56	11	Witt	1	1	0
Streator	30	25	5	Wood Dale	52	34	18
Sugar Grove	9	8	1	Woodhull	1	1	0

Table 78

Full-time Law Enforcement Employees as of October 31, 2002
by City by State—Continued

City by state	Total law enforcement employees	Total officers	Total civilians	City by state	Total law enforcement employees	Total officers	Total civilians
ILLINOIS—Continued				**INDIANA—Continued**			
Woodridge	72	50	22	Goshen	60	53	7
Wood River	26	19	7	Greencastle	17	15	2
Woodstock	44	32	12	Greendale	15	11	4
Worden	1	1	0	Greenfield	36	29	7
Worth	27	25	2	Greensburg	27	18	9
Yates City	1	1	0	Greenwood	76	54	22
Yorkville	20	18	2	Griffith	39	31	8
Zeigler	2	2	0	Hagerstown	5	5	0
Zion	60	44	16	Hammond	256	207	49
				Hartford City	12	10	2
INDIANA				Hebron	9	8	1
				Highland	50	42	8
Albion	5	5	0	Hobart	69	54	15
Alexandria	17	13	4	Huntingburg	10	9	1
Anderson	151	130	21	Huntington	44	33	11
Angola	20	16	4	Indianapolis	2,665	1,589	1,076
Attica	6	6	0	Jasonville	5	5	0
Auburn	28	21	7	Jasper	25	18	7
Aurora	12	8	4	Jeffersonville	57	49	8
Austin	6	6	0	Kendallville	25	18	7
Batesville	15	10	5	Kingsford Heights	2	2	0
Bedford	41	32	9	Knox	8	8	0
Beech Grove	41	30	11	Kokomo	137	99	38
Berne	6	6	0	Kouts	4	4	0
Bicknell	11	7	4	Lafayette	137	106	31
Bloomington	108	78	30	Lake Station	28	23	5
Bluffton	30	20	10	La Porte	52	47	5
Boonville	14	13	1	Lawrence	60	53	7
Brazil	16	12	4	Lawrenceburg	21	17	4
Bremen	16	12	4	Lebanon	29	28	1
Brookville	10	9	1	Ligonier	9	9	0
Brownsburg	39	28	11	Linton	13	9	4
Burns Harbor	2	2	0	Logansport	54	44	10
Cambridge City	5	5	0	Long Beach	6	5	1
Carmel	89	75	14	Loogootee	7	5	2
Cedar Lake	18	14	4	Lowell	19	14	5
Charlestown	17	12	5	Madison	34	27	7
Chesterfield	6	6	0	Marion	89	73	16
Chesterton	25	20	5	Martinsville	26	19	7
Clarksville	44	35	9	Merrillville	64	52	12
Clinton	11	7	4	Michigan City	103	88	15
Columbia City	19	17	2	Mishawaka	125	97	28
Columbus	79	73	6	Mitchell	14	9	5
Connersville	39	37	2	Monticello	16	12	4
Corydon	7	7	0	Mooresville	26	20	6
Covington	6	6	0	Mount Vernon	15	14	1
Crawfordsville	43	29	14	Muncie	128	120	8
Crown Point	42	31	11	Munster	46	35	11
Culver	5	4	1	Nappanee	21	15	6
Decatur	21	17	4	New Albany	78	61	17
Delphi	11	7	4	New Castle	39	36	3
Dunkirk	10	6	4	New Chicago	5	1	4
Dyer	32	25	7	New Haven	24	18	6
East Chicago	149	117	32	New Whiteland	11	7	4
Edinburgh	14	9	5	Noblesville	71	61	10
Elkhart	150	116	34	North Liberty	4	4	0
Elwood	21	17	4	North Manchester	15	11	4
Evansville	323	285	38	North Vernon	19	16	3
Fairmount	9	5	4	Oakland City	5	5	0
Fishers	67	60	7	Peru	30	28	2
Fort Wayne	549	413	136	Petersburg	5	5	0
Fowler	3	3	0	Plainfield	37	34	3
Frankfort	38	29	9	Plymouth	30	24	6
Franklin	46	33	13	Portage	69	51	18
Garrett	15	11	4	Portland	17	13	4
Gary	374	284	90	Princes Lakes	4	4	0
Gas City	16	12	4	Princeton	17	16	1
Georgetown	3	3	0	Rensselaer	14	9	5

Table 78

Full-time Law Enforcement Employees as of October 31, 2002

by City by State—Continued

City by state	Total law enforcement employees	Total officers	Total civilians	City by state	Total law enforcement employees	Total officers	Total civilians
INDIANA—Continued				**IOWA—Continued**			
Richmond	93	79	14	Cresco	8	8	0
Rochester	20	14	6	Creston	16	12	4
Rushville	18	13	5	Davenport	202	159	43
Salem	20	14	6	Decorah	18	13	5
Schererville	63	50	13	Denison	17	12	5
Scottsburg	15	13	2	Des Moines	495	359	136
Sellersburg	16	11	5	De Witt	9	9	0
Seymour	51	36	15	Dubuque	108	102	6
Shelbyville	53	40	13	Dyersville	11	6	5
South Bend	326	256	70	Eagle Grove	7	7	0
Speedway	40	31	9	Eldora	6	6	0
St. John	19	14	5	Eldridge	7	7	0
Sullivan	8	8	0	Emmetsburg	7	6	1
Tell City	18	13	5	Estherville	12	12	0
Terre Haute	151	128	23	Evansdale	8	7	1
Tipton	16	12	4	Fairfield	20	14	6
Trail Creek	4	4	0	Forest City	9	9	0
Union City	10	7	3	Fort Dodge	46	43	3
Valparaiso	67	48	19	Fort Madison	26	21	5
Vincennes	43	37	6	Garner	5	5	0
Wabash	31	26	5	Glenwood	13	11	2
Walkerton	12	7	5	Grinnell	17	15	2
Warsaw	47	35	12	Grundy Center	2	2	0
Washington	24	18	6	Hampton	13	8	5
Waterloo	6	5	1	Harlan	9	8	1
Westfield	27	23	4	Hawarden	4	4	0
West Lafayette	56	40	16	Hiawatha	8	8	0
West Terre Haute	12	7	5	Humboldt	6	6	0
Westville	5	4	1	Independence	15	11	4
Whitestown	1	1	0	Indianola	19	17	2
Whiting	28	22	6	Iowa City	101	72	29
Winchester	16	12	4	Iowa Falls	16	11	5
Winona Lake	5	5	0	Jefferson	8	8	0
				Johnston	14	13	1
IOWA				Keokuk	35	25	10
				Knoxville	18	13	5
Adel	8	8	0	Lake Mills	5	5	0
Albia	7	6	1	Le Claire	8	7	1
Algona	15	10	5	Le Mars	15	14	1
Altoona	22	20	2	Manchester	14	9	5
Ames	70	47	23	Maquoketa	17	12	5
Anamosa	8	7	1	Marion	47	38	9
Ankeny	44	34	10	Marshalltown	61	43	18
Atlantic	14	12	2	Mason City	57	44	13
Audubon	3	3	0	Missouri Valley	7	7	0
Belle Plaine	8	4	4	Monticello	7	6	1
Belmond	5	5	0	Mount Pleasant	16	14	2
Bettendorf	60	45	15	Mount Vernon	6	6	0
Bloomfield	5	5	0	Muscatine	51	38	13
Boone	22	17	5	Nevada	10	9	1
Burlington	61	45	16	New Hampton	6	6	0
Camanche	7	7	0	Newton	34	27	7
Carlisle	5	5	0	North Liberty	3	3	0
Carroll	16	15	1	Norwalk	12	10	2
Carter Lake	10	9	1	Oelwein	15	10	5
Cedar Falls	44	41	3	Ogden	3	3	0
Cedar Rapids	237	196	41	Onawa	7	7	0
Centerville	19	14	5	Orange City	7	7	0
Chariton	7	6	1	Osage	5	5	0
Charles City	13	12	1	Osceola	11	10	1
Cherokee	10	9	1	Oskaloosa	19	17	2
Clarinda	15	11	4	Ottumwa	43	36	7
Clarion	7	6	1	Pella	17	14	3
Clear Lake	19	14	5	Perry	19	13	6
Clinton	52	43	9	Pleasant Hill	11	11	0
Clive	22	19	3	Polk City	5	5	0
Coralville	33	29	4	Red Oak	12	11	1
Council Bluffs	135	116	19	Rock Rapids	3	3	0

Table 78

Full-time Law Enforcement Employees as of October 31, 2002

by City by State—Continued

City by state	Total law enforcement employees	Total officers	Total civilians	City by state	Total law enforcement employees	Total officers	Total civilians
IOWA—Continued				**KANSAS—Continued**			
Sac City	4	4	0	Cherryvale	6	6	0
Sergeant Bluff	9	8	1	Chetopa	4	4	0
Sheldon	12	8	4	Cimarron	3	3	0
Shenandoah	14	10	4	Claflin	2	2	0
Sioux Center	7	7	0	Clay Center	7	6	1
Sioux City	164	133	31	Clearwater	6	6	0
Spencer	27	20	7	Coffeyville	29	23	6
Spirit Lake	8	7	1	Colby	17	12	5
St. Ansgar	1	1	0	Columbus	10	8	2
Storm Lake	22	18	4	Colwich	3	3	0
Story City	5	5	0	Concordia	16	10	6
Tama	6	6	0	Conway Springs	3	3	0
Tipton	6	6	0	Council Grove	5	5	0
Urbandale	44	40	4	Derby	45	34	11
Vinton	7	7	0	Dodge City	55	42	13
Washington	11	11	0	Eastborough	7	7	0
Waterloo	131	121	10	Edwardsville	16	15	1
Waukee	11	9	2	El Dorado	25	23	2
Waukon	7	7	0	Elkhart	3	3	0
Waverly	16	15	1	Ellinwood	5	5	0
Webster City	21	14	7	Ellis	5	5	0
West Burlington	10	9	1	Ellsworth	6	5	1
West Des Moines	70	58	12	Elwood	3	3	0
West Liberty	6	5	1	Emporia	70	49	21
West Union	5	5	0	Enterprise	1	1	0
Williamsburg	5	5	0	Erie	3	3	0
Wilton	5	5	0	Eskridge	1	1	0
Windsor Heights	12	11	1	Eudora	8	8	0
Winterset	9	8	1	Fairway	9	8	1
				Florence	1	1	0
KANSAS				Fort Scott	22	17	5
				Fredonia	6	5	1
Abilene	16	14	2	Frontenac	9	6	3
Alma	1	1	0	Galena	14	9	5
Altamont	4	4	0	Galva	1	1	0
Andover	19	14	5	Garden City	81	53	28
Anthony	5	5	0	Garden Plain	2	2	0
Arkansas City	31	23	8	Gardner	22	21	1
Arma	4	4	0	Garnett	12	8	4
Atchison	25	23	2	Girard	7	7	0
Attica	1	1	0	Goddard	4	4	0
Atwood	1	1	0	Goodland	11	10	1
Augusta	32	24	8	Grandview Plaza	4	4	0
Baldwin City	8	7	1	Great Bend	37	32	5
Basehor	6	5	1	Halstead	6	5	1
Baxter Springs	14	10	4	Harper	3	3	0
Bel Aire	9	8	1	Haven	3	3	0
Belle Plaine	4	4	0	Hays	43	29	14
Belleville	5	5	0	Haysville	32	24	8
Beloit	14	9	5	Herington	11	6	5
Bird City	1	1	0	Hesston	7	6	1
Blue Rapids	2	2	0	Hiawatha	7	6	1
Bonner Springs	23	21	2	Highland	3	3	0
Buhler	3	3	0	Hill City	4	4	0
Burlingame	3	3	0	Hillsboro	6	6	0
Burlington	9	7	2	Hoisington	10	7	3
Burrton	1	1	0	Holcomb	4	3	1
Bushton	1	1	0	Holton	11	7	4
Caldwell	4	4	0	Hope	1	1	0
Caney	9	5	4	Horton	10	6	4
Canton	2	2	0	Hoxie	2	2	0
Carbondale	3	3	0	Hugoton	6	6	0
Cawker City	1	1	0	Humboldt	6	6	0
Cedar Vale	1	1	0	Hutchinson	98	72	26
Chanute	22	19	3	Independence	31	23	8
Chapman	2	2	0	Inman	2	2	0
Cheney	3	3	0	Iola	27	17	10
Cherokee	1	1	0	Junction City	66	50	16

Table 78

Full-time Law Enforcement Employees as of October 31, 2002
by City by State—Continued

City by state	Total law enforcement employees	Total officers	Total civilians	City by state	Total law enforcement employees	Total officers	Total civilians
KANSAS—Continued				**KANSAS—Continued**			
Kansas City	408	338	70	Rose Hill	8	7	1
Kechi	2	2	0	Rossville	3	3	0
Kingman	6	6	0	Russell	19	8	11
Kinsley	3	3	0	Sabetha	5	5	0
Kiowa	3	3	0	Salina	104	76	28
La Crosse	3	3	0	Scott City	12	7	5
La Cygne	2	2	0	Scranton	1	1	0
Lake Quivira	2	2	0	Sedan	2	2	0
Lansing	13	11	2	Sedgwick	2	2	0
Larned	9	9	0	Seneca	4	4	0
Lawrence	164	131	33	Sharon Springs	1	1	0
Leavenworth	84	62	22	Shawnee	108	87	21
Leawood	75	54	21	Silver Lake	2	2	0
Lebo	1	1	0	Smith Center	3	3	0
Lenexa	117	73	44	South Hutchinson	9	7	2
Le Roy	1	1	0	Spearville	1	1	0
Liberal	46	35	11	Spring Hill	8	7	1
Lindsborg	7	6	1	Stafford	4	4	0
Little River	1	1	0	Sterling	5	5	0
Louisburg	9	9	0	St. Francis	5	4	1
Lyndon	3	3	0	St. George	1	1	0
Lyons	8	7	1	St. John	4	4	0
Macksville	1	1	0	St. Marys	5	5	0
Maize	7	5	2	Stockton	4	4	0
Maple Hill	1	1	0	Tonganoxie	8	7	1
Marion	3	3	0	Topeka	344	286	58
Marquette	1	1	0	Towanda	3	3	0
Marysville	7	6	1	Troy	1	1	0
McLouth	1	1	0	Udall	2	2	0
McPherson	30	25	5	Ulysses	12	11	1
Meade	3	3	0	Valley Center	12	7	5
Medicine Lodge	6	6	0	Valley Falls	2	2	0
Merriam	30	26	4	Victoria	2	2	0
Minneapolis	5	5	0	Wa Keeney	5	5	0
Mission	23	22	1	Wakefield	1	1	0
Moran	1	1	0	Wamego	11	6	5
Moundridge	3	3	0	Waterville	1	1	0
Mount Hope	2	2	0	Wathena	2	2	0
Mulberry	1	1	0	Waverly	1	1	0
Mulvane	17	12	5	Weir	1	1	0
Neodesha	8	7	1	Wellington	18	14	4
Newton	33	29	4	Wellsville	3	3	0
Nickerson	5	5	0	Westwood	8	7	1
North Newton	2	2	0	Wichita	830	636	194
Norton	5	5	0	Wilson	1	1	0
Oakley	11	6	5	Winfield	29	22	7
Oberlin	3	3	0	Yates Center	4	4	0
Olathe	183	143	40				
Osage City	6	6	0	**KENTUCKY**			
Osawatomie	17	11	6				
Osborne	4	4	0	Adairville	1	1	0
Oswego	6	5	1	Albany	11	10	1
Ottawa	29	26	3	Alexandria	13	12	1
Overbrook	2	2	0	Allen	1	1	0
Overland Park	256	207	49	Anchorage	14	10	4
Oxford	3	3	0	Ashland	56	48	8
Paola	21	15	6	Auburn	3	3	0
Park City	17	15	2	Audubon Park	6	6	0
Parsons	29	21	8	Augusta	3	3	0
Peabody	3	3	0	Barbourville	16	13	3
Pittsburg	52	38	14	Bardstown	25	20	5
Plainville	5	5	0	Bardwell	1	1	0
Pleasanton	2	2	0	Beattyville	7	5	2
Prairie Village	52	40	12	Beaver Dam	6	6	0
Pratt	21	14	7	Bellefonte	2	2	0
Quinter	1	1	0	Bellevue	10	9	1
Roeland Park	16	14	2	Benham	5	4	1
Rolla	1	1	0	Benton	9	7	2

Table 78

Full-time Law Enforcement Employees as of October 31, 2002

by City by State—Continued

City by state	Total law enforcement employees	Total officers	Total civilians	City by state	Total law enforcement employees	Total officers	Total civilians
KENTUCKY—Continued				**KENTUCKY—Continued**			
Berea	31	25	6	Greenup	3	3	0
Bloomfield	1	1	0	Greenville	9	9	0
Booneville	2	2	0	Guthrie	6	5	1
Bowling Green	118	87	31	Hardinsburg	4	4	0
Brandenburg	4	4	0	Harlan	15	11	4
Brodhead	1	1	0	Harrodsburg	28	18	10
Brooksville	1	1	0	Hartford	5	5	0
Brownsville	1	1	0	Hawesville	1	1	0
Burkesville	9	5	4	Hazard	26	20	6
Burnside	4	4	0	Henderson	67	59	8
Butler	1	1	0	Hickman	3	3	0
Cadiz	10	9	1	Highland Heights	11	10	1
Calhoun	2	2	0	Hillview	11	11	0
Calvert City	6	5	1	Hindman	2	2	0
Campbellsburg	1	1	0	Hodgenville	7	7	0
Campbellsville	32	21	11	Hopkinsville	75	67	8
Campton	1	1	0	Horse Cave	5	5	0
Caneyville	1	1	0	Hustonville	1	1	0
Carlisle	8	6	2	Independence	25	23	2
Carrollton	12	11	1	Indian Hills	8	7	1
Catlettsburg	8	8	0	Inez	2	2	0
Cave City	6	6	0	Irvine	7	7	0
Central City	13	12	1	Irvington	4	4	0
Clarkson	2	2	0	Jackson	11	10	1
Clay	1	1	0	Jamestown	5	5	0
Clay City	3	3	0	Jeffersontown	58	50	8
Clinton	5	5	0	Jenkins	5	5	0
Cloverport	2	2	0	Junction City	5	5	0
Cold Spring	9	9	0	La Center	2	2	0
Columbia	10	10	0	La Grange	13	12	1
Corbin	28	21	7	Lakeside Park-Crestview Hills	9	8	1
Covington	143	113	30	Lancaster	8	8	0
Crab Orchard	2	2	0	Lawrenceburg	24	17	7
Crescent Springs	9	9	0	Lebanon	23	15	8
Crofton	1	1	0	Lebanon Junction	5	5	0
Cumberland	10	7	3	Leitchfield	16	15	1
Cynthiana	16	15	1	Lewisburg	1	1	0
Danville	24	23	1	Lewisport	3	3	0
Dawson Springs	10	6	4	Lexington	651	496	155
Dayton	8	8	0	Liberty	4	4	0
Earlington	2	2	0	Livermore	2	2	0
Edgewood	12	12	0	Livingston	1	1	0
Edmonton	6	6	0	London	33	30	3
Elizabethtown	53	39	14	Lone Oak	2	2	0
Elkhorn City	5	4	1	Louisa	7	7	0
Elkton	8	8	0	Louisville	927	709	218
Elsmere	12	11	1	Loyall	4	1	3
Eminence	6	6	0	Ludlow	10	8	2
Erlanger	40	32	8	Lynch	2	2	0
Eubank	1	1	0	Lynnview	1	1	0
Evarts	5	5	0	Madisonville	48	38	10
Falmouth	7	6	1	Manchester	13	13	0
Flatwoods	14	10	4	Marion	7	7	0
Fleming-Neon	3	3	0	Martin	5	5	0
Flemingsburg	7	7	0	Mayfield	36	28	8
Florence	57	53	4	Maysville	31	25	6
Fort Mitchell	13	12	1	McKee	2	2	0
Fort Thomas	23	22	1	Middlesboro	28	24	4
Fort Wright	10	10	0	Millersburg	3	3	0
Frankfort	58	53	5	Monticello	9	9	0
Franklin	23	20	3	Morehead	29	20	9
Fulton	15	11	4	Morganfield	13	8	5
Gamaliel	1	1	0	Morgantown	4	4	0
Georgetown	49	42	7	Mortons Gap	1	1	0
Glasgow	48	36	12	Mount Olivet	1	1	0
Graymoor-Devondale	3	3	0	Mount Sterling	28	19	9
Grayson	10	10	0	Mount Vernon	8	8	0
Greensburg	6	6	0	Mount Washington	14	13	1

Table 78

Full-time Law Enforcement Employees as of October 31, 2002
by City by State—Continued

City by state	Total law enforcement employees	Total officers	Total civilians
KENTUCKY—Continued			
Muldraugh	3	3	0
Munfordville	5	5	0
Murray	35	30	5
New Castle	1	1	0
New Haven	1	1	0
Newport	68	53	15
Nicholasville	56	53	3
Nortonville	1	1	0
Oak Grove	16	12	4
Olive Hill	7	7	0
Owensboro	139	105	34
Owenton	3	3	0
Owingsville	3	3	0
Paducah	91	77	14
Paintsville	21	13	8
Paris	23	22	1
Park City	1	1	0
Park Hills	6	6	0
Pembroke	1	1	0
Perryville	1	1	0
Pikeville	28	20	8
Pineville	8	8	0
Pioneer Village	5	5	0
Pippa Passes	1	1	0
Powderly	3	2	1
Prestonsburg	15	15	0
Princeton	17	15	2
Prospect	10	9	1
Providence	6	6	0
Raceland	6	5	1
Radcliff	51	36	15
Ravenna	2	2	0
Richmond	61	47	14
Russell	13	13	0
Russell Springs	8	7	1
Russellville	26	24	2
Sadieville	2	2	0
Salyersville	4	4	0
Science Hill	1	1	0
Scottsville	20	15	5
Sebree	2	2	0
Shelbyville	22	21	1
Shepherdsville	17	16	1
Shively	28	22	6
Silver Grove	1	1	0
Somerset	32	29	3
Southgate	6	6	0
South Shore	2	2	0
Springfield	8	8	0
Stamping Ground	1	1	0
Stanford	9	8	1
Stanton	10	10	0
St. Matthews	37	31	6
Sturgis	5	5	0
Taylor Mill	9	8	1
Taylorsville	4	4	0
Tompkinsville	11	8	3
Trenton	1	1	0
Uniontown	2	2	0
Vanceburg	6	6	0
Versailles	32	22	10
Villa Hills	9	8	1
Vine Grove	7	7	0
Warsaw	4	4	0
Wayland	1	1	0
West Buechel	11	11	0
West Liberty	9	4	5
West Point	4	4	0

City by state	Total law enforcement employees	Total officers	Total civilians
KENTUCKY—Continued			
Wheelwright	1	1	0
Whitesburg	6	6	0
Wickliffe	1	1	0
Wilder	7	7	0
Williamsburg	12	11	1
Williamstown	6	6	0
Wilmore	9	8	1
Winchester	42	29	13
Wingo	1	1	0
Worthington	4	4	0
Wurtland	1	1	0
LOUISIANA			
Abita Springs	8	7	1
Addis	6	5	1
Alexandria	188	154	34
Amite	20	20	0
Baker	31	31	0
Baldwin	9	8	1
Ball	5	4	1
Basile	14	8	6
Bastrop	49	44	5
Baton Rouge	749	593	156
Bernice	6	6	0
Berwick	10	10	0
Blanchard	4	4	0
Bogalusa	58	38	20
Bossier City	204	150	54
Breaux Bridge	22	22	0
Broussard	16	14	2
Brusly	10	9	1
Church Point	17	17	0
Clinton	7	7	0
Coushatta	6	6	0
Covington	42	32	10
Crowley	33	32	1
Cullen	5	5	0
Denham Springs	42	27	15
De Quincy	13	13	0
De Ridder	25	24	1
Dixie Inn	3	3	0
Dubach	2	2	0
Elton	5	5	0
Erath	10	7	3
Eunice	45	40	5
Farmerville	13	13	0
Ferriday	16	11	5
Folsom	3	2	1
Franklin	22	21	1
Franklinton	19	13	6
French Settlement	2	2	0
Glenmora	6	6	0
Golden Meadow	5	4	1
Gonzales	30	30	0
Grambling	18	13	5
Gramercy	7	7	0
Gretna	101	80	21
Hammond	96	71	25
Harahan	25	25	0
Haughton	6	6	0
Haynesville	8	8	0
Homer	11	11	0
Houma	86	71	15
Independence	7	7	0
Iota	4	4	0
Iowa	12	10	2
Jackson	7	6	1

Table 78

Full-time Law Enforcement Employees as of October 31, 2002

by City by State—Continued

City by state	Total law enforcement employees	Total officers	Total civilians	City by state	Total law enforcement employees	Total officers	Total civilians
LOUISIANA—Continued				**LOUISIANA—Continued**			
Jeanerette	15	11	4	Westwego	38	37	1
Jena	5	5	0	Winnfield	23	15	8
Jennings	40	32	8	Youngsville	10	8	2
Jonesboro	15	11	4	Zachary	34	33	1
Kaplan	22	22	0				
Kenner	256	176	80	**MAINE**			
Kentwood	10	10	0				
Kinder	13	13	0	Ashland	3	3	0
Krotz Springs	8	3	5	Auburn	59	51	8
Lafayette	287	212	75	Augusta	57	42	15
Lake Arthur	10	10	0	Baileyville	8	8	0
Lake Charles	177	170	7	Bangor	88	73	15
Lake Providence	11	11	0	Bar Harbor	13	9	4
Leesville	28	28	0	Bath	24	19	5
Lockport	5	5	0	Belfast	14	12	2
Mamou	18	15	3	Berwick	11	10	1
Mandeville	46	37	9	Bethel	4	4	0
Mansfield	15	11	4	Biddeford	68	48	20
Many	14	13	1	Boothbay Harbor	7	5	2
Marksville	22	14	8	Brewer	19	17	2
McNary	2	1	1	Bridgton	12	8	4
Minden	34	33	1	Brownville	2	2	0
Monroe	234	186	48	Brunswick	47	33	14
Morgan City	57	47	10	Bucksport	11	7	4
Napoleonville	3	3	0	Buxton	13	8	5
Natchitoches	67	54	13	Calais	12	8	4
New Iberia	85	69	16	Camden	15	11	4
New Orleans	2,000	1,613	387	Cape Elizabeth	17	13	4
New Roads	19	17	2	Caribou	16	14	2
Norwood	2	1	1	Carrabassett Valley	7	1	6
Oakdale	25	25	0	Clinton	2	2	0
Olla	3	3	0	Cumberland	16	11	5
Opelousas	73	57	16	Damariscotta	6	5	1
Patterson	19	18	1	Dexter	6	5	1
Pearl River	10	6	4	Dixfield	4	4	0
Pineville	48	43	5	Dover-Foxcroft	5	5	0
Plaquemine	24	20	4	East Millinocket	5	5	0
Pollock	2	2	0	Eastport	4	4	0
Ponchatoula	21	16	5	Eddington	1	1	0
Port Allen	23	19	4	Eliot	8	8	0
Port Vincent	4	3	1	Ellsworth	17	13	4
Rayne	25	24	1	Fairfield	13	12	1
Rayville	10	10	0	Falmouth	23	16	7
Richwood	13	6	7	Farmington	15	14	1
Ruston	50	41	9	Fort Fairfield	4	4	0
Shreveport	638	499	139	Fort Kent	9	5	4
Sicily Island	3	2	1	Freeport	17	12	5
Simmesport	5	5	0	Fryeburg	5	5	0
Slidell	112	76	36	Gardiner	16	11	5
Sorrento	5	5	0	Gorham	28	20	8
Springhill	13	13	0	Gouldsboro	1	1	0
Sterlington	5	5	0	Greenville	4	3	1
St. Gabriel	15	7	8	Hallowell	5	5	0
St. Martinville	23	15	8	Hampden	12	11	1
Stonewall	1	1	0	Houlton	18	13	5
Sulphur	61	57	4	Jay	11	7	4
Tallulah	16	16	0	Kennebunk	26	20	6
Thibodaux	69	55	14	Kennebunkport	12	11	1
Tickfaw	7	7	0	Kittery	27	19	8
Vidalia	22	16	6	Lewiston	96	83	13
Ville Platte	23	23	0	Limestone	5	5	0
Vinton	12	12	0	Lincoln	7	6	1
Vivian	12	9	3	Lisbon	21	16	5
Washington	5	5	0	Livermore Falls	11	7	4
Waterproof	8	6	2	Machias	4	4	0
Welsh	13	13	0	Madawaska	7	6	1
Westlake	21	20	1	Madison	6	5	1
West Monroe	76	71	5	Mechanic Falls	5	5	0

Table 78

Full-time Law Enforcement Employees as of October 31, 2002
by City by State—Continued

City by state	Total law enforcement employees	Total officers	Total civilians	City by state	Total law enforcement employees	Total officers	Total civilians
MAINE—Continued				**MARYLAND—Continued**			
Mexico	4	4	0	Cheverly	15	13	2
Milbridge	2	2	0	Cottage City	3	3	0
Millinocket	9	9	0	Crisfield	15	12	3
Milo	3	3	0	Cumberland	58	47	11
Monmouth	5	5	0	Delmar	11	10	1
Mount Desert	10	6	4	Denton	10	9	1
Newport	5	5	0	District Heights	10	8	2
North Berwick	9	8	1	Easton	62	47	15
Norway	8	7	1	Edmonston	6	6	0
Oakland	10	9	1	Elkton	40	30	10
Ogunquit	9	8	1	Fairmount Heights	5	4	1
Old Orchard Beach	25	17	8	Federalsburg	11	10	1
Old Town	19	15	4	Forest Heights	4	3	1
Orono	15	13	2	Frederick	161	128	33
Oxford	5	4	1	Frostburg	20	16	4
Paris	9	8	1	Fruitland	13	12	1
Phippsburg	1	1	0	Glenarden	7	5	2
Pittsfield	6	6	0	Greenbelt	63	49	14
Portland	218	152	66	Greensboro	3	3	0
Presque Isle	22	18	4	Hagerstown	119	98	21
Rangeley	3	3	0	Hampstead	9	8	1
Richmond	5	5	0	Hancock	5	4	1
Rockland	21	18	3	Havre de Grace	36	27	9
Rockport	8	7	1	Hurlock	8	7	1
Rumford	16	16	0	Hyattsville	41	32	9
Sabattus	8	7	1	Landover Hills	3	2	1
Saco	45	33	12	La Plata	11	10	1
Sanford	45	32	13	Laurel	57	42	15
Scarborough	46	31	15	Luke	2	2	0
Searsport	3	3	0	Manchester	4	4	0
Skowhegan	17	12	5	Morningside	12	9	3
South Berwick	11	7	4	Mount Rainier	16	13	3
South Portland	68	51	17	North East	8	7	1
Southwest Harbor	9	5	4	Oakland	7	6	1
Swan's Island	1	1	0	Ocean City	113	93	20
Thomaston	5	5	0	Ocean Pines	19	14	5
Topsham	18	14	4	Oxford	4	4	0
Van Buren	4	4	0	Pocomoke City	17	12	5
Veazie	8	7	1	Port Deposit	4	4	0
Waldoboro	6	5	1	Preston	2	2	0
Washburn	2	2	0	Princess Anne	10	9	1
Waterville	37	29	8	Ridgely	4	4	0
Wells	31	23	8	Rising Sun	7	5	2
Westbrook	43	31	12	Riverdale Park	28	19	9
Wilton	5	5	0	Rock Hall	3	3	0
Windham	29	22	7	Salisbury	105	79	26
Winslow	9	8	1	Seat Pleasant	14	9	5
Winter Harbor	1	1	0	Smithsburg	3	2	1
Winthrop	12	8	4	Snow Hill	9	8	1
Wiscasset	6	5	1	St. Michaels	5	4	1
Yarmouth	17	12	5	Sykesville	8	7	1
York	34	24	10	Takoma Park	51	37	14
				Taneytown	7	7	0
MARYLAND				Thurmont	10	10	0
				University Park	7	7	0
Aberdeen	48	39	9	Westernport	2	2	0
Annapolis	148	108	40	Westminster	53	41	12
Baltimore	3,888	3,316	572				
Baltimore City Sheriff	147	127	20	**MASSACHUSETTS**			
Bel Air	42	30	12				
Berlin	20	15	5	Abington	32	30	2
Berwyn Heights	7	6	1	Acton	37	31	6
Bladensburg	22	18	4	Acushnet	19	17	2
Brunswick	12	10	2	Adams	24	18	6
Cambridge	54	45	9	Agawam	59	50	9
Capitol Heights	12	10	2	Amesbury	40	33	7
Centreville	7	7	0	Amherst	60	50	10
Chestertown	13	11	2	Andover	71	52	19

Table 78

Full-time Law Enforcement Employees as of October 31, 2002

by City by State—Continued

City by state	Total law enforcement employees	Total officers	Total civilians	City by state	Total law enforcement employees	Total officers	Total civilians
MASSACHUSETTS—Continued				**MASSACHUSETTS—Continued**			
Aquinnah	3	3	0	Edgartown	16	15	1
Arlington	82	69	13	Egremont	2	2	0
Ashburnham	9	8	1	Erving	3	3	0
Ashby	6	6	0	Essex	9	8	1
Ashfield	2	2	0	Everett	97	89	8
Ashland	30	23	7	Fairhaven	35	30	5
Athol	25	20	5	Fall River	291	232	59
Attleboro	79	66	13	Falmouth	73	65	8
Auburn	41	31	10	Fitchburg	106	88	18
Avon	17	14	3	Foxborough	34	30	4
Ayer	20	15	5	Framingham	128	114	14
Barnstable	131	111	20	Franklin	57	46	11
Barre	10	6	4	Freetown	22	17	5
Becket	1	1	0	Gardner	43	34	9
Bedford	34	26	8	Georgetown	12	9	3
Belchertown	22	17	5	Gill	3	3	0
Bellingham	38	31	7	Gloucester	65	61	4
Belmont	54	50	4	Grafton	23	15	8
Berkley	4	4	0	Granby	11	10	1
Berlin	11	7	4	Great Barrington	16	15	1
Bernardston	3	3	0	Greenfield	52	39	13
Beverly	75	72	3	Groton	23	17	6
Billerica	86	66	20	Groveland	12	7	5
Blackstone	17	15	2	Hadley	11	10	1
Bolton	13	8	5	Halifax	15	11	4
Boston	2,771	2,143	628	Hamilton	21	15	6
Bourne	40	33	7	Hampden	14	10	4
Boxborough	11	10	1	Hanover	32	29	3
Boxford	14	13	1	Hanson	25	20	5
Boylston	12	9	3	Hardwick	3	3	0
Braintree	87	78	9	Harvard	13	8	5
Brewster	25	19	6	Harwich	41	35	6
Bridgewater	42	38	4	Hatfield	2	2	0
Brockton	220	188	32	Haverhill	99	88	11
Brookfield	3	3	0	Hingham	53	42	11
Brookline	152	134	18	Hinsdale	2	2	0
Buckland	2	2	0	Holbrook	22	21	1
Burlington	68	60	8	Holden	24	23	1
Canton	45	44	1	Holland	2	2	0
Carlisle	14	11	3	Holliston	22	21	1
Carver	18	13	5	Holyoke	151	128	23
Charlton	22	18	4	Hopedale	15	11	4
Chatham	28	22	6	Hopkinton	25	20	5
Chelmsford	71	56	15	Hubbardston	9	5	4
Chelsea	101	85	16	Hudson	37	31	6
Chicopee	127	123	4	Hull	31	29	2
Clinton	34	29	5	Ipswich	30	25	5
Cohasset	24	18	6	Kingston	30	22	8
Concord	41	34	7	Lakeville	19	14	5
Dalton	12	10	2	Lancaster	10	10	0
Danvers	63	47	16	Lanesboro	6	6	0
Dartmouth	86	62	24	Lawrence	172	146	26
Dedham	62	60	2	Lee	12	11	1
Deerfield	7	6	1	Leicester	22	17	5
Dennis	50	41	9	Lenox	10	10	0
Dighton	9	9	0	Leominster	88	72	16
Douglas	15	11	4	Leverett	1	1	0
Dover	17	16	1	Lexington	65	52	13
Dracut	47	42	5	Lincoln	19	13	6
Dudley	20	16	4	Littleton	17	16	1
Dunstable	7	7	0	Longmeadow	35	30	5
Duxbury	40	31	9	Lowell	327	249	78
East Bridgewater	27	24	3	Ludlow	39	33	6
East Brookfield	3	3	0	Lunenburg	13	13	0
Eastham	20	14	6	Lynn	208	189	19
Easthampton	28	27	1	Lynnfield	23	19	4
East Longmeadow	24	22	2	Malden	111	100	11
Easton	34	30	4	Manchester-by-the-Sea	16	14	2

Table 78

Full-time Law Enforcement Employees as of October 31, 2002
by City by State—Continued

City by state	Total law enforcement employees	Total officers	Total civilians	City by state	Total law enforcement employees	Total officers	Total civilians
MASSACHUSETTS—Continued				**MASSACHUSETTS—Continued**			
Mansfield	42	32	10	Revere	101	93	8
Marblehead	46	37	9	Rochester	10	10	0
Marion	14	14	0	Rockland	45	34	11
Marlborough	76	65	11	Rockport	17	16	1
Marshfield	45	42	3	Rowley	18	14	4
Mashpee	41	32	9	Rutland	6	5	1
Mattapoisett	17	17	0	Salem	102	92	10
Maynard	24	22	2	Salisbury	20	16	4
Medfield	22	17	5	Sandwich	34	33	1
Medford	129	124	5	Saugus	81	61	20
Medway	26	21	5	Scituate	35	28	7
Melrose	52	49	3	Seekonk	40	34	6
Mendon	19	14	5	Sharon	29	26	3
Merrimac	11	7	4	Sheffield	6	6	0
Methuen	98	84	14	Shelburne	2	2	0
Middleboro	52	42	10	Sherborn	14	14	0
Middleton	12	11	1	Shirley	17	11	6
Milford	50	46	4	Shrewsbury	51	38	13
Millbury	22	17	5	Somerset	40	32	8
Millis	19	15	4	Somerville	158	132	26
Millville	7	4	3	Southampton	7	7	0
Milton	71	56	15	Southborough	20	15	5
Monson	17	12	5	Southbridge	38	35	3
Montague	20	15	5	South Hadley	32	27	5
Monterey	1	1	0	Southwick	21	16	5
Nahant	12	12	0	Spencer	21	17	4
Nantucket	34	30	4	Springfield	651	553	98
Natick	67	53	14	Sterling	15	10	5
Needham	58	49	9	Stockbridge	6	6	0
New Bedford	321	271	50	Stoneham	51	41	10
Newbury	15	10	5	Stoughton	65	58	7
Newburyport	39	33	6	Stow	16	11	5
Newton	174	146	28	Sturbridge	23	18	5
Norfolk	19	17	2	Sudbury	33	27	6
North Adams	34	27	7	Sunderland	6	5	1
Northampton	65	59	6	Sutton	17	13	4
North Andover	51	39	12	Swampscott	37	35	2
North Attleboro	59	49	10	Swansea	36	30	6
Northborough	27	20	7	Taunton	123	117	6
Northbridge	25	20	5	Templeton	11	10	1
North Brookfield	6	6	0	Tewksbury	71	54	17
Northfield	4	4	0	Tisbury	11	10	1
North Reading	32	30	2	Topsfield	14	10	4
Norton	29	27	2	Townsend	18	16	2
Norwell	25	23	2	Truro	16	11	5
Norwood	72	61	11	Tyngsboro	28	25	3
Oak Bluffs	17	14	3	Upton	16	12	4
Orange	14	13	1	Uxbridge	23	18	5
Orleans	26	20	6	Wakefield	45	44	1
Oxford	22	18	4	Walpole	43	37	6
Palmer	27	21	6	Waltham	187	140	47
Paxton	9	8	1	Ware	18	18	0
Peabody	110	94	16	Wareham	54	45	9
Pembroke	30	28	2	Warren	11	7	4
Pepperell	18	17	1	Watertown	86	72	14
Petersham	2	2	0	Wayland	32	23	9
Phillipston	1	1	0	Webster	33	29	4
Pittsfield	91	78	13	Wellesley	55	41	14
Plainville	17	13	4	Wellfleet	18	13	5
Plymouth	121	102	19	Wenham	11	10	1
Plympton	5	5	0	Westborough	34	27	7
Princeton	8	5	3	West Boylston	18	13	5
Provincetown	24	17	7	West Bridgewater	22	21	1
Quincy	238	204	34	West Brookfield	6	6	0
Randolph	56	55	1	Westfield	84	75	9
Raynham	31	23	8	Westford	51	40	11
Reading	48	38	10	Westminster	16	11	5
Rehoboth	25	21	4	West Newbury	12	7	5

Table 78

Full-time Law Enforcement Employees as of October 31, 2002

by City by State—Continued

City by state	Total law enforcement employees	Total officers	Total civilians	City by state	Total law enforcement employees	Total officers	Total civilians
MASSACHUSETTS—Continued				**MICHIGAN—Continued**			
Weston	32	27	5	Buchanan	9	8	1
Westport	32	27	5	Buena Vista Township	17	15	2
West Springfield	93	83	10	Burr Oak	1	1	0
West Tisbury	10	10	0	Burton	46	40	6
Westwood	32	25	7	Cadillac	19	16	3
Weymouth	123	106	17	Calumet	2	2	0
Whately	2	2	0	Cambridge Township	2	2	0
Whitman	27	26	1	Canton Township	109	79	30
Wilbraham	30	29	1	Capac	5	4	1
Williamsburg	1	1	0	Carleton	4	3	1
Williamstown	17	13	4	Caro	10	9	1
Wilmington	47	45	2	Carrollton Township	8	7	1
Winchendon	16	12	4	Carson City	2	2	0
Winchester	45	38	7	Carsonville	1	1	0
Winthrop	32	30	2	Caseville	3	3	0
Woburn	80	74	6	Caspian	1	1	0
Worcester	509	449	60	Cass City	4	4	0
Wrentham	20	18	2	Cassopolis	6	5	1
Yarmouth	58	52	6	Cedar Springs	7	7	0
				Center Line	35	29	6
MICHIGAN				Charlevoix	7	7	0
				Charlotte	19	18	1
Adrian	38	33	5	Cheboygan	11	10	1
Albion	35	28	7	Chelsea	13	9	4
Algonac	9	8	1	Chesterfield Township	49	37	12
Allegan	10	9	1	Chikaming Township	4	4	0
Allen Park	59	53	6	Chocolay Township	5	4	1
Alma	13	12	1	Clare	9	8	1
Almont	10	9	1	Clawson	21	17	4
Alpena	20	18	2	Clay Township	21	15	6
Ann Arbor	230	167	63	Clinton	4	4	0
Argentine Township	6	5	1	Clinton Township	142	110	32
Armada	3	3	0	Clio	7	7	0
Auburn	3	2	1	Coldwater	19	18	1
Auburn Hills	64	50	14	Coleman	2	2	0
Bad Axe	10	10	0	Coloma City	3	3	0
Bangor	6	6	0	Coloma Township	7	6	1
Baraga	3	3	0	Colon	3	3	0
Barry Township	2	2	0	Concord	3	3	0
Bath Township	11	10	1	Constantine	7	6	1
Battle Creek	149	122	27	Corunna	5	5	0
Bay City	77	69	8	Covert Township	7	7	0
Belding	11	9	2	Croswell	6	6	0
Bellaire	3	3	0	Crystal Falls	5	5	0
Belleville	12	10	2	Davison	13	11	2
Bellevue	3	3	0	Davison Township	19	17	2
Benton Harbor	34	23	11	Dearborn	220	193	27
Benton Township	34	27	7	Dearborn Heights	112	91	21
Berkley	32	27	5	Decatur	4	4	0
Berrien Springs-Oronoko Township	9	8	1	Denmark Township	1	1	0
Beverly Hills	32	27	5	Denton Township	4	4	0
Big Rapids	20	19	1	Detroit	4,656	4,006	650
Birch Run	7	6	1	Dewitt	7	6	1
Birmingham	53	35	18	Dewitt Township	16	15	1
Blackman Township	32	30	2	Douglas	9	8	1
Blissfield	5	5	0	Dowagiac	16	15	1
Bloomfield Hills	30	26	4	Dryden Township	3	3	0
Bloomfield Township	98	74	24	Durand	7	6	1
Bloomingdale	1	1	0	East Grand Rapids	33	30	3
Boyne City	8	7	1	East Jordan	6	5	1
Breckenridge	3	3	0	East Lansing	99	66	33
Bridgeport Township	9	8	1	Eastpointe	58	53	5
Bridgman	4	4	0	East Tawas	7	6	1
Brighton	18	16	2	Eaton Rapids	12	11	1
Bronson	5	5	0	Eau Claire	2	1	1
Brooklyn/Columbia	5	4	1	Ecorse	27	26	1
Brown City	2	2	0	Edmore-Home	3	3	0
Brownstown Township	50	39	11	Elk Rapids	5	5	0

Table 78

Full-time Law Enforcement Employees as of October 31, 2002
by City by State—Continued

City by state	Total law enforcement employees	Total officers	Total civilians	City by state	Total law enforcement employees	Total officers	Total civilians
MICHIGAN—Continued				**MICHIGAN—Continued**			
Elkton	2	2	0	Hopkins	3	3	0
Elsie	1	1	0	Houghton	8	8	0
Emmett Township	16	14	2	Howard City	3	3	0
Erie Township	6	5	1	Howell	22	20	2
Escanaba	48	35	13	Hudson	3	3	0
Essexville	8	8	0	Hudsonville	10	9	1
Evart	4	4	0	Huntington Woods	18	17	1
Fair Haven Township	1	1	0	Huron Township	30	23	7
Farmington	28	22	6	Imlay City	10	9	1
Farmington Hills	169	118	51	Inkster	85	69	16
Fenton	20	15	5	Ionia	21	19	2
Ferndale	58	48	10	Iron Mountain	14	14	0
Flat Rock	29	25	4	Iron River	8	7	1
Flint	268	237	31	Ironwood	15	13	2
Flint Township	47	41	6	Ishpeming	14	13	1
Flushing	14	13	1	Ishpeming Township	1	1	0
Flushing Township	10	9	1	Ithaca	4	4	0
Forsyth Township	7	6	1	Jackson	94	69	25
Fowlerville	6	6	0	Jonesville	5	5	0
Frankenmuth	8	8	0	Kalamazoo	308	250	58
Frankfort	5	5	0	Kalamazoo Township	40	33	7
Franklin	11	10	1	Kalkaska	7	6	1
Fraser	62	48	14	Keego Harbor	7	6	1
Fremont	9	8	1	Kentwood	85	69	16
Frost Township	1	1	0	Kingsford	20	20	0
Gagetown	1	1	0	Kinross Township	4	4	0
Galesburg	4	3	1	Laingsburg	4	4	0
Garden City	55	43	12	Lake Angelus	2	2	0
Gaylord	14	12	2	Lake Linden	3	3	0
Genesee Township	26	22	4	Lake Odessa	4	4	0
Gerrish Township	7	7	0	Lake Orion	8	4	4
Gibraltar	14	13	1	Lakeview	2	2	0
Gladstone	13	12	1	L'anse	5	5	0
Gladwin	5	5	0	Lansing	366	258	108
Grand Beach	3	3	0	Lansing Township	17	16	1
Grand Blanc	23	20	3	Lapeer	24	20	4
Grand Blanc Township	46	41	5	Lathrup Village	12	11	1
Grand Haven	37	33	4	Laurium	4	4	0
Grand Ledge	16	15	1	Lawrence	4	3	1
Grand Rapids	442	366	76	Lawton	6	6	0
Grandville	34	28	6	Lennon	1	1	0
Grant	1	1	0	Leoni Township	6	5	1
Grayling	6	6	0	Leslie	3	3	0
Green Oak Township	15	13	2	Lexington	4	4	0
Greenville	26	17	9	Lincoln Park	71	61	10
Grosse Ile Township	25	18	7	Lincoln Township	13	11	2
Grosse Pointe	27	25	2	Linden	5	5	0
Grosse Pointe Farms	45	35	10	Litchfield	5	5	0
Grosse Pointe Park	50	44	6	Livonia	191	164	27
Grosse Pointe Shores	23	21	2	Lowell	9	7	2
Grosse Pointe Woods	53	40	13	Ludington	17	15	2
Hamburg Township	14	13	1	Luna Pier	4	4	0
Hampton Township	12	11	1	Mackinac Island	6	5	1
Hamtramck	46	43	3	Mackinaw City	5	5	0
Hancock	7	7	0	Madison Heights	78	61	17
Harbor Beach	4	4	0	Madison Township	2	2	0
Harbor Springs	6	5	1	Mancelona	4	3	1
Harper Woods	40	35	5	Manistee	17	15	2
Hart	4	4	0	Manistique	10	9	1
Hartford	6	6	0	Manton	1	1	0
Hastings	17	15	2	Marenisco Township	1	1	0
Hazel Park	44	37	7	Marine City	10	9	1
Hesperia	3	3	0	Marion	1	1	0
Highland Park	65	56	9	Marlette	5	5	0
Hillsdale	19	16	3	Marquette	42	36	6
Holland	74	62	12	Marshall	21	16	5
Holly	17	12	5	Marysville	19	16	3
Homer	3	3	0	Mason	14	13	1

City by state	Total law enforcement employees	Total officers	Total civilians	City by state	Total law enforcement employees	Total officers	Total civilians
MICHIGAN—Continued				**MICHIGAN—Continued**			
Mattawan	6	6	0	Plymouth	19	17	2
Mayville	2	2	0	Plymouth Township	45	30	15
Melvindale	31	28	3	Pontiac	217	169	48
Memphis	4	4	0	Portage	74	58	16
Mendon	1	1	0	Port Austin	2	2	0
Menominee	19	17	2	Port Huron	74	53	21
Meridian Township	49	43	6	Portland	7	6	1
Metamora Township	6	6	0	Potterville	3	3	0
Michiana	3	3	0	Prairieville Township	2	2	0
Midland	52	49	3	Raisin Township	1	1	0
Milan	16	12	4	Reading	3	3	0
Milford	24	18	6	Redford Township	91	74	17
Millington	3	3	0	Reed City	4	4	0
Monroe	55	46	9	Reese	2	2	0
Montague	5	5	0	Richfield Township (Genesee County)	11	9	2
Montrose Township	13	12	1	Richfield Township (Roscommon County)	5	5	0
Morenci	5	5	0	Richland	2	2	0
Morrice	2	2	0	Richland Township	4	4	0
Mount Clemens	47	36	11	Richmond	12	9	3
Mount Morris	9	8	1	River Rouge	29	27	2
Mount Morris Township	37	33	4	Riverview	33	29	4
Mount Pleasant	39	33	6	Rochester	29	21	8
Mundy Township	21	18	3	Rockford	13	10	3
Munising	6	6	0	Rockwood	9	8	1
Muskegon	91	83	8	Rogers City	7	7	0
Muskegon Heights	32	29	3	Romeo	12	8	4
Muskegon Township	16	15	1	Romulus	79	64	15
Napoleon Township	4	3	1	Roosevelt Park	7	6	1
Nashville	3	3	0	Rose City	3	3	0
Negaunee	11	10	1	Roseville	100	88	12
Newaygo	5	4	1	Ross Township	1	1	0
New Baltimore	17	16	1	Royal Oak	118	97	21
Newberry	3	3	0	Saginaw	131	115	16
New Buffalo	6	6	0	Saginaw Township	47	43	4
New Haven	7	6	1	Saline	18	13	5
Niles	33	22	11	Sand Lake	1	1	0
Niles Township	7	7	0	Sandusky	6	6	0
North Branch	4	4	0	Sault Ste. Marie	32	27	5
Northfield Township	12	10	2	Schoolcraft	2	2	0
North Muskegon	8	7	1	Scottville	3	3	0
Northville	19	16	3	Sebewaing	3	3	0
Northville Township	39	29	10	Shelby	3	3	0
Norton Shores	31	29	2	Shelby Township	81	62	19
Norvell Township	2	2	0	Shepherd	2	2	0
Novi	91	59	32	Somerset Township	1	1	0
Oak Park	78	65	13	Southfield	199	156	43
Olivet	3	3	0	Southgate	49	38	11
Onaway	1	1	0	South Haven	26	19	7
Ontwa Township-Edwardsburg	7	6	1	South Lyon	19	17	2
Orchard Lake	9	8	1	South Rockwood	3	3	0
Oscoda Township	13	12	1	Sparta	8	7	1
Otisville	1	1	0	Spaulding Township	2	2	0
Otsego	8	7	1	Spring Arbor Township	2	2	0
Ovid	3	3	0	Springfield	17	15	2
Owosso	22	21	1	Spring Lake-Ferrysburg	10	9	1
Oxford	8	5	3	Stanton	1	1	0
Parchment	3	3	0	St. Charles	4	4	0
Parma-Sandstone	5	4	1	St. Clair	12	10	2
Paw Paw	11	9	2	St. Clair Shores	106	88	18
Pentwater	3	3	0	Sterling Heights	223	166	57
Perry	8	7	1	St. Ignace	7	6	1
Petoskey	20	18	2	St. Johns	13	11	2
Pigeon	3	2	1	St. Joseph	25	19	6
Pinckney	4	4	0	St. Joseph Township	12	11	1
Pinconning	4	4	0	St. Louis	7	6	1
Pittsfield Township	48	37	11	Sturgis	23	17	6
Plainwell	11	9	2	Sumpter Township	16	13	3
Pleasant Ridge	7	7	0				

Table 78

Full-time Law Enforcement Employees as of October 31, 2002
by City by State—Continued

City by state	Total law enforcement employees	Total officers	Total civilians	City by state	Total law enforcement employees	Total officers	Total civilians
MICHIGAN—Continued				**MINNESOTA—Continued**			
Suttons Bay	1	1	0	Biwabik	4	4	0
Swartz Creek	9	8	1	Blaine	64	47	17
Sylvan Lake	5	5	0	Blooming Prairie	3	3	0
Taylor	135	106	29	Bloomington	144	110	34
Tecumseh	17	15	2	Blue Earth	7	7	0
Thomas Township	9	8	1	Brainerd	32	25	7
Three Oaks	3	3	0	Breckenridge	11	7	4
Three Rivers	21	17	4	Brooklyn Center	55	41	14
Tittabawassee Township	4	4	0	Brooklyn Park	98	75	23
Traverse City	35	33	2	Buffalo	18	15	3
Trenton	46	44	2	Burnsville	86	68	18
Troy	194	137	57	Caledonia	5	4	1
Tuscarora Township	8	7	1	Cambridge	11	10	1
Ubly	2	2	0	Cannon Falls	6	6	0
Unadilla Township	3	3	0	Centennial Lakes	20	17	3
Union City	4	4	0	Champlin	26	22	4
Utica	21	16	5	Chaska	23	19	4
Van Buren Township	46	34	12	Chisago City	6	5	1
Vassar	5	5	0	Chisholm	12	11	1
Vernon	3	3	0	Cloquet	21	19	2
Vicksburg	5	5	0	Cold Spring	6	6	0
Waldron	1	1	0	Columbia Heights	31	24	7
Walker	46	37	9	Coon Rapids	70	60	10
Walled Lake	20	14	6	Corcoran	4	4	0
Warren	291	247	44	Cottage Grove	44	31	13
Waterford Township	115	89	26	Crookston	18	16	2
Waterloo Township	2	2	0	Crosby	10	6	4
Watertown Township	1	1	0	Crystal	36	27	9
Watervliet	4	4	0	Dawson	3	3	0
Wayland	7	6	1	Dayton	5	5	0
Wayne	54	42	12	Deephaven/Woodland	8	7	1
West Bloomfield Township	99	74	25	Detroit Lakes	15	13	2
West Branch	7	6	1	Dilworth	6	5	1
Westland	128	99	29	Duluth	180	150	30
White Cloud	3	2	1	Eagan	85	67	18
Whitehall	9	8	1	East Grand Forks	23	21	2
White Lake Township	34	24	10	Eden Prairie	94	61	33
White Pigeon	4	4	0	Edina	66	49	17
Williamston	5	5	0	Elk River	34	27	7
Wixom	26	22	4	Ely	12	7	5
Wolverine Lake	9	8	1	Eveleth	11	10	1
Woodhaven	40	34	6	Fairmont	21	19	2
Woodstock Township	1	1	0	Falcon Heights	22	20	2
Wyandotte	57	44	13	Faribault	37	28	9
Wyoming	143	101	42	Farmington	17	15	2
Yale	5	5	0	Fergus Falls	24	19	5
Ypsilanti	52	39	13	Floodwood	3	3	0
Zeeland	10	9	1	Forest Lake	20	18	2
Zilwaukee	2	2	0	Fridley	46	38	8
				Gilbert	6	6	0
MINNESOTA				Glencoe	10	9	1
				Glenwood	4	4	0
Albert Lea	39	30	9	Golden Valley	39	28	11
Alexandria	21	17	4	Goodview	4	4	0
Annandale	5	5	0	Grand Rapids	20	16	4
Anoka	37	29	8	Granite Falls	5	5	0
Appleton	4	4	0	Hallock	1	1	0
Apple Valley	66	46	20	Hastings	30	25	5
Aurora	4	4	0	Hermantown	12	10	2
Austin	31	27	4	Hibbing	34	31	3
Babbitt	4	4	0	Hilltop	31	24	7
Baxter	11	10	1	Hopkins	40	25	15
Bayport	5	5	0	Hoyt Lakes	5	5	0
Becker	6	5	1	Hutchinson	35	22	13
Belle Plaine	7	6	1	International Falls	13	13	0
Bemidji	27	24	3	Inver Grove Heights	37	30	7
Benson	8	7	1	Jackson	8	7	1
Big Lake	8	7	1	Janesville	5	4	1

Table 78

City by state	Total law enforcement employees	Total officers	Total civilians	City by state	Total law enforcement employees	Total officers	Total civilians
MINNESOTA—Continued				**MINNESOTA—Continued**			
Jordan	10	8	2	Savage	30	24	6
Kasson	8	8	0	Shakopee	34	29	5
La Crescent	9	8	1	Silver Bay	5	5	0
Lake City	9	8	1	Slayton	4	4	0
Lakefield	3	3	0	Sleepy Eye	6	6	0
Lakeville	61	45	16	South Lake Minnetonka	16	14	2
Lauderdale	22	20	2	South St. Paul	27	25	2
Le Sueur	8	7	1	Springfield	5	5	0
Lindstrom	7	6	1	Spring Lake Park	13	11	2
Lino Lakes	25	22	3	St. Anthony	22	20	2
Litchfield	10	9	1	Staples	5	5	0
Little Falls	14	12	2	St. Cloud	107	89	18
Long Prairie	6	6	0	St. Francis	11	9	2
Madison	3	3	0	Stillwater	24	19	5
Mankato	58	47	11	St. James	8	7	1
Maple Grove	66	55	11	St. Joseph	7	6	1
Maplewood	66	47	19	St. Louis Park	69	50	19
Marshall	24	21	3	St. Paul	817	571	246
Medina	8	7	1	St. Paul Park	8	8	0
Melrose	8	5	3	St. Peter	19	14	5
Mendota Heights	18	16	2	Thief River Falls	18	16	2
Minneapolis	1,132	836	296	Tracy	4	4	0
Minnetonka	74	55	19	Two Harbors	8	7	1
Minnetrista	9	9	0	Virginia	22	21	1
Montevideo	10	9	1	Wabasha	6	4	2
Moorhead	72	48	24	Wadena	9	8	1
Moose Lake	4	4	0	Waite Park	15	12	3
Mora	9	8	1	Warroad	6	5	1
Morris	9	8	1	Waseca	15	13	2
Mound	14	11	3	Wayzata	10	9	1
Mounds View	17	16	1	Wells	4	4	0
Mountain Iron	5	5	0	West Hennepin	10	8	2
Mountain Lake	4	4	0	West St. Paul	37	26	11
New Brighton	32	27	5	White Bear Lake	36	29	7
New Hope	37	29	8	Willmar	36	32	4
Newport	8	8	0	Windom	9	8	1
New Prague	10	8	2	Winona	45	39	6
New Ulm	23	20	3	Woodbury	57	49	8
North Branch	10	9	1	Worthington	30	22	8
Northfield	29	22	7	Wyoming	6	6	0
North Mankato	13	12	1	Zumbrota	4	4	0
North St. Paul	18	16	2				
Oakdale	38	28	10	**MISSISSIPPI**			
Oak Park Heights	10	9	1				
Olivia	5	5	0	Aberdeen	23	18	5
Orono	21	18	3	Amory	23	18	5
Ortonville	5	4	1	Batesville	47	38	9
Osseo	6	5	1	Bay St. Louis	37	29	8
Owatonna	29	27	2	Belzoni	15	9	6
Park Rapids	8	7	1	Biloxi	191	136	55
Paynesville	4	4	0	Booneville	24	20	4
Plainview	5	5	0	Brandon	38	26	12
Plymouth	74	59	15	Brookhaven	34	30	4
Princeton	10	9	1	Bruce	5	5	0
Prior Lake	22	19	3	Byhalia	12	8	4
Proctor	8	7	1	Clarksdale	43	38	5
Ramsey	21	17	4	Cleveland	45	35	10
Red Wing	32	26	6	Clinton	62	45	17
Redwood Falls	10	9	1	Collins	13	9	4
Richfield	56	43	13	Columbia	32	28	4
Robbinsdale	28	21	7	Columbus	85	77	8
Rochester	167	121	46	Corinth	52	39	13
Roseau	7	6	1	Durant	11	11	0
Rosemount	20	17	3	Edwards	3	3	0
Roseville	53	45	8	Eupora	9	7	2
Sartell	14	12	2	Florence	18	10	8
Sauk Centre	9	6	3	Flowood	47	37	10
Sauk Rapids	13	12	1	Fulton	10	10	0

Table 78

Full-time Law Enforcement Employees as of October 31, 2002
by City by State—Continued

City by state	Total law enforcement employees	Total officers	Total civilians
MISSISSIPPI—Continued			
Gloster	7	5	2
Greenville	119	82	37
Greenwood	74	53	21
Grenada	45	40	5
Gulfport	256	191	65
Hattiesburg	180	108	72
Heidelberg	6	5	1
Hernando	25	21	4
Hollandale	12	8	4
Horn Lake	71	56	15
Houston	14	10	4
Indianola	32	24	8
Itta Bena	13	8	5
Iuka	12	9	3
Jackson	668	436	232
Kosciusko	20	20	0
Laurel	84	57	27
Leakesville	2	2	0
Leland	23	18	5
Lexington	11	10	1
Long Beach	50	31	19
Louisville	24	17	7
Lucedale	18	12	6
Macon	11	10	1
Madison	47	34	13
Magee	17	13	4
Magnolia	6	6	0
Marks	5	5	0
McComb	52	33	19
McLain	2	1	1
Meridian	119	103	16
Moorhead	6	6	0
Morton	14	10	4
Natchez	80	51	29
New Albany	24	22	2
Newton	16	11	5
Ocean Springs	43	32	11
Okolona	7	7	0
Olive Branch	66	51	15
Oxford	57	48	9
Pascagoula	87	56	31
Pass Christian	27	21	6
Pearl	64	50	14
Pelahatchie	8	6	2
Petal	23	18	5
Philadelphia	34	24	10
Picayune	48	30	18
Pickens	2	2	0
Poplarville	11	10	1
Port Gibson	12	9	3
Purvis	11	8	3
Quitman	12	12	0
Raymond	6	6	0
Richland	36	24	12
Ridgeland	75	51	24
Ripley	12	11	1
Rolling Fork	6	6	0
Ruleville	13	5	8
Sandersville	5	4	1
Senatobia	21	17	4
Shelby	11	6	5
Southaven	90	74	16
Starkville	50	43	7
Summit	7	6	1
Sunflower	3	3	0
Tchula	4	4	0
Tupelo	123	108	15
Tylertown	7	6	1

City by state	Total law enforcement employees	Total officers	Total civilians
MISSISSIPPI—Continued			
Utica	6	6	0
Verona	9	9	0
Vicksburg	94	71	23
Water Valley	11	10	1
Waveland	27	22	5
Waynesboro	24	16	8
West Point	37	28	9
Wiggins	14	11	3
Winona	13	11	2
Yazoo City	47	30	17
MISSOURI			
Adrian	2	2	0
Advance	4	4	0
Alma	3	3	0
Alton	2	2	0
Anderson	4	4	0
Appleton City	3	3	0
Arbyrd	1	1	0
Archie	3	3	0
Arnold	57	45	12
Ash Grove	4	3	1
Ashland	4	4	0
Augusta	2	2	0
Aurora	17	11	6
Auxvasse	1	1	0
Ava	8	6	2
Ballwin	68	53	15
Bates City	2	2	0
Battlefield	4	4	0
Bella Villa	1	1	0
Bellefontaine Neighbors	27	26	1
Bel-Nor	9	9	0
Bel-Ridge	16	15	1
Belton	61	41	20
Berkeley	55	44	11
Bernie	9	5	4
Bethany	6	6	0
Beverly Hills	9	7	2
Billings	4	4	0
Birch Tree	1	1	0
Bloomfield	3	3	0
Blue Springs	98	71	27
Bolivar	24	16	8
Bonne Terre	11	11	0
Boonville	27	20	7
Bourbon	5	5	0
Bowling Green	10	7	3
Branson	55	40	15
Branson West	5	5	0
Breckenridge Hills	19	18	1
Brentwood	31	25	6
Bridgeton	66	54	12
Brookfield	17	10	7
Brunswick	1	1	0
Bucklin	1	1	0
Buckner	6	5	1
Bunker	1	1	0
Butler	16	10	6
Byrnes Mill	5	5	0
Cabool	11	6	5
California	6	5	1
Calverton Park	7	6	1
Camdenton	14	11	3
Cameron	19	15	4
Campbell	7	4	3
Canton	8	4	4

Table 78

Full-time Law Enforcement Employees as of October 31, 2002
by City by State—Continued

City by state	Total law enforcement employees	Total officers	Total civilians	City by state	Total law enforcement employees	Total officers	Total civilians
MISSOURI—Continued				**MISSOURI—Continued**			
Cape Girardeau	100	74	26	Fredericktown	10	9	1
Carl Junction	13	9	4	Freeman	1	1	0
Carrollton	7	6	1	Frontenac	25	19	6
Carterville	7	7	0	Fulton	30	24	6
Carthage	34	26	8	Gainesville	2	2	0
Caruthersville	21	20	1	Galena	1	1	0
Cassville	8	8	0	Gallatin	4	4	0
Center	1	1	0	Garden City	5	5	0
Centralia	12	7	5	Gerald	5	5	0
Chaffee	9	5	4	Gideon	3	3	0
Charlack	9	9	0	Gladstone	53	40	13
Charleston	17	12	5	Glasgow	3	3	0
Chesterfield	95	85	10	Glendale	14	11	3
Chillicothe	21	15	6	Golden City	1	1	0
Clarence	1	1	0	Gower	4	4	0
Clarkton	4	4	0	Grain Valley	14	12	2
Claycomo	10	10	0	Granby	5	5	0
Clayton	63	48	15	Grandin	1	1	0
Clever	2	2	0	Grandview	68	55	13
Clinton	20	19	1	Greenwood	11	10	1
Cole Camp	3	3	0	Hallsville	2	2	0
Columbia	169	136	33	Hamilton	3	3	0
Concordia	6	6	0	Hannibal	46	34	12
Cool Valley	11	10	1	Harrisonville	29	21	8
Cooter	1	1	0	Hartville	2	2	0
Cottleville	11	10	1	Hawk Point	1	1	0
Country Club Hills	9	9	0	Hayti	9	8	1
Crane	6	5	1	Hayti Heigths	6	5	1
Crestwood	44	35	9	Hazelwood	70	54	16
Creve Coeur	59	48	11	Herculaneum	10	9	1
Crocker	3	3	0	Hermann	12	7	5
Crystal City	19	15	4	Higbee	1	1	0
Cuba	13	11	2	Higginsville	14	9	5
Dellwood	19	17	2	Hillsboro	6	6	0
De Soto	21	16	5	Hillsdale	12	11	1
Des Peres	50	40	10	Holcomb	2	2	0
Dexter	22	16	6	Holden	9	8	1
Diamond	2	2	0	Hollister	18	12	6
Dixon	7	4	3	Holt	1	1	0
Doniphan	12	9	3	Holts Summit	8	7	1
Drexel	2	2	0	Hornersville	2	2	0
Duenweg	3	3	0	Houston	5	5	0
Duquesne	7	4	3	Houston Lake	5	5	0
East Lynne	1	1	0	Humansville	2	2	0
East Prairie	12	8	4	Huntsville	2	2	0
Edgerton	1	1	0	Iberia	2	2	0
Edina	4	3	1	Independence	273	189	84
Edmundson	10	9	1	Iron Mountain Lake	1	1	0
Eldon	13	11	2	Ironton	4	4	0
El Dorado Springs	12	8	4	Jackson	28	22	6
Ellington	3	3	0	JASCO Metropolitian	5	4	1
Ellisville	22	21	1	Jasper	2	2	0
Elsberry	4	4	0	Jefferson City	106	78	28
Eureka	27	23	4	Jennings	69	46	23
Excelsior Springs	29	21	8	Jonesburg	1	1	0
Exeter	1	1	0	Joplin	86	76	10
Fair Grove	3	3	0	Kahoka	4	4	0
Fair Play	1	1	0	Kansas City	1,927	1,211	716
Farmington	33	24	9	Kearney	12	11	1
Fayette	8	8	0	Kennett	28	21	7
Ferguson	62	52	10	Kimberling City	9	6	3
Ferrelview	1	1	0	Kimmswick	1	1	0
Festus	33	23	10	Kingsville	1	1	0
Florissant	102	81	21	Kirksville	28	26	2
Foley	1	1	0	Kirkwood	70	57	13
Fordland	1	1	0	Knob Noster	14	7	7
Foristell	6	6	0	La Belle	1	1	0
Forsyth	6	6	0	Ladue	35	28	7

Table 78

Full-time Law Enforcement Employees as of October 31, 2002

by City by State—Continued

City by state	Total law enforcement employees	Total officers	Total civilians	City by state	Total law enforcement employees	Total officers	Total civilians
MISSOURI—Continued				**MISSOURI—Continued**			
La Grange	12	8	4	New London	2	2	0
Lake Lotawana	8	7	1	New Madrid	9	9	0
Lake Ozark	15	11	4	New Melle	1	1	0
Lakeshire	4	4	0	Nixa	29	21	8
Lake St. Louis	30	23	7	Noel	5	5	0
Lake Tapawingo	1	1	0	Norborne	1	1	0
Lake Waukomis	1	1	0	Normandy	21	20	1
Lake Winnebago	4	4	0	North Kansas City	57	41	16
Lamar	11	9	2	Northmoor	9	9	0
Lanagan	2	2	0	Northwoods	16	14	2
La Plata	1	1	0	Norwood	1	1	0
Lathrop	5	4	1	Oak Grove	9	8	1
Laurie	6	6	0	Oakland	70	57	13
Lawson	7	6	1	Oakview	14	4	0
Leadington	6	5	1	Odessa	10	10	0
Leadwood	4	4	0	O'Fallon	119	90	29
Lebanon	35	26	9	Olivette	28	22	6
Lee's Summit	151	103	48	Oran	1	1	0
Leeton	1	1	0	Osage Beach	35	22	13
Lexington	9	8	1	Osceola	2	2	0
Liberal	2	2	0	Otterville	1	1	0
Liberty	52	36	16	Overland	54	41	13
Licking	5	5	0	Owensville	10	8	2
Lincoln	3	3	0	Ozark	23	19	4
Linn	2	2	0	Pacific	24	17	7
Linn Creek	3	3	0	Pagedale	18	17	1
Lockwood	2	2	0	Palmyra	10	7	3
Lone Jack	4	3	1	Park Hills	13	12	1
Louisiana	16	9	7	Parkville	12	11	1
Macon	12	11	1	Peculiar	8	7	1
Malden	14	12	2	Perry	1	1	0
Manchester	41	38	3	Perryville	24	23	1
Mansfield	5	5	0	Pevely	19	14	5
Maplewood	30	25	5	Piedmont	6	6	0
Marble Hill	5	4	1	Pierce City	4	4	0
Marceline	10	6	4	Pilot Grove	1	1	0
Marquand	1	1	0	Pilot Knob	2	2	0
Marshall	34	23	11	Pine Lawn	27	23	4
Marshfield	7	7	0	Pineville	4	4	0
Marston	3	3	0	Platte City	11	11	0
Marthasville	1	1	0	Platte Woods	3	3	0
Maryland Heights	90	75	15	Plattsburg	5	5	0
Maryville	21	17	4	Pleasant Hill	16	10	6
Mayview	1	1	0	Pleasant Hope	2	2	0
Memphis	5	4	1	Pleasant Valley	11	8	3
Merriam Woods	1	1	0	Poplar Bluff	54	43	11
Mexico	34	30	4	Portageville	14	12	2
Milan	5	5	0	Potosi	14	10	4
Miner	12	7	5	Puxico	2	2	0
Moberly	48	35	13	Randolph	2	2	0
Moline Acres	7	7	0	Raymore	30	20	10
Monett	28	19	9	Raytown	71	54	17
Monroe City	5	5	0	Reeds Spring	5	4	1
Montgomery City	6	6	0	Republic	30	19	11
Montrose	1	1	0	Rich Hill	4	4	0
Morehouse	1	1	0	Richland	9	5	4
Mosby	3	3	0	Richmond	22	14	8
Moscow Mills	4	4	0	Richmond Heights	49	41	8
Mound City	2	2	0	Risco	1	1	0
Mountain Grove	14	10	4	Riverside	23	18	5
Mountain View	7	7	0	Riverview	11	10	1
Mount Vernon	9	9	0	Rockaway Beach	2	2	0
Napoleon	3	3	0	Rock Hill	15	11	4
Neosho	27	24	3	Rock Port	2	2	0
Nevada	27	20	7	Rogersville	6	6	0
New Florence	3	3	0	Rolla	49	29	20
New Franklin	3	2	1	Salem	18	13	5
New Haven	7	7	0	Salisbury	7	3	4

Table 78

Full-time Law Enforcement Employees as of October 31, 2002
by City by State—Continued

City by state	Total law enforcement employees	Total officers	Total civilians	City by state	Total law enforcement employees	Total officers	Total civilians
MISSOURI—Continued				**MISSOURI—Continued**			
Sarcoxie	4	4	0	Wentzville	46	36	10
Savannah	4	4	0	Weston	4	4	0
Scott City	16	11	5	West Plains	26	21	5
Sedalia	56	44	12	Wheaton	3	2	1
Senath	3	3	0	Willard	8	7	1
Seneca	7	7	0	Willow Springs	8	7	1
Seymour	4	4	0	Windsor	6	6	0
Shelbina	5	5	0	Winfield	3	3	0
Shrewsbury	20	17	3	Winona	3	3	0
Sikeston	73	60	13	Woodson Terrace	19	17	2
Slater	9	5	4	Wright City	6	6	0
Smithville	16	15	1				
Sparta	2	2	0	**MONTANA**			
Springfield	409	326	83				
Stanberry	1	1	0	Baker	3	3	0
St. Ann	57	45	12	Belgrade	11	9	2
St. Charles	138	106	32	Billings	156	125	31
St. Clair	14	12	2	Boulder	3	3	0
Steelville	6	6	0	Bozeman	49	41	8
Ste. Genevieve	12	11	1	Bridger	2	2	0
St. George	5	5	0	Chinook	4	4	0
St. James	7	6	1	Columbia Falls	14	8	6
St. John	25	23	2	Conrad	5	5	0
St. Joseph	152	112	40	Cut Bank	7	6	1
St. Louis	2,055	1,460	595	Dillon	8	7	1
St. Marys	1	1	0	East Helena	4	4	0
Stover	4	4	0	Eureka	3	3	0
St. Peters	103	83	20	Fort Benton	3	3	0
Strafford	5	5	0	Glasgow	8	7	1
St. Robert	23	17	6	Glendive	15	9	6
Sturgeon	2	2	0	Great Falls	115	78	37
Sugar Creek	19	14	5	Hamilton	14	13	1
Sullivan	24	16	8	Havre	25	19	6
Summersville	2	2	0	Helena	71	50	21
Sunrise Beach	2	2	0	Hot Springs	2	2	0
Sunset Hills	29	22	7	Joliet	2	2	0
Sweet Springs	3	3	0	Kalispell	39	30	9
Tarkio	3	3	0	Laurel	15	11	4
Thayer	8	6	2	Lewistown	20	14	6
Tipton	3	3	0	Libby	6	6	0
Town and Country	42	34	8	Livingston	17	12	5
Trenton	16	10	6	Manhattan	2	2	0
Troy	20	18	2	Miles City	17	12	5
Truesdale	4	1	3	Missoula	102	82	20
Union	19	17	2	Plains	3	3	0
Unionville	2	2	0	Plentywood	5	4	1
University City	98	78	20	Polson	11	10	1
Van Buren	2	2	0	Poplar	4	4	0
Vandalia	8	3	5	Red Lodge	7	7	0
Velda City	10	9	1	Ronan City	4	4	0
Versailles	11	11	0	Sidney	11	10	1
Viburnum	3	3	0	Stevensville	3	3	0
Vinita Park	13	12	1	St. Ignatius	3	3	0
Walnut Grove	2	2	0	Thompson Falls	3	3	0
Wardell	1	1	0	Three Forks	3	3	0
Warrensburg	34	31	3	Troy	3	3	0
Warrenton	17	14	3	West Yellowstone	11	6	5
Warsaw	6	6	0	Whitefish	17	12	5
Warson Woods	8	7	1	Whitehall	3	2	1
Washburn	1	1	0	Wolf Point	8	6	2
Washington	29	25	4				
Waverly	1	1	0	**NEBRASKA**			
Waynesville	10	10	0				
Weatherby Lake	4	4	0	Albion	3	3	0
Webb City	22	17	5	Alliance	28	20	8
Webster Groves	51	42	9	Ashland	5	5	0
Wellston	16	15	1	Auburn	6	6	0
Wellsville	4	4	0	Aurora	7	7	0

Table 78

Full-time Law Enforcement Employees as of October 31, 2002
by City by State—Continued

City by state	Total law enforcement employees	Total officers	Total civilians	City by state	Total law enforcement employees	Total officers	Total civilians
NEBRASKA—Continued				**NEVADA**			
Bayard	4	4	0	Boulder City	41	29	12
Beatrice	33	22	11	Carlin	7	5	2
Bellevue	83	75	8	Elko	39	35	4
Blair	16	14	2	Fallon	34	22	12
Bridgeport	3	3	0	Henderson	374	284	90
Broken Bow	7	6	1	Las Vegas Metropolitan Police			
Central City	6	5	1	Department	3,880	1,951	1,929
Chadron	18	12	6	Lovelock	6	5	1
Columbus	49	34	15	Mesquite	36	20	16
Cozad	9	5	4	North Las Vegas	294	205	89
Crete	16	11	5	Reno	470	311	159
David City	6	5	1	Sparks	136	93	43
Elkhorn	13	12	1	West Wendover	21	13	8
Fairbury	8	7	1	Winnemucca	18	14	4
Falls City	13	9	4	Yerington	8	7	1
Fremont	44	36	8				
Geneva	2	2	0	**NEW HAMPSHIRE**			
Gering	19	16	3				
Gordon	6	5	1	Alstead	2	2	0
Gothenburg	10	6	4	Alton	13	11	2
Grand Island	83	75	8	Amherst	16	14	2
Hastings	53	38	15	Andover	1	1	0
Holdrege	15	9	6	Antrim	4	4	0
Imperial	4	4	0	Ashland	6	6	0
Kearney	52	43	9	Auburn	9	7	2
Kimball	6	5	1	Barnstead	5	5	0
La Vista	28	24	4	Barrington	9	8	1
Lexington	14	12	2	Bartlett	5	4	1
Lincoln	406	301	105	Bedford	39	27	12
Lyons	2	2	0	Belmont	17	14	3
Madison	4	4	0	Bennington	2	2	0
McCook	19	15	4	Berlin	29	20	9
Milford	5	5	0	Bethlehem	6	3	3
Minatare	2	2	0	Boscawen	5	4	1
Minden	5	4	1	Brentwood	4	4	0
Mitchell	5	5	0	Bristol	9	7	2
Nebraska City	14	13	1	Campton	5	4	1
Neligh	3	3	0	Candia	6	5	1
Norfolk	57	38	19	Canterbury	1	1	0
North Platte	66	41	25	Carroll	3	3	0
Ogallala	12	11	1	Charlestown	8	5	3
Omaha	952	766	186	Chester	3	2	1
O'Neill	8	7	1	Chesterfield	5	4	1
Ord	7	4	3	Claremont	25	21	4
Papillion	32	28	4	Colebrook	4	4	0
Plainview	2	2	0	Concord	103	79	24
Plattsmouth	18	15	3	Conway	29	20	9
Ralston	13	12	1	Danville	2	2	0
Schuyler	8	6	2	Deerfield	8	7	1
Scottsbluff	36	32	4	Deering	2	2	0
Seward	11	10	1	Derry	71	59	12
Sidney	14	12	2	Dublin	3	3	0
South Sioux City	28	27	1	Enfield	7	6	1
Superior	4	4	0	Epping	12	11	1
Syracuse	3	3	0	Epsom	6	5	1
Tecumseh	4	3	1	Exeter	32	23	9
Tekamah	3	3	0	Farmington	15	13	2
Valentine	4	4	0	Fitzwilliam	4	3	1
Valley	5	5	0	Franconia	3	3	0
Wahoo	6	6	0	Franklin	20	15	5
Wayne	11	7	4	Freedom	2	2	0
West Point	7	6	1	Fremont	3	3	0
Wilber	4	4	0	Gilford	22	16	6
Wymore	3	3	0	Gilmanton	5	4	1
York	20	14	6	Goffstown	40	28	12
				Gorham	10	7	3
				Grantham	4	3	1
				Greenland	6	6	0

Table 78

Full-time Law Enforcement Employees as of October 31, 2002
by City by State—Continued

City by state	Total law enforcement employees	Total officers	Total civilians	City by state	Total law enforcement employees	Total officers	Total civilians
NEW HAMPSHIRE—Continued				**NEW HAMPSHIRE—Continued**			
Greenville	6	6	0	Wakefield	9	8	1
Hampstead	6	6	0	Walpole	4	3	1
Hampton	43	34	9	Warner	5	4	1
Hancock	3	3	0	Waterville Valley	7	6	1
Hanover	31	19	12	Weare	8	7	1
Henniker	10	8	2	Webster	2	2	0
Hillsborough	16	10	6	Winchester	6	5	1
Hinsdale	8	7	1	Windham	24	18	6
Holderness	5	5	0	Wolfeboro	15	10	5
Hooksett	35	23	12				
Hopkinton	7	6	1	**NEW JERSEY**			
Hudson	58	43	15				
Jaffrey	14	11	3	Aberdeen Township	41	34	7
Keene	59	45	14	Absecon	31	26	5
Kensington	3	3	0	Allendale	19	14	5
Kingston	9	8	1	Allenhurst	12	8	4
Laconia	44	33	11	Allentown	5	5	0
Langdon	1	1	0	Alpha	4	4	0
Lebanon	39	28	11	Alpine	14	14	0
Lincoln	11	6	5	Andover Township	17	12	5
Lisbon	3	3	0	Asbury Park	85	72	13
Litchfield	11	9	2	Atlantic City	525	410	115
Littleton	14	11	3	Atlantic Highlands	20	15	5
Londonderry	59	44	15	Audubon	19	17	2
Loudon	7	6	1	Audubon Park	6	5	1
Manchester	270	202	68	Avalon	28	20	8
Marlborough	3	3	0	Avon-by-the-Sea	11	11	0
Meredith	17	13	4	Barnegat Township	39	29	10
Merrimack	49	37	12	Barrington	16	15	1
Middleton	3	3	0	Bay Head	9	8	1
Milford	24	21	3	Bayonne	285	243	42
Milton	6	5	1	Beach Haven	19	13	6
Mont Vernon	3	3	0	Beachwood	20	18	2
Moultonboro	11	9	2	Bedminster Township	18	17	1
New Boston	4	3	1	Belleville	144	104	40
New Castle	3	3	0	Bellmawr	26	24	2
New Durham	5	4	1	Belmar	29	21	8
Newfields	2	2	0	Belvidere	6	6	0
New Hampton	6	6	0	Bergenfield	51	45	6
Newington	10	9	1	Berkeley Heights Township	34	27	7
Newmarket	18	13	5	Berkeley Township	92	70	22
Newport	18	14	4	Berlin	18	17	1
Newton	4	3	1	Berlin Township	21	19	2
Northfield	10	9	1	Bernards Township	43	35	8
North Hampton	11	10	1	Bernardsville	24	18	6
Northwood	6	5	1	Beverly	8	6	2
Nottingham	6	5	1	Blairstown Township	11	10	1
Ossipee	8	7	1	Bloomfield	139	121	18
Peterborough	12	10	2	Bloomingdale	17	16	1
Pittsfield	8	7	1	Bogota	20	15	5
Plymouth	15	9	6	Boonton	27	22	5
Portsmouth	86	65	21	Boonton Township	12	12	0
Raymond	26	18	8	Bordentown	12	10	2
Rindge	8	7	1	Bordentown Township	32	23	9
Rochester	63	47	16	Bound Brook	27	22	5
Rollinsford	4	4	0	Bradley Beach	19	15	4
Sandown	6	6	0	Branchburg Township	26	24	2
Sandwich	2	2	0	Brick Township	154	121	33
Somersworth	31	24	7	Bridgeton	78	66	12
Springfield	1	1	0	Bridgewater Township	89	72	17
Strafford	3	3	0	Brielle	15	14	1
Stratham	10	9	1	Brigantine	48	38	10
Sugar Hill	1	1	0	Brooklawn	6	6	0
Swanzey	13	10	3	Buena	15	9	6
Thornton	4	4	0	Burlington	34	31	3
Tilton	14	12	2	Burlington Township	51	43	8
Troy	3	3	0	Butler	18	17	1
Tuftonboro	3	3	0	Byram Township	15	14	1

Table 78

Full-time Law Enforcement Employees as of October 31, 2002

by City by State—Continued

City by state	Total law enforcement employees	Total officers	Total civilians	City by state	Total law enforcement employees	Total officers	Total civilians
NEW JERSEY—Continued				**NEW JERSEY—Continued**			
Caldwell	24	20	4	Fairview	31	27	4
Califon	2	2	0	Fanwood	22	21	1
Camden	492	420	72	Far Hills	4	4	0
Cape May	28	22	6	Flemington	15	14	1
Carlstadt	32	28	4	Florence Township	31	25	6
Carney's Point Township	25	20	5	Florham Park	37	31	6
Carteret	60	50	10	Fort Lee	119	98	21
Cedar Grove Township	35	32	3	Franklin	14	13	1
Chatham	28	22	6	Franklin Lakes	27	22	5
Chatham Township	31	24	7	Franklin Township (Gloucester County)	27	24	3
Cherry Hill Township	166	133	33	Franklin Township (Hunterdon County)	6	6	0
Chesilhurst	10	10	0	Franklin Township (Somerset County)	115	96	19
Chester	9	8	1	Freehold	41	31	10
Chesterfield Township	6	6	0	Freehold Township	79	63	16
Chester Township	16	15	1	Frenchtown	3	3	0
Cinnaminson Township	37	32	5	Galloway Township	70	56	14
Clark Township	54	42	12	Garfield	69	59	10
Clayton	19	17	2	Garwood	18	16	2
Clementon	12	11	1	Gibbsboro	6	6	0
Cliffside Park	48	42	6	Glassboro	56	50	6
Clifton	177	148	29	Glen Ridge	34	27	7
Clinton	10	10	0	Glen Rock	24	21	3
Clinton Township	23	20	3	Gloucester City	31	28	3
Closter	24	20	4	Gloucester Township	128	107	21
Collingswood	34	30	4	Green Brook Township	27	22	5
Colts Neck Township	19	18	1	Greenwich Township (Gloucester County)	22	17	5
Cranbury Township	17	16	1	Greenwich Township (Warren County)	9	8	1
Cranford Township	69	50	19	Guttenberg	27	23	4
Cresskill	26	21	5	Hackensack	130	108	22
Deal	19	15	4	Hackettstown	20	19	1
Delanco Township	9	8	1	Haddonfield	27	25	2
Delaware Township	8	7	1	Haddon Heights	18	17	1
Delran Township	32	28	4	Haddon Township	32	30	2
Demarest	14	14	0	Haledon	22	18	4
Denville Township	39	31	8	Hamburg	9	8	1
Deptford Township	69	63	6	Hamilton Township (Atlantic County)	70	53	17
Dover	41	36	5	Hamilton Township (Mercer County)	210	180	30
Dover Township	192	149	43	Hammonton	41	29	12
Dumont	38	30	8	Hanover Township	39	32	7
Dunellen	21	17	4	Harding Township	15	14	1
Eastampton Township	17	16	1	Hardyston Township	22	16	6
East Brunswick Township	124	93	31	Harrington Park	10	10	0
East Greenwich Township	17	15	2	Harrison	64	54	10
East Hanover Township	39	34	5	Harrison Township	17	16	1
East Newark	8	6	2	Harvey Cedars	8	7	1
East Orange	281	246	35	Hasbrouck Heights	34	32	2
East Rutherford	36	32	4	Haworth	12	11	1
East Windsor Township	61	47	14	Hawthorne	37	32	5
Eatontown	44	35	9	Hazlet Township	55	47	8
Edgewater	32	31	1	Helmetta	4	4	0
Edgewater Park Township	12	11	1	High Bridge	6	6	0
Edison Township	250	204	46	Highland Park	34	28	6
Egg Harbor City	19	14	5	Highlands	18	14	4
Egg Harbor Township	110	84	26	Hightstown	20	15	5
Elizabeth	467	344	123	Hillsborough Township	68	57	11
Elk Township	10	10	0	Hillsdale	23	20	3
Elmer	1	1	0	Hillside Township	87	73	14
Elmwood Park	35	35	0	Hi-Nella	2	2	0
Emerson	23	18	5	Hoboken	175	150	25
Englewood	98	77	21	Ho-Ho-Kus	17	15	2
Englewood Cliffs	29	28	1	Holland Township	7	6	1
Englishtown	6	6	0	Holmdel Township	48	38	10
Essex Fells	17	13	4	Hopatcong	38	29	9
Evesham Township	81	72	9	Hopewell Township	42	33	9
Ewing Township	99	84	15	Howell Township	104	86	18
Fairfield Township	46	40	6	Independence Township	9	8	1
Fair Haven	17	13	4	Interlaken	5	5	0
Fair Lawn	68	57	11				

Table 78

Full-time Law Enforcement Employees as of October 31, 2002

by City by State—Continued

City by state	Total law enforcement employees	Total officers	Total civilians	City by state	Total law enforcement employees	Total officers	Total civilians
NEW JERSEY—Continued				**NEW JERSEY—Continued**			
Irvington	205	178	27	Midland Park	15	13	2
Island Heights	5	5	0	Millburn Township	64	52	12
Jackson Township	96	78	18	Milltown	16	13	3
Jamesburg	17	12	5	Millville	84	68	16
Jefferson Township	45	38	7	Monmouth Beach	12	11	1
Jersey City	987	826	161	Monroe Township (Gloucester County)	74	62	12
Keansburg	22	18	4	Monroe Township (Middlesex County)	56	40	16
Kearny	129	121	8	Montclair	142	108	34
Kenilworth	31	30	1	Montgomery Township	39	28	11
Keyport	25	19	6	Montvale	24	22	2
Kinnelon	16	15	1	Montville Township	48	42	6
Lacey Township	55	41	14	Moonachie	20	17	3
Lakehurst	10	9	1	Moorestown Township	48	39	9
Lakewood Township	140	114	26	Morris Plains	22	17	5
Lambertville	12	10	2	Morristown	67	59	8
Laurel Springs	9	7	2	Morris Township	50	40	10
Lavallette	17	12	5	Mountain Lakes	18	14	4
Lawnside	11	9	2	Mountainside	28	23	5
Lawrence Township	85	70	15	Mount Arlington	12	11	1
Lebanon Township	10	9	1	Mount Ephraim	14	13	1
Leonia	27	20	7	Mount Holly Township	30	27	3
Lincoln Park	27	25	2	Mount Laurel Township	82	69	13
Linden	142	132	10	Mount Olive Township	57	49	8
Lindenwold	44	41	3	Mullica Township	15	14	1
Linwood	24	20	4	National Park	7	7	0
Little Egg Harbor Township	46	37	9	Neptune City	23	17	6
Little Falls Township	30	24	6	Neptune Township	82	73	9
Little Ferry	31	26	5	Netcong	10	9	1
Little Silver	20	15	5	Newark	1,563	1,361	202
Livingston Township	81	71	10	New Brunswick	168	135	33
Lodi	52	39	13	Newfield	5	5	0
Logan Township	18	17	1	New Hanover Township	3	3	0
Long Beach Township	51	39	12	New Milford	39	35	4
Long Branch	116	97	19	New Providence	31	25	6
Long Hill Township	36	29	7	Newton	32	21	11
Longport	18	13	5	North Arlington	44	35	9
Lopatcong Township	13	12	1	North Bergen Township	128	109	19
Lower Alloways Creek Township	18	12	6	North Brunswick Township	99	84	15
Lower Township	59	44	15	North Caldwell	21	17	4
Lumberton Township	33	29	4	Northfield	25	24	1
Lyndhurst Township	53	49	4	North Haledon	21	16	5
Madison	40	36	4	North Hanover Township	10	9	1
Magnolia	12	11	1	North Plainfield	51	45	6
Mahwah Township	63	54	9	Northvale	14	13	1
Manalapan Township	74	58	16	North Wildwood	35	30	5
Manasquan	23	17	6	Norwood	15	14	1
Manchester Township	79	64	15	Nutley Township	73	64	9
Mansfield Township (Burlington County)	13	13	0	Oakland	34	29	5
Mansfield Township (Warren County)	14	13	1	Oaklyn	15	13	2
Mantoloking	7	7	0	Ocean City	78	64	14
Mantua Township	27	25	2	Ocean Gate	8	7	1
Manville	26	22	4	Oceanport	19	14	5
Maple Shade Township	42	34	8	Ocean Township (Monmouth County)	73	57	16
Maplewood Township	73	59	14	Ocean Township (Ocean County)	22	16	6
Margate City	46	35	11	Ogdensburg	7	7	0
Marlboro Township	90	72	18	Old Bridge Township	140	104	36
Matawan	28	22	6	Old Tappan	14	13	1
Maywood	27	23	4	Oradell	21	20	1
Medford Lakes	9	8	1	Orange	126	106	20
Medford Township	51	41	10	Oxford Township	5	4	1
Mendham	12	10	2	Palisades Park	34	28	6
Mendham Township	16	14	2	Palmyra	19	17	2
Merchantville	16	14	2	Paramus	113	92	21
Metuchen	33	27	6	Park Ridge	19	18	1
Middlesex	34	32	2	Parsippany-Troy Hills Township	135	109	26
Middle Township	63	46	17	Passaic	186	156	30
Middletown Township	132	106	26	Paterson	517	429	88
				Paulsboro	21	19	2

Table 78

Full-time Law Enforcement Employees as of October 31, 2002
by City by State—Continued

City by state	Total law enforcement employees	Total officers	Total civilians	City by state	Total law enforcement employees	Total officers	Total civilians
NEW JERSEY—Continued				**NEW JERSEY—Continued**			
Peapack and Gladstone	10	9	1	South Amboy	29	24	5
Pemberton	5	4	1	South Belmar	10	10	0
Pemberton Township	67	57	10	South Bound Brook	13	12	1
Pennington	7	6	1	South Brunswick Township	111	76	35
Pennsauken Township	123	91	32	South Hackensack Township	20	19	1
Penns Grove	18	14	4	South Harrison Township	5	4	1
Pennsville Township	27	25	2	South Orange	61	55	6
Pequannock Township	31	26	5	South Plainfield	72	56	16
Perth Amboy	161	124	37	South River	38	31	7
Phillipsburg	43	35	8	South Toms River	13	12	1
Pine Beach	7	6	1	Sparta Township	42	34	8
Pine Hill	22	20	2	Spotswood	22	18	4
Pine Valley	8	6	2	Springfield	43	39	4
Piscataway Township	109	88	21	Springfield Township	10	9	1
Pitman	16	15	1	Spring Lake	18	14	4
Plainfield	193	163	30	Spring Lake Heights	13	10	3
Plainsboro Township	44	31	13	Stafford Township	72	50	22
Pleasantville	61	50	11	Stanhope	7	6	1
Plumsted Township	9	8	1	Stillwater Township	4	3	1
Pohatcong Township	10	9	1	Stone Harbor	24	18	6
Point Pleasant	41	33	8	Stratford	16	15	1
Point Pleasant Beach	31	23	8	Summit	57	48	9
Pompton Lakes	28	24	4	Surf City	9	9	0
Princeton	45	34	11	Swedesboro	9	8	1
Princeton Township	43	35	8	Teaneck Township	114	100	14
Prospect Park	15	14	1	Tenafly	35	29	6
Rahway	102	89	13	Tewksbury Township	12	11	1
Ramsey	39	31	8	Tinton Falls	39	38	1
Randolph Township	44	39	5	Totowa	27	26	1
Raritan	23	18	5	Trenton	423	361	62
Raritan Township	37	35	2	Tuckerton	10	9	1
Readington Township	24	22	2	Union Beach	18	14	4
Red Bank	50	40	10	Union City	225	184	41
Ridgefield	36	27	9	Union Township	173	123	50
Ridgefield Park	38	29	9	Upper Saddle River	23	18	5
Ridgewood	47	42	5	Ventnor City	50	38	12
Ringwood	30	24	6	Vernon Township	39	29	10
Riverdale	19	15	4	Verona	35	31	4
River Edge	29	22	7	Vineland	153	134	19
Riverside Township	14	14	0	Voorhees Township	64	50	14
Riverton	7	6	1	Waldwick	25	20	5
River Vale Township	23	21	2	Wallington	25	24	1
Rochelle Park Township	25	20	5	Wall Township	79	66	13
Rockaway	15	14	1	Wanaque	26	22	4
Rockaway Township	62	51	11	Warren Township	33	26	7
Roseland	28	25	3	Washington	12	11	1
Roselle	60	52	8	Washington Township (Bergen County)	25	25	0
Roselle Park	40	34	6	Washington Township (Gloucester County)	93	84	9
Roxbury Township	55	48	7	Washington Township (Mercer County)	35	27	8
Rumson	21	17	4	Washington Township (Morris County)	45	32	13
Runnemede	22	20	2	Washington Township (Warren County)	13	12	1
Rutherford	47	43	4	Watchung	34	27	7
Saddle Brook Township	34	33	1	Waterford Township	25	23	2
Saddle River	22	17	5	Wayne Township	142	114	28
Salem	35	29	6	Weehawken Township	58	53	5
Sayreville	100	81	19	Wenonah	6	6	0
Scotch Plains Township	53	46	7	Westampton Township	25	22	3
Sea Bright	13	11	2	West Amwell Township	6	5	1
Sea Girt	16	12	4	West Caldwell Township	30	28	2
Sea Isle City	27	20	7	West Deptford Township	44	37	7
Seaside Heights	29	22	7	Westfield	73	59	14
Seaside Park	17	13	4	West Long Branch	23	19	4
Secaucus	63	56	7	West Milford Township	55	48	7
Ship Bottom	10	9	1	West New York	130	123	7
Shrewsbury	20	15	5	West Orange	121	104	17
Somerdale	14	13	1	West Paterson	27	26	1
Somers Point	31	25	6	Westville	11	10	1
Somerville	39	32	7				

Table 78

Full-time Law Enforcement Employees as of October 31, 2002
by City by State—Continued

City by state	Total law enforcement employees	Total officers	Total civilians	City by state	Total law enforcement employees	Total officers	Total civilians
NEW JERSEY—Continued				**NEW MEXICO—Continued**			
West Wildwood	5	5	0	Red River	9	4	5
West Windsor Township	54	44	10	Rio Rancho	136	91	45
Westwood	35	29	6	Roswell	103	77	26
Wharton	23	22	1	Ruidoso	35	23	12
Wildwood	58	46	12	Ruidoso Downs	18	10	8
Wildwood Crest	28	22	6	Santa Clara	3	3	0
Willingboro Township	85	68	17	Santa Fe	178	137	41
Winfield Township	9	9	0	Santa Rosa	13	7	6
Winslow Township	88	71	17	Silver City	32	27	5
Woodbridge Township	244	198	46	Socorro	30	17	13
Woodbury	29	26	3	Springer	3	3	0
Woodbury Heights	8	7	1	Sunland Park	24	18	6
Woodcliff Lake	19	18	1	Taos	30	14	16
Woodlynne	10	9	1	Taos Ski Valley	3	3	0
Wood-Ridge	25	22	3	Tatum	7	2	5
Woodstown	9	8	1	Texico	4	4	0
Woolwich Township	12	11	1	Truth or Consequences	20	15	5
Wyckoff Township	34	26	8	Tucumcari	22	16	6
				Tularosa	11	6	5
NEW MEXICO							
				NEW YORK			
Alamogordo	107	63	44				
Albuquerque	1,209	893	316	Addison Town and Village	3	3	0
Angel Fire	4	3	1	Albany	431	329	102
Artesia	42	25	17	Albion Village	13	12	1
Aztec	19	15	4	Alexandria Bay Village	3	3	0
Bayard	6	6	0	Alfred Village	6	6	0
Belen	31	20	11	Allegany Village	2	2	0
Bernalillo	20	14	6	Altamont Village	1	1	0
Bloomfield	20	17	3	Amherst Town	184	151	33
Bosque Farms	11	9	2	Amity Town and Belmont Village	1	1	0
Capitan	4	3	1	Amityville Village	28	25	3
Carlsbad	77	53	24	Amsterdam	41	40	1
Carrizozo	6	4	2	Angola Village	3	3	0
Chama	7	7	0	Arcade Village	6	6	0
Cimarron	2	2	0	Ardsley Village	19	19	0
Clayton	16	5	11	Asharoken Village	3	3	0
Cloudcroft	3	3	0	Attica Village	3	3	0
Clovis	82	62	20	Auburn	78	70	8
Corrales	26	20	6	Avon Village	5	5	0
Cuba	2	2	0	Baldwinsville Village	16	13	3
Deming	39	31	8	Ballston Spa Village	11	7	4
Dexter	4	4	0	Batavia	34	29	5
Espanola	36	32	4	Beacon	41	39	2
Estancia	2	1	1	Bedford Town	51	45	6
Eunice	10	6	4	Bethlehem Town	57	39	18
Farmington	156	106	50	Binghamton	158	148	10
Gallup	94	58	36	Blooming Grove Town	18	16	2
Grants	26	18	8	Bolivar Village	1	1	0
Hatch	7	5	2	Boonville Village	3	3	0
Hobbs	122	80	42	Brant Town	4	1	3
Hurley	5	4	1	Briarcliff Manor Village	20	20	0
Jal	8	4	4	Brighton Town	47	41	6
Jemez Springs	2	2	0	Brockport Village	15	11	4
Las Cruces	211	143	68	Bronxville Village	29	22	7
Las Vegas	61	45	16	Caledonia Village	3	3	0
Lordsburg	13	10	3	Cambridge Village	2	2	0
Los Alamos	47	26	21	Camden Village	7	4	3
Los Lunas	34	26	8	Camillus Town and Village	26	23	3
Lovington	24	17	7	Canajoharie Village	5	5	0
Melrose	2	1	1	Canisteo Village	3	3	0
Mesilla	5	5	0	Canton Village	12	10	2
Milan	11	7	4	Carmel Town	41	33	8
Moriarty	8	7	1	Catskill Village	16	16	0
Mountainair	4	3	1	Cayuga Heights Village	7	6	1
Portales	39	25	14	Chester Town	9	9	0
Questa	3	3	0	Chester Village	10	9	1
Raton	26	18	8	Chittenango Village	7	6	1

Table 78

Full-time Law Enforcement Employees as of October 31, 2002

by City by State—Continued

City by state	Total law enforcement employees	Total officers	Total civilians	City by state	Total law enforcement employees	Total officers	Total civilians
NEW YORK—Continued				**NEW YORK—Continued**			
Cicero Town	5	4	1	Gowanda Village	1	1	0
Clarkstown Town	188	166	22	Granville Village	6	6	0
Clayton Village	4	3	1	Great Neck Estates Village	14	12	2
Clay Town	23	18	5	Greece Town	92	84	8
Clifton Springs Village	2	2	0	Greenburgh Town	129	113	16
Clyde Village	5	4	1	Greene Village	3	2	1
Cobleskill Village	11	11	0	Green Island Village	3	2	1
Coeymans Town	14	10	4	Greenwich Village	2	2	0
Cohoes	45	33	12	Greenwood Lake Village	13	9	4
Colchester Town	1	1	0	Guilderland Town	49	34	15
Colonie Town	150	107	43	Hamburg Town	81	65	16
Cooperstown Village	4	4	0	Hamburg Village	16	14	2
Corfu Village	1	1	0	Hamilton Village	4	4	0
Corinth Village	6	6	0	Harriman Village	7	7	0
Corning	29	25	4	Harrison Town	84	75	9
Cornwall-on-Hudson Village	5	5	0	Hastings-on-Hudson Village	21	20	1
Cornwall Town	16	12	4	Haverstraw Town	48	44	4
Cortland	44	42	2	Hempstead Village	141	115	26
Coxsackie Village	1	1	0	Highland Falls Village	14	11	3
Crawford Town	11	10	1	Highlands Town	1	1	0
Croton-on-Hudson Village	20	20	0	Hoosick Falls Village	3	3	0
Dansville Village	12	9	3	Hornell	23	22	1
Delhi Village	3	3	0	Horseheads Village	16	13	3
Depew Village	37	29	8	Hudson	27	22	5
Deposit Village	1	1	0	Hudson Falls Village	16	12	4
Dewitt Town	41	37	4	Hunter Town	2	2	0
Dobbs Ferry Village	29	27	2	Hyde Park Town	16	13	3
Dryden Village	6	6	0	Ilion Village	20	18	2
Dunkirk	35	34	1	Inlet Town	3	2	1
East Aurora-Aurora Town	19	15	4	Irondequoit Town	68	56	12
Eastchester Town	56	49	7	Irvington Village	25	23	2
East Fishkill Town	34	25	9	Ithaca	86	72	14
East Greenbush Town	31	23	8	Jamestown	77	62	15
East Hampton Town	68	49	19	Johnstown	26	25	1
East Hampton Village	39	23	16	Kensington Village	6	6	0
East Rochester Village	9	8	1	Kent Town	26	21	5
East Syracuse Village	11	9	2	Kings Point Village	27	25	2
Eden Town	5	4	1	Kingston	85	79	6
Ellenville Village	14	12	2	Kirkland Town	7	6	1
Ellicott Town	12	11	1	Lackawanna	68	49	19
Ellicottville	2	2	0	Lake Placid Village	17	14	3
Elmira	97	85	12	Lake Success Village	25	22	3
Elmira Heights Village	10	10	0	Lakewood-Busti	10	9	1
Elmira Town	4	4	0	Lancaster Town	39	31	8
Elmsford Village	18	17	1	Lancaster Village	21	15	6
Endicott Village	39	35	4	Larchmont Village	30	27	3
Fairport Village	11	10	1	Le Roy Village	13	10	3
Fallsburg Town	21	17	4	Lewisboro Town	3	2	1
Floral Park Village	46	36	10	Lewiston Town and Village	10	9	1
Fort Edward Village	5	5	0	Liberty Village	20	17	3
Frankfort Town	1	1	0	Liverpool Village	6	5	1
Franklinville Village	3	3	0	Lloyd Harbor Village	13	12	1
Fredonia Village	19	16	3	Lloyd Town	8	8	0
Freeport Village	108	91	17	Lockport	55	52	3
Freeville Village	1	1	0	Long Beach	86	73	13
Friendship Town	1	1	0	Lowville Village	5	5	0
Fulton City	38	35	3	Lynbrook Village	55	46	9
Garden City Village	68	55	13	Lyons Village	13	11	2
Gates Town	41	33	8	Macedon Town and Village	3	3	0
Geddes Town	18	16	2	Malone Village	18	18	0
Geneva	40	35	5	Malverne Village	24	24	0
Glen Cove	57	53	4	Mamaroneck Town	40	39	1
Glens Falls	36	30	6	Mamaroneck Village	57	51	6
Glenville Town	37	24	13	Manlius Town	45	37	8
Gloversville	40	38	2	Marcellus Village	1	1	0
Goshen Town	7	7	0	Marlborough Town	7	4	3
Goshen Village	16	15	1	Massena Village	27	22	5
Gouverneur Village	11	8	3	Mechanicville	13	12	1

Table 78

Full-time Law Enforcement Employees as of October 31, 2002
by City by State—Continued

City by state	Total law enforcement employees	Total officers	Total civilians	City by state	Total law enforcement employees	Total officers	Total civilians
NEW YORK—Continued				**NEW YORK—Continued**			
Menands Village	13	10	3	Rochester	860	688	172
Middleport Village	3	3	0	Rockville Centre Village	61	52	9
Middletown	74	63	11	Rome	78	74	4
Monroe Village	21	16	5	Rosendale Town	5	4	1
Montgomery Town	6	5	1	Rotterdam Town	64	43	21
Monticello Village	28	26	2	Rouses Point Village	2	2	0
Moravia Village	1	1	0	Rye	44	40	4
Moriah Town	2	2	0	Rye Brook Village	29	28	1
Mount Morris Village	6	6	0	Sag Harbor Village	13	12	1
Mount Pleasant Town	56	47	9	Salamanca	14	14	0
Nassau Village	1	1	0	Sands Point Village	20	20	0
Newark Village	20	19	1	Saranac Lake Village	14	14	0
New Berlin Town	1	1	0	Saratoga Springs	83	70	13
Newburgh	99	88	11	Saugerties Village	11	11	0
Newburgh Town	64	51	13	Scarsdale Village	43	38	5
New Hartford Town and Village	32	21	11	Schenectady	207	160	47
New Paltz Town and Village	24	20	4	Schodack Town	11	10	1
New Rochelle	234	178	56	Schoharie Village	1	1	0
New Windsor Town	45	33	12	Scotia Village	14	13	1
New York	53,774	37,240	16,534	Seneca Falls Village	22	16	6
Niagara Falls	159	144	15	Shawangunk Town	4	4	0
Niagara Town	4	4	0	Shelter Island Town	10	8	2
Niskayuna Town	41	31	10	Sherrill	4	4	0
Nissequogue Village	3	3	0	Sidney Village	9	9	0
North Castle Town	39	36	3	Silver Creek Village	6	5	1
North Greenbush Town	16	14	2	Skaneateles Village	5	5	0
Northport Village	18	14	4	Sleepy Hollow Village	24	24	0
North Syracuse Village	14	12	2	Solvay Village	14	14	0
North Tonawanda	59	50	9	Southampton Town	131	99	32
Norwich	19	18	1	South Glens Falls Village	6	6	0
Ocean Beach Village	2	2	0	South Nyack Village	7	7	0
Ogdensburg	32	27	5	Southold Town	68	51	17
Old Brookville Village	51	40	11	Southport Town	2	1	1
Old Westbury Village	29	24	5	Spring Valley Village	70	66	4
Olean	40	39	1	St. Johnsville Village	2	2	0
Olive Town	1	1	0	Stony Point Town	30	29	1
Oneida	26	23	3	Suffern Village	32	27	5
Oneonta City	29	26	3	Syracuse	544	473	71
Orangetown Town	95	86	9	Tarrytown Village	42	35	7
Orchard Park Town	38	33	5	Ticonderoga Town	8	8	0
Ossining Town	16	16	0	Tonawanda	34	29	5
Ossining Village	65	57	8	Tonawanda Town	161	106	55
Oswego City	50	45	5	Troy	128	114	14
Owego Village	10	7	3	Trumansburg Village	1	1	0
Oxford Village	2	2	0	Tuckahoe Village	28	25	3
Oyster Bay Cove Village	11	11	0	Tuxedo Park Village	7	4	3
Painted Post Village	4	4	0	Tuxedo Town	16	12	4
Palmyra Village	6	5	1	Ulster Town	26	22	4
Peekskill	73	57	16	Utica	180	167	13
Pelham Manor Village	29	28	1	Vernon Village	1	1	0
Pelham Village	27	26	1	Vestal Town	39	35	4
Penn Yan Village	14	13	1	Wallkill Town	28	23	5
Perry Village	9	8	1	Walton Village	6	5	1
Piermont Village	7	7	0	Wappingers Falls Village	7	4	3
Plattsburgh City	51	46	5	Warwick Town	33	27	6
Pleasantville Village	21	21	0	Washingtonville Village	16	13	3
Port Chester Village	66	63	3	Waterford Town and Village	14	11	3
Port Dickinson Village	5	4	1	Waterloo Village	8	7	1
Port Jervis	32	32	0	Watertown	66	62	4
Portville Village	1	1	0	Watervliet	31	27	4
Port Washington	71	64	7	Watkins Glen Village	4	4	0
Potsdam Village	18	14	4	Wayland Village	1	1	0
Poughkeepsie	120	98	22	Webb Town	5	5	0
Poughkeepsie Town	92	81	11	Webster Town and Village	39	33	6
Pulaski Village	2	2	0	Wellsville Village	16	12	4
Quogue Village	15	15	0	Westfield Village	7	6	1
Ravena Village	2	1	1	Westhampton Beach Village	18	16	2
Riverhead Town	95	74	21	West Seneca Town	78	64	14

Table 78

Full-time Law Enforcement Employees as of October 31, 2002

by City by State—Continued

City by state	Total law enforcement employees	Total officers	Total civilians	City by state	Total law enforcement employees	Total officers	Total civilians
NEW YORK—Continued				**NORTH CAROLINA—Continued**			
Whitehall Village	5	5	0	Chapel Hill	123	102	21
White Plains	245	203	42	Charlotte-Mecklenburg[1]	2,002	1,501	501
Whitesboro Village	7	7	0	Cherryville	18	14	4
Whitestown Town	5	5	0	China Grove	13	12	1
Windham Town	2	2	0	Chocowinity	2	2	0
Woodbury Town	26	22	4	Claremont	9	8	1
Yonkers	687	620	67	Clarkton	4	4	0
Yorktown Town	59	51	8	Clayton	38	31	7
Yorkville Village	4	4	0	Cleveland	4	4	0
				Clinton	36	32	4
NORTH CAROLINA				Clyde	4	4	0
				Coats	7	5	2
Aberdeen	21	19	2	Concord	143	126	17
Ahoskie	21	16	5	Conover	24	23	1
Albemarle	51	45	6	Conway	1	1	0
Andrews	7	6	1	Cooleemee	3	3	0
Angier	10	10	0	Cornelius	43	31	12
Apex	43	33	10	Cramerton	10	10	0
Archdale	25	20	5	Creedmoor	17	13	4
Asheboro	71	66	5	Dallas	17	13	4
Asheville	207	161	46	Davidson	17	16	1
Atlantic Beach	23	18	5	Denton	7	7	0
Aulander	1	1	0	Dobson	4	4	0
Aurora	1	1	0	Drexel	5	5	0
Ayden	19	15	4	Dunn	49	37	12
Badin	4	4	0	Durham	549	444	105
Bailey	2	2	0	East Bend	2	2	0
Bakersville	2	1	1	East Spencer	4	4	0
Bald Head Islands	12	11	1	Eden	56	47	9
Banner Elk	6	6	0	Edenton	17	14	3
Beaufort	14	13	1	Elizabeth City	58	49	9
Beech Mountain	13	9	4	Elizabethtown	17	16	1
Belhaven	10	7	3	Elkin	21	18	3
Belmont	34	29	5	Elon	13	12	1
Benson	16	13	3	Emerald Isle	22	17	5
Bethel	7	7	0	Enfield	12	10	2
Beulaville	5	5	0	Erwin	10	9	1
Biltmore Forest	14	13	1	Fair Bluff	3	3	0
Biscoe	8	7	1	Fairmont	17	13	4
Black Creek	1	1	0	Faison	2	2	0
Black Mountain	22	18	4	Farmville	18	15	3
Bladenboro	6	6	0	Fayetteville	362	282	80
Blowing Rock	14	10	4	Fletcher	12	11	1
Boiling Spring Lakes	5	5	0	Forest City	36	30	6
Boiling Springs	6	6	0	Four Oaks	7	6	1
Bolton	1	1	0	Foxfire Village	2	2	0
Boone	43	35	8	Franklin	17	17	0
Boonville	2	2	0	Franklinton	8	8	0
Brevard	28	23	5	Fremont	4	4	0
Broadway	4	4	0	Fuquay-Varina	28	23	5
Brookford	1	1	0	Garland	2	2	0
Bryson City	6	6	0	Garner	52	46	6
Bunn	1	1	0	Garysburg	1	1	0
Burgaw	10	9	1	Gaston	2	2	0
Burlington	141	107	34	Gastonia	189	167	22
Burnsville	6	6	0	Gibson	2	2	0
Butner	45	38	7	Gibsonville	17	14	3
Cameron	1	1	0	Glen Alpine	2	2	0
Candor	4	4	0	Goldsboro	115	103	12
Canton	16	11	5	Graham	32	29	3
Cape Carteret	5	5	0	Granite Falls	14	12	2
Carolina Beach	29	23	6	Granite Quarry	4	4	0
Carrboro	35	32	3	Greensboro	667	499	168
Carthage	10	9	1	Greenville	191	151	40
Cary	153	125	28	Grifton	7	7	0
Caswell Beach	4	4	0	Hamlet	20	17	3
Catawba	1	1	0	Havelock	28	22	6
Chadbourn	10	9	1	Haw River	8	8	0

Table 78

Full-time Law Enforcement Employees as of October 31, 2002

by City by State—Continued

City by state	Total law enforcement employees	Total officers	Total civilians	City by state	Total law enforcement employees	Total officers	Total civilians
NORTH CAROLINA—Continued				**NORTH CAROLINA—Continued**			
Henderson	62	54	8	Monroe	80	69	11
Hendersonville	46	34	12	Montreat	5	5	0
Hertford	8	7	1	Mooresville	55	45	10
Hickory	133	106	27	Morehead City	42	35	7
Highlands	11	11	0	Morganton	101	73	28
High Point	222	190	32	Morrisville	27	25	2
Hillsborough	25	23	2	Mount Airy	50	38	12
Holden Beach	6	6	0	Mount Gilead	7	6	1
Holly Ridge	4	4	0	Mount Holly	38	32	6
Holly Springs	29	23	6	Mount Olive	17	14	3
Hope Mills	36	26	10	Murfreesboro	14	10	4
Hudson	13	12	1	Murphy	11	8	3
Huntersville	59	54	5	Nags Head	23	20	3
Indian Beach	4	4	0	Nashville	15	14	1
Jackson	2	1	1	Navassa	3	3	0
Jacksonville	118	96	22	New Bern	113	82	31
Jefferson	3	3	0	Newland	5	5	0
Jonesville	11	10	1	Newport	6	6	0
Kannapolis	95	73	22	Newton	44	35	9
Kenansville	4	4	0	Newton Grove	3	3	0
Kenly	9	9	0	Norlina	5	5	0
Kernersville	65	49	16	North Topsail Beach	10	9	1
Kill Devil Hills	29	24	5	Northwest	3	3	0
King	19	17	2	North Wilkesboro	27	24	3
Kings Mountain	36	30	6	Norwood	7	6	1
Kingstown	2	1	1	Oakboro	4	4	0
Kinston	84	73	11	Oak Island	32	24	8
Kitty Hawk	17	15	2	Ocean Isle Beach	11	11	0
Knightdale	16	15	1	Old Fort	8	7	1
Kure Beach	9	8	1	Oxford	38	31	7
La Grange	7	7	0	Parkton	3	3	0
Lake Lure	10	9	1	Pembroke	16	12	4
Lake Royale	7	3	4	Pikeville	2	2	0
Lake Waccamaw	3	3	0	Pilot Mountain	8	7	1
Landis	10	9	1	Pinebluff	2	2	0
Laurel Park	6	6	0	Pinehurst	26	21	5
Laurinburg	40	34	6	Pine Knoll Shores	9	9	0
Leland	13	12	1	Pine Level	3	3	0
Lenoir	69	54	15	Pinetops	8	6	2
Lexington	75	64	11	Pineville	37	28	9
Liberty	9	9	0	Pink Hill	1	1	0
Lilesville	1	1	0	Pittsboro	9	9	0
Lillington	10	10	0	Plymouth	14	14	0
Lincolnton	32	28	4	Princeton	4	4	0
Littleton	3	3	0	Raeford	16	15	1
Locust	6	6	0	Raleigh	714	620	94
Longview	15	15	0	Ramseur	7	7	0
Louisburg	13	12	1	Randleman	9	9	0
Lowell	8	8	0	Ranlo	6	6	0
Lucama	3	3	0	Red Springs	21	17	4
Lumberton	90	78	12	Reidsville	49	40	9
Madison	16	15	1	Rhodhiss	1	1	0
Maggie Valley	7	6	1	Richlands	7	7	0
Magnolia	1	1	0	Rich Square	1	1	0
Maiden	16	15	1	River Bend	4	4	0
Manteo	9	8	1	Roanoke Rapids	41	38	3
Marion	24	19	5	Robbins	8	7	1
Marshall	3	3	0	Robersonville	6	6	0
Mars Hill	5	5	0	Rockingham	35	30	5
Marshville	8	8	0	Rockwell	1	1	0
Matthews	60	49	11	Rocky Mount	169	132	37
Maxton	14	9	5	Rolesville	5	5	0
Mayodan	15	12	3	Roseboro	5	5	0
Maysville	1	1	0	Rose Hill	4	4	0
McAdenville	4	4	0	Rowland	7	6	1
Mebane	18	15	3	Roxboro	36	31	5
Middlesex	4	4	0	Rutherfordton	14	14	0
Mocksville	15	14	1	Salemburg	1	1	0

Table 78

Full-time Law Enforcement Employees as of October 31, 2002
by City by State—Continued

City by state	Total law enforcement employees	Total officers	Total civilians
NORTH CAROLINA—Continued			
Salisbury	97	80	17
Saluda	3	3	0
Sanford	88	70	18
Scotland Neck	9	8	1
Seagrove	1	1	0
Selma	27	22	5
Seven Devils	5	5	0
Shallotte	11	10	1
Sharpsburg	9	8	1
Shelby	79	64	15
Siler City	22	17	5
Smithfield	36	33	3
Southern Pines	34	26	8
Southern Shores	10	10	0
Southport	10	9	1
Sparta	5	5	0
Spencer	13	12	1
Spindale	13	13	0
Spring Hope	6	6	0
Spring Lake	23	17	6
Spruce Pine	10	10	0
Stanfield	3	3	0
Stanley	14	10	4
Stantonsburg	3	3	0
Star	4	4	0
Statesville	87	70	17
Stoneville	5	5	0
St. Pauls	17	12	5
Sugar Mountain	5	5	0
Sunset Beach	12	12	0
Surf City	12	11	1
Swansboro	7	7	0
Sylva	13	12	1
Tabor City	8	7	1
Tarboro	35	29	6
Taylorsville	11	11	0
Taylortown	1	1	0
Thomasville	74	67	7
Topsail Beach	8	7	1
Trent Woods	4	4	0
Troutman	5	5	0
Troy	10	9	1
Tryon	12	7	5
Valdese	13	12	1
Vanceboro	2	2	0
Vass	3	3	0
Wadesboro	30	25	5
Wagram	2	2	0
Wake Forest	37	32	5
Wallace	16	13	3
Walnut Cove	6	6	0
Warrenton	6	5	1
Warsaw	15	12	3
Washington	37	28	9
Waxhaw	9	8	1
Waynesville	37	31	6
Weaverville	11	10	1
Weldon	9	8	1
Wendell	16	12	4
West Jefferson	7	7	0
Whispering Pines	7	7	0
Whitakers	5	5	0
White Lake	5	5	0
Whiteville	26	22	4
Wilkesboro	23	22	1
Williamston	21	20	1
Wilmington	286	248	38
Wilson	128	108	20

City by state	Total law enforcement employees	Total officers	Total civilians
NORTH CAROLINA—Continued			
Windsor	8	8	0
Wingate	8	8	0
Winston-Salem	571	430	141
Winterville	15	14	1
Winton	2	2	0
Woodfin	8	8	0
Woodland	1	1	0
Wrightsville Beach	28	22	6
Yadkinville	10	9	1
Yanceyville	3	3	0
Youngsville	7	6	1
Zebulon	21	20	1
NORTH DAKOTA			
Beulah	7	6	1
Bismarck	110	84	26
Bowman	2	2	0
Cando	3	3	0
Carrington	3	3	0
Carson	1	1	0
Cavalier	4	4	0
Crosby	2	2	0
Devils Lake	16	14	2
Dickinson	33	23	10
Elgin	1	1	0
Fargo	150	111	39
Fessenden	1	1	0
Grafton	11	10	1
Grand Forks	93	77	16
Harvey	3	3	0
Hazen	4	4	0
Hillsboro	2	2	0
Jamestown	33	29	4
Lamoure	1	1	0
Lisbon	3	3	0
Mandan	36	28	8
Mayville	3	3	0
Minot	82	60	22
Napoleon	2	2	0
Northwood	2	2	0
Oakes	4	3	1
Powers Lake	1	1	0
Rugby	4	4	0
South Heart	1	1	0
Steele	1	1	0
Thompson	1	1	0
Valley City	17	12	5
Wahpeton	14	13	1
Watford City	4	4	0
West Fargo	36	25	11
Williston	29	21	8
Wishek	2	2	0
OHIO			
Aberdeen	1	1	0
Ada	11	7	4
Addyston	1	1	0
Akron	548	504	44
Alliance	56	43	13
Amberley Village	19	15	4
Amherst	26	20	6
Ansonia	2	2	0
Arcanum	4	4	0
Archbold	9	8	1
Arlington Heights	4	3	1
Ashtabula	42	35	7

Table 78

Full-time Law Enforcement Employees as of October 31, 2002

by City by State—Continued

City by state	Total law enforcement employees	Total officers	Total civilians	City by state	Total law enforcement employees	Total officers	Total civilians
OHIO—Continued				**OHIO—Continued**			
Athens	33	27	6	Cleveland Heights	122	109	13
Aurora	31	24	7	Cleves	3	3	0
Austintown	55	43	12	Clinton Township	9	8	1
Avon	28	22	6	Clyde	18	14	4
Bainbridge Township	29	21	8	Coitsville Township	4	4	0
Barberton	56	43	13	Coldwater	6	6	0
Barnesville	11	7	4	Columbiana	16	12	4
Bath Township	26	19	7	Columbus	2,191	1,811	380
Bay Village	25	22	3	Conneaut	28	20	8
Beach City	2	2	0	Copley Township	24	18	6
Beachwood	56	43	13	Cortland	9	9	0
Beavercreek	64	48	16	Covington	6	5	1
Beaver Township	17	12	5	Crestline	14	10	4
Bedford	74	30	44	Creston	4	4	0
Bedford Heights	66	35	31	Crooksville	5	4	1
Bellaire	11	11	0	Cuyahoga Falls	120	95	25
Bellbrook	18	12	6	Dalton	2	2	0
Bellefontaine	30	23	7	Dayton	619	503	116
Bellevue	17	13	4	Deer Park	15	11	4
Bellville	3	3	0	Defiance	39	30	9
Belpre	16	11	5	Delaware	56	40	16
Berea	39	32	7	Delhi Township	35	31	4
Bethel	5	4	1	Delta	7	7	0
Bethesda	1	1	0	Dennison	6	6	0
Beverly	4	3	1	Deshler	3	3	0
Bexley	35	28	7	Donnelsville	1	1	0
Blanchester	8	8	0	Dover	21	20	1
Blendon Township	13	12	1	Doylestown	7	6	1
Bluffton	7	7	0	Dublin	79	61	18
Boardman	70	55	15	East Cleveland	79	64	15
Bowling Green	57	43	14	Eastlake	50	37	13
Bradford	3	3	0	East Liverpool	30	25	5
Brecksville	38	31	7	East Palestine	11	8	3
Brewster	4	4	0	Eaton	22	15	7
Bridgeport	11	7	4	Elmwood Place	9	8	1
Broadview Heights	45	32	13	Elyria	139	92	47
Brookfield Township	9	8	1	Englewood	27	18	9
Brooklyn	41	33	8	Euclid	169	99	70
Brooklyn Heights	17	17	0	Evendale	22	20	2
Brook Park	50	42	8	Fairborn	58	43	15
Brookville	16	11	5	Fairfax	9	9	0
Brunswick	53	39	14	Fairfield	78	60	18
Bryan	28	20	8	Fairfield Township	13	12	1
Buckeye Lake	6	6	0	Fairlawn	32	22	10
Bucyrus	29	21	8	Fairport Harbor	7	6	1
Burton	2	2	0	Fairview Park	30	28	2
Butler Township	13	12	1	Fayette	3	3	0
Cadiz	6	6	0	Findlay	92	73	19
Cambridge	32	25	7	Forest Park	40	33	7
Canal Fulton	8	7	1	Fort Recovery	2	2	0
Canfield	22	16	6	Fort Shawnee	5	4	1
Canton	219	182	37	Franklin	29	23	6
Carey	11	7	4	Franklin Township	16	11	5
Carlisle	8	7	1	Fredericktown	4	4	0
Carrollton	7	7	0	Fremont	39	34	5
Celina	21	15	6	Gahanna	63	53	10
Centerville	56	43	13	Galion	25	19	6
Chagrin Falls	20	12	8	Gallipolis	15	14	1
Chardon	18	10	8	Garfield Heights	79	61	18
Chauncey	2	1	1	Gates Mills	16	12	4
Chester Township	15	14	1	Geneva	16	12	4
Cheviot	10	10	0	Genoa	5	5	0
Chillicothe	57	50	7	Germantown	16	11	5
Cincinnati	1,272	990	282	German Township (Clark County)	3	3	0
Circleville	38	26	12	German Township (Montgomery County)	6	6	0
Clayton	15	15	0	Gibsonburg	4	4	0
Clearcreek Township	13	12	1	Girard	20	18	2
Cleveland	2,370	1,878	492	Glendale	8	7	1

Table 78

Full-time Law Enforcement Employees as of October 31, 2002
by City by State—Continued

City by state	Total law enforcement employees	Total officers	Total civilians	City by state	Total law enforcement employees	Total officers	Total civilians
OHIO—Continued				**OHIO—Continued**			
Golf Manor	8	7	1	Mansfield	135	92	43
Goshen Township	11	9	2	Maple Heights	63	45	18
Grandview Heights	24	19	5	Mariemont	11	10	1
Granville	13	10	3	Marietta	39	32	7
Greenfield	14	12	2	Marion	89	68	21
Greenhills	9	9	0	Marlboro Township	4	4	0
Greenville	32	24	8	Martins Ferry	15	11	4
Greenwich	4	4	0	Marysville	36	30	6
Grove City	67	51	16	Mason	35	32	3
Hamilton	142	115	27	Massillon	53	49	4
Harrison	24	21	3	Maumee	59	44	15
Hartville	8	7	1	Mayfield Heights	43	33	10
Heath	27	20	7	Mayfield Village	24	16	8
Hebron	5	4	1	McClure	1	1	0
Hicksville	9	7	2	Mc Comb	5	4	1
Highland Heights	28	22	6	McConnelsville	7	5	2
Highland Hills	12	11	1	Mechanicsburg	3	3	0
Hilliard	65	46	19	Medina	50	38	12
Hillsboro	22	18	4	Medina Township	2	2	0
Holgate	1	1	0	Mentor	112	77	35
Howland	20	19	1	Mentor-on-the-Lake	16	11	5
Hubbard	16	13	3	Miamisburg	50	39	11
Huber Heights	57	52	5	Miami Township	44	40	4
Hudson	36	30	6	Middlefield	12	7	5
Hunting Valley	13	13	0	Middleport	7	5	2
Huron	19	14	5	Middletown	144	93	51
Independence	51	36	15	Milford	17	14	3
Indian Hill	24	19	5	Millersburg	9	9	0
Ironton	20	14	6	Milton Township	1	1	0
Jackson	24	18	6	Minerva	14	9	5
Jackson Township	47	37	10	Minerva Park	5	5	0
Jefferson	6	5	1	Mingo Junction	11	10	1
Johnstown	17	9	8	Mogadore	9	9	0
Kalida	1	1	0	Monroe	23	18	5
Kelleys Island	2	2	0	Monroeville	5	5	0
Kent	55	41	14	Montgomery	23	21	2
Kenton	16	16	0	Montpelier	9	8	1
Kettering	111	83	28	Montville Township	7	7	0
Kirtland	14	9	5	Moraine	42	33	9
Kirtland Hills	9	8	1	Mount Gilead	6	6	0
Lagrange	5	5	0	Mount Healthy	12	11	1
Lakemore	7	7	0	Mount Sterling	11	7	4
Lake Township	13	12	1	Mount Vernon	31	26	5
Lakewood	110	87	23	Munroe Falls	9	8	1
Lancaster	88	67	21	Napoleon	21	16	5
Lawrence Township	6	6	0	Navarre	5	5	0
Lebanon	36	27	9	Nelsonville	12	9	3
Leipsic	3	3	0	New Albany	21	16	5
Lexington	12	8	4	New Boston	14	10	4
Liberty Township	28	23	5	Newburgh Heights	10	7	3
Lima	106	87	19	Newcomerstown	15	10	5
Lincoln Heights	11	11	0	New Lebanon	7	7	0
Lisbon	10	6	4	New Lexington	12	8	4
Lockland	14	13	1	New Matamoras	1	1	0
Logan	22	17	5	New Middletown	3	3	0
London	19	14	5	New Paris	4	4	0
Lorain	128	97	31	New Philadelphia	26	22	4
Lordstown	13	9	4	New Richmond	6	5	1
Loudonville	8	4	4	Newton Falls	11	7	4
Louisville	12	12	0	Newtown	5	5	0
Loveland	20	18	2	Niles	45	35	10
Lowellville	3	3	0	North Baltimore	5	5	0
Lyndhurst	37	29	8	North Canton	33	25	8
Macedonia	28	22	6	North College Hill	13	12	1
Madeira	13	12	1	North Kingsville	5	5	0
Madison Township	22	20	2	North Olmsted	77	57	20
Magnolia	3	3	0	North Randall	19	16	3
Malvern	5	5	0	North Ridgeville	45	37	8

Table 78

Full-time Law Enforcement Employees as of October 31, 2002

by City by State—Continued

City by state	Total law enforcement employees	Total officers	Total civilians	City by state	Total law enforcement employees	Total officers	Total civilians
OHIO—Continued				**OHIO—Continued**			
North Royalton	61	40	21	South Charleston	4	4	0
Northwood	28	21	7	South Euclid	49	39	10
Norton	22	16	6	South Russell	10	9	1
Norwalk	32	24	8	South Solon	2	2	0
Norwood	50	48	2	South Zanesville	3	3	0
Oak Harbor	6	4	2	Spencerville	4	4	0
Oakwood Village	17	13	4	Springboro	29	22	7
Oberlin	21	16	5	Springdale	47	37	10
Olmsted Falls	18	12	6	Springfield	155	130	25
Olmsted Township	18	15	3	Springfield Township (Hamilton County)	50	43	7
Ontario	25	19	6	Springfield Township (Mahoning County)	6	5	1
Oregon	58	45	13	St. Bernard	19	18	1
Orrville	20	15	5	Steubenville	57	47	10
Ottawa	7	7	0	St. Henry	2	2	0
Ottawa Hills	11	11	0	St. Marys	19	15	4
Oxford	28	26	2	Stow	42	33	9
Painesville	42	38	4	Strasburg	4	4	0
Parma	159	102	57	Streetsboro	30	23	7
Parma Heights	40	34	6	Strongsville	96	75	21
Pataskala	17	17	0	Struthers	21	16	5
Paulding	5	4	1	Sugarcreek Township	20	13	7
Payne	1	1	0	Swanton	8	7	1
Peninsula	6	5	1	Sylvania	39	32	7
Pepper Pike	25	19	6	Sylvania Township	62	45	17
Perkins Township	28	22	6	Tallmadge	37	25	12
Perrysburg	39	31	8	Terrace Park	7	6	1
Perry Township (Franklin County)	14	9	5	Thornville	1	1	0
Perry Township (Montgomery County)	6	6	0	Tiffin	43	30	13
Perry Township (Stark County)	33	24	9	Tipp City	21	17	4
Pierce Township	16	15	1	Toledo	811	692	119
Piqua	41	33	8	Toronto	10	10	0
Plain City	8	8	0	Trenton	20	13	7
Plymouth	3	3	0	Trotwood	55	51	4
Poland Township	15	13	2	Troy	45	39	6
Poland Village	6	6	0	Twinsburg	47	34	13
Port Clinton	17	12	5	Uhrichsville	8	8	0
Portsmouth	45	41	4	Union	6	6	0
Powell	17	16	1	Union City	4	4	0
Reading	23	18	5	Uniontown	12	9	3
Reminderville	7	6	1	Union Township (Clermont County)	53	43	10
Reynoldsburg	64	50	14	Union Township (Licking County)	2	2	0
Richfield	24	17	7	University Heights	38	30	8
Richland Township	2	2	0	Upper Arlington	59	48	11
Richmond Heights	29	22	7	Upper Sandusky	18	13	5
Richwood	6	6	0	Urbana	25	20	5
Rittman	12	9	3	Valley View	21	19	2
Riverside	33	32	1	Vandalia	35	28	7
Rossford	18	17	1	Van Wert	29	22	7
Russell Township	9	8	1	Vermilion	23	18	5
Sagamore Hills	13	9	4	Vienna Township	4	4	0
Salem	25	24	1	Village of Leesburg	3	3	0
Salineville	3	3	0	Wadsworth	35	26	9
Sandusky	66	55	11	Waite Hill	6	6	0
Sebring	11	8	3	Walbridge	7	3	4
Seven Hills	19	18	1	Walton Hills	17	13	4
Seville	7	6	1	Wapakoneta	18	13	5
Shadyside	10	6	4	Warren	98	78	20
Shaker Heights	97	67	30	Warrensville Heights	53	39	14
Sharon Township	9	9	0	Warren Township	8	8	0
Sharonville	48	39	9	Washington Court House	27	22	5
Shawnee Township	16	10	6	Waterville	13	12	1
Sheffield Lake	16	12	4	Waterville Township	6	6	0
Shelby	19	15	4	Wauseon	15	13	2
Shreve	3	3	0	Waverly	17	12	5
Sidney	50	39	11	Waynesville	5	4	1
Silverton	13	10	3	Wellington	8	6	2
Smith Township	5	4	1				
Solon	74	45	29				

Table 78

Full-time Law Enforcement Employees as of October 31, 2002
by City by State—Continued

City by state	Total law enforcement employees	Total officers	Total civilians	City by state	Total law enforcement employees	Total officers	Total civilians
OHIO—Continued				**OKLAHOMA—Continued**			
Wellston	12	9	3	Cleveland	7	7	0
Wellsville	5	5	0	Clinton	25	17	8
West Carrollton	31	24	7	Coalgate	7	6	1
West Chester Township	82	73	9	Colbert	8	4	4
Westerville	81	70	11	Collinsville	18	12	6
West Jefferson	15	11	4	Comanche	4	4	0
Westlake	69	50	19	Commerce	5	5	0
West Union	7	7	0	Cordell	8	5	3
Whitehall	57	45	12	Coweta	20	12	8
Wickliffe	42	31	11	Crescent	12	7	5
Willard	19	15	4	Cushing	25	17	8
Willoughby	60	45	15	Davis	11	9	2
Willoughby Hills	26	19	7	Del City	39	29	10
Willowick	35	25	10	Dewey	8	8	0
Wilmington	23	22	1	Drumright	5	5	0
Winchester	2	2	0	Duncan	49	37	12
Windham	7	5	2	Durant	38	27	11
Wintersville	10	9	1	Edmond	120	100	20
Woodlawn	18	17	1	Elk City	37	27	10
Woodsfield	7	7	0	El Reno	37	28	9
Woodville	4	4	0	Enid	130	88	42
Wooster	44	39	5	Erick	3	3	0
Worthington	43	34	9	Eufaula	12	9	3
Wyoming	20	16	4	Fairfax	7	3	4
Xenia	72	47	25	Fairview	8	5	3
Yellow Springs	11	8	3	Fletcher	2	2	0
Youngstown	227	186	41	Fort Gibson	12	10	2
Zanesville	95	55	40	Frederick	11	9	2
				Geary	9	4	5
OKLAHOMA				Glenpool	19	13	6
				Goodwell	3	3	0
Ada	47	34	13	Granite	1	1	0
Agra	1	1	0	Grove	26	19	7
Altus	59	42	17	Guthrie	30	24	6
Alva	14	9	5	Guymon	29	18	11
Anadarko	28	20	8	Haileyville	3	3	0
Antlers	10	6	4	Harrah	12	12	0
Apache	3	3	0	Hartshorne	5	5	0
Ardmore	64	47	17	Haskell	6	6	0
Arkoma	8	4	4	Healdton	9	5	4
Atoka	15	14	1	Heavener	14	8	6
Barnsdall	6	4	2	Henryetta	18	13	5
Bartlesville	68	52	16	Hinton	5	5	0
Beaver	2	2	0	Hobart	16	9	7
Beggs	8	5	3	Holdenville	14	9	5
Bethany	37	26	11	Hollis	12	8	4
Bixby	23	12	11	Hominy	8	4	4
Blackwell	23	15	8	Hooker	4	4	0
Blanchard	8	5	3	Howe	3	2	1
Boise City	2	2	0	Hugo	19	15	4
Bokoshe	2	2	0	Hulbert	5	5	0
Bristow	16	12	4	Hydro	2	2	0
Broken Arrow	144	104	40	Idabel	26	20	6
Broken Bow	17	12	5	Inola	10	4	6
Buffalo	3	3	0	Jay	11	7	4
Caddo	4	4	0	Jenks	19	14	5
Calera	8	5	3	Jones	4	4	0
Carnegie	11	5	6	Kingfisher	9	7	2
Catoosa	15	14	1	Kingston	7	7	0
Chandler	12	8	4	Konawa	7	5	2
Checotah	15	10	5	Krebs	4	4	0
Chelsea	8	5	3	Laverne	6	2	4
Cherokee	6	3	3	Lawton	178	153	25
Chickasha	43	32	11	Lexington	12	7	5
Choctaw	13	11	2	Lindsay	8	4	4
Chouteau	7	5	2	Locust Grove	10	5	5
Claremore	52	37	15	Lone Grove	9	6	3
Clayton	5	3	2	Luther	4	4	0

Table 78

Full-time Law Enforcement Employees as of October 31, 2002

by City by State—Continued

City by state	Total law enforcement employees	Total officers	Total civilians	City by state	Total law enforcement employees	Total officers	Total civilians
OKLAHOMA—Continued				**OKLAHOMA—Continued**			
Madill	11	10	1	Talihina	11	5	6
Mangum	9	6	3	Tecumseh	16	10	6
Mannford	13	9	4	Temple	1	1	0
Marietta	6	6	0	The Village	26	20	6
Marlow	14	12	2	Tishomingo	7	7	0
Maysville	4	3	1	Tonkawa	12	8	4
McAlester	60	46	14	Tulsa	944	792	152
McLoud	9	6	3	Tushka	4	3	1
Meeker	6	6	0	Tuttle	12	8	4
Miami	42	30	12	Valliant	5	4	1
Midwest City	118	95	23	Vian	4	4	0
Minco	4	4	0	Vinita	21	17	4
Moore	63	58	5	Wagoner	17	11	6
Mooreland	2	2	0	Walters	4	4	0
Morris	4	4	0	Warner	3	3	0
Mountain View	1	1	0	Warr Acres	31	22	9
Muldrow	12	8	4	Watonga	11	8	3
Muskogee	112	88	24	Waukomis	3	3	0
Mustang	26	19	7	Waurika	3	3	0
Newcastle	17	12	5	Waynoka	3	3	0
Newkirk	7	6	1	Weatherford	29	18	11
Nichols Hills	17	13	4	Weleetka	4	4	0
Nicoma Park	7	7	0	Westville	12	7	5
Noble	16	10	6	Wetumka	5	5	0
Norman	179	125	54	Wewoka	18	10	8
Nowata	9	7	2	Wilburton	10	6	4
Oilton	3	3	0	Wilson	4	4	0
Okeene	2	2	0	Woodward	27	19	8
Okemah	12	8	4	Wright City	3	3	0
Oklahoma City	1,298	1,056	242	Wynnewood	5	4	1
Okmulgee	41	28	13	Yale	6	2	4
Oologah	4	3	1	Yukon	48	34	14
Owasso	46	34	12				
Pauls Valley	20	14	6	**OREGON**			
Pawhuska	11	6	5				
Pawnee	6	6	0	Albany	76	55	21
Perkins	4	4	0	Amity	2	2	0
Perry	18	13	5	Ashland	42	29	13
Piedmont	10	8	2	Astoria	24	15	9
Pocola	8	5	3	Athena	2	2	0
Ponca City	67	55	12	Aumsville	5	4	1
Porum	2	2	0	Aurora	3	2	1
Poteau	27	21	6	Baker City	17	17	0
Prague	10	6	4	Bandon	8	7	1
Pryor	30	22	8	Banks	3	3	0
Purcell	19	19	0	Beaverton	138	114	24
Ringling	2	2	0	Bend	93	69	24
Roland	23	17	6	Black Butte	7	6	1
Rush Springs	4	4	0	Boardman	9	8	1
Sallisaw	31	19	12	Brookings	19	13	6
Sand Springs	46	34	12	Burns	9	5	4
Sapulpa	52	42	10	Butte Falls	2	2	0
Sayre	11	7	4	Canby	22	20	2
Seiling	3	3	0	Cannon Beach	8	7	1
Seminole	18	13	5	Carlton	4	3	1
Shawnee	74	53	21	Central Point	24	20	4
Skiatook	17	12	5	Clatskanie	5	4	1
Snyder	4	4	0	Coburg	8	7	1
Spencer	10	9	1	Columbia City	1	1	0
Spiro	5	5	0	Condon	2	1	1
Stigler	13	8	5	Coos Bay	38	28	10
Stillwater	102	70	32	Coquille	10	8	2
Stilwell	20	13	7	Cornelius	13	12	1
Stratford	6	3	3	Corvallis	83	56	27
Stringtown	8	7	1	Cottage Grove	22	15	7
Stroud	14	9	5	Culver	1	1	0
Sulphur	15	10	5	Dallas	20	19	1
Tahlequah	36	28	8	Dundee	4	4	0

Table 78

Full-time Law Enforcement Employees as of October 31, 2002
by City by State—Continued

City by state	Total law enforcement employees	Total officers	Total civilians	City by state	Total law enforcement employees	Total officers	Total civilians
OREGON—Continued				**OREGON—Continued**			
Eagle Point	8	7	1	Shady Cove	4	3	1
Elgin	3	3	0	Sherwood	21	18	3
Enterprise	4	4	0	Silverton	15	14	1
Eugene	299	172	127	Springfield	92	61	31
Fairview	11	10	1	Stanfield	5	5	0
Florence	21	13	8	Stayton	18	15	3
Forest Grove	29	26	3	St. Helens	20	18	2
Gaston	1	1	0	Sutherlin	15	12	3
Gearhart	3	3	0	Sweet Home	18	11	7
Gervais	3	3	0	Talent	9	8	1
Gladstone	24	17	7	The Dalles	22	20	2
Gold Beach	6	5	1	Tigard	71	56	15
Grants Pass	66	40	26	Tillamook	11	9	2
Gresham	154	108	46	Toledo	12	7	5
Hermiston	30	21	9	Troutdale	22	18	4
Hillsboro	145	109	36	Tualatin	36	31	5
Hines	4	3	1	Turner	2	2	0
Hood River	17	14	3	Umatilla	10	9	1
Hubbard	6	5	1	Vernonia	5	5	0
Independence	15	13	2	Warrenton	9	8	1
Jacksonville	5	4	1	West Linn	32	27	5
John Day	10	5	5	Weston	2	2	0
Junction City	13	8	5	Winston	9	8	1
Keizer	46	39	7	Woodburn	35	27	8
King City	3	3	0	Yamhill	2	2	0
Klamath Falls	44	40	4				
La Grande	32	18	14	**PENNSYLVANIA**			
Lake Oswego	65	39	26				
Lakeview	6	6	0	Abington Township	112	89	23
Lebanon	30	22	8	Adams Township (Butler County)	4	4	0
Lincoln City	27	18	9	Adams Township (Cambria County)	4	4	0
Madras	10	9	1	Akron	5	5	0
Manzanita	3	3	0	Albion	2	2	0
McMinnville	40	32	8	Alburtis	3	3	0
Medford	145	97	48	Aldan	4	4	0
Milton-Freewater	16	10	6	Aleppo Township	9	5	4
Milwaukie	43	31	12	Aliquippa	24	24	0
Molalla	14	10	4	Allegheny Township (Blair County)	7	7	0
Monmouth	15	13	2	Allegheny Township (Westmoreland County)	9	8	1
Mount Angel	6	5	1	Allentown	248	223	25
Myrtle Creek	13	7	6	Altoona	86	76	10
Myrtle Point	6	6	0	Ambler	14	12	2
Newberg	32	22	10	Ambridge	13	13	0
Newport	28	23	5	Amity Township	11	10	1
North Bend	25	19	6	Annville Township	4	4	0
North Plains	3	3	0	Arnold	11	10	1
Nyssa	7	7	0	Ashland	5	5	0
Oakridge	9	4	5	Ashley	2	2	0
Ontario	29	22	7	Aspinwall	7	6	1
Oregon City	39	32	7	Aston Township	18	16	2
Pendleton	25	22	3	Athens	8	7	1
Philomath	9	8	1	Athens Township	9	9	0
Phoenix	9	8	1	Avalon	6	6	0
Pilot Rock	3	3	0	Baden	5	5	0
Portland	1,319	1,046	273	Baldwin Borough	31	25	6
Powers	1	1	0	Baldwin Township	5	5	0
Prairie City	2	2	0	Bally	1	1	0
Prineville	25	16	9	Bangor	8	7	1
Rainier	7	6	1	Barrett Township	7	7	0
Redmond	37	28	9	Beaver	15	11	4
Reedsport	16	11	5	Beaver Falls	11	5	6
Rockaway Beach	3	3	0	Bedford	7	6	1
Rogue River	6	5	1	Bedminster Township	6	5	1
Roseburg	40	35	5	Bell Acres	4	4	0
Salem	267	175	92	Bellefonte	11	9	2
Sandy	13	10	3	Bellevue	17	14	3
Scappoose	9	8	1	Bellwood	3	3	0
Seaside	21	16	5				

Table 78

Full-time Law Enforcement Employees as of October 31, 2002

by City by State—Continued

City by state	Total law enforcement employees	Total officers	Total civilians
PENNSYLVANIA—Continued			
Bensalem Township	88	68	20
Bentleyville	2	2	0
Berks-Lehigh Regional	21	21	0
Berlin	1	1	0
Bern Township	10	10	0
Berwick Township	7	7	0
Bethel Park	42	36	6
Bethel Township (Delaware County)	2	2	0
Bethlehem	165	143	22
Bethlehem Township	30	28	2
Birdsboro	6	6	0
Birmingham Township	3	3	0
Blairsville	4	4	0
Blair Township	4	4	0
Blakely	4	4	0
Blawnox	4	4	0
Bloomsburg Town	19	15	4
Boyertown	8	7	1
Brackenridge	5	5	0
Bradford	21	21	0
Bradford Township	5	5	0
Brandywine Regional	14	13	1
Brecknock Township	3	3	0
Brentwood	18	14	4
Bridgeport	10	9	1
Bridgeville	9	8	1
Bridgewater	2	2	0
Brighton Township	6	6	0
Bristol	11	10	1
Bristol Township	85	69	16
Brockway	2	2	0
Brookhaven	10	9	1
Brookville	7	6	1
Brownsville	5	5	0
Bryn Athyn	5	5	0
Buckingham Township	23	21	2
Bushkill Township	12	10	2
Butler	26	26	0
Butler Township (Butler County)	25	21	4
Butler Township (Luzerne County)	8	7	1
California	8	7	1
Caln Township	20	18	2
Cambria Township	4	4	0
Cambridge Springs	3	3	0
Camp Hill	12	11	1
Canonsburg	16	16	0
Carbondale	15	15	0
Carlisle	39	33	6
Carnegie	14	13	1
Carroll Township (Washington County)	3	3	0
Carroll Township (York County)	9	9	0
Carroll Valley	4	3	1
Castle Shannon	12	11	1
Catawissa	2	2	0
Catawissa Township	2	2	0
Center Township	26	26	0
Centerville	4	4	0
Central Berks Regional	13	12	1
Chalfont	7	6	1
Chambersburg	33	30	3
Chartiers Township	11	11	0
Cheltenham Township	92	83	9
Chester	113	103	10
Chester Hill	1	1	0
Cheswick	3	3	0
Chippewa Township	15	14	1
Churchill	9	9	0
Clairton	12	11	1
PENNSYLVANIA—Continued			
Clarion	9	8	1
Clarks Summit	8	7	1
Claysville	2	2	0
Clearfield	7	7	0
Cleona	4	4	0
Clifton Heights	9	8	1
Cochranton	2	2	0
Colebrookdale District	10	9	1
Collegeville	9	8	1
Collier Township	12	11	1
Collingdale	10	8	2
Colonial Regional	24	22	2
Columbia	21	18	3
Colwyn	2	2	0
Conemaugh Township (Cambria County)	2	2	0
Conemaugh Township (Somerset County)	6	5	1
Conestoga Township	3	3	0
Conewago Township	7	6	1
Conewango Township	4	4	0
Conneaut Lake Regional	3	3	0
Connellsville	18	17	1
Conshohocken	17	15	2
Conway	3	3	0
Conyngham	2	2	0
Coopersburg	6	6	0
Coplay	4	4	0
Coraopolis	12	9	3
Cornwall	8	7	1
Corry	16	12	4
Covington Township	2	2	0
Crafton	10	9	1
Cranberry Township	26	23	3
Cresson	1	1	0
Cresson Township	3	3	0
Cressona	2	2	0
Croyle Township	1	1	0
Cumberland Township (Adams County)	6	6	0
Dale	1	1	0
Dallas	5	5	0
Dallas Township	8	8	0
Darby	19	16	3
Derry	2	2	0
Derry Township (Dauphin County)	42	36	6
Dickson City	13	13	0
Donegal Township	2	2	0
Dormont	16	15	1
Douglass Township (Berks County)	5	5	0
Douglass Township (Montgomery County)	12	11	1
Downingtown	17	15	2
Doylestown	20	15	5
Doylestown Township	20	17	3
Du Bois	10	10	0
Duboistown	2	2	0
Duncannon	3	3	0
Dunmore	9	8	1
Duquesne	16	15	1
Duryea	3	3	0
Earl Township	12	11	1
East Berlin	1	1	0
East Bethlehem Township	2	2	0
East Brady	1	1	0
East Cocalico Township	23	21	2
East Conemaugh	2	2	0
East Coventry Township	5	5	0
East Deer Township	1	1	0

Table 78

Full-time Law Enforcement Employees as of October 31, 2002

by City by State—Continued

City by state	Total law enforcement employees	Total officers	Total civilians
PENNSYLVANIA—Continued			
East Earl Township	5	5	0
Eastern Adams Regional	7	7	0
East Fallowfield Township	5	5	0
East Hempfield Township	32	28	4
East Lampeter Township	38	34	4
East Lansdowne	4	2	2
East McKeesport	3	3	0
East Norriton Township	31	28	3
East Pennsboro Township	20	19	1
East Pikeland Township	7	7	0
Easttown Township	15	14	1
East Vincent Township	6	6	0
East Washington	1	1	0
East Whiteland Township	20	18	2
Ebensburg	4	4	0
Economy	13	12	1
Eddystone	8	7	1
Edgewood	5	5	0
Edgeworth	6	4	2
Edinboro	10	9	1
Edwardsville	6	6	0
Elizabeth	2	2	0
Elizabeth Township	16	15	1
Elkland	2	2	0
Ellwood City	12	11	1
Emmaus	17	16	1
Emporium	1	1	0
Emsworth	8	7	1
Ephrata	26	22	4
Ephrata Township	11	10	1
Erie	251	205	46
Etna	7	6	1
Everett	3	3	0
Exeter Township (Berks County)	33	32	1
Fairview Township (Luzerne County)	5	5	0
Fairview Township (York County)	15	13	2
Falls Township (Bucks County)	59	51	8
Fawn Township	4	4	0
Ferguson Township	18	16	2
Ferndale	1	1	0
Findlay Township	22	15	7
Fleetwood	6	6	0
Folcroft	9	9	0
Ford City	4	4	0
Forest City	2	2	0
Forest Hills	14	11	3
Forks Township	16	15	1
Forty Fort	6	5	1
Foster Township	4	4	0
Fountain Hill	8	8	0
Frackville	7	7	0
Franconia Township	13	12	1
Franklin	23	18	5
Franklin Park	10	9	1
Franklin Township (Carbon County)	8	4	4
Freeland	1	1	0
Gallitzin	1	1	0
Gettysburg	16	14	2
Girard	5	4	1
Glenolden	10	9	1
Granville Township	7	7	0
Greencastle	4	4	0
Greensburg	37	27	10
Green Tree	12	11	1
Greenville	12	11	1
Greenwood Township	1	1	0
Grove City	7	6	1
Halifax	1	1	0
PENNSYLVANIA—Continued			
Hamburg	6	5	1
Hampden Township	22	21	1
Hampton Township	19	18	1
Hanover	26	24	2
Hanover Township (Luzerne County)	18	17	1
Harmar Township	7	7	0
Harmony Township	4	4	0
Harrisburg	230	179	51
Harrison Township	16	12	4
Hatboro	18	14	4
Hatfield Township	29	23	6
Haverford Township	82	65	17
Hazleton	35	32	3
Heidelberg	2	2	0
Hellam Township	9	9	0
Hellertown	11	10	1
Hemlock Township	1	1	0
Hempfield Township	8	6	2
Highspire	5	5	0
Hilltown Township	19	16	3
Homestead	14	14	0
Honesdale	11	9	2
Honey Brook Township	3	3	0
Hooversville	1	1	0
Horsham Township	49	40	9
Hughesville	3	3	0
Hummelstown	7	7	0
Huntingdon	13	12	1
Independence Township	1	1	0
Indiana Township	10	10	0
Ingram	4	4	0
Irwin	5	5	0
Jackson Township (Butler County)	5	5	0
Jackson Township (Cambria County)	1	1	0
Jackson Township (Luzerne County)	3	3	0
Jackson Township (York County)	9	8	1
Jeannette	18	17	1
Jefferson Hills Borough	17	16	1
Jenkins Township	2	2	0
Jenkintown	10	10	0
Jersey Shore	7	6	1
Johnsonburg	4	4	0
Johnstown	51	43	8
Kane	3	3	0
Kennett Square	14	12	2
Kidder Township	8	8	0
Kilbuck Township	4	3	1
Kingston	26	21	5
Kingston Township	12	11	1
Kittanning	9	8	1
Kline Township	2	2	0
Kutztown	10	9	1
Laflin Borough	3	3	0
Lake City	2	2	0
Lancaster	206	161	45
Lancaster Township (Butler County)	2	2	0
Lansdale	30	24	6
Lansdowne	19	16	3
Latrobe	14	13	1
Lawrence Park Township	8	7	1
Lawrence Township	8	8	0
Lebanon	50	47	3
Leetsdale	3	3	0
Leet Township	5	5	0
Lehighton	9	8	1
Lehigh Township (Northampton County)	11	10	1
Lehman Township	4	4	0

Table 78

Full-time Law Enforcement Employees as of October 31, 2002

by City by State—Continued

City by state	Total law enforcement employees	Total officers	Total civilians	City by state	Total law enforcement employees	Total officers	Total civilians
PENNSYLVANIA—Continued				**PENNSYLVANIA—Continued**			
Lewisburg	8	8	0	Monessen	12	12	0
Ligonier Township	3	3	0	Monongahela	12	10	2
Limerick Township	19	17	2	Monroeville	57	52	5
Lincoln	2	2	0	Montgomery Township	43	34	9
Linesville	1	1	0	Montoursville	7	7	0
Lititz	13	10	3	Moon Township	35	29	6
Littlestown	7	7	0	Moore Township	9	8	1
Lock Haven	15	13	2	Morris-Cooper Township	1	1	0
Locust Township	3	3	0	Morton	4	4	0
Logan Township	17	15	2	Mount Holly Springs	3	3	0
Lower Allen Township	21	18	3	Mount Jewett	2	2	0
Lower Burrell	17	17	0	Mount Joy	12	10	2
Lower Gwynedd Township	19	18	1	Mount Joy Township	8	7	1
Lower Heidelberg Township	6	6	0	Mount Lebanon	56	45	11
Lower Makefield Township	35	31	4	Mount Pleasant	5	5	0
Lower Merion Township	143	138	5	Mount Union	6	6	0
Lower Moreland Township	26	21	5	Muhlenberg Township	29	27	2
Lower Paxton Township	52	47	5	Munhall	23	19	4
Lower Pottsgrove Township	15	13	2	Murrysville	24	19	5
Lower Providence Township	33	27	6	Nanticoke	14	13	1
Lower Salford Township	19	17	2	Narberth	7	7	0
Lower Saucon Township	15	13	2	Neshannock Township	7	7	0
Lower Southampton Township	31	28	3	Nether Providence Township	16	14	2
Lower Swatara Township	11	10	1	Neville Township	9	6	3
Lower Windsor Township	6	6	0	Newberry Township	13	12	1
Luzerne Township	1	1	0	New Bethlehem	1	1	0
Macungie	4	4	0	New Britain	4	3	1
Mahoning Township (Carbon County)	5	5	0	New Britain Township	14	12	2
Mahoning Township (Montour County)	7	6	1	New Castle	33	30	3
Malvern	6	5	1	New Cumberland	9	8	1
Manheim	8	7	1	New Hanover Township	9	8	1
Manheim Township	64	51	13	New Holland	12	11	1
Manor	3	3	0	New Hope	8	6	2
Manor Township	23	21	2	New Kensington	30	24	6
Mansfield	5	5	0	Newport	2	2	0
Marlborough Township	5	4	1	Newport Township	1	1	0
Marple Township	38	32	6	New Sewickley Township	10	9	1
Marysville	4	4	0	Newtown	4	4	0
Mayfield	1	1	0	Newtown Township (Bucks County)	30	26	4
McAdoo	1	1	0	Newtown Township (Delaware County)	18	16	2
McCandless	29	27	2	Newville	1	1	0
McDonald Borough	3	3	0	New Wilmington	3	3	0
McKeesport	63	60	3	Norristown	75	65	10
McSherrystown	4	4	0	Northampton	13	12	1
Meadville	28	22	6	Northampton Township	46	40	6
Mechanicsburg	16	15	1	North Catasauqua	3	3	0
Media	21	15	6	North Cornwall Township	10	9	1
Mercer	5	5	0	North Coventry Township	10	9	1
Mercersburg	2	2	0	North East	7	6	1
Meyersdale	4	4	0	Northeastern Regional	11	10	1
Middlesex Township (Butler County)	5	5	0	Northern Berks Regional	14	13	1
Middlesex Township (Cumberland County)	9	8	1	Northern Cambria Regional	3	3	0
Middletown	16	15	1	Northern York Regional	46	41	5
Middletown Township	59	51	8	North Fayette Township	23	19	4
Midland	5	5	0	North Franklin Township	8	8	0
Mifflin County Regional	25	24	1	North Huntingdon Township	43	36	7
Mifflin Township	4	4	0	North Lebanon Township	10	9	1
Mifflinburg	5	5	0	North Londonderry Township	7	6	1
Milford	2	2	0	North Middleton Township	9	8	1
Millcreek Township	75	59	16	North Sewickley Township	2	2	0
Millersburg	4	4	0	North Strabane Township	17	16	1
Millersville	15	13	2	Northumberland	6	6	0
Millville	1	1	0	North Versailles Township	23	20	3
Milton	11	10	1	North Wales	7	6	1
Minersville	6	6	0	Norwegian Township	1	1	0
Mohnton	5	5	0	Norwood	7	7	0
Monaca	6	6	0	O'Hara Township	14	13	1
				Oakmont	7	7	0

Table 78

Full-time Law Enforcement Employees as of October 31, 2002

by City by State—Continued

City by state	Total law enforcement employees	Total officers	Total civilians	City by state	Total law enforcement employees	Total officers	Total civilians
PENNSYLVANIA—Continued				**PENNSYLVANIA—Continued**			
Ohioville	2	2	0	Robeson Township	6	5	1
Oil City	24	1⁹	5	Robinson Township (Allegheny			
Old Forge	5	5	0	County)	20	15	5
Old Lycoming Township	9	8	1	Rochester	13	11	2
Oley Township	3	3	0	Rochester Township	2	2	0
Olyphant	5	5	0	Rockledge	5	5	0
Orangeville	1	1	0	Rosslyn Farms	2	2	0
Orwigsburg	4	4	0	Ross Township	45	43	2
Oxford	9	8	1	Royersford	8	7	1
Paint Township	2	2	0	Salisbury Township	14	12	2
Palmer Township	27	24	3	Sandy Township	7	7	0
Palmerton	9	8	1	Sayre	11	9	2
Palmyra	9	8	1	Schuylkill Haven	7	7	0
Parkesburg	8	8	0	Schuylkill Township	10	9	1
Parkside	3	3	0	Scott Township (Allegheny County)	19	18	1
Patterson Area	4	4	0	Scott Township (Columbia County)	5	5	0
Patton Township	17	15	2	Scottdale	7	7	0
Paxtang	3	3	0	Scranton	186	169	17
Pen Argyl	5	5	0	Selinsgrove	6	5	1
Penbrook	6	6	0	Seven Springs	6	6	0
Penn Hills	65	56	9	Sewickley	9	8	1
Pennridge Regional	23	15	8	Sewickley Heights	8	7	1
Penn Township (Butler County)	4	3	1	Shaler Township	29	27	2
Penn Township (Lancaster County)	8	7	1	Shamokin	13	13	0
Penn Township (Westmoreland County)	22	20	2	Sharon	34	30	4
Penn Township (York County)	23	21	2	Sharon Hill	8	7	1
Pequea Township	3	3	0	Sharpsburg	7	7	0
Perkasie	15	13	2	Sharpsville	7	6	1
Peters Township	23	21	2	Shenandoah	8	7	1
Philadelphia	7,850	6,931	919	Shenango Township (Lawrence County)	4	4	0
Philipsburg	2	2	0	Shenango Township (Mercer County)	6	5	1
Phoenixville	26	24	2	Shillington	8	8	0
Pine-Marshall-Bradford Woods	17	16	1	Shippensburg	9	8	1
Pitcairn	3	3	0	Shippingport	2	2	0
Pittsburgh	1,156	1,071	85	Shiremanstown	2	2	0
Plainfield Township	8	8	0	Silver Spring Township	12	11	1
Plains Township	14	13	1	Sinking Spring	4	4	0
Pleasant Hills	20	16	4	Slippery Rock	5	5	0
Plumstead Township	13	11	2	Solebury Township	12	11	1
Plymouth Township (Luzerne County)	2	2	0	South Beaver Township	4	4	0
Plymouth Township (Montgomery				South Centre Township	4	4	0
County)	53	44	9	South Fayette Township	17	16	1
Pocono Mountain Regional	41	38	3	South Fork	1	1	0
Pocono Township	14	14	0	South Greensburg	2	2	0
Point Township	5	5	0	South Heidelberg Township	6	6	0
Portage	2	2	0	South Lebanon Township	8	7	1
Port Allegany	3	3	0	South Londonderry Township	5	5	0
Port Carbon	2	2	0	South Park Township	16	15	1
Pottstown	48	39	9	South Pymatuning Township	2	2	0
Pottsville	33	32	1	South Strabane Township	12	11	1
Prospect Park	9	9	0	South Waverly	3	3	0
Punxsutawney	11	7	4	Southwest Greensburg	2	2	0
Pymatuning Township	3	3	0	Southwest Mercer County Regional	15	14	1
Quakertown	17	15	2	South Williamsport	7	6	1
Radnor Township	54	43	11	Spring City	4	3	1
Rankin	1	1	0	Springdale	1	1	0
Reading	227	200	27	Springettsbury Township	30	28	2
Reynoldsville	2	2	0	Springfield Township (Bucks County)	5	5	0
Rice Township	4	4	0	Springfield Township (Delaware			
Richland	2	2	0	County)	43	36	7
Richland Township (Allegheny County)	12	11	1	Springfield Township (Montgomery			
Richland Township (Bucks County)	8	7	1	County)	28	27	1
Richland Township (Cambria County)	18	17	1	Spring Garden Township	20	18	2
Ridgway	7	7	0	Spring Township (Berks County)	23	22	1
Ridley Park	11	9	2	Spring Township (Centre County)	7	6	1
Ridley Township	41	33	8	State College	71	61	10
Rimersburg	1	1	0	St. Clair Township	1	1	0
Robesonia	2	2	0	Steelton	9	8	1

Table 78

Full-time Law Enforcement Employees as of October 31, 2002
by City by State—Continued

City by state	Total law enforcement employees	Total officers	Total civilians	City by state	Total law enforcement employees	Total officers	Total civilians
PENNSYLVANIA—Continued				**PENNSYLVANIA—Continued**			
Stewartstown	5	5	0	Washington (Washington County)	31	28	3
St. Marys City	13	12	1	Washington Township (Fayette County)	3	3	0
Stonycreek Township	2	2	0	Washington Township (Franklin			
Strasburg	4	4	0	County)	13	12	1
Stroud Area Regional	59	55	4	Washington Township (Westmoreland			
Sugarcreek	5	5	0	County)	6	6	0
Sugarloaf Township (Luzerne County)	4	3	1	Watsontown	5	5	0
Summerhill Township	3	3	0	Waynesboro	17	16	1
Summit Hill	3	3	0	Waynesburg	9	8	1
Sunbury	16	13	3	Weatherly	3	3	0
Susquehanna Township (Dauphin				Wellsboro	5	5	0
County)	39	37	2	Wernersville	2	2	0
Swarthmore	9	9	0	Wesleyville	4	4	0
Swatara Township	33	31	2	West Alexander	2	2	0
Swissvale	11	11	0	West Brandywine Township	6	6	0
Swoyersville	5	5	0	West Conshohocken	11	10	1
Sykesville	1	1	0	West Deer Township	11	10	1
Tamaqua	11	10	1	West Donegal Township	7	7	0
Tarentum	12	8	4	West Earl Township	5	5	0
Terre Hill	5	5	0	West Elizabeth	17	16	1
Throop	6	6	0	West Goshen Township	33	26	7
Tinicum Township (Bucks County)	5	5	0	West Hempfield Township	22	20	2
Tinicum Township (Delaware County)	14	13	1	West Hills Regional	12	11	1
Titusville	14	14	0	West Homestead	9	6	3
Towamencin Township	33	25	8	West Lampeter Township	14	13	1
Towanda	7	7	0	West Lebanon Township	10	9	.1
Trafford	4	4	0	West Manchester Township	27	25	2
Trainer	8	7	1	West Manheim Township	6	6	0
Tredyffrin Township	59	51	8	West Mifflin	39	33	6
Troy	3	3	0	West Norriton Township	29	25	4
Tullytown	7	6	1	West Pikeland Township	1	1	0
Tunkhannock	5	5	0	West Pittston	3	3	0
Tunkhannock Township (Wyoming				West Pottsgrove Township	9	8	1
County)	3	3	0	West Reading	14	12	2
Tyrone	4	3	1	West Salem Township	12	11	1
Union City	1	1	0	West Shore Regional	12	10	2
Uniontown	19	16	3	Westtown-East Goshen Township	26	23	3
Union Township (Lawrence County)	3	2	1	West View	10	9	1
Union Township (Washington County)	7	7	0	West Whiteland Township	29	27	2
Upland	2	2	0	West Wyoming	2	2	0
Upper Allen Township	16	15	1	Whitehall	26	21	5
Upper Chichester Township	23	20	3	Whitehall Township	58	49	9
Upper Darby Township	131	121	10	White Haven Borough	2	2	0
Upper Dublin Township	36	30	6	Whitemarsh Township	39	34	5
Upper Gwynedd Township	22	20	2	White Oak	14	13	1
Upper Makefield Township	12	11	1	Whitpain Township	36	29	7
Upper Merion Township	83	62	21	Wilkes-Barre	86	78	8
Upper Moreland Township	49	39	10	Wilkes-Barre Township	15	13	2
Upper Pottsgrove Township	5	5	0	Wilkinsburg	37	30	7
Upper Providence Township				Williamsport	57	53	4
(Delaware County)	12	11	1	Willistown Township	17	15	2
Upper Providence Township				Windber	3	2	1
(Montgomery County)	19	17	2	Wright Township	7	7	0
Upper Saucon Township	18	17	1	Wyoming	7	7	0
Upper Southampton Township	26	23	3	Wyomissing	27	22	5
Upper St. Clair Township	35	28	7	Yardley	4	3	1
Upper Uwchlan Township	9	9	0	Yeadon	14	12	2
Upper Yoder Township	5	5	0	York Area Regional	44	39	5
Uwchlan Township	26	24	2	York Springs-Latimore Township	2	2	0
Vandergrift	8	8	0	Youngsville	2	2	0
Vernon Township	3	3	0				
Verona	2	1	1	**RHODE ISLAND**			
Versailles	2	2	0				
Warminster Township	56	47	9	Barrington	29	24	5
Warren	18	14	4	Bristol	47	37	10
Warrington Township	32	29	3	Burrillville	33	25	8
Warwick Township (Bucks County)	18	16	2	Central Falls	41	34	7
Warwick Township (Lancaster County)	16	15	1	Charlestown	25	20	5

Table 78

Full-time Law Enforcement Employees as of October 31, 2002
by City by State—Continued

City by state	Total law enforcement employees	Total officers	Total civilians	City by state	Total law enforcement employees	Total officers	Total civilians
RHODE ISLAND—Continued				**SOUTH CAROLINA—Continued**			
Coventry	67	54	13	Coward	1	1	0
Cranston	171	139	33	Cowpens	7	7	0
Cumberland	55	47	8	Darlington	27	23	4
East Greenwich	41	32	9	Due West	6	6	0
East Providence	112	92	20	Duncan	15	13	2
Foster	16	7	9	Easley	46	34	12
Glocester	17	13	4	Eastover	2	2	0
Hopkinton	21	16	5	Edgefield	9	9	0
Jamestown	18	13	5	Ehrhardt	2	2	0
Johnston	87	69	18	Elgin	5	5	0
Lincoln	40	32	8	Estill	7	5	2
Little Compton	14	10	4	Eutawville	3	3	0
Middletown	42	38	4	Fairfax	7	7	0
Narragansett	49	38	11	Florence	123	99	24
Newport	107	84	23	Folly Beach	16	11	5
New Shoreham	10	4	6	Forest Acres	31	25	6
North Kingstown	66	53	13	Fort Lawn	4	3	1
North Providence	93	71	22	Fort Mill	26	20	6
North Smithfield	25	21	4	Fountain Inn	29	21	8
Pawtucket	179	148	31	Gaffney	42	38	4
Portsmouth	33	31	2	Georgetown	47	39	8
Providence	580	483	97	Goose Creek	59	46	13
Richmond	14	10	4	Great Falls	6	6	0
Scituate	24	18	6	Greeleyville	3	3	0
Smithfield	48	36	12	Greenville	208	167	41
South Kingstown	70	52	18	Greenwood	59	51	8
Tiverton	35	26	9	Greer	62	48	14
Warren	28	22	6	Hampton	9	8	1
Warwick	230	174	56	Hanahan	28	21	7
Westerly	57	47	10	Harleyville	4	4	0
West Greenwich	16	10	6	Hartsville	37	33	4
West Warwick	68	57	11	Hemingway	7	4	3
Woonsocket	118	101	17	Honea Path	16	12	4
				Inman	6	6	0
SOUTH CAROLINA				Irmo	20	18	2
				Isle of Palms	24	16	8
Abbeville	22	19	3	Iva	4	3	1
Aiken	102	83	19	Jamestown	2	1	1
Allendale	9	8	1	Johnsonville	5	4	1
Anderson	133	86	47	Kingstree	19	17	2
Andrews	12	9	3	Lake View	3	3	0
Aynor	4	3	1	Lamar	3	3	0
Bamberg	11	10	1	Lancaster	45	37	8
Beaufort	54	48	6	Landrum	9	8	1
Belton	20	15	5	Latta	11	10	1
Bennettsville	38	34	4	Laurens	34	28	6
Bethune	1	1	0	Lexington	30	26	4
Blackville	8	7	1	Liberty	14	9	5
Bluffton	10	10	0	Lyman	7	6	1
Bonneau	3	3	0	Lynchburg	4	4	0
Briarcliffe Acres	1	1	0	Marion	33	26	7
Burnettown	2	2	0	McColl	7	6	1
Calhoun Falls	11	10	1	McCormick	7	7	0
Camden	28	24	4	Moncks Corner	23	21	2
Central	10	10	0	Mount Pleasant	153	112	41
Chapin	7	6	1	Mullins	23	21	2
Charleston	491	359	132	Newberry	29	25	4
Cheraw	30	24	6	Ninety Six	8	7	1
Chesnee	3	3	0	North	3	2	1
Chester	29	25	4	North Augusta	64	47	17
Chesterfield	6	5	1	North Charleston	330	258	72
Clemson	31	25	6	North Myrtle Beach	96	74	22
Clinton	35	28	7	Norway	8	3	5
Clio	5	4	1	Olar	1	1	0
Clover	16	12	4	Orangeburg	88	74	14
Columbia	330	288	42	Pacolet	5	5	0
Conway	65	51	14	Pawleys Island	4	3	1
Cottageville	7	5	2	Pendleton	9	8	1

Table 78

Full-time Law Enforcement Employees as of October 31, 2002
by City by State—Continued

City by state	Total law enforcement employees	Total officers	Total civilians	City by state	Total law enforcement employees	Total officers	Total civilians
SOUTH CAROLINA—Continued				**SOUTH DAKOTA—Continued**			
Perry	1	1	0	Eagle Butte	2	2	0
Pickens	14	13	1	Elk Point	3	2	1
Pine Ridge	2	1	1	Estelline	1	1	0
Port Royal	19	17	2	Eureka	3	3	0
Prosperity	3	3	0	Faith	2	1	1
Ridgeland	9	8	1	Garretson	1	1	0
Ridgeville	2	2	0	Gettysburg	2	2	0
Ridgeway	2	2	0	Gregory	3	3	0
Rock Hill	135	95	40	Groton	3	3	0
Saluda	11	11	0	Harrisburg	1	1	0
Santee	13	9	4	Hot Springs	8	7	1
Scranton	2	2	0	Huron	28	22	6
Sellers	3	2	1	Kadoka	1	1	0
Seneca	44	33	11	Kimball	1	1	0
Simpsonville	46	37	9	Lake Andes	4	4	0
Society Hill	7	5	2	Lead	6	5	1
South Congaree	7	6	1	Lemmon	4	4	0
Spartanburg	143	123	20	Madison	11	10	1
Springdale	8	7	1	McLaughlin	3	2	1
St. George	10	9	1	Milbank	5	5	0
St. Matthews	7	7	0	Miller	4	4	0
Sullivans Island	8	7	1	Mitchell	37	27	10
Summerton	9	8	1	Mobridge	12	7	5
Summerville	76	57	19	Murdo	1	1	0
Sumter	142	104	38	North Sioux City	8	7	1
Surfside Beach	18	13	5	Parkston	2	2	0
Swansea	3	3	0	Philip	2	2	0
Tega Cay	12	8	4	Pierre	35	24	11
Travelers Rest	21	15	6	Platte	2	2	0
Turbeville	3	3	0	Rapid City	124	97	27
Union	39	36	3	Salem	2	2	0
Vance	2	2	0	Selby	1	1	0
Wagener	3	3	0	Sioux Falls	210	182	28
Walhalla	14	12	2	Sisseton	7	7	0
Walterboro	31	23	8	Spearfish	23	17	6
Ware Shoals	10	9	1	Sturgis	18	15	3
Wellford	5	5	0	Tea	3	3	0
West Columbia	48	38	10	Tripp	1	1	0
Westminster	9	9	0	Vermillion	18	17	1
West Pelzer	3	3	0	Watertown	42	31	11
West Union	2	2	0	Webster	4	4	0
Whitmire	4	4	0	Whitewood	2	2	0
Williamston	21	16	5	Winner	13	8	5
Williston	9	8	1	Yankton	46	26	20
Winnsboro	26	24	2				
Yemassee	6	4	2	**TENNESSEE**			
York	35	29	6				
				Adamsville	9	6	3
SOUTH DAKOTA				Alamo	3	3	0
				Alcoa	43	37	6
Aberdeen	46	38	8	Alexandria	4	4	0
Alcester	1	1	0	Algood	8	8	0
Armour	1	1	0	Ardmore	13	6	7
Belle Fourche	10	9	1	Ashland City	14	13	1
Beresford	8	4	4	Athens	31	29	2
Box Elder	9	7	2	Atoka	8	8	0
Brandon	8	7	1	Baileyton	1	1	0
Brookings	35	27	8	Bartlett	116	86	30
Buffalo	1	1	0	Baxter	3	3	0
Burke	1	1	0	Bean Station	7	6	1
Canistota	1	1	0	Belle Meade	21	17	4
Canton	5	5	0	Bells	5	5	0
Castlewood	1	1	0	Benton	6	5	1
Chamberlain	5	5	0	Berry Hill	17	13	4
Chancellor-Davis	1	1	0	Bethel Springs	1	1	0
Clark	2	2	0	Big Sandy	2	2	0
Colman	1	1	0	Blaine	2	2	0
Deadwood	12	9	3	Bluff City	9	9	0

Table 78

Full-time Law Enforcement Employees as of October 31, 2002
by City by State—Continued

City by state	Total law enforcement employees	Total officers	Total civilians	City by state	Total law enforcement employees	Total officers	Total civilians
TENNESSEE—Continued				**TENNESSEE—Continued**			
Bolivar	28	22	6	Gibson	2	2	0
Bradford	4	4	0	Gleason	6	5	1
Brentwood	67	54	13	Goodlettsville	51	37	14
Brighton	5	5	0	Gordonsville	4	4	0
Bristol	83	67	16	Grand Junction	1	1	0
Brownsville	36	31	5	Graysville	6	4	2
Bruceton	4	4	0	Greenbrier	12	11	1
Burns	4	4	0	Greeneville	44	42	2
Calhoun	1	1	0	Greenfield	8	7	1
Camden	17	12	5	Halls	7	7	0
Carthage	11	7	4	Harriman	24	23	1
Caryville	5	5	0	Henderson	14	13	1
Celina	5	4	1	Hendersonville	89	69	20
Centerville	18	13	5	Henning	4	4	0
Chapel Hill	5	5	0	Henry	1	1	0
Charleston	3	3	0	Hohenwald	13	13	0
Chattanooga	676	471	205	Hollow Rock	2	2	0
Church Hill	9	8	1	Hornbeak	2	1	1
Clarksville	246	213	33	Humboldt	33	27	6
Cleveland	100	89	11	Huntingdon	16	12	4
Clifton	7	7	0	Huntland	6	6	0
Clinton	24	23	1	Jacksboro	5	5	0
Collegedale	16	14	2	Jackson	236	182	54
Collierville	111	73	38	Jamestown	8	7	1
Collinwood	5	5	0	Jasper	8	8	0
Columbia	86	78	8	Jefferson City	21	19	2
Cookeville	89	68	21	Jellico	11	10	1
Coopertown	2	2	0	Johnson City	185	157	28
Copperhill	1	1	0	Jonesborough	20	15	5
Cornersville	7	3	4	Kenton	5	5	0
Covington	26	25	1	Kimball	7	7	0
Cowan	6	6	0	Kingsport	140	99	41
Cross Plains	3	3	0	Kingston	12	11	1
Crossville	35	32	3	Kingston Springs	6	5	1
Crump	3	2	1	Knoxville	479	380	99
Cumberland City	2	2	0	Lafayette	25	16	9
Cumberland Gap	2	2	0	La Follette	29	17	12
Dandridge	9	9	0	La Grange	2	2	0
Dayton	17	15	2	Lake City	10	7	3
Decatur	5	5	0	Lakewood	7	7	0
Decaturville	1	1	0	La Vergne	49	32	17
Decherd	13	12	1	Lawrenceburg	45	39	6
Dickson	61	42	19	Lebanon	80	64	16
Dover	7	7	0	Lenoir City	21	20	1
Dresden	8	8	0	Lewisburg	37	28	9
Dunlap	10	9	1	Lexington	31	26	5
Dyer	6	6	0	Livingston	21	16	5
Dyersburg	80	61	19	Lookout Mountain	20	16	4
Eagleville	4	2	2	Loretto	4	4	0
East Ridge	44	36	8	Loudon	15	14	1
Elizabethton	40	37	3	Lynnville	1	1	0
Elkton	2	1	1	Madisonville	15	13	2
Englewood	5	5	0	Manchester	35	30	5
Erin	6	6	0	Martin	37	30	7
Erwin	10	10	0	Maryville	52	42	10
Estill Springs	6	6	0	Mason	6	6	0
Ethridge	1	1	0	Maynardville	4	4	0
Etowah	14	10	4	McEwen	5	4	1
Fairview	17	16	1	McKenzie	22	17	5
Fayetteville	25	23	2	McMinnville	40	35	5
Franklin	122	101	21	Medina	6	6	0
Friendship	1	1	0	Memphis	2,867	1,935	932
Gainesboro	4	4	0	Middleton	3	3	0
Gallatin	71	50	21	Milan	29	24	5
Gallaway	6	6	0	Millersville	17	13	4
Gates	3	3	0	Millington	34	27	7
Gatlinburg	49	41	8	Minor Hill	3	2	1
Germantown	99	79	20	Monteagle	10	6	4

Table 78

Full-time Law Enforcement Employees as of October 31, 2002

by City by State—Continued

City by state	Total law enforcement employees	Total officers	Total civilians	City by state	Total law enforcement employees	Total officers	Total civilians
TENNESSEE—Continued				**TENNESSEE—Continued**			
Monterey	8	8	0	Tellico Plains	5	5	0
Morristown	81	76	5	Tiptonville	6	6	0
Moscow	4	4	0	Toone	1	1	0
Mountain City	11	9	2	Townsend	3	3	0
Mount Carmel	9	8	1	Tracy City	6	5	1
Mount Juliet	33	26	7	Trenton	25	19	6
Mount Pleasant	12	11	1	Trezevant	1	1	0
Munford	13	12	1	Trimble	5	5	0
Murfreesboro	199	160	39	Troy	4	4	0
Nashville	1,695	1,248	447	Tullahoma	40	35	5
Newbern	18	13	5	Tusculum	2	2	0
New Hope	1	1	0	Union City	45	37	8
New Johnsonville	3	3	0	Vonore	8	7	1
New Market	2	2	0	Wartburg	3	3	0
Newport	33	27	6	Wartrace	1	1	0
New Tazewell	10	10	0	Watauga	1	1	0
Niota	4	4	0	Watertown	4	3	1
Nolensville	1	1	0	Waverly	13	11	2
Norris	7	7	0	Waynesboro	9	8	1
Oakland	11	9	2	Westmoreland	9	5	4
Oak Ridge	70	58	12	White Bluff	3	3	0
Obion	4	4	0	White House	30	20	10
Oliver Springs	15	11	4	White Pine	9	8	1
Oneida	20	14	6	Whiteville	8	8	0
Paris	36	26	10	Whitwell	12	7	5
Parsons	7	7	0	Winchester	29	22	7
Petersburg	2	2	0	Winfield	3	3	0
Pigeon Forge	64	53	11	Woodbury	9	8	1
Pikeville	4	4	0				
Pittman Center	2	2	0	**TEXAS**			
Portland	28	21	7				
Pulaski	29	26	3	Abernathy	3	3	0
Puryear	2	2	0	Abilene	234	173	61
Red Bank	21	19	2	Addison	78	58	20
Red Boiling Springs	5	5	0	Alamo	32	23	9
Ridgely	6	5	1	Alamo Heights	31	21	10
Ridgetop	6	6	0	Alice	48	33	15
Ripley	33	26	7	Allen	103	79	24
Rockwood	15	14	1	Alpine	14	8	6
Rogersville	12	12	0	Alto	3	3	0
Rossville	4	4	0	Alton	13	8	5
Rutherford	5	5	0	Alvarado	18	12	6
Rutledge	4	4	0	Alvin	67	44	23
Savannah	27	16	11	Amarillo	356	276	80
Scotts Hill	4	4	0	Andrews	21	15	6
Selmer	18	17	1	Angleton	46	35	11
Sevierville	59	47	12	Anson	5	4	1
Sewanee	13	9	4	Anthony	7	7	0
Sharon	3	3	0	Aransas Pass	25	18	7
Shelbyville	46	36	10	Arcola	5	4	1
Signal Mountain	16	14	2	Argyle	7	7	0
Smithville	25	12	13	Arlington	733	565	168
Smyrna	76	55	21	Arp	3	3	0
Sneedville	1	1	0	Athens	34	25	9
Soddy-Daisy	25	20	5	Atlanta	20	15	5
Somerville	18	14	4	Austin	1,811	1,251	560
South Carthage	4	4	0	Azle	29	20	9
South Fulton	9	8	1	Baird	2	2	0
South Pittsburg	12	8	4	Balch Springs	39	28	11
Sparta	16	15	1	Balcones Heights	17	12	5
Spencer	2	2	0	Ballinger	8	6	2
Spring City	10	9	1	Bangs	3	3	0
Springfield	50	38	12	Bastrop	18	15	3
Spring Hill	21	20	1	Bay City	46	35	11
St. Joseph	1	1	0	Bayou Vista	6	6	0
Surgoinsville	4	4	0	Baytown	176	124	52
Sweetwater	20	18	2	Beaumont	324	255	69
Tazewell	6	6	0	Bedford	118	75	43

Table 78

Full-time Law Enforcement Employees as of October 31, 2002
by City by State—Continued

City by state	Total law enforcement employees	Total officers	Total civilians	City by state	Total law enforcement employees	Total officers	Total civilians
TEXAS—Continued				**TEXAS—Continued**			
Beeville	29	21	8	Commerce	21	15	6
Bellaire	56	40	16	Conroe	109	84	25
Bellmead	24	17	7	Converse	32	26	6
Bellville	12	10	2	Coppell	69	53	16
Belton	33	24	9	Copperas Cove	64	49	15
Benbrook	45	36	9	Corinth	25	24	1
Bertram	2	2	0	Corpus Christi	645	446	199
Beverly Hills	14	8	6	Corrigan	9	6	3
Big Sandy	6	5	1	Corsicana	59	45	14
Big Spring	65	44	21	Cottonwood Shores	2	2	0
Bishop	9	5	4	Crane	12	7	5
Blanco	4	4	0	Crockett	19	16	3
Blue Mound	10	6	4	Crowell	1	1	0
Boerne	36	22	14	Crowley	24	18	6
Bogata	3	3	0	Crystal City	14	10	4
Bonham	27	21	6	Cuero	14	13	1
Borger	32	25	7	Daingerfield	7	6	1
Bovina	2	2	0	Dalhart	22	15	7
Bowie	17	12	5	Dallas	3,401	2,846	555
Brady	14	8	6	Dalworthington Gardens	11	9	2
Brazoria	13	7	6	Danbury	4	4	0
Breckenridge	18	12	6	Dayton	17	12	5
Brenham	43	30	13	Decatur	18	13	5
Bridge City	17	12	5	Deer Park	72	53	19
Bridgeport	16	10	6	De Kalb	6	6	0
Brookshire	11	7	4	De Leon	5	5	0
Brookside Village	5	5	0	Del Rio	84	67	17
Brownfield	22	17	5	Denison	55	45	10
Brownsville	286	206	80	Denton	166	131	35
Brownwood	53	33	20	Denver City	13	7	6
Bruceville-Eddy	3	3	0	DeSoto	73	60	13
Bryan	141	103	38	Devine	10	8	2
Bullard	5	4	1	Diboll	19	13	6
Burkburnett	23	17	6	Dickinson	35	27	8
Burleson	55	40	15	Dilley	5	4	1
Burnet	13	12	1	Dimmitt	9	7	2
Caddo Mills	2	2	0	Donna	31	23	8
Caldwell	11	10	1	Double Oak	6	6	0
Cameron	13	8	5	Dublin	11	9	2
Caney City	5	2	3	Dumas	28	24	4
Canton	20	15	5	Duncanville	74	60	14
Canyon	23	20	3	Eagle Lake	10	9	1
Carrollton	211	148	63	Eagle Pass	83	66	17
Carthage	21	14	7	Early	7	6	1
Castle Hills	28	21	7	Earth	2	2	0
Cedar Hill	62	51	11	Eastland	11	9	2
Cedar Park	64	49	15	East Mountain	1	1	0
Celina	7	7	0	Edcouch	14	9	5
Center	20	14	6	Eden	3	3	0
Childress	14	9	5	Edgewood	4	4	0
Cisco	8	7	1	Edinburg	104	73	31
Clarksville	7	7	0	Edna	11	9	2
Cleburne	60	42	18	El Campo	33	23	10
Cleveland	27	17	10	Electra	10	5	5
Clifton	6	5	1	Elgin	17	13	4
Clint	3	3	0	El Paso	1,488	1,145	343
Clute	32	23	9	Elsa	22	15	7
Clyde	5	4	1	Ennis	36	31	5
Cockrell Hill	16	11	5	Euless	114	79	35
Coffee City	2	2	0	Everman	16	11	5
Coleman	15	9	6	Fairfield	9	8	1
College Station	138	98	40	Fair Oaks Ranch	11	11	0
Colleyville	41	31	10	Farmers Branch	107	71	36
Collinsville	2	2	0	Farmersville	7	7	0
Colorado City	13	7	6	Farwell	1	1	0
Columbus	10	9	1	Ferris	16	12	4
Comanche	8	7	1	Flatonia	4	4	0
Combes	9	8	1	Florence	2	2	0

Table 78

Full-time Law Enforcement Employees as of October 31, 2002

by City by State—Continued

City by state	Total law enforcement employees	Total officers	Total civilians	City by state	Total law enforcement employees	Total officers	Total civilians
TEXAS—Continued				**TEXAS—Continued**			
Floresville	14	13	1	Hillsboro	28	20	8
Flower Mound	97	67	30	Hitchcock	23	18	5
Floydada	5	5	0	Holliday	2	2	0
Forest Hill	30	22	8	Hollywood Park	8	8	0
Forney	18	12	6	Hondo	17	15	2
Fort Stockton	24	17	7	Hooks	5	5	0
Fort Worth	1,582	1,243	339	Horizon City	10	9	1
Frankston	4	3	1	Horseshoe Bay	11	10	1
Fredericksburg	32	29	3	Houston	7,084	5,360	1,724
Freeport	31	23	8	Howe	5	5	0
Freer	9	5	4	Hubbard	4	4	0
Friendswood	59	44	15	Hudson	4	4	0
Friona	10	6	4	Hudson Oaks	7	7	0
Frisco	82	62	20	Humble	69	53	16
Gainesville	59	41	18	Huntington	5	5	0
Galena Park	22	16	6	Huntsville	48	42	6
Galveston	193	157	36	Hurst	113	69	44
Ganado	3	3	0	Hutchins	18	12	6
Garland	422	291	131	Hutto	8	8	0
Gatesville	19	14	5	Idalou	3	3	0
Georgetown	64	43	21	Ingleside	22	15	7
Giddings	18	12	6	Ingram	7	6	1
Gilmer	22	19	3	Iowa Park	17	11	6
Gladewater	22	17	5	Irving	439	292	147
Glenn Heights	17	11	6	Italy	5	5	0
Godley	3	3	0	Itasca	3	3	0
Gonzales	20	15	5	Jacinto City	21	15	6
Gorman	5	4	1	Jacksboro	13	8	5
Graham	19	18	1	Jacksonville	32	25	7
Granbury	26	22	4	Jamaica Beach	5	5	0
Grand Prairie	287	189	98	Jasper	26	18	8
Grand Saline	7	7	0	Jefferson	8	7	1
Granger	3	3	0	Jersey Village	31	21	10
Granite Shoals	7	7	0	Johnson City	4	4	0
Grapeland	2	1	1	Jones Creek	3	3	0
Grapevine	127	94	33	Joshua	16	14	2
Greenville	77	47	30	Jourdanton	6	6	0
Gregory	5	4	1	Junction	5	5	0
Groesbeck	7	7	0	Karnes City	7	6	1
Groves	18	17	1	Katy	59	43	16
Gruver	2	2	0	Kaufman	25	18	7
Gun Barrel City	22	17	5	Keene	23	9	14
Hale Center	5	4	1	Keller	63	44	19
Hallettsville	6	5	1	Kemah	27	22	5
Haltom City	91	65	26	Kemp	6	6	0
Hamlin	9	5	4	Kenedy	9	7	2
Harker Heights	42	34	8	Kennedale	23	17	6
Harlingen	143	106	37	Kermit	15	9	6
Hart	1	1	0	Kerrville	61	47	14
Haskell	3	3	0	Kilgore	40	31	9
Hawk Cove	1	1	0	Killeen	189	145	44
Hawkins	6	6	0	Kingsville	62	45	17
Hawley	2	2	0	Kirby	17	13	4
Hearne	16	10	6	Kirbyville	3	3	0
Heath	10	9	1	Knox City	2	2	0
Hedwig Village	24	17	7	Kountze	5	5	0
Helotes	12	11	1	Kress	1	1	0
Hemphill	3	3	0	Kyle	11	10	1
Hempstead	13	11	2	Lacy-Lakeview	22	14	8
Henderson	49	41	8	La Feria	15	11	4
Hereford	27	21	6	Lago Vista	18	12	6
Hewitt	29	21	8	La Grange	8	8	0
Hickory Creek	10	10	0	La Joya	17	12	5
Hico	4	4	0	Lake Dallas	17	10	7
Hidalgo	43	32	11	Lake Jackson	59	41	18
Highland Park	67	53	14	Lakeside	4	4	0
Highland Village	31	23	8	Lakeview	16	12	4
Hill Country Village	10	10	0	Lakeway	32	27	5

Table 78

Full-time Law Enforcement Employees as of October 31, 2002

by City by State—Continued

City by state	Total law enforcement employees	Total officers	Total civilians	City by state	Total law enforcement employees	Total officers	Total civilians
TEXAS—Continued				**TEXAS—Continued**			
Lake Worth	28	20	8	Mount Pleasant	37	26	11
La Marque	34	26	8	Muleshoe	12	7	5
Lamesa	24	17	7	Munday	2	2	0
Lampasas	25	16	9	Mustang Ridge	4	4	0
Lancaster	56	36	20	Nacogdoches	70	54	16
La Porte	97	72	25	Naples	2	2	0
Laredo	422	341	81	Nash	9	8	1
La Vernia	4	4	0	Nassau Bay	18	13	5
Lavon	5	4	1	Navasota	20	13	7
League City	100	65	35	Nederland	32	21	11
Leander	34	22	12	Needville	7	7	0
Leon Valley	32	24	8	New Boston	12	9	3
Levelland	28	20	8	New Braunfels	82	61	21
Lewisville	169	118	51	New Deal	2	2	0
Lexington	4	4	0	Nocona	7	6	1
Liberty	20	12	8	Nolanville	4	4	0
Lindale	15	12	3	Northlake	6	6	0
Linden	5	5	0	North Richland Hills	158	109	49
Littlefield	21	13	8	Oak Ridge	1	1	0
Live Oak	36	27	9	Oak Ridge North	14	14	0
Livingston	20	13	7	Odessa	208	161	47
Llano	8	6	2	O'Donnell	2	2	0
Lockhart	34	27	7	Olmos Park	11	11	0
Lockney	3	3	0	Olney	9	5	4
Lone Star	5	4	1	Olton	3	3	0
Longview	162	140	22	Onalaska	7	7	0
Lorena	6	5	1	Orange	53	41	12
Lorenzo	2	2	0	Orange Grove	10	10	0
Los Fresnos	16	10	6	Ore City	4	4	0
Lubbock	362	301	61	Overton	11	6	5
Lufkin	99	77	22	Ovilla	9	8	1
Luling	23	14	9	Oyster Creek	9	5	4
Lumberton	17	14	3	Palacios	12	8	4
Lytle	5	5	0	Palestine	44	36	8
Madisonville	10	9	1	Palmer	8	7	1
Magnolia	16	11	5	Pampa	30	20	10
Malakoff	7	6	1	Panhandle	3	3	0
Manor	7	6	1	Pantego	15	10	5
Mansfield	66	49	17	Paris	87	64	23
Manvel	8	7	1	Parker	6	6	0
Marble Falls	30	20	10	Pasadena	338	269	69
Marfa	5	3	2	Pearland	99	75	24
Marshall	68	52	16	Pearsall	12	10	2
Mart	3	3	0	Pecos	38	19	19
Martindale	5	5	0	Pelican Bay	4	4	0
Mathis	12	7	5	Penitas	6	4	2
McAllen	374	235	139	Perryton	14	8	6
McGregor	17	12	5	Pflugerville	51	39	12
McKinney	104	84	20	Pharr	114	82	32
Meadows Place	15	15	0	Pilot Point	6	6	0
Melissa	4	3	1	Pinehurst	9	5	4
Memorial Villages	38	32	6	Pittsburg	14	12	2
Memphis	4	4	0	Plainview	42	34	8
Mercedes	28	21	7	Plano	464	326	138
Meridian	3	2	1	Pleasanton	22	16	6
Merkel	5	4	1	Point Comfort	2	2	0
Mesquite	273	202	71	Port Aransas	21	13	8
Mexia	26	19	7	Port Arthur	138	108	30
Midland	201	152	49	Port Isabel	23	18	5
Midlothian	30	24	6	Portland	31	22	9
Mineola	12	11	1	Port Lavaca	24	18	6
Mineral Wells	34	27	7	Port Neches	21	18	3
Mission	130	100	30	Poteet	6	5	1
Missouri City	74	57	17	Pottsboro	6	6	0
Monahans	17	10	7	Premont	5	5	0
Mont Belvieu	15	10	5	Primera	6	6	0
Montgomery	8	7	1	Princeton	6	5	1
Morgans Point Resort	7	7	0	Progreso	6	6	0

Table 78

Full-time Law Enforcement Employees as of October 31, 2002
by City by State—Continued

City by state	Total law enforcement employees	Total officers	Total civilians	City by state	Total law enforcement employees	Total officers	Total civilians
TEXAS—Continued				**TEXAS—Continued**			
Quanah	3	3	0	Sinton	9	8	1
Queen City	6	6	0	Slaton	16	10	6
Quinlan	5	5	0	Smithville	17	10	7
Quitman	6	6	0	Snyder	20	18	2
Ranger	5	5	0	Socorro	23	18	5
Ransom Canyon	2	2	0	Somerset	5	4	1
Raymondville	21	14	7	Somerville	4	4	0
Red Oak	17	11	6	Sonora	7	5	2
Refugio	8	6	2	Sour Lake	6	5	1
Reno	5	4	1	South Houston	40	31	9
Richardson	220	136	84	Southlake	58	55	3
Richland Hills	24	16	8	South Padre Island	31	24	7
Richmond	35	26	9	Southside Place	10	7	3
Richwood	6	5	1	Spearman	3	3	0
Riesel	3	2	1	Springtown	13	9	4
Rio Grande City	28	22	6	Spring Valley	21	16	5
Rising Star	2	2	0	Spur	2	2	0
River Oaks	23	17	6	Stafford	50	37	13
Roanoke	24	17	7	Stamford	11	7	4
Robinson	22	15	7	Stanton	5	5	0
Robstown	34	26	8	Stephenville	38	28	10
Rockdale	16	11	5	Stratford	1	1	0
Rockport	26	19	7	Sugar Land	135	101	34
Rollingwood	7	7	0	Sulphur Springs	38	30	8
Roma	27	22	5	Sunrise Beach Village	2	2	0
Roman Forest	6	6	0	Sunset Valley	10	10	0
Ropesville	2	2	0	Surfside Beach	6	5	1
Roscoe	2	2	0	Sweeny	7	7	0
Rose City	1	1	0	Sweetwater	24	20	4
Rosenberg	83	65	18	Taft	6	6	0
Round Rock	148	107	41	Tahoka	4	4	0
Rowlett	89	61	28	Taylor	41	29	12
Royse City	10	9	1	Teague	5	5	0
Runaway Bay	5	4	1	Temple	141	117	24
Rusk	10	9	1	Terrell	45	33	12
Sabinal	4	4	0	Terrell Hills	13	13	0
Sachse	32	23	9	Texarkana	103	90	13
Saginaw	30	26	4	Texas City	102	81	21
Salado	3	3	0	The Colony	55	41	14
San Angelo	177	150	27	Thorndale	2	2	0
San Antonio	2,543	2,036	507	Thrall	4	4	0
San Augustine	7	6	1	Three Rivers	8	6	2
San Benito	49	42	7	Tioga	3	2	1
San Diego	7	6	1	Tolar	1	1	0
Sanger	11	10	1	Tomball	38	32	6
San Juan	40	28	12	Tool	7	7	0
San Marcos	105	83	22	Trinity	11	7	4
San Saba	4	3	1	Trophy Club	16	15	1
Sansom Park Village	13	9	4	Troup	4	4	0
Santa Anna	3	2	1	Tulia	12	6	6
Santa Fe	23	17	6	Tye	4	3	1
Santa Rosa	5	5	0	Tyler	235	180	55
Schertz	50	32	18	Universal City	34	25	9
Seabrook	35	29	6	University Park	47	35	12
Seadrift	1	1	0	Uvalde	35	26	9
Seagoville	24	17	7	Van	6	6	0
Seagraves	4	3	1	Van Alstyne	10	8	2
Sealy	15	13	2	Vernon	30	22	8
Selma	16	14	2	Victoria	134	92	42
Seminole	12	10	2	Vidor	28	21	7
Seven Points	13	8	5	Waco	288	213	75
Seymour	9	7	2	Waelder	3	3	0
Shallowater	5	5	0	Wake Village	7	6	1
Shamrock	3	3	0	Waller	8	7	1
Shavano Park	12	11	1	Wallis	4	4	0
Shenandoah	19	18	1	Walnut Springs	1	1	0
Sherman	81	57	24	Watauga	45	36	9
Silsbee	21	16	5	Waxahachie	58	46	12

Table 78

Full-time Law Enforcement Employees as of October 31, 2002
by City by State—Continued

City by state	Total law enforcement employees	Total officers	Total civilians
TEXAS—Continued			
Weatherford	66	48	18
Webster	58	40	18
Weimar	8	7	1
Wells	1	1	0
Weslaco	95	65	30
West	6	6	0
West Columbia	14	7	7
West Lake Hills	22	16	6
West Orange	10	9	1
Westover Hills	14	11	3
West Tawakoni	6	5	1
West University Place	35	25	10
Westworth	13	9	4
Wharton	30	21	9
Whitehouse	21	15	6
White Oak	17	13	4
Whitesboro	11	7	4
White Settlement	42	29	13
Whitney	8	7	1
Wichita Falls	260	183	77
Willow Park	10	9	1
Wills Point	10	9	1
Wilmer	16	11	5
Windcrest	22	16	6
Wink	1	1	0
Winnsboro	13	9	4
Winters	4	4	0
Wolfforth	5	5	0
Woodville	8	7	1
Woodway	32	22	10
Wortham	4	3	1
Wylie	28	26	2
Yoakum	16	9	7
Yorktown	3	3	0
UTAH			
Alpine/Highland	15	15	0
Alta	10	4	6
American Fork	39	34	5
Blanding	7	6	1
Bountiful	44	33	11
Brian Head	5	5	0
Brigham City	29	24	5
Cedar City	34	29	5
Centerville	19	16	3
Clearfield	40	28	12
Clinton	12	11	1
East Carbon	4	4	0
Ephraim	5	5	0
Fairview	2	2	0
Farmington	14	11	3
Garland	4	4	0
Grantsville	10	8	2
Gunnison	3	3	0
Harrisville	6	5	1
Heber	13	12	1
Helper	6	5	1
Hildale	5	5	0
Hurricane	14	10	4
Kamas	2	2	0
Kanab	8	6	2
Kaysville	20	18	2
Layton	82	61	21
Lehi	26	24	2
Logan	87	58	29
Mantua	1	1	0
Mapleton	9	7	2

City by state	Total law enforcement employees	Total officers	Total civilians
UTAH—Continued			
Midvale	48	44	4
Minersville	1	1	0
Moab	14	12	2
Monticello	5	4	1
Moroni	1	1	0
Mount Pleasant	5	5	0
Murray	79	62	17
Naples	4	3	1
Nephi	11	9	2
North Ogden	18	15	3
North Park	9	8	1
North Salt Lake	12	10	2
Ogden	152	127	25
Orem	117	82	35
Park City	31	23	8
Parowan	4	2	2
Payson	15	14	1
Perry	4	4	0
Pleasant Grove/Lindon	33	29	4
Pleasant View	7	6	1
Price	18	16	2
Provo	155	100	55
Richfield	15	13	2
Riverdale	21	17	4
Roosevelt	11	10	1
Roy	41	37	4
Salem/Woodland Hills	7	7	0
Salina	5	4	1
Salt Lake City	551	397	154
Sandy	150	106	44
Santaquin/Genola	6	6	0
Smithfield	8	7	1
South Jordan	38	34	4
South Ogden	27	23	4
South Salt Lake	70	60	10
Spanish Fork	23	21	2
Springville	32	24	8
St. George	98	75	23
Stockton/Rush Valley	2	2	0
Sunset	9	8	1
Syracuse	13	11	2
Tooele	32	27	5
Tremonton	11	9	2
Vernal	18	16	2
Wellington	4	4	0
Wendover	6	5	1
West Bountiful	6	5	1
West Jordan	116	93	23
West Valley	217	180	37
Willard	2	2	0
Woods Cross	12	10	2
VERMONT			
Barre	25	18	7
Barre Town	8	7	1
Bellows Falls	12	8	4
Bennington	30	25	5
Berlin	8	7	1
Brandon	6	6	0
Brattleboro	38	23	15
Bristol	4	4	0
Burlington	133	97	36
Castleton	3	3	0
Chester	5	4	1
Colchester	31	25	6
Dover	6	5	1
Essex	32	26	6

Table 78

Full-time Law Enforcement Employees as of October 31, 2002
by City by State—Continued

City by state	Total law enforcement employees	Total officers	Total civilians	City by state	Total law enforcement employees	Total officers	Total civilians
VERMONT—Continued				**VIRGINIA—Continued**			
Fair Haven	3	3	0	Clifton Forge	15	11	4
Hardwick	5	4	1	Clintwood	4	3	1
Hartford	28	20	8	Coeburn	8	7	1
Hinesburg	3	3	0	Colonial Beach	13	8	5
Ludlow	9	5	4	Colonial Heights	53	49	4
Manchester	12	8	4	Courtland	3	1	2
Middlebury	15	13	2	Covington	28	15	13
Milton	13	12	1	Crewe	4	4	0
Montgomery	1	1	0	Culpeper	36	30	6
Montpelier	23	16	7	Damascus	4	4	0
Morristown	9	8	1	Danville	140	133	7
Newport	13	11	2	Dayton	5	5	0
Northfield	7	6	1	Dublin	9	8	1
Norwich	6	5	1	Dumfries	15	13	2
Randolph	5	5	0	Edinburg	3	2	1
Richmond	6	5	1	Elkton	7	6	1
Rutland	51	41	10	Emporia	30	21	9
Shelburne	15	10	5	Exmore	5	5	0
South Burlington	41	36	5	Fairfax City	77	59	18
Springfield	15	10	5	Falls Church	38	29	9
St. Albans	21	13	8	Farmville	34	24	10
St. Johnsbury	17	11	6	Franklin	44	32	12
Stowe	14	12	2	Fredericksburg	81	56	25
Swanton	5	4	1	Fries	1	1	0
Thetford	1	1	0	Front Royal	43	33	10
Vergennes	5	5	0	Galax	38	24	14
Vernon	4	3	1	Gate City	3	3	0
Waterbury	4	4	0	Glade Spring	3	3	0
Weathersfield	2	1	1	Glen Lyn	2	2	0
Williston	12	10	2	Gordonsville	5	5	0
Wilmington	6	5	1	Gretna	2	2	0
Windsor	10	6	4	Grottoes	5	5	0
Winhall	5	5	0	Grundy	7	6	1
Winooski	19	15	4	Halifax	5	4	1
Woodstock	6	5	1	Hampton	352	254	98
				Harrisonburg	90	70	20
VIRGINIA				Haymarket	4	3	1
				Haysi	2	2	0
Abingdon	21	19	2	Herndon	68	52	16
Alexandria	426	292	134	Hillsville	12	11	1
Altavista	11	11	0	Honaker	5	4	1
Amherst	5	5	0	Hopewell	64	49	15
Appalachia	6	6	0	Hurt	3	3	0
Ashland	22	20	2	Independence	2	2	0
Bedford	23	21	2	Jonesville	3	2	1
Berryville	8	7	1	Kenbridge	8	8	0
Big Stone Gap	18	16	2	Kilmarnock	4	4	0
Blacksburg	72	56	16	La Crosse	3	3	0
Blackstone	18	13	5	Lawrenceville	5	5	0
Bluefield	18	14	4	Lebanon	13	12	1
Bowling Green	2	2	0	Leesburg	68	52	16
Boykins	1	1	0	Lexington	18	16	2
Bridgewater	8	8	0	Louisa	4	4	0
Bristol	77	57	20	Luray	16	14	2
Broadway	4	4	0	Lynchburg	193	153	40
Brookneal	4	4	0	Manassas	108	85	23
Buena Vista	14	13	1	Manassas Park	30	21	9
Burkeville	1	1	0	Marion	20	18	2
Cape Charles	5	5	0	Martinsville	59	53	6
Cedar Bluff	3	3	0	McKenney	1	1	0
Charlottesville	141	111	30	Middleburg	3	3	0
Chase City	10	9	1	Middletown	3	2	1
Chatham	4	4	0	Mount Jackson	4	4	0
Chesapeake	461	353	108	Narrows	4	4	0
Chilhowie	6	6	0	New Market	7	7	0
Chincoteague	14	10	4	Newport News	522	384	138
Christiansburg	55	41	14	Norfolk	887	760	127
Clarksville	9	8	1	Norton	22	16	6

Table 78

Full-time Law Enforcement Employees as of October 31, 2002
by City by State—Continued

City by state	Total law enforcement employees	Total officers	Total civilians	City by state	Total law enforcement employees	Total officers	Total civilians
VIRGINIA—Continued				**WASHINGTON—Continued**			
Occoquan	2	2	0	Blaine	15	13	2
Onancock	3	3	0	Bonney Lake	30	20	10
Onley	2	2	0	Bothell	79	53	26
Orange	14	13	1	Bremerton	77	62	15
Parksley	3	3	0	Brewster	8	6	2
Pearisburg	8	7	1	Brier	7	6	1
Pembroke	2	2	0	Buckley	19	9	10
Pennington Gap	7	6	1	Burien	26	25	1
Petersburg	154	115	39	Burlington	23	18	5
Pocahontas	3	3	0	Camas	27	23	4
Poquoson	25	20	5	Carnation	3	3	0
Portsmouth	325	213	112	Castle Rock	5	5	0
Pound	5	5	0	Centralia	31	26	5
Pulaski	32	24	8	Chehalis	19	15	4
Purcellville	9	8	1	Chelan	15	9	6
Quantico	1	1	0	Cheney	15	11	4
Radford	45	32	13	Chewelah	6	5	1
Rich Creek	1	1	0	Clarkston	14	13	1
Richlands	20	15	5	Cle Elum	10	8	2
Richmond	807	632	175	Clyde Hill	9	8	1
Roanoke	288	231	57	Colfax	5	5	0
Rocky Mount	17	16	1	College Place	14	11	3
Rural Retreat	1	1	0	Colton	1	1	0
Salem	88	63	25	Colville	14	12	2
Saltville	9	8	1	Connell	7	7	0
Shenandoah	4	4	0	Cosmopolis	6	5	1
Smithfield	20	18	2	Coulee Dam	6	6	0
South Boston	31	27	4	Coupeville	5	5	0
South Hill	25	20	5	Covington	9	9	0
Stanley	3	3	0	Des Moines	55	43	12
Staunton	65	49	16	Dupont	6	6	0
Stephens City	3	3	0	Duvall	11	10	1
St. Paul	3	3	0	East Wenatchee	15	13	2
Strasburg	15	13	2	Eatonville	7	6	1
Suffolk	183	139	44	Edgewood	8	8	0
Tappahannock	10	9	1	Edmonds	69	52	17
Tazewell	11	10	1	Ellensburg	32	23	9
Timberville	3	3	0	Elma	9	7	2
Victoria	6	5	1	Elmer City	2	2	0
Vienna	49	39	10	Enumclaw	30	19	11
Vinton	28	20	8	Ephrata	16	13	3
Virginia Beach	922	758	164	Everett	217	180	37
Warrenton	24	21	3	Everson	5	5	0
Warsaw	3	2	1	Federal Way	154	109	45
Waverly	12	7	5	Ferndale	18	15	3
Waynesboro	57	50	7	Fife	29	22	7
Weber City	5	5	0	Fircrest	10	9	1
West Point	9	8	1	Forks	10	9	1
Williamsburg	49	36	13	Garfield	1	1	0
Winchester	76	64	12	Gig Harbor	15	13	2
Wise	12	11	1	Goldendale	10	9	1
Woodstock	15	14	1	Grand Coulee	3	3	0
Wytheville	30	24	6	Grandview	21	16	5
				Granger	11	9	2
WASHINGTON				Granite Falls	8	7	1
				Hoquiam	27	21	6
Aberdeen	48	36	12	Issaquah	54	28	26
Airway Heights	10	9	1	Kalama	5	4	1
Albion	1	1	0	Kelso	32	28	4
Algona	8	6	2	Kenmore	13	13	0
Anacortes	32	24	8	Kennewick	105	87	18
Arlington	23	19	4	Kent	179	121	58
Auburn	115	83	32	Kettle Falls	5	4	1
Bainbridge Island	26	22	4	Kirkland	96	63	33
Battle Ground	19	16	3	Kittitas	2	2	0
Bellevue	266	169	97	La Center	7	6	1
Bellingham	161	107	54	Lacey	52	45	7
Black Diamond	10	10	0	Lake Forest Park	26	22	4

Table 78

Full-time Law Enforcement Employees as of October 31, 2002

by City by State—Continued

City by state	Total law enforcement employees	Total officers	Total civilians	City by state	Total law enforcement employees	Total officers	Total civilians
WASHINGTON—Continued				**WASHINGTON—Continued**			
Lake Stevens	11	10	1	SeaTac	30	29	1
Lakewood	100	89	11	Seattle	1,746	1,266	480
Langley	4	4	0	Sedro Woolley	16	12	4
Long Beach	7	6	1	Selah	12	11	1
Longview	62	53	9	Sequim	16	13	3
Lynden	17	13	4	Shelton	35	20	15
Lynnwood	94	66	28	Shoreline	45	43	2
Mabton	4	4	0	Snohomish	25	21	4
Maple Valley	10	10	0	Snoqualmie	17	14	3
Marysville	67	38	29	Soap Lake	4	4	0
Mattawa	3	3	0	South Bend	5	4	1
McCleary	4	4	0	Spokane	397	293	104
Medical Lake	6	4	2	Springdale	1	1	0
Medina	11	9	2	Stanwood	12	10	2
Mercer Island	42	32	10	Steilacoom	12	11	1
Mill Creek	23	19	4	Sultan	9	8	1
Milton	15	13	2	Sumas	5	5	0
Monroe	37	29	8	Sumner	25	17	8
Montesano	10	8	2	Sunnyside	40	26	14
Morton	2	2	0	Tacoma	387	351	36
Moses Lake	34	27	7	Tekoa	2	2	0
Mossyrock	1	1	0	Tenino	6	5	1
Mountlake Terrace	39	31	8	Tieton	2	2	0
Mount Vernon	54	43	11	Toledo	2	2	0
Moxee	2	2	0	Tonasket	6	5	1
Mukilteo	26	23	3	Toppenish	23	17	6
Napavine	5	4	1	Tukwila	85	70	15
Newcastle	7	7	0	Tumwater	29	25	4
Newport	6	5	1	Twisp	4	3	1
Normandy Park	14	13	1	Union Gap	23	18	5
North Bend	5	5	0	Uniontown	3	2	1
Northport	1	1	0	University Place	25	24	1
Oakesdale	1	1	0	Vader	2	2	0
Oak Harbor	37	25	12	Vancouver	202	174	28
Oakville	2	2	0	Walla Walla	52	43	9
Ocean Shores	15	12	3	Wapato	21	14	7
Odessa	2	2	0	Warden	8	4	4
Olympia	100	72	28	Washougal	16	14	2
Omak	14	11	3	Wenatchee	64	40	24
Oroville	6	5	1	Westport	9	7	2
Orting	6	6	0	West Richland	14	12	2
Othello	17	12	5	White Salmon	9	9	0
Pacific	13	9	4	Wilbur	2	2	0
Palouse	2	2	0	Winlock	2	2	0
Pasco	56	47	9	Winthrop	3	3	0
Pe Ell	2	2	0	Woodinville	8	8	0
Port Angeles	52	28	24	Woodland	9	7	2
Port Orchard	20	18	2	Yakima	155	110	45
Port Townsend	17	14	3	Yelm	12	10	2
Poulsbo	20	17	3	Zillah	10	8	2
Prosser	18	11	7				
Pullman	35	28	7	**WEST VIRGINIA**			
Puyallup	86	51	35				
Quincy	12	10	2	Alderson	1	1	0
Rainier	5	5	0	Anmoore	2	2	0
Raymond	6	5	1	Ansted	2	2	0
Reardan	1	1	0	Athens	1	1	0
Redmond	102	71	31	Barboursville	20	18	2
Renton	123	87	36	Barrackville	1	1	0
Republic	3	3	0	Beckley	67	45	22
Richland	56	50	6	Belington	2	2	0
Ridgefield	6	6	0	Belle	4	4	0
Ritzville	4	4	0	Benwood	6	5	1
Rosalia	1	1	0	Berkeley Springs	2	2	0
Roy	3	3	0	Bethlehem	5	5	0
Royal City	3	3	0	Bluefield	33	27	6
Ruston	2	2	0	Bradshaw	3	3	0
Sammamish	22	21	1	Bramwell	3	3	0

Table 78

Full-time Law Enforcement Employees as of October 31, 2002
by City by State—Continued

City by state	Total law enforcement employees	Total officers	Total civilians	City by state	Total law enforcement employees	Total officers	Total civilians
WEST VIRGINIA—Continued				**WEST VIRGINIA—Continued**			
Bridgeport	22	20	2	Montgomery	12	11	1
Buckhannon	8	7	1	Moorefield	7	7	0
Burnsville	1	1	0	Morgantown	62	53	9
Cameron	3	2	1	Moundsville	22	16	6
Capon Bridge	2	2	0	Mount Hope	6	5	1
Cedar Grove	2	2	0	Mullens	5	5	0
Ceredo	9	6	3	New Cumberland	2	2	0
Chapmanville	3	3	0	New Haven	4	4	0
Charleston	180	155	25	New Martinsville	13	9	4
Charles Town	17	15	2	Nitro	17	16	1
Chesapeake	3	3	0	Northfork	4	4	0
Chester	5	5	0	Nutter Fort	6	6	0
Clarksburg	44	37	7	Oak Hill	16	14	2
Clendenin	4	4	0	Oceana	5	5	0
Danville	3	3	0	Paden City	5	4	1
Delbarton	1	1	0	Parkersburg	77	64	13
Dunbar	17	14	3	Parsons	1	1	0
East Bank	1	1	0	Paw Paw	1	1	0
Eleanor	1	1	0	Petersburg	3	3	0
Elkins	16	10	6	Philippi	6	6	0
Fairmont	42	31	11	Piedmont	3	3	0
Fairview	1	1	0	Pineville	3	3	0
Fayetteville	6	6	0	Point Pleasant	10	9	1
Follansbee	7	7	0	Pratt	2	2	0
Fort Gay	2	2	0	Princeton	22	19	3
Gary	1	1	0	Rainelle	3	3	0
Gassaway	2	2	0	Ranson	7	7	0
Gauley Bridge	2	2	0	Ravenswood	9	8	1
Gilbert	4	4	0	Reedsville	1	1	0
Glasgow	3	3	0	Rhodell	2	2	0
Glen Dale	6	5	1	Richwood	6	5	1
Glenville	2	2	0	Ridgeley	3	3	0
Grafton	7	6	1	Ripley	9	8	1
Grantsville	1	1	0	Rivesville	1	1	0
Grant Town	1	1	0	Romney	4	3	1
Hamlin	2	2	0	Ronceverte	2	2	0
Handley	2	2	0	Salem	3	3	0
Harpers Ferry/Bolivar	3	3	0	Shepherdstown	7	5	2
Harrisville	1	1	0	Shinnston	6	6	0
Henderson	1	1	0	Sistersville	4	4	0
Hinton	6	6	0	Smithers	6	6	0
Huntington	82	75	7	Sophia	3	3	0
Hurricane	16	14	2	South Charleston	41	29	12
Iaeger	2	2	0	Spencer	8	7	1
Kenova	11	7	4	St. Albans	23	19	4
Kermit	2	2	0	Star City	6	5	1
Keyser	14	9	5	St. Marys	4	4	0
Keystone	3	3	0	Stonewood	3	3	0
Kimball	1	1	0	Summersville	20	18	2
Kingwood	4	4	0	Sutton	3	2	1
Lewisburg	12	10	2	Terra Alta	2	2	0
Logan	9	7	2	Vienna	19	15	4
Lumberport	2	2	0	War	2	2	0
Mabscott	2	2	0	Wardensville	1	1	0
Madison	6	5	1	Wayne	4	2	2
Man	3	3	0	Webster Springs	2	2	0
Mannington	4	4	0	Weirton	49	40	9
Marlinton	1	1	0	Welch	11	9	2
Marmet	5	5	0	Wellsburg	4	4	0
Martinsburg	46	34	12	West Logan	1	1	0
Mason	3	3	0	West Milford	2	2	0
Masontown	1	1	0	Weston	7	6	1
Matewan	2	2	0	Westover	7	7	0
Matoaka	6	6	0	West Union	1	1	0
McMechen	3	3	0	Wheeling	83	82	1
Milton	5	5	0	White Sulphur Springs	5	4	1
Mitchell Heights	1	1	0	Whitesville	2	2	0
Monongah	1	1	0	Williamson	8	7	1

Table 78

Full-time Law Enforcement Employees as of October 31, 2002

by City by State—Continued

City by state	Total law enforcement employees	Total officers	Total civilians	City by state	Total law enforcement employees	Total officers	Total civilians
WEST VIRGINIA—Continued				**WISCONSIN—Continued**			
Williamstown	6	5	1	Everest	25	23	2
Winfield	3	3	0	Fennimore	5	5	0
				Fitchburg	41	34	7
WISCONSIN				Fond du Lac	83	69	14
				Fontana	8	7	1
Algoma	5	5	0	Fort Atkinson	27	20	7
Altoona	10	9	1	Fox Lake	3	3	0
Amery	7	6	1	Fox Point	19	17	2
Antigo	20	17	3	Fox Valley	29	26	3
Appleton	136	107	29	Franklin	78	59	19
Arcadia	5	5	0	Geneva Town	7	6	1
Ashwaubenon	52	44	8	Genoa City	5	4	1
Augusta	4	4	0	Germantown	41	30	11
Bangor	3	3	0	Glendale	49	48	1
Baraboo	31	25	6	Green Bay	223	185	38
Barron	7	7	0	Greendale	36	28	8
Bayfield	4	4	0	Greenfield	78	57	21
Beaver Dam	39	29	10	Hallie	7	6	1
Belleville	4	4	0	Hartford	27	22	5
Beloit Town	16	10	6	Hartland	18	15	3
Berlin	15	13	2	Hayward	8	7	1
Black River Falls	9	8	1	Hazel Green	2	2	0
Blanchardville	1	1	0	Holmen	9	8	1
Bloomer	7	6	1	Horicon	12	9	3
Boscobel	6	6	0	Hudson	22	19	3
Brillion	7	7	0	Independence	2	2	0
Brookfield	83	60	23	Iron Ridge	1	1	0
Brown Deer	35	30	5	Jackson	11	10	1
Burlington	27	21	6	Janesville	116	103	13
Burlington Town	8	8	0	Jefferson	17	13	4
Butler	8	7	1	Juneau	5	4	1
Caledonia	36	28	8	Kaukauna	25	24	1
Campbellsport	2	2	0	Kenosha	264	186	78
Cedarburg	30	20	10	Kewaskum	7	7	0
Chenequa	9	9	0	Kewaunee	6	6	0
Chetek	6	5	1	Kiel	12	7	5
Chilton	7	7	0	Kohler	8	7	1
Chippewa Falls	35	27	8	Lac du Flambeau	12	11	1
Cleveland	3	2	1	La Crosse	120	97	23
Colby-Abbotsford	7	6	1	Lake Delton	14	13	1
Columbus	16	11	5	Lake Geneva	28	20	8
Cornell	3	3	0	Lake Mills	14	12	2
Cottage Grove	10	9	1	Lancaster	7	6	1
Crandon	4	3	1	Lodi	6	5	1
Cuba City	5	4	1	Luxemburg	2	2	0
Cudahy	44	31	13	Madison	462	382	80
Darien	7	6	1	Manitowoc	76	66	10
Darlington	5	5	0	Maple Bluff	5	5	0
Deerfield	3	3	0	Marinette	31	24	7
DeForest	13	11	2	Markesan	3	3	0
Delafield	15	14	1	Marshall Village	8	7	1
Delavan Town	11	10	1	Marshfield	53	38	15
Denmark	2	2	0	Mauston	9	8	1
De Pere	38	34	4	Mayville	12	10	2
Dodgeville	11	10	1	McFarland	13	12	1
Durand	4	4	0	Medford	10	9	1
Eagle River	6	6	0	Menomonee Falls	69	58	11
Eagle Village	2	2	0	Menomonie	33	26	7
East Troy	7	7	0	Merrill	25	21	4
Eau Claire	129	99	30	Middleton	38	30	8
Eleva	1	1	0	Milton	10	9	1
Elkhart Lake	3	3	0	Milwaukee	2,425	1,977	448
Elkhorn	20	16	4	Mineral Point	6	6	0
Elk Mound	1	1	0	Minocqua	16	11	5
Ellsworth	7	6	1	Mondovi	4	4	0
Elm Grove	25	17	8	Monona	23	19	4
Elroy	2	2	0	Monroe	35	26	9
Evansville	9	8	1	Mosinee	7	6	1

Table 78

Full-time Law Enforcement Employees as of October 31, 2002

by City by State—Continued

City by state	Total law enforcement employees	Total officers	Total civilians	City by state	Total law enforcement employees	Total officers	Total civilians
WISCONSIN—Continued				**WISCONSIN—Continued**			
Mount Horeb	12	10	2	Stoughton	24	19	5
Mount Pleasant	40	31	9	Sturgeon Bay	22	21	1
Mukwonago	19	12	7	Sturtevant	16	10	6
Muskego	47	36	11	Summit	8	8	0
Neenah	51	41	10	Sun Prairie	67	44	23
Neillsville	7	6	1	Superior	64	57	7
New Berlin	94	74	20	Theresa	2	2	0
New Glarus	5	5	0	Thiensville	8	7	1
New Holstein	11	7	4	Three Lakes	5	5	0
New Lisbon	3	3	0	Tomah	25	19	6
New Richmond	13	12	1	Tomahawk	8	7	1
Niagara	5	5	0	Town of East Troy	7	6	1
North Fond du Lac	14	11	3	Town of Madison	18	16	2
North Hudson	7	6	1	Twin Lakes	14	10	4
Oak Creek	66	49	17	Two Rivers	32	26	6
Oconomowoc	13	12	1	Valders	1	1	0
Oconto	9	9	0	Verona	13	12	1
Oconto Falls	6	6	0	Viroqua	9	8	1
Omro	6	5	1	Walworth	5	5	0
Onalaska	31	28	3	Washburn	4	4	0
Oregon	15	14	1	Waterloo	8	7	1
Osceola	5	5	0	Watertown	52	38	14
Oshkosh	114	97	17	Waukesha	144	104	40
Palmyra	5	5	0	Waunakee	17	15	2
Park Falls	8	7	1	Waupun	23	17	6
Pepin	1	1	0	Wausau	71	64	7
Peshtigo	7	6	1	Wautoma	6	5	1
Pewaukee	16	14	2	Wauwatosa	120	91	29
Pewaukee Township	22	20	2	West Allis	160	134	26
Phillips	5	4	1	West Bend	76	57	19
Platteville	27	21	6	West Milwaukee	24	19	5
Pleasant Prairie	27	26	1	West Salem	7	6	1
Plover	18	15	3	Whitefish Bay	25	22	3
Plymouth	15	15	0	Whitehall	4	4	0
Portage	29	21	8	Whitewater	33	23	10
Port Washington	24	19	5	Williams Bay	7	6	1
Poynette	6	5	1	Winneconne	6	5	1
Prairie du Chien	17	12	5	Wisconsin Dells	16	11	5
Prescott	7	6	1	Wisconsin Rapids	49	38	11
Pulaski	5	5	0	Woodruff	6	5	1
Reedsburg	23	16	7				
Rhinelander	24	17	7	**WYOMING**			
Rice Lake	26	23	3				
Richland Center	13	11	2	Afton	4	4	0
Ripon	20	14	6	Baggs	1	1	0
River Falls	25	22	3	Basin	4	4	0
River Hills	13	13	0	Buffalo	15	9	6
Rothschild	12	10	2	Casper	124	81	43
Sauk Prairie	14	13	1	Cheyenne	114	87	27
Saukville	11	9	2	Cody	19	17	2
Shawano	24	20	4	Diamondville	4	3	1
Sheboygan	117	90	27	Douglas	20	13	7
Sheboygan Falls	15	13	2	Evanston	33	28	5
Shorewood	34	25	9	Evansville	13	8	5
Shorewood Hills	6	5	1	Gillette	61	41	20
Silver Lake	3	2	1	Glenrock	11	6	5
Siren	3	3	0	Green River	35	26	9
Slinger	10	9	1	Greybull	5	4	1
Somerset	6	5	1	Guernsey	4	4	0
South Milwaukee	40	34	6	Hanna	7	4	3
Sparta	21	16	5	Jackson	30	21	9
Spencer	3	3	0	Kemmerer	10	8	2
Spooner	7	6	1	La Barge	1	1	0
Spring Green	4	3	1	Lander	19	17	2
Stanley	3	3	0	Laramie	74	47	27
St. Croix Falls	4	4	0	Lovell	9	6	3
Stevens Point	58	44	14	Lusk	4	4	0
St. Francis	24	19	5	Lyman	7	5	2

Table 78

Full-time Law Enforcement Employees as of October 31, 2002
by City by State—Continued

City by state	Total law enforcement employees	Total officers	Total civilians	City by state	Total law enforcement employees	Total officers	Total civilians
WYOMING—Continued				**WYOMING—Continued**			
Mills	10	9	1	Saratoga	11	6	5
Moorcroft	4	3	1	Sheridan	48	28	20
Newcastle	14	8	6	Sundance	5	5	0
Pine Bluffs	5	2	3	Thermopolis	13	7	6
Powell	22	14	8	Torrington	21	15	6
Rawlins	31	21	10	Wheatland	11	10	1
Riverton	35	23	12	Worland	11	11	0
Rock Springs	57	37	20				

[1] The data in this table are provided for Charlotte Police Department, North Carolina, only. However, Charlotte Police Department reports its crime figures combined with those of Mecklenburg County; they can be found in Table 8 under Charlotte-Mecklenburg.

Table 79

Full-time Law Enforcement Employees as of October 31, 2002
by University and College by State[1]

University/College by state	Total law enforcement employees	Total officers	Total civilians	University/College by state	Total law enforcement employees	Total officers	Total civilians
ALABAMA				**CALIFORNIA—Continued**			
				San Marcos	14	9	5
Auburn University:				Stanislaus	21	10	11
Main Campus	55	32	23	College of the Sequoias	7	6	1
Montgomery	22	11	11	Contra Costa Community College	29	18	11
Calhoun Community College	6	4	2	Cuesta College	8	6	2
Faulkner University	10	10	0	El Camino College	22	16	6
Jacksonville State University	19	15	4	Foothill-De Anza College	18	11	7
Talladega College	6	3	3	Humboldt State University	17	11	6
Troy State University	8	6	2	Long Beach City College	20	17	3
University of Alabama:				Marin Community College	7	5	2
Huntsville	15	11	4	Pasadena Community College	18	9	9
Tuscaloosa	48	40	8	Riverside Community College	24	17	7
University of Montevallo	14	9	5	San Bernardino Community College	8	4	4
University of North Alabama	12	11	1	San Diego State University	37	30	7
University of South Alabama	40	28	12	San Francisco State University	41	19	22
				San Jose/Evergreen Community College	8	5	3
ALASKA				Santa Rosa Junior College	19	12	7
				Sonoma State University	17	12	5
University of Alaska:				State Center Community College	14	11	3
Anchorage	22	14	8	University of California:			
Fairbanks	13	10	3	Berkeley	118	62	56
				Davis	92	45	47
ARIZONA				Irvine	29	21	8
				Lawrence-Livermore Laboratory	7	2	5
Arizona State University:				Los Angeles	84	45	39
Main Campus	68	44	24	Riverside	31	23	8
West	14	9	5	San Diego	51	28	23
Arizona Western College	5	4	1	San Francisco	48	31	17
Central Arizona College	6	5	1	Santa Barbara	42	30	12
Northern Arizona University	29	19	10	Santa Cruz	41	18	23
Pima Community College	36	29	7	West Valley-Mission College	11	9	2
University of Arizona	78	46	32				
Yavapai College	6	6	0	**COLORADO**			
ARKANSAS				Adams State College	2	2	0
				Arapahoe Community College	7	6	1
Arkansas State University	23	18	5	Auraria Higher Education Center	34	21	13
Henderson State University	8	7	1	Colorado School of Mines	8	7	1
Northwest Arkansas Community College	7	4	3	Colorado State University	29	22	7
Southern Arkansas University	7	6	1	Fort Lewis College	9	7	2
University of Arkansas:				Pikes Peak Community College	17	15	2
Fayetteville	35	26	9	Red Rocks Community College	2	1	1
Little Rock	31	25	6	University of Colorado:			
Medical Sciences	40	35	5	Boulder	59	39	20
Monticello	7	6	1	Colorado Springs	26	13	13
Pine Bluff	17	12	5	Health Sciences Center	79	34	45
University of Central Arkansas	26	23	3	University of Northern Colorado	19	12	7
				University of Southern Colorado	3	2	1
CALIFORNIA							
				CONNECTICUT			
Allan Hancock College	6	5	1				
California State Polytechnic University:				Central Connecticut State University	27	21	6
Pomona	23	12	11	Eastern Connecticut State University	19	13	6
San Luis Obispo	35	16	19	Southern Connecticut State University	37	27	10
California State University:				University of Connecticut:			
Bakersfield	14	10	4	Health Center	22	13	9
Channel Islands	18	12	6	Storrs, Avery Point, and Hartford	69	55	14
Chico	17	12	5	Western Connecticut State University	23	15	8
Dominguez Hills	23	11	12	Yale University	85	71	14
Fresno	25	15	10				
Fullerton	28	20	8	**DELAWARE**			
Hayward	25	13	12				
Long Beach	31	24	7	University of Delaware	76	46	30
Los Angeles	27	17	10				
Monterey Bay	18	13	5	**FLORIDA**			
Northridge	30	20	10				
Sacramento	22	16	6				
San Bernardino	22	14	8	Florida A&M University	37	28	9
San Jose	65	34	31	Florida Atlantic University	47	31	16

Table 79

Full-time Law Enforcement Employees as of October 31, 2002
by University and College by State[1]—Continued

University/College by state	Total law enforcement employees	Total officers	Total civilians	University/College by state	Total law enforcement employees	Total officers	Total civilians
FLORIDA—Continued				**ILLINOIS—Continued**			
Florida Gulf Coast University	17	12	5	Northwestern University:			
Florida International University	63	42	21	Chicago	20	16	4
Florida State University:				Evanston	31	22	9
Panama City	3	2	1	Oakton Community College	11	10	1
Tallahassee	74	55	19	Parkland College	15	10	5
New College of Florida	16	12	4	Rock Valley College	14	12	2
Pensacola Junior College	19	15	4	Southern Illinois University:			
Santa Fe Community College	22	15	7	Carbondale	47	37	10
Tallahassee Community College	25	14	11	Edwardsville	41	32	9
University of Central Florida	62	43	19	School of Medicine	11	2	9
University of Florida	162	91	71	South Suburban College	16	12	4
University of North Florida	38	25	13	Triton College	14	9	5
University of South Florida:				University of Illinois:			
St. Petersburg	14	10	4	Chicago	103	61	42
Tampa	60	43	17	Springfield	17	11	6
University of West Florida	31	22	9	Urbana	69	55	14
				Waubonsee College	3	3	0
GEORGIA				Western Illinois University	30	25	5
				William Rainey Harper College	14	8	6
Abraham Baldwin Agricultural College	10	9	1				
Albany State University	27	12	15	**INDIANA**			
Armstrong Atlantic State University	16	12	4				
Augusta State University	17	14	3	Ball State University	40	30	10
Berry College	16	11	5	Indiana State University	34	25	9
Clark Atlanta University	34	16	18	Indiana University:			
Clayton College and State University	19	13	6	Bloomington	55	45	10
Coastal Georgia Community College	6	6	0	Gary	14	10	4
Columbus State University	14	13	1	Indianapolis	51	33	18
Dalton State College	7	7	0	New Albany	10	8	2
Fort Valley State University	19	13	6	Marian College	5	3	2
Georgia College and State University	19	12	7	Purdue University	42	35	7
Georgia Institute of Technology	50	35	15				
Georgia Perimeter College	50	10	40	**IOWA**			
Georgia Southern University	34	27	7				
Georgia State University	118	83	35	Iowa State University	34	31	3
Gordon College	8	7	1	University of Iowa	50	27	23
Kennesaw State University	34	23	11	University of Northern Iowa	24	17	7
Mercer University	7	7	0				
Middle Georgia College	9	8	1	**KANSAS**			
Morehouse College	32	28	4				
Morris-Brown College	41	18	23	Emporia State University	10	9	1
North Georgia College	12	8	4	Fort Hays State University	11	10	1
Piedmont College	4	4	0	Kansas State University	49	21	28
Savannah State University	21	10	11	Pittsburg State University	16	13	3
Southern Polytechnic State University	20	14	6	University of Kansas:			
South Georgia College	7	7	0	Main Campus	46	26	20
University of Georgia	71	58	13	Medical Center	52	27	25
University of West Georgia	23	16	7	Wichita State University	33	23	10
Valdosta State University	26	18	8				
Wesleyan College	5	5	0	**KENTUCKY**			
				Eastern Kentucky University	26	19	7
ILLINOIS				Kentucky State University	13	7	6
				Morehead State University	20	11	9
Black Hawk College	9	8	1	Murray State University	20	14	6
Chicago State University	28	21	7	Northern Kentucky University	25	14	11
College of DuPage	19	13	6	University of Kentucky	44	36	8
College of Lake County	17	9	8	University of Louisville	36	23	13
Eastern Illinois University	25	22	3	Western Kentucky University	31	20	11
Governors State University	11	8	3				
Illinois State University	26	22	4	**LOUISIANA**			
John A. Logan College	4	3	1				
Joliet Junior College	15	7	8	Delgado Community College	20	15	5
Loyola University of Chicago	32	15	17	Grambling State University	14	13	1
Morton College	6	4	2	Louisiana State University:			
Northeastern Illinois University	18	13	5	Baton Rouge	62	60	2
Northern Illinois University	55	38	17	Health Sciences Center, New Orleans	59	58	1
				Health Sciences Center, Shreveport	58	38	20

Table 79

Full-time Law Enforcement Employees as of October 31, 2002
by University and College by State[1]—Continued

University/College by state	Total law enforcement employees	Total officers	Total civilians
LOUISIANA—Continued			
Shreveport	9	9	0
Louisiana Tech University	19	17	2
McNeese State University	17	10	7
Nicholls State University	18	12	6
Northwestern State University	15	14	1
Southeastern Louisiana University	33	26	7
Southern University and A&M College:			
Baton Rouge	42	28	14
New Orleans	8	8	0
Shreveport	8	8	0
Tulane University	47	34	13
University of Louisiana:			
Lafayette	24	23	1
Monroe	25	20	5
University of New Orleans	38	29	9
MAINE			
University of Maine:			
Farmington	4	4	0
Orono	30	21	9
University of Southern Maine	26	18	8
MARYLAND			
Bowie State University	25	13	12
Coppin State College	20	16	4
Frostburg State University	20	16	4
Morgan State University	41	33	8
Salisbury University	21	17	4
St. Mary's College	12	2	10
Towson University	52	35	17
University of Baltimore	41	9	32
University of Maryland:			
Baltimore City	128	58	70
Baltimore County	32	26	6
College Park	104	76	28
Eastern Shore	13	11	2
MASSACHUSETTS			
Boston College	60	41	19
Boston University	59	51	8
Brandeis University	18	15	3
Bristol Community College	10	7	3
Emerson College	15	12	3
Fitchburg State College	16	14	2
Framingham State College	14	12	2
Harvard University	106	66	40
Holyoke Community College	9	9	0
Lasell College	16	15	1
Massachusetts College of Art	21	5	16
Massachusetts College of Liberal Arts	12	8	4
Massachusetts Institute of Technology	63	60	3
Massasoit Community College	14	12	2
Mount Holyoke College	22	15	7
Northeastern University	73	51	22
North Shore Community College	18	16	2
Quinsigamond Community College	9	9	0
Salem State College	22	20	2
Springfield College	31	14	17
Tufts University, Medford	63	41	22
University of Massachusetts:			
Amherst	69	54	15
Dartmouth	36	24	12
Harbor Campus, Boston	32	23	9
Medical Center, Worcester	26	21	5
Wellesley College	17	13	4

University/College by state	Total law enforcement employees	Total officers	Total civilians
MASSACHUSETTS—Continued			
Wentworth Institute of Technology	27	13	14
Western New England College	21	12	9
Westfield State College	18	12	6
MICHIGAN			
Central Michigan University	29	19	10
Delta College	9	7	2
Eastern Michigan University	30	24	6
Ferris State University	19	13	6
Grand Rapids Community College	13	10	3
Grand Valley State University	16	13	3
Hope College	9	7	2
Lansing Community College	10	9	1
Macomb Community College	35	28	7
Michigan State University	97	62	35
Michigan Technological University	12	9	3
Mott Community College	4	4	0
Northern Michigan University	17	14	3
Oakland Community College	20	19	1
Oakland University	20	16	4
Saginaw Valley State University	9	7	2
University of Michigan:			
Ann Arbor	99	52	47
Flint	20	8	12
Western Michigan University	62	30	32
MINNESOTA			
University of Minnesota:			
Duluth	8	8	0
Twin Cities	58	37	21
MISSISSIPPI			
Coahoma Community College	7	6	1
Jackson State University	56	48	8
Mississippi State University	36	26	10
University of Mississippi:			
Medical Center	89	56	33
Oxford	46	30	16
MISSOURI			
Central Missouri State University	21	16	5
Lincoln University	12	5	7
Mineral Area College	5	4	1
Northwest Missouri State University	16	10	6
Southeast Missouri State University	22	16	6
St. Louis Community College, Meramec	12	9	3
Truman State University	9	8	1
University of Missouri:			
Columbia	45	29	16
Kansas City	44	26	18
Rolla	11	9	2
St. Louis	17	16	1
Washington University	36	23	13
MONTANA			
Montana State University	30	15	15
University of Montana	18	14	4
NEBRASKA			
University of Nebraska:			
Kearney	8	6	2
Lincoln	32	26	6

Table 79

Full-time Law Enforcement Employees as of October 31, 2002
by University and College by State[1]—Continued

University/College by state	Total law enforcement employees	Total officers	Total civilians	University/College by state	Total law enforcement employees	Total officers	Total civilians
NEVADA				**NEW YORK—Continued**			
Truckee Meadows Community College	6	5	1	Utica-Rome	16	11	5
University of Nevada:				Syracuse University	59	54	5
Las Vegas	41	28	13	**NORTH CAROLINA**			
Reno	26	21	5				
				Appalachian State University	30	19	11
NEW JERSEY				Beaufort County Community College	2	2	0
				Belmont Abbey College	5	5	0
Brookdale Community College	20	11	9	Davidson College	9	8	1
Essex County College	58	15	43	Duke University	133	54	79
Kean University of New Jersey	38	26	12	East Carolina University	55	42	13
Middlesex County College	16	10	6	Elizabeth City State University	16	10	6
Monmouth University	26	15	11	Elon University	9	8	1
Montclair State University	37	24	13	Fayetteville State University	21	13	8
New Jersey Institute of Technology	59	26	33	Mars Hill College	4	4	0
Richard Stockton College	23	18	5	Methodist College	23	7	16
Rowan University	42	3	39	North Carolina Agricultural and			
Rutgers University:				Technical State University	33	26	7
Camden	38	18	20	North Carolina Central University	37	22	15
Newark	59	26	33	North Carolina School of the Arts	14	13	1
New Brunswick	132	62	70	North Carolina State University, Raleigh	54	41	13
The College of New Jersey	29	16	13	Pfeiffer University	5	5	0
University of Medicine and Dentistry:				Queens College	9	3	6
Camden	18	17	1	Saint Augustine's College	11	4	7
Newark	120	48	72	University of North Carolina:			
Piscataway	33	27	6	Asheville	16	8	8
William Paterson University	37	22	15	Chapel Hill	82	44	38
				Charlotte	43	36	7
NEW MEXICO				Greensboro	45	30	15
				Pembroke	15	11	4
Eastern New Mexico University	8	7	1	Wilmington	35	27	8
New Mexico Highlands University	8	2	6	Wake Forest University	41	18	23
New Mexico State University	31	20	11	Western Carolina University	17	13	4
University of New Mexico	47	31	16	Winston-Salem State University	19	13	6
Western New Mexico University	2	2	0				
				NORTH DAKOTA			
NEW YORK							
				North Dakota State University	11	10	1
Cornell University	56	45	11	University of North Dakota	15	11	4
Ithaca College	30	17	13				
Rensselaer Polytechnic Institute	30	20	10	**OHIO**			
State University of New York:							
Albany	71	35	36	Baldwin-Wallace College	12	1	11
Albany (Plaza)	15	3	12	Bowling Green State University	30	24	6
Binghamton	43	29	14	Cleveland State University	33	25	8
Buffalo	68	61	7	Columbus State Community College	28	23	5
Downstate Medical Center	119	29	90	Cuyahoga Community College	36	31	5
Stony Brook	121	55	66	Kent State University	34	28	6
State University of New York				Lakeland Community College	13	9	4
Agricultural and Technical College:				Marietta College	7	6	1
Alfred	18	12	6	Miami University	38	28	10
Canton	9	8	1	Ohio State University	56	45	11
Cobleskill	10	9	1	Ohio University	32	25	7
Farmingdale	16	15	1	Sinclair Community College	24	20	4
Morrisville	12	11	1	University of Akron	39	32	7
State University of New York College:				University of Cincinnati	122	50	72
Brockport	18	16	2	University of Toledo	42	33	9
Buffalo	35	29	6	Wright State University	23	14	9
Cortland	19	18	1	Youngstown State University	27	22	5
Environmental Science and Forestry	13	11	2				
Fredonia	15	14	1	**OKLAHOMA**			
Geneseo	19	15	4				
New Paltz	26	21	5	Cameron University	8	7	1
Old Westbury	21	18	3	East Central University	5	5	0
Oneonta	24	17	7	Murray State College	1	1	0
Optometry	13	5	8	Northeastern Oklahoma A&M College	9	7	2
Oswego	28	22	6	Northeastern State College	12	10	2
Plattsburgh	19	14	5				
Potsdam	24	11	13				

Table 79

Full-time Law Enforcement Employees as of October 31, 2002
by University and College by State[1]—Continued

University/College by state	Total law enforcement employees	Total officers	Total civilians	University/College by state	Total law enforcement employees	Total officers	Total civilians
OKLAHOMA—Continued				**SOUTH CAROLINA—Continued**			
				Columbia	74	54	20
Oklahoma State University:				Spartanburg	7	7	0
Main Campus	42	32	10	Winthrop University	20	14	6
Okmulgee	5	5	0				
Tulsa	6	4	2	**SOUTH DAKOTA**			
Rogers State University	3	3	0				
Seminole State College	5	5	0	South Dakota State University	16	9	7
Southeastern Oklahoma State University	7	6	1				
Southwestern Oklahoma State University	8	7	1	**TENNESSEE**			
Tulsa Community College	18	10	8				
University of Central Oklahoma	23	17	6	Austin Peay State University	18	12	6
University of Oklahoma:				Chattanooga State Technical			
Health Sciences Center	63	37	26	Community College	12	8	4
Norman	45	32	13	East Tennessee State University	25	19	6
				Middle Tennessee State University	28	24	4
PENNSYLVANIA				Tennessee State University	45	40	5
				Tennessee Technological University	20	12	8
Bloomsburg University	20	17	3	University of Memphis	36	30	6
California University	16	14	2	University of Tennessee:			
Cheyney University	14	14	0	Chattanooga	22	16	6
Clarion University	17	12	5	Knoxville	62	49	13
East Stroudsburg University	16	14	2	Martin	15	12	3
Edinboro University	15	14	1	Memphis	38	24	14
Elizabethtown College	14	9	5	Vanderbilt University	92	71	21
Indiana University	28	21	7	Volunteer State Community College	6	5	1
Kutztown University	17	11	6	Walters State Community College	7	7	0
Lehigh University	26	18	8				
Lock Haven University	10	9	1	**TEXAS**			
Mansfield University	12	12	0				
Millersville University	17	15	2	Alamo Community College District	69	44	25
Moravian College	11	7	4	Alvin Community College	13	11	2
Pennsylvania State University:				Amarillo College	17	15	2
Altoona	9	8	1	Angelo State University	12	9	3
Beaver	4	4	0	Austin College	8	7	1
Behrend	9	6	3	Baylor Health Care System	122	40	82
Berks	9	8	1	Baylor University, Waco	31	20	11
Harrisburg	8	7	1	Central Texas College	9	8	1
McKeesport	3	3	0	College of the Mainland	7	6	1
Mont Alto	3	3	0	Eastfield College	12	10	2
University Park	59	50	9	El Paso Community College	40	33	7
Shippensburg University	19	17	2	Grayson County College	4	3	1
Slippery Rock University	17	15	2	Hardin-Simmons University	7	4	3
University of Pittsburgh:				Houston Baptist University	11	9	2
Bradford	6	5	1	Lamar University, Beaumont	33	19	14
Pittsburgh	119	73	46	Laredo Community College	14	13	1
West Chester University	36	19	17	McLennan Community College	10	5	5
				Midwestern State University	9	8	1
RHODE ISLAND				Mountain View College	7	7	0
				North Lake College	14	13	1
Brown University	59	29	30	Paris Junior College	3	3	0
University of Rhode Island	32	18	14	Prairie View A&M University	30	16	14
				Rice University	38	24	14
SOUTH CAROLINA				Richland College	12	11	1
				Southern Methodist University	41	23	18
Aiken Technical College	7	1	6	South Plains College	6	6	0
Bob Jones University	3	3	0	Southwestern University	7	6	1
Clemson University	49	30	19	Southwest Texas State University	62	29	33
Coastal Carolina University	29	12	17	Stephen F. Austin State University	39	22	17
College of Charleston	53	28	25	St. Mary's University	17	11	6
Columbia College	12	9	3	St. Thomas University	5	1	4
Francis Marion University	11	11	0	Sul Ross State University	8	6	2
Lander University	11	10	1	Tarleton State University	13	11	2
Medical University of South Carolina	54	34	20	Texas A&M International University	18	12	6
Presbyterian College	9	8	1	Texas A&M University:			
South Carolina State University	33	21	12	College Station	135	54	81
The Citadel	13	8	5	Commerce	26	15	11
Trident Technical College	20	18	2	Corpus Christi	24	14	10
University of South Carolina:				Galveston	7	6	1
Aiken	6	6	0				

Table 79

Full-time Law Enforcement Employees as of October 31, 2002
by University and College by State[1]—Continued

University/College by state	Total law enforcement employees	Total officers	Total civilians	University/College by state	Total law enforcement employees	Total officers	Total civilians
TEXAS—Continued				**VIRGINIA—Continued**			
Texas Christian University	31	21	10	Northern Virginia Community College	35	35	0
Texas Southern University	37	26	11	Old Dominion University	56	31	25
Texas State Technical College:				Radford University	23	18	5
Harlingen	13	9	4	Thomas Nelson Community College	10	8	2
Waco	16	14	2	University of Richmond	32	16	16
Texas Technological University, Lubbock	64	41	23	University of Virginia	120	54	66
Texas Woman's University	30	14	16	University of Virginia, College at Wise	8	7	1
Trinity University	24	11	13	Virginia Commonwealth University	92	67	25
Tyler Junior College	12	5	7	Virginia Military Institute	6	6	0
University of Houston:				Virginia Polytechnic Institute and			
Central Campus	61	39	22	State University	53	35	18
Clearlake	21	13	8	Virginia State University	32	18	14
Downtown Campus	20	13	7	Virginia Western Community College	6	6	0
University of Mary Hardin-Baylor	6	6	0				
University of North Texas:				**WASHINGTON**			
Denton	56	33	23				
Health Science Center	20	11	9	Central Washington University	14	12	2
University of Texas:				Eastern Washington University	11	11	0
Arlington	64	22	42	Evergreen State College	15	11	4
Austin	132	60	72	University of Washington	62	50	12
Dallas	37	17	20	Washington State University:			
El Paso	54	20	34	Pullman	18	17	1
Health Science Center, San Antonio	86	36	50	Vancouver	3	3	0
Health Science Center, Tyler	22	5	17	Western Washington University	20	14	6
Houston	237	68	169				
Medical Branch	86	34	52	**WEST VIRGINIA**			
Pan American	26	17	9				
Permian Basin	10	4	6	Bluefield State College	1	1	0
San Antonio	66	30	36	Concord College	6	5	1
Southwestern Medical School	97	39	58	Fairmont State College	9	8	1
Tyler	10	4	6	Glenville State College	7	2	5
West Texas A&M University	11	8	3	Marshall University	26	22	4
				Potomac State College	5	5	0
UTAH				West Liberty State College	6	6	0
				West Virginia State College	12	10	2
Brigham Young University	39	27	12	West Virginia Tech	5	5	0
College of Eastern Utah	2	2	0	West Virginia University	51	44	7
Salt Lake Community College	17	15	2				
Southern Utah University	6	5	1	**WISCONSIN**			
University of Utah	90	31	59				
Utah State University	18	12	6	University of Wisconsin:			
Utah Valley State College	8	6	2	Eau Claire	12	10	2
Weber State University	12	10	2	Green Bay	9	5	4
				La Crosse	9	7	2
VIRGINIA				Madison	100	54	46
				Milwaukee	37	30	7
Christopher Newport University	12	11	1	Oshkosh	13	11	2
College of William and Mary	22	19	3	Parkside	13	9	4
Emory and Henry College	1	1	0	Platteville	7	6	1
Ferrum College	7	7	0	Stout	10	9	1
George Mason University	52	38	14	Whitewater	12	11	1
Hampton University	36	20	16				
James Madison University	27	21	6	**WYOMING**			
Longwood College	20	12	8				
Mary Washington College	19	12	7	Sheridan College	2	2	0
Norfolk State University	54	24	30	University of Wyoming	22	13	9

[1] These agencies have no resident population associated with them.

Table 80

Full-time Law Enforcement Employees as of October 31, 2002
by Suburban County by State

County by state	Total law enforcement employees	Total officers	Total civilians	County by state	Total law enforcement employees	Total officers	Total civilians
ALABAMA				**CALIFORNIA—Continued**			
Autauga	46	19	27	Santa Clara	750	558	192
Baldwin	97	72	25	Santa Cruz	272	132	140
Blount	68	39	29	Shasta	244	155	89
Calhoun	37	31	6	Solano	462	110	352
Colbert	43	28	15	Sonoma	665	245	420
Dale	19	16	3	Stanislaus	554	439	115
Elmore	70	27	43	Sutter	77	51	26
Houston	73	47	26	Tulare	609	447	162
Jefferson	636	507	129	Ventura	1,386	807	579
Lauderdale	72	31	41	Yolo	214	70	144
Lawrence	51	27	24	Yuba	158	74	84
Limestone	73	36	37				
Madison	212	103	109	**COLORADO**			
Morgan	127	46	81				
Shelby	143	92	51	Adams	424	288	136
St. Clair	37	31	6	Arapahoe	627	427	200
Tuscaloosa	195	85	110	Boulder	310	200	110
				Broomfield	174	92	82
ARIZONA				Douglas	373	243	130
				El Paso	536	364	172
Coconino	196	60	136	Jefferson	623	426	197
Maricopa	2,298	626	1,672	Larimer	354	221	133
Mohave	210	82	128	Mesa	182	103	79
Pima	1,195	464	731	Pueblo	250	142	108
Pinal	314	142	172	Weld	226	104	122
Yuma	291	64	227				
				DELAWARE			
ARKANSAS							
				New Castle County Police Department	532	335	197
Benton	158	70	88				
Craighead	32	24	8	**FLORIDA**			
Crawford	54	22	32				
Crittenden	149	31	118	Alachua	407	242	165
Faulkner	73	33	40	Bay	263	181	82
Jefferson	47	42	5	Brevard	845	415	430
Lonoke	32	18	14	Broward	4,733	1,621	3,112
Miller	38	24	14	Charlotte	352	244	108
Pulaski	503	398	105	Clay	496	268	228
Saline	61	41	20	Collier	1,056	566	490
Sebastian	126	30	96	Escambia	1,092	399	693
Washington	150	82	68	Flagler	107	75	32
				Gadsden	65	49	16
CALIFORNIA				Hernando	314	205	109
				Hillsborough	2,961	1,107	1,854
Alameda	1,560	927	633	Lake	568	233	335
Butte	235	101	134	Lee	810	464	346
Contra Costa	1,080	670	410	Leon	301	217	84
El Dorado	372	179	193	Manatee	808	386	422
Fresno	1,085	482	603	Marion	731	240	491
Kern	1,116	508	608	Martin	526	227	299
Los Angeles	14,949	8,989	5,960	Miami-Dade	4,758	3,158	1,600
Madera	107	77	30	Nassau	195	127	68
Marin	290	198	92	Okaloosa	309	233	76
Merced	231	165	66	Orange	1,928	1,312	616
Monterey	461	344	117	Osceola	411	276	135
Napa	115	84	31	Palm Beach	2,730	1,142	1,588
Orange	4,249	1,873	2,376	Pasco	618	379	239
Placer	415	225	190	Pinellas	2,738	996	1,742
Riverside	2,801	1,417	1,384	Polk	1,403	527	876
Sacramento	2,146	1,497	649	Santa Rosa	216	144	72
San Bernardino	2,733	1,558	1,175	Sarasota	924	399	525
San Diego	1,453	1,047	406	Seminole	815	326	489
San Francisco	965	830	135	St. Johns	357	207	150
San Joaquin	718	301	417	St. Lucie	491	218	273
San Luis Obispo	377	159	218	Volusia	649	434	215
San Mateo	589	426	163				
Santa Barbara	659	469	190				

Table 80

Full-time Law Enforcement Employees as of October 31, 2002

by Suburban County by State—Continued

County by state	Total law enforcement employees	Total officers	Total civilians	County by state	Total law enforcement employees	Total officers	Total civilians
GEORGIA				**ILLINOIS —Continued**			
				Peoria	193	63	130
Augusta-Richmond	697	495	202	Rock Island	153	61	92
Bartow	207	158	49	Sangamon	224	74	150
Bibb	279	240	39	St. Clair	175	163	12
Bryan	62	29	33	Tazewell	76	41	35
Catoosa	115	56	59	Will	443	260	183
Chattahoochee	9	4	5	Winnebago	266	121	145
Cherokee	258	226	32	Woodford	41	34	7
Clayton	337	136	201				
Clayton County Police Department	241	222	19	**INDIANA**			
Cobb	580	374	206				
Cobb County Police Department	666	527	139	Adams	38	16	22
Columbia	288	185	103	Allen	293	124	169
Coweta	169	90	79	Boone	53	24	29
Dade	37	20	17	Clark	93	32	61
DeKalb	679	513	166	Clay	24	11	13
DeKalb County Police Department	1,215	882	333	Clinton	54	15	39
Dougherty County Police Department	46	44	2	Dearborn	67	24	43
Douglas	257	179	78	Delaware	110	43	67
Fulton	915	631	284	Elkhart	168	63	105
Fulton County Police Department	326	245	81	Floyd	76	23	53
Gwinnett County Police Department	752	516	236	Hamilton	71	57	14
Harris	36	34	2	Hancock	70	35	35
Henry	143	68	75	Harrison	66	21	45
Henry County Police Department	168	145	23	Hendricks	104	41	63
Houston	246	99	147	Howard	115	35	80
Jones	66	33	33	Huntington	39	13	26
Lee	71	31	40	Johnson	109	47	62
Madison	39	27	12	Lake	496	173	323
McDuffie	23	17	6	Madison	119	51	68
Newton	108	69	39	Monroe	95	30	65
Paulding	180	113	67	Morgan	64	20	44
Peach	45	23	22	Ohio	8	8	0
Pickens	45	30	15	Porter	166	63	103
Rockdale	184	102	82	Posey	29	12	17
Spalding	137	84	53	Scott	21	7	14
Twiggs	31	12	19	Shelby	82	29	53
Walker	106	72	34	St. Joseph	281	130	151
Walton	134	90	44	Tippecanoe	165	46	119
				Tipton	18	9	9
IDAHO				Vanderburgh	223	105	118
				Vermillion	24	17	7
Ada	343	111	232	Vigo	99	37	62
Bannock	70	38	32	Warrick	78	55	23
Canyon	106	59	47	Wells	37	13	24
				Whitley	40	14	26
ILLINOIS							
				IOWA			
Boone	82	33	49				
Champaign	59	53	6	Black Hawk	137	105	32
Clinton	30	13	17	Dallas	36	12	24
Cook	6,276	2,409	3,867	Dubuque	54	46	8
De Kalb	79	42	37	Johnson	84	55	29
Du Page	562	453	109	Linn	177	118	59
Grundy	50	30	20	Polk	326	167	159
Henry	72	24	48	Pottawattamie	141	45	96
Jersey	19	16	3	Scott	139	42	97
Kane	151	94	57	Warren	32	22	10
Kankakee	113	58	55	Woodbury	112	35	77
Kendall	86	78	8				
Lake	416	165	251	**KANSAS**			
Macon	146	44	102				
Madison	150	72	78	Butler	68	47	21
McHenry	274	89	185	Douglas	117	75	42
McLean	67	54	13	Harvey	34	15	19
Menard	14	8	6	Johnson	498	381	117
Monroe	29	14	15	Leavenworth	98	75	23
Ogle	65	49	16				

Table 80

Full-time Law Enforcement Employees as of October 31, 2002
by Suburban County by State—Continued

County by state	Total law enforcement employees	Total officers	Total civilians	County by state	Total law enforcement employees	Total officers	Total civilians
KANSAS —Continued				**MARYLAND**			
Miami	33	20	13	Allegany	26	21	5
Sedgwick	453	167	286	Anne Arundel	100	74	26
Shawnee	148	115	33	Anne Arundel County Police			
Wyandotte	130	40	90	Department	886	655	231
				Baltimore County Police Department	2,093	1,769	324
KENTUCKY				Baltimore County Sheriff	86	66	20
				Calvert	91	77	14
Boone	126	113	13	Carroll	65	52	13
Bourbon	5	4	1	Cecil	175	65	110
Boyd	19	17	2	Charles	346	224	122
Bullitt	36	31	5	Frederick	191	148	43
Campbell	11	9	2	Harford	290	233	57
Campbell County Police Department	30	29	1	Howard	59)	35	24
Carter	7	5	2	Howard County Police Department	485	342	143
Christian	20	18	2	Montgomery	147	120	27
Christian County Police Department	8	7	1	Montgomery County Police Department	1,480	1,111	369
Clark	15	13	2	Prince George's	234	124	110
Daviess	52	38	14	Prince George's County Police			
Fayette	81	48	33	Department	1,547	1,326	221
Gallatin	5	4	1	Queen Anne's	47	44	3
Grant	21	19	2	Washington	192	71	121
Greenup	14	13	1				
Henderson	24	21	3	**MICHIGAN**			
Jefferson	263	216	47				
Jefferson County Police Department	642	484	158	Allegan	109	64	45
Jessamine	28	23	5	Bay	87	39	48
Kenton	35	32	3	Berrien	164	65	99
Kenton County Police Department	43	41	2	Calhoun	162	59	103
Madison	17	16	1	Clinton	60	26	34
Oldham	19	18	1	Eaton	130	70	60
Oldham County Police Department	32	29	3	Genesee	279	143	136
Pendleton	7	6	1	Ingham	215	120	95
Scott	31	29	2	Jackson	115	55	60
Woodford	6	6	0	Kalamazoo	191	153	38
Woodford County Police Department	19	17	2	Kent	320	167	153
				Lapeer	81	52	29
LOUISIANA				Lenawee	98	49	49
				Livingston	125	71	54
Acadia	111	89	22	Macomb	446	212	234
Ascension	253	193	60	Midland	61	35	26
Bossier	187	187	0	Monroe	209	100	109
Caddo	623	412	211	Muskegon	120	54	66
Calcasieu	726	237	489	Oakland	914	764	150
East Baton Rouge	780	647	133	Ottawa	131	119	12
Jefferson	2,559	1,666	893	Saginaw	135	84	51
Lafayette	501	370	131	St. Clair	147	69	78
Lafourche	311	169	142	Van Buren	83	42	41
Livingston	185	185	0	Washtenaw	178	137	41
Ouachita	318	318	0	Wayne	1,317	834	483
Plaquemines	208	194	14				
Rapides	403	322	81	**MINNESOTA**			
St. Bernard	349	253	96				
St. Charles	347	249	98	Anoka	195	96	99
St. James	103	73	30	Benton	59	21	38
St. John the Baptist	215	214	1	Carver	133	68	65
St. Martin	232	197	35	Chisago	65	35	30
St. Tammany	575	489	86	Clay	31	27	4
Terrebonne	318	289	29	Dakota	149	72	77
Webster	128	28	100	Hennepin	735	305	430
West Baton Rouge	163	133	30	Houston	21	11	10
				Isanti	52	17	35
MAINE				Olmsted	116	52	64
				Polk	30	25	5
Androscoggin	25	16	9	Ramsey	383	255	128
Cumberland	54	50	4	Scott	116	36	80
				Sherburne	159	47	112
				Stearns	132	52	80
				St. Louis	182	89	93

Table 80

Full-time Law Enforcement Employees as of October 31, 2002

by Suburban County by State—Continued

County by state	Total law enforcement employees	Total officers	Total civilians	County by state	Total law enforcement employees	Total officers	Total civilians
MINNESOTA—Continued				**NEW JERSEY—Continued**			
				Essex County Police Department	42	41	1
Washington	215	81	134	Gloucester	119	102	17
Wright	161	99	62	Hudson	258	198	60
				Hunterdon	33	28	5
MISSISSIPPI				Mercer	140	97	43
				Middlesex	235	195	40
Forrest	83	77	6	Monmouth	660	438	222
Harrison	341	147	194	Morris	330	245	85
Hinds	406	96	310	Ocean	193	84	109
Jackson	135	71	64	Passaic	768	590	178
Lamar	39	25	14	Salem	150	130	20
Madison	89	37	52	Somerset	213	168	45
Rankin	142	68	74	Sussex	144	122	22
				Union	178	154	24
MISSOURI				Warren	20	16	4
Andrew	14	10	4	**NEW MEXICO**			
Boone	58	46	12				
Buchanan	71	50	21	Bernalillo	313	253	60
Cass	59	47	12	Dona Ana	149	126	23
Christian	66	42	24	Sandoval	46	40	6
Clay	168	114	54	Santa Fe	95	73	22
Clinton	18	11	7	Valencia	47	37	10
Franklin	138	115	23				
Greene	215	132	83	**NEW YORK**			
Jackson	126	90	36				
Jasper	112	93	19	Albany	145	109	36
Jefferson	207	139	68	Broome	64	53	11
Lafayette	35	24	11	Cayuga	56	34	22
Lincoln	93	40	53	Chautauqua	119	81	38
Newton	57	39	18	Chemung	50	43	7
Platte	110	79	31	Dutchess	128	109	19
Ray	23	12	11	Genesee	58	40	18
St. Charles	198	136	62	Herkimer	11	6	5
St. Louis County Police Department	985	744	241	Livingston	62	45	17
Warren	53	26	27	Madison	36	29	7
Webster	25	14	11	Monroe	320	260	60
				Montgomery	38	26	12
MONTANA				Nassau	3,244	2,579	665
				Oneida	183	85	98
Cascade	111	31	80	Onondaga	291	247	44
Missoula	175	48	127	Ontario	89	58	31
Yellowstone	152	50	102	Orange	101	89	12
				Orleans	42	28	14
NEBRASKA				Oswego	78	67	11
				Putnam	97	78	19
Cass	49	25	24	Rensselaer	35	29	6
Dakota	14	12	2	Rockland	79	71	8
Douglas	184	121	63	Saratoga	103	73	30
Lancaster	88	70	18	Schenectady	14	8	6
Sarpy	173	117	56	Schoharie	25	14	11
Washington	40	21	19	Suffolk	360	240	120
				Tioga	49	36	13
NEVADA				Warren	90	67	23
				Washington	38	32	6
Nye	117	82	35	Wayne	63	51	12
Washoe	691	423	268	Westchester Public Safety	320	262	58
NEW JERSEY				**NORTH CAROLINA**			
Atlantic	116	88	28	Alamance	127	76	51
Bergen	469	389	80	Alexander	35	23	12
Bergen County Police Department	148	85	63	Brunswick	101	82	19
Burlington	83	67	16	Buncombe	309	210	99
Camden	215	187	28	Burke	102	80	22
Cape May	119	109	10	Cabarrus	150	145	5
Cumberland	58	50	8	Caldwell	102	55	47
Essex	537	451	86				

Table 80

Full-time Law Enforcement Employees as of October 31, 2002

by Suburban County by State—Continued

County by state	Total law enforcement employees	Total officers	Total civilians	County by state	Total law enforcement employees	Total officers	Total civilians
NORTH CAROLINA—Continued				**OHIO—Continued**			
Catawba	107	99	8	Montgomery	457	189	268
Chatham	68	52	16	Pickaway	79	30	49
Cumberland	456	266	190	Portage	133	53	80
Currituck	50	36	14	Richland	115	52	63
Davidson	175	120	55	Stark	240	119	121
Davie	60	30	30	Summit	476	387	89
Durham	389	141	248	Trumbull	140	54	86
Edgecombe	105	47	58	Warren	154	80	74
Forsyth	441	205	236	Washington	52	35	17
Franklin	77	38	39	Wood	118	113	5
Gaston[1]	191	99	92				
Gaston County Police Department[1]	213	136	77	**OKLAHOMA**			
Guilford	441	222	219				
Johnston	160	83	77	Canadian	59	30	29
Lincoln	131	72	59	Cleveland	97	48	49
Madison	21	13	8	Comanche	50	26	24
Mecklenburg[2]	1,182	306	876	Creek	27	23	4
Nash	118	70	48	Garfield	38	16	22
New Hanover	262	233	29	Logan	20	9	11
Onslow	143	101	42	McClain	23	10	13
Orange	129	101	28	Oklahoma	671	146	525
Pitt	244	102	142	Osage	59	32	27
Randolph	196	132	64	Pottawatomie	43	14	29
Rowan	137	96	41	Rogers	30	23	7
Stokes	56	40	16	Sequoyah	21	7	14
Union	161	125	36	Tulsa	181	156	25
Wake	514	302	212	Wagoner	20	11	9
Wayne	125	68	57				
Yadkin	54	33	21	**OREGON**			
				Benton	36	31	5
NORTH DAKOTA				Clackamas	236	192	44
				Columbia	20	17	3
Burleigh	62	36	26	Jackson	66	47	19
Cass	118	59	59	Lane	116	65	51
Grand Forks	29	23	6	Marion	94	74	20
Morton	33	20	13	Multnomah	122	97	25
				Polk	29	24	5
OHIO				Washington	254	185	69
				Yamhill	44	37	7
Allen	156	75	81				
Ashtabula	79	41	38	**PENNSYLVANIA**			
Auglaize	53	20	33				
Belmont	70	57	13	Allegheny	204	174	30
Brown	53	36	17	Allegheny County Police Department	213	189	24
Butler	314	167	147	Beaver	32	25	7
Carroll	26	19	7	Centre	12	10	2
Clark	157	132	25	Cumberland	30	25	5
Clermont	208	86	122	Lancaster	49	39	10
Columbiana	30	22	8	Washington	32	28	4
Crawford	69	20	49	York	72	61	11
Cuyahoga	1,056	172	884				
Delaware	134	74	60	**SOUTH CAROLINA**			
Fairfield	127	95	32				
Franklin	769	398	371	Aiken	137	105	32
Fulton	33	22	11	Anderson	172	134	38
Geauga	96	47	49	Berkeley	159	100	59
Greene	156	134	22	Charleston	640	245	395
Jefferson	94	33	61	Cherokee	87	39	48
Lake	180	52	128	Dorchester	102	68	34
Lawrence	38	30	8	Edgefield	47	23	24
Licking	186	129	57	Florence	218	111	107
Lorain	235	77	158	Greenville	430	351	79
Lucas	485	304	181	Horry	203	51	152
Madison	30	25	5	Horry County Police Department	215	194	21
Mahoning	240	230	10	Lexington	379	219	160
Medina	163	71	92	Pickens	117	82	35
Miami	140	50	90				

Table 80

Full-time Law Enforcement Employees as of October 31, 2002

by Suburban County by State—Continued

County by state	Total law enforcement employees	Total officers	Total civilians	County by state	Total law enforcement employees	Total officers	Total civilians
SOUTH CAROLINA—Continued				**TEXAS—Continued**			
				Harris	3,434	2,543	891
Richland	563	437	126	Harrison	88	38	50
Spartanburg	303	279	24	Hays	231	93	138
Sumter	113	106	7	Henderson	94	60	34
York	263	117	146	Hidalgo	494	203	291
				Hood	76	27	49
SOUTH DAKOTA				Hunt	85	31	54
				Jefferson	403	97	306
Lincoln	9	8	1	Johnson	178	69	109
Minnehaha	129	70	59	Kaufman	96	37	59
Pennington	151	57	94	Liberty	61	42	19
				Lubbock	235	134	101
TENNESSEE				McLennan	276	112	164
				Midland	173	77	96
Anderson	102	42	60	Montgomery	410	270	140
Blount	258	219	39	Nueces	312	98	214
Carter	63	57	6	Orange	135	60	75
Cheatham	60	26	34	Parker	102	54	48
Chester	22	10	12	Potter	191	106	85
Dickson	103	45	58	Randall	133	62	71
Fayette	55	32	23	Rockwall	86	25	61
Hamilton	377	149	228	San Patricio	86	40	46
Hawkins	55	52	3	Smith	266	106	160
Knox	683	399	284	Tarrant	1,163	460	703
Loudon	60	59	1	Taylor	162	71	91
Madison	198	191	7	Tom Green	148	37	111
Marion	32	17	15	Travis	1,359	633	726
Montgomery	207	193	14	Upshur	62	27	35
Robertson	89	75	14	Victoria	166	100	66
Rutherford	313	128	185	Waller	50	23	27
Sevier	121	75	46	Webb	264	162	102
Shelby	2,588	538	2,050	Wichita	161	38	123
Shelby County Police Department	39	30	9	Williamson	292	169	123
Sullivan	127	99	28	Wilson	68	24	44
Sumner	139	69	70				
Tipton	39	35	4	**UTAH**			
Unicoi	37	22	15				
Union	31	18	13	Davis	237	184	53
Washington	174	76	98	Kane	21	14	7
Williamson	94	82	12	Salt Lake	1,230	392	838
Wilson	137	131	6	Utah	269	195	74
				Weber	364	272	92
TEXAS							
				VERMONT			
Archer	12	7	5				
Bastrop	132	47	85	Chittenden	12	8	4
Bell	234	89	145	Grand Isle	4	3	1
Bexar	1,581	444	1,137				
Bowie	49	44	5	**VIRGINIA**			
Brazoria	265	116	149				
Brazos	166	73	93	Albemarle County Police Department	122	99	23
Caldwell	79	27	52	Amherst	68	63	5
Cameron	259	102	157	Arlington County Police Department	482	343	139
Chambers	67	31	36	Bedford	72	71	1
Collin	433	120	313	Botetourt	80	63	17
Comal	210	93	117	Campbell	55	52	3
Coryell	52	19	33	Charles City	18	11	7
Dallas	1,623	426	1,197	Chesterfield County Police Department	507	411	96
Denton	434	133	301	Clarke	22	13	9
Ector	189	83	106	Culpeper	76	60	16
Ellis	160	61	99	Dinwiddie	58	47	11
El Paso	1,016	236	780	Fairfax County Police Department	1,702	1,258	444
Fort Bend	443	275	168	Fauquier	111	94	17
Galveston	317	224	93	Fluvanna	30	21	9
Grayson	124	60	64	Gloucester	88	73	15
Gregg	144	69	75	Goochland	32	25	7
Guadalupe	159	44	115	Greene	20	14	6
Hardin	64	35	29				

Table 80

Full-time Law Enforcement Employees as of October 31, 2002
by Suburban County by State—Continued

County by state	Total law enforcement employees	Total officers	Total civilians	County by state	Total law enforcement employees	Total officers	Total civilians
VIRGINIA—Continued				**WEST VIRGINIA—Continued**			
Hanover	189	173	16	Jefferson	17	15	2
Henrico County Police Department	744	541	203	Jefferson-Kearneysville State Police	20	13	7
Isle of Wight	31	25	6	Kanawha	84	66	18
James City County Police Department	71	68	3	Kanawha State Police:			
King George	38	23	15	Parkway Authority	7	7	0
Loudoun	392	326	66	Quincy	7	6	1
Mathews	18	11	7	South Charleston	31	21	10
New Kent	33	23	10	Marshall	26	24	2
Pittsylvania	124	65	59	Marshall-Moundsville State Police	14	5	9
Powhatan	45	31	14	Mineral	13	8	5
Prince George County Police				Mineral-Keyser State Police	5	4	1
Department	56	44	12	Ohio	27	26	1
Prince William County Police				Ohio-Wheeling State Police	6	5	1
Department	531	423	108	Putnam	38	34	4
Roanoke County Police Department	149	112	37	Putnam State Police:			
Scott	40	39	1	Teays Valley	5	4	1
Spotsylvania	102	96	6	Winfield	4	3	1
Stafford	122	107	15	Wayne	35	22	13
Warren	67	66	1	Wayne-Wayne State Police	9	8	1
Washington	87	71	16	Wood	64	37	27
York	88	83	5	Wood-Parkersburg State Police	16	9	7
WASHINGTON				**WISCONSIN**			
Benton	72	52	20	Brown	304	140	164
Clark	194	129	65	Calumet	44	23	21
Franklin	24	21	3	Chippewa	64	52	12
Island	42	36	6	Douglas	51	47	4
King	807	516	291	Eau Claire	95	49	46
Kitsap	154	122	32	Kenosha	315	107	208
Pierce	298	241	57	La Crosse	102	36	66
Snohomish	316	235	81	Marathon	171	62	109
Spokane	282	226	56	Milwaukee	990	676	314
Thurston	115	90	25	Outagamie	207	76	131
Whatcom	86	73	13	Ozaukee	103	77	26
Yakima	101	67	34	Pierce	48	44	4
				Rock	183	92	91
WEST VIRGINIA				Sheboygan	168	75	93
				St. Croix	73	39	34
Berkeley	50	41	9	Washington	155	63	92
Berkeley-Martinsburg State Police	22	18	4	Waukesha	309	151	158
Brooke	23	16	7	Winnebago	181	125	56
Brooke-Wellsburg State Police	4	3	1				
Cabell	104	38	66	**WYOMING**			
Cabell-Huntington State Police	16	11	5				
Hancock	37	25	12	Laramie	77	45	32
Hancock-New Cumberland State Police	4	3	1	Natrona	51	42	9

[1] The data are listed separately for both Gaston County and Gaston County Police Department. North Carolina. However, Gaston County reports its crime figures combined with those of the Gaston County Police Department; they can be found in Table 10 under Gaston County Police Department.

[2] The data in this table are provided for Mecklenburg County, North Carolina, only. However, Mecklenburg County reports its crime figures combined with those of the Charlotte Police Department; they can be found in Table 8 under Charlotte-Mecklenburg.

Table 81

Full-time Law Enforcement Employees as of October 31, 2002
by Rural County by State

County by state	Total law enforcement employees	Total officers	Total civilians
ALABAMA			
Barbour	29	12	17
Bibb	13	11	2
Bullock	5	5	0
Butler	21	9	12
Chambers	54	18	36
Choctaw	13	5	8
Cleburne	18	7	11
Coffee	42	15	27
Coosa	17	8	9
Covington	48	24	24
Crenshaw	10	10	0
Dallas	51	26	25
Escambia	46	19	27
Franklin	40	20	20
Geneva	12	10	2
Greene	20	9	11
Hale	9	6	3
Henry	12	8	4
Jackson	72	32	40
Lowndes	38	11	27
Macon	35	19	16
Marengo	29	11	18
Marion	24	11	13
Marshall	82	38	44
Monroe	45	22	23
Perry	17	9	8
Pickens	20	7	13
Pike	28	16	12
Randolph	11	11	0
Tallapoosa	52	22	30
Walker	75	30	45
Washington	15	8	7
Wilcox	18	7	11
Winston	22	9	13
ARIZONA			
Apache	75	37	38
Cochise	164	73	91
Gila	114	46	68
Graham	50	20	30
Greenlee	26	12	14
La Paz	89	33	56
Navajo	125	58	67
Santa Cruz	69	38	31
Yavapai	293	108	185
ARKANSAS			
Arkansas	46	12	34
Ashley	26	14	12
Baxter	42	28	14
Boone	34	21	13
Bradley	5	4	1
Calhoun	12	6	6
Carroll	34	17	17
Chicot	7	6	1
Clark	27	11	16
Clay	19	8	11
Cleburne	26	15	11
Cleveland	11	6	5
Columbia	29	14	15
Conway	30	12	18
Cross	34	14	20
Dallas	27	6	21
Desha	9	7	2
Drew	11	10	1
Franklin	16	10	6
ARKANSAS—Continued			
Fulton	11	6	5
Garland	112	39	73
Grant	10	8	2
Greene	42	11	31
Hempstead	38	14	24
Hot Spring	33	29	4
Howard	20	9	11
Independence	75	49	26
Izard	23	18	5
Jackson	21	11	10
Johnson	28	11	17
Lafayette	13	7	6
Lawrence	18	9	9
Lee	6	5	1
Lincoln	18	7	11
Little River	22	8	14
Logan	25	12	13
Madison	14	7	7
Marion	18	10	8
Mississippi	86	26	60
Monroe	15	7	8
Montgomery	16	8	8
Nevada	17	6	11
Newton	11	7	4
Ouachita	32	14	18
Perry	16	7	9
Phillips	9	7	2
Pike	12	6	6
Poinsett	42	13	29
Polk	22	10	12
Pope	74	29	45
Prairie	14	7	7
Randolph	12	10	2
Scott	14	7	7
Searcy	12	5	7
Sevier	20	11	9
Sharp	16	9	7
St. Francis	36	15	21
Stone	19	8	11
Union	55	24	31
Van Buren	27	14	13
White	79	32	47
Woodruff	13	6	7
Yell	21	12	9
CALIFORNIA			
Alpine	18	14	4
Amador	89	48	41
Calaveras	95	56	39
Colusa	63	35	28
Del Norte	59	30	29
Glenn	66	29	37
Humboldt	234	84	150
Imperial	276	187	89
Inyo	70	39	31
Kings	203	82	121
Lake	159	61	98
Lassen	93	71	22
Mariposa	66	53	13
Mendocino	165	130	35
Modoc	27	16	11
Mono	47	25	22
Nevada	194	71	123
Plumas	74	41	33
San Benito	63	32	31
Sierra	17	11	6
Siskiyou	131	60	71

Table 81

Full-time Law Enforcement Employees as of October 31, 2002
by Rural County by State—Continued

County by state	Total law enforcement employees	Total officers	Total civilians	County by state	Total law enforcement employees	Total officers	Total civilians
CALIFORNIA—Continued				**FLORIDA—Continued**			
Tehama	112	83	29	Franklin	84	66	18
Trinity	33	26	7	Gilchrist	38	24	14
Tuolumne	131	67	64	Glades	52	26	26
				Gulf	54	30	24
COLORADO				Hamilton	53	15	38
				Hardee	88	39	49
Alamosa	34	23	11	Hendry	124	93	31
Archuleta	34	13	21	Highlands	230	106	124
Baca	9	3	6	Holmes	19	15	4
Bent	19	6	13	Indian River	394	180	214
Chaffee	39	15	24	Jackson	67	48	19
Cheyenne	8	5	3	Jefferson	43	18	25
Clear Creek	44	20	24	Lafayette	8	7	1
Conejos	14	7	7	Levy	132	66	66
Costilla	15	8	7	Liberty	24	13	11
Crowley	12	8	4	Madison	64	53	11
Custer	21	10	11	Monroe	489	223	266
Delta	44	18	26	Okeechobee	164	74	90
Dolores	7	4	3	Putnam	147	100	47
Eagle	84	71	13	Sumter	142	76	66
Elbert	37	27	10	Suwannee	90	51	39
Fremont	79	57	22	Taylor	46	33	13
Garfield	85	23	62	Union	18	14	4
Gilpin	34	25	9	Wakulla	75	51	24
Grand	57	34	23	Walton	168	128	40
Gunnison	27	12	15	Washington	62	29	33
Hinsdale	5	4	1				
Huerfano	21	9	12	**GEORGIA**			
Jackson	8	5	3				
Kiowa	4	3	1	Atkinson	15	7	8
Kit Carson	19	6	13	Bacon	17	7	10
Lake	15	8	7	Baker	3	3	0
La Plata	101	78	23	Banks	29	20	9
Las Animas	41	13	28	Ben Hill	38	20	18
Lincoln	17	5	12	Bleckley	22	11	11
Logan	41	23	18	Brantley	19	12	7
Mineral	4	3	1	Brooks	29	18	11
Moffat	37	34	3	Bulloch	67	37	30
Montezuma	52	23	29	Butts	53	34	19
Montrose	104	73	31	Candler	16	6	10
Morgan	55	41	14	Charlton	23	11	12
Otero	22	22	0	Chattooga	44	25	19
Ouray	7	6	1	Clinch	20	9	11
Park	66	45	21	Coffee	79	35	44
Phillips	3	3	0	Colquitt	81	41	40
Pitkin	41	22	19	Cook	47	20	27
Prowers	31	11	20	Crawford	18	11	7
Rio Blanco	20	14	6	Crisp	64	46	18
Rio Grande	23	8	15	Dawson	69	46	23
Routt	46	27	19	Decatur	31	27	4
Saguache	17	8	9	Dodge	28	18	10
San Juan	5	4	1	Early	49	24	25
San Miguel	35	31	4	Echols	8	7	1
Sedgwick	9	4	5	Elbert	25	23	2
Summit	52	45	7	Emanuel	34	15	19
Teller	74	38	36	Evans	16	8	8
Washington	36	10	26	Fannin	29	28	1
Yuma	16	7	9	Floyd County Police Department	79	72	7
				Franklin	43	24	19
FLORIDA				Glynn County Police Department	121	107	14
				Greene	45	31	14
Baker	77	54	23	Greene County Police Department	45	29	16
Bradford	30	19	11	Habersham	48	28	20
Calhoun	23	14	9	Hall	325	213	112
Citrus	283	172	111	Hancock	34	13	21
Columbia	167	122	45	Haralson	37	22	15
DeSoto	85	66	19	Hart	26	23	3
Dixie	54	18	36	Jackson	74	48	26

Table 81

Full-time Law Enforcement Employees as of October 31, 2002

by Rural County by State—Continued

County by state	Total law enforcement employees	Total officers	Total civilians	County by state	Total law enforcement employees	Total officers	Total civilians
GEORGIA—Continued				**IDAHO—Continued**			
Jeff Davis	21	18	3	Gem	21	11	10
Jenkins	8	4	4	Gooding	15	9	6
Johnson	12	9	3	Idaho	29	20	9
Lamar	41	22	19	Jefferson	26	15	11
Laurens	91	52	39	Jerome	17	14	3
Liberty	86	58	28	Kootenai	109	73	36
Lincoln	26	8	18	Latah	39	27	12
Lumpkin	64	40	24	Lewis	11	6	5
Marion	12	5	7	Lincoln	6	5	1
Meriwether	31	17	14	Minidoka	22	14	8
Murray	61	29	32	Nez Perce	36	23	13
Pierce	30	12	18	Oneida	12	8	4
Pike	25	19	6	Owyhee	20	12	8
Polk	57	16	41	Payette	28	16	12
Polk County Police Department	37	34	3	Power	14	9	5
Pulaski	20	11	9	Shoshone	33	19	14
Putnam	54	25	29	Teton	11	7	4
Quitman	4	3	1	Twin Falls	62	39	23
Rabun	19	18	1	Valley	26	14	12
Schley	8	3	5	Washington	17	9	8
Screven	22	20	2				
Seminole	19	11	8	**ILLINOIS**			
Stephens	30	24	6				
Stewart	4	4	0	Adams	27	24	3
Talbot	10	5	5	Alexander	7	6	1
Tattnall	31	15	16	Bond	18	9	9
Taylor	20	11	9	Brown	6	5	1
Thomas	67	63	4	Bureau	39	23	16
Tift	112	105	7	Calhoun	8	4	4
Towns	26	12	14	Carroll	23	9	14
Troup	104	54	50	Cass	7	6	1
Turner	27	11	16	Christian	29	16	13
Upson	58	31	27	Clark	13	8	5
Ware	92	32	60	Clay	13	7	6
Ware County Police Department	14	1	13	Coles	48	25	23
Warren	4	4	0	Crawford	21	9	12
Webster	7	4	3	Cumberland	18	8	10
Wheeler	8	3	5	De Witt	29	16	13
White	50	31	19	Douglas	23	9	14
Wilkes	24	23	1	Edgar	19	9	10
Worth	32	21	11	Edwards	9	4	5
				Effingham	43	21	22
HAWAII				Fayette	24	10	14
				Ford	27	9	18
Hawaii Police Department	515	385	130	Franklin	43	17	26
Kauai Police Department	160	123	37	Fulton	43	21	22
Maui Police Department	423	318	105	Gallatin	4	4	0
				Greene	13	6	7
IDAHO				Hamilton	8	4	4
				Hancock	20	10	10
Adams	12	8	4	Hardin	3	3	0
Bear Lake	11	5	6	Henderson	14	9	5
Benewah	16	8	8	Iroquois	27	16	11
Bingham	47	32	15	Jackson	67	22	45
Blaine	32	18	14	Jasper	19	9	10
Boise	17	11	6	Jefferson	45	24	21
Bonner	84	47	37	Jo Daviess	36	18	18
Bonneville	76	51	25	Johnson	12	6	6
Boundary	19	10	9	Knox	55	21	34
Butte	14	7	7	La Salle	74	57	17
Camas	5	3	2	Lawrence	13	7	6
Caribou	15	8	7	Lee	42	23	19
Cassia	50	33	17	Livingston	57	28	29
Clark	7	3	4	Logan	37	20	17
Clearwater	25	16	9	Macoupin	56	39	17
Custer	11	7	4	Marion	38	14	24
Elmore	31	20	11	Marshall	17	8	9
Fremont	22	10	12	Mason	20	9	11

Table 81

Full-time Law Enforcement Employees as of October 31, 2002
by Rural County by State—Continued

County by state	Total law enforcement employees	Total officers	Total civilians
ILLINOIS—Continued			
Massac	29	11	18
McDonough	25	14	11
Mercer	23	11	12
Montgomery	23	13	10
Morgan	38	15	23
Moultrie	19	10	9
Perry	32	10	22
Piatt	25	10	15
Pike	25	10	15
Pope	10	5	5
Pulaski	18	13	5
Putnam	10	5	5
Randolph	20	10	10
Richland	21	8	13
Saline	40	10	30
Schuyler	9	3	6
Scott	8	4	4
Shelby	24	12	12
Stark	13	4	9
Stephenson	38	28	10
Union	14	8	6
Vermilion	78	33	45
Wabash	9	4	5
Warren	19	11	8
Washington	18	6	12
Wayne	17	8	9
White	7	7	0
Whiteside	56	24	32
Williamson	64	35	29
INDIANA			
Bartholomew	66	37	29
Benton	19	6	13
Blackford	28	9	19
Brown	33	13	20
Crawford	12	7	5
Daviess	32	14	18
Decatur	26	8	18
Dubois	31	15	16
Fayette	38	35	3
Fountain	18	8	10
Fulton	18	10	8
Gibson	40	16	24
Grant	147	46	101
Greene	35	13	22
Henry	58	29	29
Jackson	52	14	38
Jasper	41	19	22
Jay	34	10	24
Jefferson	29	12	17
Jennings	39	14	25
Knox	27	26	1
Kosciusko	75	32	43
LaGrange	52	17	35
La Porte	134	57	77
Lawrence	58	25	33
Marshall	47	20	27
Martin	18	8	10
Miami	31	15	16
Montgomery	37	17	20
Newton	39	14	25
Noble	69	19	50
Orange	29	8	21
Owen	30	11	19
Parke	36	9	27
Perry	13	6	7
Pulaski	41	11	30

County by state	Total law enforcement employees	Total officers	Total civilians
INDIANA—Continued			
Putnam	34	13	21
Randolph	41	15	26
Ripley	10	10	0
Rush	23	10	13
Spencer	49	13	36
Starke	26	12	14
Steuben	57	20	37
Sullivan	34	10	24
Switzerland	10	8	2
Union	11	7	4
Wabash	35	15	20
Warren	20	7	13
Washington	26	14	12
Wayne	89'	30	59
IOWA			
Adair	8	6	2
Adams	9	5	4
Allamakee	14	8	6
Appanoose	16	9	7
Audubon	9	5	4
Boone	20	10	10
Bremer	23	11	12
Buchanan	28	13	15
Buena Vista	17	10	7
Butler	17	11	6
Calhoun	11	7	4
Carroll	14	10	4
Cass	9	6	3
Cedar	34	9	25
Cerro Gordo	50	17	33
Cherokee	15	5	10
Chickasaw	12	8	4
Clarke	19	5	14
Clay	15	9	6
Clayton	21	11	10
Clinton	48	31	17
Crawford	12	10	2
Davis	6	5	1
Decatur	10	5	5
Delaware	11	10	1
Des Moines	25	20	5
Dickinson	18	9	9
Emmet	14	8	6
Fayette	31	11	20
Floyd	18	10	8
Franklin	9	6	3
Fremont	19	7	12
Greene	13	8	5
Grundy	15	11	4
Guthrie	10	5	5
Hamilton	11	9	2
Hancock	9	7	2
Hardin	31	10	21
Harrison	21	9	12
Henry	24	11	13
Howard	13	6	7
Humboldt	12	9	3
Ida	16	8	8
Iowa	16	11	5
Jackson	11	9	2
Jasper	36	13	23
Jefferson	26	7	19
Jones	23	10	13
Keokuk	8	4	4
Kossuth	23	8	15
Lee	28	13	15

Table 81

Full-time Law Enforcement Employees as of October 31, 2002
by Rural County by State—Continued

County by state	Total law enforcement employees	Total officers	Total civilians
IOWA—Continued			
Louisa	19	9	10
Lucas	12	5	7
Lyon	21	9	12
Madison	15	6	9
Mahaska	25	10	15
Marion	21	11	10
Marshall	56	18	38
Mills	28	10	18
Mitchell	15	6	9
Monona	20	8	12
Monroe	12	5	7
Montgomery	21	8	13
Muscatine	65	22	43
O'Brien	27	11	16
Osceola	15	10	5
Page	12	7	5
Palo Alto	16	8	8
Plymouth	19	9	10
Pocahontas	13	7	6
Poweshiek	17	10	7
Ringgold	11	6	5
Sac	13	7	6
Shelby	14	8	6
Sioux	23	14	9
Story	77	33	44
Tama	21	13	8
Taylor	10	6	4
Union	12	5	7
Van Buren	10	5	5
Wapello	40	9	31
Washington	30	13	17
Wayne	10	5	5
Webster	33	17	16
Winnebago	12	5	7
Winneshiek	17	8	9
Worth	15	6	9
Wright	18	6	12
KANSAS			
Allen	13	6	7
Anderson	16	10	6
Atchison	22	10	12
Barber	8	3	5
Barton	31	16	15
Bourbon	8	6	2
Brown	22	9	13
Chase	5	5	0
Chautauqua	9	4	5
Cherokee	35	22	13
Cheyenne	4	3	1
Clark	9	4	5
Clay	14	6	8
Cloud	15	9	6
Coffey	29	13	16
Comanche	4	4	0
Cowley	37	14	23
Crawford	65	31	34
Decatur	7	3	4
Dickinson	25	15	10
Doniphan	10	4	6
Edwards	8	4	4
Elk	7	3	4
Ellis	24	16	8
Ellsworth	15	8	7
Finney	95	41	54
Ford	46	22	24
Franklin	41	20	21

County by state	Total law enforcement employees	Total officers	Total civilians
KANSAS—Continued			
Geary	56	23	33
Gove	5	4	1
Graham	7	3	4
Grant	15	6	9
Gray	11	5	6
Greeley	6	2	4
Greenwood	20	11	9
Hamilton	14	7	7
Harper	18	6	12
Haskell	16	11	5
Hodgeman	9	4	5
Jackson	41	17	24
Jefferson	42	23	19
Jewell	8	4	4
Kearny	19	10	9
Kingman	16	7	9
Kiowa	15	15	0
Labette	36	18	18
Lane	7	4	3
Lincoln	12	7	5
Linn	24	13	11
Logan	4	3	1
Lyon	67	15	52
Marion	9	7	2
Marshall	16	7	9
McPherson	36	15	21
Meade	17	17	0
Mitchell	11	9	2
Montgomery	28	18	10
Morris	12	7	5
Morton	10	6	4
Nemaha	17	8	9
Neosho	28	13	15
Ness	11	6	5
Norton	9	4	5
Osage	36	18	18
Osborne	12	9	3
Ottawa	20	5	15
Pawnee	15	7	8
Phillips	14	9	5
Pottawatomie	34	20	14
Pratt	13	8	5
Rawlins	8	3	5
Reno	67	55	12
Republic	9	4	5
Rice	10	9	1
Riley County Police Department	161	92	69
Rooks	6	6	0
Rush	9	4	5
Russell	17	10	7
Saline	94	38	56
Scott	5	4	1
Seward	45	11	34
Sheridan	6	3	3
Sherman	10	4	6
Smith	8	4	4
Stafford	10	4	6
Stanton	13	5	8
Stevens	12	6	6
Sumner	26	17	9
Thomas	10	8	2
Trego	4	3	1
Wabaunsee	13	7	6
Wallace	2	1	1
Washington	5	5	0
Wichita	9	4	5
Wilson	23	10	13
Woodson	10	6	4

Table 81

Full-time Law Enforcement Employees as of October 31, 2002
by Rural County by State—Continued

County by state	Total law enforcement employees	Total officers	Total civilians	County by state	Total law enforcement employees	Total officers	Total civilians
KENTUCKY				**KENTUCKY—Continued**			
Adair	5	4	1	Metcalfe	4	2	2
Allen	10	9	1	Monroe	7	6	1
Anderson	8	7	1	Montgomery	18	16	2
Anderson County Police Department	2	2	0	Morgan	5	4	1
Ballard	11	11	0	Muhlenberg	11	11	0
Barren	16	13	3	Nelson	26	21	5
Bath	6	3	3	Nicholas	4	3	1
Bell	16	9	7	Ohio	18	16	2
Boyle	8	7	1	Owen	6	4	2
Bracken	3	2	1	Owsley	3	2	1
Breathitt	5	4	1	Perry	15	15	0
Breckinridge	7	7	0	Pike	30	19	11
Butler	8	6	2	Powell	10	9	1
Caldwell	8	6	2	Pulaski	32	24	8
Calloway	22	21	1	Robertson	1	1	0
Carlisle	3	3	0	Rockcastle	6	5	1
Carroll	5	5	0	Rowan	13	10	3
Casey	6	5	1	Russell	11	10	1
Clay	6	4	2	Shelby	18	17	1
Clinton	5	4	1	Simpson	12	12	0
Crittenden	3	2	1	Spencer	5	4	1
Cumberland	5	4	1	Taylor	14	12	2
Edmonson	7	5	2	Todd	4	3	1
Elliott	4	4	0	Trigg	6	6	0
Estill	4	3	1	Trimble	3	3	0
Fleming	6	6	0	Union	9	8	1
Floyd	20	12	8	Warren	56	48	8
Franklin	14	14	0	Washington	4	4	0
Fulton	4	4	0	Wayne	7	6	1
Garrard	6	5	1	Webster	7	6	1
Graves	13	11	2	Whitley	7	4	3
Grayson	11	8	3	Wolfe	5	4	1
Green	3	2	1				
Hancock	7	6	1	**LOUISIANA**			
Hardin	31	29	2				
Harlan	18	18	0	Allen	45	29	16
Harrison	8	8	0	Assumption	79	41	38
Hart	7	7	0	Beauregard	71	54	17
Henry	6	6	0	Bienville	41	38	3
Hickman	3	3	0	Caldwell	21	21	0
Hopkins	9	7	2	Cameron	76	66	10
Jackson	9	7	2	Catahoula	91	32	59
Johnson	13	9	4	Claiborne	92	20	72
Knott	9	7	2	Concordia	203	202	1
Knox	8	6	2	De Soto	82	74	8
Larue	6	5	1	East Carroll	179	166	13
Laurel	34	30	4	East Feliciana	62	44	18
Lawrence	6	4	2	Evangeline	59	25	34
Lee	3	2	1	Franklin	75	75	0
Leslie	7	4	3	Grant	48	48	0
Letcher	7	6	1	Iberia	226	118	108
Lewis	7	5	2	Iberville	148	86	62
Lincoln	7	6	1	Jackson	32	32	0
Livingston	7	7	0	Jefferson Davis	43	30	13
Logan	16	15	1	La Salle	48	43	5
Lyon	4	4	0	Lincoln	50	50	0
Magoffin	6	4	2	Madison	57	57	0
Marion	7	6	1	Morehouse	153	153	0
Marshall	18	16	2	Natchitoches	59	51	8
Martin	6	4	2	Pointe Coupee	108	39	69
Mason	12	10	2	Red River	47	40	7
McCracken	32	31	1	Richland	123	110	13
McCracken County Police Department	2	1	1	Sabine	67	65	2
McCreary	8	7	1	St. Helena	53	23	30
McLean	6	5	1	St. Mary	150	111	39
Meade	9	7	2	Tangipahoa	277	277	0
Menifee	3	3	0	Tensas	135	22	113
Mercer	8	8	0	Union	56	37	19

Table 81

Full-time Law Enforcement Employees as of October 31, 2002
by Rural County by State—Continued

County by state	Total law enforcement employees	Total officers	Total civilians
LOUISIANA—Continued			
Vermilion	99	54	45
Vernon	131	131	0
Washington	104	104	0
West Carroll	19	19	0
West Feliciana	75	72	3
Winn	26	26	0
MAINE			
Aroostook	19	14	5
Franklin	26	15	11
Hancock	44	13	31
Kennebec	30	20	10
Knox	20	18	2
Lincoln	22	19	3
Oxford	14	12	2
Penobscot	23	20	3
Piscataquis	15	7	8
Sagadahoc	17	15	2
Somerset	17	15	2
Waldo	16	14	2
Washington	22	12	10
York	31	27	4
MARYLAND			
Caroline	27	23	4
Dorchester	32	26	6
Garrett	41	19	22
Kent	22	20	2
Somerset	20	17	3
St. Mary's	201	104	97
Talbot	22	20	2
Wicomico	103	80	23
Worcester	48	41	7
MICHIGAN			
Alcona	25	14	11
Alger	13	9	4
Alpena	30	16	14
Antrim	49	20	29
Arenac	24	15	9
Baraga	6	6	0
Barry	34	31	3
Benzie	42	15	27
Branch	46	24	22
Cass	76	41	35
Charlevoix	34	16	18
Cheboygan	35	18	17
Chippewa	18	14	4
Clare	27	23	4
Crawford	27	15	12
Delta	32	15	17
Dickinson	33	17	16
Emmet	24	21	3
Gladwin	31	20	11
Gogebic	21	15	6
Grand Traverse	118	64	54
Gratiot	36	19	17
Hillsdale	43	28	15
Houghton	30	19	11
Huron	24	23	1
Ionia	58	20	38
Iosco	25	5	20
Iron	9	8	1
Isabella	52	25	27
Kalkaska	42	25	17

County by state	Total law enforcement employees	Total officers	Total civilians
MICHIGAN—Continued			
Keweenaw	6	6	0
Lake	55	17	38
Leelanau	38	18	20
Luce	4	3	1
Mackinac	9	7	2
Manistee	30	15	15
Marquette	57	30	27
Mason	41	21	20
Mecosta	48	25	23
Menominee	30	14	16
Missaukee	26	13	13
Montcalm	76	28	48
Montmorency	13	10	3
Newaygo	29	26	3
Oceana	34	19	15
Ogemaw	36	16	20
Ontonagon	14	10	4
Osceola	22	19	3
Oscoda	16	11	5
Otsego	27	14	13
Presque Isle	26	14	12
Roscommon	24	24	0
Sanilac	54	23	31
Schoolcraft	12	5	7
Shiawassee	67	33	34
St. Joseph	53	26	27
Tuscola	47	29	18
Wexford	50	25	25
MINNESOTA			
Aitkin	48	18	30
Becker	47	21	26
Beltrami	66	25	41
Big Stone	7	4	3
Blue Earth	54	22	32
Brown	35	9	26
Carlton	43	23	20
Cass	51	29	22
Chippewa	16	7	9
Clearwater	18	7	11
Cook	17	12	5
Cottonwood	17	6	11
Crow Wing	88	35	53
Dodge	29	20	9
Douglas	65	22	43
Faribault	20	9	11
Fillmore	31	18	13
Freeborn	41	20	21
Goodhue	102	39	63
Grant	10	5	5
Hubbard	28	13	15
Itasca	66	65	1
Jackson	18	7	11
Kanabec	23	11	12
Kandiyohi	104	33	71
Kittson	10	5	5
Koochiching	18	10	8
Lac Qui Parle	9	6	3
Lake	28	14	14
Lake of the Woods	10	5	5
Le Sueur	28	14	14
Lincoln	10	4	6
Lyon	37	13	24
Mahnomen	15	10	5
Marshall	18	11	7
Martin	29	10	19
McLeod	58	21	37

Table 81

Full-time Law Enforcement Employees as of October 31, 2002
by Rural County by State—Continued

County by state	Total law enforcement employees	Total officers	Total civilians
MINNESOTA—Continued			
Meeker	34	14	20
Mille Lacs	56	19	38
Morrison	48	15	33
Mower	47	20	27
Murray	9	4	5
Nicollet	23	10	13
Nobles	32	9	23
Norman	8	5	3
Otter Tail	70	29	41
Pennington	32	7	25
Pine	47	26	21
Pipestone	20	10	10
Pope	14	6	8
Red Lake	11	6	5
Redwood	17	9	8
Renville	16	9	7
Rice	45	19	26
Rock	16	11	5
Roseau	14	9	5
Sibley	21	9	12
Steele	22	16	6
Stevens	11	6	5
Swift	15	7	8
Todd	26	14	12
Traverse	7	5	2
Wabasha	27	15	12
Wadena	16	6	10
Waseca	24	11	13
Watonwan	21	9	12
Wilkin	8	6	2
Winona	49	19	30
Yellow Medicine	19	7	12
MISSISSIPPI			
Adams	52	50	2
Alcorn	25	13	12
Attala	12	7	5
Benton	12	6	6
Calhoun	10	5	5
Chickasaw	16	16	0
Claiborne	21	9	12
Clarke	27	13	14
Clay	22	12	10
Coahoma	18	17	1
Covington	14	8	6
Greene	15	7	8
Grenada	14	12	2
Holmes	47	9	38
Issaquena	4	4	0
Itawamba	19	10	9
Jasper	20	6	14
Lauderdale	130	46	84
Lawrence	22	10	12
Lee	127	44	83
Leflore	58	23	35
Lincoln	49	41	8
Lowndes	49	41	8
Marion	26	26	0
Marshall	37	18	19
Monroe	27	20	7
Montgomery	7	6	1
Noxubee	8	4	4
Oktibbeha	21	19	2
Panola	47	16	31
Pearl River	70	40	30
Perry	15	6	9
Pike	49	25	24
MISSISSIPPI—Continued			
Pontotoc	17	14	3
Quitman	12	11	1
Scott	56	17	39
Sharkey	10	5	5
Simpson	17	16	1
Smith	14	8	6
Stone	15	13	2
Sunflower	29	7	22
Tallahatchie	27	11	16
Tate	37	16	21
Tippah	22	8	14
Tishomingo	22	14	8
Union	40	30	10
Walthall	23	19	4
Warren	29	23	6
Washington	53	31	22
Wayne	20	5	15
Webster	9	6	3
Wilkinson	15	8	7
Winston	7	6	1
Yalobusha	12	7	5
Yazoo	13	10	3
MISSOURI			
Adair	28	9	19
Atchison	8	4	4
Audrain	35	26	9
Barry	32	19	13
Barton	15	7	8
Bates	13	8	5
Benton	21	14	7
Bollinger	11	6	5
Butler	48	32	16
Caldwell	12	7	5
Callaway	22	20	2
Camden	94	47	47
Cape Girardeau	62	39	23
Carroll	14	6	8
Carter	10	5	5
Cedar	19	13	6
Chariton	13	10	3
Clark	17	8	9
Cole	43	33	10
Cooper	8	7	1
Crawford	24	18	6
Dade	11	6	5
Dallas	16	13	3
Daviess	5	4	1
De Kalb	9	5	4
Dent	11	7	4
Douglas	13	9	4
Dunklin	24	8	16
Gasconade	9	8	1
Gentry	10	6	4
Grundy	10	5	5
Harrison	4	4	0
Henry	22	11	11
Hickory	13	9	4
Holt	7	4	3
Howard	11	6	5
Howell	37	31	6
Iron	14	7	7
Johnson	61	39	22
Knox	5	2	3
Laclede	27	15	12
Lawrence	25	18	7
Lewis	9	4	5

Table 81

Full-time Law Enforcement Employees as of October 31, 2002
by Rural County by State—Continued

County by state	Total law enforcement employees	Total officers	Total civilians	County by state	Total law enforcement employees	Total officers	Total civilians
MISSOURI—Continued				**MONTANA—Continued**			
Linn	6	5	1	Golden Valley	2	2	0
Livingston	19	10	9	Granite	9	5	4
Macon	13	11	2	Hill	24	11	13
Madison	10	7	3	Jefferson	21	11	10
Maries	8	6	2	Judith Basin	5	4	1
Marion	37	14	23	Lake	44	20	24
McDonald	17	14	3	Lewis and Clark	66	40	26
Mercer	8	3	5	Liberty	10	4	6
Miller	24	20	4	Lincoln	35	19	16
Mississippi	7	7	0	Madison	10	7	3
Moniteau	8	5	3	McCone	6	3	3
Monroe	14	9	5	Meagher	8	4	4
Montgomery	13	12	1	Mineral	18	7	11
Morgan	32	17	15	Musselshell	9	7	2
New Madrid	27	20	7	Park	20	11	9
Nodaway	23	9	14	Petroleum	1	1	0
Oregon	10	5	5	Phillips	11	7	4
Osage	7	6	1	Pondera	10	8	2
Ozark	18	6	12	Powder River	7	3	4
Pemiscot	51	23	28	Powell	19	11	8
Perry	28	18	10	Prairie	3	3	0
Pettis	31	18	13	Ravalli	75	30	45
Phelps	31	24	7	Richland	19	7	12
Pike	26	11	15	Roosevelt	15	9	6
Polk	30	21	9	Rosebud	35	17	18
Pulaski	20	18	2	Sanders	19	7	12
Putnam	6	3	3	Sheridan	10	5	5
Ralls	7	6	1	Silver Bow	77	43	34
Randolph	33	20	13	Stillwater	11	7	4
Reynolds	12	7	5	Sweet Grass	13	7	6
Ripley	9	7	2	Teton	12	9	3
Saline	30	18	12	Toole	20	12	8
Schuyler	5	4	1	Treasure	2	2	0
Scotland	6	3	3	Valley	15	4	11
Shannon	9	5	4	Wheatland	9	5	4
Shelby	9	5	4	Wibaux	2	2	0
St. Clair	60	15	45				
Ste. Genevieve	45	34	11	**NEBRASKA**			
St. Francois	60	51	9				
Stone	45	36	9	Adams	19	17	2
Sullivan	6	5	1	Antelope	11	6	5
Taney	60	29	31	Arthur	1	1	0
Texas	9	4	5	Banner	1	1	0
Vernon	21	8	13	Blaine	1	1	0
Washington	30	16	14	Boone	9	3	6
Wayne	16	8	8	Box Butte	20	6	14
Worth	3	2	1	Boyd	4	4	0
Wright	13	5	8	Brown	10	5	5
				Buffalo	40	22	18
MONTANA				Burt	11	6	5
				Butler	9	5	4
Beaverhead	17	7	10	Cedar	9	4	5
Big Horn	28	13	15	Chase	8	3	5
Blaine	19	8	11	Cherry	11	5	6
Broadwater	11	7	4	Cheyenne	8	7	1
Carbon	10	6	4	Clay	9	4	5
Carter	2	2	0	Colfax	10	5	5
Chouteau	14	9	5	Cuming	6	5	1
Custer	12	6	6	Custer	7	6	1
Daniels	7	3	4	Dawes	8	3	5
Dawson	58	6	52	Dawson	24	16	8
Deer Lodge	28	20	8	Deuel	5	4	1
Fallon	8	2	6	Dixon	12	7	5
Fergus	19	9	10	Dodge	24	17	7
Flathead	102	46	56	Dundy	9	5	4
Gallatin	67	38	29	Fillmore	11	5	6
Garfield	3	3	0	Franklin	3	3	0
Glacier	18	12	6	Frontier	8	5	3

Table 81

Full-time Law Enforcement Employees as of October 31, 2002
by Rural County by State—Continued

County by state	Total law enforcement employees	Total officers	Total civilians	County by state	Total law enforcement employees	Total officers	Total civilians
NEBRASKA—Continued				**NEVADA—Continued**			
Furnas	13	8	5	Lincoln	19	17	2
Gage	13	11	2	Lyon	93	66	27
Garden	9	4	5	Mineral	22	16	6
Garfield	2	2	0	Pershing	19	12	7
Gosper	5	4	1	Storey	19	18	1
Grant	1	1	0	White Pine	32	26	6
Greeley	3	2	1				
Hall	36	29	7	**NEW HAMPSHIRE**			
Hamilton	14	7	7				
Harlan	8	4	4	Cheshire	22	9	13
Hitchcock	7	4	3	Merrimack	27	17	10
Holt	11	5	6				
Hooker	1	1	0	**NEW MEXICO**			
Howard	12	6	6				
Jefferson	6	5	1	Catron	10	6	4
Johnson	6	2	4	Chaves	54	36	18
Kearney	12	7	5	Cibola	20	13	7
Keith	9	8	1	Colfax	8	6	2
Keya Paha	2	1	1	Curry	18	15	3
Kimball	9	3	6	De Baca	17	5	12
Knox	12	5	7	Eddy	53	39	14
Lincoln	45	24	21	Grant	24	22	2
Logan	1	1	0	Guadalupe	5	4	1
Loup	1	1	0	Harding	2	2	0
Madison	47	22	25	Hidalgo	23	7	16
McPherson	1	1	0	Lea	58	42	16
Merrick	9	4	5	Lincoln	26	17	9
Morrill	8	3	5	Luna	31	27	4
Nance	8	7	1	McKinley	42	31	11
Nemaha	8	5	3	Mora	7	4	3
Nuckolls	7	4	3	Otero	36	30	6
Otoe	20	11	9	Quay	7	7	0
Pawnee	4	3	1	Rio Arriba	22	19	3
Perkins	9	5	4	Roosevelt	13	10	3
Phelps	15	7	8	San Juan	105	86	19
Pierce	8	4	4	San Miguel	13	10	3
Platte	34	16	18	Sierra	16	14	2
Polk	12	8	4	Socorro	14	13	1
Red Willow	7	5	2	Taos	21	16	5
Richardson	12	7	5	Torrance	22	20	2
Rock	8	3	5	Union	4	3	1
Saline	12	10	2				
Saunders	18	11	7	**NEW YORK**			
Scotts Bluff	24	14	10				
Seward	21	11	10	Allegany	48	37	11
Sheridan	5	4	1	Chenango	22	22	0
Sherman	6	5	1	Clinton	37	24	13
Stanton	8	7	1	Columbia	54	44	10
Thayer	10	6	4	Cortland	48	31	17
Thomas	1	1	0	Delaware	22	14	8
Thurston	10	5	5	Essex	29	28	1
Valley	4	1	3	Franklin	17	13	4
Wayne	5	4	1	Fulton	52	35	17
Webster	8	5	3	Greene	26	24	2
Wheeler	2	2	0	Jefferson	61	33	28
York	22	9	13	Lewis	28	19	9
				Otsego	20	17	3
NEVADA				Schuyler	40	36	4
				Seneca	42	26	16
Carson City	127	91	36	Steuben	54	41	13
Churchill	44	37	7	St. Lawrence	40	36	4
Douglas	110	95	15	Sullivan	47	37	10
Elko	62	51	11	Tompkins	43	38	5
Esmeralda	16	11	5	Ulster	75	71	4
Eureka	16	13	3	Wyoming	43	32	11
Humboldt	46	20	26	Yates	42	23	19
Lander	32	21	11				

Table 81

Full-time Law Enforcement Employees as of October 31, 2002

by Rural County by State—Continued

County by state	Total law enforcement employees	Total officers	Total civilians	County by state	Total law enforcement employees	Total officers	Total civilians
NORTH CAROLINA				**NORTH DAKOTA**			
Alleghany	25	10	15	Adams	3	3	0
Anson	49	29	20	Barnes	7	6	1
Ashe	32	16	16	Benson	4	4	0
Avery	28	20	8	Billings	4	3	1
Beaufort	73	47	26	Bottineau	13	9	4
Bertie	26	19	7	Bowman	2	2	0
Bladen	67	42	25	Burke	4	4	0
Camden	13	12	1	Cavalier	11	5	6
Carteret	81	41	40	Dickey	6	5	1
Caswell	44	28	16	Divide	2	2	0
Cherokee	28	20	8	Dunn	4	3	1
Chowan	36	17	19	Eddy	5	5	0
Clay	17	10	7	Emmons	3	3	0
Cleveland	119	80	39	Foster	3	2	1
Columbus	86	53	33	Golden Valley	5	4	1
Craven	115	60	55	Grant	2	2	0
Dare	127	54	73	Griggs	4	4	0
Duplin	77	49	28	Hettinger	4	4	0
Gates	17	11	6	Kidder	2	1	1
Graham	12	11	1	Lamoure	5	4	1
Granville	68	38	30	Logan	3	2	1
Greene	28	22	6	McHenry	6	5	1
Halifax	72	49	23	McIntosh	3	3	0
Harnett	117	71	46	McKenzie	12	5	7
Haywood	69	47	22	McLean	23	19	4
Henderson	152	119	33	Mercer	19	7	12
Hertford	63	24	39	Nelson	5	4	1
Hoke	34	19	15	Oliver	3	2	1
Hyde	14	9	5	Pembina	14	8	6
Iredell	169	123	46	Pierce	7	3	4
Jackson	42	36	6	Ramsey	7	6	1
Jones	15	10	5	Ransom	5	5	0
Lee	69	34	35	Renville	4	4	0
Lenoir	80	48	32	Richland	22	13	9
Macon	51	36	15	Rolette	12	9	3
Martin	31	28	3	Slope	1	1	0
McDowell	55	37	18	Stark	13	10	3
Mitchell	15	13	2	Stutsman	10	8	2
Montgomery	49	29	20	Towner	3	2	1
Moore	102	60	42	Traill	7	4	3
Northampton	41	16	25	Walsh	18	12	6
Pamlico	26	13	13	Ward	42	20	22
Pasquotank	39	34	5	Wells	4	3	1
Pender	70	39	31	Williams	29	22	7
Perquimans	10	9	1				
Person	64	37	27	**OHIO**			
Polk	32	19	13				
Richmond	67	42	25	Adams	33	25	8
Robeson	212	102	110	Ashland	76	56	20
Rockingham	121	89	32	Athens	26	21	5
Rutherford	100	69	31	Champaign	33	27	6
Sampson	75	48	27	Clinton	67	39	28
Scotland	56	33	23	Coshocton	65	52	13
Stanly	55	36	19	Darke	72	40	32
Surry	89	51	38	Defiance	32	20	12
Swain	25	13	12	Erie	74	37	37
Transylvania	57	41	16	Fayette	42	31	11
Tyrrell	12	7	5	Guernsey	47	20	27
Vance	81	38	43	Hancock	93	39	54
Warren	30	22	8	Hardin	26	19	7
Washington	30	13	17	Harrison	20	15	5
Watauga	50	29	21	Henry	22	22	0
Wilkes	93	57	36	Highland	55	55	0
Wilson	114	66	48	Hocking	20	19	1
Yancey	23	14	9	Holmes	48	45	3
				Huron	77	28	49
				Jackson	45	16	29
				Knox	67	52	15

Table 81

Full-time Law Enforcement Employees as of October 31, 2002
by Rural County by State—Continued

County by state	Total law enforcement employees	Total officers	Total civilians	County by state	Total law enforcement employees	Total officers	Total civilians
OHIO—Continued				**OKLAHOMA—Continued**			
Logan	84	36	48	Mayes	37	17	20
Marion	39	28	11	McCurtain	26	21	5
Meigs	8	7	1	McIntosh	20	13	7
Mercer	43	30	13	Murray	11	4	7
Monroe	28	23	5	Muskogee	26	21	5
Morgan	16	11	5	Noble	10	5	5
Morrow	58	21	37	Nowata	20	14	6
Muskingum	118	84	34	Okfuskee	13	5	8
Noble	30	7	23	Okmulgee	14	11	3
Ottawa	60	57	3	Ottawa	36	16	20
Paulding	25	11	14	Pawnee	19	10	9
Perry	18	12	6	Payne	42	36	6
Pike	21	18	3	Pittsburg	30	21	9
Preble	72	22	50	Pontotoc	16	9	7
Putnam	40	31	9	Pushmataha	17	7	10
Sandusky	62	45	17	Roger Mills	13	8	5
Scioto	65	51	14	Seminole	29	24	5
Seneca	67	20	47	Stephens	20	10	10
Shelby	68	33	35	Texas	36	9	27
Tuscarawas	101	30	71	Tillman	14	4	10
Union	63	39	24	Washington	35	17	18
Van Wert	39	18	21	Washita	13	7	6
Vinton	16	15	1	Woods	5	5	0
Wayne	82	70	12	Woodward	17	9	8
Williams	24	21	3				
Wyandot	21	10	11	**OREGON**			
				Baker	22	11	11
OKLAHOMA				Clatsop	29	25	4
				Coos	52	32	20
Adair	17	12	5	Crook	18	13	5
Alfalfa	9	4	5	Curry	23	15	8
Atoka	9	5	4	Deschutes	86	69	17
Beaver	13	8	5	Douglas	105	70	35
Beckham	16	8	8	Gilliam	5	4	1
Blaine	10	6	4	Grant	6	5	1
Bryan	28	14	14	Harney	5	5	0
Caddo	28	15	13	Hood River	20	18	2
Carter	55	18	37	Jefferson	25	16	9
Cherokee	32	20	12	Josephine	74	40	34
Choctaw	19	7	12	Klamath	37	30	7
Cimarron	7	4	3	Lake	8	7	1
Coal	9	6	3	Lincoln	28	26	2
Cotton	13	8	5	Linn	93	61	32
Craig	19	10	9	Malheur	26	16	10
Custer	25	12	13	Morrow	28	15	13
Delaware	31	12	19	Sherman	5	4	1
Dewey	10	4	6	Tillamook	26	24	2
Ellis	10	3	7	Umatilla	28	15	13
Garvin	22	19	3	Union	11	9	2
Grady	56	16	40	Wallowa	14	8	6
Grant	9	5	4	Wasco	19	17	2
Greer	7	3	4	Wheeler	5	3	2
Harmon	3	3	0				
Harper	12	4	8	**PENNSYLVANIA**			
Haskell	12	7	5				
Hughes	11	6	5	Bradford	9	7	2
Jackson	18	9	9	Clarion	10	7	3
Jefferson	10	5	5	Clearfield	10	8	2
Johnston	13	7	6	Elk	6	5	1
Kay	28	14	14	Huntingdon	6	5	1
Kingfisher	14	6	8	Jefferson	6	6	0
Kiowa	12	8	4	Warren	50	21	29
Latimer	13	10	3				
Le Flore	23	12	11	**SOUTH CAROLINA**			
Lincoln	20	10	10				
Love	19	6	13	Abbeville	50	23	27
Major	9	3	6	Allendale	11	10	1
Marshall	14	5	9				

Table 81

Full-time Law Enforcement Employees as of October 31, 2002
by Rural County by State—Continued

County by state	Total law enforcement employees	Total officers	Total civilians	County by state	Total law enforcement employees	Total officers	Total civilians
SOUTH CAROLINA—Continued				**SOUTH DAKOTA—Continued**			
Bamberg	13	11	2	Meade	48	15	33
Barnwell	36	23	13	Mellette	5	4	1
Beaufort	196	175	21	Miner	4	3	1
Calhoun	21	19	2	Moody	10	5	5
Chesterfield	54	34	20	Perkins	3	2	1
Clarendon	30	25	5	Potter	6	2	4
Darlington	67	61	6	Roberts	9	3	6
Dillon	69	30	39	Sanborn	3	2	1
Fairfield	50	48	2	Spink	15	8	7
Georgetown	130	77	53	Stanley	6	5	1
Greenwood	102	64	38	Sully	3	3	0
Hampton	49	27	22	Todd	1	1	0
Jasper	32	28	4	Tripp	3	2	1
Kershaw	54	47	7	Turner	5	4	1
Lancaster	101	61	40	Union	19	6	13
Laurens	98	56	42	Walworth	10	2	8
Lee	26	23	3	Yankton	10	9	1
Marion	35	31	4	Ziebach	2	2	0
Newberry	82	39	43				
Saluda	53	21	32	**TENNESSEE**			
Union	46	29	17				
				Bedford	73	26	47
SOUTH DAKOTA				Benton	39	16	23
				Bledsoe	15	10	5
Aurora	4	3	1	Bradley	89	81	8
Beadle	20	6	14	Campbell	44	37	7
Bennett	10	6	4	Cannon	32	12	20
Bon Homme	8	4	4	Carroll	29	15	14
Brookings	20	11	9	Claiborne	40	38	2
Brown	48	16	32	Clay	22	12	10
Brule	11	3	8	Cocke	65	34	31
Buffalo	1	1	0	Coffee	62	58	4
Butte	6	5	1	Crockett	29	12	17
Campbell	2	2	0	Cumberland	81	38	43
Charles Mix	10	4	6	Decatur	16	10	6
Clark	2	2	0	DeKalb	36	17	19
Clay	10	6	4	Dyer	53	27	26
Codington	9	6	3	Fentress	22	13	9
Corson	3	2	1	Franklin	56	31	25
Custer	10	9	1	Gibson	40	32	8
Davison	6	4	2	Giles	54	20	34
Day	6	3	3	Grainger	24	15	9
Deuel	8	4	4	Greene	145	60	85
Dewey	3	2	1	Grundy	18	9	9
Douglas	2	2	0	Hamblen	61	60	1
Edmunds	6	4	2	Hancock	27	18	9
Fall River	14	5	9	Hardeman	42	21	21
Faulk	8	3	5	Hardin	29	13	16
Grant	4	3	1	Hartsville-Trousdale	29	16	13
Gregory	3	2	1	Haywood	31	13	18
Haakon	2	2	0	Henderson	24	21	3
Hamlin	2	2	0	Henry	64	28	36
Hand	3	2	1	Hickman	31	18	13
Hanson	1	1	0	Houston	19	8	11
Harding	1	1	0	Humphreys	23	12	11
Hughes	22	7	15	Jackson	21	13	8
Hutchinson	3	3	0	Jefferson	47	28	19
Hyde	1	1	0	Johnson	32	16	16
Jackson	1	1	0	Lake	19	8	11
Jerauld	2	2	0	Lauderdale	49	19	30
Jones	2	2	0	Lawrence	48	34	14
Kingsbury	5	4	1	Lewis	31	14	17
Lake	9	4	5	Lincoln	54	21	33
Lawrence	36	14	22	Macon	56	21	35
Lyman	4	3	1	Marshall	44	19	25
Marshall	9	4	5	Maury	111	60	51
McCook	4	3	1	McMinn	65	38	27
McPherson	1	1	0	McNairy	28	14	14

Table 81

Full-time Law Enforcement Employees as of October 31, 2002
by Rural County by State—Continued

County by state	Total law enforcement employees	Total officers	Total civilians	County by state	Total law enforcement employees	Total officers	Total civilians
TENNESSEE—Continued				**TEXAS—Continued**			
Meigs	23	12	11	Deaf Smith	37	13	24
Monroe	46	43	3	Delta	17	10	7
Moore	21	12	9	Dewitt	25	10	15
Morgan	32	14	18	Dickens	6	2	4
Obion	56	22	34	Dimmit	21	10	11
Overton	51	18	33	Donley	8	5	3
Perry	17	11	6	Duval	32	19	13
Pickett	12	12	0	Eastland	25	8	17
Polk	35	17	18	Edwards	9	4	5
Putnam	104	49	55	Erath	42	20	22
Rhea	46	46	0	Falls	14	9	5
Roane	51	28	23	Fannin	39	15	24
Scott	44	31	13	Fayette	37	18	19
Sequatchie	18	11	7	Fisher	9	5	4
Smith	35	19	16	Floyd	11	3	8
Stewart	26	12	14	Foard	4	3	1
Van Buren	13	7	6	Franklin	19	9	10
Warren	72	37	35	Freestone	30	17	13
Wayne	21	10	11	Frio	20	11	9
Weakley	38	18	20	Gaines	19	9	10
White	47	22	25	Garza	14	8	6
				Gillespie	32	18	14
TEXAS				Glasscock	3	3	0
				Goliad	24	12	12
Anderson	53	27	26	Gonzales	45	16	29
Andrews	31	11	20	Gray	38	14	24
Angelina	91	44	47	Grimes	43	24	19
Aransas	50	22	28	Hale	49	48	1
Armstrong	7	3	4	Hall	9	3	6
Atascosa	72	27	45	Hamilton	21	9	12
Austin	42	22	20	Hansford	9	4	5
Bailey	8	4	4	Hardeman	10	5	5
Bandera	34	21	13	Hartley	4	4	0
Baylor	11	3	8	Haskell	8	2	6
Bee	33	16	17	Hemphill	13	7	6
Blanco	16	9	7	Hill	43	19	24
Borden	3	2	1	Hockley	23	9	14
Bosque	21	10	11	Hopkins	51	25	26
Brewster	23	9	14	Houston	26	13	13
Briscoe	3	2	1	Howard	30	14	16
Brooks	30	12	18	Hudspeth	22	12	10
Brown	50	21	29	Hutchinson	30	12	18
Burleson	27	15	12	Irion	8	4	4
Burnet	69	32	37	Jack	14	9	5
Calhoun	40	23	17	Jackson	25	12	13
Callahan	12	8	4	Jasper	33	17	16
Camp	17	6	11	Jeff Davis	4	3	1
Carson	13	6	7	Jim Hogg	40	22	18
Cass	35	13	22	Jim Wells	54	34	20
Castro	18	6	12	Jones	17	6	11
Cherokee	52	25	27	Karnes	16	8	8
Childress	12	4	8	Kendall	43	29	14
Clay	19	11	8	Kenedy	11	10	1
Cochran	13	8	5	Kent	4	2	2
Coke	6	5	1	Kerr	90	44	46
Coleman	11	5	6	Kimble	12	7	5
Collingsworth	9	5	4	King	1	1	0
Colorado	40	18	22	Kinney	16	7	9
Comanche	33	9	24	Kleberg	69	25	44
Concho	9	4	5	Knox	7	4	3
Cooke	48	21	27	Lamar	70	23	47
Cottle	2	2	0	Lamb	29	12	17
Crane	11	8	3	Lampasas	32	20	12
Crockett	18	13	5	La Salle	20	15	5
Crosby	12	6	6	Lavaca	22	11	11
Culberson	13	7	6	Lee	16	10	6
Dallam	10	4	6	Leon	33	15	18
Dawson	17	6	11	Limestone	54	19	35

County by state	Total law enforcement employees	Total officers	Total civilians	County by state	Total law enforcement employees	Total officers	Total civilians
TEXAS—Continued				**TEXAS—Continued**			
Lipscomb	9	5	4	Walker	62	30	32
Live Oak	23	12	11	Ward	32	12	20
Llano	39	20	19	Washington	56	31	25
Loving	3	2	1	Wharton	61	37	24
Lynn	18	6	12	Wheeler	10	6	4
Madison	23	8	15	Wilbarger	16	7	9
Marion	17	11	6	Willacy	34	17	17
Martin	7	3	4	Winkler	28	9	19
Mason	10	5	5	Wise	91	46	45
Matagorda	70	36	34	Wood	62	26	36
Maverick	76	33	43	Yoakum	20	10	10
McCulloch	9	5	4	Young	34	14	20
McMullen	3	3	0	Zapata	97	32	65
Medina	53	19	34				
Menard	9	5	4	**UTAH**			
Milam	23	11	12				
Mills	8	5	3	Beaver	40	13	27
Mitchell	11	5	6	Box Elder	72	28	44
Montague	20	8	12	Cache	95	77	18
Moore	39	13	26	Carbon	39	17	22
Morris	20	9	11	Daggett	26	6	20
Motley	2	2	0	Duchesne	39	15	24
Navarro	110	62	48	Emery	36	24	12
Newton	17	10	7	Garfield	26	7	19
Nolan	24	11	13	Grand	28	20	8
Ochiltree	17	7	10	Iron	59	48	11
Oldham	10	5	5	Juab	18	7	11
Palo Pinto	48	19	29	Millard	48	30	18
Panola	36	19	17	Morgan	12	11	1
Parmer	13	5	8	Piute	3	3	0
Pecos	25	15	10	Rich	9	3	6
Polk	69	43	26	San Juan	33	28	5
Presidio	25	6	19	Sanpete	24	19	5
Rains	20	8	12	Sevier	61	51	10
Reagan	15	9	6	Summit	73	38	35
Real	7	3	4	Tooele	67	48	19
Red River	27	12	15	Uintah	46	37	9
Reeves	498	12	486	Wasatch	38	18	20
Refugio	34	13	21	Washington	136	61	75
Roberts	5	4	1	Wayne	6	5	1
Robertson	23	9	14				
Runnels	26	7	19	**VERMONT**			
Rusk	57	35	22				
Sabine	18	8	10	Bennington	17	12	5
San Jacinto	29	13	16	Franklin	19	11	8
San Saba	9	4	5	Lamoille	15	7	8
Schleicher	10	5	5	Orleans	7	4	3
Scurry	23	9	14	Rutland	31	26	5
Shackelford	12	3	9	Washington	12	10	2
Shelby	29	11	18				
Sherman	8	3	5	**VIRGINIA**			
Somervell	41	20	21				
Starr	90	28	62	Accomack	62	53	9
Stephens	11	5	6	Alleghany	53	42	11
Sterling	3	3	0	Amelia	19	12	7
Stonewall	7	3	4	Appomattox	33	30	3
Sutton	13	4	9	Augusta	120	58	62
Swisher	9	7	2	Bath	17	17	0
Terrell	5	3	2	Bland	15	8	7
Terry	41	7	34	Brunswick	41	18	23
Throckmorton	7	3	4	Buchanan	48	37	11
Titus	52	23	29	Buckingham	21	16	5
Trinity	16	11	5	Caroline	41	32	9
Tyler	27	20	7	Carroll	33	27	6
Upton	17	9	8	Charlotte	30	28	2
Uvalde	28	15	13	Craig	13	8	5
Val Verde	47	32	15	Cumberland	16	11	5
Van Zandt	63	22	41	Dickenson	40	31	9

Table 81

Full-time Law Enforcement Employees as of October 31, 2002
by Rural County by State—Continued

County by state	Total law enforcement employees	Total officers	Total civilians
VIRGINIA—Continued			
Essex	13	13	0
Floyd	27	17	10
Franklin	88	73	15
Frederick	99	85	14
Giles	28	18	10
Grayson	26	20	6
Greensville	30	21	9
Halifax	48	36	12
Henry	119	106	13
Highland	12	7	5
King and Queen	15	8	7
King William	27	16	11
Lancaster	31	25	6
Lee	46	46	0
Louisa	47	34	13
Lunenburg	21	14	7
Madison	22	12	10
Mecklenburg	35	31	4
Middlesex	18	12	6
Montgomery	107	92	15
Nelson	20	14	6
Northampton	46	36	10
Northumberland	26	17	9
Nottoway	21	14	7
Orange	35	28	7
Page	48	41	7
Patrick	44	30	14
Prince Edward	25	25	0
Pulaski	51	41	10
Rappahannock	21	21	0
Richmond	16	10	6
Rockbridge	29	22	7
Rockingham	156	49	107
Russell	57	47	10
Shenandoah	62	54	8
Smyth	54	54	0
Southampton	74	62	12
Surry	15	10	5
Sussex	39	35	4
Tazewell	86	76	10
Westmoreland	30	21	9
Wise	85	72	13
Wythe	34	27	7
WASHINGTON			
Adams	23	15	8
Asotin	14	12	2
Chelan	67	49	18
Clallam	50	37	13
Columbia	13	8	5
Cowlitz	52	42	10
Douglas	42	28	14
Ferry	24	9	15
Garfield	13	7	6
Grant	58	43	15
Grays Harbor	80	40	40
Jefferson	27	22	5
Kittitas	33	29	4
Klickitat	43	15	28
Lewis	57	40	17
Lincoln	26	15	11
Mason	56	43	13
Okanogan	37	32	5
Pacific	20	16	4
Pend Oreille	31	11	20
San Juan	26	16	10
Skagit	102	53	49
WASHINGTON—Continued			
Skamania	25	21	4
Stevens	35	30	5
Wahkiakum	8	7	1
Walla Walla	25	22	3
Whitman	32	17	15
WEST VIRGINIA			
Barbour	8	3	5
Barbour-Philippi State Police	5	4	1
Boone	24	22	2
Boone State Police:			
Danville	6	5	1
Whitesville	5	4	1
Braxton	12	11	1
Braxton-Sutton State Police	6	5	1
Calhoun	2	2	0
Calhoun-Grantsville State Police	4	3	1
Clay	7	6	1
Clay-Clay State Police	7	6	1
Doddridge	2	2	0
Doddridge-West Union State Police	4	3	1
Fayette	36	32	4
Fayette State Police:			
Gauley Bridge	4	3	1
Oak Hill	10	9	1
Parkway Authority	9	9	0
Gilmer	5	5	0
Gilmer-Glenville State Police	5	4	1
Grant	6	6	0
Grant-Petersburg State Police	1	1	0
Greenbrier	23	21	2
Greenbrier State Police:			
Lewisburg	8	7	1
Rainelle	4	3	1
Hampshire	10	8	2
Hampshire-Romney State Police	19	7	12
Hardy	9	6	3
Hardy-Moorefield State Police	5	4	1
Harrison	37	35	2
Harrison-Bridgeport State Police	16	15	1
Jackson	18	13	5
Jackson-Ripley State Police	5	4	1
Lewis	11	9	2
Lewis-Weston State Police	6	5	1
Lincoln	7	7	0
Lincoln-Hamlin State Police	8	7	1
Logan	19	13	6
Logan-Logan State Police	19	12	7
Marion	35	25	10
Marion-Fairmont State Police	7	6	1
Mason	28	17	11
Mason-Point Pleasant State Police	5	4	1
McDowell	17	15	2
McDowell-Welch State Police	8	7	1
Mercer	31	24	7
Mercer State Police:			
Parkway Authority	6	6	0
Princeton	13	10	3
Mingo	19	17	2
Mingo State Police:			
Gilbert	4	3	1
Williamson	5	4	1
Monongalia	50	28	22
Monongalia-Morgantown State Police	24	15	9
Monroe	6	6	0
Monroe-Union State Police	4	3	1
Morgan	9	8	1

Table 81

Full-time Law Enforcement Employees as of October 31, 2002
by Rural County by State—Continued

County by state	Total law enforcement employees	Total officers	Total civilians	County by state	Total law enforcement employees	Total officers	Total civilians
WEST VIRGINIA—Continued				**WISCONSIN—Continued**			
Morgan-Berkeley Springs State Police	5	4	1	Green Lake	42	18	24
Nicholas	24	19	5	Iowa	32	20	12
Nicholas State Police:				Iron	20	20	0
Richwood	4	3	1	Jefferson	120	97	23
Summersville	4	3	1	Juneau	52	41	11
Pendleton	3	3	0	Kewaunee	38	36	2
Pendleton-Franklin State Police	5	4	1	Lafayette	23	14	9
Pleasants	7	6	1	Langlade	41	17	24
Pleasants-St. Marys State Police	4	3	1	Lincoln	48	28	20
Pocahontas	17	6	11	Manitowoc	103	61	42
Pocahontas-Buckeye State Police	6	5	1	Marinette	59	30	29
Preston	29	14	15	Marquette	37	37	0
Preston-Kingwood State Police	7	6	1	Menominee	7	6	1
Raleigh	50	39	11	Monroe	51	48	3
Raleigh State Police:				Oconto	55	23	32
Beckley	20	12	8	Pepin	16	10	6
Parkway Authority	10	9	1	Portage	85	43	42
Randolph	7	7	0	Price	32	20	12
Randolph-Elkins State Police	23	15	8	Sauk	116	87	29
Ritchie	7	6	1	Shawano	83	38	45
Ritchie-Harrisville State Police	4	3	1	Taylor	36	17	19
Roane	8	7	1	Trempealeau	45	23	22
Roane-Spencer State Police	6	5	1	Vernon	26	26	0
Summers	5	4	1	Vilas	69	34	35
Summers-Hinton State Police	5	4	1	Walworth	211	82	129
Taylor	19	6	13	Washburn	27	13	14
Taylor-Grafton State Police	3	2	1	Wood	78	44	34
Tucker	5	4	1				
Tucker-Parsons State Police	4	3	1	**WYOMING**			
Tyler	9	4	5				
Tyler-Paden City State Police	4	3	1	Albany	26	20	6
Upshur	8	8	0	Big Horn	15	8	7
Upshur-Buckhannon State Police	8	7	1	Campbell	57	37	20
Webster	4	4	0	Carbon	36	15	21
Webster-Upperglade State Police	5	4	1	Converse	17	10	7
Wetzel	8	8	0	Crook	17	5	12
Wetzel-Hundred State Police	4	3	1	Fremont	93	28	65
Wirt	3	2	1	Goshen	8	7	1
Wirt-Elizabeth State Police	4	3	1	Hot Springs	5	3	2
Wyoming	18	17	1	Johnson	9	8	1
Wyoming-Jesse State Police	4	3	1	Lincoln	35	15	20
				Niobrara	15	4	11
WISCONSIN				Park	41	18	23
				Platte	10	9	1
Adams	52	52	0	Sheridan	23	17	6
Ashland	25	25	0	Sublette	39	23	16
Barron	7	7	0	Sweetwater	50	31	19
Bayfield	34	21	13	Teton	42	22	20
Buffalo	21	10	11	Uinta	37	24	13
Burnett	30	15	15	Washakie	7	6	1
Clark	51	46	5	Weston	9	7	2
Columbia	74	38	36				
Crawford	27	26	1	**OTHER AGENCIES**			
Dodge	149	48	101				
Door	56	42	14	American Samoa	250	200	50
Dunn	51	23	28	Guam	331	273	58
Florence	10	10	0	Puerto Rico	19,274	17,297	1,977
Fond du Lac	117	53	64	Virgin Islands	631	459	172
Forest	37	35	2				
Grant	45	24	21	National Institutes of Health	117	57	60
Green	49	38	11				

Table 82

Full-time Law Enforcement Employees as of October 31, 2002
by Other Agencies by State

Other agency by state	Total law enforcement employees	Total officers	Total civilians	Other agency by state	Total law enforcement employees	Total officers	Total civilians
ALABAMA				**ILLINOIS—Continued**			
				Lake County Forest Preserve	9	9	0
City of Montgomery, Housing Authority, Investigative Unit	7	6	1	Springfield Park District	8	8	0
Huntsville International Airport	24	19	5	Will County Forest Preserve	12	11	1
Marshall County Drug Enforcement	7	6	1				
				INDIANA			
ALASKA							
				St. Joseph County Airport Authority	16	16	0
Anchorage International Airport	65	63	2				
Fairbanks International Airport	27	26	1	**KANSAS**			
CALIFORNIA				Johnson County Park	15	14	1
				Metropolitan Topeka Airport Authority	25	19	6
East Bay Regional Parks, Alameda County	65	51	14	Shawnee Mission Public Schools	10	10	0
Fontana Unified School District	22	13	9	Topeka Fire Department, Arson Investigation	1	1	0
Grant Joint Union High School	23	20	3	Unified School District:			
Monterey Peninsula Airport	5	5	0	Goddard	4	4	0
Port of San Diego Harbor	147	127	20	Maize	5	3	2
San Bernardino Unified School District	75	22	53	Wyandotte County Parks and Recreation	9	9	0
San Francisco Bay Area Rapid Transit, Contra Costa County	258	180	78				
Stockton Unified School District	18	18	0	**KENTUCKY**			
DISTRICT OF COLUMBIA				Buffalo Trace-Gateway Narcotics Task Force	4	4	0
				Cincinnati-Northern Kentucky International Airport	60	43	17
Metro Transit Police	457	347	110	Fayette County Schools	30	26	4
National Zoological Park	21	21	0	FIVCO Area Drug Task Force	6	5	1
				Jefferson County Board of Education	24	18	6
FLORIDA				Land Between The Lakes	9	9	0
				Lexington Bluegrass Airport	28	20	8
Florida School for the Deaf and Blind	15	9	6	Northern Kentucky Narcotics Enforcement	3	1	2
Fort Lauderdale Airport	139	88	51	Pennyrile Narcotics Task Force	9	9	0
Jacksonville Airport Authority	33	32	1				
Lee County Port Authority	47	32	15	**MAINE**			
Melbourne International Airport	12	11	1				
Miami-Dade County Public Schools	204	177	27	Penobscot Indian Island	18	7	11
Miccosukee Tribal	51	38	13				
Palm Beach County School District	207	134	73	**MICHIGAN**			
Pinellas County Schools	21	16	5				
Sarasota-Bradenton International Airport	16	16	0	Bishop International Airport	6	6	0
Seminole Tribal	79	55	24	Capitol Region Airport Authority	25	21	4
Tampa International Airport	138	64	74	Hudson Mills Metropark	8	8	0
Volusia County Beach Management	72	62	10	Kensington Metropark	8	7	1
				Lower Huron Metropark	7	7	0
GEORGIA				Metro Beach Metropark	6	6	0
				Stoney Creek Metropark	6	6	0
Augusta Board of Education	42	38	4	Wayne County Airport	182	177	5
Bibb County Board of Education	33	28	5				
Cherokee County Marshal	12	6	6	**MINNESOTA**			
Cobb County Board of Education	34	32	2				
Fayette County Marshal	10	9	1	Minneapolis-St. Paul International Airport	110	71	39
Fulton County Marshal	68	61	7	Three Rivers Park District	32	18	14
Gwinnett County Marshal	1	1	0				
Gwinnett County Public Schools	20	17	3	**MISSOURI**			
Macon County Schools	4	4	0				
Metropolitan Atlanta Rapid Transit Authority	306	268	38	Clay County Park Authority	6	5	1
Mitchell County Drug Unit	9	8	1	Jackson County Park Rangers	20	18	2
Richmond County Marshal	32	26	6	Lambert-St. Louis International Airport	120	93	27
Troup County Marshal	8	7	1	St. Charles County Park Rangers	3	3	0
Washington County Board of Education	5	5	0				
				NEVADA			
ILLINOIS							
				Clark County School District	130	116	14
Cook County Forest Preserve	125	116	9				
Du Page County Forest Preserve	28	24	4				

Table 82

Full-time Law Enforcement Employees as of October 31, 2002
by Other Agencies by State—Continued

Other agency by state	Total law enforcement employees	Total officers	Total civilians
NEVADA—Continued			
Washoe County School District	31	29	2
NEW JERSEY			
Park Police:			
Camden County	45	44	1
Morris County	32	31	1
Union County	364	318	46
Prosecutor:			
Atlantic County	125	76	49
Bergen County	262	124	138
Burlington County	136	51	85
Camden County	261	168	93
Cape May County	61	19	42
Cumberland County	63	20	43
Essex County	449	303	146
Gloucester County	83	24	59
Hudson County	221	96	125
Hunterdon County	47	19	28
Mercer County	155	101	54
Middlesex County	199	128	71
Monmouth County	283	80	203
Morris County	151	103	48
Ocean County	149	68	81
Passaic County	197	81	116
Salem County	38	17	21
Somerset County	113	50	63
Sussex County	51	32	19
Union County	223	67	156
Warren County	59	34	25
NEW MEXICO			
Acoma Tribal	16	8	8
Jicarilla Tribal	38	20	18
Laguna Tribal	27	18	9
Santa Clara Tribal	11	5	6
Taos Pueblo Tribal	15	8	7
Zuni Tribal	48	22	26
NEW YORK			
Onondaga County Parks	2	2	0
Staten Island Rapid Transit	25	24	1
Suffolk County Parks	40	34	6
NORTH CAROLINA			
Asheville Regional Airport	15	15	0
Caswell Center Hospital	3	3	0
Cherokee Tribal	36	36	0
Piedmont Triad International Airport	29	18	11
Raleigh-Durham International Airport	34	31	3
Wilmington International Airport	15	13	2
OHIO			
Cleveland Metropolitan Park District	78	68	10
Greater Cleveland Regional Transit Authority	116	103	13
Hamilton County Park District	35	32	3
Port Columbus International Airport	57	35	22
Wood County Park District	6	6	0
OKLAHOMA			
Norman Public Schools	6	5	1
Putnam City Campus	25	20	5

Other agency by state	Total law enforcement employees	Total officers	Total civilians
OREGON			
Port of Portland	58	45	13
PENNSYLVANIA			
Allegheny County District Attorney, Criminal Investigation Division	28	24	4
Allegheny County Port Authority	65	45	20
County Detective:			
Butler County	4	4	0
Cumberland County	9	7	2
Dauphin County	15	12	3
Lebanon County	7	6	1
Lehigh County	8	8	0
Westmoreland County	60	16	44
Delaware County District Attorney, Criminal Investigation Division	38	31	7
Delaware County Park	50	49	1
Harrisburg International Airport	19	14	5
Tyrone Area School District	3	2	1
Westmoreland County Park	22	22	0
RHODE ISLAND			
Narragansett Tribal	11	10	1
SOUTH CAROLINA			
Charleston County Aviation Authority	34	25	9
Columbia Metropolitan Airport	16	15	1
Whitten Center	3	3	0
TENNESSEE			
Chattanooga Metropolitan Airport	22	14	8
Knoxville Metropolitan Airport	44	26	18
Memphis International Airport	52	41	11
Metropolitan Board of Parks and Recreation (Nashville-Davidson)	19	19	0
Nashville International Airport	80	66	14
Tri-Cities Regional Airport	18	17	1
TEXAS			
Amarillo International Airport	15	15	0
Cameron County Park Rangers	10	10	0
Dallas-Fort Worth International Airport	338	305	33
Hospital District:			
Dallas County	92	62	30
Tarrant County	64	32	32
Houston Metropolitan Transit Authority	239	152	87
Independent School District:			
Aldine	44	35	9
Alvin	15	13	2
Angleton	5	4	1
Austin	77	53	24
Bay City	8	7	1
Brownsville	97	15	82
Conroe	78	54	24
Corpus Christi	57	29	28
East Central	13	12	1
Ector County	26	23	3
El Paso	38	30	8
Fort Bend	44	39	5
Hempstead	1	1	0
Judson	8	7	1
Katy	32	24	8

Table 82

Full-time Law Enforcement Employees as of October 31, 2002

by Other Agencies by State—Continued

Other agency by state	Total law enforcement employees	Total officers	Total civilians	Other agency by state	Total law enforcement employees	Total officers	Total civilians
TEXAS—Continued				**WASHINGTON**			
Killeen	12	12	0				
Klein	37	24	13	Colville Tribal	35	23	12
Midland	23	8	15	Lummi Tribal	22	20	2
North East	42	36	6	Nisqually Tribal	12	11	1
Pasadena	32	24	8	Port of Seattle	134	108	26
Raymondville	4	4	0	Skokomish Tribal	6	5	1
Socorro	18	16	2	Swinomish Tribal	12	9	3
Spring	28	27	1				
Spring Branch	40	31	9	**WEST VIRGINIA**			
Taft	2	2	0				
Tyler	5	5	0	Kanawha County Parks and Recreation	2	2	0
Weslaco	15	15	0				
				WISCONSIN			
UTAH							
				Menominee Tribal	34	26	8
Granite School District	22	16	6	Oneida Tribal	31	24	7
VIRGINIA							
Chesapeake Bay Bridge-Tunnel	85	42	43				

SECTION VII

Agencies that contribute to the Uniform Crime Reporting (UCR) Program forward crime data through the state UCR Programs in 46 states and the District of Columbia. Local agencies in states that do not have a state Program submit statistics directly to the FBI, which provides continuing guidance and support to individual contributing agencies. State UCR Programs are very effective liaisons between local contributors and the FBI. Many of the Programs have mandatory reporting requirements and collect data beyond the national UCR scope to address crime problems germane to their particular locales. In most cases, these state agencies also provide more direct and frequent service to participating law enforcement agencies, make information more readily available for use at the state level, and contribute to more streamlined operations at the national level.

With the implementation of state crime reporting Programs, the national UCR Program ceased direct collection of data from individual law enforcement agencies within those states. Currently, the state data collection agency forwards information it receives from local agencies to the national Program.

The criteria established for state Programs ensure consistency and comparability in the data submitted to the national Program, as well as regular and timely reporting. These criteria are: (1) The state Program must conform to national UCR Program standards, definitions, and information requirements. The states are not, of course, prohibited from collecting other statistical data beyond the national requirements. (2) The state criminal justice agency must have a proven, effective, statewide Program and demonstrate acceptable quality control procedures. (3) Coverage within the state by a state agency must be, at least, equal to that attained by the national UCR Program. (4) The state agency must have adequate field staff assigned to conduct audits and to assist contributing agencies in recordkeeping practices and crime-reporting procedures. (5) The state agency must furnish the FBI with all of the detailed data

regularly collected by the FBI in the form of duplicate returns, computer printouts, and/or magnetic tapes. (6) The state agency must have the proven capability (tested over a period of time) to supply all the statistical data required in time to meet deadlines established for publication of the national Uniform Crime Reports.

To fulfill its responsibilities in connection with the UCR Program, the FBI continues to edit and review individual agency reports for both completeness and quality. National UCR Program staff have direct contact with individual contributors within the state as necessary in connection with crime reporting matters, coordinating such contact with the state agency. On request, staff members conduct training programs within the state on law enforcement recordkeeping and crime-reporting procedures. Following audit standards established by the federal government, the FBI conducts an audit of each state's UCR data collection procedures once every 3 years. Should circumstances develop whereby the state agency does not comply with the aforementioned requirements, the national Program may reinstitute a direct collection of Uniform Crime Reports from law enforcement agencies within the state.

Reporting Procedures

Based on records of all reports of crime received from victims, officers who discover infractions, or other sources, law enforcement agencies across the country tabulate the number of Crime Index (Part I) offenses brought to their attention each month. Specifically, the Index crimes reported to the FBI are murder and nonnegligent manslaughter, forcible rape, robbery, aggravated assault, burglary, larceny-theft, motor vehicle theft, and arson.

Whenever complaints of crime are determined through investigation to be unfounded or false, they are eliminated from an agency's count. Agencies report to the FBI the number of actual offenses known regardless of whether anyone is arrested for the crime, stolen property is recovered, or prosecution is undertaken.

Another integral part of the monthly submission is the total number of actual Crime Index offenses cleared. Crimes are cleared in one of two ways: by arrest of at least one person, who is charged and turned over to the court for prosecution, or by exceptional means, when some element beyond law enforcement control precludes the arrest of a known offender. Law enforcement agencies also report the number of Index crime clearances that involve only offenders under the age of 18, the value of property stolen and recovered in connection with the offenses, and detailed information pertaining to criminal homicide and arson.

In addition to its primary collection of Crime Index (Part I) offenses, the UCR Program solicits monthly data on persons arrested for all crimes except traffic violations. The age, sex, and race of arrestees are reported by crime category, both Part I and Part II. Part II offenses include all crimes not classified as Part I.

Monthly data are also collected on law enforcement officers killed or assaulted. The number of full-time sworn and civilian personnel are reported as of October 31 of each year.

At the end of each quarter, summarized information is collected on hate crimes, i.e., specific offenses that were motivated by an offender's bias against the race, religion, ethnic origin, sexual orientation, or physical or mental disability of the victim. Hate crime data from those agencies participating in the National Incident-Based Reporting System (NIBRS) are submitted monthly.

Editing Procedures

Each report submitted to the UCR Program is thoroughly examined for arithmetical accuracy and for deviations that may indicate errors. To identify any unusual fluctuations in an agency's crime count, UCR staff compare monthly reports with previous submissions of the agency and with those for similar agencies. Large variations in crime levels may indicate modified records procedures, incomplete reporting, or changes in the jurisdiction's geopolitical structure.

Data reliability is a high priority of the Program, which brings to the attention of the state UCR Program or the submitting agency

any noted deviations or arithmetical adjustments. A standard FBI procedure is to study the monthly reports and to evaluate periodic trends prepared for individual reporting units. Any significant increase or decrease becomes the subject of a special inquiry. Changes in crime reporting procedures or annexations can influence the level of reported crime. When this occurs, the figures for specific crime categories or totals, if necessary, are excluded from trend tabulations.

To assist contributors in complying with UCR standards, the national Program provides training seminars and instructional materials on crime reporting procedures. Throughout the country, the national UCR Program maintains liaison with state Programs and law enforcement personnel and holds training sessions to explain the purpose of the Program, the rules of uniform classification and scoring, and the methods of assembling the information for reporting. When an individual agency has specific problems in compiling its crime statistics and its remedial efforts are unsuccessful, personnel from the FBI's Criminal Justice Information Services Division may visit the contributor to aid in resolving the difficulties.

The *Uniform Crime Reporting Handbook*, which details procedures for classifying and scoring offenses, is supplied to all contributors as the basic resource document for preparing reports. To enhance communication among Program participants, letters to UCR contributors and UCR *State Program Bulletins* are produced as needed. These provide policy updates and new information, as well as clarification of reporting issues.

The final responsibility for data submissions rests with the individual contributing law enforcement agency. Although the Program makes every effort through its editing procedures, training practices, and correspondence to assure the validity of the data it receives, the accuracy of the statistics depends primarily on the adherence of each contributor to the established standards of reporting. Deviations from these established standards, which cannot be resolved by the national UCR Program, may be brought to the attention of the Criminal Justice Information Systems Committees of the

International Association of Chiefs of Police and the National Sheriffs' Association.

Arrest Data

Florida state arrest data are not included in Tables 30–68. Limited arrest data were received from Illinois, Kentucky, Nevada, and South Carolina. No 2002 arrest data were received from the District of Columbia and no population is attributed to the two agencies for which 12 months complete arrest data were received. Complete 12-month arrest figures for New York City were not available for inclusion in this book. Arrest totals for these areas, however, were estimated for inclusion in Table 29, "Estimated Arrests, United States, 2002."

Population

For the 2002 edition of *Crime in the United States*, the UCR Program obtained current population estimates from the Bureau of the Census to estimate 2002 population counts for all contributing law enforcement agencies. The Bureau of the Census provided revised 2001 state/national population estimates and 2002 state/national population estimates. Using these provisional census data, the national UCR Program updated the 2001 Bureau of the Census city and county estimates and calculated the 2002 state growth rates. Subsequently, the Program updated population figures for individual jurisdictions by applying the 2002 state growth rates to the updated 2001 Bureau of the Census data.

NIBRS Conversion

Several states provide their UCR data in the expanded NIBRS format. For presentation in this book, NIBRS data were converted to the historical summary UCR formats. The NIBRS database was constructed to allow for such conversion so that UCR's long-running time series could continue.

Crime Trends

By showing fluctuations from year to year, trend statistics offer the data user an added perspective from which to study crime. Percent change tabulations in this publication are computed only for reporting agencies that provided comparable data for the periods under consideration. The Program excludes from the trend calculations all figures except those received for common months from common agencies. Also excluded are unusual fluctuations that the Program determines are due to variables such as improved records procedures, annexations. etc.

Data users should exercise care in making any direct comparison between data in this publication and those in prior issues of *Crime in the United States*. Due to differing levels of participation from year to year and transient reporting problems that require the Program to estimate crime counts for certain contributors, the data are not comparable from year to year.

Offense Estimation

Tables 1 through 5 and 7 of this publication contain statistics for the entire United States. Because not all law enforcement agencies provide data for complete reporting periods, the UCR Program includes estimated crime counts in these presentations. Offense estimation occurs within each of three areas: Metropolitan Statistical Areas (MSAs), cities outside MSAs, and rural counties. Using the known crime experiences of similar areas within a state, the national Program computes estimates by assigning the same proportional crime volumes to nonreporting agencies. The size of agency; type of jurisdiction, e.g., police department versus sheriff's office; and geographic location are considered in the estimation process.

Various circumstances require the national Program to estimate certain state offense totals. For example, some states do not provide forcible rape figures in accordance with UCR guidelines; reporting problems at the state level have, at times, resulted in no usable data. Additionally, the conversion of summary reporting to NIBRS has contributed to the need for unique estimation procedures. A summary of state-specific and offense-specific estimation procedures follows.

Year	State(s)	Reason for Estimation	Estimation Method
1985	Illinois	The state UCR Program was unable to provide forcible rape figures in accordance with UCR guidelines.	The rape totals were estimated using national rates per 100,000 inhabitants within the eight population groups and assigning the forcible rape volumes proportionally to the state.
1986	Illinois	The state UCR Program was unable to provide forcible rape figures in accordance with UCR guidelines.	The rape totals were estimated using national rates per 100,000 inhabitants within the eight population groups and assigning the forcible rape volumes proportionally to the state.
1987	Illinois	The state UCR Program was unable to provide forcible rape figures in accordance with UCR guidelines.	The rape totals were estimated using national rates per 100,000 inhabitants within the eight population groups and assigning the forcible rape volumes proportionally to the state.
1988	Florida, Kentucky	Reporting problems at the state level resulted in no usable data.	State totals were estimated by updating previous valid annual totals for individual jurisdictions, subdivided by population group. Percent changes for each offense within each population group of the geographic divisions in which the states reside were applied to the previous valid annual totals. The state totals were compiled from the sums of the population group estimates.
	Illinois	The state UCR Program was unable to provide forcible rape figures in accordance with UCR guidelines.	The rape totals were estimated using national rates per 100,000 inhabitants within the eight population groups and assigning the forcible rape volumes proportionally to the state.
1989	Illinois	The state UCR Program was unable to provide forcible rape figures in accordance with UCR guidelines.	The rape totals were estimated using national rates per 100,000 inhabitants within the eight population groups and assigning the forcible rape volumes proportionally to the state.
1990	Illinois	The state UCR Program was unable to provide forcible rape figures in accordance with UCR guidelines.	The rape totals were estimated using national rates per 100,000 inhabitants within the eight population groups and assigning the forcible rape volumes proportionally to the state.
1991	Illinois	The state UCR Program was unable to provide forcible rape figures in accordance with UCR guidelines.	The rape totals were estimated using national rates per 100,000 inhabitants within the eight population groups and assigning the forcible rape volumes proportionally to the state.
	Iowa	NIBRS conversion efforts resulted in estimation for Iowa.	State totals were estimated by updating previous valid annual totals for individual jurisdictions, subdivided by population group. Percent changes for each offense within each population group of the West North Central Division were applied to the previous valid annual totals. The state totals were compiled from the sums of the population group estimates.
1992	Illinois	The state UCR Program was unable to provide forcible rape figures in accordance with UCR guidelines.	The rape totals were estimated using national rates per 100,000 inhabitants within the eight population groups and assigning the forcible rape volumes proportionally to the state.
1993	Illinois	NIBRS conversion efforts resulted in estimation for Illinois.	Since valid annual totals were available for approximately 60 Illinois agencies, those counts were maintained. The counts for the remaining jurisdictions were replaced with the most recent valid annual totals or were generated using standard estimation procedures. The results of all sources were then combined to arrive at the 1993 state total for Illinois.
		The state UCR Program was unable to provide forcible rape figures in accordance with UCR guidelines.	The rape totals were estimated using national rates per 100,000 inhabitants within the eight population groups and assigning the forcible rape volumes proportionally to the state.
	Kansas	NIBRS conversion efforts resulted in estimation for Kansas.	State totals were estimated by updating previous valid annual totals for individual jurisdictions, subdivided by population group. Percent changes for each offense within each population group of the West North Central Division were applied to the previous valid annual totals. The state totals were compiled from the sums of the population group estimates.
	Michigan, Minnesota	The state UCR Programs were unable to provide forcible rape figures in accordance with UCR guidelines.	The rape totals were estimated using national rates per 100,000 inhabitants within the eight population groups and assigning the forcible rape volumes proportionally to each state.
1994	Illinois	NIBRS conversion efforts resulted in estimation for Illinois.	Illinois totals were generated using only the valid crime rates for the East North Central Division. Within each population group, the state's offense totals were estimated based on the rate per 100,000 inhabitants within the remainder of the division.

Year	State(s)	Reason for Estimation	Estimation Method
		The state UCR Program was unable to provide forcible rape figures in accordance with UCR guidelines.	The rape totals were estimated using national rates per 100,000 inhabitants within the eight population groups and assigning the forcible rape volumes proportionally to the state.
	Kansas	NIBRS conversion efforts resulted in estimation for Kansas.	State totals were generated using only the valid crime rates for the West North Central Division. Within each population group, the state's offense totals were estimated based on the rate per 100,000 inhabitants within the remainder of the division.
	Montana	The state UCR Program was unable to provide complete 1994 offense figures in accordance with UCR guidelines.	State totals were estimated by updating previous valid annual totals for individual jurisdictions, subdivided by population group. Percent changes for each offense within each population group of the Mountain Division were applied to the previous valid annual totals. The state totals were compiled from the sums of the population group estimates.
1995	Illinois	The state UCR Program was unable to provide complete 1995 offense figures in accordance with UCR guidelines.	Valid Crime Index counts were available for most of the largest cities. For other agencies, the only available counts were generated without application of the UCR Hierarchy Rule. (The Hierarchy Rule requires that only the most serious offense in a multiple-offense criminal incident is counted.) To arrive at a comparable state estimate to be included in national compilations, the total supplied by the Illinois State Program (which was inflated because of the nonapplication of the Hierarchy Rule) was reduced by the proportion of multiple offenses reported within single incidents in the available NIBRS data. Valid totals for the large cities were excluded from the reduction process.
	Kansas	The state UCR Program was unable to provide complete 1995 offense figures in accordance with UCR guidelines.	The state UCR Program was able to provide valid 1994 state totals which were then updated using 1995 crime trends for the West North Central Division.
	Montana	The state UCR Program was unable to provide complete 1995 offense figures in accordance with UCR guidelines.	State estimates were computed by updating the previous valid annual totals using the 1994 versus 1995 percent changes for the Mountain Division.
1996	Florida	The state UCR Program was unable to provide complete 1996 offense figures in accordance with UCR guidelines.	The state UCR Program was able to provide an aggregated state total; data received from 94 individual Florida agencies are shown in the 1996 jurisdictional figures presented in Tables 8 through 11.
	Illinois	The state UCR Program was unable to provide complete 1996 offense figures in accordance with UCR guidelines.	Valid Crime Index counts were available for most of the largest cities. For other agencies, the only available counts were generated without application of the UCR Hierarchy Rule. (The Hierarchy Rule requires that only the most serious offense in a multiple-offense criminal incident is counted.) To arrive at a comparable state estimate to be included in national compilations, the total supplied by the Illinois State Program (which was inflated because of the nonapplication of the Hierarchy Rule) was reduced by the proportion of multiple offenses reported within single incidents in the available NIBRS data. Valid totals for the large cities were excluded from the reduction process.
	Kansas	The state UCR Program was unable to provide complete 1996 offense figures in accordance with UCR guidelines.	The Kansas state estimate was extrapolated from 1996 January-June state totals provided by the Kansas State UCR Program.
	Kentucky, Montana	The state UCR Programs were unable to provide complete 1996 offense figures in accordance with UCR guidelines.	The 1995 and 1996 percent changes within each geographic division were applied to valid 1995 state totals to generate 1996 state totals.
1997	Illinois	The state UCR Program was unable to provide complete 1997 offense figures in accordance with UCR guidelines.	Valid Crime Index counts were available for most of the largest cities. For other agencies, the only available counts were generated without application of the UCR Hierarchy Rule. (The Hierarchy Rule requires that only the most serious offense in a multiple-offense criminal incident is counted.) To arrive at a comparable state estimate to be included in national compilations, the total supplied by the Illinois State Program (which was inflated because of the nonapplication of the Hierarchy Rule) was reduced by the proportion of multiple offenses reported within single incidents in the available NIBRS data. Valid totals for the large cities were excluded from the reduction process.

Year	State(s)	Reason for Estimation	Estimation Method
	Kansas	The state UCR Program was unable to provide complete 1997 offense figures in accordance with UCR guidelines.	The Kansas state estimate was extrapolated from 1996 January-June state totals provided by the Kansas State UCR Program.
	Kentucky, Montana, New Hampshire, Vermont	The state UCR Programs were unable to provide complete 1997 offense figures in accordance with UCR guidelines.	The 1996 and 1997 percent changes registered for each geographic division in which the states of Kentucky, Montana, New Hampshire, and Vermont are categorized were applied to valid 1996 state totals to effect 1997 state totals.
1998	Delaware	The state UCR Program was unable to provide forcible rape figures in accordance with national UCR guidelines.	The 1998 forcible rape total for Delaware was estimated by reducing the number of reported offenses by the proportion of male forcible rape victims statewide.
	Illinois	The state UCR Program was unable to provide complete 1998 offense figures in accordance with UCR guidelines.	Valid Crime Index counts were available for most of the largest cities. For other agencies, the only available counts were generated without application of the UCR Hierarchy Rule. (The Hierarchy Rule requires that only the most serious offense in a multiple-offense criminal incident is counted.) To arrive at a comparable state estimate to be included in national compilations, the total supplied by the Illinois State Program (which was inflated because of the nonapplication of the Hierarchy Rule) was reduced by the proportion of multiple offenses reported within single incidents in the available NIBRS data. Valid totals for the large cities were excluded from the reduction process.
	Kansas	The state UCR Program was unable to provide complete 1998 offense figures in accordance with UCR guidelines.	To arrive at 1998 estimates, 1997 state totals supplied by the Kansas State UCR Program were updated using 1998 crime trends for the West North Central Division.
	Kentucky, Montana, New Hampshire, Wisconsin	The state UCR Programs were unable to provide complete 1998 offense figures in accordance with UCR guidelines.	State totals were estimated by using the 1997 figures for the nonreporting areas and applying 1997 versus 1998 percentage changes for the division in which each state is located. The estimates for the nonreporting areas were then increased by any actual 1998 crime counts received.
	Vermont	Due to changes in reporting procedures, the 1997 Vermont Crime Index offense totals were not comparable to those for 1998.	The 1998 Vermont Crime Index offense totals were excluded from Table 4. The 1997 Vermont state estimates were, however, retained in the aggregate national, regional, and divisional volume and rate totals.
1999	Illinois	The state UCR Program was unable to provide complete 1999 offense figures in accordance with UCR guidelines.	Valid Crime Index counts were available for most of the largest cities. For other agencies, the only available counts were generated without application of the UCR Hierarchy Rule. (The Hierarchy Rule requires that only the most serious offense in a multiple-offense criminal incident is counted.) To arrive at a comparable state estimate to be included in national compilations, the total supplied by the Illinois State Program (which was inflated because of the nonapplication of the Hierarchy Rule) was reduced by the proportion of multiple offenses reported within single incidents in the available NIBRS data. Valid totals for the large cities were excluded from the reduction process.
	Kansas, Kentucky, Montana	The state UCR Programs were unable to provide complete 1999 offense figures in accordance with UCR guidelines.	To arrive at 1999 estimates for Kansas, Kentucky, and Montana, 1998 state totals supplied by each state's Uniform Crime Reporting Program were updated using 1999 crime trends for the divisions in which each state is located.
	Maine	The state UCR Program was unable to provide complete 1999 offense figures in accordance with UCR guidelines.	The Maine Department of Public Safety forwarded monthly January through October crime counts for each law enforcement contributor; since 12 months of data were not received, the national Program estimated for the missing data following standard estimation procedures to arrive at a 1999 state total.
	New Hampshire	The state UCR Program was unable to provide complete 1999 offense figures in accordance with UCR guidelines.	The state total for New Hampshire was estimated by using the 1998 figures for the 1999 nonreporting areas and applying the 2-year percent change for the New England Division.
2000	Illinois	The state UCR Programs were unable to provide complete 2000 offense figures or forcible rape figures in accordance with UCR guidelines.	Valid Crime Index counts were available for most of the largest cities. For other agencies, the only available counts were generated without application of the UCR Hierarchy Rule. (The Hierarchy Rule requires that only the most serious offense in a multiple-offense criminal incident be counted.) To arrive at a comparable state estimate to be included in national compilations, the total supplied by the Illinois State Program (which was inflated due to the nonapplication of the

Year	State(s)	Reason for Estimation	Estimation Method
			Hierarchy Rule) was reduced by the proportion of multiple offenses reported within single incidents in the available NIBRS data. Valid totals for the large cities were excluded from the reduction process.
	Kansas	The state UCR Program was unable to provide complete 2000 offense figures in accordance with UCR guidelines.	To arrive at 2000 estimates for Kansas, 1999 state estimates were updated using 2000 crime trends for the West North Central Division.
	Kentucky, Montana	The state UCR Programs were unable to provide complete 2000 offense figures in accordance with UCR guidelines.	To arrive at 2000 estimates for Kentucky and Montana, 1999 state totals supplied by each state's UCR Program were updated using 2000 crime trends for the divisions in which each state is located.
2001	Illinois	The state UCR Program submitted complete data for only seven agencies within the state. Additionally, the state UCR Program was unable to provide forcible rape figures in accordance with UCR guidelines.	Valid Crime Index counts were available for most of the largest cities. For other agencies, the only available counts were generated without application of the UCR Hierarchy Rule. (The Hierarchy Rule requires that only the most serious offense in a multiple-offense criminal incident is counted.) To arrive at a comparable state estimate to be included in national compilations, the total supplied by the Illinois State Program (which was inflated because of the nonapplication of the Hierarchy Rule) was reduced by the proportion of multiple offenses reported within single incidents in the available NIBRS data. Valid totals for the large cities were excluded from the reduction process.
	Kentucky	The state UCR Program was unable to provide complete 2001 offense figures in accordance with UCR guidelines.	To arrive at the 2001 estimate for Kentucky, the 2000 state estimates were updated using 2001 crime trends reported for the East South Central Division.
2002	Kentucky	The state UCR Program was unable to provide complete 2002 offense figures in accordance with UCR guidelines.	To obtain the 2002 state crime count, the state UCR Program was contacted, and the state agency was able to provide their latest state total, 2000. Therefore, the 2001 state estimate was updated for inclusion in the 2002 edition of *Crime in the United States* by using the 2001 crime trends for the division in which the state is located. To derive the 2002 state estimate, the 2002 crime trends for the division were applied to the adjusted 2001 state estimate.
	Illinois	The state UCR Program was unable to provide complete 2002 offense figures in accordance with UCR guidelines.	Valid Crime Index counts were only available for most of the largest cities. For other agencies, the only available counts were generated without application of the UCR Hierarchy Rule. (The Hierarchy Rule requires that only the most serious offense in a multiple-offense criminal incident is counted.) To arrive at a comparable state estimate to be included in national compilations, the total supplied by the Illinois State Program (which was inflated because of the nonapplication of the Hierarchy Rule) was reduced by the proportion of multiple offenses reported with single incidents in the available NIBRS data. Valid totals for the large cities were excluded from the reduction process.

Table Methodology

Although most law enforcement agencies submit crime reports to the UCR Program, not all agencies send 12 months of complete data for the reporting year. To be included in this publication's Tables 8 through 11, which show specific jurisdictional statistics, figures for all 12 months of the reporting year must have been received by the FBI prior to established publication deadlines. Other tabular presentations are aggregated on varied levels of submission. With the exception of the tables that consist of estimates for the total United States population, each table in this publication shows the number of agencies reporting and the extent of population coverage.

Designed to assist the reader, this table explains the construction of many of this book's tabular presentations.

(1) Table	(2) Database	(3) Table Construction	(4) General Comments
1	All law enforcement agencies in the UCR Program. Crime statistics include estimated offense totals for agencies submitting less than 12 months of offense reports for each year.	The 2002 statistics are consistent with Table 2. Pre-2002 crime statistics may have been updated and, hence, may not be consistent with prior publications. Population statistics represent July 1 provisional estimations for each year except 1990 and 2000, which are Bureau of the Census decennial census data. (See the Population section in this appendix.)	Represents an estimation of national reported crime activity from 1983 to 2002.
2	All law enforcement agencies in the UCR Program. Crime statistics include estimated offense totals for agencies submitting less than 12 months of offense reports for 2002.	Statistics are aggregated from individual state statistics as shown in Table 5. Population statistics for 2002 represent estimates based upon the percent change in state population from Bureau of the Census 2001 revised estimates and 2002 provisional estimates. (See the Population section in this appendix.)	Represents an estimation of national reported crime activity in 2002.
3	All law enforcement agencies in the UCR Program (including those submitting less than 12 months of offense reports for 2002).	Regional offense distributions are computed from volume figures as shown in Table 4. Population distributions are based on Bureau of the Census provisional estimates for 2002.	Represents the 2002 geographical distribution of estimated Crime Index offenses and population.
4	All law enforcement agencies in the UCR Program. Crime statistics include estimated offense totals for agencies submitting less than 12 months of offense reports for 2001 and 2002.	The 2002 statistics are aggregated from individual state statistics as shown in Table 5. Population statistics represent Bureau of the Census 2001 revised estimates and 2002 provisional estimates.	Represents an estimation of reported crime activity for Index offenses at the: 1. national level 2. regional level 3. division level 4. state level Any comparison of UCR statistics should take into consideration demographic factors.
5	All law enforcement agencies in the UCR Program. Crime statistics include estimated offense totals for agencies submitting less than 12 months of offense reports for 2002.	Population statistics for 2002 represent estimates based upon the percent change in state population from Bureau of the Census 2001 revised estimates and 2002 provisional estimates. (See the Population section in this appendix.) Statistics under the heading Area Actually Reporting represent reported offense totals for agencies submitting 12 months of offense reports and estimated totals for agencies submitting less than 12 but more than 2 months of offense reports. The statistics under the heading Estimated Totals represent the above plus estimated offense totals for agencies submitting 2 months or less of offense reports.	Represents an estimation of reported crime activity for Index offenses at the state level. Any comparison of UCR statistics should take into consideration demographic factors.
6	All law enforcement agencies in the UCR Program. Crime statistics include estimated offense totals for agencies submitting less than 12 months of offense reports for 2002.	Statistics are published for all Metropolitan Statistical Areas (MSAs) having at least 75% reporting and for which the central city/cities submitted 12 months of data for 2002. Population statistics for 2002 represent estimates based upon the percent change in state population from Bureau of the Census 2001 revised estimates and 2002 provisional estimates. (See the Population section in this appendix.) The statistics under the heading Area Actually Reporting represent reported offense	Represents an estimation of the reported crime activity for Index offenses at the individual MSA level. Any comparison of UCR statistics should take into consideration demographic factors.

(1) Table	(2) Database	(3) Table Construction	(4) General Comments
		totals for agencies submitting all 12 months of offense reports plus estimated offense totals for agencies submitting less than 12 but more than 2 months of offense reports. The statistics under the heading Estimated Total represent the above plus the estimated offense totals for agencies submitting 2 months or less of offense reports. The tabular breakdowns are according to UCR definitions. (See App. II.)	
7	All law enforcement agencies in the UCR Program. Crime statistics include estimated offense totals for agencies submitting less than 12 months of offense reports for 1998 through 2002.	Offense totals are for all Index offense categories other than aggravated assault.	Represents an estimation of national reported crime activity from 1998 to 2002. Aggravated assault is not included in the data source from which this table is derived.
8	All law enforcement agencies submitting 12 months of complete offense reports for 2002.	Cities and Towns are agencies in Population Groups I through V. Population statistics for 2002 represent estimates based upon the percent change in state population from Bureau of the Census 2001 revised estimates and 2002 provisional estimates. (See the Population section in this appendix.)	Represents reported crime activity of individual agencies in cities and towns 10,000 and over in population. Any comparison of UCR statistics should take into consideration demographic factors.
9	All university/college law enforcement agencies submitting 12 months of complete offense reports for 2002.	The 2000 student enrollment figures, which are provided by the U.S. Department of Education, are the most recent available. They include full- and part-time students. No adjustments to equate part-time enrollments into full-time equivalents have been made.	Represents reported crime from those individual university/college law enforcement agencies contributing to the UCR Program. These agencies are listed alphabetically by state. Any comparison of these UCR statistics should take into consideration size of enrollment, number of on-campus residents, and other demographic factors.
10	All law enforcement agencies submitting 12 months of complete offense reports for 2002.	Suburban Counties are the areas covered by noncity agencies within an MSA. (See App. III.) Population classifications of suburban counties are based on 2002 UCR estimates for individual agencies. (See the Population section in this appendix.)	Represents crime reported to individual law enforcement agencies in suburban counties, i.e., the individual sheriff's office, county police department, highway patrol, and/or state police. These figures do not represent the county totals since they exclude city crime counts. Any comparison of UCR statistics should take into consideration demographic factors.
11	All law enforcement agencies submitting 12 months of complete offense reports for 2002.	Rural Counties are those outside MSAs whose jurisdictions are not covered by city police agencies. (See App. III.) Population classifications of rural counties are based on 2002 UCR estimates for individual agencies. (See the Population section in this appendix.)	Represents crime reported to individual rural county law enforcement agencies covering populations 25,000 and over, i.e., the individual sheriff's office, county police department, highway patrol, and/or state police. These figures do not represent the county totals since they exclude city crime counts. Any comparison of UCR statistics should take into consideration demographic factors.
12-15	All law enforcement agencies submitting at least 6 common months of complete offense reports for 2001 and 2002.	The 2002 crime trend statistics are 2-year comparisons based on 2002 reported crime activity. Only common reported months for individual agencies are included in 2002 trend calculations. Population statistics for 2002 represent estimates based upon the percent change in state population from Bureau of the Census 2001 revised estimates and 2002 provisional estimates. (See the Population section in this appendix.) See Appendix III for UCR population breakdowns. Note that Suburban and Nonsuburban Cities are all municipal agencies other than central cities in MSAs.	
16-19	All law enforcement agencies submitting 12 months of complete offense reports for 2002.	The 2002 crime rates are the ratios, per 100,000 inhabitants, of the aggregated 2002 crime volumes and the aggregated 2002 populations of the contributing agencies. Population statistics for 2002 represent estimates based upon the percent change in state population from Bureau of the Census 2001 revised estimates and 2002 provisional estimates. (See the Population section in this appendix.) See Appendix III for UCR population breakdowns. Note that Suburban and Nonsuburban Cities are all municipal agencies other than central cities in MSAs.	The forcible rape figures furnished by the Delaware and Illinois state UCR Programs were not in accordance with national guidelines. For inclusion in these tables, the Delaware and Illinois forcible rape figures were estimated by using the national rates for each population group applied to the population by group for Delaware and Illinois agencies supplying all 12 months of data. There is a slight decrease in national coverage for Table 19 due to editing procedure and lower submission rate.

(1) Table	(2) Database	(3) Table Construction	(4) General Comments
20	All law enforcement agencies submitting Supplementary Homicide Report (SHR) data for 2002.	The weapon totals are the aggregate for each murder victim recorded on the SHRs for calendar year 2002.	The SHR is the monthly report form concerning homicides. It details victim and offender characteristics, circumstances, weapons used, etc.
21, 22	All law enforcement agencies submitting 12 months of complete offense reports for 2002.	The weapon totals are aggregated 2002 totals. Population statistics represent 2002 UCR estimates.	
23, 24	All law enforcement agencies submitting at least 6 months of complete offense reports for 2002.	Offense total and value lost total are computed for all Index offense categories other than aggravated assault. Percent distribution is derived based on offense total of each Index offense. Trend statistics are derived based on agencies with at least 6 common months complete for 2001 and 2002.	Aggravated assault is excluded from Table 23. For UCR Program purposes, the taking of money or property in connection with an assault is reported as robbery.
25-28	All law enforcement agencies submitting at least 6 months of complete offense reports for 2002.	The 2002 clearance rates are based on offense and clearance volume totals of the contributing agencies for 2002. Population statistics for 2002 represent estimates based upon the percent change in state population from Bureau of the Census 2001 revised estimates and 2002 provisional estimates. (See the Population section in this appendix.) See Appendix III for UCR Program population breakdowns.	
29	All law enforcement agencies in the UCR Program (including those submitting less than 12 months of complete data for 2002).	The arrest totals presented are national estimates based on the arrest statistics of all law enforcement agencies in the UCR Program (including those submitting less than 12 months). The Total Estimated Arrests statistic is the sum of estimated arrest volumes for each of 28 offenses, not including suspicion. Each individual arrest total is the sum of the estimated volumes within each of the eight population groups. (See App. III.) Each group's estimate is the reported volume (as shown in Table 31) divided by the percent of total group population reporting, according to 2002 UCR estimates for individual agencies. (See the Population section in this appendix.)	
30, 31	All law enforcement agencies submitting complete reports for 12 months of 2002.	The 2002 arrest rates are the ratios, per 100,000 inhabitants, of the aggregated 2002 reported arrest statistics and population. The population statistics for 2002 represent estimates based upon the percent change in state population from Bureau of the Census 2001 revised estimates and 2002 provisional estimates. (See the Population section in this appendix.) See Appendix III for UCR population classifications and geographical configuration.	
32, 33	All law enforcement agencies submitting 12 months of complete reports for 1993 and 2002.	The arrest trends are the percentage differences between 1993 and 2002 arrest volumes aggregated from all common agencies. The population statistics for 2002 represent estimates based upon the percent change in state population from Bureau of the Census 2001 revised estimates and 2002 provisional estimates. (See the Population section in this appendix.) Population statistics for 1993 are based upon the percent change in state population from Bureau of the Census 1992 and 1993 provisional estimates.	
34, 35	All law enforcement agencies submitting 12 months of complete reports for 1998 and 2002.	The arrest trends are the percentage differences between 1998 and 2002 arrest volumes aggregated from common agencies. The population statistics for 2002 represent estimates based upon the percent change in state population from Bureau of the Census 2001 revised estimates and 2002 provisional estimates. (See the Population section in this appendix.) Population statistics for 1998 are based upon the percent change in state population from the Bureau of the Census 1997 and 1998 provisional estimates.	

(1) Table	(2) Database	(3) Table Construction	(4) General Comments
36, 37	All law enforcement agencies submitting 12 months of complete reports for 2001 and 2002.	The arrest trends are 2-year comparisons between 2001 and 2002 arrest volumes aggregated from common agencies. Population statistics for 2001 represent estimates based upon the percent change in state population from Bureau of the Census 2000 decennial counts and provisional 2001 estimates. Population statistics for 2002 represent estimates based upon the percent change in state populations from the Bureau of Census 2001 revised estimates and 2002 provisional estimates. (See the Population section in this appendix.)	
38-43	All law enforcement agencies submitting 12 months of complete reports for 2002.	Population statistics for 2002 represent estimates based upon the percent change in state population from Bureau of the Census 2001 revised estimates and 2002 provisional estimates. (See the Population section in this appendix.)	
44, 45	All city law enforcement agencies submitting 12 months of complete reports for 2001 and 2002.	The 2002 city arrest trends represent the percentage differences between 2001 and 2002 arrest volumes aggregated from common city agencies. City Agencies are all agencies within Population Groups I-VI. (See App. III.) Population statistics for 2001 represent estimates based upon the percent change in state population from Bureau of the Census 2000 decennial counts and provisional 2001 estimates. Population statistics for 2002 represent estimates based upon the percent change in state population from Bureau of the Census 2001 revised estimates and 2002 provisional estimates. (See the Population section in this appendix.)	
46-49	All city law enforcement agencies submitting 12 months of complete reports for 2002.	City Agencies are all agencies within Population Groups I-VI. (See App. III.) Population statistics for 2002 represent estimates based upon the percent change in state population from Bureau of Census 2001 revised estimates and 2002 provisional estimates. (See the Population section in this appendix.)	Slight decrease in coverage for Table 49 due to editing procedure and lower submission of race data.
50, 51	All suburban county law enforcement agencies submitting 12 months of complete reports for 2001 and 2002.	The 2002 suburban county arrest trends represent percentage differences between 2001 and 2002 volumes aggregated from contributing agencies. Suburban Counties are the areas covered by noncity agencies within an MSA. (See App. III.) Population statistics for 2001 represent estimates based upon the percent change in state population from Bureau of the Census 2000 decennial counts and provisional 2001 estimates. Population statistics for 2002 represent estimates based upon the percent change in state populations from the Bureau of Census 2001 revised estimates and 2002 provisional estimates. (See the Population section in this appendix.)	
52-55	All suburban county law enforcement agencies submitting 12 months of complete reports for 2002.	Suburban Counties are the areas covered by noncity agencies within an MSA. (See App. III.) Population statistics for 2002 represent estimates based upon the percent change in state population from the Bureau of the Census 2001 revised estimates and 2002 provisional estimates. (See the Population section in this appendix.)	Slight decrease in coverage for Table 55 due to editing procedure and lower submission of race data.
56, 57	All rural county law enforcement agencies submitting 12 months of complete reports for 2001 and 2002.	The 2002 rural county arrest trends represent percentage differences between 2001 and 2002 volumes aggregated from contributing agencies. Rural Counties are noncity agencies outside MSAs. (See App. III.) Population statistics for 2001 represent estimates based upon the percent change in state population from Bureau of the Census 2000 decennial counts and provisional 2001 estimates. Population statistics for 2002 represent estimates	

(1) Table	(2) Database	(3) Table Construction	(4) General Comments
		based upon the percent change in state populations from the Bureau of Census 2001 revised estimates and 2002 provisional estimates. (See the Population section in this appendix.)	
58-61	All rural county law enforcement agencies submitting 12 months of complete reports for 2002.	Rural Counties are noncity agencies outside MSAs. (See App. III.) Population statistics for 2002 represent estimates based upon the percent change in state population from the Bureau of the Census 2001 revised estimates and 2002 provisional estimates. (See the Population section in this appendix.)	
62, 63	All suburban area law enforcement agencies submitting 12 months of complete reports for 2001 and 2002.	The 2002 suburban area arrest trends represent percentage differences between 2001 and 2002 arrest volumes aggregated from contributing agencies. Suburban Area includes agencies within a metropolitan area excluding those that cover central cities as defined by the Office of Management and Budget. (See App. III.) Population statistics for 2001 represent estimates based upon the percent change in state population from Bureau of the Census 2000 decennial counts and provisional 2001 estimates. Population statistics for 2002 represent estimates based upon the percent change in state populations from the Bureau of Census 2001 revised estimates and 2002 provisional estimates. (See the Population section in this appendix.)	
64-67	All suburban area law enforcement agencies submitting 12 months of complete reports for 2002.	Suburban Area includes agencies within a metropolitan area excluding those that cover central cities as defined by the Office of Management and Budget. (See App. III.) Population statistics for 2002 represent estimates based upon the percent change in state population from Bureau of the Census 2001 revised estimates and 2002 provisional estimates. (See the Population section in this appendix.)	
68	All law enforcement agencies submitting 12 months of complete reports for 2002.	Population statistics for 2002 represent estimates based upon the percent change in state population from Bureau of the Census 2001 revised estimates and 2002 provisional estimates. (See the Population section in this appendix.)	Data furnished are based upon individual state age definitions for juveniles.
69	All law enforcement agencies submitting 12 months of complete reports for 2002.	Arrest totals are aggregated for individual agencies within each state. Population statistics represent Bureau of the Census provisional estimates for 2002. (See the Population section in this appendix.)	Any comparison of statistics should take into consideration variances in arrest practices, particularly for Part II crimes.

The Uniform Crime Reporting Program classifies offenses into two groups, Part I and Part II crimes. Each month, contributing agencies submit information on the number of Part I offenses (Crime Index) known to law enforcement; those offenses cleared by arrest or exceptional means; and the age, sex, and race of persons arrested. Contributors provide only arrest data for Part II offenses.

The **Part I** offenses, those that comprise the Crime Index due to their seriousness and frequency, are defined below:

Criminal homicide—a.) Murder and nonnegligent manslaughter: the willful (nonnegligent) killing of one human being by another. Deaths caused by negligence, attempts to kill, assaults to kill, suicides, and accidental deaths are excluded. The Program classifies justifiable homicides separately and limits the definition to: (1) the killing of a felon by a law enforcement officer in the line of duty; or (2) the killing of a felon, during the commission of a felony, by a private citizen. b.) Manslaughter by negligence: the killing of another person through gross negligence. Traffic fatalities are excluded. While manslaughter by negligence is a Part I crime, it is not included in the Crime Index.

Forcible rape—The carnal knowledge of a female forcibly and against her will. Rapes by force and attempts or assaults to rape regardless of the age of the victim are included. Statutory offenses (no force used—victim under age of consent) are excluded.

Robbery—The taking or attempting to take anything of value from the care, custody, or control of a person or persons by force or threat of force or violence and/or by putting the victim in fear.

Aggravated assault—An unlawful attack by one person upon another for the purpose of inflicting severe or aggravated bodily injury. This type of assault usually is accompanied by the use of a weapon or by means likely to produce death or great bodily harm. Simple assaults are excluded.

Burglary (breaking or entering)—The unlawful entry of a structure to commit a felony or a theft. Attempted forcible entry is included.

Larceny-theft (except motor vehicle theft)—The unlawful taking, carrying, leading, or riding away of property from the possession or constructive possession of another. Examples are thefts of bicycles or automobile accessories, shoplifting, pocket-picking, or the stealing of any property or article which is not taken by force and violence or by fraud. Attempted larcenies are included. Embezzlement, confidence games, forgery, worthless checks, etc., are excluded.

Motor vehicle theft—The theft or attempted theft of a motor vehicle. A motor vehicle is self-propelled and runs on the surface and not on rails. Motorboats, construction equipment, airplanes, and farming equipment are specifically excluded from this category.

Arson—Any willful or malicious burning or attempt to burn, with or without intent to defraud, a dwelling house, public building, motor vehicle or aircraft, personal property of another, etc.

The **Part II** offenses, for which only arrest data are collected, are defined below:

Other assaults (simple)—Assaults and attempted assaults where no weapons are used and which do not result in serious or aggravated injury to the victim.

Forgery and counterfeiting—Making, altering, uttering, or possessing, with intent to defraud, anything false in the semblance of that which is true. Attempts are included.

Fraud—Fraudulent conversion and obtaining money or property by false pretenses. Confidence games and bad checks, except forgeries and counterfeiting, are included.

Embezzlement—Misappropriation or misapplication of money or property entrusted to one's care, custody, or control.

Stolen property; buying, receiving, possessing—Buying, receiving, and possessing stolen property, including attempts.

Vandalism—Willful or malicious destruction, injury, disfigurement, or defacement of any public or private property, real or personal, without consent of the owner or persons having custody or control. Attempts are included.

Weapons; carrying, possessing, etc.—All violations of regulations or statutes controlling the carrying, using, possessing, furnishing, and manufacturing of deadly weapons or silencers. Attempts are included.

Prostitution and commercialized vice—Sex offenses of a commercialized nature, such as prostitution, keeping a bawdy house, procuring, or transporting women for immoral purposes. Attempts are included.

Sex offenses (except forcible rape, prostitution, and commercialized vice)— Statutory rape and offenses against chastity, common decency, morals, and the like. Attempts are included.

Drug abuse violations—State and/or local offenses relating to the unlawful possession, sale, use, growing, and manufacturing of narcotic drugs. The following drug categories are specified: opium or cocaine and their derivatives (morphine, heroin, codeine); marijuana; synthetic narcotics—manufactured narcotics that can cause true addiction (demerol, methadone); and dangerous nonnarcotic drugs (barbiturates, benzedrine).

Gambling—Promoting, permitting, or engaging in illegal gambling.

Offenses against the family and children—Nonsupport, neglect, desertion, or abuse of family and children. Attempts are included.

Driving under the influence—Driving or operating any vehicle or common carrier while drunk or under the influence of liquor or narcotics.

Liquor laws—State and/or local liquor law violations except drunkenness and driving under the influence. Federal violations are excluded.

Drunkenness—Offenses relating to drunkenness or intoxication. Driving under the influence is excluded.

Disorderly conduct—Breach of the peace.

Vagrancy—Begging, loitering, etc. Includes prosecutions under the charge of suspicious person.

All other offenses—All violations of state and/or local laws except those listed above and traffic offenses.

Suspicion—No specific offense; suspect released without formal charges being placed.

Curfew and loitering laws (persons under age 18)—Offenses relating to violations of local curfew or loitering ordinances where such laws exist.

Runaways (persons under age 18)—Limited to juveniles taken into protective custody under provisions of local statutes.

This publication presents crime statistics by area, enabling data users to analyze local crime counts in relation to other areas of a like geographic location or population size. The Nation is divided into regions, divisions, and states. Data are also broken down using population figures and proximity to metropolitan areas. Sheriffs, county police, and state police generally report crimes within counties but outside cities; local police report crime in city limits.

Community Types

The Uniform Crime Reporting (UCR) Program displays data aggregated by three types of communities:

1. Metropolitan Statistical Areas (MSAs)—Each MSA has a central city with at least 50,000 inhabitants or an urbanized area of at least 50,000 in population. MSAs include the county of the central city and other contiguous counties that have substantial economic and social ties to the central city and county. For UCR purposes, counties in an MSA are considered suburban. An MSA may cross state lines. Establishing reporting units representing major population centers assists data users in analyzing and presenting uniform statistical data on metropolitan areas. The Program discourages data users from making year-to-year comparisons of MSA data because of changes in the geographic composition of MSAs.

New England MSAs are comprised of cities and towns instead of counties. In this publication's tabular presentations, New England cities and towns are assigned to the proper MSA. However, statistics for the areas outside of these MSAs are compiled in county data presentations. In the counties that have both suburban and rural portions, data for state police and sheriffs are included in statistics for the *rural* areas.

About 80 percent of the Nation's population inhabited MSAs in 2002. Some presentations in this publication refer to suburban areas, which include cities with under 50,000 population as well as unincorporated areas within the MSA and exclude central cities. The suburban area concept is important because of the unique crime conditions in the communities around the United States' largest cities.

2. Cities Outside MSAs—Cities outside MSAs are mostly incorporated areas and made up 8 percent of the Nation's population in 2002.

3. Rural Counties Outside MSAs—Most rural counties are composed of unincorporated areas. Law enforcement agencies in rural counties cover areas that are not under the jurisdiction of city police departments. Some 12 percent of the population in 2002 were served by rural law enforcement agencies.

Community types are illustrated below:

	MSA	NON-MSA
CITIES	CENTRAL CITIES 50,000 AND OVER	CITIES OUTSIDE METROPOLITAN AREAS
	SUBURBAN CITIES	
COUNTIES (including unincorporated areas)	SUBURBAN COUNTIES	RURAL COUNTIES

Population Groups

The UCR Program uses the following population group classifications:

Population Group	Political Label	Population Range
I	City	250,000 and over
II	City	100,000 to 249,999
III	City	50,000 to 99,999
IV	City	25,000 to 49,999
V	City	10,000 to 24,999
VI	City[1]	Less than 10,000
VIII (Rural County)	County[2]	N/A
IX (Suburban County)	County[2]	N/A

[1] Includes universities and colleges to which no population is attributed.

[2] Includes state police to which no population is attributed.

Individual law enforcement agencies are the major source of UCR data. Annually, the number of agencies included in each population group varies because of population growth, geopolitical consolidation, municipal incorporation, etc. In noncensus years, the UCR Program estimates population figures for individual jurisdictions. A more comprehensive explanation of population estimations is located in Appendix I.

The table below displays the number of agencies contributing to the UCR Program within each population group for 2002.

Population Group	Number of Agencies	Population Covered
I	71	53,175,169
II	171	25,571,226
III	423	29,153,832
IV	803	27,912,096
V	1,867	29,581,897
VI[1]	8,735	26,310,716
VIII (Rural County)[2]	3,437	34,517,436
IX (Suburban County)[2]	1,817	62,146,326
Total	17,324	288,368,698

[1] Includes universities and colleges to which no population is attributed.

[2] Includes state police to which no population is attributed.

Regions and Divisions

The accompanying map depicts the four regions of the United States: the Northeastern States, the Midwestern States, the Southern States, and the Western States. Further, the regions are split into nine divisions. The table lists the regional, divisional, and state organization of the Nation for the UCR Program's purposes.

NORTHEASTERN STATES

New England
  Connecticut
  Maine
  Massachusetts
  New Hampshire
  Rhode Island
  Vermont

Middle Atlantic
  New Jersey
  New York
  Pennsylvania

MIDWESTERN STATES

East North Central
  Illinois
  Indiana
  Michigan
  Ohio
  Wisconsin

West North Central
  Iowa
  Kansas
  Minnesota
  Missouri
  Nebraska
  North Dakota
  South Dakota

SOUTHERN STATES

South Atlantic
  Delaware
  District of Columbia
  Florida
  Georgia
  Maryland
  North Carolina
  South Carolina
  Virginia
  West Virginia

East South Central
  Alabama
  Kentucky
  Mississippi
  Tennessee
West South Central
  Arkansas
  Louisiana
  Oklahoma
  Texas

WESTERN STATES

Mountain
  Arizona
  Colorado
  Idaho
  Montana
  Nevada
  New Mexico
  Utah
  Wyoming

Pacific
  Alaska
  California
  Hawaii
  Oregon
  Washington

Regions and Divisions of the United States, 2002

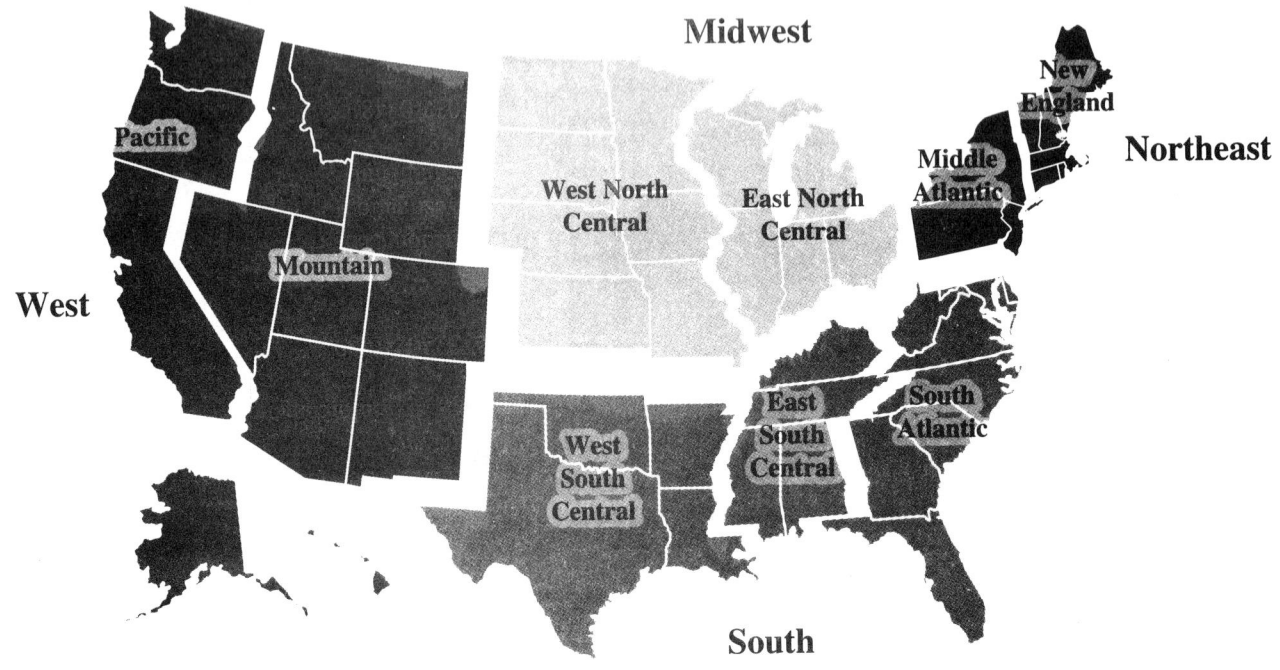

The U.S. Department of Justice administers two statistical programs to measure the magnitude, nature, and impact of crime in the Nation: the Uniform Crime Reporting (UCR) Program and the National Crime Victimization Survey (NCVS). Each of these programs produces valuable information about aspects of the Nation's crime problem. Because the UCR and NCVS programs are conducted for different purposes, use different methods, and focus on somewhat different aspects of crime, the information they produce together provides a more comprehensive panorama of the Nation's crime problem than either could produce alone.

Uniform Crime Reports

The FBI's UCR Program, which began in 1929, collects information on the following crimes reported to law enforcement authorities: homicide, forcible rape, robbery, aggravated assault, burglary, larceny-theft, motor vehicle theft, and arson. Law enforcement agencies report arrest data for 21 additional crime categories.

The UCR data are compiled from monthly law enforcement reports or individual crime incident records transmitted directly to the FBI or to centralized state agencies that then report to the FBI. Each report submitted to the UCR Program is examined thoroughly for reasonableness, accuracy, and deviations that may indicate errors. Large variations in crime levels may indicate modified records procedures, incomplete reporting, or changes in a jurisdiction's boundaries. To identify any unusual fluctuations in an agency's crime counts, monthly reports are compared with previous submissions of the agency and with those for similar agencies.

In 2002, law enforcement agencies active in the UCR Program represented approximately 288.4 million United States inhabitants—93.4 percent of the total population.

The UCR Program provides crime counts for the Nation as a whole, as well as for regions, states, counties, cities, and towns. This permits studies among neighboring jurisdictions and among those with similar populations and other common characteristics.

UCR findings for each calendar year are published in a preliminary release in the spring of the following calendar year, then succeeded by a detailed annual report, *Crime in the United States*, issued in the fall. In addition to crime counts and trends, this report includes data on crimes cleared, persons arrested (age, sex, and race), law enforcement personnel (including the number of sworn officers killed or assaulted), and the characteristics of homicides (including age, sex, and race of victims and offenders; victim-offender relationships; weapons used; and circumstances surrounding the homicides). Other periodic reports are also available from the UCR Program.

The UCR Program is continually converting to the more comprehensive and detailed National Incident-Based Reporting System (NIBRS). NIBRS can provide detailed information about each criminal incident in 22 broad categories of offenses.

National Crime Victimization Survey

The Bureau of Justice Statistics' NCVS, which began in 1973, provides a detailed picture of crime incidents, victims, and trends. After a substantial period of research, the survey completed an intensive methodological redesign in 1993. The redesign was undertaken to improve the questions used to uncover crime, update the survey methods, and broaden the scope of crimes measured. The redesigned survey collects detailed information on the frequency and nature of the crimes of rape, sexual assault, personal robbery, aggravated and simple assault, household burglary, theft, and motor vehicle theft. It does not measure homicide or commercial crimes (such as burglaries of stores).

Two times a year, U.S. Bureau of the Census personnel interview all household members at least 12 years old in a nationally representative sample of approximately 49,000 households (about 80,000 people). Approximately 160,000 interviews are conducted annually. Households stay in the sample for 3 years. New households rotate into the sample on an ongoing basis.

The NCVS collects information on crimes suffered by individuals and households, whether or not those crimes were reported to law enforcement. It estimates the proportion of each crime type reported to law enforcement, and it summarizes the reasons that victims give for reporting or not reporting.

The survey provides information about victims (age, sex, race, ethnicity, marital status, income, and educational level), offenders (sex, race, approximate age, and victim-offender relationship), and the crimes (time and place of occurrence, use of weapons, nature of injury, and economic consequences). Questions also cover the experiences of victims with the criminal justice system, self-protective measures used by victims, and possible substance abuse by offenders. Supplements are added periodically to the survey to obtain detailed information on topics like school crime.

The first data from the redesigned NCVS were published in a BJS bulletin in June 1995. BJS publication of NCVS data includes *Criminal Victimization in the United States*, an annual report that covers the broad range of detailed information collected by the NCVS. BJS publishes detailed reports on topics such as crime against women, urban crime, and gun use in crime. The NCVS data files are archived at the National Archive of Criminal Justice Data at the University of Michigan to enable researchers to perform independent analyses.

Comparing UCR and NCVS

Because the NCVS was designed to complement the UCR Program, the two programs share many similarities. As much as their different collection methods permit, the two measure the same subset of serious crimes, defined alike. Both programs cover rape, robbery, aggravated assault, burglary, theft, and motor vehicle theft. Rape, robbery, theft, and motor vehicle theft are defined virtually identically by both the UCR and NCVS. (While rape is defined analogously, the UCR Crime Index

measures the crime against women only, and the NCVS measures it against both sexes.)

There are also significant differences between the two programs. First, the two programs were created to serve different purposes. The UCR Program's primary objective is to provide a reliable set of criminal justice statistics for law enforcement administration, operation, and management. The NCVS was established to provide previously unavailable information about crime (including crime not reported to police), victims, and offenders.

Second, the two programs measure an overlapping but nonidentical set of crimes. The NCVS includes crimes both reported and not reported to law enforcement. The NCVS excludes, but the UCR includes, homicide, arson, commercial crimes, and crimes against children under age 12. The UCR captures crimes reported to law enforcement, but it excludes simple assaults and sexual assaults other than forcible rape from the Crime Index.

Third, because of methodology, the NCVS and UCR definitions of some crimes differ. For example, the UCR defines burglary as the unlawful entry or attempted entry of a structure to commit a felony or theft. The NCVS, not wanting to ask victims to ascertain offender motives, defines burglary as the entry or attempted entry of a residence by a person who had no right to be there.

Fourth, for property crimes (burglary, theft, and motor vehicle theft), the two programs calculate crime rates using different bases. The UCR rates for these crimes are per capita (number of crimes per 100,000 persons), whereas the NCVS rates for these crimes are per household (number of crimes per 1,000 households). Because the number of households may not grow at the same rate each year as the total population, trend data for rates of property crimes measured by the two programs may not be comparable.

In addition, some differences in the data from the two programs may result from sampling variation in the NCVS and from estimating for nonresponse in the UCR. The NCVS estimates are derived from interviewing a sample and are, therefore, subject to a margin of error. Rigorous statistical methods are used to calculate confidence intervals around all survey estimates. Trend data in NCVS reports are described as genuine only if there is at least a 90 percent certainty that the measured changes are not the result of sampling variation. The UCR data are based on the actual counts of offenses reported by law enforcement jurisdictions. In some circumstances, UCR data are estimated for nonparticipating jurisdictions or those reporting partial data.

Apparent discrepancies between statistics from the two programs can usually be accounted for by their definitional and procedural differences or resolved by comparing NCVS sampling variations (confidence intervals) of those crimes said to have been reported to police with UCR statistics.

For most types of crimes measured by both the UCR and NCVS, analysts familiar with the programs can exclude from analysis those aspects of crime not common to both. Resulting long-term trend lines can be brought into close concordance. The impact of such adjustments is most striking for robbery, burglary, and motor vehicle theft, whose definitions most closely coincide.

With robbery, annual victimization rates are based only on NCVS robberies reported to the police. It is also possible to remove UCR robberies of commercial establishments such as gas stations, convenience stores, and banks from analysis. When the resulting NCVS police-reported robbery rates are compared to UCR noncommercial robbery rates, the results reveal closely corresponding long-term trends.

Each program has unique strengths. The UCR provides a measure of the number of crimes reported to law enforcement agencies throughout the country. The UCR's Supplementary Homicide Reports provide the most reliable, timely data on the extent and nature of homicides in the Nation. The NCVS is the primary source of information on the characteristics of criminal victimization and on the number and types of crimes not reported to law enforcement authorities.

By understanding the strengths and limitations of each program, it is possible to use the UCR and NCVS to achieve a greater understanding of crime trends and the nature of crime in the United States. For example, changes in police procedures, shifting attitudes towards crime and police, and other societal changes can affect the extent to which people report and law enforcement agencies record crime. NCVS and UCR data can be used in concert to explore why trends in reported and police-recorded crime may differ.

APPENDIX V – Directory of State Uniform Crime Reporting Programs

Alabama

Alabama Criminal Justice Information Center
Suite 350
770 Washington Avenue
Montgomery, Alabama 36104
334-242-4900

Alaska

Uniform Crime Reporting Section
Department of Public Safety Information System
5700 East Tudor Road
Anchorage, Alaska 99507
907-451-5166

American Samoa

Department of Public Safety
Post Office Box 1086
Pago Pago, American Samoa 96799
684-633-1111

Arizona

Access Integrity Unit
Uniform Crime Reporting Program
Arizona Department of Public Safety
Post Office Box 6638
Phoenix, Arizona 85005-6638
602-223-2263

Arkansas

Arkansas Crime Information Center
One Capitol Mall, 4D-200
Little Rock, Arkansas 72201
501-682-2222

California

Criminal Justice Statistics Center
Department of Justice
Post Office Box 903427
Sacramento, California 94203-4270
916-227-3282

Colorado

Uniform Crime Reporting
Colorado Bureau of Investigation
Suite 3000
690 Kipling Street
Denver, Colorado 80215
303-239-4300

Connecticut	Uniform Crime Reporting Program Post Office Box 2794 Middletown, Connecticut 06457-9294 860-685-8030
Delaware	Delaware State Bureau of Identification Post Office Box 430 Dover, Delaware 19903 302-739-5875
District of Columbia	Metropolitan Police Department 300 Indiana Avenue, N.W. Washington, D.C. 20001 202-727-1077
Florida	Criminal Justice Information Services Uniform Crime Reports Florida Department of Law Enforcement Post Office Box 1489 Tallahassee, Florida 32302-1489 850-410-7121
Georgia	Georgia Crime Information Center Georgia Bureau of Investigation Uniform Crime Reporting Unit Post Office Box 370748 Decatur, Georgia 30037-0748 404-244-2840
Guam	Guam Police Department Planning, Research and Development Building #233 Central Avenue Tiyan, Guam 96913 671-475-8421
Hawaii	Crime Prevention and Justice Assistance Division Department of the Attorney General Suite 401 235 South Beretania Street Honolulu, Hawaii 96813 808-586-1416 ·
Idaho	Bureau of Criminal Identification Idaho Department of Law Enforcement Post Office Box 700 Meridian, Idaho 83680 208-884-7156

Illinois	Uniform Crime Reporting Division of Administration; Crime Statistics Illinois State Police 3rd Floor 400 Iles Park Place Springfield, Illinois 62708 217-782-5794
Iowa	Iowa Department of Public Safety Wallace State Office Building East Ninth and Grand Des Moines, Iowa 50319 515-281-8494
Kansas	Criminal Justice System Kansas Bureau of Investigation Crime Data Information Center 1620 Southwest Tyler Street Topeka, Kansas 66612 785-296-8200
Kentucky	Criminal Identification and Records Branch Kentucky State Police 1250 Louisville Road Frankfort, Kentucky 40601 502-227-8790
Louisiana	Louisiana Commission on Law Enforcement Uniform Crime Reporting 12th Floor 1885 Wooddale Boulevard Baton Rouge, Louisiana 70806 225-925-7465
Maine	Records Management Services Uniform Crime Reporting Division Maine Department of Public Safety Maine State Police 36 Hospital Street, Station 42 Augusta, Maine 04333 207-624-7003
Maryland	Central Records Division Maryland State Police 1711 Belmont Avenue Baltimore, Maryland 21244 410-298-3883

Massachusetts	Crime Reporting Unit Uniform Crime Reports Massachusetts State Police 470 Worcester Road Framingham, Massachusetts 01702 508-820-2111
Michigan	Uniform Crime Reporting Section Criminal Justice Information Center Michigan State Police 7150 Harris Drive Lansing, Michigan 48913 517-322-1424
Minnesota	Criminal Justice Information Systems Bureau of Criminal Apprehension Minnesota Department of Public Safety 1246 University Avenue St. Paul, Minnesota 55104 651-642-0670
Missouri	Missouri State Highway Patrol 1510 East Elm Street Post Office Box 568 Jefferson City, Missouri 65102-0568 573-526-6278
Montana	Montana Board of Crime Control Post Office Box 201408 Helena, Montana 59620-1408 406-444-4298
Nebraska	Uniform Crime Reporting Section The Nebraska Commission on Law Enforcement and Criminal Justice Post Office Box 94946 Lincoln, Nebraska 68508 402-471-3982
Nevada	Criminal Information Services Nevada Highway Patrol 808 West Nye Lane Carson City, Nevada 89703 775-687-1600
New Hampshire	Uniform Crime Reporting Unit New Hampshire State Police New Hampshire Department of Public Safety 10 Hazen Drive Concord, New Hampshire 03305 603-271-2509

New Jersey	Uniform Crime Reporting Unit
	New Jersey State Police
	Post Office Box 7068
	West Trenton, New Jersey 08628-0068
	609-882-2000 x 2392
New York	Statistical Services
	New York State Division of Criminal Justice Services
	8th Floor, Mail Room
	4 Tower Place
	Albany, New York 12203
	518-457-8381
North Carolina	Crime Reporting and Criminal Statistics
	State Bureau of Investigation
	Post Office Box 29500
	Raleigh, North Carolina 27626-0500
	919-662-4509
North Dakota	Information Services Section
	Bureau of Criminal Investigation
	Attorney General's Office
	Post Office Box 1054
	Bismarck, North Dakota 58502
	701-328-5500
Ohio*	Office of Criminal Justice Services
	Suite 300
	400 East Town Street
	Columbus, Ohio 43215
	614-644-6797
Oklahoma	Uniform Crime Reporting Section
	Oklahoma State Bureau of Investigation
	Suite 300
	6600 North Harvey
	Oklahoma City, Oklahoma 73116
	405-879-2533
Oregon	Law Enforcement Data System Division
	Oregon State Police
	3225 State Street
	Salem, Oregon 97301
	503-378-3055
Pennsylvania	Bureau of Research and Development
	Pennsylvania State Police
	1800 Elmerton Avenue
	Harrisburg, Pennsylvania 17110
	717-783-5536

*National Incident-Based Reporting System Only

Puerto Rico	Statistics Division
	Puerto Rico Police
	Post Office Box 70166
	San Juan, Puerto Rico 00936-8166
	787-793-1234 x 3113
Rhode Island	Rhode Island State Police
	311 Danielson Pike
	North Scituate, Rhode Island 02857
	401-444-1121
South Carolina	South Carolina Law Enforcement Division
	Post Office Box 21398
	Columbia, South Carolina 29221-1398
	803-896-7016
South Dakota	South Dakota Statistical Analysis Center
	500 East Capitol Avenue
	Pierre, South Dakota 57501-5070
	605-773-6310
Tennessee*	Tennessee Bureau of Investigation
	901 R.S. Gass Boulevard
	Nashville, Tennessee 37216-2639
	615-744-4014
Texas	Uniform Crime Reporting
	Crime Information Bureau
	Texas Department of Public Safety
	Post Office Box 4143
	Austin, Texas 78765-9968
	512-424-2734
Utah	Data Collection and Analysis
	Uniform Crime Reporting
	Bureau of Criminal Identification
	Utah Department of Public Safety
	Post Office Box 148280
	Salt Lake City, Utah 84114-8280
	801-965-4566
Vermont	Vermont Crime Information Center
	103 South Main Street
	Waterbury, Vermont 05671-2101
	802-241-5220

*National Incident-Based Reporting System Only

Virginia	Criminal Justice Information Services Division
	Virginia State Police
	Post Office Box 27472
	Richmond, Virginia 23261-7472
	804-674-2023
Virgin Islands	Virgin Islands Police Department
	Criminal Justice Complex
	Saint Thomas, Virgin Islands 00802
	809-774-2211
Washington	Uniform Crime Reporting Program
	Washington Association of Sheriffs and Police Chiefs
	Suite 200
	3060 Willamette Drive, Northeast
	Lacey, Washington 98516
	360-486-2380
West Virginia	Uniform Crime Reporting Program
	West Virginia State Police
	725 Jefferson Road
	South Charleston, West Virginia 25309
	304-746-2159
Wisconsin	Office of Justice Assistance
	Suite 202
	131 West Wilson Street
	Madison, Wisconsin 53702-0001
	608-266-0936
Wyoming	Uniform Crime Reporting
	Criminal Records Section
	Division of Criminal Investigation
	316 West 22nd Street
	Cheyenne, Wyoming 82002
	307-777-7625

APPENDIX VI – National Uniform Crime Reporting Directory

Administration   304-625-3691
    Program administration; management; policy

Crime Analysis, Research and Development   304-625-3600
    Statistical models; special studies and analyses; crime forecasting

Information Dissemination   304-625-4995
    Requests for published and unpublished data; printouts, magnetic tapes, and books

National Incident-Based Reporting System (NIBRS)   304-625-2998
    Information for law enforcement agencies regarding the NIBRS certification process;
    federal funding for NIBRS-compliant records management systems; and data submission specifications

Quality Assurance   304-625-2941
    Assistance in confirming statistical validity and ensuring agency reporting integrity

Statistical Processing   304-625-4830
    Processing of summary and incident-based reports from data contributors; reporting problems;
    requests for reporting forms; data processing; data quality

Training/Education   304-625-3691
    Requests for training of law enforcement personnel; information on police reporting systems;
    technical assistance

      Send correspondence to: Federal Bureau of Investigation
                                       Criminal Justice Information Services Division
                                       Attention: Uniform Crime Reports
                                       1000 Custer Hollow Road
                                       Clarksburg, West Virginia   26306

Crime in the United States (annual)*

Law Enforcement Officers Killed and Assaulted (annual)*

Hate Crime Statistics (annual)*

Killed in the Line of Duty: A Study of Selected Felonious Killings of Law Enforcement Officers (special report)

In the Line of Fire: Violence Against Law Enforcement—A Study of Felonious Assaults on Law Enforcement Officers (special report)

Uniform Crime Reports: Their Proper Use (brochure)

National Incident-Based Reporting System (brochure)

Preliminary Semiannual Uniform Crime Report, January–June

Preliminary Annual Uniform Crime Report

Uniform Crime Reporting Handbook:
   National Incident-Based Reporting System (NIBRS)
   Summary System

NIBRS:
   Data Collection Guidelines
   Data Submission Specifications
   Error Message Manual
   Addendum to the NIBRS Volumes
   Conversion of NIBRS Data to Summary Data
   NIBRS Addendum for Submitting LEOKA Data
   Supplemental Guidelines for Federal Participation

Manual of Law Enforcement Records

Hate Crime:
   Hate Crime Data Collection Guidelines
   Hate Crime Magnetic Media Specifications for Tapes & Diskettes
   Hate Crime Statistics, 1990: A Resource Book
   Training Guide for Hate Crime Data Collection

Age-Specific Arrest Rates and Race-Specific Arrest Rates for Selected Offenses

Periodic Press Releases:
   Hate Crime
   Law Enforcement Officers Killed and Assaulted

* These publications are available on the FBI's Internet site at www.fbi.gov/ucr/ucr.htm.

Evaluation Form For
Crime in the United States, 2002

1. For what purpose did you use this issue of *Crime in the United States?*

2. Was the publication adequate for that purpose?
    - —— Quite adequate
    - —— Somewhat adequate
    - —— Quite adequate
    - —— Adequate
    - —— Not adequate

3. Are there presentations not included that you would find particularly useful?

4. What changes, if any, would you recommend for subsequent issues?

5. Can you point out specific table notes or presentations which are not clear or additional terms which need to be defined?

6. In what capacity did you use *Crime in the United States?*
    - —— Criminal justice/law enforcement agency employee *(specify functional area)*
    - —— Researcher
    - —— Student
    - —— Other government employee
    - —— Legislator
    - —— Private citizen
    - —— Media
    - —— Educator
    - —— Other *(specify)*

7. Add any additional comments you care to make.